AUSTRALIAN DICTIONARY OF BIOGRAPHY

VOLUME 15 : 1940-1980

Kem - Pie

General Editor
JOHN RITCHIE

Deputy General Editor
DI LANGMORE

MELBOURNE UNIVERSITY PRESS

MELBOURNE UNIVERSITY PRESS
PO Box 278, Carlton South, Victoria 3053, Australia

First published 2000

Typeset by Syarikat Seng Teik Sdn. Bhd., Malaysia
Printed in Australia by Brown Prior Anderson Pty Ltd

National Library of Australia Cataloguing-in-Publication entry

Australian dictionary of biography. Volume 15, 1940–1980, Kem-Pie.

ISBN 0 522 84236 4 (set).
ISBN 0 522 84843 5.

1. Australia—Biography—Dictionaries. 2. Australia—History—1940–1980—Biography. I. Ritchie, John, 1941–. II. Langmore, Diane, 1941–.

920.094

PREFACE

In 1940 a nondescript, weatherbeaten factory in Melbourne, which had previously produced lipstick cases, was converted into a munitions-making plant for the duration of World War II. In 1980, after much toing and froing, members of the Australian Olympic Federation decided that Australian athletes should compete in the Olympic Games in Moscow. Many of the events that occurred and the people who rose to prominence in the intervening years provide the subject matter for Volume 15 of the *Australian Dictionary of Biography*. It contains 682 entries by 543 authors and is the third of four in the 1940-1980 section.

Incorporating the lives of some 2700 individuals, volumes 13 to 16 illustrate such topics as immigration, accelerating industrialism, urbanization and suburbanization, and war (World War II, Korea, Malaya and Vietnam). While other themes are also illuminated—material progress, increasing cultural maturity, conservative and radical politics, conflict and harmony, loss of isolation and innocence—the emphasis of the biographies is on the individuals. The entries throw light on the complexity of the human situation, and on the greatness and the littleness of moral response and actual behaviour which this can evoke. In Volume 15 the subjects range from Errol Noack, a national serviceman who died at the age of 21, to Grace Perrier, a librarian who lived until she was 103. Although the majority of the men and women included in this volume flourished in the 1940-1980 period, a minority of the lives, like that of the solicitor and patron of the arts, Alexander Melrose, who was born in 1865, reveal facets of Australian history long before 1940.

The two volumes of the 1788-1850 section, the four of the 1851-1890 section and the six of the 1891-1939 section were published between 1966 and 1990. Volumes 13 and 14, the first two of the 1940-1980 section, were published in 1993 and 1996 respectively. Douglas Pike was general editor for volumes 1 to 5, Bede Nairn for Volume 6, Nairn and Geoffrey Serle for volumes 7 to 10, Serle for Volume 11, and John Ritchie for volumes 12 to 15. An index to volumes 1-12 was published in 1991, and the *A.D.B.* was produced on CD-ROM in 1996. The chronological division was designed to simplify production, for 7211 entries have been included in volumes 1-12 (volumes 1-2, for 1788-1850, had 1116 entries; volumes 3-6, for 1851-1890, 2053; volumes 6-12, for 1891-1939, 4042). For the period from 1788 to 1939, the placing of each individual's name in the appropriate section was determined by when he/she did his/her most important work (*floruit*). In contrast, the 1940-1980 section only includes individuals who died in this period. Volume 13 thus marked a change from the *floruit* to the 'date of death' principle. When Volume 16 has been completed, the A.D.B. will begin work on the period 1981-1990.

The choice of subjects for inclusion required prolonged consultation. After quotas were estimated, working parties in each State, and the Armed Services and Commonwealth working parties, prepared provisional lists which were widely circulated and carefully amended. Many of the names were obviously significant and worthy of inclusion as leaders in politics, business, the armed services, the church, the professions, the arts and the labour movement. Some have been included as representatives of ethnic and social minorities, and of a wide range of occupations; others have found a place as innovators, notorieties or eccentrics. A number had to be omitted through pressure of space or lack of material, and thereby joined the great mass whose members richly deserve a more honoured place, but thousands of these names, and information about them, have been gathered in the biographical register at the A.D.B.'s headquarters at the Australian National University.

Most authors were nominated by working parties. The burden of writing has been shared almost equally by the staff of universities and by a variety of other specialists.

The *A.D.B.* is a project based on consultation and co-operation. The Research School of Social Sciences at the A.N.U. has borne the cost of the headquarters staff, of much research and of occasional special contingencies, while other Australian universities have supported the project in numerous ways. The A.D.B.'s policies were initially determined by a national committee composed mainly of representatives from the departments of history in each Australian university. That committee's successor, the editorial board, has kept in touch with historians at many universities, and with working parties, librarians, archivists and other local experts, as well as with research assistants in each Australian capital city and correspondents abroad. With such varied support, the *A.D.B.* is truly a national project.

ACKNOWLEDGMENTS

The Australian Dictionary of Biography is a programme supported by the Research School of Social Sciences at the Australian National University. Special thanks are due to Professor Jill Roe for guidance as chair of the editorial board, and to Professors Geoffrey Brennan and Ian McAllister, successive directors of the R.S.S.S., and Mrs Pauline Hore, the school's business manager. Those who helped in planning the shape of the work have been mentioned in earlier volumes.

Within Australia, the A.D.B. is indebted to many librarians and archivists, schools, colleges, universities, institutes, historical and genealogical societies, and numerous other organizations; to the National Library of Australia, the Australian War Memorial, the Commonwealth Scientific and Industrial Research Organization, the Australian Institute of Aboriginal and Torres Strait Islander Studies, and the National Archives of Australia; to public libraries, archives and record offices in the various States and Territories, and to registrars of probates and of the Supreme and Family courts whose co-operation has solved many problems; to various town and shire clerks; to the Returned & Services League of Australia, the Australian Department of Defence, and State education departments; to the Royal Society of New South Wales, the Royal College of Pathologists of Australasia, the Australian Orthopaedic Association, the *Medical Journal of Australia*, the Linnean Society of New South Wales, the Royal Art Society of New South Wales, the Media, Entertainment and Arts Alliance, the Australian Institute of Mining and Metallurgy, the Australian Federation of University Women, the Sisters of Charity of Australia, the Big Brother Movement, the Union Club, the Aisling Society of Sydney, the Law Courts Library, the Whitlam Library, the Coalfields Heritage Group, the United Grand Lodge of New South Wales, the Professional Golfers' Association of Australia, the New South Wales Cricket Association, all in Sydney; and to the Snowy Mountains Hydro-Electric Authority, Cooma, the Pioneer Women's Hut, Tumbarumba, and the Dubbo Rural Lands Protection Board, New South Wales; to the Royal Australasian College of Surgeons, the Australian Society for Microbiology, the Walter and Eliza Hall Institute of Medical Research, the Baker Medical Research Institute, Commonwealth Serum Laboratories Ltd, the Australian Council for Educational Research, the Royal Australian Air Force Association (Victorian Division), the Royal Australian Institute of Architects, the Australian Institute of Agricultural Science and Technology, the Australian Institute of Management and Public Administration, the Royal Humane Society of Australasia, the Christian Brothers Provincial, the Society of Jesus, the Salvation Army, the Menzies Foundation, the Victorian Bar, the National Australia Bank, the Lyceum Club, the Melbourne Savage Club, the Municipal Association of Victoria, Preston and Northcote Community Hospital, and Kingston Heath Golf Club, all in Melbourne; to the Australian College of Education, the Australian Institute of International Affairs, the Law Council of Australia, the Institution of Engineers, Australia, the National Heart Foundation of Australia, the National Health and Medical Research Council, the Commonwealth Club, and the Air Power Studies Centre, all in Canberra; to the National Trust of Queensland, the Royal Society of Queensland, the Queensland Art Gallery Society, the Royal Australian Planning Institute (Queensland Division), the Australian Institute of Landscape Architects, the Housing Industry Association, and the Brisbane Golf Club, all in Brisbane; and to the Queensland Master Builders' Association, Townsville, the Maryborough and Wide Bay Club, Maryborough, and the Caledonian Lodge, Mackay, Queensland; to the Young Women's Christian Association of Perth, the Liquor Licensing Court, the Pastoralists' and Graziers' Association of Western Australia, all in Perth; to the Benedictine Community of New Norcia, Western Australia; and to the Australian and New Zealand Association for the Advancement of Science, the South Australian Police Library and the Grand Lodge of Freemasons, Adelaide.

Thanks for the free gift of their time and talents are due to contributors, to past and present members of the editorial board, and to the working parties. For particular assistance the A.D.B. owes much to Margy Burn, Justin Corfield, Don Fairweather, Bill Gammage, Bryan Gandevia, Paul Hammond, Cameron Hazlehurst, Robert Hyslop, Jenny Mills, John Molony, Bruce Moore, Norm Neill, Hank Nelson, Robert O'Neill, Peter Sack, F. B. Smith, R. J. M. Tolhurst, Peter Yeend and Norbert Zmijewski.

Essential assistance with birth, death and marriage certificates has been provided by the co-operation of registrars in New South Wales, Queensland, South Australia, Tasmania, Victoria, Western Australia, the Northern Territory and the Australian Capital Territory; by the General Register offices in London and Edinburgh; by the registrars-general in Fiji and Papua New Guinea; by the Department of Home Affairs, South Africa, and the registrar of births and deaths in Hong Kong and at Calcutta, India; by the bureaux of vital statistics in the State Health departments in California, Hawaii, Massachusetts, Michigan, New York, Pennsylvania and Virginia, United States of America; by the registrars-general, Vancouver and Manitoba, Canada; by the Public Registry, Valetta, Malta; by the City Archives, Bergen, Kristiansand, Oslo and Stavanger, Norway; by the mayors of Antibes, Noumea, and the 16e arrondissement, Paris; by civil status offices in Rome and Fermo, Italy; by the registry offices at Hamburg, Munich, Schöneberg and Trier, Germany; by the civil registration offices at Amsterdam and Eindhoven, The Netherlands; by the Lithuanian State Archives; by the consuls-general for the Czech Republic and Poland, in Sydney, and for Lithuania, in Melbourne, and by the consul for Greece, in Darwin; by the Belgian, Croatian, Egyptian, Greek, Hungarian, Italian, Netherlands, Polish and Spanish embassies, and by the South African High Commission, Canberra.

For other assistance overseas, thanks are due to Pauric Dempsey and William Murphy, Dublin, Betty Iggo, Edinburgh, and Roger Joslyn, New York; to the universities of Birmingham, Cambridge, Leeds, London, Newcastle, Oxford and Sheffield, King's College, London, Jesus College, Cambridge, and The Queen's College, Oxford; to the universities of Aberdeen, Edinburgh, Glasgow, St Andrew's and Strathclyde, Scotland; to the National University of Ireland and Trinity College, Dublin, and the Queen's University of Belfast; to Humboldt-Universität, Berlin, Ludwig-Maximilians-Universität, Munich, Ruprecht-Karls-Universität, Heidelberg, Friedrich-Schiller-Universität, Jena, and the Technische Universität, Darmstadt, Germany; to the universities of Warsaw and Wroclaw, Poland; to Columbia University, New York, the Catholic University of America, Washington D.C., Yale University, Connecticut, Smith College, Massachusetts, Michigan Technological University, the universities of Wisconsin and Iowa, and Notre Dame University, Indiana, U.S.A.; to the University of British Columbia, Canada; to Massey University, Palmerston North, and the universities of Auckland, Canterbury and Otago, New Zealand.

Gratitude is also due to the Royal Society, the Royal Society of Arts, the Royal College of Art, the Royal College of Music, the Royal Academy of Music, the Royal College of Organists, the Associated Board of the Royal Schools of Music, the Guild Hall, the Royal College of Physicians, the Royal College of Surgeons, England, the Royal College of Pathologists, the Royal London Hospital, the Royal Free Hospital, the Royal Society for the Promotion of Health, the British Orthopaedic Association, the Institute of Psychiatry, the London School of Hygiene and Tropical Medicine, the

Royal Veterinary College, the Royal Geographical Society, the Royal Historical Society, the Royal Philatelic Society, the British Ecological Society, the Royal Entomological Society, the Royal Institute of British Architects, the Institution of Electrical Engineers, the Institute of Chartered Secretaries and Administrators, the Honourable Society of Gray's Inn Trust Fund, the Clothworkers' Company, the Young Women's Christian Association, the British Architectural Library, and the Air Historical Branch, R.A.F., all in London; to the Ministry of Defence, Hayes, the Office of the Second Sea Lord and Commander-in-Chief Naval Home Command, Portsmouth, the Fleet Air Arm Museum, Ilchester, the King's Own Scottish Borderers, Berwick-upon-Tweed, the Commonwealth War Graves Commission, Maidenhead, and the Museum, Devizes, England; to the Royal College of Surgeons, Edinburgh, Scotland; to the King's Inn Library, Dublin, Ireland, the Grande Chancellerie de la Légion d'Honneur, Paris, the Office of the High Commission for Refugees, Geneva, the Secretariat of the Chapter of Orders and the Royal Danish Theatre Archives and Library, Copenhagen, the Norwegian Society of Chartered Engineers, Oslo, the Nederlandsi Gilde van Kunstmeden, Nieuwegein, The Netherlands; to KZ Gedenkstaette, Dachau, Carl Zeiss, Jena, and Deutsche Dienstelle, Berlin, Germany; to the Österreichisches Staatarchiv, Vienna, Miroslav Krieza Lexicographic Institute, Zagreb, and the Yad Vashem Archives, Jerusalem; to the staffs of the *Northern Territory Dictionary of Biography*, *Österreichisches Biographisches Lexikon*, Vienna, *Dictionary of Canadian Biography*, Toronto, and *Dictionary of New Zealand Biography*, Wellington, to the Royal Society of New Zealand, the New Zealand Institute of Architects, the Auckland City Libraries, and the New Zealand Defence Force, Wellington; and to other individuals and institutions who have co-operated with the A.D.B.

The A.D.B. deeply regrets the deaths of such notable contributors as Fred Alexander, John Barrett, Jan Bassett, W. S. Benwell, Barbara Bolton, Paul Bourke, P. L. Brown, J. H. Calaby, David Denholm, Warren Derkenne, Gwyneth Dow, Don Dunstan, Ken Elford, Renée Erdos, G. C. Fendley, J. F. Firth, R. M. H. Garvie, J. C. H. Gill, Charles Glyn-Daniel, J. Barton Hack, Bobbie Hardy, Victoria Hobbs, Kathleen Dunlop Kane, A. I. Keenan, B. R. Keith, Max Kelly, Hazel King, H. C. C. Langdon, Winston G. Lewis, F. M. McGuire, Ian McNeill, Ronald McNicoll, E. J. O'Brien, Katherine M. O'Brien, N. J. Plomley, Joan T. Radford, Don Rawson, Gordon Reid, Margaret Rilett, Geoffrey Sawer, Geoffrey Serle, R. P. Serle, E. K. Sinclair, Neil Smith, R. J. Southey, A. C. Staples, John M. Tregenza, Syd Trigellis-Smith, Marjorie Waite, James R. H. Watson, Douglas J. Whalan and Lionel Wigmore.

Grateful acknowledgment is due to the director and staff of Melbourne University Press, and to Chris Cunneen, Suzanne Edgar, Margaret Steven, Helga Griffin, Alison Pilger, Jenny Newell, Gerard Oakes, Maureen Brooks, Margot Harker, Nicole McLennan, Mimi Colligan, Wendy Birman, Leigh Edmonds and Syd Trigellis-Smith who worked for the A.D.B. while Volume 15 was being produced.

The A.D.B. expresses its deep appreciation of financial assistance from Mrs Caroline Simpson of Sydney and the Myer Foundation, Melbourne, which helped in the production of this volume.

xi

WORKING PARTIES

Armed Services
Peter Burness, John Coates, Alec Hill, David Horner (chair), John McCarthy, Perditta McCarthy, Philip Mulcare, Anthony Staunton, Alan Stephens, D. Stevens, A. J. Sweeting.

Commonwealth
Nicholas Brown, David Carment, Patricia Clarke, Bill Gammage, Tom Griffiths (chair), Ian Hancock, Robert Hyslop, C. J. Lloyd, Graeme Powell, Libby Robin, John Thompson.

New South Wales
J. J. Carmody, C. Cunneen, R. Curnow, F. Farrell, S. Garton, E. M. Goot, Beverley Kingston (chair), J. K. McLaughlin, A. J. Moore, N. B. Nairn, Heather Radi, Jill Roe, Dagmar Schmidmaier, G. Souter, Alan Ventress.

Queensland
Ysola Best, Pat Buckridge, M. D. Cross, Marion Diamond, M. W. French, Helen Gregory, Jennifer Harrison, I. F. Jobling, W. R. Johnston (chair), Lorna McDonald, Dawn May, S. J. Routh, C. G. Sheehan.

South Australia
John Bannon, Joyce Gibberd, R. M. Gibbs, P. A. Howell (chair), Helen Jones, J. H. Love, Katharine Massam, Judith Raftery, Jenny Tilby Stock, Patricia Stretton, R. E. Thornton.

Tasmania
G. P. R. Chapman, Shirley Eldershaw, Margaret Glover, Elizabeth McLeod, S. Petrow, Anne Rand, O. M. Roe (chair), G. T. Stilwell.

Victoria
G. R. Browne, Mimi Colligan, B. J. Costar, Jim Davidson, G. J. Davison, David Dunstan, F. J. Kendall, J. F. Lack (chair), Janet McCalman, R. A. Murray, J. R. Poynter, Carolyn Rasmussen, J. D. Rickard, Judith Smart, F. Strahan.

Western Australia
Wendy Birman, D. Black, G. C. Bolton (chair), Michal Bosworth, Dorothy Erickson, Charles Fox, Sue Graham-Taylor, Jenny Gregory, Lenore Layman, John McIlwraith, Jenny Mills, Jill Milroy, C. Mulcahy, Jan Ryan, Tom Stannage.

As to time and place, Geoffrey Serle was born on 10 March 1922, almost within sight and sound of Glenferrie Oval, Hawthorn, son of Melbourne-born parents, Percival Serle (1871-1951), accountant and scholar, and his wife Dora Beatrice, née Hake (1875-1968), an artist. In the year of Serle's birth, Henry Lawson died and Melbourne University Press was founded. Schooled at Scotch College, Serle proceeded in 1941 to the University of Melbourne, where he read history. He suspended his studies and enlisted in the Melbourne University Regiment on 13 October 1941; he transferred to the Australian Imperial Force on 15 September 1942; during his thirty-two months service he was seriously wounded in action at Finschhafen, New Guinea. Discharged from the army on 7 June 1944, he resumed his undergraduate course, and numbered Max Crawford, Kathleen Fitzpatrick and Manning Clark among his mentors. Serle joined the Labour Club, helped to found the Victorian Fabian Society and co-edited (with Ken Gott) *Melbourne University Magazine*. After completing his B.A.(Hons) degree in 1946, he won a Rhodes Scholarship and entered University College, Oxford, where he graduated D.Phil. in 1950. He returned to the University of Melbourne, taught Australian history there and, from 1961, at Monash University, and edited (1955-63) *Historical Studies Australia and New Zealand*. On 12 January 1955 he married Jessie Macdonald, who became an art historian; they were to have a daughter, Oenone, and three sons, Donald, Jamie and Richard.

In a career that was as multifaceted as it was creative, Serle established his name as historian, biographer and editor. His first book of history, *The Melbourne Scene, 1803-1956*, co-edited with James Grant, was a collection of documents, published in 1957. It was followed by two general histories of the colony of Victoria, *The Golden Age* (1963) and *The Rush to be Rich* (1971). The former focused on the goldrushes of the 1850s, the latter on the boom of the 1880s. In 1973 he produced *From Deserts the Prophets Come*, a history of Australian literature, art, music, theatre, architecture and science. His biographies included *John Monash* (1982), which won four major awards, *Percival Serle* (1988), the most sensitive, self-revealing and elegant of all his works, *Sir John Medley* (1993) and *Robin Boyd* (1995). In addition to these full-scale studies, he also completed forty-nine entries for the *Australian Dictionary of Biography*. Most of them are jewels. Varying in length from 500 to 6000 words, these articles cover subjects ranging from John Curtin to the McInnes brothers, Graham and Colin. Serle's 'brief lives' reveal the span of his interests and expertise, the humanity of his judgement, and the precision of his prose. In 1975 he and Bede Nairn were appointed joint general editors of the *A.D.B.* One came from a middle-class, Protestant and Melburnian background; the other, by upbringing, was working-class, Catholic and a Sydneysider. They made a marvellous team. Together, they produced volumes 7 to 10; after Bede's retirement, Geoff edited Volume 11 alone.

Serle also contributed a great deal to libraries, magazines, the arts and sport. In 1966, with Professor A. G. L. Shaw, he founded the Friends of the La Trobe Library to promote development of the library's research collections; he was, in turn, secretary, president and vice-president of the Friends, foundation editor of the *La Trobe Library Journal*, and vice-president (1989-94) of the council of the State Library of Victoria. Conscious of the merits of other repositories, he supported the National Library of Australia, the Australian War Memorial and the National Gallery of Australia. Serle's love of Australian literature, and his friendship with Clem Christesen and Stephen Murray-Smith, led him to be closely associated with *Meanjin* and *Overland*: he contributed to both magazines, edited *Meanjin* in 1957, and chaired its board and that of *Overland*. Absorbing 'high culture' all his life, he read prodigiously and developed a passion for the novel—in all its forms. He inherited an enduring love of painting, especially that of the Heidelberg School. For many years he belonged to the Buildings (Classification) Committee of the Victorian branch of the National Trust of Australia. In his youth Serle was an excellent hurdler and hockey-player, and a capable cricketer and Australian Rules footballer; in middle age he was an enthusiastic spectator at all these sports; even in his sixties he continued to play a wily game of tennis against members of the A.D.B. staff, a number of whom were nearly a generation younger. He eventually acknowledged the merits of Rugby Union football, yet showed next to no interest in horse-racing.

A fellow of the Australian academies of the Humanities and of the Social Sciences, and of the Royal Victorian and Royal Australian Historical societies, Serle was appointed AO in 1986. He had been promoted to a readership in 1963, but neither sought nor accepted a chair. Incisive and insightful, pragmatic and down-to-earth, left-leaning in his political sympathies without being dogmatic, he was gentle in nature, thoughtful in temperament, egalitarian in outlook, exceptionally hard-working, and a loyal friend. He enjoyed a can of beer, a glass of wine, a cigarette and his pipe. In private life, he succeeded in the three things that matter most, as a son, a husband and a father. Family tradition traced his ancestry to the Conquest, and Norman elements could be discerned in his features, but his laconic voice and distinctive drawl were outward signs that he was 'unapologetically Australian'. When I sent him a letter from London in 1972 extolling the virtues of England, he sent a postcard in reply: on one side it had a painting by Tom Roberts, on the other he wrote, 'aut Australia, aut nihil'. Serle died on 27 April 1998 at Epworth Hospital, Richmond. The nation that he loved has lost one of its finest sons, one who left to family, friends and colleagues an abundant legacy. As the Reverend Dr Davis McCaughey said in his eulogy, Geoff took the 'fragments of a useable past' and wove them into 'the stuff of consciousness and conscience'. Through his understanding of our past, he has helped us to understand ourselves.

J. R.

AUTHORS

AARONS, Eric:
Makinson.
ALLEN, Maree G.:
O'Neill, M.
ALLEN, Margaret:
Macghey.
ANDERSON, Hugh:
McDonald, S.
ANDERSON, Jaynie:
Philipp.
ANDRÉ, Roger:
Lewis, G.
ANGAS, Hamish:
Lawson, G. G.
ANNABLE, Rosemary:
Nicol, P.
ARNOLD, John:
Kerr, D.; Moir.
ATCHISON, John:
Lea, M.; McMorran; Miller, Sir R.;
Mulley.
AUSTEN, T. E.:
Macartney, J.

BAKER, E. R.:
Opas.
BALLARD, Chris:
O'Malley.
BANNON, J. C.:
O'Halloran.
BASSETT, Jan*:
Muntz; Parker.
BATE, Weston:
Pickworth.
BAUME, Peter:
McKenna, N.
BEAUMONT, Joan:
Kevin.
BECKETT, Jeremy:
Newton, W.; Nona.
BELL, Roger:
Moore, A.
BENJAMIN, Ruth:
Lush, M.
BENNET, Darryl:
Lawrenson; Morrow, J.; Olsen;
Parkes, E.
BERTRAND, Ina:
Liddell.
BEST, Ysola:
Moonlight; O'Shane.
BETTISON, Margaret:
Newson.
BHATHAL, R.:
Lemberg.

* deceased

BIRMAN, Wendy:
Lefroy, Sir A. & Sir E.; Meares; Nicholas;
Phillips, L.
BISHOP, Catherine:
Lock.
BLACK, David:
Leslie; MacDonald, A.
BLENCOWE, M.:
Mander-Jones.
BOADLE, Donald:
Merrylees.
BOARDMAN, N. Keith:
Pennefather, R.
BODYCOMB, John F.:
Northey.
BOLAND, T. P.:
O'Donnell.
BOLTON, G. C.:
McDonald, Sir R.; Moseley.
BOLTON, H. C.:
Matthaei.
BONGIORNO, Frank:
Mattner.
BONNIN, Nancy:
Lamond.
BOSWORTH, Michal:
Lester; McCall, J.; Paul.
BOTT, Tony:
Pearce, M.
BOURKE, Helen:
Northcott, C.
BOXALL, Helen:
O'Connor.
BOYAN, W.:
McGrowdie.
BRADY, Veronica:
Mackenzie, K.
BRANAGAN, D. F.:
McBride.
BRANDON, Peter:
Martin, A.
BRETT, Judith:
Lazar Geroe.
BREWARD, Ian:
Macaulay.
BROOKE, Marion:
Mills, B.
BROOME, Richard:
Mulga Fred.
BROWN, Bruce:
Peacock.
BROWN, Gavin:
McCallum, N.
BROWNE, Geoff:
Kennedy, Sir J.; Leggatt.
BROWNRIGG, Jeff:
Le Gallienne; Pardey, E. & M.

BUCKRIDGE, Patrick:
Penton; Picot.
BUNDOCK, Anthea:
Nunan.
BURNESS, Peter:
Milson.
BURNS, Creighton:
Perkin.
BURROWS, E.:
Luisini.
BUTTERSS, Philip:
Mudie.
BUTTON, John N.:
Lovegrove.
BYRNE, Geraldine:
Kilfoyle.

CABLE, K. J.:
Kerrigan; Mowll.
CAMERON, Cecily:
Macdonald, A.
CARMODY, John:
Loewenthal; Mathy.
CARNELL, Ian:
McGovern; McLaren, W.
CARROLL, V. J.:
McKay, C. E.
CARRON, L. T.:
McAdam; McArthur, A.
CASHMAN, R. I.:
Mairinger.
CASTLES, Ian:
Nixon.
CAWLEY, Sally:
Nevile.
CHAPPELL, Louise:
O'Keeffe.
CHITTLEBOROUGH, Jon:
Monsoor; Norman.
CIGLER, Beryl:
Osman.
CLOSE, Cecily:
Lothian.
CLUNE, David:
McGirr.
COATES, H. J.:
Northcott, Sir J.
COCHRAN, I. C.:
McDonald, Allan.
COCHRANE, Peter:
Kirby, Sir J.
COHEN, Kay:
Kemp; McCracken.
COLE, John:
Morris, W.
COLE, Keith:
Lamilami.
COLLIGAN, Mimi:
Kingston.
COMPTON, J. S.:
Oom.
CONNELL, W. F.:
McLean, D.

CONNOLLY, P. D.:
Macrossan.
CONSANDINE, Marion:
Kirke; Legg; Molesworth.
COOKE, Glenn R.:
Molvig.
COOPER, Alastair:
Mould.
CORFIELD, Justin J.:
Lempriere, G., W. & P.
CORNISH, Selwyn:
McFarlane.
CORRIS, Peter:
McConnell, W.; Miller, H.
COSTAR, B. J.:
McDonald, Sir J.; Martin, Sir N.; Moss; Phelan.
COSTIGAN, Michael:
Murtagh.
COULSON, Helen:
Lambert, V.
COULTHARD-CLARK, C. D.:
Letcher; Lloyd, C.; Malley; Packer, G.
COWLEY, R. E.:
Matthews.
CRAYFORD, Michael:
Lewers, G. & H.
CROCKETT, Cheryl:
Officer, D.
CROFT, Julian:
Norway.
CROSS, Manfred:
Lawson, G.; Maguire; Milliner.
CROSS, Roger:
Marston.
CRYLE, Mark:
Krimmer.
CUNNEEN, Chris:
Kulakowski; Magnus, W.
CUSHING, Nancy:
Lamb.
CUTHILL, W. J.:
McLean, C.

DAMOUSI, Joy:
Lee, J.
d'APICE, Richard J. W.:
McClemens.
DAVIS, R. P.:
Lonergan.
DE GARIS, B. K.:
Paltridge.
DENHOLM, David*:
Palazzi.
DENHOLM, Zita:
McLean, C. M.
DERMODY, Kathleen:
Officer, Sir F.
DEWAR, Mickey:
Lockwood.
DEWDNEY, J. C. H.:
Martin, N.

* deceased

xvi

DILGER, David:
O'May.
DIXON, Marion:
McRae, W.
DONOVAN, Peter:
Murray, Sir J. S.
DRINKWATER, Derek:
McVey; Moroney.
DRURY, Nevill:
Norton, R.
DUGGAN, John M.:
McCaffrey.
DUNCAN, Alan T.:
Page, W.
DUNCAN, Bruce:
Lombard.
DUNSTAN, David:
Luke; McEncroe; Myer; O'Shea.
DUTTON, Tom:
Lammon.
DYSTER, Tom:
Miljanovic.

EASSON, Michael:
Kenny; McCallum, J.
EDGAR, Suzanne:
Kleeman; Logue; Mansom; Melrose; Moses.
EDMONDS, Leigh:
Middleton.
EDWARDS, W. H.:
MacDougall, W.
EGAN, Bryan:
Morgan, F.
EKINS, Ashley:
Kirby, J. W.
ELIAS, Ann:
Murray, J. F.
ELLIS, Julie-Ann:
Morgan, Sir E.
ERICKSON, Dorothy:
Kotai.
EVANS, Kate:
Nutt.
EYLAND, Ann:
Magoffin.

FAHEY, Charles:
Lienhop; Pethard.
FAIRWEATHER, D. F.:
Lyster; McKeown; Parish.
FALK, Barbara:
Lloyd, G.
FANNING, Pauline:
Lynravn.
FARQUHARSON, John:
McDonald, Sir W.; Nott.
FARRELL, Frank:
King, R. A.; McAlpine; Nugan.
FERRALL, R. A.:
McIntyre, W. & M.; Nettlefold.
FIRTH, Beverley:
MacDougall, J.
FLETCHER, Meredith:
Marx.

FLETCHER, Philippa L.:
Octoman.
FLOREANI, Carmel:
Moses.
FLYNN, Michael:
Maddocks.
FOGARTY, Mike:
McCarthy, B.
FOWLER, Kenneth F.:
Neumann.
FOYLE, Lindsay:
Nicholls.
FRAENKEL, G. J.:
Lindon.
FRANCIS, Charles:
Monahan.
FRASER, Alan:
King, E. R.
FREDMAN, L. E.:
McLarty, D.; Morris, I.
FREESTONE, Robert:
Luker.
FRENCH, M.:
O'Brien, T.

GALLAGHER, Neil:
Morrow, Sir A.
GAMMAGE, Bill:
Kibby; Mitchell, G.
GARDINER, Lyndsay*:
Keogh.
GARTON, Stephen:
McGeorge.
GIBBERD, Joyce:
Krischock; McCarthy, M.; O'Brien, L.; Peters, J.
GIBBS, Desmond:
Lyttle.
GIBBS, R. M.:
McGregor, Sir J. & H.
GILBERT, L. A.:
Kent Hughes, E.
GILLESPIE, James:
Lilley; Morris, E.
GISTITIN, Carol:
Perrier.
GOLDRING, John:
Mackay, R. W.
GOLLAN, Robin:
Palmer.
GOODALL, Heather:
Maynard, C.
GOOT, Murray:
McNair.
GORDON, Harry:
Marshall, J.
GOWER, S. N.:
Milford.
GRAHAME, Rachel:
Magnus, E.; Main; Oppen.
GREENWOOD, John:
Mansfield, Sir A.

* deceased

GREGORY, C. A.:
Mackay, D.
GREVILLE, P. J.:
Lucas; Madden.
GREY, Jeffrey:
King, R.; Mackay, Sir I.
GRIFFEN-FOLEY, Bridget:
McNulty; Mills, B.; Monson; Packer, Sir F.
GRIFFIN, James:
Mason, P.; O'Dea, P.
GRIGGS, Peter D.:
O'Brien, C.
GROVES, Murray:
Oala-Rarua.
GRUNDY, Peter C.:
Lambert, C.
GUEST, J. S.:
MacCallum, Sir P.

HAINES, Gregory:
McDonald, Sir C.
HANCOCK, I. R.:
Kent Hughes, Sir W.; McConnell, J.
HANKEL, Valmai A.:
Mortlock, J. & D.
HANNA, Bronwyn:
Nosworthy.
HANSEN, I. V.:
Langley, H.
HARDISTY, Sue:
McEwan.
HARDWICK, G. A.:
Packard.
HARDY, Bobbie*:
Moysey.
HARRISON, Jennifer:
Marlay.
HAY, John:
King, A.
HAYMAN, Charlotte:
Perry, A.
HAYSOM, Noel M.:
Marshall, T.
HAZLEHURST, Cameron:
Mockridge.
HEAGNEY, Brenda:
Little.
HEATHER, Neil:
May.
HENRY, Margaret:
McDougall.
HERCUS, Luise:
McLean, M.
HILL, A. J.:
Moriarty; Morshead; Murray, J. J.
HILL, Jennifer:
Phillips, D.
HOHNEN, Peter:
Money.
HOLDEN, Colin:
Moore, R. H.
HOLLAND, H. G.:
Morrison, F.
* deceased

HOLROYD, J. P.:
Peters, C.
HOME, R. W.:
Martyn; Parnell.
HONEY, Andrew:
Moore, A.
HONOUR, Vic:
Lockie.
HOOD, Robin K.:
Moore, M. L.
HOPLEY, J. B.:
MacDonald, H.
HORNE, Julia:
Munro; O'Neill, J.
HORNER, D. M.:
Lavarack; MacArthur.
HOWARD, Keith D.:
Lloyd, J.
HOWARTH, Jim:
Nilsen, N.
HOWE, Renate:
Penington.
HOWELL, P. A.:
Napier; Norrie.
HOWIE-WILLIS, Ian:
Marou Mimi; Onus.
HUGGONSON, David:
Lockyer.
HURLEY, John V.:
King, E. S.
HURST, Doug:
McDonald, Angus.
HUTCHINGS, Karen:
Patterson.
HYSLOP, Robert:
Perry, P.

INDER, Stuart:
Kennedy, E.
IRVING, T. H.:
Mortimer.

JAGGARD, E.:
Martinovich.
JAMES, Bob:
Longworth; O'Toole.
JENKIN, John:
Mitchell, Sir M.
JINKS, Brian:
Murray, Sir J. K.
JOHNSTON, Elizabeth:
O'Brien, E.
JOHNSTON, W. Ross:
O'Sullivan, M.
JONES, Barry O.:
Partridge.
JONES, Helen:
Leal; McDonnell; Marshall, D.
JONES, Philip:
Mountford.
JOSKE, W. D.:
Orr, S.
JUPP, James:
Kosovich.

KANE, Kathleen Dunlop*:
O'Neill, P.
KAYE, William:
Menhennitt.
KELEHER, Helen:
Kincaid.
KENNEDY, John:
McMahon.
KENNY, Catherine:
McGregor, K.
KERLEY, Margot:
McCallum, F.; Moore, R. C.
KERR, John D.:
Pearce, E.
KERR, Ruth S.:
Lack; Morrison, A.; Newman, J.
KERVILLE, D.:
McKay, R.
KINGSLAND, Richard:
Langslow; Mighell.
KINGSTON, Beverley:
Lord; McDowell.
KIRKPATRICK, Peter:
Lynch, F.; Macdonald, A. J.; Macdougall.
KIRKPATRICK, Rod:
Macfarlan, C.; Macleod; Manning, H.
KLEINERT, Sylvia:
Namatjira.
KNOTT, John:
Mason, (G.) W.; Noack.
KNOWLES, Beth:
Petrie.
KOLENBERG, Hendrik:
Lymburner.
KOLENBERG, Julianna:
Lymburner.
KOSCHARSKY, Halyna:
Pelensky.
KOWALD, Margaret:
McLeod.

LACK, John:
McKay, C. N.; McKay, R.; Old.
LAKE, Max:
Phillips, G.
LANDIS, Alan:
Lipscombe.
LANDIS, Louise:
Lipscombe.
LANE, Terence:
Krimper.
LANGMORE, Diane:
Kernot.
LAVERTY, John:
Nixon-Smith.
LAWRENCE, T. F. C.:
Loder.
LAWSON, Valerie:
Norton, E.
LAX, Mark:
McLean, W.
LAYMAN, Lenore:
McLarty, Sir D.; Meagher, Sir T.
* deceased

LEAVEY, Margaret Carmel:
Mackinlay.
LEE, David:
Lawson, J.; McCall, W.
LEMON, Andrew:
Manifold.
LEVERINGTON, K. C.:
Mungomery.
LEVI, J. S.:
Michaelis.
LEWIS, Julie:
Martin, M.
LINDSAY, Neville:
Paine, D.
LITHGOW, Shirley:
Page, R.
LIVINGSTONE, Stanley E.:
Mellor; Nyholm.
LLOYD, C. J.:
McEwen.
LOCKWOOD, Kim:
Lockwood.
LOMAS, L.:
McGarvie.
LONERGAN, John P.:
Penman.
LOUKAKIS, Angelo:
Palmos.
LOVE, Peter:
Monk; Paine, A.
LOVERING, J. F.:
Mitchell, S.
LOXTON, Alan H.:
Loxton.
LYON, John L.:
Lyon.

MCALLESTER, James C.:
Kingsbury.
McCalman, Janet:
Kumm.
MCCARTHY, Janice:
Paschke.
MCCARTHY, John:
McCormack.
MCCARTHY, Louella:
McNeill.
MCCARTHY, W. J.:
Pierce.
MCCAUGHEY, Davis:
Maclean, H.; Owen, J.
MCDONALD, G. L.:
MacMahon.
MCDONALD, Neil:
Parer.
MCEVOY, K. P.:
Paine, Sir K.
MACFARLING, Ian:
Pearce, C.
MCGILLICK, Paul:
Paramor.
MCINTYRE, Darryl:
McIlveen.

MACINTYRE, Stuart:
Miles.
McKENNA, C. W. F.:
Mewton-Wood.
McKERN, H. H. G.:
Morrison, F.
McKINNEY, Judith Wright:
McKinney.
McLAUGHLIN, John Kennedy:
Manning, Sir J.; Maxwell, A.
McLENNAN, N. T.:
Perrett.
McLEOD, G. R. C.:
Murphy, Sir A.
McMINN, W. G.:
Newbold.
McNEILL, Dorothy:
McKay, C. N.
McNEILL, Ian*:
Kirby, J. W.
McPHERSON, Albert B.:
Maynard, F.
MAHER, Laurence W.:
Menzies, F.; Phillips, Sir P.
MAJOR, K. W.:
Nankervis.
MALEZER, Les:
O'Leary.
MALLORY, Greg:
Macdonald, A.
MALONE, Betty:
Leggett, E. & J.
MARGINSON, Ray:
Mendelsohn.
MARKUS, Andrew:
Kramer.
MARSDEN, Susan:
Perry, Sir F.
MARTIN, A. W.:
Menzies, Sir R.
MASSAM, Katharine:
McGuire, D.
MATHER, Patricia:
McKeon.
MAXWELL, Virginia:
Mackinnon, C.
MAY, Dawn:
Maruff.
MEDCALF, M.:
Laing; Murray, J. D.
MELLOR, Elizabeth J.:
Pendred.
MENGHETTI, Diane:
McConachy; Paterson.
MENZ, Christopher:
Le Grand.
MERRETT, D. T.:
McConnan.
MICHAELIDES, Jean:
Laurantus.
MILLS, Jenny:
Mackinnon, D. de B.

* deceased

MITCHELL, Bruce:
Letters; Pearson.
MOORE, Bruce:
Niland.
MORGAN, John:
Marshall, B.
MORONEY, Tim:
Nolan, F.
MORRIS, Richard:
Nielsen.
MOSELY, Philip:
Masters.
MOSSENSON, David:
Masel.
MULCAHY, Clement:
Lynch, A.
MULVANEY, D. J.:
Massola; O'Brien, J. L.
MURRAY, Robert:
Maltby; Montgomery.

NELSON, H. N.:
McCarthy, J.; Murray, H. L.
NEWELL, Jenny:
McClure Smith.
NOLAN, Judith:
Murphy, R. J.

OAKES, Gerard:
Lee, S.
O'BRIEN, Anne:
Moyes, J. & A.
OGILVIE, June:
Macdonald, A. M.
O'GORMAN Perusco, Anne:
McConnel.
O'GRADY, Desmond:
Nibbi.
O'GRADY, Frank:
McGarry.
O'NEIL, Bernard:
Ling.
O'NEILL, Sally:
Kirsova; Nolan, V. C.
OPPENHEIMER, Jillian:
Nivison.
OPPENHEIMER, Melanie:
McKerihan.
OVERBERG, Henk:
Leddy; Maas.

PAGE, Vilma:
Mullens.
PANG, Mae Anna Quan:
Kent.
PARNABY, Owen:
Mitchell, Sir A.
PATMORE, Greg:
O'Brien, M.
PATRICK, Alison:
Kiddle.
PEEL, Geoffrey W.:
Nilsen, O.
PEGRUM, Roger:
Oliphant.

PERKINS, Elizabeth:
Moore, T.
PERKINS, John:
Lewis, A. C.; Locke; Parry Okeden.
PERRY, Warren:
Lloyd, H.
PETROW, Stefan:
Miller, Dame M.
PHILLIPS, Harry C. J.:
McGibbon.
PHILP, Angela:
Payne.
PIERCE, Peter:
Leonski; McAuley.
PILGER, Alison:
Millington; Oberg.
PIZZEY, Graham:
Morrison, P.
POOLE, Peter N.:
McGuire, J.
POPE, Brian:
McKean.
PORTER, Muriel:
Kerr, E.
POWELL, Alan:
McLaren, R.; Murray, H. J.
POYNTER, J. R.:
Lowe.
PRENTICE, S. A.:
L'Estrange.
PRENTIS, M. D.:
McLucas; Maitland.
PRESLAND, Gary:
Mackay, K.
PREST, Wilfrid:
Oldham, W.
PRICE, Barry:
O'Connell, T.
PROUST, Anthony:
North.

RADBOURNE, Jennifer:
Mahoney.
RADFORD, Robin:
Löhe.
RADI, Heather:
Long, M.
RAFTERY, Judith:
McCutcheon, A. & M.
RAINBIRD, Stephen:
Macqueen.
RAMSLAND, John:
Martin, E.
RASMUSSEN, Carolyn:
Kirkhope; Kisch; Lush, D.
READ, Peter:
Perkins.
REECE, R. H. W.:
McKenna, C.
REFSHAUGE, W. D.:
Metcalfe.
REGAN, Kerry:
McGrath, V.

REID, Maree:
Murphy, I.
REIGER, Kerreen M.:
Meredith.
REYNOLDS, Peter:
Parkes, C.
RICH, Jenny:
Lampungmeiua.
RICH, Joe:
Nickson.
RICHARD, E.*:
Kindler; Nimmo.
RICHARDS, Eric:
McLeay.
RICHMOND, Katy:
Martin, J.
RICHMOND, Mark:
Loewe.
RICKARD, John:
Macartney, K.; Muir; Percy.
RICKARD, Suzanne L. G.:
Mackinnon, D.
RICKARDS, R. W.:
Lions.
RITCHIE, John:
McClure.
RITTER, Leonora:
Melville.
ROBERTS, Jan:
Latour.
ROBERTSON, Peter:
Pawsey.
ROE, J. I.:
McDonald, N.; Newson.
ROE, Michael:
Kessell.
RONALD, Heather B.:
Lort Smith; Maclean, D.
ROSE, P. I.:
Opas.
ROUND, Kerrie:
Lindsay, H.
ROURKE, Arianne:
Mansell.
ROUTH, S. J.:
Phillips, S.
RUSHBROOK, Peter:
Kepert.
RUTLAND, Suzanne D.:
Klein; Newman, H.
RUTLEDGE, Martha:
Kinsella; Kirsova; Louat; Lynton, W. & N.;
Martin, D.; Meagher, J.; Penfold Hyland.

SADLEIR, David:
Lloyd, E.
ST LEON, Mark Valentine:
Lindsay, M.
SARGESON, A. M.:
Lions.
SCHNEIDER, Russell:
McKellar.

* deceased

SCHUMANN, Ruth:
Leworthy.
SEARS, J. S.:
McGuffog.
SELLECK, R. J. W.:
McDonell.
SEMMENS, Kelman:
Mészáros.
SERLE, Geoffrey*:
Keogh; Macartney, F.; McCue; McInnes,
G. & C.; Mack; Mackay, R. R.; Mackenzie,
A.; Medley.
SHANAHAN, Martin:
O'Grady.
SHAW, Bruce:
Nemarluk.
SHEARER, I. A.:
O'Connell, D.
SHEPHERD, Michael*:
Lewis, Sir A.
SHERINGTON, G. E.:
Mackintosh.
SHIELDS, John:
McGuirk; O'Dea, E.
SHORTER, Tresna:
McDonald, Sir R.
SIMMONS, H. L. N.:
Papathanasopoulos.
SIMMS, Roger:
Kornweibel.
SIMPSON, Caroline:
Ogilvy.
SINNAMON, Ian:
Langer.
SISSONS, D. C. S.:
Murakami.
SMIBERT, James:
Newton, Sir W.
SMITH, Bernard:
Marsden.
SMITH, Colin:
Kilvington.
SMITH, David I.:
McCarthy, Sir E.
SMITH, E. J.:
Marriott.
SMITH, I. H.:
Orr, J.
SOLOMON, G. D.:
MacAdie.
SOUTER, Gavin:
Osborne.
SPARKS, Cameron:
Medworth.
SPAULL, Andrew:
Kepert; Madgwick.
SPEARRITT, Peter:
Northfield.
SPREADBOROUGH, E. F.:
Moore, M. S.
STAUNTON, Anthony:
Mills, T.

* deceased

STELLA, Leonie:
Mofflin.
STEPHENS, Alan:
Lukis; Mackinolty; Newton, W. E.
STEVEN, Margaret:
Mauldon.
STEVENSON, Brian F.:
Morris, Sir K.; Nicklin; O'Sullivan,
Sir N.
STEWART, E. D. J.:
Morgan, W.
STODDART, Brian:
Kirkwood.
STONE, Jonathan:
Macintosh.
STRAHAN, Frank:
McBrien; McPherson; Mawby.
STRANO, A.:
Luisini.
STRAUSS, Jennifer:
Learmonth.
STRAWHAN, Peter:
Mills, F.
STURMA, Michael:
O'Keefe.
SULLIVAN, Martin:
Lewis, S.
SULLIVAN, Rodney:
Kern.
SUTTON, R.:
Moten.
SWEENEY, Kay:
Ord.
SWEETING, A. J.:
Long, G; Morris, B.; O'Brien, J. W.
SWIFT, Robert S.:
Maiden; Murphy, J.
SWINDEN, Leonard B.:
Lindell.
SYMES, Jim:
Mingay.
SYNAN, Peter:
Lyons.

TANNER, Howard:
Mansfield, J.
TAPLIN, Harry:
Mackey.
TASSELL, Margaret:
King, H. J.
TATE, Audrey:
Ludowici; McMillan.
TAYLOR, Chris:
Massey.
TAYLOR, Helen:
McLeish.
TAYLOR, Robert I.:
Patten.
TAYLOR, Robyn:
Kohler.
TEMPLETON, Jacqueline:
Morgan, A.
THEARLE, M. John:
Meehan.

THOMAS, James B.:
Philp.
THOMPSON, John R.:
Nan Kivell.
THOMSON, Tess:
Moore, Sir R.
THWAITE, Joy:
Langley, E.
TOWNSLEY, W. A.:
Morris, Sir J.
TREMBATH, Richard:
Philip.
TRIOLI, Cecile:
Laidlaw, D.
TRONSER, Sue:
McDonald, P.
TRUMBLE, Robert:
Lambert, R.
TURNBULL, Malcolm J.:
Munz.
TURNER, J. Neville:
O'Driscoll.
TYQUIN, Michael B.:
MacCallum, W.

VELLA, Maeve:
Nicol, W.
VINES, Patricia C.:
Laidlaw, A.

WALKER, D. R.:
Lambert, E.
WALLACE-CRABBE, Chris:
Maxwell, I.
WALSH, G. P.:
Leahy; McCaughey, S. & Sir D.; Manchee;
Mathews, W. J. O. & W. J.; Mills, A.;
Nothling; O'Loghlen; Pennefather, H.
WARDELL, V. A.*:
Owen, E.
WARREN, James W.:
Marshall, A. J.
WATERHOUSE, D. F.:
Nicholson.
WATERHOUSE, Jill:
McIntosh.
WATERHOUSE, Richard:
McCarten; McGrath, F.
WATERSON, D. B.:
Kinsela.
WEATHERBURN, Hilary:
Nelson.
WEEKS, Phillipa:
Owen, Sir W.
WHARTON, Geoff:
MacKenzie.
WHIFFEN, Neville:
Murphy, R. K.
WHITE, Paul:
Martin, C.
WHITE, Peter:
Lawson, A.

* deceased

WHITE, Richard:
Lea, H.
WHITE, Sally A.:
Maxwell, M.
WHITEHEAD, Sally:
Mockridge.
WHITLAM, E. G.:
Lazzarini.
WHITMORE, Raymond L.:
Kindler; Nimmo.
WILD, Stephen:
Morgan, J.
WILLIAMS, Brian:
McRae, C.
WILLIAMS, Howard:
Latham.
WILLIAMS, John M.:
Menzies, Sir D.
WILLIAMS, Lesley:
Mackerras, I. & M.
WILLIAMS, Paul D.:
Pie.
WILSON, Helen J.:
Paspalis.
WIMBORNE, Brian:
Le Messurier, A. & F.; Murray, P.
WINTER, Barbara:
Long, R.
WINTER, Gillian:
Oldaker.
WOOD, James:
Mitchell, J.
WOODWARD, Judith M.:
Moreno.
WOOKEY, Ann:
Miller, G.
WOOLSTON, Hazel:
McCready.
WRIGHT, Barclay:
Luscombe.
WRIGHT, Don:
Lew.
WRIGHT, R.:
McArthur, Sir G.; Macfarlan, I.; Oldham, T.

YIANNAKIS, John N.:
Mandalis; Manessis; Perivolaris.
YORK, Barry:
Madirazza.
YOUNG, J. McI.:
O'Bryan.
YOUNG, John:
Lampe.
YULE, Valerie:
Morey.

ZAINU'DDIN, A. G. Thomson:
Marshall, A. E.
ZELLING, Howard:
Ligertwood; Mayo.
ZONGOLLOWICZ, Bogumila:
Kleeberg.

A NOTE ON SOME PROCEDURES

Differences of opinion exist among our authors, readers and the editorial board as to whether certain information should normally be included—such as cause of death, burial or cremation details, and value of estate. In this volume our practices have been as follows:

Cause of death: usually included, except in the case of those aged over 70.

Burial/cremation: included when details available.

Value of estate: included where possible for categories such as businessmen, and if the amount is unusually high or low. In recent years, when the practice developed of distributing assets early to avoid estate and probate duties, the sum is not always meaningful; moreover, at times it is impossible to ascertain full details. Hence we have resorted to discretionary use.

Some other procedures require explanation:

Measurements: as the least unsatisfactory solution we have used imperial system measurements (as historically appropriate), followed by the metric equivalent in brackets.

Money: we have retained £ for pounds for references prior to 14 February 1966 (when the conversion rate was A£1 = A$2).

Religion: stated whenever information is available, but there is often no good evidence of actual practice, e.g. the information is confined to marriage and funeral rites.

[q.v.]: the particular volume is given for those included in volumes 1-14, but not for those in this volume. Note that the cross-reference [q.v.] now accompanies the names of all who have separate articles in the *A.D.B.* In volumes 1-6 it was not shown for royal visitors, governors, lieutenant-governors and those Colonial Office officials who were included.

Small capitals: used for relations and others when they are of substantial importance, though not included in their own right; these people are also q.v.'d.

Floruit and 'date of death': for the period 1788 to 1939, the placing of subjects in volumes 1 to 12 was determined by when they flourished; in contrast, volumes 13 to 16 (for the period 1940 to 1980) only include people who died in those years.

CORRIGENDA

Every effort is made to check every detail in every article, but a work of the *A.D.B.*'s size and complexity is bound to contain some errors.

Corrigenda have been published with each volume. A consolidated list, including corrections made after the publication of Volume 12 (1990), forms part of the *Index* (1991). A list of corrigenda compiled since 1996 accompanies Volume 15.

Only corrections are shown; additional information is not included; nor is any reinterpretation attempted. The exception to this procedure occurs when new details about parents, births, marriages and deaths become available.

Documented corrections are welcomed. Additional information, with sources, is also invited, and will be placed in the appropriate files for future use. In both cases, readers should write to:

The General Editor
Australian Dictionary of Biography
Research School of Social Sciences
Australian National University
CANBERRA ACT 0200
Australia.

REFERENCES

The following and other standard works of reference have been widely used, though not usually acknowledged in individual biographies:

Australian Encyclopaedia, 1-2 (Syd, 1925), 1-10 (1958), 1-12 (1983)

Biographical registers for various Australian parliaments: A. W. Martin & P. Wardle *and* H. Radi, P. Spearritt & E. Hinton *and* C. N. Connolly—New South Wales; D. Black & G. Bolton—Western Australia; K. Thomson & G. Serle *and* G. Browne—Victoria; D. B. Waterson *and* D. B. Waterson & J. Arnold—Queensland; H. Coxon, J. Playford & R. Reid—South Australia; S. & B. Bennett—Tasmania; and J. Rydon—Commonwealth

O'M. Creagh and E. M. Humphris (eds), *The V.C. and D.S.O.: a complete record . . .* 1-3 (Lond, 1934)

Dictionary of National Biography (Lond, 1885-1990)

C. A. Hughes and B. D. Graham, *A Handbook of Australian Government and Politics 1890-1964* (Canb, 1968) and *1965-1974* (1977); *Voting for the Australian House of Representatives 1901-1964*, with corrigenda (Canb, 1975), *Queensland Legislative Assembly 1890-1964* (Canb, 1974), *New South Wales . . .* (1975), *Victoria . . .* (1975), and *South Australian, Western Australian and Tasmanian Lower Houses . . .* (1976); D. Black, *An Index to Parliamentary Candidates in Western Australian Elections 1890-1989* (Perth, 1989)

J. Thomas (ed), *South Australians 1836-1885*, 1-2 (Adel, 1990); J. Statton (ed), *Biographical Index of South Australians 1836-1885*, 1-4 (Adel, 1986)

F. Johns, *Johns's Notable Australians* (Melb, 1906), *Fred Johns's Annual* (Lond, 1914); *An Australian Biographical Dictionary* (Melb, 1934); P. Serle, *Dictionary of Australian Biography*, 1-2 (Syd, 1949); D. Carment et al (eds), *Northern Territory Dictionary of Biography*, 1 (Darwin, 1990), 2 (Darwin, 1992); D. Horton (ed), *The Encyclopaedia of Aboriginal Australia*, 1-2 (Canb, 1994)

S. Sadie (ed), *The New Grove Dictionary of Music and Musicians*, 1-20 (Lond, 1980); W. Bebbington (ed), *The Oxford Companion to Australian Music* (Melb, 1997); P. Parsons (ed), *Companion to Theatre in Australia* (Syd, 1995)

W. Moore, *The Story of Australian Art*, 1-2 (Syd, 1934); (Syd, 1980), A. McCulloch, *Encyclopedia of Australian Art* (Lond, 1968), 1-2 (Melb, 1984), revised S. McCulloch (Syd, 1994)

E. M. Miller, *Australian Literature . . . to 1935* (Melb, 1940), extended to 1950 by F. T. Macartney (Syd, 1956); H. M. Green, *A History of Australian Literature*, 1-2 (Syd, 1961, 2nd edn 1971), revised by D. Green (Syd, 1984-85); W. H. Wilde, J. Hooton & B. Andrews, *The Oxford Companion to Australian Literature* (Melb, 1985), 2nd edn (1994)

Who's Who (Lond) and *Who's Who in Australia* (Syd, Melb), present and past edns

Jobson's Year Book of Public Companies (Syd, Melb), present and past edns

ABBREVIATIONS USED IN BIBLIOGRAPHIES

AA	Australian Archives	ed	editor
AAA	Amateur Athletic Association	Edinb	Edinburgh
ABC	Australian Broadcasting Commission/Corporation	edn	edition
		Eng	England
ACT	Australian Capital Territory		
ADB	Australian Dictionary of Biography, Canb	Fr	Father (priest)
Adel	Adelaide		
ADFA	Australian Defence Force Academy, Canb	Geog	Geographical
		Govt	Government
Agr	Agriculture, Agricultural	HA	House of Assembly
AIF	Australian Imperial Force	Hist	History, Historical
AJCP	Australian Joint Copying Project	Hob	Hobart
ALP	Australian Labor Party	HR	House of Representatives
AMPA	Arts, Music and Performing Library, Melb.	HSSA	Historical Society of South Australia
ANU	Australian National University, Canb	Inc	Incorporated
ANUABL	ANU Archives of Business and Labour	Inst	Institute, Institution
		intro	introduction, introduced by
ANZAAS	Australian and New Zealand Association for the Advancement of Science	*J*	*Journal*
		JCU	James Cook University of North Queensland, Townsville
A'sia/n	Australasia/n		
Assn	Association	LA	Legislative Assembly
Aust	Australia/n	LaTL	La Trobe Library, Melb
AWM	Australian War Memorial, Canb	Launc	Launceston
		LC	Legislative Council
Bass L	Adolph Basser Library, Australian Academy of Science, Canb	L	Library
		Lond	London
Bd	Board		
BHP	Broken Hill Proprietary Co. Ltd	*Mag*	*Magazine*
bib	bibliography	MDHC	Melbourne Diocesan Historical Commission (Catholic), Fitzroy
biog	biography, biographical		
BL	J. S. Battye Library of West Australian History, Perth	Melb	Melbourne
		mf	microfilm/s
Brisb	Brisbane	*MJA*	*Medical Journal of Australia*
		ML	Mitchell Library, Syd
c	circa	Mort L	Mortlock Library of South Australiana
CAE	College of Advanced Education		
Canb	Canberra	ms/s	manuscript/s
cat	catalogue	mthly	monthly
CO	Colonial Office, Lond		
co	company	nd	date of publication unknown
C of E	Church of England	NFSA	National Film and Sound Archive, Canb
Com	Commission/er		
comp	compiler	NL	National Library of Australia, Canb
Corp	Corporation/s		
CSIRO	Commonwealth Scientific and Industrial Research Organization	no	number
		np	place of publication unknown
cte	committee	NSW	New South Wales
Cwlth	Commonwealth	NSWA	The Archives Authority of New South Wales, Syd
Dept	Department	NT	Northern Territory
DNB	*Dictionary of National Biography*	NY	New York

ABBREVIATIONS USED IN BIBLIOGRAPHIES

NZ	New Zealand
OL	John Oxley Library, Brisb
p, pp	page, pages
pc	photocopy
PD	*Parliamentary Debates*
PIM	*Pacific Islands Monthly*
PNG	Papua New Guinea
PP	*Parliamentary Papers*
PRGSSA	*Proceedings of the Royal Geographical Society of Australasia (South Australian Branch)*
priv pub	private publication
PRO	Public Record Office
Procs	*Proceedings*
pt	part/s
PTHRA	*Papers and Proceedings of the Tasmanian Historical Research Association*
pub	publication, publication number
Q	*Quarterly*
QA	Queensland State Archives, Brisb
Qld	Queensland
RAHS	Royal Australian Historical Society (Syd)
RG	Registrar General's Office
RGS	Royal Geographical Society
RHSQ	Royal Historical Society of Queensland (Brisb)
RHSV	Royal Historical Society of Victoria (Melb)
RMIT	Royal Melbourne Institute of Technology
Roy	Royal
RWAHS	Royal Western Australian Historical Society (Perth)
1st S	First Session

2nd S	Second Session
SA	South Australia/n
Sel	Select
SLNSW	State Library of New South Wales
SLSA	State Library of South Australia
SLT	State Library of Tasmania
SLV	State Library of Victoria
SMH	*Sydney Morning Herald*
Soc	Society
SRSA	State Records Office, South Australia
supp	supplement
Syd	Sydney
TA	Tasmanian State Archives, Hob
T&CJ	*Australian Town and Country Journal*
Tas	Tasmania/n
Trans	*Transactions*
ts	typescript or transcript
UK	United Kingdom
UNE	University of New England, Armidale
Univ	University
UNSW	University of New South Wales
UPNG	University of Papua New Guinea
US	United States of America
V&P	*Votes and Proceedings*
VHM(J)	*Victorian Historical Magazine (Journal)*
v, vol	volume
Vic	Victoria/n
WA	Western Australia/n
WAA	Western Australian State Archives
*	deceased

K

KEMP, SIR JOHN (WINTERBURN) ROBERT (1883-1955), engineer and public servant, was born on 6 October 1883 at Yendon, Victoria, son of native-born parents John Winterburn Kemp, schoolteacher, and his wife Elizabeth, née McClelland. Young John attended state schools and studied engineering (1903 and 1905-06) at the University of Melbourne. He worked (1905-07) as a draftsman and cadet engineer in the Victorian Department of Public Works before becoming assistant-examiner in the patents branch of the Commonwealth Department of Trade and Customs. An appointment (1910) as shire engineer of Karkarooc Shire, in north-west Victoria, gave him a grounding in local government administration. Three years later he joined the Victorian Country Roads Board. On 23 April 1913 at Christ Church, Hawthorn, he married with Anglican rites Iva Estelle Maude Lilley (d.1952); they were to remain childless.

The C.R.B. was at the forefront of Australian road-making and Kemp's experience earned him the post of foundation chairman (1920) of the Queensland Main Roads Board. In 1925 the board was replaced by the Main Roads Commission, with Kemp as sole commissioner. He initiated a State-wide road-survey and liaised with local government authorities on long-term planning for the construction and maintenance of declared 'main' roads.

From the outset Kemp developed a reputation among his staff for counting 'the shekels'. Aware of the need to balance funds with objectives, he gave priority to the length of roads over their width, and was not averse to private or toll roads if they added miles to the system. From 1923 the Commonwealth government granted money to the States for road-making. Commonwealth-State road-funding then expanded to encompass 'development' and 'tourist' roads. Kemp proved a persuasive advocate for continued Federal financial support and represented Queensland at Commonwealth-State discussions, such as the 1926 Federal Aid (Roads) conference of State ministers and their chief engineers. Throughout the 1920s and 1930s, when horses provided most of the work-power, he was a familiar sight to road-gangs during his tours of inspection, often conducted in the knee-deep mud of Central Queensland's black-soil plains.

Kemp's persistent efforts to improve professional standards led to increasing numbers of Main Roads engineers being employed by local councils. He encouraged his staff to study for formal qualifications at the Central Technical College and, after 1930, at the University of Queensland where he assisted in developing the curriculum for the faculty of engineering. That year he became a board-member of the Professional Engineers of Queensland. He was vice-chairman (1925) and chairman (1927) of the Brisbane division of the Institution of Engineers, Australia, and a councillor (1923-34), vice-president (1928-30) and president (1931-32) of the national body. Unusually for public servants of that time, he delivered numerous papers at specialist and public forums. In 1938 he was the Australian delegate to the international road congress in The Hague, and made an extensive tour of Europe and the United States of America to observe new road technology.

With his knowledge of infrastructure requirements, transport economics and local conditions, Kemp became the Queensland government's chief development adviser. He chaired (1935-36) the royal commission on electricity and was a member (1936-37) of the royal commission on transport. Chairman (1932-38) of the industry, mining and works committee of the State Employment Council (which assessed development projects for unemployment relief), he headed the Stanley River Works Board, formed to build Somerset Dam, and the Bridge Board, on which his drive and enthusiasm contributed to the early completion (1940) of Brisbane's (J.D.) Story [q.v.12] Bridge. From 1939 he held office as Queensland's co-ordinator-general of works.

In 1942 Kemp became deputy director-general of allied works, Queensland, and supervised hundreds of defence projects, ranging from airstrips to naval bases. To meet military deadlines, he overcame shortages of manpower and equipment, and the logistical problems of moving plant and workers throughout Queensland. During construction of the Inland Defence Road (Ipswich to Charters Towers) and the road from Mount Isa to Tennant Creek, Northern Territory, he showed considerable tact in dealing with allied forces representatives who did not comprehend the difficulties involved. Begun in August 1942, the Brisbane Graving Dock was completed in twenty-two months, despite wartime shortages.

Kemp was awarded the W. C. Kernot [q.v.5] medal (1932) by the University of Melbourne and the (Sir) Peter Nicol Russell [q.v.6] medal (1942) by the Institution of Engineers. As chairman (1937-46) of the Works Board, he was involved in building the University of Queensland at St Lucia. A member (1927-55) of the university's senate, he received the honorary degree of master of engineering in 1949, the year he retired as Main Roads commissioner. In 1951 he was knighted. Held in awe for his achievements, Sir John was never aloof and retained the respect of colleagues and staff. His work was his life. With little leisure time, he found relaxation in reading; after World War II he took up golf.

At the Presbyterian Church, Armadale, Melbourne, on 23 October 1954 Kemp married 56-year-old Annie Janet Tulloch, his former secretary. Survived by his wife, he died on 28 February 1955 in Brisbane and was cremated. In the eulogy given at his funeral service in St John's Anglican Cathedral, Archbishop (Sir) Reginald Halse [q.v.14] described Kemp as 'a man of very great gifts' and 'extraordinary versatility' who was 'a national benefactor'.

C. Lack (comp), *Three Decades of Queensland Political History, 1929-1960* (Brisb, 1962); R. L. Whitmore (ed), *Eminent Queensland Engineers* (Brisb, 1984); K. Cohen, *Australia Remembers: The Main Roads Commission Construction Works during World War Two, Cloncurry District* (Brisb, 1995); Qld Main Roads Bd, *Annual Report*, 1922; Qld Main Roads Com, *Annual Report*, 1945; *J of the Inst of Engineers, Aust*, 27, no 3, 1955; *Courier-Mail*, 1, 3 Mar 1955; A. J. Wheeler, To be a Superman (M.Pub.Ad. thesis, Dept of Government, Univ Qld, 1975); J. E. England, Memoirs, ts, 1970, *and* F. S. Parkes, Past Experiences—No.1, ts, nd (Qld Main Roads Com, Brisb); J. R. Kemp papers (held at Inst of Engineers, Canb, *and* Qld Transport Dept Archives and Heritage Unit, Brisb).   KAY COHEN

KENNEDY, ERIC THOMSON (1897-1974), journalist and newspaper executive, was born on 1 March 1897 at Albury, New South Wales, elder son of native-born parents James Kennedy, drover, and his wife Charlotte, née Thompson. Educated at country schools and—after his parents separated—in Sydney, Eric was employed as a clerk. On 8 September 1915 he enlisted in the Australian Imperial Force. He served on the Western Front with the 5th Field Artillery Brigade (1916-18) and at General Headquarters (1918-19), rose to temporary staff sergeant (1918), was mentioned in dispatches and was awarded the Meritorious Service Medal (1919).

Discharged in Sydney on 18 January 1920, Kennedy joined the *Sunday Times* as a junior reporter before moving to the *Evening News* in 1921. At St Paul's Anglican Church, Rose Bay, on 21 January 1922 he married Gwendolen Bartley Hughes. In 1924 he accepted an advertising post in Melbourne with the *Evening Sun*. He enjoyed combining his journalistic experience with advertising, and when the *Evening Sun* failed in April 1925 he

returned to Sydney as advertising representative and motor editor for Sir Hugh Denison's [q.v.8] *Sun*. In 1934 Sir Keith Murdoch [q.v.10] attracted Kennedy back to Melbourne as assistant general manager of the *Herald*. Appointed advertising-manager of Denison's Associated Newspapers Ltd in 1937, Kennedy was welcomed back to Sydney with a dinner. His *Herald* colleagues telegraphed: 'We have lost a good bloke and you have got him. Treat him well. They are scarce'.

The good bloke became chief executive-officer of Associated Newspapers in 1942 and managed the group until 1953. 'E.K.' extended his extraordinarily wide range of friends and contacts, who kept him well-informed on local and national affairs. He and his wife were part of the Sydney social scene. A confident, self-made man, physically imposing, he was cheerful and fit, and enjoyed golf, tennis and swimming. Tolerant, readily offering sound counsel, he was also a witty companion and conversationalist.

Kennedy was chairman (1942-46) of the Audit Bureau of Circulations, a member (1942-45) of the Commonwealth's Press Censorship Advisory Committee, a director (1942-53) of Australian Associated Press Pty Ltd and an executive-member (1950-51) of the Commonwealth Jubilee Celebrations Council. He was president (1947-49) of the Australian Newspaper Proprietors' Association, having been warmly nominated by R. A. G. Henderson, general manager of John Fairfax & Sons [qq.v.4,8] Pty Ltd, who publicly praised his 'capacity and wisdom'. But in 1953, following the Fairfax takeover of Associated Newspapers, Henderson decided there was no room either for Kennedy's capacity or his wisdom.

Using his generous payout to develop a successful public relations consultancy, Kennedy remained active—president (1960-66) of the Psychiatric Rehabilitation Association, vice-chairman (1963-74) of St Luke's Hospital board, a committee-member of the Australian-American Association, and a member of the Australian, American National and Australian Golf clubs. He died on 5 January 1974 while playing golf at Elanora Country Club and was cremated; his wife and daughter survived him. An old colleague Jim Macdougall wrote in his *Daily Mirror* column, 'In a savagely competitive world of newspapers, Eric Kennedy had too much humanity, too much kindness'.

Newspaper News (Syd), 10 Dec 1947; *SMH*, 28 Aug 1942, 21 Nov 1947, 3 June 1950, 9 Jan 1974; *Daily Mirror* (Syd), 7 Jan 1974; *Wentworth Courier*, 16 Jan 1974; Kennedy papers (ML); information from Mrs J. Reed, Kensington, and Mr H. Stevens, Mosman, Syd; personal information.

STUART INDER

KENNEDY, FREDA EVELYN; *see* GIBSON

KENNEDY, SIR JAMES ARTHUR (1882-1954), accountant, secretary and politician, was born on 5 February 1882 at Parkville, Melbourne, youngest of six children of James Kennedy (d.1885), a builder from Scotland, and his English-born wife Emma, née Page. From Errol Street State School, North Melbourne, Jim won a scholarship to Parkville Grammar School; from there he won another to Scotch College. Growing up opposite Royal Park, he spent much of his time playing football and cricket. He and his brother Ted were 'dashing' wingers with both the Essendon and Carlton clubs in the Victorian Football League: Jim kicked 30 goals in 41 games in 1901 and 1905-07, while Ted was a member of three successive Carlton premiership sides in 1906-08. A 'forceful bat' for the Carlton Cricket Club, Jim was later president of the Brighton Cricket Club and a trustee (1945) of the Melbourne Cricket Ground.

On leaving Scotch in 1897, Jim Kennedy was employed by the British Australasian Tobacco Co. Ltd. He gained accountancy qualifications and in 1903 joined the Melbourne Electric Supply Co. On 15 October 1913 at the Congregational Church, Carlton, he married a costumier Annie Taylor Biggins. A fellow of the Commonwealth Institute of Accountants and of the Chartered Institute of Secretaries, he became chief accountant of the M.E.S.C. in 1920 and secretary in 1927; he also served as secretary of the company's subsidiary, the Melbourne Investment Trust. Although the M.E.S.C.'s enterprises were taken over by the State Electricity Commission in 1930, Kennedy continued as secretary of the company and the trust, presiding over their gradual liquidation. In 1940 he established a public accountancy practice in Collins Street.

Kennedy was a member (1928-45) of Brighton City Council and mayor in 1932-33. He did 'good work' as chairman of the council's finance committee and as Brighton's representative on the Municipal Association. In addition, he was treasurer of Brighton Community Hospital. As mayor in a Depression year, he cancelled the annual ball, using the money saved to buy shoes for children of the unemployed.

In 1937, representing the United Australia Party, Kennedy was elected to the Legislative Council for the province of Higinbotham and later led his party in the Upper House. He held the portfolios of transport and mines in the Dunstan-Hollway [qq.v.8,14] coalition of 1943-45. Commissioner of public works in Hollway's ministries of 1947-50, he was minister of electrical undertakings and of mines in December 1948. He was knighted in 1950.

As a minister Kennedy's major achievement reflected his long involvement with local government. A keen advocate of centralized town planning, he wanted to expand the powers of the Melbourne and Metropolitan Board of Works to make it the city's planning authority. His intentions were embodied in the Town and Country (Metropolitan Area) Act (1949). Believing in co-operative housing societies, he 'campaigned ceaselessly' for their extension, acted as adviser and auditor to many societies, introduced the 1944 co-operative housing societies bill to the Upper House and became chairman of the Deakin Co-operative Housing Society which was established to assist immigrants in particular.

Christianity was 'the first and dominant loyalty' of Kennedy's life. He was a Sunday School teacher (from 1902), secretary (from 1916) of the Brighton Congregational Church, vice-president of the Sunday Christian Observance Council and a strict teetotaller. Treasurer of the Victorian Congregational Union for over twenty years, he was its chairman in 1940-41. Kennedy took a strong interest in the Church's youth and welfare work, chairing a young people's committee and working for the establishment of the Metropolitan Missions of the Congregational Union and the Tanderra Home for the Aged.

Sir James was committed to the ideals of service and duty. Until the last weeks of his life he never missed a parliamentary sitting and never left before the day's business was completed. Some 5 ft 8 ins (173 cm) tall, stocky and broad-shouldered, he was genial and even-tempered. He and his wife were enthusiastic ballroom dancers. Despite his busy workload, his daughters recalled an especially happy family life and a 'very nice, kind Dad'. He read widely, his tastes ranging from Gibbon to Zane Grey. Dickens, Scott, Thackeray and Dumas were his favourite authors. Survived by his two daughters, Kennedy died on 20 November 1954 at Brighton and was buried in Melbourne general cemetery. In 1957 a memorial window was unveiled in the Brighton Congregational Church.

J. S. Gawler, *A Roof Over My Head* (Syd, 1963); *PD* (Vic), 23 Nov 1954, p 1965; *Listener In*, 26 June-2 July 1943; *Southern Congregationalist*, Dec 1954; *Herald* (Melb), 18 Sept 1932, 25 Nov 1954; *Age* (Melb), 30 Apr 1940, 22 Nov 1954; information from Mrs M. Mossman, Camberwell, and Mrs N. Dinsmore, Brighton, Melb.   GEOFF BROWNE

KENNY, JAMES DENIS (1906-1967), glassworker and trade union official, was born on 27 November 1906 at Waterloo, Sydney, fourth child of native-born parents James Kenny, wagon driver, and his wife Margaret, née Rowley. Educated at the Patrician Brothers' School, Glebe, 14-year-old James started work in a felt-hat enterprise. At the Church of Our Lady of Mount Carmel, Waterloo, on 8 November 1926 he married 19-year-old Bessy May Kenny with Catholic rites. About 1928 he joined the Australian Glass Workers' Union; he was successively State secretary (1936-47), treasurer, federal secretary and State president (1950-67).

A delegate to the Labor Council of New South Wales in the 1930s, he aligned himself to the group centred on R. A. King [q.v.]. Kenny was elected vice-president (1945), president (1946) and, a few months later, assistant-secretary (re-elected until 1958). He began to wield significant influence and was credited by B. A. Santamaria in his autobiography, *Against The Tide* (Melbourne, 1981), with being a major force supporting the industrial groups in the mid-1940s. Kenny ensured that no union affiliated with the Australian Labor Party in New South Wales switched its allegiance to the Democratic Labor Party—unlike in Victoria.

Despite his anti-communist beliefs—he had denounced the miners' leadership for the 1949 coal strikes—Kenny opposed the Menzies [q.v.] government's proposal to ban the Communist Party of Australia. Although he regularly broadcast on radio-station 2KY, he gained most of his popularity from industrial campaigns and from his involvement in disputes in the metal, steel, building, construction and coal industries. In the early 1950s he cautiously advocated incentive payments in Australian industry, a measure fiercely opposed by many sections of the labour movement.

Kenny was a member (from 1948) of the Legislative Council, an executive-member (1951-57) and vice-president (1957-67) of the Australasian Council of Trade Unions, and junior vice-president (c.1952-57) of the federal executive of the A.L.P. He served on the Commonwealth Immigration Advisory Council, the council of the University of New South Wales, the Technical Education Advisory Council, the Sydney Opera House and Sydney Cricket Ground trusts, and the Commonwealth Ministry of Labour Advisory Council. Widely travelled, he was a delegate to conferences of the International Labor Organization, held in Geneva (1954 and 1964), the New Zealand Federation of Labour (1956 and 1962) and, controversially, the All-China Federation of Trade Unions, Peking (Beijing, 1957).

In 1958 Kenny succeeded King as secretary of the Labor Council. His main achievement was to promote better industrial conditions, including long-service leave, workers' compensation and associated benefits. He was involved in public protests against the régime in South Africa, campaigns for higher wages for Aboriginal workers, and peace and disarmament rallies. The American vice-president Richard Nixon had visited him in October 1953 at his cramped offices in the Trades Hall. In the 1960s Kenny commissioned the purchase of land and raised funds for the development of a new Labor Council building in Sussex Street. He was general manager (from 1960) of 2KY, and a director of Television Corporation Ltd (forging close relationships with the Packer [q.v.] family) and of Air Sales Broadcasting Co. Pty Ltd (radio 2HD, Newcastle).

An appealing leader, Kenny had the common touch and won grudging respect from his most bitter opponents. He died of coronary vascular disease on 12 October 1967 at his Maroubra home and was buried in Waverley cemetery. His wife survived him, as did their son Alan who worked (1962-88) at the Labor Council as a property manager.

R. Markey, *In Case of Oppression* (Syd, 1994); *PD* (NSW), 12 Oct 1967, p 2342; Labor Council of NSW, *Yearly Report*, 1922-23, *and* Minutes, 23 Nov 1922, 23 Jan 1930 (ML); *ACTU Bulletin*, May 1957, p 37, July-Dec 1967, p 3; *SMH*, 16 Jan 1958, 13 Oct 1967; *Sun-Herald*, 28 Feb 1960.   MICHAEL EASSON

KENT, HERBERT WADE (1877-1952), collector of Chinese art, was born on 28 September 1877 at South Yarra, Melbourne, son of Robert George Kent, a civil servant from England, and his Victorian-born wife Fanny Isabel, née Wade. Herbert was educated (1893-97) at Melbourne Church of England Grammar School. Stimulated by the decorative Chinese export wares in his family's home, he developed an interest in Chinese art and a wish to live in the East. He worked for shipping companies, from 1898 to 1904 with Orient Steam Navigation Co. in Melbourne and London, and from 1905 to 1936 with Butterfield & Swire in China and Japan. On 8 January 1913 at St John's Anglican Church, Toorak, he married Irene Lenore Simson.

While in the East, Kent developed an understanding of Chinese aesthetics. With an impeccable eye, he formed a collection of ceramics, and a few items of archaic bronze, jade, lacquer, painting and furniture. The outstanding pieces were early ceramics, particularly those of the T'ang (A.D.618-907) and Sung (Song) (A.D.960-1279) dynasties, which reflected his taste for pure form and colour, and his love of horses.

Returning to Melbourne in 1937, Kent was eager to share his passion for Chinese art, which he considered one of the greatest expressions of the human mind and imagination. With the support of the trustees of the National Gallery of Victoria he arranged an exhibition of his collection of 129 objects. It generated interest and excitement, and was hailed by the art critic Basil Burdett [q.v.7] as a stimulating and important exhibition. Moved by public enthusiasm, the Kents presented their collection to the N.G.V. where it became the nucleus of the gallery's holdings of Chinese art. Kent was proud that his collection represented 'Chinese taste' and contained 'no specimen made specially for the export trade'.

In 1938 Kent became a trustee of the gallery and its first curator of Oriental art. Having secured the support of the Felton [q.v.4] Bequests' Committee to travel to London to purchase works of art, he acquired an excellent range of Chinese ceramics and established useful contacts. Other overseas collectors and dealers, inspired by Kent's enthusiasm, donated gifts which the N.G.V. exhibited in March 1939. The Society of Artists, Sydney, awarded Kent its medal in 1943 in recognition of his services to Australian art; in 1948 the gallery housing Oriental art at the N.G.V. was renamed in his honour.

Devoted to his collection, Kent described his other hobbies as golf and riding; he lived at Toorak and belonged to the Melbourne Club. He made two further trips to England, the last in May 1951. At the end of that year he retired as treasurer of the council of trustees due to ill health. Survived by his wife and daughter, he died on 7 April 1952 at Preston and was cremated. In 1961 his wife presented his favourite piece, a Sung dynasty white vase, to the gallery.

L. B. Cox, *The National Gallery of Victoria, 1861 to 1968* (Melb, 1970); *Trans of the Oriental Ceramic Soc*, 39, 1971-73, p 30; *Apollo*, 97, Mar 1973, p 217; *Art in Aust*, 15 Nov 1937; National Gallery of Vic Archives.   MAE ANNA QUAN PANG

KENT HUGHES, ELLEN MARY (1893-1979), medical practitioner and alderman, was born on 29 August 1893 at Fitzroy, Melbourne, eldest of seven children of Wilfred Kent Hughes, a Victorian-born surgeon, and his wife Clementina Jane, née Rankin (d.1916), a nurse from England. Ellen was a niece of Rev. Ernest Selwyn Hughes [q.v.9], and a sister of (Sir) Wilfrid Kent Hughes and Gwenda Lloyd [qq.v.]. She attended Ruyton Girls' School, Kew, then remained at home in 1912 until her mother was discharged from a tuberculosis sanatorium. In the following year Ellen entered Trinity College Hostel, University of Melbourne (M.B., B.S., 1917). On 31 July 1917 at St Monica's Catholic Pres-

bytery, Footscray, she married Paul René Loubet, a divorcee from France and a medical-assistant at the Children's Hospital, Melbourne. Widowed three months later, Ellen bore Paul's son. Colleagues found her temporary work at the Queen Victoria Memorial Hospital for Women and Children; they also found her a nanny, Alice Pickup, who remained an esteemed member of Ellen's household for fifty-four years.

In 1918 Dr Kent Hughes, as she was known professionally, was appointed resident medical officer at the Hospital for Sick Children, Brisbane, on a salary of £50 a year. Mother and baby lived in quarters, with Alice nearby. One year later Ellen accepted a locum tenency at Mitchell at a time when the State was gripped by drought and the pneumonic influenza epidemic. There, on 26 August 1920, at All Saints Anglican Church she married Francis Garde Wesley Wilson (d.1970), a returned soldier and auctioneer; they were to have a son and three daughters. In 1921 the Wilsons went to Kingaroy where Mrs Wilson was elected (1923) to the shire council.

In 1928 the family moved to Armidale, New South Wales. With extraordinary energy, 'a co-operative husband' and Alice ('Nanny'), Dr Kent Hughes combined medical practice (with Roger Mallam) and community service. She 'never found that being a woman had the slightest adverse effect' on her career. Honorary paediatrician at the Armidale and New England Hospital, government medical officer and a justice of the peace, she was 'tireless in her ministrations', 'firm in her admonitions' and resolute in answering calls. She published two articles in the *Medical Journal of Australia*, 'Observations on Congenital Syphilis' (1919) and 'The Role of the Private Practitioner in Preventive Medicine' (1967).

Aboriginal women had nursed her Hughes grandmother near Armidale after the loss of her first child. Ellen felt a long-standing debt to their people. One of her chief cares was the health of the local Aboriginal community, especially the mothers and children. Although she was criticized for her moral and maternalistic views, she retained wide respect and affection: her twinkling eyes and wide smile softened her brusque manner. She worshipped for fifty years at St Peter's Cathedral and was a member of its parish council. A devout Anglo-Catholic, she donated Eucharistic vestments to St Mary's Church and invited home a succession of curates to give them 'the once over'!

As Alderman Wilson she served (1937-68) on the Armidale City Council (deputy-mayor 1963-64); she pursued such causes as urban beautification and housing for Aborigines with characteristic persistence, especially if she sensed male indifference. In 1968 she was appointed M.B.E. Dr Kent Hughes qualified

5

as a fellow of the Royal Australian College of General Practitioners in 1971 and was granted the freedom of the city of Armidale in 1975. Her physician ordered her to retire in 1977. Survived by her five children, she died on 16 May 1979 at Armidale and was cremated with Anglican rites. In 1990 her residence was opened as Kent House, a community centre.

F. Howard, *Kent Hughes* (Melb, 1972); L. M. Hellstedt (ed), *Women Physicians of the World* (Washington, 1978); M. A. Franklin, *Assimilation in Action* (Armidale, NSW, 1995); *Queenslander*, 28 July, 4 Aug 1923; *SMH*, 10, 16 Jan 1957; *Armidale Express*, 3 Jan 1968, 16 Nov 1970, 22 Aug 1975, 16, 18 May 1979; information from Mrs J. Crew, Mrs P. Wilson and Dr H. Royle, Armidale, NSW.

L. A. GILBERT

KENT HUGHES, SIR WILFRID SELWYN (1895-1970), soldier and politician, was born on 12 June 1895 in East Melbourne, second of seven children of Wilfred Kent Hughes, a Victorian-born surgeon, and his English-born wife Clementina Jane, née Rankin (d.1916). Ellen Kent Hughes and Gwenda Lloyd [qq.v.] were his sisters. Billy attended Trinity Grammar School until the age of 13 when he won a scholarship to Melbourne Church of England Grammar School. The brightest boy of his year, he became school captain, an officer in the cadets, and captain of athletics and football.

On 17 August 1914 he enlisted in the Australian Imperial Force and was posted to the 7th Battalion. In Egypt, Sergeant Kent Hughes learned that he had won a Rhodes scholarship. Commissioned in April 1915, he transferred to the headquarters of the 3rd Light Horse Brigade, commanded by his uncle F. G. Hughes. Billy was to serve at Gallipoli, and in the Sinai, Palestine and Syria. In 1917 he won the Military Cross for his work as staff captain. He was promoted major and appointed deputy adjutant and quartermaster general, Australian Mounted Division. Mentioned in dispatches four times, he wrote his first book, *Modern Crusaders* (Melbourne, 1918), describing the exploits of the Light Horse.

At war's end, Kent Hughes entered Christ Church, Oxford (B.A., 1922). He threw himself into undergraduate life, represented Australia in the 400-m hurdles at the 1920 Olympic Games at Antwerp, Belgium, and pursued a well-born American girl Edith Kerr, nearly seven years his junior, whom he married on 3 February 1923 at the 1st Congregational Church, Montclair, New Jersey, United States of America.

In April 1923 Kent Hughes returned to Australia and joined his father's publishing firm. Standing for the Legislative Assembly as a Progressive Nationalist, he won the seat of Kew in 1927; he was to retain it until 1949. He was appointed secretary to Sir William McPherson's [q.v.10] cabinet in November 1928 but, with his friend (Sir) Robert Menzies [q.v.], resigned in July 1929. Rebels against the conservative establishment and the mediocrity of State politics, in 1930 Kent Hughes and Menzies formed the Young Nationalist Organisation which became a major force in Victorian non-Labor politics.

Kent Hughes held various portfolios in the United Australia Party-Country Party ministry of 1932-35, among them railways, labour and transport; his responsibilities also included unemployment relief. For arranging the Duke of Gloucester's [q.v.14] tour, he was appointed M.V.O. in 1934. In November 1933 Kent Hughes had published four articles in the Melbourne *Herald* explaining why he had become 'a Fascist—without a shirt'! Spurning 'domineering dictators, picturesque uniforms, and Roman salutes', he admired fascism as 'the spirit of the age' and, with its emphasis on economic planning, as the 'half-way house' between *laissez faire* and socialism.

In August 1939 he resigned as deputy-leader of the Opposition and was appointed major in the Militia. He was seconded to the A.I.F. in June 1940 and was D.A. & Q.M.G. of the 8th Division in Malaya by April 1941. Colonel Kent Hughes was captured at the fall of Singapore in February 1942 and spent six months at Changi before being transferred to Formosa (Taiwan) and later to Manchuria. Released in August 1945, and appointed O.B.E. (1947) for his 'inspiration' to all ranks during his incarceration, he brought home a recurring amoebic complaint, an enduring interest in Asia, and a long poem written in captivity which was published as *Slaves of the Samurai* (Melbourne, 1946).

Tall, lean, his hair and moustache turning grey, Kent Hughes joined the recently formed Liberal Party and became deputy-premier to Tom Hollway [q.v.14] in 1948. In the following year he was elected to the House of Representatives for the seat of Chisholm; he was to hold it until his death. Menzies elevated Kent Hughes to the ministry in May 1951, handing him the portfolios of the interior and of works and housing. But the man who liked to get things done was given too much to do. Frustrated and outspoken, he upset important people by criticizing 'masses of red tape, inefficiency and bumbledom', and by telling Canberra's voters, as their 'uncrowned king', that they should rise above 'parish pump' politics. Privately, he complained of being the 'junior office boy' who dealt with hedge-cutting and the installation of water meters.

One public duty gave him the greatest satisfaction. As chairman (from 1951) of the organizing committee, he overcame the squabbling which threatened the removal of the 1956 Olympic Games from Melbourne and presided over their success. Offered a knighthood, he accepted a K.B.E. (1957) only after assurances that other committee-members would receive awards.

After the 1955 elections Menzies had dropped Kent Hughes from the ministry, citing administrative inefficiency and the need to bring in new men. Perhaps he was also re-acting to public comments that Kent Hughes had made in Tokyo criticizing government foreign policy. Billy was now unmuzzled, and a potential trouble-maker. Restrained only by his sense of propriety, and by an idiosyncratic view of party loyalty, he became a prophet of gloom on the communist threat in Asia and Africa; he accused Menzies of knowing nothing about the 'Far East' and caring less; and he attacked the government's de-ficiencies in preparing Australia's defences. Kent Hughes relished chairing (1956-61) the Joint Parliamentary Committee on Foreign Affairs and, from 1960, regularly issued, and paid for, some three hundred copies of his own 'Intelligence Bulletin' to fellow par-liamentarians and selected Liberal Party branches. Frequent trips to London, Oxford, Washington and Asia, and his close contacts with Thai and Taiwanese leaders, meant that he was often better informed than the min-isters he interrogated. Billy also managed to irritate his party chieftains by supporting the Netherlands' retention of West Irian, calling for the removal of 'White' from Australia's immigration policy, and attacking Britain's Labour government for imposing economic sanctions against Rhodesia while trading with communist countries.

Mostly, he walked alone, neither seeking nor attracting a following among the back-bench conservatives and malcontents. Looking and sounding like a survival of an earlier age, when Melbourne Grammar boys rushed to serve king and country, he sat erect on his mount on Anzac Day in 1968 wearing the uniform of the Light Horse. Friends and political opponents recognized in the man a dignity, integrity, vitality and kindliness. Those closest also knew that behind the formal exterior was a devotion to family, a capacity to talk to anyone, and a dry sense of humour which dictated hiding the best whisky when visited by his sister Gwenda, the 'family communist'.

Sir Wilfrid retained his involvement in sport, and stayed fit by skiing, tramping in Gippsland and jog-trotting around Lake Burley Griffin. Survived by his wife and three daughters, he died on 31 July 1970 at Kew; he was accorded a state funeral and was cre-mated with Anglican rites. His estate was sworn for probate at $107 670. Three portraits are held privately.

F. Howard, *Kent Hughes* (Melb, 1972); P. Hasluck, *The Chance of Politics*, N. Hasluck ed and intro (Melb, 1997); Kent Hughes *and* Menzies *and* Liberal Party of Aust papers (NL); information from Mrs J. Derham, and Mrs M. and Mr H. A. Sasse, Kew, Melb.   I. R. HANCOCK

KEOGH, ESMOND VENNER ('BILL') (1895-1970), soldier, medical scientist and administrator, was born on 2 November 1895 at Malvern, Melbourne, third of four children of Esmond Joseph Keogh, financial agent, and his wife Helen Beatrice, née Moore, both Victorian born. The father's estate agency foundered, the parents separated about 1900 and the father worked as a bush labourer in Western Australia. Supporting the family, Helen found congenial employment looking after four orphaned children. Esmond and his brother lived for a time with an uncle, then with their mother again. Helen was deter-mined that her children should have access to higher education. Esmond attended a Catholic parish school before becoming a boarder at the Sisters of Mercy school at Mornington. He was later sent to St Stanislaus' College, Bathurst, New South Wales, where he dis-covered an interest in art and music.

To the consternation of the wider Keogh family, Esmond won a scholarship to Mel-bourne Church of England Grammar School and enrolled in 1910, a shy, quiet Catholic boy. His academic performance was mediocre and the school left little mark on him. He had fallen under the guidance of his beloved elder sister Lesbia [q.v.9 Harford], a law student and poet who introduced him to Frederick Sinclaire's [q.v.11] Free Religious Fellowship and the Victorian Socialist Party. By 1914 he was calling himself a Unitarian and was deeply concerned about inequality and social justice. He had uncertainly enrolled in agricultural science at the University of Melbourne. On 13 November, just 19, he enlisted in the Australian Imperial Force and was posted to the 3rd Light Horse Field Ambulance.

Keogh embarked for Egypt on 2 February 1915. At Heliopolis he nursed some of the first British casualties following the Gallipoli land-ings. From late May to late June his unit was employed at Anzac as a labour force before retiring to Lemnos. Early in August they re-turned to Anzac and were immediately en-gaged in the chaotic rescue of casualties from the 4th Brigade, A.I.F. On 10 November the 3rd L.H.F.A. was withdrawn to Lemnos for rest, then to Egypt on Boxing Day. After three months at Heliopolis, Keogh returned to Melbourne, claiming to be a medical student. He rejected his former semi-pacifist outlook and was posted to No.9 Company of the 3rd [Division] Australian Machine Gun Battalion. In August 1916 he sailed for England.

From then on 'Es' was known to his digger mates and—family apart—to his adult associates as 'Bill' Keogh. He was sent to the Western Front in November and in 1917 took part in the battle of Messines, Belgium (while attached to the 9th Field Ambulance), and in the advances in the Ypres salient. Promoted temporary corporal, he was wounded in his right hand on 12 October and spent a month in hospital in England. His Military Medal was gazetted in February 1918. Returning to his unit in April, he was promoted temporary sergeant in July and took part in the victorious advance from August (including the capture of Mont St Quentin, France). On 29 September at Quennemont Farm he led a section without an officer, setting an 'example of the highest courage and devotion to duty', and was awarded the Distinguished Conduct Medal. Embarking for home in March 1919, he was discharged on 9 July. His sister Estelle had served in Queen Alexandra's Military Nursing Service and was awarded the Royal Red Cross (1918).

Keogh rarely spoke of his war experiences, once remarking that Martin Boyd [q.v.13] had written all that needed to be said about the prolongation of the war and the 'brutes in authority' who kept 'the blood-lust simmering'. He was emotionally and nervously drained, and for more than a year lived aimlessly on the fringe of bohemia, taking up his left-wing friends again, who now included Guido Baracchi [q.v.13]. Bill spent most of 1921 working on a dairy-farm which his alcoholic father briefly held as a soldier settler, six miles from Maffra, Gippsland. In 1922 he began the medical degree at the University of Melbourne (M.B., B.S., 1927). He struggled through the first three years, but graduated with honours. Inspired by Professor (Sir) Peter MacCallum [q.v.], he was largely responsible for a masterly student report on desirable reforms in the curriculum, including much greater attention to pathology. A month before his finals, Lesbia had died. His mother, with whom he usually lived, was his constant charge until her death in 1951.

Deciding that development of medical research, especially graduate training in microbiology, biochemistry and bacteriology, was all-important, Keogh joined the Commonwealth Serum Laboratories, Parkville, in May 1928 and became a pathologist 'training at the bench'. Until 1934, however, he spent most of his time working as a relieving officer at interstate stations. Thus at Kalgoorlie, Western Australia, and Bendigo, Victoria, he was faced with the problem of miners' phthisis and other matters of public health. He developed a sense of mission, retaining his political sympathies but sceptical of any political nostrum. Although he was to remain an atheist, his career would be based on the teachings of Christianity, with public medicine as his chosen practical means of service.

Late in 1935 Keogh established his own unit in the C.S.L. and was seconded part time to the Walter and Eliza Hall [qq.v.9] Institute to work on viruses. A firm friendship grew with the director Charles Kellaway [q.v.9] whose deputy (Sir) Macfarlane Burnet sensed a rival. In 1936-41 Keogh published eighteen papers on viruses, two in collaboration with Burnet.

During World War II, Burnet later remarked, Keogh 'went up like a rocket'. On the war's outbreak he was attending medical conferences in the United States of America. He made many valuable contacts, while revelling in galleries, concerts and the theatre; he also formed friendships with Katharine Hepburn and John Steinbeck. Hurrying home, he was gazetted major in the Australian Army Medical Corps on 13 October and in November was appointed in charge of pathology in the 2nd/2nd Australian General Hospital, which arrived in the Middle East in April 1940. Disease was the immediate problem: a generation of modern Australian pathologists was bred in the hospitals there. Keogh and two others wrote an important paper identifying the type of local dysentery. With R. R. Andrew and (Sir) Ian Wood he attended a course on tropical medicine given by Professor Saul Adler, a fellow of the Royal Society, which had effects of the utmost importance. In support of Major General (Sir) Samuel Burston, to whom he was in practice 'first assistant', and (Sir) Neil Fairley [qq.v.13,14], he contributed to dissuading General (Earl) Wavell from committing any large force in Macedonia, for fear of malaria. By the time casualties began to pour in from North Africa, Keogh had worked on solving the problem of storing blood serum and the provision of blood banks. He also co-operated with the young (Sir) Benjamin Rank in developing plastic surgery. Keogh was considerate to his subordinates, developing his gift for choosing the right man for the right job. He was known affectionately as 'the old feller'.

Before returning to Australia in March 1942, Keogh was appointed army adviser in pathology. He became director of pathology (from October) in charge of preventive medicine and was promoted lieutenant colonel (November). He was also given charge of hygiene (May 1943) and entomology (March 1944). Based at Victoria Barracks, Melbourne, he constantly travelled, controlling the establishment of pathology laboratories in hospitals and appointments thereto. Malaria was the critical problem: casualties in 1942-43 were catastrophic. Via the Land Headquarters Medical Research Unit at Cairns, Queensland, Fairley planned the strategy, Keogh the tactics, and daily atebrin was forced on the troops—the result a triumph. Keogh's other major achievement was to follow his hunch about penicillin, as yet unproven, and appoint P. L. Bazeley to supervise its production, thus enabling Australia to be among the first in the world to use it extensively.

In April 1945-January 1946 Keogh was medical adviser on the Australian Military Mission to Washington. He was both seeking the most advanced knowledge and creating opportunities for his 'kindergarten'. He spent much of his time in the Pentagon, conferring with senior medical administrators, incidentally arranging Carnegie and Rockefeller grants and, in January-February in England, Nuffield grants, for medical research by Australians. That year, when the government appointed him observer of experimental testing at Bikini Atoll, he was prevented from attending by American authorities, presumably because of his left-wing background.

Keogh returned to the C.S.L. and in the next four years contributed five major articles, three of them in *Nature*. At the beginning of large-scale development of medical research, he joined the advisory committee of the Australian National Health and Medical Research Council, and was prominent in discussions of the role of the new John Curtin [q.v.13] School of Medical Research at the Australian National University, Canberra. He and Burnet formed a close working arrangement. Burnet recognized Keogh's strengths, especially in advising on human problems, and referred to him as both 'a guardian angel and a grey eminence'. Keogh was reaching the peak of his influence as an 'enabler' on many Commonwealth and State funding bodies, and dominating selections for appointments. His particular interest was Fairfield Hospital; he was appointed its consultant microbiologist in 1947 and encouraged research on infectious diseases.

In order to head Victoria's contribution to the national campaign against tuberculosis, Keogh resigned from the C.S.L. in 1949 to join the Department of Health. The structure of the campaign, notably mass chest X-rays, was in place; his task was to make it work. He kept power in his own hands, summoning his consultative committee only once. When he was satisfied that, although morbidity figures had not yet markedly declined, it was statistically clear that the campaign was successful, he resigned in 1955. Keogh had also been co-operating with Burnet on the viral infection, poliomyelitis. Jonas Salk of the University of Pittsburgh, U.S.A., discoverer in 1950 of the appropriate vaccine, contacted Burnet. He and Keogh sent Bazeley to Pittsburgh to equip himself for the campaign. In 1955 Keogh spent six weeks in the U.S.A. ensuring agreement on production methods. He then helped to arrange production at the C.S.L. and double-checking at Fairfield, where he had been responsible for creating an Epidemiological Research Unit under A. A. Ferris, and joined the N.H.M.R.C. supervising committee. Immunization began in July 1956. Within a few years polio cases notified Australia-wide dropped virtually to zero.

From 1950 Keogh had been an executive-member of the Anti-Cancer Council of Victoria. In 1955 he was appointed part-time medical adviser, in effect director. The council was largely inert; Keogh saw that it needed leadership and money. He recruited (Sir) William Kilpatrick as fund-raiser; within five years the council's annual budget was almost ten times as large, and a huge voluntary support-movement had been gathered. The council's emphases were on research, patient care and public education; much of the public fear and ignorance about cancer was dispersed. Keogh wrote innumerable compassionate letters to those stricken. Extensive smear-testing for early detection of cancer of the cervix was introduced in his time. One of his last protégés was the distinguished researcher Donald Metcalf. Keogh retired in 1968 but remained busy, especially in pursuing his lasting interest in statistics.

Keogh's chief pastime was racing and betting. He worked hard at form and perhaps more than paid his way; he even backed Wotan at 100/1 to win the 1936 Melbourne Cup. But his 'infallible' system failed him in the end. Bridge and poker were other favourite relaxations. He also had wide cultural interests: his taste in art was modernist and he knew most of the 'rebels and precursors' of the 1920s-40s, his love for music (classical and jazz) was deep, and he was uncommonly widely read.

He had great capacity for making friends, among them the wives and children of his friends. He was 'everybody's Uncle Bill', giving frequent lavish presents and helping the young in their troubles. His one remaining close family association was with his sister Estelle and her daughters. Keogh had homosexual inclinations. When at last in the 1950s he had a flat to himself, he had one loving relationship which lasted for several years, and there were probably other liaisons. If he had earlier associations, they were very discreet indeed. Bill Keogh accepted no honours: he despised the trappings of status and authority, and avoided publicity. He destroyed his own papers. In May 1970 he joined the huge Anti-Vietnam Moratorium March, and laboured to finish the distance. He died, of cancer, on 30 September that year at Parkville. His body was bequeathed to the anatomy department, University of Melbourne. He had asked that no obituaries be written and no memorial raised, but his friends and colleagues arranged a memorial gathering at which Rank gave the address. The Anti-Cancer Council named its headquarters after Keogh. He had never been interested in accumulating money; he gave nearly all his *objets d'art* to his friends and left an estate of a mere $6460.

L. Gardiner, *E. V. Keogh* (Melb, 1990), *and* for bibliog.   LYNDSAY GARDINER*
                                               GEOFFREY SERLE*

KEPERT, JOHN LESLIE (1903-1970), technical educationist, was born on 14 November 1903 at Bendigo, Victoria, fourth of six children of Australian-born parents Louis Kepert, a schoolteacher of Bohemian descent, and his wife Florence Agnes, née Coleman, a former schoolteacher. Jack attended his father's schools at East Shelbourne and Neerim South, and obtained a diploma of engineering (1924) from Footscray Technical School. He continued his studies at the University of Melbourne (B.E.E., 1928; B.M.E., 1929; M.M.E., 1936). In 1928-29 he was officer-in-charge of the development of the State Electricity Commission's Rubicon A hydroelectric power station; the project formed the subject of his master's thesis. At the Baptist Church, Footscray, on 24 May 1930 he married Ivy Rebecca Durber, a stenographer.

In 1929 Kepert had joined the Education Department of Victoria as a senior instructor at South Melbourne Technical School. He transferred to Footscray Technical School in 1937 and became vice-principal in 1944. Kepert was an energetic teacher whose rapport with staff, students and the business community was assisted by 'his ready smile, his relaxed manner, his sense of humour and his natural ability to be a man among all manner of men'. Behind his *bonhomie* lay 'a highly perceptive and very resourceful mind, a rapier wit and an obdurate adherence' to principles.

Because teaching was a reserved occupation, Kepert was refused entry into the Australian Imperial Force in World War II; in December 1941, however, he was commissioned in the Reserve of Officers as honorary captain, Ordnance Mechanical Engineers. After the war he was principal (1945-59) of Caulfield Technical College. In spite of administrative and lecturing demands, he served as president of the Institution of Automotive and Aeronautical Engineers, and sat on the council of the Institution of Engineers, Australia, the University of Melbourne's standing committee of convocation and Monash University's council.

In 1959 Kepert was appointed assistant chief inspector of technical schools. Four years later he was promoted to chief inspector. His informal contacts with engineers and industrialists at his 'other office', the Kelvin Club, ensured that the 'voice of industry' was heard in the reform of Victoria's technical education curriculum. In 1966 he led the Australian delegation to a conference at Huddersfield, England, on the education of technicians. As director of technical education in 1967-68, Kepert presided over a period of change which saw the removal of the colleges from Education Department control. He served on the council of the new Victorian Institute of Colleges and restructured vocational education within the department before he retired on 14 November 1968.

Always a keen sportsman, Kepert had been an outstanding young athlete and a regular entrant in the annual River Yarra swim. He died of coronary vascular disease on 9 September 1970 at Mont Albert and was cremated; his wife and four sons survived him. Footscray Technical College (Victoria University of Technology) named a scholarship and a building after him.

Education Dept (Vic), *Vision and Realisation*, 1, L. J. Blake ed (Melb, 1973); *Education Gazette and Teachers' Aid* (Vic), 14 July 1969, 27 Oct 1970; P. W. J. Rushbrook, Straws in the Wind: the construction of technical and further education in Victoria 1945-1985 (Ph.D. thesis, Monash Univ, 1995); information from Prof D. Kepert, Univ WA.
                                               ANDREW SPAULL
                                               PETER RUSHBROOK

KERN, RONALD GERALD (1922-1976), builder and real-estate developer, was born on 27 December 1922 at Subiaco, Perth, eldest of four sons of Australian-born parents Ernest Stanley Kern (d.1936), a tram conductor who became a timber-feller, and his wife Grace Margaret, née Collins (d.1938). After their parents died, the boys lived with relations and Ron helped to raise his brothers, Stanley, Lionel and Bernard, who were 14, 12 and 11 years old in 1938. Ron worked as a telegraph messenger before joining the Australian Imperial Force on 24 October 1941. He fought with the 2nd/28th Battalion in North Africa (1942), New Guinea (1943) and British North Borneo (1945), and was twice wounded. Earlier, while training in North Queensland, he had decided to live there after the war. Discharged from the army on 7 March 1946, he made for Charters Towers with his brothers. Ron, Stanley and Lionel soon moved to Townsville and went into business, progressing from repairing and renovating houses to building them. On 15 August 1954 at the Church of Mary Immaculate, Aitkenvale, Ron married with Catholic rites Maureen Lillian Ross, a nurse.

Kern Bros Ltd (with almost one hundred employees) was floated on the Brisbane stock exchange in June 1956; Ron was its chairman and managing director. Within a year the firm secured a contract to construct the massive foundations for a plant at Mary Kathleen to treat uranium ore. Ron lived on site. The work was completed ahead of schedule, with larger profits than anticipated. Further contracts followed. Kern's caution and far-sightedness in diversifying ensured consistent profitability and created one of Queensland's major construction enterprises. Eventually fourteen subsidiary companies were involved in building houses, quarrying stone, preparing ready-mixed concrete and developing land in Brisbane, Townsville, Gladstone, Ipswich and Rockhampton.

Kern founded and chaired the North Queensland Permanent Building Society (later the Northern Building Society Ltd). He was chairman (1969-71) of the North Queensland division of the Queensland Master Builders' Association, and foundation chairman (1973) and a life member (1976) of the North Queensland division of the Housing Industry Association. As deputy-chairman of the North Queensland Self-Government League, he criticized ineffective State and Federal planning. Politically, he was a 'self-effacing' conservative with an affinity for the development ideology of the National Party, though he prudently donated to the Liberal and Labor parties as well. He also supported a wide range of educational, cultural and sporting groups, and won numerous trophies for lawn bowling.

Handsome and upright, with a direct, confident gaze, Kern was a practising and charitable Catholic who guided his children with love and authority. He understood 'money and its workings', despite his lack of formal training. An astute judge of character, he chose his close friends 'irrespective of their station in life'. His companies were noted for their high morale and good industrial relations. Kern died of cancer on 1 October 1976 at Townsville and was buried in Belgian Gardens cemetery. His wife, daughter and son survived him. In 1988 he was honoured as an 'Unsung Hero' by the Australian Stockman's Hall of Fame and Outback Heritage Centre, Longreach. Renamed the Kern Corporation Ltd, his firm moved to Brisbane in 1979, shed its house-building operations in 1986 and passed into receivership in 1991.

North Qld Register, 1 Mar 1975; Townsville Bulletin, 5 Oct 1976, 6 Sept 1986, 14 Sept 1991, 27 May 1995; S. Ariotti, Recollections of Ronald G. Kern (ms, held by author, James Cook Univ); Kern family scrapbook (held by Mr M. Kern, Townsville, Qld); Kern file (Townsville City L); Kern file (Aust Stockman's Hall of Fame and Outback Heritage Centre, Longreach, Qld); information from Mrs M. Kern and Mr J. Daniel, Townsville, Mr S. Ariotti, Buderim, Qld, and Mrs A.-M. Eames, Mitchelton, Brisb.   RODNEY SULLIVAN

KERNOT, EDITH LATHAM (1877-1967), community worker, was born on 4 December 1877 at Geelong, Victoria, second of eight surviving children of Henry James Hobday, a clerk from England, and his Sydney-born wife Charlotte Amelia, née Walters. She began her education at Geelong and completed it at Miss Watson's Hadleigh College, Malvern. Musically gifted as a child, Edith took weekly steamer trips to Melbourne for violin lessons and, as an 8-year-old, made her début at a charity concert for the Ladies' Benevolent Association. From the age of 14, her most treasured possession was an eighteenth-century Duke violin. She continued to play at church and charity concerts for most of her life.

On 5 March 1901 at Christ Church, Geelong, she married Walter Charles Kernot (d.1941) with Anglican rites. Walter was one of a large Geelong family which supplied that city and Melbourne with a number of chemists and engineers. Charles Kernot [q.v.5] was his uncle; William Charles, Wilfred Noyce and Maurice Edwin Kernot [qq.v.5,9] were his cousins. He himself was a chemist who was to become a councillor of both the Pharmaceutical Council of Victoria and the Pharmacy College, Melbourne. Like his wife he was active in local affairs, as a foundation councillor (1905-31) of Geelong Church of England Girls' Grammar School (the Hermitage), honorary treasurer to the city council, vice-president of the Geelong and District Hospital, vestryman at Christ Church, and worshipful master (1898) of the Geelong Masonic Lodge of Unity and Prudence.

Besides raising their three children, Edith was an indefatigable worker for numerous community organizations. From the early 1900s she participated in the development of the District Nursing Society, of which she was later vice-president for twenty years. An original member of the Geelong branch of the Australian Red Cross Society, she was president for three years and, on completing fifty years service, was awarded its laurel wreath. She was also vice-president of the City Mission for a decade. In 1933-48 Mrs Kernot served on the Charities Board of Victoria, chairing its country standing committee in 1945-47. Elected to the committee of management of the Geelong and District Hospital in 1934, she sat on its house and building committees (1937-65), and was a vice-president (1951-65) of the hospital. In 1958 she was appointed M.B.E.

Much of Edith Kernot's work was directed towards the welfare of women and children. She served on the council of the Geelong Female Refuge for ten years and on the Girls' Friendly Society provincial council for eight. A long-standing member of the Ladies' Benevolent Association, she was president in 1932-52. In addition, she was a foundation member and president (1921-58) of the Geelong Baby Health Centres Association, and for thirty-four years a vice-president of the Baby Health Centres Association of Victoria.

Vital and energetic, Mrs Kernot carried herself erectly until old age. Those who observed her in her public duties remarked on her dignity, discipline and foresight. She was brisk and efficient, and could be formidable when occasion warranted, but her descendants also remember her sense of fun. Survived by her son and two daughters, she died on 23 March 1967 at Geelong and was cremated.

W. G. Volum, *The Volum Family* (Melb, 1992); Hospitals and Charities Com (Vic), *Your Hospitals*, Aug 1964; Geelong District Hospital, *Annual Report*, 1964-65; *Geelong Advertiser*, 1 Jan 1958, 25 Mar 1967; information from Mr W. G. Volum, Beaumaris, Melb.   DIANE LANGMORE

KERR, DORIS BOAKE (1889-1944), writer, was born on 29 August 1889 at Summer Hill, Sydney, elder daughter of native-born parents Gregory Augustine Kerr, civil servant, and his wife Adelaide Eva, née Boake. Her maternal grandfather Barcroft Capel Boake (1838-1921) had emigrated to Australia in the late 1850s and established himself as a professional photographer, first in Melbourne and then in Sydney. His son was the poet Barcroft Boake [q.v.3]. Doris was later to use 'Capel Boake' as her pseudonym. When her father—described by his father-in-law 'as a helpless creature'—lost his job with the Railways Department, the Kerrs moved to Melbourne about 1893. Hindered by a club foot which was subsequently amputated, Gregory probably never had regular employment in Melbourne, although he was for a time draughts correspondent for the *Age*. Doris's mother supported the family by working for a commercial photographer. By 1915 they had settled at Caulfield.

Although she attended a state school, Doris claimed that 'she was self-educated at the Prahran Public Library'. She left school relatively early and worked as a shop-assistant before becoming in turn a typist and a librarian. Her first story was published in the *Australasian* in January 1916. It was followed by other stories and poems, some of which appeared in the Victorian *School Paper*. Her first novel, *Painted Clay* (Melbourne, 1917), was published by the Australasian Authors' Agency and reprinted by Virago (London, 1986). It tells the story of a shop assistant's fight for independence in a period when menial work or marriage were the only choices for a majority of young women. In 1923 the New South Wales Bookstall Co. published *The Romany Mark*, her novel about circus life. Kerr's best book, *The Dark Thread*, was released under the Hutchinson imprint in London in 1936. It was one of the few interwar Australian novels to deal with urban everyday life. Her last novel, *The Twig is Bent*, written with the aid of a Commonwealth literary grant but published posthumously (Sydney, 1946), was a rather wooden historical tale set in early Melbourne.

Kerr remained single and continued to live in the family home. Active in P.E.N. International and a foundation member of the Society of Australian Authors, by the early 1940s she was working as secretary to J. K. Moir [q.v.] who was credit manager at Paynes Bon Marché Pty Ltd in Bourke Street and a noted supporter of Australian literature. Kerr died suddenly of a cerebral haemorrhage on 5 June 1944 at Caulfield and was cremated. Her friend Myra Morris [q.v.10] wrote immediately to Moir: 'There'll never be anyone else like Doris—so generous, so full of understanding, with so rare a mind'.

A collection of Kerr's verse with a foreword by Morris was published in 1949 as *The Selected Poems of Capel Boake*. Although her work, with that of her Melbourne contemporaries 'Georgia Rivers' (Marjorie Clark) and Jean Campbell, is passed over in studies of Australian women's writing in the interwar period, her two main novels, *Painted Clay* and *The Dark Thread*, deserve to be more widely known.

J. Arnold (ed), *The Imagined City* (Syd, 1983); C. Boake, *Painted Clay*, intro C. Downer (Lond, 1986); J. Kerr (ed), *Dictionary of Australian Artists* (Melb, 1992); *Listener In*, 17-23 Feb 1940; *Australasian*, 27 May 1939; *Herald* (Melb), 5 June 1944; 'Capel Boake' material, J. K. Moir collection (SLV).
                                                          JOHN ARNOLD

KERR, EDITH AMELIA (1893-1975), missionary and headmistress, was born on 6 June 1893 at Patyah, Edenhope, Victoria, ninth of ten children of James Kerr, a grazier from Scotland, and his Victorian-born wife Mary Taylor, née Gardiner. Educated at the Melbourne Continuation School, Edith began work as a primary school teacher. After the death of her fiancé on active service in 1917, she decided to become a missionary. She attended the Deaconess and Missionary Training Institute of the Presbyterian Church and in 1920 was made deaconess. In 1921 she was sent to Korea as a missionary, under the auspices of the Presbyterian Women's Missionary Union.

Miss Kerr spent the next twenty years in Korea where she concentrated on educational initiatives for disadvantaged women and girls. From 1935 she was principal of the Tongnai Farm School, near Pusan, which rehabilitated destitute women through vocational training. She was recalled in 1941 when conditions under the Japanese occupation grew increasingly dangerous. Back home on leave and deputation work, Kerr had attended the University of Melbourne (B.A., 1933). Again in Melbourne during World War II, she entered the Presbyterian Theological Hall, Ormond College, and in 1946 was the first woman in the Presbyterian Church of Australia to gain a bachelor of divinity.

While studying, Kerr earned her living by teaching at Methodist Ladies' College, Kew. In 1944 she applied to be accepted as a formal candidate for the ministry of the Presbyterian Church, then not open to women. Despite support from the Victorian assembly, her Melbourne North presbytery opposed her. The matter went to the general assembly, but her application was dismissed. Although no Presbyterian woman minister in Australia would be ordained for another thirty years, Kerr was the one who first brought this subject into discussion. Following her rejection, she wrote a persuasive and comprehensive defence of the ordination of women (in the form of a booklet published in 1948) during a two-year stint as principal of the Presbyterian Deaconess Training Institute, Dunedin, New Zealand.

In 1949 she returned to Victoria to prepare for further missionary work in Korea. She had been invited to join the academic staff of the Ewha Women's University in Seoul. To her disappointment, however, she was rejected on medical grounds. She resumed teaching, at Penleigh Presbyterian Girls' School, Essendon, and in 1950 was appointed headmistress of Clarendon Presbyterian Ladies' College, Ballarat. Leaving that post in 1955, she lectured in theology at Rolland [q.v.11] House Deaconess Training College, Melbourne, for six years.

A gifted woman with a vibrant personality and considerable personal warmth and charm, Kerr was an engaging public speaker, particularly in the service of the Christian faith. She was also accomplished in music, poetry, embroidery and painting. In retirement she took an active role in the temperance movement within the Presbyterian Church, and created a library and recreational club at the Hedley Sutton home for the aged, Canterbury. She died there on 2 April 1975 and was buried in Box Hill cemetery.

J. Clarke and M. Cochran, *The Lamp Burns Brightly* (Ballarat, Vic, 1970); Presbyterian Churches of Vic and Qld, *Missionary Chronicle*, Sept 1921, May 1941, Sept 1945, Feb, June, Sept 1949; Presbyterian Church of Aust, Deaconess Council, Minutes, 6 Sept 1955, 5 Feb 1957, 1 Dec 1959 (Presbyterian Church Archives, Melb); family papers (held by Miss R. Richardson, Surrey Hills, Melb).   MURIEL PORTER

KERRIGAN, ALAN BEVLY (1899-1977), barrister, was born on 19 March 1899 at Singleton, New South Wales, second child of native-born parents Walter Andrew Kerrigan, mercantile clerk, and his wife Ada Albenia, née Hobden. Alan's boyhood was spent at Dulwich Hill: he was the second pupil enrolled at Trinity Grammar School, founded by the rector of the parish (Bishop) G. A. Chambers who had a decisive influence on him. School and sports captain, Kerrigan won an exhibition to the University of Sydney (B.A., 1921). He then taught history at The King's School, Parramatta. Following his father's death in 1926, he decided to read law. Associate to Justice (Sir) Langer Owen [q.v.11], he passed the Barristers' Admission Board examinations and was admitted to the Bar on 4 June 1930. At St John's Anglican Church, Parramatta, on 9 July that year he married Anne Brownrigg Cowper, a descendant of William Cowper [q.v.1].

Kerrigan built up a large Equity practice, and was prominent in the taxation field and in appellate cases. Appointed Q.C. in October 1954, he appeared several times before the Privy Council and served (1941-48 and 1957-60) on the council of the New South Wales Bar Association. It was in the field of ecclesiastical law that he made his most emphatic contribution. The Church of England in Australia had long been involved in complex legal issues. Kerrigan brought a clear, analytical mind and a remorseless energy to elucidating the Church's legal problems and seeking solutions. First appointed to the Sydney diocesan synod in 1938, and later to its standing committee, he played a prominent role in the famous 'Red Book' case over ritual.

As a leading jurist, Kerrigan was appointed chancellor of the diocese of Grafton in 1943. This honorary office involved giving legal advice to the bishop and synod. Three years later he succeeded Professor Sir John Peden [q.v.11] as chancellor of Newcastle. There the former and incumbent bishops—G. M. Long and F. De W. Batty [qq.v.10,7]—were leaders in the movement for a constitution for an autonomous Church, as drafted by Peden. Kerrigan inherited his predecessor's role, and worked with Batty and other Australian

bishops to that end. The proposed constitution had met many obstacles and Kerrigan
found the going hard.

Batty despaired in 1950, but the visiting
archbishop of Canterbury encouraged a fresh
start, warning that Australia would soon be
unable to rely on earlier English legislation.
Kerrigan played a major part in reviving the
constitutional movement, becoming, in the
process, the trusted adviser of many leading
churchmen. The efforts were crowned by
the acceptance of the new constitution, following many amendments, in 1961. Thereafter,
Kerrigan was an important member of the
new general synod. In 1976 he was appointed
C.B.E. He served on Trinity Grammar's council for thirty-five years, and belonged to the
Australasian Pioneers', Australian and Newcastle clubs. Survived by his wife and three
sons, he died on 31 January 1977 at Hornsby
and was cremated.

C of E (NSW), *Procs of General Synod*, 1945-75;
Aust Law J, 50, Aug 1976, p 429; *Anglican Encounter*,
Apr 1977; *SMH*, 22 Oct 1954, 12 June 1976, 2, 4 Feb
1977; *Newcastle Morning Herald*, 3 Feb 1977; infor-
mation from Mrs J. West, Trinity Grammar School,
Summer Hill, Syd; family information.
                                                              K. J. CABLE

KESSELL, STEPHEN LACKEY (1897-
1979), forester and administrator, was born
on 17 March 1897 at Wollongong, New South
Wales, second child of Stephen Kessell, a
Primitive Methodist minister from England,
and his native-born wife Annie Jane, née
Lackey. The family moved to South Australia
about 1905. Young Stephen attended Adelaide
High School and studied forestry at the
University of Adelaide (B.Sc., 1917; M.Sc.,
1927). He enlisted in the Australian Imperial
Force on 18 December 1917 and reached
England in August 1918. In the following
year he was granted leave to further his
studies and entered the University of Oxford
(Dip.For., 1919). Discharged from the army in
April 1920, he then worked with the forests
department of Western Australia under the
conservator C. E. Lane-Poole [q.v.9], whose
unsuccessful attempts to persuade government to endorse his policies ended in resignation. Kessell acted in his stead from
October 1921 and was confirmed in the position in January 1923. He was to hold that
appointment for a further twenty-two years.
On 20 August 1924 at Christ Church, Claremont, he married with Anglican rites Barbara
Morton Sawell (d.1978), a pharmacist.

Following Lane-Poole's lead, Kessell developed 'working plans' for most timber, but
jarrah especially, on accessible crown land,
seeking to curb over-cutting and to regener-

ate earlier damage. While never so acerbic as
his precursor, Kessell yet lamented that 'the
Anglo-Saxon settlers who populated Australia
brought with them no traditions of forestry as
a rural industry, and for 100 years or more
the forests were looked upon as an enemy to
be slaughtered'. His fame became greatest
for developing defences against bushfire,
although he was also innovative in using fire
as a silvicultural tool. Kessell's widespread
use of unskilled labour during the Depression
aided regeneration and pine plantation. Application of science and technology suffused all
the department's work, as did pursuit of the
best standards in forester training. Kessell
insisted on skilled and specialized direction in
a report on forestry written for the New South
Wales government in 1934. That concern also
inspired his moves to establish (1935) the
Institute of Foresters of Australia, of which he
was founding president (1936-38).

In May 1941 Kessell was seconded to the
Commonwealth Department of Munitions as
controller of timber. He fulfilled the job's
potential, prompting L. T. Carron's judgement
that 'if Australia ever had a "national forest
policy" . . . it had one during World War II'. In
1944 Kessell advised the Tasmanian government on forest policy, remarking that the
State's bargains with business interests 'have
been largely at the expense of the forests and
the Forestry Department'. Some of his criticisms bore especially on Australian Newsprint Mills Pty Ltd which in 1941 had begun
production at Boyer. Seeking to redeem the
situation, A.N.M. appointed Kessell its managing director in 1946. The newcomer called
upon his workforce to build an industry
'which will contribute for all time to the essential needs of the community'. Under Kessell's
administration A.N.M. weathered shortages
and dislocations to join the ebullience of the
Menzies [q.v.] years. Throughout the 1950s
production and employment rose steadily.
Chemical and silvicultural work advanced.
Mill management heeded welfare and
amenity. Kessell was disappointed by the
board's decision (1958) not to support plans
for further expansion. He retired in 1962.

A member (chairman 1944-64) of the Australian universities' board of higher forestry
education since its inception in 1931, Kessell
promoted the Australian Forestry School's
inclusion within the Australian National University, Canberra, an incorporation achieved
in 1965. He served on the councils of the
A.N.U. (1960-63) and the University of
Tasmania (1947-48 and 1952-62), showing at
the latter institution but marginal sympathy
for academic dissidence in general and less
for the upholders of S. S. Orr [q.v.]. In 1951
Kessell was appointed M.B.E. He was also
deputy-president (1967-71) of the National
Safety Council of Australia.

Retiring to Melbourne, he served on the board of A.N.M. and other companies. He belonged to the Australian Club, complementing his earlier membership of the Weld (Perth) and the Tasmanian. An able sportsman, 'Kim' Kessell was ever urbane and courteous, and often charming. Many found him aloof, some self-effacing. His very ease of style might have contributed to his historical standing being unduly small. Yet, in all he did, Kessell went beyond supreme competence towards creativity. Survived by his daughter, he died on 29 June 1979 at Armadale, Melbourne, and was cremated. His estate was sworn for probate at $519 292.

WA Forests Dept, *50 Years of Forestry in Western Australia* (Perth, 1969); L. T. Carron, *A History of Forestry in Australia* (Canb, 1985); A. Meyer, *The Foresters* (Hob, 1985); S. J. Pyne, *Burning Bush* (NY, 1991); *PP* (NSW), 1934-35, 1, p 445; *J & PP* (Tas), 1944-45 (42); *Newsprint Log*, 1, no 2, Mar 1946; *Aust Forestry*, 42, no 3, 1979, p 138; CRS CP43/1 file 10A/1943/638, CRS AA1975/154/1 (AA, Canb); Univ Tas Archives.   MICHAEL ROE

KEVIN, JOHN CHARLES GEORGE (1909-1968), diplomat, was born on 9 October 1909 at Forbes, New South Wales, eldest of three sons of native-born parents Edward Kevin, chemist, and his wife Edith Emily May, née Hutchinson. His grandfather was 'Mr Kevin' in a version (1900) of Henry Lawson's [q.v.10] poem, 'The Old Bark School'. Educated at St Stanislaus' College, Bathurst, St Joseph's College, Hunters Hill, and St John's College, University of Sydney (LL.B., 1932), Charles was admitted to the Bar on 25 May 1932. In 1935 he joined the staff of the Australian High Commission in London. He edited *Some Australians Take Stock* (London, 1939) which included his essay on foreign policy. On 1 July 1939 at the Church of Our Lady of Victories, Kensington, he married Hermine Schick with Catholic rites; they were to have a son before being divorced.

In 1940 Kevin returned to Australia. While working with the Department of the Army, Melbourne, he helped to establish (1941) the Commonwealth Security Service. On 23 February 1942 he was appointed sub lieutenant, Royal Australian Naval Volunteer Reserve. He was promoted lieutenant and went to sea in H.M.A.S. *Horsham* before returning to the security service in 1943. A report on the C.S.S. by the British intelligence officer Captain A. H. Hillgarth, Royal Navy, described Kevin as 'the brains of the concern'.

Entering the Department of External Affairs in June 1945, Kevin was initially based in Canberra. He served as official secretary in New Delhi (1947-50), then was called to Canberra where he took charge of the admin-

istrative and general division. Alan Watt described this position as a thankless one, in which the occupant never achieved 'fame or glory; indeed, he is lucky if he keeps any friends amongst his colleagues'. It was a tribute to Kevin's fairness, urbanity and accessibility—to those who shared his daily custom of a quiet drink in the back bar of the Hotel Canberra—that he was less harmed by his tenure of this post than most who held it.

Apart from a further term in Canberra in 1955-59, Kevin spent the rest of his career abroad: he was Australian minister to Indonesia (1953-55), high commissioner to Ceylon (Sri Lanka) (1959-61), high commissioner to Pakistan (1961-62) and ambassador to South Africa (from September 1962). With his bearing, presence, elegance and imperturbability, he was very much a diplomat in the British Foreign Office tradition. His legal background and personal skills were put to good use in the negotiation of the Antarctic Treaty (1959) and the Vienna convention on diplomatic relations (1961). He was appointed C.B.E. in 1964.

On 6 May 1963 Kevin married Mary Therese Wilson, an Englishwoman he had met in Ceylon, two of whose daughters (Tammy and Naomi) he adopted. He died of cancer on 13 February 1968 in Pretoria, South Africa, and was buried in Zandfontein cemetery. His wife and daughters survived him, as did Anthony, the son of his first marriage, who also pursued a diplomatic career.

A. Watt, *Australian Diplomat* (Syd, 1972); F. Cain, *The Origins of Political Surveillance in Australia* (Syd, 1983); Dept of External Affairs, *Current Notes on International Affairs*, 39, no 2, Feb 1968; A. Hillgarth Report (PREM 3 159/10, PRO, Lond).

JOAN BEAUMONT

KIBBY, WILLIAM HENRY (1903-1942), soldier and plasterer, was born on 15 April 1903 at Winlaton, Durham, England, second of three children of John Robert Kibby, draper's assistant, and his wife Mary Isabella, née Birnie. Early in 1914 the family migrated to Adelaide where Bill attended Mitcham Public School. He had various jobs before he was employed to design and fix plaster decorations at the Perfection Fibrous Plaster Works, Edwardstown. In 1926 he married Mabel Sarah Bedmead Morgan, a 19-year-old typist, in her father's house at Glenelg; they lived at Helmsdale and had two daughters.

Short—5 ft 6 ins (168 cm)—and strong, Kibby loved outdoor activity. He was assistant-scoutmaster of the 2nd Glenelg Sea Scouts and sailed in their lifeboat; he took his family on walks and picnics; and he played golf on public courses. In 1936 he joined the 48th Field Battery, Royal Australian Artillery

(Militia). He liked taking part in military tattoos. His considerable artistic talent found expression not only in his plaster designs but in water-colours and drawings. He took art classes briefly at the School of Mines and Industries, and painted and sketched at home while the family listened to the radio.

On 29 June 1940 Kibby enlisted in the Australian Imperial Force. Posted to the original 2nd/48th Battalion, he was promoted sergeant on 17 November, the day before the unit sailed. The 2nd/48th reached Palestine in December, but, on New Year's Eve, Kibby fell into a slit trench and fractured his leg. His convalescence and retraining lasted more than a year, during which he made at least forty delicately worked water-colours and pencil drawings. They showed a fondness for Palestine's countryside and a feeling for its people. In February 1942 Kibby rejoined the 2nd/48th in Syria and in June moved with his battalion to Egypt. He remained with it for the rest of his life, being involved in the battles of Tel el Eisa in July and El Alamein in October.

At El Alamein Kibby showed extraordinary and persistent courage. On the night of 23 October 1942 his platoon was ordered to destroy a nest of machine-guns and mortars on Miteiriya Ridge. Calling 'Follow me!', Kibby charged it with a Tommy-gun, killing three enemy soldiers, capturing twelve, and clearing the post. On the night of the 25th he repaired his platoon's signal wires at least five times in the face of heavy fire. His company commander Captain Peter Robbins intended to recommend him for the Distinguished Conduct Medal, but was killed. On the night of the 26th, while under heavy artillery fire and repeated tank and infantry attack at Trig 29, Kibby moved boldly into the open, directing his men's fire and co-ordinating and inspiring their defence. Before dawn on the 31st, Kibby's platoon fought through the German lines at Ring Contour 25, then came under intense machine-gun and mortar fire as it attempted to reach the coast. Most of the platoon were killed or wounded. After reorganizing the survivors, Kibby charged forward and attacked a number of machine-guns which were firing directly at him from a few yards away. He must have known that he would die, but he kept on, silencing with grenades gun after gun until a burst killed him. His Victoria Cross citation stated, 'he left behind him an example and memory of a soldier who fearlessly and unselfishly fought to the end to carry out his duty'.

The position he died to win was given up, and the Germans buried Kibby and other platoon dead in a common grave. After retaking the ground and searching for ten days, his mates found the grave and reburied their comrades in line. 'We couldn't say much', one recalled early in 1943, 'but I guess we all knew

... that if it hadn't been for Bill Kibby we might have been lying there with them'. In January 1944 Kibby's remains were reinterred in El Alamein war cemetery. A club at the Woodside army camp, near Adelaide, commemorates his name. Money was raised by public appeal to buy a house at Helmsdale for Kibby's widow. She never remarried, and never ceased to mourn her husband, a man whom his daughters recall as never raising his voice, a father whose curly hair, brilliant blue eyes and quiet smile stay with them still.

J. G. Glenn, *Tobruk to Tarakan* (Adel, 1960); L. Wigmore (ed), *They Dared Mightily* (Canb, 1963); B. Maughan, *Tobruk and El Alamein* (Canb, 1966); *Advertiser* (Adel), 29 Jan, 1 Feb, 4 Mar 1943; *Glenelg Guardian*, 20 May, 3 June 1943; information from Mrs C. Massey, Kingston Park, and Mr J. Huckstepp, Glenelg, Adel.   BILL GAMMAGE

KIDDLE, MARGARET LOCH (1914-1958), historian, was born on 10 September 1914 at South Yarra, Melbourne, eldest of four children of John Beacham Kiddle, solicitor, and his wife Mauna Loa, née Burrett. Town-bred, Margaret was fourth-generation Australian, proud of her pioneering forebears. Like her father's family, she was tall, carried herself beautifully and was superb on horseback. A grimmer inheritance was the kidney-disease that was to kill her.

She was educated privately and at St Catherine's School (1921-26), Melbourne Church of England Girls' Grammar School (1927-33) and the University of Melbourne (B.A. Hons, 1938; M.A., Dip.Ed., 1947). During World War II she worked on prices-policy research for (Sir) Douglas Copland [q.v.13]. In 1946 Kiddle became a tutor (later senior tutor) in the department of history. She stayed there for the rest of her life, save for a year (1952) spent document-hunting in Britain and another (1954) working as a research fellow at the Australian National University, Canberra. Her publications included *Caroline Chisholm* (1950), three books for children—*Moonbeam Stairs* (1945), *West of Sunset* (1949) and *The Candle* (1950)—and her posthumous masterpiece, *Men of Yesterday, A Social History of the Western District of Victoria 1834-1890* (1961), defiantly completed just before she died.

Kiddle earned most of her living by university teaching, which she took seriously and greatly enjoyed. Nevertheless she always said that she was 'not an academic'. She may have meant that her foreshortened future precluded any career-planning, as it excluded marriage; certainly she meant that she had no taste for 'academic' theorizing about history. She enjoyed her time at the A.N.U., where she predictably made many friends, but she would not take seriously her colleagues' admiration for her work.

Her talent took time to mature. Despite Kiddle's love for history, which was encouraged by Gwenda Lloyd [q.v.] at M.C.E.G.G.S. and then by Professor Max Crawford, her examination results, affected by illness, were mediocre. The Chisholm biography was rather wooden, perhaps because she could not find the private papers which might have transformed it. In 1949 a family friend suggested that she write a book about Western District society. Kiddle had a vision of the questions that might be answered if the settlers' own letters and diaries could be collected to throw light both on their Anglo-Celtic origins and on their colonial experiences. It took her the rest of her life to convert that vision into the manuscript that became *Men of Yesterday*.

Her letters show how well equipped she was for her work. Helping her siblings through family crises, she revealed herself as courageous, generous, commonsensical and indomitably realistic. She was a gifted raconteur, recognizing the tragic, and savouring the comic and the preposterous. She had a penetrating eye for people and a loving, attentive eye for landscape, which she had to see for herself: 'imagination is not enough'. In the search for documents, her 'true-blue merino' ancestry and her father's gift for friendship opened many doors. Burdened by illness, she was astonished in 1954 at the work she had already done.

At times the book seemed uncontrollable, 'an amorphous mass'. Then it crystallized: 'the people . . . are almost speaking for themselves now'—and their world took shape. With an impressive control of illuminating detail, she wrote about the relationships between human beings and the land into which they came. She took in her stride the most outrageous of personalities—'I seem to have an affinity for publicans and sinners'. The Aborigines were integral to her history, and despite the title (a quotation) so were the women. She did not romanticize. The settlers' faults and follies were part of their reality, and though she agonized over the chapter on morality, she refused to soften it.

Kiddle planned other books, but by 1957 time was running short. Sustained by blood-transfusions, she held on until her manuscript was finished. The least vain of authors, she then listed some essential revisions, and told her literary executors to use their own judgement. She died of renal failure caused by polycystic kidneys on 3 May 1958 at Richmond and was cremated.

Friends (notably Professor John La Nauze) prepared her draft for publication. The royalties on her books, bequeathed to the history department, have among other things en-dowed an essay prize named in her honour, but her best memorial remains *Men of Yesterday*, of which she wrote: 'if I've done nothing else, I've at least tried to cock a snook at destiny, & that, I think, is a good thing to do'. It sold 15 000 copies and has become an Australian classic.

R. M. Crawford, biog intro in M. Kiddle, *Men of Yesterday* (Melb, 1961); L. Gardiner, 'Margaret Kiddle', in H. Radi (ed), *200 Australian Women* (Syd, 1988); *Hist Studies*, 31, Nov 1958; *MCEGGS Mag*, 1958; Kiddle papers (LaTL); Kiddle files (Melb Univ Press); Kiddle papers *and* L. Gardiner, notes and papers concerning Kiddle, including an unpublished biog article (1983) *and* Crawford papers (Univ Melb Archives); Kiddle letters (held by the estate of the late Dr A. G. Serle, Hawthorn, Melb); information from Mrs K. Bush, Berwick, Vic.   ALISON PATRICK

KILFOYLE, JOHN AUGUSTUS CHARLES (1893-1962), pastoralist, was born on 9 December 1893 at Palmerston (Darwin), only child of Thomas Kilfoyle, a grazier from Ireland, and his native-born wife Catherine, née Byrne. In 1882-83 Tom had led an overlanding party with his relations, the Duracks [qq.v.4,8] and the Byrnes, and established Rosewood station which extended from the eastern Kimberley region of Western Australia into the present Northern Territory. Jack was educated (1901-14) at Christian Brothers' College, Perth. Although he had lost the sight in one eye as the result of an insect bite which became infected, he proved an excellent athlete. On his father's death in 1908, he inherited a half-share in Rosewood; he worked on the property from 1915 and took over its management in March 1922.

During the next twenty-five years Kilfoyle built a reputation as a successful owner-manager on a medium-sized property (734 000 acres, 297 000 ha) on what was known as a 'big man's frontier' increasingly dominated by companies and absentee proprietors. Having improved his beef Shorthorns with a strain of 'milk' bulls acquired from Nestlé & Anglo Swiss Condensed Milk Co. (Australasia) Ltd, he put his profits into improving the property by fencing, paddocking and providing watering-places. He also welcomed technological innovations. A Federal board of inquiry into land policy in 1937 praised Kilfoyle's thorough management and close supervision of Rosewood.

To Kilfoyle's neighbours he seemed prone to 'tarry-diddle' in that he was too enterprising in branding cleanskin calves found on his boundaries. In 1932 he was charged with the theft of some part-Devon bulls from the Wyndham Freezing, Canning & Meat Works. He was sentenced to two years imprisonment in Wyndham gaol, but allowed his liberty during the day. At a retrial the sentence was commuted to a fine. As a result of the incident his sleeping partners, Holmes Bros Ltd, withdrew from the pastoral company. The Devon strain became a feature of Rosewood cattle.

Kilfoyle's manner was disarming. His strongest oath was 'By Jove'; he neither smoked nor drank alcohol; and his worst habit was chewing the corners of his handkerchief. At the age of 40 he seemed a model bachelor, but in 1938 he was sued for breach of promise by May Dorothy Hayes, daughter of his father's former partner: she sought damages of £10 000 and received £850. Kilfoyle's only comment was, 'Oh dear ... these women are expensive'. On 23 February 1939 at St Mary's Catholic Cathedral, Perth, he married a divorcee Thelma Ada Hope Ryan, née Dutton. His fortunes prospered during World War II and in 1947 he sold Rosewood, fully stocked, for £92 000. He established an £8000 trust for the Aborigines on his property, then moved with his wife in turn to Sydney and Melbourne. His collection of Australian stamps was to be valued at £35 000 in 1961. The Kilfoyles lived in Berkeley Square, London, from 1952, but returned to Perth in 1961. Survived by his wife and stepson, Kilfoyle died of emphysema and bronchitis on 26 May 1962 in Perth and was buried in Karrakatta cemetery. His estate was sworn for probate at £94 608.

M. Durack, *Sons in the Saddle* (Lond, 1983); *PP* (Cwlth), 1937-40, 3, p 813; *West Australian*, 12, 23, 25 Feb 1932, 22 Nov 1947; G. C. Bolton, The Kimberley Pastoral Industry from 1885 to the present (M.A. thesis, Univ WA, 1953); G. F. Byrne, An analysis of the social profiles of the Kilfoyles of Rosewood Station (M.A. thesis, Edith Cowan Univ, 1996); Kilfoyle papers (held by author, Claremont, Perth); Dame Mary Durack papers (BL).

GERALDINE BYRNE

KILVINGTON, BASIL (1877-1947), surgeon and medical researcher, was born 6 August 1877 at Hartlepool, Durham, England, son of Rev. James Kilvington, Wesleyan minister, and his wife Jane, née Glover. The family emigrated to Victoria in 1888. Basil was educated at Camberwell Grammar School and the University of Melbourne (M.B., 1898; B.S., 1900; M.D., 1901; M.S., 1902). He was a resident medical officer (1899) at the Melbourne Hospital and established a practice at Camberwell. On 16 March 1904 he married Lucy May Watsford at the Methodist Church, Canterbury.

While working as a demonstrator at the university, Kilvington began his study of the regeneration of nerves for which he won the David Syme [q.v.6] research scholarship in 1908. He experimented on dogs to disprove

—contemporaneously with J. N. Langley and H. K. Anderson—the claim of (Sir) Charles Ballance and (Sir) James Purves Stewart that cut distal nerves could auto-regenerate. He also showed that nerve fibre regrowth from a proximal stump bifurcated along various channels, suggested ways of reducing aberrant reconnections, established that sensory and motor nerve material was interchangeable for nerve bridging, but that autografts were much superior to allografts and xenografts, and advocated operating before healing.

In 1918 Kilvington was elected honorary surgeon to in-patients at the Melbourne Hospital; he later practised at Prince Henry's and Epworth hospitals. At the university he was a tutor at Trinity College, Stewart lecturer in surgery (1922-35) and chairman of the board of examiners in surgery. He served as president of the Melbourne Hospital Clinical Society (1920), the Victorian branch of the British Medical Association (1921), the Surgical Association of Melbourne (1926) and the surgical section of the Australasian Medical Congress, at Dunedin, New Zealand (1927). In 1926 he was one of the founders of the College of Surgeons of Australasia.

Although he mourned the loss of the 'early days' when he had ample time for research, from 1905 to 1942 Kilvington published eighteen papers on nerves (some in the *British Medical Journal*), including reports on healing a boy with Erb's palsy and relieving trigeminal neuralgia by injecting alcohol into nerves. He also wrote on hydatids, radium, cancer, decapsulation of the kidneys, prostatectomy, goitre, ulcers and orthopaedics. After becoming an honorary consulting surgeon at the Royal Melbourne Hospital in 1934, he resumed experiments on animals at the Walter and Eliza Hall [qq.v.9] Institute. World War II obliged him to fill in at the R.M.H., preventing further research.

Younger colleagues remembered Kilvington's goodwill. As a surgeon he worked 'calmly and smoothly ... skilfully and neatly', and was very quick. That he was a little casual about asepsis reflected, perhaps, his training under such pre-Listerians as Sir Thomas FitzGerald [q.v.4]. Kilvington was apprehensive but open-minded about nationalized medicine. A member of Melbourne Rotary from 1935, he was its president in 1942-43. He undertook historical research in Tasmania, collected stamps and pictures, and enjoyed play-readings. Kilvington maintained his famous 'puckish humour' to the end. He died of congestive cardiac failure on 28 June 1947 at Richmond and was buried in Boroondara cemetery; his wife and two sons survived him. A portrait by Paul Fitzgerald hung at the Basil Kilvington medical centre in St Kilda Road until that building's demolition and is now held by the Royal Australasian College of Surgeons, Melbourne.

Kilvington's initial work—funded by the British Medical Association and the Royal Society—was published in the *British Medical Journal* in 1905-12 and is among the earliest cited in (Sir) Sydney Sunderland's *Nerves and Nerve Injuries* (1968). Sir George Syme [q.v.12] said it was 'widely recognised as of the highest order'. Kilvington's supervisor W. A. Osborne [q.v.11] praised his 'noble urge for research' and skill in its execution. (Sir) Albert Coates [q.v.13] thought that Kilvington 'tended to hide his light'. None of his contemporaries went as far, however, as the British neurosurgeons M. A. Glasby and T. E. J. Hems who described him in 1993 as the 'father of peripheral nerve surgery' whose 'substantial and prophetic discoveries' were 'to nerve repair what [Nobel prize-winner Alexis] Carrel's [were] to vascular surgery'. That those discoveries were scarcely recognized suggests that they were generations ahead of the means to apply them through microsurgical techniques.

P. Kenny (ed), *The Founders of the Royal Australasian College of Surgeons* (Melb, 1984); Univ Melb, *Speculum*, Nov 1960, p 27; *MJA*, 1947, 2, p 317; *J of Hand Surgery* (British and European vol), 1993, 18B, p 461; Roy A'sian College of Surgeons Archives, Melb.   COLIN SMITH

KINCAID, HILDA ESTELLE (1886-1967), medical practitioner, was born on 15 December 1886 at Fitzroy, Melbourne, third daughter of John Kincaid, a stock agent from England, and his Victorian-born wife Maria Ann, née Avery. Hilda was educated at Methodist Ladies' College, Kew (dux 1902). A contemporary remembered her as 'a thin wisp of a girl' with a lisp, who 'had grey matter in abundance but was neither arrogant nor a prig'.

In 1905 Kincaid entered the University of Melbourne (B.Sc., 1908; M.Sc., 1910; D.Sc., 1912). The scientific work for her doctoral thesis, 'Biochemical significance of phosphorus', was conducted in the laboratory of Professor W. A. Osborne [q.v.11]. Awarded a government research scholarship, she was employed at the university as a demonstrator and as an assistant in bacteriology, but turned to studying medicine and graduated (M.B., B.S.) in 1920. She was a resident medical officer at the Melbourne Hospital in 1920 before working in Sydney at the Renwick [q.v.6] Hospital for Infants and at the Scarba children's home; she was also a demonstrator in physiology at the University of Sydney and an assistant-physician to out-patients at the Rachel Forster Hospital for Women and Children.

From 1927 until her retirement in 1952 Kincaid was medical officer (child welfare) for the Melbourne City Council. Working in a team with Dr John Dale [q.v.8] and Dr Hilda Bull (the wife of Louis Esson [q.v.8]), Kincaid awakened public interest in the health of pre-school children at a time when others were preoccupied with infant mortality. She examined the effects of environment and nutrition on the growth and development of underprivileged children. During the Depression she tried to alleviate iron deficiency in mothers which was exacerbated by malnutrition and poverty. A pamphlet outlining a low-cost, nutritionally balanced diet was distributed through baby health centres. She also investigated haemoglobin levels in infants and methods of providing iron supplements.

A committee-member of the Demonstration Nursery School which established the Lady Gowrie [q.v.9] Child Centre in Melbourne in 1939, Kincaid served with Dr Vera Scantlebury Brown, Christine Heinig [qq.v.11,14] and Frances Derham on a subcommittee which planned and lobbied successfully for the foundation of similar centres interstate. Much of Kincaid's work was conducted at the Lady Gowrie Centre where she and her staff recorded pre-school children's height, weight and nutrition. Her research was thorough, exact and detailed. She was troubled by the levels of malnourishment, tooth decay, bone deformities and anaemia, which she saw as largely preventable. Her interest in the posture of young children led her to design suitable chairs and tables for them.

Kincaid attended meetings and conferences of the Victorian branch of the British Medical Association and of the Victorian Paediatric Society. She published her research in the proceedings of the Royal Society of Victoria, the Australian and New Zealand Association for the Advancement of Science, the Pan-Pacific Women's Congress and in the *Medical Journal of Australia*. Small in stature and meticulous in appearance, she was a modest, likeable woman with a sense of humour. She was fond of motoring, travelling, theatre-going and dancing; she also took pleasure in helping to raise her sister's children. Her colleagues Dale and Bull were close friends who shared her love of the arts. Kincaid died on the night of 31 March/1 April 1967 at her East Malvern flat and was cremated.

A. G. T. Zainu'ddin, *They Dreamt of a School* (Melb, 1982); Roy Soc Vic, *Procs*, 23, 1911; *MJA*, 16 Aug 1930, 23 Feb 1935, 26 Mar, 30 July 1938, 8 June 1940; Methodist Ladies' College, Kew, Melb, Archives; City of Melb Archives (Nth Melb L).

HELEN KELEHER

KINDLER, JOHN ERNEST (1906-1968), civil engineer and public servant, was born on 21 October 1906 at Nuriootpa, South Australia, third child of Carl Gustav Ernst Kindler, blacksmith, and his wife Selma Amalia, née Basedow. Educated at Gawler District and Adelaide high schools, and the University of Adelaide (B.E., 1928; M.E., 1930), John joined (1928) J. J. C. Bradfield's [q.v.7] Sydney Harbour Bridge branch of the New South Wales Department of Public Works. On 5 October 1931 at the Lutheran rectory, Undercliffe, he married Sara Kathleen (Kit) Way, a clerk. Next year he transferred to the main roads section of the Department of Transport.

In 1933 the Queensland Bureau of Industry established a board to construct a bridge across the Brisbane River from Fortitude Valley to Kangaroo Point. Bradfield was retained as consulting engineer and Kindler was employed (from 1934) as an assistant to the project's supervising engineer (Sir) James Holt. The Story [q.v.12] bridge, opened in 1940, remains the largest steel bridge in the country to be designed and built by Australians from local materials. Seconded to the Allied Works Council in 1942, Kindler built coastal defences and marine facilities under the direction of (Sir) John Kemp [q.v.], Queensland's wartime deputy director-general of allied works. In 1946 Kindler was made principal designing engineer under Holt, who became chief engineer of the bridges (later structures) branch in the office of the co-ordinator-general of public works. Three years later Holt was elevated to chief engineer, responsible for hydraulics as well as structures, and Kindler was promoted his deputy.

The co-ordinator-general's engineering office gained a high reputation for the quality of its work. Kindler was ideally suited to head the structures branch. Thoroughly trained by Holt, he kept himself informed of overseas developments and was open to new ideas, provided that they passed his rigorous examination. What was more, he had the knowledge, confidence and courage to criticize—publicly, if necessary—accepted practices, and to pioneer new techniques in design and construction. In 1954 Holt succeeded Kemp as co-ordinator-general and Kindler was promoted chief engineer.

Among his numerous hydraulic projects, Kindler was involved in the Tully Falls and Barron River hydro-electric schemes and in supplying water to the Collinsville power-station. He was also involved in the development of university campuses at St Lucia and Townsville, and in the design and construction of the township of Weipa. But it was the designing and building of bridges that fired his imagination and demonstrated the range of his talents. Some twenty major bridges were designed under his supervision, and he took particular care to integrate design with construction.

Kindler was committed to advancing his profession. The Institution of Engineers, Australia, published six of his papers and awarded him the Warren [q.v.6] memorial prize—with co-author William Hansen in 1957 and as sole author in the following year. Kindler won the institution's R. W. (Sir Robert) Chapman [q.v.7] medal in 1958. Chairman (1955) of the institution's Brisbane division, he had been active in founding (1947) the Association of Professional Engineers, Australia, and in preparing the Professional Engineers' case (1958-61) before the Commonwealth Conciliation and Arbitration Commission. He was closely associated with the University of Queensland through his friends, his co-operation in technical investigations and his membership (1955-68) of the board of the faculty of engineering. As convener of the civil engineering sub-committee of the Queensland government's advisory committee on engineering education (formed 1964), he helped to found (1965) the Queensland Institute of Technology.

Stern in appearance, scrupulous by habit and sincere in his dealings with people, Kindler was a sympathetic but exacting taskmaster who earned the respect of his staff and the admiration of his peers. Outside his working hours he enjoyed bushwalking, gardening and classical choral music, and worshipped at St Stephen's Anglican Church, Coorparoo. He died suddenly of myocardial infarction on 25 June 1968 at his desk in the Administration Building, Brisbane, and was cremated; his wife and two daughters survived him. On the day of his death the government was about to announce his appointment as co-ordinator-general of public works. The Q.I.T. named a lecture theatre and a medal after him.

Inst of Engineers, Aust, *Author and Subject Index of Publications 1920-1968* (Syd, 1968); R. L. Whitmore (ed), *Eminent Queensland Engineers* (Brisb, 1984); Brisbane City Council, *Story Bridge* (Brisb, 1992); Co-ordinator General's report, in Dept of Public Works (Qld), *Annual Report*, 1964-65; information from Mrs L. Greenhalgh, Chapel Hill, Brisb, and Mrs P. Madsen, North Carlton, Melb.
RAYMOND L. WHITMORE
E. RICHARD*

KING, ALEXANDER (1904-1970), professor of English, was born on 22 May 1904 at Sherborne, Dorset, England, second son of Rev. Henry Robinson King, a master at Sherborne School, and his wife Emily Constance, née Gray, a schoolteacher. Educated at Sherborne School and New College,

Oxford, Alec obtained third-class honours in classics (B.A., 1928; M.A., 1931). He decided to become a schoolteacher and enrolled at the London Day Training College (Dip.Ed., 1928). There he met Catherine Helen, daughter of (Sir) Walter Murdoch [q.v.10]. He followed her to Western Australia. They were married with Anglican rites on 17 December 1929 at Perth College chapel. King taught French and classics for two years at Guildford Grammar School, but was retrenched during the Depression.

In 1933 he joined Murdoch's department of English at the University of Western Australia as a part-time assistant-lecturer. King progressed to lecturer (1941), senior lecturer (1946) and reader (1952). His principal publications included a school text, co-authored with Martin Ketley, *The Control of Language* (London, 1939); a children's book, *Australian Holiday* (Melbourne, 1945), which King wrote with his wife; W*ordsworth and the Artist's Vision* (London, 1966); and a collection of essays, edited and subsequently published by his son Francis, *The Unprosaic Imagination* (Perth, 1975). King's major writings reflected his preoccupation with the importance of the creative imagination, with the interrelated literary, spiritual and secular significance of poetry, and, above all, with the vital importance of 'the life of the mind', a phrase that recurred in his conversation.

The influence of Wordsworth and the English Romantics were equally discernible in his teaching of literature, for which he was celebrated and best remembered. His was a quiet and wise voice, dedicated to nourishing and affirming the essentially interpretative function of reading and criticism. In an English department which moved from the belletristic approach of his father-in-law to the Leavisite practices of Professor W. A. Edwards, King's voice provided a subtly different and alternative discourse.

Edwards's enthusiasms for Freud were matched by King's more Jungian notions; the Leavisite's idea of the self-sufficiency of the literary text was counterpointed by King's reluctance to embrace ideology or theory. He preferred to deal with seamless linkings of poetry, the visual arts and music. Beyond the tutor's study, he was a fine violinist, president of the university's orchestral society, and a member of its choral and Bach societies. With Catherine established as a leading radio broadcaster and Alec a regular contributor to the city's cultural life, they turned their Claremont home into a vital and often crowded meeting-place for visiting and local artists, performers and community leaders. For many of Alec's colleagues and honours students, his home came to embody the idea of that fusion of literature, life and creative imagination which informed his teaching.

Louis Kahan's sketch (1942) of King caught precisely the quietly contemplative demeanour of an inspiring teacher and scholar.

In 1966 King took up the second chair of English at Monash University, Melbourne. Ill health marred his tenure. Survived by his wife, daughter and two sons, he died of cancer on 7 March 1970 at Canterbury and was cremated.

Gazette of Univ WA, 16, no 1, 1966; *Monash Univ Gazette*, 7, no 7, 1970; *West Australian*, 18 Jan 1966, 14 Mar 1970; Univ WA Archives.   JOHN HAY

KING, ALICE GORDON; *see* ELLIOTT

KING, CHARLES STANLEY; *see* ELLIOTT, ALICE

KING, EDGAR SAMUEL JOHN (1900-1966), surgeon and pathologist, was born on 10 June 1900 at Mosgiel, Otago, New Zealand, son of John King, an English-born bootmaker, and his New Zealand-born wife Beatrice Margaret, née Thomson. During Edgar's childhood the family emigrated to Victoria. He was educated at Melbourne High School and the University of Melbourne (M.B., B.S., 1923; M.D., 1926; M.S., 1931). Determined to become a surgeon, he spent two years as a resident medical officer at the Alfred Hospital, then went to England where he worked in the Middlesex and Guy's hospitals. He qualified as a fellow of the Royal College of Surgeons (1927) and, on his return to Melbourne, as a fellow of the (Royal) Australasian College of Surgeons (1930). At Scots Church, Collins Street, on 28 January 1930 he married with Presbyterian forms Leonora (Lorna) Jane Shaw, a nurse. That year he joined the surgical staff of the Alfred before transferring to the (Royal) Melbourne Hospital in 1931 as surgeon to out-patients.

King's ambition was to advance surgical knowledge and technique rather than to develop a large practice. In the absence of a department of surgery at the University of Melbourne, he combined surgery with research and teaching in the department of pathology. He was Stewart lecturer (1928-31 and 1933-34), senior lecturer (1932) and acting-professor (1934). By 1941 he had published two books and forty-nine papers on a wide range of pathological topics which earned him three Jacksonian essay prizes from the Royal College of Surgeons, England (1930, 1933 and 1938), the David Syme [q.v.6] research prize (1931) and a D.Sc. (1933) from his university. King's chief surgical interest lay in fields then little developed—ischaemic heart disease and carcinoma of the oesophagus.

On 13 October 1939 King was appointed major, Australian Army Medical Corps, Australian Imperial Force. In April 1940 he sailed for the Middle East with the 2nd/2nd Australian General Hospital. Among several temporary attachments to other units, he served with the 2nd/1st Casualty Clearing Station in January 1941, heading a surgical team which treated soldiers wounded in the battles of Bardia and Tobruk, Libya. In August-October he had charge of a special thoracic unit at the 2nd/1st A.G.H. Back home from March 1942, he was promoted temporary lieutenant colonel in January 1944 and placed in command of the 2nd/2nd A.G.H.'s surgical division. From November 1945 to January 1946 he performed the same duties with the 2nd/7th A.G.H. at Lae, New Guinea. He was admitted to hospital in Australia in February 1946 and was transferred to the Retired List on 16 October.

Severe pulmonary tuberculosis forced King to abandon surgery and return to pathology. He was appointed pathologist to the R.M.H. in 1947 and succeeded (Sir) Peter MacCallum [q.v.] in the chair of pathology at the university in 1951. King inherited a department stretched by the postwar influx of students and depleted of equipment and experienced staff. Over the next ten years he created his ideal department, a place where teaching and research in morbid anatomy flourished side by side with experimental pathology. Young people came in increasing numbers for intellectual stimulus and to use facilities previously unavailable in Australia. King was elected a fellow of the Royal Australasian College of Physicians (1949) and of the Australian Academy of Science (1954); the latter honour gave him special pleasure as recognition of the scientific nature of modern pathology. He served on the National Health and Medical Research Council (1956-69), the board of the Walter and Eliza Hall [qq.v.9] Institute (1951-66), the National Radiation Advisory Committee (1959-66), the Commonwealth Serum Laboratories Commission (1961-66), and the Anti-Cancer Council of Victoria whose executive committee he chaired (1963-66). In 1950-58 he was a councillor and chairman of the editorial board of the Royal Australasian College of Surgeons. He was appointed C.M.G. in 1965.

Throughout his career King's chief characteristics were infectious enthusiasm and an enormous capacity for hard work. His earlier studies had made him an outstanding morbid anatomist and histopathologist, but he was at heart a biologist with a wide range of interests and a well-developed scepticism of theories based on tradition rather than adequate evidence. He believed that disease provided opportunities for more subtle and complex experiments than any devised in a laboratory; his instinctive reaction to any new finding was to ponder its wider biological significance. A logical and lucid lecturer, his real strength as a teacher was revealed in small groups where his Socratic and iconoclastic approach was both intimidating and stimulating. He was at his best in leading an informal discussion, often over lunch, about medical or general topics. While invariably friendly and polite, he rarely failed to identify and correct errors of fact or reasoning.

With Lorna and their four daughters, King shared a happy home life. For years after he was struck by illness, his wife helped him to conserve his energy for work by serving him dinner in bed. He was never interested in sport and, apart from reading, had only one absorbing hobby: his stamp collection was among the finest in Australia.

By the end of his life King had published three monographs and more than one hundred papers. In his later years he had little time for original work, but he provided informed criticism even in fields in which he had no personal expertise. Colleagues remembered him as a sage adviser, a confidant of unselfish integrity and a charming companion who showed concern for every member of his department. Despite an incurable illness, he worked on plans for the new department of pathology until a few days before his death. Survived by his wife and daughters, he died of chronic lymphatic leukaemia on 31 January 1966 in East Melbourne and was cremated. His portrait by (Sir) William Dargie is held by the department of pathology, University of Melbourne.

Dept of Pathology, Univ Melb, *The Melbourne School of Pathology* (Melb, 1962); G. L. McDonald (ed), *Roll of the Royal Australasian College of Physicians* (Syd, 1988); *MJA*, 9 July 1966, 20 Aug 1966; *Aust and NZ J of Surgery*, Aug 1966; *Records of the Aust Academy of Science*, 6, no 2, Dec 1967; *Age* (Melb), 1 Feb 1966; personal knowledge.
JOHN V. HURLEY

KING, ELWYN ROY (1894-1941), airman and engineer, was born on 13 May 1894 at The Grove, near Bathurst, New South Wales, eldest child of Richard King, a native-born labourer, and his English-born wife Elizabeth Mary, née Miller. Educated at public schools, Roy studied mechanical engineering by correspondence. He found work repairing bicycles, shearing machinery and motorcars. Enlisting in the Australian Imperial Force on 20 July 1915, he sailed for Egypt in October and served with the 12th Light Horse Regiment from February 1916.

In December King transferred as an air mechanic to the Australian Flying Corps. Sent to England in the following month and selected for pilot training, he was commissioned in October 1917 and joined No.4 Squadron, A.F.C., in France on 21 March 1918. The squadron was then engaged in the difficult and dangerous work of attacking targets on the ground, and it was not until 20 May that King gained his first victory in aerial combat. His flying had at first displeased his commanding officer Major W. A. McCloughry [q.v.10]. Due to King's height (6 ft 3 ins, 191 cm) and bulk, he had difficulty in bringing the control column of his Sopwith Camel far enough back to effect a good landing. The problem diminished when the squadron converted to the roomier Sopwith Snipe.

Promoted captain and appointed flight commander in September, King proved a brilliant patrol leader. His aerial combat record of twenty-six victories, and his tactical skill and daring in attacking ground targets at low level, earned him the Distinguished Flying Cross (1918), the Distinguished Service Order (1919) and a mention in dispatches (1919). Firm and energetic, he was conspicuous in wartime photographs for his broad smile which reflected his genial nature. His colleagues called him 'Bo' or 'Beau', and held him in high regard.

After his A.I.F. appointment terminated in Melbourne on 11 August 1919, King engaged in civil aviation, chiefly with the Larkin [q.v.9]-Sopwith Aviation Co. of Australasia Ltd. He made a number of notable commercial flights, including many 'firsts' in the transport of mail, newspapers and photographs for the press. In 1920 he indignantly declined an invitation to join the Australian Air Corps (later the Royal Australian Air Force) because, at that stage, the authorities had failed to offer an appointment to Frank McNamara [q.v.10], a Victoria Cross winner.

In the early 1920s King left aviation. He and another pilot formed Shipman, King & Co. Pty Ltd which manufactured and imported machinery at its Port Melbourne and Sydney premises. The business suited Roy's engineering talents, and it prospered. He spent much of his time restoring and racing motorcars. On 31 March 1925 he married 20-year-old Josephine Vida Livingston at St John's Anglican Church, Camberwell, Melbourne. Called up for R.A.A.F. service in December 1939, he was initially designated a pilot, but was transferred to the Administrative and Special Duties Branch in 1940. He commanded three flying training schools before taking charge of the R.A.A.F. Base, Point Cook, in October 1941 as acting group captain. Survived by his wife, son and daughter, he died of cerebral oedema on 28 November 1941 at Point Cook and was cremated. Hun-

dreds of mourners from military and civil aviation circles attended his funeral.

E. J. Richards (comp), *Australian Airmen* (Melb, 1918); F. M. Cutlack, *The Australian Flying Corps* (Syd, 1923); A. H. Cobby, *High Adventure* (Melb, 1942); C. Shores et al, *Above the Trenches* (Lond, 1990); embarkation roll, 12th Light Horse Regiment *and* War diary, 4th Squadron, Aust Flying Corps (AWM); information from Mrs P. King, Yamba, Mr R. King, Port Macquarie, NSW, and Mr F. S. Livingston, Brighton, Melb.   ALAN FRASER

KING, HERBERT JOHN (1892-1973), photographer and field naturalist, was born on 31 May 1892 in Hobart, third son of John King, cycle manufacturer, and his wife Susannah, née Robinson. In 1900 the Kings moved to Launceston where Herbert attended the Commercial College. Thereafter he was employed in the family business which manufactured and imported bicycles and motorcycles. He enjoyed riding motorbikes, both in competitive events and as a means of exploring Tasmania; in particular, he came to love the remote wilderness areas. His companion in these travels was his wife Lucy Minna, née Large, whom he had married at the registrar's office, Hobart, on 23 December 1918. Like her husband, she was a devout Christadelphian. In 1922 King was a member of the first party to use motorcycles to reach Gustav Weindorfer's [q.v.12] Waldheim resort at Cradle Mountain. From 1932 until his retirement in 1951 King managed the family firm, but, at heart, work simply gave him the resources to support his outside interests.

Having taken up photography as a boy, King joined the Northern Tasmanian Camera Club in 1912. That year he won awards for his published photographs. These were the first of his many pictorial black-and-white compositions to win prizes or to be exhibited in Australia and abroad. A self-taught amateur, technically innovative and painstaking, King experimented with a range of colour processes (for slides and 16-mm movies) and with specialized techniques, including panorama, infra-red, aerial and time-lapse photography. During the years of World War II he produced a series of colour-movies on natural history for the Queen Victoria Museum and Art Gallery, where he was to be honorary photographer (1958-62). In 1947 he helped to establish the Launceston Cine Society.

King's interest in Tasmania's natural history developed into a passion that came to dominate his photography and his life. He was a member (1942-63) of the Royal Society of Tasmania, and a founding member (1949), president (1950-64) and life member (1955) of the Launceston Field Naturalists' Club. His photographs illustrated several books, in his lifetime and after it. King's pioneering efforts in listing, collecting and photographing Tasmania's flora prompted Lord Talbot de Malahide to finance and publish in six parts *The Endemic Flora of Tasmania* (London, 1967-78). Part IV (1973) was dedicated to King.

Widely known as 'H.J.', King suffered as a youth from a stammer which he later overcame. He gave numerous illustrated lectures —some as community fund-raisers—largely on photography, Tasmanian landscapes and natural history. Of average build, with a fair complexion, an upright brush of hair, a long face and a rather serious expression, he was reserved by nature but held strong views, a combination which sometimes resulted in an abruptness of manner. Yet he was generous and patient when sharing his passions and expertise, especially with the young and the disabled. Survived by his wife and two daughters, King died on 18 February 1973 at Launceston and was cremated.

H. J. King, *Tasmania Remembered*, eds G. W. Cox and E. V. Ratcliff (Launc, Tas, 1974); R. A. Ferrall, *Tasmanians All* (Launc, 1982); J. G. Branagan and M. Woodroffe, *Tasmania Revisited* (Launc, 1990); C. Long, *Tasmanian Photographers 1840-1940*, ed G. Winter (Hob, 1995); *Launceston Naturalist*, 6, no 5, Mar 1973, p 1; *Sunday Examiner-Express*, 17 June 1972; King papers *and* information from Mrs M. Cameron (Queen Victoria Museum & Art Gallery, Launc); family papers and collections, held by Mrs D. Glennie, Launc.

MARGARET TASSELL

KING, ROBERT ARTHUR (1886-1960), saddler, labour official and politician, was born on 9 April 1886 at Launceston, Tasmania, son of Robert King, tailor, and his wife Louisa, née Barrett. Young Bob left school at 13 and was apprenticed to a saddler, but he found limited opportunities in that trade and took work in coastal shipping. At St John's Anglican Church, Launceston, on 2 November 1910 he married Florence (Floss) May Mullins. Persuaded by E. H. Farrar [q.v.8] to join the Australian Saddlery Trade Employees' Federation, King moved to Sydney late that year. As A.S.T.E.F. president he was involved in the union's restructuring and modernization, inspired by a whirl of socialist ideas.

Joining the executive of the Labor Council of New South Wales, King was its assistant-secretary (1923-30) and organizer (1930-34). He saw the labour movement as needing that style of open discussion engineered by the visit of the British socialist Tom Mann [q.v.10]. King succeeded J. S. Garden [q.v.8] as secretary of the Labor Council in 1934. Two years later they prevented an attempted takeover of radio 2KY by their former political

hero J. T. Lang [q.v.9]. As secretary of the board of control, King extricated 2KY from its financial difficulties and 'was bookkeeper and everything else, except the technician and announcer'. He was to be president of the Australian Federation of Commercial Broadcasting Stations in the 1940s.

The revival of militancy on the industrial front was matched by a growth of united front politics on the left. In 1938 King attended the May Day celebrations in the Soviet Union. He also worked with A. S. McAlpine [q.v.] to involve labour in progressive social action. Bob, as he was known to friends and acquaintances, combined with the Catholic right against the communists after 1945 and managed to remain unopposed as secretary in successive elections until the bitter years of conflict preceding his retirement in 1958. In his prime he was 'a blunt, forceful speaker' and a relentless, quiet achiever.

King had always seen politics as important in pursuing the interests of organized workers. He served on the Australian Labor Party's State executive (1927-28, 1939-52). Nominated to the Legislative Council in 1931 during the dramatic confrontation between Lang and Governor Sir Philip Game [q.v.8], he was elected to the reconstituted council for twelve years in 1934 and re-elected until 1960. King had been briefly expelled from the Labor Party by a special conference in August 1936. He supported R. J. Heffron [q.v.14] in manoeuvres against Lang's leadership of the parliamentary party, and was a delegate to most A.L.P. federal conferences between 1936 and 1953. In the postwar era of rising anti-communism King co-operated with the right, but, as a committee-member of the Australian-Russian Society until his resignation in 1948, he was under surveillance by the Commonwealth Investigation Service.

His extensive commitments included serving as vice-president (1935-57) of the Australasian Council of Trade Unions, and as a member of the Commonwealth War Workers' Housing Trust (1939-45), the New South Wales Committee of Advice on Man Power (from 1941) and the Commonwealth's Immigration Advisory Committee (1945). King attended the meeting of the World Federation of Trade Unions in Paris in 1945 and conferences in Geneva of the International Labor Organization (1945 and 1947). He served on the royal commission of inquiry into the gas industry in 1948-49.

In his sixties King's brown hair had whitened; a slight stoop and hesitant walk suggested failing health, but he was alert and still in control. Grasping their historical significance, in 1955 he persuaded the Labor Council to donate its pre-1940 records to the Mitchell [q.v.5] Library. When he retired as secretary of the Labor Council in 1958 he was appointed manager of radio 2KY and a director of radio 2HD, Newcastle. He died on 27 February 1960 in Prince Henry Hospital, Little Bay, and was cremated; his wife and two daughters survived him. In a public tribute Heffron praised King for being 'an excellent type of Australian citizen' who had given 'a lifetime of service in the interests of trade unionism and Labor politics'.

F. Farrell, *International Socialism & Australian Labour* (Syd, 1981); B. Nairn, *The 'Big Fella'* (Melb, 1986); G. Freudenberg, *Cause for Power* (Syd, 1991); R. Markey, *In Case of Oppression* (Syd, 1994); *PD* (NSW), 8 Mar 1960, p 2774; Labor Council of NSW, *Yearly Report*, 1922-23, *and* Minutes, 23 Nov 1922, 23 Jan 1930 (ML); *SMH*, 27, 29 Feb 1960; *Sun-Herald*, 28 Feb 1960; AG 119/79 item 935 (AA, Canb).   FRANK FARRELL

KING, ROY (1897-1959), army officer, was born on 27 August 1897 at Tighes Hill, Newcastle, New South Wales, fourth child of native-born parents James King, miner, and his wife Bessie, née Sharpe. Roy attended Cooks Hill Public School and entered the Royal Military College, Duntroon, Federal Capital Territory, in February 1916. He graduated in December 1919, too late to serve in World War I, and was commissioned lieutenant in the Permanent Military Forces.

In 1920-21 King trained in England. Receiving a round of staff and regimental postings which was the lot of regular officers, he served in Queensland as adjutant and quartermaster to the 42nd Battalion (1921-25), the 26th Battalion (1925-27) and the 11th Light Horse Regiment (1931-34). During a term as a staff officer at the 1st District Base he was honorary aide-de-camp (1928-29) to the governor. On 12 March 1929 at the Albert Street Methodist Church, Brisbane, King married a divorcee Florence Lorna Grainger, née Reynolds, who had two sons from her first marriage. In 1934 he was posted to the 8th L.H.R. at Benalla, Victoria, and in 1936 to Army Headquarters, Melbourne. Next year he was promoted major.

Seconded to the Australian Imperial Force, King sailed for the Middle East in May 1940 as brigade major to the 19th Brigade. In December he was promoted lieutenant colonel and given command of the 2nd/5th Battalion. He led the unit in the advance across Libya (January-March 1942) and in the attempt to defend Greece (April). For his conduct of the rearguard and a flank-guard which covered the withdrawals from Kalabáka on 18 April and Brállos on the 23rd, he was awarded the Distinguished Service Order. His commander Brigadier (Sir) Stanley Savige [q.v.] described King's handling of his battalion as 'masterly'. Evacuated on 26 April, King and his men were sent to Syria in June. They took part in the battle of Damour and the defeat of Vichy-French forces in July. King was promoted colonel in November and was seconded to the staff of the 7th Division. He was twice mentioned in dispatches. In March 1942 he returned to Australia.

Two months later King was given command of the 3rd Brigade, located near Darwin. On 18 February 1943 he took charge of the 16th Brigade which had returned from the Papuan campaign. The 16th trained extensively in North Queensland and moved to Aitape, New Guinea, in December 1944. Operating over difficult terrain and in monsoonal rains, the brigade advanced 30 miles (48 km) in January-February 1945, inflicting heavy losses on strong Japanese forces. At the end of the arduous Wewak campaign in August, King was admitted to hospital and brought home to Australia. In 1946 he was appointed C.B.E.

King was director (1945-47) of military training at A.H.Q. and commandant (1947-49) of the Australian Staff College, Queenscliff, before joining the British Commonwealth Occupation Force in Japan as brigadier in charge of administration and commander of the Australian military component. With the outbreak of the Korean War in June 1950, his workload increased considerably: the existing organization in Japan was used to support all Commonwealth forces operating in Korea. Promoted temporary major general in August 1951 (substantive March 1952), King was appointed principal administrative officer, B.C.O.F., in Japan and Korea. He returned to Australia in November 1951 and commanded military districts in Queensland (1951-52) and South Australia (1952-54). Following his retirement on 28 August 1954, he lived in Sydney.

Although King's later appointments were significant, his most important contribution to the army was made during World War II when he demonstrated—against the prejudices of some senior Militia officers—that regular officers could make excellent unit and formation commanders. Major General (Sir) Jack Stevens [q.v.], King's divisional commander in New Guinea, had judged him 'a good trainer of men', but 'an introvert and an isolationist'. From a more detached perspective, the war historian Gavin Long [q.v.] described him as a 'shy man really, sceptical, keen on his job, without affectation, resolute'. Survived by his wife and stepsons, King died of a coronary occlusion on 24 September 1959 in his home at Collaroy Plateau and was cremated with Anglican rites.

G. Long, *To Benghazi* (Canb, 1952) and *Greece, Crete and Syria* (Canb, 1953) and *The Final Campaigns* (Canb, 1963); AWM 67 and 3DRL 3561 (AWM).   JEFFREY GREY

KINGSBURY, BRUCE STEEL (1918-1942), soldier and real-estate agent, was born on 8 January 1918 in Melbourne, second child of English-born parents Philip Blencowe Kingsbury, estate agent, and his wife Florence Annie, née Steel. Bruce was educated at Windsor State School and (on a scholarship) at Melbourne Technical College. At the outset of his career he preferred life in the bush and left the city for a job as caretaker on a farm at Boundary Bend by the Murray River. He and his boyhood friend Alan Avery later worked on sheep-stations in New South Wales. Kingsbury returned to Melbourne, entered his father's real-estate business at Northcote and played in the Jika Cricket Association.

Enlisting in the Australian Imperial Force on 16 May 1940, Kingsbury was posted to the 2nd/2nd Pioneer Battalion before obtaining a transfer to Avery's unit, the 2nd/14th Battalion. The two young men were assigned to No.9 Platoon and formed a close friendship with Harry Saunders, brother of the Aboriginal soldier Captain Reg Saunders. The battalion embarked for the Middle East in October. After training in Palestine and garrisoning Mersa Matruh, Egypt, the unit took part in the invasion of Syria which began on 8 June 1941. On the 24th, at Jezzine in the Lebanese mountains, Kingsbury's platoon attacked a rocky peak, known as Hill 1284, which was held by the Vichy French. Although the assault failed, the French commander was to describe the courage and endurance of the Australian infantrymen that day as 'incomparable'.

The members of the 2nd/14th Battalion returned to Australia in March 1942. Five months later they were sent to Papua to halt the Japanese on the Kokoda Track. At Isurava on 27 and 28 August the Japanese, with superior numbers, repeatedly attacked the battalion's positions. On the 29th they broke through the right flank, threatening the Australians' headquarters. It was essential to regain lost ground immediately. No.9 Platoon had suffered heavy losses, but its survivors volunteered to join in a counter-attack. On his own initiative Kingsbury rushed forward with a Bren gun, shooting from the hip against terrific enemy machine-gun fire and inflicting many casualties. He waited for his comrades to catch up, but, before they did, he moved ahead again, still firing, until he was killed by a sniper's bullet.

For his coolness, determination, complete disregard for his own safety, and devotion to duty in the face of great odds, Kingsbury was awarded the Victoria Cross. The battalion's second-in-command Major P. E. Rhoden recorded that Kingsbury's valour had demonstrated that the previously undefeated Japanese could be beaten, and that it also inspired the 2nd/14th's opposition to the enemy over the succeeding weeks. Kingsbury was buried in Bomana war cemetery, Port Moresby. A Melbourne suburb was named after him and a commemorative plaque was unveiled at his old primary school.

W. B. Russell, *The Second Fourteenth Battalion* (Syd, 1948); D. McCarthy, *South-West Pacific Area —First Year* (Canb, 1959); H. Gordon, *The Embarrassing Australian* (Melb, 1962); J. C. McAllester, *Men of the 2/14 Battalion* (Melb, 1990); information from Mr T. A. Cochrane, Clontarf, Brisb.

JAMES C. MCALLESTER

KINGSTON, NATHANIEL CLAUDE (1886-1978), musician and theatre manager, was born on 19 July 1886 at Richmond, Melbourne, only child of Tasmanian-born parents Nathaniel Kingston, contractor, and his second wife Isabella, née Stanley. Educated initially at state schools in Melbourne and at Goulburn, New South Wales, Claude was sent to Wesley College, Melbourne, but left at 15 and enrolled at Bradshaw's Business College. He worked as a piano salesman and later for a grainbroker.

Determined to become a musician, Kingston studied piano and organ with Frederick Mewton and Professor Joshua Ives [q.v.9] and taught music in his spare time. In 1905 he was appointed organist-choirmaster at Christ Church, Ormond; he transferred to the Presbyterian Church, Elsternwick, in 1908. Next year he acquired from Charles MacMahon [q.v.10] rights to the film, *For the Term of His Natural Life*, which he successfully exhibited in Victoria and New Zealand.

In September 1910 Kingston was appointed organist at the Collins Street Baptist Church; he was soon given charge of the choir. At that church on 13 May 1916 he married Mabel Ella Thompson who, as Madame Ella Kingston, was to have a successful Australian concert and oratorio career, and to direct (1924-40) the church choir. Kingston produced many oratorios and cantatas at the church and at the Melbourne Town Hall, including the first Australian performance (1921) of Massenet's *Marie Magdeleine*, with Ella singing the leading role.

A new career opened up for Kingston after he visited the United States of America in 1919-20. On his return he worked as concert manager in Western Australia for the entrepreneur Hugh D. McIntosh [q.v.10]. In 1921 he became director of celebrity tours for J. & N. Tait [qq.v.12] who had recently joined J. C. Williamson [q.v.6] Ltd. Kingston spent much of his time promoting grand opera, Gilbert and Sullivan, ballet and musical comedies for 'the Firm'. Based in Sydney for nearly twenty years, he managed the Melba [q.v.10]-Williamson opera tours of 1924 and 1928, and the visits of such stars as Yehudi (Baron) Menuhin, Mischa Levitzki, (Dame) Clara Butt and Feodor Chaliapin.

In 1940 Kingston came back to Melbourne as general manager of the organization's theatrical business. A director (from 1948) of J. C. Williamson Theatres Ltd, he was made its executive-director (1958) and a director (1963) of the parent company, J. C. Williamson Ltd. In 1963 he was appointed O.B.E. He worked part time in his Comedy Theatre office until he was 85, and published his memoirs, *It Don't Seem a Day Too Much*, in 1971.

Some saw Kingston as a shy, charming, slightly old-fashioned figure. Others regarded him as a shadowy presence who exerted power behind the scene. In a wider sphere Kingston showed a keen interest in horse-racing and the stock market. He died on 24 January 1978 in East Melbourne and was buried in Brighton cemetery. His wife predeceased (1966) him. There were no children.

D. M. Himbury, *Theatre of the Word* (Melb, 1993); *Aust Musical News*, 1 May 1920, 1 Jan 1923, July-Oct 1934; Collins Street Baptist Church, Deacons' Minute-books, 1910-44; information from Mr J. McCallum, Pitt Water, NSW, Mr C. Dorning, Frankston, Mr L. Fiander, Kew, Lady Tait, South Yarra, and Ms J. Youlden, North Caulfield, Melb.

MIMI COLLIGAN

KINSELA, CHARLES HENRY WILLIAM (1886-1944), funeral director, was born on 8 April 1886 in Sydney, second son of native-born parents Charles Kinsela (d.1900), undertaker, and his wife Ellen Elizabeth, née Milham. His paternal great-grandparents were both convicts. Educated privately and at Rockdale College, young Charles served (1903-08) in the 1st Light Horse Regiment (New South Wales Lancers). In 1906 he became manager of the undertaking firm (founded by his grandfather in 1830) which was under his mother's proprietorship. At St Michael's Anglican Church, Surry Hills, on 26 October 1910 he married Beatrice Veronica Hope De Bello, a milliner.

Shrewdly moving away from the Victorian image of undertaking as a somewhat seedy but necessary craft, the family prospered through a combination of service and respectability. When Kinsela took control of the firm in 1914 he claimed to have 'the most up to date plant in the Commonwealth providing Reform Funerals at a LOWER RATE than any other in the trade'. As a lucrative sideline he provided carriages or motor vehicles for weddings. The first undertaker in Sydney to purchase (1920) motor hearses and a mortuary ambulance, he established a large complex at 116 Oxford Street, near the Victoria Barracks.

After World War I Kinsela transformed himself from undertaker to funeral director and visited California several times, bringing home some of the most advanced manifestations of the American way of death. His daughter Beatrice was a pioneer female embalmer. Kinsela designed a gleaming, open-cabined Packard hearse and deployed a cortège of glassed-in Cadillac motorcars. He engaged the architect C. B. Dellit [q.v.13] to convert (1932-33) a multi-storeyed building in Taylor Square into Art Deco funeral premises containing Protestant and Catholic chapels, offices and 'storerooms'. This 'building with a soul'—with its Rayner Hoff [q.v.9] statues, 'Fan of Life' shrine, 'Sunset of Life' amber glass, delicate colours and cinema-style lighting—was a veritable secular temple 'to help the bereaved bear their trouble by a greater understanding of the mystery of the great Beyond'.

On 6 May 1938 the firm was registered as a private company, Charles Kinsela Pty Ltd, with a capital of £100 000 in £1 shares; it had thirty-eight branches and agencies (mainly in the eastern suburbs of Sydney), modern equipment and a solid reputation. Moreover, the firm's metropolitan market-share had expanded from about 9 per cent in 1920 to 15 per cent in the late 1930s when Kinselas conducted between 1700 and 1900 funerals a year. A relatively stable price structure after 1921 produced increasing profits through added volume and government and military contracts, despite the decline in infant mortality.

Kinsela was a dynamic, flamboyant and affable businessman. A foundation committee-member (1935-44) of the Australian Funeral Directors' Association, he did what he could to 'control . . . erroneous public opinion about the funeral director'. He was 5 ft 10 ins (178 cm) tall and solidly built, with a square face, and blue eyes framed by spectacles; his wavy grey hair was complemented by a toothbrush moustache. Immaculately dressed in a double-breasted suit and luxuriant buttonhole, Kinsela combined the service traditions of the family firm with the skills and business attributes of a Californian funeral director. His expansive traits and expensive tastes were restrained by a shrewd company secretary. Kinsela was a keen motor yachtsman, a lawn bowler, a show-horse judge and a trotting-horse owner who belonged to Tattersall's, the New South Wales Masonic, the St George's Motor Boat and the Rose Bay Bowling and Recreation clubs.

Survived by his wife, daughter and two sons, he died of chronic nephritis on 24 November 1944 at his Bondi home and was cremated with Anglican and Masonic rites. His estate was sworn for probate at £21 924. Following internal disputes, Charles Kinsela Pty Ltd went into voluntary liquidation in

1982. The Taylor Square edifice became a restaurant and then a bar and nightclub, still with 'Kinselas' in neon lights above the entrance.

Aust Funeral Directors' Assn, *Report of Conference* (Melb, 1936); *Aust Funeral Director*, May, July, Aug 1935; *SMH*, 5 June 1883, 22, 23 Oct 1900, 20 Dec 1932, 25 Nov 1944, 5 Dec 1981, 17 Feb 1982; *Propeller*, 11 Oct 1934; Charles Kinsela Pty Ltd, records (held by Aust Securities Com, Syd) *and* funeral registers, address and account books (ML); information from Mr A. Contini, Syd, and Mr R. Allison, Melb; family information.

D. B. WATERSON

KINSELLA, EDWARD PARNELL (1893-1967), judge, was born on 10 June 1893 at Glen Innes, New South Wales, second of six children of Patrick Kinsella, a sheriff's officer from Ireland, and his native-born wife Mary Jane, née Shannon. Patrick had twelve children from a previous marriage. Educated at St Patrick's College, Goulburn, Ted joined the Department of Lands as a cadet draughtsman on 10 June 1910 and was stationed at Wagga Wagga, Moree and Glen Innes.

He enlisted in the Australian Imperial Force on 28 August 1914, embarked for Egypt with the 2nd Battalion and served in the Gallipoli campaign from the landing to the evacuation. Transferred to the 54th Battalion, Sergeant Kinsella sailed for France in June 1916 and was commissioned on 23 August (lieutenant 28 December). He took leave in Australia in June-July 1918 and returned to France in November where he was posted to the 56th Battalion. On 2 August 1919 he married Marie Louise Josephine Graff at the Town Hall, Marchienne-au-Pont, Belgium.

Back in Sydney, Kinsella returned to the Department of Lands in February 1920. His A.I.F. appointment terminated on 25 July. From June 1923 he worked as a clerk in the returned soldiers' settlement branch. Despite bouts of illness, he continued to study part time at the University of Sydney (LL.B., 1927) and was admitted to the Bar on 5 May 1927. As the Australian Labor Party's candidate, he was elected to the Legislative Assembly for George's River in 1930, but was defeated in 1932 and 1935 when he supported the Lang [q.v.9] Labor Party.

In the 1930s Kinsella developed a sound practice from Chancery and University chambers, mainly in common law and industrial work. On 19 January 1943 he was appointed a District Court judge. He joined the Industrial Commission of New South Wales from 7 October; his work included chairing the Crown Employees' Appeal Board. Six ft 4 ins (193 cm) tall, he wore striped trousers, a black coat and a homburg. On 18 January

1950 he was elevated to the Supreme Court bench. Austere and dignified, with a passion for justice, he ran a tight court and wrote careful judgements. Kinsella twice served as royal commissioner, inquiring in 1951-52 into Frederick Lincoln McDermott's conviction for murder and in 1962-63 into off-course betting. He was also judge in Admiralty from 1961 until he retired on 6 June 1963.

A leading Catholic layman, Kinsella was a foundation member (1952) and chairman (1961-67) of St Vincent's Hospital's advisory board and president of the Anti-Tuberculosis Association of New South Wales. He was a keen racegoer and was elected to the Australian Jockey Club in 1942. Although he also belonged to the University Club, the Sydney Cricket Ground and the Hunters Hill Bowling Club, he was not gregarious and most enjoyed fishing. In 1964 he was appointed C.B.E. Kinsella died on 20 December 1967 at Darlinghurst and was buried in Northern Suburbs cemetery; his wife, two daughters and two of their three sons survived him.

Aust Law J, 27 June 1963, p 60; *Sunday Telegraph* (Syd), 15 Apr 1962; *Daily Telegraph* (Syd), 21 Dec 1967; *SMH*, 27 Oct 1930, 20 Jan, 7 Oct 1943, 25 Nov 1952, 4 Sept, 23 Nov 1962, 5 Apr 1963, 21 Dec 1967; information from Mrs M. P. Sexton, Deakin, Canb.

MARTHA RUTLEDGE

KIRBY, SIR JAMES NORMAN (1899-1971), industrialist and philanthropist, was born on 15 June 1899 in Sydney, fifth child of Victorian-born parents Louis Kirby, plasterer, and his wife Margaret, née Gartner. Educated at Newtown Public School and Francis Street Catholic School, Marrickville, in 1914 James was apprenticed to a motor mechanic at 7s. 6d. a week. He completed his training with the Howarth Petrol Economiser Co. Drawn to manufacturing machine tools, he set up his own automative-engine reconditioning business, James N. Kirby Pty Ltd, in 1924. At St Paul's Catholic Church, Dulwich Hill, on 21 November 1925 he married a saleswoman Agnes Ann Wessler whom he later described as his greatest asset.

A foundation member (1931) of the Metals Treatment Society of New South Wales (Australian Institute of Metals), Kirby appropriated the micrometer as his advertising symbol. His firm reground cylinders in the engines of Sir Charles Kingsford Smith's [q.v.9] aeroplanes. Kirby's reputation for precision engineering led to his involvement in the Commonwealth government's manufacture of military aircraft; in 1940 he was appointed manager of the Commonwealth Aircraft Corporation Pty Ltd. During his tenure he formed connexions with the British air industry and began a long friendship with

Lord Hives, chairman of Rolls Royce Ltd. Kirby's factories made field-guns and aircraft components.

After World War II Kirby started to manufacture consumer goods (Crosley refrigerators and television sets, Bendix washing machines, Pye transistor radios and high-fidelity equipment, lawnmowers and other household goods). He sensed a big future in industry based on suburban expansion and home-making. Strengthening his British links, he was appointed a director of Nuffield (Australia) Ltd by Lord Nuffield—another dear friend—and with George A. Lloyd set up a car assembly plant (the British Motor Corporation (Australia) Pty Ltd) in Sydney to build Morris Oxfords.

Founding chairman (1958) of the Manufacturing Industries Advisory Council, Kirby attended the eleventh Australian Citizenship Convention in Canberra in 1960: he spoke in favour of sensitive assimilation strategies and opposed the formation of ethnic 'cliques' in factories; he also warned against the 'high sounding' New Citizens Council of Australia, agreeing with Albert Monk [q.v.] that it was connected with 'Communists, crooks and tyrants of the unions'. Although Kirby received limited formal education, he formed strong university ties. He was a foundation council-member (1947) of the New South Wales University of Technology, and of the Nuclear Research Foundation at the University of Sydney where he became a friend of Professor Harry Messel.

In the latter part of his life the bulky-framed, ruddy-faced and laconic Kirby served as a director of many companies, including Qantas Empire Airways Ltd. He was appointed C.B.E. in 1956 and knighted in 1962. His idiosyncratic armorial crest bore the sign of a marlin to indicate his love of fishing, a motto in an Aboriginal dialect— 'Ngaben-Bidjigarme' ('I all hands hold')—and the words 'For God and Empire'. He was an honoured Rotarian, a director of the Australian Elizabethan Theatre Trust and deputy-chairman of the Winston Churchill Memorial Trust (Australia) for many years.

Kirby belonged to the New South Wales, American National and Australian Golf clubs and to Royal Sydney Yacht Squadron. He was also a record-holding fisherman, and an orchid grower. His horse, Home James, won the Grafton Cup in 1963 and 1964, and its owner developed a close association with Clarence River Jockey Club, of which he became patron. In keeping with his preference for close working ties outside the spotlight, he enjoyed the relaxed fraternity of the country track more than the members' stand at Randwick. He was made an honorary citizen of Grafton in 1970. Sir James died at his Vaucluse home on 30 July 1971 and was cre-

mated with Anglican rites; his wife and two sons survived him.

Paternalistic and charitable, Kirby had long admired American industry's culture of patronage. In 1967 he had established the James N. Kirby Foundation for educational and charitable work, with a grant of $2 million, most of his personal fortune. 'I came up the hard way', he said, 'I suppose it is because of that I felt I had to plough something back'. The foundation, chaired by one of his sons, has distributed more than $5 million since its inception.

J. Gunn, *High Corridors* (Brisb, 1988); H. Beran, *'I Feel I Should Plough Something Back'* (Syd, 1993); James N. Kirby Foundation, *Annual Report*, 1992; *SMH*, 30 May 1957, 4 July 1958, 11, 12 Feb 1960, 28 Mar, 22 Sept 1961, 19, 20 Oct 1967, 31 July, 4 Aug 1971; *Aust Financial Review*, 19 Oct 1967; *Daily Examiner* (Grafton), 15 July 1970, 31 July, 3 Aug 1971; records of the School of Physics *and* Sir Leslie Herron, 'Valedictory Address' at the funeral of Sir James Kirby, Box 85, G47 (Univ Syd Archives); Nuclear Research Foundation papers, Box 212, G47 (Univ Syd Archives).   PETER COCHRANE

KIRBY, JOHN WILLIAM (1935-1967), soldier, was born on 11 February 1935 in Sydney, only child of Australian-born parents John Edward Kirby, dealer, and his wife Alice Kathleene, née Casson. Young Jack was raised at Lewisham and attended Petersham Presbyterian Church where he was a leader in the Boys' Brigade. He was apprenticed to a motor mechanic and rose to sergeant in the Citizen Military Forces' regimental cadets.

Enlisting in the Australian Regular Army on 18 May 1953, Kirby served in the Republic of (South) Korea with the 1st Battalion, Royal Australian Regiment, in 1954-55. He was in Malaya with 3RAR in 1957-59, for part of the Emergency. Corporal Kirby was mentioned in the press in May 1959 for his bravery in leading three men on a forced march to obtain supplies for comrades at a remote jungle camp. On 10 June 1961 at St John Vianney's Catholic Church, Manly, Queensland, he married Beverley Anne Bailey, an assistant-chemist; they were to remain childless. Promoted sergeant that year, he served as an instructor (1963-65) at the Far East Land Forces Jungle Warfare School at Kota Tinggi, Johore, Malaysia. In June 1964 and March-April 1965 he was detached for service in Sarawak, Borneo.

Kirby was posted to 6RAR in July 1965 and promoted temporary warrant officer, class two, in March 1966. The battalion began a tour of duty in the Republic of Vietnam (South Vietnam) in June, operating from Nui Dat in Phuoc Tuy province. Appointed company sergeant major to 'D' Company, Kirby soon became popular with national servicemen and regular soldiers alike; they respected him for his experience and abilities, and affectionately nicknamed him 'Big Jack'.

On 18 August 1966, while on patrol in a dense rubber plantation, the 108 men of 'D' Company encountered a formation of People's Liberation Armed Forces (Viet Cong) and North Vietnamese regular troops, estimated at 2500 in number. In the resulting three-hour 'fire-fight', later known as the battle of Long Tan, Kirby was a mainstay of the besieged Australians. Under continuous fire, he moved among the soldiers, distributing ammunition, organizing the collection and evacuation of the wounded, steadying and encouraging the men and even joking with them on occasions. At one stage he rushed from the company's defensive position and silenced an enemy machine-gun post being set up 50 metres from the perimeter. Immediately after the battle Sergeant Jim Myles, who arrived with the relief force, encountered Kirby carrying two Australian casualties—one over each shoulder. For his bravery and leadership, he was awarded the Distinguished Conduct Medal.

During Operation Tamborine misdirected artillery rounds from the 161st New Zealand Field Battery landed on 'D' Company's position on 6 February 1967. Kirby was hit in the chest and died before he could be evacuated. Private Ron Eglinton recalled: 'He was a big, gruff, heavy man, a real father figure to us all and he was dead ... It was just so bloody pointless'. Kirby's remains were returned to Australia and cremated with Presbyterian forms. His wife survived him.

T. Burstall, *The Soldiers' Story* (Brisb, 1986); L. McAulay, *The Battle of Long Tan* (Melb, 1986); S. Rintoul, *Ashes of Vietnam* (Melb, 1987); I. McNeill, *To Long Tan* (Syd, 1993); I. McNeill with A. Ekins, *A Province for a Battlefield* (Syd, 1998); *Australian*, 18 Aug 1988, special edn.

ASHLEY EKINS
IAN MCNEILL

KIRKE, BASIL EVERALD WHARTON (1893-1958), radio broadcaster and manager, was born on 29 March 1893 at Armidale, New South Wales, fourth child of Australian-born parents Samuel Wharton Kirke, draftsman, and his wife Ellen, née Clements. The family moved to Manly, Sydney, in the early 1900s. Basil attended Fort Street Model School and played Rugby Union football. About 1910 he sailed to Fiji where he worked in turn as an overseer and manager of the Viria Estate sugar-plantation. While on leave, he joined (1911) the Manly Life Saving Club and in February 1914 participated in a mass surf-rescue.

On 19 February 1915 Kirke enlisted in the Australian Imperial Force and was posted to the 2nd Australian General Hospital. Wounded at Gallipoli in October, he was invalided home and discharged on 21 February 1916. That year he entered the British Colonial Service. After being stationed in Fiji, he was sent to the British Solomon Islands Protectorate as inspector, armed constabulary. He spent some time in Malaya before managing (1919) the Jawarare rubber-plantation in Papua. At St Monica's Catholic Church, Footscray, Melbourne, on 21 February 1920 he married Margaret Tunney (d.1926); they were to have one child. Kirke was employed by the New South Wales Department of Lands as temporary manager (from 1920) of the Mullumbimby Soldiers' Settlement and as an inspector (1922-23). He then farmed his own sugar-plantation at Condong, Tweed River.

In 1924 Kirke obtained a post with radio-station 2BL, Sydney. Full of energy and drive, he wrote all 2BL's advertising copy, filled the roles of chief studio announcer and sports commentator, and, as 'Uncle Bas', broadcast popular children's programmes. In June 1928 he and his engineer Ray Alsop stayed on air for eighteen hours to report the final leg (Fiji-Australia) of (Sir) Charles Kingsford Smith's [q.v.9] historic trans-Pacific flight.

Kirke moved to Western Australia in 1929 as manager of the national station 6WF, operated by the Australian Broadcasting Co. (Commission from 1932). On 6 November 1929 at Scots Church, Fremantle, he married with Presbyterian forms 24-year-old Jessie Craig Cahill. Disparagingly dubbed 'the wise man from the East', he soon won over his critics and attracted listeners with daring antics such as broadcasting from the seabed off Cottesloe and from inside Yallingup caves. Despite the Depression, he was credited with increasing the State's radio licences to almost 50 000. He was manager for Victoria in 1936-37, then manager for New South Wales. In the latter post he helped to found (1938) the A.B.C. Senior Officers' Association; he organized (1940) a short-wave service which broadcast in several languages; and he employed women announcers so that men could be released for the armed forces.

When the Papua and New Guinea service of the A.B.C. went to air on 9PA Port Moresby in July 1946, Kirke was its station manager and local controller. Disappointed at the service's slow development, he returned to Sydney and was inspector (from 1951) at head office. In 1953 he returned to Western Australia as manager, and lobbied tirelessly for new offices and studios. He fell seriously ill in 1957. Survived by his wife and their son, and by the son of his first marriage, he died of hypertensive heart disease on 8 January 1958 in Perth and was cremated with Congregational forms. A studio in the A.B.C.'s new building in Perth was named (1961) after him.

NSW Broadcasting Co. Ltd, *A Memento of the World's Greatest Achievement in Aviation and Broadcasting, June 9th 1928* (Syd, 1928); K. S. Inglis, *This is the ABC* (Melb, 1983); *Wireless J of Aust*, 29 Feb 1928; *Wireless Weekly*, 6 Apr 1928; *Broadcaster*, 13-20 Jan 1940; *ABC Weekly*, 22 Jan 1958; *Herald* (Melb), 13 Dec 1919; *West Australian*, 9 Jan 1958; ABC Document *and* Radio archives (Syd); family information provided by Mr E. Kirke, Applecross, Perth.
                                              MARION CONSANDINE

KIRKHOPE, ELIZABETH KILGOUR (1896-1978), headmistress, and JOHN HENDERSON (1900-1979), company director, were born on 8 February 1896 and 19 August 1900 at Carlton, Melbourne, the first and fourth of nine children of John Kirkhope, clergyman, and his wife Elizabeth Kilgour, née Corr, who had both emigrated from Scotland in 1895 to establish a branch of the Catholic Apostolic Church in Victoria. Elizabeth attended Lauriston Girls' School, Malvern, run by the Irving sisters, granddaughters of Edward Irving, founder of the Catholic Apostolic Church, and daughters of M. H. Irving [q.v.4]. In 1914 Elizabeth was dux and head prefect. She majored in mathematics at the University of Melbourne (B.A., 1918; Dip.Ed., 1919; M.A., 1920) before returning to Lauriston as a teacher.

Having taught in London, in 1928 Miss Kirkhope was appointed headmistress of Lowther Hall Church of England Girls' Grammar School, Essendon, where she managed to raise academic standards while keeping the ailing school afloat during the Depression. In late 1933 she went back to Lauriston, purchasing it outright in 1935 and taking up residence. She guided and strengthened the school until 1948 when, with the aid of her brothers John and William, she incorporated it as a non-profit-making company. In 1956 she handed over the academic affairs of the school to a former pupil, but remained resident principal until 1964.

A highly qualified teacher for a girls' school of the 1920s, Miss Kirkhope was active in the development of her profession. For many years she was a senior executive-officer of the Association of Headmistresses of Girls' Secondary Schools of Victoria; in addition, she served on the hard-won Women Teachers' Wages Board from its establishment in 1946 until 1960. Closely involved with Invergowrie Homecraft Hostel, Hawthorn—of which her sister Margaret Ellen (1899-1983) was principal in 1938-67—and with the training of teachers for independent schools at Mercer House, she was also a member of the Council of Public Education. She helped to arrange the first school broadcasts by the Australian Broadcasting Commission.

Miss Kirkhope was a skilled administrator who encouraged girls with academic potential, but not at the expense of educating the whole person or of other students. An innately family-oriented and frugal woman, she possessed a warm, genuine interest in her pupils which did not diminish with time. She could appear forbidding and aloof, but was generally remembered with affectionate respect for being fair and progressive. In her younger years she played hockey; in later life she developed her skills in needlework, tapestry, crochet and knitting. She died on 26 November 1978 at Canterbury and was buried with Anglican rites in Fawkner cemetery.

John Kirkhope, the eldest son, was educated at University High School. In 1916 he began work with Holmes & McCrindle, chartered accountants, while studying at the Working Men's College, Melbourne. He became a partner in the firm in 1924. At the Catholic Apostolic Church, Carlton, on 4 February 1937 he married Beatrice Lindley Perry; she died in childbirth the following year. In 1939 John commenced separate practice and thereafter accepted a succession of directorships. A councillor (1955-64) and vice-chairman (1962-64) of the Victorian branch of the Institute of Chartered Accountants in Australia, he played a prominent role in successful moves to reform the Victorian Companies Act (1958, 1961) and in the implementation of uniform company legislation throughout Australia in the 1960s. He was a keen fisherman, an enthusiastic golfer and tennis player, and a dedicated member of his church. Survived by his son, he died on 17 November 1979 at Gordon, Sydney, and was buried in Northern Suburbs cemetery.

His younger brother WILLIAM (1902-1983) was also a chartered accountant. He served in the Australian Imperial Force in 1939-44 and rose to temporary colonel in the pay corps. In 1942 he was appointed O.B.E. After World War II he was treasurer (1945-57) of the Victorian branch of the Liberal Country Party and a member (1955-57) of the board of business administration of the Department of Defence. A director of numerous companies, he was chairman of Mayne Nickless Ltd and a commissioner (1968-75) of the State Savings Bank of Victoria. He died on 1 August 1983; his sister Margaret died four days later.

J. N. Marshall, *A Jubilee History 1928-1978* (Melb, 1978); A. D. Pyke, *The Gold, the Blue* (Melb, 1983); *Lauristonian*, 1964, 1967; *Age* (Melb), 18 Apr 1964; Lauriston Girls' School Archives; information from the Kirkhope family, Miss G. Davies, Kilsyth, Mr N. Marshall, Prahran, Melb, and the late Mrs L. Gardiner.   CAROLYN RASMUSSEN

KIRKPATRICK, CATHERINE MABEL JOYCE; *see* ALLAN

KIRKWOOD, JOSEPH HENRY (1897-1970), professional golfer, was born on 3 April 1897 at Canterbury, Sydney, second son of English-born parents Thomas William Kirkwood, labourer, and his wife Effie Clara, née Broome, late Hardwick. Educated at Manly, Joe became a caddy at Manly Golf Club and was later apprenticed to D. G. Soutar, the club's professional from Scotland. In 1916 Kirkwood was temporary professional at Brisbane Golf Club, Yeerongpilly, before being appointed the professional at Riversdale Golf Club, Melbourne. He married Maud Lucy Woods on 2 January 1918 with Catholic rites in the Church of Our Lady Star of the Sea, Watsons Bay, Sydney; they were later divorced.

In 1920 Kirkwood won the Australian Open championship with a record (until 1934) score of 290 for four rounds. During a public subscription to help to send him to Britain, he was criticized for his failure to enlist for war service. At St Andrews, Scotland, Kirkwood was in contention for the 1921 Open, but faded to tie for sixth place; he claimed that he had been sabotaged by bookmakers who disrupted his concentration. Next year he beat the best professionals in Britain by an astonishing thirteen strokes in a tournament at Lossiemouth. He again looked certain to win the Open in 1923, but lost by three stokes to finish fourth, and in 1927 tied for third. He never won another major tournament, perhaps because he lacked the necessary temperament, but he was to gain numerous professional titles.

Kirkwood took up permanent residence in the United States of America in 1926 and was increasingly involved in exhibition matches with such players as Walter Hagen, Gene Sarazen and Bobby Jones. Attached as a professional to several leading American golf clubs—including Huntingdon Valley Country Club, Pennsylvania—Kirkwood spent much of his time touring the world, giving trick-shot exhibitions. He could play superbly both left and right handed, drive a ball off a watchface (once hitting a hole-in-one while so doing) or off prone assistants' noses, hit two balls at once in different directions, and hit a ball long distances from under an onlooker's foot. He and Hagen travelled extensively in Asia, Africa and the Americas; Kirkwood reckoned that he played on more than 6000 courses. The pair claimed to have popularized the use of wooden tees instead of placing the ball on small mounds of sand or dirt. Their life on tour became legendary, combining Hagen's love of drink and Kirkwood's of women.

Kirkwood had presented a cup to the Professional Golfers' Association of Australia in 1922; he returned to Australia in 1928, 1930, 1934, 1937 and 1954; in the 1930s, with Hagen and Sarazen, he attracted large crowds.

Although he transformed himself into a well-dressed, well-groomed and fast-talking showman, with a pronounced American accent and turn of phrase, Kirkwood always introduced himself as an Australian. Among his acquaintances and pupils were W. C. Fields, Harold Lloyd, the Duke and Duchess of Windsor, Dwight D. Eisenhower, Richard Nixon, J. H. Scullin [q.v.11], rajahs and aristocrats. In World War II he was allegedly investigated on suspicion of being an enemy agent —he had taught Japanese soldiers to play golf in the 1930s. He remained an excellent golfer throughout his life and at the age of 63 recorded 62 on a par-72 course, breaking his age for the first time.

Kirkwood had remarried and divorced at least two wives in America: Cathy, and Loretto Hartnett. His somewhat apocryphal memoirs were published posthumously as *Links of Life* (Oklahoma City, 1973). He died on 29 October 1970 at Burlington, Vermont, and was buried in Stowe cemetery. A daughter and four sons survived him; Joe junior played Joe Palooka in ten films about the comic-strip character.

W. Hagen, *The Walter Hagen Story* (Lond, 1957); J. Pollard, *Australian Golf* (Syd, 1990); C. de Groot and J. Webster, *Pro Golf Out of the Rough* (Syd, 1991); *Golf in Aust*, 1920-24; *Herald* (Melb), 26 May, 21 June 1926, 21 Nov 1928, 10 Oct 1934, 1 Jan 1985; *Argus*, 8 Dec 1928, camera supp; *Age* (Melb), 22 Nov 1930, 15 Oct 1943; *SMH*, 15, 23 Oct 1943, 7 July 1944; *New York Times*, 15 Nov 1970; *Sunday Telegraph* (Syd), 22 Nov 1970.   BRIAN STODDART

KIRSOVA, HELENE (1910-1962), prima ballerina and choreographer, was born on 18 June 1910 in Copenhagen and named Ellen Elisabeth Kirsten Wittrup, youngest child of the large family of Sophus Christian Ferdinand Hansen, directeur, and his wife Ingeborg, née Wittrup. Using her mother's maiden name, Ellen attended the ballet schools of Emilie Walbom and Jenny Møller in Copenhagen. At 18 she began tuition in Paris under Olga Preobrajenska, Léo Staats and, particularly, Lubov Egorova. In 1929 Wittrup joined Le Ballet Franco Russe and toured South America. She then danced with Madame Ida Rubenstein in Paris and in July 1931 at Covent Garden, London.

Later that year, as 'Hélène Kirsova', she joined the Ballets Russes de Monte-Carlo under René Blum and Colonel de Basil. When they split up, she stayed with Blum and worked closely with Michel Fokine. Although overshadowed by the 'baby ballerinas', she achieved personal success as a principal dancer in the company's seasons at the Alhambra Theatre, London, in 1933 and 1936. To the critic Arnold Haskell, Kirsova appeared to be of 'finely-tempered steel' in the role created for her by Léonide Massine in *Choreartium* (1933). Her most celebrated part was the Butterfly in Fokine's *L'Epreuve d'Amour* in 1936.

Rejoining de Basil's Ballets Russes de Monte Carlo (led by Léon Woizikovsky), Kirsova toured Australia in 1936-37 as prima ballerina. From the opening night (13 October 1936) in Adelaide she felt the audience's enthusiasm and was to create a tremendous public following. Her grace, 'perfect musical sense' and flawless technique made her interpretation as principal soloist in *Les Sylphides* one of her greatest successes, displaying her 'gifts of elevation, strength and precision'. She was perhaps better remembered for roles requiring dramatic depth—as the puppet ballerina in *Petrouchka*, Columbine in *Le Carnaval* and the Street Dancer in *Le Beau Danube*. Haskell described her 'dancing of the exacting role of the shy, brilliant bird' in *The Firebird* as 'one of the most perfect things seen in this or any other season'.

Kirsova left with the company for Europe, but returned to Sydney in December 1937. At St Mark's Anglican Church, Darling Point, on 10 February 1938 she married 38-year-old Erik Fritz Emil Fischer, the Danish vice-consul. She claimed to have given up dancing 'for ever', and rejoiced at the prospect of riding horses and 'no more dieting'. Her son was born in 1939.

In June 1940 Madame Kirsova founded a school to teach Russian ballet in Sydney. Her pupils soon provided the dancers for her own ballet company. As a teacher, she was a strict disciplinarian 'without being a martinet'; the classes were mentally and physically demanding. Her rivals claimed that she concentrated on her soloists, whom she developed superbly, while allowing less precise work from the ensemble. Dynamic and energetic, she could be rude and cutting to lesser talents, but was always warm to her favourites. Among her protégés were the young Australian dancers Strelsa Heckelman, Rachel Cameron, Helene ffrance, Henry Legerton and Paul 'Clementin' (Hammond), and the New Zealander Peggy Sager. Steeped in the Diaghilev concept of 'music, decor, ballet, drama, being made a total entity', Kirsova was a great collector of contemporary art and had an 'extensive knowledge of it'. She encouraged artists and musicians to come to her studio to watch classes and rehearsals. (Sir) William Dobell [q.v.14], Wolfgang Cardamatis, Frank Hutchens [q.v.9] and Lindley Evans became

habitués. Other supporters included (Sir) Warwick Fairfax and Thyne Reid [q.v].

The Kirsova Ballet gave its first performance on 8 July 1941 as part of a five-week season at the New South Wales State Conservatorium of Music. Although the company was at first strengthened by four former de Basil dancers, its achievements were hailed as evidence that it was possible to stage ballets of professional standard without importing large, expensive companies from abroad. The programme included two original ballets choreographed by Kirsova, *A Dream—and a Fairy Tale* and *Vieux Paris*, with scenery and costumes by Loudon Sainthill [q.v.]. Music was provided by two pianists as Kirsova spurned second-rate orchestras. By the time of the November season at the Minerva Theatre, the thirty-five dancers were paid trade-union rates. Kirsova herself paid their dues to Actors' Equity of Australia, which registered them as professional performers. She gave generous donations from the proceeds of her seasons to the Australian Red Cross Society and the Legacy Club of Sydney, and paid for children's playgrounds at Erskineville (a project dear to her).

Despite wartime difficulties and shortages —among them the mobilization of male dancers, problems in obtaining coupons for rationed material, travel restrictions and scarcity of theatres—the company managed to tour, opening a season on 31 January 1942 at His Majesty's Theatre, Melbourne. The repertoire was increased each season by ballets which Kirsova had created, such as *Faust* and *Revolution of the Umbrellas*. She commissioned young Australian artists to paint sets and design costumes that she had specially made, and sometimes young musicians—(Sir) Charles Mackerras and Henry Krips—to write the scores. Her choreography was minimalist, influenced by the clean lines of modern art. The only revivals she staged were *Les Sylphides* and *Swan Lake* (Act II), each of which had the advantage of requiring only one male dancer. She herself returned to the stage after six years to perform the slow waltz movement in her ballet, *Capriccio*.

Following the 1944 New Year season in Melbourne, the Kirsova Ballet went on to Adelaide, and gave what turned out to be its final performance in Brisbane on 6 May 1944. Kirsova cherished her independence. Reluctant to compromise, she refused the offer of backing from J. C. Williamson [q.v.6] Ltd which would have made her in effect a salaried producer-director. She was unable to compete when Williamson formed a full-time professional company under the direction of Edouard Borovansky [q.v.13]. Although she had paid award rates, she could not provide full-time employment. Her best dancers joined

Borovansky. The Kirsova Ballet School continued until 1946.

Hélène returned that year to Copenhagen, where she obtained a divorce on 16 October 1947. At the British Consulate, Paris, on 3 April 1948 she married Peter Buchard Bellew. A grandson of the actor Kyrle Bellew [q.v.7], Peter had written a history of the Kirsova Ballet and had joined the United Nations Educational, Scientific and Cultural Organization secretariat. They lived in the village of St Prix outside Paris (later moving to an apartment in Rue Galilee near the Arc de Triomphe) and visited Australia regularly. Remembered as 'still slim, her blonde hair untinged by time', and always beautifully dressed in simple grey or black clothes (often from Dior), she entertained visiting Australian artists, musicians and former students. She remained a keen photographer and art-collector: her paintings included works by Justin O'Brien, Wallace Thornton and (Sir) Sidney Nolan. Following a visit to Moscow, Hélène Bellew published a book, *Ballet in Moscow Today* (London, 1956); she also contributed to *A Dictionary of Modern Ballet* (London, 1959).

Survived by her husband and their son, and by the son of her first marriage, Kirsova died of cancer on 22 February 1962 in Guy's Hospital, London, and was cremated. Her achievements—as a dancer and choreographer, in founding a professional company in wartime, and by attaining box-office success —had lighted the way for those who followed her in establishing a permanent ballet company in Australia.

P. Bellew, *Pioneering Ballet in Australia* (Syd, 1946); F. Salter, *Borovansky* (Syd, 1980); E. H. Pask, *Ballet in Australia* (Melb, 1982); *Table Talk*, 5, 12, 19, 26 Nov, 3, 10, 17 Dec 1936; *Argus*, 24 June 1937, 29 Jan 1942; *SMH*, 8 Jan, 11 Feb, 17 Mar, 18 Aug 1938, 20 May 1940, 9 July 1941, 3 Jan, 20 June 1942, 20 Sept 1943, 13 Jan 1952, 28 Mar 1957, 25 Feb 1962; *Herald* (Melb), 17 Jan 1938; interview with Paul Hammond, Esso Performing Arts Collection (ts, NL); information from Mr O. Fischer, Eagleby, Qld, and Ms K. Vedel, Valby, Denmark.

SALLY O'NEILL
MARTHA RUTLEDGE

KISCH, EGON ERWIN (1885-1948), journalist and communist, was born on 29 April 1885 in Prague, Austria-Hungary, second of five sons of Jewish parents Hermann Kisch, owner of a textile shop, and his wife Ernestine, née Kuh. Egon briefly attended the German Technical College and the German University of Prague before serving for a year in the Imperial army. He began a career as a journalist and continued his education informally as lecture-reporter for the *Prager Tageblatt*. In 1906-13 he worked for the major German-language newspaper, *Bohemia*, developing his skills in *reportage*—journalism as a form of social critique intended to arouse public concern. His experiences as a corporal on the Serbian front during World War I led him to seek a more systematic analysis of society's ills, resulting in a lifelong involvement with international communism.

In November 1918 Kisch participated in the revolution in Vienna. Soon after, he left for Berlin where he became involved in organizing 'popular front' bodies on behalf of the Comintern. The publication of *Der Rasende Reporter* in 1924, followed by accounts of trips to the Soviet Union (1926), the United States of America (1929) and China (1933)—'all written from the Communist point of view, but sparkling with wit and colour'—established his reputation as the most significant and successful writer of *reportage* in German.

Following the Reichstag fire on 27 February 1933, Kisch was imprisoned by the Nazis. They exiled him to Czechoslovakia whence he made his way to Paris. He lived with his wife, the 'faithful, complacent, horse-teethed Giesl, who looked like a schoolmistress and worked for the G.P.U.' (Soviet political police). Kisch's opposition to war and fascism sprang from personal conviction and experience, not simply from his involvement with the Communist Party. He lied about his communist affiliation when sent by the Movement Against War and Fascism to attend an anti-war congress, to be held in Melbourne in November 1934. The Australian organizers had wanted someone better known, but they soon learned why this ebullient, good-humoured man was one of the 'most popular characters' among exiled communist intellectuals in Europe.

Acting on advice from London, the Lyons [q.v.10] government declared Kisch a prohibited immigrant and refused him permission to land at Fremantle, Western Australia. The warmth and enthusiasm of supporters who visited him when his ship berthed in Melbourne, and the flurry of legal activity undertaken on his behalf, tempted the adventurer to jump on to the wharf on 13 November, breaking his leg. Rushed on board and taken to Sydney, he was able to disembark there because Justice H. V. Evatt [q.v.14], sitting alone, found the prohibition order to be illegal. The authorities gave Kisch a 'dictation test' in Scottish Gaelic; after he failed, he was convicted on the 28th of being a prohibited immigrant and sentenced to be deported.

To the embarrassment of the Federal government, the High Court of Australia ruled on 19 December that Scottish Gaelic was not a European language within the meaning of the Immigration Act (1901-25). Kisch was free to exercise his wit and charm on large crowds. The government's inept attempts to keep him out of Australia had succeeded in making the name of a previously unknown journalist a household word. Kisch was a consummate propagandist, inclined to be cynical, but undoubtedly likeable. He was dark, short, and 'fat around the midriff', a 'vivacious little man, fluent of speech, sparkling of eye, restless in spirit, quick of thought and action'. His gallantry and good humour made the government's vendetta against him seem the more crass.

While relatively few Australians had any sympathy for communists, the 'Kisch Affair' created widespread fears that, by using the Immigration Act to curtail free speech, the government was resorting to tactics similar to those undermining democracy in Europe. The government made a second declaration, overcoming the technical shortcoming which Evatt had found in the first, and on 21 January 1935 Kisch was again convicted of being a prohibited immigrant. None the less, the government offered to remit his sentence of three months imprisonment and to pay costs if he left Australia promptly. He did so on 11 March after a final blaze of public appearances, including a torchlight procession in Melbourne to commemorate the Reichstag fire.

For the small group of anti-war campaigners, Kisch's visit was a boost to morale. The incident alerted numerous Australians to the fascist threat and ways of combating it, and led to the formation of the Australian Writers' League. Kisch's account of his experiences, *Australian Landfall* (London, 1937), was a lively, entertaining addition to his long list of publications. Back in Europe, he took part in the Spanish Civil War. After the Germans occupied France in 1940, he found refuge in Mexico until he returned to Czechoslovakia at the end of World War II. His draft for a large book on his native land remained unfinished. He died of a stroke on 31 March 1948 in Prague and was cremated.

J. Smith, *On the Pacific Front* (Syd, 1936); A. Koestler, *The Invisible Writing* (Lond, 1969); R. Throssell (ed), *Straight Left* (Syd, 1982); R. Gibson, *The People Stand Up* (Melb, 1983); U. von Felbert, *China und Japan als Impuls und Exempel Fernostliche Ideen und Motive bei Alfred Doblin, Bertolt Brecht und Egon Erwin Kisch* (Frankfurt, 1986); *APSA News*, 9, no 3, Sept 1964, p 6; *Labour Hist*, no 32, May 1977, p 27, no 36, May 1979, p 94; *Herald* (Melb), 13 Nov 1934; *Age* (Melb), 27 Sept 1969.

CAROLYN RASMUSSEN

KLEEBERG, JULIUSZ EDWARD (1890-1970), army officer and Polish leader, was born on 30 March 1890 at Trembowla, Galicia, Austria-Hungary (Poland), third of four children of Colonel Emil Kleeberg (d.1908), army officer, and his wife Józefa, née Kuschée. The family moved to Vienna in 1898. Juliusz attended military schools at St Pölten and at Weiss-Kirchen before graduating (1910) as second lieutenant at the Theresianische Militärakademie, near Vienna. After World War I began he served in the cavalry on the Eastern Front. He was a staff officer (1915-17) in the Polish Legion, and later performed training duties in Warsaw. Promoted major (1918) and lieutenant colonel (1920), he took part in the Russo-Polish War as chief of staff of the Polish Legion in 1919 and deputy chief of staff, 5th Polish Army, in 1920. In Warsaw on 15 February 1919 he had married Halina Anna Olszynska.

After studying (1920-22) at the École Superieure de Guerre, Paris, Kleeberg was appointed Polish military and naval attaché in that city in 1923. He was a noted horseman and won many competitions. As colonel (1924) and brigadier general (1937), he held increasingly important cavalry commands in Poland. Awarded the Cross of Valour with two Bars and the gold Cross of Merit with Swords, he was appointed (c.1937) to the Order of Polonia Restituta (fourth class).

In August 1939 Kleeberg was made deputy-commander of the Lublin Army Corps 'B', to be raised from reserves. The Germans invaded before the formation could be mobilized. Once Poland was overrun, Kleeberg escaped to Paris where he headed the government in exile's military mission to the Allies. He went to Belgrade in November and organized the movement of some 40 000 Polish soldiers to France. Following the French capitulation in June 1940, he was briefly military attaché at Vichy. He then led a resistance cell which smuggled servicemen to Britain, for which he was appointed to the Légion d'honneur (1941) and awarded the Croix de Guerre (1947). In 1943 he was forced to flee across the Pyrénées to Spain. Promoted major general, he performed liaison duties with allied forces in the Mediterranean (1943-45) and commanded Polish troops in Scotland (1945-47). He retired from the army in July 1948.

Having farmed in Wales for three years, Kleeberg and his wife followed their son to Australia, reaching Melbourne on 3 February 1952. They settled at Kogarah, Sydney, and bought (with a bank loan) the shop in St George Hospital. The shop was rundown, but cheap, with a three-room flat above. Although lacking commercial experience, they managed to make a living. A devout Catholic, Kleeberg was a bookworm and loved music. He was naturalized in 1956.

Tall, fair and distinguished looking, Kleeberg was prominent in the Polish community and president (1954-58 and 1960-70) of the Federal Council of Polish Associations in

Australia. He impressed Roman Wierzbicki 'as a man who had a stern sense of duty and skill in negotiations and handling of people ... compatible with a strong personality and courage'. His 'charm and courtesy were invaluable assets'. Kleeberg wanted 'a *Polonia* [Poles living permanently abroad] loyal to Australia as citizens of this country, yet mindful of their origins and cultural traditions'.

As federal president, Kleeberg fostered the development of Polish organizations, such as the one which helped to build an orphanage and school at Marayong in 1954. He visited most of the Polish centres in 1958 and took part in their celebrations to commemorate the 'Millennium of Christianity' in Poland. In the late 1960s he welcomed a number of eminent Polish visitors to Sydney, among them Cardinal Wojtyla, later Pope John Paul II. Kleeberg was killed on 4 July 1970 when struck by a car at Mount Vincent. Survived by his wife and son, he was buried in the Polish section of Eastern Creek cemetery.

T. Kryska-Karski and S. Zurakowski, *Generalowie Polski Niepodleglej* (Warsaw, 1991); C. Lezenski and C. Kukawski, *O Kawalerii Polskiej XX Wieku* (Wroclaw, 1991); A. Kleeberg, *Who was General Julius Edward Kleeberg?* (Canb, 1995); Z. Mierzwinski, *Generalowie II Rzeczypospolitej*, 2 (Warsaw, 1995); R. Treister, A copy of statement after the death of Juliusz Kleeberg for the New South Wales Police, 4 July 1970 (held by author, Rowville, Melb); naturalization file A446/179, item 56/24073 (AA, Canb); Polish war records, information and papers provided by Mr A. Kleeberg, Holder, Canb; War Archives (Austrian State Archives, Vienna).

BOGUMILA ZONGOLLOWICZ

KLEEMAN, REGINALD THEODORE (1901-1979), engineer, was born on 4 May 1901 at Mile End, Adelaide, only child of native-born parents Theodore Richard Kleemann, clerk, and his wife Mary Jane, née Wadey. Reginald attended Woodville Public and Adelaide High schools before studying mechanical engineering, both at the School of Mines and Industries and the University of Adelaide (B.E., 1923). He represented the university in Australian Rules football. Blue eyed and fair haired, 'Snow' was a tall young man, with a jutting jaw and a strong brow. In January 1923 he joined the Broken Hill Proprietary Co. Ltd as a draughtsman at Whyalla, a place he would help to transform from saltbush plains to steel city.

Two hills, Iron Monarch and Iron Knob, lay 33 miles (53 km) north-west of Whyalla and contained rich deposits of ore. Kleeman was assistant (from 1924) to the quarry officer at Iron Knob and officer-in-charge (from 1927). The demand for iron soon exceeded the scope of the old steam-shovel and hand-loading methods. Kleeman's task was to over-

see the installation of modern plant. In 1928 bench 'E' went into production at Iron Monarch, with electric locomotives, revolving shovels producing 400 tons of ore an hour, and a primary crusher capable of breaking down 1000 tons an hour. The ore was taken by rail to Whyalla and thence by ship to the company's steel works at Newcastle, New South Wales. Kleeman revised quarry practices and directed improvements for the settlement at Iron Knob. Streets were paved and trees were carefully cultivated. On 23 April 1927 at St James's Anglican Church, West Adelaide, he married Stella Mary Coligan (d.1960).

In 1930 Kleeman moved to Whyalla as assistant to the superintendent; within three years he was chief engineer. During the Depression he supervised relief work which involved regrading part of the Iron Knob 'tramway' and tunnelling to determine ore reserves in Iron Prince and Iron Baron, 28 miles (45 km) south-west of Whyalla. He was close to the managing director Essington Lewis [q.v.10] who, after visiting Japan in 1934, planned an immense war effort for the company. Kleeman spent 1937 at head office, Melbourne, and was promoted acting-superintendent at Whyalla in 1938. The annual output of two million tons of ore from Iron Knob and Iron Baron stimulated the iron and steel industries, and their subsidiaries, providing employment for 30 000 people throughout Australia. In 1940 Kleeman took on the new position of superintendent of B.H.P.'s South Australian operations. He was later responsible for constructing plant to mine iron ore on Cockatoo Island, Western Australia.

At Whyalla a munitions annexe, heavy forging plant and heavy machine shop were built. In 1938 work on a blast furnace had commenced, and in 1940 the harbour was dredged to allow slipways for shipbuilding which began in 1940. After the State government passed the Northern Areas and Whyalla Water Supply Act (1940), a start was made on the Morgan-Whyalla pipeline to bring River Murray water, vital for the works and town. In 1941 the blast furnace was lit and four corvettes were launched; forty-three vessels were built over the next twenty-five years.

The town grew rapidly through the years of World War II due to the co-operation of its citizens, the company, and the Federal and State governments. Kleeman's diplomacy with the premier (Sir) Thomas Playford and key public servants was crucial: he had a knack of getting to know people and invariably allowed others to state their case. Kind and generous, and a man's man, Snow had a sense of humour so dry that seconds could pass before listeners grasped the effect of his remark.

He came to be seen as the man at the heart of Whyalla, partly because municipal government was non-existent before the Whyalla

Town Commission was established in 1945. Until then he ran the works, the company town and the essential services. The South Australian Housing Trust and B.H.P. introduced an extensive construction programme to provide residential accommodation, and the company also built hostels for single men. Recreational facilities were created; Kleeman promoted an aero-club to train pilots; noisy industries were separated from domestic areas; and a brick factory, an abattoir and a model dairy were set up. B.H.P. subsidized the building of Whyalla Hospital (1940) and Whyalla Technical High School (1943); Kleeman chaired the hospital board and the school council. President (1962-70) of the council of the South Australian Institute of Technology, he was its first honorary fellow (1974) and encouraged the institute to establish branches at The Levels and at Whyalla.

Kleeman had been appointed O.B.E. in 1946. In the following year he travelled abroad to investigate modern machinery. A member of the Australasian Institute of Mining and Metallurgy (1936), and of the American Institute of Mining and Metallurgical Engineers (1943), he was a fellow (1949) of the Institution of Engineers, Australia. From 1960 he was vice-chairman of Australian Mineral Development Laboratories.

In 1956 he had become B.H.P.'s South Australian manager, and visited North and South America. Back home in 1957, he organized new blasting and drilling methods: by using ammonium nitrate and fuel oil, the size of the blast was increased five-fold. Work on the site for a steel plant at Whyalla began in 1961 and the first steel was produced in 1965. On 2 November 1960 Kleeman had married Doris Edith Pocock, née Goerecke, at the Wesley Methodist Church, Wollongong, New South Wales. He retired in 1966, took up several directorships and consultancies, and had time to follow horse-racing and go sailing. In 1959 he had joined the Adelaide Club.

Snow Kleeman oversaw Whyalla's massive expansion whereby raw material was converted to final product within South Australia. Although he maintained meticulous standards, he delegated responsibility, shunned publicity and protected his employees' welfare. Survived by his wife, and by the daughter and son of his first marriage, he died on 31 May 1979 at Largs Bay and was cremated. The Institute of Technology holds his portrait by David Dridan.

BHP Recreation Review, Sept 1933; *PRGSSA*, 42, 1940-41; *BHP Review*, Feb 1940, June 1946, June 1947, Oct 1956; *Advertiser* (Adel), 13 June 1946, 2 Sept 1966, 4 June 1979; *Whyalla News*, 6 June 1979; BHP Co Ltd Archives, PM/1105 (Port Melb); information from Mrs L. M. Torr, Pymble, Syd, and Mr D. G. Edgar, Rapid Bay, SA.   SUZANNE EDGAR

KLEIN, LOUIS (1917-1975), clothing manufacturer and Jewish leader, was born on 5 November 1917 at Spitalfields, London, one of four sons of Solomon Klein, a journeyman tailor from Eastern Europe, and his wife Fanny, née Gilbert. His parents were Jewish and strictly orthodox. Louis attended a *cheder* (afternoon religious school) and a general English school in the East End, and later a polytechnic and classes at the University of London. He worked with his father in the manufacturing section of the clothing firm, Simpson (Piccadilly) Ltd. At the register office, Holborn, on 28 October 1940 he married Mona Freda Finegold. While serving (1941-46) in the British Army he was wounded twice and mentioned in dispatches (1945).

Tall and distinguished looking, Klein dressed immaculately. In 1948 he emigrated with his family to New South Wales and settled at Parramatta. That year, with his cousin Sidney Sinclair, he founded and became managing director of Anthony Squires Pty Ltd, which was to grow to be one of the country's largest manufacturers of quality men's suits. Vice-president of the Australian Confederation of Apparel Manufacturers, he chaired several investment companies. As a founder and later president of the Australia-Israel Chamber of Commerce, he fostered Australian trade with Israel.

Klein was prominent in the formation of the Parramatta Synagogue. After moving to the North Shore, he served on the local synagogue's board of management (president 1968-70). He also helped to establish the Jewish Memorial Centre in Canberra and, in 1967, the Joint (later Jewish) Communal Appeal to raise funds for organizations in Sydney. By the early 1970s Klein was a prominent leader of Australian Jewry. He had been State chairman and president of the United Israel Appeal (a major fund-raising organization for Israel), executive-chairman of its federal branch and vice-president of the New South Wales Jewish Board of Deputies. In October 1972 he was elected president of the Executive Council of Australian Jewry. He was sometime vice-president of the New South Wales Friends of the Hebrew University, Jerusalem, and of Shalom College, University of New South Wales.

Disenchanted with the standard of the Jewish press, Klein had bought the *Australian Jewish Times* in 1968. The newspaper developed rapidly under his leadership and with the capital he provided. In 1973 he bought out the *Sydney Jewish News*. Klein was a board-member of the Hakoah Eastern Suburbs Soccer Club, a member of the State branch of the National Trust of Australia and a benefactor of the Australian Opera. He belonged to the Royal Automobile Club of Australia, the Royal Motor Yacht Club of New South Wales and Tattersall's Club in Sydney, and to Curzon House in London. In 1973 he was appointed C.B.E.

Klein died of myocardial infarction on 31 July 1975 in his apartment at Toft Monks, Elizabeth Bay, and was buried in Northern Suburbs cemetery. He was survived by his wife, son and daughter; they later ran the *Australian Jewish Times* (the *Australian Jewish News* from 1990).

S. D. Rutland, *Seventy-Five Years* (Syd, 1970) and *Pages of History* (Syd, 1995); *Aust Jewish Times*, Dec 1968, Feb 1973, Aug 1975; information from Mrs M. Klein and Ms S. Bures, Dover Heights, Syd.

SUZANNE D. RUTLAND

KOHLER, EDWARD FREDERICK (1890-1964), sculptor, was born on 27 May 1890 at Tarampa, near Lowood, Queensland, son of Prussian-born parents August Friedrich Kohler, carpenter, and his wife Annie Hilda Limprich. Lured by the discovery of gold, Gus left for Kalgoorlie, Western Australia, about 1893; Hilda and her four children followed him six months later. The Kohlers led an itinerant life in the backblocks and Edward's formal education was minimal. A shy young man, with a talent for music and art, he was apprenticed to a blacksmith at Narrogin. After his parents separated, he joined his father at Korrelocking.

On 18 February 1915 Kohler enlisted in the Australian Imperial Force. He fought with the 11th Battalion at Gallipoli (from June) and on the Western Front (from March 1916). In November 1916 he was posted to I Anzac (later Australian) Corps schools as an instructor in gunnery. Promoted company sergeant major in January 1917, he was awarded the Meritorious Service Medal for his diligence and for using his spare time to make sectional drawings of gun-parts. He was discharged in England on 15 April 1919. During the war he had married Denise Marie Louise Devacht (d.1936), a 24-year-old Belgian; they were to have twin sons. In 1921-28 he performed clerical duties with the Imperial War Graves Commission in France.

Kohler attended the Académie des Beaux-Arts, Lille, from 1928. He also studied the modelling of animals, particularly horses, under René Joire. In 1930-32 he worked for M. Subricas, a French sculptor, and spent eight months at Pierre de Soete's studio in Brussels, producing war memorials, busts, medals and trophies. Due to the breakdown of his marriage, and to regulations which prevented foreigners from obtaining government commissions in France and Belgium, Kohler returned to Western Australia in 1932. He became chief sculptor at the Ajax Plaster Co. Ltd's studios in West Perth where he received

the most prosaic of assignments, such as garden ornaments and heads (based on Hollywood movie-stars) for hat shops. At the chapel of the Churches of Christ, Perth, on 17 November 1937 he married Eileen Hazel Cook, a 31-year-old artist.

After he won a national competition with his equestrian statue of King George V, which was unveiled in 1938 outside the Brisbane City Hall, numerous public and private commissions came Kohler's way: they included the Sir Talbot Hobbs [q.v.9] memorial (1940) on Riverside Drive, Perth, and bas-relief panels for buildings such as the Piccadilly Theatre, Karrakatta Crematorium, the Institute of Agriculture at the University of Western Australia and the Collie Mine Workers' Institute (1952). Kohler was the second professionally trained sculptor to practise successfully in the State (Pietro Porcelli [q.v.11] was the first). During World War II he was employed as a camouflage officer with the Department of Home Security. In the postwar period his figurative style was no longer fashionable, but he continued to receive commissions from his major patron, the Catholic Church. His religious works are located throughout Australia, among them the beautiful 'Joseph the Carpenter and the Boy Jesus' (1949-50) at Corpus Christi College, Werribee, Victoria. Survived by his wife and their two daughters, and by the twins of his first marriage, Kohler died on 28 June 1964 in Perth and was buried with Anglican rites in Karrakatta cemetery.

R. Taylor, 'Edward F. Kohler, Perth sculptor, 1890-1964', in D. Bromfield (ed), *Essays on Art and Architecture in Western Australia* (Perth, 1988); E. Kohler, Mr E. F. Kohler . . . since 1914 (undated typescript) and K. Kohler, Edward F. Kohler (unpublished essay, Mar 1995) held by Mrs K. Van Raak, Gosnells, Perth; family information.

ROBYN TAYLOR

KONDOM; *see* AGAUNDO

KORNWEIBEL, ALBERT HUBERT CARL (1892-1980), journalist and music critic, was born on 22 December 1892 at Hornsey, London, eldest of three children of August Theodor Hubert Kornweibel, a commission merchant from Germany, and his English-born wife Gertrude Rose, née Leaver (d.1893), a music teacher. Educated in a convent school at Southampton, Hampshire, and at St George's College, Weybridge, Surrey, Albert worked as a clerk in his father's office. He suffered from a 'weak chest' and, at the age of 19, emigrated to Western Australia where he was employed as cadet reporter on the *Western Mail*. Transferring to the *West Australian*, he developed into an accomplished all-rounder, doing everything from court reporting to sub-editing.

An enthusiastic music lover and pianist who had attended concerts in London, Kornweibel became the *West Australian*'s music critic in 1916. From the early 1920s he adopted the pen-name, 'Fidelio', because he 'revered' Beethoven's only opera. He studied music theory with Alexander Leckie [q.v.10] and tried his hand at composing, albeit with little success. He also read widely, listened to his extensive record collection and played masses of sheet music. To improve his journalism, he visited the United States of America in 1921 and attended lectures at the University of Western Australia in 1926. At Mount Hawthorn, Perth, on 21 April 1923 he had married with Presbyterian forms Alma Woodhouse, née Lindner (d.1967), a former nurse and a divorcee with three children.

Kornweibel played a significant part in the development of music in Western Australia. His fifty years as a music critic (and as a reviewer of books, dance and drama) coincided with several key stages in that development: the influential years of the Metropolitan Orchestral Society (founded 1913); the time of strong community interest in choral groups, especially in the 1920s; the changes that flowed from the establishment (1928) of the Perth (later West Australian) Symphony Orchestra and from the advent (1932) of the Australian Broadcasting Commission; and the creation (1958) of a department of music at the university.

Increasing deafness obliged Kornweibel to stand aside as a music critic in the mid-1940s. The use of a large hearing-aid for concert work meant that after a twelve-month break 'Fidelio' was back in business. His small figure carrying a case containing valves and batteries for his hearing-aid was a familiar sight at concerts. Following his retirement in 1957, he continued reviewing until deafness and poor eyesight forced a halt. Despite these difficulties, he published *Apollo and the Pioneers* (1973), a history of one hundred years of music-making in Western Australia. In its foreword (Sir) Frank Callaway wrote that the author's knowledge of music and its allied arts had informed and enlightened the public. Although 'Korny' encouraged amateurs and professionals, he maintained unflinching standards. He died on 7 March 1980 at Claremont and was cremated; his daughter Donna Sadka (a drama critic) survived him, as did his stepdaughter and one of his stepsons. Jill Crommelin's obituary described Kornweibel as a gentleman, 'everything a man should be—kind, cultivated and wittily self-deprecating'.

National Theatre News (Perth), May 1958; *Newspaper House News*, June 1980; *Music Maker*, Nov-

Dec 1989; *West Australian*, 4 May 1921, 23 Jan 1973, 8, 10 Mar 1980 and 30 June 1983 (Fremantle supplement); J. Ambrose, interview with Kornweibel, 31 May 1977 (Oral Hist Project, NL); L. Fisher, taped interview with Enid Scott and Donna Sadka (BL); information from Mrs D. Sadka, Claremont, Perth.

ROGER SIMMS

KOSOVICH, IVAN (1913-1975), journalist and political organizer, was born on 31 January 1913 at Zaostrog, Dalmatia, Austria-Hungary (Croatia), son of Jure Kosovich, peasant farmer, and his wife Iva, née Banovich. Many immigrants came to Australia from this region before and after its inclusion in the kingdom of Yugoslavia in 1918. The Kosovichs reached Western Australia in 1926 and Jure later bought a vineyard at Millendon in the Swan Valley. Ivan had various jobs in Perth, in addition to helping in the vineyard. Studious and serious in appearance and manner, he was largely self-educated.

Kosovich moved to Sydney in 1935 when elected secretary of the Savez Jugoslavenskih Iseljenika Australije (Union of Yugoslav Immigrants in Australia). He was also the first editor of its newspaper, *Napredak* (Progress), published in Serbo-Croatian. Because of its pro-communist origins, *Napredak* did not obtain the attorney-general's licence necessary for foreign language newspapers until 1937. The paper was forced to suspend publication in 1940 but allowed to resume in 1942. Following the German and Italian occupation of Yugoslavia in April 1941, Kosovich actively supported the resistance movement. He led the Liberate Yugoslavia Aid Committee which promoted the communist-led partisans under Tito, collected aid for postwar reconstruction in Yugoslavia and funded an orphanage at Bihać.

In May 1945 Tito's government appointed Kosovich consul in Sydney for Yugoslavia. On 10 November that year at St James's Anglican Church, Sydney, he married Frances (Frana) Elizabeth Tomasich, a typist from Dalmatia. As consul, Kosovich facilitated the repatriation of Yugoslavs: over one thousand left early in 1948, yet many returned in the 1950s. By then the Yugoslav communities in Australia had expanded due to the number of anti-Tito refugees. Kosovich's increasingly difficult position was exacerbated by the split between Tito and Stalin in 1948. In the Soviet-Yugoslav dispute the Savez sided with Moscow while Kosovich as consul remained loyal to Belgrade.

Recalled to Yugoslavia in late 1950, Kosovich came back to Sydney with his family in 1953 and was naturalized in 1964. He operated a small grocery with his brother at Bass Hill and in 1960 launched another newspaper, the *Yugoslav-Australian Journal* (*Novo Doba* from 1970), which he edited at night. His son

Steven later co-edited the paper. Ivan suffered from chronic asthma, but remained involved in community affairs as president of the Yugoslav-Australian Club at St Johns Park, State chairman of the co-ordinating committee of National Communities from Yugoslavia and chairman of the Yugoslav languages group at Special Broadcasting Service's radio 2EA. Disillusioned with communism, he was a member of the Australian Labor Party's State migrant advisory committee and secretary (later president) of the party's Bass Hill branch.

Although he disdained all sport except the traditional Dalmatian game, *bocce*, Kosovich enjoyed reading, chess and films. He was neat in his habits and frugal in his tastes. Survived by his wife and two sons, he died of heart disease on 15 October 1975 at his Chester Hill home and was buried in the Catholic section of Rookwood cemetery.

C. A. Price, *Southern Europeans in Australia* (Melb, 1963); M. Gilson and J. Zubrzycki, *The Foreign Language Press in Australia, 1848-1964* (Canb, 1967); J. Jupp (ed), *The Australian People* (Syd, 1988); M. Tkalcevic, *Croats in Australia* (Melb, 1989); A1068/1, item IC47/15/1/13/1 (AA); information from Mr S. Kosovich, Chester Hill, Syd.
                                                         JAMES JUPP

KOTAI, FERENC (FRANCIS) LAJOS (1908-1970), potter and teacher, was born on 26 July 1908 in Budapest, Austria-Hungary, son of István Michl, businessman, and his wife Katalin, née Kota. Deferring to the wishes of the Hungarian government, in 1936 the Michls changed their Austrian surname to the more Slavic-sounding Kotai. Trained in fine arts, ceramics and sculpture at the School of Applied Arts, Ferenc became known for the work he exhibited in the Hungarian National Gallery. On 6 January 1934 in Budapest he married Julia Csökönyi; they were to have six children. In 1946 the family fled from the 'Iron Curtain' which was beginning to descend on their country. After three years as displaced persons in West Germany, they emigrated to Australia, arriving in 1950.

Kotai was assigned a job in a whaling station at Carnarvon, Western Australia, while his family remained at the Graylands Migrant Centre. When his two-year term had been completed, he set up a pottery at Bassendean, Perth, and took private students. An inspiring teacher who worked up to eighty hours a week, he was one of the State's most important ceramists in the early postwar period. From 1954 he taught pottery and clay-sculpture at Fremantle Technical School; housed in its Finnerty Street annexe, his workshop was located in a near-derelict asylum (now the Fremantle Arts Centre).

Experimenting, sharing and making-do were the norm. Kotai's wartime scavenging experience proved invaluable, particularly in finding material from which to build kilns. Most of his early students were mature-aged women, part of a worldwide resurgence of interest in the crafts. Kotai encouraged them to be independent—to mix their own glazes and learn from their mistakes. 'He was quite ruthless with nondescript work. It was simply dropped into the clay bin to be recycled'.

Many of his students achieved a professional level, among them Jean Ewers, Doris Harms, Tedye McDiven, Meg Brent-White (Sheen) and Michiko Love. When Kotai's teaching position seemed to be under threat, he urged them to set up the Perth Potters' Club to continue working together. Formed about 1957, it continues today. Although Kotai was something of a martinet, his pupils were devoted to him. Ewers described him as 'a gifted man, with a great breadth of knowledge, technical ability, artistry, generosity and wit. All this with a good leaven of Hungarian temperament'. His only solo exhibition in Perth was held in 1964 at the Skinner [q.v.] Galleries.

Kotai despaired of completing a thesis in order to retain his senior lectureship. In 1969 he was forced to retire because of his lack of formal qualifications. Survived by his wife, three sons and three daughters, he died of myocardial infarction on 5 February 1970 at Shenton Park and was buried with Lutheran forms in Karrakatta cemetery. His daughter Evelyn drew two portraits of Kotai which are held by the family. His son Bela, whom Francis had trained as a potter, studied at the Western Australian Institute of Technology and exhibited internationally; in 1995 he became foundation head of the Western Australian School of Art and Design.

J. Ewers, 'Francis Kotai', *Pottery in Aust*, 18, no 1, 1979, p 13; *Weekend News* (Perth), 28 Nov 1964; *West Australian*, 9 Feb 1970; F., E. and B. Kotai, artists' files *and* F. Kotai collection (Art Gallery of WA); family objects and papers (held by Mrs G. Hohnen, East Fremantle, Mr P. Kotai, Nedlands, Ms T. Kotai-Ewers, Kardinya, and Mrs J. Kotai, Palmyra, Perth); archives of the late Mrs J. Ewers (held by Ms T. Kotai-Ewers).
                                                    DOROTHY ERICKSON

KRAMER, ERNEST EUGENE (1889-1958), missionary, was born on 10 May 1889 at Basel, Switzerland, son of German-born parents Karl Friedrich Kramer, storekeeper, and his wife Maria Elisabeth, née Reinhardt. Educated locally, Ernst became fluent in French and German, and trained as a milling engineer. In 1909 he emigrated to South Australia where he began work in a mill at Salisbury. On 21 March 1912 at Bena, Victoria, he married

Euphemia Buchanan (d.1971) with Presbyterian forms.

In 1912 Kramer became convinced of his calling to take the word of God to settlers and Aborigines in the interior. Between 1913 and 1921 he made three extended journeys on his self-appointed mission. Reputedly a fine bushman and a skilled mechanic, he travelled with his wife and infant children in a covered wagon, pulled by donkeys, over some of the driest and most isolated parts of South and Central Australia. Kramer had no regular income and was dependent on donations of food and money. He interpreted his capacity to survive as a sign of divine providence and recorded his experiences in *Australian Caravan Mission to Bush People and Aboriginals* (1922?).

Having visited Alice Springs, Northern Territory, on his travels, Kramer returned there in 1923. In 1925 the Aborigines' Friends' Association appointed him its missionary for Central Australia. Kramer kept the A.F.A. informed of the Aborigines' condition. Assisted by his wife and eldest daughter Mary, he ministered to the needs of Aborigines who had 'come in' from the surrounding country. He built a non-denominational church where he held regular prayer-meetings and used an Arrernte translation of the Gospels. In the cooler months he toured by camel-team and later by motorcar, proselytizing and dispensing food and medicine. In 1928-29 he supervised the Jay Creek 'half-caste' children's home. Scientists and clergymen valued his services as a guide.

Kramer was popular among the Aborigines. Rather than aiming to 'civilize' them, he brought them 'The Light of Life'—knowledge of Jesus. He did, however, urge them to cease fighting among themselves and to leave cattle alone. In 1932 he called for police intervention to protect Aboriginal women and children from the violent behaviour of their men. In preference to sentencing Aborigines to prison, he advocated the use of corporal punishment, administered under medical supervision.

At a time of extreme racism Kramer spoke for the humanity of the Aboriginal people. He entreated the government to increase its spending, and on numerous occasions drew attention to the suffering of those deprived of land and access to watering places. Professor (Sir) John Cleland [q.v.8] praised Kramer for 'doing as much as anyone in Australia to protect' the Aborigines. Yet, Kramer also accepted the right of Europeans to appropriate land in semi-arid and arid regions, publicly supported the pastoralists' interests and tempered his criticism of the way that Aborigines were treated.

After resigning from his post in 1934, Kramer worked as a representative of the British and Foreign Bible Society, in Melbourne for fifteen years and then in Adelaide. He died of acute leukaemia on 16 February 1958 in Adelaide and was buried in Mitcham cemetery; his wife, son and three daughters survived him.

Aborigines' Friends' Assn, *Annual Report*, 1925-1929, *and* papers (Mort L).   ANDREW MARKUS

KRIMMER, WILLIAM CHARLES (1867-1944), businessman, was born on 28 July 1867 at German Station (Nundah), near Brisbane, second son of Johann Philip Krimmer, a labourer from Württemberg, and his Prussian-born wife Maria, née Braun. Educated at the local school, William was initially employed as a carpenter at J. C. Hutton Pty Ltd, ham and bacon curers, Zillmere. On 10 August 1903 he married with Presbyterian forms Jane Eliza Handford in her parents' home at Zillmere. He later worked as an engineer in the bacon factory of Foggitt Jones & Co. Ltd, Oxley, in which he had a financial interest.

Moving to the Darling Downs in 1906, Krimmer bought a small bacon factory at Black Gully, Toowoomba, and managed it in partnership with Harold A. Reed whom he had known from his time at Hutton's. They soon launched their 'K.R.' brand of ham and bacon, and found a market for it. In June 1916 Krimmer was invited to take charge of the Darling Downs Co-operative Bacon Co. Ltd. A primary producers' co-operative, the enterprise had been registered as a company in 1911 and was to become an association in 1932. Its factory at Willowburn, Toowoomba, produced hams, bacon, smallgoods and canned food. The directors appointed Krimmer general manager at a salary of £10 a week and engaged his brother Benjamin as sub-manager. Having agreed to close the operation at Black Gully on condition that he could bring the K.R. brand with him, Krimmer received £1500 for the goodwill of his former business and one hundred shares in the new concern.

The arrival of the Krimmers reversed the fortunes of the ailing farmers' co-operative which had lost £5500 in the first half of 1916. Despite having to dispose of substandard stock, it made a profit of £4200 in the second half of the year. By 1918 three more Krimmer brothers—Otto, Ernest and Charles—had joined the firm. The company continued to prosper, its products winning prizes at local agricultural shows. Extensions to the factory were completed in 1922. The effects of a severe drought in 1923 and a major fire in January 1924 were overcome. Premises were opened at Roma Street (1932) and Doboy

(1934), Brisbane, and at Ultimo, Sydney (1938). Selling its goods throughout Australia and abroad, the business proved an outstanding success in the co-operative marketing of agricultural produce.

William Krimmer was known for his firm managerial style, for his reluctance to enter into discussions with representatives of organized labour and for his neat appearance. Invariably dressed in a suit and tie, he drove a sulky to work from his home in Russell Street, Toowoomba. He was also known for his familiarity with the day-to-day workings of every aspect of the business he ran. As a hobby he kept show horses and thoroughbreds: Highstrung, which he had bred in 1942, was to win the Doomben Ten Thousand in 1947. Krimmer died on 8 March 1944 at Toowoomba and was cremated with Anglican rites; his wife, two sons and three daughters survived him.

B. Hinchcliffe (ed), *They Meant Business* (Toowoomba, Qld, 1984); *Qld Country Life*, 13 Nov 1958; *Toowoomba Chronicle*, 24 Jan 1924, 7 Oct 1943, 9 Mar 1944.   MARK CRYLE

KRIMPER, SCHULIM (1893-1971), cabinetmaker, was born on 28 July 1893 at Sereth, Bukovina, Austria-Hungary (Rumania), youngest of five children of Rabbi Jacob Wolf Neutuch. Orphaned at the age of 9, Schulim lived with his eldest married sister for three years before being apprenticed to a local cabinet-maker. He completed his articles and remained with his master until the outbreak of World War I, in which he served with the Austro-Hungarian artillery.

After the war Krimper travelled through central Europe, working in such centres as Prague and Vienna. In the early 1920s he settled in Berlin. As a Jew, he suffered from the rise to power of Hitler and the National Socialists and was thwarted in his plans to set up his own business. He married Elsbeth Leipziger on 25 January 1938 in Berlin. By August he was employed in the joinery of a training centre for Jews who wished to emigrate.

In November the Krimpers were granted permission to emigrate to Australia. *En route* they spent six months in England where Schulim helped to supervise the building of a refugee camp. They arrived in Melbourne on 17 August 1939. Krimper was naturalized in 1945. The war and immediate postwar years were difficult for him, but his friendship with Robert Haines, assistant-director of the National Gallery of Victoria, led the gallery to acquire two of his major cabinets in 1948, to an important exhibition at Georges Gallery in 1951 and to another at the Rockefeller Centre,

New York, in 1956. A retrospective exhibition followed at the N.G.V. in 1959.

During the 1950s and 1960s Krimper was Melbourne's premier supplier of custommade furniture in the modern style. His ability to reveal the beauties of his timbers was legendary, as was the finesse of construction of his furniture. He was the first cabinetmaker in Victoria to demand—and receive—for his craft the respect which had previously been accorded only to painters and sculptors.

Even in his earliest days in Melbourne a certain mystique surrounded his name. Many of his customers—often fellow immigrants—were in awe of him, and his demeanour did little to put them at ease. When they visited his St Kilda workshop he was rarely to be found at work. Eventually he emerged from the office, wearing a smock or dustcoat, a French beret and—when the mood took him—a monocle. He liked to be known simply by his surname.

Krimper suffered his first heart attack in the mid-1960s. Although his output had been steadily declining since the peak in the late 1950s, when he employed six assistants, he continued working every day until his death. Survived by his wife and daughter, he died on 18 August 1971 at St Kilda and was buried in Springvale cemetery. The N.G.V. held a memorial exhibition in 1975. His work is represented in the National Gallery of Australia, Canberra, the art galleries of Queensland and South Australia, and the Powerhouse Museum, Sydney.

T. Lane and M. Strizic, *Schulim Krimper* (Melb, 1987) and for bib; *Herald* (Melb), 19 Dec 1955, 20 Sept 1956, 7 May 1969, 25 Aug 1971, 9 Apr 1975; *Age* (Melb), 7 Apr 1975; *Australian*, 15 Oct 1981.
                                              TERENCE LANE

KRISCHOCK, HENRY LUDWIG FRANK (1875-1940), photographer, was born on 1 September 1875 in Adelaide, sixth child of Carl Ludwig Daniel Franz Krischock, a bootmaker from Germany, and his English-born wife Mary, née Richardson. In his boyhood Harry sold his textbooks and bought a camera, thus ending his education at Pulteney Street School. By 1897 he was working for Hutchison [q.v.9], Craker & Smith, publishers of *Quiz and the Lantern*. He gave his occupation as clerk when he married Ethelinda Cornelius on 20 July 1899 at the Primitive Methodist manse, Norwood. Four years later he advertised himself as H. Krischock, photographer, of Gresham Street; carrying a camera on his back, he cycled to many locations for his assignments. On 7 March 1903 the *Critic* published a page of his photographs of a race-meeting in Melbourne and his work remained prominent in that weekly until 1907. South Australian photographer (1906-09) for the *Australasian* and *Garden and Field*, Krischock worked under contract, supplying, developing and processing his own film.

In 1911 the Wondergraph Co. began making local news and feature films. Krischock's first cinematographic film, *Adelaide in a Hurry*, showed city people in their daily activities. He was Wondergraph's contract cameraman in 1912 and his film of the Melbourne Cup that year was shown in Adelaide one night after the race was run. The Wondergraph Picture Pavilion opened in Hindley Street, Adelaide, in 1913; Krischock was commissioned to make a documentary film, *From Pasture to Table*, on how Adelaidians obtained their meat. Competition between film companies increased after 1914 and he sold his films of horse-racing to Wondergraph, West's Pictures, and the Empire and Star theatres.

Krischock continued shooting newsreels and documentaries for Wondergraph until the 1920s. He was photographer for four South Australian feature films: *Remorse, a Story of the Red Plague* (1917), *Our Friends, the Hayseeds* (1917), *What Happened to Jean* (1918) and *Why Men Go Wrong* (1922). The National Film and Sound Archive, Canberra, holds eight examples of his work. The Mortlock Library of South Australiana has more than one hundred of Krischock's photographs: some of them are aerial shots, others panoramas, and a number feature floods, fires, soldiers and royalty. His contract with the *Advertiser* lasted thirty years; it included work for the *Express and Journal* and the *Chronicle*; and it involved travel throughout South Australia. In the 1920s his sons Keith and Bill joined Krischock Studios. The *Advertiser* took over their business in 1950.

A stocky man with piercing eyes, Krischock was kind and generous, but also quick tempered, garrulous and extroverted. He was best-known for his photographs of sport and twice fell foul of football umpires by intruding on the ground and querying their decisions. Whereas other press photographers were sparing in their use of reels, Krischock sat high in the stand at Adelaide Oval during cricket matches and snapped incessantly with a telescopic lens. Survived by his wife, three sons and two daughters, he died on 25 October 1940 at Kingswood and was cremated. His profession was more a 'ruling passion' than a means of livelihood and he enjoyed the hurly-burly of photographing the unexpected. To him, 'a chance missed was a picture lost'.

A. Pike and R. Cooper, *Australian Film, 1900-1977* (Melb, 1980); A. D. McCredie (ed), *From Colonel Light into the Footlights* (Adel, 1988); *News* (Adel), 27 Sept 1924; *Advertiser* (Adel), 26 Oct 1940; Personalities Remembered, radio talk 5CL, 8 Aug 1971 (Mort L); information from Mr R. Krischock, Novar Gardens, and Mr S. Perceval, Kent Town, Adel.   JOYCE GIBBERD

KULAKOWSKI, MIECZYSLAW (1915-1978), businessman, was born on 15 January 1915 in Warsaw, eldest of three sons of Julian Stanislaw Kulakowski, businessman, and his wife Anna, née Chmielewska. Educated at the Higher School of Commerce, Warsaw, Mieczyslaw served as an officer cadet in the Polish Army in September 1939. He was captured and taken to Germany as a prisoner of war. Escaping to France in 1942, he joined the Polish Red Cross at Lyons, unsuccessfully attempted to cross to England, and eventually reached Berne where he worked for Pro Polonia which aided Polish prisoners of war. Later, he remained in Switzerland, helping to provide food and clothing for war-devastated Poland.

On 14 February 1948 at the Polish Church, 16th Arrondissement, Paris, Kulakowski married Nathalie Starza-Miniszewska, who had also worked for the Polish Red Cross in France. Although neither spoke English, they emigrated to Sydney, arriving on 13 December 1949. Having completed their contract to work for the immigration department for two years, they began to search for a productive occupation. Michael found it by supplying the needs of thousands of new Australian citizens who longed for music and memories of their homelands, and whose radio or gramophone was their only luxury. He sold this equipment, as well as records in the European languages. The business flourished and in 1952 Carinia Co. Pty Ltd (named after an Aboriginal word meaning 'home') was founded to sell continental records previously unavailable in Australia. The trademark was a victorious mermaid (the symbol of Warsaw) rising from a map of Australia. Importing the matrices from Europe, the company produced vinyl discs and cassettes—in over thirty languages —at their Willoughby factory. For thirteen years Carinia's 'Continental Cabaret', a weekly radio programme, was broadcast on radio 2KY.

Michael and Nathalie were naturalized in 1955. Six ft 2 ins (188 cm) tall, he wore glasses and had brown hair, a moustache and grey-blue eyes. Generous and endowed with 'charm and old world courtesy', he was devoted to his clients. Kulakowski was an outstanding example of the contribution postwar immigrants made to Australia. He enjoyed sport (particularly cycling in his youth) and acquired a knowledge of cricket. Possessing a good singing voice, he was an enthusiast for classical music. In 1962 the company acquired the exclusive Australian distribution of German Telefunken recordings. Other labels were added to its catalogue, and classical music comprised 65 per cent of sales by 1977. That year the business celebrated its twenty-fifth anniversary by presenting a bronze bust of Chopin to the Australian National Gallery.

Carinia became the largest, privately owned record company in the country. From 1954 Kulakowski travelled frequently to Europe and the United States of America, but his love of his adopted country was deep. The couple lived at Castlecrag and had a holiday home on Dangar Island, in the Hawkesbury River, where Michael enjoyed fishing. About 1973 he suffered a serious heart attack, but continued to work at his usual pace. While travelling in France on business, Kulakowski died on 8 July 1978 at Antibes and was cremated; his ashes were placed under a blue spruce at Northern Suburbs crematorium, Sydney. A Catholic memorial service was held at the Polish church, Marayong. Nathalie continued to run Carinia until 1988. The Kulakowskis and their clients had helped to change the sound of Australia.

Sun (Syd), 17 Mar 1977; *Financial Review*, 28 July 1978; naturalization files, A446/178, item 55/25486, A446/179, item 56/24073 (AA, Canb); information from and papers held by Mrs N. Kulakowski, Castlecrag, Syd.   CHRIS CUNNEEN

KUMM, FRANCES GERTRUDE (1886-1966), churchwoman and philanthropist, was born on 8 April 1886 at Collingwood, Melbourne, eldest of eight children of Frederick John Cato [q.v.7], a Victorian-born merchant, and his wife Frances, née Bethune, who came from New Zealand. In partnership with his cousin Thomas Edwin Moran, Cato was steadily building a grocery empire. When Gertrude was 2 he bought a house at Toorak in which she was to spend much of her life.

Gertrude was educated at home until the age of 14. She then entered Methodist Ladies' College (wearing a ruby-red dress) where she was conspicuous as one of the few from wealthy homes. The Cato family was deeply Methodist, and, despite the demands of business, her father spent so much time working for the Wesleyan Church that he was 'almost its unpaid employee'. Hence Gertrude absorbed from birth the ideals of service to the Church and of philanthropic work.

Fred Cato's international missionary involvement brought to the family home in 1911 Dr Hermann Karl William Kumm, a missionary and explorer. Born in Prussia and later based in England, Kumm was a fellow of the Royal Geographical Society who had traversed the north-central African divide between the Niger River and the Nile. His wife had died in 1906, leaving him with two young sons. Within a fortnight of announcing their engagement, Gertrude and Karl were married with Methodist forms on 12 January 1912 at Hawthorn.

The couple travelled to England. From there Dr Kumm continued his work for the Sudan United Mission. On the outbreak of World War I they moved to New Jersey, United States of America, where their son John and daughter Lucy (d.1934) were born. Their American life was more settled: Karl was restricted by heart disease and Lucy was a diabetic.

Dr Kumm died in 1930. His widow was distraught. Her sister Una (later Dr Porter) was sent to bring Gertrude and the children back to Australia and the family home. Mrs Kumm threw herself into Christian public life, serving the Young Women's Christian Association as national president (1945-51) and as vice-president (1951-55) of the World Y.W.C.A for the South Pacific Area. Other commitments ranged from the Australian Red Cross Society and the National Council of Women (president 1945-53) to various agencies of the Methodist Church, the Victorian Diabetic Association (president 1953-57) and the Women's Hospital, Melbourne (president 1938-42). Her greatest service was to postwar refugees and immigrants as a member (1952-61) of the Commonwealth Immigration Advisory Council. In 1948 she was appointed O.B.E.

Mrs Kumm possessed a loving and gracious disposition which endeared her to the many people with whom she worked around the world. Survived by her son, she died on 4 June 1966 at South Yarra and was cremated. A wing of the Royal Women's Hospital, Carlton, is named after her; the Y.W.C.A.'s Cato conference centre in Melbourne commemorates the work of Gertrude, Una and their mother.

A. Blainey, *If God Prospers Me* (Melb, 1990); YWCA, *Association News*, Mar 1947; *Aust YWCA*, Dec 1951, July 1966; *Sun News-Pictorial*, 11 Sept 1947; *Age* (Melb), 6 June 1966; *Herald* (Melb), 7 June 1966.   JANET MCCALMAN

L

LACK, CLEM LLEWELLYN (1900-1972), journalist, public servant and historian, was born on 19 December 1900 at Bundaberg, Queensland, son of William Lack, an overseer who came from England, and his Queensland-born wife Elizabeth, née Evans. Educated locally, Clem began work in 1918 as a cadet with the *Gympie Times*, then moved to the Brisbane *Courier* (later *Courier-Mail*) in 1922 as a 'C' grade reporter. On 18 December 1923 at the Surface Hill Methodist Church, Gympie, he married 28-year-old Ivy Beatrice Latimer (d.1971).

As political columnist and chief of the parliamentary-gallery staff for the *Courier-Mail* and *Sunday Mail*, Lack wrote a daily commentary on proceedings in the Legislative Assembly. He studied part time at the University of Queensland, obtaining a diploma of journalism (1928) and a B.A. (1934). In 1935-70 he lectured on journalism intermittently at the university. Between 1940 and 1944 he was special writer, leader-writer and book reviewer on the Brisbane *Telegraph*. He spent the next three years with the Melbourne *Age*, but found the experience unrewarding. Returning to Brisbane, he joined (1948) and headed (from 1953) the public relations bureau of the Chief Secretary's Department.

Lack became increasingly involved in the (Royal from 1959) Historical Society of Queensland as a member (1949), councillor (1958), chairman of the editorial committee and editor of publications (1959), fellow (1962) and vice-president (1968). The society wielded considerable influence, publishing periodicals and monographs, promoting the establishment of affiliated branches in regional areas of the State, participating in public functions in Brisbane and gathering a photographic collection. Office-bearers of the R.H.S.Q. were prominent on government committees which organized Queensland's centenary celebrations in 1959, with Lack chairing the publications committee. He helped Sir Raphael Cilento, the society's president, to compile a centenary history, *Triumph in the Tropics* (1959), and edited *Queensland, Daughter of the Sun* (1959), a survey marking one hundred years of responsible government.

Although Lack was notable for the volume of his historical writing, his first book had been a collection of verse, *The Fields of Amaranth and Other Poems* (1936). His most significant work was in compiling and editing *Three Decades of Queensland Political History* (1962). An exhaustive review of the period from 1929 to the parliamentary session of 1960, the book drew on his close observation of events and personal knowledge of the participants. One of his numerous articles in the R.H.S.Q.'s journal, '"Wild White Men" in Queensland'—co-authored with Cilento—dealt with Whites living among the Aborigines; the society released it as a monograph in 1959.

With Harry Stafford, Lack wrote *The Rifle and the Spear* (1964), a dramatic account of frontier battles between Aborigines and Europeans. Late in life Lack expressed his view that history was the 'master study of humanity and progress': rather than merely recording 'wars and the reigns of kings', it should be all-embracing in covering 'the development of human civilisation'. *A Bookman's Essays*, a collection of his writings on the Celtic and English peoples, was published in 1969.

Lack was tall, bulky and bespectacled. After retiring in 1966, he engaged in freelance journalism, edited the Queensland Country Party's monthly magazine, and remained active in the R.H.S.Q. as research officer and editor of its journal. Survived by his son and daughter, he died on 20 March 1972 at his Teneriffe home and was cremated. His preoccupations and values belonged to Brisbane's cultural milieu of the 1950s. The R.H.S.Q. inaugurated the Clem Lack memorial oration in 1973. Delivering the second oration, Cilento described his friend as a 'competent, romantic, indefatigable and lovable man' who had treasured his Celtic inheritance and sympathized with downtrodden groups.

RHSQ, *J*, 7, no 1, 1962-63, p 33, 9, no 5, 1973-74, p 50; *Telegraph* (Brisb), 21 Mar 1972.

RUTH S. KERR

LAIDLAW, ANNIE INA (1889-1978), navy matron, was born on 23 January 1889 at Lake Wallace, near Edenhope, Victoria, second of three daughters of native-born parents James Adam Laidlaw, grazier, and his wife Annie, née Gilchrist. Ina was educated at Alexandra Ladies' College, Hamilton. On 11 November 1913 she started training at the (Royal) Children's Hospital, Melbourne; three years later she was retained as a staff nurse.

Appointed to the Australian Army Nursing Service on 30 June 1917, Laidlaw was immediately sent to India where she served in military hospitals at Bombay and Poona. She returned to Melbourne in March 1919 and her A.A.N.S. appointment terminated on 21 May. Back at the Children's Hospital, she worked as a ward sister until 1925 when she was granted leave to undertake midwifery training at the Royal Hospital for Women, Sydney. She resumed her post at the Children's Hospital and in January 1926 became assistant lady superintendent (assistant-matron). In 1930 she was promoted to lady superintendent of the hospital's orthopaedic section at Frankston, where she worked under the medical superintendent Dr John Colquhoun.

The Royal Australian Naval Nursing Service was formed in 1942. Surgeon Captain W. J. Carr, who knew Miss Laidlaw socially, nominated her to head the new service; on 20 April she was appointed superintending sister, with the equivalent rank of lieutenant commander. She assisted in the selection of qualified nurses suitable for recruitment as R.A.N.N.S. officers. Initially, twelve were chosen in Melbourne and twelve in Sydney. Their numbers rose to sixty before World War II ended. They served in naval hospitals in Sydney and Darwin, at Milne Bay, Papua, and at Flinders Naval Depot, Westernport, Victoria; they staffed naval sick-quarters in Brisbane and Canberra, at Townsville and Cairns, Queensland, and at Fremantle, Western Australia; some of them were attached to army and air force hospitals. Laidlaw visited her staff at their various postings.

Based at Flinders Naval Depot, she had charge of the establishment's hospital in addition to her responsibilities for the whole of the R.A.N.N.S. In March 1943 she was promoted matron. Laidlaw and her colleagues shared their living-quarters with officers of the Women's Royal Australian Naval Service, but had their own officers' mess where meals and services were provided by W.R.A.N.S. cooks and stewards. The nurses' duties included training men as sick-berth attendants to prepare them for employment at sea. There was some resentment among male members of the Medical Branch who felt that their positions were being usurped. Laidlaw overcame the difficulty. One nursing officer recalled that she 'was of sterling worth . . . a born leader—a woman of tremendous courage'.

After Laidlaw's R.A.N.N.S. appointment ended on 15 March 1946, she returned to her position at the orthopaedic division of the Children's Hospital and remained there until 1950. She had a large circle of friends, belonged to the Peninsula Country Golf Club, Frankston, enjoyed a game of cards and drove a baby Austin motorcar.

In 1951-52 Laidlaw was home sister at the Queen Elizabeth Hospital for Children, London. She then worked in Melbourne as resident matron at the Freemasons' Homes of Victoria, Prahran. Following her retirement in 1957, she lived in the Returned Sailors', Soldiers' and Airmen's Imperial League of Australia's home for nurses at R.S.L. (St Kilda) House. She died on 13 September 1978

at McKinnon and was cremated with the forms of the Uniting Church. Nora Heysen's portrait of Laidlaw is held by the Australian War Memorial, Canberra.

A. S. Walker, *Medical Services of the R.A.N. and R.A.A.F.* (Canb, 1961); L. Gardiner, *Royal Children's Hospital, Melbourne, 1870-1970* (Melb, 1970); Roy Children's Hospital, Melb, Archives; information from Mrs C. Eckersley, Hawthorn, Melb, and the late Miss E. Emms.   PATRICIA C. VINES

LAIDLAW, DAVID KERSELL (1902-1979), businessman, was born on 16 August 1902 at Brunswick, Melbourne, ninth child of Adam Laidlaw, painter, and his wife Johanna Trisia, née Moriarty, both Melbourne born. The family lived in Edward Street, Brunswick, where Johanna made garments for the clothing trades. Educated at Stewart Street State School, at the age of 16 David went to Newcastle, New South Wales, to work with a relation who manufactured shirts. Laidlaw returned to Melbourne in 1922 and joined Castle Clothing, Brunswick, where he rose from foreman to manager. On 18 April 1927 at Scots Church, Melbourne, he married with Presbyterian forms Jessie Irene Barnes, a 19-year-old machinist.

In 1935 he decided to form his own company, D. K. Laidlaw & Sons Pty Ltd. Seeking to promote its Australian image, the firm adopted the name 'Yakka', an Aboriginal word meaning 'hard work'. The word had entered the Australian vocabulary in the late nineteenth century as synonymous with strength and endurance, qualities promoted by the company for its industrial-wear products. In 1939 the firm moved to its first industrial premises at 153 Weston Street, Brunswick, to produce combination overalls. Within a few years Yakka transferred to larger premises at 260 Lygon Street, East Brunswick. During World War II the company won several large government contracts, the main one with the Royal Australian Air Force. A welfare capitalist model of factory management was adopted and trade union support was advertised as part of company promotion: 'Hard Yakka, 100 per cent union made'. By the end of the war Yakka employed eighty workers.

The 1950s saw a period of rapid expansion in manufacturing in general and for Yakka in particular. A factory which made boys' shorts was opened at Sunbury, and in 1955 a third factory was built in Ballarat Street, Brunswick, to make jeans, and bib-and-brace and combination overalls. Yakka produced its own label jeans: 'Brand Em' was followed by 'Keyman' in 1962. In 1960 the company moved to larger premises at Broadmeadows, expanding operations interstate and distributing products directly to industry. Further expansion ensued, with factories established at Wangaratta and Wodonga, Victoria, and at Albury and Darlinghurst, New South Wales.

By the 1960s Laidlaw had begun to withdraw from the business, leaving it largely to his sons John and Brian who were made joint managing directors. John became sole managing director in 1976, Brian having taken the managing directorship of H. D. Lee Australia. Next year Yakka became the major sponsor of Collingwood Football Club, providing the players with special training guernseys that bore a large Yakka logo.

Five ft 8 ins (178 cm) tall and sturdily built, David Laidlaw was an active sportsman who played 150 games of Australian Rules football with the East Brunswick club. He had a bright, outgoing personality and a keen sense of humour. For many years he was involved in local community activities as a Brunswick city councillor, president of the Bing Boys' Club and a life governor of Mount Royal home for the aged. Survived by his wife, daughter and two sons, he died on 20 February 1979 at Brunswick and was cremated; his estate was sworn for probate at $60 960.

Australian, 22 Mar 1994; Hard Yakka—the history of D. K. Laidlaw & Sons Pty Ltd (ts, nd, held by ADB); information from Mr J. D. Laidlaw, Broadmeadows, Melb.   CECILE TRIOLI

LAING, HUGH BOYD (1889-1974), headmaster and Gaelic scholar, was born on 11 October 1889 at Stoneybridge on the island of South Uist, Inverness-shire, Scotland, son of Donald John Laing, farmer, and his wife Ann, née Boyd. Educated at Kingussie Higher Grade School, and the University of Glasgow (M.A., 1911) where he studied arts and then divinity, Hugh taught for one year at Skerry's College, Edinburgh. In 1913 he emigrated to Western Australia and continued his career at Scotch College, Perth. During World War I he was four times rejected for service in the Australian Imperial Force because of his flat feet.

Joining the Western Australian Education Department on 6 April 1915, Laing was posted to the Goldfields High School, Kalgoorlie, Perth Modern School (1918) and Bunbury High School (1925). He was first assistant and head of the English department (from 1929) at Albany High School. At St Andrew's Presbyterian Church, Perth, on 4 January 1929 he married Marion Stibbs, a 21-year-old stenographer. While at Albany he gained a diploma of education (1937) from the University of Western Australia. Laing held the headmastership at Albany High School (1942-43), Northam High School (1944-49) and again at Albany (1950-54). During his time at Albany he set a high academic standard for the

school, re-stocked the library, and promoted co-operation between school and town. A lover of hockey, he encouraged sport and promoted the building of an oval and its use by outside groups. In 1954, the year of his retirement, he was also acting-superintendent of English in secondary schools; for a further ten years he was a member of the examining panel for Leaving certificate English.

Laing was an outstanding, talented teacher, with a logical approach and a quizzical sense of humour; he took a keen interest in his students and had a strong influence on many of them. The nicknames he was given, 'Whizz-Bang' and 'Whizzy', stemmed from his Gaelic Christian name, Uisdean. His rather craggy appearance and unusual accent made him a butt of student humour, which he took in good part. Laing's greatest strengths were his knowledge of language and the pleasure he took in it, particularly the teaching and appreciation of English literature.

In 1964 Laing published a book of poetry and prose, written predominantly in Gaelic: it was entitled *Gu Tir Mo Luaidh* ('To the land of my praise'). For 'The Fever That Will Never Die' he won the poetry section of the Gaelic Mod and was appointed national bard of Scotland for 1965-66. The most significant and unusual request for his knowledge of Gaelic had occurred at Bunbury in 1927 when three 'coloured' seamen from South Africa jumped ship. The Immigration Act (1901) prescribed a dictation test for 'undesirable aliens'. A local customs official asked Laing to administer the test in Gaelic. All three seamen failed. The case foreshadowed that of Egon Kisch [q.v.] in 1934. Laing contributed prolifically to newspapers in Australia and abroad on historical, literary and educational topics. Survived by his wife, son and three daughters, he died on 22 September 1974 in Perth and was cremated with Anglican rites. D. McGregor Whyte's portrait (1919) of Laing is held by the family.

Scottish Educational J, Sept 1968; *Aust Women's Weekly*, 7 Jan 1970; *Western Teacher*, 9 Feb 1972; *South Western Times*, 3 May 1927; *Albany Advertiser*, 18 Dec 1953, 2 Feb 1954; *West Australian*, 5 June 1959, 30 Jan, 19 Mar, 14 May 1960, 7 Oct 1965, 25 Sept 1974; *Glasgow Herald*, 4 Aug 1959; *Living Today* (Perth), 23 Mar 1972; Education Dept (WA), files 7064/13 and 1975/35, and Laing's record of service (PRO, Perth); information from Mr I. G. Medcalf, Nedlands, Miss M. J. Laing, Shenton Park, Perth, and the late Mr A. C. Staples.
                                                          M. MEDCALF

LAMB, JOHN (1885-1974), businessman, was born on 22 August 1885 at Arbroath, Forfarshire, Scotland, son of John Lamb, railway stoker, and his wife Jane, née Cameron.

Trained as a tailor's cutter, young John emigrated to Australia in 1911. He worked at Peapes & Co. Ltd, tailors and shirtmakers, in George Street, Sydney, before settling at Newcastle. On Christmas Day 1915 he married with Presbyterian forms Adelaide Crawford, daughter of a master tailor, at her mother's home at Boolaroo. Lamb joined T. A. Braye, a solicitor, as a partner in Elliott & Cowman, a Newcastle firm of tailors and mercers founded by the Lasker brothers in 1887. The business was promoted as 'The House that Value built' and was expanded to include a second shop in 1917. By 1920 the company had become Elliotts Ltd, menswear outfitters. An early form of consumer credit was available through the Workers Cash Order & Finance Co. Ltd which operated out of the main store.

Success in these ventures permitted investment in broadcasting. In 1947 Lamb bought Newcastle radio station 2KO from (Sir) Allen Fairhall. Having purchased radio 2UE Sydney Pty Ltd for £165 000 from John Fairfax & Sons [qq.v.4,8] Pty Ltd in 1954, he took over as director of the ailing company. Under the Lambs' management 'it soon became a goldmine'. The Lamb family secured Newcastle's commercial television licence in 1960, two years before their station NBN-3 began broadcasting. After a court battle was fought to gain rights to broadcast (Sir Frank) Packer [q.v.] and Fairfax programmes, substantial shareholdings in Newcastle Broadcasting & Television Corporation Ltd were sold to Consolidated Press Ltd and News Ltd in August 1963.

Ability and astute investments enabled John Lamb to acquire other broadcasting interests in Adelaide, at Kempsey, New South Wales, and at Port Macquarie through his family company, Broadcast Investments Pty Ltd. He did not flaunt his wealth and influence, travelling by bus to work and by train to Sydney for 2UE board-meetings. Lamb was modest and quiet about his achievements, and generous in sharing the benefits they conferred. Few of his 'employees could understand a word of his thick Scottish burr'; his 'largely unintelligible speech' at the annual 2KO Christmas party was a cause of merriment.

Lamb attended St Andrew's Presbyterian Church, Cooks Hill. He was an active member of the Rotary Club of Newcastle, the Masonic and the Newcastle City Bowling clubs; a bowling green was named after him. A rare photograph of Lamb in public shows him as a small, frail figure, bowling with his three admiring sons. He was a long-time resident of the Lake Macquarie suburb of Speers Point, but moved to Bar Beach, Newcastle, following the death of his wife in 1953. There he enjoyed a daily swim in the ocean until 1973. Lamb died on 16 January 1974 at Lingard Hospital, Mere-

wether, and was buried in Sandgate cemetery. He was survived by his three sons: John (Jack) and Hugh worked in Elliotts until the business was sold in 1978; Stewart moved to Sydney to look after their interests in 2UE.

G. Souter, *Company of Heralds* (Melb, 1981); *Newcastle Morning Herald*, 18 Jan 1974, 15 Mar 1986; *Newcastle Sun*, 3 July 1978; *Sun-Herald*, 7 Oct 1979; *Good Weekend*, 28 Dec 1991.

NANCY CUSHING

LAMBERT, CECIL RALPH ('ESKI') (1899-1971), bank officer and public servant, was born on 6 January 1899 at Leichhardt, Sydney, third of twelve children of William Addison Lambert, a dairyman from England who officiated (1920-23 and 1925) as mayor of Leichhardt, and his native-born wife Edith, née Barrell. Educated at Cleveland Street Intermediate High School, Cecil entered the Commonwealth Public Service at the age of 16. He worked first in the Treasury's taxation branch and then in the Attorney-General's Department.

Short and stocky, Lambert had an olive complexion, black hair and dark eyes. From childhood he had disliked the name Cecil and embraced his nickname 'Eski', accepting that he looked like an Eskimo. He represented New South Wales in baseball in 1919, 1921-26 and 1928, and captained the State side in 1921-24. When a team from Stanford University, California, United States of America, visited in 1928, he captained Australia (once) and New South Wales (once) in matches against them. In the 1927-28 cricket season he achieved the best bowling average for Petersham district club. At St Paul's Anglican Church, Scarborough, on 9 March 1929 he married Jessie Marshall, a 24-year-old schoolteacher; they had one daughter before Jessie died in 1935. He married 25-year-old Bronwen Evans on 12 June 1937 at the Presbyterian Church, Mosman.

In 1933 Lambert had joined the Rural Bank of New South Wales as an executive-officer; he was appointed a deputy-director to implement the Farmers' Relief Act (1932). From December 1939 he served as chairman and director of the Rural Reconstruction Board of New South Wales. Seconded to the Commonwealth Rural Reconstruction Commission between February 1943 and September 1945, he resumed his post with the reconstruction board and became a member (1947) of the economic advisory committee which considered proposals to divert waters of the Snowy River. Returning again to the Commonwealth public service, he was appointed director of regional development in the Department of Post-war Reconstruction in August 1948. In the following year he was made director (later assistant-secretary) of Northern Territory affairs, Department of the Interior, an office he held until 11 May 1951 when he took up the duties of secretary, Department of Territories.

As head of this department, Lambert served only one minister—(Sir) Paul Hasluck —for more than a decade. He was selected in preference to J. R. Halligan [q.v.14] because Hasluck believed that, unlike Halligan, Lambert possessed capacities and qualities which he himself lacked. In addition, Hasluck knew of Lambert's reputation for solving problems 'in an intensely practical way', and understood that he was 'forceful, perpetually industrious and widely experienced in public service practice'.

The ambitious Hasluck was sometimes impatient with his departmental officers and complained that preparation of advice was often protracted. He appreciated the position of public servants, but his frustration grew to anger on occasions. Hasluck claimed that Lambert never fully understood what he had in mind for increasing the participation of Papuans and New Guineans in the advancement of their country. Moreover, although Hasluck wrote a long memorandum on social and community development in the Territory, he doubted that he 'really got through to' Lambert on the subject.

An unusually demanding minister, Hasluck continued to hold his secretary in regard. Lambert had qualified as a fellow (1946) of the Federal Institute of Accountants and Hasluck praised the presentation of the department's financial submissions. Hasluck also recognized Lambert's capacity for hard work—despite his narrow vision—and valued his expertise in agricultural development. In 1955 Lambert was appointed C.B.E. From March 1961 he represented the government on the board of Commonwealth-New Guinea Timbers Ltd.

Lambert retired on 15 May 1964 and pursued his interests in Freemasonry and horse-racing. He died on 21 July 1971 in Canberra Hospital and was cremated with Presbyterian forms; his wife and their daughter survived him, as did the daughter of his first marriage.

P. Hasluck, *A Time for Building* (Melb, 1976); information from Ms J. Tompsett, Cook, and Mr R. S. Swift, Kingston, Canb, Cr M. Sheehan, Leichhardt, and Mr B. Davis, Eastwood, Syd; author's research notes and papers, held in ADB file, Canb.

PETER C. GRUNDY

LAMBERT, ERIC FRANK (1918-1966), novelist, was born on 19 January 1918 at Upper Clapton, Hackney, London, son of Frank Lambert, commercial traveller, and his wife Marion Rosina, née Bean. The family emigrated to Sydney in 1919 and settled at Manly. Eric was educated at Manly Public, Sydney Boys' High and Manly Boys' Intermediate High schools. At 17 he left school, denied the university education he craved, and worked in a garage. On 10 June 1940 Lambert enlisted in the Australian Imperial Force. He saw action in the Middle East with the 2nd/2nd Machine-Gun Battalion (January 1941-October 1942) and the 2nd/15th Battalion (to January 1943) before sailing for Australia. From August 1943 he was in Papua with the 2nd/15th, returning home in March 1944. Throughout his service he was in and out of hospital. While in Singapore (September-October 1945) assisting the repatriation of prisoners of war from Changi, he was promoted sergeant. He was discharged in Melbourne on 7 December 1945.

The novelist Frank Hardy, one of Lambert's closest friends in the late 1940s, persuaded him to join the Communist Party of Australia in 1947. Hardy was best man when Lambert married with Unitarian forms Joyce Margaret Boyd Smith, a schoolteacher, on 6 April 1950 in East Melbourne. The Lamberts were later divorced. Eric joined the Melbourne Realist Writers' Group and was a founder (1954) of the radical nationalist journal, *Overland*, but fell out with its editor Stephen Murray-Smith. Unpredictable and disputative, Lambert had a growing reputation as an awkward customer, troubled by war memories, poor health and disabling jealousies.

In 1949 Lambert was awarded a Commonwealth Literary Fund fellowship. He privately published his first novel, *The Twenty Thousand Thieves* (1951), based on his war experiences in the Middle East. The book was soon accepted by a commercial publisher—Frederick Muller Ltd in London—and was to sell over 750 000 copies. Lambert's communism shaped the politics of the novel, as well as its reception in the sharply polarized world of the Cold War. *The Veterans* (London, 1954) was set in the jungles of New Guinea and also enjoyed huge sales. Both works drew clear distinctions between the common soldiers, invariably radicals and free spirits, and the officer-class, which was, just as invariably, venal and inept. Even so, the novels remain powerful and often moving accounts of World War II.

Following the 1955 World Assembly for Peace (held in Helsinki) at which Lambert was an Australian delegate, he remained based in London. In 1956 he went to Hungary, joined the revolutionaries and broke with the communists over the Russian invasion. His articles on Hungary in the Sydney *Daily Telegraph* further alienated the left. Lambert wrote seventeen novels under his own name, and as 'D. Brennan' retold film stories. He drew on the war in *Glory Thrown In* (1959) and *Hiroshima Reef* (1967), and on his second-ment to Changi in *MacDougal's Farm* (1965). Nationalist and anti-authoritarian sympathies permeate his novels about Eureka, Ballarat and Ned Kelly [q.v.5]: *The Five Bright Stars* (Melbourne, 1954), *Ballarat* (1962) and *Kelly* (1964). On 5 March 1963 at the register office, Wood Green, Middlesex, Lambert married a divorcee Phyllis Daphne Hogarth, née Pamplin. Survived by his wife and their two daughters, he died of acute hypertensive heart failure on 16 April 1966 at Little Maplestead, Essex.

Z. O'Leary, *The Desolate Market* (Syd, 1974); D. Walker, 'The Writers' War', in J. Beaumont (ed), *Australia's War 1939 to 1945* (Syd, 1996); *SMH*, 7 Oct 1949, 29 Aug, 13, 24, 25 Sept 1952, 20 Apr 1966; S. Murray-Smith papers, box 113 (LaTL).

D. R. WALKER

LAMBERT, RAYMOND EDOUARD (1908-1966), musician, was born on 13 June 1908 at Ostende, Belgium, son of Edouard Joseph Lambert, musician, and his wife Marie Catherine, née Crabbe, an operatic soprano known as 'Maria Ramberti'. Raymond graduated from the Brussels conservatorium at the age of 15, then continued his pianoforte studies at Liège under Arthur de Greef, a former pupil of Franz Liszt. While in Belgium, he appeared in public recitals with his father, a prominent violinist.

In 1926 the Lamberts emigrated to Australia where Edouard was appointed concert master of the Melbourne Symphony Orchestra. Raymond went back to Belgium in 1930, for military training and musical performances. After returning to Melbourne in 1932, he became chief study-teacher of piano at the University Conservatorium of Music, a position he held until his death. At St Patrick's Catholic Cathedral, East Melbourne, on 24 December 1934 he married Ruth Ferguson ('Jill'), daughter of T. J. Ryan [q.v.11]; they were to be divorced in 1948.

In addition to teaching, Lambert established a reputation in the fields of solo-playing, chamber music and accompanying. He was noted for his interpretation of French piano music, and of the music of Chopin, Liszt and other Romantic composers. His repertoire, however, extended through the range of keyboard music from Bach and Handel to the contemporary work of Olivier Messiaen.

With the establishment of the Australian Broadcasting Commission in 1932, Lambert was soon in demand for studio recitals of singers and instrumentalists. In 1936 he was made the official A.B.C. accompanist in Melbourne for radio studio performances and for visiting artists from abroad. Having toured Australia in 1933 with the baritone John

Brownlee [q.v.7], Lambert became accompanist and associate artist to many distinguished singers, including Florence Austral, Marjorie Lawrence [qq.v.7,10], Dame Clara Butt, Elizabeth Rethberg, Ezio Pinza, Alexander Kipnis and (Dame) Joan Hammond. Among the instrumentalists with whom he gave sonata recitals were Jeanne Gautier, Wolfgang Schneiderhan, Christian Ferras, Ruggiero Ricci and Ricardo Odnoposoff. Lambert toured Australia with the young American violinist Michael Rabin; he also accompanied him on two tours (1953-55) of the United States of America and in recitals in Scandinavia, Italy and France. He was, as well, associate artist during Ricci's European tour in 1963.

Lambert found special joy and fulfilment in chamber music. With his colleagues he ranged through a considerable part of the repertoire from the early classic period to the contemporary. Informed critics referred not only to his technical ability and musicianship, but also to his artistic integrity. Lambert gave Vincent d'Indy's piano sonata its first Australian performance in 1965, in a studio recital pre-recorded for the A.B.C. and later released on disc. He appeared on television as solo artist, as accompanist, and with orchestra, giving the first performances in Australia of works by Prokofiev, d'Indy and Gershwin, and playing concertos by Brahms, Liszt, Tchaikovsky and Rachmaninov.

At the office of the government statist, Queen Street, Melbourne, on 7 August 1951 Lambert married Beatrice Gwendoline McCaul, a 24-year-old public servant. Following an operation for cancer, he died of a pulmonary embolism on 17 January 1966 in East Melbourne and was buried in Cheltenham cemetery; his wife survived him, as did the daughter and two sons of his first marriage. A special radio tribute on the A.B.C. on 21 January that year recognized his contribution to performing, broadcasting and teaching.

J. Glennon, *Australian Music and Musicians* (Adel, 1968); *Canon*, 9, no 9, Apr 1956; *Australasian*, 2 Apr 1927; *SMH*, 13, 18, 22 Aug 1932, 9 June 1933, 11, 12 Jan, 14, 18 Feb 1935, 30 Mar 1938, 16, 19, 25 Sept 1944, 6 Aug 1957, 18 Jan 1966; *Herald* (Melb), 17 Jan 1966; *Age* (Melb), 18 Jan 1966; ABC Archives (Melb); information from Mrs M. Schofield, Kew, Melb; personal knowledge.   ROBERT TRUMBLE

LAMBERT, VIOLET BARRY (1898-1975), grazier and shire councillor, was born on 4 February 1898 at Footscray, Melbourne, younger daughter of Victorian-born parents Robert Gustavus John James Powell, horse-shipper, and his wife Maria Ada May, née Barry. Educated at Aldworth Girls' Grammar

School, Malvern, Violet was a competent pianist and needleworker, and a fine horse-woman. During World War I she helped to promote enlistment and also joined the Purple Cross Society, a group of young women dedicated to the care of horses used in war.

At St George's Anglican Church, Malvern, on 12 July 1922 Violet married George Frederick Lambert, who acted as her father's agent in India until 1925. When the couple returned to Victoria they bought a grazing property at Lysterfield, which she named Chandanagore. After her husband's death in 1930, Violet ran it alone. When her father died in 1934, she also took over the management of Netherlea at Fern Tree Gully, his Red Poll stud and dairy-farm. Throughout World War II Mrs Lambert ran her own property almost single-handed, producing wool and fat lambs. In addition, she was president of the local Red Cross and fire brigade units, senior air-raid warden for the district and a member of the Volunteer Air Observer Corps. She had been appointed (1936) a special magistrate of the Children's Court, Caulfield, and was made a justice of the peace (1946); she was, as well, foundation president (1936) of the Fern Tree Gully branch of the Country Women's Association.

One of the first women councillors in Victoria, Lambert was elected to the Shire of Fern Tree Gully council in 1931. She represented the south riding for twenty-eight years and was shire president in 1946-47. A founder (1951) of the Australian Local Government Women's Association, she presided over its Victorian branch in 1952-56.

Mrs Lambert was one of the council's leading policy-makers for almost three decades. Her slight stature and ladylike manner belied her authority, tenacity and fluency in debate. She was largely responsible for the shire's first permanent baby health centre, its first emergency housekeeping service and for visits by the Melbourne District Nursing Service. While shire president, she founded the Fern Tree Gully and District Agricultural and Horticultural Society. In 1954, as founding president of the Fern Tree Gully Aged People's Welfare Association, she led moves to establish homes for the elderly, which were opened in 1956 and later known as Glengollan Village. She remained its president until her death. In 1957 she was appointed O.B.E. The Glengollan Village hostel was named after her in 1978.

While fighting an unsuccessful battle against compulsory acquisition of Chandanagore as part of the catchment area for Lysterfield reservoir, Lambert suffered a heart attack and moved in 1950 to Netherlea to live with her sister. Following her sister's death in 1971, she lived there alone and re-established its Red Poll stud. Survived by her daughter, she died on 15 August 1975 at Berwick and was buried in Springvale cemetery.

H. Coulson, *Story of the Dandenongs, 1838-1959* (Melb, 1959); A. V. Smith, *Women in Australian Parliaments and Local Governments* (Canb, 1975); A. Cerutty, *A History of Glengollan Village* (Melb, 1981); *Pakenham Gazette*, 20 Aug 1975; papers held by and information from Mrs H. B. Ronald, Sth Yarra, Melb.   HELEN COULSON

LAMILAMI, LAZARUS (1913?-1977), Methodist preacher, was born probably in 1913 at Brogden Beach, Arnhem Land, Northern Territory, son of Nangurulur and his wife Ngalmajulwun. Lamilami's parents belonged to the Maung language group of Aborigines whose territory included the Goulburn Islands and the adjacent coast of north-western Arnhem Land. Ngalmajulwun had been given in marriage to Nangurulur as recompense for an injury her people had done to his brother; that brother sailed with Indonesian trepang fishermen bound for Macassar (Ujung Pandang) in the Celebes (Sulawesi) and never returned.

Moving back and forward from South Goulburn Island to the mainland, Lamilami was reared in the customs of his people. He received an elementary education at the school founded (1916) by the Methodist Overseas Mission on South Goulburn Island. At the same time, like almost all his Maung contemporaries, he was initiated into full membership of the tribe. He trained as a carpenter and served for some years in the M.O.M.'s luggers which plied between Darwin and the missions along the north Arnhem Land coast.

About 1930 Lamilami married Magumiri in the Methodist Church, Goulburn Island. The marriage had been arranged by the elders according to Maung custom but it ended some five years later. Lamilami then sailed in naval patrol vessels sent to monitor Japanese pearlers operating in northern Australian waters. During World War II he lived on Croker Island where he built mission houses. In 1947 at South Goulburn Island he married Ilidjili in accordance with Maung rites; they were to have a daughter, Ruby (Nanguri-nyara), and two sons, Ronald (Ilugilug) and Lloyd (Dabidjara).

From 1947 Lamilami was employed as a carpenter at the mission on Goulburn Island. Involving himself in the work of the Church, he went on several tours for the M.O.M. and visited churches and centres in Australia where he spoke about his people and his life. His addresses, delivered in a 'slow, deliberate and well-modulated voice', were well received. He also became a visiting evangelist to the Maung. In 1964 the M.O.M. transferred him to the Croker Island mission as a builder and local preacher. Next year he was accepted as a candidate for the ministry. After studying in Adelaide, he was ordained on 5 November 1966. He was posted to Minjilang, on Croker Island, and won the respect both of his own people and the White missionaries. In 1968 he was appointed M.B.E. 'for service to the community'.

Genial, thoughtful and kind, Lamilami was a prominent figure in the traditional and religious life of Croker and Goulburn islands, and in the Methodist Church in the Northern Territory. He did much to promote harmony between Europeans and Aborigines, believing that they should 'walk hand in hand together'. His autobiography, *Lamilami Speaks* (Sydney, 1974), described the social organization and kin classification of his people, and gave an account of their traditional way of life. The book emphasized 'their struggle to retain their own heritage in the face of internal and external pressures that were intensifying all along the Arnhem Land coast'. To him, the availability of liquor and the prospect of uranium mining were fraught with danger.

In January 1977 Lamilami joined the staff of Nungalinya College, Darwin, as lecturer in Aboriginal studies; his teaching contributed to a cross-cultural understanding of Christianity. He was a member (1974-78) of the council of the Institute of Aboriginal Studies, Canberra. Survived by his wife and three children, he died of septicaemia on 21 September 1977 in Darwin and was buried in Minjilang cemetery with the forms of the Uniting Church. Numerous Aborigines and Europeans attended his funeral on Croker Island, testimony to his friendship with people of different races. A plaque in his memory was placed in the Nungalinya College chapel.

M. McKenzie, *Mission to Arnhem Land* (Adel, 1976); K. Cole, *The Aborigines of Arnhem Land* (Adel, 1979); E. Shepherdson, *Half a Century in Arnhem Land* (Adel, 1981); *Aust Inst of Aboriginal Studies Newsletter*, Jan 1978; Uniting Church of Aust, Methodist Overseas Mission records (ML).

KEITH COLE

LAMMON, THOMAS (c.1869-1965), indentured labourer, was born about 1869 on the island of Lamenu (also Lamen or Lamon), New Hebrides (Vanuatu), after which he was named. As a youth he was recruited to work on sugar plantations in Queensland. Labourers such as he were commonly known as Kanakas. Even though all but a handful came from Melanesia, they were officially referred to as Polynesians. Tom initially worked in the Ayr district as house-boy, stoker and blacksmith's offsider. He learned to com-

municate with his European overseers and fellow workers in a form of pidgin English which is now virtually extinct in Queensland, but a derivative, Bislama, has become the national language of Vanuatu.

After his first contract expired, Lammon spent a brief period at home before signing on again and returning to Queensland. What happened next is unclear. Tom said that he worked for a time at the Victoria mill, near Ingham, but other family members claim that he had additional jobs, including that of assistant to a recruiting officer, before he moved to Cairns. There, about 1890, he married Annie Anita (Netta) Bukabuka (or Booka Booka), probably from Buka Island in the Solomons. She had also come to Queensland as an indentured labourer and worked as a domestic servant. She and her husband were to have three sons and two daughters. Before the turn of the century the Lammons had returned to Ingham. Tom worked for the Lynn family at Farnham, near Gairloch Bridge on the Herbert River. He later leased land from the Lynns and grew his own sugarcane. A very religious man, he joined the Anglican Church and became a lay preacher or catechist. As a result he learned to read and write, to a limited degree.

In 1901 the Federal government's Pacific Island Labourers Act prohibited further recruiting of Kanakas after 31 March 1904 and provided for the repatriation of those in Australia by 31 December 1906. Nevertheless, 1500 to 2000 Melanesians were allowed to stay in Queensland. Tom and his family were among them. By 1919 he was one of the Victoria mill's long-term growers, supplying an estimated 150 tons each year. He gained a reputation as an upright and hard-working man. Having rented different parcels of land from the Lynns until about 1930, the Lammons moved to Ayr. Living beside Plantation Creek with a number of linked New Hebridean families, they eked out an existence selling vegetables and fruit in the streets, and eating wild game and fish caught in the swamps. When Netta died in 1955, Tom moved in with his relations. Aged about 96, he died on 11 August 1965 in Ayr District Hospital and was buried in the local cemetery; a son and a daughter survived him.

J. W. Davidson and D. Scarr (eds), *Pacific Islands Portraits* (Canb, 1970); T. Dutton, *Queensland Canefields English of the Late Nineteenth Century* (Canb, 1980); C. Moore, *Kanaka* (Port Moresby, Papua New Guinea, 1985).

TOM DUTTON

LAMOND, HENRY GEORGE (1885-1969), writer, was born on 13 June 1885 at Carl Creek in Queensland's Gulf country, second of three children of Scottish-born James

Lamond, a sub-inspector of police, and his wife Amy Brooke, née Shadforth, from Victoria. Educated at state schools, Brisbane Grammar School and Queensland Agricultural College, Gatton, in 1902 Henry became a jackeroo on Maneroo station, near Longreach. On 27 June 1910 at Maneroo he married with Anglican rites Eileen Meta Olive (d.1968), daughter of William McMillan, the former owner. Lamond worked on western Queensland properties in various jobs from horse-breaker to manager before leasing the six Molle Islands, off Proserpine, in 1927. He farmed on South Molle and began a mail service to the mainland, then moved to a farm at Lindum, Brisbane, in 1937.

In the 1920s Lamond (who pronounced his surname to rhyme with Hammond) had begun writing short stories, articles on natural history, and advice on handling cattle and sheep. His work appeared in journals such as *Queensland Country Life*, *Walkabout*, the *Bulletin*, *Farmer and Settler* and the *Pastoral Review*; in the United States of America his writings were published in *Atlantic Monthly, Adventure* and *Short Stories*. His first monograph, *Horns and Hooves* (London, 1931), was followed by a collection of tales, *Tooth and Talon* (Sydney, 1934), and by *An Aviary on the Plains* (Sydney, 1934). He published more than a dozen books, mostly novels about animals, among them *Brindle Royalist* (Sydney, 1947) and *Red Ruin Mare* (London, 1956). His work won popularity in Australia, England and the U.S.A. Regarded as classics of their genre, his novels were studied in Australian schools.

During the Depression Lamond had supported his family by subsistence farming and writing. From the mid-1930s he augmented his income by giving talks on the wireless for the Australian Broadcasting Commission; like his books, his speech was 'littered with bush colloquialisms'. A recognized authority on the early history of the large Australian stations, he had an unrivalled knowledge of the Queensland outback. John Hetherington [q.v.14] considered him 'exactly what you would expect an author of action stories to be. He is about 6 ft [183 cm] tall, with massive shoulders … his face is craggy … Using a salty idiom and punctuating his narrative with racy anecdotes, he talks in a strong, rather rough-throated outdoor man's voice'. Lamond scoffed at pretentiousness and was a master of the flippant comment. With scant respect for those who placed great store in their ancestors, he wrote of his forebear Thomas Shadforth [q.v.2]: 'He may have been in charge [of convicts], or he may have been one of them. I neither know nor care'. Lamond was appointed M.B.E. in 1968.

Survived by his daughter and one of his two sons, he died on 12 July 1969 in his home at Greenslopes, Brisbane, and was cremated. A plaque on Lamond Hill, South Molle, commemorates him, his wife and their son Hal who was killed in 1942 while serving with the Royal Australian Air Force.

C. Hadgraft, *Queensland and its Writers* (Brisb, 1959); S. Torre, *The Australian Short Story, 1940-1980* (Syd, 1984); *Age Literary Supplement*, 11 Mar 1961, p 18; *Hoofs and Horns*, Aug 1969; *Pastoral Review*, 18 Aug 1969, p 681; *Telegraph* (Brisb), 12 July 1969; *Sunday Mail* (Brisb), 13 July 1969; Lamond papers (OL); H. G. Lamond, Contributions towards a bibliography (Fryer L, Univ Qld); information from Mrs E. A. Edgell, Greenslopes, Brisb.

NANCY BONNIN

LAMPE, FREDERIC ERNEST (1892-1972), retailer and businessman, was born on 27 February 1892 at Elsternwick, Melbourne, fifth (second surviving) child of Victorian-born parents Hermann Ernst Franz Lampe, schoolteacher, and his wife Mary Pechina, née West. Educated at a state school and a business college, Eric worked in an indenting business. On 22 September 1914 he enlisted in the Australian Imperial Force and in December sailed for the Middle East. He served with the A.I.F. Records Section in Egypt, France and Britain, rising through the ranks to quartermaster and honorary captain (1917). At the parish church of St George, Islington, London, on 23 June 1919 he married Hilda Sheehan. That year he was appointed M.B.E. and became a member of the A.I.F. Disposals Board. In 1920 he returned to Melbourne where his appointment terminated on 8 August.

Within the year he was governing director (1920-34) of Lampe, Moffat Pty Ltd in Flinders Lane, an importer and supplier to the garment trade. The experience gave him a thorough understanding of the supply side of retailing. In 1934 Lampe was invited to join the board of Manton & Sons Pty Ltd, drapers in Bourke Street. The firm acquired the adjoining site (occupied by the Theatre Royal) and built a modern department store. Within three years the site was further enlarged. While Manton senior continued as chairman of directors, Lampe supplied much of the drive and organizing skill for the business. As deputy-chairman (from 1943) he presided at annual general meetings. He was appointed joint managing director in 1946 and succeeded Manton as chairman in 1954.

After being elected deputy-president of the Master Drapers' and Traders' Association in 1940, Lampe was president in 1941-43, 1948 and 1949-50. During his first term of office the association advocated the cause of city retailers who were striving to satisfy civilians' needs in the face of wartime rationing and austerity. In addition, Lampe was president

(1943-44, 1948 and 1949-50) of the Australian Council of Retailers. Following World War II the retail clothing trade was faced with unprecedented demand and its representatives lobbied the Commonwealth government to relinquish price control and restore normal market conditions. President (1948-58) of the French Chamber of Commerce in Australia, Lampe was appointed to the Légion d'honneur by the French government for his work in fostering relationships between France and Australia. He also promoted trade with Japan.

Lampe had become a foundation member of the Institute of Public Affairs, Victoria, established in 1943 to promote private enterprise. He served on its industrial committee which produced *Looking Forward* (c.1943), a statement on basic political and economic problems. As chairman (1951-57) of the editorial committee, he read and commented on every article published in the *I.P.A. Review*. He succeeded Sir George Coles [q.v.13] as president of the institute and held office from 1957 to 1971. In chairing meetings, Lampe 'dispensed with stiff formality' and displayed 'his warmth, friendliness and natural breeziness of manner'. In 1968 Coles, Sir Ian Potter and Lampe were invited to serve on the finance committee of the Victorian branch of the Liberal Party, not least for their fund-raising contacts.

Coveting Mantons' prime site with its 115-ft (35 m) frontage, G. J. Coles & Co. Pty Ltd launched a takeover bid in 1955. When the Manton sons accepted, Lampe resigned, ending thirty-five years involvement in the garment trade. In the following year he took up a directorship of Alex. Cowan (Australia) Pty Ltd, papermakers and wholesale stationers, and was the firm's chairman (from 1958). In 1956 Lampe was appointed a life governor of the Retail Traders' Association of Victoria, and to an economic advisory committee by the Menzies [q.v.] government.

The theatre 'was one of the great loves of his life'. Lampe was director of the Australian Elizabethan Theatre Trust (1954-71) and of the Australian Ballet (1962-71); he was also deputy-chairman of the Union Theatre Repertory Company (Melbourne Theatre Company from 1968). To them he brought 'his own special brand' of 'infectious optimism'. The Lampes travelled abroad 'frequently and extensively'. In 1960 they visited Moscow. Shortly after returning home he published his observations in *Two Eyes on Moscow* (1960), crediting the Soviet economy with giving its citizens a better standard of living than he had expected. A member of the Athenaeum and Australian clubs, Lampe was appointed C.B.E. in 1970. He died on 20 November 1972 in his home at Toorak and was cremated. His wife predeceased (1969) him; they had no children.

H. Iverson (comp and ed), *The Leaders of Industry and Commerce in Australia* (Melb, 1963); *IPA Review*, Oct-Dec 1971, p 78, Oct-Dec 1972, p 82; *Herald* (Melb), 23 Nov 1972; Manton files (Coles Myer Archives, Melb).   JOHN YOUNG

LAMPUNGMEIUA (TIPPAKLIPPA), CHARLIE ONE (1920?-1974), coastwatcher, was born probably in 1920 on Melville Island. Belonging to the Ironwood and Tukkarinna (mullet) groups, he was affiliated with the Munupi country, and spoke Tiwi, English and Malay.

In 1942 Lampungmeiua was one of thirty-nine Aborigines recruited for coastwatching work around Bathurst and Melville islands by Jack Gribble, a patrol officer based near Snake Bay, Melville Island. Gribble was commissioned in the Royal Australian Naval Volunteer Reserve, but his men were not formally enlisted. Selected for their local knowledge and bush skills, the Aborigines received no wages; they were given a few rations, clothing, clay pipes and tobacco, and were told that they would be paid after World War II had ended.

Issued with naval uniforms and weapons, the Aborigines practised drill, and were trained to use rifles, machine-guns, grenades and two-way radios. They also learned to identify Japanese aircraft and ships. One visitor patronizingly reported that they acquitted themselves 'in a manner comparable with white servicemen'. The Aborigines carried out armed patrols in the motor vessel, *Amity*, and in dugout canoes; they performed guard duty, built a jetty, dam, store and huts, and made bricks and cultivated gardens at their base. Lampungmeiua was a machine-gunner in the *Amity*. He and 'Strangler' McKenzie made several secret trips by submarine to Japanese-occupied Timor to assist in landing small parties of allied troops and stores. They were chosen because they spoke Malay.

The main tasks of Gribble's Aboriginal patrol were to watch for enemy invaders, and to search for downed planes and airmen. Members of the group escorted several allied airmen to safety, including the crew of a Dutch bomber and an American fighter pilot. They also rescued eleven survivors from an American supply ship which was sunk off Melville Island. In addition, they warned authorities about a number of Japanese submarines, piloted visiting ships and located enemy sea-mines. In one fifteen-month period they patrolled over 2250 miles (3600 km) by boat and 1150 miles (1800 km) by foot to provide security for the two airstrips and the radar stations in the area. They were taken to Darwin for a special parade.

After the war Charlie One lived near Garden Point, Melville Island. A 'strong and determined leader' who insisted that his 'people respect and maintain their culture', he was held in high regard. He refused a party of miners access to his land to explore for mineral sands. His woven-flax ropes—attached to harpoons for catching dugong and turtle—were valued by the Tiwi. He married three sisters Dorie, Elizabeth and Gladys Puruntatameri. In August 1962 the R.A.N. honoured surviving Aboriginal coastwatchers in a ceremony on Melville Island. Tippaklippa received £200 and was awarded the Defence, War and Australian Service medals. Accidentally spiking his head on a nail, he died on 22 September 1974 at Nguiu and was buried in Garden Point (Pirlangimpi) cemetery. Gladys survived him, as did the daughter of his marriage to Elizabeth.

S. Baldwin (ed), *Unsung Heroes and Heroines of Australia* (Melb, 1988); R. Hall, *The Black Diggers* (Syd, 1989); *NT News*, 28 Aug 1962, 27 Sept 1974; Dept of Defence (Navy Office), Canb, file 307/201/22; NTAC 1980/111 NN and F1 1965/2637 (AA, Darwin); information from Tiwi Land Council, Winnellie, Darwin.   JENNY RICH

LANGER, KARL (1903-1969), architect and town planner, was born on 28 July 1903 in Vienna, only son and elder child of Karl Langer, locksmith, and his wife Magdalena, née Loitsch. Karl senior's manual and technical skills fostered his son's interest in design. Young Karl attended the Staatsgewerbeschule until 1923, worked for various architects and became a member (1926) of the Austrian Guild of Architects. Professionally and intellectually restless, he undertook further study and entered architectural competitions. He consolidated his skills through his association with leading progressives, including Heinrich Schmid and Herman Aichinger, on those public housing projects which established the socialist credentials of 'Red Vienna' in the turbulent postwar years.

Peter Behrens, pioneer modernist and director of the Wagnerschule, had admitted Langer (in 1923) to his renowned school of architecture within the Akademie der Bildenden Künste in Wien (Vienna Academy of Fine Arts). Langer's work appeared in the catalogues of a school exhibition which toured Europe in 1926. He graduated in 1928. That year Behrens employed him to head his architectural atelier in Vienna. Langer was responsible for some celebrated buildings attributed to Behrens and his partner Alexander Popp, most notably the massive tobacco factory at Linz and additions to the historic St Peter's group at Salzburg. In his spare hours Langer studied at the Technische Hochschule (later Technical University of Vienna) for the qualification of zivilarchitekt (1931) and at the University of Vienna for his doctorate in art history (1933).

In Vienna on 14 May 1932 Langer married a fellow doctoral student Gertrude Fröschel; they were to remain childless. He left Behrens' firm in 1934 and began a small practice, assisted by his wife. His work, modest in scale, was well reviewed in Austrian and British journals, but it was not an auspicious time to launch himself as an architect. The rise of Nazism generated a cultural climate inimical to creative expression and threatened the Langers personally. He was a social democrat; she was Jewish. *Kristallnacht* (November 1938) confirmed their determination to emigrate, a difficult task for Karl who was eligible for military service. Adopting a ruse, they travelled to Greece whence they sailed for Australia. They reached Sydney in 1939. About this time Karl's former student contemporaries and lifelong professional confidants Rudi Baumfeld and Victor Gruenbaum emigrated to the United States of America; Gruenbaum founded the firm of Victor Gruen Associates at Los Angeles.

There was little demand for *avant-garde* architects in Sydney, though Langer's peers received him cordially. He found temporary employment with the architects H. M. Cook & W. J. Kerrison in Brisbane, where he and Gertrude settled. Under wartime manpower regulations, he was soon transferred to a mundane post with the Queensland Railways. Brisbane was then a mixture of provincial city and strategic centre. The Langers' modernist achievements and sophistication contributed considerably to the city's cultural life, and a youthful literary and artistic group gathered around them. Karl lectured part time in architecture and architectural design at the University of Queensland, studied the local landscape and flora, and published his short but influential *Sub-Tropical Housing* (1944). Gertrude gave public lectures for the Queensland Art Fund and later became art critic for the *Courier-Mail*.

In 1944 the Brisbane City Council offered Langer the position of assistant town planner. His selection in preference to a returned serviceman became a political issue and manpower controls were invoked to block his release from his railways job for the duration of the war. The protracted, nationwide publicity attending this episode brought him an impressive waiting-list of commissions that ranged from revising the town plan for the city of Mackay to advising on the site for a civic centre in Perth.

Langer also obtained a consultancy with the Cumberland County Council (the planning authority for Sydney) which commissioned him in 1947 to examine the development of the city, and advise on a comprehensive list of civic and regional planning issues. He was able to find two periods in 1947 and 1948 for this work, totalling four months; his fee was set at six guineas a day, plus a guinea a day for living expenses. His proposals included a plan to replace the Fort Macquarie (Bennelong Point) Tram Depot with an opera house. On his way to Australia, one of the last places in his beloved Attica that he had visited and sketched was the ancient temple of Poseidon on the tip of Cape Sounion—a combination of landscape and landmark which remained with him when he thought about the Sydney Harbour of the future.

Projects for Darwin, for Ingham, Too-woomba, Yeppoon, Kingaroy and Mount Isa, Queensland, and for the National Capital Development Commission, Canberra, were among Langer's other town-planning tasks. He advised Senator Ian Wood, his old friend and mayor of Mackay, in his work with the Senate Select Committee on the Development of Canberra (1954-55) and the Joint Parliamentary Committee on the Australian Capital Territory (1957-68). In the controversy over where the new Federal Parliament House should be located, Langer advocated the Capital Hill site: in *Architecture in Australia* (1959) he pondered over the problems of placing a building there, particularly how to make the flagstaff topping W. B. Griffin's [q.v.9] design appear significant in the scale of that landscape.

Commissions which Langer undertook included economical domestic buildings, the first Gold Coast canal developments and coastal tourist projects. The best known of these was Lennons Hotel (1956) at Broadbeach, Gold Coast, then generously set in wilderness between highway and beach. His favourite building was the chapel (1966) at St Peter's Lutheran College, Indooroopilly, Brisbane. Built on the edge of a small hill, it embodied the lessons he had learned from classical Greece.

Langer's reserve and courtesy accompanied a deep belief in community responsibilities, particularly in cultural matters. His campaigns for more creative use of the Brisbane River as a civic asset, for a Queen Street mall and other facilities for pedestrians were rejected, not always politely; when they were later adopted, others received the credit. After being naturalized in November 1945, Langer was deemed eligible to join professional bodies. He was active in the Royal Australian Institute of Architects, first president (1952) of the Queensland division of the Royal Australian Planning Institute, a founder and chairman (1966-68) of the Queensland Association of Landscape Architects and a member (1963-69) of the National Trust of Queensland. The Queensland Art Gallery Society elected him its president for 1961-62 and 1967; Gertrude held the same office in 1965-66 and 1974-75.

At the University of Queensland, Langer lectured in town planning; he also taught at the Queensland Institute of Technology. Both institutions were to award student prizes in his memory. In 1968 he was appointed to the Australian Council for the Arts and elected vice-chairman of its music board. He died of myocardial infarction on 16 October 1969 in Brisbane. Following a service at St Peter's chapel, he was cremated at Mount Thompson crematorium, another of his buildings. His wife survived him.

K. Bittman (ed), *Strauss to Matilda* (Syd, 1988); M. Jurgensen and A. Corkhill (eds), *The German Presence in Queensland* (Brisb, 1988); Soc of Architectural Historians, Aust and NZ, *Nuts and Bolts, or Berries*, 1993 Annual Conference (Perth, 1993); Aust Inst of Landscape Architects, *Landscape Aust*, 7, no 1, 1984, p 48; I. Sinnamon, Karl Langer in Queensland (paper presented to the Soc of Architectural Historians Aust and NZ Conference on Modernism, Perth, 1993, copy held by author, Dept of Architecture, Univ Qld); Langer papers (Fryer L and OL) *and* architectural drawings (OL); information from the late Karl and Gertrude Langer.

IAN SINNAMON

LANGLEY, EVE (1904-1974), novelist, was born on 1 September 1904 at Forbes, New South Wales, and registered as Ethel Jane, elder daughter of Arthur Alexander Langley (d.1915), carpenter, and his wife Myra, née Davidson, both from Victoria. By 1914 her mother was a hotelkeeper at Crossover, Gippsland; in 1916 she married Patrick Cullen. 'Eve', as Ethel called herself, attended Crossover, Brunswick Central and Dandenong state schools and Dandenong High School before working as a domestic servant and later as a printer's devil. During the late 1920s she and her sister 'June' (Lillian May, b.1905) defiantly dressed as boys and wandered about the countryside, picking peas and hops.

In 1930 Eve tried share-farming at Metung, Gippsland, but by 1932 had followed her family to Auckland, New Zealand. With Douglas Stewart, Gloria Rawlinson and Robyn Hyde, she built up a considerable reputation for verse in New Zealand's little magazines. On 6 January 1937 at the registrar's office, Auckland, she married Hilary Roy Clark, a 22-year-old art student. By 1941 they had a daughter Bisi Arilev, and two sons, Langley Rhaviley and Karl Marx. Eve's husband had her admitted to Auckland Mental Hospital in August 1942 when she was emotionally disturbed. She was released into her sister's care in March 1949 and divorced in 1952.

Langley had published a semi-autobiographical novel, *The Pea-Pickers* (Sydney, 1942), narrated by the central character Steve. The book was fashioned from journals, letters and memories of the time she had spent in Gippsland. In full control of her material, she evoked a landscape and an era through highly charged, intensely imagistic prose. *The Pea-Pickers* was the novel upon which the Langley legend was founded. Its author was hailed by Stewart as 'the Judith Wright of New Zealand' and awarded the Prior [q.v.11] memorial prize. This early potential was strangely thwarted. Eve was already equating creativity and artistic freedom with masculinity, while yearning constantly for sexual fulfilment. *White Topee* (Sydney, 1954) was a more loosely structured novel, an impressionistic diary recording Steve's reincarnation as Oscar Wilde. (Langley changed her name by deed poll to Oscar Wilde in 1954.)

In 1950-55 Langley worked as a book-repairer at Auckland Public Library. She visited Australia in 1956-57 and travelled as far as Cairns. In 1960 she returned to New South Wales where she remained, apart from one abortive trip to Greece in search of inspiration in 1965. Penniless, and spiritually and physically debilitated, she was bailed out by Stewart. She lived her remaining years in a lonely hut, Iona Lympus, at Katoomba, with her numerous dolls and a clutch of cats for company.

Still she wrote and painted tirelessly. Indecipherable novels were found on hoarded brown paper and Weeties packets. Langley sent over 4000 pages of single-spaced typescript on rose-coloured paper to Angus & Robertson [qq.v.7,11] Ltd. None of it was published. The material was repetitive, difficult, at times inaccessible. She increasingly dwelt on her constant wish to be a man, and habitually wore her sola topi and a long fur coat over a gentleman's pinstripe suit in winter, and over white shorts and a singlet in summer. Eve Langley-Clark died alone between 1 and 13 June 1974 at Katoomba and was buried in the local cemetery with Anglican rites. Her body had lain undiscovered for a month, the face gnawed by rats. Her children survived her. The sheer lyric detail and impassioned textural density of Langley's prose is rare in Australian fiction.

J. L. Thwaite, *The Importance of Being Eve Langley* (Syd, 1989) *and* for bibliog; Langley papers (ML).   JOY THWAITE

LANGLEY, HENRY THOMAS (1877-1968), Church of England clergyman, was born on 30 March 1877 at the parsonage, Windsor, New South Wales, sixth of twelve children of HENRY ARCHDALL LANGLEY (1840-1906), an Irish-born clergyman, and his native-born wife Elizabeth Mary, née Strachan. After studying at Moore Theological College, Henry Archdall was made deacon on 11 June 1865, and ordained priest on 27 May 1866 by Bishop Barker [q.v.3]. He served in various Sydney parishes before moving to Melbourne in 1878 where he ministered at St Matthew's, Prahran. Successively archdeacon of Gippsland, and of Melbourne and Geelong, he was elected first bishop of Bendigo in 1902. He died on 5 August 1906 and was succeeded in the bishopric by his elder brother John Douse Langley (1836-1930), a graduate of Trinity College, Dublin.

Henry Thomas Langley proceeded from Caulfield Grammar School to Trinity College, University of Melbourne (B.A., 1899; M.A., 1904). While at university he helped to found the Student Christian Movement. Made deacon on 10 June 1900, he was ordained priest on 2 June 1901 by Bishop Goe [q.v.9]. At St Mark's Church, Rosedale, on 4 September that year Langley married Ethel Maud Du Vé (d.1957). He was curate of parishes in Sydney before returning to Victoria as rector of St James's, Traralgon. During his incumbency (1911-42) at St Mary's, Caulfield, he was appointed a chaplain in the Australian Military Forces in 1916 and a canon of St Paul's Cathedral, Melbourne, in 1918. He set up (1920) a board to superintend religious education in Anglican communions in Australia and New Zealand. In 1921 he founded Shelford Church of England Girls' School. A council-member of Melbourne Church of England and Caulfield Grammar schools, he had something of his father's drive and interest in education. He was also much involved in the Mission of St James and St John, and in the Church of England Boys' and Men's, the Church Missionary and the Bush Church Aid societies.

In 1942 Langley was elected dean of Melbourne. He associated himself with socialist movements and marched annually in the May Day procession. Conscious of his status as dean, he was inclined to be prickly and difficult in domestic ecclesiastical matters, but he had his father's ecumenical spirit and was a good churchman. After retiring in 1947, he took a leading part in 1950 in negotiating an amendment to the Victorian Education Act (1928), allowing government schools to engage chaplains. In addition, he chaired the Council for Christian Education in Schools. Langley enjoyed gardening, fishing, tennis (when younger) and excursions in the country. Survived by his daughter and three of his four sons, he died on 28 November 1968 at Hawthorn and was cremated.

His sister MINNIE RUTH (1878-1973) was born on 24 June 1878 at Windsor and educated at the Clergy Daughters' School (St

Catherine's), Waverley, Sydney. She taught (1896-1901) in Melbourne at Miss Isabella McComas's [q.v.10] Glamorgan Preparatory School for Boys, Toorak. In 1903 Ruth and her younger sister Nona—both in their twenties —took over the Castlemaine Ladies' College and renamed it St Catherine's Girls' College. Ruth was registered as a secondary school-teacher on 11 April 1907. She instilled in the girls her own love of botany and English literature. In 1920 she moved the school to Toorak, Melbourne, and entered into partner-ship with Flora, daughter of William Temple-ton [q.v.6]. The school continued to provide a broad-based education, a homely atmosphere and cultural opportunities.

The fifth Langley daughter, Aphra, served as school-housekeeper for twelve months. When the school bought Beaulieu, the Mars Buckley [q.v.3] mansion in Heyington Place, the widowed Aphra provided money and furniture. By the early 1930s the school was well established. Energetic, with a sparkling personality, Ruth Langley was a member of the Young Women's Christian Association's national board, the Melbourne Diocesan Board of Education and the Australian Women's National League. She died of acute pulmonary oedema on 17 December 1933 at Toorak and was buried in Box Hill cemetery.

Her place as principal was immediately assumed by her elder sister Hilda Sarah (1874-1951). Two of her brothers, Henry Thomas and Arthur Theodore (a medical practitioner), became trustees of the school; another brother, Frank Ernest, was also a medical practitioner and captained (1905) the Melbourne Football Club. The Langley con-nexion with St Catherine's was severed in 1947 when the school was sold and came under the control of a corporation.

K. Cole, *A History of the Diocese of Bendigo, 1902-1976* (Bendigo, Vic, 1991); D. E. and I. V. Hansen (eds), *St Catherine's* (Melb, 1996); *A'sian Post,* 9 Mar 1950; Langley file (Diocesan Archives, Cath-edral Church of St Paul, Melb); family papers and scrapbooks (held by Mrs M. Pritchard, Glen Iris, Melb).   I. V. HANSEN

LANGSLOW, MELVILLE CECIL (1889-1972), public servant, was born on 20 June 1889 at Maldon, Victoria, sixth child of Richard Charles Langslow, butcher, and his wife Marion, née McArthur, both Victorian born. Nothing is known of Melville's edu-cation. Joining the Commonwealth Public Service in December 1908, he worked as a clerk in the Treasury. On 11 August 1914 he enlisted in the Australian Imperial Force; he served in Cairo (1915-16) and London

with the Australian Army Pay Corps. Rising through the ranks, he was commissioned in 1917 and promoted major in 1920.

Before hostilities ceased, it was planned that the Commonwealth government would pay for 940 aircraft and associated equipment, stores and services provided by Britain to the Australian Flying Corps. Langslow was given the task of handling Australia's involvement in the financial arrangements, but his assign-ment ended when the British offered to settle the debt by taking back the remaining equip-ment. Appointed M.B.E. (1919), Langslow returned to Melbourne in 1922. His A.I.F. appointment terminated on 5 September and he joined the finance branch of the Depart-ment of Defence. At St Andrew's Anglican Church, Brighton, on 14 September 1933 he married Clyde Helene Hooper Merry; they were to remain childless.

From 1936 Langslow was finance member of both the Civil Aviation Board and the Air Board. His 'insistence on the limitation of expenditure' contributed to a delay in testing new navigational beacons for commercial air-craft. Had the devices been operational in 1938, they might have given vital guidance to the DC-2 airliner, *Kyeema*. While flying through low cloud on 25 October, *Kyeema* overshot Essendon airport, Melbourne, and crashed into Mount Dandenong. Fourteen passengers and four crew were killed in the worst air disaster in Australian aviation history to that date. In its report on the inci-dent, the air accident investigation committee blamed the controller-general of civil aviation, Captain E. C. Johnston, and Langslow for bungling the installation of the beacons. A later government inquiry found that all mem-bers of the Civil Aviation Board were respon-sible. The initial casting of blame on Langslow left him lastingly embittered.

Major Langslow—as he encouraged some and directed others to call him—was ap-pointed secretary of the Department of Air on its formation in November 1939; he was to remain in the post until he retired from the public service in 1951. While his principal role was to ensure the most economical expen-diture of public funds, uniformed members of the Air Board were more interested in obtain-ing the best available equipment and logistic support. Animosities were therefore likely to arise, irrespective of the individuals con-cerned, but Langslow's uncompromising nature ensured his unpopularity with senior R.A.A.F. officers. His long memory, his tough stance on the financial aspects of every Air Board decision and the fact that he was better briefed on administrative details than the uni-formed members often frustrated the plans of senior air force officers. They usually re-sponded with mild to strong dislike of him, or, occasionally, with reluctant deference.

Continuing to serve at Air Force Headquarters as other members of the board came and went, Langslow built up a detailed understanding of the workings of government and a deep academic knowledge of aviation. Successive ministers for air sought his opinion on financial affairs and service matters. During World War II Arthur Drakeford [q.v.14] consulted him on factionalism within the R.A.A.F. which the government was too indecisive to handle. Langslow was also well placed to monitor dealings between R.A.A.F. officers and the minister. In 1949 he and the chief of the Air Staff, Air Marshal (Sir) George Jones, amicably devised principles to determine which positions in the Department of Air should be held by public servants and which by members of the R.A.A.F.

Although Langslow was regarded as an *éminence grise*, he generally exercised power for the good of the air force. Survived by his wife, he died on 31 March 1972 in East Melbourne and was buried in Brighton cemetery.

D. Gillison, *Royal Australian Air Force 1939-1942* (Canb, 1962); R. Williams, *These are Facts* (Canb, 1977); J. E. Hewitt, *Adversity in Success* (Melb, 1980); H. Rayner, *Scherger* (Canb, 1984); C. D. Coulthard-Clark, *The Third Brother* (Syd, 1991); A. Stephens, *Going Solo* (Canb, 1995); *SMH*, 5 Apr 1972; information from Mr F. S. Lovie, Isaacs, Canb; personal knowledge.   RICHARD KINGSLAND

LATHAM, ELEANOR MARY (1878-1964), charity worker, was born on 10 October 1878 at Northcote, Melbourne, only child of English-born parents, Richard Tobin and his wife Fanny Louisa, née Matthews, both of whom were schoolteachers. Richard and Fanny involved themselves in issues of public health, welfare and adult education. Ella was educated at T. Palmer's [q.v.11] University High School and the University of Melbourne (B.A., 1904). On 19 December 1907 at her parents' Northcote home she married with Methodist forms (Sir) John Greig Latham [q.v.10]; they were to have two sons and a daughter.

During her early married life and throughout World War I Ella found herself relatively isolated as her husband built his legal career, extended his political connexions and undertook wartime responsibilities. She furthered her education and social interests by joining the Catalysts, a group of professional women, and by becoming a foundation member (1912) of the Lyceum Club, which she served as secretary (1918-22), vice-president (1922-23 and 1926-27) and president (1925-26).

In 1923 Ella Latham began a long-standing commitment to the (Royal) Children's Hospital, Melbourne, first as president of its new Hawthorn auxiliary, then as a member (from 1926) of the hospital's committee of manage-

ment and finally as president (1933-54). In these positions she showed foresight, initiative and administrative ability in completely changing the role, structure and functioning of the hospital. With the support of the medical director Vernon Collins and the lady superintendent Lucy de Neeve [qq.v.13], she transformed it from a charity hospital to an institution that provided medical services of the highest quality, education and training facilities for staff, a research organization in both curative and preventive medicine, and a link with the university.

In 1935 Lady Latham (her husband was knighted that year) founded the Victorian Society for Crippled Children. Soon after, she developed a model rehabilitation centre in the grounds of the orthopaedic section of the Children's Hospital, located at Frankston. From 1932, while her husband served as councillor, deputy-chancellor and chancellor of the University of Melbourne, she was active in university affairs. She was president of a women's fund-raising committee and, during World War II, co-patron with Lady Gowrie [q.v.9] of a university women's patriotic fund. In her varied activities she was influential in furthering her husband's career; at the same time, she was an excellent foil to his acerbic nature.

Lady Latham was one of the most creative and highly respected women of her generation in public life. She was appointed C.B.E. in 1954. An unselfish woman who never sought publicity or recognition, she allowed others to take her place once her plans were established. After her retirement in 1954, her life was rather lonely. Rheumatism prevented her from indulging her love of gardening. She had lost her own family—her gifted first-born son Richard [q.v.10] in World War II, her daughter Freda from premature death (1953) and her younger son Peter through estrangement. Survived (for four months) by her husband, she died on 26 March 1964 in Melbourne and was cremated; her estate was sworn for probate at £49 388.

L. Gardiner, *Royal Children's Hospital, Melbourne, 1870-1970* (Melb, 1970); A. Norris, *The Society* (Melb, 1974); J. M. Gillison, *A History of the Lyceum Club* (Melb, 1975); H. Williams, *From Charity to Teaching Hospital* (Melb, 1989); Roy Children's Hospital, Melb, Archives; Latham papers, MS 6409, box 2, folder 17 (NL).

HOWARD WILLIAMS

LATOUR, LOMA KYLE (1902-1964), sculptor, was born on 16 May 1902 at Mellool station, Moulamein, New South Wales, daughter of Victorian-born parents George Stewart Turnbull, station manager, and his wife Louisa, née Scott (d.1903), a writer and china painter. At her mother's wish Loma was not baptized. 'Farmed out' to relations in England, she was educated by governesses and at boarding school. At the age of 12 she returned to Australia with three enduring characteristics: a cultivated English accent, a rebellious spirit and a passion for art. Her father had remarried, but Loma never met her stepmother. She was sent to stay with relations and repeatedly ran away. After one blazing row, she went to Sydney and changed her name to 'Latour' (also spelt 'Lautour'). Concealing her age, she acted in melodramas and took walk-on parts in Shakespearian plays with Alan Wilkie's [q.v.12] company. As actor, model and artist, she led a bohemian existence. On 28 December 1928 at the registrar general's office, Sydney, she married Raymond, second son of Norman Lindsay [q.v.10]; they separated in the mid-1930s.

With her unconventional direct speech and stylish good looks, Latour was regularly interviewed and photographed in her Kings Cross studio, chain-smoking and briefly clad. Influenced by Jacob Epstein and trained by Rayner Hoff [q.v.9], she became well known as a sculptor. She worked hard to earn her living, often for eighteen hours a day, making everything from china dolls' heads to large papier-mâché figures for the 1938 Sydney sesquicentenary floats; she also produced masks, bronze and terracotta busts of friends like Dulcie Deamer [q.v.8], lino-cuts, jewellery and Art Deco chrome-metal lights. Her output was prodigious, and original.

In Sydney in the 1930s Latour exhibited with the Women's Industrial Art Society, the Society of Artists, the Contemporary Art Society and the Royal Art Society. In 1936 the National Art Gallery of New South Wales purchased 'The Egoist', her glazed earthenware bust of George Bernard Shaw. She taught modelling and pottery, and was employed at Mashman [q.v.10] Bros Ltd's pottery works in 1936; in addition, she executed numerous large-scale plaster, brass or concrete murals and fountains, as for the Minerva Theatre, Kings Cross, in 1938. The nude was her favourite subject and Holly Farram her favourite model.

In 1940 Latour moved to Lansvale intending to breed dogs, to garden and to write. At St Columba's Presbyterian Church, Woollahra, on 28 March 1941, the day her previous marriage was dissolved, she married Victor Clarence ('Jamie') Jamieson, a fitter in the Australian Imperial Force. He left for Singapore on 10 April and became a prisoner of war. For a time Latour made camouflage at Bankstown before returning to inner Sydney. Jamieson was discharged from the army in June 1946; his health was poor, the marriage shaky, and he was drinking heavily (as was Loma). He died at her studio 'on or about' 21 July 1946 after accidentally drinking cyanide from a beer bottle. She eventually secured a war-widow's pension.

Moving to Brisbane in 1950, Latour immediately attracted favourable reviews when she exhibited her masks, pottery and jewellery with the Royal Queensland Art Society, the Moreton Galleries and the Half Dozen Group of Artists. She formed new friendships, especially with the antique dealer Cecilia McNally, who sold her jewellery. Latour soon bought a waterfront acreage on Stradbroke Island. There she lived contentedly in a studio-shack with assorted animals and 'cousin Roy' Needrie, a jeweller. She established a vineyard and orchard, going about naked or in a lap-lap. In 1962 she suffered a vicious sexual assault from which she never fully recovered. Latour died of emphysema and asthma on 19 December 1964 at the Repatriation General Hospital, Greenslopes; she bequeathed her eyes to the Eye Bank and her body to the University of Queensland.

J. Kerr (ed), *Heritage* (Syd, 1995); *Clay Products J*, Dec 1935, July 1936, July 1937, July 1939, Nov 1940; *People* (Syd), 9 Apr 1950, p 34, 10 May 1950, p 41; *Aust Antique Collector*, 1986, p 70; *SMH*, 30 June, 9, 30 July 1936, 5 Aug 1937, 21 June, 7, 21 July 1938, 5 Jan, 16 Feb, 10 July 1939, Women's Supp, 30 Apr 1940; *Telegraph* (Brisb), 22 Aug 1950, 14 Dec 1953; *Courier-Mail*, 15 Dec 1953, 21 Dec 1964; L. K. Latour database and scrapbook (Qld Art Gallery); information from Mrs E. Durbidge, Stradbroke Island, Qld, and Mrs A. Barker-Richardson, Brisb.

JAN ROBERTS

LAURANTUS, SIR NICHOLAS (1890-1980), businessman and philanthropist, was born on 5 February 1890 on the island of Kythera, Greece, third of twelve children of Panayiotis Lourantos, contractor, and his wife Angeliki, née Marsellos. After seven years of schooling, Nicholas helped his father as an apprentice carpenter and blacksmith. Letters from relations overseas stimulated his desire to emigrate. When a cousin at Grenfell, New South Wales, offered to look after him, Nick and his younger brother George sailed for Australia in the *Seidlich*, reaching Sydney on 1 November 1908.

George remained there with friends. Nick began work in the Thermopylae Café at Grenfell for 7s. 6d. a week, with accommodation above the shop. He determined to learn English in three months and kept a dictionary beside his bed, constantly checking and memorizing new words. 'I knew I was in a good country', he later said, 'and I wanted to stay here'. By the time he was naturalized in 1911 he had Latinized the spelling of his surname to Laurantus. He was then a short, good-looking young man with alert brown eyes and an outgoing personality. Frugal and hardworking, by 1913 he had saved enough money to buy the café in partnership with an American relation and to establish Laurantus & Co. He sent for George, who was to be a partner in many of his later business ventures.

In 1914 Nicholas Laurantus acquired the lease of the Albion Hotel at Young. At St John's Anglican Church, Cowra, on 29 March 1920 he married Clare May Barker (d.1954), a 33-year-old housekeeper. Three hotels later, in 1921, he decided to try farming, and took his wife and baby daughter to a small wheat farm near Cowra. He chose a bad year and almost lost his money. In 1922 he moved to Narrandera where he acquired the lease of the open-air Globe Theatre, announcing his intention in the local newspaper 'to show before Narrandera audiences the best and latest productions in the way of moving pictures'. The Globe marked the start of a successful chain of cinemas across southwestern New South Wales which he ran with the aid of George and other family members whom he brought from Kythera.

In 1938 Laurantus bought Windella station near Narrandera; he later acquired other properties, including Lake Midgeon station which reputedly had the largest shearing shed in New South Wales. In a few years he was very wealthy. One of his managers said of him, 'Nick was purely a financier but he did have this love of the land. His knowledge was such that he could look into the future and say, "Wool's going to be good, so we'll grow sheep", or, at another time, "Wheat's going to be good, so we'll farm country"'.

Laurantus went out of his way to advise young Greek immigrants and assist them financially. By breaking out of the café circuit and venturing into cinemas, hotels and grazing, and by being completely at ease in both Greek and Anglo-Australian society, he set an example for other Greeks: if they learned English, mixed with Australians and worked hard, they too could succeed. At the same time he felt that Greek immigrants should know and love their own language and culture. In 1968 he gave $100 000 to establish a chair of modern Greek at the University of Sydney. During the 1970s he donated about $450 000 to St Basil's Homes in Australia for aged people. Lourantos Village at Lakemba was named after him.

Appointed M.B.E. in 1977, Laurantus was overjoyed to be knighted in 1979 and described his investiture at Government House, Canberra, as the happiest day of his life. From 1968 he had lived in Sydney at the Masonic Club. A frail but stubborn old man, still fond of jokes and good company, Sir Nicholas died on 26 July 1980 at Greenacre and was buried in the Greek section of Botany cemetery. His only child Helen survived him.

J. Michaelides, *Portrait of Uncle Nick* (Syd, 1987), and for bibliog; *To Yofiri*, 3-4, 1978, p 16; *Narrandera Argus*, 17 Oct 1922; *Sun* (Syd), 10 Sept 1968; *SMH*, 11 Sept 1968, 31 Dec 1976, 16 June 1979, 28 July 1980; naturalization file A1/1 item 11/17987 (AA, Canb); information from Mr J. Colhoun, Narrandera, NSW.   JEAN MICHAELIDES

LAURIE-RHODES, IAN; *see* Rhodes

LAVARACK, SIR JOHN DUDLEY (1885-1957), army officer and governor, was born on 19 December 1885 at Kangaroo Point, Brisbane, third child of English-born parents Cecil Wallace Lavarack, a draughtsman who became a major in the Queensland Defence Force, and his wife Jessie Helen, née Mackenzie. Educated at Brisbane Grammar School, John was a prominent member of the cadets. He gained high marks in the examination for a commission in the Permanent Military Forces and on 7 August 1905 was appointed lieutenant, Royal Australian Artillery. His junior regimental postings took him to Sydney, Brisbane, Townsville, Thursday Island and Queenscliff, Victoria.

On 10 October 1912 at St George's Anglican Church, Queenscliff, Captain Lavarack married Sybil Nevett Ochiltree. He attended the Staff College, Camberley, England, from early 1913 until the outbreak of World War I. After working at the War Office, London, he was promoted brigade major of the 22nd (British) Divisional Artillery in February 1915. The division was sent to France in September; in November it was redeployed to Salonica (Thessaloniki), Greece. By May 1916 Major Lavarack was staff officer, royal artillery, at the XVI Corps' headquarters.

Lavarack had been appointed to the Australian Imperial Force in February 1915. Although he made many requests, he was not permitted to leave Macedonia and link up with his countrymen until July 1916 when he joined the 2nd Division for the operations at Pozières, France. He commanded two field batteries and was brigade major of the 5th Divisional Artillery during the subsequent fighting on the Somme and the advance to the Hindenburg line. One of the few Australian officers with staff-college training, he was transferred in May 1917 to the headquarters of the 1st Division where he worked under Colonel (Sir) Thomas Blamey [q.v.13]: it was probably in this period that an antipathy developed between the two officers that continued for the remainder of their careers.

By December Lavarack was a lieutenant colonel and general staff officer, 1st grade, of the 4th Division, commanded by Major General E. G. Sinclair-Maclagan [q.v.11]. Lavarack took part in battles at Dernancourt (April

1918), Villers-Bretonneux (April), Hamel (July) and Amiens (August). Maclagan and he had taken the major hand in planning the operation at Hamel which set the pattern for later Australian successes. For his war service Lavarack was awarded the Distinguished Service Order (1918) and the French Croix de Guerre (1919); he was also appointed C.M.G. (1919) and thrice mentioned in dispatches.

Returning to Australia in September 1919, Lavarack was posted to the Royal Military College, Duntroon, Federal Capital Territory, as director of military art. In 1924 he served as a staff officer on the headquarters of the 2nd (Militia) Division, Sydney. In March 1925 he was made director of military training at Army Headquarters, Melbourne. Promoted brevet colonel in 1926, at the end of the following year he went to London to attend the Imperial Defence College. He was the first Australian army officer to complete the course; a fellow student was (Sir) Frederick Shedden [q.v.].

Back home, in early 1929 Lavarack was given the post of director of military operations and intelligence at Army Headquarters. He found himself in keen debate with Shedden who was secretary of the defence committee. Shedden and the Naval Staff claimed that Australia's defence should rest on the Royal Navy. Lavarack, as adviser to the chief of the General Staff, argued that Japan would attack in the Far East when Britain was preoccupied in Europe. Therefore, he contended, the Australian army had to be prepared to deal with a possible invasion. He published his views in the *Army Quarterly* (1933).

In January 1933 Lavarack became commandant of the R.M.C. On 21 April 1935 he was promoted temporary major general (substantive in June) and took over as C.G.S., superseding a number of more senior officers. Intelligent, with a quick and incisive mind, Lavarack was impressive in appearance. He was 5 ft 11½ ins (182 cm) tall, with a dark complexion and blue eyes. Lieutenant General (Sir) Sydney Rowell [q.v.], who had worked under Lavarack, recalled that he 'had a fine brain; he wrote brilliantly and spoke convincingly'. While he 'did not possess the most equable of temperaments and could be a difficult master ... at other times he was a delightful character with a wide range of interests'.

As C.G.S., Lavarack renewed his arguments with the navy and Shedden, and also challenged successive ministers for defence —Sir Archdale Parkhill, H. V. C. Thorby and G. A. Street [qq.v.11,12]—over the government's reliance on the Royal Navy and its insistence that army funds be spent on coastal defences rather than the field force. Lavarack found himself increasingly at odds with the government. The release (apparently by senior army officers) of information to the press that was critical of government policy led ministers to mistrust the army. Lavarack's appointment as C.B. (1937) was delayed because politicians were dissatisfied with him.

In 1938 the government appointed a British officer, Lieutenant General E. K. Squires [q.v.12], as inspector general of the Australian Military Forces. John Hetherington [q.v.14] claimed that 'some Ministers had begun to suspect soon after [Lavarack] became C.G.S. that his reports were framed to tell them less what they should know than what he believed they would like to know'. Yet, as Brett Lodge has argued persuasively, it 'would be more accurate to say that Lavarack was telling the government too much of what it did not want to hear: that its defence policy was bankrupt'. He had pressed his case strongly, but he might have achieved more with a different approach.

Lavarack worked closely with Squires to prepare the army for war before departing in May for a tour of Britain. He returned in September, after hostilities had begun. Squires was appointed C.G.S. and Blamey was selected to command the new 6th Division, A.I.F. Still out of favour with the government, Lavarack was promoted lieutenant general and given Southern Command. To add to his difficulties, Blamey saw him as a potential rival, and was able to use Lavarack's temperament as a justification for denying him a series of important appointments. 'Joe' Lavarack, as he was known, certainly had an unpredictable and 'wicked temper which rose like a flash and often subsided quickly'. He was passionately fond of sport, such as golf and tennis, but, when he lost, there was often an extraordinary display of bad humour. For all that, he could be charming and personable. Essentially a shy man, he was sensitive to any perceived slight to his rank or position.

When the government decided in March 1940 to raise the 7th Division and Blamey was given the newly formed I Corps, he refused to have Lavarack as commander of the 6th Division because of his 'defects of character'. Against Blamey's wishes, the government chose Lavarack to command the 7th and he reverted to major general to accept the appointment. He arrived in the Middle East in November. At the end of March 1941 Axis forces under General Erwin Rommel attacked in Libya. The 18th Brigade of the 7th Division was rushed to Tobruk to support the 9th Australian Division under Major General (Sir) Leslie Morshead [q.v.].

Faced with a rapidly deteriorating situation, General Sir Archibald (Earl) Wavell, the commander-in-chief in the Middle East, ordered Lavarack to Tobruk in early April as head of Cyrenaica Command. He organized the defence of the fortress, deploying Morshead's division on the perimeter. On 13 and 14 April the garrison repelled a strong assault by Rommel's forces. Wavell directed Lavarack to take over Western Desert Force, but Blamey advised that Lavarack was unsuitable for high command. On 14 April Lavarack returned to his division in Egypt.

The remaining two brigades of the 7th Division played a major role in the allied invasion of the French mandated territory of Syria in June 1941. Lavarack exercised effective leadership over his formation which advanced in two columns, one on the coast and the other inland near Merdjayoun. Seizing an opportunity, he changed the axis of the advance, thrusting towards Jezzine and catching the Vichy French commander unawares. The French counter-attacked and Lavarack had to reconstitute a force at Merdjayoun.

In the midst of these battles Lavarack was promoted (18 June) lieutenant general to command I Corps, Blamey having become deputy commander-in-chief in the Middle East. The corps took responsibility for conducting almost the whole of the Syrian campaign. Reorganizing his force, which included British, Indian and Free French troops as well as the 7th Division, Lavarack supervised the capture of Damascus and Damour. An armistice came into effect on 12 July. For his commands at Tobruk and in Syria, in which Wavell said that he had shown 'abilities of a high order', Lavarack was appointed K.B.E. (1942) and mentioned in dispatches.

Following the outbreak of war with Japan, plans were made for I Corps to sail to the Far East. By late January 1942 Lavarack and his senior staff were in Java, ahead of the troops. Lavarack cabled the Australian government, endeavouring to prevent the first of his units from being retained in Java. He was unsuccessful in this effort, but the remainder of his men were diverted to Australia. His support of a British proposal to deploy the corps in Burma annoyed the Australian government. He left Java by aeroplane and arrived in Melbourne on 26 February. In March he was acting commander-in-chief of the Australian Military Forces before Blamey assumed the appointment on his return from the Middle East. Next month Lavarack took command of the First Army with responsibility for the defence of Queensland and New South Wales. His two years in the post were a time of frustration. Blamey overlooked him when an army commander was required in New Guinea.

In February 1944 Lavarack flew to Washington to become head of the Australian Military Mission. He was military adviser to the Australian delegation at the United Nations Conference on International Organiz-

ation held at San Francisco in April-June 1945. As the war progressed he became increasingly disappointed by his lack of active command, and was anxious to preserve his military reputation. Some politicians accused Blamey of shelving him. Lavarack claimed that he had always been loyal to Blamey and, contrary to Blamey's assertions, had never coveted his position. Lavarack returned to Australia in August 1946 and retired on 18 September.

That month it was announced that he had been appointed governor of Queensland. He was sworn in on 1 October 1946, the first Australian-born to hold the post. In 1951 his term was extended for another five years and there was to be a further extension of one year from 1 October 1956. He was appointed K.C.V.O. in 1954 and K.C.M.G. in 1955. Because of ill health he was relieved of his duties on 25 January 1957. Sir John died on 4 December 1957 in his home at Buderim, Queensland. He was accorded a state funeral and was cremated; his estate was sworn for probate at £38 024. His wife, who had been president of the A.I.F. Women's Association during World War II, survived him, as did his three sons, all of whom served in that war.

According to the Brisbane *Courier-Mail*, Lavarack had discharged his duties as governor 'with a quiet and modest dignity' and had 'impressed all who met him with his soldierly sense of duty, his friendly accessibility in social intercourse, and his desire to be of service to people in all parts of the State'. He had, moreover, made a substantial contribution to the Australian army. Despite a fiery temperament, he was an educated and articulate officer, and, as a commander, 'showed himself to be a determined and competent leader'. The Lavarack Barracks at Townsville are named after him. His portraits by George Bell [q.v.7] (1919) and (Sir) Ivor Hele (1941) are held by the Australian War Memorial, Canberra.

G. Long, *Greece, Crete and Syria* (Canb, 1953); J. Hetherington, *Blamey, Controversial Soldier* (Canb, 1973); S. F. Rowell, *Full Circle* (Melb, 1974); D. M. Horner (ed), *The Commanders* (Syd, 1984); B. Lodge, *Lavarack* (Syd, 1997); *VHJ*, 46, no 2, May 1975, p 365; *J of the Roy United Services Inst of Aust*, 5, no 1, Apr 1982, p 49; *Courier-Mail*, 5 Dec 1957; Lavarack papers (ADFA L).   D. M. HORNER

LAWRENSON, FREDERICK JAMES (1921-1952), air force officer, was born on 8 March 1921 at Carlton, Sydney, younger of twin sons of Harry Whalley Lawrenson, a labourer from England, and his native-born wife Jessie Robina, née Yeoman. Educated at Arncliffe and Camdenville public schools, Frederick began work as an insurance clerk. He surfed, played Rugby Union football and ice hockey, and enjoyed woodwork and reading.

On 19 July 1941 Lawrenson enlisted in the Citizen Air Force. He trained as a pilot in Australia and Rhodesia, and was commissioned in February 1943. Sent to the Middle East in April, he served (from July) with the Royal Air Force's No.6 Squadron, flying Hurricanes on 'tank-busting' and anti-shipping sorties. In May 1944 he transferred to No.450 Squadron, Royal Australian Air Force, which was operating in Italy. Lawrenson was promoted acting flight lieutenant in October and made a flight commander. On 29 December he was ordered to dive-bomb a target at Nervesa della Battáglia, near Venice. As he descended, an enemy shell hit his Kittyhawk, blowing away the cockpit's canopy, smashing part of the windscreen and wounding him in the face. Undeterred, he pressed home his attack and flew the aircraft back to base, talking and shouting to himself in order to stay conscious. He was awarded the Distinguished Flying Cross for his conduct that day and later mentioned in dispatches.

In March 1945 Lawrenson was promoted acting (substantive 1952) squadron leader. He briefly commanded a forward fighter-bomber control post before returning to Australia in November. For most of 1946-47 he was stationed with units in Canberra. At St Philip's Anglican Church, Sydney, on 7 February 1948 he married Yvonne Jean Turner, a 19-year-old stenographer. He served with No.76 and No.77 squadrons in Japan in 1948-49 and during this period was appointed to the Permanent Air Force. Back home, he was posted as flight lieutenant to No.78 (Fighter) Wing, Williamtown, New South Wales, in June 1949. After Vampire fighters had been involved in two fatal crashes, he was one of four pilots who 'exhibited considerable courage' in 1951 by test-flying the wing's remaining aeroplanes to prove that they were airworthy.

No.2 Operational Training Unit was formed in April 1952. Lawrenson was appointed its chief flying instructor, responsible for the tactical training of all pilots proceeding to the Republic of (South) Korea for active service with No.77 Squadron. Because he had to teach complicated manoeuvres to inexperienced aviators, the job entailed substantial personal risk. He won the Air Force Cross for the 'exemplary manner' in which he performed his duties.

Lawrenson was posted to No.77 Squadron in August 1952. On Christmas Eve that year, while leading four Meteors on an armed reconnaissance over the Imjim River and Koksan Valley region of the Democratic People's Republic of (North) Korea, he was shot down by ground-fire and was presumed to have been killed. His wife and daughter survived him. Freddie's friends remembered his cheerfulness, sincerity and honesty. Yvonne wrote of their 'short but very happy time together'.

R. O'Neill, *Australia in the Korean War 1950-53*, 2 (Canb, 1985); AWM 65 (AWM); A705/15, item 166/24/1043 (AA, Canb); information from Mrs Y. J. Lawrenson, Penshurst, Col L. J. Jewson, Killarney Heights, Syd, and Wing Cdr J. J. O'Donnell, Fisher, Canb.

DARRYL BENNET

LAWSON, AUBREY (1914-1977), motorcycle rider, was born on 5 April 1914 near Warialda, New South Wales, second son of native-born parents John Stafford Lawson, grazier, and his wife Blanche Ethel, née Atkins. In 1924 the family moved to Sydney. On leaving Naremburn Junior Technical School, Aub worked in the Postmaster-General's Department as a telegraph messenger (from 1929) and motor driver (from 1936). In 1933 he joined the Australian Corps of Signals, Militia. He made an immediate impact in 1937 as a motorcycle racer for World Speedways Pty Ltd with a flamboyant leg-trailing style and a long tartan scarf billowing behind him. Contracted to the Wembley Lions team, he went to London in March 1939; at his mother's insistence, his sister accompanied him as chaperone. He was a sensation in Britain and qualified for the world championship final, but the title was abandoned on the outbreak of war.

Back in Australia, Lawson enlisted in the Australian Imperial Force on 13 July 1940. Seven days later at St Clement's Anglican Church, Marrickville, he married Mary Ann Pulbrook, a 19-year-old salesgirl; they were to have five children before being divorced in 1969. Lawson served as a dispatch rider with the 8th Divisional Signals and embarked for Singapore in February 1941. Sailing from that island on special duty on 13 February 1942, he was rescued after his ship was bombed, and succoured by the Dutch on Sumatra. He reached Australia on 6 March. In Melbourne he joined Land Headquarters staff and was commissioned acting lieutenant on 3 July. Assigned to the 7th Divisional Signals, he took part in the invasion of Balikpapan, Borneo, in 1945 and on 24 January 1946 was transferred to the Reserve of Officers.

Lawson was a founding director (1946) of a promotional company to race at the Sydney Sports Ground. With slicker track surfaces (less dirt), he used his left leg in a foot-forward stance. Returning to London, he rode for the West Ham club in 1947-51; he was the team's top scorer in 1949, 1950 and 1951. During the English winters he rode in Australia. He took a break in 1952 and bought a 240-acre (97 ha) farm at Quirindi, New South Wales. Lured back to racing, he captained the Norwich club in England from 1953 to 1960 and was the team's top scorer in 1953, 1957 and 1959. Lawson qualified for ten world championship finals at Wembley—in 1939, 1949-51, 1953-54 and 1957-60. His best result was third place in 1958. He competed in eighty-four Test matches (mostly as captain of the Australian team), scored a record 680 points, and won five Australian and five New South Wales championships.

Retiring from speedway racing in 1960, Lawson made a one-off comeback at Kembla Grange in 1963 to win the New South Wales title. From 1957 he was involved with the Claremont Speedway in Perth, where he settled in 1967. On 13 November 1972 he married a divorcee Roma Domenica Gasman, née Haas, at the registry office, Perth. Survived by his wife, and by the two sons and two of the three daughters of his first marriage, he died of a coronary occlusion on 20 January 1977 at Northam and was buried in Karrakatta cemetery with Presbyterian forms.

J. W. Jacobs and R. J. Bridgland (eds), *Through: the Story of Signals 8 Australian Division and Signals A.I.F. Malaya* (Syd, 1949); *Motor Cycling in Australia*, 1, Apr 1947, p 25, May 1947, p 23, Sept 1947, p 14, Nov 1947, p 23; *Sports Novels*, 10, Mar 1951, p 64; *SMH*, 26 June, 21 Nov, 18 Dec 1947, 12 Dec 1949, 25 Feb 1950, 13 Dec 1952; *Sun* (Syd), 7 Dec 1957, 17 Jan 1959.   PETER WHITE

LAWSON, GEORGE (1880-1966), trade union official and politician, was born on 14 August 1880 at South Pine River, Caboolture district, Queensland, eighth child of Irish-born parents Alexander Lawson, farmer, and his wife Ellen, née Rilley. Educated at Warner State School, George drove three-horse teams for R. Jackson, a Brisbane carrier. In 1901-02 he fought in South Africa with the 5th (Queensland Imperial Bushmen) Contingent and was mentioned in dispatches. At her father's South Brisbane home on 16 January 1907 he married with Presbyterian forms Rebecca Jane Buchanan, a civil servant; they were to have two sons before she died in 1918.

In 1907 Lawson founded the Brisbane Trolleymen, Draymen and Carters' (later Carters and Drivers') Union and in the following year became its secretary. The union affiliated with the Australian Labour Federation in 1911. During the 1912 general strike Lawson served on the strike committee. Later that year, at the union's first State conference, he was elected general secretary, a position he held unopposed for almost twenty years. He was a capable administrator, and the union grew in numbers and influence. Expanding his activities, he attended (1910-31) the Queensland Trade Union Congress (president 1927), joined the amalgamation com-

mittee which established the Trades and Labour Council of Queensland in 1922 (president 1924 and 1927), attended the seventh International Labour Conference in Geneva (1925), and was a delegate (1930-32) to the executive of the Australian Council of Trade Unions.

An alderman (1916-21) of Windsor Town Council, Lawson had joined (1916) the central political executive of the Queensland Labor Party. In 1919 he was appointed to the Legislative Council, the Labor majority of which voted for its abolition in 1922. Lawson attended six Labor-in-Politics conventions. On 19 December 1931 he won the seat of Brisbane in the House of Representatives. An energetic parliamentarian, he was Opposition whip in 1934-41. He married 30-year-old Kathleen Lally on 14 September 1935 at St Stephen's Catholic Cathedral, Brisbane.

In October 1941 Lawson was appointed minister for transport, but lost his portfolio when the ministry was reconstructed in September 1943. He attended the twenty-seventh I.L.C. in Paris in 1945, then toured Europe as a member of Les Haylen's [q.v.14] Commonwealth immigration advisory committee. In 1947 Lawson moved in caucus to increase the number of members in Federal parliament; the change was implemented by the time of the 1949 elections in which Labor was defeated. Thereafter, Lawson played the part of an elder statesman until his retirement in 1961. A strong opponent of both the communists and the 'groupers', he supported the leadership of Dr H. V. Evatt [q.v.14].

Lawson served as a bridge between the industrial and political wings of the labour movement. He was loyal to the principles and policies of his party, and forthright in expressing his views. A devoted family man, he enjoyed reading, gardening and a modest bet on the horses. He died on 25 November 1966 in his home at Ashgrove, Brisbane, and was buried with Catholic rites in Pinaroo lawn cemetery; his wife survived him, as did the sons of his first marriage.

M. Cross, 'George Lawson, Portrait of a Union Leader', *RHSQJ*, 10, no 1, 1975-76, p 116; Transport Workers Union records (Newstead, Brisb); TLCQ records (Fryer Memorial L, Univ Qld); information from the late Mrs M. E. Carroll; personal knowledge.   MANFRED CROSS

LAWSON, GEORGE GAVIN (1882-1953), architect, was born on 27 May 1882 at Leith, Edinburgh, third of five children of William Lawson, corn merchant, and his wife Jessie Muller, née Wilson. Educated in Edinburgh, George was apprenticed for five years to the architects Hamilton, Patterson & Rhind. He emigrated to South Africa and practised at Johannesburg, where he designed the Wanderers' Club. While employed in the Police Works Department, Pretoria, he won a competition to design the city's town hall and post office. He later worked in Salisbury, Rhodesia (Harare, Zimbabwe), before emigrating to Australia. At St Silas's Anglican Church, Albert Park, Melbourne, on 18 November 1910 he married Edith McDowall Davies, a 28-year-old bookbinder. After submitting (1911) an unsuccessful entry for the Federal Capital Design Competition for Canberra, Lawson moved to Queensland. On 19 August 1914 he enlisted in the Australian Imperial Force; he served in Egypt with the 2nd Divisional Ammunition Column and on the Western Front with the 4th Field Artillery Brigade. He was sent to Australia on leave in September 1918 and discharged in Melbourne on 24 January 1919.

Appointed senior draughtsman in the South Australian architect-in-chief's office in November 1920, Lawson designed the dental school (1922) at the University of Adelaide, the (Sir John) Bice [q.v.7] building (1923) at the (Royal) Adelaide Hospital and the Hartley [q.v.4] building (1924) at the Teachers' Training College on Kintore Avenue. In 1925 he entered into partnership with Charles W. Rutt and designed the offices of the Burnside City Council. He began his own practice in 1926 and represented (from 1927) a Melbourne architectural firm in Adelaide, under the name of Barlow, Hawkins & Lawson, later Barlow & Lawson. In 1928 they designed the Edments building in Rundle Street, and planned the Lister building on North Terrace in commercial gothic style.

That year Lawson also drew the plans for Adelaide's first parking-station (now demolished), on the corner of Pulteney Street and North Terrace. Another of the firm's projects in 1928 was the Springfield estate, in association with Springfield Ltd, the State government and the Mitcham City Council; it was a garden suburb intended for the *nouveaux riches*. Lawson designed Raymond Begg's home in Brookside Road (modelling it on a house in Pasadena, California), and Joseph Crompton's house in Springfield Avenue. As a result of his work in this suburb, he received other commissions for homes in the south-eastern foothills, some of which were built in his favourite Dutch colonial style. In 1929 he introduced discarded clinker bricks for external and internal facings of domestic residences. Lawson was probably the first architect in South Australia to specify the use of mud bricks—for Walter Birks's holiday house at Macclesfield.

Jack D. Cheesman joined Lawson in 1932 and became a partner in the following year. Maurice Doley entered the partnership during World War II and, with the addition of

Newell Platten, R. A. Brabham and A. L. Brownell, the firm was named (1953) Lawson Cheesman Doley & Partners. Survived by his wife, Lawson died on 9 June 1953 at his Sefton Park home and was cremated. The South Australian chapter of the Royal Australian Institute of Architects named a fellowship after him.

M. Page, *Sculptors in Space* (Adel, 1986); *Roy Aust Inst of Architects (SA Chapter) Q Bulletin*, Apr-June 1953, pp 13, 15.   HAMISH ANGAS

LAWSON, JOHN NORMAN (1897-1956), politician, was born on 24 March 1897 in Sydney, third son of James Lawson, a native-born contractor (general carrier), and his wife Eleanor, née Day, who came from England. Educated at Sydney Boys' High School and the University of Sydney (B.V.Sc., 1920), John worked as a veterinarian in New Zealand until 1926 when he took up Kidgery, a small sheep-station near Nyngan, New South Wales. At St Stephen's Presbyterian Church, Sydney, on 21 November 1925 he married Jessie Alicia, daughter of R. B. Orchard [q.v.11]. In 1930 Lawson stood unsuccessfully as the Nationalist candidate for the seat of Cobar in the Legislative Assembly.

The United Australia Party endorsed him to contest the House of Representatives seat of Macquarie, held by J. B. Chifley [q.v.13], minister for defence in J. H. Scullin's [q.v.11] Australian Labor Party government. Macquarie contained the towns of Penrith, Katoomba, Lithgow and Bathurst, and encompassed a diverse region of farming, grazing, coalmining and manufacturing. At the general elections in December 1931, Lawson fought a tough but fair campaign against Chifley, whom he later praised as 'one of the ablest men in the Commonwealth'. Lawson was helped by the A.L.P. vote being divided between Chifley and A. S. Luchetti, a member of the Labor splinter group led by J. T. Lang [q.v.9]; after Luchetti was eliminated from the count, Lawson defeated Chifley by 456 votes in a poll of 41 086.

The new back-bencher expressed his opinions forcefully in parliament. Among other matters, he supported the proposal to establish a shale-oil undertaking at Newnes, north of Lithgow, and advocated measures to improve conditions on the land. At the elections in 1934 he increased his margin to 3263. He was appointed temporary chairman of committees in November. In the following year he visited England—as a member of the Commonwealth delegation, Empire Parliamentary Association—for King George V's silver jubilee. Retaining Macquarie in 1937, Lawson was appointed a parliamentary secretary in July 1938; he assisted the treasurer

R. G. (Baron) Casey [q.v.13] and (from November) the minister for industry (Sir) Robert Menzies [q.v.].

Dissatisfaction in the U.A.P. with the performance of J. A. Lyons [q.v.10] as prime minister was brought to a head in March 1939 when Menzies resigned his portfolios in protest at the prime minister's refusal to proceed with a scheme for national insurance. A fervent supporter of Menzies, Lawson relinquished his parliamentary secretaryships. Following Lyons's death in April, Menzies became prime minister. The Country Party decided against joining his government, and he took the opportunity to reward Lawson's loyalty by appointing him minister for trade and customs on 26 April.

With the outbreak of World War II in September 1939, the government assumed sweeping new powers under the National Security Act. Lawson's responsibilities included import licensing, price control and censorship. He also implemented minor reforms on the waterfront, and reached a gentleman's agreement with Japan whereby that country would limit its export of piece-goods to Australia and take two-thirds of its imported wool from Australia. Lawson was appointed to the Economic Cabinet in December.

The government planned to establish a motorcar industry in Australia and authorized Lawson to negotiate an agreement with Australian Consolidated Industries Ltd which gave that company a virtual monopoly. This proposal incurred strong criticism, particularly from the Country Party. The ministry was embarrassed when it was revealed that Lawson had leased a racehorse from W. J. Smith [q.v.11], managing director of A.C.I. Menzies reprimanded Lawson for making a 'foolish blunder', but did not ask him to resign. Lawson, however, convinced himself that the government would be jeopardized if he retained his portfolio. He drove from Sydney to Melbourne and tendered his resignation to Menzies on 23 February 1940.

At the Federal elections in September, Lawson lost his seat to Chifley. During his remaining years Lawson owned and managed Arrowfield, a stud-farm at Jerrys Plains, New South Wales. Survived by his wife, daughter and two sons, he died of myocardial infarction on 14 August 1956 in Singleton District Hospital and was cremated. Friends and opponents alike respected him as a man of ability and fairness.

P. Hasluck, *The Government and the People 1939-1941* (Canb, 1952); L. F. Crisp, *Ben Chifley* (Melb, 1961); *PD* (Cwlth), 30 Aug 1956, p 15; *SMH*, 30 Dec 1931, 26 Apr 1932, 15 July, 11 Nov 1938, 21, 25 Feb, 17 Mar, 15, 20, 28 June 1939, 9, 13 Jan, 15, 24 Feb 1940, 16 Aug 1956; Lawson papers (NL).

DAVID LEE

LAZAR GEROE, CLARA (1900-1980), psychiatrist, was born on 4 October 1900 at Pápa, Hungary, daughter of Adolf Adam Lazar, wholesale grocer, and his wife Ilona, née Lusztig. Although Jewish, Clara completed her secondary schooling at the local Calvinist college. Her tertiary education was disrupted by the political turmoil in Hungary at the end of World War I; after attending a number of universities, she graduated in medicine from the University of Pecs in 1924. She had become interested in psychoanalysis during the war, when Dr Sandor Ferenczi was garrisoned in her home town and the leading bookshop stocked his books. Her family bought one and she secretly read it. In 1926 she joined a training course at the Hungarian Psycho-analytical Society, Budapest, becoming a member in 1931 and a training analyst in 1938. Having studied under Michael Balint, she practised privately in Budapest from 1932 to 1939.

At the International Psycho-Analytical Congress, held in Paris in 1938, Clara had explored the possibility of six Hungarian analysts emigrating to New Zealand. Their applications were refused. A group of Australians—including Bishop E. H. Burgmann, the doctors R. S. Ellery, R. C. Winn [qq.v.13,14,12] and Paul Dane, and (Sir) Charles Moses—took up their case with the Commonwealth Department of Immigration. Of the six, only Clara was accepted. She later surmised that she was selected because she had a child. With her husband Vilmos Gerö (William Geroe)—whom she had married on 27 August 1927 in Budapest—and their son, she arrived in Melbourne on 14 March 1940.

Dr Geroe, as she was generally known, began clinical work as training analyst at the new Melbourne Institute for Psychoanalysis, Collins Street, in February 1941. She soon established a regular series of seminars to discuss the works of Freud, organized seminars for teachers, parents and staff of the Children's Court clinic, and ran a special clinic for those who could not afford private fees. Particularly interested in children, she acted as an adviser to Margaret Lyttle [q.v.] at Preshil, Kew. Geroe lectured in the department of psychology at the University of Melbourne and served as honorary psychoanalyst to the Royal Melbourne Hospital. Her medical qualifications were not accepted until 1956, when she became a member of the Australasian Association of Psychiatrists. She was also a foundation fellow of the (Royal) Australian and New Zealand College of Psychiatrists, and a president of the Australian Psychoanalytical Society.

A warm-hearted, motherly woman, Geroe brought to the establishment of psychoanalysis in Australia the experience of its beginnings in Central Europe. Like Freud's, her couch was covered with a Turkish rug, and she carried a lifelong nostalgia for the early days of the psychoanalytic movement in Europe, with its camaraderie and intellectual radicalism. She also had wide cultural interests and seldom missed a Musica Viva concert, a film festival or an art exhibition. Judy Cassab painted her portrait in 1965. Survived by her husband and son, Geroe died on 12 February 1980 at Parkville and was cremated.

MJA, 26 July 1980, 2, no 2, p 106; *International Review of Psycho-Analysis*, 7, pt 4, 1980, p 522; *Meanjin Q*, 41, no 3, 1982, p 342; *J of the International Assn for the Hist of Psychoanalysis*, no 2, Winter 1986, p 9; D. Kirsner, interviews with Clara Geroe (1977 and 1979, tapes held by author, LaTrobe Univ); information from Dr G. Geroe, Castlemaine, Vic, Dr R. Rothfield, Malvern, Dr O. H. D. Blomfield, Hawthorn, Dr W. Brumley, Richmond, Melb, and Dr R. Martin, Hunters Hill, Syd.   JUDITH BRETT

LAZZARINI, HUBERT PETER (1884-1952), politician, was born on 8 September 1884 at Young, New South Wales, ninth child of Italian-born Pietro Lazzarini, a labourer who became an orchardist, and his native-born wife Annie, née Stubbs. Carlo Camillo Lazzarini [q.v.10] was his brother. Pietro had emigrated after the fall (1849) of the Roman republic, first to the United States of America and then to Australia. Bert received a Catholic education at Young, worked as a draper at Germanton (Holbrook from 1915), joined the trade-union movement and set up his own store at Wellington. On 14 June 1916 at the Catholic Church, Holbrook, he married Constance Maude Williams, a dressmaker; her father was Prussian and her mother Irish.

In 1919 Bert and Maude moved to Dulwich Hill, Sydney. That year the Australian Labor Party's branch at Young nominated Lazzarini to stand for the House of Representatives seat of Werriwa. The New South Wales executive chose him in October, ahead of nominees from the Grenfell and Cootamundra branches. Two months later he defeated (by 466 votes) John Lynch who had won the seat for the A.L.P. in 1914 and held it for the Nationalists in 1917. An electoral redistribution before the 1922 polls moved Werriwa eastward, taking from it the Young, Grenfell and Cootamundra regions, and adding the coastal strip from Shellharbour to Botany Bay. Lazzarini was to hold the seat (with increasing majorities) at the elections in 1922, 1925, 1928 and 1929. In 1927 he and his family shifted to Fairfield.

Labor's J. H. Scullin [q.v.11] was commissioned prime minister in October 1929, the month that the New York Stock Exchange collapsed. One year later the A.L.P. was elected to office in New South Wales under J. T. Lang

[q.v.9]. Acute differences arose between the two governments on methods to counter the Depression. In March 1931 a special federal conference expelled the New South Wales branch and Lazzarini became a member of J. A. Beasley's [q.v.13] Lang Labor Party in Federal parliament. On 25 November Beasley's group, with the support of the Opposition, brought down Scullin's government. At the elections in December Lazzarini was defeated. Another redistribution in 1934 moved Werriwa northwards, with the loss of Goulburn and the addition of Liverpool. Lazzarini won the seat in September that year.

The Langites rejoined the Federal Parliamentary Labor Party in 1936 and in the following year Lazzarini was elected to the executive. In 1940 Lang formed the Australian Labor Party (Non-Communist). On 2 May Beasley unveiled a party of that name in the House of Representatives. This time Lazzarini remained with the F.P.L.P. He immediately and furiously countered the charge that those who would not again follow Beasley and Lang were pro-communist. In private Lazzarini mocked New South Wales members who sat on the fence 'with both ears to the ground'. At the polls in September he defeated seven candidates, including Rex Connor [q.v.13]. The F.P.L.P. re-elected him to its executive.

When Labor gained power under John Curtin [q.v.13] in October 1941, Lazzarini became minister for home security and minister assisting the treasurer J. B. Chifley [q.v.13]. He shed his treasury responsibilities in September 1943, but Curtin gave him the additional portfolio of works in February 1945. In July that year his title was changed to minister for works and housing so that he could administer the pioneering Commonwealth and State Housing Agreement which provided homes for low-income families. The Department of Home Security was abolished in February 1946 and Lazzarini was not elected to Chifley's second ministry (formed in November 1946).

Under the 1949 electoral redistribution, Werriwa was moved farther northward, losing most of the area south of Helensburgh and Liverpool, and gaining a large portion of the municipality of Fairfield. Lazzarini at last lived in his electorate. Following the April 1951 polls, he announced that he would not contest the next. Chifley thought that a local candidate should replace him. In a protracted contest E. G. Whitlam emerged from a final scrum of nine. Lazzarini died of a cerebral haemorrhage on 1 October 1952 at Fairfield and was buried in Liverpool cemetery; his wife, son and two daughters survived him. Parliamentary colleagues paid tribute to 'Laz', emphasizing his integrity and commitment to Labor principles.

P. Weller (ed), *Caucus Minutes 1901-1949*, 3 (Melb, 1975); *PD* (Cwlth), 2 May 1940, p 490, 1 Oct 1952, p 2495; *Holbrook Courier*, 16 June 1916; *Southern Mail* (Bowral), 9, 16 Sept 1919; *SMH*, 8 Oct, 11 Nov, 15 Dec 1919, 2 Oct 1952; *Goulburn Evening Penny Post*, 18, 23 Oct, 4 Nov 1919; *Young Witness*, 21, 24, 31 Oct 1919.   E. G. WHITLAM

LEA, HARRY (1876-1957), confectioner, was born on 22 February 1876 at Spitalfields, London, within sound of Bow Bells, and named Monascher, son of Harris Levy, boot finisher and tailor, and his wife Hannah, née Emanuel. Emigrating with the family to Western Australia when he was aged 12, 'Harry' went to work rolling cigars in a factory —the only time he would receive wages. After his parents paid for him to learn to make confectionery, he pushed a barrow, peddling his wares around Perth and Fremantle. He later sold bottles for recycling and did some gold-prospecting.

On 30 March 1905 Levy married 19-year-old Esther Goldman at her mother's Adelaide home. The young couple initially settled at Kalgoorlie, Western Australia. They ran a refreshment room and catering business at Kadina, South Australia, for two years before beginning various enterprises in Melbourne and at Puckapunyal. With a growing family, they reached Sydney by 1916 and opened a fruit store on The Corso at Manly where their eldest son Maurice later demonstrated a prize-winning flair for fruit displays. To enhance the slower winter trade, Harry revived his confectionery skills, selling toffees as well as fruit.

The sideline prospered. In 1924 Levy opened a small milk bar and confectionery shop in Castlereagh Street, Sydney, to cater for trade from the Haymarket Theatre next door. He manufactured his products at the rear of the premises. By this time his elder children were involved in the business. In June 1930 Depression rents allowed them to take over a Pitt Street shirt shop. Levy changed his name to 'Lea' and called the firm 'Darrell Lea' after his youngest son. The style of confectionery display that came to be identified with Darrell Lea was quickly established. The shirt-racks, the experience with fruit-selling and Maurice's flair led to a focus on heaped pyramids of their thirty lines of chocolate. Darrell Lea offered, like Busby Berkeley, a kaleidoscopic overabundance and extravagance seemingly at odds with Depression stringency, and in sharp contrast to the more refined displays of competitors such as Newman's or California. Equally significant was the decision to sell at half their competitors' price, so they were effectively mass-marketing what had previously been a luxury. High turnover also maintained the reputation for freshness, based on individual batch cooking and the close integration of manufacturing and retailing. The uniform for their hand-picked salesgirls was developed from the ticket-writer's smock, an overlarge bow added for effect.

Harry, handsome and dapper, sporting his bowler and umbrella or motoring to golf in his Riley, left the development of the business to his sons who opened more stores in Sydney. The Darrell Lea Chocolate Co. Ltd was registered in 1935. Next year the firm successfully tendered for premises at No.1 York Street, under the first arch of the new Harbour Bridge, and manufactured there until a new factory was opened at Kogarah in 1962. In 1940 a branch of the business had been set up in Melbourne. Survived by his wife, daughter and four sons, Harry Lea died on 24 July 1957 at Marrickville and was cremated with Jewish rites. The company remained a family concern and his grandchildren joined the firm.

National Times, 14-20 Mar 1982, p 28; *Woman's Day*, 14 Jan 1985, p 14; Darrell Lea Chocolate Shops Pty Ltd (ts history of the company) *and* company records; information from Mr M. Lea, Kogarah, Syd.   RICHARD WHITE

LEA, MORRIS JAMES (1917-1980), engineer and surveyor, was born on 19 August 1917 at Northcote, Melbourne, son of Victorian-born parents James Hugh Lea, soldier, and his wife Sarah Louisa, née Moorhouse. Morrie attended Ripponlea State and Brighton Technical schools, and won a scholarship to Melbourne Technical College where he obtained a diploma of civil engineering in 1933. Deciding against accepting a scholarship to the University of Melbourne because of the Depression, he entered into articles with F. J. Walters, working as an assistant to Donald Macdonald. In 1937 Lea was licensed as a surveyor and won the Victorian Institute of Surveyors' prize. Qualifying as a municipal engineer in 1939, he was elected to the Institution of Engineers, Australia, in 1940. On 11 December that year at St Paul's Anglican Church, Caulfield, he married Mavis Louise Parsons, a stenographer.

Commissioned in the Citizen Military Forces in August 1940, Lea was seconded to the Australian Imperial Force on 27 July 1941. Following military-engineering and staff training in Australia, he served in Papua and New Guinea, mostly in staff posts, in 1943-45. He was promoted major (1943) and mentioned in dispatches (1946). His A.I.F. appointment terminated in Australia on 26 November 1945. In 1948-54 he was again involved with the C.M.F., commanding No.2 Movement Control Training Group and rising to temporary lieutenant colonel.

When Lea returned to civilian life he and Walters established a company, F. J. Walters & Lea Pty Ltd. Lea conducted an extensive practice in engineering, surveying and planning. Keenly involved in the affairs of his profession, he was a council-member (1947-52) and president (1949-50) of the Victorian Institute of Surveyors, and its nominee (1954-59) on the Surveyors' Board of Victoria. He was largely responsible for forming the Institution of Surveyors, Australia, of which he was foundation member, treasurer, president (1960-62) and honorary fellow (1966).

As one who constantly advocated that surveyors should take an active role in town planning, Lea served on the council of the (Royal) Australian Planning Institute, of which he was treasurer for many years, and on the Melbourne divisional committee (president 1956). In 1958 the National Capital Planning Committee was set up: the Institution of Engineers, with the support of the council of the Institution of Surveyors, chose Lea as its nominee on that body. On his retirement from the committee in 1970, he was appointed O.B.E. He was also a member of the Town and Country Planning Board (1968-71) and the Town Planning Appeals Tribunal (1974-80).

Lea's work was technically sound and he expressed himself well. These qualities, combined with his integrity, forthrightness and humour, made him a valued counsellor. Five ft 11 ins (180 cm) tall and of medium build, he was a proficient sportsman, an honorary life member of the Woodlands and Yarra Yarra golf clubs, and a member of Alma Bowling Club; he also belonged to the Rotary Club of Melbourne. A Freemason, he was a past master of the United Service Lodge. He died of cancer on 5 June 1980 at Prahran and was cremated; his wife, son and one of his two daughters survived him.

Aust Surveyor, Dec 1960, Sept 1980; R. Smith, M. J. Lea (ms, nd, Sunbury, Vic); information from Mrs S. Lea-Wood, Ocean Grove, Vic, Sir John Overall, Kingston, Canb, and Brig D. Macdonald, Mosman, Syd.   JOHN ATCHISON

LEAHY, JOHN JEREMIAH (1875-1959), grazier, stock-dealer and racehorse owner, was born on 19 May 1875 at Gundaroo, New South Wales, fourth child and youngest son of native-born parents Jeremiah Leahy, butcher and farmer, and his first wife Eliza, née Reynolds (d.1887). While being educated at nearby Mugwill Public School, Leahy raised and sold turkeys to a travelling buyer. He left school at 14, worked for his father, carted firewood and travelled the district with a draught stallion, serving farmers' mares. In 1910 Leahy set up as a stock-dealer and grazier. Helped at first by his brother Daniel,

he soon owned a considerable amount of land around Gunning, including Keswick. At St Francis's Catholic Church, Gunning, on 7 May 1913 he married Mary Elizabeth Grovenor; they were to have nine children.

J. J. Leahy assembled a pastoral empire which rivalled that of A. B. Triggs [q.v.12], and his numerous stock and land deals became legendary. He owned or leased one hundred or more properties in all, mainly in central and western New South Wales. Although he was a cattleman from the mid-1930s, his wool clip was reputedly one of the largest in Australia. The stations he owned at various times included Cultowa, 212 000 acres (86 000 ha) on the Darling River near Wilcannia, Oxley, 50 000 acres (20 000 ha) at the head of the Macquarie Marshes, Burra, 20 000 acres (8000 ha) at Tumbarumba, and—in Queensland—Mount Sturgeon, 706 square miles (1830 km^2) near Hughenden, and Oban, 1100 square miles (2850 km^2) at Dajarra.

His operations followed a strategic plan, centred on his favourite property, Manna Park, near Condobolin, New South Wales. Experience taught him that frontage country was not always the best: thus much of his fattening country was back from the rivers, with depots near a railhead for rapid movement of fat or store stock. Leahy also had a stock depot with an airstrip at Lansvale, opposite Warwick Farm racecourse. He mostly sold his stations bare, and bought them on a walk-in walk-out basis.

Essentially a 'hands on' man, Leahy travelled vast distances, first by horse and rail, and later by car and aeroplane. His passion for efficiency demanded that a fleet of cars was always on hand, and he was one of the first to use aircraft extensively, enabling him to assess the state of the country. He owned numerous aeroplanes, among them two converted World War I Bristol fighters; he retained the services of a pilot, but invariably did his own navigation. By 1940 he was flying about 50 000 miles a year and was one of the biggest suppliers of prime stock to the Sydney and Melbourne markets. A ready innovator, he used wire-netting on a large scale to rabbit-proof his runs.

Leahy was a member of the Australian Jockey Club and other sporting bodies, and a keen follower of the ring, but his main recreation was breeding and racing thoroughbreds. He owned the Ardsley and Woodlands (Bundilla) studs near Bathurst. Among his horses, Speciality won the Doncaster Handicap (1921) and Metropolitan Stakes (1922), and Akuna the Sydney Cup in 1935. His large number of brood mares included Sarcherie (which he bred). Sarcherie came second in the Melbourne Cup in 1934 and 1935, and third in 1937 (after winning the Doncaster). In 1927 Leahy had visited England—where he watched racing from the Royal enclosure at Ascot—Ireland and Europe.

A big man physically and in outlook, Leahy was always well dressed, but lived quietly and unostentatiously. He was honest, well respected and shrewd. Buying for cash and selling on terms, he never had a mortgage. He helped many to get a start in the pastoral industry, and was a benefactor of Lewisham Hospital and St Ignatius' College, Riverview, Sydney. Although he had country homes at Bathurst and Forbes, the family lived at Wellbeck, Strathfield, until 1942, and then at Roseville Chase. In 1953 his wife sued him for alimony pending her suit for judicial separation, and Leahy sued two of his sons for £44 000 in payment for stock and plant. Survived by his wife, five of his seven sons and one of his two daughters, Leahy died on 2 June 1959 at Roseville and was buried in Forbes cemetery. His son William Charles was killed in September 1945 while serving with the Royal Australian Air Force.

Pastoral Review, 14 Apr 1925, 16 Aug 1926, 16 May 1928, 16 Aug, 16 Dec 1937, 17 July 1959; *SMH* 14 Apr 1935, 30 Aug 1937, 24 Nov 1939, 27, 28 May, 23, 24, 26, 27, 30 June 1953; information from Mr P. Leahy, Tenterfield, NSW.

G. P. WALSH

LEAL, CHARLOTTE MARY CLARINA (1881-1961), community worker, was born on 20 June 1881 at Clare, South Australia, second of five daughters of John Harry, schoolteacher, and his wife Kate, née Hancock. Raised in her parents' Methodist faith, Lottie was educated at public schools in Clare and Gawler, and at the Advanced School for Girls, Adelaide. She studied painting under Rose McPherson (Margaret Preston [q.v.11]) and became an associate of the (Royal) South Australian Society of Arts on exhibiting 'Roses' in its 1903 federal exhibition. After McPherson went abroad next year, Lottie took over her studio in Gilbert Place and taught drawing, painting and outdoor sketching. On 6 July 1911 at the Methodist Church, Archer Street, North Adelaide, she married James Leonard Leal, a stationer from England; they were to have five children.

The employment of a resident housekeeper enabled Mrs Leal to embark on voluntary public service and to use her debating skills; her husband also participated in civic affairs, serving as mayor (1919-22) of Thebarton. In June 1921 Mrs Leal formed the Thebarton Women's Service Association to develop philanthropic and educational activities in the town. She was its president in 1921-33 and later vice-president. Its members raised funds, distributed relief to 'distress cases', especially during the Depression, and supported mu-

nicipal projects. As 'mother' of the first and twelve subsequent metropolitan associations, Leal kept them in touch and espoused their causes. Foundation president (1921-33) of the Thebarton School for Mothers Institute and Baby Health Centre, she led T.W.S.A. efforts to buy a motorcar in 1930 for the centre's nurse. She was a committee-member (1921-39) of the District Trained Nursing Society's Thebarton branch, a member (1922-28) of the executive-committee of the Minda Home for the Feeble-Minded and Epileptic, and founding president (1923) of the Thebarton Girl Guide Company.

A T.W.S.A. delegate to the National Council of Women of South Australia, Leal began an exacting role in the council's activities: she was an executive-member (1923-29), president (1929-34 and 1940-41) and life vice-president (from 1937). With particular concern for country families, she headed the N.C.W. through the worst years of the Depression and represented it on the Local Industries Promotion Council in 1930-35. She and Jean Bonython [q.v.7] were the only women members in 1934-35 on the executive-committee for the State's centenary celebrations, to which Leal submitted N.C.W. proposals. As vice-president of the Women's Centenary Council of South Australia, she worked closely with Adelaide Miethke [q.v.10]. In 1936 Leal was appointed M.B.E. Two years later she joined a committee of inquiry into the situation of delinquent children and other wards of the state; its report (1939) was humane and thoroughly researched.

Leal's 'devout and generous work' helped the Methodist Church, both at the suburban level and through the Women's Home Mission League. In addition, she assisted the Resthaven Home for Lonely Women and in 1938 founded and presided over the Brighton (later Kate Cocks [q.v.8]) Babies' Home Aid. Survived by a son and two daughters, she died on 13 August 1961 at Woodville and was cremated. The Charlotte Leal chapel (1967) at the Kate Cocks Babies' Home commemorated her.

Thebarton Women's Service Assn, *Constitution and By-Laws* (Adel, 1930) and Minutes, 1923-58 (held by Mrs C. Allen, Mile End, Adel); National Council of Women of SA, *Annual Report*, 1921-37, *and* Methodist Church, Women's Home Mission League of SA, Cte Minutes, 1937-48 (Mort L); State Centenary Celebrations Executive Cte (SA), Minutes, 1932-35 (SRSA); *SA Methodist*, 15 Sept 1961; information from Miss M. Leal, Millswood, and Mrs C. Allen, Mile End, Adel.   HELEN JONES

LEARMONTH, NOEL FULFORD (1880-1970), farmer, naturalist and local historian, was born on 22 February 1880 at Ettrick, the family property near Tyrendarra, Victoria, son of Tasmanian-born John Ralston Learmonth, grazier, and his wife Mary Jane Marshall, née Fulford, from South Australia. William Learmonth [q.v.5] was his grandfather. Noel completed his education (1895-98) at Geelong Church of England Grammar School. He worked for the Victorian Railways (notably on the Mildura survey), served (1902-03) as private secretary to M. K. McKenzie, the commissioner of crown lands, and took up a pastoral block near Gayndah, Queensland. After his father's death in 1911, he returned to Victoria, named the land he inherited Carramar and began farming there. On 26 August 1914 at St Alban's Anglican Church, Armadale, Melbourne, he married Edith Mary Salter (d.1964); they were to have four children.

Throughout his life Learmonth developed his skills as a naturalist and local historian. While working on the Mildura survey, he had sent paragraphs to the *Bulletin* which were published under the pen-name, 'Leo'. In 1910-11 the *Geelong Grammar School Quarterly* included two of his articles. Learmonth's contributions to the ornithology of south-west Victoria, especially its seabirds, continued in articles in the *Emu*, the *Victorian Naturalist* and the *Bird Observers' Club Notes*, culminating in *The Birds of the Portland District* (1966). In this work, and in activities such as the campaigns for national parks at Mount Richmond (proclaimed 1960) and Lower Glenelg (proclaimed 1969), he was assisted by members of the Portland Field Naturalists' Club which he had helped to found in 1945. His interest in bird-life earned him an associate-fellowship of the National Museum of Victoria.

Learmonth's first full-scale historical project had been *The Portland Bay Settlement* (1934), prepared to mark Portland's centenary. Following his retirement to that city in 1952, his responses to various requests for local histories included *The Story of St Stephens* (1956), *The Story of a Port* (1960) and *Portland 1800 to 1920* (1966). His final book, *Four Towns and a Survey* (1970), included studies of several local towns, first published in the *Portland Guardian*, and an account of his time on the Mildura railway survey. His pioneering work, meticulously detailed and lucidly written, was recognized by life membership of the Melbourne Anglican Diocesan Historical Society and a fellowship (1962) of the Royal Historical Society of Victoria.

Colleagues found Learmonth a stimulating companion, 'his forthrightness ... tempered with courtesy, his knowledge with wit'. He was a member of the Bread and Cheese Club, and the Melbourne Cricket Club. Survived by his daughter, he died on 9 September 1970 at Portland and was cremated. One of his sons

had died in infancy, the other two in World War II. The elder was the subject of John Manifold's poem, 'The Tomb of Lt. John Learmonth, A.I.F.'; the younger, Wing Commander Charles Cuthbertson Learmonth, D.F.C., had an air force base in Western Australia named after him.

G. Serle, 'Foreword' in N. Learmonth, *Four Towns and a Survey* (Melb, 1970); Geelong C of E Grammar School, *Corian*, Dec 1970, p 538; *Vic Naturalist*, 88, no 2, Feb 1971, p 39; *Emu* (Melb), 71, pt 2, Apr 1971, p 88; *VHM*, 43, no 4, Nov 1972, p 956; *Portland Observer*, 11 Sept 1970.
                                                            JENNIFER STRAUSS

LEDDY, FRANCISCUS NICOLAAS (1903-1964), company director, was born on 20 April 1903 at Rotterdam, the Netherlands, son of Franciscus Nicolaas Leddy, director of prisons, and his wife Cornelia, née Delabrie. Educated at Leyden high school and the Nederlandse Economische Hogeschool, Rotterdam, young Leddy began his professional career in 1929 in the export department of Philips' Gloeilampenfabrieken at Eindhoven. On 22 August 1928 at The Hague he had married Johanna Philippine Nagelkerke; they had one son before being divorced in 1931. Leddy's second marriage also ended in divorce. After serving as manager (from 1933) of Philips Vienna, he was transferred to Cairo in 1938 as managing director of Philips Orient. World War II brought out the improviser in him: he established a workshop which employed Arab boys and wounded Australian servicemen whom he trained to make direction-finding loops for the soldiers, using scrap material from aircraft that had been shot down near Tobruk. In May 1942 he was promoted governing director of Philips Lamps (Australasia) Pty Ltd. At St Stephen's Presbyterian Church, Sydney, on 31 December 1945 he married Gertrude Kay Lamond, née Brookes, a 21-year-old divorcee.

On reaching Sydney, Leddy had found a curious collection of Philips' plants scattered throughout New South Wales to manufacture and assemble electronic communication equipment. The opportunity to consolidate and expand came late in 1945 when he bought the old munitions factory at Hendon, Adelaide, at a bargain price. In the following year he shifted all Philips' operations to the Hendon site, which was opened on 21 April 1947 by the premier (Sir) Thomas Playford. By 1956 some 3200 workers were employed there. Philips' expansion prompted other industries to set up in Adelaide.

Leddy diversified Philips Electrical Industries Pty Ltd. The first experimental television transmitter in Australia was built at Hendon in 1955. By mid-1956 the first locally made

Philips television receivers were marketed, heralding the introduction of television. Leddy became a technical adviser to the Federal government on television issues and was a director of (Sir) Frank Packer's [q.v.] Television Corporation Ltd (TCN-9, Sydney). He was also a key figure in bringing the first frequency modulation broadcasts to Australia in the late 1950s. Under his leadership Philips' engineers successfully completed the coaxial cable between Sydney and Melbourne in April 1962. Prominent in industry, Leddy was a life governor of the Sydney division of the Australian Institute of Management, and a councillor of the New South Wales Chamber of Manufactures and of the Nuclear Research Foundation, University of Sydney. In 1953 he had been appointed to the Order of Oranje-Nassau.

Although his health was never strong, Leddy cut an imposing figure. He was the prototype of the authoritarian manager, arousing deep feelings either of loyalty or antipathy in those he met. Individuals with the courage to stand up to him often earned his respect. On the evening of 24 August 1955, as he was leaving his Sydney office, he was shot in the arm and chest by an unknown assailant; the gunman was never found. Leddy had some of the hallmarks of the European *homme civilisé*. He was fluent in five languages, he collected paintings and antiques, and he had an abiding interest in music and photography. His skills as a gardener were legendary: in 1958 his garden at Pymble won first prize in the open section of the *Sydney Morning Herald* competition. He belonged to the Royal Sydney Yacht Squadron, and to the American National and Killara Golf clubs.

Leddy left Sydney on 13 June 1962 to take up the presidency of the Philips' group in Italy. He died on 23 June 1964 at Milan and was buried at Eindhoven, the Netherlands. His wife and their two daughters survived him, as did the son of his first marriage.

F. P. Dickson, *Philips in Australia* (np, priv pub, 1926); Philips Electrical Industries Pty Ltd in Australia, *Announcer*, 1, no 9, 1947, 6, no 1, 1952, 8, no 9, 1954; *SMH*, 30 Apr 1946, 24 Nov 1952, 27 Oct 1953, 28 Aug 1955, 7 Oct 1958, 26 June 1964; *Daily Telegraph* (Syd), 26 June 1964. HENK OVERBERG

LEE, JEAN (1919-1951), murderer, was born on 10 December 1919 at Dubbo, New South Wales, fifth and youngest child of Australian-born parents Charles Wright, railway ganger, and his wife Florence, née Peacock. Her names were registered as Marjorie Jean Maude. After the family moved to Sydney in 1927, she was educated at Chatswood Public School, at a convent in North Sydney and at Willoughby Central Domestic High School (1932-33). She did not sit her Intermediate certificate examinations.

Jean Wright turned her hand to a number of jobs, working as a milliner, waitress, stenographer and as a labourer in a canned-goods factory. Aged 18, on 19 March 1938 at the Methodist Church, South Chatswood, she married Raymond Thomas Brees, a 25-year-old house-painter; their daughter was born in April 1939. From the beginning the marriage was strained by financial difficulties; Brees was regularly out of work and drinking heavily. The couple separated and were divorced in April 1949.

As a single mother, Jean Brees found it difficult to make ends meet. Increasingly she became caught in a cycle of poverty, petty crime and prostitution in Sydney and Brisbane, using numerous aliases, among them 'Jean Lee'. In 1943 she had begun an association with Morris Dias, a criminal who managed her earnings from prostitution. Three years later she met Robert David Clayton, a 'con man' and gambler with whom she formed an enduring, if violent, relationship. Between May 1945 and July 1948 she appeared twenty-three times at Sydney's Central Police Court, mostly on charges of offensive behaviour.

In October 1949 Lee travelled to Melbourne with Clayton, who had just been released from gaol. There they teamed up with another criminal, Norman Andrews. The three committed minor offences which brought them into further conflict with the law. On 8 November a 73-year-old, part-time bookmaker William ('Pop') Kent was found murdered in the front room of his house in Dorrit Street, Carlton. The police alleged that Clayton, Andrews and Lee had accompanied Kent to his home, bashed him, tortured him to find where he had hidden his money, and finally strangled him. Angry and bitter about the charge, Lee pleaded innocence and insisted she was an onlooker rather than an active participant in the crime.

On 25 March 1950, after a long and dramatic trial in the Supreme Court, the three were found guilty of murder and sentenced to death. The media and a majority of people were in favour of the sentence being carried out, but, spearheaded by the Labor Women's Organising Committee and groups opposed to capital punishment, some public sympathy emerged for Lee. No woman had been hanged in Victoria for fifty-six years. Telegrams of protest were sent to the McDonald [q.v.] government, but a subsequent legal appeal failed to reverse the decision. At 8 a.m. on 19 February 1951 Jean Lee was carried to the scaffold and hanged at Pentridge prison, Coburg, while protesters and the press gathered outside. Clayton and Andrews were hanged two hours later. Survived by her daughter, Lee was buried within the prison walls. She was the last woman to suffer the death penalty in Australia.

J. Holledge, *Australia's Wicked Women* (Lond, 1963); M. Cannon, *The Woman as Murderer* (Melb, 1994); P. Wilson et al, *Jean Lee* (Syd, 1997); *People* (Syd), 28 Mar 1951; *Herald* (Melb), 8 Nov 1949, 23 Mar, 14 Dec 1950, 12, 13, 19 Feb 1951.

JOY DAMOUSI

LEE, SAMUEL (1912?-1975), nightclub and restaurant owner, was born probably in 1912 at Winnipeg, Manitoba, Canada, son of Samuel Levi, broker, and his wife Flora, née Davis. From playing the xylophone in his school band, young Levi progressed to the vibraphone in big bands touring the west coast of North America. He adopted the stage-name 'Sammy Lee', and became a band-leader and a club-owner in Canada. After touring Australia in 1937 as a drummer with the Americanadians band, he returned to Melbourne before settling at Potts Point, Sydney. He opened the Roosevelt nightclub at Potts Point in 1939, but sold out in 1946. Next year, with Perce Galea [q.v.14], he opened Sammy Lee's Theatre Restaurant in Oxford Street. By 1950 he also operated other clubs.

A large man, with a North American accent and a thin moustache, Lee smoked Cuban cigars and was known for his flamboyant clothes—bright coloured jackets worn over black shirts and trousers. He was described as generous, excitable and as hard as nails, and built his reputation on a high standard of service and entertainment featuring overseas artists and 'nubile nymphs' in singing and dancing acts. Divorced from his Canadian wife Rachel, he married Joy Florence Joynton Rolfe on 29 April 1941 at the Court House, Manly. He changed his surname by deed poll to Lee on 23 January 1951.

Adverse publicity from his appearances in court affected Lee's business. In 1952 his first wife sued for arrears of maintenance; his company, Lee Enterprise Pty Ltd, was found to have used employees' tax deductions for its own purposes. He gave evidence before the royal commission of inquiry into the liquor laws: Judge Maxwell [q.v.] found that the Roosevelt and Sammy Lee's had sold black-market liquor; Lee was indicted for perjury and eventually acquitted in 1954.

Lee's ventures soon prospered: he brought Disney's Mousketeers to Australia in 1959 and added the Latin Quarter Restaurant in Pitt Street to his holdings. In 1963, in part-nership with Lee Gordon [q.v.14] and Reg Boom, he opened his most famous nightclub, Les Girls Restaurant, at Kings Cross. Men, dressed as women, mimed and danced in its all-male revue. Lee took over the sole running of Les Girls in 1964. He displayed a talent for discovering and naming 'drag queens', like the legendary 'Carlotta', and turned the club and the show into a Sydney institution. By the early 1960s, however, Lee's clubs were suf-fering through competition from suburban Returned Service League and Rugby League clubs. In 1965 he turned the Latin Quarter into a discotheque, but business fell off dra-matically following the shooting there of an underworld figure in 1967. Lee was forced to turn the club into the Cheetah Room. The problems he faced at the Latin Quarter were symptomatic of the growth of illegal casinos and gang wars in the entertainment industry.

Divorced again in January 1957, Lee married a 26-year-old actress Maureen Ethel Grant on 18 September that year at the office of the government statist, Melbourne. By 1963 he had moved his family from Greenowe Avenue, Potts Point, to Watsons Bay. Once known as 'the King of the Cross', Lee found himself out of touch and described the area as 'bloody dangerous' for unescorted women. He died of myocardial infarction on 21 July 1975 in a Vaucluse hospital and was buried in the Jewish section of Rookwood cemetery. His wife, their son and daughter, and the son of his first marriage survived him.

Royal Commission of Inquiry into the Liquor Laws and Allied Subjects, 2 (Syd, 1954); D. Hickie, *The Prince and the Premier* (Syd, 1985); C. and J. Cockington, *He did it her way* (Syd, 1994); *SMH*, 19, 20 Feb, 5, 8, 30 Apr, 2, 4 July, 19-21 Oct, 25 Nov 1952, 20 Jan 1953, 23 Feb, 19 Mar, 22-24 June 1954, 10 June 1959, 22 July 1975; *Sun-Herald* (Syd), 24 Oct 1954, 7 Aug 1955, 7 Mar 1965.   GERARD OAKES

LEFROY, SIR ANTHONY LANGLOIS BRUCE (1881-1958) and SIR EDWARD BRUCE HENRY (1887-1966), pastoralists, were born on 20 April 1881 and 22 May 1887 in Perth, first and second sons of (Sir) Henry Bruce Lefroy [q.v.10], pastoralist and later premier, and his first wife Rose Agnes, née Wittenoom, grand-daughter of J. B. Witte-noom [q.v.2]. A. O. Lefroy [q.v.5] was their grandfather. The boys were educated at the High (later Hale [q.v.4]) School, Perth, and Haileybury College, Hertfordshire, England. Returning to Western Australia, Edward worked as a jackeroo on his uncle Frank Wittenoom's [q.v.12] Boolardy station, then being managed by Langlois. In 1906 Witte-noom obtained merino ewes and lambs from the Boonoke stud in New South Wales and in 1909 Edward moved to the Midlands to develop Cranmore Park, some 10 000 acres (4050 ha) of virgin country near Walebing, his father's property. Langlois bought Coodardy station in the Murchison district in 1913 and later acquired Hillview farm at Chittering. On

26 June 1915 at the bishop's chapel, Perth, Edward married with Anglican rites Beatrice Edith Vincent.

In England, on 18 December 1915, Langlois was commissioned in the (Royal) Army Service Corps. Serving on the Western Front as adjutant, 31st Divisional Train, he was promoted captain and awarded the Military Cross. On 7 June 1919 at the register office, Kensington, London, he married French-born Callista Adèle Charlotte Emilie Courouble. Meanwhile in 1917 Edward had transferred sheep from the Boonoke stud to Walebing where they provided the nucleus of the Cranmore Park flock. A leading Australian sheep stud, Cranmore Park was also noted for its production of superior grain. In the 1920s Edward's pastoral interests expanded to include Badja station at Yalgoo and the Mount Malcolm Pastoral Co. Ltd. He aimed to improve his stock as a whole, rather than preparing individual sheep for exhibition, and his multiple-pen entries excelled at the Royal Agricultural Society of Western Australia's annual shows throughout the 1930s. In 1939 he introduced into Western Australia a technique of mulesing as a measure against flystrike; he consistently used genetic breeding to strengthen his sheep for dry conditions; and in 1949 he underwrote the visit to Australia of the Dutch geneticist A. L. Hagedoorn.

After World War I Langlois Lefroy had managed his properties from Perth. An astute businessman, he became a director (1918) and chairman (from 1944) of the West Australian Trustee Executor & Agency Co. Ltd. He also chaired the board of advice of the State branch of the Bank of New South Wales. Elected (1924) to the executive-committee of the Western Australian Pastoralists' Association (president 1936-53), he represented the State on the Australian Wool Board. In his youth Langlois had been a skilled horseman; he retained a long association with polo, and with hunting and racing. He and Wittenoom owned Coolbarro, winner of the 1930 Perth Cup, and Yaringa which won the Western Australian Derby (1935) and St Leger (1936). Langlois commanded (1940-43) the 19th Garrison Battalion in Western Australia and rose to temporary lieutenant colonel. In 1944 he chaired the State division of the Australian Red Cross Society. Tall and athletic, and distinguished in appearance, he was known as 'one of the finest members of one of the finest families'. As chairman of directors of West Australian Newspapers Ltd he handled its affairs firmly and with habitual tact.

Edward Lefroy had served on the Moora Road Board for twenty-five years (chairman 1921 and 1930-35), and been active in the Moora Agricultural Society and the Midlands District Sheepbreeders' Association. The on-set of arthritis restricted his participation in sport, but he supported the Bindi Bindi Aboriginal cricket team founded by his father. Resenting the continuation of protective tariffs as the Depression deepened, he was vice-chairman (1930-33) of the State's secessionist Dominion League. He was a member (from 1929) and chairman (1934-43) of the State committee of the (Commonwealth) Council for Scientific and Industrial Research and was co-opted (1945) to the council of the Commonwealth Scientific and Industrial Research Organization; he was also a member (1945-57) of the senate of the University of Western Australia, a board-member of the Fairbridge [q.v.8] Farm School and a fellow of the Royal Society of Arts, London.

The Lefroys were influential in founding the university's Institute of Agriculture. Edward donated money for research into medicine, sheep and clover. A thoughtful man of quiet demeanour, he belonged to the Weld Club, and was generally liked and respected. Langlois was knighted in 1952 and Edward in 1955. Sir Langlois died on 2 November 1958 in Perth; his wife survived him. Sir Edward died on 10 September 1966 at Colvin House, Round Hill; his wife and three sons survived him. Both brothers were buried in Karrakatta cemetery. Their estates were sworn for probate at £286 758 and $290 223 respectively.

G. H. Burvill, *Agriculture in Western Australia* (Perth, 1979); *Pastoralist and Grazier* (Perth), Nov 1958; Univ WA, *Univ News*, 16, no 1, 1966; *West Australian*, 3 Nov 1958, 27 Mar 1978; *Countryman* (Perth), 15 Sept 1966; news-clippings (West Australian Newspapers L); information from Dr R. B. Lefroy, Mosman Park, Perth, and Mr P. Lefroy, Chittering, WA.   WENDY BIRMAN

LE GALLIENNE, DORIAN LEON MARLOIS (1915-1963), composer, was born on 19 April 1915 at Armadale, Melbourne, only child of Dorian Reginald Harold Ronald Le Gallienne, a French-born actor, and his wife Charlotte Edith Estella, née White, daughter of the assistant-astronomer at the Melbourne Observatory. Stella, as she was known, had studied piano and conducting with G. W. L. Marshall-Hall [q.v.10]. A committed suffragette, she met Le Gallienne in 1914 at a meeting of the Women's Social and Political Union in Melbourne and married him that year. The relationship broke up in 1924, a year after the family had travelled to England. Stella returned home with her son in 1928 and enrolled him at Melbourne Church of England Grammar School. He completed the Intermediate certificate in 1930.

At the age of 16 Dorian was diagnosed as a diabetic. Excused regular attendance at school, he studied privately. The Le Gallienne home was 'a cultured household of refined values' and, under his mother's guidance, he took to reading, especially the poetry of Blake, Donne and Shakespeare. His imagination also ranged into an emerging world of musical possibilities, again prompted and encouraged by his mother.

In 1938 and 1939, following basic training at the University Conservatorium of Music, Le Gallienne studied at the Royal College of Music, London, first with Arthur Benjamin [q.v.7] and later with Herbert Howells. Back in Australia, he worked during World War II for the Commonwealth Department of Information in the overseas broadcasting service. After the war he joined the staff of the Australian Broadcasting Commission and taught materials of music at the University Conservatorium.

From about 1937 Le Gallienne had composed intermittently. His early works included sonatas for flute (1943) and violin (1945), *Contes Heraldiques* (1947), and *Four Divine Poems of John Donne* (1950). He also wrote small ensemble pieces for amateur productions of Shakespeare. In 1951 he won a Commonwealth Jubilee music scholarship which enabled him to study (1951-53) with the English composer Gordon Jacob. Some commentators argue that this further exposure to English music had a debilitating effect, leading to a derivative and unsatisfactory musical style. There is no doubt that Le Gallienne was influenced by a pastoral Englishness, but his works show a sophisticated independent spirit and liveliness that was not present in many Australian composers who preceded him.

On his return to Melbourne, Le Gallienne taught harmony and composition at the University Conservatorium, wrote as music critic (1954-63) for the *Age*, and continued to compose. His most important compositions of this period included *Overture* in E flat (1952), a symphony (1953), *Voyageur*, a ballet (1954), *Duo* for violin and viola (1956), *Sinfonietta* (1956), and a trio for oboe, violin and viola (1957). In addition to these substantial compositions, there were numerous occasional scores and incidental music for plays.

Towards the end of his life Le Gallienne lived with Professor Richard Downing [q.v.14] in a mud-brick house built for them by the architect Alistair Knox on 300 acres (120 ha) that they had jointly purchased at Eltham in 1948. Le Gallienne had known Downing for many years and had travelled with him in Europe in 1939. At Eltham, in conjunction with Tim Burstall and Patrick Ryan, who had formed Eltham Films, Le Gallienne had the opportunity of returning to the composition of occasional music. Eltham's cosmopolitan atmosphere, tolerance and gentle bohemianism suited the composer.

Le Gallienne's life at this time was stable and contented, qualities that are reflected in his self-assured film scores. His music for Burstall's *The Prize* (1960), a film which won a bronze medal at the Venice Film Festival, was the first of a number of significant film and television scores. The music for *The Dance of the Angels* (1962), which presented several ceramic sculptures of John Perceval in a stylish A.B.C. documentary, quickly followed, as did that for a similar documentary treatment of 'The Crucifixion' (1962), Matchum Skipper's sculptured Stations of the Cross. Both of these scores demonstrate a confident, eclectic style well matched to the filmed images: there is a raucous medievalism evident in the music for the dancing angels, while the score for 'The Crucifixion' is angular and scarifying. Working closely with the films' director, Le Gallienne was able to craft scores which became a crucial component of the whole conception. Music for an episode of an A.B.C. children's television series, 'Sebastian and the Sausages', was among his last compositions.

Suffering from coronary sclerosis, Le Gallienne died suddenly on 27 July 1963 at South Yarra and was buried in Eltham cemetery, below the towers of Justus Jorgensen's [q.v.14] Montsalvat. In 1967 the music critic Roger Covell argued that Le Gallienne's symphony was 'still the most accomplished and purposive . . . written by an Australian'. The *Sinfonietta* and *Contes Heraldiques* were recorded by the A.B.C. and frequently broadcast in the 1960s and 1970s. One of Le Gallienne's earliest compositions, *Nocturne* for piano (1937), has remained popular and was recorded by Vera Bradford for the Columbia Co.'s Australian label. The *Duo* for violin and viola is still included in recital programmes. Sound recordings of the film music, the *Voyageur* ballet, the *Four Divine Songs of John Donne* (with the contralto Lauris Elms and the pianist Marie Van Hove) and a number of orchestral compositions recorded by the A.B.C. (under the baton of John Hopkins) have also helped to keep some of Le Gallienne's compositions alive in the years since his death.

R. Covell, *Australia's Music* (Melb, 1967); J. Murdoch, *Australia's Contemporary Composers* (Melb, 1972); G. Loughlin, *Cities of Departure* (Melb, priv print, 1984); J. M. Brownrigg, 'Seeking the Prize: Some Background to the Film Music of Dorian Le Gallienne', in N. Brown (ed), *One Hand on the Manuscript* (Canb, 1995); Le Gallienne papers (LaTL).   JEFF BROWNRIGG

LEGG, FRANK HOOPER (1906-1966), journalist and broadcaster, was born on 26 June 1906 at Walmer, Kent, England, son of

Francis Ellis Legg, schoolmaster, and his wife Ethel Annie, née Hooper. Frank was educated (1916-24) at Sir Roger Manwood's School, Sandwich; he passed the London General Schools' honours certificate in 1922 and gained full colours for soccer, hockey, Rugby and cricket. Employed by the Bank of England, he 'was a banker by day and writer by night'. He reached Brisbane on 28 June 1927 in the *Largs Bay*, having earned his passage as a supervisor for the Big Brother Movement. Arriving penniless, he worked in Sydney, Melbourne and Adelaide as a free-lance writer and insurance officer. On 4 July 1929 he married with Anglican rites Evelyn Amy Bragg at Christ Church, St Kilda, Melbourne; they were later divorced and he was estranged from his only child Richard. In 1937 Legg joined the Adelaide *News*. As 'The Prattler' he began giving talks for the Australian Broadcasting Commission, and, with Horace Miller, conducted the 'Early Morning Session' and 'Hospital Half-Hour' which were relayed nationally.

On 26 July 1940 Legg enlisted in the Australian Imperial Force. He served as a sergeant in the 2nd/48th Battalion, saw action at Tobruk, Libya, and Tel El Eisa, Egypt, and by September 1942 was regimental sergeant major. His series of articles, 'Tales of Tobruk', appeared in the *A.B.C. Weekly*. In a broadcast, 'The Worst Day', made in Australia in April 1943, he related his experiences on 31 October 1942 in the battle of El Alamein: with shells screaming overhead, blasting his ear-drums and wrenching his teeth, he had prayed for courage to meet his end decently. In this, and in future reports, he revealed his admiration for and understanding of fighting men as he described their tears, death, deser-tion and bravery. At El Alamein his battalion had sustained 346 casualties, yet he said he '*couldn't* hate' the Germans.

Commissioned lieutenant in September 1943, Legg was training in Queensland when he was asked to be the A.B.C.'s war corre-spondent in the Pacific. His A.I.F. appoint-ment terminated on 15 December. He was happily surprised to receive a good salary and reached New Guinea on 6 January 1944. 'The bulky equipment and hot humid conditions made recording extremely difficult as Legg and his radio operator, Bill MacFarlane, joined the 9th Division on the Huon Cam-paign'. Recording at the front and reporting hand-to-hand fighting with the Japanese, Legg praised the footsloggers' courage, ten-acity and humour in the jungle conditions. He especially admired the heroism and dedi-cation of the stretcher-bearers. On 1 May 1945 he recorded material for a documentary on the invasion of Tarakan, Borneo: it included soldiers in the troopship, *Manoora*, singing to the tune, *Lili Marlene*, and interviews with

General Sir Thomas Blamey and the Victoria Cross winner Tom Derrick [qq.v.13]. On 15 August Legg left Manila for Tokyo where he witnessed the Japanese surrender aboard the U.S.S. *Missouri* on 2 September.

After the war Legg built up a reputation from Sydney as a radio and television panel chairman and compere—his voice became one of the best known on A.B.C. radio. His popular programmes included 'Week-End Magazine' (1946-59), 'Film Review' (1949-66) and 'Any Questions' (1955-64). He also made documentary and feature programmes, par-ticularly on wartime subjects. In 1961 he was co-editor and associate-producer of the television series, 'Anzac', shown on ATN-7 to mixed reviews. He published several books, among them *The Eyes of Damien Parer* (Adelaide, 1963), *War Correspondent* (Adelaide, 1964), *The Gordon Bennett Story* (1965) and *Cats on Velvet* (1966). Legg post-humously shared the 1964-65 Journalists' Club award for his biography of Frank Hurley [q.v.9], *Once More on my Adventure*, written with Hurley's daughter Toni.

Elegant, warm and self-effacing, with a strong sense of mateship, Legg was closely associated with the Spastic Centre, Mosman. His reports of the human face of war showed compassion for man's vulnerability. Legg had married 33-year-old Elva Henrietta Gregory on 8 October 1949 at St Stephen's Presby-terian Church, Macquarie Street. He died on 30 March 1966 at Hornsby hospital from injuries received as a passenger in a motorcar accident and was cremated with Methodist forms; his wife survived him, as did the son of his first marriage.

B. Maughan, *Tobruk and El Alamein* (Canb, 1966); K. S. Inglis, *This is the ABC* (Melb, 1983); *ABC Weekly*, 1940; *ABC Radio Guide*, 12 Apr 1966; *SMH*, 31 Mar, 1, 6 Apr, 14 June 1966; ABC Docu-ment *and* Radio Archives, Syd; F. Legg papers (ML); information from Mr R. Legg, Forestville, Syd, and Sir Roger Manwood's School, Sandwich, Kent, Eng.
MARION CONSANDINE

LEGGATT, SIR WILLIAM WATT (1894-1968), soldier, lawyer and politician, was born on 23 December 1894 on Malekula Island, New Hebrides (Vanuatu), eldest child of Thomas Watt Leggatt, a missionary from Scot-land, and his Australian-born wife Margaret Muter, née Wilson. Thomas was to become moderator (1931) of the Presbyterian Church of Victoria. Bill received his early education in the New Hebrides. In 1907 the family moved to Victoria where he entered Geelong College and Ormond [q.v.5] College, University of Melbourne (B.A., 1915; LL.B., 1920). He gained a scholarship to study for the ministry, but suspended his course and enlisted in the Australian Imperial Force on 6 August 1915.

After serving in Egypt, Leggatt was sent to the Western Front in June 1916. In the following month he was commissioned and posted to the 60th Battalion. A further promotion to lieutenant came in May 1917. Employed as a signalling officer, he won the Military Cross for maintaining communications while under heavy shell-fire at Villers Bretonneux, France, on 8 August 1918. He was transferred to the 59th Battalion on 25 September. Two days later he was wounded in the right arm. His A.I.F. appointment terminated in Melbourne on 22 June 1919.

Leggatt re-entered university determined to pursue law rather than theology, a decision which placed him in financial difficulties. A loan from the Department of Repatriation enabled him to complete his studies, and he eventually repaid his scholarship money to the Presbyterian Church. Admitted as a solicitor on 1 March 1921, he practised successively at Kyabram, Rushworth and Murrayville. In 1926 he moved to Mornington which remained his home town. At Burwood, Melbourne, on 21 September that year he married Dorothy Meares Andrews, a 32-year-old schoolteacher; his father conducted the service. A university graduate (B.A., 1916; M.A., Dip.Ed., 1918), Dorothy had edited (1917) *Melbourne University Magazine* and advocated the establishment of a women's college. She became a prominent member of the Lyceum Club.

From 1934 Leggatt was active in the Citizen Military Forces. On 1 July 1940 he was appointed major in the A.I.F. He served in Rabaul, Mandated Territory of New Guinea, from March 1941 as second-in-command of the 2nd/22nd Battalion. Promoted lieutenant colonel, he took command of the 2nd/40th Battalion in November. One month later the unit sailed from Darwin to reinforce the Dutch and Portuguese garrisons on Timor. Leggatt also had under his command elements of the 2nd/2nd Australian Independent Company and a battery of coast artillery, the combined body being known as 'Sparrow Force'.

Leggatt set up his headquarters near Koepang, the Dutch administrative centre, and soon found that his formation was seriously deficient in weapons, ammunition and communications. He also had to make the best of an impossible strategic position: although he realized that the Japanese might invade in large numbers, he lacked air and naval support necessary to combat such an assault. Leggatt was forthright in describing the military weaknesses of Sparrow Force to his superiors.

Plans for reinforcements were belatedly put in train, and Brigadier W. C. D. Veale [q.v.] reached Timor on 12 February 1942 to assume command of an expanded Sparrow Force. The Japanese invaded on the 20th, preventing the dispatch from Australia of the bulk of the additional troops. Leggatt's men made a 'spirited' defence. They successfully counter-attacked and captured the village of Babau, before succumbing to sustained air and ground assaults from superior enemy forces. The 2nd/2nd commandos continued to wage guerrilla warfare in Portuguese Timor until December.

When Leggatt had surrendered on 23 February 1942 he was virtually without food or ammunition. Communications failures had hampered his ability to make informed decisions about the best disposition of his troops. Like his fellow senior officers, he was untrained in tactics appropriate to mobile defence. None the less, the achievement of the 2nd/40th had been 'remarkable' in that heavy casualties had been inflicted on the enemy at relatively little cost.

In captivity at Usapa-Besar, Leggatt displayed skilful leadership in protecting the interests of his men and ensuring that discipline was maintained. He also seized on the lax security at the camp to encourage foraging and intelligence-gathering expeditions. In July 1942 he and other officers were taken to Java before being sent to Changi camp, Singapore.

Renowned for paying little attention to 'spit and polish' presentation, or to the traditional formalities of rank, Bill Leggatt discomfited his senior officer (Sir) Frederick Galleghan [q.v.14] at Changi by wearing a 'broken peaked cap, old golf shoes and shorts with a hip pocket torn down and his bottle of chilli sauce in it'. Leggatt suffered many privations, but maintained a certain dignity and a sense of humour. He kept a nominal roll of all 2nd/40th Battalion prisoners who passed through Singapore. Released in September 1945, he was awarded the Distinguished Service Order (1947) and mentioned in dispatches. In 1958, when he revisited Changi, he remarked: 'it wasn't all bad. I learned a lot there . . . you learn tolerance. You learn reliance—to maintain yourself on the resources of your own mind'.

From April to September 1946 Leggatt was based in Melbourne as officer-in-charge of war-crimes investigations. He transferred to the Reserve of Officers in October. Resuming his legal practice, he was admitted to the Bar on 1 November. In 1947 he won the seat of Mornington in the Victorian Legislative Assembly for the Liberal Party. He served in the Hollway [q.v.14] ministry as chief secretary (7 December 1948 to 19 June 1950), and briefly held responsibility for works, lands and soldier settlement (19-27 June 1950). As chief secretary, Leggatt supported prison reform and the easing of liquor laws, but the government fell before legislation could be introduced. He was more conservative on the question of film censorship, declaring in 1950 that 'there is no place for anti-British films in Victorian theatres'.

In (Sir) Henry Bolte's government, Leggatt held the portfolios of education and immigration (8 June 1955-2 February 1956); for two days in June 1955 he was attorney-general and minister of labour and industry. Active in the Mornington community, he was a founder (1937) of the King George V Memorial Bush Nursing Hospital, and a member (1947-55) and president (1952-53) of the shire council.

Leggatt resigned from parliament in February 1956 to become Victorian agent-general in London. He did not treat the post as a sinecure and proved a vigorous promoter of his State. In 1957 he was knighted. Solidly built and of ruggedly distinguished appearance, he possessed an easy-going charm and was a fluent speaker. At the conclusion of his term in 1964, the *Age* commended him for his 'imagination and drive'. Retiring to Mornington, Sir William died on 27 November 1968 in the Repatriation General Hospital, Heidelberg; he was accorded a state funeral and was cremated. His wife, daughter and two sons survived him.

'Timor' in P. Dennis et al (eds), *The Oxford Companion to Australian Military History* (Melb, 1995); P. Henning, *Doomed Battalion* (Syd, 1995); *PD* (Vic), 28 Nov 1968, p 2333; *Age* (Melb), 7 July 1955, 5 Jan 1956, 10 July 1964, 28, 29 Nov 1968.

GEOFF BROWNE

LEGGETT, EMILY (1875-1949) and JOSEPH HENRY (1876-1960), ballroom-dancing promoters, were wife and husband. Emily was born on 14 April 1875 in Melbourne, fifth child of English-born parents Henry Cohen, saddler, and his wife Mary Ann, née Eggleton. Harry was born on 20 April 1876, also in Melbourne, tenth child of Samuel Leggett, a coachsmith from England, and his Irish-born wife Rosina, née Nangle. The Leggett family was poor. Harry grew up on the streets of the city learning many of the skills he later used as a professional entertainer. He entered competitions and played at several Melbourne theatres where he earned a name as a promising dancer and comedian.

Henry Cohen taught his children to play musical instruments. He formed a troupe of young musicians, the Premier Juvenile Variety Company, which performed in the suburbs. In 1892 Harry Leggett was invited to join the troupe; he remained with it until the company was disbanded after Cohen's death in 1895. Harry often appeared at Melbourne's Bijou and at the Opera House (later the Tivoli). Emily, who showed talent as a dancer, teamed up with him. As a duo, they performed variety acts in Melbourne, Brisbane and Sydney. They were married on 7 March 1899 at 422 Queen Street, Melbourne, with the forms of the Free Christian Church. Both continued their stage careers, and Emily taught music; their son and daughter were part of theatrical life from infancy.

Harry and Emily attempted several ventures of their own: they taught dancing at Collingwood, staged variety shows at the local town hall and operated an unsuccessful open-air cinema in Johnston Street. Following some financial set-backs, they moved to Hampton. Harry then took an engagement in Hobart while Emily stayed and taught dancing. When he returned in 1907, they moved to Windsor where they opened a dancing academy. The venture prospered and they organized balls at the Albert Hall, Windsor, and at the Prahran and St Kilda town halls.

During World War I the Leggetts supported the Australian Red Cross Society and the Prahran Patriotic Society. In 1920 they built a ballroom of their own in Greville Street, Prahran. Over the next decade they acquired more property nearby. The family lived on the premises and many of their staff were housed in the cottages they bought. The ballroom was gradually enlarged until it could accommodate four thousand people. There they trained thousands of dancers, organized national and international competitions, introduced new dances, and staged variety shows and balls. About one hundred dancers were hired to assist them and the ballroom was crowded six nights a week. Formal dress was obligatory in the evenings and behaviour was monitored. No intoxicating liquor was allowed on the premises. Half an hour before the official dancing began, free tuition was given.

The Leggetts showed their public spiritedness in numerous ways. In the Depression they organized free dancing in the afternoons, and at night those without the full admission price of 1s. 6d. (two shillings on Saturdays) were never turned away. In World War II the Leggetts organized patriotic shows and balls, paying the costs from their own pockets. Those in uniform were admitted free, and many servicemen were bedded down and served breakfast next morning. Constant innovation made Leggett's a popular ballroom. On particular nights the hall was decorated to illustrate such themes as 'A Night in Hades', 'An Evening in Paris', or 'Circus Night'. Prizes were generous. In the early 1950s Leggett's became the heart of Melbourne's square-dance boom.

It was very much a family business. Emily and Harry managed the ballroom until their retirement in 1942, after which their son Phillip took over. The Leggetts continued to offer hospitality to friends and young artists, and to show interest in dancing and entertainment. Harry was a justice of the peace and a police magistrate; Emily was vice-president of the St John's Home for Boys. She died on 29 January 1949 at her Brighton home. Survived by their son, Harry died on 2 January 1960 in East Melbourne. Both were buried in Melbourne general cemetery.

P. Leggett, *The Leggett Family and their Famous Ballroom in Prahran* (Melb, 1988) and *Select Your Partners*, L. McCalman and B. Malone eds (Melb, 1991); *Age* (Melb), 11 Nov 1946, 31 Jan 1949; *A'sian Post*, 6 July 1950; *Sun News-Pictorial*, 6 Oct 1956.

BETTY MALONE

LE GRAND, HENRICUS ALEXANDER THEODORUS (1921-1978), potter and teacher, was born on 10 May 1921 at Zevenaar, the Netherlands, son of French-Dutch parents Petrus Egidius Hubertus Le Grand, labourer, and his wife Elisabetha Antoinetta, née van Haren. After studying (1938-42) art and ceramics at the Instituut voor Kunstnijverheidsonderwijs te Amsterdam, Henri gained practical experience with the potter Emile Regout at Maastricht and in the Goedewagen factory at Gouda. He also worked as a sculptor, and his early interest in sculptural form continued to influence his pots throughout his career. Le Grand became a member of the Dutch Guild of Potters and began to use the seal which appears on some of his work. On 11 May 1944 at Amsterdam he married Hendrika Engelina Rademaker; they were to have five children before being divorced.

Emigrating from the Netherlands in 1950, the Le Grands initially settled in Sydney. Henri took a number of jobs until 1954 when he was appointed to the staff of East Sydney Technical College. In the following year he was transferred to the Canberra Technical College as part-time ceramics teacher. He was naturalized in 1955. By 1961 he was chief art teacher at the college. A capable and efficient teacher, he also designed a kick-wheel, suitable for children, which was produced commercially.

Le Grand had been trained in the tradition of well-designed, functional, high-fired stoneware; he disliked casting and the type of decoration which relies on applied appendages and bright glazes for its effect. Placing emphasis on sure, firm shapes, achieved by hand-building or throwing on a wheel, he was admired for his restrained use of glaze for decoration and for his simple, strong and elegantly shaped pots. From the mid-1960s his work showed increasing differentiation between purely functional ware and art pots, and he also experimented with surface decoration.

In addition, Le Grand liked to produce his own clay bodies and used clay from Black Mountain, Canberra—sometimes mixed with commercial bases and other ingredients—to produce a medium for students' work. His use of local clays and minerals, and of native timbers for firing, interested critics of his own work. He experimented with clays and minerals found near Yass, New South Wales, and even brought clay from the Northern Territory. In 1956 his pots were included in the Fine Arts Exhibition of the Melbourne Olympic Arts Festival. Thenceforward he exhibited extensively. Reviews of his work were generally favourable.

On 23 February 1968, at Canberra Community Hospital, Le Grand married Jean Margaret Bastin, née Andrews, a library officer and a divorcee. Retiring in November due to poor health, he lost interest in pottery, partly due to the physical demands of the medium, and turned to restoring vintage cars. In 1969 he was appointed M.B.E. for services to the arts. That year a retrospective exhibition of his work was held at the Canberra Theatre Gallery. Survived by his wife, and by the three sons and two daughters of his first marriage, Le Grand died of myocardial infarction on 29 November 1978 at Canberra Hospital and was cremated with Anglican rites. His work is represented in the National Gallery of Australia, Canberra, and other public collections.

Retrospective Exhibition of the Pottery of Henri Le Grand, exhibition cat (Canb, 1969); C. Menz, 'Henri Le Grand—Potter and Teacher', *Pottery in Aust*, 27, Aug 1988, p 27; *Territorial*, 9 Mar 1961; *Canb Times*, 25 Nov 1966, 23 May 1969; National Gallery of Aust (Canb) files.

CHRISTOPHER MENZ

LEMBERG, MAX RUDOLF (1896-1975), biochemist, was born on 19 October 1896 at Breslau, Germany (Wroclaw, Poland), elder son of Justizrat Dr Arthur Lemberg, lawyer, and his wife Margarethe, née Wendriner. Rudi came from a liberal, cultured home where adherence to the Jewish religion was more 'a matter of decent loyalty to one's forebears than a religious conviction'. Although law 'was a family tradition', there were scientists among his relations, including Albert Neisser who discovered the bacterium that causes gonorrhoea. A frail and over-protected child, Rudi was educated at home by a tutor and loved to roam the countryside. Soon his parents' flat was full of butterflies, lizards, frogs and tortoises. He attended the Johannes-Gymnasium and from May 1914 studied natural sciences at the University of Breslau (Ph.D., *summa cum laude*, 1922). His summers were spent at the universities of Munich (1915) and Heidelberg (1916). Lemberg had been initially rejected by the army on medical grounds, but was accepted on 2 June 1917. He served with the artillery in the German offensive of March 1918, was wounded, and won the Iron Cross (2nd class). While in France he became a Lutheran.

After World War I Lemberg returned to Breslau university, studied organic chemistry under Heinrich Biltz and submitted his doctoral thesis in October 1921. He was employed as Biltz's private assistant and published three papers with him. Poor prospects at German universities for a scientist of Jewish descent led Lemberg in 1923 to join Boehringer & Soehne, Mannheim, as an industrial chemist. In 1925 he was retrenched. He had married Hanna Adelheid Claussen on 23 December 1924 at Wroclaw; they were to remain childless.

Lemberg returned to the university at Heidelberg in 1926 to obtain a qualification which would allow him to lecture. In 1930 he was habilitated as *privatdozent*. On the recommendation of Professor Karl Freudenberg, he obtained a Rockefeller Foundation fellowship to work (1930-31) under Sir Frederick Gowland Hopkins at the Sir William Dunn Institute of Biochemistry, Cambridge, England, in the company of such outstanding scientists as Joseph Barcroft, David Keilin and Robin Hill. Back at Heidelberg in 1931, Lemberg established himself as one of the few experts on bile pigments. In 1933 the *Beamtengestez* ended his academic career in Germany. English friends and the Freudenbergs arranged for him to return to Cambridge and the haven of the Dunn Institute. He continued to systematize various bile pigment classes, but turned his attention 'from chemical structural to metabolic and functional aspects'. Thus began his gradual conversion from organic chemist to biochemist.

As the number of refugees increased, it became evident that not all of them could stay at Cambridge. In 1935 Lemberg accepted an appointment as director of the biochemical laboratories at Royal North Shore Hospital, Sydney. The decision was difficult and he saw it as the 'end' of his scientific career. He wrote: 'I went into the wilderness, for I did not expect inspiration from my Australian colleagues at that time. For many years I worked in an almost complete vacuum with little response'. At first he concentrated on the research he had initiated at Cambridge on the *in vitro* transformation of haemoglobin into bile pigments and summarized his ideas on the bile pigment problem in an article, 'Disintegration of haemoglobin in the animal body', in *Perspectives in Biochemistry* (Cambridge, 1937).

With colleagues such as J. W. Legge and W. H. Lockwood, Lemberg continued to study biological haemoglobin breakdown. When World War II had ended, he and Legge began

writing *Hematin Compounds and Bile Pigments* (New York, 1949). An immediate success, the book became a standard text for workers in the tetrapyrrole field and established Lemberg as a leading biochemist. It also attracted gifted co-workers to his laboratory, particularly when the National Health and Medical Research Council supported his research programme. From 1949 he studied the structure of prosthetic groups, especially those of cytochrome oxidase and cytochrome, and the biochemistry and chemical pathology of porphyrias. In these fields he made significant contributions which stimulated other investigators worldwide. Lemberg was assistant-director of the hospital's Institute of Medical Research from 1952 until he retired in 1972. With J. Barrett he published *Cytochromes* (London, 1973); like his earlier book, it was thoroughly researched and presented.

Although Lemberg worked independently, he was active in scientific circles and recognized as a world authority in his field. He was elected a fellow (1952) of the Royal Society, a foundation fellow (1954) and council-member (1956-58) of the Australian Academy of Science, foundation president (1955) of the Australian Biochemical Society, and president (1955) of the Royal Society of New South Wales which awarded him its James Cook [q.v.1] medal (1964) and Burfitt [q.v.7] prize (1971). Other distinctions included the H. G. Smith [q.v.11] medal (1948) of the Royal Australian Chemical Institute, appointment (1956) as professor emeritus by the University of Heidelberg, the Britannica Australia award for science (1966) and an honorary D.Sc. from the University of Sydney (1970).

Naturalized in 1937, Lemberg had sponsored the emigration of his brother Walter to Sydney in 1939. Rudi had built a home in an acre of virgin bush at Wahroonga. While he cherished native flora and enjoyed bushwalking in the national parks and Snowy Mountains in the wild-flower season, he cultivated a garden of camellias, rhododendrons and azaleas. He was vice-president of the Occupied Europe Relief Society; he and his wife worked with Camilla Wedgwood [q.v.] to assist refugees.

Apart from his scientific research, Lemberg was engrossed in the fields of philosophy and religion. He reconciled his belief in science and religion through the concept of complementarity. A member of the Society of Friends, he delivered its 1966 James Backhouse [q.v.1] lecture and was prominent in public discussions of mankind's use of science. Lemberg was an idealist who spoke his mind forthrightly. He was also a dedicated pacifist (under continuing surveillance by Australian security), but, when it came to the question of Israel, his Jewishness clashed with the Quaker in him. Survived by his wife, he died on 10 April 1975 at his Wahroonga home and was cremated.

Encounter with Rudi Lemberg (priv print, Syd, 1975); *Annual Review of Biochemistry*, 34, 1965, p 1; *Records of the Aust Academy of Science*, 4, no 1, 1978, p 132; *Biog Memoirs of Fellows of Roy Soc* (Lond), 22, 1976, p 257, *and* for Lemberg's publications; *Search* (Syd), 6, no 10, 1975, p 404; Roy Soc of NSW, *J and Procs*, 1975, p 166; Roy Soc of NSW Archives, Syd; naturalization file A1/1 item 37/9065, *and* ASIO file, A6119/64 item 502 (AA, Canb); Lemberg papers (Basser L).   R. BHATHAL

LE MESSURIER, ALFRED ROY (1886-1946), company director, and FREDERICK NEILL (1891-1966), paediatrician, were born on 19 February 1886 and 12 January 1891 at Semaphore, Adelaide, third and fifth surviving children of South Australian-born parents Alfred Le Messurier, agent, and his wife, Jane Sinclair, née Neill. Both boys were educated at the Collegiate School of St Peter. At 16 Roy entered his father's shipping agency, A. & E. Le Messurier, where he specialized in importing timber from Tasmania for local furniture-makers and developed it into a significant enterprise. He later joined Thorold Wilhelm Gunnersen, a Melbourne-based importer of Baltic and North American softwoods. In 1915 they formed Gunnersen Le Messurier Ltd, an indent agency arranging direct sales from suppliers to South Australian clients for an agreed commission. Until 1920 the company had no premises; as managing director, Le Messurier operated from the offices of the family firm. At St Bede's Anglican Church, Semaphore, on 17 April 1912 he had married Margaret Galway Saunders.

Despite World War I, Gunnersen Le Messurier grew steadily. Demand for timber from South Australia's fledgling car industry, as well as the cooperage, building and furniture trades, provided scope for Le Messurier who, by 1921, was the main shareholder in his father's company. He imported quality timbers, such as Tasmanian oak, blackwood, sassafras, King Billy pine and beech. To supply Baltic pine to Melbourne, he helped to found (1925) Alstergren Pty Ltd, brokers and agents.

In July 1926 Le Messurier bought shares in Mathias & Co., furniture-makers, and in Lloyd's Timber Mills Ltd; both became important clients of Gunnersen Le Messurier Ltd. That year he backed a new retail timber merchant, Wadlow Ltd. Le Messurier also funded promising young timbermen and was described by an associate as 'the best picker of men he had ever met'. In 1927 he helped Norman Moore to buy Rosenfeld & Co. (South Australia) Ltd and a few months later assisted in the establishment of Cullity Timbers Ltd, Perth. He invested in South Australian and Western Australian salvage companies, and founded Moore Le Messurier Pty Ltd in Sydney in 1932.

On his father's death in 1927, Le Messurier had succeeded him as chairman, a position he retained for life. By the age of 41 he was a formidable figure in the timber industry. Although the sale of Tasmanian wood was the main source of Gunnersen Le Messurier's prosperity in the late 1930s, the import of North American oregon and hemlock, and New Zealand white pine, kauri pine and rimu also proved profitable. During World War II, when American hemlock was unavailable, Le Messurier investigated the use of locally grown *Pinus radiata*. With plywood, too, in short supply, he helped to establish Tasmanian Plywood Mills and Westralian Plywoods.

Outside office hours, Le Messurier led a comfortable but unostentatious life. He liked to mix work with relaxation and many of his business associates were his closest friends. As a young man he had enjoyed cricket and lacrosse; in addition, he played football for Port Adelaide and North Adelaide, and was vice-captain of the latter team in 1911 and 1913. In 1908 he had represented South Australia at an interstate Australian Rules football carnival held in Melbourne. Survived by his wife, and by three of his five sons, he died of cancer on 5 October 1946 at his Fitzroy home and was buried in Cheltenham cemetery; his estate was sworn for probate at £61 254. At St Mark's College, University of Adelaide, a bursary and a room are named after him.

Unlike his elder brother who was not scholastically minded, Frederick was a fine all-round student at St Peter's. A lieutenant in the cadets, a member of the debating society, a prefect (1907-08) and school captain (1908), he represented the school in athletics and skippered its football and cricket teams. He was Farrell scholar in 1905 and Young [q.v.6] exhibitioner in 1908. Le Messurier played for the North Adelaide Football Club in 1908-10 and 1913-14. Studying medicine at the University of Adelaide, he graduated with first-class honours (M.B., B.S., 1913; M.D., 1920) and became a resident medical officer at the (Royal) Adelaide Hospital.

On 7 October 1914 Le Messurier was appointed captain, Australian Army Medical Corps, Australian Imperial Force. He served at Gallipoli and in Egypt before joining the 12th Field Ambulance on the Western Front in March 1917. East of Hamel, France, on 8-10 August 1918 he evacuated wounded soldiers while under fire and won the Distinguished Service Order. Next month he was promoted temporary lieutenant colonel and placed in command of the field ambulance. Mentioned in dispatches, he returned to Adelaide where his A.I.F. appointment terminated on 17 April 1919.

Le Messurier accepted a post as a resident medical officer at the Children's Hospital, Melbourne, and developed an interest in paediatrics. At the chapel of his old school on 9 November 1920 he married Frieda Gwendoline James with Anglican rites. In 1922 he joined the staff of Mareeba Babies' Hospital, Adelaide, and later became an honorary medical officer. Ward 6A was to be named after him. He was honorary assistant-physician (from 1924) and honorary physician (1926-47) at Adelaide Children's Hospital; a member of the hospital's board, he served as deputy-president in 1947-58.

In the mid-1920s Le Messurier had observed the use of lactic-acid milk feeding at Washington University, St Louis, United States of America, a process which involved scalding cows' milk and adding a solution of glucose and lactic acid to make the milk more sterile and digestible for infants. He introduced the practice in South Australia and popularized it. Specializing as a paediatrician, he took particular interest in parent education, infant feeding and the management of pre-school children. He retained a connexion with St Peter's as its school doctor (1927-61). At the University of Adelaide he lectured (from 1935) on the medical diseases of children and was an occasional demonstrator in anatomy.

Mobilized in 1940, Le Messurier began full-time duty in command of the 105th Australian General Hospital, Adelaide, in December 1941. He was promoted temporary colonel in October 1942. His task was to establish the unit and supervise the construction of what later became the Repatriation General Hospital, Springbank (Daw Park). His personal contacts, including members of his family, were useful in obtaining building materials for the hospital, beyond those provided under contract, and his efforts and sense of purpose led to the successful completion of the project. He remained in command of the hospital until 1946. In an attempt to make the R.G.H. self-sufficient and to provide a form of therapy, staff and patients grew food and raised animals. Among his other achievements were the enclosure of eight sunrooms for the wards, and the construction of a bowling-green, bathing-box and canteen.

Le Messurier was a stocky man, widely known as Freddy and sometimes irreverently as 'Freddo the Frog'. Gifted with a keen sense of humour, he inspired confidence, and could be considerate and kind. Yet, he remained a strong disciplinarian, obsessed with detail and reluctant to delegate. Some thought him difficult and 'stuffed up with his own importance'. Despite being considered petty and pernickety, he was usually fair, reasonable

and popular. Survived by his only son, Le Messurier died on 20 May 1966 in Calvary Hospital, North Adelaide, and was cremated. His estate was sworn for probate at $94 994.

M. Barbalet, *The Adelaide Children's Hospital, 1876-1976* (Adel, 1975); J. Tregenza, *Le Messuriers of Port Adelaide* (Adel, 1991); P. Last, *The Repat* (Adel, 1994); Univ Adel, *Calendar*, 1914, 1921, 1926; *St Peter's College Mag*, May, Aug, Dec 1908, 1909, Dec 1961; *Aust Timber J*, Oct 1946; *MJA*, 1 Oct 1966; *Advertiser* (Adel), 21 May 1966; Univ Adel, staff records; information from Dr H. Jones, Beaumont, Adel.   BRIAN WIMBORNE

LEMPRIERE, GEOFFREY RAOUL (1904-1977), WILLIAM HENRY (1905-1979) and PETER LELAND (1910-1976), woolbuyers, were born on 3 May 1904, 5 August 1905 and 17 June 1910, the two eldest at Elsternwick and the youngest at Sandringham, Melbourne, sons of Victorian-born parents Audley Raoul Lemprière, woolbroker, and his wife Adelaide Maude, née Greene. T. J. Lemprière [q.v.2] was their great-grandfather. Geoffrey and William attended Grange Hill Open Air School, Sandringham, and Peter spent some time at Melbourne Church of England Grammar School before the three brothers were sent to Geelong Church of England Grammar School, Corio.

In 1921 Geoffrey travelled to Europe to study at L'Ecole de Commerce, Neuchâtel, Switzerland; he also gained experience in the wool industry in Italy, Belgium and Britain. Back in Australia, he joined his father's wool-buying firm, A. R. Lemprière Pty Ltd, spending most of his time at the Sydney office. Elected a director when his father died in 1931, he became the European representative, based in Belgium.

Geoffrey returned to Australia on the outbreak of World War II, served in the Australian Imperial Force for twelve months, then transferred to the Royal Australian Air Force in July 1941. He was promoted flying officer and posted to Rabaul as No.24 Squadron's intelligence officer shortly before New Britain fell to the Japanese in January 1942. During the allied evacuation he was separated from his comrades, captured and sent to Japan. Although ill-treated, he worked to maintain the morale of his fellow prisoners and was mentioned in dispatches. His R.A.A.F. appointment terminated in Australia on 22 February 1946.

After the war, an event that traumatized him, he resumed his work as the European representative of the family company. He retired in 1955. Two years later he served on the Australian trade mission to India. Living at Roger River in north-west Tasmania, he was State president of the Liberal Party, a member (1961-65) of its federal executive, president of the Tasmanian Arts Council and a breeder of horses. In 1969 he was appointed O.B.E. He died, unmarried, on 20 March 1977 at Shearwater and was cremated.

Like Geoffrey, William Lemprière had gone to Europe to study the wool industry. He joined the family firm in 1926 and was appointed a director in 1931. On 29 December 1932 he married Kathleen Elizabeth Griffiths with Anglican rites at All Saints Church, East St Kilda. A committee-member (1938-47) of the Victorian and South Australian Woolbuyers' Association, he was supervising wool appraiser for the Central Wool Committee in 1939-46. William was mobilized in the Militia in May 1941, but was released as a temporary sergeant in January 1942 because of his reserved occupation.

Chairman (1949-52 and 1955-57) of the Australian Council of Woolbuyers, William was a representative (1950-51) on the Commonwealth-United States of America Wool Conference. In 1951 he was appointed to deal with the British wool stockpile, a post he held until 1953; he was later a director (1963-70) of Containers Ltd. In 1961 he published *Matthew Flinders Square*, a plan for the civic development of Melbourne. He was appointed O.B.E. in 1964. Survived by his wife, daughter and son, he died on 20 September 1979 at Parkville and was cremated.

Peter Lemprière, the youngest brother, began his career in the wool industry with Gollin & Co. Pty Ltd. On 20 July 1937 at All Saints Church, East St Kilda, he married Lula Elizabeth Collins. He enlisted in the R.A.A.F. on 2 August 1940 and rose through the ranks as a wireless-telegraphy operator. Commissioned in December 1943, he was promoted flying officer and served at R.A.A.F. Headquarters, Melbourne, before his appointment terminated on 2 October 1945. After the war he joined the family company, Lemprière (Australia) Pty Ltd, and was chairman (1960-63) of the Australian Council of Wool Buyers. The establishment of the Australian Wool Industry Tripartite Council stemmed largely from his initiative, and he subsequently became its chairman. He was also a director of numerous companies, and chairman of John Foster (Australia) Pty Ltd and South Pacific Canneries Pty Ltd.

After his retirement Peter Lemprière worked as a spokesman for the Victorian Society for Crippled Children and Adults, of which he was a benefactor. A keen golfer, he was a committee-member of the Barwon Heads Golf Club. He died of coronary vascular disease on 27 September 1976 at Burnley and was cremated; his wife, son and two daughters survived him.

J. B. Payne and W. D. Lemprière, *A Monograph of the House of Lemprière* (priv pub, Melb, 1979); J. J. and R. S. Corfield and M. Collins Persse (comps), *Geelong Grammarians*, 2 (Geelong, Vic, 1998); *Corian*, June 1977; *Mercury* (Hob), 21 Mar 1977.

JUSTIN J. CORFIELD

LEONSKI, EDWARD JOSEPH (1917-1942), soldier and murderer, was born on 12 December 1917 at Kenvil, New Jersey, United States of America, sixth child of Russian-born parents John Leonski, labourer, and his wife Amelia, née Harkavitz. The family moved to East 77th Street, New York, during Edward's infancy. Leaving junior high school in 1933, he took a secretarial course and finished in the top 10 per cent of his class. He held several clerical jobs before working for Gristede Bros Inc. Superior Food Markets. When called up for military service on 17 February 1941, he left behind an unhappy family: a mother mentally unstable, two brothers with prison records and a third in a psychiatric hospital.

While stationed with the 52nd Signal Battalion at San Antonio, Texas, Leonski began to drink heavily, preferring such concoctions as whisky laced with hot peppers; he displayed his strength by vaulting on to bar counters and walking along them on his hands. About this time he tried to strangle a woman. The American authorities failed to comprehend the problem that they shipped to Australia in January 1942.

Arriving in Melbourne in February, Leonski was quartered at Camp Pell, Royal Park. He resumed his ferocious drinking and allegedly attempted to rape a woman in her St Kilda flat. Drunkenness led to thirty days in the stockade, but release was followed by another binge. On 3 May Mrs Ivy McLeod was found murdered in the doorway of a shop next to the Bleak House Hotel, Albert Park. Melbourne newspapers immediately dubbed it a 'Brownout Crime'. The unpopular wartime reduction of street lighting helped Leonski to commit two more murders undisturbed: of Mrs Pauline Thompson outside a city boarding-house on 9 May and of Mrs Gladys Hosking in Royal Park on the 18th. All three were throttled; all were older than the killer; and, though their genitals were exposed, none was sexually assaulted.

Efficient detective work and the evidence of a soldier in whom Leonski had confided led to his arrest on 22 May. Sensitive to relations with its American ally, the Curtin [q.v.13] government decided—after consultation with Britain and in the face of some strenuous opposition—that Leonski could be tried by a United States court martial. Following some dispute, he was declared sane, and was tried and found guilty on 17 July. Fair haired and of middle height, Leonski was powerfully built, boyish in appearance and cheerful in demeanour. He gave no explanation for his crimes, other than to say of one of his victims, 'I wanted that voice. I choked her'.

Held in the city watchhouse, he corresponded with a woman at Eltham, learned Oscar Wilde's 'The Ballad of Reading Gaol' and became a communicant of the Catholic Church. Leonski was hanged at Pentridge prison on 9 November 1942. His remains were finally buried in a military cemetery in Honolulu. Albert Tucker's painting, 'Memory of Leonski' (in his 'Image of Evil' series, 1943), is privately owned; Leonski was also the subject of a novel by Andrew Mellan (1979) and of a feature film, *Death of a Soldier* (1986).

I. Chapman, *Private Eddie Leonski, the Brownout Strangler* (Syd, 1982); M. McKernan, *All In!* (Melb, 1983); *People*, 30 Aug 1950; *Argus*, 4, 11-15, 20-29 May, 14-15 and 17-18 July 1942.　　PETER PIERCE

LESLIE, HUGH ALAN (1900-1974), newspaper editor and politician, was born on 17 April 1900 at Durban, Natal, South Africa, son of Charles Howard Roberts Leslie, a Scottish-born surgeon, and Helen Gibson. Hugh's parents died when he was very young and he was raised in an institution. Educated in South Africa at King Williams Town and at Grahamstown College, he raised his age and served in the South African armed forces in 1916-19. He worked as a railway clerk and journalist before emigrating to Victoria in 1923 and moving to Western Australia about four years later. By 1928 he was secretary of the Wyalkatchem branch of the Country Party. At St Saviour's Anglican Church, Wyalkatchem, on 26 December 1931 he married 21-year-old Isabel Margaret Dawson; they were to have seven children. He became editor of the *North-Eastern Wheatbelt Tribune* in 1931 and later its proprietor.

Selling Wheatbelt Press Ltd in 1939, Leslie took up the chairmanship of the Wyalkatchem District Patriotic Committee and the presidency of the local branch of the Returned Sailors' and Soldiers' Imperial League of Australia. He enlisted in the Australian Imperial Force on 29 June 1940 and was stationed in the Middle East with the 2nd/28th Battalion. An injury at Tobruk, Libya, in May 1941 led to his return to Australia and the amputation of his right leg. Discharged from the army on 7 March 1943, he won the Legislative Assembly seat of Mount Marshall for the Country Party on 20 November. He officiated as party whip and parliamentary party secretary, and was a member of the select committee that inquired into wool handling at appraisement centres in 1945. On 30 October 1949 he resigned from State parliament and on 10 December won the seat of Moore in the House of Representatives.

In 1952-58 Leslie was a member of the parliamentary Public Accounts Committee. His main opposition at the hustings came from the Liberal Party. He lost his seat to H. V. Halbert in 1958, but regained it—on preferences—in 1961. He stood down in 1963 because of his wife's ill health. In the aftermath of the 1964 Senate elections, Leslie was suspended from the County Party for five months for authorizing unofficial how-to-vote cards which were said to resemble Liberal Party pamphlets.

Outside parliament, Leslie belonged to the Rats of Tobruk and to the Civilian Maimed and Limbless Association. A co-founder, president and long-standing member of the State branch of the Spastic Welfare Association, he was also president of the British Commonwealth paraplegic games council. He chaired the committee of the first Commonwealth and Empire Paraplegic Games, held in Perth in 1962. Despite his disability, he gave 'boundless energy' to fishing, shooting and golf. Late in life he was active in the Gingin community while living at Lancelin. In 1967 he was appointed O.B.E.

Leslie was a 'peppery-tongued' but cheerful man with a quick sense of humour. He had worked hard in his electorate and as campaign manager for other Country Party politicians, including E. B. Johnston [q.v.9]. Survived by his wife, five daughters and one of his two sons, Leslie died on 2 September 1974 at the Repatriation General Hospital, Hollywood, and was cremated with the forms of the Churches of Christ.

J. C. Rice, *Wyalkatchem* (Wyalkatchem, WA, 1993); *West Australian*, 22 Oct 1963, 11 May 1965, 10 June 1967, 4 Sept 1974; information from the Hon. N. Baxter, Wooroloo, WA, and Mrs R. Stott, Viveash, Perth.　　DAVID BLACK

LESTER, MARY GRACE (1911-1980), political activist, was born on 23 January 1911 in Perth, daughter of Francis Scott, a clerk from Scotland, and his Sydney-born wife Grace Mary, née Turrell. Mary worked in a number of jobs before becoming a typiste. At St Mary's Catholic Cathedral, Perth, on 24 February 1936 she married Bernard Murtough Terry, a 30-year-old clerk. He served as a squadron leader in the Royal Australian Air Force during World War II and was killed in North Africa on 16 November 1942. To provide for their three sons, Mary returned to work. On 27 October 1944 at All Saints Church, Osborne Park, she married with Anglican rites Cecil Lester, a 26-year-old mechanic who had enlisted in the army. She gave birth to a daughter in 1946, but separated from her husband two years later. Mary's father moved in with her to help care for the children while she held a secretarial post at Royal Perth Hospital. Her petition for divorce was to be granted in 1955. In the late 1940s, having campaigned against the Cold War and called for nuclear disarmament, she joined the Communist Party of Australia.

The Western Australian branch (formed 1951) of the Union of Australian Women agitated against nuclear weapons. Lester became its secretary in 1955. In the following year she was appointed vice-president of the U.A.W.'s national committee. The union had links in Perth with the Native Welfare Council, the Combined Equal Pay Committee, the Western Australian Association for Children's Film and Television, and the women's committees of the Seamen's and Waterside Workers' federations. Women marched in Labour Day and May Day processions in that city and at Fremantle. In 1957 Lester joined other U.A.W. members in lunchtime marches on Fridays through the streets of Perth. They wore aprons and scarves, made from flour-sacks or shopping bags, which were inscribed with such slogans as 'Danger! Stop all bomb tests', 'Ban the A-bomb' and 'Mothers Join Us, Protest Too'. Street protests were forbidden under the Western Australia Police Act (1892). On 13 September 1957 five marchers, including Lester, were arrested. They were convicted on 10 October of carrying 'printed notices without permission in a public place'. Their appeal against the fines was upheld by the Supreme Court. The lunchtime marches continued until 6 August 1958, the thirteenth anniversary of the bombing of Hiroshima.

In June that year Lester visited Vienna as a national delegate to the World Congress of Women; she travelled to Moscow before returning home in November. As secretary (1960) of the International Women's Day committee, she invited German, French and Indonesian women activists to speak to U.A.W. members. In 1962 three Soviet women visited Perth for International Women's Day. Lester stood unsuccessfully (1963 and 1964) for election to the Perth Shire Council as a communist candidate.

In poor health, and perhaps sensing that it was time to make room for a younger woman, Lester resigned as State secretary of the U.A.W. in 1965. She travelled to Libya in 1979 to see the grave of her first husband. Survived by her four children, she died of myocardial infarction on 14 August 1980 in Royal Perth Hospital and was cremated.

L. Layman and J. Goddard, *Organise* (Perth, 1988); UAW (Melb), *Our Women*, Mar-May 1956, Sept-Nov 1959, Mar-May 1960, June-Aug 1961, Feb 1963, Mar 1964; *West Australian*, 11 Oct, 20 Nov 1957; UAW (WA branch) papers (PRO, Perth); Gilchrist papers (BL); information from Mr B. Terry, Wanneroo, Perth.   MICHAL BOSWORTH

L'ESTRANGE, WILLIAM MANDEVILLE ELLIS (1868-1951), electrical engineer and administrator, was born on 11 December 1868 in Dublin, son of Edgar William L'Estrange, solicitor, and his wife Mary Frances, née Henderson. Educated at Arnold House, Chester, England, William emigrated to Queensland in 1886. He worked as an assistant to the surveyor C. D. Dunne in 1887-93 before being employed by a relation, E. G. C. Barton [q.v.13], senior partner of Barton, White & Co. (later the Brisbane Electric Supply Co. Ltd and from 1904 the City Electric Light Co. Ltd). In 1898 L'Estrange visited England to negotiate purchases of equipment for the company. He studied electrical engineering in London and at Cologne, Germany, and gained professional experience in the United States of America.

Appointed secretary of Barton's firm in 1900, L'Estrange became its joint-manager and engineer in 1912. At St Philip's Anglican Church, Auburn, Sydney, on 20 March 1901 he had married Mary Emmeline Alder. He chaired the Queensland State Repatriation Board in 1915-20. When the Ipswich Electric Supply Co. Ltd was formed in association with C.E.L. in 1917, he was its secretary; he rose to managing director (1927) and chairman (1933). His wise and conservative leadership ensured that his companies were well placed to meet the increasing demand for electricity. Granted leave of absence in 1935, he retired in 1938.

L'Estrange had been a member of the Queensland Electrical Association and president (1911) of the Queensland Institute of Engineers. As a member of a committee formed by the Q.I.E. in 1914 to consider schemes for improved road construction and as president (1915-16) of the (Royal) Automobile Club of Queensland, he proposed the formation of a department of highways to control road-making. He also advocated a change in legislation to allow the reticulation of electricity supply by overhead rather than underground mains. In 1933-34 he was chairman of the Brisbane division of the Institution of Engineers, Australia. From 1922 he had been the institution's representative on the Great Barrier Reef Committee. He was a member (1913) of the Institution of Electrical Engineers and a fellow (1919) of the Chartered Institute of Secretaries, London.

Described as quiet and unassuming, L'Estrange took a close interest in Brisbane's public life. He was involved in the development of the University of Queensland as warden (1922-27) of the standing committee of council, a member (1927-35) of the senate and chairman (1928-34) of the buildings and grounds committee. In retirement he lived at Toowoomba. His recreations included golf and yachting. A widower, on 20 October

1949 at St Patrick's Catholic Cathedral, Toowoomba, L'Estrange married 57-year-old Elizabeth Mary McGee; like her husband, she was a former secretary of the Ipswich Electric Supply Co. Ltd. Survived by his wife, and by the son and three daughters of his first marriage, he died on 20 December 1951 at Toowoomba and was cremated; his estate was sworn for probate at £100 297.

Aust Hist Publishing Co, *Queensland and Queenslanders* (Brisb, 1936); R. L. Whitmore (ed), *Eminent Queensland Engineers* (Brisb, 1984); M. I. Thomis, *A History of the Electricity Supply Industry in Queensland*, 1 (Brisb, 1987); *Queenslander*, 9 June 1927; *Courier-Mail*, 21 Dec 1951, 23 Apr 1952; W. I. George and S. A. Prentice, Some References to Early Professional Engineering Societies in Queensland (1890-1919) (ms, 1989, Univ Qld L).

S. A. PRENTICE

LETCHER, VICTOR FREDERICK (1892-1968), public servant, was born on 22 July 1892 at Prahran, Melbourne, second son of Victorian-born parents John Hosking Letcher, clerk, and his wife Annie Marie, née Dale. Educated at Prahran College, he joined the Victorian Railways in 1910. After successively serving as secretary to commissioners E. B. Jones and W. M. Shannon, in 1925 he was appointed 'special officer' on the staff of (Sir) Harold Clapp [q.v.8], the chairman of commissioners. On 18 April that year Letcher married Sylvia Maie Ford at All Saints Anglican Church, St Kilda; they were to remain childless. In 1926-27 he spent eight months in the United States of America studying railway administration. He was promoted chief clerk for the Victorian Railways in 1929 and manager of publicity and tourist services in 1933.

In July 1939 an aircraft construction branch was formed within the Commonwealth Department of Supply and Development to manage the local manufacture of Beaufort bombers for the Royal Australian Air Force. Clapp was appointed general manager of the new branch and he made Letcher superintendent of administration. From March 1940 aircraft manufacture was under the control of a statutory body, the Aircraft Production Commission, with Letcher as its secretary. In January 1942 the A.P.C. was replaced by the aircraft advisory committee, of which Letcher was a member in his capacity as director of administration in the Department of Aircraft Production (established June 1941).

On 3 June 1946 Letcher was promoted departmental secretary, but in November the D.A.P. became a division of the Department of Munitions (later Supply) and he reverted to the status of assistant-secretary and director of aircraft production; he was also deputy-chairman of the board of aircraft factory administration which was established to provide technical direction. In the immediate postwar period he facilitated the introduction of jet aircraft into the R.A.A.F. and helped to negotiate licences for the local manufacture of Rolls Royce Nene and Avon turbo-jet engines, and the Canberra bomber. He accompanied (Sir) Lawrence Wackett, manager of the Commonwealth Aircraft Corporation Pty Ltd, on a visit to Britain and America in 1950. Their findings led the government to abandon the planned purchase of a British jet fighter in favour of the American Sabre, powered by Avon engines. Letcher again completed the legal and financial details to permit the aircraft's manufacture in Australia.

In 1953 he went to England to handle liaison duties for Australia's production of aircraft, munitions and guided weapons. Retiring from the public service in 1959, he founded French Aeronautics Pty Ltd which became the local representative of the Office Français D'Exportation de Matériel Aéronautique. Letcher's business interests took him on several trips to France, although travel aggravated his chronic asthma. Survived by his wife, he died on 17 April 1968 at his Toorak flat and was cremated. His estate was sworn for probate at $336 209. A tall, slim figure of neat and impressive appearance, Victor Letcher was remembered by those who worked with him as a remote and intensely private person.

D. P. Mellor, *The Role of Science and Industry* (Canb, 1958); L. J. Wackett, *Aircraft Pioneer* (Syd, 1972); A. T. Ross, *Armed and Ready* (Syd, 1995); *Herald* (Melb), 26 Jan 1927, 16 May 1942, 5 June 1946; *Argus*, 9 Jan 1942, 31 Jan 1947; *Age* (Melb), 18 Apr 1968; information from Mr L. F. Bott, Templestowe, and Mr E. R. Bennet, St Kilda, Melb.

C. D. COULTHARD-CLARK

LETTERS, FRANCIS JOSEPH HENRY (1897-1964), classicist and writer, was born on 6 December 1897 at Gympie, Queensland, eldest of four sons of Francis Lawrence Letters, a pharmacist from Scotland, and his Melbourne-born wife Sophie, née Bastian. His father had been educated in Belgium and his mother in Vienna. The family moved to Brisbane in 1906 (where Frank attended a Catholic school) and to Sydney in 1910. Continuing his education at Christian Brothers' College, Waverley, and the University of Sydney (B.A., 1918; M.A., 1921; LL.B., 1926), he graduated with first-class honours in Latin. He was coached in Greek by Christopher Brennan [q.v.7], whom he admired.

Disappointed at not being offered a position at the university, Letters studied law and coached students. He visited Europe in 1926. In addition to classical languages, he was fluent in French and German, and acquired some Spanish, sufficient Italian to master Dante and enough Hebrew to read the Old Testament. Back in Sydney, he was admitted to the Bar on 28 July 1927 and practised until 1937, while applying in vain for university posts. He coached Governor Sir Philip Game's [q.v.8] son, and enjoyed vice-regal patronage of his first slim book, *Darkness and Light and other Poems* (1934). At St Martha's Catholic Church, Strathfield, on 5 October 1933 he married Kathleen Mary Logue, a 23-year-old violinist.

In 1937 Letters obtained an acting-lectureship in Greek at the university. Early in 1938 he was appointed foundation lecturer in English and Latin at New England University College, Armidale; his salary of £400 was about half his combined earnings from the Bar and coaching. Greek was not taught at the college and he wrote acidly of the 'Greekless Athens of the North'. Letters published— sometimes privately—a scholarly work, *Virgil* (c.1943, revised, New York, 1946), poetry, *The Great Attainer* (1943) and *Aurora Australis* (Sydney, 1963), and one book of essays, *In a Shaft of Sunlight* (Sydney, 1948). He contributed verse and essays to *Southerly*, *Quadrant*, *Twentieth Century*, *A.B.C. Weekly* and *Catholic Weekly*, and also wrote for the Church. Only his major academic publication, *The Life and Work of Sophocles* (London, 1953), was well received in academic circles. In 1956 the National University of Ireland conferred on him an honorary D.Litt.

Widely read and enormously knowledgeable, Letters had a lively interest in all matters of the mind. His manner was gentle, his sense of humour quizzical and his laugh boisterous. He was 5 ft 8 ins (173 cm) tall, with brown, wavy hair which turned white in later years. He cultivated his legendary reputation as the 'absent-minded professor' because it left him largely free from the distractions of university politics, about which he cared not a whit. All the while he watched as men he believed less qualified obtained promotion. Appointed associate-professor in 1957, he was overlooked when the chair of classics was created in 1959. His indifference to administration counted against him, as did his attacks in the early 1950s on the ascendancy of economists and the 'rise of barbarism' in Australian universities.

Letters' Catholic faith was central to his life and work, and contemporaries remarked on the serenity it gave him. He shared with many Catholics a sense of being alienated from the culture of the majority and believed that anti-Catholic prejudice had blighted his academic career. In 1960 Pope John XXIII appointed him a knight of the Order of Saint Gregory the Great. Letters retired at the end of 1963. Survived by his wife and four daughters, he died of cancer on 23 September 1964 at Armidale and was buried in the local cemetery.

M. Kelly (ed), *For Service to Classical Studies* (Melb, 1966); K. Letters, *History Will Out* (priv pub Armidale, NSW, 1997); *UNE External Studies Gazette*, Oct 1964; *SMH*, 27 Apr 1960; *Northern Daily Leader*, 24 Sept 1964; Letters papers (NL); information from Mrs K. Letters, Armidale, NSW.
BRUCE MITCHELL

LEVANTE, THE GREAT; *see* COLE, LESLIE

LEW, ROBERT BATHURST (1891-1970), Methodist minister, was born on 2 January 1891 at West Tamworth, New South Wales, second child of native-born parents Robert Lew, railway-engine cleaner, and his wife Annie, née Jelbart. Educated at Lithgow, at Newcastle and at the Theological Institution, Newington College, Sydney, young Robert played football and tennis, and developed a lifelong interest in sport. The Church sent him to Coraki, Lismore and Gloucester as a probationary minister. From 1 May 1916 he served as a Young Men's Christian Association representative with the 9th Infantry Brigade, Australian Imperial Force; he also acted as a stretcher-bearer at Passchendaele, Belgium. Lew was ordained at Wesley's Chapel, London. On 1 May 1918 he was commissioned honorary lieutenant; from March 1919 he was a chaplain 4th class in the A.I.F.

Demobilized on 30 December, Lew completed his degree at the University of Sydney (B.A., 1923) while serving in the Bankstown, Waverley, Ballina, Five Dock, Katoomba, Lismore and Wollongong circuits. On 6 September 1924 at the Methodist Church, Summer Hill, he married Sylvia Jean Hay, who held a diploma from the New South Wales State Conservatorium of Music. Lew had continued as a part-time army chaplain and served full time with the Militia in 1942-44 before returning to work in the Chatswood and Manly circuits. A forceful preacher and a faithful pastor, he believed that the Church spent too much time in abstruse speculation about details of ritual and organization instead of getting on with the 'supreme function' of presenting Christ 'as He was and is'.

In 1948 Lew was appointed principal of Methodist Ladies' College, Burwood, a post he held until his retirement in 1959. Known as a good administrator, he presided over a period that saw increasing numbers of students, considerable physical expansion and the financial consolidation of the school. Sylvia Lew's work for the boarding-house and with the boarders' choir (which she founded) drew even more attention. Under her leadership the choir flourished and took part in Australian Broadcasting Commission programmes.

Secretary (1946-48) and president (1949-50) of the New South Wales Conference, Lew was secretary-general (1951-54) and president-general (1954-57) of the Methodist Church of Australasia. He chaired the Methodist Overseas Missions board, the Federal Methodist Inland Mission council and the federal council of the Methodist Mission to the Nation. A member of the central committee of the World Council of Churches and vice-president of its Australian council, he represented (1954) Australian Methodism at the second assembly of the W.C.C. at Evanston, United States of America. In addition, he was a delegate (1956) to the World Methodist Conference at Lake Junaluska, North Carolina, U.S.A., an executive-member of the World Methodist Council and vice-chairman of the Australian commission for Inter-Church Aid and Service to Refugees.

Lew received an honorary D.D. from the Baldwin-Wallace College, Ohio, in 1956 and was appointed O.B.E. in 1959. Survived by his wife and three daughters, he died on 20 October 1970 at Gordon and was cremated.

S. and R. Coupe, *Walk in the Light* (Syd, 1986); Methodist Church of A'sia, *NSW Conference Minutes*, 1959, p 161, 1970, p 62; Methodist Ladies' College (Burwood, Syd), *Excelsior*, Dec 1959, Dec 1970; *SMH*, 5 Nov 1927, 25 Apr 1936; *Sun* (Syd), 24 May 1954, 21 Oct 1970; *Methodist* (Syd), 7 Nov 1970; information from Miss H. Lew, Turramurra, Syd.

DON WRIGHT

LEWERS, GERALD FRANCIS (1905-1962), sculptor and construction engineer, and HETTIE MARGARET ERNESTINE (1908-1978), artist, were husband and wife. Gerald was born on 1 July 1905 in Hobart, seventh of eight children of Robert David Lewers (d.1911), a bank manager from Ireland, and his Tasmanian-born wife Maria Bispham, née Propsting, both of whom were Quakers. By 1906 Robert had been transferred to Sydney, where he settled on the North Shore. Gerry's early interest in the bush was nurtured by his parents. He attended Chatswood Public School, the Friends' High School, Hobart (as a boarder in 1920), and Barker College (1920-23), Sydney. In 1924 he sailed in a lugger with A. F. B. Hull's [q.v.9] zoological expedition to the Great Barrier Reef. Two years later Lewers joined his brother-in-law Mervyn Farley in a construction and quarry business which was mainly engaged in building roads and installing sewerage works; he studied part time at (East) Sydney Technical College and played first-grade Rugby Union for Northern Suburbs.

Margo was born on 23 April 1908 at Mosman, Sydney, second of three children of Gustav Adolf Plate (d.1913), a German-born grazier and artist, and his English-born wife Elsie Gill, née Burton. Having learned to type, Margo worked successively as a secretary, as a cadet commercial artist with the *Daily Telegraph*, and with a small firm that produced hand-made wooden articles with Australian motifs. She soon established her own studio and made hand-printed textiles and pottery. Later, she designed pots for R. Fowler [q.v.4] Ltd.

Gerald and Margo met at Dattilo Rubbo's [q.v.11] evening art-classes in the late 1920s. In 1931 he travelled in Europe and studied at the Kunstgewerbeschule, Vienna. Back in Sydney, on 6 October 1932 he married Margo at the district registrar's office, Mosman. In 1934 they went abroad and enrolled at the Central School of Arts and Crafts, London. Gerald studied under John Skeaping and exhibited (1934) with 'Six Colonial Artists' at the Cooling galleries, New Bond Street. Margo worked at textile design, painting and drawing with John Farleigh. They saw exhibitions with Gerald's brother-in-law Arthur Wheen [q.v.12] and also journeyed through Europe.

In Sydney in 1935 Margo established the Notanda Gallery, an interior-decorating shop in Rowe Street, and continued to design hand-printed fabrics. Her daughters Darani and Tanya were born in 1936 and 1940. The shop closed in 1939. An active member of the Sydney branch of the Contemporary Art Society of Australia, Margo was a pupil (1945-50) in Desiderius Orban's evening painting-classes. Gerald had returned to Farley & Lewers which built (1937) the Port Pirie-Port Augusta railway line in South Australia. About 1942 he took over the management of the firm's quarry at Castlereagh, New South Wales.

During his spare time Lewers carved animals and birds in wood and stone, creating a large number of realistic and semi-abstract sculptures. These intimate and small-scale works (mainly in private collections) captured the physical characteristics and movement of penguins, ants, numbats, kangaroos, giraffes, dolphins and fish. They included 'Camel's Head' and 'Tortoise' (Art Gallery of New South Wales), and 'Pelican Birdbath' (Lewers gallery). Margel Hinder, a close friend, said that Lewers' 'love and understanding for the wood and stone of his own land, coupled with his sensitivity for the inner life of wild animals and birds, carried out with his assured craftsmanship, led to some of his finest and most distinguished works'.

In 1950 Gerald retired from Farley & Lewers to become a full-time sculptor. Next year the family moved to his farmhouse on the Nepean River, where Margo was to make a garden of trees and river boulders. Patrick White wrote that in 'the house at Emu Plains ideas hurtled, argument flared, voices shouted, sparks flew. It was a place in which people gathered spontaneously'. J. D. Pringle recalled that guests 'were rewarded by exquisite food cooked by Margo and a great deal of wine provided by Gerry'. Quiet and gentle, Lewers 'always remained an all-round man—an excellent rider and bushman, a practical engineer who could turn his hand to anything, a skilled craftsman'. Margo gave an 'enduring impression of warmth, tenacity, candour and intelligence', although Pringle found her 'slightly terrifying with her hoarse voice and black stare'.

A member of the Society of Artists, Sydney, and of the Contemporary Art Society, Lewers took part in solo and group exhibitions. He helped to establish the Society of Sculptors and Associates in 1951 and was its founding treasurer. From 1953 until his death Lewers received over fifteen major commissions, among them 'Relaxation', a reclining 'sandstone figure of heroic size' (University House, Canberra), and the sandstone relief on the York Street front of the Commonwealth Bank of Australia (Sydney, 1954). He and Margo were jointly commissioned to create a garden of pebbles, cacti and sandstone shapes for the M.L.C. Building, North Sydney (1957). Lewers worked with swiftness and certainty, and later began to use metal, especially for public fountains 'whose shapes mirrored and reflected the moving waters' (I.C.I. House, Melbourne; Macquarie Place, Sydney).

From 1950 Margo worked in a variety of mediums including painting, textiles, sculpture and mosaic. She won recognition as a leading postwar abstract expressionist. Her early compositions explored colour and formal geometric abstraction; her work became more fluid and expressionistic by the early 1960s. She showed extensively in Australia and in several international travelling exhibitions; she received numerous public commissions (including the mosaic wall for the Canberra-Rex Hotel (1957) and the Aubusson tapestry (1968) for the Reserve Bank of Australia's boardroom); and she won at least fourteen awards and prizes.

While holidaying at Chillagoe, Queensland, Lewers was thrown from a horse and fractured his skull. He died of a brain haemorrhage on 9 August 1962 at Cairns hospital and was cremated. A major memorial exhibition was held at the A.G.N.S.W. in 1963. At the wish of Dr H. C. Coombs, Margo completed (1965) Gerald's design for a huge copper relief in the Reserve Bank, Canberra.

Margo Lewers died of cancer on 20 February 1978 at her Emu Plains home and was cremated. Through the generosity and persistence of her daughters, the Emu Plains property and collection of artworks was offered to Penrith City Council. In 1981 the Lewers Bequest and Penrith Regional Art Gallery was opened. The Lewers' work is represented in most national and State galleries, as well as in regional and university collections.

Margo's brother CARL OLAF PLATE (1909-1977) was born on 19 December 1909 in South Perth and was brought to Sydney in 1913. He worked in advertising, studied art at (East) Sydney Technical College and travelled extensively (1936-40) in Europe, visiting Paris, several Scandinavian countries and the Soviet Union. In London he attended St Martin's School of Art and the Central School of Arts and Crafts. Upon returning to Sydney (1940), he re-established the Notanda Gallery, where he exhibited British and Australian modern art, and sold art books and posters. He married Jocelyn Brittain Zander on 13 August 1945 at the office of the government statist, Melbourne.

Like his sister, Plate was represented in many solo, group and travelling exhibitions, and was responsible for bringing to Australia several important exhibitions by British artists. He used collage as a form of drawing: he often found it the most efficient way of documenting ideas and impressions for future works. Plate believed that 'Ambivalence, contradiction and paradox are the factors of life which affect me most'. His early influences were the British Surrealists, Graham Sutherland and Paul Nash, but from the late 1950s his work was more aligned to the philosophies and practices of Australian and European abstract expressionism. He died of cancer on 15 May 1977 at his Woronora River home and was cremated; his wife, son and three daughters survived him.

L. Thomas, *Gerald Lewers Memorial Exhibition* (Syd, 1963); A. Watson, *Carl Plate 1909-1977*, exhibition cat (Syd, 1977); K. Scarlett, *Australian Sculptors* (Melb, 1980); D. Hickey, *Gerald and Margo Lewers, their lives and their work* (Syd, 1982); *Art and Aust*, 7, no 2, Sept 1969, p 144, 7, no 3, Dec 1969, p 235, 16, no 2, Dec 1978, p 131; *SMH*, 26 Aug 1929, 1 Nov 1934, 12 Jan, 26 June 1954, 1 Aug 1957, 10, 18 Aug 1962, 19, 22 June 1963, 22 Feb, 3 Nov 1978, 12 July 1980, 26 June 1982; *Sun News-Pictorial*, 14 Apr 1954; *Sun-Herald*, 21 July 1963, 11 July 1965, 29 Oct 1967; *Sunday Telegraph* (Syd), 11 Sept 1960; *Australian*, 21 Oct 1967, 30 Aug 1969; *National Times*, 21-27 Jan 1979, p 28; H. de Berg, Conversations with Margo Lewers, 1962 and 1965 (taped interviews, NL); M. *and* G. Lewers *and* Carl Plate papers (Lewers Bequest and Penrith Regional Art Gallery, NSW).   MICHAEL CRAYFORD

LEWIS, ALLEN CHARLES (1891-1970), businessman, was born on 16 April 1891 at Chatham, Kent, England, son of Allen Lewis, builder's clerk, and his wife Ann Jane, née Platt. Young Allen was educated at Frogmore School. He described himself as a man of 'independent means' when he married Beatrice Monica Atkinson on 13 July 1912 at the register office, Kingston, Surrey. Soon after, he sailed for Australia as the representative of the Indented Bar & Concrete Engineering Co. Ltd, London. He helped to form (initially as company secretary) Country Concrete Constructions Ltd (registered 1916). Most of its contracts were for rural projects.

In 1920 the firm was reconstituted as Concrete Constructions Ltd but it remained a private company. Lewis built up a substantial shareholding and served as chairman. Projects in the 1920s included the reconstruction of Mark Foy [q.v.8] Ltd's store in Liverpool Street, the grandstand at the Royal Agricultural Society showground, the Government Savings Bank building in Martin Place, the Menzies Hotel, Melbourne, and reinforced concrete highways. Dubbed 'Concrete Lewis' by the *Bulletin*, he visited the United States of America in 1927. On his return he opened relations with insurance companies and in the depressed 1930s won contracts for office buildings, including the new headquarters of Colonial Mutual Life Assurance Society Ltd at Durban, which was the basis for Concrete Construction's development as a major building firm in southern Africa.

Under Lewis's control as chairman and managing director, Concrete Constructions operated as a contractor for building projects rather than as a 'developer'. The company submitted tenders, used subcontractors and relied on progress payments to finance its projects. 'A.C.' (as he preferred to be known) acquired a thorough knowledge of developments in construction methods and a considerable interest in finance. He was an associate of the Institution of Civil Engineers, London. Nevertheless, his skills were essentially in the areas of information, costing and organization, and in negotiating contracts, supervising large construction projects and selecting personnel.

Lewis was a director of Colonial Mutual, the Perpetual Trustee Co. Ltd and Australia Hotel Co. Ltd; he was later to become chairman of Mercantile Mutual Insurance Co. Ltd and a State director of the National Bank of Australasia. In October 1939 he was appointed to the Commonwealth government's Capital Issues Advisory Board. Thirteen months later he was made honorary 'business manager' of the Australian Army, with a seat on the Military Board. His responsibilities incorporated the acquisition, storage and distribution of military equipment, other than ordnance and explosives. After a month he became seriously ill and retired. By that time, however, he had produced an interim report on the army's supply organization and some of his recommendations were subsequently adopted. His entrepreneurial talents were subsequently applied to constructing Fairmile motor launches for the navy. In the postwar period the impact of his company on Sydney was even more pronounced: among his projects was the Australian Mutual Provident Society Ltd's building on Circular Quay, described as Australia's first 'skyscraper'.

For relaxation, Lewis enjoyed tennis in his younger days, followed an almost daily routine of a few rounds of boxing with Joe Wallis [q.v.] at his gymnasium, took morning swims in the surf with the Bronte Splashers and played golf. He acquired an enduring passion for horse-racing and won the 1952 Caulfield Cup with Peshawar, which he owned jointly with Sir Sydney Snow [q.v.12]. Lewis belonged to the Australian and Royal Sydney Golf clubs. Survived by his wife, daughter and two sons, he died on 6 December 1970 at his Bellevue Hill home and was cremated with Anglican rites. His estate was sworn for probate at £1 523 707.

P. Angly, *Concrete Constructions* (np, nd); *SMH*, 11 Nov 1927, 7 Jan 1930, 17 Oct 1968, 9 Apr 1971; [M. Zvirblis], submission to the Australian Bicentennial Authority, '200 Greatest Stories Never Told' (MS 7461, 1988, NL); information from Mr J. Rankin, Point Piper, Mrs A. Lewis, Rose Bay, Mrs N. Platt Hall, Vaucluse, and Miss J. Barnard, Drummoyne, Syd.   JOHN PERKINS

LEWIS, SIR AUBREY JULIAN (1900-1975), professor of psychiatry, was born on 8 November 1900 at Kent Town, Adelaide, only child of Jewish parents George Solomon Lewis, an accountant from England, and his South Australian-born wife Ré, née Isaacs, an elocution teacher. A highly gifted child, Aubrey was educated (1911-17) at Christian Brothers' College, Wakefield Street, where his intellectual abilities rapidly matured. He completed his medical studies at the University of Adelaide with distinction (M.B., B.S., 1923; M.D., 1931), worked at the (Royal) Adelaide Hospital for two years, undertook anthropological research on Aborigines and accepted (1926) a Rockefeller Foundation fellowship in psychological medicine.

After two years postgraduate study in the United States of America and Germany, Lewis joined (1929) the staff of the Maudsley Hospital, London. In 1946 the hospital was designated the Institute of Psychiatry under the auspices of the University of London. Through peace and war, the quality of Lewis's work was widely appreciated; in 1946 he was appointed to the chair of psychiatry at the institute, a post he held until his retirement in 1966. On 22 February 1934 at the Liberal Jewish Synagogue, St Marylebone, he had married Hilda North Stoessiger (d.1966), a psychiatrist.

Lewis was a fellow (1938) of the Royal College of Physicians and an honorary fellow (1972) of the Royal College of Psychiatrists. In 1959 he was knighted. As a leader, educator and administrator, he built a reputation in association with the institute, which he constructed as a model of scientific research and teaching. In the process he became a trusted adviser to general medical bodies, national and international research councils, and political organizations, thereby raising the status of his discipline. These activities tended to overshadow his contributions as a clinician, scholar and researcher whose investigations embraced social inquiries, genetics, clinical phenomenology and biology. His studies of melancholia and obsessional illness were his best-known work. In his collected papers— *The State of Psychiatry, Inquiries in Psychiatry* (London, 1967) and *The Later Papers of Sir Aubrey Lewis* (Oxford, 1977)—the substance of his thought is expressed clearly by his mastery of language.

Sir Aubrey's austere appearance, well captured in Ruskin Spear's official portrait of 1966 (held by the institute) was misleading. High standards of personal and professional integrity went with a warm, kindly, humorous disposition which earned him the affection of colleagues and friends. In Emerson's sense of the term he was a representative man, and recognized as such in his lifetime, except, paradoxically, in his native land, until recently.

Survived by his two daughters and two sons, Lewis died on 21 January 1975 in Charing Cross Hospital, London. A memorial service was held in April at the synagogue in which he had been married. Fifteen years later an Aubrey Lewis unit was opened at Royal Park Hospital, Melbourne. The occasion prompted the appearance of a newspaper article, 'The man Adelaide forgot'. It began: 'Had Aubrey Lewis gone to St Peter's College and been interested in field sports his name would probably be well known to generations of South Australians. But he was Jewish, went to a Catholic school, his father was a nobody and he lived up the east end of Rundle St—definitely the wrong side of the tracks for a prejudicial, parochial Adelaide of the 1920s'. To these reasons might have been added the traditionally inferior status of his discipline and his inability through illness to revisit the country of his birth.

M. Shepherd and D. L. Davies (eds), *Studies in Psychiatry* (Lond, 1968); M. Shepherd, *A Representative Psychiatrist* (Cambridge, Eng, 1986) and *Sir Aubrey Lewis* (Melb, 1991); *Psychiatry and Social Science Review*, 3, 1969, p 6; *J of Psychiatric Research*, 17, 1983, p 93; *The Times*, 22 Jan 1975; *Advertiser* (Adel), 10 Mar 1990.

MICHAEL SHEPHERD*

LEWIS, GRACE MARGARET (GRETTA) (1892-1968), community worker, was born on 2 February 1892 at Hamilton, Victoria, third child of Victorian-born parents Thomas Halliburton Laidlaw, a stock and station agent who became a pastoralist, and his wife Margaret, née Thomson. Gretta was educated at Alexandra College, Hamilton (1905-07), and Toorak College, Melbourne (1908-10); as a young woman she loved sport, especially riding, motoring, shooting and rowing. At Scots Church, Melbourne, on 12 April 1921 she married with Presbyterian forms Lancelot Ashley Lewis (d.1938), a company director; he was a son of John Lewis [q.v.10] and had served (1914-17) in the Australian Imperial Force. In 1924 the couple moved from Adelaide's fashionable East Terrace to Benacre, the Lewis family's Italianate mansion at Glen Osmond.

Handsome rather than pretty, and always smartly tailored, Mrs Lewis possessed prodigious energy and a flair for organization. It was said of her that she rarely refused an office. She was vice-president (1932-33) and a council-member (until 1944) of the District and Bush Nursing Society. An ardent flower-lover who won the Lady Hore-Ruthven [q.v.9 Gowrie] cup in 1932, 1935 and 1937, she was principal planner of the 1936 Floral Pageant: it was a spectacular component of South Australia's centenary celebrations and the precursor to Adelaide's annual National Flower Day, inaugurated (1938) at her suggestion.

In November 1939 Premier (Sir) Thomas Playford appointed Mrs Lewis to chair the executive-committee of the Women's Defence Services in South Australia, which had responsibility for the Women's Voluntary National Register. Her most constructive war effort, however, was in administering the Girl Guides' Thrift Campaign which raised some £72 000 between 1939 and 1946 to support a range of projects. A vice-president (1925-52) and life member (1942) of the Girl Guides' Association of South Australia, she was appointed O.B.E. in 1942.

After World War II had ended, Mrs Lewis addressed herself to the world problem of tuberculosis control. Vice-president (from 1943) of the South Australian Tuberculosis Association, she visited North America in 1947 to investigate methods for the rehabilitation of patients. She represented the National Association for the Prevention of Tuberculosis in Australia at conferences held at Boston, Massachusetts, and in London (1952), in Istanbul (1959), and again in Britain and the United States of America (1963). In 1956 the South Australian branch of the National Safety Council of Australia awarded her a certificate of merit for designing an improved reflector for bicycles, but her efforts to patent the device proved unsuccessful. Late in life she took up painting and exhibited (1963) at the City of Hamilton Art Gallery, Victoria. In 1966 she made a final tour of the U.S.A. to lecture on gardening with native flora. After returning, she worked on the preservation of Charles Sturt's [q.v.2] house at Grange. Survived by her daughter and two sons, she died on 23 May 1968 at Benacre and was cremated; her estate was sworn for probate at $93 753. Gretta's elder son Thomas Lancelot was premier (1974-76) of New South Wales; her younger son Alexander Ashley was a member (1972-89) of the Western Australian parliament.

Annual Record of Patent Office Procs, Canb, 1956, 1958; *Adventuring*, 30, no 10, July 1968, p 2; *Advertiser* (Adel), 1 June 1939, 3 Oct 1947, 3 May 1955, 24 Mar, 7 Sept 1966, 25 May 1968; Governor's despatches to the Secretary of State, 25 Feb 1942 (Government House, Adel); Lewis papers (Mort L); information from Miss M. S. Douglas, Nth Adel.

ROGER ANDRÉ

LEWIS, SAMUEL PHINEAS (1901-1976), schoolteacher, was born on 15 June 1901 in Sydney, eldest child of native-born parents Judah Henry Lewis, hairdresser, and his wife Rebecca Caroline, née Myers. Sam won a bursary to Cleveland Street Intermediate and Sydney Boys' High schools. After a year at the University of Sydney (B.Ec., 1934) studying economics, and another at Teachers' College, he began teaching at Bondi Public School in 1921. That year he attended the council-meeting of the New South Wales Public School Teachers' Federation. He was posted to other Sydney schools before being sent to Narrabri where he campaigned for J. T. Lang [q.v.9] in the 1925 State elections. Lewis believed that his transfer to Atholwood, a one-teacher school near the Queensland border, was a punishment for his political activities.

He returned to Sydney in 1929, taught at Maroubra Junction Junior Technical School and attended university part time. Meanwhile, he was foundation secretary of the Educational Workers' League, a small group of teachers who wanted to abolish public examinations, weekly tests, homework and corporal punishment, and who sought the active participation of every teacher in the governance of schools. Lewis was also involved with the assistants' branch of the Teachers' Federation, of which he was for some years vice-president. In 1933-34 he vigorously disputed the policies of the president C. H. Currey [q.v.13] and attacked the federation's hierarchy for its inactivity as teachers' salaries declined and their working conditions deteriorated. Lewis organized the Conference on Education for a Progressive Democratic Australia (1938) which urged

numerous reforms, including Federal funding for schools.

Although Lewis had celebrated his bar mitzvah, his faith in Judaism lapsed. At the district registrar's office, Randwick, on 20 December 1940 he married Ethel Caroline Nelson Teerman (d.1985), a 32-year-old schoolteacher. In the early 1930s Lewis had become secretary of the Coogee branch of the Communist Party of Australia. As organizer of the militant minority group in the Teachers' Federation he attracted such attention that he attended a Communist Party conference in 1935 under the assumed name of Samuel 'Curtis'; as Curtis he was elected to the district committee of the Communist Party in 1938. He unsuccessfully contested the seat of Barton for R. J. Heffron's [q.v.14] State Labor Party at the 1940 Federal elections and the seat of Randwick at the State elections in 1941.

Lewis was elected deputy-president of the Teachers' Federation in 1943 and president in 1945. He and his supporters became engaged in a bitter struggle against conservative and anti-communist forces within the federation and in the wider political arena. The Commonwealth Investigation Service examined his activities. In Federal parliament Lang persistently attacked Lewis as a notorious communist after the Chifley [q.v.13] government accredited him as a delegate to the United Nations Educational, Scientific and Cultural Organization meeting in Mexico City in 1947.

In 1952 Lewis was defeated for the presidency of the Teachers' Federation, even though the federation had won significant salary increases for teachers during his term of office. With his radicalism undiminished, he taught for several years at Paddington and Newtown junior technical schools. At Newtown he was reprimanded in 1955 for slapping an insolent boy on the face; despite the reprimand, Lewis received widespread support from fellow teachers who considered that he had been provoked by a racist slur. In 1958 he was re-elected deputy-president of the federation, a post he held until re-elected president in 1964.

Believing that implementation of the federation's policies needed the militant, united action of teachers, Lewis supported publicity campaigns, petitions and mass meetings. Witty, ironic and forceful, he was recognized as one of the finest public speakers of his generation. He aggressively upheld women teachers in their long campaign for equal pay; he fought for the federation's acceptance of and by the trade union movement; and he achieved for teachers the right to have their complaints about working conditions heard in the Industrial Commission of New South Wales instead of being controlled by the fiat of the Public Service Board. In his last address as president in January 1968 he told an adulatory audience that the 'unity of teachers can be and should be part of the greater unity of the peoples—the People's Symphony'.

Lewis suffered from diabetes and was partially paralysed by a stroke in 1974. He died on 16 August 1976 at his Maroubra home and was cremated; his wife survived him, as did their daughter Jeannie who is well known in Australia and Latin America for her stage appearances. In 1983 the Teachers' Federation instituted Sam Lewis peace awards.

J. T. Lang, *Communism is Treason* (Syd, 1948); B. A. Mitchell, *Teachers, Education and Politics* (Brisb, 1975); NSW Teachers' Federation, *Sam Lewis Memorial Booklet* (Syd, 1976); *SMH*, 25 Nov, 11 Dec 1955, 20 Jan 1956; A. D. Spaull, Teachers and Politics: a comparative study of State teachers' organizations in Victoria and New South Wales since 1940 (Ph.D. thesis, Monash Univ, 1972); Lewis papers (ML *and* held by Ms J. Lewis, Maroubra, Syd); A467/1 item SP42/40 (AA, Canb).

MARTIN SULLIVAN

LEWORTHY, BETTY CAROLINE (1877-1962), church and community worker, was born on 13 January 1877 at Riverton, Southland, New Zealand, elder daughter of Malcolm Henry Leworthy (d.1891), a station-manager from England, and his Irish-born wife Eleanor, née Sutherland. In the late 1870s the family settled at Victor Harbor, South Australia. Educated locally, Betty trained as a shorthand-typist at the Remington Agency Ltd's business college, Adelaide, then opened a small copying agency in Waymouth Street. In 1901 she was appointed senior instructor in typing at the School of Mines and Industries; next year she took over the shorthand classes and taught both subjects until 1904. She was the founding principal (from 1905) of the Remington Agency Ltd schools (Remington Training College) which merged in 1912 with Muirden [q.v.10] College Ltd. In 1920 she opened Miss Leworthy's Business College for Girls, in Hindmarsh Square; two years later she set up a local branch of Zercho's [q.v.12] Business College; and in 1923 she managed the Typewriter Co. Ltd.

Meanwhile, Leworthy had become involved in community work. Converted from her Anglican faith, she was founding honorary secretary (1914) of the Catholic Women's League, whose patron was Lady Galway [q.v.14]. The league undertook a range of war-work and raised funds to build a recreational hall at Keswick for returned servicemen. Despite protests from some of the C.W.L., Leworthy was a staunch advocate of conscription. Over the next thirty years she broadened the league's activities in the field of social work, and extended the religious and intellectual interests of its members by involving them in organizations outside their own denomination.

Having visited England where she inspected hostels, in 1916 Leworthy accepted the post of resident secretary of St Mary's Hostel and Club Café for young women, in Pirie Street (relocated to East Terrace in 1918), Adelaide. It was founded under the auspices of the C.W.L. When the hostel experienced financial difficulties, she served as matron (1932-40), and remained on the board until 1959. The Bruce-Page [qq.v.7,11] government had invited her in 1924 to report on aspects of emigration from England and Italy. During the Depression the league endeavoured to find work for unemployed Catholic women and provided soup kitchens at poorer Catholic schools. In 1940 Leworthy again took charge of the league's war effort and headed a committee to assist the Australian Comforts Fund. She was appointed M.B.E. in 1949. Late in life she managed a ladies' employment agency.

Leworthy's manner was dynamic and determined, yet she was sensitive and kindly by disposition. She was small and slender in build, cultivated in her tastes and conservative in dress. Generous and practical in her concern for the disadvantaged, she fought for social justice and saw women as agents of change. Her ecumenical outlook challenged the segregationist attitudes of the Catholic hierarchy. She died on 17 February 1962 at Parkside Mental Hospital and was buried in West Terrace cemetery.

Catholic Women's League Mag, Oct 1935, Nov 1941; R. Schumann, '"Charity, Work, Loyalty" The Catholic Women's League in South Australia', *JHSSA*, 11, 1983; *Observer* (Adel), 28 Feb 1891; *Southern Cross* (Adel), 31 Mar, 11 Aug, 27 Oct 1916, 20 Dec 1918, 15 Feb 1924; *Advertiser* (Adel), 20 Feb 1962; H. P. Jones, The History of Commercial Education in South Australia with Special Reference to Women (M.A. thesis, Univ Adel, 1967); Catholic Women's League (Adel), Minutes, 25 Oct 1914, 13 Feb 1931, 23 July 1934, 13 May 1935, 9 Aug 1940; St Mary's Hostel Bd, Minutes, 1952-59 (Catholic Archives, Adel); personal information.

RUTH SCHUMANN

LIDDELL, MARY WHERRY (1877-1967), journalist, was born on 22 October 1877 at Inniskirk, near Lisnaskea, County Fermanagh, Ireland, daughter of Thomas Bullock, house steward, and his wife Mary, née Wherry. On 18 June 1902 she married a merchant James Crothers Liddell (d.1946) at the Church of the Holy Trinity, Kinawley, with the rites of the Church of Ireland; their sons Edward and Leslie were born in 1904 and in 1907 respectively. The Liddells settled in Sydney about 1910.

Mary's conservative political opinions were apparent from her first public position as secretary of the Women's Loyal Service Bureau, which was formed to organize middle-class women as a strikebreaking force during the August-September 1917 general strike in Sydney. At the same time she was also a feminist. A member of the Lyceum and Feminist clubs in Sydney, she represented the latter on the National Council of Women of New South Wales in 1918-19 and was the club's secretary in 1922.

Her career as a journalist included working (1920-29) on the literary staff of the *Evening News* and as social editor of the *Sunday News*. Mrs Liddell was the only woman invited to contribute in 1929 to teaching the short-lived diploma course in journalism at the University of Sydney. For a brief time (1932-33) she worked for *Truth* in Melbourne. She maintained continuous membership (from 1920) of the New South Wales Institute of Journalists, of which she was a committee-member (1923-31, 1935-39 and 1942-50) and vice-president (1929-30 and 1951-55). When the organization was wound up in 1956, she graciously declined a proffered financial gift for 'preeminent help to the Institute'.

On 1 September 1925 Liddell was one of four 'distinguished women journalists' who had convened the first meeting of the Society of Women Writers of New South Wales. She became foundation vice-president, represented (from 1926) the society on the National Council of Women and was a member (1928-30) of the N.C.W.'s executive-committee. In 1929 Liddell was honorary treasurer of the New South Wales Women Voters' Association: she supported its amalgamation with other organizations to form the United Associations of Women, and was a member (1930-31) of the U.A.W.'s executive.

As a justice of the peace, as a member of respectable bodies like the English-Speaking Union, and as a prominent journalist with impeccable feminist credentials and a reputation for being tolerant and fair-minded, Liddell was a popular choice for the woman representative on the first Commonwealth film censorship appeal board. She took up her duties in January 1929 and was widely expected to be re-appointed, but after a change of government she was replaced in 1930 by (Dame) Mary Gilmore [q.v.9].

Survived by her sons, Liddell died on 3 October 1967 at Randwick and was cremated with Anglican rites.

NSW Inst of Journalists, *Annual Report*, 1912-55; National Council of Women of NSW, *Biennial Report*, 1913-38; *Journalist*, 20 July 1928, p 97, 24 Sept 1928, p 134, 24 May 1929, p 85, 23 July 1929, p 110; *Everyone's*, 5 Dec 1928, p 4, 18 Dec 1929, p 6, 15 Jan 1930, p 6; *SMH*, 30 Nov, 3 Dec 1928; L. A. Heath, Sydney Literary Societies of the Nineteen Twenties: cultural nationalism and the promotion of Australian literature (Ph.D. thesis, Univ NSW, 1996); Premier's Dept (NSW), Correspondence, box 9/4748, A17/5711 (NSWA).   INA BERTRAND

LIENHOP, SIR JOHN HERMAN (HENRY) (1886-1967), stock-and-station agent, pastoralist and politician, was born on 3 February 1886 at Kangaroo Flat, Victoria, seventh child of Albert Lienhop, a licensed victualler from Germany, and his Irish-born wife Bridget, née Nash. When her husband died in 1896, Bridget took over the running of their hotel. Educated at Kangaroo Flat State School, John worked as a clerk before establishing himself as a stock-and-station agent at Bendigo. On 23 June 1910 at All Saints Pro-Cathedral, Bendigo, he married with Anglican rites 28-year-old Rosetta Wirth (d.1928).

About 1912 Lienhop bought an 8000-acre (3240 ha) grazing property, The Springs, at Womboota near Deniliquin, where he specialized in raising lambs for export and became a successful stock-breeder. He later acquired extensive properties throughout Victoria. An active supporter of the woollen industry, he helped to found the State Wool Committee and served on the Australian Wool Council.

Lienhop was a foundation member of the United Country Party. He was president of the Bendigo branch, a member (1932-38) of the central council and a director of the party's journal, the *Countryman*. In 1937 he was elected to the Legislative Council for Bendigo Province. As a member of parliament he maintained a long-standing interest in rural industry and local development.

Appointed minister without portfolio in (Sir) Albert Dunstan's [q.v.8] government in April 1942, Lienhop was promoted in September 1943 to commissioner of public works, a position he was to hold until the defeat of the Dunstan-Hollway [q.v.14] coalition in October 1945. During World War II he was chairman of the Location of Industries Committee and was elected (1943) to the council of the University of Melbourne. In the Hollway-McDonald [q.v.] government he served (November 1947-December 1948) as minister in charge of electrical undertakings and minister of mines. For two years he was government leader in the Legislative Council.

With other members, including fellow Bendigonian (Sir) George Lansell [q.v.9], Lienhop resigned from the United Country Party in February 1949, following its decision to sit in opposition against Hollway's Liberal and Country Party government. After condemning Dunstan's actions, he joined a committee to oversee the formation of the L.C.P. in the Bendigo district. In the June elections for the Legislative Council the contest was seen to be between Lienhop and Dunstan, rather than between Lienhop and his Country Party opponent, Allan Brownbill, whom he defeated. At the declaration of the poll Lienhop announced: 'Today in his old erstwhile stronghold and throughout the State he [Dunstan] is a spent force'.

In December 1950 Lienhop resigned from parliament to become Victorian agent-general in London. At St John's Church, Toorak, on 18 January 1951 he married Catherine Mary Dalton, a 33-year-old nursing sister; they sailed for England soon after. Lienhop was knighted in 1952 and retired to Melbourne in 1956. Throughout his life he owned racehorses. President of the Bendigo Jockey Club and of the Northern Districts Racing Association, he was also an active member of the Victoria Racing, the Victorian Amateur Turf and the Moonee Valley Racing clubs. Sir John died on 27 April 1967 in East Melbourne and was buried in Bendigo cemetery; his wife survived him, as did the two sons of his first marriage.

Mining and Geological J, Mar 1948; *Annals of Bendigo*, 5, 1921-35, 6, 1936-50, 7, 1951-70; *Bendigo Advertiser*, 18 Sept, 1 Oct 1928, 6 July 1937, 1 Feb 1949; *Age* (Melb), 22 Feb 1944, 20 June 1949, 28 Apr 1967.   CHARLES FAHEY

LIGERTWOOD, SIR GEORGE COUTTS (1888-1967), judge, was born on 15 October 1888 at Maylands, Adelaide, third child of William Leith Ligertwood, a builder from Scotland, and his native-born wife Margaret, née Anderson. George was educated at Norwood Public and the Pupil Teachers' schools, and at the University of Adelaide (B.A., 1908; LL.B., 1910). He was admitted to the Bar on 15 December 1910. An associate (from 1911) to Sir Samuel Way [q.v.12], Ligertwood became acting-master of the Supreme Court in 1914. At the Methodist Church, Upper Sturt, on 6 April 1915 he married Edith Emily Naismith, a former nurse; they were to have two daughters and two sons.

On 6 May 1918 Ligertwood enlisted in the Australian Imperial Force; he was undergoing training in England when World War I ended. He returned to South Australia in 1919 and was a partner in the firm Baker, McEwin, Ligertwood & Millhouse. President (1935-37 and 1941-43) of the Law Society of South Australia, Ligertwood was also a member (1937 and 1942-43) of the executive-committee of the Law Council of Australia. Appointed K.C. on 28 August 1930, he served on the bench of the Supreme Court from 12 July 1945 until his retirement in 1958; barristers found him able, pleasant and courteous.

The Federal government appointed Ligertwood to three royal commissions. In 1945 he inquired into Major General Gordon Bennett's [q.v.13] controversial escape from Singapore in World War II; Ligertwood found that Bennett had not been justified in vacating his command. In the 1949 royal commission into timber-leases in New Guinea, Ligertwood exonerated the minister for external territories E. J. Ward [q.v.]. In 1954-55 Ligertwood was one of three commissioners who examined espionage in Australia; their report on the Petrov affair concluded that the Soviet Union had directed spying operations from its embassy in Canberra. Ligertwood was knighted in 1956. The government of Western Australia appointed him a royal commissioner in 1959 to inquire into betting. He also chaired the Federal committee on taxation (1959-61), the South Australian committee on assessment for land tax (1962-64) and a committee on the salaries of South Australian parliamentarians.

Ligertwood was an active Presbyterian, a governor (1930-67) of Scotch College, Adelaide, a prominent Freemason and a member (from 1929) of the Adelaide Club. At the University of Adelaide he had been examiner in wrongs (1913-15) and in property (1917 and 1919-26); he was a member of council from 1942 and warden (1945-59) of the senate. He received an honorary LL.D. from the University of Western Australia in 1963 and from his own university in 1964. Deputy-chancellor (1958-61) and chancellor (1961-66) of the University of Adelaide, he chaired the planning committee for the Flinders University of South Australia (founded 1966). Ligertwood died on 13 October 1967 in Adelaide and was cremated; his wife, two daughters and a son survived him. (Sir) Ivor Hele's portrait of Ligertwood is held by the University of Adelaide where the Ligertwood building commemorates him.

D. Hilliard, *Flinders University* (Adel, 1991); *Public Service Review* (SA), Jan 1917; *Advertiser* (Adel), 17 July 1945, 1 Mar 1948, 1 Jan, 25 June 1949, 4 Dec 1959, 16 Oct 1967; Ligertwood papers (Mort L); Law Soc of SA *and* Supreme Court of SA Archives; information from Assoc Prof A. Ligertwood, Univ Adel, *and* Grand Lodge of Freemasons of SA *and* Univ Adel archivist; personal information.
                                          HOWARD ZELLING

LILLEY, ALAN BRUCE (1895-1976), hospital administrator, was born on 8 May 1895 at Fitzroy, Melbourne, third child of Victorian-born parents Henry William Lilley, printer, and his wife Lillias, née Bull. The family moved to Subiaco, Perth. Educated at Scotch College, on 11 May 1911 Alan became a junior clerk in the audit branch of the Treasury. He enlisted in the Australian Imperial Force (probably on 11 September 1914) and in 1915 served as a sergeant with the 2nd Australian

Field Ambulance in Egypt, at Gallipoli and on Mudros. From October 1916 he was on the Western Front. Commissioned and posted to the 13th Battalion in August 1917, Lieutenant Lilley was seriously wounded in the leg in June 1918 at Vaire Wood, France. He returned to Perth, and to the Treasury; his A.I.F. appointment terminated on 1 April 1919. At the Baptist Church, West Leederville, on 22 November that year he married Mabel Fishburne Reid.

In 1921 Lilley enrolled in medicine at the University of Sydney (M.B., Ch.M., 1926). After graduating, he worked at Royal Prince Alfred Hospital (as a resident medical officer), at the Commonwealth Serum Laboratories, Melbourne, and as acting-director of the Australian Institute of Tropical Medicine, Townsville, Queensland, where he extended his bacteriological studies. Lilley headed (from 1928) R.P.A.H.'s bacteriology department in Sydney. He quickly showed his administrative talents, founding and directing the hospital's blood-transfusion service. In 1933 he was appointed chief executive officer and general superintendent. Under Lilley and (Sir) Herbert Schlink [q.v.11], chairman of the board from 1934, R.P.A.H. consolidated its position as the most innovative public hospital in Sydney; by 1943 its number of beds had increased from 330 to 1200. Lilley toured Europe and America in 1938 and North America in 1947, strengthening his faith in the further planning of medical services. Although his colleagues complained that Lilley had 'a certain aloofness which limited intimate friendships' and that he was 'somewhat short of a sense of humour', he worked harmoniously with the domineering Schlink, despite a widening gulf in their views on state intervention.

In 1943 Lilley had chaired the medical survey committee of the Commonwealth Joint Parliamentary Committee on Social Security. He collected data on hospitals and advocated greater central planning of hospital and private health services, with a more direct role for the Commonwealth. The government largely ignored his proposals. Appointed chairman of the Hospitals Commission of New South Wales in 1944, he successfully juggled the pressures imposed by ministers, hospital boards and the changing policies emanating from the Commonwealth. He resigned in 1958 to become the first medical director of the New South Wales State Cancer Council. A fellow (1939) of the American College of Hospital Administrators and a founding fellow (1945) of the Australian Hospital Association, he was appointed C.B.E. in 1959.

Lilley had maintained his military connexions, serving as lieutenant colonel (1929-33) of his university's regiment. After his retirement in 1967, he published *Sydney Uni-*

versity Regiment (1974). A member of the Australian Club, he enjoyed golf, tennis and photography. He died on 23 July 1976 at the Repatriation General Hospital, Concord, and was cremated; his wife and two sons survived him.

C. E. W. Bean, *The A.I.F. in France*, 1918, 5 (Syd, 1937); G. E. Hall and A. Cousins (eds), *Book of Remembrance of the University of Sydney in the War 1914-1918* (Syd, 1939); K. Maddox, *Schlink of Prince Alfred* (Syd, 1978); J. A. Gillespie, *The Price of Health* (Melb, 1991); *MJA*, 23 Oct 1976, p 656; *RPA*, Spring 1976, p 28; *SMH*, 29 July 1939, 17, 24 Aug 1944, 1 Jan 1959.   JAMES GILLESPIE

LINDELL, JOHN HENRY STOCKTON (1908-1973), health administrator, was born on 17 March 1908 at Moonee Ponds, Melbourne, third child of John Lindell, a manager from Sweden, and his Victorian-born wife Georgina Henrietta, née Stockton. Educated at Essendon Primary and Melbourne High schools, young John completed his Intermediate certificate in 1921. He was apprenticed to a pharmacist and studied at the Melbourne College of Pharmacy, but was considered too young at 18 to sit the final examinations.

On 2 May 1927 Lindell enlisted as a cadet in the Royal Australian Air Force. After qualifying as a pilot at Point Cook, he held a short-service commission (1928-32) in the Royal Air Force, with which he flew bombers and flying boats in England. A crash caused permanent injuries to both his legs and ankles, and left him with a slight rolling gait. Having completed his commission, he returned to Australia and was placed on the R.A.A.F. Reserve as a flying officer.

In 1933 Lindell briefly managed a pharmacy in Surrey Hills before enrolling in medicine at the University of Melbourne (M.B., B.S., 1940; M.S., 1947; M.D., 1948). He struggled to finance his courses with part-time work and assistance from his widowed mother. In third year he gained a residential scholarship to Ormond [q.v.5] College. He came equal top in his final year. On 10 December 1941 Lindell married Margaret Annie Rolland at the Presbyterian Church, East Malvern. That year he had joined the Royal Melbourne Hospital as a resident medical officer. In 1942 he was made deputy medical superintendent and in the following year medical superintendent.

When the Cain [q.v.13] government replaced the Hospitals and Charities Board with the Victorian Hospitals and Charities Commission in 1953, it appointed Lindell as chairman. In this post, which he held for almost twenty years, he became the most influential and respected health administrator in the

State, and a leader at national and international levels. Although the system he inherited was soundly based, additional hospitals were sorely needed, especially in the outer metropolitan area, and major institutions in the inner city—among them the Royal Women's, Royal Children's, the Dental, Alfred, Mercy and Austin hospitals—required rebuilding or remodelling. Lindell tackled these tasks with enthusiasm, courage, wisdom and foresight, tempered by a sensitivity that enabled him to establish priorities and to reconcile compelling but often conflicting interests. His term of office saw a ring of general hospitals built on the suburban periphery, aimed at meeting local needs and diverting routine cases from city hospitals. Similar work occurred in rural towns throughout Victoria.

Lindell was concerned to prevent or correct costly duplication of high-technology functions. He concentrated many services in particular hospitals, or shared them between two institutions—radiotherapy for the treatment of cancer, spinal operations, plastic surgery, open-heart surgery, renal transplants, renal dialysis and laboratory functions like cytology and tissue typing. He attempted to develop the concept of regionalization by interrelating institutions in a functional way within a specific locality, and paid particular attention to the needs of the aged and disabled. Further developments saw the establishment by the University of Melbourne of professorial clinical units in major teaching hospitals and the foundation of Victoria's second medical school, at Monash University. His tactful presence facilitated such initiatives.

About 5 ft 10 ins (178 cm) tall and physically strong, with eyes that sparkled with dash and interest, Lindell exuded an air of authority and purpose. He could be firm when necessary, but was conciliatory and prepared to listen to opinions contrary to his own. His humanitarian approach helped to lower the barriers that separated hospitals from society, making them an integral part of the communities they served.

A fellow of the Pharmaceutical Society of Australia and of the Australian Institute of Hospital Administrators, Lindell also belonged to the Beefsteak and Royal Melbourne Golf clubs. He retired in 1972 and was appointed C.M.G. in 1973. Survived by his wife, two sons and two daughters, he died of cancer on 24 August 1973 at Eaglemont and was cremated.

K. S. Inglis, *Hospital and Community* (Melb, 1958); T. Hewat, *The Florey* (Syd, 1990); *MJA*, 2, 1973, p 984; *Hospital J of Aust*, Jan 1973; *Herald* (Melb), 2 Feb 1957, 12 Aug 1967; *Sun News-Pictorial*, 23 Nov 1972; *Age* (Melb), 27 Aug 1973.

LEONARD B. SWINDEN

LINDON, SIR LEONARD CHARLES EDWARD (1896-1978), neurosurgeon, was born on 8 February 1896 in North Adelaide, second son of James Hemery Lindon (d.1897), a schoolmaster from England, and his Queensland-born wife Mary Ellen Cockburn, née Mayne, grand-daughter of W. C. Mayne [q.v.5]. James Lindon had founded Queen's School, North Adelaide. Leonard was educated at Geelong Church of England Grammar School, Victoria, the Collegiate School of St Peter, Adelaide, and (on a scholarship) the University of Adelaide (M.B., 1919; M.S., 1923). On 11 March 1915 he enlisted in the Australian Imperial Force; he served with the 1st Australian Stationary Hospital in the Gallipoli campaign, but was sent home in March 1916 and discharged to resume his medical studies.

Lindon won a Rhodes scholarship in 1918 which he took up in 1920. His time at Balliol College, Oxford, overlapped that of (Sir) Hugh Cairns [q.v.7] who later influenced him greatly. Lindon worked as a house-surgeon at the Radcliffe Infirmary and was elected a fellow of the Royal colleges of Surgeons (England and Edinburgh, 1922). On 12 December 1921 at Holy Trinity Church, Brompton, London, he married Jean Monteith Marten whose father had built up Adelaide's largest medical practice and occasionally performed brain surgery. In 1923 Lindon returned home. He assisted his father-in-law and brother-in-law, (Sir) Henry Newland [q.v.11], and developed interests in tuberculosis and neurological surgery.

In 1929-30 Lindon studied neurosurgery, with Harvey Cushing at Boston, United States of America, and Cairns in London. He published twenty articles, eleven on neurosurgery, which were characterized by a self-criticism unusual in that period. Keeping abreast of international developments by reading and travelling, he depended on general surgery for his living and practised at the Children's Hospital and the (Royal) Adelaide Hospital. At the latter institution he established a neurosurgical clinic in 1931 and was among the first in Australia to obtain X-rays of blood vessels in the brain. In 1940 he helped to found the Society of Australasian Neurological Surgeons. Lindon held various offices in the University of Adelaide, the South Australian branch of the British (later Australian) Medical Association and the Royal Australasian College of Surgeons (vice-president 1956-58, president 1959-61).

As lieutenant colonel, Australian Army Medical Corps, A.I.F., he served in the Middle East in 1940-41 and had charge of the neurosurgical centre at the 2nd/2nd Australian General Hospital. For this work he was mentioned in dispatches. Back in Adelaide, he performed part-time military duties in 1942.

Following his retirement from the Royal Adelaide Hospital in 1951, Lindon maintained his practice. In 1964 he was knighted. The modesty so prominent in his publications was not always apparent in his conduct, but he avoided controversy. He rowed in his youth, played cricket and tennis, and took golfing holidays with his friends. Troubled by arthritis, he gave up neurosurgery in 1971. After his wife's death in 1974, his health deteriorated. Survived by his daughter and two sons, he died on 28 August 1978 in North Adelaide and was cremated. His portrait (1964) by Rex Bramleigh is held by the Royal Australasian College of Surgeons, Melbourne.

J. E. Hughes, *Henry Simpson Newland* (Adel, 1972); *Aust and NZ J of Surgery*, July 1974; *MJA*, 11 Aug 1979; *Advertiser* (Adel), 23 June 1959, 31 Aug 1978; Roy A'sian College of Surgeons Archives, Melb; Rhodes Trust, Oxford, Univ Adel records (Mort L); information from Prof D. Simpson, Univ Adel, and Mr T. Dinning, Mylor, SA.

G. J. FRAENKEL

LINDSAY, HAROLD ARTHUR (1900-1969), author and conservationist, was born on 13 November 1900 at Hyde Park, Adelaide, eldest of three children of South Australian-born parents George Stuart Lindsay, sharebroker, and his second wife Anna, née Wilberth. Harold was educated at Kyre College (1911-14) and the Collegiate School of St Peter (1915), but the fees left little money to clothe him in the style of his schoolmates or to provide those extras they took for granted. He developed an acute sense of inferiority and left school at 15 to work in an office, which he hated. George Lindsay, who had accompanied his brother-in-law David Lindsay [q.v.10] on several expeditions, taught Harold bushcraft.

From the age of 19 Harold (nicknamed 'Bill') performed various jobs in the country. In 1928 he turned to bee-keeping. On 25 February 1933 at the Congregational Church, Highgate, Adelaide, he married Margaret Hilda McDonald. He supplemented his income by contributing to the *Bulletin* and other magazines for which he wrote short stories, humorous pieces and articles about nature. Enlisting in the Australian Imperial Force on 23 February 1942, Lindsay rose to warrant officer, class one, in the Australian Army Education Service: he taught bushcraft to servicemen in Australia, New Guinea and New Britain. After he was discharged on 23 November 1945, he earned his living solely from writing. *The Bushman's Handbook* and *Halliday's Quest* appeared in 1948, and were followed by five novels for adults and four books for children. *The First Walkabout*, written with Norman Tindale, was named the best

Australian children's book for 1955 by the Children's Book Council of Australia. Lindsay used the pen-names 'Larrapinta', 'Bert the Carpenter', 'A. B. Carrick', 'Lucerne Flea', 'Bogaduck', 'Ex R.S.M.' and 'Archaean'.

For some years his 'Naturalist's Diary' column was published in the Melbourne *Age* and the *Sunday Advertiser*, Adelaide. In the 1920s Lindsay had become passionately interested in conservation and called for Heywood, an Unley Park estate, to be converted to a reserve for native birds and scrub. Recurring illness prevented him from mixing with people and promoting his ideas. When he joined the army his sickness was identified as an allergy and he was desensitized. On his return to civilian life he made the environment his crusade and founded the Adelaide Bushwalkers in 1946 to help his cause. This group replanted part of the Mount Bold reservoir reserve with endangered native species, and sought areas of isolated country that could be designated as sanctuaries and national parks. In 1947 Lindsay read about the English National Trust for Places of Historic Interest or Natural Beauty; largely through his efforts, the National Trust of South Australia was established in 1955.

Although Lindsay had his supporters, some people thought that he was opinionated and others regarded him as a bore. His *Handbook* had offended many conservationists by describing how a bushman could trap and kill birds and animals for survival; his later suggestion that eucalypts in the Mount Lofty ranges should be replaced by commercially viable, less flammable, imported trees alarmed field naturalists in the Royal Society of South Australia. Yet, without him, South Australia would have lost much of its natural and historic environment. Survived by his daughter, Lindsay died of coronary artery disease on 4 December 1969 at Highgate and was buried in Centennial Park cemetery.

G. Dutton, *Out in the Open* (Brisb, 1994); *Adel Review*, Mar 1996; *SMH*, 20 Sept 1948, 7 Aug 1955, 13 Feb, 16 July 1960, 9 Dec 1961, 11 Jan 1964; *Advertiser* (Adel), 14 Mar 1950, 26 June 1954, 21 July 1960, 6 Dec 1969; H. de Berg, Harold Arthur Lindsay (taped interview, 15 Mar 1960, NL); H. A. Lindsay papers (Mort L) *and* scrap-books (Barr Smith L, Univ Adel).

KERRIE ROUND

LINDSAY, LOMA; *see* LATOUR

LINDSAY, MARY ANN JOSEPHINE (1892-1975), circus artiste, was born on 7 February 1892 at Wentworth, New South Wales, eldest of six children of native-born parents William Alfred Sole, circus bandsman, and his wife

Eliza Jane, daughter of William George Perry, a circus performer known as 'W. G. Eroni'. In 1890 the four Sole brothers had joined Eroni Bros Circus as bandsmen. The circus travelled by road: a glittering band-carriage led a procession of splendid Dallinger living-wagons, an extensive menagerie and as many as 135 horses.

Born 'in the business', Mary trained as a performer with her siblings and cousins. At 12 she was taught the trapeze by Charlie Harris who had been a 'gear man' for 'the Flying Herberts'. She soon perfected her own balancing act on the high trapeze, and also became an accomplished wirewalker and acrobatic equestrienne. Meanwhile, she learned to read and write in the horse-tent with a slate and chalk.

As the Perry family grew in numbers and diverged in ambitions, the Eroni circus began to fragment. Mary went with Gus St Leon's Circus in 1913-15. By late 1916 the Sole family was touring the northern rivers region of New South Wales as Sole Bros Circus under the direction of Bill Sole. On 4 February 1919 at St Mary's Catholic Cathedral, Sydney, Mary married Albert Spencer Lindsay, an acrobat in the circus. Next year, after performing throughout Australia and New Zealand on the Fuller [qq.v.8] circuit, the Lindsays sailed for South Africa and thence for England. As 'La Belle Marie', Mary thrilled vaudeville audiences in London with her balancing trapeze act. When her father and uncle were killed by an explosion in June 1923, the Lindsays hurried home. Bert took over the management of the circus.

In 1926-29 Sole Bros Circus toured southern and central Africa; the troupe gave a special performance in the Congo for the King of the Belgians. Returning to Australia during the Depression, the circus re-established its name and reputation, and briefly combined with Ashton's [q.v.7] Circus in 1932. Mary 'walked the wire . . . flew on the flying trapeze . . . walked up a pyramid of swords, was the queen of the Roman rings, and worked the horses'. She also sold tickets, organized finances, negotiated with councils for sites, oversaw the canvas-making and supervised transport by truck or train.

Mary and Bert retired to their home at Manly, Sydney, in 1964. They handed over direction of the circus to their daughter Jean and her husband Joseph Perry. After Bert died, at the age of 81 Mary took up residence in a caravan on the family's 200-acre (80 ha) farm at Dunmore where she tended a range of animals. A slight but stocky woman, energetic and forthright, 'Aunty' Mary was widely known and respected by Australia's circus and show people. She died on 17 April 1975 at Kiama and was buried in Frenchs Forest lawn cemetery; her daughter survived her.

M. St Leon (comp), *The Circus in Australia 1842-1921* (Syd, 1981) and *Australian Circus Reminiscences* (Syd, 1984); *Music Maker*, 20 June 1945; *Hillston Spectator*, 14 Sept 1906; *Bulletin*, 9 July 1914; *Kiama Independent*, 18 Apr 1975; *Daily Telegraph* (Syd), 23 Apr 1975; M. St Leon, research notes (NL); information from the late Mrs M. Lindsay, and the late Mr M. Perry.

MARK VALENTINE ST LEON

LING, HAROLD EUSTACE HILL (1907-1966), manufacturer, was born on 27 September 1907 at Petersham, Sydney, fourth of five sons of native-born parents Harry Hill Ling, auditor, and his first wife Alma, née Cafe. Educated at Mosman Superior Public School and, in Melbourne, to Intermediate certificate level, Harold worked in Adelaide from 1924 as a clerk, salesman and book-keeper for Goldsbrough, Mort [qq.v.4,5] & Co. Ltd. At St Paul's Anglican Church, Adelaide, on 2 November 1929 he married Eileen Winifred Hill. Called up for full-time service in the Militia on 18 May 1942, Ling transferred to the Australian Imperial Force and joined the Central Australia Transport Column as a clerk. He was promoted sergeant in October 1943 and discharged on 7 February 1946.

About this time Lance Leonard Hill, Ling's brother-in-law and neighbour at Glenunga, Adelaide, built an outdoor rotary clothes-hoist for his wife. As friendly requests turned to orders for similar hoists, and as advertising increased demand, the backyard activity became better organized. Ling joined Hill to manage the accounts and marketing. Gilbert Toyne's wind-up hoist, patented in South Australia in 1925, had been manufactured and distributed by L. L. Lambert. When Toyne's patent lapsed in 1946, Hill and Ling secured their own patents. That year they formed a partnership, rented a small factory at Fullarton and expanded production. Lack of materials threatened the viability of the enterprise. Faced with postwar restrictions and shortages, and the reluctance of British Tube Mills Ltd to sell them iron and steel, they bought salvage items and later imported pipe from France.

On 15 January 1948 Hills Hoists Ltd was formed with Hill its chairman, Ling a director, and only £12 226 in assets. They raised additional money from their families and some of the workers, thereby establishing a team tradition. Staff received the first shares. On 17 March Ling was appointed managing director. One month later the Fullarton property was purchased. Within a year of operating, the company returned a dividend of £1262. Ling treated the firm as a large family, with a mixture of paternalism, benevolence and mateship. He championed the cause of the underdog, gave and expected loyalty, and shared profits with his staff through a bonus system. In June 1949 the company established a non-contributory superannuation scheme and £750 was invested for the first seventy employees. By 1954 Hills began issuing shares to all workers with more than three years service.

Improvisation, adaptation and tenacity were fundamental to the sustained growth and success of Hills Hoists. The firm boosted the popularity of rotary clothes-lines by introducing a lever-action model which was one-third cheaper than existing types. From 1950 Hills acquired subsidiaries in the fields of galvanizing, tube-manufacture and storage. By 1954 the company had branches throughout Australia; by 1959 there were outlets in New Zealand and Britain. Hills consolidated its activities at Edwardstown, and widened its range of manufactures to include laundry-prams, folding chairs, ironing-tables, and playground equipment such as swings and basketball-poles. Steel tubing was sold to other manufacturers. Having undertaken research and development before the introduction of television in 1956, Hills anticipated the demand for aluminium tubes for antennas. A television rental and repair service followed.

When Hill retired from the board in 1956, Ling became chairman of directors. The company had a turnover of £2 million in 1957 and employed 600 staff. Publicly listed as Hills Industries Ltd in 1958, the firm was less paternalistic under the scrutiny of the Stock Exchange of Adelaide, although Ling maintained regular Friday-night gatherings around a keg of beer. Due to ill health, he resigned as managing director in 1965, but remained chairman of the board. In less than twenty years his drive, initiative, vision and enthusiasm had built a multi-million-dollar business with 1400 employees. Survived by his wife, son and two daughters, Ling died of cirrhosis of the liver on 12 December 1966 at his Urrbrae home and was buried with Catholic rites in Centennial Park cemetery. His son Bob succeeded him as managing director. Ling's estate was sworn for probate at $71 416.

D. Harris, *What a Line!* (Adel, 1996); *Hills Herald*, 4, no 10, July 1978; *News* (Adel), 4 Oct 1961; *Australian*, 8 Aug 1965; *Advertiser* (Adel), 13 Dec 1966; information from Mrs P. MacDonald, Auckland, NZ, and Mr R. H. Ling, Mitcham, Adel.
BERNARD O'NEIL

LIONS, FRANCIS (1901-1972), organic chemist, was born on 30 November 1901 in Perth, second son of John Maximillian Lions, a Swedish-born engineer, and his wife Mary, née McDonald, who came from Scotland. The

family moved to Sydney in 1903. Frank attended Sydney Boys' High School, where he was dux and captain of the school. In the Leaving certificate examination (1918) he came first in the State in chemistry and second in physics. At the University of Sydney (B.Sc., 1923), he excelled at various sports, including cycling, rugby, boxing and diving; his face displayed the scars of these activities. He graduated with first-class honours and the university medals in chemistry (1922) and organic chemistry (1923).

Awarded an 1851 Exhibition scholarship in 1923, Lions worked in England at the Victoria University of Manchester (Ph.D., 1925) under Professor (Sir) Robert Robinson and accompanied him to Brasenose College, Oxford. In 1926 Lions returned to the University of Sydney as lecturer and demonstrator in chemistry. At St Stephen's Presbyterian Church, Macquarie Street, on 2 November 1935 he married Wilga Oscella Moore. She died in 1950. On 18 August 1951 he married with Presbyterian forms Jean Elizabeth Ross at her father's Haberfield home. Both his wives were chemists and schoolteachers.

His first research paper, published with Robinson in 1925, had concerned model synthetic compounds related to the molecular structure of the plant alkaloid brucine. It was the forerunner of an extensive series of publications, up to 1968, dealing primarily with the synthesis and reactions of heterocyclic organic compounds. Lions's knowledge of heterocyclic chemistry was monumental, and he usually lectured without notes. He recognized that certain heterocyclic compounds would bind to metals, and in the late 1940s began to think about the design of organic molecules which would encapsulate metals tightly. Small molecules able to bind metals at one or two sites were well known, but the possibility of wrapping up a metal with a single molecule binding at six sites had been recognized in only one instance, that of Komplexon (1,2-ethanediamine tetraacetic acid), and this discovery was then not widely known.

Lions discussed his ideas with an inorganic chemist Francis Dwyer [q.v.14] who was enthusiastic; the two men began a significant and fruitful scientific collaboration. They and their students synthesised the organic compounds and their metal chelate complexes, and established their properties. These molecules became justly famous because of their design elements and high stabilities. It is a tribute to Lions's knowledge and foresight that he recognized all the ingredients essential for success with such molecules, including the necessary types of binding atoms, the atoms needed to link them, and the spatial requirements of the metal and the binding atoms. It was grand design some twenty years ahead of its time, and a milestone in the chemical literature. Proud of his classical linguistic knowledge, Lions called the molecules 'sexidentates' (six-toothed), and was offended when the editor of the *Journal of the American Chemical Society* changed this to 'sexadentates' because he thought they would be confused with contraceptives. In the 1950s he toured the United States of America, informing many inorganic chemists about these important compounds and their variants.

Frank Lions was an imaginative chemist and an enthusiastic teacher, remembered with admiration and affection by his students and colleagues. His rational views on science and human affairs influenced not only the students but also the conduct of the university. Promoted senior lecturer in 1944 and reader in 1946, he deserved appointment to a university chair, but 'imported' professors were preferred for such positions. As the sole fellow of the university senate elected by the graduates from 1949 to 1959, Lions was a significant force for inducing change in the university, and was one of the first to recognize the need for a student health service.

His contributions to science were officially acknowledged by his election as president of the Royal Society of New South Wales in 1946 and the award of its medal for 1965. Lions died of a coronary artery occlusion on 13 March 1972 at Hornsby hospital and was cremated with Methodist forms; his wife survived him, as did the daughter and two of the three sons of his first marriage.

Roy Soc of NSW, *J and Procs*, 100, 1966, p 93, 105, 1972, p 56; *Reviews of Pure and Applied Chemistry*, 19, 1969, p 177; *SMH*, 27 Jan 1919, 18, 27 July 1923, 16 Apr 1932, 3 Oct 1936, 10 Mar 1943, 6 Nov 1946, 10 Nov 1949, 26 Mar 1966.

R. W. Rickards
A. M. Sargeson

LIPSCOMBE, STANLEY ROBERT (1918-1980), antique dealer, was born on 15 December 1918 at Paddington, Sydney. When he was 2 years old he and his twin brother Edwin were adopted by Samuel Edwin Lipscombe, an engine driver from England, and his Australian-born wife Ethel, née English. Stanley was educated at Villawood and Lidcombe Commercial public schools. In his youth he started to buy and sell furniture, quickly learning how to differentiate between antiques and reproductions.

After leaving school at the age of 16, Lipscombe was employed by Fred Naylor at the Antique Furniture Co., 40 Market Street, where he learned the art of French polishing. This skill became his entrée to many dealers' shops and their clientele. An avid reader with a photographic memory, he acquired enough knowledge to open his own shop in Goulburn

Street in 1942. He dealt mainly in Victorian antiques and pieces of early Australiana—which came largely from outer Western Sydney—and restored most of the furniture that he received.

Lipscombe increased his knowledge of the Georgian period. In 1943 he moved to Castlereagh Street and built an attractive neo-Georgian façade on his shop. His courtly manners, quick wit and well-measured ways were business assets, and he took elocution lessons to correct his high-pitched speech. From 1946 his friend Arthur Grimwade of Christie's silver department acquired suitable pieces for him at English sales before new fiscal controls made the cost of importing silver almost prohibitive. By the late 1940s Lipscombe's clients included the prominent collector Gladys Penfold Hyland [q.v.] and her husband.

A generous man, Lipscombe donated prizes for raffles, helped to organize exhibitions, and initiated valuation days for the Australian Red Cross Society and other charities; he entranced the ladies with his wealth of knowledge, valuing and often buying their pieces. He was a Freemason, and belonged to St John Ambulance Brigade's auxiliary and the Rotary Club of Sydney. From 1960 to 1973 he answered questions in an irregular column, 'Collector's Corner', in the *Australian Women's Weekly*.

In 1962 Lipscombe visited England. There he was described as resembling a 'little boy in a lollipop shop'. Next year he opened another shop in Bathurst Street, Sydney. Many famous antiques passed through his hands, including a painting of foxhounds by George Stubbs (now in the Tate gallery, London) and the Caernarvon glass, a spectacular mirror. Lipscombe's knowledge spanned paintings, furniture, silver and porcelain. A founding member (1949) of the Ceramic Collectors' Society, he advised the Art Gallery of New South Wales on the purchase of antique Oriental ceramics and lectured (1970-79) on arts and crafts at the University of New South Wales.

In 1976 Lipscombe moved from Woollahra to the Park Regis apartments in the city. Very much a loner, he had a passion for horse-racing. On 6 September 1980 he suffered a cerebral haemorrhage at Rosehill Racecourse; he died that day at Westmead hospital and was cremated. In conducting his business Lipscombe rarely issued receipts: he knew who had given him stock on consignment or for repairs. On his death his executors found it difficult to determine what belonged to whom.

Sun-Herald, 29 Nov 1964; *Daily Examiner* (Grafton), 3 Aug 1971; *SMH*, 26 Apr 1973, 23 Feb 1979, 8 Sept 1980, 21 Dec 1991; *Aust Financial Re-*

view, 23 Sept 1980, 2 Jan 1981, 7 Jan 1987; J. Pagan, obituary, 10 Sept 1980 (ms, held by Mrs F. Campbell, Syd); information from Messrs W. F. Bradshaw, Woollahra, Syd, E. Lipscombe, Toukley, NSW, and A. Grimwade, St James's, Lond.

LOUISE LANDIS
ALAN LANDIS

LITTLE, ELAINE MARJORY (1884-1974), pathologist, was born on 2 June 1884 in Brisbane, second of four daughters of Joseph Henry Little, an Irish-born medical practitioner, and his English-born wife Agnes Elisabeth, née Mellor. After his wife died in 1890, Dr Little took his family to England for several years; back in Australia, he practised at Armidale, New South Wales, and then in Brisbane. Marjory attended private schools in Brisbane and England, and the Girls' High School, Armidale. A small legacy enabled her to enrol (1906) in science at the University of Sydney (B.Sc., 1911; M.B., 1915). She lived in Women's College (1906-10) and was a resident tutor (1914-15) there while demonstrating in pathology.

Junior (1915) and senior (1916-17) resident medical officer at Royal Prince Alfred Hospital, Little replaced A. H. Tebbutt (who was on active service) as the hospital's pathologist. Following his return, she wanted to enlist. As the Australian Army Medical Corps did not admit female medical officers, she paid her own fare to England and began work at the Lister Institute of Preventive Medicine, London. She was appointed captain, Royal Army Medical Corps, in April 1918. The institute's director (Sir) Charles Martin [q.v.10], then working in France, called her to Rouen where she served as pathologist with the 25th Stationary Hospital. She co-authored a report on fatal influenza cases in British army hospitals in France which was published by the Medical Research Council (Great Britain). Later she took charge of the isolation hospital (46th S.H.) laboratory at Étaples, earning the praise of her commanding officer Colonel S. R. Cummins. When the cold and discomforts of winter had given way to spring, Marjory found solace in the adjoining pine forest: 'those to whom the forest had become like a close friend knew where to find the glades where the primroses and lilies-of-the-valley flowered'.

Having returned to Sydney in January 1920, Dr Little resumed her post as a demonstrator at the university, set up private practice as a pathologist in Macquarie Street, and published 'Life in a Lab in France' in the *Sydney University Medical Journal* (1923) and an article on dysentery in the *Medical Journal of Australia* (1923). She was appointed consulting haematologist at Sydney and Royal North Shore hospitals, and honorary pathologist at the Rachel Forster Hospital for Women and Children (she was to be a board-member in 1949-62). President (1935-36) of the Medical Women's Society of New South Wales and one of the few women invited to become a foundation fellow of the Royal Australasian College of Physicians in 1938, she also became a fellow (1956) of the Royal College of Pathologists of Australia.

In 1958 Little gave the annual postgraduate oration of the faculty of medicine in the university's Great Hall. It was entitled 'Some pioneer medical women of the University of Sydney' and was based on the careers of her friends, among them Elsie Dalyell, Margaret Harper and Susie O'Reilly [qq.v.8,9,11]. Marjory was tall, with a severe hair-style, and seemed forbidding, but beneath her stern exterior she was kind and friendly, and dedicated to encouraging younger medical women. Retiring from practice in 1952, she spent her remaining years enjoying her house and garden at Pymble. She died on 2 May 1974 at Lane Cove and was cremated.

G. E. Hall and A. Cousins (eds), *Book of Remembrance of the University of Sydney in the Great War 1914-1918* (Syd, 1939); A. G. Butler (ed), *Official History of the Australian Army Medical Services in the War of 1914-1918*, 3 (Canb, 1943); L. Cohen, *Rachel Forster Hospital* (Syd, 1972); G. L. McDonald (ed), *Roll of the Royal Australasian College of Physicians*, 1 (Syd, 1988); *MJA*, 31 Aug 1974, p 338; Roy A'sian College of Physicians Archives (Syd); information from Mrs S. R. Simpson, Bowral, NSW, and Dr J. Edwards, Waverley, Syd.

BRENDA HEAGNEY

LLOYD, CHARLES EDWARD MAURICE (1899-1956), army officer, was born on 2 February 1899 at South Fremantle, Western Australia, second and sole surviving child of Thomas Edward Lloyd, postmaster, and his wife Edith, née Lock, both native-born. His parents separated in 1901 and his father committed suicide two years later. Edith worked as a telephone attendant at Coolgardie and Fremantle (from 1909) while raising her son. Educated at Beaconsfield, Fremantle Boys' Central and Perth Modern schools, Charles entered the Royal Military College, Duntroon, Federal Capital Territory, in February 1915. Fellow cadets nicknamed him 'Gaffer' because of his serious demeanour.

Graduating as lieutenant in 1918, Lloyd was sent to complete his training with British Army units in England (1919) and India (1920), following which he held staff appointments with the field artillery in Victoria and New South Wales. At St Stephen's Presbyterian Church, Caulfield West, Melbourne, on 31 December 1921 he married Sybil Drummond. He studied at the University of Sydney (LL.B., 1925) and, after attending the Staff

College at Camberley, England (1932-33), was appointed brigade major of the 4th Divisional Artillery in Melbourne; he was promoted major in 1937. Next year he was posted to Army Headquarters as deputy assistant director (later assistant-director) of artillery.

On 13 October 1939 Lloyd was seconded to the Australian Imperial Force and was assistant quartermaster general, I Corps, when he sailed for the Middle East in May 1940. As a colonel on 9th Division headquarters (from 24 December) he was chief of staff to Major General (Sir) Leslie Morshead [q.v.] during the siege of Tobruk (April to October 1941); he subsequently served as chief liaison officer at A.I.F. Headquarters, Middle East. His record in North Africa cemented his reputation as a capable professional and a staff officer 'of uncommon intellectual gifts'. He was appointed C.B.E. (1941). In January-February 1942 he was deputy intendant-general in General Sir Archibald (Earl) Wavell's Australian-British-Dutch-American Command, Netherlands East Indies. He held the temporary rank of major general in the post and Wavell judged him 'a staff officer of great quality'.

Back in Melbourne, Lloyd reverted to brigadier and had two brief postings before July 1942 when he was made director of staff duties, Allied Land Forces Headquarters, South-West Pacific Area. In September Lieutenant General (Sir) Sydney Rowell [q.v.] asked for him as brigadier, general staff, I Corps, in Papua, but in February 1943 the commander-in-chief General Sir Thomas Blamey [q.v.13] appointed him adjutant-general at L.H.Q. Once more a temporary major general, Lloyd was entrusted with rejuvenating this key staff branch. He flew to London in July 1945 to represent Australia at a conference on the reorganization of the S.W.P.A. Home again, in December he was an expert witness before (Sir) George Ligertwood's [q.v.] inquiry into Lieutenant General Gordon Bennett's [q.v.13] escape from Singapore.

Blamey's successor Lieutenant General (Sir) Vernon Sturdee [q.v.] decided to send Lloyd to Washington as head of the Australian Military Mission—allegedly in retaliation for perceived earlier obstructiveness. Because the post was of reduced military importance in peacetime, Lloyd believed that his prospects of advancement were at an end. He left the army and was placed on the Reserve of Officers on 25 February 1946 as honorary major general; he had been thrice mentioned in dispatches in 1941-42.

Deputy managing director of the Melbourne Argus and Australasian Ltd for eight months in 1946, Lloyd found the newspaper world uncongenial. His attempt to gain Liberal Party pre-selection that year for a seat in Federal parliament proved abortive. Family evidence suggests that he suffered a breakdown at this point, brought on by regret at his hasty resignation from the army. Appointment as a member of the government committee which reported in 1948 on the administration of the British Commonwealth Occupation Force in Japan marked his recovery. From August he represented the International Refugee Organization in Australia. He was in the Republic of (South) Korea in 1951-53 as chief of mission for the United Nations Korean Reconstruction Agency. Gripped by anything to do with postwar reconstruction, he returned to Australia and was vice-chairman of Navcot (Aust.) Pty Ltd which was associated with shipping refugees from Europe.

Lloyd's hobbies were woodworking and model engineering. On a visit to relations in Western Australia, he died of jaundice on 31 May 1956 in the Repatriation General Hospital, Hollywood, Perth. He was buried with Anglican rites in Karrakatta cemetery; his wife, daughter and two sons survived him. A portrait (1944) of Lloyd by (Sir) Ivor Hele is held by the Australian War Memorial, Canberra.

G. Long, *To Benghazi* (Canb, 1952) and *The Final Campaigns* (Canb, 1963); L. Wigmore, *The Japanese Thrust* (Canb, 1957); B. Maughan, *Tobruk and El Alamein* (Canb, 1966); J. Hetherington, *Blamey, Controversial Soldier* (Canb, 1973); S. F. Rowell, *Full Circle* (Melb, 1974); D. M. Horner, *High Command* (Canb, 1982); A. B. Lodge, *The Fall of General Gordon Bennett* (Syd, 1986); *Reveille* (Syd), 1 Nov 1939; *SMH*, 2 Jan, 11 Mar 1942; *West Australian*, 1 June 1956; records held by and information from Mrs S. M. Todner, Sth Fremantle, Perth, and Mrs J. M. Lloyd, Brighton, Melb.

C. D. COULTHARD-CLARK

LLOYD, ERIC EDWIN LONGFIELD (1890-1957), soldier, intelligence officer and diplomat, was born on 13 September 1890 at Marrickville, Sydney, son of George Thrift Lloyd, a banker from Ireland, and his native-born wife Amelia Sarah, née Hunter. The family moved to Ireland when Eric was aged 12 and he attended St Andrew's College, Dublin. He joined the Union Bank of Australia Ltd in London and served for two years in the King Edward's Horse. The bank transferred him to Sydney in 1912.

Commissioned in the 29th Infantry (Australian Rifles), Militia, in 1913, Lloyd was appointed second lieutenant in the Australian Imperial Force on 27 August 1914. He landed at Gallipoli on 25 April 1915 with the 1st Battalion. Awarded the Military Cross for leading a raid against a Turkish trench on 5 June, he was promoted captain (July), mentioned in dispatches, and twice named in divisional orders for 'gallantry and valuable service'. In January 1916 he was invalided to Australia suffering from typhoid fever. On 2 May that year at St Andrew's Anglican Cathedral, Sydney, he married Elsie Lilian Wilkinson. His A.I.F. appointment terminated in December, but he remained on full-time duty with the Intelligence Section of the General Staff, 2nd Military District, Sydney, until his demobilization in 1920.

Lloyd joined the Pacific branch of the Prime Minister's Department and began learning Japanese. In May 1921 he was appointed to the investigation branch of the Attorney-General's Department and posted as inspector-in-charge, Sydney. He kept communists, fascists and Nazis under surveillance, and monitored the activities of the New Guard. In addition, he performed part-time military intelligence work (1921-35) before transferring to the Reserve of Officers as honorary lieutenant colonel. In 1925-30 he was also aide-de-camp to the State governor Sir Dudley de Chair [q.v.8]. On 30 April 1932 Lloyd was one of three Commonwealth officials who successfully argued against (Sir) Walter Massy-Greene's [q.v.10] plan to break into the State taxation office to obtain documents being guarded by supporters of Premier J. T. Lang [q.v.9].

In 1934 Lloyd was political adviser and interpreter to (Sir) John Latham [q.v.10] on his mission to the Netherlands East Indies, China and Japan. Recommended by Latham, in the following year he was appointed Australian trade (later government) commissioner, Tokyo. Frank Clune [q.v.13] visited Lloyd and found him 'quiet, dignified, and cultured ... a worthy representative'. Others referred to his charm, his strong character, and his capacity for hard work, and were impressed by his sympathetic understanding of his hosts, with whom he got on well (though he later admitted detesting Japanese food). Lloyd proved to be a reliable reporter on Japanese politics and international ambitions. In 1938 he judged that the Japanese were preparing for 'a protracted state of war'; he noted Japan's interest in expanding southward, as far as Australia. Posted home in 1940, he rejoined the investigation branch as deputy-director.

A conflict between the armed services and the Attorney-General's Department over control of Australia's internal security appeared to be resolved in March 1941 with Lloyd's appointment as director of the new Commonwealth Security Service. Dissension between the armed services and the C.S.S. began, and disputes between the army, navy and air force continued. The government asked A. M. Duncan [q.v.14], the Victorian chief commissioner of police, to review the security service. Following claims that Lloyd was too closely linked to the army, Duncan recommended in January 1942 that W. J. MacKay [q.v.10], the New South Wales police commissioner, be appointed to head the C.S.S. as director-general. Continuing as director, Lloyd was second-in-charge to MacKay, and to his successor W. B. Simpson.

In January 1944 Lloyd replaced H. E. Jones [q.v.9] as director of the investigation branch and superintending peace officer, while retaining his position in the security service. He was appointed director-general of security in 1945. When the investigation branch and security service merged later that year, he was made director, Commonwealth Investigation Service. Among its various functions the C.I.S. inquired into security and financial irregularities, carried out surveillance and conducted character checks. In early 1946 Lloyd took leave and went to Tokyo as counsellor to William Macmahon Ball, the British Commonwealth member of the Allied Council for Japan. Although Ball thought that Lloyd was considerate, loyal and eager, he described him as a poor linguist who lacked understanding of Japan and who was 'wholly unequipped for the position he occupied'.

Lloyd returned to Australia and his C.I.S. post in 1947. The security situation was deteriorating. Classified information was being leaked to the Soviet embassy; Opposition politicians accused the government of allowing communists to penetrate defence research establishments; and the United States of America placed an embargo on intelligence exchanges with Australia. These developments undermined confidence in the C.I.S. which had insufficient resources to fulfil its roles. In 1949 the government formed the Australian Security Intelligence Organization to investigate subversion, to maintain central security records, to carry out checks on immigrants, and to liaise with other authorities at home and abroad. Lloyd had not been consulted on the decision and did not want his agency emasculated. His health began to suffer and he retired in 1952.

Living in Canberra and at Castle Hill, Sydney, Lloyd pursued his hobbies of motoring, forestry and Oriental studies. All the while he continued to believe that Japan remained expansionist. He belonged to the Imperial Service Club, Sydney, and the Barton, Canberra, sub-branch of the Returned Sailors', Soldiers' and Airmen's Imperial League of Australia. In the early 1950s he was patron of the Australian Rifles Old Comrades' Association. Survived by his wife and three sons, he died of tuberculosis on 18 July 1957 in Canberra Community Hospital and was cremated.

Longfield Lloyd was a softly spoken, self-effacing, modest and cautious man, and a dependable public servant. One journalist sensed that he was uncomfortable in the spotlight, and that he spoke quickly and used humour to deflect questions. (Sir) Kenneth Bailey [q.v.13] wrote that Lloyd displayed the qualities of a 'gallant soldier': 'courage, loyalty, unassuming dignity, the ability to set the call of duty above all personal considerations', and 'the unswerving acceptance of the decisions of his Government and his Department'.

F. Cain, *The Origins of Political Surveillance in Australia* (Syd, 1983); and *The Australian Security Intelligence Organization* (Melb, 1994); W. M. Ball, *Intermittent Diplomat*, A. Rix ed (Melb, 1988); W. Gobert, *The Origins of Australian Diplomatic Intelligence in Asia 1933-1941* (Canb, 1992); *JRAHS*, 59, pt 4, Dec 1973, p 247; *Sunday Telegraph* (Syd), 2 Mar 1947; *SMH*, 19 July 1957, 12 Aug 1970; Lloyd papers (NL); A367/4 items C23512 and C23512 pt 2, A367/1 item C15000A, A432/15 item 55/4432 and A7359/84 item MS238 (AA, Canb).

DAVID SADLEIR

LLOYD, GWENDOLEN KENT (1899-1965), educationist, was born on 16 July 1899 at South Yarra, Melbourne, third of seven children of Wilfred Kent Hughes, a Victorian-born surgeon, and his English-born wife Clementina Jane, née Rankin (d.1916). Wilfrid and Ellen [qq.v.] were her brother and sister. Gwenda was educated (1909-15) at Melbourne Church of England Girls' Grammar School, where she was captain. For two years she cared for her terminally ill mother, then worked as a member of a Voluntary Aid Detachment at the repatriation hospital, Macleod. In 1919 she enrolled at the University of Melbourne (B.A., 1922; Dip.Ed., 1923); after graduating, she travelled abroad.

In 1925 Miss Kent Hughes joined the staff of the middle school at M.C.E.G.G.S. as assistant house mistress to Dorothy Ross. She participated in an early attempt—by means of the Howard Plan—to solve the problems of a school with non-selective entry, taught history at the middle and senior levels, and in 1928 wrote a history of the school for its silver jubilee.

At Holy Trinity Church, Kew, on 6 September 1930 Gwenda married with Anglican rites JOHN VICTOR REGINALD LLOYD (1895-1964). Born on 24 May 1895 at Carlton, Melbourne, he was named Victor Reginald. He enlisted in the Australian Imperial Force under the name of John Lloyd, served (1915-17) in the 21st Battalion, and saw action at Gallipoli and on the Western Front. Before and after the war he was employed in the State government's titles office; on retirement, he set up his own office to search company titles. He brought to his marriage a cultivated knowledge of music, and a deep concern for peace and for a more egalitarian society: he had strong ties to the trade union movement and belonged to the Communist Party of Australia. Chairman of the Council for Education, Music and the Arts, and secretary of the Society for the Promotion of Australian Art, he fought for the retention of the site near the Yarra River for the Victorian Arts Centre.

Having suspended her teaching career in 1934 to care for her two children, Gwenda returned to M.C.E.G.G.S. in 1940 to begin a creative working relationship with Dorothy Ross, the recently appointed headmistress who, like Lloyd, was a member of the New Education Fellowship. Their objective was to ensure that all pupils, academic and non-academic, received an education which equipped them to be thoughtful, concerned citizens. The administration of the school became an education in democratic habits and values. With the students, Gwenda played a part in drawing up a constitution for the school's executive-council in 1948. From 1940 she had fought for social studies as a matriculation subject, seeing it as preparation for citizenship in a democracy.

When the school returned to South Yarra in 1945 after its wartime evacuation, Gwenda entered a flowering period of her career. That year the young Aboriginal singer Harold Blair [q.v.13] entered the Lloyds' life. Providing him with a home when he was in Melbourne was an example of the communal conscience that Gwenda strove to create in her professional work. John became Blair's official manager and organized his 1949 Australian tour; Gwenda tutored him at night. She also trained teachers at the Kindergarten Training College (1948-49 and 1959) and at the Associated Teachers' Training College (Mercer House) in 1948-62. Mrs Lloyd became joint chief of staff of M.C.E.G.G.S. in 1951 and in the following year served as a consultant to the Australian Broadcasting Commission's youth-education course in social studies. In 1953 she wrote the school's golden jubilee history and encouraged pupils to write and perform a play, 'The Building of the House'. In 1955 she was involved in making the school film, 'Learning and Living Together'. When Edith Mountain succeeded Ross as headmistress, the abrupt change of policy prompted Gwenda's resignation in 1958, with thirty-two other staff. She continued to fight for her principles as federal secretary (1958-60) of the N.E.F.

Colleagues and pupils noted Gwenda's fine profile and upright bearing; her manner of speaking retained something of the bluff, authoritative formality of some Anglican women of her generation. Survived by her daughter and son, she died of a pulmonary embolism on 19 October 1965 at Kew and was cremated. Her husband had died of a coronary occlusion on 7 July 1964. Gwenda Lloyd's life and teaching exemplified the belief, nourished between the wars, that education was the key to the peaceful co-existence of nations and individuals. With her husband, she was commemorated by a trust established for the educational benefit of Aborigines and part-Aborigines.

K. Harrison, *Dark Man, White World* (Melb, 1975); J. Epstein, *A Golden String* (Melb, 1981); R. McCarthy and M. Theobald (eds), *Melbourne Girls Grammar School Centenary Essays, 1893-1993* (Melb, 1993); *New Horizons in Education*, 35, Autumn 1966; *MCEGGS Mag*, 1966; Lloyd papers (Univ Melb Archives); information from Mrs J. Crew, Armidale, NSW, Prof A. McBriar, Breamlea, Vic, Mr B. Taft, Mr J. Arrowsmith and Ms N. Muir, Melb.   BARBARA FALK

LLOYD, HERBERT WILLIAM (1883-1957), public servant, army officer and politician, was born on 18 November 1883 at South Yarra, Melbourne, only child of Irish-born parents William Lloyd, a mounted constable (later sergeant) in the Victoria Police, and his wife Fanny Henrietta, née Mills. Educated at Thomas Palmer's [q.v.11] University High School and at Wesley College, Lloyd joined the Commonwealth Treasury as a clerk on 26 June 1902. He was commissioned in the Australian Field Artillery in 1906, appointed militia adjutant, A.F.A., Victoria, in 1908 and promoted captain in the following year. On 31 March 1910 he resigned from the public service; next day he entered the Permanent Military Forces.

While serving with the artillery in Sydney, Lloyd married Meredith Pleasents (d.1952) on 27 May 1914 at the Methodist Church, Redfern. Appointed captain, Australian Imperial Force, on 18 August, he sailed for Egypt in October as adjutant of the 1st Field Artillery Brigade. At Gallipoli in May 1915 he was promoted major and made a battery commander; for his conduct during the campaign (April-December) he won the Distinguished Service Order. Back in Egypt, he was promoted lieutenant colonel and sent to France in March 1916 as commander of the 22nd Howitzer Brigade. Transferred to the 5th F.A.B. in April, he led it with 'ability, initiative and energy', attributes he also displayed when he was acting commander of the 2nd Divisional Artillery in February-March 1917. That year he was appointed C.M.G. and a member of the Serbian Order of the White Eagle.

Having briefly commanded the 6th (Army) Brigade, A.F.A., from November 1917, Lloyd took command of the 12th in February 1918: the unit distinguished itself in the Lys operations (April to July) and in battles along the

Somme (from August). Three days before the Armistice Lloyd was promoted temporary brigadier general and given command of the 5th Divisional Artillery. He was appointed C.B. (1919) and mentioned in dispatches four times. After his A.I.F. appointment terminated on 15 July 1919 in Melbourne, he took on training and staff duties at Army Headquarters. In 1920 he served as transport officer for the Prince of Wales's visit to Australia, for which he was appointed C.V.O. Lloyd attended the Staff College, Quetta, India, in 1920-21 before being posted to 1st Division headquarters in Sydney. He resigned from the P.M.F. on 26 August 1925 and was transferred to the Citizen Military Forces.

Lloyd obtained a post with Vacuum Oil Co. Pty Ltd, but severed his connexion with that company on winning the Legislative Assembly seat of Parramatta for the Nationalists in 1929. Next year he became managing director of Australian Soaps Ltd. Defeated in the 1930 general elections, he was deputy-commander of the New Guard before his re-election in 1932 as the United Australia Party member for Mosman, a seat he was to retain until 1941. Following the outbreak of World War II, he held the civil post of director-general of army recruiting in May-July 1940.

In August Lloyd was mobilized in the Australian Military Forces and posted to Army Headquarters as deputy adjutant-general. Promoted temporary major general, he took over the 2nd Division in October. In April-July 1941 he was also director-general of recruiting. His division was garrisoning Western Australia in September 1943 when he transferred to the 1st Division in Sydney. Between May 1945 and January 1946 he administered command of the Second Army. On 1 February 1946 he retired as honorary major general. Again in civilian life, he was a board-member of several companies, including the Adelaide Steamship Co. Ltd.

Urbane and amiable, but firm and determined, Bertie Lloyd was a brilliant conversationalist and a good listener. His resonant voice enhanced his skills as a public speaker and his fund of anecdotes enlivened his after-dinner speeches. In his social relations he had flair and adapted quickly to new circumstances. An oarsman in his youth, he later took up golf and hunting. He was a member of the Naval and Military Club, Melbourne (from 1906), and of the Union and Imperial Service clubs, Sydney. Survived by his daughter and two sons, he died on 10 August 1957 at the Repatriation General Hospital, Concord, and was cremated with Anglican rites and military honours. M. H. Ellis [q.v.14] described Lloyd as 'one of the historic figures of the A.I.F. in World War I' and observed that no soldier had 'ever turned to him for help in vain'.

W. Perry, *The Naval and Military Club, Melbourne* (Melb, 1981); W. Perry, 'Major-General Herbert William Lloyd (1883-1957): A Gunner Officer of another Era', *Sabretache*, 34, no 1, Jan-Mar 1993, p 3; *SMH*, 16 Feb 1929, 14 June 1930; *Herald* (Melb), 24 July 1931, 23 May 1940; *Bulletin*, 21 Aug 1957; personal knowledge.   WARREN PERRY

LLOYD, JOHN EDWARD (1894-1965), soldier, farmer and licensing magistrate, was born on 13 April 1894 at Ascot Vale, Melbourne, second son of Australian-born parents Walter Edwin Russell Lloyd, clerk, and his wife Gustavia Anne Louise Whipple, née Lamb. Educated at the Grange Preparatory School, South Yarra, and Brighton Grammar School, John joined the Mount Lyell Mining & Railway Co. Ltd in 1910; he worked as an accounts clerk before being trained as an analytical chemist. On 1 January 1914 he was commissioned in the 49th Battalion, Militia. Sixteen months later he was appointed lieutenant in the Australian Imperial Force and sailed for Egypt with the 23rd Battalion.

In September 1915 Lloyd reached Gallipoli. Evacuated with typhoid fever in November, he recuperated in Australia before joining the 24th Battalion on the Western Front in December 1916. The unit took part in the attack on the Hindenburg line near Bullecourt, France, on 3 May 1917. Because senior officers were unavailable, 23-year-old Captain Lloyd took command. During the battle's appalling carnage his rapidly diminishing force became isolated, but he held his ground and managed to fight off five counter-attacks. He won the Military Cross. On 4 October he led the battalion's 'A' Company in the assault on Broodseinde Ridge, Belgium, and, although twice wounded, refused to be evacuated for forty-eight hours. Awarded a Bar to his M.C., he was promoted major in October while in hospital in London.

Lloyd's A.I.F. appointment was terminated on 12 February 1918 to enable him to transfer to the Indian Army. He performed regimental and staff duties in India, first as a lieutenant and then as a captain, and fought in the Afghan War of 1919. Taking leave in Western Australia, he married with Anglican rites Margaret Muriel Robinson on 1 March 1920 at St George's Cathedral, Perth; they had met in London when he was in hospital and she was a voluntary nursing aide. With the reduction of the Indian Army, he reluctantly resigned in September 1922. John and Muriel bought a farm in the Walebing district, near Moora, Western Australia, but were forced to sell it in 1928. He found a job in Perth as an administrative clerk with a land and estate agent.

In 1936 Lloyd resumed his service in the Citizen Military Forces and was posted to the 16th Battalion which he led in 1939-40 as temporary lieutenant colonel. Seconded to the A.I.F., on 1 July 1940 he was appointed to raise and command the 2nd/28th Battalion. By February 1941 he and his men were in Palestine. From April to September they helped to defend Tobruk, Libya. The 2nd/28th carried out raids against the enemy and mounted fighting patrols; Lloyd continuously moved among his forward troops by day and night. Fearless, cheery and untiring, he instilled efficiency and high morale in the battalion. He was awarded the Distinguished Service Order and twice mentioned in dispatches.

Promoted temporary brigadier in March 1942, Lloyd took over the 16th Brigade. The 16th garrisoned Ceylon (Sri Lanka) in March-July and, after a brief period in Australia, sailed to Papua in September. Between October and December the brigade helped to push Japanese forces across the Owen Stanley Range to the Sanananda area. Contending with weariness, hunger and tropical diseases, as well as determined foes, Lloyd's soldiers were spurred to success by his leadership and encouragement. He was appointed C.B.E. (1943) for his part in the campaign.

Lloyd contracted malaria and was evacuated to Australia. In March 1943 he was reassigned as chief instructor at the Land Headquarters Tactical School, Beenleigh, Queensland. He spent the seven months until June 1944 in India and Burma, lecturing to the British on Australian methods of jungle warfare. He later performed staff duties in New Guinea. As commander of the 2nd Prisoner of War Reception Group in August-December 1945, he arranged the repatriation of some 13 000 Australian prisoners and internees. On 21 December he transferred to the Reserve of Officers as honorary brigadier.

Resuming land agency work in Perth, Lloyd bought a farm at Mayanup in 1948 in partnership with his son Robin, but subsequently returned to live in the capital. In 1949 he was appointed a magistrate of the licensing court; he resigned in 1961 due to incipient blindness. He had been honorary colonel (1955-60) of his old C.M.F. unit, and was patron of the Rats of Tobruk Association in Western Australia and of the 16th and 2nd/28th battalions' associations. A man of presence, Lloyd had tanned features, a clipped, grizzled moustache, twinkling eyes and bushy brows. Many citizens of Perth recognized his upright figure leading old comrades in Anzac Day parades.

Survived by his wife, daughter and two sons, Lloyd died on 24 December 1965 at Mayanup and was buried with military honours in Karrakatta cemetery; the funeral was said to have been the largest since John Curtin's [q.v.13] in 1945. Lloyd's son Russell rose to brigadier in the Australian Regular Army, and his daughter Margaret married (Sir) Francis Burt, the State governor (1990-93). One of Lloyd's former soldiers wrote of him: 'if I wore a hat I would, like the old soldiers of Charles XII of Sweden, take it off whenever his name was mentioned'.

E. G. Keogh, *South West Pacific, 1941-45* (Melb, 1965); C. E. W. Bean, *Anzac to Amiens* (Canb, 1968); *Reveille* (Syd), 1 May 1933, 1 Feb 1966; *Tobruk to Borneo*, 52, no 204, Mar 1996, p 4; J. E. Lloyd papers held by Brig R. D. F. Lloyd, Fremantle, WA.

KEITH D. HOWARD

LOCK, ANN (1876-1943), missionary, was born on 1 August 1876 at Rhynie, South Australia, seventh child of English-born parents Walter Lock, share-farmer, and his wife Ann, née Stokes. Young Ann had little education and worked as a dressmaker before 1901 when she entered Angas [q.v.1] College, Adelaide, a 'Missionary Training Home for Ladies'. Raised as a Methodist, she joined (1903) the interdenominational Australian Aborigines' Mission (United Aborigines' Mission from 1929). She was to devote thirty-four years to nursing, feeding and clothing Aborigines, providing them with spiritual instruction, and educating and caring for their children.

In 1905-09 Lock was based at Forster, New South Wales. Moving to Western Australia, she successively served (1909-12) as assistant and matron of the A.A.M.'s Dulhi-Gunyah Orphanage for Aboriginal children in Perth. She founded a mission at Katanning, then worked at the Carrolup Native Settlement, 20 miles (32 km) away, until personality clashes led her to leave in 1917. As A.A.M. representative, she joined an independent evangelist Sydney Hadley at Sunday Island Mission, near Derby, where she remained until 1923. After two years at Oodnadatta in South Australia she felt called to the Northern Territory in 1927. Lacking the full support of the A.A.M. and encountering opposition from officials and settlers, she toiled alone at Harding Soak, 100 miles (160 km) north of Alice Springs. Drought forced her to retreat to Katherine in October 1928.

Two months earlier a number of Aborigines had murdered a White man Fred Brooks near Harding Soak. A police party subsequently killed at least seventeen and possibly seventy Aborigines. In 1929 Lock was recalled to Alice Springs to give evidence to a board of inquiry investigating the massacre. She achieved temporary prominence when newspapers reported H. A. Heinrich's allegation that she had told him she would be 'happy to marry a black'. In its report the board blamed the racial unrest in part on 'a

woman Missionary living amongst naked blacks thus lowering their respect for the whites'. The U.A.M. condoned Lock's unusual preference for working alone as a missionary. Independent and forthright, she retained an unshakeable faith in God and her calling in the face of hostility from European society.

Ryan's Well station, some 78 miles (125 km) north of Alice Springs, was her base from June 1929. Next year the owner asked her to leave and she travelled 200 miles farther north by buggy to Boxer Creek in the Murchison Range. She stayed at what is now known as Annie Loch Waterhole until September 1932. Back in South Australia in 1933, she made another long buggy trip, driving from Crystal Brook to Ooldea where she pioneered a mission until 1936. After marrying a widower James Johansen on 15 September 1937 at the registrar's office, Port Augusta, she resigned from the U.A.M. Johansen belonged to the Plymouth Brethren and ministered to Whites living on Eyre Peninsula; despite suffering from diabetes, Annie accompanied him on his travels. She died of pneumonia on 10 February 1943 at Cleve and was buried in the local cemetery. Her estate was sworn for probate at £95 18s.

C. Bishop, 'a woman Missionary living amongst naked blacks': Annie Lock, 1876-1943 (M.A. thesis, ANU, 1991), and for bibliog. CATHERINE BISHOP

LOCKE, CHARLES HERBERT (1910-1977), company director and fund-raiser for charity, was born on 21 September 1910 at Turramurra, Sydney, fifth of seven children of William Henry Locke, an insurance manager from London, and his Victorian-born wife Alice Henrietta, née Westcott. Charles came from a Methodist background. Educated at Newington College (1920-25) and at Wrekin College, a public school in Shropshire, England, he joined his father in the Sydney office of the Royal Exchange Assurance Co. of London. After a brief stint as a jackeroo, young Locke worked for the Prudential Assurance Co. Ltd and rose to be its Sydney managing agent with power of attorney for the British Equitable Assurance Co. Ltd from mid-1938. On 14 April 1936 he had married Lesley Alison Vine (d.1972) at All Saints Church, St Kilda, Melbourne; they were to have three sons and a daughter.

Commissioned (1938) in the Militia, Locke transferred to the Australian Imperial Force on 27 April 1940 and was promoted captain, Australian Army Service Corps, in July. He served with 9th Division headquarters in the Middle East in 1941-43: he took part in the defence of Tobruk, Libya, and was mentioned in dispatches. Based in Australia from February 1943, he was sent to New Guinea in

Locke

A.D.B.

October that year. In January 1945 he was appointed to command 'Z' Special Unit which operated behind enemy lines; one month later he was promoted temporary lieutenant colonel (confirmed in September). He transferred to the Reserve of Officers on 4 May 1946 and resumed his career in the insurance business. With Warren Carpenter, he established Carpenter Locke Pty Ltd in 1948 and became managing director of this underwriting agency which later added a brokerage business.

From 1953 Locke's business career was essentially that of a non-executive, independent director of numerous Australian companies, including Toohey's [q.v.6] Ltd (chairman from 1971), the Australia Hotel Co. Ltd, Newcastle Wallsend Coal Co. Ltd (Peko-Wallsend Ltd), Commercial & General Acceptance Ltd, Australian Equity Corporation Ltd, Permanent Trustee Co. of New South Wales Ltd and the local board of Colonial Mutual Life Assurance Society Ltd. He was appointed chairman when Gerardus Dusseldorp established Lend Lease Corporation Ltd in 1958 and was deputy-chairman from 1962. Locke was later chairman of International Computers (Australia) Pty Ltd and of Louis Klein's [q.v.] clothing manufacturers, Anthony Squires Pty Ltd.

On the basis of his obvious talents as a businessman, his connexions, his organizing abilities and a long-standing commitment to serving the community, Locke proved an active fund-raiser for such endeavours as Cranbrook, Frensham and St Andrew's Cathedral Choir schools, and for various causes connected with medical research and services (including the National Heart Foundation, the Children's Medical Research Foundation and the Sydney District Nursing Association). In 1965 he succeeded Rear Admiral Buchanan [q.v.13] as chairman of the Australian Outward Bound Memorial Foundation, a position he was to hold until 1977. In 1968 Locke was appointed O.B.E. From the early 1950s he was an active parishioner of St Mark's Anglican Church, Darling Point—as church council-member (from 1954), churchwarden (from 1960) and rector's warden (from 1971).

At St Mark's on 10 May 1973 he married Mary Clare Gregory, née Luya, a widow and close family friend. Locke's major recreational activity was golf, combined with an enthusiasm for horse-racing. These interests were reflected in his membership of the Australian, Union, Tattersall's, the Australian Jockey, Royal Sydney Golf and Elanora Country clubs, as well as the Melbourne Club and the Royal and Ancient Golf Club of St Andrews, Scotland. While visiting the United States of America, he died of myocardial infarction on 15 May 1977 at San Francisco and was cremated; his ashes were interred in St

Mark's, Sydney. He was survived by his wife and by the children of his first marriage.

SMH, 29 June 1938, 29 Mar 1958, 29 Nov 1965, 17 May 1977; funeral address by the late Canon J. Whild, St Mark's Church, Darling Point (held by author, UNSW, Syd); information from Dr P. Swain, archivist, Newington College, Syd, and from Messrs S. Locke, Hoskinstown, NSW, T. Locke, Queens Park, and N. Locke, Darling Point, Syd.

JOHN PERKINS

LOCKIE, GEORGE WILLIAM (1910-1971), schoolmaster, was born on 18 February 1910 at Tipperary Point, Mount Morgan, Queensland, son of George Lockie, a carter from Scotland, and his native-born wife Tessie Esther, née Nelson. Educated locally, George won a scholarship to the Teachers' Training College, Brisbane, where he qualified in 1928. In May that year he was posted to Virginia State School. He continued to study part time in 1936-42, 1947, 1951-52 and 1955 at the University of Queensland (B.A., 1943).

Well known as a sportsman, Lockie captained both the Queensland and Brisbane Rugby League football teams in 1933-34. He played cricket for the Toombul club (life member 1943) and for Queensland in 1945-46; a sound batsman, he also bowled medium-paced teasers. In September 1933 he transferred to Ascot State School. On 4 August 1934 at the Methodist Church, Northgate, he married Keziah May Thomas, a 24-year-old shop-assistant. At Brisbane State High School (from 1940), he was appointed sports master.

In 1946 Lockie and his fellow-teacher V. G. Honour published *Graphic Geography*, a six-volume series for secondary students; these texts ran to numerous editions and were used in high schools throughout Australia. Honour and Lockie also wrote *Graphic Social Studies: Third Grade* (1952), an activities book for primary students. In 1948-52, for three afternoons each week, Lockie instructed young prisoners at Brisbane's Boggo Road gaol. Promoted acting-principal at Nambour High School in 1953, in the following year he became deputy-principal of Ipswich High School and Technical College. He was successively principal of Salisbury (1954-55), Mount Isa (1956-57) and Bundaberg (1958-60) high schools. In 1961 he returned to Brisbane State High as principal.

Lockie's term at B.S.H. saw the greatest expansion in the school's history: student numbers increased from 1091 in 1960 to 2183 in 1967. The Commonwealth Science Block and the Library Building were part of an extensive construction programme. During this period of change pupils achieved high academic standards and excelled at sport. Lockie often referred to the school as a team, and it was said of him that his captaincy made the team function smoothly and effectively. With an energetic personality and an authoritative manner, he was able to enforce discipline while retaining popularity with staff and students. He was a splendid leader who drew out the best in those under him, and many young sportsmen owed their success to his encouragement.

In 1971 Lockie won a scholarship to study at the University of London, but he was too ill to take it up. Survived by his wife and three daughters, he died of Hodgkin's disease on 2 November that year at his Northgate home and was cremated. He was posthumously awarded a fellowship by the Australian College of Education in May 1972.

Annual Magazine of the Brisbane State High School, 1971; *Courier-Mail* and *Telegraph* (Brisb), 3 Nov 1971; Teachers' staff cards (Hist Unit, Qld Dept of Education, Brisb); information from Toombul Cricket Club *and* Qld Cricket Assn, Brisb; personal information.   Vic Honour

LOCKWOOD, DOUGLAS WRIGHT (1918-1980), journalist, soldier and author, was born on 9 July 1918 at Natimuk, Victoria, second child of native-born parents Alfred Wright Lockwood [q.v.10], journalist, and his second wife Ida Dorothea, née Klowss, daughter of a German immigrant. Alfred had four children by a previous marriage. Educated at Natimuk State School, Douglas worked on his father's newspaper, the *West Wimmera Mail*, and on newspapers at Camperdown, Tatura and Mildura.

In 1941 Lockwood joined the Melbourne *Herald*. On 4 October that year at the Methodist Church, Wangaratta, he married Ruth Hay, a clerk. Soon afterwards he was sent to Darwin and in February 1942 saw the first enemy bombs fall on Australian soil. Enlisting in the Australian Imperial Force on 15 June, he trained in intelligence and security duties. He served in New Guinea and on Bougainville in 1944-45 with 'V' and 'Z' Field Security sections, and was promoted warrant officer. Following his discharge on 15 June 1945 in Melbourne, he was a war correspondent for the *Herald*, reporting from the Netherlands East Indies. In 1946 he returned to Darwin and, except for postings to the *Herald*'s Melbourne (1947-48) and London (1954-56) offices, was to remain there until 1968.

With the Northern Territory, the north of Western Australia and north-west Queensland as his beats, Lockwood reported bizarre events in the region, recorded everyday occurrences and wrote social history. In April 1954 he broke the news that Evdokia Petrov had sought asylum at Darwin airport. His 1957 account of how a Timorese boy Bas Wie had succeeded (in 1946) in flying from Koepang to Darwin (by stowing away in an aircraft's wheel-housing) won a competition in the London *Evening News* for 'the world's strangest story'. Lockwood received the 1958 (Sir William) Walkley [q.v.] award for his report on Ruth Daylight, an Aboriginal girl who was living in squalor after being sent to Canberra to meet the Queen Mother. Accompanying a government expedition to the Gibson and Great Victoria deserts in 1963, he helped to find drought-stricken Pintupi Aborigines who had had no previous contact with Europeans. He was banned for life from Vestey-owned cattle-stations for exposing the company's treatment of Aboriginal stockmen and their families.

Appointed managing-editor of South Pacific Post Pty Ltd, Lockwood moved to Port Moresby in 1968. He retained his role when the newspaper was amalgamated with the New Guinea *Times-Courier* next year to form the *Post-Courier*. In 1971 he went to Melbourne as assistant to the editor-in-chief of the Herald and Weekly Times Ltd, and was later editorial-manager. Lockwood was manager of the *Herald* in 1973 before resuming his former job in Port Moresby in 1974. He returned to Australia in 1975 for reasons of health, settled in Victoria and was to be managing-editor of the Bendigo *Advertiser* until his death.

As sole author, Lockwood published *Crocodiles and Other People* (London, 1959), *Fair Dinkum* (London, 1960), *I, the Aboriginal* (Adelaide, 1962)—which won the Adelaide *Advertiser*'s award for literature in 1962 and was later made into a television film—*We, the Aborigines* (Melbourne, 1963), *The Lizard Eaters* (Melbourne, 1964), *Up the Track* (Adelaide, 1964), *Australia's Pearl Harbour* (Melbourne, 1966), *The Front Door* (Adelaide, 1968), *My Old Mates and I* (Adelaide, 1979) and *Northern Territory Sketchbook* (Adelaide, 1968) which featured drawings by Ainslie Roberts. He co-wrote *Life on the Daly River* (London, 1961) with Nancy Polishuk, *The Shady Tree* (Adelaide, 1963) with Bill Harney [q.v.14] and *Alice on the Line* (Adelaide, 1965) with Doris Blackwell. A number of his books were translated into German, Danish, Russian or Polish.

Lockwood's style was sceptical, humorous, understated and distinctly Australian; he understood the Territory and its people, and wrote for general readers unfamiliar with the region. His books were well researched: for *Australia's Pearl Harbour* he interviewed Japanese and American as well as Australian veterans of the air assault on Darwin. *The Front Door* surveyed Darwin's settlement and its social and economic development. He admired his friend Harney's laconic wit and skill as a raconteur, and encouraged and supported his subsequent writing. When Harney died, Lockwood began editing selections from his books; the work was to be completed by Ruth Lockwood and published as *A Bushman's Life* (Melbourne, 1990).

Survived by his wife, son and daughter, Lockwood died of myocardial infarction on 21 December 1980 at Bendigo and was cremated. His son Kim, also a journalist and author, scattered Lockwood's ashes over Kakadu National Park.

D. Carment and B. James (eds), *Northern Territory Dictionary of Biography*, 2 (Darwin, 1992); *Bulletin*, 10 Nov 1962; *Herald* (Melb), 23 Dec 1980; family information.
                                             MICKEY DEWAR
                                             KIM LOCKWOOD

LOCKYER, ARNOLD ALEXANDER (1915-1945), airman, was born on 4 May 1915 at Wootha (Woother) Station, near Port Hedland, Western Australia, second son of native-born parents Samuel Lockyer, stationhand, and his wife Sylvia Burns. Arnold was of Aboriginal and European descent. Educated until the age of 13 at Roebourne and Whim Creek state schools, he was strongly built and proved a good athlete. For recreation, he boxed, ran, swam, and rode horses. On 16 March 1936 he married Sussanna Philomena Clarke with Catholic rites at Port Hedland. He worked as a stationhand, wood-cutter, general labourer and driver in the North-West before moving to Perth and starting a business as a contract-carrier. Bob Ive, a former employer, had found him trustworthy and capable. Fascinated by internal-combustion engines, Lockyer made all mechanical repairs to the trucks he drove.

Early in World War II it was deemed to be 'neither necessary nor desirable' to enlist Aborigines in the Australian Imperial Force. In contrast, the Royal Australian Air Force accepted qualified non-Europeans to meet the manpower needs of the Empire Air Training Scheme. Finding himself without a job, Lockyer enlisted in the R.A.A.F. on 5 May 1942. He was 5 ft 9½ ins (177 cm) tall, weighed 10 st. 12 lb. (69 kg) and had a medium complexion, brown eyes and brown hair. Having qualified for mechanical ground-staff, in April 1943 he was posted to No.17 Repair and Servicing Unit, Cunderin, Western Australia. He longed to be accepted for aircrew, and in July-November 1944 undertook an air-gunnery course at Sale, Victoria, and operational training at Tocumwal, New South Wales. On completion, he was promoted sergeant.

From December 1944 to January 1945 Lockyer was attached to the Heavy Bomber Refresher Training Unit at Nadzab, New Guinea. After a number of short postings in Australia, he joined No.24 Squadron at Fenton, Northern Territory, on 6 April 1945 as a flight engineer. He was promoted flight sergeant on 23 May. The squadron moved to Morotai, Netherlands East Indies, in June, and to Balikpapan, Borneo, in July. Lockyer was a member of the crew of Liberator A72-92 (belonging to No.21 Squadron) on an operation over the Celebes on 27 July. The bomber was shot down and crashed near Tomohon village. Lockyer managed to parachute to the ground, but was taken prisoner and clubbed to death by the Japanese on 21 August 1945. He was later buried in Ambon (Amboina) war cemetery, Indonesia. His wife and three sons survived him.

R. Hall, *The Black Diggers* (Syd, 1989); M. V. Nelmes, *Tocumwal to Tarakan* (Canb, 1994); note by Mr B. Ive, Perth, 19 Oct 1939 (copy on ADB file, Canb).
                                             DAVID HUGGONSON

LODER, SIR LOUIS FRANCIS (1896-1972), civil engineer and public servant, was born on 30 December 1896 at Sale, Victoria, eldest son of James Edward Loder, a watchmaker from England, and his native-born wife Marie Dorothea, née Jensen. From his primary school at Sale, Louis won a scholarship to Wesley College, Melbourne, and thence another to Queen's College, University of Melbourne (B.C.E., 1923; M.C.E., 1926). On 26 April 1916 he suspended his studies and enlisted in the Australian Imperial Force. He sailed for England in August and began training as a pilot in December.

In April 1917 Loder completed his course and was commissioned in the Australian Flying Corps. Two months later he was grounded for medical reasons, but remained with the A.F.C. as an assistant machine-gun instructor and armament officer. Promoted lieutenant in July, he was sent to the Western Front in October. He served with No.2 Squadron and was mentioned in dispatches. His A.I.F. appointment terminated in Melbourne on 15 May 1919, but he remained on the Reserve of Officers until 1945. Loder graduated from university with first-class honours and was awarded the Stawell [q.v.6] research scholarship for 1923. That year he worked as a designing engineer with (Peter) Johns [q.v.4] & Waygood Ltd before joining the Victorian Country Roads Board in November. On 5 April 1924 at Trinity Church, Camberwell, he married with Presbyterian forms Jean Arnot, daughter of G. A. Maxwell [q.v.10].

At the C.R.B., Loder helped to design and supervise the building of bridges, including a timber structure, 295 ft (90 m) long, at Echuca, and another of steel and timber, some 300 ft in length, at Stratford. Promoted highway engineer (1925), he oversaw the development of hundreds of miles of cheap, bituminized roads suitable for heavy traffic. He was promoted again in 1928, to chief engineer, and held this post until he was appointed chairman of the board in 1940. When the Allied Works Council was formed in 1942 he became its co-ordinator of State instrumentalities in Victoria. Complying with the council's request, in 1942-45 the C.R.B. surfaced with bitumen 787 miles (1267 km) of the Stuart Highway in the Northern Territory. In 1944 Loder succeeded E. G. Theodore [q.v.12] as director-general of allied works.

In February 1945 Loder was appointed director-general of the Commonwealth Department of Works (Department of Works and Housing from July 1945 to June 1952) with responsibility for the design, costing, supervision and execution of all architectural and engineering works for the Federal government. He saw the completion (1945) of the Captain Cook [q.v.1] Graving Dock in Sydney Harbour, the building (from 1947) of the rocket range at Woomera, South Australia, and the start (1961) of construction of the 'beef' roads programme in northern Australia. Loder chaired the joint Commonwealth-States technical committee which reported in 1948 and 1949 on the proposed Snowy Mountains project, and the committee which investigated the Western Australian comprehensive water-supply scheme. In 1950-61 he was deputy-commissioner representing the Commonwealth on the River Murray Commission.

Having begun as part-time lecturer in 1937, Loder remained a member of the engineering faculty of the University of Melbourne until 1961. He was an associate-member (1920) of the Institution of Engineers, Australia, serving (from 1934) on the committee of its Melbourne division (chairman 1941); he became a full member of the institution in 1935, was elected to the council in 1941 (president 1947) and in 1966 was made an honorary member (honorary fellow from 1968). Loder delivered several papers to meetings of the institution, including a dissertation in 1931 on low-cost road construction in Victoria and another in 1949 on the planned Snowy Mountains project. The institution awarded him its (Sir) Peter Nicol Russell [q.v.6] memorial medal for 1954; the University of Melbourne named him the (W. C.) Kernot [q.v.5] medallist in 1955; and the University of Western Australia conferred on him an honorary doctorate of engineering in 1949.

Loder retired in 1961. He had been appointed C.B.E. (1953) and was knighted in 1962. From 1963 he chaired a sub-committee of the Melbourne transportation committee; he later reported to the Commonwealth

government on transportation requirements in northern Australia. A teetotaller, Sir Louis was a tall, sparsely built man with a resonant voice and a finely tuned sense of propriety. As a youth he had been a keen footballer and an accomplished sprinter; in his advanced years he enjoyed tennis. He died on 11 February 1972 at Healesville, Victoria, and was cremated; his wife and three sons survived him.

W. K. Anderson, *Roads for the People* (Melb, 1994); *J of the Inst of Engineers, Aust*, Dec 1954, Dec 1966; *Chartered Engineer*, Nov 1966; family information.   T. F. C. LAWRENCE

LOEWE, FRITZ PHILIPP (1895-1974), meteorologist, was born on 11 March 1895 at Schöneberg, Berlin, son of Eugen Loewe, judge, and his wife Hedwig, née Makower. Educated (1904-13) at the Königliches Joachimthalsches Gymnasium, in 1913-14 Fritz began to study law and French at the universities of Grenoble, France, and of Berlin. His love of heights and interest in ice and snow had begun in 1909 on a visit to the Swiss Alps. At Grenoble he first observed the diminution in the substance of glaciers, which became an enduring preoccupation. He served (1914-18) in the German Army as a wireless operator, rose to corporal and was awarded the Iron Cross (first class).

Having qualified as a physical-education teacher, Loewe returned to the University of Berlin (Ph.D., 1926); he studied (1919-23) geography, physics, mathematics and meteorology, and graduated *magna cum laude*. He took part (1924-25) in the first direct measurement of oceanic depth currents, worked at meteorological observatories at Davos, Switzerland, and in Germany, headed (1925-28) the aeroplane branch of the Prussian Meteorological Institute, and joined (1928) the weather service, Tempelhof Airport, Berlin. On 3 September 1927 in Berlin he had married Else Koester, a geography student; their honeymoon in Central Anatolia, Turkey, included geological and hydrological studies.

Loewe accompanied Professor Alfred Wegener, pioneer of continental-drift theory, on his last Greenland expeditions. In 1929, with Ernst Sorge, he made the first seismic measurements of the surprising thickness of the ice-cap close to its margin. During the over-wintering (1930-31) Loewe's toes were crudely amputated at Eismitte camp when gangrene followed frostbite. He and Wegener observed that the bulk of snowdrift transport occurs at considerable heights above the surface. When Wegener died attempting to reach the coast, Loewe became acting-leader. With Else, he returned to Greenland in 1932 as adviser for the film, *S.O.S. Eisberg*. He was to assist Wegener's widow to publish *Greenland Journey* (London, 1939), an account of the 1930-31 expedition.

Because he was Jewish, Loewe lost his civil-service position in 1933. After a brief incarceration he left Germany with his wife and daughters. He investigated (1934-37) meteorology at the Scott Polar Research Institute, Cambridge, England, where contact with (Sir) Raymond Priestley [q.v.11] led to his emigration to Victoria on a Carnegie grant. Loewe reached Melbourne with his family on 1 March 1937. At the University of Melbourne (M.Sc., 1959) he established the meteorology department in 1939. Priestley admired 'his really fine attitude to a world which has deprived him of all his toes, of his livelihood, and of his country'.

Although he continued to produce papers, Loewe devoted his time to teaching. The exigencies of World War II increased demands on his aerial meteorological expertise; he also trained Royal Australian Air Force navigators. Initially classified as an enemy alien, he helped to have the new category 'refugee alien' recognized, and was naturalized in 1944. When the war ended he made several research expeditions to Antarctica. On the aborted voyage of H.M.A.S. *Wyatt Earp* in 1947, he studied the pack-ice which blocked their progress. He accompanied the French *Commandant Charcot* expeditions and in 1950-51 wintered in Terre Adélie. There he drew up a detailed mass balance of the Antarctic ice-sheet: his measurements of the intense but shallow layer were described as 'classic'. In 1955 he was awarded the Polar medal.

Loewe was seconded to the United Nations Educational Scientific and Cultural Organization in 1958 to establish meteorological training in Karachi. He surveyed glaciers in Pakistan's Nanga Parbat region, again observing glacier diminution in contrast to the increasing substance of the Antarctic ice-sheet. In 1960 he retired as senior lecturer-in-charge, but continued to spend time at the university until his death. From 1961 he was a visiting professorial research fellow with the Institute of Polar Studies, Ohio State University (Hon. D.Sc., 1970), United States of America, and 'showed great resource in finding odd and unexpected routes' to and from his Melbourne base. He revisited Greenland in 1962, 1964 and 1967.

'Most learned, tolerant, and kindly', Loewe was tall, with a domed forehead, prominent teeth and a goatee, and recognizable in later life by his awkward gait. He was a conscientious liberal who worked with Rabbi Herman Sanger [q.v.] in the Association of Jewish Refugees to win recognition for 'refugee aliens'. Loewe chaired (1944) the Temple Beth Israel's religious-school parents' committee and contributed to the Jewish press.

He wrote romantic verse using imagery drawn from his experience 'on the heights'; his prose revealed a vivid appreciation of the power and beauty of place, and a gift for its evocation.

As a teacher, Loewe produced Australia's first generation of graduate meteorologists. As a researcher, he was an empiricist with a passion to measure natural phenomena at the extremes of latitude and altitude. He reported his findings in several articles a year. 'In each case his measurements opened new horizons on known conditions'. His overview of meteorological science emphasized his conviction that theoretical 'justifications' should succeed empirical results. 'One of the great men of the heroic age of geophysical exploration', Loewe died on 27 March 1974 at Heidelberg, Melbourne, and was buried in Fawkner cemetery; his wife and two daughters survived him. A lecture theatre at the University of Melbourne was named after him in 1976.

E. Wegener (ed), assisted by F. Loewe, *Greenland Journey* (Lond, 1939); *Neue Deutsche Biographie*, 15 (Berlin, 1986); P. G. Law, *The Antarctic Voyage of HMAS Wyatt Earp* (Syd, 1995); *People* (Syd), 11 Mar 1953, p 24; *Zeitschrift für Gletscherkunde und Glazialgeologie*, 10, 1974, p 259, *and* for publications by Loewe; *J of Glaciology*, 14, no 70, 1975, p 191; *SMH*, 3 Mar 1955; R. E. Priestley, Diary 1936, *and* Loewe collection (Univ Melb Archives); Univ Melb, Registrar's correspondence, *and* Science Faculty minutes, 1937-74, *and* Council Minute-books, 1936-38 (Univ Melb Archives); naturalization file A446/172 item 61/24003, A367 item C82613 (AA, Canb).   MARK RICHMOND

LOEWENTHAL, SIR JOHN ISAACS (1914-1979), military surgeon and academic, was born on 22 December 1914 at Bondi, Sydney, seventh and youngest child of native-born parents Abraham Marcus Loewenthal, commercial agent, and his wife Carlotta Minnie, née Cohen. John attended Bondi Public and Sydney Grammar schools; for winning first place in literary subjects in 1931, he was made school captain. Despite showing little interest in science at school, he enrolled in medicine at the University of Sydney (M.B., B.S., 1938); he graduated with second-class honours and the Clayton and F. Norton Manning [q.v.5] prizes for clinical medicine and for psychiatry.

A resident medical officer (1938-39) at Royal Prince Alfred Hospital, Loewenthal was house surgeon to (Sir) Hugh Poate [q.v.11] and house physician to (Sir) Charles McDonald [q.v.]. In late 1939 he became senior resident pathologist. Next year he was awarded a fellowship in surgery at the recently established postgraduate school, Prince Henry Hospital (Little Bay); his fellowship lasted a mere eight weeks before he was mobilized as captain, Australian Army Medical Corps, on 3 June 1940. Appointed to the Australian Imperial Force in July, he was posted to the 2nd/9th Field Regiment, I Corps Artillery. He sailed for the Middle East in April 1941 and served in Palestine, Syria and Egypt. In November he was in hospital with malaria-induced jaundice. By January 1942 he had joined the 2nd/1st Casualty Clearing Station; he returned to Australia with the unit in March.

In September Loewenthal was promoted major and immediately embarked for Milne Bay, Papua. Like many other personnel in that region, he contracted malaria and was sent to hospital in Australia in January 1943. Resuming duty next month, he served on the staff of the 116th Australian General Hospital, Charters Towers, Queensland, until leaving for New Guinea in August—one day before he and his 22-year-old fiancée Anne June Stewart, a voluntary aide, intended to be married. They eventually wed on 12 September 1944 at the Scots' Church, West Maitland, New South Wales.

As officer-in-charge of a mobile surgical team in the Markham and Ramu valleys, Loewenthal carried a heavy load of cases. He dealt with casualties on the spot at advanced positions. The main dressing-station under his command at Dumpu routinely held about 250 patients. Despite the risk from enemy fire, he saved the lives of many soldiers who would not have survived being transported even over short distances. Appointed senior surgeon in the 2nd/3rd C.C.S. in November, he took part in the Finschhafen and Huon Peninsula campaigns. After falling ill again in December, he gradually recovered and in April 1944 was transferred to the 115th A.G.H., Heidelberg, Melbourne, with an attachment to the Directorate of Medical Services. He performed general, urological and orthopaedic surgery, and (with Major Robert Officer and Captain J. W. Perry) undertook research on the clinical use of penicillin; for this work he was to be awarded an M.S. (1946) by the University of Melbourne. In October 1945 he was posted to the 113th Military Hospital, Concord, Sydney. His A.I.F. appointment terminated on 11 December.

In mid-1946 Loewenthal went to London on a Nuffield travelling fellowship and as chief assistant to Professor (Sir) James Ross at St Bartholomew's Hospital; later that year he qualified as a fellow of the Royal College of Surgeons, England. In June 1947 he was appointed lecturer in surgery at the Victoria University of Manchester and deputy-director, surgical professorial unit, at the Manchester Royal Infirmary. Shortly after delivering the Hunterian lecture to the R.C.S. in July 1948, he resigned to return to Sydney where he began private practice. Despite the hostility of some of the surgeons at R.P.A.H., he was appointed honorary assistant-surgeon there in 1949, tutor in surgery (1948) at the University of Sydney and honorary consulting surgeon (1950) at Ryde District Soldiers' Memorial Hospital.

In March 1956 Loewenthal succeeded Sir Harold Dew as Bosch [qq.v.13,7] professor of surgery at the university. He began to build up the research and teaching of his almost non-existent department—which resembled 'an empty house . . . likened . . . to the *Marie Celeste*'—especially in the teaching hospitals beyond the citadel of R.P.A.H. He was really only 'an average sort of teacher'. His students were in awe of him; one of them said, 'He terrified me, like a clipped English colonel'. Loewenthal, however, made significant appointments at Royal North Shore, St Vincent's and Concord hospitals, a number of them new chairs. He also supported the work of the R. Gordon Craig [q.v.8] Research Laboratories, and expanded the scope of his department with a lectureship in diagnostic radiology, and a chair in orthopaedic and traumatic surgery (with its associated Raymond Purves Research Laboratories). Although his own interests developed in the fields of vascular and transplantation surgery, he performed a diminishing number of operations and did little research after his academic appointment, but he was a great internationalist who travelled the world presenting the research of his colleagues and subordinates. He was dean (1965-71) of the faculty of medicine, a fellow (1965-66) of the senate and acting-dean (1977).

Loewenthal had his critics, but his charm, his ease in dealing with people of all social levels and his capacities as a committee-man were widely acknowledged. He lacked humbug, and was described as 'a happy, genial (yet forceful) personality' and one of 'the most generous' of men. Various colleagues believed that he was partial to those who supported him; they thought that, while he made good appointments, he was cool and often unhelpful to those who disagreed with him. At the university he tended to do things first and advise people later. Described as a 'wheeler-dealer', he wanted to be 'top cookie, at the centre of things'. He remained a fiercely loyal Sydney university man and was hostile to important figures in the fledgling medical faculty at the University of New South Wales, as well as its vice-chancellor (Sir) Philip Baxter.

Having retained an association with the army, Loewenthal was promoted colonel and appointed consulting surgeon to Army Headquarters, Melbourne, in 1957. During the Vietnam War he was so shocked that repatriated Australian casualties were not being sent to Concord and to major teaching hospitals that he demanded that the minister for the army visit Ingleburn military camp to see the conditions to which the injured men were being subjected.

Elected a fellow of the Royal Australasian College of Surgeons in 1955, Loewenthal was a councillor (1961-74) and president (1971-74). He had the reputation of being an outward-looking and reformist president who sought to alter the Melbourne dominance in that college; he was also associated with its journal, the *Australian and New Zealand Journal of Surgery*. He was a founder (1960) and national president (1975-79) of the National Heart Foundation of Australia, and a member of the Cancer Council of New South Wales, the National Health and Medical Research Council, and several other governing bodies. In addition, he was vice-chairman of the Ludwig Institute of Cancer Research, and an honorary fellow of the American College of Surgeons, the R.C.S., Edinburgh, the Cardiac Society of Australia and New Zealand, and the College of Physicians, Surgeons and Gynaecologists of South Africa. Although he did not initially share the enthusiasm of the younger staff at Sydney Hospital for building a new hospital at Westmead, he changed his position, became an active member of its board and received much of the credit for its development. He also served on the boards of Royal North Shore Hospital and the Royal Alexandra Hospital for Children. Appointed C.M.G. in 1975, he was knighted in 1978.

Sir John enjoyed gardening, and belonged to the Australian Club, Legacy Club of Sydney, Royal Sydney Yacht Squadron and Bowral Golf Club. He collapsed on 17 August 1979 at a dinner held in the university's Great Hall in honour of his impending retirement. Survived by his wife, two sons and two daughters, he died of complications of myocardial infarction on 25 August at R.P.A.H. After a funeral at St Luke's Presbyterian Church, Roseville, he was cremated. He had long abandoned any interest in Judaism, but had never been baptized a Christian. His estate was sworn for probate at $408 826.

One of the generation of great Australian surgeons who learned their craft in the demanding conditions of World War II, Loewenthal had been outstanding. In the words of Professor Alexander Boyd, he was 'a really good, safe and dependable clinician; a neat and careful operator who [paid] great attention to technique'. Of all the Sydney university men of his generation, he was the closest to being a 'national figure'. He is commemorated by the John Loewenthal research fellowship of the R.A.C.S. and the Sir John Loewenthal award of the National Heart Foundation. The R.A.C.S. holds his portrait by Robert ('Alfie') Hannaford.

A. S. Walker, *The Island Campaigns* (Canb, 1957); J. A. Young et al (eds), *Centenary Book of the University of Sydney Faculty of Medicine* (Syd, 1984); *Lives of the Fellows of the Royal College of Surgeons of England, 1974-1982* (Lond, 1988); *Lancet*, 2 Sept 1979; *Aust and NZ J of Surgery*, 49, Dec 1979, 50, no 1, Feb 1980; *MJA*, 3 Nov 1979, p 481; Roy A'sian College of Surgeons Archives, Melb; Univ Syd Archives; information from Lady Loewenthal, Mr W. Forsyth, Profs C. R. B. Blackburn, J. B. Hickie, P. I. Korner, J. M. Little, W. H. McCarthy and F. O. Stephens, Syd.   JOHN CARMODY

LOGUE, LIONEL GEORGE (1880-1953), speech therapist, was born on 26 February 1880 at College Town, Adelaide, eldest of three children of South Australian-born parents George Edward Logue, clerk, and his wife Lavinia, née Rankin. Educated (1889-96) at Prince Alfred College, Lionel studied elocution with Edward Reeves who purged his voice of much of its Australian accent. In 1902 he became Reeves's secretary and assistant-teacher, and studied at the Elder [q.v.4] Conservatorium of Music. He later worked on a gold mine at Kalgoorlie, Western Australia. At St George's Anglican Cathedral, Perth, on 20 March 1907 he married Myrtle Gruenert, a 21-year-old clerk.

Settling in Perth, Logue taught elocution, public speaking and acting. He staged plays, recited Shakespeare and Dickens at concerts, and founded a public-speaking club. He also taught part time at the Young Men's Christian Association, at Scotch College and, from 1910, at Perth Technical School. In the following year he toured the world. A Christian Scientist, Logue was dedicated to healing. In World War I he treated returned soldiers afflicted with speech impediments caused by shell-shock. Using humour, patience and 'super-human sympathy', he taught them exercises for the lungs and diaphragm, and to breathe sufficiently deeply to complete a sentence fluently.

Logue practised at 146 Harley Street, London, from 1924: the fees paid by his wealthy clients enabled him to accept poorer patients without charge. In 1926 the Duke of York consulted Logue about his stammer. The therapist diagnosed poor co-ordination between larynx and diaphragm, and asked him to spend an hour each day practising rigorous exercises. The duke came to his rooms, stood by an open window and loudly intoned each vowel for fifteen seconds. Logue restored his confidence by relaxing the tension which caused muscle spasms. The duke's stammer diminished to occasional hesitations. Resonantly and without stuttering, he opened the Australian parliament in Canberra in 1927.

Using tongue-twisters, Logue helped the duke to rehearse for his major speeches and coached him for the formal language of his coronation in 1937. At Westminster Abbey on 12 May, wearing the M.V.O. decoration given to him by King George VI on the previous night, Logue sat in the apse to encourage him during the ceremony. Before the King's radio broadcast that evening, Logue whispered to him: 'Now take it quietly, Sir'. Logue was a founder (1935) of the British Society of Speech Therapists and a founding fellow (1944) of the College of Speech Therapists; a Freemason, he was speech therapist to the Royal Masonic School, Bushey. He retained his love of music and the theatre, and enjoyed walking and gardening. In World War II his practice shrank and he acted as an air-raid warden three nights a week. The 'slow, measured pace' which he had afforded the King's diction proved affecting in His Majesty's wartime broadcasts and speeches. Elevated to C.V.O. in 1944, Logue was with the King for the V.E.-Day broadcast on 8 May 1945. Their friendship was 'the greatest pleasure' of Logue's life. After his wife's death that year, Logue took up spiritualism. Survived by his three sons, he died on 12 April 1953 in London and was cremated.

R. Pound, *Harley Street* (Lond, 1967); D. Judd, *King George VI 1895-1952* (Lond, 1982); A. Morrow, *The Queen Mother* (Lond, 1984); S. Bradford, *King George VI* (Lond, 1989); *Quiz and the Lantern*, 8 Mar, 8 Aug 1902; *Advertiser* (Adel), 20 Mar 1902, 13 Apr 1953; *Western Mail* (Perth), 29 Jan 1910, 9 Dec 1911, 1 Mar 1913, 1 Nov 1918, 17 Jan 1929; *SMH*, 11 Feb 1952; *The Times*, 13, 17 Apr 1953; information from Prof V. and Mr A. L. Logue, Lond.

SUZANNE EDGAR

LÖHE, FRIEDRICH MAX IMMANUEL (1900-1977), Lutheran minister, was born on 26 May 1900 at Tanunda, South Australia, eldest son of German-born parents Johannes Paul Löhe, the Lutheran pastor of Steinfeld (Stonefield), and his wife Thusnelde Bertha Hildegard, née Völter. In 1902 the family moved to Natimuk, Victoria, where Max attended primary school. He pursued his ambition to be a farmer until he decided in 1915 to proceed to secondary school in South Australia where he completed his senior certificate at Immanuel College, Point Pass. His Wimmera boyhood had given him a 'pro-Australian outlook' which, he later wrote, resented in the more conservative atmosphere of Point Pass. Löhe returned to farming until 1921 when he felt called to the ministry. He began his theological training at the Wartburg Seminary, Tanunda, in the first class of the newly formed United Evangelical Lutheran Church in Australia, of which his father was foundation president. In 1923 the seminary was relocated at Immanuel College,

North Adelaide, with his father as principal. Löhe was ordained on 2 August 1925 at St Stephen's Church, Adelaide, and installed in the parish of Mackay, North Queensland. At Nazareth Church, South Brisbane, on 29 April 1926 he married Hedwig Adelheid Rechner (d.1988), a 31-year-old milliner from Tanunda. He was pastor at Nazareth Church from 1932 to 1953.

Emphasizing 'a changeless Christ for a changing world', Löhe believed that education was 'the keystone of all church work', and 'intelligent lay leadership' its greatest need. He maintained his commitment to education and the printed word throughout his ministry, preparing teaching materials for Sunday School, serving as a member of college and seminary boards, and editing (1934-48) *Lutheran Youth*. In addition, he undertook editorial work in Queensland for the *Lutheran Herald* (1927-34) and the *Queensland Lutheran* (1943-53), chaired (1943-53) his church's publications board, helped to revise the Lutheran hymnal and edited the devotional book, *Lord Teach us to Pray*. Keenly interested in architecture, he promoted the renovation and preservation of church buildings. He also supported the Hope Vale Mission in North Queensland, and Lutheran missions elsewhere in Australia and in New Guinea. His fluency in English and German enabled him to be an effective intermediary between the two cultures in both secular and church affairs. He worked for greater understanding and reconciliation—at the parish level, between the two major Lutheran synods in Australia, with Federal and State governments during World War II, and in assisting German-speaking immigrants in the years after 1945.

Löhe was secretary (1933-40) and president (1940-53) of the Queensland district of the U.E.L.C.A. In 1953 he became president-general and returned to North Adelaide. A staunch advocate of Church unity, he was president of the Lutheran Church of Australia from its formation in 1966 until his retirement in 1972. The Wartburg Seminary of Dubuque, Iowa, United States of America, had conferred a D.D. (1955) on him for his services to the Church. He was appointed C.B.E. in 1976.

After travelling widely in Europe, India, North America and Papua New Guinea, Löhe ministered in Canberra and East Melbourne in his retirement. Interested in history, the preservation of church records, and bookbinding, he was influential in the building and establishment of the Lutheran Archives in North Adelaide and became its archivist.

Max Löhe was tall, broad shouldered and imposing. A vigorous and dynamic man, he was conservative in his theology, but sensitive in his handling of difficult issues. His 'strong and insightful leadership' provided a 'stabilising influence' during the first years of the

L.C.A. and his 'clear and forthright (sometimes brusque) opinions' gave direction to his colleagues. His home was noted for its hospitality. Most of his personal library was bequeathed to the Luther Seminary and archives in North Adelaide. He was a keen follower and former player of Australian Rules football. Survived by his wife, he died on 23 July 1977 at his North Adelaide home and was buried in Langmeil cemetery, Tanunda. He had no children.

T. Hebart, *The United Evangelical Lutheran Church in Australia*, English version, ed J.J. Stolz (Adel, 1938); E. Leske, *For Faith and Freedom* (Adel, 1996); *Lutheran*, 15 Aug 1977, pp 338, 340; Löhe papers (Lutheran Archives, Nth Adel); information from Rev H. F. W. Proeve, Tanunda, SA.

ROBIN RADFORD

LOMBARD, FRANCIS WILLIAM (1911-1967), Catholic priest, was born on 26 April 1911 at Brighton, Melbourne, third son and youngest of five children of John Lombard, police constable, and his wife Bridget, née Collins, both from County Cork, Ireland. Frank spent his childhood at Brighton and Berwick before his father was posted to Ivanhoe police station about 1923. He was educated at Berwick State School, Christian Brothers' College, East Melbourne, and St Kevin's College, Toorak. In 1927 he decided to become a priest and returned to St Kevin's to study Latin. Over 6 ft (183 cm) tall and 17 stone (108 kg) in weight, he was a splendid sportsman, but tuberculosis in 1933 forced him to spend twelve months in the Greenvale Sanatorium. He studied for the priesthood at Corpus Christi College, Werribee, and was ordained by Archbishop Mannix [q.v.10] on 26 July 1936 at St Patrick's Cathedral, Melbourne.

While assistant-priest at Northcote, Lombard served part time as an army chaplain in 1939-40. Impressed by the youth movement established by the Belgian priest Joseph Cardijn, he received Mannix's approval in 1940 to establish the Young Christian Workers movement in Melbourne and was named its chaplain. In 1942 he was appointed priest in charge of the parish of Collingwood to test the Y.C.W. in an industrial area. When the movement spread to other States under the direction of the coadjutor archbishop Dr Justin Simonds [q.v.], Lombard was made national chaplain.

Despite his inherently shy disposition, Lombard developed a more extroverted side to his nature. He was a superb public speaker, especially to large crowds, and had a particular appeal for the young. By October 1943 the Y.C.W. had expanded to forty-seven leaders' groups and over four thousand members in

Melbourne. It also ran recreational and sporting activities, and later sponsored housing and trading co-operatives.

During 1949-50 Lombard visited Europe. He met Cardijn and other Y.C.W. officials who confirmed his view that the organization aimed to influence the mass of workers and not merely their leaders. None the less, Lombard staunchly resisted B. A. Santamaria's attempts to use the Y.C.W. as a recruiting-ground for his anti-communist Catholic Social Studies Movement and insisted that the Y.C.W. avoid politics and act independently in factories. In England, in March 1950, he secured British agreement for young immigrants to come to Australia.

In January 1955, having retired from the Y.C.W. in ill health, Lombard became parish priest at Clayton. There he built up the premises, fittings and equipment, and a lively community. Following a heart attack in 1960, he remained totally invalided. He died of coronary vascular disease on 28 July 1967 at Clayton and was buried in Melbourne general cemetery. The Y.C.W. Co-operative Centre in Melbourne was named after him.

Dedicated to youth and popular with them, Lombard had emphasized religious practice. He was a tough and strong-willed activist who read little and left no writings. Some considered him authoritarian and found it difficult to work with him, but most admired his energy, self-discipline and frugality. According to Bishop John Kelly, 'he under-estimated his own very considerable, intellectual abilities', but compensated for this by his gift for leadership.

Advocate (Melb), 15 June, 3, 17 Aug 1967; *Herald* (Melb), 31 July 1967; D. Kehoe, History of the Young Christian Workers (YCW) in Melbourne (ms, YCW Holdings, Melb); Lombard file (MDHC); YCW Archives (Phillip Island, Vic).

BRUCE DUNCAN

LONERGAN, JOHN THOMAS (1902-1979), trade union official, was born on 29 May 1902 in Hobart, eleventh child of David Lonergan, labourer, and his wife Louisa, née Coe. Educated at the Central School, Hobart, Jack went to work on the waterfront at the age of 17. On 24 July 1926 he married Effie Gladys Mary Sherrin in Hobart with Catholic rites; they were to remain childless. He was increasingly active in the Tasmanian branch of the Waterside Workers' Federation of Australia and was elected vice-president in 1935. Succeeding to the presidency that year, he retained the office until 1970, with only two breaks (1951-52 and 1956-57) when he chose not to stand.

In 1936 Lonergan was elected branch representative on the union's federal council.

Three years later he became federal president of the W.W.F. He held this part-time position throughout a vital period in the union's development. Working closely with the general secretary Jim Healy [q.v.14], he presided over negotiations with the Curtin [q.v.13] government that led to the establishment (1942) of the Stevedoring Industry Commission with worker representation. After a campaign of stoppages that closed fifty-two Australian ports on 11 December 1946, Lonergan proudly reported the securing of an annual two-week paid holiday for all watersiders.

Lonergan maintained a remarkable popularity with Tasmanian dockers and was frequently unchallenged in annual elections for the State presidency; when the post was contested he usually scored easy victories. Yet, he had opponents within the union and sometimes incurred criticism for his efforts to reach compromise settlements. Even in his final year as federal president of the W.W.F. he and Jim Healy were accused of supporting the Australian Council of Trade Unions' policy rather than that of their union. Handing over the federal presidency to Jack Beitz in 1950, Lonergan continued for several years as a federal councillor.

When the occasion warranted strong action he was a tough upholder of union principles. Lonergan was branch president in Hobart during a celebrated case (1956-59) when two W.W.F. members, Frank and Denis Hursey, objected to paying a political levy for the Australian Labor Party. Following protracted litigation, the High Court of Australia finally accepted the legality of political levies and union expulsion for non-payment, but prohibited exclusion of non-unionists from the workplace.

Short and stocky, Jack Lonergan was an excellent public speaker, capable of swinging a public meeting by oratorical devices such as variations of tone and emotional appeals. He remained a staunch unionist: content to represent his members at State A.L.P. conferences, he sought neither party nor political office. In 1970 he escorted Queen Elizabeth II and the Duke of Edinburgh during their inspection of the Hobart waterfront. Survived by his wife, he died on 16 April 1979 at Lindisfarne and was cremated.

T. Bull, *Politics in a Union* (Syd, 1977); R. Davis, *Eighty Years' Labor* (Hob, 1983); *Maritime Worker*, 8 May 1979; *Mercury*, 18 Apr 1979; Waterside Workers' Federation of Aust, Tas Branch records (Maritime Union of Aust, Hob); information from Mr L. Brown, Moonah, Hob.   R. P. DAVIS

LONG, GAVIN MERRICK (1901-1968), journalist and historian, was born on 31 May 1901 at Foster, Victoria, eldest of six children of George Merrick Long [q.v.10], clergyman, and his wife Felecie Alexandra, née Joyce, both Victorian born. Gavin was educated at Trinity Grammar School, Kew, All Saints College, Bathurst, New South Wales, and the University of Sydney (B.A., 1922; Dip.Ed., 1925). He planned to follow his father into the Anglican priesthood, but turned to teaching (1922-23) at The King's School, Parramatta, where he also coached rowing. In 1924 he tried his hand as a jackeroo.

Next year Long travelled to England. He worked for nine months in the migration and settlement office at Australia House, London. The trip abroad had been largely prompted by his courtship of Mary Jocelyn Britten, daughter of a master at King's, who was holidaying in Britain. Gavin and Jocelyn were quietly married on 5 September 1925 at the register office, Kensington. She sailed for Australia a fortnight later; he left for Europe and returned home in March 1926. They were remarried on 24 September that year at St Peter's Anglican Church, Melbourne.

Long's interest in journalism had been stimulated by the publication of his casual contributions to newspapers and journals. Following a stint with the *Daily Guardian* in Sydney, he was employed (1926-31) as a junior on the Melbourne *Argus*. Even in that tough field his talent for accurate and objective reporting shone out, as did his enterprise and broadening versatility. His earnings from spare-time journalism for the *Argus* and the *Australasian* were considerable, amounting to about two-thirds of his salary. From June 1927 he wrote a weekly column on films for the *Australasian*. In November 1928 the *Argus* promoted him to general reporter. Little more than a year later he rose to senior reporter, only to be reduced to his former status because of the Depression. Accepting an offer of appointment as a senior with the *Sydney Morning Herald*, he began work as a sub-editor in July 1931.

In 1932 Long began writing a weekly page on films for the *Sydney Mail* and soon branched into theatre, music and art criticism for the *Herald*. He served (1933-34) on the federal council of the Australian Journalists' Association. From 1936 he was chief cable sub-editor on the *Herald*, handling major stories from overseas. Leaders, articles on defence issues and book reviews came within his ambit. In 1938 he was posted to the *Herald*'s London office. Shortly after the outbreak of World War II he was appointed a war correspondent with the British Expeditionary Force in France. Evacuated from Boulogne in May 1940, he then reported on operations involving the Royal Navy. In November the *Herald* sent him to Egypt; he covered the campaigns of the 6th Australian Division in Libya (December 1940-February 1941) and

Greece (March-April). In mid-1941 he was recalled to Australia. He resumed his articles and editorials on defence, and visited Darwin and Port Moresby.

In March 1943, on the recommendation of C. E. W. Bean [q.v.7], Long was appointed general editor of the official history of Australia in World War II. Based at the Australian War Memorial, Canberra, he spent the last thirty months of the war in planning, consulting, and recruiting authors and staff. He also drafted a narrative of the Syrian campaign to test the adequacy of the official records and his own capacity to write about a theatre in which he had not witnessed events. When not thus engaged, he went back and forth to the front, staying at different headquarters and interviewing participants from past and present campaigns. More than one hundred of his notebooks and diaries—a treasure trove of information about Australia and Australians at war—were filled in this way.

The official history eventually comprised five series which totalled twenty-two volumes —seven on the army, two on the navy, four on the air force, five on the home front and four on medical matters. It was the largest historical project ever undertaken in Australia. Long was to write three of the army volumes; thirteen other authors were to write the remaining nineteen volumes. A concise volume was also planned, to be written by Long. With the task barely under way, he contracted cancer but continued to work.

Long was 6 ft 2 ins (188 cm) tall, dark and slender, with hooded brown eyes. He had poor eyesight and looked straight ahead when he walked, conveying an aloofness which was foreign to his nature. In the 1940s he had strong black hair and a close-clipped moustache which contributed to his youthful looks. Although grave and scholarly in appearance, he had a ready wit and a lively sense of humour. He was generous, yet lived austerely. His patched trousers—the repairs only partly concealed beneath a striped, unfashionable, double-breasted coat—and the cold showers which he took until late in life were the products of his upbringing and his aversion to waste. With a preference for simple things, he deplored the passing of the 'horse and buggy' days; he did not like motorcars and did not drive. Shy and sensitive, he recognized those feelings in others.

In conveying messages to his writers and staff, Long used homely phrases: 'too much dressing spoils the salad' (to one author fond of colourful prose); 'hard writing makes easy reading' (to another). And he applied such principles to his own work from the outset. He wrote brisk, clear narrative, with an unerring sense for the appropriate word. His style was 'robust and eminently readable'. By leaving the facts 'to speak for themselves', he stirred the reader's imagination 'to produce the comment which [he] had inspired but left unwritten'. Usually accessible, he established a friendly but cautious relationship with his team of writers, winning their respect with wise guidance and quiet encouragement. He thought nothing of drafting a chapter or chapters for a struggling author. His close involvement imposed on the separate monographs a unity of purpose and method which brought the massive detail into perspective while preserving the individuality of each of his authors.

The first two of Long's own volumes, *To Benghazi* and *Greece, Crete and Syria*, were published in Canberra in 1952 and 1953 respectively. Both were thrice reprinted, with sales exceeding 20 000 copies. The acclaim which they received on publication was echoed, thirty-four years later, by David Horner in his introduction to the third reprint of *To Benghazi*. He described Long's handling of the battle of Bardia as 'thrilling, lucid, vividly realistic' and 'told from the perspective of the men in the front-line'. *To Benghazi* 'set the tone and standards for each of the subsequent volumes of the official history'. These appeared in steady progression until 1977. Each was the subject of a leader-page article or the principal book review in almost every Australian metropolitan newspaper. In Britain most were warmly and widely reviewed. Long was appointed O.B.E. (1953) and a member of the Greek Order of the Phoenix (1956).

In March 1963 Long retired, 'characteristically dismissing' himself when he decided that the history had reached the stage at which his full-time employment was no longer justified. The third of his volumes, *The Final Campaigns*, was published that year. In 1963-65 he was a research fellow with the Australian Dictionary of Biography at the Australian National University. A member (1943-68) of the War Memorial's board of management (later trustees), he was that institution's principal adviser on history and films, and an initiator of its research scholarship and grants programmes. He had been critical of the standard of Australian government publications and joined other experts in producing the official *Style Manual* (Canberra, 1966). A prolific contributor to the *Canberra Times*, he wrote over ninety articles and book reviews. His *MacArthur as Military Commander* (London, 1969) examined General Douglas MacArthur [q.v.] from an Australian viewpoint. *The Six Years War* (Canberra), Long's concise history of Australian involvement in the 1939-45 conflict, though finished much earlier, was not published until 1973.

Survived by his wife, son and daughter, Long died of lung cancer on 10 October 1968 at his Deakin home and was cremated. He had been struggling to finish *MacArthur* and was sedated against discomfort and pain: discomfort, he said, was when he was unable to sleep at night; pain, when he had to bite his lips to stop himself from screaming. He had taken his death sentence quietly, expressing the hope that he would not linger and risk being charged with 'loitering'. When his time arrived he left without fuss, 'closing the door quietly behind him', as (Sir) Paul Hasluck remarked, 'like the gentleman he always was'. Long's brief death notice in the *Canberra Times* was devoid of padding and humbug. It lacked the customary public declarations of devotion, but it would be hard to find a man who privately was more loved. His bust by John Dowie is held by the Australian War Memorial.

Stand-To (Canb), 8, no 2, Mar-Apr 1963, p 3; S. Jamieson, Gavin Long—An Appreciation (ts) *and* Long papers, 1937-78, *and* Official History 1939-45 War: Records of Gavin Long, General Editor (AWM); Long family papers (held by Mr J. Long, Glebe, Syd).   A. J. SWEETING

LONG, MARGARET (RETTA) JANE (1878-1956), missionary, was born on 5 April 1878 at Ultimo, Sydney, only daughter and eldest child of Matthew Dixon (d.1935), carpenter and joiner, and his wife Matilda, née Brown, both Irish-born Baptists. Retta was educated at a small private school. She joined the New South Wales Christian Endeavour Union and began evangelizing at La Perouse Aborigines' Reserve where Christian Endeavour conducted Sunday services. Her father built two rooms on to the church, and, at the age of 19, she moved in as the first resident missionary.

In 1899 the mission was reconstituted as the New South Wales Aborigines' Mission. The Aborigines at La Perouse helped to secure Retta's welcome when she contacted Aboriginal communities on the south coast, the Hawkesbury and the Macleay. Public transport and whatever the Christian Endeavour network supplied were her only means of travel. In 1899 she walked seventy miles during one visit to south-coast communities. Retta held a profound belief in the power of the Gospel to transform the lives of 'sinners' and thought that the Aborigines were in no way 'inferior to the white race'. She came to admire their spirituality, generosity and endurance. As a young missionary she was happy to accept their hospitality and their company on her journeys.

Unable to pay in full the money it owed, the N.S.W.A.M. resolved in 1902 to function as a 'faith mission' and to rely on God to supply its needs. Retta's role was supervisory in the field, and inspirational there and elsewhere. She was an able publicist and her success encouraged support. The evangelical press reported in detail her travel, her needs (a lady's bicycle), her appearances at Sunday services, and the 'bright singing and testimonies' of Aborigines with whom she worked. In 1905 she left the N.S.W.A.M. to form—with support from its Singleton committee—the Aborigines Inland Mission of Australia. On 11 January 1906 at the Baptist Church, Singleton, she married Leonard William Long; he was a Wesleyan and a fellow member of Christian Endeavour. Five of their seven children were to survive infancy. William and Retta became co-directors of A.I.M. They appear to have operated in absolute harmony, sharing the supervisory role, travelling extensively to visit A.I.M. stations, occasionally relieving a hard-pressed missionary, attending mission conferences and investigating a new field interstate.

The burden of maintaining the complex organizational structure essential in a faith mission fell more heavily on Retta. Her prayers were often directed to the matter of recruitment. She encouraged the Christian Endeavour connexion, sought the support of prayer circles, attended church services and addressed meetings. In 1907 A.I.M. began publishing *Our Aim*, a monthly magazine edited and partly written by Mrs Long. She maintained a voluminous correspondence: her outstanding gift was her 'ability to write helpful encouraging letters'.

Retta's mission assisted dispossessed and semi-urban Aborigines. When she began her work, Aboriginal communities were reforming on recently gazetted reserves, and in camps on town commons and river banks. This resulted in the physical separation and isolation of their communities. With government permission, the A.I.M. built a church and a missionary residence on many of the reserves. Its missionaries lived among the Aborigines, often in similar material circumstances.

In 1910 the Longs moved A.I.M.'s headquarters to Sydney. An advisory council was formed in 1917, followed by local and interstate auxiliaries. During the 1930s interstate advisory councils took responsibility for local recruitment. A.I.M. was remarkably successful: there were forty-three missionaries in 1931 and fifty-two by 1940. In 1924 Retta had rejoiced that 'the most striking feature' of the year's work was the 'appearance of a Native Ministry. With almost unique suddenness simultaneously all over our field, God has laid his separating hands upon at least twelve men and women'. Although the numbers were small and some were backsliders, men and women continued to come forward.

After Leonard died from ptomaine poisoning on 28 December 1928, Retta continued as sole director. She reorganized the field into districts under a senior missionary and instituted a council to advise on placements. With her missionary son Arnold at the wheel of the A.I.M. van, she spent years pursuing the goal of a native ministry. In 1929 she began the *Australian Evangel*, a monthly paper designed for an Aboriginal readership.

From 1930 Mrs Long held a series of conventions for deepening the spiritual life of 'Native Christians', each extending over several days, and attended by hundreds. These were the 'great revivalist rallies' which a later generation recalled with 'reverence and nostalgia'. At these conventions she promoted her plan for a native training college. A fund was opened and negotiations commenced for suitable premises, but it was not until 1938 that the first two students entered the Native Training College, Port Stephens. Another of her initiatives was the publication of a book of hymns written by Aborigines.

Retta was physically frail. In 1935, partly for her health, she became less active. She began to write about the mission: *Providential Channels* (1935) was in the nature of a testimony; *In the Way of His Steps* (1936) a brief history; *The Aboriginal as a Subject of the Kingdom of God* (1938) a warm, but not uncritical, appraisal of the 'much maligned and misunderstood original inhabitants'. In 1937 she visited Britain to attend the Keswick Convention; she also went to Glasgow to inspect the Bible Training Institute and to Belfast to meet relations.

Mrs Long was emphatic that the mission's sole concern was salvation. It taught from the Bible and had helped those 'eager to read God's word' to learn to read. But it was not a mission which sought to 'civilize the native'. In practice, however, A.I.M.'s fundamentalist morality made many demands on its adherents. None the less, A.I.M. was in general less intrusive on Aboriginal culture than other missions, and it avoided involvement in institutions that took children from their parents. When A.I.M.'s missionaries in Darwin were evacuated during World War II and asked to care for Aboriginal evacuees, they did so. On their return in 1946 they received a subsidy and were given premises for the Retta Dixon Home. Mrs Long hoped that this was a new beginning, but the home was to have a troubled history. The Training College had also been evacuated during the war. Retta negotiated to rent premises at Dalwood, and in 1946 bought Minimbah House, Singleton. For a few years the college was little more than a training centre for Sunday School teachers, but by the 1950s a trickle of applicants for the ministry began. The college was renamed the A.I.M. Bible Training Institute in 1953 and opened to applicants from other missions.

Retta continued as director of A.I.M. until 1953, though frequently unwell; her family relieved her of much of the responsibility. Survived by her three daughters and two of her four sons, she died on 18 October 1956 at her Normanhurst home and was buried with Baptist forms in Rookwood cemetery. Mrs Long had achieved more than she intended. When Peter Read interviewed a later generation of the Wiradjuri he found that the Gospel brought by A.I.M. had become part of an 'old-fashioned but nonetheless respected Aboriginality'.

E. L. Telfer, *Amongst Australian Aborigines* (Syd, 1939); A. E. Gerard, *United Aborigines' Mission* (Adel, nd, 1945?); I. Lindsay and H. Miles, *Bringing Christ to Aboriginal Australia* (Lawson, NSW, 1989); J. Harris, *One Blood* (Syd, 1994); *Roll Call*, 1897-1905; *NSW Aborigines' Advocate*, 1, 1901-05; *Our Aim*, 26 Jan 1929, 22 Oct 1931, 15 June, 16 Aug 1938, 16 Nov 1946, Nov 1956; *Land Rights News*, July 1988, p 24; P. Read, A History of the Wiradjuri People of New South Wales 1883-1969 (Ph.D. thesis, ANU, 1983); Conference with Mission Authorities, Darwin, 1948, A431 1948/1670, *and* Aborigines' Inland Mission, Retta Dixon Home, A452 1956/162 (AA, Canb).

HEATHER RADI

LONG, RUPERT BASIL MICHEL (1899-1960), naval officer and businessman, was born on 19 September 1899 at North Carlton, Melbourne, youngest of eight children of Victorian-born parents Charles Richard Long [q.v.10], inspector of schools, and his wife Louisa Catherine, née Michel. Educated at Princes Hill State School, Rupert entered the Royal Australian Naval College, Osborne House, Geelong, with the first intake of cadets in 1913. He went to sea in H.M.A.S. *Australia* (1917-18) as a midshipman and in H.M.A.S. *Huon* (1918-19) as a sub lieutenant.

Sent to England in 1919 for further training, Long gained the maximum of five first-class certificates for his lieutenant's courses. He joined H.M.S. *Ramillies* and qualified as a torpedo specialist before returning to Australia in 1924. Following postings to H.M.A. ships *Platypus* (1924-25) and *Anzac* (1925-26), he served in the Mediterranean and on the China Station in H.M.S. *Dauntless*. On 29 October 1927 at St Clement's parish church, Oxford, England, he married Heather Mary Macrae (d.1935). Promoted lieutenant commander in January 1928, he was squadron torpedo officer when the new *Australia* was commissioned three months later. In 1933 he passed the course at the Royal Naval Staff College, Greenwich.

Next year Long took up duties as district intelligence officer and staff officer to the captain superintendent, Sydney. He improved and expanded the local intelligence organization. In April 1936 he was posted to Navy Office, Melbourne, as assistant-director of naval intelligence and staff torpedo officer. Among his most important tasks was the strengthening of the coastwatcher network, especially in the islands north of Australia. Fleet Admiral William F. Halsey, United States Navy, was to credit the coastwatchers with saving Guadalcanal in 1942.

At the Presbyterian Church, Lindfield, Sydney, on 19 August 1937 Long married a divorcee Frances Vera Cliff, daughter of Sir Walter Carpenter [q.v.7]. Appointed director of naval intelligence on 25 August 1939, Long was promoted acting commander on 6 April 1940. Influenced by his father to be proudly Australian, he recognized the necessity of working closely with allied intelligence agencies. He represented Britain's Military Intelligence 5 and M.I.6 in Australia, receiving the benefit of their worldwide connexions.

The linchpin of Australian intelligence and security work, Long set up an espionage system in the Netherlands East Indies and South-West Pacific. In 1940 he advocated the formation of the Combined Operational Intelligence Centre, Melbourne, and in January 1941 became its first director, in addition to his role as D.N.I. He founded the Special Intelligence Bureau under Commander (Captain) T. E. Nave to help break Japanese consular and merchant-navy codes, and received 'Ultra' material (intercepted and decrypted enemy messages) from Britain. Long formed close contacts with cryptanalysts in Singapore, Batavia and Canada, and with the Far East Security Service.

He played a role in the formation (March 1941) of the Commonwealth Security Service. In 1942 he persuaded General Sir Thomas Blamey [q.v.13] to set up the Far Eastern Liaison Office for psychological warfare. General Douglas MacArthur [q.v.] accepted Long's proposal to establish the Allied Intelligence Bureau, which co-ordinated the activities of coastwatchers and other intelligence and sabotage parties operating in Japanese-occupied territory. Long had attended a conference on cryptanalysis and espionage in Singapore in November 1941, and in September 1944 went to London for a Joint Intelligence Committee conference. In January-February 1945 he visited Washington, New York and Ottawa to discuss postwar security with the Federal Bureau of Investigation, British Security Co-ordination, the Royal Canadian Mounted Police and Canadian naval intelligence. He had been appointed O.B.E. in 1944.

Leaving the navy in December 1945, Long embarked on a business career in Sydney, establishing engineering and precision-instruments firms, and dabbling in the mining of mineral sands. In 1949 he unsuccessfully sought Liberal Party pre-selection for the Federal seat of Mackellar. For a time he was connected with the Association, a secretive, anti-communist organization. A heavy smoker,

he died of cancer on 8 January 1960 at his Manly home and was cremated with Anglican rites; his wife and their son and daughter survived him. Allison Ind described Long as 'a stocky man with a cupid's-bow mouth and a steel-trap mind'. Known as 'Cocky' or 'Von', he supported his men and their families, and won their devotion. Paul McGuire wrote that British naval intelligence officers regarded Long as 'one of the ablest of them all'. Eric Feldt [q.v.14] considered that, in a war in which it was often said that 'too little' was done 'too late', Long 'did enough and he did it *in time*'.

B. Winter, *The Intrigue Master* (Brisb, 1995), and for bibliog; *PIM*, Feb 1960; *Age* (Melb), 11 Jan 1960; *Herald* (Melb), 13 Jan 1960; R. B. M. Long papers (AWM); information from Mr P. Long, Wahroonga, Syd, Lt Cdr L. D. Emerson-Elliott, Charnwood, Canb, and the late Mr A. A. Fisher.

BARBARA WINTER

LONGFIELD LLOYD, ERIC EDWIN; *see* LLOYD, ERIC

LONGWORTH, ISABEL FRANCES (1881-1961), dentist and peace-activist, was born on 1 June 1881 at Temora, New South Wales, sixth daughter of William Swann, a schoolteacher from England, and his native-born wife Elizabeth, née Devlin. Isabel was brought up from childhood 'to think war evil'. Registered as a dentist on 20 June 1902, she practised at Parramatta. From 1907 she had several city addresses before setting up at Buckland Chambers, Liverpool Street, in 1912. Her patients included Miles Franklin [q.v.8], Jennie Scott Griffiths [q.v.] and other social and political reformers. She joined the Australian Freedom League in 1912. Disappointed with Rose Scott [q.v.11] and her supporters whom she believed were advocating war in the name of defence, she sought out militant anti-conscriptionists in the Domain.

In 1917-20 Swann spoke at Socialist Sunday Schools, offered dental services to imprisoned Industrial Workers of the World, embroiled herself in controversies over compulsory saluting of the flag at schools, became secretary of the Women's Peace Army and founded a local branch of the Howard Prison Reform League (life member 1938). She corresponded with Henry Holland [q.v.9] in New Zealand, and, as part of an Anglo-Indian committee, claimed to have ended indentured labour in Fiji. She also worked on the New Guinea Natives' Welfare Committee which hid native seamen in Sydney until their shipboard conditions were improved.

Representing the Women's International League for Peace and Freedom, Swann attended the interstate conference organized by the Australian Peace Alliance in 1921. On 23 August 1924 at the district registrar's office, Randwick, she married William Longworth, a universal grinder; they were to have one daughter. Mrs Longworth continued to practise in Sydney, at Wyong (from 1932)—while they tried to grow passionfruit commercially near Toukley—and at Newcastle where the family settled in 1936. In that year she helped the Christian Socialist Movement to organize a broad-based peace conference at the Newcastle Town Hall at which she argued that fascism was anti-women. She published a pamphlet, *An Open Road to International Order*, in 1938 and established the Newcastle branch of the Australian League of Nations Union, which she recast as a branch of the Australian Association for the United Nations after World War II.

In 1941 Longworth had arranged a northern meeting of the Congress for Friendship and Aid to the Soviet Union. Standing for the House of Representatives as an Independent ('Scientific Socialist'), she unsuccessfully contested the seats of Newcastle (1946) and Shortland (1949). Her prodigious plans to influence educators, politicians and workers in the 1950s produced radio programmes, letters to newspapers, questions in State and Federal parliament, and school lessons on international affairs. Recognized as the longest-practising dentist in Australia, at the age of 78, small, frail and grey haired, she worked to establish a Cessnock branch of A.A.U.N. She attended (as an observer) congresses of the (United Nations) Economic Commission for Asia and the Far East, held in Queensland (1959) and in Karachi (1960). Survived by her daughter, she died on 13 January 1961 at Newcastle and was cremated with Congregational forms.

R. W. Halliday, *A History of Dentistry in New South Wales 1788 to 1945*, A. O. Watson ed (Syd, 1977); *Newcastle Morning Herald*, 6 Sept 1951, 18 Mar 1954, 14 Jan 1961; *Cessnock Eagle*, 17 Nov 1959; *SMH*, 21 Jan 1960; Longworth papers (ML); Longworth folder (Newcastle Regional L); B8023-4, A5200 (Univ Newcastle Archives). BOB JAMES

LORD, KEITH EDWARD (1922-1978), discount furniture retailer, was born on 3 June 1922 at Punchbowl, Sydney, second son of native-born parents Henry Edward Lord, fitter's labourer, and his wife Jessie Elenor, née Skinner. Trained as an assistant boilermaker, Keith was employed by Anderson's [q.v.13] Sausages Pty Ltd when he raised his age by three years and enlisted in the Australian Imperial Force on 6 June 1940. He attended Eastern Command Cooking School and in June 1941 embarked for the Middle East where he was attached to the 2nd/6th Field Regiment. From March 1942 he was based in Australia. On 13 January 1943 at St Andrew's Anglican Church, Sans Souci, Sydney, he married Jean Tingle, a 17-year-old office-assistant. He served with his regiment in New Guinea from 1 July 1943 until embarking for Brisbane in January 1944. Several bouts of malaria kept him in Queensland until he was discharged from the A.I.F. on 29 September 1945.

Lord worked as a truck driver and as a door-to-door salesman before opening a vacuum-cleaner service at Sans Souci in 1950. Some ten years later he set up as an electrical retailer and in 1962 established Keith Lord Pty Ltd in Parramatta Road, Ashfield. In addition to electrical goods, he soon sold quality furniture and furnishings at discount prices in spacious and well-lit premises. Another store, Bill Lord Pty Ltd, run by his son, was opened at Carlton. In 1970 Keith Lord Holdings Ltd acquired John Hicks & Co. Ltd, a Brisbane furniture retailer; the Brisbane store was quickly sold and the capital used for expansion in Sydney. By the early 1970s the Ashfield store, with its 110-yard (100 m) frontage on Parramatta Road, was a landmark.

In 1975 Lord was operating five discount stores—one in the city and four in the suburbs. The spectacular growth of his business reflected growing opportunities for discount selling due to television advertising, increasing affluence, and a growing enthusiasm for electrical appliances and home decoration. Lord joined a national purchasing group to buy locally and overseas on favourable terms, and became prominent in a prolonged battle for the abolition of resale price maintenance. The company stayed under the control of Lord, his family and a few business associates. He supervised his stores meticulously and emphasized salesmanship. Despite his reputation as an aggressive discounter, he remained an old-fashioned salesman who studied his customers closely. Interior decorators were employed as consultants, his furniture carried a five-year warranty, and a fleet of radio-controlled vans provided after-sales service.

Wiry, with a receding hairline and huge, capable hands, by the 1970s Lord appeared older than his years. He planned to retire late in 1978 and to spend more time sailing his boat and fishing on the Georges River near his home at Blakehurst. During a business visit to the United States of America he suffered a heart attack at San Francisco airport and died on 13 July 1978 in the Peninsula Hospital, Burlingame. Survived by his wife, four sons and three daughters, he was cremated in Sydney. The company went into voluntary liquidation in 1994.

Keith Lord Holdings Limited. A Corporate Fact Book (Syd, c1971); *Rydge's*, Nov 1970, p 53, Aug 1978, p 52; *Sun-Herald*, 16 July 1978; *SMH*, 23 May, 19 July 1978; *Aust Financial Review*, 24 June, 24 Aug 1994.   BEVERLEY KINGSTON

LORT SMITH, LOUISA ELEANOR (1875-1956), animal-welfare advocate and administrator, was born on 12 March 1875 at Sale, Victoria, tenth of eleven children of William Montgomery, a grazier who came from Ireland, and his Australian-born wife Elizabeth Wilhelmina, née Du Moulin. Louisa was educated at Sale at Miss Jane Geoghegan's school and Madame Beausire's Ladies' High School. Her father's reversal of fortune in the 1880s forced the family to leave their property for suburban Caulfield.

In the early 1900s Louisa and her younger sister Marion (d.1940) began to teach ballroom dancing to students of some of Melbourne's private schools. They continued for over twenty-five years, thus gaining financial security. By the early 1920s they had a spacious home in Toorak and the wherewithal to devote much of their time to the care and welfare of animals.

These two women and others interested in such work met in May 1928 to form the Animal Welfare League of Victoria. An executive-committee, mainly comprising socially prominent women from South Yarra and Toorak, managed the administration and called on others to assist with fundraising activities. On 19 December 1925 at St George's Anglican Church, Malvern, Louisa had married Charles Lort Smith; he was 69 years old and a respected Melbourne solicitor. Charles incorporated many of her ideas in a constitution for the league. With the closure of the veterinary school at the University of Melbourne in 1929, its free clinic was transferred in the following year to the Animal Welfare League on the initiative of Mrs Lort Smith. Dr E. F. J. Bordeaux, president of the Veterinary Association of Victoria, was appointed to take charge. Louisa became honorary secretary to the league and (Dame) Mabel Brookes [q.v.13] was president. In the first year 2150 animals were treated, including 188 horses. Widowed in 1931, Lort Smith worked almost full time at the clinic, where volunteers were a vital part of its operation. The title of honorary director gave her complete authority over the league's activities from 1933.

Believing that there was sufficient demand for a public animal-hospital, Mrs Lort Smith and Frances Lyle (wife of Sir Thomas Lyle [q.v.10])—who had joined the executive-committee in 1930—secured land in Villiers Street, North Melbourne. Lady Lyle, a passionate animal lover, donated £5000, and the Lort Smith-Lyle Hospital for Sick and Injured Animals was opened in April 1936. Later, after a difference of opinion, Lady Lyle asked for her name to be removed, but she continued her financial support and bequeathed a trust fund to help the hospital. She died in 1949.

Although Lort Smith was often criticized for being over-sentimental in her devotion to animals, she showed a hard-headed business ability in ensuring the stability of the league's finances and the management of the hospital. Appointed a justice of the peace in the 1940s, when manpower and material shortages were making the work of the league difficult, she became a well-known figure in Melbourne, associated with almost every animal-welfare deputation to successive Victorian governments. She persistently advocated improved means of transporting livestock and better methods at abattoirs—in particular, use of the 'captive-bolt' pistol instead of the poleaxe. Years of pressure finally brought legislation in 1949 permitting such a device; by 1952 its use in Victoria was mandatory. That year Lort Smith took over the presidency of the Animal Welfare League. No important decisions had been made without her approval and she had exercised full powers in running the hospital.

Petite and impeccably groomed, Lort Smith was a woman of courage and determination, with the ability to win the interest and support of influential people. Her clear blue eyes missed nothing. She had style and an air of authority: even when she was 80 there was some apprehension felt while 'Mrs Lort' was on the hospital premises. In 1953 she was awarded Queen Elizabeth II's coronation medal. Lort Smith retired as president of the league six weeks before her death. She died on 15 July 1956 in East Melbourne and was cremated. The bulk of her estate, sworn for probate at £61 382, was used to set up 'The Lort Smith Trust for Animals'. Her portrait by Violet Teague [q.v.12] is held by the Lort Smith hospital.

A. Henderson (ed), *Early Pioneer Families of Victoria and Riverina* (Melb, 1936); *People* (Syd), 19 Dec 1951, p 14; *Parade*, June 1974, p 12; *Herald* (Melb), 28 Sept 1936, 19 Aug 1954, 15 Oct 1955, 26 May, 16, 18 July 1956; *Age* (Melb), 16 July 1956; Animal Welfare League, Minute-books, 1925-1957; information from Mr J. M. Dale, Robe, SA.
                                    HEATHER B. RONALD

LOTHIAN, ELIZABETH INGLIS (1881-1973), teacher of classics, was born on 22 October 1881 at Gateshead, Durham, England, second child and eldest daughter of John Inglis Lothian, a publisher's cashier, and his wife Lillias, née Smith. Thomas Carlyle Lothian [q.v.10] was her brother. The family arrived in Melbourne in 1888. Elizabeth attended St Kilda State School until 1895 when she entered Presbyterian Ladies' College, East Melbourne, on a half-scholarship. In the following year she passed the matriculation examination in eight subjects, but remained at school and obtained exhibitions in 1898-99.

A non-resident student of Ormond [q.v.5] College, Lothian read classics at the University of Melbourne (B.A. Hons, 1903; M.A., 1908; Dip.Ed., 1914). After teaching for a year at Healesville, she shared the Wyselaskie [q.v.6] scholarship in classical and comparative philology and logic. She entered Newnham College, Cambridge, in 1905, and completed part one of the classics tripos with second-class honours in 1907. That year she returned to Melbourne.

In 1908 Miss Lothian became classics mistress at Tintern Ladies' College, Hawthorn. Joining the staff of (Melbourne) Church of England Girls' Grammar School in 1914, she was soon made senior classics mistress. She was appointed to the Victorian School Board's classics standing committee in 1922. Retiring from teaching in 1946, she was remembered for her ability to bring classical civilization to life. Her own love of the subject was nourished by contact with the Classical Association of Victoria—of which she was a member (from 1913) and councillor (1927-60) —and by a five-month sojourn in Greece with Jessie Webb [q.v.12] in 1923.

From her schooldays Lothian had been associated with groups providing support and companionship to educated women. At P.L.C. she had been one of 'The '98 Brigade of Friendship', which included Marion Phillips [q.v.11] and Elizabeth's early academic rival and lifelong friend Enid Derham [q.v.8]. Lothian belonged to the Princess Ida Club at university, the Catalysts (1910), the Lyceum Club (1914) and the Victorian Women Graduates' Association (1920). Having been a Fabian at Cambridge, she joined the Fabian Society of Victoria in 1908 and served on its executive. She remained in touch with university life by teaching classics at Queen's (1914-54) and Ormond (1918-19) colleges. Co-secretary (1917-37) of a provisional committee dedicated to the foundation of University Women's College, she served the college as a councillor (1938-50), member (1938-60) of the education committee and classics tutor (1938-53).

For most of her life Lothian lived with members of her family and was a kindly aunt to her brother's children. Bed-ridden in her final years, she retained vigour of mind and an interest in the institutions for which she had worked. She died on 6 May 1973 at Box Hill

and was cremated with Presbyterian forms. In 1932 she had spoken of 'The Modern Woman' as progressing 'from clothes to politics', with the possibility of the 'strongest willed' breaking away from what had been expected of them. She did not herself seek to lead or break with custom, but by quiet and purposeful activity smoothed the way for those who wished to travel farther.

K. Fitzpatrick, *PLC Melbourne* (Melb, 1975); F. Kelly, *Degrees of Liberation* (Melb, 1985); R. Mathews, *Australia's First Fabians* (Melb, 1993); Presbyterian Ladies College (Melb), *Patchwork*, 1895-1910, *and* enrolment record; *MCEGGS Mag*, 1973, *and* Archives.   CECILY CLOSE

LOUAT, FRANK RUTLEDGE (1901-1963), barrister, was born on 30 December 1901 at Merrylands, Sydney, eldest child of James Rutledge Louat, a native-born architect, and his wife Mabel Frances Horton, née Busby, from New Zealand. A great-nephew of (Sir) Arthur Rutledge [q.v.11], Frank was proud of his French descent and pronounced his surname in the French manner. He was educated at Sydney Church of England Grammar School (Shore) and the University of Sydney (LL.B., 1925; LL.D., 1933). Interested in politics, he was elected to the council of the National Party at the age of 21 and awarded the university's Morven Nolan prize for political science in 1923. On 14 May 1925 he was admitted to the Bar; he established his practice in University Chambers. Well known as a member of the university's debating team in 1925-26, Louat was a leader-writer (1926-28) for the *Sydney Morning Herald* and joint honorary secretary (1928) of the local branch of the United Association of Great Britain and France. With Selwyn Betts [q.v.7] he published a much-used commentary, *The Practice of the Supreme Court of New South Wales at Common Law* (1928).

At St Stephen's Presbyterian Church, Sydney, on 27 June 1931 Louat married a divorcee Marian Julia Mackie, née Ellis-Oates; they were to be divorced in 1937. On 9 July 1938 he married another divorcee Isobel Anne Wearne, née Hamilton, at the Scots Church, Sydney. They lived at Greenknowe Avenue, Potts Point. From 1938 Louat frequently wrote for the *Daily Telegraph* and commented on current affairs for the Australian Broadcasting Commission. He was an executive-member of the United Australia Party and in 1940 unsuccessfully contested the Federal seat of Eden-Monaro.

For many years the only doctor of laws practising at the New South Wales Bar, Dr Louat projected an image of 'cheerful fussiness' in court: he was a stickler for procedure and involved himself 'with all the relevant details'. He appeared good-tempered and used his rich and mellow voice in the manner of an accomplished actor. Having written his doctoral thesis on 'A survey of the executive power of the Commonwealth', he frequently appeared before the High Court of Australia in constitutional cases. President (1940-46) of the Constitutional Association of New South Wales, he advised the Commonwealth government on the Constitutional Convention in Canberra in 1942 and sat on the National Security Regulations Advisory Committee in 1944. Throughout World War II he was active in defence of civil liberties and free speech, and in May 1946 helped to organize protest meetings against strikes by industrial pressure groups. He was nominated by the Court of International Justice as an observer for the 1950 referendum in the French territories in India. On 16 July 1952 he took silk.

'A man of innumerable interests of an intellectual, artistic and social nature', Louat was a past president and life member of the Dante Alighieri Art and Literary Society, a trustee (from 1959) of the Art Gallery of New South Wales, and a member of the Australasian Pioneers' Club and Royal Sydney Yacht Squadron. He enjoyed sailing, reading, writing and fishing. Louat was honorary vice-president of the French Chamber of Commerce in Australia. In 1958 he was appointed (chevalier) to the Légion d'honneur for furthering Australian-French relations, and habitually wore its discreet red ribbon in his buttonhole. Plump and clean shaven, he was proud of his culinary expertise and was president (1953-54) of the Wine and Food Society of New South Wales. Louat was on holiday in France when he died of heart disease on 26 January 1963 at Dijon. His wife survived him.

J. Gleeson, *William Dobell* (Syd, 1981); P. Buckridge, *The Scandalous Penton* (Brisb, 1994); NSW Bar Assn, *Bar Gazette*, no 6, June 1963, p 13; *SMH*, 21 Apr, 22 Dec 1925, 27, 29 Apr 1926, 4 May 1933, 3 June 1938, 18, 20 Sept, 8 Nov 1940, 19 Aug 1941, 28 July 1942, 24 Sept 1943, 7 May 1945, 2 and 3 May 1946, 3 Dec 1947, 14 Jan 1950, 17 July 1952, 15 July 1958, 29 Jan 1963; information from Messrs M. Broun, QC, Syd, and D. M. Selby, Wahroonga, Syd.

MARTHA RUTLEDGE

LOVEGROVE, DENIS (1904-1979), trade unionist, party official and politician, was born on 25 September 1904 at Carlton, Melbourne, only child of Violet Lovegrove who came from Tasmania. Educated at Faraday Street State School, 'Dinny' left at an early age and followed a variety of manual occupations. He lost his job as a plasterer with the onset of the Depression. On 28 January 1928 at the Baptist manse, Collingwood, he had married Irene Chinn (d.1946); they were to have two children.

In 1930 Lovegrove joined the Communist Party of Australia (under the name 'Denis Jackson') and became secretary of the Unemployed Workers' Movement. A skilled orator and a leading activist, he was regarded by the authorities as a dangerous agitator and was arrested several times following violent demonstrations. He was expelled from the Communist Party in 1933, probably because he fell foul of Ernest Thornton [q.v.]. By nature Lovegrove was fiercely independent, and it is likely that he reacted against stern party discipline. He later alleged that, after his expulsion, communists had 'bashed [him] with bike chains at the back of the Fitzroy Town Hall'.

As secretary (1935-47) and president (1955-78) of the Fibrous Plaster and Plaster Workers' Union, Lovegrove was prominent in the Victorian Trades Hall Council (president 1938), in the Australian Council of Trade Unions, and increasingly in the Australian Labor Party which he joined in 1936. He was an executive-member (1938-55), president (1943-44), organizing secretary (1947-50) and secretary (1950-55) of the State branch of the A.L.P. In 1953-54 he was the party's federal president.

By the early 1940s Lovegrove had become staunchly identified with anti-communism, both politically and in the trade unions; he was subsequently involved with the organization and activities of the anti-communist industrial groups. As A.L.P. State secretary he was a key right-wing figure in events leading up to the party split in 1955. He then sided with the party's new national executive, believing that narrowly based splinter groups were doomed to fail.

In the Victorian elections of 1955 Lovegrove won the seat of Carlton, defeating Bill Barry [q.v.13], the sitting member and candidate for the Anti-Communist Labor Party. The campaign was characterized by violence and acrimony: Lovegrove described his opponent as 'a man with a crucifix in one hand and a dagger in the other'. Remaining in parliament until 1973—as member for Fitzroy (1958-67) and Sunshine (1967-73)—Lovegrove was deputy-leader of the Opposition in 1958-67. Both sides of the House regarded him as an outstanding debater. His speeches were hard-hitting, passionate and well researched, but his past associations with the 'groupers' militated against his becoming leader.

Even Lovegrove's enemies conceded that he was a man of considerable intelligence, capacity and courage, who espoused causes with conviction. He could be charming when he chose, but essentially he was tough. As early as 1941 political associates had described him as a man with a 'bitter streak' and this trait became more obvious as he grew older. Certainly he had a sardonic wit and a strong disregard for what he regarded as political hypocrisy. He was consumed by politics. Music was one of his few distractions, and he was a competent and enthusiastic violinist. In 1964-68 he served on the council of the University of Melbourne. Having retired from parliament, he became a director of the Industrial Printing & Publicity Co. Ltd. Lovegrove had married a divorcee Eileen Delaney, née Collins, on 27 February 1951 at the Collins Street Baptist Church. He died on 25 January 1979 in East Melbourne and was cremated; his wife survived him, as did the son of his first marriage.

R. McMullin, *The Light on the Hill* (Melb, 1991); *Sun News-Pictorial*, 19 Apr 1973; *Age* (Melb), 29 Jan 1979; information from Mr J. Arrowsmith, Fitzroy, Mr B. Taft, Clifton Hill, the Hon. R. McLellan, Melb, Mr L. Short, Mosman, Syd, and the Hon. J. R. McClelland, Wentworth Falls, NSW; personal knowledge.   JOHN N. BUTTON

LOWE, SIR CHARLES JOHN (1880-1969), judge and university chancellor, was born on 4 October 1880 at Panmure, near Warrnambool, Victoria, sixth of eight children of English-born parents Thomas Lowe, schoolteacher, and his wife Mary Ann Amelia, née Barnett. Thomas had emigrated from his native Lancashire in 1864, aged 22; he married in 1866, and became an assistant-teacher in a 'national' school at Bendigo before taking charge of the Panmure school in 1873. An eye injury led to his total blindness in 1880. The Lowes ran a few cows and a small store to supplement Thomas's meagre pension; although life was hard, especially after the store was destroyed by fire, the family was happy and the children well schooled. Charles, who greatly admired his indomitable father, was appointed a temporary monitor at the Panmure school on £10 a year after taking his merit certificate. He won a scholarship to Surrey College in suburban Melbourne, but had to quit after a year to earn money when the Panmure business finally failed. An assistant-master at Hawksburn Grammar School and (from 1897) at St Paul's Cathedral Choir School, he also succeeded in matriculating, determined to do arts and law.

At the University of Melbourne (B.A. Hons, 1900; M.A., 1902; LL.B. Hons, 1904), Lowe was the model of the able poor student. Alexander Leeper [q.v.10], the warden of Trinity College, gave him a £10 non-resident scholarship, but seven hours a day spent teaching prevented him attending university lectures; fortunately his brilliant fellow student (Sir) John Behan [q.v.7] lent him his lecture notes. After graduating, Lowe borrowed £100 from an uncle to pay to take articles with W. R.

Rylah, father of (Sir) Arthur [q.v.]. Admitted to the Bar on 1 August 1905, Lowe supplemented his modest initial earnings by teaching at Bradshaw's Business College and publishing a handbook on commercial law (1911). He also learned shorthand—a skill which was to prove useful on the bench—and worked as a court reporter. Lowe progressed slowly as a barrister, working mainly in the Court of Petty Sessions and then the County Court (where he became leader of the Bar); he had Supreme Court briefs, but none in the High Court, and never took silk. Not a creative lawyer like his friend (Sir) Owen Dixon [q.v.14], he nevertheless, in two decades at the Bar, became extraordinarily proficient in common and criminal law.

Tall, lean and lithe, though with a characteristic family stoop, Lowe was a dapper young man; his stiffly waxed moustache, at first dashing, grew smaller over the years. He was keen on sport, rarely missing an important cricket match. On 15 January 1908 at St Stephen's Anglican Church, Richmond, he married Clara Rhoda Dickason, a 26-year-old schoolteacher. Charles and Clara had a close understanding, which endured; they lived first in modest comfort at Westgarth, and later moved to Malvern and finally Toorak. Methodical at home as at work, Lowe walked to the morning train, teaching his daughter her tables on her way to school. Returning at 6 p.m., he would dine, play fifty-up at billiards with his wife, and work in his personal law library until midnight, with cocoa at 10. Saturday was for sport, watching, or playing tennis and golf. Sunday was seldom for church—he supported though rarely attended the local Anglican church—but always for the family, with organized outings. In time he gave the family the travel he had missed in his youth, including trips to North America in 1927 and to Europe in 1935. He loved the theatre, and reading, including the *Times Literary Supplement* and *Punch*, and a French novel every holiday. He joined the Melbourne, the Australian and the Royal Melbourne Golf clubs. His family was said to have discouraged him from entering politics.

In 1926 a vacancy occurred on the Supreme Court bench. Dixon urged Lowe to make himself available. Though at first reluctant, he was sworn in on 28 January 1927 to acclamation he did not expect. 'No Judge has commenced his duties with such an assurance of sympathetic and appreciative assistance from the Bar', wrote (Sir) Robert Menzies [q.v.]. Panmure celebrated for a week. In the same year Lowe joined the council of the University of Melbourne, emerging immediately as a strong advocate of a 'permanent' vice-chancellor, a reform achieved in 1933. He also served (1927-35) on the council of Trinity College.

During a record (for Victoria) thirty-seven years on the bench, Lowe won a reputation as 'one of the notable judges of the twentieth century' by meticulous application of the law. His decisions were seldom overturned, and he was pleased to find them surviving the Privy Council itself in the famous murder trial of John Bryan Kerr in 1951. Lowe's judgements were plain: he avoided added observations and general legal theory, yet he said that he admired the creative 'insouciance' with which Dixon could ignore precedents. He was impatient of academic lawyers 'insufficiently schooled in court practice'. He was firm with counsel, and good at deflating the pompous (such as the counsel in a divorce case who laboriously proved a husband a 'perjurer' for claiming to be teetotal while drinking up to six beers a night; 'I suppose that makes the condition of being teetotal a little more tolerable', Lowe interjected).

Lowe assumed Victorian values, including a 'manly sort of modesty'. He showed unusual insight into the circumstances of everyday life which brought citizens into the court, whether in dispute or charged with crime. A tragic case early in his term, of a deserted wife convicted of manslaughter after killing her children and attempting suicide, long influenced him, but he was not sentimental, especially to those he thought justly convicted. He was extraordinarily patient, notably in 1953 when a man accused of murder tried to prevent his trial proceeding by continually abusing the judge; Lowe eventually had him removed, but postponed sentence until an appeal had confirmed that trial in the accused's absence was valid. His well-publicized judgements included the 'Pyjama Girl' case (1944)—in which he clearly thought that the belatedly accused husband Antonio Agostini [q.v.13] was lucky to escape with manslaughter—and a 'wrong baby' case (1949).

Although Lowe was to act thrice as chief justice, he was not the senior puisne judge when the chief justiceship fell vacant in 1944, and the government chose to appoint Sir Edmund Herring from outside the court. Lowe approved of Herring's efforts to increase judicial efficiency; he himself argued for a separate court for divorce and a board to deal with motor-vehicle compensation cases.

Lowe's unforgettably judicious style was carefully controlled. 'No one could be as wise as Sir Charles Lowe looks', Menzies cribbed from the eighteenth century, but Lowe's colleague (Sir) Kevin Anderson thought his impassive expression a 'studied pose'. His solemnity, even while joking, contributed to his reputation as a great wit, but not all courtroom quips remain amusing in plain air. A juror asked to be excused because his wife was about to conceive; counsel, amending, said she was about to be confined: Lowe ruled that 'in either case the presence of the husband is highly desirable'. A very self-regarding speech from recently knighted Sir John Latham [q.v.10] provoked him to pun that 'the night has a thousand eyes'.

Presiding over four major commissions of inquiry, three for the Commonwealth and one for the State, Lowe became a national figure. 'I have no special competence to conduct an inquiry beyond the desire to arrive at the truth of matters according to the evidence, irrespective of whether or not it fits into any preconceived pattern', he wrote about one of the commissions, expressing his approach to all. He was both praised and criticized for thus narrowing his focus.

On the morning of 13 August 1940 a Royal Australian Air Force Hudson approaching Canberra airport crashed with three members of the Commonwealth cabinet and the chief of the general staff on board. Lowe was asked to chair an R.A.A.F. court of inquiry. The resentment of the professionals was eased by his thoroughness, which included a familiarization trip—his first flight—in a Hudson. His report decided the aircraft had stalled, and found no evidence of sabotage, poor maintenance, inadequate pilot training, or that a passenger was at the controls.

When World War II took Latham overseas, Lowe served as chancellor (1941-54) of the University of Melbourne. Unlike earlier incumbents (including Sir James Barrett [q.v.7], who nominated him), he immediately insisted that his role as chancellor was not 'to decide questions of policy, which were vested in the permanent Vice-Chancellor. His influence was mainly limited to the persuasive weight of the views expressed by him at Council meetings'. He worked easily with the liberal-minded (Sir) John Medley [q.v.].

On 3 March 1942 Lowe was appointed to inquire into 'all the circumstances' of the Japanese air-raids on Darwin on 19 February which had shocked Australia into an unprecedented sense of vulnerability. The day after his arrival in Darwin he telegraphed the minister for defence co-ordination: 'absolutely imperative Darwin be strengthened; vulnerable to any major attack'. Lowe's report concentrated on poor co-ordination between civilian and military authorities, on the delay in giving warning of the impending raids, and on lack of leadership in the panic which followed. Twenty-four years later Lowe defended himself against claims by the journalist Douglas Lockwood [q.v.] that he had deliberately narrowed his report to conceal the truth about 'Australia's Pearl Harbour'.

In June 1943 Lowe was named royal commissioner to investigate an allegation by E. J. Ward [q.v.], minister for labour and national service, that the Menzies government had prepared a 'defeatist' plan—by then, Ward claimed, missing from official files—to retreat beyond a 'Brisbane Line'. In fact a contingency plan to withdraw to south-eastern Australia had been laid before the Labor government, not its predecessor, and Ward's own prime minister John Curtin [q.v.13] denied that any files were missing. Ward claimed privilege and did not appear before the royal commission, preventing Lowe from ruling on his statement, but the judge none the less concluded that there was no substance in the charges.

Lowe's last investigation, another royal commission, was undertaken for the State of Victoria. In April 1949 the prominent communist Cecil H. Sharpley published in the Melbourne *Herald* 'revelations' of the party's activities, including rigged union elections and espionage. On 19 May Lowe was appointed to report on the 'origins, aims, objects and funds of the Communist Party in Victoria' and its 'activities and operations'. He sat from June 1949 to March 1950, examining 159 witnesses and compiling 10 000 pages of record. Scrupulous as always, Lowe never allowed his investigation to become a witch-hunt. Ralph Gibson, who spent eight days in the box as the party's first witness, wrote that Lowe, 'contrary to our fears and to the Government's hopes, displayed a certain genuine interest in Communist theory and a certain respect for evidence'.

Reporting with 'painstaking fair-mindedness', Lowe found that 'The Communist Party is prepared to use any means to achieve what it thinks to be a desirable object', and that it 'does not hold itself bound to obey laws which it regards as oppressive'. His 'meticulous sifting' of allegations of rigging of union elections found some proved but not all; and, on the issue of the party's purported allegiance to a foreign power, he found no evidence of direction from overseas and insufficient to support Sharpley's allegations of espionage. Party-members praised Lowe, but others have criticized him for failing to uncover acts of espionage since revealed. Gibson claimed that Lowe 'was punished for his honesty by the virtual burial of his report'. In reality it was overtaken by events. While the royal commission was sitting, Menzies won a Federal election undertaking to ban the Communist Party of Australia. He introduced his Communist Party dissolution bill the day before Lowe's report was issued on 28 April 1950.

With Medley, Lowe had defended university staff against allegations of 'Redness' made in the State parliament, and protested in favour of freedom of speech in the Teachers' College adjacent to the university, but when a meeting was held on 13 September 1951 at which a number of professors urged a 'No'

vote in the referendum on the banning of the Communist Party, Lowe protested to the new vice-chancellor (Sir) George Paton that the university had been identified with a party political cause. Consequent attempts to regulate such meetings were resented by staff and students, and attacked as illiberal in the press. Lowe claimed that his position was not understood: he was concerned that the university 'should not appear to enter the arena of controversy' on 'party political questions'. It proved easier said than done.

A discreet but creative chancellor, Lowe spoke out for better conditions for professors, publicly supported research, international academic intercourse, 'liberal education', and co-residential colleges ('as a result of my experience in the divorce court, they've got to live together and the sooner they start trying to do it the better'). He championed poor students, especially from the country, and lamented (though accepting) the closure of the university's short-lived Mildura branch in 1949. He was unhappy with quotas, insisting that 'all who have qualified' should be accepted. Lowe stood down as chancellor in 1954. He received an honorary LL.D. (1956). The citation stated that 'Precise and learned, he nevertheless commands the common touch', and praised 'The wit that sparkles behind a grave and deliberate front'. At the university's centenary celebrations Medley described him as 'one of the greatest men who have served this University'.

In 1959 Lowe broke the former record of thirty-two years as a judge of the Victorian Supreme Court. He did not formally retire until 1964, but presided over his last case on 17 December 1962, at the age of 82; every one of the forty-three judges gathered in the court for his official farewell had appeared before him as a barrister.

Before 1946 Lowe had spent seven years as president of the English Speaking Union, writing regularly on Australian issues for its London newsletter. In 1956 he agreed to be president of the new Australian-Asian Association of Victoria, when requested by R. G. (Baron) Casey [q.v.13]. Although in 1959 he publicly championed the cause of an Asian student whose father had been unjustly charged medical fees, threatening to resign as president until Casey gave redress, he was thought over-scrupulous in refusing to admit to membership citizens of countries not in diplomatic relations with Australia (such as China), and in distancing the association from campaigns against the White Australia policy; the cautious foreword he wrote for the abolitionist pamphlet, *Control or Colour Bar*, was withdrawn by mutual consent. His strict legalism again emerged during the public campaign against the hanging of Ronald Ryan [q.v.]; he argued in the *Age* that the cabinet's discretion was limited to details of the particular case and that it could not consider general principles against capital punishment, a distinction he claimed was 'of prime constitutional importance'.

Lowe was much honoured. He was knighted in 1948, and in December 1953 was called to the bar of the Legislative Assembly to be thanked for his services to the State and to parliament, especially as administrator of Victoria, a role in which he later made an official visit to Warrnambool, and spectacularly to Panmure. In 1956 he was appointed K.C.M.G.

Living quietly in retirement, Lowe kept up a number of activities, including golf. He died on 20 March 1969 in East Melbourne and was cremated; his wife, son and daughter survived him. At a memorial function held in the Supreme Court on 24 March, Chief Justice Sir Henry Winneke quoted from Lowe's own farewell speech: 'The moral I draw from my own career is that in this community, provided a boy has a modicum of ability and sufficient pertinacity, there is scarcely any position he may not reach'.

(Sir) David Low [q.v.10] drew a fine cartoon of Lowe in 1916. The university holds a portrait of Sir Charles, in chancellor's robes, by Paul Fitzgerald. Of the two portraits in the Victorian Bar, Judy Cassab's portrayal, in mufti, looks persuasively tough, but Lowe much preferred the portrait, also by Fitzgerald, showing him bewigged and benign.

Speeches at a Gathering in the Law Courts of Melbourne on Wednesday 19 December 1962 . . . to farewell the Honourable Sir Charles Lowe (Melb, 1963); N. Rosenthal, *Sir Charles Lowe* (Melb, 1968); K. Anderson, *Fossil in the Sandstone* (Melb, 1986); A. Inglis, *The Hammer & Sickle and the Washing Up* (Melb, 1995); *Quadrant*, Jan-Feb 1969, p 77; V. Rastrick, The Victorian Royal Commission on Communism 1949-1950 (M.A. thesis, ANU, 1973); Lowe papers (Supreme Court of Vic L).

J. R. POYNTER

LOXTON, MERLIN FORSTER (1895-1972), barrister and army officer, was born on 7 June 1895 in North Sydney, second of five children of native-born parents Edward James Loxton, barrister and member (1920-25) of the Legislative Assembly, and his wife Jane (Jeanie) Rosa Hamilton, née Marshall. Educated (1905-13) at Barker College, Hornsby, Merlin played Rugby and cricket in the school's first XV and XI. He was the State's champion rifle-shooter among the Commonwealth senior cadets and, on leaving school, was appointed cadet lieutenant in the 26th Battalion, Militia. In 1914 he enrolled in arts at the University of Sydney (LL.B, 1923).

Sailing for England in April 1915, Loxton was commissioned in the Royal Field Artillery Special Reserve on 5 June. Three months later he was sent to the Western Front with the 114th Battery. He saw action at Loos and on the Somme, France, and at Ypres, Belgium. In 1917 he was wounded at Wystchaete and evacuated to England. Next year he was promoted acting captain, and commanded his battery in France and with the Army of Occupation in Germany. Awarded the Military Cross (1919) and thrice mentioned in dipatches, he returned to Sydney in July 1919.

Although Loxton greatly loved horses and hankered for life on the land, he returned to the university to study law and was admitted to the Bar on 10 May 1923. He developed a solid practice in most jurisdictions and in 1935 inherited his father's rooms in University Chambers. A strong cross-examiner, he respected people who were honest and straightforward and despised those who were not. He aggressively questioned any witness whom he perceived to be prevaricating or disregarding the truth, and he was quick to react if he believed that his opponent, a presiding judge or a magistrate had been unfair to his clients. While respectful and disciplined in his dealings with others, he was never overawed by status or reputation. He took silk on 24 June 1953.

Loxton was president (1928-31) of Barker College Old Boys' Union. As a member (1932-70) of the college council, he established a high level of co-operation between the Old Boys' Union and the council to solve financial, leadership and management problems that threatened the school's existence. Loxton represented Barker in the college's unsuccessful attempt to be included in the Athletic Association of the Great Public Schools of New South Wales. When the A.A.G.P.S. remained adamant, those schools refused admission formed their own group which became the Associated Schools of New South Wales.

In the 1920s Loxton had become interested in skiing. Surfing before the days of surfboards was another of his passions. That Wamberal, his home beach, was open and unpatrolled did not worry him unduly: he learned to take sensible precautions and taught others to do likewise. A member of the Australian Club for many years and of the Warrawee Bowling Club, he had warmth, a capacity for steadfast friendship and a restrained—if occasionally pointed—sense of humour. At his successive houses at Wahroonga and Turramurra he established gardens that were much admired. He also built up a significant art collection, principally of Australian Impressionists. Loxton died on 24 November 1972 at Hornsby and was cremated with Presbyterian forms. He never married.

G. E. Hall and A. Cousins (eds), *Book of Remembrance of the University of Sydney in the War 1914-1918* (Syd, 1939); S. Braga, *Barker College* (Syd, 1978); *London Gazette*, supp, 1 Jan 1919, p 27; *SMH*, 25 June 1953, 13 Jan 1973; Barker College Archives, 1911-70; Loxton family papers (held by author, Wahroonga, Syd); family information.

ALAN H. LOXTON

LUCAS, LEONARD CUTHBERT (1894-1978), soldier, architect and public servant, was born on 6 November 1894 at Townsville, Queensland, eldest son of Robert Lucas, a sawmill manager from Ireland, and his Scottish-born wife Thomasina, née Cuthbert. Leonard attended state school at Charters Towers and became a senior cadet. He tried his hand at canecutting and journalism while studying engineering at the local school of mines. Joining the 2nd Infantry Regiment (Kennedy Battalion) in 1912, he progressed rapidly through the ranks to second lieutenant.

On the outbreak of World War I Lucas was sent with his unit to Thursday Island in August 1914. Taking 'unofficial leave', he enlisted in the Australian Imperial Force on 9 March 1915 and was posted to the 18th Battalion as a signaller. In June he was promoted sergeant and sailed for Egypt. On 20 August he landed at Gallipoli. Wounded in that month, he was evacuated with jaundice in October. He was commissioned in Egypt in February 1916 and embarked for France in March. For his work as battalion signals officer on the Somme in August, he was mentioned in dispatches.

In February 1917 Lucas was transferred to the 2nd Divisional Signal Company as lieutenant. On 3 May, during an attack on the Hindenburg line, he repaired telephone wires while under heavy artillery fire and won the Military Cross. Wounded again in November, he was hospitalized in England before he returned to France in April 1918. He was promoted captain in June. At St John's parish church, Glasgow, Scotland, on 28 March 1919 he married his cousin Whilhemina Shields, a 19-year-old typist. Lucas furthered his technical education through an attachment to Bridgman & Bridgman, architects and surveyors, at Torquay, England. His A.I.F. appointment terminated in Australia on 14 March 1920. Employed that year as an assistant in the office of the architect H. J. Brownlee in Sydney, and as a draughtsman with the Commonwealth War Service Homes Commission from 1922, he was registered as an architect on 26 June 1923.

Lucas had resumed his Militia service in 1921. He rose to lieutenant colonel (1933) and commanded the engineers of the 1st Division in 1933-39. The Department of the Interior posted him to Darwin in 1939 to supervise the construction of Larrakeyah Barracks. He was appointed to the 7th Military District headquarters staff in August and took up full-time duty in the following month. On 4 April 1940 he joined the A.I.F. as commander, Royal Australian Engineers, 6th Division, and sailed for the Middle East; his men served throughout the 1941 campaigns in Libya, Greece and Crete. Lucas was awarded the Distinguished Service Order for his leadership in Libya.

After helping to garrison Ceylon (Sri Lanka) from March 1942, he arrived home in May. As temporary brigadier, he was deputy engineer-in-chief (1942-45) at Land Headquarters and Advanced L.H.Q., and travelled extensively in the South-West Pacific Area. In 1945 he commanded the 1st R.A.E. Training Centre, Kapooka, New South Wales. He co-authored a booklet, *The Royal Australian Engineers—Lessons from The War 1939-45*. Demobilized in November, he held the office of (honorary) colonel commandant, R.A.E., in 1955-60 and maintained a keen interest in the corps. Following a term (1946-50) as Commonwealth director of works in the Northern Territory—where he was an official member (1948) of the Legislative Council—Lucas transferred to Western Australia. In 1953 he was seconded to take charge of construction of the atomic test site at Emu, South Australia; for this work he was appointed O.B.E. (1954). He retired in 1957.

A short, slight, energetic man, genuine and fair-minded, 'Luke' was 'brimful of bush humour, with twinkling blue eyes and steel-wire moustaches'. He wrote a pamphlet, *Man Management*, which summarized his vast experience in thirty-two pithy commandments, among them, 'Have a plan but don't let it choke you', and 'Don't piss in pockets—they leak'. He was fond of quoting the Bible, and enjoyed fishing, sketching and water-colour painting. Survived by his daughter and one of his two sons, Lucas died on 3 September 1978 at St Leonards, Sydney, and was cremated. His son John served as an officer in the R.A.E.

L. Beadell, *Blast the Bush* (Adel, 1967); R. McNicoll, *The Royal Australian Engineers 1919 to 1945* (Canb, 1982); D. O. Magee, *Sappers at the A-Bomb Tests* (Syd, 1994); *Sapper*, 1, no 6, 1974, p 4; 2, no 2, Dec 1978, p 34.   P. J. GREVILLE

LUCY, SYLVIA ROSE; *see* ASHBY

LUDOWICI, FREDERICK JOHN (1873-1969), businessman and conservationist, was born on 27 November 1873 at Willoughby, Sydney, eighth child of John Charles Ludowici, a tanner from Prussia, and his London-born wife Elizabeth, née Fay. Educated at Sydney Grammar School, Frederick began work at the age of 16 as an apprentice in his father's firm, J. C. Ludowici & Son Ltd, 'Mill Belt Manufacturers, Tanners, Curriers and Importers'. In 1891 he became its secretary on a salary of £13 per month. At St Philip's Anglican Church, Sydney, on 30 April 1902 he married Annie Maria Yates. Ludowici was appointed a director of the company in 1905 and general manager in 1914. Tall, fair haired and unaffected, he had a lively interest in the leather business and allied fields, and a genuine concern for people. Before World War I he went 'stagecoaching out West to find . . . the uses and abuses of belting in the ever-growing industry'.

Several times president of the Master Tanners and Leather Manufacturers' Association, in 1940 Ludowici deplored the difficulty of obtaining permits to import hides from New Zealand in a period when Australian cattlemen continued to brand their stock on the rump which led to excessive waste. Despite a quick temper, he was a much-loved employer. He retired as managing director in 1959, and resigned as chairman in 1962 and as a board-member in 1966 (at the age of 92). By the 1950s the business employed some 300 people at its 10-acre (4 ha) site at Lane Cove and its factory at Marrickville.

·Ludowici was a complex man, shy and diffident, yet fond of company, with 'great personal charm which covered a strong, determined inner character'. Known to colleagues and friends as 'Ludo' or 'Jack Ludo', he loved literature and music, and delighted in unobtrusively helping people, including, it is said, Henry Lawson's [q.v.10] wife, Bertha. He was sympathetic to Aborigines, and supported the Royal Blind Society of New South Wales, the (Royal) Flying Doctor Service and the Church of England's Carlingford Boys' Home. A Freemason and Rotarian, he also belonged to the Commercial Travellers' Association, the Royal Australian Historical Society and the Royal Australasian Ornithologists' Union, and was sometime president of the Royal Horticultural and Naturalists' societies of New South Wales.

His absorbing interest, outside work, was horticulture, especially the propagation of native wildflowers, trees and shrubs. Ludowici donated trees to Sydney City Council, to catchment areas and to Balls Head Reserve where, from 1930 until he was in his nineties, he worked voluntarily to restore the area. On his retirement, he humorously identified his interests as 'belts, beetles, bugs and birds'. In 1967 a ceremony was arranged by the Wildlife Preservation Society of Australia and North Sydney Municipal Council to unveil a plaque dedicating the F. J. Ludowici Grove. Survived by two of his three sons, Ludowici

died on 7 August 1969 at Hornsby and was cremated. His friend P. J. Hurley ('Waratah', gardening writer for the *Sydney Morning Herald*) described him as 'a man who loved trees with a great intensity'.

B. Henderson (ed), *Monuments and Memorials* (Syd, 1988); *Aust Leather J*, 15 Dec 1958; *SMH*, 25 Mar 1924, 10, 14 Feb 1940, 11 Mar 1959, 8 Aug 1969; *North Shore Times*, 28 Dec 1967; information from and family papers held by Mrs M. Rhodes-White, Wootton, NSW.   AUDREY TATE

LUISINI, EZIO (1891-1964), shopkeeper and winemaker, was born on 14 February 1891 at Ferentillo, Umbria, Italy, only child of Tobia Luisini, share-farmer, and his wife Arduina, née Rosati (d.1906), a domestic servant. Tobia emigrated to Western Australia in 1895. Ezio attended school at Ferentillo until grade five. In 1909 he joined his father, clearing bushland in the State's south-west. They worked together for a sawmill at Worsley before Ezio set up as a sub-contractor with his own team of workers. Fearing that he would be forced to enlist in the Australian or Italian armies, he hid in the outback, possibly near New Norcia, until World War I had ended. In 1918 he took a job with the State Saw Mill, Manjimup.

Following several attempts, dating from 1913, Luisini was naturalized in 1920. At St Patrick's Catholic Church, Fremantle, on 7 September 1921 he married a 17-year-old Italian, Antonietta Fanesi (d.1931); their only child, a daughter, was stillborn in 1922. Soon after, Luisini bought a wine saloon, with living quarters upstairs, at 215 William Street, Perth; the area came to be known as 'Little Italy' and he lived there for the rest of his life.

Luisini's business acumen helped him to assist Italian immigrants, especially those who had recently arrived: he answered their questions, gave them advice and offered favourable credit. He extended his premises next door, opened a mercery and stocked a wide range of goods, including equipment for rural work. In 1924 he bought 100 acres (40 ha) near Wanneroo, 12 miles (20 km) north-west of Perth. Four years later his pioneering vineyard paid dividends. On 29 January 1936 at St Brigid's Catholic Church, West Perth, he married 32-year-old Carmela ('Lina') Strano, a Calabrian; it was an 'arranged marriage' and they were to have no children. During World War II Luisini was interned at Kalgoorlie in April 1942 on the ground that he held fascist sympathies; he denied the allegation and was released in September. He eventually acquired more land and established a second vineyard which was flourishing by 1958. The Wanneroo council was to name a park after him.

'Mr Luisini', as he was known, was courteous and kindly. Sturdily built, intelligent and humorous, he was warm-hearted to children and those in genuine need, but was not easily duped. He avoided conspicuous spending, preferring shabby, comfortable clothes and a simple way of life. Labouring in his vineyards was his weekend recreation. His humility, frugality, simplicity and loyalty endeared him to members of the Italian community. Politicians valued his opinion. He gave large sums of money, anonymously, to worthy causes.

An obsession with making money was rooted in Luisini's childhood poverty. Although he was a self-made man, he was often sad, the deaths of his mother and first wife having deprived him of the love he sorely wanted. Survived by his wife, he died on 7 May 1964 at Subiaco and was buried in Karrakatta cemetery. He bequeathed most of his estate, sworn for probate at £233 905, to two nephews of his first wife and left Carmela £35 a week for her maintenance; in 1965 she successfully challenged the terms of the will, and was awarded £10 000 as well as £50 maintenance per week. She outlived her husband by twenty-one years.

A. Strano, *Luck Without Joy* (Perth, 1986); *Wanneroo Times*, 14, 16 Aug 1989, 22 Nov 1993; D. Gava, Italian Immigrants in Osborne-Wanneroo 1900-1950 (M.A. thesis, Univ WA, 1978); naturalization file A435/1 item 45/4/5758, internment file A367/1 item C26084 (AA, Canb); personal information.
                                                A. STRANO
                                                E. BURROWS

LUKE, SIR KENNETH GEORGE (1896-1971), manufacturer and sporting administrator, was born on 11 November 1896 in Port Melbourne, son of London-born parents George Edwin Luke, labourer, and his wife Minnie Annie, née Bensley. Ken attended South Brunswick State School and Ballarat High School before being apprenticed to an engraver in a silver factory at the age of 14.

Diligent and ambitious, he saved enough from his wages to become a partner (1921) in a small metal-spinning and silverware business at Carlton. By 1925 he was its proprietor and an employer of seven. For them there was no Depression. They were still with him thirty years later—with 650 others—making an ever-increasing range of products: silverware, stainless-steel surgical equipment, plated goods and glass-washing machines. For ten years Luke never knew an evening or a weekend off; he had an alarm clock to wake him at regular intervals at night so that he could keep the machinery going. In 1929 he bought a larger factory in Queen's Parade, Fitzroy, doubled his staff and introduced new lines. At the outbreak of World War II production was again stepped up and Luke became an honor-ary adviser to the Department of Supply and Shipping. On 11 February 1939 he had married 29-year-old Valda Richardson with Anglican rites at the Church of the Annunciation, St Marylebone, London.

Luke extended his interests after 1945. He had purchased the property, Deepfields, at Romsey as a weekend retreat, but the city-bred industrialist developed a passion for farming and made it a champion Dorset Horn and Poll Hereford stud. In November 1949 the Hollway [q.v.14] government appointed him a trustee of the (Royal) Exhibition Building. During his terms as chairman (1954-57 and 1961-63) trade exhibitions came to the fore, the stadium annexe was constructed for the 1956 Olympic Games, unwanted tenants were removed, and a new western annexe was built for an international trade fair in 1963. Luke had founded (1952) the White Ensign Club for sailors. He became a notable supporter of many other charitable causes. In the 1950s and 1960s he travelled abroad to keep abreast of manufacturing trends, such as automation. By then a millionaire, he still maintained a craftsman's as well as a proprietor's eye over the workings of his plants. K. G. Luke (Australasia) Ltd was registered as a public company in 1953.

A cricketer, motorcyclist and yachtsman in his youth, Luke also enjoyed racing and owned the successful 'FF' horses, with names like Fighting Force and Feeling Fine. In his view, sport bred character. He was best known, however, for his involvement with Australian Rules football. In 1938-55 he was president of the Carlton Football Club. A delegate (from 1935) to the Victorian Football League, he was its vice-president (1946-55) and president (1956-71). With postwar growth generating record crowds, he consolidated central administration and professionalized the game for players. In 1962 the V.F.L. bought land at Waverley for a new ground, which Luke envisaged as an alternative to the Melbourne Cricket Ground for football finals. V.F.L. Park, his legacy, opened in 1970.

'KG', as he was known, was a self-made man, hard-working and disciplined, but also far-sighted, courteous and even-tempered. The range of his interests and the number of his involvements was remarkable—he believed that a busy man could always take on another job. He was a councillor of the Royal Agricultural Society of Victoria and a member of at least fourteen clubs, including the Savage, the Victoria Racing and the Melbourne Cricket clubs. Luke was appointed C.M.G. in 1954 and knighted in 1962. Survived by his wife and daughter, Sir Kenneth died on 13 June 1971 at his Hawthorn home and was cremated. By that time K. G. Luke Group Industries Ltd, with twelve subsidiaries, had sales of $17.2 million and an annual profit of nearly $3 million. Luke's estate was sworn for probate at $412 156. A stand at Waverley Park is named after him and a portrait by Paul Fitzgerald is held by the Australian Football League.

K. Dunstan, *The Paddock that Grew* (Melb, 1974); D. Dunstan, *Victorian Icon* (Melb, 1995); *Herald* (Melb), 26 Nov 1955, 13 June 1964; *Age* (Melb), *Australian* and *SMH*, 14 June 1971; Aust Football League Archives, Jolimont; Roy Exhibition Building Archives, Museum of Vic, Melb.

DAVID DUNSTAN

LUKER, SIDNEY LAND (1890-1952), civil engineer and town planner, was born on 10 February 1890 at Madras, India, third son of Thomas Luker, journalist and merchant, and his wife Ellen, née Clark. Educated in England at Wycliffe College, Gloucestershire, and the University of Birmingham (B.Sc. Civil Eng., 1911), Sidney was employed by the engineers, Tulloch & Weaver, at Gloucester. Early in 1913 he came to Australia to join the works branch of the Commonwealth Department of Home Affairs. Initially engaged on planning Canberra's drainage, he assisted (1913-14) with engineering works for the Royal Australian Naval College, Jervis Bay. Back in India in 1915, he was assistant-engineer with the Corporation of Madras. He revisited Sydney where, on 19 April 1917 at Strathfield, he married with Baptist forms Annie Luker Morris, a distant cousin and a kindergarten teacher. Returning to England, he was commissioned in the Royal Engineers on 12 January 1918; he was wounded in action in France and demobilized in June 1919.

Luker worked briefly with a firm at Manchester, England, to gain experience with ferro-concrete. This modern building technology he first employed in the design and construction of godowns, wharves, and foreshore reclamation and protection works along the Yangtze River, China, for Butterfield & Swire. At the end of his three-year contract, he left Shanghai for Sydney in November 1922. An expert in reinforced-concrete design, he was appointed engineer for the reconstruction of the main road from Redfern to Botany and helped to transform a 'running sore' to a model thoroughfare. In 1925 he worked as a private consultant to various Sydney councils, upgrading the arterial road system.

In March 1926 Luker joined the Main Roads Board (Department of Main Roads from 1932). For many years he was the senior maintenance engineer for the metropolitan and (from 1938) the country divisions. In 1930 he undertook a study tour of the United States of America with H. M. Sherrard, representing the board at the International Road Congress in Washington, D.C. Luker succeeded

Sherrard as assistant chief engineer in 1941. From 1942 he served in turn as chief engineering consultant to the United States Army Services of Supply and as an area controller of technical services to the Commonwealth Department of Labour and National Service. On 2 January 1946 Luker took up duties as first chief planner for the Cumberland County Council. He oversaw the preparation of Australia's first statutory metropolitan planning scheme—a blueprint for Sydney in the British town and country planning tradition—which was completed within three years.

Active in professional and community circles, Luker was a fellow of the Institute of Public Administration, and a member of the institutions of engineers of Britain (from 1918), China (1919) and Australia (1925). In 1941 he chaired the Sydney division of the Institution of Engineers, Australia; he served on its national council in 1945. He had contributed to and been an associate-editor (1924-28) of the *Shire and Municipal Record*.

The development of Canberra quickened Luker's interest in planning. A foundation member (1934) and president (1943) of the Town and Country Planning Institute of New South Wales, he served on six of its committees. He also lectured part time (1950-52) on town and country planning at the University of Sydney. In 1951 he spent five months in Europe, attending conferences of the International Federation for Housing and Town Planning and of the Town Planning Institute, London. With his engineering background, Luker approached planning as a technical-bureaucratic activity which focused on better arrangement of land-use patterns. His major achievement was co-ordinating the County of Cumberland Planning Scheme.

Of average height and stocky build, Luker was both a consummate professional and a man of great warmth and charm. He died of a cerebral haemorrhage on 28 July 1952 at the Mater Misericordiae Hospital, North Sydney, and was cremated; his wife, two sons and two daughters survived him. The Sydney division of the (Royal) Australian Planning Institute has sponsored (since 1956) the biennial Sidney Luker memorial medal and lecture.

D. Winston, *Sydney's Great Experiment* (Syd, 1957); NSW Dept of Main Roads, *The Roadmakers* (Syd, 1976); *Civic Development*, July 1952; *Aust Planner*, 21, Apr-May 1983, p 29; *SMH*, 10 Apr 1947, 16 Aug 1949, 29 July 1952; Cumberland County Council, chairman's minute, 1 Aug 1952 (NSWA); NSW Roads and Traffic Authority Archives (Syd); information from Mr P. Luker, Syd, and Ms C. Havilland, Lond. ROBERT FREESTONE

LUKIS, FRANCIS WILLIAM FELLOWES (1896-1966), air force officer, was born on 27 July 1896 at Balingup, Western Australia, second child of William Fellowes Lukis, a farmer and grazier from England, and his Victorian-born wife Jean, née Campbell. Educated at the High School, Perth, Francis worked on the family property. He enlisted in the Australian Imperial Force on 7 December 1914, served at Gallipoli with the 10th Light Horse Regiment, and saw action in Egypt with that regiment and the 3rd Machine-Gun Squadron.

Commissioned in July 1916, Lukis transferred to No.1 Squadron, Australian Flying Corps, in Palestine on 25 February 1917. He flew as an observer (April-September) and as a pilot (from February 1918) on corps and army reconnaissance duties. In August 1918 he was promoted temporary captain and became a flight commander. Twice mentioned in dispatches, he embarked for Australia in March 1919 and remained in uniform as a member of the Australian Air Corps. Lukis joined the (Royal) Australian Air Force (formed on 31 March 1921) as one of its original twenty-one officers and was posted to No.1 Flying Training School, Point Cook, Victoria.

Gregarious, personable and a 'wonderful' leader, 'Luke' was a popular figure in the air force. He had a wide circle of acquaintances and a remarkable knowledge of notable Australian families. People liked to see him. His somewhat avuncular manner was reinforced by his solid stature and bristling moustache. At St Mary's Anglican Church, West Perth, on 21 January 1925 he married Florence St Aubyn Allen. He commanded No.3 Squadron and the new R.A.A.F. Station at Richmond, New South Wales (1925-30), No.1 Squadron (1930, 1932-34), No.1 Aircraft Depot, Laverton, Victoria (1936-38), No.1 F.T.S. (1938-39) and the R.A.A.F. Station at Laverton (1939-41). A graduate (1931) from the Royal Air Force Staff College, Andover, England, he was promoted group captain and appointed O.B.E. in 1938.

When the R.A.A.F. was reorganized into regional commands to meet the emerging Japanese threat, Lukis was made acting air commodore in May 1941 and posted to Townsville, Queensland. As air officer commanding Northern Area, he was responsible for the air defences of northern Australia and the adjacent territories. The resources available were hopelessly inadequate, but his enthusiasm and efficiency impressed Major General L. H. Brereton, the commander of the American Far East Air Force. In January 1942 Northern Area was divided: Lukis was promoted temporary air commodore and remained at Townsville in command of North-Eastern Area. For his success in conducting operations during a period which included the battle of the Coral Sea, he was appointed C.B.E. (1943). From August 1942 he was air

member for personnel at Air Force Headquarters, Melbourne.

In December 1943 Lukis took command of the R.A.A.F.'s premier strike force in the South-West Pacific Area, No.9 Operational Group (Northern Command from April 1944). Personalities and timing, however, conspired against him. Two senior air force officers in the theatre—the Americans General George Kenney and Major General Ennis Whitehead—doubted his abilities. Moreover, about the time Lukis took over No.9 O.G., the supreme commander General Douglas MacArthur [q.v.] effectively consigned Australian forces to a mopping-up role. Instead of being in the vanguard of the drive against Japan, Lukis found himself relegated to the task of garrisoning New Guinea. Despite his efforts to secure more satisfying work for his command, No.9 O.G. had become known in the R.A.A.F. as the 'Non-Ops Group'.

After the war the R.A.A.F.'s officer corps was reduced by about 90 per cent. Lukis was placed on the Retired List on 2 May 1946. He worked for Australian National Airways Pty Ltd as aerodrome-manager at Essendon, Melbourne, until 1952 when he was appointed A.N.A.'s manager in Canberra. From 1957 he headed the Canberra office of the stockbroking firm Ian Potter & Co. Active and popular, he had been president (1947-48) of the Air Force Association (Victoria division) and a member of the Naval and Military and the Australian clubs in Melbourne. Following his move to Canberra he was a foundation member (1954) of the Commonwealth Club, and was prominent in the Services Club, Manuka, the Canberra Club and the Royal Canberra Golf Club. He died of cancer on 18 February 1966 in Melbourne and was cremated; his wife and two sons survived him.

G. Odgers, *Air War Against Japan 1943-1945* (Canb, 1957); D. Gillison, *Royal Australian Air Force 1939-1942* (Canb, 1962); F. M. Cutlack, *The Australian Flying Corps* (Brisb, 1984); C. D. Coulthard-Clark, *The Third Brother* (Syd, 1991); A. W. Stephens, *Power Plus Attitude* (Canb, 1992) and 'RAAF Operational Commanders', in *Proceedings of the 1993 RAAF History Conference* (Canb, 1994); *RAAF News*, Mar 1966; *Herald* (Melb), 18 Feb 1966; *Canb Times*, 19 Feb 1966; information from Air Cdre W. H. Garing, Turramurra, Syd, and Air Cdre A. D. J. Garrisson, Kingston, Canb.

ALAN STEPHENS

LUSCOMBE, LENNARD EARL MAX (1893-1957), pianist and piano-roll manufacturer, was born on 19 August 1893 in East Melbourne, son of Max Luscombe (d.1914), a watchmaker from Berlin, and his Victorian-born wife Elsie, née Drake. Living at Fitzroy, Max played the trumpet in theatre orchestras and Elsie taught music. Their son's piano lessons began when he was aged 3. Extremely shy and reserved, Len was dominated by his mother, with whom he lived for most of his life. She was determined that he become a child prodigy. He, however, preferred popular dance music and by 1911 was conductor-violinist and arranger for a Melbourne theatre orchestra.

Fascinated by the new medium of piano-roll recording, about 1916 Luscombe made some of the earliest to be produced in Australia, using brown wrapping-paper carefully cut by hand with a pen-knife. In 1917 he left for the United States of America where he performed, held the post of music director at the Century Theatre, New York, took lessons from the composer T. M. Tobani and visited piano-roll companies, especially that of the Connor family at Chicago.

Back in Melbourne and with the financial support of his mother, Luscombe founded the Anglo-American Player Roll Co. in 1921. It produced piano-rolls under the 'Broadway' label. He imported machines for roll-production (including an electric cutter) from the Acme Machine Co., Newark, New Jersey. In addition to running the company, Luscombe was its sole artist, recording in the quiet of the night. He used names such as 'Dan Rawlins', 'Art Kaplan' and 'Earl Lester' to create the impression of a larger staff of pianists. The Acme company later supplied him with quantities of American masters. Initially these were rather plain and uninteresting, but soon works by the great arrangers of the Q.R.S. Music Co. were sent from America and issued on the Broadway label.

Like those of his rival George Henry Horton, manufacturer of the Mastertouch label in Sydney, Luscombe's rolls provided home-made, mechanically-generated entertainment for thousands of Australian households. From the player-piano's heyday in the late 1920s until the coming of television in the 1950s, countless unskilled but enthusiastic 'players' pumped pianola pedals, while onlookers sang the words printed on the paper roll. A dark, good-looking man, Luscombe was a committed artist, whose work never lost its freshness. Of all the Australian pianola musicians—among them Edith and Laurel Pardey [qq.v.] and Lettie Keyes—he made the best transition to recording the new rhythms of popular music after World War II.

At the Unitarian Manse, East Melbourne, on 4 September 1957 Luscombe married Eugenie Victorine, née Dineley; she was a postmistress and a divorcee. He died of cancer on 8 December 1957 and was cremated; his wife and his mother survived him. The Broadway label, plant and library of masters were purchased by Horton's firm. Luscombe's rolls have survived and reveal a remarkable musicianship: his cleverness was that he used few notes. Pianola-roll enthusiasts still search diligently for his arrangements.

Mastertouch Piano Roll Co, *Mastertouch*, golden jubilee cat (Syd, 1969); W. M. Denham, publisher's note (ts on ADB file, Canb); personal information.
                                                  BARCLAY WRIGHT

LUSH, DORA MARY (1910-1943), bacteriologist, was born on 31 July 1910 at Hawthorn, Melbourne, daughter of Victorian-born parents John Fullarton Lush, clerk, and his wife Dora Emma Louisa, née Puttmann. Mabel Mary Hailes Lush [q.v.] was her aunt. Educated at Fintona Girls' School, Dora pursued a conventional course of study for a girl until 1928 when she took physics and chemistry. She was dux, and won the exhibition in geography and a free place to the University of Melbourne (B.Sc., 1932; M.Sc., 1934). In 1933, at the university's department of bacteriology, she studied bacillary dysentery.

In the following year Miss Lush joined the staff of the Walter and Eliza Hall [qq.v.9] Institute as a bacteriological research fellow. She worked closely with (Sir) Macfarlane Burnet in a small team examining viruses and the human immune system. Employing a method largely devised by Burnet for studying viruses, she undertook path-breaking research with E. V. Keogh [q.v.] and others. Lush collaborated in the search for an influenza vaccine, the early development of myxomatosis and the identification of the herpes simplex virus. Burnet considered her the 'most outstandingly competent' bacteriologist with whom he had ever worked.

Early in 1939 Lush proceeded to the National Institute for Medical Research, London. There she hoped to follow through work on the poliomyelitis virus which she could not pursue in Melbourne. The outbreak of World War II interrupted her plans and she joined a team, led by Sir Patrick Laidlaw, investigating air-borne infections. For two years, through the darkest days of the air-raids on London, she applied her laboratory skills to the influenza virus 'with an excursion into the practical problems of dust control in hospital wards'. In 1942 she was diverted into work on immunization against typhus.

Lush returned to Australia in September that year. Scrub typhus was causing havoc among Australian servicemen in the tropics and Burnet was pleased to have her support in work on a vaccine. The rickettsia microbe could only be maintained by inoculation of blood through a series of animals. Although there was a known element of risk in such work, Lush had complete mastery of a wide range of laboratory techniques. In any case, it was wartime. Lush had previously recovered from a mild case of typhus when she worked in London. On 27 April 1943 she accidentally pricked the index finger of her left hand while inoculating a mouse with scrub typhus. The strain of virus proved a particularly malignant one. She died on 20 May that year in Royal Melbourne Hospital and was cremated. Her insistence that regular blood samples be taken to assist further research into the disease and its treatment caught the public imagination. She was hailed as a martyr to science and the war effort. Within three years it was discovered that the disease could be treated with antibiotics and that a vaccine was unnecessary.

A tall, slim woman with wavy auburn hair, Lush was athletic, energetic and direct. She was an exceptionally good dancer, 'a near champion at squash' and a passionate skier. Immaculately groomed, she wore three-inch (7.6 cm) heels, even in the laboratory. From an early age she had demonstrated a remarkable capacity for sustained application to detailed tasks. In the laboratory she was careful, methodical and keenly analytical, but her career was cut short before she could realize her full potential as an independent researcher. Her life and work have been honoured by the National Health and Medical Research Council's biomedical scholarships, and by her old school which offers Dora Lush scholarships for mathematics and science.

M. Burnet, *Walter and Eliza Hall Institute 1915-1965* (Melb, 1971); Walter and Eliza Hall Inst, *Annual Report*, 1943, p 6; *Aust J of Science*, June 1943, p 193; *Age* (Melb), *Argus* and *Sun News-Pictorial*, 21 May 1943.   CAROLYN RASMUSSEN

LUSH, MABEL MARY HAILES (1881-1958), kindergarten teacher, was born on 30 June 1881 in East Melbourne, third child of George Lush (1846-1932), a Victorian-born merchant and later philanthropist, and his Scottish-born wife Mabel Mary Elizabeth Nicol, née Fullarton. Her mother died three days after Mary's birth and George Lush remarried in 1886. Educated (1892-97) to matriculation level at Ruyton Girls' School, Kew, Mary studied and taught piano. In 1905 she gained a diploma of music from the University of Melbourne.

A devout Christian and a member of the Collins Street Baptist Church, Miss Lush began her teaching career in 1906 as a volunteer at Melbourne's first free kindergarten, in Bouverie Street, Carlton. Showing aptitude for the work, she trained as a kindergarten teacher in 1909-10 and as an infant teacher in 1911. She studied the latest kindergarten methods with John Dewey at Columbia University, New York (1917), and with the McMillan sisters in London (1927). In her work at Carlton as assistant-director (1911-16), director (1916-28) and co-ordinator of student training (1912-28), she achieved a reputation for a high standard of teaching and leadership. She was loved and trusted by the families of Carlton and admired by her students.

Lush became a leader of the Free Kindergarten Union of Victoria. She served as an acting-supervisor (1914 and 1916), president of the directors' association, and lecturer (1915-34 and 1940) at the Kindergarten Training College. In 1926 she published her *avant-garde* curriculum, *Progressive Kindergarten Methods*. From 1937 she held positions on the F.K.U.V. executive (acting-president 1942-44, president 1944-48), and on the college council and education committee. She represented the F.K.U.V. on the Australian Association of Preschool Child Development (from 1937) and the Lady Gowrie [q.v.9] centres (from 1939), and lectured on kindergarten education and child development in many forums.

Throughout her professional life Lush balanced a strong belief in the value of early childhood education with a philanthropic ideal. She gave her time and knowledge generously, accepted no salary, and made substantial donations to the Carlton Kindergarten, the F.K.U.V. and other related organizations. Unmarried, she combined family life and professional expertise with humanitarian concern. She adhered firmly to traditional values and obligations, nursing her father, sister and stepmother through their final illnesses in the family home at Kew. Academically qualified and displaying competence, commitment and leadership, she was compassionate in her work for the welfare of disadvantaged women and children.

When she retired from Carlton Kindergarten in 1928 a stained-glass window was erected in her honour. Lush was made life vice-president of the F.K.U.V. in 1948 and was appointed O.B.E. in 1954. Following a long illness, she died on 1 October 1958 at Richmond and was cremated with Presbyterian forms; her estate was sworn for probate at £49 366. Dora Mary Lush [q.v.] was her niece.

L. Gardiner, *The Free Kindergarten Union of Victoria 1908-1980* (Melb, 1982); FKUV, *Annual Report*, 1915-16, 1927-28, 1928-29, 1958-59, *and* Mthly News Sheet, Oct 1948 (held Univ Melb Archives); R. Benjamin, Mary Lush, 1881-1958: a pioneer in early childhood (ts, 1991, held by author, Caulfield, Melb).   RUTH BENJAMIN

LYMBURNER, STANLEY FRANCIS (1916-1972), artist, was born on 11 June 1916 at Albion, Brisbane, elder child of Australian-born parents Edmund Lymburner, surveyor, and his wife Gladys Bacon, née Jones. Francis was educated at Brisbane Grammar School and at Brisbane Technical College where he studied art under F. Martyn Roberts and won (1936) the Godfrey Rivers [q.v.11] medal. He shared a studio, read widely, listened to classical music and was fascinated by the sea.

In 1939, against his parents' wishes, and with the financial support of Mrs Constance Beven, Lymburner moved to Sydney. He sketched at Taronga Zoological Park, joined a students' sketch club and attended evening-classes in etching at East Sydney Technical College. In 1940 he took rooms at The Rocks. Next year an article in *Art in Australia* featured his drawings of animals and he held his first solo exhibition, at the Notanda Gallery. Mobilized in the Militia on 1 July 1942, Lymburner was posted to the 120th Australian Special Hospital as a nursing orderly. He was discharged medically unfit on 27 November 1944.

Considered by many to be at the forefront of developments in contemporary art in Sydney in the 1940s, Lymburner belonged to the Sydney Art Group (formed in 1945). Tom Bass was a friend, as were the artists who lived at Merioola. Lymburner was good looking, bohemian and strongly attractive to women. His son Julian was born to Mavis Mace on 29 September 1944. Francis's romantic paintings—mainly of dancers, circus people and views of Sydney—were often associated with the 'Sydney Charm School', as it was called. Sydney Ure Smith [q.v.11] published *Fifty Drawings by Francis Lymburner* in 1946 and (Sir) Warwick Fairfax of the *Sydney Morning Herald* was an early admirer, collector and patron of Lymburner's work. In 1951 Lymburner wrote reviews for the *S.M.H.* and won the Mosman jubilee art prize.

Following a farewell exhibition at David Jones's [q.v.2] Art Gallery in 1952, Lymburner left for England. His years in London were lean and disappointing; he lived on the meagre sales of works sold at exhibitions in Australia, where his reputation declined in his absence. Haunting the world of theatre and music, and the Soho district, he mixed with many well-known actors, writers and artists—and Australian expatriates such as Barry Humphries—but exhibited only in a few group shows in London.

Lymburner returned to Sydney in February 1964. He exhibited widely, though without success. His style had become 'painterly' and powerfully expressionistic. In 1966 he suffered a cerebral haemorrhage which paralysed his left side. There are no known paintings dated after that year, but he continued to teach at his Park Street studio and published *Lymburner* (1970), a second book of drawings,

introduced by George Molnar. Lymburner spent his last year in a nursing home at Narrabeen. He died of ischaemic heart disease on 10 October 1972 while lunching at Jonah's Villa Al Mare restaurant at Whale Beach. Survived by his son, he was cremated. The Art Gallery of New South Wales organized a touring retrospective exhibition of his paintings and drawings in 1992.

L. Klepac and H. Kolenberg, *Francis Lymburner Drawings* (Hob, 1986); H. Kolenberg and B. Pearce, *Francis Lymburner* (Syd, 1992), and for bib and exhibitions; *Meanjin Q*, Winter 1950, p 111; *SMH*, 18 Sept 1951, 28 May 1952, 1 July 1970, 22 Oct 1972; H. de Berg, Francis Lymburner (taped interview, 20 Nov 1965, NL).   HENDRIK KOLENBERG
                                                  JULIANNA KOLENBERG

LYNCH, ALBERT EDWIN (1900-1976), Catholic priest and musician, was born on 10 December 1900 at Collie, Western Australia, eldest child of Ernest Edwin Lynch, a miner from India, and his Victorian-born wife Elizabeth, née Stewart. Raised as an Anglican and educated at state schools, young Albert received his first musical training from the redoubtable Sister Monica at St Joseph's Convent, Boulder, before taking a job as a clerk. In the early 1920s his talent as a violinist earned him a place in orchestras supporting silent movies and enabled him to perform solo recitals on the wireless. Joseph Nowotny became his mentor. The Rivervale Progress Association sponsored the first of a series of concerts to raise the £1000 needed to send Lynch to Belgium in 1923 to study under Emile Marchot at the Conservatoire Royal de Musique de Bruxelles for three and a half years. During this period he was converted to Catholicism. Back in Perth, he led a fifteen-piece orchestra at the Ambassadors Theatre, Hay Street.

In 1930 Lynch began training for the priesthood at the Pontifical Urban College of Propaganda Fide, Rome. He also studied the Palestrina school of polyphonic music, as well as Gregorian chant. In the following year he performed Schubert's *Ave Maria* before Pope Pius XI. Lynch was ordained priest in St John Lateran Basilica on 16 March 1935. In the Benedictine abbey at Solesmes, France, he encountered the revival of plainsong stimulated by Pope Pius X's liturgical reforms. Appointed curate of Palmyra, Perth, on 6 July 1935, he returned to Western Australia in October. In 1938 he formed an all-male choir at St Mary's Cathedral, Perth, which he conducted for fifteen years. In conjunction with Christian Brothers' College, St George's Terrace, he established Western Australia's first Catholic choir school. As diocesan director (from 1938) of Gregorian chant, he travelled zealously throughout the State, assisting convent schools to establish plainsong choirs, and organizing examinations and competitions. He served on the music examinations board of the University of Western Australia, and collaborated with the Benedictine Abbey Nullius of New Norcia and its musicians, notably Dom Stephen Moreno [q.v.] and Dom Eladio Ros. Lynch was chaplain (1938-42) of Aquinas College, Manning, and, later, of other institutions. Founding parish priest (1952) of Applecross, he dedicated the parish to St Benedict and ministered there until he retired in 1973.

Following the Second Vatican Council's directives regarding use of the vernacular, in the 1960s Lynch had begun to write church music with English lyrics. For Pope Paul VI's visit to Australia in 1970, he wrote music for the Mass in St Mary's Cathedral, Sydney, and *Mass of the Unsung Saints* for a service held at Randwick racecourse where he conducted the choir. His compositions were used at the International Eucharistic Congress in Melbourne in 1973. Lynch died on 23 August 1976 at Applecross and was buried in Karrakatta cemetery. He bequeathed his violin, viola and bows to the University of Western Australia, his piano to the Applecross parish school, and his records of polyphonic music and Gregorian chant to the archbishop of Perth.

Centenary of the Catholic Church in Western Australia, 1846-1946 (Perth, 1946); D. F. Bourke, *The History of the Catholic Church in Western Australia* (Perth, 1979); *Record* (Perth), 21 Jan, 13 Apr 1935, 9 May, 27 June, 18 July 1936, 9 Jan 1937, 17 Dec 1939, 7 Mar 1940, 23 July, 22 Sept 1943, 4 Feb 1949, 22 July 1976, 16 July 1980; *Catholic Weekly* (Syd), 4 July 1968; *West Australian*, Melville Sth Perth supp, 7 Dec 1970, 24 Aug 1976; Lynch papers (Catholic Archdiocesan Archives, Perth); Benedictine Abbey of New Norcia, Archives (WA).

CLEMENT MULCAHY

LYNCH, FRANCIS ENNIS ('GUY') (1895-1967), sculptor, was born on 23 September 1895 at North Carlton, Melbourne, son of Joseph Patrick Lynch, mason, and his wife Annie, née Connor, both Victorian born. Frank was educated at Christian Brothers' College, East Melbourne, before the family moved to Auckland, New Zealand. Giving his occupation as plasterer, Lynch enlisted in the New Zealand Expeditionary Force on 17 April 1915 and was allocated to the artillery. He fought at Gallipoli that year. In France from April 1916, he was posted to the New Zealand Divisional Signal Company, awarded the Military Medal (July 1917) 'for acts of gallantry in the field' and promoted sergeant. On 28 December 1918 Lynch married Doris Louise Hannen in the parish church at Stevenage, Hertfordshire, England. She died in childbirth in October 1919; their son predeceased him.

Discharged in New Zealand on 26 February 1920, Lynch received commissions to sculpt war memorials in Wellington and at Devonport, Auckland. In 1922 George Finey persuaded him to come to Sydney where he entered the bohemian community 'for ever bawling in honour of Michelangelo'. On one drunken evening the damp clay of a commissioned bust of Sir Joynton Smith [q.v.11] provided material for a studio mud-fight. 'Guy', as Frank was known, studied under Rayner Hoff [q.v.9], and exhibited works such as 'Australian Venus' and 'The Digger'. 'The Satyr', shown at the Society of Artists' younger group exhibition in 1924, created a sensation, being hailed as a masterpiece and damned as 'a pagan work'. It was bought for the National Art Gallery of New South Wales. That year Lynch was commissioned by Dame Nellie Melba [q.v.10] to make a bust of her grand-daughter Pamela and a garden sculpture, 'Victory of Orpheus'. He later created the figures for the battle diorama, 'Pozières', at the Australian War Memorial, Canberra. At St Francis's Catholic Church, Paddington, on 27 April 1927 Lynch married Marjorie Cush, a 27-year-old secretary.

'The Satyr' had been modelled on Frank's younger brother JOSEPH YOUNG LYNCH (1897-1927), a black-and-white artist. Joe had worked with the British Red Cross Society in London and France in World War I. He abandoned study at the Elam School of Arts & Design, Auckland, and developed his drawing by sketching street-life alongside his friend C. J. ('Unk') White. Arriving in Sydney with his brother, Joe established himself as a freelance cartoonist and by 1925 was drawing for Melbourne *Punch*, where he met Kenneth Slessor. In 1926 he was back in Sydney as the youngest member of the *Smith's Weekly* art staff. On 14 May 1927, while drunk, Joe threw himself off a Mosman-bound ferry near Fort Denison, fought off a would-be rescuer and drowned; his body was never recovered. Joe's unruly life and tragic death inspired Slessor's elegy, 'Five Bells'.

Guy 'went to pieces' after Joe's death. In 1929, however, he studied in London at the Royal College of Art, under Benjamin Clemens. At the Royal Academy of Arts he exhibited a bust of the writer Beverley Nichols in 1931, and one of Sir Isaac Isaacs [q.v.9] in 1938 (purchased by the Commonwealth government in 1945). He also visited Paris and completed a bust of Lieutenant General Baron Birdwood [q.v.7] before returning to Sydney in November 1938.

In 1941 Lynch completed a commission to depict Aboriginal life for one of the bronze panels on the west doors of the Public Library of New South Wales. Mobilized in the Militia in October, he performed clerical duties in Australia until discharged for reasons of age and fitness in October 1944. He was a member of the Royal Art Society of New South Wales. Suffering from arthritis and arteriosclerosis, by 1950 he had retired to a poultry-farm at Buxton, near Picton. In 1959 he joined the Gallipoli Legion of ANZACS Club.

To his second wife, Guy was 'a very direct and honest man', though White found him dogmatic, especially in matters of art. Jack Lindsay described Lynch as having 'an Irish-Australian face, rough and tough and of the wildwood, yet sensitive'. As a sculptor he was 'practically self-taught'. Joe was 'a looser and wilder version' of his brother. Survived by his wife, Guy Lynch died on 13 May 1967 at Picton and was cremated. In 1977 his widow paid for 'The Satyr' to be cast in bronze. Placed in the Royal Botanic Gardens, Sydney, it is a memorial to the unfulfilled promise of both brothers.

K. Slessor, *Bread and Wine* (Syd, 1970); D. Stewart, *A Man of Sydney* (Melb, 1977); K. Scarlett, *Australian Sculptors* (Melb, 1980); J. Lindsay, *Life Rarely Tells* (Melb, 1982); *Daily Telegraph Sunday Pictorial*, 15 May 1927; *SMH*, 24 July 1924, 15 Nov 1938, 30 June 1977; E. Muspratt, ms biog of Unk White, Frank Johnson papers (ML); information from the late Mr C. J. ('Unk') White.

PETER KIRKPATRICK

LYNRAVN, NORMAN SÖREN (1912-1970), librarian and author, was born on 26 April 1912 in South Melbourne, fourth child of Jens Sörensen Lyng, draughtsman, and his Victorian-born wife Gertrude Eleanor, née Burrowes. Jens had come to Australia from Denmark in 1891, worked in turn as a newspaper editor and public servant, and published several books, two of them on non-British immigrants in Australia. Norman was educated at the Central School, Caulfield North, Melbourne High School and Canberra University College (B.A., 1937). In 1929 he joined the Federal Capital Commission, Canberra, as a junior clerk and in the following year transferred to the Parliamentary Library of which the Commonwealth National Library (later National Library of Australia) formed part.

In 1938 he changed his surname to Lynravn: one of the reasons was that he wanted to make a career on his own merits rather than being always known as 'old Lyng's son'. At St Saviour's Cathedral, Goulburn, New South Wales, on 23 December 1939 he married with Anglican rites Joan Meredith Dart, a 19-year-old stenographer; she later became known as a contributor of satirical verse to the *Canberra Times*. Under-

stating his age, Lynravn enlisted in the Australian Imperial Force on 19 December 1941 and was posted to the 2nd/14th Light Field Ambulance. In 1943 he transferred to the Australian Army Education Service. He served in Papua and New Guinea in 1944-45 where he contracted a liver infection which permanently affected his health. Back in Australia, he was commissioned lieutenant in September 1945 and transferred to the Reserve of Officers in March 1946.

Lynravn's wartime experience of trying to meet diverse educational needs in remote areas led him to seek responsibility for the National Library's service to outlying territories. His first assignment was to re-establish the public library in Port Moresby. From 1947 he was the National Library's chief preparation officer. In 1953-56 he was its liaison officer in London; his duties included oversight of the transfer to Australia of the Gayer-Anderson collection and the papers of John Grant [q.v.1]. He was director of publications when he retired in 1968 due to ill health.

A foundation member (1937) of the Australian Institute of Librarians (later Library Association of Australia), Lynravn contributed regularly to professional literature, his *Libraries in Australia* (Melbourne, 1948) being an overall survey. In addition, he wrote general articles, reviews, entries for the *Australian Dictionary of Biography*, short stories and crime fiction, such as (with L. W. Martin) *Murder on Mount Capita* (Sydney, 1944). He was a member of the Canberra Fellowship of Australian Writers and, while in London, of the Society of Australian Authors.

Lynravn was 5 ft 9 ins (175 cm) tall, with blue eyes and a fair complexion. As a young man he had played (1929-40) Australian Rules football for Ainslie. An able librarian and a competent, considerate administrator, he was a strong advocate of a wide-ranging educational role for his profession. His laconic manner of speech, puckish humour and occasional practical jokes endeared him to his colleagues. Survived by his wife and son, he died from complications of Banti's syndrome on 30 October 1970 at Queanbeyan, New South Wales, and was cremated.

Canb Times, 17 Sept 1938, 26 Mar 1969, 31 Oct 1970; A. T. Bolton, Interview with Cliff Burmester, 20 Nov-24 Dec 1988 (sound recording, Oral Hist Project, NL); C. A. Burmester, Memoirs (ts, NL); File A3901 (NL); Ainslie Football Club records; family papers held by, and information from, Mr G. Lynraven, Wynnum, Brisb.   PAULINE FANNING

LYNTON, WILLIAM MAYNE (1885-1965) and NANCYE DORIS (1893-1973), actors, were husband and wife. William was born on 4 May 1885 at Bowness, Cumberland,

England, son of John Linton, general labourer, and his wife Catherine, née Mains. Educated at Glasgow, he moved south, trod the boards in music halls and pestered theatrical managements until given a part in *Rob Roy* in 1905. He travelled with (Sir) Frank Benson's Shakespearian Company in 1906-07 and was subsequently based in London. At the register office, St Giles, on 2 July 1912 he married Annie Lenon (otherwise 'Hughes'), née Gass, a 42-year-old divorcee and an actress; they were later divorced. A strong, good-looking man with a trim moustache, Lynton had worked in the United States of America from 1911: he went on Shakespearian tours, supported Douglas Fairbanks and George Arliss, appeared in silent films, and toured the country lecturing on 'Scott of the Antarctic'. Lynton was commissioned honorary lieutenant in the British Army on 27 June 1917; after carrying out recruiting duties at Toronto, Canada, he was attached to the Military Control Office, New York. In 1919 he returned to the stage.

Nancye was born on 19 June 1893 at Chingford, Essex, England, daughter of theatrical parents George Musgrove and Nellie Stewart [qq.v.5,12]. Brought to Australia in September, she was mainly educated in her mother's dressing-room by a governess who travelled with the company. At school at Lausanne, Switzerland, she trained as a pianist and made friends with (Dame) Cicely Courtneidge. She was later taught dancing by Edouard Espinosa in London and fencing by Frank Stuart in Sydney. In 1910-11 she conducted the orchestra for her mother's eight-month tour of Australia. Nancye Stewart made her stage début on 14 February 1914 in *Joseph and his Brethren* at the Theatre Royal, Melbourne. Over the next five years she appeared under various managements, sometimes with her mother. In 1916 she joined Marie Tempest's company, playing five roles as well as understudying her. Nancye acted in the farce, *Pretty Soft*, at the Morosco Theatre, New York, in 1919, then played in repertory at the Copley Street Theatre, Boston.

Stewart and Lynton met in New York in 1920 when they were cast in George M. Cohan's production of *Genius and the Crowd*. They claimed to have married there on 5 March 1920 before crossing the U.S.A. with Walker Whiteside in *The Master of Ballantrae*. Nancye returned home in 1921. Mayne followed her next year to take up a contract with J. C. Williamson [q.v.6] Ltd which lasted on and off for twenty years. He played the detective in *The Bat*, and had leading roles with Pauline Frederick, Gertrude Elliott, Muriel Starr and Emélie Polini [q.v.11]. At the registrar general's office, Sydney, Mayne and Nancye were married on 15 September 1924. Between giving birth to three sons, she per-

formed in stage shows such as *De Luxe Annie* and *My Old Dutch*. Lynton appeared (1924-59) in five Australian films, notably as Lieutenant Bligh [q.v.1] in Charles Chauvel's [q.v.7] *In the Wake of the Bounty* (1933).

Among the earliest actors to pioneer (from 1925) radio drama, the Lyntons were more active in radio than the theatre throughout the 1930s. During the Depression Mayne broadcast poetry readings with musical accompaniments provided by Nancye. In 1934 he adapted and directed plays (which starred his wife) for radio 2UW. By 1935 he was producing for F. W. Thring's [q.v.12] radio 3XY in Melbourne. Next year he and Nancye negotiated contracts with the Australian Broadcasting Commission in Melbourne at a joint salary of £25 a week. Mayne was soon held to be a bad influence in the studio; 'consistently halting', he 'fluffed' his lines and treated the producer 'cavalierly by his late arrival and behaviour'. In 1938 he complained to William Cleary [q.v.8]: 'I went over to the Melbourne National Stations an established success, both as Producer and Player—finished literally carrying a Spear before the Microphone, discredited both as Producer and Player'. He took up directing for 3XY.

Performing 'everything from evanescent variety to the unquenchable classics', Nancye Stewart excelled as a character actress. Throughout her career she appeared in more than five hundred radio plays. She enjoyed gardening, cooking, jam-making, dressmaking, reading and travel, treasured the briar-rose patterned china from her mother's house in England, and had 'an intense interest in the renovation of old houses and old furniture'. Nancye was a practical person with 'a direct no-nonsense manner'. The family returned to Sydney in 1945.

By then Lynton was a 'big, heavy-looking man very much in the mould of the old actor-manager'. The things he liked doing did not pay much. Shakespeare was his real love. In 1946-49 he produced matinées for Leaving certificate students, among them *The Tempest* and *Julius Caesar*. The Lyntons went to Britain in 1949. Nancye was to comment that: we 'were only successful in our careers when we were touring separately'. They squabbled when together and wrote each other love letters when apart. Mayne appeared in (Sir) Tyrone Guthrie's production (1949) of *The Three Estates* at the Edinburgh Festival of Music and Drama, and Nancye in London in Terence Rattigan's *Who is Sylvia?* She toured (1951-52) Australia with the John Alden [q.v.13] Company in three Shakespearian plays, then returned to Britain. While Mayne acted in London in *Ring Round the Moon* and other plays, Nancye appeared with the Old Vic Theatre Company (1953-54) under the Oliviers and with the Shakespeare Memorial

Theatre Company, Stratford-on-Avon (1954-55). Her parts included Gertrude in Richard Burton's *Hamlet*, which they also performed at Kronborg Castle, Elsinore, Denmark.

Mayne did little professionally after they came back to Sydney in 1955. He died on 20 May 1965 in North Sydney and was cremated with Presbyterian forms. Nancye had supported (Dame) Margaret Rutherford in *The Happiest Days of Your Life* and Leo McKern in *Ned Kelly* for the Australian Elizabethan Theatre Trust. Her last stage role was Aunt Julie in *Hedda Gabler* (Hobart, 1969), but she continued to perform in television and radio plays, and as Mabel in the long-running radio serial 'Blue Hills'. Survived by two of her sons, Nancye Stewart died on 8 August 1973 at her Neutral Bay home and was cremated with Anglican rites.

N. Stewart, *My Life's Story* (Syd, 1923); H. Porter, *Stars of Australian Stage and Screen* (Adel, 1965); M. Skill, *Sweet Nell of Old Sydney* (Syd, 1974); R. Lane, *The Golden Age of Australian Radio Drama 1923-1960* (Melb, 1994); *Wireless Weekly*, 16 Feb 1934, p 12, 25 Oct 1935, p 23; *Weekly Times*, 20 Sept 1941; *New York Times*, 19 Sept 1911, 17 Dec 1912; *Argus*, 14 Feb 1914; *SMH*, 5 Apr 1922, 7 July, 5, 10 Aug 1933, 13 Apr 1946, 21 June 1956, 30 May 1965; ABC files, SP1558/2 box 20 (AA, Syd); information from, and papers held by, Mr M. Lynton, Neutral Bay, Syd.   MARTHA RUTLEDGE

LYON, MARJORIE JEAN (1905-1975), surgeon and prisoner of war, was born on 13 February 1905 at Northam, Western Australia, fourth child of Australian-born parents Patrick Pearson Lyon, barrister, and his wife Jeanie Dunlop, née MacMaster. J. L. Lyon [q.v.10] was her grandfather. Marjorie attended Northam State School and Methodist Ladies' College, Perth, where she was twice dux. She won the Dagmar Berne prize in the year that she graduated from the University of Sydney (M.B., B.S., 1928), then served as a resident medical officer at several city hospitals. While studying in Britain, she qualified as a member (1934) of the Royal College of Obstetricians and Gynaecologists, and as a fellow (1936) of the Royal College of Surgeons, Edinburgh.

On 30 July 1937 Lyon joined the Malayan Medical Service. She was stationed at Johore Bahru in January 1942 at the time of the Japanese advance. Ordered to Singapore, she joined her English friend Dr Elsie Crowe at the general hospital and took charge of a shock ward. When evacuation orders were received, she embarked in the *Kuala* with Crowe and other personnel. Bombers sank the vessel near Pompong Island in the Lingga Archipelago. Injured herself, Lyon swam one-quarter of a mile (400 m) to the island, treated

Crowe—whom she had saved from drowning —and cared for the wounded. Days later she, Crowe and others were rescued by the *Kafuku Maru* (*Krait*) and taken to Sumatra, Netherlands East Indies. They subsequently made their way to Padang. Although the arrival of the Japanese was imminent, Lyon chose to remain with the wounded and was interned as a prisoner of war. She assumed medical responsibility for approximately 50 British and 2500 Dutch women and children, initially located at a Salvation Army hospital, then at a Catholic monastery and later at a gaol. Finally, the internees were moved to a jungle camp at Bangkinang.

For three and a half years they endured food shortages, overcrowding and poor sanitation which caused malnutrition and disease. Some of the Dutch internees challenged Lyon's authority, but, due to her unstinting care and rigorous measures, the camp recorded only 160 deaths. Despite being only 5 ft 1 in. (155 cm) tall, she 'gave the Japanese hell. She was always demanding medicine and getting slapped for asking'. Crowe was impressed with Lyon's integrity and by the way she regarded 'each and every patient' as 'sacrosanct'. After the Japanese had surrendered, Lyon was evacuated to Singapore. Lady Mountbatten met her there and described her as 'an outstanding woman doctor ... whose work ... will make history, and who succeeded in commanding and controlling the Japanese and seeing that they carried out *her* orders.'

Dr Lyon was appointed O.B.E. in 1946. She practised with the Malayan Medical Service until 1950. Following a brief period as a private specialist, she joined the Western Australian Schools Medical Services in 1951. She retired in 1970. Lyon was a reserved and selfless woman who helped her relations, friends and acquaintances; she lived quietly at her Nedlands home and was devoted to her dog and garden. Suffering from cancer, she died of coronary vascular disease on 27 March 1975 at Nedlands and was cremated with Presbyterian forms.

G. M. Walton, *The Building of a Tradition* (Perth, 1949); A. Coates and N. Rosenthal, *The Albert Coates Story* (Melb, 1977); S. Baldwin (ed), *Unsung Heroes and Heroines of Australia* (Melb, 1988); L. R. Silver, *Krait* (Syd, 1992); *Aust Women's Digest*, Dec 1945; *Weekend News*, 29 Mar 1975; *West Australian*, 18 Feb 1984; *Bulletin*, 29 Mar 1988; M. J. Lyon diaries (held by author, Mt Claremont, Perth).   JOHN L. LYON

LYONS, PATRICK FRANCIS (1903-1967), Catholic bishop, was born on 6 January 1903 in North Melbourne, second child of Patrick Joseph Lyons, a Victorian-born labourer, and his wife Catherine Cecilia, née McMahon, who came from Ireland. Young Patrick was educated at St Mary's School, West Melbourne, and St Joseph's Christian Brothers' College, North Melbourne. After matriculating, he joined the Department of the Navy as a clerk. Four years later he resigned and undertook ecclesiastical training at St Columba's College, Springwood, New South Wales, St Patrick's College, Manly, Sydney, and (from 1923) the Pontifical Urban College of Propaganda Fide, Rome. Ordained in Rome on 6 January 1927, he was awarded a doctorate of divinity in June that year. He returned to Victoria where he served successively as assistant-priest at Collingwood, Geelong and Brunswick before being appointed in 1935 to the staff of St Patrick's Cathedral, Melbourne. In 1938 he was promoted administrator of the cathedral, chancellor of the archdiocese and secretary to Archbishop Daniel Mannix [q.v.10]; in 1939 he was made vicar-general.

While at St Patrick's, Lyons organized celebrations in 1939 to mark the centenary of the Catholic Church in Melbourne, the principal event being the completion of the cathedral's spires. In the same year he helped to establish St Patrick's Cathedral Boys' Choir and choir school, using as a nucleus members of the Vienna Mozart Boys' Choir who had been stranded by the outbreak of World War II. In 1940 he was appointed cavaliere della Corona d'Italia in recognition of his services to the Italian community in Victoria.

On 2 July 1944 at St Patrick's Cathedral Lyons was consecrated bishop of Christchurch, New Zealand. He was transferred to the titular see of Cabasa, becoming auxiliary bishop to Cardinal (Sir) Norman Gilroy [q.v.14] in Sydney on 5 April 1950. A passionate admirer of Mannix, Lyons acted as the episcopal leader (1950-54) of the Catholic Social Studies Movement in Sydney. There, his authoritarian style and testy personality occasioned resentment, especially when he dismissed Fr P. J. Ryan [q.v.] from the C.S.S.M. chaplaincy. In 1954 Gilroy removed Lyons from his position with 'the Movement' and replaced him with James Carroll, the newly consecrated auxiliary archbishop. While in Sydney, Lyons made submissions on behalf of the Catholic Church to the Royal Commission on Television (1953-54).

Appointed coadjutor bishop of Sale on 11 October 1956, Lyons was elevated to bishop in the following year. In 1959 he negotiated an extension of the diocese of Sale to the west: eight parishes were detached from the Melbourne archdiocese, thus concluding a campaign begun by Bishop Patrick Phelan [q.v.11] to make the thinly populated diocese more viable. During Lyons's episcopacy the Catholic population of Sale grew rapidly through immigration, refugee settlement and industrial development. He attended sessions of Vatican Council II in 1962-65.

Intelligent, conservative, meticulous and forthright, Bishop Lyons seemed aloof to many of his parishioners, though his close friends found him engaging. At Sale he presided cautiously over a Church in transition. He died of cancer on 13 August 1967 in East Melbourne and was buried in St Mary's Cathedral, Sale.

P. Ormonde, *The Movement* (Melb, 1972); G. Henderson, *Mr Santamaria and the Bishops* (Syd, 1983); *Gippsland Heritage*, 1, June 1983; *Catholic Life*, Dec 1993, special supp; *Advocate* (Melb), 9 May 1940, 5 July 1944, 11 Oct 1956, 17 Aug 1967; *Gippsland Times*, 29 Oct 1959, 22 July 1965, 14, 21 Aug 1967; *Age* (Melb), 1 Apr 1944, 11, 14 Aug 1967; Bishop Patrick Lyons—chronology of his career (Bishop's Office, Diocese of Sale, Sale, Vic).
                                                      PETER SYNAN

LYONS, WALTER JOSEPH; *see* ATHALDO, DON

LYSTER, FLEURY JAMES (1872-1948), metallurgist, was born on 24 February 1872 at Kilmore, Victoria, sixth child of Irish-born parents John Lyster, carpenter, and his wife Mary Ann, née Fleury. Orphaned when he was about 11 years old, Jim finished his schooling and learned the trade of carpenter with his uncle, a builder and undertaker at Seymour. During the depressed 1890s Lyster travelled to Denmark, Western Australia. He married his childhood sweetheart Mary Hannah Byrne on 13 July 1897 at St Joseph's Catholic Church, Albany; she had arrived by ship, chaperoned by her brother. The young couple went to the Coolgardie and Kalgoorlie goldfields, and then to Leonora where Lyster worked in the Sons of Gwalia Ltd's mine which was managed by Herbert Hoover [q.v.9], a young engineer who later became president of the United States of America. Moving to New South Wales, in May 1907 Lyster began work at the Broken Hill South Blocks mine, constructing a new mineral processing mill of which he was appointed foreman. He worked directly for the Zinc Corporation Ltd (founded by Hoover in 1905 to buy and treat zinc-rich tailings at Broken Hill) which had absorbed the South Blocks company in 1911.

Flotation, an important mineral separation process, was pioneered at Broken Hill. By 1912 the Delprat-Potter [qq.v.8,11] method was in use at several of the mines, but the problem remained of floating the lead or the zinc mineral independently from the ore mixture. Lyster was again associated with Hoover who was a director and responsible for the elusive metallurgical success critical to the survival of the company. Noting that particles of the lead mineral floated naturally in froth in his gravity ore-treatment plant, Lyster began experiments which culminated in his application for patent no.5040 on 21 May 1912. By September that year the Zinc Corporation was operating the first commercial selective flotation plant in the world, using Lyster's process.

In August 1913 Minerals Separation Ltd negotiated an agreement with the Zinc Corporation and Lyster for the rights to the process: Lyster received £2375, at a time when unskilled labourers in the mines earned about nine shillings a day. Luck, as well as keen observation and intelligent experimenting, had contributed to his success. The ore he used was fresh and finely ground, and the mine water was alkaline which prevented the naturally contained copper sulphate from activating the zinc.

Tall and of medium build, Lyster had blue eyes, dark hair and a generous moustache. He read widely and was interested in sport. In all he did his aim was perfection. After serving many years as mill superintendent, he retired to Vaucluse, Sydney, in 1935. He received from the Zinc Corporation's directors a letter of gratitude, four months paid leave and a cheque for £1000. At Broken Hill the corporation established the annual James Lyster scholarship. Survived by his daughter and three of his four sons, he died on 14 October 1948 at Lewisham Hospital and was buried in South Head cemetery.

O. H. Woodward, *A Review of the Broken Hill Lead-Silver-Zinc Industry* (Melb, 1952, Syd, 1965); G. Blainey, *The Rush that Never Ended* (Melb, 1963) and *The Rise of Broken Hill* (Melb, 1968); W. S. Robinson, *If I Remember Rightly*, G. Blainey ed (Melb, 1967); A. Lynch, *Leslie Bradford Golden Jubilee Oration*, J. Burns ed (Melb, 1987); R. J. Solomon, *The Richest Lode* (Syd, 1988); *Barrier Daily Truth*, 15 Oct 1948; *Barrier Miner* and *Sun* (Syd), 16 Oct 1948; Univ Melb Archives; Lyster family records (held by Mr B. J. Lyster, Silverwater, Syd); information from Mrs D. Lyster, Myrtle Bank, and Mr J. F. Lyster, Grange, Adel.

D. F. FAIRWEATHER

LYTTLE, MARGARET (GRETA) JANE RUTH (1875-1944), educationist, was born on 1 July 1875 at Hinton, New South Wales, sixth of nine children of Sydney-born parents John Thomas Lyttle, a Baptist minister of Northern Irish descent, and his wife Margaret Purves, née McNeilly. Greta was educated in state schools. Commencing her career in 1891 as a pupil-teacher at Prahran, Melbourne, she worked in various government primary

schools, mostly as infant mistress, and used 'modern methods'. She was praised by school inspectors and by Emmeline Pye [q.v.11] of the Melbourne Training College. Miss Lyttle supported Mary Lush [q.v.] in her work at Melbourne's first free kindergarten, at Carlton.

In 1914 Lyttle moved to nearby Queensberry Street State School, where she managed the Montessori room. She resigned in 1917 to set up a Montessorian school, the School of the Pathfinder, at South Yarra, with the help of the progressive educationist and social reformer Rev. John Thomas Lawton [q.v.10]. She continued to collaborate with Lawton as directress of the junior school of St Andrew's College, Kew, which he founded in 1921. Following several years of financial insecurity and excessive hard work—which included bringing up her three nieces and a nephew—her health declined and she left in 1929, somewhat disillusioned with the way the school was run. For extra income she took in student boarders. Preshil began when several St Andrew's parents persuaded her to teach their children in her own home at Kew.

Named after Priesthill farm on the Scottish moors where a family ancestor, John Brown the Covenanter, was executed for his religious beliefs in the reign of Charles I, Preshil adopted a golden eagle as its symbol and 'courage' as its motto. Lyttle was strongly influenced by the writings of Friedrich Froebel and Maria Montessori, and by the work of the New Education Fellowship in Australia. She was a brilliant teacher of 'instinctive genius' who went back to first principles: her aim was to develop the child's feelings, sense of independence, security and self-confidence. Believing that the best learning took place through self-directed activity, she produced a prospectus which stated: 'Preshil aims at being a school which fits itself to the needs of the child'. Like Constance Tisdall [q.v.12] and Dorothy Ross, she was a pioneer of the 'progressive movement'.

With little financial backing and approaching the age of 58, Lyttle pushed ahead with her new venture. Preshil Preparatory School was registered in 1933, with twenty students between 6 and 10 years old. The fees covered only the basic running expenses, and there were constant money worries and personal sacrifice. By 1937, however, Preshil had outgrown its premises and Lyttle secured a loan to move to Arlington, Kew, one of the school's four present campuses.

To some, Miss Lyttle was formidable and outspoken; to others, she was kind and reassuring. She was decidedly eccentric in manner and in dress. Unmarried by choice, she was, according to one relation, attractive and feminine with 'a soft warm face' and dimples. In her last years she suffered poor health and did little teaching. She died of chronic nephritis on 2 August 1944 at Kew and was cremated. From 1946 to 1994 her niece Margaret Lyttle was headmistress of Preshil, which added to its title 'the Margaret Lyttle Memorial School'.

N. R. White, *School Matters* (Melb, 1995); *Aust J of Education*, 14, no 1, Mar 1970; R. C. Petersen, Experimental Schools and Educational Experiments in Australia, 1906-1948 (Ph.D. thesis, Univ Syd, 1968); D. R. Gibbs, John Thomas Lawton (1878-1944); biography of an educational and social reformer (M.Ed. thesis, Univ Melb, 1978); taped interviews with Miss M. Lyttle and others, May 1976 (held by author, Camberwell, Melb); family and school papers (held by Mr D. Lyttle, Kew, Melb).

DESMOND GIBBS

M

MAAS, CHRISTIANUS LEONARDUS MARIA (1911-1973), Catholic priest, was born on 24 December 1911 at Helmond, the Netherlands, fourth of seven children of Petrus Hubertus Maas, textile worker, and his wife Petronella Maria, née Bombay, both devout Catholics. Leo was educated at the Canisius and Hogere Burger schools, and the seminary of St Willibrord, Uden. In 1931 he began his novitiate at St Franciscus Seminary of the Society of the Divine Word, Teteringen. He was ordained priest on 22 August 1937. Commissioned as a missionary priest on 31 July 1938, he reached the island of Flores, Netherlands East Indies (Indonesia), in December. On 15 July 1942 he was captured by the Japanese and later interned as a prisoner of war at Pare, Celebes (Sulawesi).

Following his release in November 1945, Maas spent seven months recuperating in Melbourne before returning to the Netherlands. On 11 December 1948 he was again posted to Flores. While in transit in Melbourne, he was persuaded by Archbishop Mannix and Arthur Calwell [qq.v.10,13] to remain as migrant chaplain to the growing Dutch Catholic community in Victoria.

Despite his frail health, Maas unleashed astonishing energy and activity in Melbourne, although he retained his longing for Indonesia, which he never saw again. He encouraged Dutch immigrants to come to Australia, providing them with initial accommodation. In 1950 he bought a large house at Kew which he converted into a reception hostel for young, single male immigrants (about 3000 men passed through the hostel before it closed in 1973). In 1951 he devised a scheme to bring out some 300 migrant farmers and their families, and place them as sharefarmers throughout Victoria. Next year he converted an old boarding-house, The Gables, at Daylesford into a reception centre and proceeded to sponsor the emigration of a further 278 Dutch families between 1952 and 1958.

Pastoral care of Dutch settlers constituted a further aspect of Maas's activities. He clearly understood that successful settlement was best based on continuing the old patterns of life. To be able to celebrate Christmas in the accustomed Dutch manner, he formed a church-choir which became the St Gregorius Dutch Male Choir in November 1952. Maas founded (1949) a monthly newsletter, *Onze Gids*, and established (1952) the Catholic Dutch Migrant Association. He encouraged it to set up Providence Hostel, a home for abandoned children, at Bacchus Marsh in 1957. In the late 1960s Maas raised the issue of an ageing community; by the time of his death Providence Hostel was changing from a child-care to an elderly-care complex.

Known as an expert on settlement, both within Australia and abroad, Maas was appointed to the Order of Oranje-Nassau on 30 April 1955. Among his fellow countrymen in Australia he became a folk-hero. No theologian, but a practical man, he was more at home begging for money than with the niceties of theological debate. Nevertheless, the Catholic *aggiornamento* of the 1960s, in which his Dutch colleagues took such a leading part, affected him deeply, and he repeatedly expressed dissatisfaction with the conservatism of the Australian Catholic Church in his annual reports to his order.

Taciturn and persistent, Maas was inclined to keep his own counsel and only lowered his guard with his confrères in the Netherlands. He died of cerebrovascular disease on 8 July 1973 in St Vincent's Hospital, Fitzroy, and was buried in Melbourne general cemetery. The Dutch national anthem was sung at his requiem Mass celebrated at St Patrick's Cathedral.

T. van der Meel, *Geschreven portretten van Nederlandse Emigrantenpriesters in Australië* (The Hague, 1994); *Onze Gids*, 1950; Soc of the Divine Word, *Annual Report*, 1961, 1963, 1968; *Dutch Societies Courier*, Aug 1973; correspondence between C. L. M. Maas and his sister, 1935-73 (held by Sister Christiana Maas, Baexem, The Netherlands).   HENK OVERBERG

McADAM, JAMES BANNISTER (1910-1959), forester and soldier, was born on 6 February 1910 at Preesall with Hackinsall, Lancashire, England, son of John George McAdam, railway cashier, and his wife Elizabeth Ann, née Bannister. The family emigrated to Queensland. James was sent to state schools and to Toowoomba Grammar School. In 1929 he joined the Queensland Forest Service as a cadet. He proceeded to the University of Queensland, Brisbane, and the Australian Forestry School, Canberra (Dip.For., 1934), where he was awarded the Schlich medal as the outstanding student in his final year. Athletic and of robust build, he excelled at sport, particularly Rugby Union football. From 1934 he undertook field-work in Queensland. At St Paul's Anglican Church, Maryborough, on 19 January 1938 he married Eileen Alexandra Ewing, a schoolteacher. That month he was appointed a forest officer in the public service of the Mandated Territory of New Guinea.

With the threat of war in the Pacific, McAdam enlisted in the Australian Military Forces on 19 September 1940 at Wau. He began full-time duty with the New Guinea Volunteer Rifles on 22 January 1942 and was promoted sergeant within a fortnight. After the Japanese invaded Salamaua in March, he led a party of scouts which established an observation post within a mile (1.6 km) of enemy positions. The intelligence which the team gathered was crucial to the success of the Australian raid on the town in June. McAdam acted as a guide in the foray. Transferred to the Australian New Guinea Administrative Unit in September, he was awarded the Military Medal for his outstanding service at Salamaua. In April 1943 he was commissioned lieutenant.

Promoted temporary major, McAdam was appointed commander, Royal Australian Engineers (New Guinea Forests), in February 1944. His unit's task was to assess and map the forest resources of Papua, New Guinea, Bougainville and Manus Island for war needs and for future management in peacetime. He relinquished the appointment in September 1945. Following a brief attachment to Army Headquarters, Melbourne, he transferred to the Reserve of Officers on 8 February 1946 and settled in Port Moresby as acting-secretary (later director) of the Department of Forests, Territory of Papua-New Guinea. Keen and industrious, he had a 'passion for protecting the trees'. In 1949 he visited Australia to give evidence to the royal commission into timber rights. He was a member (1949-59) of the Territory's Executive Council and an official member (1951-59) of its Legislative Council.

McAdam was active in the affairs of the Papua and New Guinea Scientific Society (president 1951). His main hobby was woodcraft. While on leave, he died of hypertensive coronary vascular disease on 27 February 1959 at Margate, Queensland, and was cremated. His wife, son and two daughters survived him. In 1963 a magnificent park of some 5000 acres (2000 ha) near Wau in the Bulolo Gorge was named after him; it includes outstanding forests of hoop and klinkii pines in which he had shown particular interest.

D. McCarthy, *South-West Pacific Area—First Year* (Canb, 1959); R. McNicoll, *The Royal Australian Engineers, 1919 to 1945* (Canb, 1982); *PIM*, Mar 1959; *Age* (Melb), 27 May 1963; Inst of Foresters of Aust records (Yarralumla, Canb); information from PNG National Parks Bd; personal knowledge.

L. T. CARRON

MACADIE, THOMAS FERGUS BUCHANAN (1919-1973), soldier and atomic-energy administrator, was born on 22 Sep-

tember 1919 at Williamstown, Melbourne, third child of Thomas Fergus MacAdie, a superintendent stevedore from Scotland, and his Queensland-born wife Amelia Mary, née Buchanan. Educated at Williamstown High School, young Fergus entered the Royal Military College, Duntroon, Federal (Australian) Capital Territory, in February 1938. He graduated as lieutenant, Australian Staff Corps, in August 1940. Although he hoped for an early transfer to the Australian Imperial Force, he was posted to a succession of training establishments.

In February 1942 MacAdie joined the Guerrilla Warfare School, Wilsons Promontory, Victoria, as an instructor. By July he was a temporary major, commanding the 2nd/7th Independent Company, A.I.F. It had been a dramatic change of fortune. With his unit, he reached Wau, New Guinea, in October. MacAdie was then 6 ft 2½ ins (189 cm) tall, 'thin and strangely hawk-like, with curiously flecked eyes set deep above a high-bridged nose'. Behind those features were characteristics which had been apparent at Duntroon and would continue to develop: an unruffled self-assurance, the ability to work with and to influence others, an engaging sophistication, a ready wit, a sense of occasion and a will to win.

The 2nd/7th was attached to Kanga Force and operated with conspicuous success around Mubo in January-March 1943. MacAdie led a daring raid on the main Japanese defences at Garrison Hill and Mat Mat in January. His men drove off a strong enemy attack in February, inflicting heavy casualties. He was awarded the Distinguished Service Order for his leadership and skill in handling the unit. The company flew to Bena Bena in May to augment Bena Force. Under MacAdie's command (as temporary lieutenant colonel from June), this formation eventually numbered more than 1100 men. They garrisoned the surrounding region, produced maps, built roads and an airfield, and engaged in skirmishes against the enemy. MacAdie was mentioned in dispatches.

Returning to Australia in November, he performed staff duties as a major. In 1945-46 he was back in the Territory as a substantive lieutenant colonel, commanding the 3rd New Guinea Infantry Battalion. Following a short posting to Army Headquarters, Melbourne, he flew to Japan in March 1947 to command the 67th Battalion. On 12 June 1948 in Tokyo he married Colleen May, daughter of Colonel Jeff Clay, United States Army; the bride and groom were driven from the ceremony in the Imperial coach. In Melbourne again, he was at the 3rd Division's headquarters from December. A review of the Staff Corps list in 1949 revised his seniority and enhanced his prospects.

MacAdie served on the Australian Joint Services Staff, Washington, in 1950-53. An appointment in the directorate of personnel administration, Army Headquarters, followed his return to Australia. In 1954 he was once more posted abroad, as services attaché, Saigon. Promoted colonel, he was appointed director of military intelligence at Army Headquarters in April 1957. Three years later he was promoted temporary brigadier (substantive in April 1963), and made director of military operations and plans. He spent 1963 as a student at the Imperial Defence College, London, and was appointed chief of staff at headquarters, Eastern Command, Sydney, in 1964. MacAdie seemed destined for higher positions in the army, but ill health forced him to retire on 11 October 1967. He was appointed C.B.E. in 1968.

On 7 November 1967 MacAdie had joined the Australian Atomic Energy Commission. He worked as a clerk in the technical policy section until 1970 when he was promoted head of international relations. In April 1972 he became counsellor (atomic energy) at the Australian Embassy in Paris, responsible for liaising with French and international nuclear organizations. Survived by his wife and daughter, he died suddenly on 21 January 1973 in Paris.

D. McCarthy, *South-West Pacific Area—First Year* (Canb, 1959); D. Dexter, *The New Guinea Offensives* (Canb, 1961); G. D. Solomon, *A Poor Sort of Memory* (Canb, 1978); *SMH*, 23 Jan 1973.

G. D. SOLOMON

McALPINE, ABNER STREPHON (1891-1958), industrial and political organizer, was born on 26 February 1891 in Sydney, second surviving child of McIntosh McAlpine, a native-born clerk, and his wife Rosa Maria, née Bannister, who came from England. Leaving Parramatta Public School at the age of 15, Abe was apprenticed as a fitter and turner with the New South Wales Government Railways and Tramways. He joined the Amalgamated Engineering Union and later became a delegate to the Labor Council of New South Wales and a member of the Australian Labor Party. On 13 June 1914 he married Eileen Barber at St Columbus's Anglican Church, Flemington. He divorced her in 1924 and on 4 April 1925 married with Presbyterian forms Zellmira Veronica Foldi at her Drummoyne home.

Drawing together right- and left-wing unions opposed to the Communist Party of Australia, McAlpine was vice-president (1931) and president (1932-35) of the Labor Council. From 1936 to 1941 he was the salaried assistant-secretary to the council and an executive-member of Radio 2KY's broadcast-

ing committee. He worked closely with R. A. King [q.v.] and other trade union leaders in the battles against J. T. Lang [q.v.9] for control of 2KY and for Lang's replacement as leader of the State Labor party. Following the success of the left wing in carrying the 'Hands Off Russia' declaration at the 1940 State Labor party conference, McAlpine was closely involved with federal intervention and was president (1940-43) of the restructured State branch.

McAlpine sought to unite the labour movement behind the wartime policies of the Federal and State parliamentary leaders, John Curtin [q.v.13] and (Sir) William McKell. In November 1942 he chaired the stormy meeting of the executive of the State A.L.P., when Curtin persuaded the delegates to accept conscription for service in the South-West Pacific. A member (1940-50) of both the Federal and New South Wales A.L.P. executives, McAlpine was junior vice-president (1941-45) and president (1946-50) of the Federal A.L.P. William Holman, the father of W. A. Holman [q.v.9], had taught McAlpine elocution: while his speeches were forceful, they lacked inspiration, partly due to his dour and humourless nature.

In 1941 McAlpine had resigned as assistant-secretary of the Labor Council to join the Australian Shipbuilding Board (chairman 1947-52). He was also a member (1943-51) of the New South Wales Broadcasting Advisory Committee. McAlpine became involved in postwar planning as a member of the Commonwealth Immigration Advisory Council (1949-58) and the Factory Welfare Board (New South Wales) (1954-58). Although he was more an administrator and bureaucrat than an activist or innovator, he constantly supported trade-union campaigns to promote daytime technical training for apprentices. In his spare time he enjoyed family life, gardening, fishing and swimming. Survived by his wife and two sons, he died of a coronary occlusion on 22 January 1958 at his Concord home and was cremated with Presbyterian forms.

L. F. Crisp, *The Australian Federal Labour Party 1901-1951* (Syd, 1978); P. Weller and B. Lloyd (eds), *Federal Executive Minutes, 1915-1955* (Melb, 1978); *SMH*, 31 July 1931, 21 Aug, 7, 24 Oct 1940, 9 May, 16 June 1941, 2 Dec 1942, 2 Dec 1946, 2 May 1947, 15 Oct 1949, 11 May 1950, 24 Jan 1958; *Smith's Weekly*, 27 June 1942; family information.

FRANK FARRELL

McARTHUR, ALAN GRANT (1923-1978), forester, was born on 21 July 1923 at Manly, Sydney, son of Cuthbert Grant McArthur, a Scottish-born storeman, and his native-born wife Vera Kathleen, née Gordon. His father had come to Australia at the age of 14 and served in the Australian Imperial Force. Growing up on a wheat-farm at Merriwagga, Alan completed his primary schooling by correspondence, then attended Yanco Agricultural High School where he established an enduring interest in Australian exploration. In 1941 he joined the Forestry Commission of New South Wales. After studying at the University of Sydney (B.Sc.For., 1945) and the Australian Forestry School, Canberra (Dip.For., 1945), he worked on plantation management in the Tumut and Orange districts.

On 18 February 1947 at St Jude's Anglican Church, Tumbarumba, McArthur married Gladys Charlotte Gardner, a 19-year-old dental nurse. Having been promoted senior forester, he was appointed the first full-time fire control officer of the Snowy Mountains area in 1951 and began his passionate, lifelong inquiry into the behaviour and control of forest and grassland fires. He devised a regional fire prevention plan which provided a model for similar operations elsewhere. In 1953 he transferred to the Commonwealth Forestry and Timber Bureau, Canberra, as fire researcher. He was promoted director of the bureau's forest research institute in 1970. Five years later he was appointed principal research officer in the Commonwealth Scientific and Industrial Research Organization's new division of forest research.

For more than twenty-five years McArthur studied the behaviour of fires in a wide range of fuel types, devising systems for rating the danger of fires under different meteorological conditions. These systems became an essential tool for rural bushfire brigades; they were adopted by the Bureau of Meteorology in forecasting fire-hazard conditions; and they were recommended by the United Nations Food and Agriculture Organization for use in developing countries. McArthur also prepared guidelines for controlled burning, a practice he regarded as essential in containing the disastrous fires to which Australian native forests are prone. Much of his data was derived from field exercises with forestry students to whom he lectured in 1954-70, first at the A.F.S. and later at the Australian National University.

The Western Australian royal commission into bushfires (1961) was one of several official inquiries to benefit from McArthur's advice. He participated in a number of international conferences, and wrote or co-authored some sixty papers on the behaviour and effects of fire and on watershed management. With R. H. Luke, he published *Bushfires in Australia* (Canberra, 1978) which remains an authoritative text.

An athlete in his youth, McArthur took up golf and enjoyed a game of bridge. He suffered from diabetes mellitus, retired in July 1978 and died of pneumonia on 9 November that year in Canberra Hospital. Survived by his wife, son and daughter, he was cremated with Presbyterian forms. He had been elected a fellow (1978) of the Institute of Foresters of Australia and was posthumously awarded the N. W. Jolly [q.v.9] medal for that year.

Aust Forestry, 41, no 4, 1978, p 189, 42, no 2, 1979, p 57; personal information.   L. T. CARRON

MacARTHUR, DOUGLAS (1880-1964), army officer, was born on 26 January 1880 at Little Rock, Arkansas, United States of America, third son of Captain Arthur MacArthur, an army officer who rose to lieutenant general, and his wife Mary Pinkney, née Hardy. Douglas entered the United States Military Academy, West Point, New York, in 1899 and graduated first in his class in 1903. As a junior engineer officer, he served in the Philippines, accompanied his father on a tour of Asia and commanded a company of engineers in Kansas. In 1913 he joined the General Staff of the War Department, Washington, and in 1914 took a prominent part in the Veracruz expedition in Mexico. He was a major at the War Department in 1917 when America entered World War I.

In August that year MacArthur was promoted colonel of infantry and made chief of staff of the 42nd ('Rainbow') Division, with which he served on operations in France from February 1918. As a brigadier-general (August 1918), he led the 84th Brigade in several offensives, then assumed command of the 42nd Division shortly before the Armistice was declared. Twice wounded, he had been conspicuous in the front line, and had won the Distinguished Service Cross (twice), the Distinguished Service Medal, the Silver Star (seven times) and various foreign decorations.

Unlike many others, MacArthur retained his wartime rank and in mid-1919 became superintendent of the military academy. He completely overhauled its structure and curriculum. In 1922-30 he held senior commands in the Philippines and the U.S.A., and was president of the American Olympic Committee for the 1928 Amsterdam games. Promoted general, he was appointed chief of staff, U.S. Army, in November 1930. He served presidents Herbert Hoover [q.v.9] and Franklin D. Roosevelt, and argued strenuously for funds during the Depression.

In 1935 MacArthur became military adviser to the new Commonwealth of the Philippines. On his retirement from the U.S. Army in 1937, he continued as field marshal in the Philippine Army. Aged 61, in July 1941 he was recalled to the U.S. Army and appointed major general (general from December), commanding all American and local forces in the Philippines. The Japanese attacked in December. MacArthur has been criticized for his conduct of the Philippines campaign, especially for allowing his air forces to be caught on the ground by Japanese bombers and for overestimating the capabilities of his Filipino troops. His men were still holding out on the Bataan Peninsula and Corregidor Island when, in March 1942, Roosevelt ordered MacArthur to go to Australia. He was awarded the Congressional Medal of Honour.

On 21 March MacArthur arrived in Melbourne. Next month he was formally appointed supreme commander of the South-West Pacific Area, with authority over all allied naval, land and air forces in the theatre. In placing the Australian forces under MacArthur, the Federal government surrendered a large measure of sovereignty, but, considering Australia's limited strength and the magnitude of the Japanese threat, there was no real alternative. MacArthur established a close relationship with Prime Minister John Curtin [q.v.13], promising him that 'we two, you and I, will see this thing through together . . . You take care of the rear and I will handle the front'. Initially, the strategic ideas and ambitions of this foreign general were almost the same as those of the Labor government.

General Sir Thomas Blamey [q.v.13] was the sole Australian to be appointed as one of MacArthur's three immediate subordinates —he was given command of the Allied Land Forces. Curtin established the Prime Minister's War Conference as the senior decision-making body, but it met rarely after July 1942. The conference consisted of Curtin, MacArthur and the secretary of the Department of Defence, (Sir) Frederick Shedden [q.v.]. Aloof, highly intelligent, variously hated and loved throughout the U.S. Army, MacArthur believed that it was his destiny to lead the Allies to victory in the Pacific, having vowed to the people of the Philippines, 'I shall return'. His air commander in 1942, Lieutenant General George H. Brett, thought that he was 'a brilliant, temperamental egoist; a handsome man, who can be as charming as anyone who ever lived, or harshly indifferent to the needs and desires of those around' him. Everything about MacArthur was on a 'grand scale'—his 'virtues and triumphs and shortcomings'.

MacArthur was also a man of personal contradictions. His first marriage, on 14 February 1922 at Palm Beach, Florida, to a divorcee Henriette Louise Cromwell Brooks, had ended in divorce in 1929. Conservative, moralistic and apparently religious, when he

was chief of staff he had kept a young Eurasian mistress Isabel Rosario Cooper in a Washington hotel while his mother lived at his official residence. On 30 April 1937 in a civil ceremony in New York he married Jean Marie Faircloth, some twenty years his junior, to whom he was devoted; their only child Arthur was born in the following year. In January 1942 MacArthur had secretly accepted $US500 000 from Manuel Quezon, the Philippines' president, as a 'recompense and reward' from the Filipino people.

While living in Australia, MacArthur became the focus of public attention. His demands were fulfilled; his press communiqués provided the main source of military information; and Australian and American forces responded to his directions. MacArthur's prestige and influence in the U.S.A. meant that large numbers of troops were dispatched to Australia where they had a considerable and long-lasting impact on its society. In July 1942 he moved his headquarters from Melbourne to Brisbane in preparation for an offensive to regain Rabaul, but the Japanese pre-empted him. Landing in the Buna-Gona region of Papua in July, they struck inland, heading for Port Moresby. MacArthur and Blamey hurried to reinforce the Territory's defences. The Australians repelled a Japanese landing at Milne Bay in August.

The Papuan campaign did not show MacArthur at his best. After the defeat in the Philippines, he feared that another failure would result in his being superseded. Questioning the fighting qualities of the poorly supplied Australian troops, who were being driven back over the Owen Stanley Range, he asked Curtin to send Blamey to Port Moresby to take personal command. The Australians had in fact fought well, but Blamey relieved Lieutenant General (Sir) Sydney Rowell [q.v.] of his command. MacArthur then directed additional forces to New Guinea, including an American division. Faced with MacArthur's demands for more speed, Blamey relieved two other senior officers. For the final stages of the campaign, MacArthur moved to Port Moresby, and in dramatic fashion told his American corps commander Lieutenant General Robert L. Eichelberger: 'If you don't take Buna, I want to hear that you are buried there!'

By contrast with the Papuan campaign, the New Guinea offensives of 1943 were a brilliant orchestration of Australian and American sea, land and air forces. Australia provided the bulk of the ground forces until April 1944, after which the Americans bore the brunt of the fighting. Taking advantage of excellent signals intelligence and of MacArthur's hunches, his troops landed in areas where the Japanese were weakest. As the Americans approached the Philippines,

MacArthur promised Curtin that Australians would take part in the islands' recapture, but that never came to pass. MacArthur was unwilling to allow the Australians to play a major role in the recovery of American territory. In September he met with Curtin in Canberra for the last time. On 20 October MacArthur went ashore on the first day of the U.S. landing at Leyte Gulf in the Philippines.

Promoted general of the army in December 1944, MacArthur directed Blamey to use more forces to garrison the Japanese-held areas of New Britain, Bougainville and New Guinea than the Australian commander thought necessary. He also ordered Australian troops to land at Tarakan and at Brunei Bay, Borneo, in May and June. Blamey opposed plans for a final landing at Balik-papan in July, but MacArthur advised the Australian government that cancelling the operation would 'disorganize completely' the strategic plan of the joint chiefs of staff. The Australian government approved the proposed landing, unaware that MacArthur had previously told the joint chiefs that, if they disallowed the operation, it would 'produce grave repercussions with the Australian government and people'.

On 2 September 1945 MacArthur accepted Japan's surrender aboard the battleship, *Missouri*, in Tokyo Bay. Blamey, and senior naval and air force officers, represented Australia. MacArthur became supreme commander for the Allied Powers, responsible for the occupation of Japan and the creation of a democracy there. An Australian, Lieutenant General (Sir) John Northcott [q.v.], commanded the British Commonwealth Occupation Force.

When the Korean War began in June 1950, MacArthur was given the United Nations Command, consisting mainly of U.S. forces. At first Australia provided two warships, an infantry battalion and—at MacArthur's express request—a fighter squadron. In an effort to break the North Korean offensive, and against all advice, he planned a daring amphibious landing at Inchon, near Seoul, far behind the North Korean front line. Conducted in September, it was an outstanding success: the North Koreans were driven back, almost to the Chinese border, with the Australian battalion playing a prominent role. MacArthur had been lucky.

Then the Chinese crossed their border in October 1950 and threw the United Nations forces back in disarray. In the New Year the U.N. line was stabilized south of Seoul. MacArthur called for bombing-raids on China. While the U.S. government was talking of a political settlement, he announced that there was 'no substitute for victory'. On 11 April 1951 President Harry S. Truman relieved him of his command.

MacArthur returned to the United States to a hero's welcome. He was 71 and his military career was over. In an address to Congress he promised to 'fade away—an old soldier who tried to do his duty as God gave him the light to see that duty'. Survived by his wife and son, he died on 5 April 1964 in Washington; his tomb is in the old court-house at Norfolk, Virginia. One of the most enigmatic military leaders of the twentieth century, MacArthur has been the subject of over fifty biographies. His *Reminiscences* were published in New York in 1964. Between 1942 and 1945 he had been the dominant figure in Australia's conduct of World War II. Few figures who have spent less than three years in this country have had such an impact on Australian life.

G. Long, *MacArthur as Military Commander* (Syd, 1969); D. C. James, *The Years of MacArthur* (Boston, 1970, 1975, 1985); W. Manchester, *American Caesar* (Boston, 1978); C. M. Petillo, *Douglas MacArthur* (Bloomington, Indiana, 1981); D. M. Horner, *High Command* (Canb, 1982); E. Rasor, *General Douglas MacArthur, 1880-1964* (Westport, Connecticut, 1994) for bib; G. Perrett, *Old Soldiers Never Die* (NY, 1996); MacArthur papers (MacArthur Memorial, Norfolk, Virginia); Blamey papers (AWM); Shedden papers (AA, Canb); Sutherland papers (US National Archives).

D. M. HORNER

McARTHUR, SIR GORDON STEWART (1896-1965), politician, grazier and barrister, was born on 7 April 1896 at South Yarra, Melbourne, third child of (Sir) William Gilbert Stewart McArthur [q.v.10], barrister, and his wife Margaret Rutherford, née Macpherson, both Victorian born. Peter McArthur, a pioneer Western District pastoralist, was his grandfather. Educated (from 1909) at Geelong College, Gordon left in 1915 to join the British Army. He was commissioned in the Royal Field Artillery on 27 August 1916. In the following year he lost his right leg in action on the Western Front. Following recuperation and demobilization in 1918, he attended Jesus College, Cambridge (B.A., 1921; M.A., 1941), from which he graduated in the mechanical science tripos.

In 1921 McArthur was recruited to Broken Hill Proprietary Co. Ltd by Essington Lewis [q.v.10]. He worked as an engineer at Newcastle, New South Wales, and at Whyalla, South Australia, until in 1926 a growing interest in the law persuaded him to resign and travel to England for further study. He was called to the Bar at the Inner Temple in 1929 and, following his return to Melbourne, admitted to the Victorian Bar on 14 February 1930. Four years later McArthur left the law to manage Meningoort, his father's 5743-acre (2324 ha) property near Camperdown, which he inherited in 1935. He built a reputation for livestock and pasture improvement, and for breeding such thoroughbreds as the champion racehorse Chicquita. On 6 August 1936 at the Presbyterian Church, Toorak, he married Theodosia, daughter of Sir George Syme [q.v.12].

Elected to the Legislative Council for South-Western Province in June 1931, he was the third McArthur family member to enter the Victorian parliament: he was preceded by his uncles John Neil McArthur [q.v.10] and Peter Campbell McArthur. Neither politically driven nor personally ambitious, Gordon McArthur found his conservative values comfortably accommodated by—successively—the United Australia Party, the Liberal Party and the Liberal-Country Party, while his affable 'country liberalism' was satisfied by his role as 'local member'. In the council he was dubbed the member who 'never missed a division' and appreciated for his thoughtful explanations of proposed legislation. A warm, easy mixer, fond of a smoke and a yarn, he knew everyone and everyone knew him. McArthur held his seat for thirty-four years.

In June 1955 McArthur's career took an unexpected turn. Premier (Sir) Henry Bolte, convinced that McArthur's abilities had been unrecognized, ignored his objections and named him minister without portfolio. On 10 April 1956 McArthur was appointed minister for forests, and of State development and decentralization. He proved a diligent administrator who refused to allow his disability to interrupt arduous forest inspections. When Bolte failed in his attempt in 1958 to win control of the Upper House by persuading the Country Party to provide the president, he again turned to McArthur. On 8 July he was sworn in as president of the Legislative Council. Tolerant, impartial, at times even mischievous, McArthur was an outstanding chairman who used charm to deflect rancour and experience to ensure procedural integrity. He was knighted in 1959. In 1960 his casting vote and, more unusually, his deliberative vote when the House was in committee, saved the government's controversial licensing (amendment) bill. But commitment to duty was not without cost and his health began to decline.

Tall, distinguished and genial, McArthur enjoyed sport. At Geelong College he had been a member of the football, cricket, athletic and rowing teams, and at Cambridge he had stroked the Jesus College Lent boat, winning fame as the 'rower with one leg'. He was later a good golfer and horseman. A clubbable man, and a witty after-dinner speaker, he was a member of the Melbourne (president 1958), Victoria Racing, Naval and Military, and Royal Melbourne Golf clubs; at Cambridge he belonged to the Leander, Pitt and Hawks clubs. He was also a member of the Geelong College council. Following a long illness and periods in hospital, Sir Gordon McArthur died of chronic pyelonephritis on 10 August 1965 in East Melbourne. He was accorded a state funeral and was buried in Camperdown cemetery; his wife, daughter and three sons survived him. His eldest son Fergus Stewart McArthur entered the House of Representatives in 1984; his nephew Peter Stewart McArthur was a member (1976-82) of the Victorian Legislative Assembly.

K. West, *Power in the Liberal Party* (Melb, 1965); *Pastoral Review*, 17 Sept 1965, p 893; *Aust Bar Gazette*, May 1966, p 18; *Age* (Melb), 9 June 1960; family information.   R. WRIGHT

MACARTNEY, FREDERICK THOMAS BENNETT (1887-1980), poet and critic, was born on 27 September 1887 in Port Melbourne, third child of Thomas Macartney, a bus driver from Northern Ireland, and his Melbourne-born wife Elizabeth Emma, née Jacob. His father died in 1892. Aided by her family and taking occasional sewing commissions, the widow raised her three children at North Fitzroy. Fred attended Alfred Crescent State School until he was 12. He held various jobs, usually as a shop-assistant, before working as a bookkeeper on a Riverina station in 1910-12.

His upbringing had been strictly Methodist; his boyhood recreations were based on the local church. By late youth he no longer wanted to be 'saved', but, 'having the gift of the gab and an orderly mind' (his words), he sharpened his self-education by joining his church's Young Men's Literary and Debating Society. He soon became its president. Reading extensively in the Public (State) Library, he took an elocution course at the Working Men's College, succeeded in impromptu-speech competitions, and learned shorthand. In 1907-10 he won nineteen prizes 'of a guinea or two' for poems, stories and essays in Australia-wide competitions for non-professional writers, and had verse published in the *Australasian*.

Macartney returned to Melbourne in 1912. Encouraged by Bernard O'Dowd [q.v.11], he developed his poetry. By then he was a rationalist, a Fabian member of the Victorian Socialist Party and later an anti-conscriptionist. He formed friendships with Frank Wilmot, Henry Tate, Guido Baracchi, the Palmers [qq.v.12,13,11] and others of the radical intelligentsia, and was a founder (1916) of the Melbourne Literary Club whose journal, *Birth*, he edited in 1919-21. Macartney also helped to reissue Joseph Furphy's [q.v.8] *Such Is Life*. He was a founding member of the

Y Club in 1918 and, from late in World War I, had been secretary of the State Wool Committee.

In 1921 Macartney went to Darwin as an assistant to the administrator of the Northern Territory, F. C. Urquhart [q.v.12], and to the government secretary. Appointed public trustee in 1922, by 1924 he was the 'legal Pooh-Bah' of the Territory: sheriff, clerk of courts and judge's associate, registrar of companies, bankruptcy, and births, deaths and marriages, and returning officer. R. I. D. Mallam, judge from 1928, became a close friend and eventually left him his modest estate. Macartney continued to contribute to the *Bulletin* and refreshed his literary associations on leave in Melbourne, where he settled again when he resigned in 1933.

For more than twenty years Macartney remained a leading literary figure, freelancing as poet, critic, lecturer, editor, biographer and autobiographer. He gave university extension lectures and radio broadcasts in 1933-34. The monthly, *All About Books*, published his cogent reviews of some 270 Australian books between 1935 and 1938; he had few peers as a reviewer, but the journal's circulation was small. In 1940-41 and later he lectured at universities on Australian literature for the Commonwealth Literary Fund, from which he received small grants for his own work. During World War II and its immediate aftermath he was a senior officer (1942-47) of the public trustee. For several years from the late 1940s he laboured on revising and updating E. Morris Miller's [q.v.10] annotated bibliography, *Australian Literature from its beginnings to 1935* (1940); 'Miller and Macartney' was published in 1956. Other important books were *Furnley Maurice (Frank Wilmot)* (1955) and his autobiography, *Proof Against Failure* (Sydney, 1967).

Macartney valued his poetry far above his other literary endeavours. He was a craftsman, ranging diversely from philosophy to light satire, with wit and irony; friendly critics admired his 'vigorous imagery' and 'intellectual subtlety'. *Preferences* (Sydney, 1941) and *Selected Poems* (Sydney, 1961) were largely choices from numerous earlier publications. Macartney denounced Hopkins, Eliot and Auden for abandoning traditional usages, especially metrical form. From the 1950s critics and historians largely ignored him.

Prominent in the Australian Literature Society and the International P.E.N. Club, Macartney was president of the Fellowship of Australian Writers (Victoria) for four years in the 1940s until he resigned because of the activity of left-wing writers. He was cantankerous in literary affairs: 'I'm the barking dog of literature in Melbourne', he proudly claimed. Highly sensitive to criticism, he replied offensively. He despised Miller's work and was infuriated by critics who did not fully recognize the worth of his revision. In the 1950s he denounced *Meanjin*'s political content. His later years were marked by a lack of appreciation of post-1950s Australian writing, and vitriolic comment on trends in the arts in general. Yet he was a learned man, with admirable literary standards, though rigid and dated.

Macartney's great love was music, on which he occasionally wrote. He produced linocuts, practised bookbinding, and was an able handyman. Swimming and tennis were his main pastimes. He had married Veronica Clarice Hannan (d.1936) on 14 August 1917 at the registry office, Collins Street, Melbourne, but they soon separated. On 5 February 1947 at the manse of the Unitarian Church, East Melbourne, he married Mavis Murray Walker (d.1979), a 43-year-old art teacher. Macartney died, childless, on 2 September 1980 at South Blackburn and was cremated.

L. Strahan, *Just City and the Mirrors* (Melb, 1984); *Meanjin Q*, 1969, no 4; *Age* (Melb), 30 Sept 1978, 4 Sept 1980; Macartney papers (LaTL *and* NL); personal knowledge.   GEOFFREY SERLE*

MACARTNEY, JAMES EDWARD (1911-1977), newspaper editor, was born on 15 July 1911 at Coolgardie, Western Australia, son of Melbourne-born parents Edward Hussey Burgh Macartney, surveyor, and his wife Constance May, née Griffith. His great-grandfather was Archdeacon Hussey Burgh Macartney [q.v.5]. Educated at the High School, Perth, Jim joined the staff of the *West Australian* in 1928 and was employed as a cadet reporter in the following year. While at the University of Western Australia in the early 1930s, he edited the student newspapers, *Pelican* and *Sruss-Sruss*, antagonized the authorities and was sent down.

On 14 December 1932 at St George's Anglican Cathedral, Perth, Macartney married 19-year-old Edith Violet Flanagan; they were to be divorced ten years later. In 1934 he was appointed editor of the new weekly, *Broadcaster*. After West Australian Newspapers Ltd bought the *Daily News*, he became its editor in 1936. Within four years his journalistic candour, business acumen and eye for brighter format lifted the paper's standing and almost doubled its sales. Macartney served (1942-45) in the Royal Australian Air Force; he rose to flight lieutenant, and flew Ansons with No.67 Squadron and Catalinas with No.42 Squadron in the South-West Pacific Area. When World War II ended he resumed his post as editor and in 1951 was promoted managing editor of the company. At John Knox Presbyterian Church, Gardenvale, Melbourne, on 15 February 1946 he had married Margaret Cosson Bessell-Browne, née Bennett, a 29-year-old divorcee.

For some ten years the firm's pyramidal management was guided by what it believed 'J.M.' wanted. The weaknesses inherent in this system were largely obscured by his sagacious and usually compassionate administration. Macartney's dailies wielded significant influence in Western Australia. He circumvented British restrictions by having his reporters cover nuclear tests in the Monte Bello islands; he dispatched expeditions to promote northern development; and he was a driving force behind the introduction of commercial television. Strenuously anti-communist, his newspapers backed Australia's involvement in the Vietnam War. They also supported free enterprise, while advocating a better deal for the less fortunate. Macartney was respected for his ability to select and train staff, among them the cartoonist Paul Rigby and the journalist B. E. Kirwan Ward.

In March 1960 Macartney was awarded a grant by the government of the United States of America to promote an exchange of ideas between the two countries. Elected president (1960) of the Australian Newspapers Council, he chaired the press, publicity and public relations committee for the Commonwealth Games (1962) in Perth. Yet, in essence he remained a shy man, virtually banning from his publications information about himself. In 1962 Macartney was appointed managing director of West Australian Newspapers. His continuing tussles with directors, penchant for calling governors and premiers to task, autocratic tendencies and chronic alcoholism exacerbated the pressures. Despite five months sick leave in 1968, he left the company in May 1969.

Macartney worked intermittently as a consultant for newspapers, journals, television and radio, and found more time to enjoy golf at the Lake Karrinyup Country Club. Throughout his life he remained something of a rebel, relishing tilts at sacred cows, humbug and hypocrisy. He died of cancer on 21 September 1977 in Perth and was cremated with Anglican rites; his wife and their two sons survived him, as did the son and two daughters of his first marriage.

Radical (Perth), 2, no 3, 1959; WA Newspapers Ltd, *Q Bulletin*, Sept 1969; *West Australian*, 17 May 1969, 22 Sept, 22 Oct 1977; *Sunday Times* (Perth), 18 May 1969; information from Mr G. Richards, Dalkeith, Miss V. Gammon, Dianella, and Mr P. Ewing, Cottesloe, Perth; personal information.

T. E. AUSTEN

MACARTNEY, KEITH LAMONT (1903-1971), academic, actor and theatre director, was born on 18 July 1903 at Moonee Ponds, Melbourne, son of Clive Lamont Macartney, traveller, and his wife Alice Maude, née Kimpton, both Victorian born. Keith was sent to Scotch College, where he was to be joint-dux (1921) and a prefect (1922). At the University of Melbourne (B.A. Hons, 1925) he won exhibitions in English each year, as well as exhibitions in French, German and the science of language, and graduated with first-class honours in English language and literature. In 1926-27 he tutored in the department of English and at Ormond [q.v.5] College, before travelling to Europe. Entering Clare College, Cambridge (B.A., 1931; M.A., 1935), he studied Anglo-Saxon and Norse in the school of archaeology and anthropology, and gained a first-class in the tripos, becoming an exhibitioner of the college and Dame Bertha Philpotts scholar.

Much as he relished Cambridge, Macartney returned in 1936 to a part-time lectureship in English language at the University of Melbourne. In the following year he was appointed lecturer. His promotion to senior lecturer in 1942 took into account his leading part in keeping the department going in difficult wartime conditions. Although he continued to contribute to teaching and course-planning, it soon became clear that his true vocation was for drama. His lectures, laced with dramatic readings, were often remembered with affection by his former students, but he was also eager to apply his theatrical talents beyond departmental boundaries. An accomplished singer, he joined Elsa Haas in providing the musical accompaniment to Lorna Stirling's lectures on the history of music: according to his colleague Ian Maxwell [q.v.], they were 'the most delightful lectures' he had ever attended. Macartney founded the university graduates' Tin Alley Players. In recognition of his role in developing student theatre, he was appointed associate-professor of drama in 1946. From 1950 he was associate-professor of English.

For several years following his return, Macartney lent the theatrical skills (and often the material) he had acquired at Cambridge to the annual student revue, and was hailed as 'Australia's answer to Jack Buchanan'. He directed many plays for the Tin Alley Players, and college and student groups. Memorable among his Shakespeare productions were *A Midsummer Night's Dream* (1941), in which he played Puck, and *Macbeth* (1947, co-directed by Joy Youlden); always promoting the dramatic role of music, he engaged Margaret Sutherland to write the incidental music for the former and Dorian Le Gallienne [q.v.] for the latter. Nor were his interests confined to the classics: his productions included Maxwell Anderson's *Winterset* and the Capek brothers' *And so ad infinitum* ('The

Insect Play'). He was an imaginative director, particularly skilled in grounding students in the techniques of speech and movement.

Macartney became something of a figure around the university. His dress, for the time, was mildly bohemian, and the silk handkerchief which, in the course of lectures, he deployed from his cuff, highlighted his theatrical manner. His discretion and exemplary manners ensured that his homosexuality, though widely assumed, was never an issue.

Plagued with intermittent illness, and finding the rapidly expanding university a less congenial place, he retired in 1964 but returned (1965-67) to help the understaffed department. He was sympathetic to the dilemmas facing the student generation, and marched in the 1970 Vietnam moratorium. Macartney published little and his lectures were not intellectually demanding. His reputation rested on the civilizing impact he had on a small university community which needed artistic stimulus. He died of a cerebral haemorrhage on 21 March 1971 at his Hawthorn home and was cremated; his estate was sworn for probate at $183 308. The night before his death he had been heard amusing himself, singing and playing the piano.

N. Macgeorge (comp), *The Arts in Australia* (Melb, 1948); *Univ Melb Mag*, 1956, p 99; *Univ Melb Gazette*, Jan 1968, Dec 1971; *Age* (Melb), 27 Mar 1971; Ian Maxwell papers *and* staff files (Univ Melb Archives); information from Prof D. Bradley, Phillip Island, Vic, and the late Mr G. Fairfax; personal knowledge.   JOHN RICKARD

MACAULAY, ROBERT WILSON (1882-1951), Presbyterian clergyman, was born on 8 October 1882 at Byker, Newcastle upon Tyne, England, son of Samuel Macaulay, surgeon, and his wife Margaret Morrison, née Wilson. Robert was educated at Ashville College, Harrogate, Jesmond College, Newcastle, and—following the family's emigration to Western Australia in 1898—at the High School, Perth. After working in the Union Bank, he attended the University of Adelaide (B.A., 1903) and studied theology at Westminster College, Cambridge, England. He was licensed in the Presbyterian Church in June 1907 and briefly assisted John Watson at Liverpool.

Returning home on a holiday, Macaulay was persuaded to serve at the Presbyterian Church, East Fremantle, where he was ordained in 1908. Two years later he was called to Elsternwick, Melbourne. There, on 14 November 1911, he married Annie Margaretha Dircks (d.1942). Endowed with ability, energy and a sense of humour, Macaulay was a sensitive pastor and a fine preacher, with a rare command of the English language. In 1912 he enrolled in divinity at Ormond [q.v.5] College, University of Melbourne, but gave up his course during World War I. Appointed a chaplain in the Australian Imperial Force on 5 August 1916, he served with the 3rd Brigade on the Western Front from February to October 1917 and suffered shell-shock.

Macaulay was a convinced internationalist: he was an executive-member (1920-48) of the Australian League of Nations Union (United Nations Association) and of the United Nations Relief and Rehabilitation Administration (1944-48). He also belonged to the Returned Sailors' and Soldiers' Imperial League of Australia, and was an active Freemason.

In 1921 Macaulay was called to Trinity Church, Camberwell; there he was a colleague of Rev. P. J. Murdoch [q.v.10], whom he succeeded in 1928. Under Macaulay the congregation grew to more than five hundred, including business, political and professional leaders. He served on numerous committees, and was business convener for both the Victorian General Assembly and the General Assembly of Australia. Appointed clerk of the latter body in 1933, he helped to guide discussions in the Samuel Angus [q.v.7] case. That year he was named moderator of the Victorian assembly; during his one-year term he travelled widely throughout the State and to Korea. In 1938-42 he was clerk of the Victorian assembly. His international vision for Australian Christianity was underlined by his ecumenism. A founding member of the Victorian committee of the Commission on Faith and Order, he was also involved in setting up what became the Australian Council of Churches. As first president (1932-38) of the Christian Social Order Movement, he helped to give it national standing and influence on postwar reconstruction.

Succeeding Rev. John Flynn [q.v.8], Macaulay was moderator-general (1942-45) of the Presbyterian Church of Australia. He and the Anglican bishop John Stoward Moyes [q.v.] were invited in 1943 to an international round table of Christian leaders at Princeton, New Jersey, United States of America, the recommendations of which went to allied leaders, once they had been presented to Cordell Hull and Wendell Wilkie. While in the U.S.A., Macaulay was awarded an honorary D.D. from the American University, Washington, D.C. Further recognition of his knowledge of international affairs came when Dr H. V. Evatt [q.v.14] invited him in 1949 to be a religious adviser to the Australian delegation to the United Nations Assembly.

Despite his many commitments, Macaulay continued to read widely. Discerning critics considered that his leadership of worship and the quality of his preaching was better than ever. Some of his addresses were published in the *Messenger* or as pamphlets. His wisdom gave him national status and influence, but he never lost his innate modesty. He loved science fiction, bowls, bridge and cricket, and was respected for his kindliness and decisiveness. Survived by his two daughters and four sons, he died of coronary vascular disease on 1 August 1951 at his Camberwell home and was buried in Boroondara cemetery, Kew.

Presbyterian Churches of Vic and Tas, *Messenger*, 10, 17 Aug 1951; *Argus*, 2 Apr 1942, 2 Aug 1951; *Sun News-Pictorial*, 18 Dec 1949, 2 Aug 1951; *Age* (Melb), 24 Jan 1950, 3 Aug 1951; family papers, held by Mr A. J. Macaulay, Nunawading, Melb.

IAN BREWARD

McAULEY, JAMES PHILLIP (1917-1976), poet, was born on 12 October 1917 at Lakemba, Sydney, third child of native-born parents Patrick Phillip McAuley, grazier, and his wife Mary Maud, née Judge. From Homebush Public School, James proceeded to Fort Street Boys' High School, where he became school captain; a contemporary was (Sir) John Kerr, later godfather to one of McAuley's children. Winning an exhibition to the University of Sydney (B.A. Hons, 1938; M.A., 1940; Dip.Ed., 1942), McAuley graduated with first-class honours in English. During his undergraduate years he was influenced by the philosophy of Professor John Anderson [q.v.7], and attracted to communism and anarchism. His first poem, 'Homage to T. S. Eliot', appeared in 1935 in *Hermes*, the university magazine he was to edit. Music was another recreation. 'Jimmy the Jazz Pianist' (in Donald Horne's fond phrase) was a fabled figure on campus, and McAuley also served as organist and choirmaster at Holy Trinity Church, Dulwich Hill. Later, he wrote hymns, besides playing a modern reproduction of the virginal.

While tutoring (1938) at a property near Bungendore, McAuley gathered his early poems under the title 'Prelude, Suite and Chorale, a *livre composé*'. His M.A. thesis, 'Symbolism: An Essay In Poetics', manifested his abiding interest in twentieth-century German and French poetry. Appointed junior housemaster at Sydney Church of England Grammar School (Shore) in 1940, he resigned when questioned about his principled refusal to volunteer for war service, took a teacher's scholarship and was appointed in 1942 to Newcastle Boys' Junior High School. Throughout his career he remained deeply concerned with standards in secondary education and became president (1971) of the Australian Association of Teachers of English.

At the district registrar's office, Newcastle, on 20 June 1942 McAuley married Norma Elizabeth Abernethy, a 22-year-old school-

teacher. In October he was appointed research consultant to a wartime advisory committee in the Prime Minister's Department, before being mobilized in the Militia on 7 January 1943. He transferred to the Australian Imperial Force that month. Following a stint in army education, Sergeant McAuley was commissioned in January 1944 and worked in Melbourne with A. A. Conlon's [q.v.13] Directorate of Research (and Civil Affairs).

On idle afternoons in the Victoria Barracks in 1944, McAuley and Harold Stewart concocted the 'Ern Malley' hoax. Intending to castigate 'the decay of meaning and craftsmanship' in much contemporary verse, they targeted the Adelaide journal *Angry Penguins*, edited by Max Harris. Using a comically eclectic array of sources, together with a fictitious biography for the hapless Ern, the hoaxers sent 'his' *The Darkening Ecliptic* to Harris, who eagerly published it. This successful and serious prank has been loosely blamed for setting back literary modernism and encouraging philistinism in Australia. Exaggerated claims were advanced for the Malley poems, but, once the hoax was exposed in a Sydney newspaper, McAuley had little to say of them.

In December 1943 he made the first of many visits to New Guinea, which became a second 'spirit country', as well as an inspiration for his thinking about post-colonial polities. From August 1945 McAuley was an instructor at the Land Headquarters School of Civil Affairs (later Australian School of Pacific Administration), first in Canberra and then in Sydney. Transferring to the Reserve of Officers in March 1946, he remained at the school as a lecturer until 1959. One of his tasks was to train officers for service in the Territory of Papua and New Guinea. Inspired by the mission of Marie Thérèse Noblet [q.v.11], McAuley adopted in 1952 the Catholic faith from which his father had lapsed.

His first volume of verse, *Under Aldebaran*, was published by Melbourne University Press in 1946. In the early 1950s he discovered the Austrian poet Georg Trakl, whose work he later translated. McAuley's poetic reputation was consolidated with *A Vision of Ceremony* (Sydney, 1956). The role as public intellectual, which he increasingly sought, found expression in *The End of Modernity* (Sydney, 1959). Anti-modernist in precept and tone, these essays argued for the spiritual dimension of the greatest art. He developed that position, while trenchantly stating his liberal-conservative political beliefs, through the journal *Quadrant*, of which he became founding editor in 1956. In 1967 it was revealed that, through its association with the Congress for Cultural Freedom, *Quadrant* received funds from the Central Intelligence

Agency. McAuley claimed, without refutation, that no consequent pressure had ever been placed on him as editor. Nevertheless, *Quadrant* continued to be demonized by its left-wing competitors, *Meanjin* and *Overland*, though all shared contributors, a constant struggle for funds, and an inclusive, liberal practice in the selection of material.

From the mid-1950s McAuley's energies were directed to ideological differences within the Australian Labor Party. Support for the anti-communist policies of the industrial groups brought him into sympathetic contact with B. A. Santamaria and the Catholic Social Studies Movement. It also placed him in conflict with the Catholic hierarchy of Sydney, notably Cardinal (Sir) Norman Gilroy [q.v.14] and Bishop James Carroll. Eventually McAuley supported the formation of the Democratic Labor Party.

In 1960 McAuley seemed to have retreated from politics, when he accepted a readership in poetry at the University of Tasmania. Next year he succeeded to the chair of English, which he held until his death, despite soundings from mainland universities. Teaching and administrative responsibilities (he was at various times chairman of the professorial board and acting vice-chancellor) did not impede his role as controversialist, nor his literary output. A monograph on Christopher Brennan's [q.v.7] poetry appeared in 1963. When, 'suddenly, unbidden, the theme [returned]', McAuley recovered his poetic drive and completed a verse epic on the Portuguese explorer, *Captain Quiros* (Sydney, 1964). Always an inspiring teacher, he instilled in students love and respect for the craft of poetry. His modestly titled *A Primer of English Versification* (Sydney, 1966) remains an exemplary, traditional introduction to this subject. It was in the fecund decade of the 1960s that he also wrote most of his hymns, many set to music by Richard Connolly. While in Europe and the United States of America in 1967, he began the sequence of poems on Sydney youth called 'On the Western Line'. In the same year he helped to form Peace With Freedom, a body of right-wing intellectuals determined to counter 'propaganda against the allied commitment in the Vietnam War'. Earlier that year he had spent a month in South East Asia, meeting Australian servicemen in Vietnam and experiencing a misplaced confidence in America's capacity 'to knock out the major forces' of its enemy.

McAuley's next volume of verse, *Surprises of the Sun* (Sydney, 1969), made as much impact as any before, being received with puzzlement and acclaim. Containing numerous autobiographical poems, it seemed to mark a shift from austere classicism towards a Romantic sensibility. In fact, few Australian poets had been more wholehearted in believing in the healing powers of nature. 'At Rushy Lagoon' the poet—characteristically at the edge of the scene—discerns 'a world of sense and use'. McAuley rejoiced in natural plenitude, as in the poem, 'In the Huon Valley', which the governor of Tasmania was to read at his funeral. This was McAuley when most like Keats, of whom he was less suspicious than of other Romantic poets, such as the radical Shelley. Distinctively, he pressed for meanings that could be made explicit and sought declarative statements:

> Life is full of returns;
> It isn't true that one never
> Profits, never learns.

A wistful hope, in this conclusion, temporarily mastered anguish, but for McAuley dread was always at hand. Like Keats, he savoured:

> joys that lie
> Closest to despair.

The latter was ever ready to announce itself, whether as terror of spiritual emptiness or political disorder at home and abroad. Teaching Shakespeare's *Henry IV*, McAuley spoke with especial relish the words 'Let order die!' The fascination of that terrible sentiment recalled the anarchic side of his nature, the youthful self which he summoned and faced down. He maintained that, without order, or belief in the structure of faith that can sustain it, there was nothingness. 'The Exile' represented the poet as a 'man repudiated, cancelled', whose life is 'without contexts, or hope' and for whom emptiness is intensified by spiritual dread.

In 1969 McAuley was elected a fellow of the Australian Academy of the Humanities. After a visit to New Delhi in January 1970 for a seminar on Australian and Indian literature, he was found to have bowel cancer. Once recovered and able to quip 'better a semicolon than a full stop', he intensified his literary and public efforts. Significantly, the poems which he wrote in 1970-76 were collected as *Time Given* (Canberra, 1976). In 1972 his achievement in the humanities was recognized by the Britannica Award of $10 000 and a gold medal. A volume of essays, *The Grammar of the Real*, and a critical anthology, *A Map of Australian Verse*, were published in 1975, the year he was appointed A.M. *Music Late at Night* (London, 1976), which contained his Trakl translations, was inspired, in part, by a visit to that poet's familiar Austrian cities of Innsbruck and Salzburg.

Early in 1976 McAuley was diagnosed as having liver cancer. Courageously and meticulously, he prepared for death. A man in whom gracefulness always consorted with rage, and whose opinion of himself was more scarifying than that of his enemies, McAuley was a bold and bitter jester. More droll than the Ern Malley hoax was his projection of Poets' Anonymous, wherein bad poets would be encouraged to discuss their affliction and be paid by the government not to write. McAuley—who often took an angry man's comfort in last things—began his testament, 'Explicit', playfully:

Fully tested I've been found
Fit to join the underground.

While he praised the discursive poetry of Dryden as 'well-bred and easy, energetic, terse', McAuley was committed to a hard-won lyric impulse. Things of the world delighted him: landscapes, political connexions, wine. Spiritual promises he affirmed passionately, but did not trust. The prescriptive McAuley who declared that Christ

cannot walk in a poem,
Not in our century

was given the lie in his resplendent poem, 'Jesus'. McAuley had the hazardous gift of turning metaphors into edicts, behind which practice lay his desperate wish that these might yet be vehicles of truth.

Survived by his wife, daughter and four sons, McAuley died on 15 October 1976 at Lenah Valley, Hobart, and was buried in Cornelian Bay cemetery. Lean, sandy haired, with grey-green eyes and a deeply lined face, he was energetic and patrician in gesture, melodious and measured in speech. His portrait, painted in 1963 by Jack Carington Smith [q.v.13], is held by the National Gallery of Australia, Canberra; another, by Nora Heysen, belongs to the University of Tasmania. Dame Leonie Kramer, a long-time friend, edited his *Collected Poems* (Sydney, 1994). The University of Tasmania established the James McAuley lecture in 1979 and named three prizes in English in his honour.

V. Smith, *James McAuley* (Melb, 1965); P. Coleman, *The Heart of James McAuley* (Syd, 1980); L. McCredden, *James McAuley* (Melb, 1992); *Mercury* (Hob), 18 Jan, 14 July, 30 Oct 1961, 30 Mar, 21 Oct 1963, 5 Mar 1966, 10 June, 30 Oct, 30 Dec 1967, 27 Dec 1969, 29 July 1970, 5 May 1971, 20 Nov, 16 Dec 1972, 24, 28 Apr, 16, 19 Oct 1976, 18 Nov 1980, 5 Nov 1982.   PETER PIERCE

McBRIDE, WILLIAM JOHN (1879-1970), metallurgist, was born on 18 February 1879 at Glenelg, Adelaide, son of English-born William John McBride, teacher of music, and his wife Teresa Lucy, née Harman. Educated at Christian Brothers' College and at the University of Adelaide (B.Sc., 1898) where he studied metallurgy and geology, he began work with the Reedy Creek Gold-Copper Co.

In 1900 McBride joined Broken Hill South Ltd as metallurgist, chief assayer and mill superintendent under W. E. Wainwright [q.v.12]. During his first year he enlarged and modified the milling plant; the increased efficiency and reduced costs that resulted helped the company to ride out a four-year decline in metal prices. He then carried out experiments on selective lead and zinc flotation methods, apparatus and reagents, training Thomas Andrew Read [q.v.] who soon took over much of the assaying. Between 1905 and 1908 McBride planned and constructed (with many technical modifications) a bigger mill which provided a high-grade lead concentrate in its first year of operation.

A controversy arose in 1908 about possible harmful effects of new explosives in use underground. McBride supervised much of the analytical work and design of apparatus, and tested and ultimately vindicated the product. Perhaps more important was his design and construction of equipment to measure suspended dust levels in underground mine air (the subject of several health surveys). To treat slime dumps containing valuable lead, silver and zinc, McBride and the engineer J. C. Cunningham devised in 1913 a sub-aeration flotation cell for T. M. Owen's mineral separation process. Their design was adopted by other Broken Hill mines and used until the 1970s.

On 17 April 1907 McBride had married Kathleen Ann Murphy (d.1952) at St Laurence's Catholic Church, North Adelaide; they were to remain childless. An efficient rifleman, mentioned as likely to represent South Australia in competitions, he was secretary of the Broken Hill Rifle Club for five years. When World War I interrupted the export of metals, he was sent to Port Pirie, South Australia, to represent the combined Broken Hill mining interests while a joint company, Broken Hill Associated Smelters Pty Ltd, was formed.

Enlisting in the Australian Imperial Force on 14 August 1915, McBride was commissioned in November and reached France in May 1916. He was posted to the 1st Tunnelling Company and promoted temporary captain (substantive in 1917). On the night of 9 April 1917 he organized the defence of the deep-mine system at Hill 60, near Ypres, Belgium, and arranged for parties to rescue men who had been gassed. For these actions he was awarded the Military Cross. He returned to Australia in 1919, having travelled through the United States of America where he visited mines and treatment works. His A.I.F. appointment terminated on 16 December.

Mining investors in Melbourne—W. S. Robinson, (Sir) Herbert Gepp and (Sir) Colin Fraser [qq.v.11,8]—had noticed McBride's abilities. Gepp considered that McBride's training and temperament fitted him to act as liaison officer, linking the Broken Hill, Port Pirie and Risdon (Tasmania) operations, particularly the zinc roasting techniques then being developed. In the following five years his main tasks were the construction and operation of blende roasters at Broken Hill, Port Pirie, Wallaroo (South Australia) and Risdon, and of acid plants at Cockle Creek, New South Wales. He also advised Robinson and the Burma Corporation Ltd in 1920 on its Namtu gravity and flotation mill in Burma. In 1925 McBride went to Britain. There he worked as consulting metallurgist for the National Smelting Co. (Swansea and Avonmouth). He published only one paper (jointly with Wainwright) on his research, being content to see the results applied. At various times he was a member of the Australasian Institute of Mining Engineers (later Australasian Institute of Mining and Metallurgy), the Institution of Mining and Metallurgy, England, and the American Institute of Mining and Metallurgical Engineers.

Back in Adelaide as a consultant in the mid-1930s, McBride experienced financial difficulties. By 1938 he had returned to England without his wife and re-established himself. In 1943 he was appointed works manager of Fullers' Earth Union Ltd, Redhill, Surrey. He lived at Highstead Farmhouse, Horan, East Sussex. In 1951 he retired to Eastbourne. On 3 December 1953 he married 62-year-old Alice Marjorie Mansfield at the local register office. Survived by his wife, he died on 27 July 1970 at Eastbourne. A plaque at Broken Hill commemorates him.

W. S. Robinson, *If I Remember Rightly*, G. Blainey ed (Melb, 1967); B. Carroll, *Built on Silver* (Melb, 1986); W. Hodder, History of the South Mines (ts, Broken Hill Archives, Charles Rasp L); Broken Hill Associated Smelters papers *and* C. Fraser papers (Baillieu L, Univ Melb); Inst of Mining and Metallurgy (Lond), membership applications and W. McBride file.   D. F. BRANAGAN

McBRIEN, LIKELY HERMAN (1892-1956), football administrator and politician, was born on 7 December 1892 in South Melbourne, sixth child of Irish-born parents John McBrien, foreman, and his wife Frances Ann, née Kittson. Educated at Middle Park Central School, Likely began work in 1906 as a messenger for the *Age* newspaper. He enlisted in the Australian Imperial Force on 2 October 1916 and undertook clerical duties at Administrative Headquarters, London, before returning to Australia where he was discharged on 13 August 1917. At St Luke's Anglican Church, South Melbourne, on 16 July 1919 he married Madge Margaret Summers. Returning to the *Age*, he became assistant circulation manager and advertising manager. In 1922-29 he was secretary of the Authorised News Agents' Association of Victoria.

A versatile sportsman, McBrien played cricket and tennis, and later golf and bowls. He also took part in the first (1913) three-mile (4.8 km) swim down the River Yarra and rowed number four in the Albert Park VIII which won the Victorian championship in 1915. But Australian Rules football was the passion of his life. From 1909 to 1911 he was a player and treasurer of the Leopold Football Club (later the South Melbourne Football Club's second XVIII); he retired after fracturing an arm in a game of ice hockey. A committee-member (from 1912) of the South Melbourne club, he was honorary secretary (1922) and president (1929).

On 28 May 1929 'Like' was appointed secretary of the Victorian Football League, a position he held until March 1956. He helped to develop the league, chaired its finance committee and arranged the purchase of Harrison [q.v.4] House, Spring Street, Melbourne, for the V.F.L.'s headquarters; what was more, he promoted an attempted amalgamation of the Victorian Football Association with the V.F.L. and endeavoured to expand the code interstate, while vigorously opposing any threat from Rugby.

During World War II McBrien was honorary administrator and senior vice-president of the Australian Comforts Fund, honorary deputy-chairman of the Returned Soldiers' War Services Fund and honorary chairman of the purchasing panel for the army's directorate of amenities. Elected to the Legislative Council in 1943 as an Independent member for the province of Melbourne North, he served as commissioner of public works and vice-president of the Board of Land and Works in Ian Macfarlan's [q.v.] short-lived ministry in 1945. His campaign for the rehabilitation of returned servicemen was one of his prime commitments. Opposed to paid entry to organized sport on Sundays, he was appointed (1948) to the Melbourne Sunday Christian Observance Council. In 1949 he was defeated in the elections for the Legislative Council. He was appointed O.B.E. in 1950.

McBrien held a string of other public posts: chairman of the Edith Cavell Fund Trust, the Homes for Aged and Infirm Society, and the Yarra Bend National Park Trust; honorary treasurer of the Travellers' Aid Society and of the Victorian Anti-Sweating and Industrial Improvement League; executive-member of the Playgrounds and Recreation Association of Victoria; and trustee of the Heidelberg branch of the Returned Sailors', Soldiers' and Airmen's Imperial League of Australia. A qualified accountant, he was a fellow of the International Institute of Accountants and of the Institute of Commerce, England. In addition, he was a director of Disher & McBrien Pty Ltd.

Survived by his wife, daughter and son, McBrien died of cerebral thrombosis on 22 December 1956 at Richmond and was cremated. Percy Taylor, the *Argus*'s sports journalist, wrote: '"Like" McBrien was a big man in every respect—a big frame, a deep booming voice, a big heart, and big ideas for the advancement of sport'.

Table Talk, 1 May 1930; *Argus*, 25 May 1929, 15 Sept 1934; *Age* (Melb), 14 Apr 1943, 9 May 1944, 24 Dec 1956; *Herald* (Melb) and *Sun News-Pictorial*, 24 Dec 1956; McBrien biog sheet (Vic Parliamentary L).
                  FRANK STRAHAN

McCAFFREY, CHRISTIAN JAMES (1901-1980), medical superintendent and radiologist, was born on 27 August 1901 at Albury, New South Wales, eldest of five children of James McCaffrey, a Melbourne-born customs officer, and his New Zealand-born wife Dorothy, née Tobin. He was named after the Boer leader Christian de Witt. When the family moved to Sydney he was sent to Christian Brothers' College, Waverley, where he became school captain and shone in studies and in sport. Awarded an exhibition and bursary in 1918, he entered St John's College, University of Sydney (M.B., 1925); his boxing prowess ended the 'hazing' of freshmen at college, and he played Rugby League football for the university.

In November 1925 McCaffrey joined the Department of Public Health. On 2 November 1926 he was appointed medical officer at the Mental Hospital, Parramatta; two years later he gained a university diploma in psychiatry. In 1932 he moved to (Royal) Newcastle Hospital. An able, largely self-taught radiologist, he was appointed medical superintendent in October 1939. At St Philip's Anglican Church, Sydney, on 22 November 1933 he had married Pearl Marie Smith (d.1960), a 32-year-old chemist; they were to have a son and daughter. From 1945 he began recruiting bright young men with war service. By 1950 the hospital was mostly run by salaried specialists, leaving the honorary medical staff largely devoid of power, despite implacable and lasting opposition from the State branch of the British Medical Association. McCaffrey also forged strong links with the Australian Labor Party, at all levels.

Due to McCaffrey's innovations, by the mid-1950s the hospital had a strong commitment to patient welfare, medical audit and efficiency. Some of his staff were to achieve distinction: Peter Hendry became president of the World Association of Societies of Pathology and deputy-chancellor of the University of Newcastle, R. M. Gibson [q.v.14] pioneered geriatric care in Australia, and Ivan Schalit, director of anaesthesia, developed one of the first intensive-care units in Australia. McCaffrey was a brilliant teacher of staff at all levels, highly literate, provocative in the Socratic tradition, and far-sighted in his views of health care. For all that, he did promote and protect his favourites.

Basic to the audits that McCaffrey instituted throughout the hospital was an emphasis on good medical records. He was much criticized for his opposition to using incubators for premature babies (the accepted view is that he was wrong) and for his promotion of 'rooming in' for full-term babies (now standard practice). His opposition to the indiscriminate use of antibiotics with the danger of patients acquiring resistance— although rejected by organized medicine at the time—has been justified. In the 1950s McCaffrey wrote a formal proposal for a medical school at Newcastle.

Tensions and antagonisms surfaced in the early 1960s: a number of the specialist staff disagreed with McCaffrey, and the board of directors was embroiled in the controversy. In 1964 an investigation by the Hospitals Commission of New South Wales into serious differences of opinion and unrest among the staff led to the dismissal of the board by the minister for health. At St Luke's Catholic Church, Cooks Hill, on 15 April 1963 McCaffrey had married Doreen Ashmel Birch (d.1975); she was aged 36, and an ear, nose and throat specialist who had been recruited from England. She later returned to Britain, followed by McCaffrey who retired in a storm of criticism in July 1965. They subsequently practised at Lincoln, England, in New Zealand, and eventually at Mount Gambier, South Australia. Survived by the daughter of his first marriage and the son of his second, McCaffrey died on 20 March 1980 at Naracoorte and was buried in Carinya Gardens cemetery, Mount Gambier.

Many found Christian McCaffrey a charismatic teacher and leader; to others he was dominating and devious; few doubted his brilliant grasp of administration. He and the team he gathered around him at the R.N.H. in the 1950s anticipated most of the modern concepts of hospital administration and health care.

L. Butler (ed), *Chris McCaffrey* (Newcastle, NSW, 1985); *SMH*, 20 Oct 1939, 27 June, 18 July 1964; *Newcastle Morning Herald*, 21 Oct 1960, 18, 21, 23 July 1964, 19 May, 3 Apr, 30 June 1965; Christian Brothers' College, Waverley, Syd, Archives; Univ Syd Archives.
             JOHN M. DUGGAN

McCALL, JAMES ARTHUR (1903-1978), schoolteacher and public servant, was born on 13 November 1903 at Kalgoorlie, Western Australia, third child of Australian-born parents James Arthur McCall, pattern-maker, and his wife Selina, née Tonkin. Jim was educated at Perth Modern School, Claremont Teachers' College and the University of Western Australia (B.A., 1925; B.A. Hons., 1929; Dip.Ed., 1941).

In 1926 McCall was posted to Northam Senior High School; he was to remain there for fifteen years, teaching and providing vocational guidance. At St George's Anglican Cathedral, Perth, on 12 May 1934 he married Amie Gwenneth Purser (d.1978), a 27-year-old schoolteacher. Seconded in June 1941 to the Education Department in Perth as a careers officer, he co-operated with the youth-employment committee of the Federal Department of Labour and National Service. His professional life was to be influenced by the reports of three commissions of inquiry—into youth employment (1937), juvenile delinquency (1943) and child welfare (c.1954). After working in the area of vocational and educational guidance from January 1943, he became district superintendent of education (guidance and handicapped children) on 25 June 1951. Transferred to the Child Welfare Department in July 1954 as a head of division, he was appointed departmental director on 9 December 1955.

At this time there were no state-owned or state-operated institutions for juvenile delinquents in Western Australia. McCall moved quickly to renovate buildings owned by the Anglican-run Swan Homes in order to establish Hillston Boys' Farm School at Stoneville. The institution encouraged boys to reform themselves, to attend trade classes and eventually to move to a less restrictive centre.

The Adult Education Board of Western Australia organized in 1958 a series of lectures on juvenile delinquency to which McCall contributed. A general meeting of the audience recommended further inquiry into the problem, and requested better funding for those institutions already caring for delinquent children. In December McCall was appointed convenor of a committee, the members of which included the commissioner of police, the inspector-general of mental-health services and the director of education. Their findings, published in 1962, stressed the need for suitable training of child-welfare personnel, and proper care and assessment of children in modern institutions or remand homes. Interest in child welfare reflected a belief in the power of scientific research to identify causes of delinquency and to remedy them.

In 1959 McCall had visited Europe and the United States of America to study the management of reform schools; he had in mind the establishment of a maximum security institution on the outskirts of suburban Perth. Riverbank Boys Reformatory was officially opened at Caversham on 12 May 1960. A new Children's Court was built in Perth in 1964 and the Longmore Remand and Assessment Centre was set up in 1965. In the following year McCall began the process of finding a site on which to construct small units to house families undergoing domestic crises.

McCall was appointed Western Australian representative on the National Literature Board of Review on 30 December 1967. Next year he retired from the Child Welfare Department. Survived by his son, he died on 16 September 1978 at Dalkeith and was cremated.

D. Mossenson, *A History of Teacher Training in Western Australia* (Melb, 1955); Child Welfare Dept (WA), *Report on Juvenile Delinquency in Western Australia* (Perth, 1962); A. R. Peterkin, *The Noisy Mansions* (Perth, 1986); Education Dept (WA), *Annual Report*, 1950-53; *West Australian*, 1 Aug 1962; Child Welfare Dept (WA), ACC1417 A3409, ACC2558 1955-66, *and* Education Dept (WA), ACC1497 618/1947 and 41/1951 and 154/1955, ACC1606 1581-58 (PRO, Perth).

MICHAL BOSWORTH

McCALL, WILLIAM VICTOR (1908-1968), politician and businessman, was born on 24 May 1908 at Chatswood, Sydney, second child of native-born parents William James McCall, bank officer, and his wife Hilda Mary, née Bowman. When his father died in 1924, Bill left Sydney Grammar School to support the family. He relied on his wits and entrepreneurial skills to establish himself in business, first as a skin-trader and then as a wool-buyer.

Tough times for business during the Depression persuaded McCall to enter politics. In 1931 he tried to gain pre-selection as the United Australia Party's candidate for the Federal seat of Martin, but was defeated by W. A. Holman [q.v.9]. Next year the U.A.P. chose McCall to contest a by-election for another Federal seat, East Sydney, traditionally a Labor stronghold. He performed well during the campaign, losing to the Lang [q.v.9] Labor Party's E. J. Ward [q.v.] by only 173 votes. On 6 June 1934 McCall married Georgina Bessie Dart (d.1961) with Presbyterian forms at her parents' Chatswood home.

After Holman died in 1934, McCall won pre-selection for Martin. Although only 26 years old, he was president of the U.A.P.'s Chatswood-Willoughby branch and an impressive public speaker. He campaigned energetically, countering Labor Party criticism of the Lyons [q.v.10] government's tariff policy and its insistence on balancing the budget, and was elected in September. McCall believed in physical fitness: he jogged in the early morning, surfed in Sydney, and played golf and tennis. He also immersed himself in local politics. Aligned with the Citizens' Reform Association and aided by his standing as a member of Federal parliament, he was elected to the Sydney Municipal Council as a representative for Fitzroy Ward in 1935.

In the House of Representatives McCall generally supported the Lyons government, but could be outspoken in opposing particular decisions. He led the back-bench protest against Thomas Paterson's [q.v.11] decision in 1936 to refuse Mrs Mabel Freer entry into Australia; McCall exposed Paterson's maladroit handling of the case and helped to persuade the government to reverse the decision in the following year. Enlisting in the Militia in late 1938, McCall was commissioned in January 1939 and transferred to the Reserve of Officers in October 1940. He had taken a keen interest in defence preparations. After World War II began, he advocated an 'all-out' effort against Germany, and later Japan.

Believing that the government lacked vigour in prosecuting the war, McCall became disillusioned with Prime Minister (Sir) Robert Menzies [q.v.]. He was even more unhappy when, following the indecisive general elections of September 1940, Menzies failed to reach agreement with the A.L.P. on forming an all-party government. McCall thought that Menzies made ministerial appointments on the basis of seniority rather than merit, which added to his frustration. From mid-1941 he and other U.A.P. backbenchers regularly found fault with Menzies' leadership. On 28 August at a joint U.A.P.-Country Party meeting McCall brought the issue to a head. He vowed that, unless Menzies stood down, he would ensure that the government was unable to command a majority in the House. Menzies resigned on the 29th.

McCall lost his seat in the 1943 general elections which produced a landslide victory for Labor. With the money he had made on the stock market and his foresight in appreciating that postwar immigration would produce a land boom, he went into real estate, buying and selling rural and residential properties. His stated philosophy was simple: if he 'did not make a quarter of a million', he would 'lose a quarter of a million'. In December 1967 he stunned the business world by offering nearly $2 million cash for a prime redevelopment site in Martin Place, Sydney.

At Wesley Church, Melbourne, on 24 October 1962 McCall married Mavis Michele Dearing, a 35-year-old secretary; they lived at Bellevue Hill, Sydney. On 19 August 1968 McCall and his chauffeur Sten Jacobssen left Pitt Water for Sydney in McCall's speedboat; the upturned vessel was found next day off Long Reef near Collaroy; no bodies were located and the two men were presumed to have drowned. McCall's wife and daughter survived him, as did the son and daughter of his first marriage. His estate was sworn for probate at $60 219.

P. Hasluck, *The Government and the People 1939-1941* (Canb, 1952); P. Spender, *Politics and a Man* (Syd, 1972); A. W. Martin, *Robert Menzies*, 1 (Melb, 1993); *SMH*, 21, 25 Jan 1932, 16, 20, 22, 30 June 1934, 11, 30 July 1935, 5, 13, 19 Nov 1936, 5 Dec 1940, 29 Aug 1941, 21 Aug 1968; *Daily Telegraph* (Syd), 25 Aug 1968.   DAVID LEE

McCALLUM, FRANK (1890-1946), medical practitioner and public-health administrator, was born on 26 May 1890 at Ararat, Victoria, son of Australian-born parents Alexander McCallum, Wesleyan minister, and his wife Lelia Agnes, née Williams. Educated at the Friends' High School, Hobart, Warrnambool College, Victoria, and Wesley College, Melbourne, Frank entered Queen's College, University of Melbourne (M.B., B.S., 1917; D.P.H., 1921; D.P.A., 1945). On 26 November 1914 he suspended his studies and enlisted in the Australian Imperial Force; after two months with the 6th Field Ambulance at Gallipoli in 1915, he was invalided home and discharged. He then completed his undergraduate course and in December 1917 was commissioned captain, Australian Army Medical Corps, A.I.F. In 1918 he served with a number of units in France. His appointment terminated on 18 March 1920 in Australia.

On the recommendation of his friend J. H. L. Cumpston [q.v.8], McCallum joined (1920) the Commonwealth Department of Trade and Customs and was posted to Brisbane as a quarantine officer. In 1922 he was awarded a Rockefeller Foundation scholarship to study public health and epidemiology in the United States of America and Britain. He attended Johns Hopkins University, Baltimore, and the London School of Tropical Medicine. The Royal College of Physicians, London, and the Royal College of Surgeons, England, jointly awarded him (1925) a diploma in tropical medicine and hygiene. Based at the Department of Health's central office in Melbourne from 1924, he was medical secretary to the international Pacific health conference in 1926. His father had officiated on 16 January that year when McCallum married a 26-year-old civil servant Kate Annie Hosking at Queen's College, Parkville. Kate died in 1929; she and Frank had no children. Following a term (1927-29) as director of epidemiology, he was appointed chief medical officer at the Australian High

Commission, London, with responsibility for the medical assessment of migrants.

While in Britain, McCallum represented Australia at world health forums and served on the committee of the Office International d'Hygiène Publique, Paris. In 1932 he returned to Melbourne and was promoted senior medical officer in Canberra. He published (either alone or in collaboration with Cumpston) articles on international hygiene, an epidemiological report on an outbreak of smallpox, and histories of smallpox and intestinal infections in Australia. His *International Hygiene* (Canberra, 1935) was based on lectures he had given over thirteen years at the School of Public Health and Tropical Medicine, Sydney.

Deputy-chairman (1943) of the medical survey committee appointed by the Joint Parliamentary Committee on Social Services, McCallum was later a member of the medical planning committee. On 19 June 1945 he succeeded Cumpston as director-general of health. Cumpston had written in support of the appointment that McCallum's 'experience —international and national, in tropical medicine, nutrition, public health, and social medical planning—has been exceptionally wide'. McCallum's potential as director-general was cut short by illness. He died of complications of pyelonephritis on 25 September 1946 at Royal Prince Alfred Hospital, Sydney, and was cremated. His colleagues and patients mourned the loss of a steadfast and humane man.

MJA, 23 Nov 1946; A1928 items 1020/20, 215/626, CP268/3 item McCallum, F. (AA, Canb).

MARGOT KERLEY

McCALLUM, JOHN ARCHIBALD (1892-1973), politician and schoolteacher, was born on 31 July 1892 at Mittagong, New South Wales, second child of Archibald Duncan McCallum, a coach-builder from Scotland, and his Welsh-born wife Catherine Margaret, née Protheroe. Educated locally and at Sydney Boys' High School, John proceeded to Teachers' College in 1912 and taught at Parramatta High School. On 27 September 1915 he enlisted in the Australian Imperial Force. He served (1916-17) with the 55th Battalion in Egypt, France and Belgium. Wounded at Polygon Wood in September 1917, he was invalided to England, repatriated and discharged on 21 April 1919. He graduated from the University of Sydney (B.A., 1921) with the university medal in history.

On 17 December 1921 at Christ Church, Sydney, McCallum married with Anglican rites Eda Lockwood, a 20-year-old teacher; they were to have four children before being divorced in 1938. He resumed teaching in 1922; except for periods (1924-27 and 1929-31) at Grafton, he was based in Sydney. Promoted examiner in 1937, he lectured in history at Balmain Teachers' College in 1947-49. At the Presbyterian Church, Grafton, on 27 November 1940 he had married Edith Ellen Ernestina Fay, a 30-year-old schoolteacher; this marriage, too, ended in divorce.

From the 1920s McCallum had been active in the Workers' Educational Association; he taught history and economics, and contributed to the *Australian Highway*. He also belonged to Round Table. After working (1922-23) with R. W. G. Mackay [q.v.] on the fortnightly magazine, *New Outlook*, McCallum became prominent in the Australian Institute of Political Science, publishing articles in its journal, *Australian Quarterly*, and presenting papers at its summer schools. His writings urged Australians to adopt an independent defence policy; they also deplored the industrial left wing's attempts to dominate the Australian Labor Party.

In 1931 McCallum was elected State president of the federal Labor Party. An article he published (1932) in *Australian Quarterly* described Labor as the party of momentum. He stood unsuccessfully for the seats of Lakemba (1932) in the Legislative Assembly and Martin (1934) in the House of Representatives. Crippled by the breakaway party of J. T. Lang [q.v.9], in the mid-1930s federal Labor was in a moribund condition in New South Wales. McCallum savagely attacked Lang's despotism and party machine: he claimed that Lang had turned to left-wing extremists for support in exchange for 'complete and arbitrary authority'.

McCallum declared that federal Labor had sold out to the rebels at the A.L.P. unity conference in 1936. Convinced that the Catholic Church had influenced the State A.L.P. conference (1937) to adopt a neutral policy on the Spanish Civil War and on fascism, and troubled by the threats posed by Japan and the European dictators, he rejected Labor's isolationism and left the party.

In the late 1930s and early 1940s McCallum regularly appeared on the Australian Broadcasting Commission's schools programme, 'The World We Live In', to give his views on international affairs. A foundation member (1944) of the Liberal Party, he was elected to the Senate in 1949 and entered that House in June 1950. His maiden speech revealed how he had drifted from his Labor principles: 'those who go on saying that the fundamental thing today is to protect the ordinary man against the monopolist ... and the entrepreneur are living in an age that is finished. I consider that the fundamental problem today is to protect everybody against the growing power of the State'. In the same speech he also advocated the establishment of the Joint Parliamentary Committee on Foreign Affairs, which he was to join on its formation in 1952. He was re-elected to parliament in 1951 and 1955, but his career was undistinguished. Chairman of the Senate Select Committee on the Development of Canberra (1954-55) and the Joint Committee on the Australian Capital Territory (from 1957), he foreshadowed changes to the Senate committee system that were introduced in the 1970s. He was a member (1952-59) of the council of the Australian National University.

Kindly, quiet and scholarly, McCallum could be fierce on some issues, particularly the danger of communism. He opposed state aid to private schools. In his last term he found it increasingly hard to enter the rough and tumble of debate; he was defeated in a Liberal pre-selection ballot in 1961 and relinquished his seat in the Senate in June 1962. Survived by the two sons and two daughters of his first marriage, he died on 30 December 1973 in his home at Lindfield, Sydney, and was cremated with Presbyterian forms.

P. Gathercole et al (eds), *Childe and Australia* (Brisb, 1995); *PD* (Cwlth, Senate), 5 Mar 1974, p 13; *SMH*, 8 Apr 1931, 7 June 1932, 29 May, 22 June 1934, 21 Sept 1938, 1 June 1940, 17 May 1949, 21 Oct 1959, 21 Oct 1961, 11 June 1964, 3 Jan 1974.
                                                    MICHAEL EASSON

McCALLUM, NORMAN ELLIOTT WHITE (1915-1976), forensic scientist, was born on 11 August 1915 at Corowa, New South Wales, second son of Australian-born parents John Ulysses McCallum, bank-teller, and his wife Olive Mary, née Elliott. Educated locally, Norman joined the Victoria Police in 1937 and became a patrol-car driver, taking night-shifts in order to continue studying by day. In 1941 he transferred to the scientific section as a chemist and began a part-time course at the University of Melbourne (B.Sc., 1946; M.Sc., 1949). His exhibition-winning research on alcohol in the blood led the courts to admit as evidence the results of chemical tests for alcohol.

At Chalmers Church, Auburn, on 23 April 1942 McCallum had married with Presbyterian forms Phillida Mary Taylor, a 22-year-old chemist. In 1949-50 he studied forensic science at the laboratory at New Scotland Yard, London, and at Interpol Headquarters, Paris. Seconded (1951) to work at the University of Melbourne with Keith Bowden (senior lecturer in forensic medicine and government pathologist), he grew frustrated with the police force's continued undervaluing of his skills and resigned in 1952 to take a lectureship in chemical pathology. His studies

on the metabolism of phenobarbitone earned him a Ph.D. in 1955.

In the following year McCallum studied modern forensic-science methods at the school of legal medicine, Harvard University, and visited laboratories associated with law enforcement in the United States of America. Back in Melbourne, he returned to the university and built up a laboratory devoted to forensic science, which in 1958 was combined with the scientific section at Russell Street Police Headquarters under his directorship. He demanded that his staff adhere meticulously to his own high standards. In 1963 the laboratories were transferred to premises (named after him) in Spring Street. McCallum remained nominal director, but retained his position at the university where he was promoted reader in chemical pathology in 1967. His teaching ability, enthusiasm and practical experience resulted in the reorganization of the course on forensic medicine.

Despite the heavy burdens of academic responsibility and indifferent health in later years, McCallum continued to practise forensic science when opportunities arose. He was frequently consulted as a reliable and impartial authority, and was called on to provide testimony in cases involving blood-alcohol determinations. Deeply interested in the law, he became a justice of the peace, chairman of the Diamond Valley-Carlton branch of the Royal Victorian Association of Honorary Justices and a member of the board of studies in criminology at the university. He was an associate-member of the Royal College of Pathologists of Australia and a fellow of the Royal Australian Chemical Institute.

McCallum died of hypertensive cardiovascular disease on 19 November 1976 at Heidelberg and was cremated; his wife, son and daughter survived him. For his work on blood alcohol, which was responsible for the introduction of the Breathalyser in Victoria in 1969, he posthumously received the Widmark award, presented by the International Committee on Alcohol, Drugs and Traffic Safety in January 1977.

A. Dower, *Crime Chemist* (Lond, 1965); Vic Police, *Police in Victoria* (Melb, 1980); R. Haldane, *The People's Force* (Melb, 1986); Vic Police, Personnel records (held at Vic Police Headquarters, Melb).
                                                    GAVIN BROWN

MacCALLUM, SIR PETER (1885-1974), professor of pathology, was born on 14 July 1885 at Maryhill, Glasgow, Scotland, son of Peter McCallum, master grocer, and his wife Annie, née Morrison. The family emigrated to New Zealand in 1886, his father to become branch manager of the Singer Sewing

Machine Co. at Christchurch. Peter attended local state schools until the age of 12 when he began work in an ironmonger's store. His health suffered and, on medical advice, he resumed his schooling, subsequently winning scholarships to Christ's College and thence to Canterbury College (B.Sc., N.Z., 1907; M.Sc., 1908; M.A., 1909). At university he gained an exhibition in biology, and Blues in athletics and Rugby.

His ambition was to study medicine. Having saved some money from part-time teaching, MacCallum worked his passage to England as a coal-trimmer in 1910. He entered the University of Edinburgh (M.B., Ch.B., 1914) where he obtained first-class honours in most subjects and prizes in three. Again awarded a double Blue (athletics and Rugby), he was disappointed not to be capped for Scotland.

Before being called up for service in the Royal Army Medical Corps, MacCallum had six months experience in general practice. On 17 March 1915 he was appointed lieutenant, R.A.M.C. Special Reserve. In October he was promoted captain. For his deeds on the Western Front he won the Military Cross and was twice mentioned in dispatches. In 1918 he was gassed and evacuated to England. He took home leave in New Zealand, then returned to Scotland with his 33-year-old fiancée Bella Dytes Jennings, née Cross; she was a widow and a doctor of science. They were married on 25 August 1919 at St Giles's Church, Edinburgh, with the forms of the Church of Scotland. He became a lecturer in pathology and she in botany. Appointed clinical pathologist at the Royal Infirmary, MacCallum undertook research at the Royal College of Physicians of Edinburgh, of which he was elected a member (1934) and fellow (1953). He also taught at the Royal College of Physicians and Surgeons, Glasgow, and obtained its diploma of public health (1923).

In 1924 MacCallum was offered chairs of pathology at Johannesburg, South Africa, and in Melbourne. He chose Melbourne. His arrival was greeted with enthusiasm by the medical profession and the university. Sir Harry Allen [q.v.7], MacCallum's predecessor, had occupied the chair for forty-two years, and Professor R. J. A. Berry and Professor W. A. Osborne [qq.v.7,11] had respectively taught anatomy and physiology for almost two decades. New blood was welcome. MacCallum met kindred spirits in Charles Kellaway at the Walter and Eliza Hall [qq.v.9] Institute, and W. J. Penfold [q.v.11] at the Commonwealth Serum Laboratories.

Not a man for rhetoric or display, MacCallum began quietly. Sincere, forthright and pertinacious, he stamped his personality on the department and ran it well. He concentrated on administration more than research,

and was fortunate in having as his associates such outstanding future professors as F. L. Apperley, E. S. J. King [q.v.] and R. D. Wright, for whom he provided a supportive research environment. His teaching was sound and thorough, though more appreciated at postgraduate level; undergraduates were often daunted by his long, unpunctuated sentences. Well known for his interest in non-curricular activities, he was president of the university's sports union and chairman of the grounds committee.

MacCallum strove to bring about change. He supported the proposal for a new medical school, with the (Royal) Melbourne Hospital being relocated closer to the university; and he encouraged the appointment (1934) of Melbourne's first full-time salaried vice-chancellor (Sir) Raymond Priestley [q.v.11]. MacCallum was dean (1939-43 and 1947-50) of the faculty of medicine, chairman (1944-46) of the professorial board and a member (1931-50 and 1953-61) of council. He delivered the Halford [q.v.4] oration—on population trends —in Canberra in 1938 and the Lady Masson [q.v.10] lecture—'Chemistry and Medicine'— in Melbourne in 1951. On his retirement in 1950, the university conferred on him an honorary M.D. and presented him with a *Festschrift*.

As temporary lieutenant colonel, MacCallum had been director of pathology at Army Headquarters, Melbourne, from September 1941 to April 1942. During World War II he 'raised and commanded the Medical Wing of the Melbourne University Rifles', and served on the physiology sub-committee of the chemical warfare experimental and research committee. In 1945 he was a sympathetic and helpful chairman of the Victorian Committee for Post-War Reconstruction which assisted the rehabilitation of ex-service personnel who wanted to resume or begin university studies. In 1946 he reported to the Western Australian government on the establishment of a medical school in that State.

A compulsive organizer and energetic committee-man, MacCallum was involved in community affairs as a foundation fellow (1938) of the Royal Australasian College of Physicians, as chairman of the Australian National Research Council (1948-51), the Australian Red Cross Society (1951-58) and the College of Dentistry (1941-63), and as president (1946) of the Victorian branch of the British Medical Association. In 1945-62 he was a member of the Medical Board of Victoria. He also chaired (1946-63) the executive-committee of the Anti-Cancer Council of Victoria, through which, with the support of staunch allies like R. Kaye-Scott, he advocated the foundation and development of a cancer institute. In 1949 the Victorian Cancer Institute was established; in the following year its out-patient sections were named the Peter MacCallum Clinic. Clinical work expanded, research and teaching increased, and the first training school in Australia for radiotherapists was set up. It became one of the world's leading centres for cancer treatment and research, and was named the Peter MacCallum Cancer Institute in 1986.

Following his wife's death in 1927, MacCallum had married with Anglican rites Ursula Lillie Grace at the Church of the Holy Nativity, Blenheim, New Zealand, on 15 August 1928. After she died in 1941, he married his former secretary Frieda Maud Davies (d.1953) at Holy Trinity Church, Kew, on 7 June 1946.

In 1953 MacCallum was knighted. Always a keen traveller, he was one of a group of doctors and academics who visited China in 1957 at the invitation of the Chinese Medical Association. On the return journey he visited Japan with his friend Dr Leonard Cox [q.v.13]. MacCallum enjoyed golf and walking. For twenty-five years he sailed and fished with another friend, (Sir) Walter Bassett [q.v.13], at Sorrento, Victoria.

Reserved and reticent at times, Sir Peter was admired by his students for his probity, kindness and generosity. Colleagues and friends who knew him more intimately enjoyed his sense of fun, and respected his compassion, tolerance and staunch principles. He had a reputation for sound judgement and, consequently, for his capacity to influence people. Survived by the three daughters of his first marriage and by the son of his second, he died on 4 March 1974 at Kew and was cremated. A portrait by Max Meldrum [q.v.10] hangs in the department of pathology, University of Melbourne; another, by Paul Fitzgerald, is held by the Peter MacCallum Cancer Institute, East Melbourne.

Dept of Pathology, Univ Melb, *The Melbourne School of Pathology* (Melb, 1962); K. F. Russell, *The Melbourne Medical School 1862-1962* (Melb, 1977); G. L. McDonald (ed), *Roll of the Royal Australasian College of Physicians*, 1, 1938-75 (Syd, 1988); *MJA*, 1951, 2, p 101, 1974, 2, p 24; MacCallum papers (Univ Melb Archives); Minutes of the Anti-Cancer Council of Vic *and* the Executive Cte of the Anti-Cancer Council of Vic *and* the Interim Cte of the Cancer Inst Bd, *and* Address by Minister of Health to the first meeting of the Cancer Inst Bd, 27 Apr 1949 (Peter MacCallum Cancer Inst Archives, Melb).   J. S. GUEST

MacCALLUM, WALTER PATON (1895-1959), army medical officer, was born on 3 April 1895 in Sydney, youngest of four children of Scottish-born (Sir) Mungo William MacCallum [q.v.10], professor of modern language and literature at the University of Sydney, and his Hanoverian-born wife Dorette Margarethe, née Peters. Walter inherited from his parents a lively interest in literature. Educated at Sydney Grammar School (1908-13), he won the Greek medal, the (Sir Daniel) Cooper [q.v.3] scholarship in classics and a university exhibition. He served in the cadets, captained boats and played in the First XI. Well built and six feet (183 cm) tall, he was school captain.

In 1914 MacCallum entered St Andrew's College, University of Sydney, and began an arts degree. On 5 May 1915 he was commissioned in the Australian Imperial Force. Posted to the 20th Battalion, he saw action at Gallipoli (August-December) and on the Western Front (from March 1916). He was appointed a general staff officer, 3rd grade, at 2nd Division headquarters in October 1916. For his 'energy and initiative', especially during the advance towards Bapaume, France, in February 1917, he won the Military Cross. In September he became brigade major of the 5th Brigade. Gaining a reputation as a brilliant organizer, he was thrice mentioned in dispatches and was awarded the Distinguished Service Order for his staff work in operations around the Somme from May to August 1918. That month he was promoted major. His A.I.F. appointment terminated in Australia on 30 April 1919.

Returning to the university, MacCallum switched to medicine (M.B., Ch.M., 1924). He held resident appointments at the Royal Prince Alfred Hospital, the Royal Alexandra Hospital for Children and the Coast Hospital before establishing his own practice at Edgecliff in 1926. On 9 June that year at St Peter's Anglican Church, Mount Victoria, he married Vida Agnes Rossell; they were to have four children. From 1920 he had either served in the Militia or been included in the general list of the Reserve of Officers; he did not transfer to the Australian Army Medical Corps Reserve until May 1933. He held teaching posts at the Royal Prince Alfred and the Royal Alexandra hospitals, became an honorary assistant-physician at the two institutions in the mid-1930s and rose to honorary consulting physician at both in 1955.

On 17 May 1940 MacCallum had joined the Australian Imperial Force. He embarked for the Middle East on 19 October as registrar of the 2nd/5th Australian General Hospital. In January 1941 he was appointed deputy assistant director of medical services, I Corps. After participating (March-April) in the campaigns in Greece and Crete, he was promoted temporary lieutenant colonel and placed in command of the A.A.M.C. Training Wing in Palestine. He was mentioned in dispatches for his work in the Middle East. In January 1942 he flew to Batavia and in the following month assisted in the evacuation of Sumatra as a member of the A.I.F. team. By March he was back in Australia.

Promoted temporary colonel, in April 1942 MacCallum was appointed deputy director general of medical services at General Headquarters, Melbourne. In August 1943 he was elevated to substantive colonel and temporary brigadier. He served with Advanced Allied Land Forces Headquarters at Hollandia, Netherlands New Guinea, and at Morotai, in 1944-45. His medical planning for the Australian operations in Borneo was rewarded when he was appointed C.B.E. (1947). MacCallum was placed on the Reserve of Officers on 8 March 1946. Having spent six months in London refreshing his clinical skills, he returned to Sydney where he built up a successful Macquarie Street practice as a consultant physician. He held numerous hospital appointments and was honorary physician (1946-50) to the governor-general.

MacCallum's courtesy and consideration made him popular with patients and nursing staff; renowned as a stickler for punctuality, he was, none the less, equally popular as a teacher of medical students. He was a fellow (1946), honorary secretary (1948-50, 1953 and 1958) and treasurer (1950-58) of the Royal Australasian College of Physicians, a member (from 1956) of the New South Wales Medical Defence Council and vice-chairman of trustees of his old school. Survived by his wife, two sons and one of his daughters, he died of a coronary occlusion on 22 November 1959 at his Edgecliff home and was cremated.

C. E. W. Bean, *The A.I.F. in France*, 1917, 1918 (Syd, 1933, 1942); A. S. Walker, *Middle East and Far East* (Canb, 1953); *MJA*, 30 July 1960, p 193.
MICHAEL B. TYQUIN

McCARTEN, MAURICE THOMAS JOSEPH (1902-1971), jockey and racehorse-trainer, was born on 17 September 1902 at Hawera, South Taranaki, New Zealand, son of John McCarten, a New Zealand-born groom, and his wife Mary, née O'Neil, from Ireland. Maurice was given trackwork from the age of 9 and apprenticed at 14 to the trainer Fred Tilley. His first winner was Merry Gain in Wellington. In the following years he won almost every major race in New Zealand and headed the jockeys' premiership twice.

In Sydney on 18 August 1923, at his first appearance on an Australian racecourse, McCarten rode three winners at Canterbury; that year he won the first of four Australian Jockey Club Derbys, on Ballymena. After returning to New Zealand, he came back again to Sydney and married with Catholic rites Mary Veronica O'Brien on 25 May 1925 at the Church of Our Lady of the Rosary, Kensington. Next year McCarten settled in

Sydney and linked with the trainers Fred Williams and George Price [q.v.11]. He rode more than a thousand winners. The Melbourne and Caulfield cups eluded him, but his victories included four Brisbane (two on Spear Chief, 1938, 1939) and two Sydney cups, two Victoria Derbys and two Epsom handicaps. He was renowned as a master of tactics, especially in the major races, but he did not achieve the Sydney jockey's premiership until 1938-39. His most famous ride was on Spear Chief which beat the 40/1-on favourite Ajax in the 1939 Rawson Stakes.

Troubled by weight problems and lured by the opportunity to acquire the ailing J. T. Jamieson's stables, horses and wealthy clients, in May 1942 McCarten was granted a trainer's licence by the A.J.C. From 1946 Neville Sellwood [q.v.] was his leading jockey. Among the most successful horses McCarten trained were (Sir) Adolph Basser's [q.v.13] Delta, (Sir) Frank Packer's [q.v.] Columnist, S. T. Wootton's Todman and Noholme, and Knave, owned by T. C. Lowry from New Zealand. As a trainer, McCarten won the 1947 Caulfield Cup with Columnist and the 1951 Melbourne Cup with Delta; he also won many of the A.J.C.'s and Victoria Racing Club's classic and weight-for-age races. The freak sprinter, Todman, won the Sydney Turf Club's inaugural Golden Slipper Stakes by eight lengths in 1957 and the tough mare, Wenona Girl, collected the Sires' Produce Stakes in Sydney and Melbourne and the A.J.C. Oaks in 1960. McCarten won the Sydney trainers' premiership four times in succession between 1948-49 and 1951-52, and finished second to T. J. Smith ten times.

His fortunes declined from the mid-1960s. The State government resumed his stables for a (still unconstructed) section of the eastern suburbs railway. Many of his racecourse friends were dead and his clients abandoned him in favour of large-scale establishments. By 1971 McCarten had only two poorly performed horses in his stables. Survived by his wife, daughter and son, he died of cancer on 10 June 1971 at his Randwick home and was buried in Botany cemetery. He was a master horseman, capable—both as a jockey and trainer—of getting the best out of his charges. Despite his outstanding skills, exemplary character and likeable disposition, his later career indicates the fickle nature of the racing fraternity.

N. Penton, *A Racing Heart* (Syd, 1987); J. Pollard, *Australian Horse Racing* (Syd, 1988); M. Painter and R. Waterhouse, *The Principal Club* (Syd, 1992); *Aust Jockey Club Racing Calendar*, Feb 1989, p 9; *SMH*, 31 July 1939, 2, 4 May 1942, 20 Feb, 18 Sept 1949, 11 June 1971; *Smith's Weekly* (Syd), 27 July 1946; *Sun-Herald* (Syd), 18 Apr 1982.
RICHARD WATERHOUSE

McCARTHY, BERNARD DENNIS (1900-1977), sailor, was born on 3 July 1900 at Woodstock, near Cape Town, South Africa, son of Harry McCarthy, building contractor, and his wife Grace Raymond. Educated at the Salesian Institute, Cape Town, Bernard became an accomplished organist. In 1918 he sailed to Britain and on his eighteenth birthday enlisted in the Royal Navy as a boy, 2nd class; he was then 5 ft 4½ ins (164 cm) tall, with cherubic features, fair hair and blue-grey eyes. In March 1919 he was posted to H.M.S. *Malaya*. He came to Australia in 1920 as a member of the crew of H.M.S. *Stalwart*, one of six destroyers given to the Royal Australian Navy.

On 9 May 1921 McCarthy transferred to the R.A.N. He served five of the next eight years at sea, with breaks in 1922, 1925 and 1926-28 at Flinders Naval Depot, Western-port, Victoria, and was promoted (1926) petty officer. Discharged on 21 August 1929, he found work with the Catholic Church Property Insurance Co. of Australasia Ltd and rose to district manager. By 1938 he was an in-surance inspector. On 11 June that year at Geelong he married 20-year-old Ellen Splatt (d.1968) in a civil ceremony. Having enrolled (1935) in the Royal Australian Fleet Reserve, he was mobilized in H.M.A.S. *Australia* when World War II broke out.

Sent to Britain, in November 1940 McCarthy was among the commissioning crew of the destroyer, H.M.A.S. *Napier*. The ship sailed to the Mediterranean in May 1941. During the battle of Crete, which began that month, she evacuated troops to Alexandria, Egypt, and fought off repeated air-attacks *en route*. As chief quartermaster, McCarthy 'took charge of the wheel-house on each occasion of the ship being bombed'; he dis-played 'great coolness' and skill in responding to numerous wheel-orders and steering 'the ship clear of destruction'; his actions won him the Distinguished Service Medal. In Septem-ber he was again posted to Flinders Naval Depot. Joining (March 1942) H.M.A.S. *Arunta*, whose first lieutenant (Rear Admiral) G. J. B. Crabb found him 'most reliable and trustworthy', McCarthy was promoted (July) acting chief petty officer. For meritorious service during the Leyte Gulf operations in the Philippines in October 1944, he was awarded a Bar to his D.S.M.

McCarthy was promoted temporary commissioned boatswain in May 1945 and was posted successively to the *Australia, Shropshire, Kanimbla* and *Sydney*. In 1950-51 he was attached to H.M.A.S. *Commonwealth*, the R.A.N.'s base in Japan, where he operated small craft and transported supplies to Korea. After returning to Australia, he served mostly at sea. A dapper figure and quite 'English' in his attitudes and bearing, he took a close interest in the younger sailors who served with him. On 30 June 1956 he left the navy; in the following year he was promoted sub lieutenant on the Retired List. He worked as a senior messenger with the Bank of Adelaide and sold his medals to a private collector. Survived by his son and daughter, he died on 27 February 1977 at the Repatriation General Hospital, Daw Park, and was buried in Centennial Park cemetery with Catholic rites.

M. Fogarty, 'Bernard Dennis McCarthy, DSM and Bar, RAN', *Sabretache*, 27, no 3, July-Sept 1986, p 33; *SMH*, 21 July 1951; PR 87/122 (AWM); cor-respondence from Rear Admiral G. J. B. Crabb *and* Mr B. McCarthy (held by author, Weston, Canb).

MIKE FOGARTY

McCARTHY, SIR EDWIN (1896-1980), public servant, was born on 30 March 1896 at Walhalla, Victoria, son of Australian-born parents Daniel McCarthy, miner, and his wife Catherine, née Kennedy. Educated at Chris-tian Brothers' College, South Melbourne, Edwin left at the age of 15 and joined the Postmaster-General's Department as a tele-graph messenger. In 1913 he moved to the Auditor-General's Office. Fourteen years later he transferred to the Department of Markets and Migration (later the Department of Com-merce, then Commerce and Agriculture) where he worked as accountant (1927-33) and senior clerk (1933-35). Meanwhile, he studied part time at the University of Melbourne (B.Com., 1932). As assistant-secretary (mar-keting) from 1935, he accompanied Prime Minister Joseph Lyons [q.v.10] on his visit to Britain that year, and again in 1937 to attend the Imperial Conference.

At St Joseph's Catholic Church, Neutral Bay, Sydney, on 4 July 1939 McCarthy mar-ried Marjorie Mary Graham, a 28-year-old nurse. After World War II broke out, he served on the Overseas Shipping Committee and travelled to England on government busi-ness. From 1941 to 1944 he was Australia's shipping representative in Washington, where he also liaised with the American authorities on other commercial subjects.

Returning to Australia, McCarthy was appointed (1945) secretary of the Depart-ment of Commerce and Agriculture and Commonwealth controller-general of food. In 1948 he helped to formulate the wheat price-stabilization scheme. Involved that year in drawing up the Havana Charter for an Inter-national Trade Organization, he was 'a fore-most exponent of the case for international commodity agreements' at gatherings of Commonwealth prime ministers and at meetings under the General Agreement on Tariffs and Trade. In July 1949 he became vice-chairman of the International Wheat Council; he was to be its chairman in 1959-60.

McCarthy was sent to London in 1949 as Australia's deputy high commissioner. In 1952 he was appointed C.B.E. In 1955 he was knighted. He was acting high commissioner when President Gamal Abd-al-Nasser nationalized the Suez Canal on 26 July 1956. With other Commonwealth representatives, McCarthy was briefed by the British prime minister Sir Anthony Eden (Earl of Avon) and senior ministers. Although it was later claimed that the high commissioners were treated with less than full candour by Eden and his ministers, McCarthy sent cables home warning that the British might use force to regain the canal. Within fourteen weeks his prediction was fulfilled.

In 1957-61 McCarthy chaired the United Nations committee that dealt with international commodity arrangements. Australian ambassador to the Netherlands in 1958-62, he was also head of the new Australian mission to Belgium in 1959-62. In addition, he was Australia's first ambassador (1960-64) to the European Economic Community, an appointment which reflected his knowledge and understanding of his country's trading interests in Europe. During this period he confronted such major issues as Britain's application to join the E.E.C. and the Netherlands' dispute with Indonesia over West New Guinea (Irian Jaya).

Sir Edwin retired from the Commonwealth Public Service on 30 March 1961. At the request of the Federal government he continued to serve in his diplomatic posts in Brussels and The Hague. In 1962 he was appointed head of the Australian Permanent Mission to the European Atomic Energy Community; based in Brussels, he held this post until 17 March 1964. Sir Garfield Barwick, the minister for external affairs, praised his 'long, distinguished and valuable career of dedicated public service' and specifically mentioned his work in the field of international commodity agreements. McCarthy chaired (1964-67) the Commonwealth Economic Committee in London and remained in that city until the mid-1970s when he settled at Double Bay, Sydney.

As one of Australia's senior trade officials from the mid-1930s to the 1960s, McCarthy was a persistent, fair and good-humoured negotiator. He exerted considerable influence 'in the early debates on the importance of commodity price stabilisation to developing countries'. Throughout his career 'he firmly believed in the right and duty of a public servant to give his minister the best advice on policy he could offer'. His staff looked up to him; his colleagues regarded him as wise and experienced. Modest and unassuming, he was a friendly, courteous and dignified man of considerable presence. Survived by his wife, son and daughter, he died on 4 September 1980 at Woden Valley Hospital, Canberra, and was buried in Gungahlin cemetery. His son John joined the Department of Foreign Affairs.

W. J. Hudson, *Blind Loyalty* (Melb, 1989); *Canb Times*, 5 Sept 1980; *SMH*, 6, 10 Sept 1980; Dept of Foreign Affairs and Trade (Canb), personnel records; Sir Garfield Barwick, Press Release, 16 Mar 1964 (copy on ADB file); information from Mr P. Flood and Mr J. McCarthy, Dept of Foreign Affairs and Trade, Canb.   DAVID I. SMITH

McCARTHY, JOHN KEITH (1905-1976), government officer, soldier and writer, was born on 20 January 1905 at St Kilda, Melbourne, son of Thomas McCarthy, a warehouseman from Galway, Ireland, and his Victorian-born wife Mary Genevieve, née Gibbs. After completing his Leaving certificate at Christian Brothers' College, St Kilda, Keith went jackerooing in New South Wales, worked at Mark Foys [qq.v.4,8] Ltd in Melbourne, and cut cane in North Queensland.

In 1927 McCarthy sailed for the Mandated Territory of New Guinea. Strongly built, 5 ft 11 ins (180 cm) tall, with wavy fair-to-reddish hair, he had found a government position that matched his natural curiosity, energy and humanity. He was introduced to the work of the Department of Native Affairs at Kokopo, near Rabaul, then travelled alone to a new station at Malutu among the Nakanai of central New Britain. In 1929 he was one of five who completed a short course at the University of Sydney in subjects thought relevant to native affairs.

Posted in 1930 to the Sepik district, McCarthy served at Ambunti and Marienberg. While extending control both north and south of the river, he had his first experience of police under his command shooting and killing a villager. When he was transferred to Kavieng on New Ireland, he antagonized the planters by encouraging villagers to make their own copra, and he was shifted again. Briefly at Salamaua, McCarthy went to Kainantu in 1932 for an encounter with eastern highlanders and was then asked to lead a major patrol through the Kukukuku territory west of the Bulolo goldfields. By Anzac Day 1933 McCarthy's men had walked 240 miles (385 km) in two and a half months, and had almost reached Otibanda when they were ambushed: seven Kukukukus were killed, a number of New Guinean police were wounded (one mortally), and McCarthy was struck by arrows in the thigh and stomach. He subsequently developed a station at Menyamya, but the government closed it to reduce expenditure, and the value of much tough pioneer patrolling was lost.

McCarthy spent his leave working his way to and from South Africa in a cargo ship. Back in the Territory, he held a short posting on the Madang coast and returned in 1935 to the Sepik as assistant district officer at Aitape. He accompanied the administrator (Sir) Walter McNicoll [q.v.10] up the Sepik beyond the Dutch border, patrolled across the Torricelli Mountains, and led the government's response when an earthquake killed more than one hundred people and destroyed gardens and houses. On leave in Victoria, McCarthy married with Anglican rites Jean Letitia Beilby on 30 April 1937 at All Saints Church, East St Kilda. They arrived in Rabaul a week before the volcanic eruptions of 29 and 30 May in which nearly 450 people died.

Taking a series of postings on Bougainville and New Britain, McCarthy was at Talasea when the Japanese invaded Rabaul in January 1942. Jean had been evacuated with other White women and children, and Keith made a dangerous journey into the Japanese-influenced area to radio the first report of the fate of Rabaul. Assisted by a few planters, missionaries and other government officers, he directed some two hundred survivors south and west by foot, canoe and small boat; they boarded the *Lakatoi*, which arrived at Cairns, Queensland, on 28 March. For his 'bravery and enterprise' he was to be appointed M.B.E. (1943).

On 12 February 1942 McCarthy enlisted in the Militia; in July he was appointed captain (temporary major 1943), Australian Imperial Force. He returned to the Territory in September, served with the Australian New Guinea Administrative Unit, and fought behind enemy lines with the Allied Intelligence Bureau's 'M' and 'Z' Special Units. Commanding an A.N.G.A.U. and native police detachment, he landed on Los Negros and Manus islands with a squadron of the 5th United States Cavalry Regiment in February 1944 and was included in the award of a Presidential Unit Citation for the action. In 1946 he was seconded to the British Borneo Civil Affairs Unit as lieutenant colonel and was military resident commissioner in Sarawak before transferring to the Reserve of Officers on 11 December.

As district officer at Madang from 1947, McCarthy oversaw war-damage reconstruction and attempted to redirect cult movements. Two years later he was appointed to the new rank of district commissioner, at Rabaul. In 1955 he went to Port Moresby as executive-officer in the Department of the Administrator and in 1960 became director of Native Affairs (District Administration from 1964). A member (from 1951) of the Legislative Council, he entered the first elected House of Assembly in 1964 as one of the most experienced official members and served as deputy-speaker until 1968. He had represented Papua and New Guinea on delegations to other countries and acted (1957) as administrator of Nauru. His memoir, *Patrol into Yesterday*, was published in Melbourne in 1963. He was appointed C.B.E. in 1965.

Following his retirement from the administration in 1967, McCarthy unsuccessfully contested the seat of Port Moresby in the 1968 elections. Three years later he and Jean left Papua New Guinea for Mount Eliza, Victoria. Survived by his wife, he died on 29 October 1976 at Frankston and was cremated with Catholic rites. A memorial to 'Makarti' stands at Rabaul, a tribute from those he saved in 1942.

Volatile, but always generous and witty, McCarthy was one of the most forward-looking and perceptive of Australian officials. His own cartooning and painting made him an appreciative collector of Melanesian art, and his capacity for story-telling translated into an engaging prose. He was one of the few officials who made the difficult transition from the adventure of exploratory patrols, to departmental head, to the willing devolution of power.

A. L. Epstein et al (eds), *Politics of Dependence* (Canb, 1971); *PIM*, Dec 1976, pp 5, 69; J. K. McCarthy papers (NL); Evacuation Scheme, AWM 54, 607/8/1 (AWM); information from Mrs J. McCarthy, Mount Eliza, Vic.   H. N. NELSON

McCARTHY, MARY AGNES (1903-1978), nurse, policewoman and welfare officer, was born on 8 March 1903 at Sevenhill, near Clare, South Australia, seventh of ten children of native-born parents Charles James McCarthy, gardener, and his wife Elizabeth, née Shinnick. Mary was educated at St Dominic's Priory College, North Adelaide, and from 1913 at St Mary's College, Adelaide. She qualified as a nurse at the Broken Hill District Hospital in 1923 and was registered in Adelaide from 1924 to September 1929. Influenced by Kate Cocks [q.v.8], McCarthy joined the Police Department on 9 December 1929 and became the twelfth person to enter the Women Police branch as a constable. Apart from a few months at country stations, she remained in Adelaide until her retirement in 1963. It was usually her calm voice that was heard when the branch was telephoned. Her duties included being on call at all hours, taking statements from female witnesses, searching prisoners and escorting them to court, patrolling the streets and beaches, taking charge of wayward girls and, in extreme cases, making an arrest.

She was awarded two honourable mentions for her 'zeal, acumen and intelligence' which led to the conviction of an abortionist for manslaughter (1935), and which was displayed in her investigation of cases of conspiracy and attempted abortion (1938). McCarthy had joined the police force because of her concern for people. Her experiences led her to remark: 'We see life in the raw. We meet with the sordid and at times stark evil. I think you need a spiritual background to give you balance. And when you meet a man, however sodden with drink or with vice he may be, you must remember he has all the dignity of a human being'. Stories abounded of the way she helped children. In one instance Constable McCarthy was made the legal guardian of a neglected girl. To comply with the regulations for women police, she learned ju-jitsu and was issued with a Browning pistol, but never had to use either.

The activities of policewomen were in some respects similar to those of later social workers. In 1960 McCarthy and five female colleagues served as welfare officers of the Supreme Court of South Australia. Following her retirement from the force, she was appointed (1964) to the staff of the court as its first part-time welfare officer. For the next decade she assisted judges and the master in cases involving the well-being, custody and guardianship of children of divorced or separated parents.

Tall, slim and elegantly dressed (South Australian policewomen did not wear uniforms until 1974), McCarthy had blue eyes, soft features and a warm smile. While compassionate, she was also determined. She was a devout Catholic and gave freely of the little money she had to those in want, but she shunned publicity. Theatre, music, ballet and reading were her interests. Her last years were spent at Flora McDonald Lodge, Cowandilla. She died there on 3 April 1978. A police escort attended her burial in Centennial Park cemetery.

SA Police Gazette, 22 May 1935, 18 May 1938; *Advertiser* (Adel), 29 June 1934, 7 Aug 1964; *News* (Adel), 6 May 1963; Nurses' Bd of SA, Register of Nurses, Mental Nurses and Midwives, 1928 (SRSA); information from Dame Roma Mitchell, Adel, and Mr J. D. Ormond, Nth Adel.   JOYCE GIBBERD

McCAUGHEY, SAMUEL (1892-1955) and SIR DAVID ROY (1898-1971), graziers, were born on 27 November 1892 and 2 October 1898 at Coree station, Jerilderie, New South Wales, third and fourth children of David McCaughey (d.1899), a grazier from Ireland, and his native-born wife Lucilla Louisa Blanche, née Gell. Sir Samuel McCaughey

[q.v.5] was their uncle. Educated at Geelong Church of England Grammar School, Victoria, and at Jesus College, Cambridge, Samuel returned to Coree in 1914. Back in England, he was commissioned in the Royal Field Artillery on 13 September 1915. He served with the 46th Battery, 1st Divisional Artillery, on the Western Front and was promoted lieutenant in 1917. At the Scottish National Church, Chelsea, London, on 3 February that year he married Victorian-born Eleanor Una McKellar; they were to have four daughters and a son.

Home again, in 1919 McCaughey bought the remaining portion (65 000 acres, 26 300 ha) of Coree from his uncle's estate, and purchased the 9000-acre (3650 ha) Tongala estate (originally part of Coree) as a settlement for his wife. Coree merino stud (registered in 1922), based on Haddon Rig blood, and Coree Pastoral Co. Pty Ltd (formed in 1938) became noted for their high quality rams and merino clip. In 1952 Samuel and his brother Roy gave 24 000 acres (9700 ha) of Coree to the nation for pastoral research and training, in memory of Samuel's son and a nephew, both killed in World War II. The McCaughey Memorial Institute was run as a commercial enterprise by a trust administered by Roy, Sir Henry Manning and J. P. Abbott [qq.v.10,13]. Survived by his daughters, Samuel McCaughey died of leukemia on 29 January 1955 at Manly and was cremated with Presbyterian forms.

Like his brother, Roy McCaughey was educated at Geelong Grammar. He sailed for England in April 1917 and served with the Royal Field Artillery. On his return, he bought Coonong from his uncle's estate in 1919 and began improving its Peppin [q.v.5] merino stud, established in 1907. In 1924 he purchased the famous sire Wanganella 9.1 (Ballymena) from the Austins' [q.v.3] Wanganella stud at Deniliquin for a world record price of 5000 guineas. Coonong merinos, noted as heavy wool cutters, were soon sold throughout Australia. They topped the Melbourne wool sales 'for the day' in 1937, 1938 and 1947. Another of McCaughey's ram purchases was Uardry 4.312, for which he paid the top price of $11 550 at Sydney in 1966.

A further profitable venture was the establishment (1925-26) of the Coonong Beef Shorthorn stud at Borambola Park, near Wagga Wagga. Regular infusions of imported blood from Scotland (including a 3600-guinea junior stock bull in 1951) kept his Shorthorns at the pinnacle of the breed in Australia: between 1916 and 1953 Coonong won more Beef Shorthorn championships in Sydney than any other stud, including ten senior championships. At the stud's dispersal sale in 1959, 173 head realized £112 397, the top eight bulls averaging £1375.

On 28 March 1944 at Potts Point, Sydney, Roy McCaughey had married with Presbyterian forms Gwendoline Patricia Camille North-Hunt, née Whelan, a 40-year-old widow. In 1951 he and his wife gave a Commonwealth Jubilee singing scholarship (valued at £500 per year) for study overseas; they were selected to host (at Coonong) an intended visit by H.R.H. Princess Elizabeth and the Duke of Edinburgh. In 1955 Patricia McCaughey published *Samuel McCaughey*, a biography of Sir Samuel.

Roy McCaughey was a director (1928-58) and chairman (from 1950) of the Commonwealth Wool & Produce Co. Ltd. When the firm merged with Elder, Smith [qq.v.4,6] & Co. Ltd in 1958 and Goldsbrough, Mort [qq.v.4,5] & Co. Ltd in 1963, he chaired the New South Wales board until 1970. A director (1959-64) of the Bank of New South Wales and a council-member (from 1962) of the New South Wales Sheepbreeders' Association, he belonged to the Australian and Union clubs (Sydney) and the Melbourne and Australian clubs (Melbourne). With James Ashton [q.v.13] and others, he was a trustee of Sir Samuel's estate. He was appointed C.M.G. in 1956 and knighted in 1963.

Tall, solidly built and hospitable, Sir Roy hated personal publicity. His collection of paintings included works by Sydney Long, Sir Arthur Streeton and Penleigh Boyd [qq.v.10,12,7]. According to an old friend, he 'never had a cross word for anyone, but he wouldn't stand any nonsense. The men at Coonong all thought the world of him'. Survived by his wife, he died on 13 September 1971 at St Vincent's Hospital, Sydney, and was cremated. His estate was sworn for probate at more than $1 million. He bequeathed $500 to each man in his employ.

C. Massy, *The Australian Merino* (Melb, 1990); *Pastoral Review*, 16 Mar, 16 July 1949, 16 Apr, 16 Dec 1953, 16 Feb, 16 July 1955, 17 June 1970, 19 Oct 1971; *People* (Syd), 5 July 1950; *Corian*, June 1972; *SMH*, 29 Aug 1950, 12 Mar, 13 Dec 1951, 4 Apr 1972, 24 June 1995.   G. P. WALSH

McCLEMENS, JOHN HENRY (1905-1975), judge, conservationist and Catholic layman, was born on 7 March 1905 at Chatswood, Sydney, son of Australian-born parents Archibald John McClemens, accountant, and his wife Mary Louisa, née Thompson. Jock was educated at Chatswood Public and North Sydney Boys' High schools, and at the University of Sydney (B.A., 1925; LL.B., 1928); he combined playing Rugby Union football with debating and an interest in public affairs. Having served articles of clerkship (from 1925) with F. C. Petrie, he was admitted as a solicitor of the Supreme Court of New South Wales on 15 March 1929. He transferred to the Bar on 14 March 1930.

Operating from 53 Martin Place, McClemens soon developed an extensive practice in the common law and industrial jurisdictions. In the archbishop's chapel at St Mary's Cathedral, Sydney, on 23 March 1935 he married with Catholic rites Florence Mary Elizabeth Jones; they were to have two children before being divorced in 1945. During World War II McClemens took part in harbour patrols. Particularly effective in difficult jury trials, he was appointed King's Counsel in 1945. He contributed to the *Australian Law Journal*, the *Sydney Law Review* and the *Australian Journal of Criminology*.

A persistent critic of delays in filling judicial vacancies, McClemens was appointed a judge of the Supreme Court on 3 September 1951. He was outspoken on the inadequacies of the accommodation of the courts, on dilatory procedures, and on the high cost of litigation, especially in claims arising from motor-vehicle accidents. As royal commissioner (1961) into allegations of brutality and theft at Callan Park Mental Hospital, he found that acts of cruelty were rare and that the medical superintendent's allegations were exaggerated, but he did recommend a reduction in patient numbers in order to overcome crowding.

Involvement in criminal law, both at the Bar and as a judge, led McClemens to become interested in criminology, the prevention of crime, and the care of released offenders. He was president of the Australian Prison After-Care and of the Australian Crime Prevention councils, a member of the advisory committee of the institute of criminology at the University of Sydney, and a founder of the Australian Institute of Criminology, Canberra. These concerns, as well as the preservation of human rights, the safeguarding of civil liberties and the promotion of law reform, occupied much of his time out of court.

McClemens was an office-bearer (usually president or chairman) in many organizations and government bodies associated with crime prevention and the treatment of discharged offenders. He represented the Australian government at the United Nations seminar on the 'Role of Police in the Protection of Human Rights' (Canberra, 1963) and at the U.N. Congress on the Prevention of Crime and Treatment of Offenders (Stockholm, 1965). In his report to the State government in 1974 on the New South Wales prison system, he concluded that custodial punishment had failed to reform prisoners or to deter them from committing further crimes.

When the Supreme Court Act (1970) came into effect in 1972, McClemens was appointed chief judge at common law, a position he relinquished shortly before he stepped down as a judge on attaining the statutory retiring age on 7 March 1975; at that time he was the longest-serving judge on the Supreme Court. He had come to be held in great affection by his colleagues. In his retirement address McClemens warned against the perils of delinquency and crime, urged the retention of judicial robes, railed for one last time against the inadequacies of court accommodation, and emphasized the need for an incorruptible judiciary. He offered his services as lecturer in support of the fledgling College of Law.

McClemens served as councillor (1959-69) and president (1961-65) of the National Trust of Australia (New South Wales), and also as foundation chairman (1962-69) of the Australian Council of National Trusts. He was an instigator of the *National Trust Register* and made significant contributions to the conservation campaign, both by his presence and his views.

A convert to Catholicism, McClemens proved active and dedicated in support of the Church, though he sometimes clashed with its hierarchy. In his early days on the bench he was known to walk from the old Supreme Court to St Mary's Cathedral to pray for men he had just sentenced to death. He and (Sir) Charles McDonald [q.v.] strove to build a strong Newman Association of Catholic Graduates and to establish a Catholic chaplaincy at the University of Sydney. McClemens was chairman of the Mater Misericordiae Hospital, North Sydney, and of the University Catholic Federation of Australia; he was also president of the St Thomas More Society of Catholic lawyers. In 1960 he was appointed (knight commander) to the Order of St Gregory the Great by Pope John XXIII. Representing three major Catholic lay organizations, McClemens invited Pope Paul VI to Australia and was chairman of the Citizens' Welcome Committee for the 1970 papal visit.

A large and kind-hearted man, McClemens was regarded as an approachable and humane judge, despite his roaring voice and somewhat intimidating manner. He formed a close relationship with Joan Raymunde Delaney, a schoolteacher and secretary of the Newman Association. Following the death of his former wife, he married Joan on 2 February 1967 at the Church of Our Lady of the Sacred Heart, Randwick. The swift and successive deaths of the son and daughter of his first marriage in 1974 devastated him. He died of a ruptured abdominal aortic aneurysm on 3 November 1975 at the Mater hospital and was buried with Catholic rites among his family in the Anglican section of Waverley cemetery. His wife, who had recently retired as headmistress of Petersham Girls' High School, survived him.

McClemens's portrait (1954) by Dora Schipper is held by the Supreme Court; an award in criminology at the department of law, University of Sydney, commemorates him.

I. F. Wyatt, *Ours in Trust* (Syd, 1987); *Aust Law J*, 49, 1975, pp 151, 700; *Aust J of Forensic Sciences*, 9, 1976, p 76; *J of the Aust Catholic Hist Soc*, 7, pt 1, 1981, p 15; *SMH*, 30 Aug, 2 Sept 1951, 13 Apr 1960; Supreme Court of NSW, farewell address 19 Feb 1975 (ts, copy held by ADB); McClemens papers (ML).   RICHARD J. W. d'APICE

McCLURE, LESLIE THOMPSON (1908-1966), pie-maker and caterer, was born on 5 October 1908 at Warrnambool, Victoria, eldest of ten children of Australian-born parents Robert Thompson McClure, labourer, and his wife Frances, née McNeil. Educated intermittently at Gnotuk State School until the age of 13, Les worked for his father before being employed by an uncle at Hamilton. He rose before dawn, helped to milk forty cows, delivered the milk in four-gallon (18 litre) drums strung over the handlebars of his bicycle, milked the cows again in the evening and knocked off at 7 p.m. Four nights a week he played the fiddle in a dance group. His uncle sold out in 1933 and the dairy's new proprietor reduced McClure's wages by ten shillings to £1 a week.

On 21 June that year at St Andrew's Presbyterian Church, Hamilton, McClure married Jessie Alice Emmett, a railwayman's daughter. With borrowed money, he had rented a nearby farm for £80. He gradually increased his milk production to 100 gallons (455 litres) a day, acquired three horses and carts, and opened milk bars at Hamilton and Portland. In February 1939 he disposed of his interests and moved to Bendigo where he established a café named Dad & Dave. A sign that read 'Looky! Looky! See Cookie' encouraged customers to peer through a window and watch the pies being made. As a newcomer, McClure survived price-cutting battles with rival pie-makers and an ice-cream war waged by his competitors. By the end of World War II he owned a string of cafés and milk bars. From 1946 he catered for Bendigo race-meetings, the Melbourne Royal Show and trotting at the showgrounds; from 1952 he did likewise at Flemington Racecourse.

His Four'n Twenty meat pies, initially made at Bendigo in 1947, were produced at the Showgrounds (from 1949) and at a purpose-built factory in Union Road, Ascot Vale (from 1953). After McClure engaged a Czech and two Germans as minority partners in 1951, the pies were so remarkably different from the traditional standard that sales outstripped production facilities. Building extensions doubled the factory's floor-space in 1955 and redoubled it in 1959. In 1956 he had built a machine which produced 1000 dozen pies an hour; by 1960 ninety-eight radio-operated vans delivered his goods. Having ceased smoking cigarettes as a 13-year-old, he took to cigars.

McClure sold his interests in Four'n Twenty Pies Pty Ltd to Peters [q.v.11] Ice Cream (Vic.) Ltd in 1960 for £600 000 and left pie-making to concentrate on public catering. In February 1962 he opened McClure's Restaurant (Come As You Are!) in St Kilda Road. Open eighteen hours a day, it had pop-up toasters on the breakfast bar and a telephone on every table to allow customers to order direct from the kitchen. Above the restaurant was a function room, the Oriana. Big hearted, cheery and down-to-earth, McClure liked to describe himself as 'just a little battler from the bush'. He died suddenly of myocardial infarction on 30 October 1966 at his Toorak home and was cremated; his wife, son and five daughters survived him. McClure's estate was sworn for probate at $157 377.

Bendigo Advertiser, 3 Aug 1938; *Bulletin*, 22 Feb 1964; *Herald* (Melb), 31 Oct 1966; newspaper-cuttings held by and information from Mrs J. Cappelletti, Hughes, Canb; information from Mrs J. McClure, Middle Brighton, Mrs J. Chapman, Brighton East, and Mr K. McClure, Malvern, Melb.
JOHN RITCHIE

McCLURE SMITH, HUGH ALEXANDER (1902-1961), newspaper editor and diplomat, was born on 14 April 1902 at Malvern, Melbourne, second child of William Andrew McClure Smith, Australian-born general manager of the Australian Estates & Mortgage Co. Ltd, and his wife Helen Louise Turnbull, née Walker, who came from Scotland. On leaving Melbourne Church of England Grammar School in 1919, Hugh went abroad to study French and history at the University of Geneva, and to read history at Balliol College, Oxford. At Oxford he shared lodgings—and an interest in foreign affairs and politics—with Cecil Whitehall and (Sir) Warwick Fairfax. McClure Smith was unable to sit his final examinations due to influenza that was to damage his heart. He spent three years confined to bed, passing the time by reading law, and was called (1929) to the Bar at the Inner Temple, London.

In 1928 McClure Smith had joined Price, Waterhouse & Co., accountants. He contributed occasional articles on economic, business and imperial affairs to newspapers, including the *Sydney Morning Herald* which he represented at the 1932 Imperial Economic Conference in Ottawa. Assistant-correspondent (1933-35) in New York and Washington for *The Times*, he joined its staff in London as principal economic leader-writer early in 1936. At St Mary Abbots parish church, Kensington, on 25 January that year he married Margaret Vincent Buddy, a 27-year-old American who was to accompany him to Sydney.

Associate-editor of the *S.M.H.* in 1937, McClure Smith was appointed editor on 1 January 1938. He began controversially by criticizing Neville Chamberlain's policy of appeasement. His unflinching stand on many issues did not necessarily please the newspaper's proprietors or his political friends, among them (Sir) Robert Menzies [q.v.]. McClure Smith had a clear and confident writing style, often quite lyrical, based on wide-ranging knowledge and strong convictions. As editor he was responsible for the leader, for some feature articles and for selecting the letters to the editor. He served as president (1939-44) of the New South Wales Institute of Journalists and belonged to the Australian Institute of International Affairs. Trying to reconcile the conflicting demands of government censorship and the right of the public to be informed made World War II a fraught time for him, as did battles over paper rationing. In 1943 he visited Britain and the United States of America to report on the war effort, and in 1945 represented the *Herald* at the United Nations Conference on International Organization, held at San Francisco.

Hugh and Margaret were avid ballet- and theatre-goers who enjoyed entertaining, particularly over late-night suppers at their Bellevue Hill home. Among their friends were theatre people—the Oliviers (with whom they stayed in England), (Sir) Noël Coward, Danny Kaye and Svetlana Beriosova—and Australian painters—Roland Wakelin, (Sir) William Dobell [qq.v.12,14], (Sir) Russell Drysdale, (Sir) Sidney Nolan, Justin O'Brien and Sali Herman—whose works they collected. Hugh once said, 'I am never happier than going back to the office in my dinner jacket after a rewarding dinner'. He had, however, a tendency for 'buttonholing', to the extent that Fairfax reprimanded him for it. McClure Smith's successor, John Douglas Pringle, described him as 'a rather Anglicised Australian', a 'charming, cultured, intelligent man'. He had a polished, well-groomed appearance, and a slight stutter. In Sydney he belonged to the Union Club, in London to the Athenaeum and the Junior Carlton clubs. Later friends included (Sir) Anthony Eden (Earl of Avon), Lady Diana Cooper, Robert Morley and (Sir) Peter Ustinov.

Advised to work shorter hours to safeguard his health, McClure Smith planned to retire from the *S.M.H.* on 31 December 1952. Fairfax and Rupert Henderson disagreed with him over the newspaper's stand on the Federal government's proposed banking legislation and in November he was asked to leave early. According to Gavin Souter, he had been the *Herald*'s best editor in the twentieth century. The reasons behind his retirement, and the issue of his fitness for work, were questioned in the House of Representatives in February 1953 after he was named Australian minister in Cairo. R. G. (Baron) Casey [q.v.13], minister for external affairs, maintained that McClure Smith was not ill (as the press had reported), and defended the appointment of an outsider on the grounds of a shortage of trained departmental staff. McClure Smith's long-standing interest in international affairs stood him in good stead. In April 1953 he embarked for Egypt. By the time he arrived, King Farouk had abdicated. It was a complex period politically. General Mohammed Naguib's Republic of Egypt was established in 1953 and fell in 1954. In Cairo McClure Smith often worked from home, calling the legation staff to him and keeping them working late into the night. He helped to arrange the departure of British troops from Suez following the fighting over the canal.

In 1955 McClure Smith was appointed ambassador to the Netherlands. He also led the Australian delegation at the tenth session of the United Nations General Assembly in New York later that year. While in The Hague he travelled extensively, learning as much as possible about the Dutch. Queen Elizabeth II appointed him C.V.O. on her royal tour of Holland in 1958. He reported on Indonesian-Dutch relations, the 1956 election, the crisis over Queen Juliana and her court allegedly falling under the influence of a faith-healer, and a new Netherlands-Australian migration agreement (1956). In February 1959 he was appointed ambassador to Italy. The 1960 Olympic Games were held in Rome, focusing international attention on that city, and he found himself busier with his representative duties than in his previous posts.

In September 1961 McClure Smith announced that he would retire at the end of November. Survived by his wife and daughter, he died of a heart attack on 8 October that year at Florence and was buried with full military honours in the Protestant cemetery, Rome, not far from the grave of John Keats. His estate was sworn for probate at £160 971. In 1963 Margaret McClure Smith presented a painting by Drysdale to the Art Gallery of New South Wales in her husband's memory. A bronze bust of McClure Smith by an Italian sculptor is held by the family.

J. D. Pringle, *Have Pen* (Lond, 1973); D. McNicoll, *Luck's a Fortune* (Syd, 1979); G. Souter, *Company of Heralds* (Melb, 1981); *SMH*, 12 Aug 1939, 25, 26 Feb 1953, 20 June 1960, supp, 30 Sept, 10, 11 Oct 1961, 1 Feb 1963, 14 Apr 1981, supp; *The Times*, 10 Oct 1961; A1838/1 1500/2/2/7, A1838/265 1500/2/15/3 and 20/4 (AA, Canb); bib of McClure Smith's articles on ADB file, Canb; information from Mrs K. Coventry, Porto Ercole, Italy.

JENNY NEWELL

McCONACHY, NORMAN GILBERT (1914-1976), prospector, was born on 25 April 1914 at Longreach, Queensland, eldest of three sons of Australian-born parents Norman Charles McConachy, drover, and his wife Annie May, née Gilbert. Educated at the local state school, he began work as a clerk. In the mid-1920s his father took over as manager of Buckingham Downs, a sheep-station 96 miles (154 km) south of Mount Isa; about ten years later he moved 46 miles (74 km) north to Ashover station, a property which was to remain in the family. Young Norman became a pastoral worker.

On 20 August 1938 at the Presbyterian Church, Mount Isa, McConachy married Mary Kathleen Brown. The couple ran a café at Longreach until the mid-1940s, then shifted to Mount Isa. Norman was employed by Mount Isa Mines Ltd as an underground timberman. His wife died of meningitis in June 1954, leaving a young family. Increasingly absorbed in prospecting for minerals, McConachy bought a Geiger counter. His brother-in-law and two other men joined him in forming a syndicate with Clem Walton (a taxi driver) and his three partners. In July McConachy's party met with spectacular success when they discovered a huge uranium deposit 35 miles (56 km) east of Mount Isa. They quickly pegged the area.

Lacking sufficient capital to develop a mine, the syndicate offered the site for sale as the Mary Kathleen uranium field. By late July 1954 Australasian Oil Exploration Ltd had tendered £250 000 (plus a royalty on all the ore extracted), until then the highest price paid for an untested Australian mine. A British mining company, Rio Tinto Co. Ltd, acquired a controlling interest and took responsibility —through its Australian subsidiary—for managing the project. The open-cut Mary Kathleen mine, complete with a model company town which housed up to 1200 workers and their families, began production in 1958 and contributed to an Australian mining boom.

McConachy's initial share of the purchase price allowed him to place his children in boarding-schools and to buy a hotel at Townsville. Some years later he retired to live there. A stocky, clean-shaven man of less than middle height, he had been a keen amateur boxer in his youth. Although he never enjoyed another successful 'find', his careful husbanding of the Mary Kathleen windfall ensured his prosperity. Unlike many prospectors, he abhorred gambling and other financial 'waste'. The only indulgences he allowed himself were a trip around the world in his retirement and an annual visit to Ashover station. He died of cancer on 3 March 1976 in Brisbane and was buried beside his wife in Mount Isa cemetery. Two of his three daughters survived him; his son Malcolm had been killed (1969) in the Vietnam War at the age of 21. McConachy's estate was sworn for probate at $342 597.

Mount Isa City Council, *Discover Mount Isa* (Mount Isa, Qld, nd, 1944?); G. Blainey, *Mines in the Spinifex* (Syd, 1960); C. Hooper, *Angor to Zillmanton* (Brisb, 1993); *Morning Bulletin*, 23, 28 July 1954; *Courier-Mail*, 5 Mar 1976; information from Mrs N. McConachy, Mount Isa, Qld.

DIANE MENGHETTI

MCCONNAN, SIR LESLIE JAMES (1887-1954), banker, was born on 15 June 1887 at the Manse, Benalla, Victoria, second son of Rev. Alexander Candlish McConnan, a Presbyterian minister from London, and his South Australian-born wife Harriet-Jane, née Don. On completing his schooling at North Eastern College, Leslie joined the local branch of the National Bank of Australasia in June 1904. He worked as a clerk at Birchip (1905-07), Hamilton (1907-09) and Melbourne before being promoted accountant (1910) at Corowa, New South Wales, and inspecting accountant (1912).

Moving to Sydney, McConnan held various responsible positions in city branches, becoming sub-manager of the George Street branch in 1920. At St Stephen's Presbyterian Church, Sydney, on 10 January 1921 he married Scottish-born Gladys Anne Hay. In 1923 he was appointed manager for South Australia. He acted as temporary manager (1928-29) of the London office, then resumed his post in Adelaide. By August 1930 he was back in Sydney as manager for New South Wales. Assistant chief manager at head office, Melbourne, from December 1934, he succeeded (Sir) Ernest Wreford [q.v.12] as chief manager on 1 May 1935.

McConnan's polished performance as a witness before the royal commission into the monetary and banking systems in February 1936 impressed the commissioners. Not surprisingly, he argued strongly that the existing relationship between the Commonwealth Bank of Australia and the trading banks—based on voluntary co-operation—provided the fledgling central bank with all the powers it required, and that legislation to give the Commonwealth Bank wider authority was both unnecessary and unworkable. He foresaw many of the practical problems that would arise from trading banks being required to hold uniform proportions of their deposits with the Commonwealth Bank. His stewardship of the National Bank was competent rather than remarkable. He lacked the outstanding technical banking skills of his predecessor, but was better liked by the staff. Due to the depressed 1930s and wartime regulations, the performance of the National was undistinguished in terms of its return on shareholder equity and its asset growth. The National's most conspicuous success was its acquisition of the Queensland National Bank in 1947 when McConnan out-manoeuvred another eager bidder.

By 1941 McConnan belonged to the Savage, Australian and Melbourne clubs, the Union Club (Sydney) and the Adelaide Club, as well as to the Royal Melbourne and Royal Sydney golf clubs. In close touch with many individuals who were to reshape conservative politics, he was deeply opposed to the 'socialist' policies of the Australian Labor Party in general, and to its proposals regarding banking in particular. He was a foundation (1942) council-member of the Institute of Public Affairs, Victoria, a connexion which brought him into contact with a wider group of businessmen. In these councils McConnan was the practical man of action with shrewd political sense rather than a political philosopher. His wider purpose was to bring about the defeat of the Labor government, and so end what he perceived as its threat to free enterprise. A range of powerful commercial interests were represented on the National Bank's board: its directors included H. G. Darling and (Sir) George Coles [qq.v.8, 13]—both foundation councillors of the I.P.A.—and Sir Frank Clarke [q.v.8], who were willing to allow their chief executive to play an overtly political role. Moreover, McConnan met regularly with (Sir) Ian Potter, the prominent stockbroker, and (Sir) Robert Menzies [q.v.].

Once the government's plans to continue the substance of its wartime banking controls into the peace became known in late 1944, it was McConnan who took the offensive. He was dismissive of his fellow-bankers who avoided a head-on confrontation. In contrast, he played directly on the fears of the banks' employees and customers about the loss of their jobs and freedom. His campaign included direct mail to customers and a series of radio broadcasts. McConnan mobilized the banking community at large, drawing on the private banks' 22 000 staff, 80 000 shareholders and 1.25 million customers as a single-issue political faction within the new Liberal Party. The Associated Banks of Victoria, of which McConnan was president (1938-39, 1942-44 and 1947-49), provided the administrative support for a co-ordinated nationwide campaign against the government, while the individual banks were generous in providing personnel and funds. McConnan revelled in the fight, particularly after the Chifley [q.v.13] government introduced legislation to nationalize the trading banks in 1947. He was absent from his desk for months at a time, travelling to lobby and organize, to galvanize his loyal troops of bank-workers, and to make public appearances.

With the defeat of the government in 1949, McConnan returned to his banking duties. A grateful board asked him to remain another three years beyond the usual retirement age. McConnan, however, had no grand plans for the bank, now free of the threat of nationalization, but still shackled by the Banking Act of 1945. The form of central banking that McConnan had argued against in 1936 had come to pass. It fell to another generation of bankers to negotiate peace with the regulators.

Knighted in 1951, McConnan eventually retired on 31 July 1952. He became a director of several companies, including the Colonial Mutual Life Assurance Society, and some investment firms associated with Potter. Sir Leslie was also a member of the central executive of the Victorian division of the Australian Red Cross Society, and of the finance and management committees of Royal Melbourne Hospital; in addition, he was a trustee of the Royal Society of Victoria, a councillor of Geelong College, Melbourne Scots club and the Australian-American Association, and president of Banks Rowing Club. His business and private worlds intersected in city clubs and on the golf links, and through his work for numerous charities. He regretted his lack of formal education, but its absence did not prevent him becoming one of the most influential men of his generation. Of middle height and medium build, he had expressive dark brown eyes, 'kindly and smiling when in a good humour, penetrating and questioning when not'. Following complications arising from a fall, he died on 22 December 1954 in the Alfred Hospital and was cremated; his wife and daughter survived him. His estate was sworn for probate at £18 843. (Sir) William Dargie's portrait of McConnan is held by the National Australia Bank, Melbourne.

A. L. May, *The Battle for the Banks* (Syd, 1958); G. Blainey, *Gold and Paper* (Melb, 1958); C. D. Kemp, *Big Businessman* (Melb, 1964); D. T. Merrett, *ANZ Bank* (Syd, 1985); C. B. Schedvin, *In Reserve* (Syd, 1992); *A'sian Insurance and Banking Record*, Feb 1945, May 1952; information from the National Aust Bank Group Archives, Springvale, Melb.

D. T. MERRETT

McCONNEL, URSULA HOPE (1888-1957), anthropologist, was born on 27 October 1888 at Cressbrook, near Toogoolawah, Queensland, fifth daughter and eighth of ten children of James Henry McConnel, grazier and farmer, and his wife Mary Elizabeth, née Kent, both Queensland born. David Cannon McConnel [q.v.5] was her grandfather. Raised at Cressbrook (the family property and Shorthorn stud), Ursula was educated at the Brisbane High School for Girls and later at New England Girls' School, Armidale, New South Wales, where she took prizes in singing and languages. From 1905 to 1907 she attended courses in history, politics, literature and music at the women's department, King's College, London. Although once engaged, she never married, and pursued a career with vigour and dedication.

In her early years McConnel's academic interests varied. At the University of Queensland (B.A. Hons, 1918; M.A., 1931) she graduated with first-class honours in philosophy and also studied psychology in her brother-in-law Elton Mayo's [q.v.10] department. In 1923 she began a doctorate in anthropology at University College, London, where she came under the influence of (Sir) Grafton Elliot Smith [q.v.11] and William Perry. Loneliness and stress brought on an illness and she returned to Australia in 1926 without finishing her thesis.

Supervised by Professor A. R. Radcliffe-Brown [q.v.11] at the University of Sydney, McConnel began ethnographic research in 1927 among the Wik-Mungkana people on Cape York Peninsula. She visited far North Queensland on 'four or five' field-trips, the last in 1934. Australian Aboriginal culture was to be the focus of the bulk of her scholarship; she published numerous articles in *Oceania* and a book, *Myths of the Munkan* (Melbourne, 1957). The early 1930s proved the most productive years of her anthropological career, but it was also a period filled with disappointment. Although she received a Rockefeller fellowship (1931-33) to study under Edward Sapir at Yale University, Connecticut, United States of America, McConnel was bitterly frustrated that she failed to be awarded a Ph.D. from University College, London, on the basis of her publications. Moreover, she resented being passed over for academic appointments in Australia.

Financially secure from her investments in wool bonds, McConnel retired to Cressbrook in the mid-1930s. Early in the following decade she moved to Eagle Heights, south of Brisbane, where she continued to examine and document her field-notes and ethnographic collections. She died of a cerebral haemorrhage on 6 November 1957 at Hillcrest Private Hospital, Kelvin Grove, and was cremated with Anglican rites. Her ashes were buried at Cressbrook. The importance of McConnel's scholarly contribution was recognized after her death. With those of Donald Thomson [q.v.], her publications form the foundations of present-day anthropological research on western Cape York Peninsula. She had devoted much of her life to this endeavour, driven by a sense of duty and justice towards the Aborigines with whom she had worked.

J. Marcus (ed), *First in Their Field* (Melb, 1993); A. O'Gorman, Ursula McConnel: the archaeology of an anthropologist (B.A. Hons thesis, ANU, 1989).

ANNE O'GORMAN PERUSCO

McCONNELL, JOHN VERRAN (1911-1971), Liberal Party official, was born on 23 October 1911 at Footscray, Melbourne, son of Victorian-born parents Herbert John McConnell, machinist, and his wife Ethel Lois, née Martin. After a Methodist upbringing and attendance at various state schools, John enrolled at Stott's Business College and then at the University of Queensland. He joined G. J. Coles [q.v.13] & Co. Ltd as an accountant in 1933.

At Wesley Chapel, Melbourne, on 19 January 1939 McConnell married Gwendolyn Ruth Hewett. On 15 July 1940 he enlisted in the Australian Imperial Force. He was commissioned lieutenant (1941), and served in New Guinea (1943-44) and New Britain (1945) with the 14th-32nd Battalion. Demobilized on Friday 10 August 1945, the former Young Nationalist began work on the following Monday as general secretary of the Victorian division of the new Liberal Party of Australia, a post he held until his death.

McConnell's shrewdness, knowledge of voting patterns, and detailed planning helped the Victorian Liberals to exploit the Labor split of 1954-55, thus launching twenty-seven years of State rule. His post-election analyses —measured and comprehensive—became the architect's drawings for the next Federal or State campaign as 'Mac' committed himself to the 'continuous campaigning' which became the Liberal byword from 1957-58. His was the sharpest mind on the federal staff planning committee; his assessments were invariably incorporated in the advice forwarded by the officials to the federal executive; and (Sir) Robert Menzies [q.v.] as well as (Sir) Henry Bolte, the Victorian premier, relied heavily on his counsel.

Ever the professional, in September 1959 McConnell undertook a study tour of Britain, Europe and the United States of America, returning with fresh ideas on organization and the use of television. Better at identifying problems than implementing solutions, McConnell was ahead of his time in developing strategies for marginal and rural seats,

and in using in-house polling to gauge voter preferences and formulate policies. He saw, before anyone else in Victoria, that the Liberals would soon be threatened electorally in the outer Melbourne suburbs where they had been so dominant in the 1950s.

Of middle height, grey and plain-featured, with a clipped moustache, Mac was seemingly self-contained, but his immediate associates were devoted to him, respecting both his integrity and political cunning. He was fond of a drink, and was once warned by a State party president against imbibing during office hours. Although children arrived late, he became a dedicated family man who enjoyed golfing, reading and visiting art galleries.

McConnell served on the Eltham Shire Council for eight years and was president in 1967-69; he was also a justice of the peace and president of the Eltham sub-branch of the Returned Services League of Australia. In 1969 he was appointed O.B.E. He stood twice —unsuccessfully—for Liberal pre-selection: in 1953 for the State seat of Malvern and in 1968 for the Senate vacancy caused by (Sir) John Gorton's move to the Lower House. The second rejection hurt. His friends on the State executive were expected to nominate their faithful and hard-working servant. Despite his disappointment, he remained steadfast while becoming slightly less guarded.

On 12 August 1971 McConnell collapsed at Princes Bridge railway station and died of myocardial fibrosis. Survived by his wife and three sons, he was cremated with Anglican rites. His estate was sworn for probate at $82 777.

P. Aimer, *Politics, Power and Persuasion* (Syd, 1974); *Age* (Melb), 14 Aug 1945, 16 Feb 1968, 14 Aug 1971; Liberal Party of Aust papers (NL and Univ Melb Archives); information from Sir John Anderson, Brighton, Prof G. Davison, Camberwell, and the late Sir Robert Southey.

I. R. HANCOCK

McCONNELL, WILLIAM (1906-1970), boxing-trainer, was born on 18 August 1906 at Paddington, Sydney, son of native-born parents William Daniel McConnell, dealer, and his wife Ruby St Clair, née Hall. After minimal education, Bill married his childhood sweetheart Millicent Miller (d.1959) on 28 June 1923 at St Francis's Catholic Church, Haymarket; he was aged 16 and she was a year older. They had three children by the time he was 20 and lived in a single room. He was employed in a brass foundry and she had worked as a chocolate-packer.

In 1926 McConnell entered a boxing tournament solely to make money. Stocky and tough, he fought as a flyweight and won through to the final by competing seven times over a total of forty-four rounds. He lost the fifteen-round final, but the purse of £40 enabled him to buy some furniture and move into a rented house. McConnell fought professionally at Leichhardt Stadium and advanced to main events until he was matched with the future lightweight champion (1931) Bobby Delaney who outweighed him by a stone. Knocked out in the fifth round, McConnell was so badly beaten that he was unable to work for several weeks. He retired from fighting and turned to training.

His gymnasium—which he opened at Newtown in 1930 and moved to Abercrombie Street, Chippendale, about 1934—became the 'Stillman's' of Sydney, where young hopefuls went in search of glory, old stagers battled to keep their careers afloat, overseas fighters trained, and the boxing fraternity gathered. Over forty years McConnell trained numerous Australian and State champions. He achieved his greatest success with the southpaw Jimmy Carruthers whom he took to the world bantamweight title in 1952. Carruthers defended the title three times, earning substantial purses and ushering in a brief period of prosperity for McConnell.

Leading American fighters such as Freddie Dawson and Archie Moore regarded McConnell's skills highly. Unlike many others in his role, he seems to have cared for and protected the boxers in his charge. During the late 1940s he was president of the Boxers', Managers' and Trainers' Guild. In 1950 a number of articles under McConnell's name, crafted from his notes by boxing journalist Ray Mitchell, appeared in the *Australian Ring Digest*: in these pieces the trainer forcefully expressed his views on honest promotion, fair refereeing and the image of boxing. After Carruthers' premature retirement in 1954, McConnell's fortunes waned. He grew disenchanted with the conduct of boxing and suffered a severe loss when his gymnasium was destroyed by fire in 1955. He opened another gym on a different site at Chippendale, turned his attention to training amateur fighters, and took a job as a cleaner to make ends meet.

Known as 'Silent Bill', an ironic reference to his loquaciousness, McConnell provided lively copy for sporting journalists. He and his rival, fellow trainer Ernest McQuillan, occasionally came to blows, but McQuillan organized a boxing show to raise money for McConnell who suffered a heart attack in 1968 and was in financial distress. On 10 September that year, while in St Vincent's Hospital, McConnell married an invalid pensioner Gloria Joyce Sproule. Survived by his wife, and by the two sons and two daughters of his first marriage, he died of myocardial infarction on 21 January 1970 in St Vincent's and was buried in Botany cemetery. Carruthers and many other fighters whom McConnell had trained attended the funeral.

G. Kieza, *Australian Boxing* (Syd, 1990); *Aust Ring Digest*, May, Nov 1950; *People*, 2 June 1954; *SMH*, 21 July, 24 Oct 1947, 28 Aug 1955, 9 Nov 1959, 22 July 1960, 25 Apr 1969; *Daily Mirror* (Syd), 4 Jan 1969, 20 Sept 1982; information from Mr R. Mitchell, Gymea, Syd.   PETER CORRIS

McCORMACK, DAVID WILLIAM (1917-1944), air force officer, was born on 27 November 1917 at Footscray, Melbourne, third child of David McCormack, a Victorian-born fitter, and his wife Maria Josephine, née Kennedy, who came from Ireland. Educated at St Coleman's School, Fitzroy, and Christian Brothers' College, East Melbourne, young David worked as a clerk, as a salesman, and as an electrical mechanic with the State Electricity Commission of Victoria. On 21 July 1940 he enlisted in the Royal Australian Air Force under the Empire Air Training Scheme. He was 5 ft 9 ins (175 cm) tall, with brown eyes and dark hair that reflected his Irish descent.

Selected as a trainee pilot, McCormack attended No.4 Elementary Flying Training School, Mascot, Sydney (August-October 1940), and No.1 Service Flying Training School, Camp Borden, Canada (November 1940-February 1941). He was commissioned in February 1941. Arriving in Britain in the following month, he completed the course at No.55 Operational Training Unit. On 26 May he was posted to No.615 Squadron, Royal Air Force, which was then equipped with the Hurricane IIa; in November he was promoted flight lieutenant. Fighter Command was on the offensive in 1941. McCormack took part in hazardous, low-level attacks in Belgium and northern France, and against enemy shipping in the North Sea. In February 1942 he was awarded the Distinguished Flying Cross: the citation noted his 'determination in the face of enemy fire' and the 'inspiring' example he set for others.

In March McCormack embarked with his squadron for India and the war against Japan. Based in Bengal, the unit adapted rapidly to new conditions of air fighting. By November McCormack was in action in the Arakan region of Burma, carrying out long-distance sorties over inhospitable terrain. For his bravery he was awarded a Bar to his D.F.C. (June 1943) and mentioned in dispatches (1945). Having been detached to training duties in April 1943, he took command of No.615 Squadron in February 1944 and was promoted squadron leader on 1 July.

The unit had converted to Spitfires which it used mainly in a ground-attack role during the second battle of the Arakan (from February 1944) and the Japanese siege of Imphal,

Manipur (March-June). On 29 May McCormack clearly demonstrated his skill as a pilot. In an engagement with enemy fighters his Spitfire's engine developed a glycol leak. With his windscreen obscured by oil and his engine barely functioning, he navigated over mountains and made a forced landing on a waterlogged airstrip.

On 10 August 1944 McCormack led sixteen Spitfires on a flight from Palel, Imphal, to the squadron's new base at Biagachi, near Calcutta. *En route* they encountered the most violent type of monsoonal storm; his aircraft was one of eight that crashed, and he was killed; his body was recovered and buried in Calcutta (Bhowanipore) war cemetery. Members of No.615 Squadron took up a subscription for a remembrance window in St Augustine's Catholic Church, Yarraville, Melbourne. McCormack had been the epitome of the aggressive World War II pilot of single-seat fighter and ground-attack aircraft.

G. Odgers, *Air War Against Japan 1943-1945* (Canb, 1957); *Age* (Melb), 26 June 1945; PR 88/083 and AWM 65 (AWM).   JOHN MCCARTHY

McCRACKEN, JOHN (1895-1956), public servant, was born on 13 September 1895 at Motherwell, Lanarkshire, Scotland, son of Joseph McCracken, a turning-machinist, and his wife Agnes, née McMaster. John completed his schooling at Dalziel High School before the family emigrated to Brisbane in 1911. That year he joined the Queensland Audit Office as a messenger. In July 1912 he was appointed a cadet-clerk with the State Public Service Board. Studying at night at the Central Technical College, he gained qualifications in accountancy. He became an associate-member (1921) of the Commonwealth Institute of Accountants and later a fellow of the Australian Society of Accountants; in the 1930s he returned to the college to teach the subject part time.

On 19 August 1915 McCracken had enlisted in the Australian Imperial Force. He served with the 13th Battery, 5th Field Artillery Brigade, in Egypt (December 1915 to March 1916) and on the Western Front. Severely wounded in the leg in April 1917, he spent several months in hospital in England; although his leg was not amputated, he was left with a permanent, painful disability. He was repatriated in March 1918 and discharged in Brisbane in the following month. On 22 February 1919 at her Hill End home he married with Baptist forms Amy Gertrude Bell, a 26-year-old public servant.

Appointed assistant-secretary (1924) in the office of the public service commissioner J. D. Story [q.v.12], McCracken was promoted senior public service inspector in 1935 and deputy public service commissioner in 1936. He was a member of the Bureau of Industry under J. B. Brigden [q.v.7], and in 1937 was one of two commissioners chosen by Premier William Forgan Smith [q.v.11] to report on the Brisbane City Council's administration. Story retired in 1939. Despite pressure on the Queensland government to expand the number of public service commissioners to three, McCracken succeeded him as sole commissioner.

During World War II McCracken's responsibilities markedly increased. He took on the duties of deputy food controller for Queensland and director of civil defence, and chaired both the public safety advisory committee and the advisory committee under the Public Service Act. In addition, he served on the Public Service and the Police Superannuation boards, and presided over the Crown Employees Patriotic Fund which raised thousands of pounds for war relief. Keenly aware of the situation of ex-servicemen, he continued to advocate their rights when the war ended.

Lack of money had prevented McCracken from studying law as a young man. He relished his role as the public service industrial-relations representative in the State Industrial Court and the Commonwealth Court of Conciliation and Arbitration. The exhaustive preparation that lay behind his regular appearances throughout the 1940s and early 1950s at the forty-hour week and basic-wage hearings won him respect, but Queensland's trade-union officials regarded him as a 'hard man' for his inflexible adherence to government directives. Publicly known as Jock, he used the term 'laddie' and a heightened Scots accent in forceful encounters.

Despite his war injury, McCracken was a keen, albeit occasional, fisherman. He dabbled in carpentry and joinery, read avidly, enjoyed testing his car on the open road and grew beautiful roses. A member (from 1954) of the senate of the University of Queensland, he assisted Story to introduce a diploma of public administration. In February 1956 he retired as public service commissioner and was appointed to the State Industrial Court. Although he was involved in a motorcar accident near Gunning, New South Wales, he acted entirely in character, accepting work until a few months before his death.

McCracken died of cancer on 4 September 1956 in St Helen's Private Hospital, South Brisbane, and was cremated with Presbyterian forms; his wife, daughter and three sons survived him. Contemporaries referred to him as the last of his kind. Loyalty and a highly developed sense of duty had been his guiding principles. Government decisions may not have always accorded with his concept of right and wrong, but he was unswerving in carrying them out. His taciturnity in public masked a sense of humour and many acts of kindness. In Story's view, he was 'one of the brightest and best of the backroom boys'.

G. Greenwood and J. Laverty, *Brisbane 1859-1959* (Brisb, 1959); G. Whitehouse and K. Wiltshire, *The History of the Queensland Professional Officers' Association* (Brisb, 1987); *Univ Qld Gazette*, Dec 1956; *Sunday Mail* (Brisb), 12 Mar 1944; information from Mr R. Howatson, Coorparoo, Mr A. Luke, Ashgrove, Dr D. I. McCracken, Chapel Hill, and Mr A. McCracken, Indooroopilly, Brisb.

KAY COHEN

McCREADY, GEORGINA (1888-1980), nurse, trade unionist and administrator, was born on 17 December 1888 at Greenock, Renfrewshire, Scotland, daughter of George Johnstone, telephone inspector, and his wife Margaret, née Gibson. The parents moved with their eight children to Glasgow and Georgina was educated there. While employed in a chartered accountant's office, she advanced to ledger-work and learned shorthand at evening-college. She then sought a new vocation, entered the Eastern District Hospital and qualified as a general nurse on 1 November 1912. Georgina accompanied her father when he visited relations in Australia in 1913. In the following year the entire family settled in the Sydney suburb of Dumbleton (Beverly Hills).

The Australasian Trained Nurses' Association required Georgina to sit for the general nurses' examination; she was registered on 11 November 1914 and worked at the Renwick [q.v.6] Hospital for Infants. Between 1919 and 1928 she was matron, in turn, of Cessnock, Maitland and Broken Hill hospitals. During this period she obtained special leave and qualified in midwifery at the Royal Hospital for Women on 14 December 1922, and in baby health at Tresillian Mothercraft Training Centre in 1928. In the mid-1920s she was of slim build and average height, with auburn hair and green eyes; she retained her strong features and soft Scottish accent.

As a supervisory nurse, Sister Johnstone assisted in checking hospital standards throughout the State, as required by the Public Hospitals Act (1929). Many fell below Nurses' Registration Board requirements and nurses had no industrial cover. Helped by Jessie Street's [q.v.] influence, Johnstone and Ione Nowland (assistant to the registrar of the N.R.B.) formed the New South Wales Nurses' Association at an emergency meeting on 27 March 1931. It was registered as a trade union on 28 April and as an industrial union on 12 August. The 1931 executive included

Nowland as president and Johnstone as honorary secretary.

At St Stephen's Presbyterian Church, Sydney, on 25 January 1932 Georgina married Samuel McCready (d.1940), a 35-year-old dairy-farmer. Deeply interested in nursing affairs, she was honorary secretary (1935) of the N.S.W.N.A.; the first award for nurses was achieved in 1936. In addition to her experience and energy, she also possessed administrative skills. Her drive to improve conditions for nurses made her the more determined to support the association through its long struggle with financial problems and lack of members. She again served (1941-45) as honorary secretary. In 1943 she was able to report an expanded membership and the first year of financial stability. The association amalgamated with the Trained Mental Nurses' Association in 1945. By the end of that year McCready was general secretary; she was subsequently assistant-secretary (1946-53). In 1953 she became one of the first two life members of the association. Throughout her years of service the N.S.W.N.A. initiated significant industrial advances for many branches of nursing.

Mrs McCready represented the N.S.W.N.A. at national and State conferences; she also participated in discussions about amalgamation with the A.T.N.A. and for a national nurses' union. She helped to promote postgraduate education for nurses. On 19 January 1949 she had chaired the inaugural meeting of the provisional council for the New South Wales College of Nursing, of which she was president (1949-50). In 1954 the association announced the McCready scholarship in honour of her work. She retired in 1960 and was appointed M.B.E. in 1963.

Georgina McCready died on 16 September 1980 at Leichhardt; her body was delivered to the University of Sydney's medical faculty. She had laboured to improve nursing standards and nurses' living and working conditions, to establish non-political and non-sectarian policies, and to bring about educational and cultural advancement.

H. Radi (ed), *Jessie Street* (Syd, 1990); M. Dickenson, *An Unsentimental Union* (Syd, 1993); *Aust Nurses' J*, 1931, Sept 1937, p 199; *Lamp*, Dec 1954, p iv, July 1963, p 3, Dec 1980, p 34, July 1989, p 14, Aug 1989, p 26; NSW Nurses' Assn Archives (Noel Butlin Archives Centre, ANU, *and* Camperdown, Syd); NSW College of Nursing Archives (Glebe, Syd); information from Miss R. Hand, Bargo, Miss E. M. Schofield, Toongabbie, NSW, and the late Miss M. Porter.

HAZEL WOOLSTON

McCUE, JOHN ROBERTSON THOMAS (1881-1975), Baptist pastor and prohibitionist, was born on 7 May 1881 at Port Campbell,

Victoria, fifth child of Michael McCue and his wife Agnes, née Robertson. Born in Ireland, Michael was a former soldier who had emigrated from India in the 1870s and turned to farming; Agnes was the daughter of a Baptist family from the Shetland Islands. Leaving school at the age of 13, Robertson found work in shearing sheds and as a woodcutter. At 16 he moved to Beulah where he had relatives, took a job in a general store, and returned to school intending to enter the ministry.

About 1902 McCue began home mission work, preaching at Kerang and Wonthaggi; he lived in a tent and played in the local cricket and football teams. After four years at the Baptist College of Victoria, during which he studied English literature and philosophy at the University of Melbourne, he was ordained in 1911. He then served as associate-minister at St Kilda. On 8 September 1914 he married Sarah Edith Annie Collins at the Baptist Church, Beulah. He was successively pastor at Kyneton, Castlemaine (where in 1920 he organized mass meetings which gained local option and the closure of four hotels), West Moreland and West Preston.

From 1930, while occasionally preaching, McCue worked almost full time for twenty-seven years as secretary and organizer of the Victorian Local Option Alliance (later the Victorian Temperance Alliance) and as editor of *Clarion Call*, its official journal. He was a prohibitionist, not a mere temperance man, who campaigned for the closure of public houses on Saturdays and believed that consumption of alcohol should be confined to those with a medical prescription. Described by the press as Victoria's most famous wowser and anti-liquor champion, he remained good-humoured and courteous in controversy.

His success was mixed. A vehement and articulate speaker and letter-writer to the newspapers, he was confident that he was following divine purpose. In the 1930 and 1938 referendums he led the campaigns for the reduction of liquor licences, but failed although polling well. In the late 1940s hundreds of barmaids recruited during World War II continued to work. McCue threatened legal action. The women were sentenced to dismissal, strike actions followed in their support, officialdom intervened, and they continued in employment.

As the Olympic Games were nigh, a referendum was called in 1956 to vote for or against the late closing of public houses. McCue was largely responsible for persuading more than 60 per cent of voters to 'Stick to Six'. In 1963, however, Premier (Sir) Henry Bolte and his deputy (Sir) Arthur Rylah [q.v.] skilfully arranged for a royal commission conducted by (Sir) Philip Phillips [q.v.] which recommended ten o'clock closing. Once Liberal Party policy had been altered, legislation enabled 10 p.m. closing from February 1966. McCue was sure that prohibition and sanity would eventually prevail in Victoria, but the cause was lost.

Mrs McCue was a founder (1924) and active member of the Victorian Women's Baptist Association, and a life governor (from 1955) of the Royal Women's Hospital. She died in 1971. Survived by his son and two daughters, Robertson McCue died on 22 April 1975 at Kew and was cremated.

F. J. Wilkin, *Baptists in Victoria . . . 1838-1938* (Melb, 1939); K. Dunstan, *Wowsers* (Melb, 1968); P. Blazey, *Bolte* (Brisb, 1972); Roy Com into the Sale, Supply, Disposal or Consumption of Liquor in the State of Victoria, PP (Vic), 1964-65, 2 (22, 23); *La Trobe Hist Studies*, no 3, 1972; *Vic Baptist Witness*, 5 June 1975; *Herald* (Melb), 14 June 1956; *Age* (Melb), 17 July 1964.   GEOFFREY SERLE*

McCUTCHEON, ARTHUR DONALD (1890-1955), Methodist minister and social worker, and MABEL MARY (1886-1942), nurse, were husband and wife. Arthur was born on 2 June 1890 at New Seaham, County Durham, England, son of John McCutcheon, coalminer, and his wife Martha Louisa, née Snowdon. Orphaned at 14, he worked in the mines for eight years and became a lay preacher. He responded to an advertisement for men willing to undertake home mission work with the Methodist Church in South Australia, reached Adelaide in 1912, and was sent to Keith. On 11 September 1914 he enlisted in the Australian Imperial Force; he served at Gallipoli and on the Western Front as a stretcher-bearer with the 4th Field Ambulance. Taking leave in England, on 2 December 1916 at the Primitive Methodist Chapel, Seaham Harbour, he married Hilda Annie Robinson (d.1923). After he was discharged from the A.I.F. on 28 February 1919 in Adelaide, he was accepted as a probationary minister. While stationed at Berri, he ministered at soldier-settler camps along the Murray River. In 1920 he was transferred to Semaphore. On 22 February 1922 he was ordained. He served at Cowell (1922), Tailem Bend (1925), Magill (1929) and Broken Hill, New South Wales (1932).

Mabel was born on 13 April 1886 at Hangleton, Sussex, England, daughter of Alfred Woolgar, a journeyman blacksmith, and his wife Jemima Florence, née Coles. Having qualified as a hospital nurse, she worked in London, Dublin and New York. From 1914 she served with Queen Alexandra's Imperial Military Nursing Service in France, Greece and Egypt. At the Wesleyan Methodist Chapel, Melcombe Regis, Dorset, England, on 8 August 1917 she married Wilfred Henry

Franks, a sapper in the A.I.F. Sailing as a war bride in the *Megantic*, she arrived in Adelaide with her infant daughter on 18 February 1920. She divorced her husband on 4 April 1922. Registered as a nurse on 29 March that year, she was matron at Clare hospital and then at Cowell where she met Arthur McCutcheon. They were married on 26 March 1925 at the Methodist Manse, Payneham, Adelaide; their son was born in December that year.

Appointed superintendent of Port Adelaide Central Methodist Mission in 1935, McCutcheon held the position until 1954. Under his leadership, the mission developed a men's hostel, employment agency, kindergarten and nursery school, gymnasium clubs, a children's 'cinema church', dressmaking and handicraft classes, a distribution point for second-hand clothing and footwear, a health clinic (founded by Mabel) and a home for the aged. McCutcheon's personal response to local need also included serving (1939-54) as a Royal Australian Naval Reserve chaplain to the naval depot at Port Adelaide and as a probation officer at the local court.

Mrs McCutcheon's innovative ideas about health earned the mission a distinguished reputation as an experimental social-service agency. Her interest in rheumatoid arthritis, prevalent among the elderly poor, and her knowledge of 'health-giving ray treatment' led her to establish a clinic at the mission. From modest beginnings in 1936, it became a major physiotherapy and chiropody service, equipped with modern electrical appliances and staffed by trained therapists. The clinic offered dietary advice and free apples to patients, and sold such 'exotic' foods as soya beans, 'unpearled' barley, unpolished rice, cracked wholewheat and vegetable juice.

Mabel also encouraged the mission to establish (1941) a health camp at Mount Barker for deprived families, especially 'poor tired mothers'. She was appointed M.B.E. in 1939. Survived by her husband and her two children, she died of cancer on 30 December 1942 in North Adelaide and was buried in North Brighton cemetery. By 1951 her clinic provided rehabilitation for injured waterside workers and a treatment centre for children suffering from poliomyelitis.

Arthur's boldness in making expansive plans for the mission attracted wide support. As much a pragmatist as a visionary, he ruffled Methodist feathers by accepting money from horse-racing interests. His earlier experiences in mining communities had turned him into a Christian Socialist and a militant supporter of trade-union causes. While standing firmly in the Evangelical mainstream, he was impatient with otherworldly complacency and conceived the mandate of the Church in the broadest terms. His humanity was evident in his regular radio talks and column in the *News*, selections from which were published as *As I See Life* (1943) and *Sparks in the Darkness* (1944). The Methodist Conference in South Australia elected him president in 1947. He gave a clear statement of his vision in his presidential address, 'Christian Responsibility for the Social Order'. McCutcheon died of coronary thrombosis on 24 June 1955 at Mount Barker and was buried beside his second wife; their son and the daughter of his first marriage survived him.

A. Hunt, *This Side of Heaven* (Adel, 1985); *PD* (SA), 1945, p 411 *et passim*; Port Adel Central Methodist Mission, *Annual Report*, 1935-55, *and* Minutes of Q Bd Meetings, minute-books, 1904-66 (Port Adel Central Mission); *News* (Adel), 22 Mar 1938, 12 June 1941, 1 Apr 1954; SA *Methodist*, 8 Jan 1943, 1 July 1955; information from Mr J. McCutcheon, Semaphore, Adel.

JUDITH RAFTERY

MACDONALD, ALEXANDER (1910-1969), ironworker and trade union official, was born on 21 May 1910 at Greenock, Renfrewshire, Scotland, third of five children of Alexander Macdonald, sawmill foreman, and his first wife Sybil, née Smith. Alexander senior worked for Scotts' Shipbuilding & Engineering Co. and presided over the Greenock Central Co-operative Society. Young Alex attended Homescroft School until the age of 13. He worked at the shipyard for a short time, but was unable to find permanent employment in Scotland. His mother had died when he was 6 and his father remarried in 1920. When relations between the children and their stepmother deteriorated, Alex followed his elder sister Anna to Australia. Emigrating under the 'Dreadnought scheme'—which aimed to train British youths to work on Australian farms—he sailed from England in the *Sophocles* on 13 August 1925. The ship was delayed at Cape Town for almost six weeks due to a worldwide seamen's strike; during this time Alex carried messages to the sailors in the *Sophocles*.

After landing in Sydney, Macdonald spent three months at a training farm at Scheyville, then worked on properties in the mid-west of New South Wales. He made his way to Western Australia with the intention of returning to Scotland, but his father dissuaded him because unemployment had risen at home. Alex 'humped his bluey' and reached Queensland in June 1932. The Depression deepened and labourers' wages were cut. He refused the ten shillings a week then being offered on small farms, preferring to take seasonal work around the State. Involved in the Unemployed Workers' Movement, he was present when the jobless clashed with the Mackay City Council in January 1933 over the issue of their shelter-shed. He learned much from this experience, and was soon committed to the U.W.M., and to organizing and educating the unemployed.

Moving to Brisbane, Macdonald laboured on government relief-projects and lived in one of many camps for those 'on the dole'—a disused tobacco factory in South Brisbane known as the 'Crystal Palace'. Late in 1933 he attended a conference of the unemployed at the Trades Hall. About this time he joined the Communist Party of Australia. Elected to the party's State committee in 1936, he became Brisbane district branch secretary in 1937 and was subsequently elected to the party's central committee. As a communist candidate, he was defeated for the Legislative Assembly seat of Kurilpa in the 1938 elections, and for the Senate in 1949 and 1951. At the general registry office, Brisbane, on 11 August 1939 he had married Molly Cassandra Neild, a 32-year-old nurse. They lived at West End.

Macdonald was employed (from 1940) as an ironworker at the Evans [q.v.8] Deakin shipyard. A member of the Federated Ironworkers Association of Australia, he was elected full-time secretary of the Queensland branch in January 1943. He took an active role in the wider trade-union movement as secretary of the Metal Trades Federation, of the central disputes committee in the Queensland railway strike (February-April 1948), and of the Labor Day committee of the Trades and Labor Council of Queensland (1943-48). In addition, he belonged (1949-69) to the interstate executive of the Australian Council of Trade Unions and later worked to secure the presidency for R. J. L. Hawke.

Although he lost the secretaryship of the F.I.A. in a court-controlled ballot in 1951, Macdonald was elected secretary of the Queensland T.L.C. in January 1952. He spoke quietly, rarely raised his voice and seldom showed anger; he was also tolerant and understanding, and a good listener. The united front he built up involved many shades of militancy and political outlook, and his judgement earned the respect of various factions. His strength lay in negotiation. Macdonald played a leading role in several major disputes, among them the Queensland meat strike (1946), the shearers' strike (1956) and the Mount Isa conflict (1964-65). When he spoke at demonstrations and meetings he presented a well-researched and logical case. Conscious of the good name of the trade-union movement, he was careful in handling and recording money received.

Macdonald prepared cases for basic-wage and equal-pay claims in the State Industrial Court, promoted youth education and employment, advocated the extension of the basic wage to Aboriginal workers, and tried to improve annual, long-service and sick-leave benefits, minimum wages, restricted hours, safety laws and pensions. From November 1968 he represented the forty unions affiliated with the T.L.C. before the State Industrial Conciliation and Arbitration Commission. He tried to establish a liaison with university students and admitted them to the Trades Hall. Passionately interested in history, he collected, preserved and indexed union records. He was a member and vice-president of the Queensland Peace Committee.

Five ft 11 ins (180 cm) tall, solidly built, with brown eyes and brown hair, Macdonald smoked heavily, enjoyed a social drink, and was interested in music, theatre, art and reading. He was a devoted husband and father, and had a host of friends. At heart he was an internationalist and a humanitarian. Survived by his wife and two daughters, he died of myocardial infarction on 18 August 1969 at Princess Alexandra Hospital, South Brisbane, and was cremated. His death shocked the union movement: thousands of mourners attended his funeral at which a piper played the lament of the clan Macdonald.

Qld Railways Central Disputes Cte, TLC, *Report and Balance Sheet of the Queensland Railway Strike, February 2nd to April 6th, 1948* (Brisb, 1948); *Telegraph* (Brisb), 9 Nov 1968, 18 Aug 1969; *Courier-Mail*, 18 Aug 1969; TLCQ records (Fryer L, Univ Qld); family papers and other documents (held by Mrs C. Cameron, Mt Gravatt, Brisb).
                                        CECILY CAMERON
                                        GREG MALLORY

MACDONALD, ALEXANDER JOHN HILTON (1916-1973), journalist, was born on 19 August 1916 at Elizabeth Bay, Sydney, only child of Alexander Macdonald, a mining engineer from Scotland, and his Sydney-born wife Naomi, née Hingston. While young Alexander boarded at the Benedictine abbey school at Fort Augustus, Scotland, his father regularly sent him books; the lad eagerly consumed everything from *The Boys' Own Annual* to Dostoyevsky, and resolved to become a writer. He returned to Sydney in 1936 and worked with his father at a goldmine near Thornborough, North Queensland. There he wrote 'Day Must Break', an improbable blank-verse tragedy set during the first Punic War; staged at the Theatre Royal, Sydney, in November 1937, it was a 'monumental flop'. By this time he was a continuity writer with the Australian Broadcasting Commission and a 'boon companion' of Peter Finch [q.v.14], sharing a series of flats with him at Kings Cross. At St Jude's Anglican

Church, Randwick, on 27 November 1943 Macdonald married Nona Maud Noble, a 25-year-old secretary.

His talent clearly lay in comedy. At the A.B.C., Macdonald wrote scripts for Dick Bentley. He then shifted to radio 2UE, and in 1945 joined the Colgate-Palmolive Radio Unit where, with Fred Parsons, he scripted the phenomenally popular 'McCackie Mansion', starring Roy Rene [q.v.11]. The pair also wrote for Jack Davey [q.v.13], Willie Fennell, and Dorothy Foster and Rita Pauncefort ('Ada and Elsie'), among many others. Macdonald began writing radio reviews for *Smith's Weekly* in 1947, and later turned his hand to film and theatre criticism. In 1952 he joined the staff of the *Daily Telegraph*. His humorous columns became such a feature that a selection was published as *Don't Frighten the Horses* (Melbourne, 1961). He had a gift for word-play and comic absurdity—the 'surly leprechaun' Chauncy Pilgarlic became a motif —but lacked the demotic touch of Lennie Lower [q.v.10], with whom he was often compared. In the 1960s he wrote and reviewed for other Sydney newspapers, including the *Daily Mirror* and *Sydney Morning Herald*.

A short man, with what Douglas Stewart described as 'extraordinary eyes like oysters', Macdonald was an old-style bohemian, 'constantly embroiled in conflicts with creditors, editors, bank managers and women'. He was unsuited to domesticity, and his marriage was dissolved in 1958. Nevertheless, on 26 July 1961 at St Mary's Cathedral, Sydney, he married with Catholic rites Beverley Jane Burnell, a 20-year-old typist. Macdonald became a fixture at the Journalists' Club. There he wrote much of his copy and for some years was an inactive board-member. With Edgar Holt, Cyril Pearl, Kenneth Slessor [q.v.] and others, he formed the Condiments Club, dedicated to good food and fine wine. In 1970 he was awarded a Commonwealth Literary Fund fellowship to write his autobiography, *The Ukulele Player Under the Red Lamp* (1972).

Survived by his wife and their two sons, and by the son and daughter of his first marriage, Macdonald died of complications of hepatic cirrhosis on 17 December 1973 at St Vincent's Hospital, Darlinghurst, and was cremated. When Finch heard of his death he kept an agreement, made in their youth, 'that the survivor should pay for a round of drinks at the Journos'.

D. Stewart, *A Man of Sydney* (Melb, 1977); E. Dundy, *Finch, Bloody Finch* (Lond, 1980); R. Campbell, *The Road to Oxalis Cottage* (Lond, 1984); D. Angel, *The Journalists' Club, Sydney* (Syd, 1985); Aust Journalists' Assn, *Copy*, Feb-Mar 1974; *Daily Telegraph* (Syd), 18 Dec 1973; *SMH*, 6 Sept 1969, 10 Dec 1970, 22 Dec 1973, 8 Apr 1974.

PETER KIRKPATRICK

McDONALD, ALLAN McKENZIE (1888-1953), farmer, auctioneer and politician, was born on 4 July 1888 at Winchelsea, Victoria, fourth child of Allan McDonald, a contractor who became a farmer, and his wife Elizabeth, née McKenzie (d.1889), both of whom came from Geelong. Educated at Winchelsea State School, young Allan worked as a farm labourer and then as a farmer. In later years he often drew on the lessons that life on the land had taught him. On 17 September 1913 at the McLennan Memorial Presbyterian Church, Birregurra, he married Sarah Mary Farquharson, a 27-year-old domestic servant; they were to have six children. Following his father's death in 1914, Allan succeeded him as a member of the Winchelsea Shire Council. He remained on the council for almost forty years, becoming a lucid, forceful and entertaining speaker.

On 6 April 1916 McDonald enlisted in the Australian Imperial Force; at that time he was described as being 5 ft 8 ins (173 cm) tall, with a fair complexion, grey eyes and brown hair. After joining the 14th Battalion in France in December, he was shot in the left arm on 11 April 1917 at Bullecourt and spent some months in hospital. He served with distinction at Polygon Wood, Belgium, in September, and was promoted sergeant in October. Next month he was transferred from the front because of his injured arm. Returning to Australia, he was discharged from the A.I.F. in October 1918.

McDonald helped to form the Winchelsea sub-branch of the Returned Sailors' and Soldiers' Imperial League of Australia and was its president in 1920-21; he also presided over the 14th Battalion and 4th Brigade associations in 1933-34. He belonged to the Independent Order of Odd Fellows of Victoria and was grand master in 1923. Elected shire president in 1921 and 1927, he was a staunch supporter of local government. He represented the council on the Municipal Association of Victoria, of which he was president (1941-42).

At the 1919 and 1922 general elections, McDonald had stood unsuccessfully for the House of Representatives as the Nationalist candidate for Corangamite. While employed (from 1924) as an auctioneer with Dalgety [q.v.4] & Co. Ltd, he increased his knowledge of stock and land values, and his understanding of rural Victoria. He worked as a party organizer and assisted the election campaigns of his uncle James McDonald who held (1917-33) the seat of Polwarth in the Legislative Assembly. When James died in August 1933, Allan won Polwarth for the United Australia Party in the ensuing by-election. He spoke regularly in parliament and gained a reputation as a constructive politician. From 1935 he was the Opposition's leading spokesman on farming issues. Although he was mentioned as a possible leader of his party in Victoria, he resigned in August 1940 to contest the Federal elections.

On 21 September 1940 McDonald won the seat of Corangamite in the House of Representatives for the U.A.P. From 26 June to 7 October 1941 he held the portfolio of external territories in the governments of (Sir) Robert Menzies [q.v.] and (Sir) Arthur Fadden [q.v.14]. McDonald contested the leadership of the U.A.P. in 1941 and 1943. Advocating the welfare of returned servicemen and their families, he served on a parliamentary committee which reported (1943) on repatriation. He strongly supported its recommendation that preference in employment be given to ex-servicemen. In 1946-49 he was Opposition whip. Subsequently, he took little part in the proceedings of the House, preferring to involve himself in discussions in the party room; always a practical man, he may have decided to make way for new and younger members eager to catch the Speaker's eye. Ill health further curtailed his activity.

McDonald was immensely popular in his electorate. Widely respected for his strength of character, courage, independence of thought and sense of justice, he had a ready wit and an easy laugh. He was a steadfast Presbyterian, proud of his Scottish ancestry, and of Australia's links with the Crown and Britain. Survived by his wife, four daughters and one of his two sons, he died of cancer on 10 June 1953 in his home at Winchelsea; he was accorded a state funeral and was buried with Masonic rites in the local cemetery.

N. Wanliss, *The History of the Fourteenth Battalion, A.I.F.* (Melb, 1929); P. Hasluck, *The Government and the People, 1939-1941* (Canb, 1952); E. B. Gregory et al, *Coast to Country* (Melb, 1985); *Herald* (Melb), 6 Oct 1937; *Argus*, 24 Apr 1943, 13 June 1953; *Age* (Melb), 11 June 1953; *Colac Herald*, 12 June 1953.   I. C. COCHRAN

MacDONALD, ALLAN NICOLL (1892-1978), accountant and politician, was born on 25 August 1892 at Lochee, Forfarshire, Scotland, son of Alexander MacDonald, a retired mill manager, and his wife Helen Christie, née Nicoll. Educated at Arbroath High School, Allan emigrated to Western Australia in 1911. He lived at Collie, and worked in a bakery and as a teamster's labourer. In 1914 he moved to Perth. Employed by the accountancy firm, Rankin, Morrison & Co., he attended evening classes in commerce and accountancy at Perth Technical School.

On 17 August 1914 MacDonald enlisted in the Australian Imperial Force. After sailing for Egypt with the 8th Battery, Australian Field Artillery, he served at Gallipoli until he fell ill and was evacuated. Apart from seven months in England in 1916-17, he spent the rest of the war in Egypt, attaining the rank of acting warrant officer, class one, in the Australian Army Pay Corps. In June 1919 he was discharged at his own request to take an appointment with the American Red Cross Commission in Palestine. At the register office, Wandsworth, London, on 4 October that year he married Christiana Hildreth, who had been a driver for the Women's Legion when he met her in 1916.

They arrived in Perth in February 1920 and MacDonald resumed his job with Rankin, Morrison & Co. In 1925 he became secretary of the Western Australian Consultative Council, a coterie of businessmen chaired by Sinclair McGibbon [q.v.]. Probably formed at the behest of Prime Minister S. M. (Viscount) Bruce [q.v.7] to raise funds for the United Party (later the National Party of Western Australia), the Consultative Council also aimed to combat communist activity and industrial lawlessness. MacDonald acted as director of the unsuccessful United-Country parties' campaign to regain office in the 1927 State elections. Notwithstanding the victory of the conservative coalition in 1930, dissatisfaction with the influence of 'outside' fund-raising bodies led to the effective disbanding of the Consultative Council. From 1930 MacDonald was general secretary of the National Party.

In 1934 he was elected to the Senate as a United Australia Party candidate. His term should have begun on 1 July 1935. When Senator Sir Walter Kingsmill [q.v.9] died in January that year, Sir James Mitchell [q.v.10], the lieutenant-governor of Western Australia, appointed MacDonald to fill the vacancy from 5 March, in accordance with section 15 of the Constitution. On 29 November 1937 Prime Minister J. A. Lyons [q.v.10] made MacDonald a minister without portfolio; he assisted the minister for commerce (to November 1938) and the treasurer (7 November 1938 to 7 April 1939). Following Lyons's death, MacDonald supported W. M. Hughes [q.v.9] against (Sir) Robert Menzies [q.v.] for the leadership of the U.A.P. Menzies omitted him from his first ministry on 26 April 1939. MacDonald's decision in December to vote against the government during the committee stage of the gold tax collection bill did not help his hopes of gaining a portfolio.

A member of the Senate standing committee on regulations and ordinances (1939-47) and the parliamentary standing committee on broadcasting (September 1943 to July 1944), MacDonald was also a member (1943) of the Empire Parliamentary Association delegation to Britain and Canada. He lost his seat in the 1946 elections, left the Senate on 30 June 1947, and did not gain endorsement for the 1949 polls. A pipe-smoking, outgoing man, he had been active in the Returned Sailors' and Soldiers' Imperial League of Australia before entering the Senate. During his years in parliament he was keenly interested in lawn bowls; back in Perth, he found recreation in tending the garden of his Mount Lawley home.

MacDonald was a member (from 1949) and chairman (1961-65) of the Western Australian Lotteries Commission. He died on 18 January 1978 at the Repatriation General Hospital, Hollywood, and was cremated with Anglican rites; his wife, two daughters and three sons survived him.

PD (Cwlth), 6 Dec 1939, p 2166; *West Australian*, 23 Jan 1978; author's interview with A. N. MacDonald, June 1964; family information.

DAVID BLACK

MACDONALD, AMELIA MORRISON FRASER (1865-1946), social reformer and women's activist, was born on 17 June 1865 at Blackburn, Linlithgowshire, Scotland, elder daughter of Peter Fraser, cooper, and his wife Isabella, née McRae. Amelia attended school at Govan, Glasgow. When she was 11 years old, her mother died, and she worked as a seamstress to support herself and her sister. At West Govan on 2 August 1886 she married with the forms of the Church of Scotland Alexander Parkinson Macdonald (d.1937), a steamship steward and caterer. They emigrated to Sydney where, for nine years, she ran a tailoring business. In 1896 the Macdonalds moved to Western Australia. Amelia opened a café in Barrack Street, Perth, which continued to operate until 1913. Her orphaned 19-year-old niece Isabella Millar had joined the childless couple in 1910; Bonnie Brae at Glen Forrest was their home from 1916.

With other newly enfranchised women— among them Jean Beadle, Muriel Chase, Edith Cowan, Roberta Jull and Bessie Rischbieth [qq.v.7,8,9,11]—Mrs Macdonald was committed to widespread reform. A long-term member of St Andrew's Presbyterian Church and, later, an Anglican Sunday School teacher, she joined the Perth branch of the Theosophical Society and became its treasurer in 1902. The society's ideals of spiritual force, service, social reform, universal education and equal citizenship were her guiding principles. Following a visit by Annie Besant, the international president, Macdonald became a founder (1909) of the Women's Service Guilds of Western Australia. The guilds endeavoured to implement the Theosophical order of service laid down by Besant. Macdonald was treasurer of the Perth guild and State president (1929). A principal

figure in establishing the Kindergarten Union, the Western Australian Girl Guides' Association and the King Edward Memorial Hospital for Women, she supported the Workers' Educational Association, the Women's Immigration Auxiliary Council and the Woman's Christian Temperance Union. She vigorously opposed legislation for the compulsory notification and treatment of venereal diseases, regarding it as ineffective; instead, she favoured state provision of health education, and free, confidential and voluntary treatment.

In 1911 Macdonald helped to found the State branch of the National Council of Women. Five years later she joined the Order of International Co-Freemasonry. On 19 August 1924 she was appointed a justice of the peace for the Swan district. Next year she formed the Western Australian Women Justices' Association (president 1925-29 and 1938-43). The association scrutinized the treatment of juveniles in court, lobbied the government to place women on juries and advocated a court of domestic relationships separate from the police court.

Five ft 2 ins (157 cm) tall, slim and red haired, Macdonald displayed an intelligent, analytical mind and a determination to alter legal, educational and social structures which oppressed women and children. In all her efforts she had the backing of her husband and niece. For recreation, she enjoyed bridge, reading and bush-walking; late in life she learned to drive a motorcar. She died on 31 August 1946 at Subiaco and was cremated with Liberal Catholic rites.

D. Popham, *Reflections* (Perth, 1978); J. Roe, *Beyond Belief* (Syd, 1986); Women's Service Guilds (WA), *Dawn*, 18 Sept 1946; records of Women Justices' Assn of WA *and* Women's Service Guilds of WA *and* Perth Theosophical Soc (BL); information from Mr D. A. Johnston, City Beach, Perth.

JUNE OGILVIE

McDONALD, ANGUS MACKENZIE (1912-1968), air force officer, was born on 4 August 1912 at Waratah, New South Wales, second child of Australian-born parents Angus Duncan McDonald, contractor, and his wife Leila Gertrude, née Jones. Educated at Scotch College, Melbourne, young Angus worked as an accountant with Goldsbrough Mort [qq.v.4,5] & Co. Ltd. On 2 February 1941 he enlisted in the Royal Australian Air Force. After training in Australia and Canada, he reached Britain in February 1942 as a sergeant observer (later navigator). His first operational tour (from September) was with No.102 Squadron, Royal Air Force, which operated Halifax heavy bombers.

On the night of 11/12 December McDonald was navigator on a mission to Turin, Italy.

Ground-fire disabled one of the aircraft's starboard engines before the target was reached. On the return trip, ice accretion on the aeroplane forced the pilot, Flight Lieutenant N. S. Milnes, to reduce altitude. Anti-aircraft fire over France crippled a port engine. McDonald opposed any suggestion that the crew abandon the aeroplane and helped Milnes to nurse the Halifax back to England. For his 'courage and technical skill' he was awarded the Distinguished Flying Medal. Commissioned one week later, he continued to demonstrate a 'high standard of navigation' in attacks on the heavily defended German cities of Cologne, Bremen, Essen, Düsseldorf and Berlin, 'as well as the more distant objective' of Genoa, Italy. He was awarded the Distinguished Flying Cross (1943).

In January 1944 McDonald was selected (with other experienced aircrew) to visit factories and tell workers what it was like to fly the aircraft and use the equipment they produced. On 3 June that year at the Presbyterian Church, Regent Square, London, he married Lesley Joyce Lobb, a 21-year-old stenographer: Lesley wore a 'wedding gown of white lace, made and presented by parachute workers' whom Angus had addressed. In the following month he was posted to No.571 Squadron, R.A.F., which was equipped with Mosquito light bombers. For consistently displaying 'great skill and utmost keenness' throughout raids on industrial cities in Germany and during mine-laying operations in the Dortmund-Ems Canal, he was awarded a Bar to his D.F.C. (1945).

In some ways McDonald was an unlikely hero. Rotund, balding and over 30, he looked nothing like the dashing, youthful aviator on recruiting posters. But he had three attributes that counted more—professional ability, courage and determination. He was also intelligent, enthusiastic and good-humoured, both at work and play. During training he had effortlessly soaked up knowledge, and approached everything he did with infectious zest and wit. Renowned for his escapades, he was seen as a 'scallywag', a 'party man' and a lover of the turf. His appetite for life was wholehearted.

Demobilized in Australia on 30 January 1946 as an acting squadron leader, McDonald returned briefly to his old job in Melbourne, then became the general manager of a firm that sold veterinary supplies. He died of complications of cerebrovascular disease on 1 October 1968 at Heidelberg and was cremated; his wife and daughter survived him.

AWM 65 (AWM); information from Mrs L. Hughes, Toorak, and Mr D. H. Jones, East Hawthorn, Melb, Mr J. McKenzie, Point Clare, and Mr C. Sutton, Tamworth, NSW, and Wg Cdr B. J. Hayes, Narrabundah, Canb. DOUG HURST

McDONALD, SIR CHARLES GEORGE (1892-1970), physician and university chancellor, was born on 25 March 1892 at Newcastle, New South Wales, seventh child and youngest of five sons of William McDonald, a publican from Ireland, and his Victorian-born wife Mary, née Slattery. Dominant and devoted, Mary had a 'blessed obsession with education' for all her ten children. Charles attended the convent school of the Sisters of Mercy, Singleton, and Singleton Superior Public School where the headmaster tutored him privately in Latin and French. After the family had moved to Sydney, he went to Sydney Boys' High School (on a scholarship). Uninterested in sport, he concentrated on his lessons, literature and debating, co-founded the school magazine, the *Record*, and was senior prefect (1909-10). Having passed the senior public examination with honours in four languages, McDonald won a bursary, wrestled with the choice of entering law or medicine, tossed a coin and enrolled in the latter at the University of Sydney (M.B., 1916; Ch.M., 1928). He debated, contributed to a student songbook, edited *Hermes* (1915-16) and the *Sydney University Medical Journal* (1916-20), presided (1917) over the medical society and penned a marvellous satire on the dour dean of medicine, Sir Thomas Anderson Stuart [q.v.12].

In 1916 McDonald began a long association with Royal Prince Alfred Hospital, initially as a resident medical officer. Appointed captain, Australian Army Medical Corps, Australian Imperial Force, on 17 June 1918, he was disappointed not to serve overseas, but worked in the army's anti-tuberculosis dispensary at Randwick, gaining experience in diseases of the chest. He transferred to the Reserve of Officers on 29 October 1919. That day, at the Sacred Heart Church, Mosman, he married with Catholic rites Elsie Isobel Hosie, a 25-year-old stenographer. After ending his military service with the rank of major in September 1920, he continued as a visiting specialist at the Randwick dispensary. He was also honorary adviser on tuberculosis to the Australian Red Cross Society and examiner for admissions to the Queen Victoria Homes for Consumptives. Meanwhile, he began general practice at Randwick (1919) and then at Hurstville (1920). He always insisted on the value of the human bond between doctor and patient, and stressed how important it was for specialists and, particularly, professors of medicine, to spend some years in general practice.

Honorary assistant-physician in the tuberculosis clinic at R.P.A.H. from 1920, McDonald encountered a team of senior physicians whose standards impressed him greatly. He learned from G. E. Rennie [q.v.11] the importance of Socratic questioning in bedside teaching; from Professor A. E. Mills [q.v.10] he gained enthusiasm for the new medicine based on biophysics and biochemistry. McDonald remained at R.P.A.H. as an honorary or consulting physician until his death, and was a member (1964-70) of its board. Other hospitals where he worked included Royal North Shore, Lewisham, St Joseph's (Auburn), Prince Henry and St George.

The infectious, slowly understood and lethal nature of tuberculosis had made McDonald's choice that of a man of courage. His work involved him with large numbers of cases: in his first year the clinic saw 510 new patients, 365 of whom lived with an infected person. He also taught on two afternoons a week. By 1924 Mills regularly used him as his deputy on teaching rounds in the hospital, and as lecturer in the university; he wrote that McDonald's 'classes are crowded, not only by those students who are allotted to him, but by others keen and eager to learn from him . . . he has the gift . . . of making his students understand the principles on which . . . knowledge is based'. That year McDonald became a tutor at the hospital. In 1928 he joined Mills and another mentor, S. A. Smith, as a specialist in Macquarie Street. He and Smith met six days a week for morning tea; their conversation on Wednesday and Saturday concentrated on the afternoon's horse-races.

McDonald had been assistant-editor (1920-22) of the *Medical Journal of Australia*; he published eight papers (mainly to do with the chest), and wrote over thirty editorials and commentaries for the journal. Despite this record, and strong references, he was unsuccessful in his application for the Bosch [q.v.7] chair of medicine at the university in 1929. From 1938 he lectured there in clinical medicine. On 1 July 1940 he was appointed lieutenant colonel, A.I.F. Attached to the 2nd/6th Australian General Hospital, he sailed for the Middle East in December. He landed in Greece in March 1941. In the following month he organized the escape of a group of nurses by destroyer, then moved with the hospital to Gaza, Palestine. Returning to Sydney on 27 February 1943, he was transferred to the Reserve of Officers on 7 June and was mentioned in dispatches. He resumed his post at the university, where he taught until 1952.

A founder (1938) of the Royal Australasian College of Physicians, McDonald was a member (1938-62) of its first council, secretary (1944-48), vice-president (1948-50), censor-in-chief (1950-54) and president (1954-56). He later chaired the editorial committee of the college's *Australasian Annals of Medicine* and its finance advisory committee. In 1956 he was elected a fellow of the Royal College of Physicians, London. Among other activities, he was a member (1946-62) of the State Medical Board and a trustee of the Public Library of New South Wales. He was chief medical officer (in time a trustee, then director) of the Mutual Life & Citizens' Assurance Co. Ltd for thirty years.

In 1942 McDonald had been elected to the Senate of the University of Sydney. Deputy-chancellor in 1953-54, he loved the university and was deeply aware of its history. He succeeded Sir Charles Blackburn [q.v.7] as chancellor in 1964. These were tumultuous years for the university—World War II and its aftermath, new universities, the Colombo plan, Commonwealth funding and student activism. McDonald defended the right of students to demonstrate against the Vietnam War, but, when some agitators went too far, he declared that the law must be upheld. In 1969 he was considering increased student representation on the senate.

McDonald's Catholic faith was central to his life. In the early 1930s he helped to establish the Catholic Medical Guild of St Luke. He became a respected counsellor—in more than medical matters—to Church leaders such as Cardinal (Sir) Norman Gilroy [q.v.14]. With J. H. McClemens [q.v.], he was a founder of the Newman Association of Catholic Graduates at the university; from 1953 he was chairman of Sancta Sophia College council. He also staunchly supported the annual university service at St Andrew's Anglican Cathedral. Archbishop (Sir) Marcus Loane noted, at McDonald's death, that his 'deep concern was to establish a Christian standard as the norm of all his activities'.

Ill health had prevented McDonald from attending the medical graduation on 19 January 1970. His prepared address, read by his deputy and successor (Sir) Hermann Black, included the following words: 'You will learn medicine and learn the wise practice of it only if you listen to your patients, are sympathetic with them as they should be with you, if you study their anxieties and their hopes and if you have a deep sense of devotion to your vocation'.

Although admired for his wit and warmth, and his culture and learning, McDonald had no ear for music. Some were wary of his hearty and determined style of arguing. He belonged to the Australian and Royal Sydney Golf clubs, and served as a councillor and president of Sydney High School Old Boys' Union. McDonald had been appointed C.B.E. (1956) and a knight commander of the papal Order of St Gregory the Great (1960); he was knighted in 1962 and elevated to K.B.E. in 1970. A chain-smoker who preferred his Capstan cigarettes in a holder, Sir Charles died on 23 April 1970 at the Repatriation General Hospital, Concord, and was buried in Northern Suburbs cemetery. He was survived by his wife, daughter and four sons, of whom Geoffrey and John became medical practitioners, and Charles, the youngest, a Jesuit priest.

Portraits of McDonald by (Sir) William Dargie are held by the Royal Australasian College of Physicians and the University of Sydney.

J. A. Young et al (eds), *Centenary Book of the University of Sydney Faculty of Medicine* (Syd, 1984); Univ Syd, *Gazette*, Apr 1970, p 290; Syd High School Old Boys' Union, *High Bulletin*, 50, June 1970, p 3; *MJA*, 17 Oct 1970, p 750; *J of the Aust Catholic Hist Soc*, 7, no 1, 1981, p 15.   GREGORY HAINES

MacDONALD, HENRY ALEXANDER (1915-1971), airman and freight operator, was born on 16 April 1915 at Glebe, Sydney, son of native-born parents Joseph MacDonald, a timekeeper with the Sydney Harbour Trust, and his wife Emily May, née Langton. Harry was educated at Drummoyne Boys' Intermediate High School. He enjoyed sailing, riding, swimming and golf. A well-dressed young man, with a fertile imagination, he appeared (1933-40) with the Kursaal Theatre and other small companies, performed in radio serials and worked for a theatrical agent. By 1939 he was employed as a soft-goods salesman. On 25 February that year at St Philip's Anglican Church, Sydney, he married Phyllis Joan Cleary; they were to have one child before being divorced in January 1948.

On 20 July 1941 MacDonald enlisted in the Royal Australian Air Force. In June 1942 he sailed to England as a sergeant pilot for further training with the Royal Air Force. Posted to North Africa in March 1943, he flew Wellington bombers on thirty-nine operations (day and night) with No.150 Squadron, R.A.F., and won the Distinguished Flying Medal for his 'outstanding' ability as an aircraft captain, and for his 'hard work' on the ground and in the air. One night in June, when fire and exploding bombs threatened parked aircraft, he ran to an aeroplane and taxied it to safety; he was awarded the British Empire Medal and commissioned that month. In September he returned to England where he served as an instructor at No.27 Operational Training Unit.

Repatriated in December 1944, MacDonald was promoted flight lieutenant in June 1945 while stationed at No.7 O.T.U., Tocumwal, New South Wales. In the following year he joined No.1 Communication Unit, Laverton, Victoria, and piloted Liberator aircraft carrying senior military and civilian passengers to India, Japan and the Pacific. Nicknamed 'Rainbow' because of his medal ribbons, he was admired as a skilled airman, and respected for the concern he showed for his crews and passengers. Yet, he was a man who kept to himself: he had asked that his decorations be posted to him to avoid the publicity of an investiture. On 5 February 1948 at John Knox Church, Gardenvale, Melbourne, he married with Presbyterian forms Dawne Gough Burton, née Waller, a 29-year-old divorcee. In April customs officers at Laverton discovered 24 000 American cigarettes in MacDonald's aircraft on its return from Japan. Evidence pointed to 'black-market trading', but no action was taken. MacDonald was demobilized in October.

In 1949 MacDonald and four partners formed Freight Wings which operated from Evans Head, New South Wales. Within a year he faced bankruptcy proceedings. His management of the wholesale butchery and carrying company owned by his wife ended with her bankruptcy in 1954. After being employed as a driver in Brisbane, he formed Cold Road Pty Ltd, a transport company. It ceased operating about 1969. He then set up as a financier and home-builder until he was obliged to execute a deed of arrangement with his creditors in January 1970.

MacDonald worked hard in the Australian refrigerated transport industry and even designed his own trucks. His business failures were largely due to poor financial management. Reading was his favourite form of relaxation, and he belonged to the Liberal Party and the United Service Club, Queensland. He died of myocardial infarction on 10 October 1971 at his Bowen Hills home and was cremated with Anglican rites; his wife and daughter survived him, as did the daughter of his first marriage.

H. A. McDonald, RAAF Service Record (AA, Canb); AWM 65, H. A. McDonald (AWM).

           J. B. HOPLEY

McDONALD, SIR JOHN GLADSTONE BLACK (1898-1977), orchardist and premier, was born on 6 December 1898 at Falkirk, Stirlingshire, Scotland, second child of Donald Macdonald, licensed grocer, and his wife Ann Elizabeth, née Henry. Educated locally at Carmuirs School, Jack emigrated to Australia in 1912 with his widowed mother, brother and two sisters. The family began farming at Shepparton East, Victoria, but lost their entire dairy herd in the drought of 1914.

On 4 March 1916 McDonald overstated his age and enlisted in the Australian Imperial Force. Posted to the 37th Battalion, he served on the Western Front from November that year until he was shot through the chest in February 1917. While in hospital he had a lung removed: he kept his condition a secret for most of his life. Discharged on 4 January 1918, he returned to Shepparton where he established an orchard in partnership with his brother Rodney. On 10 December 1932 at the Presbyterian Church, Ashfield, Sydney, he married Mary Cosser Trotter, a 24-year-old schoolteacher who was to become a community activist, involved in at least fourteen committees at Shepparton.

A 'practical irrigator' with good organizing abilities, McDonald soon participated in agricultural organizations. He was president of the Shepparton Irrigators' Association; vice-president of the Northern Victorian Fruit-growers' Association and of the Australian Canning Fruit Association; a regular delegate to the Victorian Fruit Marketing Authority; and an original shareholder in, and board-member (1937-70) and chairman (1965-70) of, the Shepparton Preserving Co. (later S.P.C. Ltd). Maintaining a long association with the Shepparton Football Club, he was president of its second XVIII. During his one term (1928-29) on the Shepparton Shire Council he clashed with other councillors.

After (Sir) Murray Bourchier [q.v.7] retired from parliament, Jack McDonald won an absolute majority over three other endorsed Country Party candidates at the by-election for the Legislative Assembly seat of Goulburn Valley on 19 September 1936; he held the seat until it was abolished in 1945 whereupon he transferred to the new seat of Shepparton. He was Country Party whip in 1938-43.

Appointed minister without portfolio in the Dunstan-Hollway [qq.v.8,14] coalition government on 28 June 1943, McDonald received the portfolios of water supply and electrical undertakings on 18 September. He maintained his commitment to irrigation and 'would talk water at the drop of a hat'. In 1945 he transferred the control of all river management to the State Rivers and Water Supply Commission; later, as premier, he signed the contract for the Big Eildon storage project which greatly increased the capacity of Eildon Reservoir.

At the elections on 10 November 1945—following the defeat of the Dunstan-Hollway government in September and Ian Macfarlan's [q.v.] ensuing 51-day premiership—the Country Party lost seven seats. A minority Labor government led by John Cain [q.v.13] was formed. Dunstan, who had been publicly criticized by his colleagues, chose not to contest the Country Party leadership and his 'protégé' McDonald was elected in his place. McDonald led the official opposition until the Cain government's defeat in October 1947. On 20 November a Liberal-Country Party coalition was formed with Hollway as premier. His deputy, McDonald, was president of the Board of Land and Works, commissioner of crown lands and survey, and minister of water supply and of soldier settlement. Portfolios were shared equally between

the parties, but Hollway was angered when Dunstan received a ministry. The coalition soon degenerated into a 'welter of cross-purposes and a tangle of jarring discords, animosities, jealousies and conflict'. Hollway accused Dunstan of disloyalty, and McDonald grew suspicious of the premier's close friendship with Cain.

Although he 'ruled the [Country] party with a rod of iron', McDonald was unable to contain differences within the cabinet when he acted as premier while Hollway was abroad in late 1948. McDonald adopted a forceful approach to a strike involving tramway workers. On his return the premier initially backed his deputy, before negotiating a compromise with his friend J. V. Stout [q.v.] of the Trades Hall Council. The Country Party alleged betrayal and withdrew from the ministry. In retaliation, the Liberals renamed (1949) themselves the Liberal and Country Party, and attempted an unsuccessful takeover of the Country Party. From 3 December 1948 Hollway remained in power and McDonald reverted to leader of the Opposition.

An agreement negotiated between the Country and Labor parties installed McDonald as premier and treasurer on 27 June 1950. His government's major achievements included the extension of adult franchise to elections for the Legislative Council and the establishment of the Mental Hygiene Authority. In 1951 his cabinet refused to commute the death sentence passed on Jean Lee [q.v.], the last woman to be hanged in Victoria. Stung by the Federal government's cut in loan funds to Victoria in 1951, McDonald openly criticized Prime Minister (Sir) Robert Menzies [q.v.]. Sections within the State Labor Party remained opposed to propping up a Country Party government and, when McDonald vacillated on the vexed issue of the abolition of rural electoral weighting, his position became precarious. He attempted to secure the premiership by an arrangement with Leslie Norman, the new leader of the Liberal and Country Party.

In September 1952 Hollway moved an unsuccessful no-confidence motion against McDonald's government and was expelled from the L.C.P. McDonald retaliated by establishing a royal commission to investigate allegations that Hollway had offered bribes to politicians to support the motion. The commission adjourned indefinitely after Hollway issued writs for libel against the *Age* newspaper. On 21 October 1952 Labor and two of Hollway's supporters blocked supply in the Legislative Council. McDonald failed to secure a dissolution and resigned. Hollway was commissioned to form a ministry. His Electoral Reform Party held office for only three days, from 28 to 31 October. McDonald was again commissioned premier, and the governor Sir Dallas Brooks [q.v.13] granted a dissolution. The elections on 6 December 1952 gave Labor its first majority government in Victoria.

McDonald remained in parliament, but was shaken by the death of his brother during the 1952 election campaign. The '2 for 1' electoral redistribution, which he had so vehemently opposed, determined in 1953 that his seat would be abolished, and his health began to be more affected by his war-wounds. He decided not to contest the 1955 election. On 27 September that year the Country Party honoured him and his deputy Keith Dodgshun [q.v.14] at a public function at the St Kilda Town Hall. McDonald was knighted in 1957.

Despite deteriorating health, Sir John remained active in his retirement. A 'dour, hard-headed and strong-minded man', he 'spoke with a rich Scottish burr'. In addition to his farming interests, he became a director of Goulburn-Murray Television Ltd and continued his close involvement with S.P.C. Ltd. When S.P.C. recorded a $1.4 million loss in 1969/70, a 'reform group' of shareholders organized proxies to remove him as chairman.

Survived by his wife, son and two daughters, McDonald died on 23 April 1977 at Mooroopna and was cremated. One week later a state memorial service was conducted at Shepparton. An undistinguished portrait of Sir John, painted from a photograph, is held at Parliament House, Melbourne.

K. West, *Power in the Liberal Party* (Melb, 1965); L. G. Houston, *Ministers of Water Supply in Victoria* (Melb, 1965); R. Wright, *A People's Counsel* (Melb, 1992); *PD* (Vic), 26 Apr 1977; *Countryman* (Melb), 4 Sept 1936, 14 Nov 1952, 22 July 1955; *Herald* (Melb), 4 July 1970; *Age* (Melb), 11 July 1970, 25 Apr 1977; *Shepparton News*, 25 Apr 1977, 8 July 1983.　　　　　　　　　　B. J. COSTAR

MCDONALD, NANCY MAY (1921-1974), poet and editor, was born on Christmas Day 1921 at Eastwood, Sydney, third child of native-born parents William James McDonald, postal engineer and returned soldier, and his first wife Beatrice May, née Hancox. Nan grew up at Eastwood, spending holidays on the Hawkesbury, and at Blackheath and Wellington. She attended (1934-38) Hornsby Girls' High School under Agnes Brewster [q.v.13] where she contributed poems to the school magazine, twice winning the Ethel Curlewis [q.v.12 Turner] prize for verse. Proceeding to the University of Sydney (B.A., 1943), she graduated with second-class honours in English.

In 1943 McDonald joined the editorial staff of Angus & Robertson [qq.v.7,11] Ltd. There she worked with such people as Alec Bolton,

Beatrice Davis and Douglas Stewart. Recalled by Rosemary Dobson as 'the best book editor in Australia', she made a considerable—though largely unacknowledged—contribution to the publication of Australian fiction and history for some thirty years. She and Davis spent 'many gruelling hours' on the manuscripts of Ion Idriess and Frank Clune [qq.v.9,13]. Several of her poems chafe at the constraints, and the pay was poor; but it was the heyday of A. & R. and professional standards were upheld.

McDonald's poetic output was small but highly regarded, with poems appearing mostly in Sydney journals from the 1940s to the 1960s. Her first collection, *Pacific Sea* (1947), praised by Stewart as 'a book of sea and bush and flowers and birds', won the first Grace Leven prize for poetry in 1947. She edited the annual, *Australian Poetry*, in 1953, thereby gaining A. D. Hope's approval. In *The Lonely Fire* (1954), which impressed Dame Mary Gilmore [q.v.9], McDonald added an urban dimension, as in 'Market Street: Friday Evening'. *The Lighthouse*, an historical verseplay influenced by T. S. Eliot and broadcast by the Australian Broadcasting Commission in 1957, was the title poem for a third publication in 1959 which contained the powerful 'The Hatters' and 'The Hawk', subsequently included in anthologies. In 1969 she published a fourth collection, *Selected Poems*, with new poetry from the Illawarra. McDonald was a practising Presbyterian; her affirmation of the east-coast Australian landscape was driven by metaphysical as well as environmental values. She shone in shorter forms, but was capable of narrative, as in the haunting 'Alison Hunt' and 'The Mail-boat's Late Again'.

From 1948 Nan McDonald corresponded with 'Dearest Rozzie' (Dobson), exchanging 'pomes' for comment and telling of her garden. After she had undergone several operations and seen the takeover (1970) of A. & R., McDonald took leave late in 1971 and freelanced for the firm thereafter. Letters to another friend in 1972-73 indicated a strained relationship with the new management: 'The old firm has certainly passed away'. Nan lived with her sister Margaret at Mount Keira, as in 'The House of Winds' (*Torch* 1936). Editing and illness left little energy even for gardening. McDonald died of cancer on 7 January 1974 at Mount Ousley and was cremated with Presbyterian forms. One late poem, *For Prisoners*, was published posthumously (Canberra, 1995). Her poems appear in most modern anthologies, but critical perspective is still lacking.

Hornsby Girls' High School, *Torch*, 1934-38; *Hemisphere*, 20, Mar 1976; *SMH*, 10 May 1956; Rosemary Dobson papers (NL); McDonald correspondence, MSS 5346, 5757 (ML).　　J. I. ROE

McDONALD, PHYLLIS MARY (1905-1977), violinist and teacher of music, was born on 27 April 1905 at Darlington, Sydney, younger daughter of Herbert John Carlyle McDonald, a native-born boiler-maker, and his wife Elizabeth, née Burke, who came from Ireland. Educated at the Sisters of Mercy Golden Grove Convent, Redfern, where she learned the violin from Sister Aquina, Phyllis played for the visiting violinist, Jascha Heifetz, who declared that she looked like a devil but played like an angel. In 1922 she won an associated board exhibition to the Royal Academy of Music, London (associate, 1924; licentiate, 1926; fellow, 1966). She studied initially with Hans Wessely and later with Edith Knocker, and was awarded numerous prizes and appointed a sub-professor at the college. McDonald formed her own string quartet and also began to establish a solo career.

Shortly after her return to Sydney, J. & N. Tait [qq.v.12] advertised a recital on 28 June 1933 by 'the brilliant violinist Miss Phyllis McDonald' at the town hall. Once settled back home, she taught violin and ensemble playing at the New South Wales State Conservatorium of Music from 1935 to 1967. She had a distinctive teaching style and a loyal following: many former colleagues and students testified to her devotion to her students. McDonald played in the Conservatorium String Quartet (which performed weekly) and with various light music ensembles. She was heard frequently on Australian Broadcasting Commission programmes, both as soloist and in ensembles. In 1942 she was one of the local artists engaged for that year's A.B.C. concert series. Critics considered her a talented performer, with a smooth, warm tone.

McDonald was a colleague and friend of several composers working at the conservatorium, especially Frank Hutchens and Raymond Hanson [qq.v.9,14], both of whom played for her diploma classes. She often performed with them and promoted their compositions. Phyllis was especially close to Hanson, who wrote his *Concerto for Violin and Orchestra* for her. When consulted by him, she told him to write what he liked, as the soloist should cope with any technical difficulties. Hanson took her at her word, and she found the result so complicated that she never found time to learn it. She did, however, record Hanson's *Sonata for Violin and Piano* and his *Three Fancies* (for violin and piano)—with the composer—for an A.B.C. broadcast in 1950.

In 1947 Willem Noske, a visiting Dutch violinist, had heard McDonald play violin sonatas by Dorian Le Gallienne [q.v.] and Hanson; he considered her 'such a fine violinist that if she were to leave Australia' he was sure 'she would be accepted in a very short time as a world violinist'. Miss McDonald was a small, rotund woman, with thick glasses. Colleagues enjoyed her company, but found her quiet and reticent, revealing little of her private life. She collapsed on her way to a concert at the Sydney Opera House and died on 12 July 1977 in Sydney Hospital; she was buried in Rookwood cemetery.

T. Radic, *Bernard Heinze* (Melb, 1986); *Aust Musical News*, 38, Nov 1947, p 19; *SMH*, 28 July 1923, 12 June, 9 July 1924, 7 Sept 1925, 31 Jan, 29 July, 31 Oct 1927; Syd Conservatorium of Music L; Dennis Wolanski L of Performing Arts, Syd Opera House; information from Sr Christina, Stella Maris Nursing Home, Cronulla, Mr F. Coe, Killara, Mr K. Miller, Lindfield, Mrs J. Taylor, Earlwood, and Miss E. Todd, Darling Point, Syd.

SUE TRONSER

McDONALD, SIR ROBERT ROSS (1888-1964), lawyer and politician, was born on 25 January 1888 at Albany, Western Australia, son of Angus McDonald, bank manager, and his wife Mary Jane, née Elder. Ross was educated at Fremantle School, Scotch College, Perth, and the University of Adelaide (LL.B., 1913). After passing Barristers' Board examinations, he was admitted to the Western Australian Bar on 15 March 1910 and in 1912 formed a partnership with L. W. Lohrman. On 15 February 1916 McDonald was commissioned in the Australian Imperial Force. He served with the 4th Division Artillery on the Western Front in 1918 and his appointment terminated on 2 November 1919.

Back in Perth, McDonald joined Robinson, Cox, Jackson & Wheatley and became a partner in 1921. His reputation in commercial law was recognized by his appointment in 1923 to the royal commission inquiring into the Kendenup land schemes of C. J. De Garis [q.v.8]. A founding member (1928) of the Law Society of Western Australia, he lectured part time at the university in 1928-31. He took silk on 10 February 1936.

One of Perth's most eligible bachelors, McDonald chose not to marry. He was honorary aide-de-camp (1925-31) to the governor Sir William Campion [q.v.7], a foundation member of Perth Rotary Club (president 1929-30), and president (for twenty years) of the local branch of the Victoria League. Elected to the Legislative Assembly as the Nationalist member for West Perth on 8 April 1933, he became party leader and deputy-leader of the Opposition in April 1938. McDonald was a polite and constructive antagonist to moderate Labor governments. In 1945 he oversaw the incorporation of the Western Australian Nationalists into the Liberal Party. Believing that the new party required rural leadership, he offered to stand down as leader early in 1946, but was persuaded to remain until replaced by (Sir) Ross McLarty [q.v.] in December.

On 1 April 1947 the Liberal-Country Party coalition took office. McLarty appointed McDonald attorney-general, minister for police and minister for native affairs; in January 1948 he exchanged the two former portfolios for housing and forests. As attorney-general, he opposed what many Western Australians saw as the encroachments of the Federal Labor government. In his other ministries he was a force for reform, showing a lively concern for the living standards of timberworkers, and infusing fresh vigour into Aboriginal policy with the appointment of the Papua-trained S. G. Middleton as commissioner for native affairs. Resigning from cabinet in October 1949, and from parliament in March 1950, he was knighted in the following June.

Well liked and respected, but marked by a gentlemanly reticence, McDonald was a trustee (1950-58) of the Public Library, Museum and Art Gallery of Western Australia, a member (1950-61) of the senate of the University of Western Australia, and chairman (1954-56) of St Catherine's, the first women's college at the university. He was also a director of numerous companies, chairman (1956-60) of the Royal Perth Hospital board and a foundation member of the State branch of the National Trust of Australia. Sir Ross died on 25 March 1964 in Perth and was buried in Karrakatta cemetery with Presbyterian forms. His estate was sworn for probate at £48 773.

P. Biskup, *Not Slaves, Not Citizens* (Brisb, 1973); P. Firkins, *A History of the Rotary Club of Perth, 1927-1987* (Perth, 1987); *West Australian*, 12 Apr 1933, 16 Dec 1946, 26, 27 Mar 1964.

G. C. BOLTON
TRESNA SHORTER

McDONALD, SIMON (1906-1968), traditional singer and bushworker, was born on 22 November 1906 at Spring Mount, near Creswick, Victoria, fourth of six children of Victorian-born parents Simon McDonald, labourer, and his wife Margaret, née Murnane. Young Simon grew up in a three-roomed bush hut built by his father on a piece of ground obtained by a miner's right, and spent almost all his life in the Creswick area. His father had once worked in the deep alluvial mines at Allendale, but mostly fossicked on his own for gold or dug potatoes seasonally for a sparse living in support of his wife and children. Songs around the fire were part of family life.

During his childhood, Simon foraged for food by picking blackberries, gathering birds'

eggs and digging bitter-tasting roots which he called yams. He contributed to the meagre family income by gardening or picking fruit in his spare time. Each winter, exempted from school for three months to dig and bag potatoes with his father, he walked miles to the paddocks to begin work at daybreak and walked home again usually in darkness.

After obtaining his merit certificate, he left Spring Mount State School at the age of 14 and continued doing odd jobs—chopping wood for his grandfather 'Wild Matty' Murnane, cutting and stooking hay, milking cows, ploughing, and digging potatoes. In the Depression, which inspired his recitation, 'The Dole', he hunted for gold and took to haircutting. Father and son made music at home, and at dances where Simon and his brother John played tin whistles in the old-time band made up of a pianist (Simon's aunt) and his father, a self-taught violinist. Simon gathered many popular songs from abroad, including *Banks of Claudy, Paddy Heggarty's Leather Britches, Grandpa's Chair is Vacant*, as well as local songs such as *The Wild Colonial Boy* and *Bill Brink*, until his repertoire comprised about fifty songs and at least seven poems of his own composition.

Work on a threshing-machine near Bannockburn and grape-picking at Mildura resulted in several recitations, 'The Thresher', 'Mildura Grapes' and 'The Union'. McDonald played football and wrote a song, *The Bloodsuckers*, about the Spring Mount team; he went woodcutting to feed the boilers at Ballarat and produced a set of verses entitled 'Two Axe Mac'; and, when he was charged with being drunk and disorderly, he created a poem, 'Locked in the Creswick Gaol'. Rejected for military service in World War II, he worked for a few months with Bayley & Grimster Pty Ltd, electrical engineers at Collingwood, Melbourne. He found the city 'too full of smoke' and headed back for the bush. Later, he joined a band which entertained visiting American servicemen at country dances; he alternated on violin and banjo, and sang popular songs.

When he was 60 McDonald looked much older, a skinny, worn-out battler on an invalid pension. Dressed in nondescript, cast-off clothes and a battered felt hat, he spent his days collecting worms and picking blackberries, and his nights cadging drinks in return for a song. While riding his overloaded bicycle near Creswick on 31 May 1968, he suffered a stroke and died. He was buried in the local cemetery with Catholic rites.

Traditional Singers and Musicians in Victoria, Wattle Records, Archive Series 2 (Syd, 1963); H. Anderson (ed), *Time Out of Mind* (Melb, 1974); *Sun News-Pictorial*, 5 Dec 1966.

HUGH ANDERSON

McDONALD, SIR WARREN D'ARCY (1901-1965), engineer, industrialist, soldier and banker, was born on 23 September 1901 at Penguin, Tasmania, son of William Patrick McDonald, a building contractor of Irish and Scottish descent, and his wife Christina Louise Gaffney. Warren spent his early childhood at Strahan. Sent to Hadspen State School, he won a scholarship to Launceston Church Grammar School. At the age of 17 he gained another to the University of Tasmania where he intended to study medicine. Because his scholarship could not be taken up until he was 18, he became a cadet-engineer with the Tasmanian Hydro-Electric Department. He relinquished his university place and never regretted his change of career, later remarking that: 'As an engineer you see what you have done. It's in concrete; it's there. I enjoy travelling over some bridge I have built ... Every bridge is different. For the fellow who built it, it has its own personality'. The simplicity and camaraderie of life in construction camps also appealed to him.

About 1925 McDonald moved to Camperdown, Victoria, as assistant-engineer of Hampden Shire. Within eighteen months he resigned to supervise the construction of houses in Canberra under a contract which the Federal Capital Commission let to his father. Warren was to become a permanent resident of the national capital, identifying himself with the community and taking pride in the city and its development. On 14 December 1927 at St Patrick's Catholic Church, Sydney, he married Christina Helen Sullivan, a 28-year-old tailoress. That year he won a contract to build a section of the Federal Highway between Canberra and Goulburn. Following the death of his father in 1936, he took over the family business, establishing McDonald Constructions Pty Ltd and, in 1948, McDonald Industries Ltd.

On 5 October 1939 McDonald had enlisted in the Militia as a sapper. Commissioned in January 1940, he was seconded to the Australian Imperial Force in May and posted to the 7th Divisional Engineers. After serving in the Middle East from November 1940 to March 1942, he was promoted lieutenant colonel and took part in the Papuan campaign as chief engineer (from April 1942) of the 6th Division. He then performed staff and training duties in Australia. In June 1945 he flew to Bougainville as temporary brigadier and chief engineer, II Corps. Returning home in October, he transferred to the Reserve of Officers on 7 December and was mentioned in dispatches (1947).

At the Federal elections in 1946, McDonald unsuccessfully contested the seat of Hume for the Country Party. Next year the Chifley [q.v.13] government asked him to advise the prices commissioner on building costs.

McDonald gradually established strong political contacts with (Sir) Robert Menzies [q.v.] and the Liberal Party. In 1952 Menzies' administration appointed him to the Australian National Airlines Commission, which operated Trans-Australia Airlines; he became vice-chairman in 1956 and chairman in February 1957. The government used the Airlines Equipment Act (1958) to block T.A.A.'s choice of new aircraft, much to the advantage of its private-enterprise competitor, Ansett-ANA. McDonald's decision to engage the public-relations firm, Eric White Associates Pty Ltd, proved important in restoring T.A.A.'s standing.

Although he knew next to nothing of banking, McDonald was selected as foundation chairman of the Commonwealth Banking Corporation in 1959. He gave the corporation 'inspired direction' which, among other things, ensured the success of the Commonwealth Development Bank of Australia. McDonald staunchly advocated developing northern Australia, in which endeavour his company played its part by constructing beef-roads in Queensland and railways in Western Australia. He was also a driving force in the campaign to increase Australian exports, and in January-February 1962 led a trade mission to countries in the Middle East and eastern Mediterranean region.

A member (1953-64) of the council of the Australian National University, McDonald chaired the buildings and grounds committee; his policy of distributing commissions to numerous architects produced a plethora of building styles. In addition, he played a key part in launching the National Heart Foundation of Australia. As its genial, but concerned, founding president (1959-64), he took hard decisions when necessary to ensure sound funding. The foundation's Warren McDonald research fellowship commemorates him.

McDonald was thickset, with silver hair and a ruddy complexion. Able, extremely energetic, well-informed and widely travelled, he was very competitive and hated to be beaten. His recreations included golf, fishing and tennis. He had represented the Australian Capital Territory in cricket, of which he was a devotee, and in Australian Rules football. In 1957 he was appointed C.B.E. He was elevated to K.B.E. in 1964 for 'public service in many fields'. Survived by his wife and three daughters, Sir Warren died of cerebral thrombosis on 12 November 1965 at Lewisham, Sydney, and was buried in Canberra cemetery.

D. McCarthy, *South-West Pacific Area—First Year* (Canb, 1959); G. Long, *The Final Campaigns* (Canb, 1963); I. Sabey, *Challenge in the Skies* (Melb, 1979); TAA, *Transair*, Aug 1952; *Age* (Melb), 13 May 1964; *Canb Times* and *SMH*, 13, 16 Nov 1965;

Cwlth Bank of Aust Archives (Syd); information from Mrs P. White, Cammeray, Mr K. Shave, Edgecliff, Syd, Mr R. Hohnen and Mr B. Owens, Forrest, Dr R. Reeder, Kingston, Mr B. Hamilton, Farrer, and Dr S. Foster, Ainslie, Canb.

JOHN FARQUHARSON

McDONELL, ALEXANDER (1900-1980), schoolteacher and educational administrator, was born on 15 March 1900 at Mildura, Victoria, third son of Melbourne-born parents George Bain McDonell, labourer, and his wife Caroline, née Anderson. Alexander retained strong memories of his country childhood in a straitened, hard-working family: living in bag houses, tents and a galvanized home without running water, watching his father shoot snakes and sulphur-crested cockatoos, having a split over his eye mended by cobwebs from a straw broom, and stacking sultanas and raisins on wooden trays for drying. Most of his primary education was obtained at the Nichols Point State School. In 1913, having completed his merit certificate, he moved to the newly opened Mildura Agricultural High School at which he won a scholarship to enable him to continue his schooling. On 1 February 1916 he was appointed as a pupil-teacher.

Driven by the hope of a predictable income as well as by patriotism, his father had enlisted in the Australian Imperial Force on 12 July 1915 and sailed for the Middle East. Alex continued at school and assisted his mother with the management of their block. When his father returned in 1918, Alex entered Melbourne Teachers' College on a secondary studentship. At the University of Melbourne (B.Sc., Dip.Ed., 1923) he was prominent as a debater and sportsman; he captained the college's football team in 1918, and its sporting team which competed against Teachers' College, Sydney, in 1920. His college report (1921) noted: 'Fine, vigorous, all round man, in study, sport, social life and teaching. Is bound to do well'. At the Presbyterian Church, Tarnagulla, on 23 May 1925 McDonell married Jean Victoria Alexander, a 24-year-old schoolteacher to whom he had been engaged for three years. They had met at college, but delayed their marriage because Alex was providing his family's only regular income while his parents developed a soldier-settlement block at Birdwoodton, near Mildura.

In 1922 McDonell had been appointed to Mildura High School (formerly the Agricultural High School). He transferred in 1926 to Bendigo High School. There he built a reputation as an outstanding teacher of mathematics and science, and played an active part in the city's sporting life, particularly its cricket and football teams. Recognition of his abilities led to his transfer in 1929 to the Teachers' College, where he worked until 1937 while studying at the University of Melbourne (B.A., 1936; B.Ed., 1937). Work and study did not prevent him from calling Australian Rules football for the Australian Broadcasting Commission in the late 1930s. McDonell's professional career blossomed and in 1937 he was made an inspector of secondary schools. His prodigious memory, which enabled him to greet teachers by name and recall their careers, became legendary. He was appointed chief inspector of secondary schools in 1953, assistant-director of education in 1958 (the first person to hold that position) and director of education in 1960.

McDonell's senior administrative career in the Victorian Education Department coincided with a period of exceptional growth and stress, and his first concerns were to build schools, to alleviate the crisis in overcrowded classrooms, and to tackle the acute shortage of qualified teachers. He remained suspicious of, and quietly resisted, the increasing involvement of parents and teachers in the administration of the school system and in the curriculum debates which developed as secondary education became part of the experience of most children. Conservative, fair-minded, wary of religious or political zealotry, efficient, and intensely dedicated to his professional duties, he held the traditional views of an educational administrator who was the product of a highly centralized system. He admired that system and its teachers, and gave them the same sort of loyalty he had given his parents.

Although McDonell retired from the department on 15 March 1965, he continued to contribute significantly to the wider educational community. At the University of Melbourne he was a member of the council (1957-65) and the Schools Board (1942-58); at Monash University he belonged to the interim council (1958) and council (1958-65). He assisted in the development of the Victoria Institute of Colleges, served (1961-64) on Sir Leslie Martin's committee on the future of tertiary education in Australia, and chaired the A.B.C.'s advisory committee on school broadcasts which introduced television into schools. Survived by his wife, son and daughter, he died on 24 February 1980 at Blackburn South and was cremated.

Education Dept (Vic), *Vision and Realisation*, L. J. Blake ed (Melb, 1973); A. McDonell, Memoirs (ms, held by Dr J. A. McDonell); teachers' and professional registers, Hist Section, Education Dept (Vic), Melb; correspondence, especially Secondary Schools Division, VPRS 10249, *and* Teachers' Colleges, VPRS 10563 (PRO, Vic); information from Dr J. A. and Mrs W. McDonell, Glen Waverley, Melb. R. J. W. SELLECK

McDONNELL, ETHEL (1876-1961), community leader, was born on 6 February 1876 at Newbridge, Staffordshire, England, daughter of John Cox Pearson, commission agent, and his wife Susannah, née Langman. Sent to the House of Education, Ambleside, Westmoreland, she then spent two years at a boarding-school in Geneva. In 1898 she began nursing as a probationer in the London Hospital. Despite the matron's belief that Ethel was more self-opinionated than competent, she was appointed a 'Holiday Sister' in June 1900 and promoted to 'Sister Victor' two months later. In 1904 she resigned from the hospital. At Christ Church, Wolverhampton, on 5 January 1909 she married John Carlile McDonnell (M.A., Cantab), a clergyman from Ireland who ministered in a London slum. They emigrated (1910) to South Australia where Carlile was appointed curate of St Bede's Anglican Church, Semaphore. At Bishop A. N. Thomas's [q.v.12] behest, he resigned his living when he could no longer subscribe to the Thirty-nine Articles. Ethel was devastated. In 1917 Carlile joined the Collegiate School of St Peter as a teacher of English. Cultivated, capable and generous, Ethel enjoyed the school milieu.

Drawn to public causes with quiet forcefulness, Mrs McDonnell took a keen interest in educational and social-welfare issues, even though some criticized her for becoming involved while raising two young children. As president (1921-24) and an executive-member (1919-46) of the Women's Non-party Association of South Australia (later League of Women Voters), she campaigned to improve the legal status of women, children and Aborigines. She was a founding member and vice-president (from 1919) of the State branch of the Australian League of Nations Union; she was also on the provisional committee of Girton School (1925-26), and a committee-member of St Mark's (1922) and St Ann's (1938-39) colleges.

McDonnell served (1923-27) on the executive of the National Council of Women of South Australia. In 1926 she was appointed a justice of the peace. The Commonwealth government chose her in 1928 as a substitute delegate to the League of Nations. Joining the social and general committee in Geneva, she 'held her own' among other female delegates: she argued against licensed brothels and praised the 'admirable work' of South Australia's policewomen; by invitation, she repeated her address to the General Assembly. In 1929, while acting-president of the Australian Federation of Women Voters, she renewed her international contacts. Spare in frame, with finely chiselled features, she spoke with 'force, eloquence and vision'.

In April 1930 McDonnell's husband died. Three years later her only son, a Royal Australian Air Force cadet, was killed in a biplane accident. Grief-stricken, she funded their memorial in St Peter's College chapel. She sought solace with relations in Melbourne and England, and benefited from intellectual companionship at the Lyceum Club, Adelaide (president 1940-42). To fund her extensive commitments, she renovated and sold houses at College Park. In 1935 she was awarded King George V's silver jubilee medal. Resuming her community activities, she assisted Lucy Morice and Doris Beeston [qq.v.10,13] on the Kindergarten Union of South Australia; in 1935-46 she sat on its executive and education committees. Under Adelaide Miethke [q.v.10], she was a vice-president (1935-36), with Charlotte Leal [q.v.], of the Women's Centenary Council of South Australia.

During World War II McDonnell worked unceasingly. In 1941, with her friend Marion Allnutt [q.v.13], she founded the South Australian unit of the Women's Australian National Services; she chaired its executive until 1947. She served (1943-47) on the University of Adelaide's board of social science. President of the A.F.W.V. in 1942-45, she coordinated lobbying on women's and children's issues, met politicians, and wrote hundreds of letters. In March 1943 she joined Common Cause, which aimed to arouse a greater sense of patriotism and self-sacrifice, and to create a better postwar society.

McDonnell spent four weeks in Melbourne after the war, caring for her grandchildren, before returning to Adelaide, troubled by ill health. Following a visit to England in 1948, she retired from public life. When her eyesight began to fail, she was helped by a housekeeper-companion. Housebound and partly bedridden, she remained hospitable and vitally interested in events. Her bed was eventually moved to the sitting-room, where she received friends. Survived by her daughter, she died on 13 July 1961 in her home at St Peters and was buried in North Road cemetery.

L. Brown et al (eds), *A Book of South Australia* (Adel, 1936); *Honorary Magistrate*, 30 June, 30 Sept 1928; *Dawn* (Perth), 21 Nov, 12 Dec 1928, 15 May 1929; *St Peter's College Mag*, May 1930, May 1933; *Observer* (Adel), 13 Mar 1926, 9 June, 22 Dec 1928; *Advertiser* (Adel), 12 Mar 1943, 23 July 1957, 18 July 1961; League of Women Voters, minutes 1919-46, and *Forward*, June 1927-Aug 1928 (Mort L); information from Mrs E. E. Yeatman, Malvern, Adel.

HELEN JONES

MACDOUGALL, AUGUSTA ('PAKIE') (1875-1945), café owner, and DUNCAN (1878-1953), actor-manager, were husband and wife. Augusta was born on Christmas Day 1875 at Waverley, Sydney, fifth child of English-born parents Benjamin Quiddington Poole, quarry-man, and his wife Clara Ann, née Wonnocott. Educated at Leichhardt Superior Public School, Augusta trained (1902-03) as a nurse at Royal Prince Alfred Hospital, Camperdown, where Henry Lawson [q.v.10] was one of her patients. While nursing, she became interested in politics and feminism.

Duncan was born on 15 February 1878 at Glasgow, Scotland, son of John Macdougall, draper's assistant, and his wife Isabella, née Mitchell. Emigrating with his family to Sydney in 1886, he was educated at Cleveland Street Superior Public School. He then worked at Angus & Robertson's [qq.v.7,11] bookshop. By the age of 22 he had set up as an elocution teacher. His first student was Augusta Poole. He also taught public speaking to candidates for the Presbyterian ministry at St Andrew's College, University of Sydney.

Duncan later wrote that he studied 'drama and prepared for stage work as an Art, not as mere industrialism'. To further his studies, he travelled to England in 1903, where he became interested in the repertory movement. Augusta followed shortly after. They were married with Congregational forms on 3 November 1904 at the City Temple, Holborn Viaduct, London. The young couple moved in socialist circles. Augusta joined the Women's Social and Political Union. She spent a fortnight in the City of London Prison, Holloway, over Christmas 1906 for refusing to leave a suffragette who had been injured by mounted police. Four months later, at the home of Ramsay MacDonald, she gave birth to a son Robin; in his early attempts at speech he gave her the name 'Pakie'.

Duncan claimed to have conducted the London Repertory Society at the New Royalty Theatre, and to have been a tutor to members of the aristocracy. Augusta obtained a diploma from the London College of Music. Together they edited two anthologies, *The Quaint Comedy of Love, Wooing & Mating* (1907) and *The Bond of Music* (1907). They visited Central Europe and by early 1913 had moved to the United States of America. Duncan became involved with the Provincetown Players: working at the Playwrights' Theatre in New York stimulated his interest in 'folk' drama—plays in the heightened demotic style of writers like Eugene O'Neill and John Millington Synge. He failed to get financial backing for a Scottish-American theatre in New York, but managed to establish (May 1919) Macdougall's Barn Theatre, though it was short-lived.

The Macdougalls returned to Sydney in November 1920. By 1922 Duncan had formed a professional company which unsuccessfully toured northern New South Wales and southern Queensland. In 1923 he estab-lished the Playbox Society in Sydney to create 'a vital Australian Theatre for the encouragement of Australian dramatists and the production of the best international drama'. His staging of Ernst Toller's *Masses and Man* in 1924 was criticized in State parliament when some of the closing-night audience sang *The Red Flag*, but the publicity increased the Playbox's fame.

In 1925 production moved from St James' Hall to the top floor of 11 Rowe Street, a tiny space seating eighty subscribers, which became the Playbox Theatre. Operating on a shoestring, Duncan produced plays by writers such as Karel Capek, Sean O'Casey, O'Neill, and Frank Wedekind, and held regular lectures and readings. Although he deplored 'stagey' acting, his own talents were debatable, especially when exposed in the leading roles he was apt to take; yet he was a gifted teacher who drew strong performances from his amateur casts. Believing that great dramatic writing needed a secure professional context in order to emerge, Duncan saw the Playbox as the nucleus of his dream of a state-sponsored national theatre and school for actors. 'Little, lean, high-strung', was how Dulcie Deamer [q.v.8] described him, with 'untidy grey hair and furrowed face'. Duncan made up for his shortness by a flamboyance that sometimes led him to exaggerate his achievements.

Pakie contributed much to the Playbox's success. She served as the society's secretary and ran its social evenings. Called 'the guiding spirit' of the theatre's most famous productions, she possessed a calm and tolerant optimism which balanced her husband's volatility. The couple's separation in December 1928 was one factor in the Playbox's demise. In mid-1929 the theatre was forced to move to larger premises in Crown Street, an unfavourable location where its following declined. Another move to Young Street in July 1931 saw the Playbox's disintegration within five months. Duncan's last performances were a series of public playreadings in 1933. Three years later he produced a prospectus for a 'Garrick Theatre', which came to nothing. Undaunted, he continued to lobby for a national theatre.

To support herself, Pakie opened (on 8 June 1929) the bohemian Pakie's Club in two large rooms on the second floor of 219 Elizabeth Street. The café, a 'little bit of Paris', was fashionable for its colourful modernist decor—designed with the assistance of Walter Burley Griffin and Roy de Maistre [qq.v.9,8] —and for monthly 'international' nights featuring aspects of the culture and cuisine of a particular country. Because it came to cater for struggling artists and writers, the standard fare was less exotic. Pakie's most famous dishes were salads and macaroni cheese (she was a vegetarian). Unlike other bohemian cafés, it sold no sly grog. Over the years Pakie's generosity, both material and emotional, became legendary. She was described as 'gentle, frail, almost to wispiness', yet 'quietly firm [and] dignified', with a face 'wrinkled by life and liveliness'.

On 8 May 1945 Pakie Macdougall died in Sydney Hospital from injuries received when hit by a military truck in Elizabeth Street the previous day; she was cremated with Presbyterian forms. Robin managed the club on more commercial lines until 1966, when a 'last reunion for old timers' took place on 2 February. A portrait of Pakie by Eric Saunders hung at the café for many years and is now held by the family.

At the Methodist Church, Chatswood South, on 27 April 1946 Duncan had married 52-year-old Vera Kathleen Montgomery. He spent his later years teaching 'voice and speech culture'. His main hobby was gardening. Survived by his wife and the son of his first marriage, he died on 19 March 1953 at Royal North Shore Hospital and was cremated with Methodist forms. The American artist Emile Derre modelled a bust of him, also held by the family.

N. Keesing, *Riding the Elephant* (Syd, 1988); *Theatre Mag*, 18, no 9, Sept 1920, no 12, Dec 1920; *Pertinent*, 13, no 3, Apr-May 1945, p 628; *NY Tribune*, 4 Apr 1915; *Sun* (Syd), 17 Nov 1929; *Daily Telegraph* (Syd), 5 Jan 1966; E. Wright, Duncan Macdougall—A Man of Theatre: a study of an important attempt to establish an art theatre in Sydney during the 1920s (B.A. Hons thesis, Univ NSW, 1981); Macdougall papers (ML); Playbox Theatre, press-clippings *and* programmes (ML); information from the late Mr R. Macdougall.

PETER KIRKPATRICK

McDOUGALL, DOUGLAS GORDON (1908-1977), accountant and lord mayor, was born on 2 July 1908 at Ballina, New South Wales, fifth child of native-born parents Alexander Thomas McDougall, engineer, and his wife Isabella Mary, née Holwell. Although severely handicapped by poliomyelitis, contracted at the age of fifteen months, Douglas became a keen swimmer. After attending Newcastle South Public and Cooks Hill Intermediate High schools, he studied accountancy part time while employed as a clerk. At St John's Anglican Church, Newcastle, on 2 May 1931 McDougall married Edith Juanita Victoria Phillips, a 30-year-old clerk; they were to remain childless. In 1934 he qualified with the Commonwealth Institute of Accountants and established a practice. During World War II he was seconded to the Department of Munitions where he served as officer-in-charge, Newcastle branch. When the war ended he joined Newstan Colliery Pty Ltd as the company's accountant. He was president of the Newcastle branch of the Australian Institute of Management, and chairman of the local branches of the Australian Society of Accountants and the Chartered Institute of Secretaries.

In 1944 McDougall had been elected to Newcastle Municipal Council for the Citizens' Group, representing the interests of the business community. As lord mayor (1956, 1958 and 1965-73) and chairman (1965) of Shortland County Council, he promoted Newcastle as an industrial capital. Believing that 'relics should not be allowed to hold up the progress of Newcastle', he advocated the demolition of several of the city's most important colonial buildings for a new office-block. The projected destruction of the historic eastern end of the city in the 1960s and its replacement with high-rise development was forestalled by widespread community opposition backed by the trade-union movement.

An accomplished pianist, McDougall supported the arts. He oversaw the establishment of the War Memorial Cultural Centre and five new branch libraries, and the installation in Civic Park of a fountain designed by the sculptor Margel Hinder. Major capital works completed during his term included an administration building for the council, suburban swimming pools, the International Sports Centre and inner-city car parks. His support for the construction of a freeway through the city's most extensive bushland reserve and a road through Birdwood Park attracted strong resistance. Aware of his waning popularity, he reluctantly retired from local government in 1973, though he returned briefly in 1977.

McDougall walked with a pronounced limp and the aid of a walking stick; he was courageous, fiercely independent and determined to overcome his disability. A small man with large schemes and the ability to carry them through, he was ambitious and enjoyed exercising power. He was a member of the boards of the State Dockyard (1968-77) and Royal Newcastle Hospital (1965-77); he held office in many community and charitable organizations; and he was an 'indefatigable guest of honour at countless functions'. A staunch Anglican who described his hobby as work, he was appointed C.B.E. in 1969. Survived by his wife, he died of myocardial infarction on 20 October 1977 in R.N.H. and was buried in Belmont cemetery. His portrait by Graeme Inson is held by Newcastle City Council.

Newcastle Morning Herald, 1 Jan 1969, 22 Oct 1977; Newcastle City Council, Minutes; Lord Mayor's clippings (Newcastle Regional L).

MARGARET HENRY

MacDOUGALL, JAMES KENNETH (1884-1960), engineer, was born on 25 September 1884 at Hawthorn, Melbourne, son of Scottish-born parents James MacDougall, importer, and his wife Elizabeth Brydie, née McRobbie. His father acquired, through an unpaid debt, a nail-manufacturing plant which was incorporated as the Austral Nail Co. Pty Ltd in 1891. Ken attended Malvern Grammar School and the Working Men's College (1901-03), gained a diploma in electrical and mechanical engineering, and was employed (from 1904) by the Melbourne City Council's electric supply department. He designed equipment for wire-drawing for the Austral Nail Co. in 1911, and was hired as a consultant when Lysaght Bros & Co. Ltd built a wire-drawing plant in Sydney in 1914.

At Christ Church, South Yarra, on 23 March 1916 MacDougall married with Anglican rites Olive Wilks Francis (d.1958). On 20 April that year he enlisted in the Australian Imperial Force. Commissioned in January 1917, he embarked for Britain in August. After serving on the Western Front with the 3rd Pioneer Battalion in February-April 1918, he was recalled to design and oversee construction work at his father's new wire-plant at Newcastle, New South Wales. His A.I.F. appointment terminated in Melbourne on 14 August.

By 1921 Austral had joined with the British firm, Rylands Bros Ltd, to form Rylands Bros (Australia) Ltd. In 1924 the Broken Hill Propriety Co. Ltd acquired Rylands; MacDougall, whose technical expertise was recognized by Essington Lewis [q.v.10], became manager. The Newcastle plant specialized in high-carbon products such as rope wires, spring wires, and nails; the three-ribbed 'star' fence-post was patented soon after MacDougall took charge. By 1935 Rylands was drawing equivalent wires twice as fast as the best American mills. A notable inventor, MacDougall devised the 'keyhole' type of self-locking tie for the binding of 'dumped' wool. Although 'Mr Ken' was known for his good relationship with employees, he left personnel and industrial matters to his deputies. Possessing a strong voice, Lieutenant Colonel MacDougall commanded (1942-45) the 32nd Battalion, Volunteer Defence Corps, which guarded the steelworks. Some Japanese shells fell on the works, but no one was killed.

His enthusiasm for the design and development of new products and techniques contributed to the world leadership of Rylands in wire-making. After his retirement in 1952, MacDougall was chairman of Lysaght Bros, the Australian Wire Rope Works Pty Ltd and Bullivants' Australian Co. Pty Ltd. A member of the Institution of Electrical Engineers, London, he was president of the Rotary Club of Newcastle and of the Newcastle branch of the New South Wales Chamber of Manufactures; he was also a member of the Technical Education Advisory Council and a foundation councillor (1949) of the New South Wales University of Technology. The university awarded him an honorary D.Sc. in 1955.

MacDougall was an engineer at heart. He enjoyed spending his weekends boating with his family on Lake Macquarie. While manager of Rylands, he lived at the Works House, the company cottage on the hill at Mayfield, designed by his wife. Survived by his daughter and two of his three sons, he died on 10 February 1960 at his New Lambton home and was cremated with Presbyterian forms.

BHP, *Newcastle Wiremill 75th Anniversary 1919-1994* (Newcastle, NSW, 1994); *BHP Review*, June-Sept 1955, p 36; *SMH*, 6 July 1949, 25 Feb 1950; *Newcastle Morning Herald*, 11 Feb 1960; A. Smith, The Australian Wire Industry: an economic, business and technical history (M.Comm. thesis, Univ Newcastle, 1982); information from Ms M. Beeston, Newcastle, Mr V. Moylan, Raymond Terrace, Mr J. Harborne, Mayfield East, NSW, and Mr R. Ellis, Roseville, Syd.　　　　　　　BEVERLEY FIRTH

MacDOUGALL, WALTER BATCHELOR (1907-1976), missionary and patrol officer, was born on 6 April 1907 at Mornington, Victoria, fifth child of Rev. Daniel Allan MacDougall, a Presbyterian minister from Scotland, and his second wife Rachel Buist, née Gibson, who was born in Tasmania. Walter was educated at Scotch College, Launceston (1914-17), and Scotch College, Melbourne (1918-22). A shy 'lanky fellow with fiery red hair', he worked on farms at Rosebery and Brim, and learned to drive a team of nine horses. In 1931-39 he served the Presbyterian Church as assistant-missionary at Port George IV (Kunmunya) in the Kimberley region of Western Australia. Second-in-charge to the superintendent J. R. B. Love [q.v.10], MacDougall managed cattle, assisted in running the garden and store, and helped with maintenance, building, church services and adult education. At the Kunmunya mission church on 10 November 1932 he married Gladys May Giles, a 31-year-old teacher. They spent their honeymoon camping in the bush and were to adopt a daughter.

In August 1938 a rifle that Walter was carrying slipped and discharged, destroying his right thumb and forefinger; he was flown to Wyndham for treatment. Next year the MacDougalls left Kunmunya. The joint endeavours of the Loves and MacDougalls have been remembered with gratitude by the Worora people. On 26 May 1940 MacDougall was appointed acting-superintendent of Ernabella mission in the north-west of South Australia. There, work with sheep provided employment opportunities for the Pitjant-jatjara people. MacDougall learned some basic Pitjantjatjara language. His responsibilities included conducting services, managing a store, supervising the use of stock, and maintaining buildings, trucks, windmills and tanks. In October he led a patrol into the Aboriginal reserve to the west. When Love took over as superintendent in 1941, MacDougall continued to oversee the sheep industry.

His attempts to join the Australian Military Forces were initially rejected because of his damaged hand. In March 1942 he left Erna-bella for Melbourne, determined to enlist. The mission diary recorded his faithful service and reported that the Aborigines wailed after he departed. Mobilized as a driver on 20 March, MacDougall was posted to No.1 General Transport Company and drove trucks in convoys through the Northern Territory from Alice Springs to Darwin. He was discharged on 28 March 1944 in Victoria. He and his wife returned to Ernabella and remained there until November 1946.

MacDougall's long and varied experience with Aborigines prepared him for employment on the Woomera Range in South Australia in 1947-72. Some people were alarmed that guided weapons would pass over Aboriginal reserves and have detrimental effects on the inhabitants. MacDougall was appointed temporary (later native) patrol officer. He lived at Woomera and acted as one of the State's protectors of Aborigines. In 1951, however, he expressed his frustration that his area of patrol was limited to Woomera itself: he had made little contact with Aborigines and was working as a driver.

Ooldea mission, near Maralinga, closed in 1952. MacDougall helped to transport Aborigines from there to the new mission at Yalata to remove them from the place where atomic bombs would be tested. In 1955 he was also appointed a protector of Aborigines in Western Australia. His area of responsibility had been extended following additions of land to the Woomera firing range, the opening of the Emu and Maralinga atomic-testing grounds in 1953, and the establishment of the Giles Meteorological Station in Western Australia in 1956. MacDougall had strenuously opposed the proposal to locate the G.M.S. on an Aboriginal reserve, arguing that the presence of its staff would adversely affect the Aborigines' traditional life. His pleas proved unavailing. In 1956 another patrol officer Robert Macaulay was based at Giles; after he moved to Woomera, the two men alternately patrolled a region of some 400 000 square miles (1 million km^2).

MacDougall spent weeks alone on patrols, trying to ensure that there were no Aborigines in areas likely to be subjected to rocket or atomic tests. He also supervised contact between Aborigines and range staff. His tall, thin figure and his vehicle became familiar sights throughout the Western Desert. Aboriginal guides, among them Tommy Dodd [q.v.14], escorted him on some patrols. He, in turn, assisted anthropologists and other researchers in the district. In the early years MacDougall made contact with nomadic tribes, took people for medical treatment and carried messages. At first, his vehicles were painted yellow so that they could be seen from the air in the event of breakdowns in the red sandhill country. His bushcraft enabled him to cope with difficult situations. Mechanical repairs were made in isolated camps and punctures were mended around his camp-fire at the end of a day's travel. The Aborigines used a system of hand gestures as one means of communication: by curling up thumb and forefinger and extending the other three fingers, they formed a symbol for the man known as Mitjamakanya (Mr Mac). In 1970 he was awarded the British Empire medal. An outcrop in Western Australia was named MacDougall's Bluff in his honour.

The MacDougalls were founding members of the Woomera United Protestant Church. Gladys taught at the local public school and held office in the Woomera branch of the Country Women's Association. Walter served as a justice of the peace and was a founding member of the Woomera Natural History Society. In the later years of his employment, there was less rocket-testing, and most Aborigines had moved to missions and settlements. MacDougall was increasingly involved in recording Aboriginal sites. On his retirement in 1972, the couple moved to Kilsyth, Melbourne. Survived by his wife and daughter, he died of pneumonia and pericarditis on 5 May 1976 at Heidelberg and was cremated; his ashes were buried at Ernabella.

MacDougall's task at Woomera had been a difficult one. Prickly and pertinacious, he dealt with Aboriginal welfare departments from two States and the Northern Territory, as well as with superiors whose priorities were scientific and military. His concern for the welfare of Aboriginal people often led to conflict. One chief scientist wrote that, while MacDougall was sincere in protecting the interests of Aborigines, he lacked balance and placed 'the affairs of a handful of natives above those of the British Commonwealth of Nations'. No epitaph could be more fitting.

M. McKenzie, *The Road to Mowanjum* (Syd, 1969); *Report of the Royal Commission into British Nuclear Tests in Australia*, 1 (Canb, 1985); M. Morey, *The Manse Folk of Kirklands, Tasmania* (Syd, 1986); P. Morton, *Fire Across the Desert* (Canb, 1989); Ernabella Mission diary, 1941-48 (pc of original) *and* G. MacDougall, Personal diary—Kunmunya, 1936-38 (held by author, Cumberland

Park, Adel); information from Mr S. Mitchell, Mount Waverley, Melb, Mrs F. Taylor, Warracknabeal, Rev E. Thomas, Wandana Heights, Vic, Mrs S. Mundy, Port Augusta, Mr P. Mason, Moonta, SA, Mr R. Macaulay, Campbell, Canb, and Mr J. Long, Glebe, Syd.   W. H. EDWARDS

McDOWELL, SIR FRANK SCHOFIELD (1889-1980), retailer, was born on 8 August 1889 at Petersham, Sydney, third child of John McDowell, a draper from Ireland, and his native-born wife Alice, née Schofield. At the age of 15 Frank joined McDowell & Hughes, drapers and costumiers of George Street (a firm which his father had established in 1889 as Denison House Drapery Co.). He was soon managing the shop. On 30 November 1911 at St Paul's Anglican Church, Burwood, he married 20-year-old Ethel Sophia Perrott; they were to have six sons and a daughter. In 1912 the partnership of McDowell & Hughes was registered as a limited company which was reconstructed as McDowell's Ltd in 1920. When the drapers W. T. Waters & Co. Ltd was acquired by McDowell's in 1925, Frank added its management to his responsibilities.

In 1935 he succeeded his father as managing director and chairman of McDowell's Ltd; he was also a trustee and committee-member (1932-67) of the Retail Traders' Association of New South Wales (of which his father had been a founder). Through astute property deals, McDowell's main store eventually dominated the corner of George and King streets. One of the first of the city retailers to recognize that shopping was moving to the suburbs, McDowell's opened stores at Hornsby and Caringbah in 1961 and at Dee Why in 1963. The company bought Mark Foys [qq.v.4,8] Ltd in 1968 and in 1970 registered McDowells Holdings Ltd. By 1971 the King Street store had been sold and demolished to provide the site for the King George tower.

McDowell's was neither a leader of fashion nor a setter of trends, but it promised friendly service, and a family atmosphere for both staff and customers. The drapery store with a staff of twelve had become a large department store with 800 'contented employees' by 1949 and 1200 by 1964. Although conservative in most respects, McDowell was capable of modernizing to keep pace with his customers. Innovations were functional and aimed at a mass market. The cafeteria, opened in 1931, could seat 600-700 people at small, linoleum-topped tables. The new suburban stores glittered with white formica, mirrors and tiles; other features included piped music, air-conditioning, 'driverless' lifts, and electric hand-driers in the washrooms. Knighted in 1967, McDowell stepped down as managing director in favour of his son John, but re-mained chairman of the board. In 1971 the company's shareholders accepted a takeover bid by Waltons Ltd.

Three generations of the family—including McDowell's sons and grandsons (enough to field a cricket team)—worked in the stores. Frank himself enjoyed cricket, played golf, took up bowls, exercised regularly in a gym in his late seventies, and was still swimming daily at the age of 87. He lived at Cronulla, and was president of Chatswood Golf Club, vice-president of the St George Veterans' Cricket Club and a member of South Cronulla Bowling Club.

As grand master (1947-51) of United Grand Lodge of New South Wales—with a lodge later named in his honour—he promoted the development of retirement and aged-care facilities through the Frank Whiddon [q.v.12] Masonic Homes. McDowell had also been grand master of Mark Master Masons and was an inspector general (1966-72) of the Superior Council of the 33° (Rose Croix). A member (from 1927) and president (1945-57) of the Rotary Club of Sydney, he remained an active senior Rotarian. He was also a trustee of the Australian Museum, a member of the advisory board of the Young Men's Christian Association and president of the All Nations Club. Survived by his children, Sir Frank died on 1 November 1980 at Calvary Hospital, Kogarah, and was cremated with Masonic rites. Sir William Dargie's portrait of McDowell is held by United Grand Lodge.

A. Mitchell, *The Rotary Club of Sydney 1921-1981* (Syd, 1981); K. Henderson, *The Masonic Grand Masters of Australia* (Melb, 1988); F. Pollon, *Shopkeepers and Shoppers* (Syd, 1989); Retail Traders' Assn of NSW, *J*, Mar 1924, Nov 1931, Sept 1949, Sept 1960, Aug, Dec 1961, Feb 1962; Rotary Club of Syd, *Directory*, 1970-71; *SMH*, 19 Apr 1964, 28 Apr 1967, 11 Aug 1968, 25 Nov 1975, 3 Nov 1980; W. McDowell, The History of McDowell's Ltd 1892-1971 (ts, held by ADB, Canb).

BEVERLEY KINGSTON

McENCROE, FRANCIS GERARD (1908-1979), inventor of the Chiko roll, was born on 11 October 1908 at Castlemaine, Victoria, second son of Victorian-born parents Pierce Francis McEncroe, wheelwright, and his wife Sarah Ann, née Desmond. Frank was educated at a local primary school and at Marist Brothers' College, Bendigo. Having obtained his merit certificate, he completed an apprenticeship in boiler-making at Thompson's [q.v.12] foundry, Castlemaine, and continued to work there for a time.

In the Depression McEncroe joined his father and two brothers, who had set up a dairy-farm and a milk-processing and distributing business at Bendigo. On 20 August 1932 he married with Catholic rites Anne Doreen Nolan at the Sacred Heart Cathedral, Bendigo. From the late 1930s he ran an outdoor catering business, selling pies, pasties and hamburgers at country shows, race meetings and other gatherings. During World War II he was licensee (1940-47) of the Court House Hotel in Pall Mall, while also working as a boiler-maker at the Bendigo Ordnance Factory.

After the war McEncroe resumed his outdoor catering business, processing, packaging and snap-freezing his products at the former dairy. In 1950, inspired by the Chinese chop-suey roll, which he saw being sold outside the Richmond football ground, he developed a similar product, subsequently called the 'Chiko roll'. Initially made by a hand-fed machine and promoted as a take-away snack, it was acclaimed in 1951 at the Wagga Wagga show, New South Wales.

That year McEncroe moved with his family to Melbourne and began producing Chiko rolls from the rear of a fish-shop in Moreland Road, Coburg. Following the success of his product, he moved into a factory at North Essendon, progressively modernized its machinery, and improved facilities for packaging, freezing and distribution. In 1960 his firm amalgamated with the neighbouring Floyds ice-works to form Frozen Food Industries Pty Ltd which became a public company in 1963.

McEncroe was fond of shooting and fishing in his early years. Later in life he was a competent golfer who played at the Medway Golf Club, Melbourne, and Tweed Heads Golf Club, New South Wales. Survived by his wife, son and daughter, he died of ischaemic heart disease on 14 March 1979 in Melbourne and was buried in Keilor cemetery. His estate was sworn for probate at $239 681.

The Chiko roll—a mixture of cabbage, barley, carrots, celery, condiments and meat (beef or mutton) wrapped in an egg-batter dough—proved a huge success in the rapidly expanding market for 'fast foods' in Australia in the 1950s and 1960s. The ingredients were diced and extruded into a long tube of pastry which was cooked as it moved along the production line. It was then deep-fried and frozen before being distributed. Further deep-frying was necessary only to reheat the roll. Typically obtained at local outlets, especially fish-and-chip shops, it was convenient both to sell and to eat in a variety of outdoor settings. At the time of McEncroe's death Australians consumed up to 40 million Chiko rolls annually, and more than a million were exported to Japan. Ownership of Frozen Food Industries of Australia Ltd subsequently passed through Provincial Traders Ltd and General Jones Pty Ltd to Petersville Sleigh Ltd.

M. Symons, *One Continuous Picnic* (Adel, 1982); *Age* (Melb), 15 Mar 1979; *Bendigo Advertiser*, 20 Mar 1979; *National Times*, 21-27 Dec 1980; information from Mr P. F. McEncroe, Essendon, Melb.

DAVID DUNSTAN

McEWAN, KATHLEEN AGNES ROSE (1894-1969), sports journalist, golfer and war-worker, was born on 15 March 1894 at Surrey Hills, Melbourne, second surviving child of Victorian-born parents John McEwan, land agent, and his wife Mary Maria ('Minnie'), née Fowler. Kitty was educated locally at Ormiston Ladies' College and developed a lifelong passion for golf. An associate-member of the Commonwealth and Riversdale golf clubs, she was Commonwealth club champion (1925-26) and captain (1926). At Riversdale she won the club trophy (1933) and once hit a hole in one. With her friend Edna Hope McLean, she visited Britain for six months in 1934. McEwan had worked (from 1929) as a freelance journalist on *Australian Home Beautiful*. She then began writing, mainly on women and golf, for the *Radiator* (1937) and the *Sun News-Pictorial* (from 1938). Five ft 4½ ins (164 cm) tall, well built, with blue-grey eyes and light reddish hair, she was public-minded, energetic and 'too modest to report her own golfing wins'.

During World War II McEwan organized fund-raising for patriotic appeals before she was appointed (June 1942) superintendent in Victoria of the Australian Women's Land Army—a national scheme for recruiting, training and placing women in rural work to redress the labour crisis. She was fully aware that—as a civilian force with less attractive conditions than those in the women's services —the A.W.L.A. could never successfully compete for recruits.

None the less, McEwan was genuinely concerned for the welfare of 'land girls' and tried to improve their lot. She continually lobbied the government to provide basic supplies, especially adequate clothing for wet and cold conditions; she also negotiated with employers, withdrew the land girls when accommodation was substandard, and supported a successful case before the Women's Employment Board for improved conditions in the flax industry. In addition, she liaised with voluntary groups to improve amenities, such as providing a mobile canteen. The deputy-director of manpower, who often deferred to her expertise, commented on her 'wise and tolerant leadership and her knowledge of rural problems'.

After being demobilized in March 1946, McEwan wrote for the *Sun* under her own name until her retirement in 1966. She encouraged women (regardless of age) to play sport, and fought for the regular inclusion of women's sporting results in the press. With wide and varied interests, she collected rare books, and served as honorary publicity officer and an executive-member of the National Council of Women of Victoria (c.1956-69) and as a councillor (1953-67) of the Royal Historical Society of Victoria.

Kitty McEwan lived in the family home at Surrey Hills. She died on 17 August 1969 at Camberwell and was buried with Presbyterian forms in the Anglican section of Box Hill cemetery. One of her last public gestures was to agree to chair the sportswomen's committee for the Queen Victoria Memorial Hospital's forthcoming (1970) building appeal. She is commemorated by the Kitty McEwan trophy at Barwon Heads Golf Club and by an award for the sportswoman of the year which was established from her bequest by the Women's Amateur Sports Council in 1974.

S. Hardisty (ed), *Thanks Girls and Goodbye* (Melb, 1990); *Aust Home Beautiful*, 7, nos 1-6 1929; *Radiator* (Melb), June 1937-Dec 1940; *VHM*, 38, no 2, May 1967; *Sun News-Pictorial*, 3 Mar 1942, 29 Mar 1946, 19 Aug 1969; *Herald* (Melb), 18 Aug 1969; AWLA B551/0 1943/110/4796 pts 1 and 2 (AA, Melb); documents provided by Ms L. Butler, Hamlyn Heights, Vic.   SUE HARDISTY

McEWEN, SIR JOHN (1900-1980), prime minister and farmer, was born on 29 March 1900 at Chiltern, Victoria, elder child of David James McEwen (d.1907), a pharmacist from Ireland, and his second wife Amy Ellen, née Porter (d.1901), who was Victorian born. David also had two children from his former marriage and another from his third. After his parents' deaths, John and his younger sister were raised in frugal circumstances by their maternal grandmother who ran a boarding-house at Wangaratta before moving to Dandenong. Educated at local state schools, he left at 13 to help support the household. He studied at night-school, qualified for clerical entry to the Commonwealth Public Service, and joined the crown solicitor's office, Melbourne, in 1916. One of his superiors was H. F. E. Whitlam [q.v.].

Although McEwen had hoped to enter the Royal Military College, Duntroon, Federal Capital Territory, he enlisted in the Australian Imperial Force on 9 August 1918. World War I ended before he could join the army in France. His A.I.F. service, however, made him eligible for the soldier-settlement scheme, a crucial factor in his subsequent career. Without any farming background, he was drawn to a way of life which he saw as 'free of a boss'.

Working as a farmhand, McEwen picked up sufficient experience to obtain a qualifying certificate and apply for land near Stanhope.

He astutely chose a larger block (86 acres, 35 ha) rather than one of the smaller holdings which beggared many of his colleagues. To obtain some capital he worked as a wharf labourer in Melbourne. He survived drought and a rabbit plague in 1919, improved his property by tenacity and unremitting hard work, and led what he recalled as a 'rough and ready' life, living in a humpy and spending solitary nights reading by the light of a kerosene lamp. At Ballavoca, Tongala, on 21 September 1921 he married with Anglican rites Annie Mills McLeod; they were to remain childless. She worked with him to develop the farm. They sold it and bought others, gradually building up a productive holding of 3000 acres (1200 ha), spread over three blocks in the Stanhope region.

At a time when many soldier settlers walked off their blocks, McEwen emerged as both a successful farmer and a leader of those who remained and those who joined them. He extended his activities through the Victorian Farmers' Union and other producers' groups. Rural activism drew him into politics. Annie was an able assistant, travelling with him constantly to meetings and functions. A member of the Country Party from the age of 19, McEwen stood unsuccessfully in 1932 for the seat of Waranga in the Legislative Assembly. At the Federal elections on 15 September 1934 he won the seat of Echuca in the House of Representatives. The Victorian Country Party had endorsed him while it was engaged in a bitter dispute with its federal paliamentary members. During the campaign McEwen clashed with (Sir) Earle Page [q.v.11], the party's federal leader. When McEwen arrived in Canberra he made peace with the federal party, thereby earning the hostility of his former colleagues in the State branch.

McEwen's maiden speech in November ranged over issues which were to preoccupy him in his parliamentary career: primary industry, commerce, trade, banking, employment and defence. It was the task of government, he said, to 'discover the basic facts upon which our national economy is founded, and search there for the root causes [of problems]'. His approach to politics and public-policy formulation was founded on this principle. He held the seat of Indi in 1937-49 and Murray in 1949-71. Harold Thorby [q.v.12] defeated him for the deputy-leadership of the party in 1937. On 29 November that year McEwen was appointed minister for the interior in Joseph Lyons' [q.v.10] United Australia Party-Country Party coalition government. The Victorian branch of the Country Party was opposed to its members participating in composite ministries and expelled McEwen. He was not readmitted to the Victorian party until 1943.

Spacious in its command of broad policy issues and diversity of administrative functions, McEwen's portfolio included Commonwealth public works, railways, immigration, the Northern and Australian Capital territories, Aborigines, electoral administration, mining, and oil exploration. He travelled widely in the Northern Territory and outback Australia, negotiated the basis of pioneering airline services in northern Australia, resumed assisted immigration from Britain and extended the policy to the Dutch, sponsored a white paper on Aboriginal policy in the Northern Territory, tried unsuccessfully to establish an all-States conference on Aboriginal welfare, and imposed an embargo on the export of iron ore which lasted until the late 1950s.

Having taken the Country Party out of the coalition on 26 April 1939, Page resigned his leadership in September. McEwen contested the position against A. G. Cameron [q.v.13] and was defeated by two votes. The exclusion of four party members from the leadership ballot—by a single vote at the party meeting —had cost McEwen victory. On 14 March 1940 (Sir) Robert Menzies [q.v.] appointed him minister for external affairs in the re-established coalition government.

McEwen's principal initiative in his new portfolio was the planning of a *coup* which removed the Vichy French government from New Caledonia and replaced it with a Gaullist administration. According to McEwen, he foresaw the entry of Japan into World War II and acted to prevent the Japanese from using New Caledonia under Vichy control as a base against Australia. With Menzies' support, and without reference to cabinet, he organized a French 'voluntary expedition' (led by a Gaullist) to sail from the New Hebrides to New Caledonia in a chartered Norwegian ship. McEwen also claimed that it was he who arranged for the old Australian cruiser, *Adelaide*, to reach Noumea at this time. Describing the *coup* in later years as a 'matter of high security done between Menzies and myself', McEwen rated it as his finest political achievement, but historians have been sceptical about the extent of his involvement in the incident.

He was given the portfolios of air and of civil aviation on 28 October 1940. Earlier that month Cameron had resigned as Country Party leader. McEwen tied with Page in the vote to elect a successor. When a second ballot failed to resolve the deadlock, the deputy-leader (Sir) Arthur Fadden [q.v.14] was appointed acting-leader. He was subsequently confirmed as leader. As minister for air, McEwen directed Australia's contribution to the crucial Empire Air Training Scheme. He also established the Women's Auxiliary Australian Air Force. After the coalition lost power in October 1941, Prime Minister John Curtin [q.v.13] appointed him to the Advisory War Council, a post he was to hold until hostilities ended. McEwen became deputy-leader of the Country Party in September 1943.

In 1945 McEwen served as a consultant with the Australian delegation to the United Nations Conference on International Organization, held at San Francisco, United States of America. He recalled the office as giving him 'a wonderful opportunity to rub shoulders with leading men from all over the world'. He was closely involved with Fadden in rebuilding the Country Party, developing its policies, and preparing it for office in partnership with Menzies' rejuvenated Liberal Party.

Following the Federal elections on 10 December 1949, McEwen was appointed minister for commerce and agriculture, ranking fifth in cabinet. He retained this ministry, shaping and extending its policies, until its functions were split on 11 January 1956. From that date he was minister for trade (trade and industry from 18 December 1963). The rural-policy elements of his previous portfolio went initially to (Sir) William McMahon who, as a junior minister, had worked amicably with McEwen. According to newspaper reports, McEwen intervened with Menzies to prevent McMahon's removal from the ministry.

McEwen succeeded Fadden as leader of the Country Party and as deputy prime minister on 26 March 1958. As party leader, he was 'revered and unchallenged'. Fadden left parliament in December and Harold Holt [q.v.14] received the treasurership. Although McEwen's supporters, among them (Sir) William Gunn, later claimed that he had rejected the Treasury, Menzies probably never offered it to him. It is possible that McEwen may have felt uncomfortable at the prospect of becoming treasurer, as he had often expressed bitterness about the department's negative role in policy-making. It is more likely that Menzies preferred to give the post to a member of the Liberal Party.

With an uninterrupted tenure of twenty-one years as minister for commerce and for trade, McEwen had a rare opportunity to command and develop a decisive sphere of national policy. There is neither precedent nor parallel in Federal politics for the dominion he exercised. In a memorable partnership with two notable public servants (Sir) John Crawford and (Sir) Alan Westerman, McEwen transformed trade policy from its crudeness in the immediate postwar years to its diversity and relative sophistication in the early 1970s.

At the beginning of his ministry McEwen did much to rejuvenate the administration of primary industry and the marketing of primary products. Bringing that sector into closer contact with government, he urged its leaders to raise their standards. He initiated schemes to stabilize export markets and to equalize returns to individual farmers from differential pricing at home and abroad.

In 1951 McEwen secured a fifteen-year agreement with Britain on meat. Over the following two decades he emerged as a conspicuous figure in numerous bilateral and multilateral trade discussions, earning international respect for his toughness and persistence. Fundamental to his achievement was the conclusion of a trade deal with Britain in 1956 to supersede the 1932 Ottawa Agreement which had begun to advantage Britain unduly. The settlement enabled Australia to relax tariff barriers against Japanese goods, a significant factor in negotiations (led by McEwen) which established the Agreement on Commerce between Australia and Japan in July 1957. In terms of detailed bargaining, much of the credit for the agreement lay with Crawford and Westerman, but it was McEwen who accepted the abundant political risks: memories of Japanese atrocities in World War II were still strong in the Australian community. In public McEwen made himself appear personally responsible for the treaty, so that he alone would fall if it proved unpopular. He dryly commented that he had 'carried the can quite consciously and no one wanted to have a share in carrying it as I remember'.

Britain's protracted negotiations for entry to the European Economic Community in the early 1960s placed pressure on Australian trade. McEwen recognized Britain's right to seek membership of the E.E.C., but criticized the timing and the manner in which entry was sought. His involvement with international trade issues and his increasing responsibility for secondary industry brought him into the area of tariff policy. At conferences under the General Agreement on Tariffs and Trade, such as the 'Kennedy Round' in the mid-1960s, he confronted external pressures to reduce tariff barriers.

At home, McEwen had to reconcile his unequivocal support for protection with the free-trade inclinations of his rural constituency, a task he performed with consummate political skill. He exploited the coalition's narrow parliamentary majorities in the early 1960s to obtain benefits and concessions for farmers, but he failed to make Prime Minister Holt devalue the Australian dollar in 1967 in line with Britain's devaluation of the pound. Holt responded with what amounted to a firm public rebuff of his deputy prime minister. Even in the final years of his ministry, however, McEwen remained a formidable political manipulator, one who obtained the establishment of the Australian Industry Development Corporation in 1971, despite two years of infuriated resistance from McMahon and the Treasury. The new corporation became known in administrative parlance as the 'McEwen Bank'.

McEwen's attitudes had been profoundly influenced by his experience of the Depression, which compelled him to place an overriding emphasis on creating and safeguarding employment. He dismissed as impracticable any notion that jobs lost by lowering the protection of Australian secondary industries could be replaced by new ones in the service sector. Foremost in his mind were the growth and economic health of the 'basic wealth-producing industries'—agriculture, mining and manufacturing. In addition, McEwen had been greatly affected by Australia's vulnerability early in World War II when deficiencies in its manufacturing industry left it unprepared for armed conflict. Thus, he was not prepared to condone policies which stripped away from existing industries a degree of protection which he considered necessary to sustain employment and contribute to national defence.

By the late 1950s McEwen was the indisputable champion of the traditional Australian view that high protection of local industry was a principal tool of economic and social policy. In the next decade he remained obdurate as this outlook crumbled and his approach was branded 'McEwenism'. More and more he found himself in conflict with the Tariff Board which, under the leadership of Sir Leslie Melville and his successor G. A. Rattigan, gradually moved the fulcrum of economic and industrial policy away from protectionism towards lower tariffs and free trade. McEwen showed characteristic resourcefulness in resisting the gathering momentum, particularly by his use of a special advisory authority to grant emergency tariff-assistance to industries and circumvent the prolonged processes of the Tariff Board. Despite his consistent and sturdy advocacy, the battle for protectionism was largely lost by the time he resigned from parliament on 1 February 1971.

McEwen had been sustained by his political intimacy with Menzies. He later recalled that in the early 1950s Menzies had hinted to him to 'get into line' for leadership of the Liberal Party and, ultimately, the prime ministership. McEwen, however, rejected any suggestion of leaving his party to gain preferment. He served as acting prime minister on ten occasions during Menzies' absences abroad. The alliance with Menzies was jeopardized only once. McEwen 'stood up' to his prime minister and threatened to end the coalition in 1962 over an electoral redistribution which would have abolished two Country Party seats and endangered another. The redistribution was cancelled.

From 1956 there had been ill-concealed animosity between McEwen and McMahon, who became treasurer in 1966 after Menzies retired and was replaced by Holt. Apart from his deep-seated antipathy to the Treasury, McEwen had long suspected that McMahon had not only leaked cabinet material unfavourable to him, but had also stirred up resentment among Liberal members over McEwen's influence in the government and the strength of the Country Party in the ministry. Following Holt's death, McEwen was appointed caretaker prime minister on 19 December 1967. McMahon was a leading aspirant for the Liberal Party leadership and therefore the prime ministership, but McEwen told him bluntly: 'Bill, I won't serve under you ... because I don't trust you'. McMahon withdrew, and (Sir) John Gorton succeeded McEwen as prime minister on 10 January 1968.

After the coalition's near defeat in the Federal elections of October 1969, Gorton faced a leadership challenge. Convinced that most of Gorton's potential successors were a 'motley' lot, and that the Liberal Party should not be denied the candidacy of its most senior minister, McEwen lifted his veto on McMahon.

Arduous negotiations and extensive travel weakened McEwen's resilience and led to a serious 'neuro-dermatitis' condition; at times he walked around Parliament House with his feet 'bleeding and bandaged'. The stress of further arguments with the Tariff Board meant that by February 1971 he had taken as much of politics as he wanted to take. By leaving then, he felt that he would prevent anyone from saying, 'Why doesn't old McEwen get out?' He was appointed a privy counsellor in 1953, C.H. in 1969 and G.C.M.G. in 1971; the Japanese appointed him to the Order of the Rising Sun in 1973.

After a long illness Dame Ann McEwen (D.B.E. 1966) had died on 10 February 1967. At Wesley Church, Melbourne, on 26 July 1968 McEwen married Mary Eileen Byrne, his personal secretary; he was aged 68, she was 46. Throughout his political career he had found relaxation in hard physical work on his cherished farm, Chilgala. He finally sold it in 1975 and moved to Toorak. In retirement he distanced himself from politics, undertook some consulting work, and travelled to Japan and South Africa. Survived by his wife, he died on 20 November 1980 at Toorak and was cremated. His estate was sworn for probate at $2 180 479. At the time of his death he was receiving a small pension from the Department of Social Security.

McEwen was about six feet (183 cm) tall and ramrod-like in bearing. His formidable public persona was complemented by the sombre suits he wore. Grimly resolute and sometimes choleric in temper, he was nicknamed 'Black Jack'. (Menzies jocularly rendered the nickname in French as *Le Noir*.)

Although awesome in presence and reputation, McEwen was generally accessible and, on occasions, jovial. His jutting jaw mingled determination with a milder, questing quality. He was an adept conversationalist who moved about the electorate with calm authority, untiring in pursuing relevant facts, but willing to listen, consult, joke, and yarn at length. A fluent, forceful and often passionate speaker, McEwen in full flight at the parliamentary dispatch box was a grand spectacle.

Although the latter years of his long political career were clouded by an increasingly bitter controversy over protectionism, a significant residue of achievement remained, particularly in the organizing and stabilizing of Australian primary industry, and the decisive shaping of international trade policies in the crucial 1950s and early 1960s. More than any other Australian political leader of his time he embodied the ethos of the traditional Australian farming community—its dogged endurance, its longing for betterment, and its aspiration for ultimate prosperity. Menzies thought that McEwen had the cast of mind of a great barrister: 'analytical, clear ... quite admirable!' Crawford, who worked closely with both leaders, concluded that while Menzies had the quicker mind, McEwen's was the surer.

John McEwen, R. V. Jackson ed (priv pub, Melb, 1983); P. Golding, *Black Jack McEwen* (Melb, 1996); *Canb Times*, 22 Nov 1980; Oral Hist Project, Sir John McEwen (ts, NL); Sir John McEwen papers (NL) *and* personal records *(*AA, Canb).

C. J. LLOYD

MACFARLAN, COLIN WILLIAM BUCHANAN (1887-1947), newspaper editor and proprietor, was born on 13 November 1887 at Gourock, Renfrewshire, Scotland, son of Dougal Carlyle Macfarlan, civil servant, and his wife Rosina, née Macintyre. Educated locally, Colin joined a brother in South Africa and worked there as a journalist on the *Cape Argus* and other newspapers. He returned home in 1910 and toured Europe before emigrating to Australia. Following a stint as a reporter on the Melbourne *Argus*, he was employed by newspaper proprietors in a number of country towns in New South Wales. In 1917 J. H. Kessell, the owner of the *Gladstone Observer*, Queensland, appointed him to edit and manage that bi-weekly. At St Saviour's Anglican Church, Gladstone, on 23 December 1919 Macfarlan married Marjorie Lilian Morgan (d.1931); they remained childless. On 9 July 1932 at Holy Rosary Church, Windsor, Brisbane, he married with Catholic rites Margaret Ethel Booth, a 28-year-old nurse.

Kessell had offered him a half-share in the *Observer*. By 1922 Macfarlan was the sole proprietor. A confrontation between Macfarlan and the Gladstone Town Council in 1929 indicated the growing independence of the provincial press. Alderman W. Ferris, the mayor, thought that the *Observer* was not reporting the council's proceedings impartially. The council invited the *Bundaberg Daily Times* to cover its meetings, offering some advertising as an incentive. For two months Macfarlan fought the decision in the columns of the *Observer* until it was reversed. Mayor Ferris 'sustained a signal defeat in his advocacy of sending the ratepayers' money out of the town in order to have reports published in an outside paper'.

In the 1929 State elections the *Observer* supported F. W. Butler, the Country and Progressive National Party candidate for Port Curtis. At the same time Macfarlan published an attack on Queensland's newspapers by William McCormack [q.v.10], the Labor premier. Macfarlan was not afraid to speak out against the conservatives when they were in power and in April 1930 condemned the Moore [q.v.10] government for breaking its contract over the Monto rail-link.

Recognizing the potential of Gladstone's port and hinterland, Macfarlan followed the provincial newspaperman's tradition of tirelessly advancing the material welfare of his town and district. A member (1921-46) and chairman (1943-44) of the Gladstone Harbour Board, he had a breadth of vision which led him to present the case at Rockhampton for a wool-appraisement centre in Central Queensland. His editorial advocacy of Gladstone fuelled the claim that the *Observer* had accomplished more for the advancement of the town than all the public bodies put together.

Macfarlan retained his Scottish brogue and was an excellent public speaker. His contemporaries regarded him as highly principled, courteous and good natured. He died of cancer on 4 June 1947 at Rockhampton and was buried with Presbyterian forms in Gladstone cemetery. His wife and daughter Carmel survived him. Carmel partnered her mother in running the *Observer*. Margaret was appointed M.B.E. (1970) for services to journalism and the community.

R. Kirkpatrick, *Sworn to No Master* (Toowoomba, Qld, 1984); *Gladstone Observer*, 9 Mar, 27 Apr, 11 May 1929, 16 Apr 1930, 11 Mar 1931, 16 July 1932, 11 June 1947, 3 Jan 1970; information from Mrs M. E. Macfarlan, Gladstone, Qld.

ROD KIRKPATRICK

MACFARLAN, IAN (1881-1964), premier, was born on 21 November 1881 at North Carlton, Melbourne, tenth child of Scottish-born parents James Macfarlan, storekeeper, and his wife Mary, née Nairn. Named John Robert, he attended Princes Hill State School and the Melbourne Education Institute. On 1 November 1897 he joined the Victorian Railways where he worked as a clerk. He won a scholarship to Ormond [q.v.5] College, University of Melbourne (LL.B., 1907), topped his final year and was awarded the Supreme Court judges' prize. From this time, possibly from a preference for the Gaelic variant of John, he called himself Ian.

Articled to E. J. Guinness, the crown solicitor, in 1907, Macfarlan was admitted as a solicitor by the Supreme Court on 4 May 1908 and to the Bar on 4 August. He earned a reputation for wide legal knowledge and telling expository skills that were the more effective for being understated. The contrast with his brother, the socially genial but judicially irascible (Sir) James Macfarlan [q.v.10], future senior puisne judge of the Supreme Court, was marked. On 12 August 1918 at St George's Presbyterian Church, East St Kilda, Ian Macfarlan married 24-year-old Beryl Johnstone Wardill King. One month earlier he had enlisted in the Royal Australian Garrison Artillery; he transferred to the Australian Imperial Force on 7 November and was discharged in December without serving abroad.

In April 1928 Macfarlan stood as a National Party candidate and won the by-election for the seat of Brighton in the Legislative Assembly, narrowly defeating the housewives' advocate Eleanor Glencross [q.v.9]. Believing that political and professional life should be separate, he accepted no further briefs. He won rapid parliamentary promotion, serving as attorney-general and solicitor-general (November 1928-December 1929) in Sir William McPherson's [q.v.10] ministry. From September 1930 he was deputy-leader of his party in opposition. He returned to the government benches as chief secretary (May 1932-April 1935) and minister in charge of electrical undertakings (May 1932-July 1934) in the Argyle-Allan [qq.v.7] coalition, but lost the deputy-leadership of the United Australia Party to (Sir) Robert Menzies [q.v.] in June 1932. Again attorney-general (July 1934-April 1935) and solicitor-general (July 1934-March 1935), he took silk on 27 November 1934. He was also a member of the 1935 select committee on the shorter working week.

At the elections on 2 March 1935, Macfarlan retained Brighton after a close and bitter contest with (Sir) Edmund Herring, the unendorsed U.A.P. candidate who was supported by a group of Young Nationalists. On 2 April (Sir) Albert Dunstan [q.v.8], leader of the parliamentary Country Party, became premier. Macfarlan led a cross-bench, country-liberal faction of the U.A.P. that advocated conditional negotiation rather than rigid opposition in dealings with Dunstan's minority government. In 1937, disenchanted with the U.A.P.'s strategic inflexibility, he left the party to serve as a liberal Independent, in which capacity he was a member (from July 1940) of the bipartisan State War Advisory Council. Persuaded to rejoin the party as deputy-leader to Thomas Tuke Hollway [q.v.14] on the formation of a Country Party-U.A.P. coalition in September 1943, he was appointed attorney-general and solicitor-general, and given the portfolio of health. As minister of public health, he set up the hospital and charities commission, introduced additional kindergartens and centres for the care of the aged and the mentally ill, and banned cigarette-smoking in cinemas (although he smoked heavily himself). His organizational abilities, lucid explanations of complex bills, and vigorous debating skills made him the dominant U.A.P. figure in the government.

Macfarlan, however, chafed under Premier Dunstan's 'do-nothing' leadership which, on 25 September 1945, provoked five dissident Liberals (the State parliamentary U.A.P. had changed its name to Liberal in March that year), two Independents and two breakaway Country Party members to combine with Labor, block supply and defeat the government. Macfarlan had voted with Dunstan, but, when party differences prevented the formation of any majority government and the passing of supply, he reluctantly agreed to head a 'stop-gap' ministry of dissidents to break the impasse, pending an election. Widely criticized, he responded that 'unity of party was of primary importance' and it had been subordinated 'only to give the people a government that would carry on lawfully until the election'.

On 2 October 1945 Macfarlan was sworn in as premier, treasurer, attorney-general and solicitor-general. With Labor support for his ten-member government on this one matter only, supply was passed. Macfarlan's 51-day premiership was competent and decisive. He settled a major tram strike in Melbourne, introduced the five-day week for Victorian public servants, and approved a State gift of £25 000 worth of war-relief foodstuffs for dispatch to England. Having been disendorsed by the State executive of the Liberal Party, he contested the general election on 10 November as leader of the Ministerial Liberals. His ministry was defeated and he lost his seat. Following an unsuccessful attempt to regain Brighton in 1947, Macfarlan retired from public life, though he privately assisted the Cain [q.v.13] government (1952-55) with legislative consolidations.

Five ft 10 ins (178 cm) tall, barrel-chested, with a fresh complexion and receding sandy-red hair, Macfarlan was devoted to his family. As a young man he had rowed in three Ormond College crews, twice represented the university in interstate races, and competed for the Civil Service Club. In middle age he exchanged rowing for a morning swim. His only social club was the Australian Natives' Association. Survived by his two sons, he died on 19 March 1964 at Sandringham and was buried in Boroondara cemetery, Kew.

E. Barbor, *They Went Their Way* (Traralgon, Vic, 1960); K. West, *Power in the Liberal Party* (Melb, 1965); P. Aimer, *Politics, Power and Persuasion* (Syd, 1974); C. Hazlehurst (ed), *Australian Conservatism* (Canb, 1979); S. Sayers, *Ned Herring* (Melb, 1980); *Aust Bar Gazette*, June 1964; *Table Talk*, 17 Jan 1929; *Age* (Melb), 1-3 Oct 1945; *Herald* (Melb), 4 Oct 1945.   R. WRIGHT

McFARLANE, STUART GORDON (1885-1970), public servant, was born on 4 May 1885 at Maldon, Victoria, ninth child of John James McFarlane, a draper from Ireland, and his English-born wife Jane, née Matthews. Stuart attended Bairnsdale State School and later acquired accountancy qualifications in Melbourne. In June 1903 he was appointed to the finance branch of the Commonwealth Treasury, on the same day as (Sir) Harry Sheehan [q.v.11]. McFarlane transferred to the Postmaster-General's Department in 1911: he served as chief ledgerkeeper in Melbourne, and then as accountant in Perth (1920), Brisbane (1921) and Melbourne (1925). From 1916 to 1919 he had been seconded to the Department of Defence as chief inspector of finances, and had held the ranks of major (1916) and lieutenant colonel (1917). In 1920 he was appointed M.B.E. At St Stephen's Catholic Cathedral, Brisbane, on 1 May 1923 he married Mary Grace McDermott (d.1952), a 36-year-old masseuse; a second wedding took place on 4 May at the Presbyterian Church, Clayfield.

With his reputation for financial prudence secured, McFarlane resumed his career in the Treasury in 1926. That year he was appointed accountant and promoted assistant-secretary (finance). Appearing before the Commonwealth Parliamentary Joint Committee of Public Accounts in 1930, he opposed Tasmania's request for increased financial assistance on the ground that adverse economic conditions were affecting every State. In 1934 he gave evidence to the Commonwealth Grants Commission on submissions by South Australia, Western Australia and Tasmania for additional help; dismissing the argument that their budgets had deteriorated because of the Financial Agreement of 1927, he rejected the States' claims. When Sheehan was promoted secretary to the Treasury in 1932, McFarlane became second-in-charge as assistant-secretary (administrative). He was appointed secretary of the Australian Loan Council and of the National Debt Commission.

McFarlane had made an 'outstanding' contribution to the premiers' conferences in 1931. E. G. Theodore [q.v.12] recorded that cabinet regarded him 'as a valuable officer' whose services were 'indispensable' to the Treasury. In 1933 McFarlane was appointed C.M.G. Fixing his sights on the post of Commonwealth auditor-general, he informed R. G. (Baron) Casey [q.v.13] in 1935 that his health had deteriorated due to the mental and physical strain of his duties during the Depression. Casey persuaded him to take the post of official secretary and financial adviser to S. M. (Viscount) Bruce [q.v.7] at Australia House, London, in April 1936. McFarlane returned to Australia in early 1938 and was gazetted on 24 February to succeed Sheehan as secretary to the Treasury. For six months in 1941 he was also secretary of the Department of War Organization of Industry.

Although McFarlane was respected as a competent administrator and accountant, his austerity—deriving perhaps from a Presbyterian background—and inflexible nature won him few close friends. His failure to understand the new doctrines of J. M. (Baron) Keynes led the government to appoint professional economists as advisers to the Treasury, among them L. F. Giblin [q.v.8] and H. C. Coombs. Following the outbreak of World War II, the treasurer (Sir) Percy Spender rejected McFarlane's advice to raise taxes to fund war expenditure, accepting instead the recommendations of the economists to draw upon under-employed resources.

McFarlane's opinions on aspects of planning for the postwar period, including the 1945 white paper on full employment, also conflicted with the ideas of the government's principal advisers. He took the view that the government should concentrate its efforts on winning the war before directing its attention to peacetime utopias. Moreover, he criticized drafts of the white paper for including controversial statistical projections and failing to acknowledge that wage and balance-of-payments pressures would inevitably accompany full employment. Perhaps his most enduring contributions were his formation of the Treasury's general financial and economic policy section in 1943, and his reorganization of the department in 1946.

In January 1948 McFarlane was appointed Australian executive-director of the International Monetary Fund and of the International Bank for Reconstruction and Development, Washington, where he took a particular interest in discussions on currency convertibility, the devaluation of sterling-area currencies in 1949, and the price of gold. His appointment expired in 1950 and he came home to Australia. After his retirement that year, he led a quiet life in Canberra. He played golf (intermittently) and bowls (regularly), and held directorships of several companies, including Anglo-Oriental Tin Consortium and Wormald Bros (Aust) Pty Ltd. In one of his incisive articles in the *Australian Financial Review* he suggested that inflation in the early 1950s stemmed more from excessive domestic demand than from international factors, such as the boom occasioned by the Korean War.

McFarlane was tall, lean and slightly stooped, with a tendency to move slowly 'as if conserving his breath before the final assault on Mt Everest'. He appeared aloof, melancholy and anxious, his tendency to anticipate the worst earning him the appellation of 'Misery Mac'. Yet he was mentally sharp, loyal, and dedicated. He was also discreet and introspective, and remained an enigma to his associates. Sir Henry Gullett [q.v.9] regarded him as 'one of the most modest men in Australian officialdom' and Spender was impressed by McFarlane's 'affable personality'. On the other hand, Sir Frederic Eggleston [q.v.8] saw him as 'shrewd, even cunning, a typical departmental officer, arrogant to outsiders, but able to get some sort of power over his Minister in the old bureaucratic manner'. Coombs echoed Eggleston's opinion when he wrote that McFarlane possessed a 'subtle, even devious mind and an intuitive sense of the line of argument likely to prove persuasive with Treasurers of different temperaments and political prejudices'.

On 9 June 1958 at St James's Anglican Church, Sydney, McFarlane married Evelyn Mary, née Bray, the 69-year-old widow of J. A. Perkins [q.v.11]. Survived by the son of his first marriage, he died on 2 November 1970 in his home at Forrest and was buried in Canberra cemetery with Presbyterian forms.

P. Spender, *Politics and a Man* (Syd, 1972); H. C. Coombs, *Trial Balance* (Melb, 1981); S. Cornish, *Full Employment in Australia* (Canb, 1981); G. Whitwell, *The Treasury Line* (Syd, 1986); *Herald* (Melb), 16 Feb 1939; F. W. Eggleston, Confidential Notes: some great public servants (ms, Menzies L, ANU); A1939/1, McFarlane, S. G. (AA, Canb).

SELWYN CORNISH

McGARRY, FRANCIS JAMES (1897-1955), lay missionary and protector of Aborigines, was born on 11 July 1897 at Wagga Wagga, New South Wales, younger of twins and sixth child of native-born parents John McGarry (d.1903), butcher, and his wife Catherine Elizabeth, née Jones. When John died, the family moved to Manly, Sydney. Educated by the Good Samaritan nuns and at Marist

Brothers' High School, Darlinghurst, Francis worked as a clerk and warehouseman. On 28 July 1917 he enlisted in the Australian Imperial Force; he joined the 45th Battalion in France in August 1918 and was discharged in Australia on 13 September 1919.

In 1922 McGarry became a member of the Society of St Vincent de Paul's Manly conference, of which he was later vice-president. From 1926 he made weekly visits to the lepers at the Coast Hospital, Little Bay, but concealed this activity from his relations and associates. Responding to a suggestion by Monsignor F. X. Gsell [q.v.9], McGarry went to Alice Springs, Northern Territory, in 1935 to assist Father P. J. Moloney in establishing a mission to the Aborigines. The Little Flower Mission, on the outskirts of the town, commenced on 3 October.

At first McGarry fed, clothed and taught Aboriginal children at the presbytery and in the local church. After a site for a permanent mission was selected about half a mile (0.8 km) to the north, a well was sunk, a windmill, tank and church-school were erected, and wurlies were built to accommodate families. McGarry travelled to Sydney and arranged for the Daughters of Our Lady of the Sacred Heart to teach at the school. He obtained most of the mission's food by begging or bargaining in the town. In the early years he acquired clothing from his relations, from the Society of St Vincent de Paul and from the proceeds of the sale of Aboriginal artefacts and weapons.

In 1942 the authorities directed that the mission and its residents be moved to Arltunga, 68 miles (109 km) east of Alice Springs. McGarry chose a site and construction began. Appointed a protector of Aborigines in September, he was the sole White living at Arltunga for the next eight months. By 1944 the mission was fully established. As a layman, McGarry thought that he had little more to contribute. He resigned in March and joined the Territory's Native Affairs Branch in September. Having served briefly at Alice Springs and Katherine, and on patrol around the Finke, he established an Aboriginal settlement at Tanami in 1945, of which he was superintendent. In the following year the community was moved, first to the Granites and then to Yuendumu, near Mount Doreen. McGarry was responsible for the welfare of approximately four hundred people at Yuendumu.

Resigning his post on 20 July 1948, McGarry returned to Sydney. After a period as a salesman-clerk with a firm of auctioneers at Manly, he became a night-watchman to keep his days free for charity work. He died of meningitis on 21 November 1955 at Wahroonga Sanatorium and was buried with Catholic rites in Frenchs Forest cemetery.

F. Flynn, *Distant Horizons* (Syd, 1947); F. O'Grady, *Francis of Central Australia* (Syd, 1977); McGarry papers (ML); information from Aust Inst of Aboriginal Studies, Canb.   FRANK O'GRADY

McGARVIE, KEITH (1891-1969), dairy-farmer and politician, was born on 13 March 1891 at Colac, Victoria, eldest of three sons of Colac-born parents William McGarvie, grazier, and his wife Jean Keith, née Archer. Keith's paternal grandfather William McGarvie, an illiterate labourer from County Donegal, Ireland, had emigrated to Australia in 1844, worked as a bullock driver at Colac and selected land at Pomborneit. His property, Greenwood, passed to William junior in 1888, and was divided between his two sons, Keith and David, on his death in 1922. The shelter provided by its stone barriers, and the richness of its volcanic soil, made Greenwood an ideal dairy-property.

Keith was educated at Pomborneit State School, Camperdown Church of England Grammar School and Dookie Agricultural College. With his father he founded the Greenwood Jersey Stud in 1908. He enlisted in the Australian Imperial Force in August 1914 and served at Gallipoli in April-May 1915 as a sergeant in the 8th Battalion; afflicted with rheumatism, he was repatriated and discharged in December.

Following his return, McGarvie gradually improved the stud. In 1933 he won an award for the best-producing Jersey cow in Victoria and Australia. He joined the Victorian branch of the Australasian (Australian) Jersey Herd Society in 1934, and was its president (1935 and 1946), vice-president (1936-38) and honorary treasurer (1958-69). In 1964 he was to become patron. Keen to further his understanding of agriculture, he travelled to the United States of America in 1926 and 1937. At the manse of St Andrew's Presbyterian Church, Colac, on 26 June 1940 he married Evelyn Johnstone, née Burrows (d.1963), a 44-year-old widow.

McGarvie's growing influence in the district stemmed from his forceful personality and firm Presbyterian convictions: although considerate and likeable, he was sometimes colourful in criticizing error or weakness. Having worked (from 1932) to transform the local co-operative dairy-factory into the Camperdown-Glenormiston Dairy Co. Ltd, he chaired its board in 1948-64. He was also chairman of the Western District Co-operative Co. Ltd (1949-64), the Co-operative Insurance Co. of Australia and the Colac Brick Co. Ltd.

Well informed about rural issues, McGarvie was president of the Camperdown Pastoral and Agricultural Society. He was elected a councillor (1940) and life councillor (1960) of the Royal Agricultural Society of Victoria, and served for many years as chairman of the dairy-cattle committee and steward-in-chief of dairy cattle. Calf clubs, the forerunners of the Young Farmers' Movement, benefited from his enthusiasm. In addition, he was president (1941-43) of the Chamber of Agriculture of Victoria and a member of the agricultural committee of the Nuffield Foundation.

McGarvie's prominence in the Camperdown region propelled him into politics. In 1933 he stood as the United Australia Party candidate and won the by-election for the seat of Warrnambool in the Legislative Assembly. Defeated in 1935, he unsuccessfully contested Warrnambool (1937 and 1940), Polwarth (by-election 1940) and Hampden (1952); he was also defeated for South-Western Province in the elections for the Legislative Council in 1952.

Outside politics and agriculture, McGarvie had diverse interests. He maintained his links with former Anzacs, belonged to several Masonic lodges, and served as a magistrate and as a Heytesbury Shire councillor (1933-36). A fine rifle-shot, he competed in England in 1937, winning a Bisley spoon and badge. McGarvie died on 5 October 1969 at Colac and was buried in Camperdown cemetery; he had no children.

H. Iverson (comp and ed), *The Leaders of Industry and Commerce in Australia* (Melb, 1963); G. A. McGarvie (ed), *The McGarvie Family History* (Horsham, Vic, 1995); *Pastoral Review*, 16 May 1941, 16 Apr 1942, 15 Apr 1943; *Camperdown Chronicle*, 10, 28 Oct 1933, 8 Oct 1969; *Colac Herald*, 9 Oct 1940, 8 Oct 1969; information from Mr G. A. McGarvie, Parkdale, Melb, Mr D. Collyer, Ballarat, and Mr J. Heath, Camperdown, Vic.   L. LOMAS

McGEORGE, JOHN ALEXANDER HUGHES (1898-1979), forensic psychiatrist, was born on 12 October 1898 at Glasgow, Scotland, son of John Matheson McGeorge, wine merchant, and his wife Martha, née George. Young John was educated at Hillhead High School, Glasgow, Newington College (1913-15), Sydney, and the University of Sydney (M.B., Ch.M., 1927; D.P.M., 1932). On 8 April 1925 at St Andrew's Anglican Cathedral he married Jean Lapish, a 26-year-old milliner; they were to remain childless. Medical officer at Parramatta Mental Hospital from 14 April 1927, he moved to Broughton Hall Psychiatric Clinic as senior medical officer on 6 May 1929. He resigned in 1936 and established himself in private practice, becoming honorary psychiatrist at Royal Prince Alfred and Sydney hospitals, and at the Women's Hospital, Crown Street.

All three armed services benefited from McGeorge's skills. After serving as an honorary major (1940-42) in the Militia, he was appointed temporary squadron leader, Royal Australian Air Force, in November 1942. Promoted wing commander in 1945, he transferred to the reserve in 1951. He continued as a consultant psychiatrist to the R.A.A.F. and held a similar position with the Royal Australian Navy from 1945.

Having passed the Barristers' Admission Board examinations, McGeorge was admitted to the Bar on 28 November 1952, but never practised. When confronted with the choice between 'neurotics in Macquarie Street' and 'bad boys in Long Bay', he opted for the latter. As consultant psychiatrist (1952-64) to the Department of Justice, he assessed many of the State's most notorious criminals, and sat (1951-57) on the Parole Board of New South Wales. His reputation spread. In 1955 he went to Honiara, Solomon Islands, to advise in the case of an English missionary who had killed a young boy with an axe. In 1962 the Victorian government, embroiled in a public outcry over its intention to hang Ronald Tait (the 'notorious vicarage murderer') invited McGeorge to assess him. He found Tait to be sane, but confounded all sides by declaring his opposition to capital punishment. That year he was publicly criticized for his role in the release of Leonard Lawson, a convicted rapist who killed two young girls after gaining his freedom. Even in his retirement McGeorge continued to assess the 'worst' offenders. Over forty years he interviewed some 7000 prisoners, including more than 500 murderers. Albert Moss, the 'mutilation murderer', was the 'most brutal' offender he encountered.

An enthusiastic public speaker and frequent contributor to the press, McGeorge was an avid popularizer of his calling. His views on the causes of juvenile delinquency, the role of alcohol in crime, homosexuality, parole, the need for permanent confinement of serious offenders, capital punishment, family life, and the mental health of famous people were well known. He was a forthright, common-sense psychiatrist, with little time for the 'idiocies' of Freud and his followers. To McGeorge, criminals were sometimes the product of overactive 'glands', but more often of 'slovenly, repressive, indulgent or broken homes'. None the less, free will could overcome determinism, except when will was eroded by alcohol. He was a firm supporter of early-closing legislation. A number of people took exception to his views. (Sir) Neville Cardus [q.v.13] dismissed McGeorge's claim that musical genius was often the result of mental instability, and (Sir) Stephen Roberts [q.v.] criticized McGeorge and other opponents of rehabilitation programmes for long-term prisoners.

McGeorge taught postgraduates at the University of Sydney (from 1950) and the

University of New South Wales (from 1958). A foundation member of the Australasian Association of Psychiatrists and its successor the (Royal) Australian and New Zealand College of Psychiatry (1964), he was president (1948-52) of the local branch of the Australian Physiotherapy Association (federal president 1952), and a member of the British Academy of Forensic Sciences and of the International Commission of Jurists. In 1962 he was appointed O.B.E.

Large and imposing, with a ruddy complexion, dark hair and a clipped moustache, McGeorge had a relaxed and assured manner. His direct opinions, however, earned him a reputation as a 'stormy petrel'. After he retired he appeared as a regular panellist on the ATN-7 television programme, 'People in Conflict', and wrote his reminiscences, *Reflections of a Psychiatrist* (1966). He belonged to the Australian Society of Authors, and to the Air Force and Royal Prince Alfred Yacht clubs. Survived by his wife, he died on 9 May 1979 at his Neutral Bay home and was buried in Northern Suburbs cemetery, unacknowledged by any obituary in the major medical journals.

MJA, 29 Feb 1936; *SMH*, 20 Feb 1944, 22 Feb 1946, 29 Nov 1952, 26 Sept 1955, 31 Jan 1956, 1 Jan, 11 Oct 1962, 28 Aug 1963, 26 Jan 1964; *Age* (Melb), 26 Dec 1964.   STEPHEN GARTON

MACGHEY, MARY VETA (c.1897-1970), headmistress, was born about 1 January 1897, probably in Adelaide. Rumours subsequently circulated that she was the daughter of a visiting Indian cricketer and a woman prominent in society, or that her mother was an opera star and her father a well-known Adelaide lawyer. It seems, however, that her father was named Filgly and her mother Mary Veta. Unable to support her illegitimate baby, Mary handed her to the South Australian State Children's Department. In February 1897 the department placed the infant with Patrick Macghey, a prison warder at Dry Creek, and his wife Martha Mary, née Winstanley, stipulating that Veta be instructed in the Catholic faith. The Macgheys cared for other state wards, but adopted Veta and raised her from 1903 as their only child. In 1911 she was sent to Adelaide High School; she excelled in academic and sporting activities, and became head prefect.

In 1916 Macghey joined the Education Department as a junior teacher. She attended Teachers' Training College and the University of Adelaide (B.A., 1919; M.A., 1930). A talented hockey player, she competed in intervarsity tournaments and also represented the State eight times. Throughout her career she encouraged girls' sport. In her youth she rode a motorcycle, wearing black leather and a red scarf, and created a sensation; she later owned a series of beautiful motorcars.

While teaching at Adelaide, Norwood and Gawler high schools, Macghey studied part time at university for the diploma of economics and political science (1923). At Kadina High School she was senior mistress (from 1931) and, at Norwood, special senior mistress (from 1943). In 1951 she was appointed founding headmistress of Adelaide Girls' High School. Although resources were limited, Miss Macghey worked energetically to establish a leading academic girls' school. She confounded expectations that her school would amount to little, and 'was tough . . . in a man's administrative world, getting just conditions for girls and teachers'. Following her retirement in 1958, she taught at Henley Beach High School and Presbyterian Girls' College, Adelaide.

Macghey had been active in the South Australian Women Teachers' Guild (president 1949). As editor (from 1942) of the *Guild Chronicle*, she wrote stirring editorials in favour of equal pay. She sat on the Teachers' Salaries Board (from 1948) and was made a fellow of the Australian College of Education. Having helped to form (1950) the South Australian Institute of Teachers, she was elected first president of its women's branch. In 1959 she was appointed O.B.E.

A generous woman, Macghey gave financial assistance to her friends and colleagues. She was short in stature and swarthy in complexion, with black, crinkly hair, dark brown eyes and a deep voice; she wore mannish suits, topped by a pussy-cat bow. Keen on a bet on the horse-races, she was also interested in art, antiques and gardening. Macghey died on 20 December 1970 at Wattle Park and was cremated; most of her estate (sworn for probate at $56 071) was bequeathed to her live-in companion Maud ('Borbie') Evans McFarlane. S.A.I.T.'s Macghey House commemorates her, as does a house at Adelaide Girls' High School.

Adel Univ Mag, 1, no 3, 2, no 1 (1919), 3, no 1 (1920); SA Women Teachers Guild, *Guild Chronicle*, 9, no 17, Sept 1947, p 3; *SAIT J*, 10, 24 Feb 1971; *News* (Adel), 26 Aug, 11 Dec 1958; *Advertiser* (Adel), 18 Dec 1958, 1 Jan 1959, 23 Dec 1970; Children Boarded Out, 1862-1908, Government Record Group 27/5 and 27/6 (SRSA); Adel High School records and magazines; St Augustine's Church, Salisbury (Adel), records.

                    MARGARET ALLEN

McGIBBON, JAMES SINCLAIR (1875-1943), accountant, political fund-raiser and tennis administrator, was born on 10 August

1875 at Kew, Melbourne, son of Scottish-born parents James McGibbon, a warehouseman who turned his hand to accountancy, and his wife Margaret Euphemia, née Nicol. Educated at Camberwell Grammar School and Auburn College, Sinclair worked with Gilmour & McGibbon until 1896 when he moved to Perth and joined the accounting firm, O. L. Haines & Co. In 1898 he established his own practice. At St George's Anglican Cathedral, Perth, on 7 August 1900 he married 20-year-old Rettie Paltridge Paterson; they were to have five children.

Although he resigned as a director of Westralian Farmers Ltd in 1915 so that McGibbon & Co. could become the firm's auditors, he maintained his rural links. In the 1917 elections for the Legislative Assembly McGibbon unsuccessfully contested the seat of Toodyay for the Country Party. The Western Australian Consultative Council was formed in 1925; McGibbon soon became its chairman. Also known as the National Union, the same name as its Melbourne counterpart, the council sought to raise funds and hold them in trust as a means of combating communist activity and industrial lawlessness. Due to its assistance to conservative political parties, the council was alleged to carry undue influence in pre-selection and policy issues. At the 1943 Federal election a public battle over these matters, with McGibbon a target, was fought on the front pages of the *Sunday Times* and *West Australian*.

State and Federal governments had made use of McGibbon's expertise. In 1909 he was appointed assistant-commissioner to Martin Edward Jull [q.v.9], the Western Australian public service commissioner who was then investigating the State's book-keeping methods. He later served as Western Australian growers' representative (1919-20) on the Australian Wheat Board. On 29 December 1939 (Sir) Eric Harrison [q.v.14], the postmaster-general, announced McGibbon's appointment as a member of the Australian Broadcasting Commission, a selection deplored by John Curtin [q.v.13], the leader of the Opposition, because of McGibbon's financial links with anti-Labor organizations. (Sir) Robert Menzies' [q.v.] government chose McGibbon in 1941 to be its business and financial representative abroad on matters relating to the armed services; he spent much of the next two years travelling overseas.

President (1927-28) of the Rotary Club of Perth, McGibbon was a director of Rotary International. While he enjoyed golf and motor-boating, his favourite recreation was tennis. He had joined the King's Park Tennis Club in 1903, and was president (1924-38) and a life member (1926) of the Western Australian Lawn Tennis Association. Practical, if domineering, he organized visits to Perth by ranked Australian players and leading teams from France, Japan, Britain and Germany. The King's Park Tennis Club named its gates and a public stand after him.

En route to New Zealand, McGibbon died of hypertensive coronary vascular disease on 8 November 1943 at the Menzies Hotel, Melbourne, and was cremated; his wife, two sons and three daughters survived him.

J. S. Battye (ed), *Cyclopedia of Western Australia*, 1 (Adel, 1912); K. S. Inglis, *This is the ABC* (Melb, 1983); H. C. J. Phillips, *Tennis West* (Syd, 1995); *Sunday Times* (Perth), 18, 25 July 1943; *West Australian*, 9 Nov 1943; D. W. Black, The National Party in Western Australia, 1917-1930: its origins and development with an introductory survey of 'Liberal' Party organisation, 1901-1916 (M.A. thesis, Univ WA, 1974).   HARRY C. J. PHILLIPS

McGINNESS, LUCY; *see* ALNGINDABU

McGIRR, JAMES (1890-1957), pharmacist and premier, was born on 6 February 1890 at Parkes, New South Wales, seventh child of Irish-born parents John Patrick McGirr, a road contractor who turned to farming, and his wife Mary Teresa, née O'Sullivan. Jim grew up on a small dairy-farm. After early schooling locally, he attended St Stanislaus' College, Bathurst. At the age of 16 he was apprenticed to his brother J. J. G. McGirr [q.v.10], a pharmacist at Parkes. Jim was an accomplished horseman and soon became a pharmacy to work at the nearby stockyards. Thrown from his horse while mustering, he badly broke his leg and spent three months in bed. After this experience he resumed his apprenticeship. Having passed chemistry (1910), botany and materia medica (1911) at the University of Sydney, and the required examinations under the Pharmacy Act (1897), he was registered as a pharmacist on 12 August 1913. McGirr was employed in a large chemist shop in Sydney and joined the Shop Assistants' Union of New South Wales before operating pharmacies in partnership with his brother Greg. He began his own pharmaceutical business at Parkes, specializing in veterinary products, and bought an 800-acre (325 ha) property in the district.

Like his brothers Greg and Patrick Michael, Jim McGirr was active in Labor politics. He joined the Parkes branch in 1906 and held various offices. In 1922 Greg vacated his Legislative Assembly seat of Cootamundra for a Sydney electorate, simultaneously arranging through party intrigue for his place to be taken by Jim, who was elected that year. The other Labor member for Cootamundra, P. F. Loughlin [q.v.10], was a strong opponent of Greg McGirr and successfully prevented Jim from being pre-selected for the 1925 election, despite appeals to the federal and State executives. In the face of some initial local resistance, Jim was selected and stood for Cumberland. A strong campaigner and a powerful orator, he was duly elected. With the return to single-member electorates in 1927, he won Bankstown, which he retained until 1950, then represented Liverpool.

When Labor under J. T. Lang [q.v.9] won the 1930 elections, McGirr—described by Lang as 'the solid type, entirely different to his brother, the flamboyant Greg'—came equal first in the ballot for the ministry with 39 out of 55 votes. He served as minister for health (4 November 1930 to 17 June 1931) and held the local government portfolio (17 June 1931 to 13 May 1932). The government combined railways, tramways, main roads and motor transport under a single portfolio and, on 22 March 1932, McGirr also became the State's first minister for transport. The press dubbed him 'Commissar for Transport'. At St Mary's Catholic Cathedral, Sydney, on 15 October that year he married 28-year-old Valerie Cecilia Armstrong.

Throughout the ensuing decade of political reverses for Labor and the bitter struggle between Lang and his opponents for control of the party, McGirr was a staunch Langite. In 1940 Lang temporarily left the Labor Party; McGirr was one of seven State parliamentarians who followed him. None the less, when Labor returned to power under (Sir) William McKell in May 1941, McGirr was included on the premier's ticket for cabinet (the only ex-Langite to be so) and became minister for local government and for housing. He attempted to implement McKell's Greater Sydney scheme and consequent local government amalgamations, but made little headway in the face of strong opposition. In 1942 he established the Housing Commission of New South Wales. Following the May 1944 elections, with housing shortages looming as a major issue, McKell made housing a separate portfolio under McGirr. With the end of World War II the problem grew more acute. McGirr tackled his responsibilities with determination and courage, winning credit for his efforts.

In February 1947 McKell resigned to serve as governor-general. The struggle for the succession was bitter, the two main contenders being McGirr and the minister for education R. J. Heffron [q.v.14] who had the support of the party executive, the majority of cabinet and McKell himself. McGirr drew his strength from the anti-McKell forces in caucus. His chief organizers were Clive Evatt and a back-bencher C. H. Matthews. The Langite rump strongly backed him. As a prac-

tising Catholic with a rural background—in contrast to the former trade-union radical Heffron—McGirr also attracted support from his co-religionists and country members. On 6 February he finally triumphed (by two votes) on the fourth ballot, and was sworn in as premier and treasurer. A number of members were so infuriated by McKell's decision to participate in the ballot that they voted against Heffron as a protest. McGirr was a leader commanding only the barest of majorities.

Straightforward, decent and humane, the new premier was personally well liked and noted for his loyalty. McGirr could be a vigorous foe and a doughty fighter when roused, but he was also given to hesitation and procrastination, and was overly suspicious of those around him. He lacked McKell's political astuteness, and his ability to master the complexities of the premiership. As McGirr's term progressed, the backlog of files in his office accumulated and increasingly disappeared into his 'refrigerator—a repository of many schemes which the Premier never bothers to defrost'.

The early days of the McGirr premiership indicated a clear break with his predecessor's style. At his first premiers' conference, McGirr made a highly publicized, intemperate attack on Prime Minister Chifley [q.v.13] over Commonwealth-State financial relations. Such outbursts were to become a recurrent feature of his administration. In addition, McGirr moved quickly to introduce the 40-hour week (something McKell had opposed) before any other State, and while the claim was still before the Commonwealth Court of Conciliation and Arbitration. Another sign of a want of restraint and careful planning was McGirr's policy speech for the 1947 elections: his party was long to regret its rash array of promises.

The new term began with an unsuccessful attempt to oust ministers who had supported Heffron for the leadership in 1947. Two McGirr supporters (Matthews and W. F. Sheahan [q.v.]) succeeded in joining the unpredictable Evatt in a cabinet still largely dominated by the McKell old guard. In regard to the 1947 election promises, the government's response was to push on as quickly as possible, whatever the consequences. Works were commenced throughout the State with more concern for political considerations than long-term implications. The public works programme began its descent into disarray. Growing industrial unrest, culminating in the 1949 coal strike, further weakened the government's position, as did constant blackouts and electricity shortages. Moreover, electoral backlash against the Federal Labor government had an impact on its New South Wales counterpart.

Internal conflict and dissension continued. The State government's attempt to shore up its electoral position through a redistribution led to a serious revolt by Labor's rural members in mid-1949. McGirr clashed publicly with his former chief supporter Evatt. The most serious split of all occurred on the eve of the 1950 elections. Four Labor members who had not followed the ticket in the ballot for the Legislative Council in 1949 were, as a result, disendorsed. McGirr unwisely took up their cause and, when rebuffed by the executive, announced that he intended to resign as leader. A week later he changed his mind.

Labor narrowly survived in office, but the balance of power was held by two of the members who had lost their endorsements, J. W. Seiffert and J. L. Geraghty. Both indicated that they would support Labor, and McGirr was thus able to form a government on 30 June 1950. Seiffert voted consistently with Labor. Geraghty, however, proved to be a more uncertain ally. He gave McGirr anxious moments as he used his key position, amid much publicity, to apply pressure on the government. The arduous demands of coping with a hung parliament, and presiding over a fractious cabinet and caucus, took an increasing toll on McGirr's health. On 2 April 1952 he resigned as premier. He left parliament on the following day to become chairman of the Maritime Services Board, a position he held until 1955, despite a furore about his lack of technical qualifications.

'Big Jim' was a physically imposing man, over six feet (183 cm) tall and weighing sixteen stone (102 kg). Although a heavy smoker, he did not drink. He never lost his love of the land, and regularly spent time on his farm near Liverpool. Survived by his wife, daughter and two sons, he died of a coronary occlusion on 27 October 1957 at Homebush and was buried in the cemetery at Parkes. His estate was sworn for probate at £52 795.

J. T. Lang, *The Great Bust* (Syd, 1962); *PD* (NSW), 29 Oct 1957, pp 1384, 1402; *SMH*, 13, 15 Mar, 4, 8 Nov 1924, 4 Nov 1930, 17 May 1941, 5, 6 Feb, 22 Aug 1947, 2 Apr 1952, 1 Jan 1955, 30 Oct 1957; *Daily Telegraph* (Syd), 14 Mar, 13 May 1924, 21 Apr 1925, 25 Jan 1947, 17 Mar 1949, 2 Apr 1952, 28 Oct 1957; *Labor Daily*, 31 Mar, 19 July 1924, 18 Apr, 5 May, 18 July 1925; *Sun* (Syd), 27 Mar 1932, 5 Feb 1947, 1 June 1950, 1 Apr 1952, 7 Feb 1955; *Daily Mirror* (Syd), 5 Feb 1947, 1 Apr 1952; *Truth* (Syd), 6 Apr 1952; D. Clune, The Labor Government in N.S.W. 1941-1965: a study in longevity in government (Ph.D. thesis, Dept of Government, Univ Syd, 1990); information from Mr R. B. Nott, Brighton-Le-Sands, Syd, and the late Messrs R. R. Downing, A. Landa and N. J. Mannix.   DAVID CLUNE

McGOVERN, SIR PATRICK SILVESTA (1895-1975), public servant, was born on 4 April 1895 at Korong Vale, Victoria, sixth of seven children of John McGovern, a farmer from Ireland, and his Victorian-born wife Elizabeth, née Carlon. Educated at state primary schools and at Beechworth College, Patrick began work in 1911 as a telegraph messenger in the Commonwealth Public Service. Following country and suburban postings, he transferred to the taxation branch of the Treasury in 1919. At St Peter's Anglican Church, Melbourne, on 22 July 1922 he married Henrietta Rose Laurissen. When a Commonwealth sales tax was hurriedly introduced in 1930, McGovern worked so unstintingly to implement it in Victoria that the strain made him seriously ill in 1932-33. As the State's chief investigating officer, sales tax, he responded to the government's increasingly complex legislation.

In 1939 McGovern was appointed deputy-commissioner, sales tax, Canberra. He later played a key role in the introduction of payroll tax (1941) and changes to entertainment tax (1942). While he was not the senior deputy-commissioner, he was 'the outstanding one'. By 1942 he had become second commissioner of taxation. The commissioner L. S. Jackson [q.v.14] concentrated on the many alterations made to income tax during World War II. McGovern oversaw other taxes, handled tax-evasion cases and performed much of the day-to-day administration. Between 1939-40 and 1944-45 the department's staff grew from 1073 to 5462, and Federal tax collections rose from £35 million to £270.5 million.

After an exhausted Jackson declined re-appointment, McGovern succeeded him as commissioner in May 1946. His early efforts centred on establishing a coherent and effective management structure, and successfully reducing wartime arrears. All the while the workload continued to increase. In the early 1950s the number of staff in the taxation office was capped at 7000 and McGovern focused on ways to maximize efficiency. (Sir) Arthur Fadden [q.v.14] appreciated the commissioner's stout defence of his wool sales deduction proposal (1950). McGovern began a second term as commissioner in 1953 and was appointed C.B.E. in 1954.

Some of his staff found him aloof, with no light touch; others thought him vain; yet everyone respected him. McGovern raised the status of the tax office significantly. He also facilitated acceptance of pay-as-you-earn and provisional-tax arrangements. Politicians who made inquiries on behalf of their constituents received 'very firm, but very just and very courteous treatment'. Socially, McGovern was more genial, but always retained his presence. Golf on Sunday mornings, gardening, powerful motorcars and woodwork were his enthusiasms. He was president (1946-47) of the Rotary Club of Canberra and a foundation member (1954) of the Common-wealth Club.

McGovern was knighted in 1959. Reluctant to retire, he was appointed commissioner for an additional year under special legislation. In April 1961 he left an office with almost 8000 staff collecting £1 billion annually. He served as honorary treasurer of the National Heart Foundation of Australia (1959-69) and of the Winston Churchill Memorial Trust (Australia) (1961-71), and as chairman of Model Dairy Industries Ltd and Canberra Crematorium Ltd. Survived by his wife and two daughters, Sir Patrick died on 18 March 1975 in his home at Forrest, Canberra, and was cremated.

A. Fadden, *They Called Me Artie* (Brisb, 1969); *PD* (Cwlth), 30 Mar 1960, p 345; *Canb Times*, 20 Mar 1975; A463/61 item 59/3737, A6899/1 item P. S. McGovern (AA, Canb).   IAN CARNELL

McGRATH, FRANCIS (1866-1947), jockey and racehorse-trainer, was born on 17 October 1866 at Boorowa, New South Wales, eldest of three sons of James McGrath, carpenter, and his second wife Catherine, née Cahill (late Kane), both from County Tipperary, Ireland. Frank learned to ride early and had his first win on his father's horse, Killarney, at the Gullen races in 1875. Apprenticed to Sydney trainer John Alsopp in 1877, he moved to Edward Keys and in 1880 joined the Newcastle stables of John Mayo, for whom he rode Prince Imperial in the 1885 Caulfield Cup: McGrath suffered head and eye injuries when sixteen of the forty-one runners fell in the straight. Although he was plagued by constant headaches, he returned to the saddle, won the 1886 Epsom Handicap on Zeno and continued to ride until 1892.

By 1898 McGrath was successfully training ponies at Canterbury, Sydney. His winnings from Stormy enabled him to buy a house and stables in Doncaster Avenue, Kensington, in 1900 and to obtain a No.1 trainer's licence from the Australian Jockey Club. On 23 July that year, at St Mary's Catholic Church, Crookwell, he married 25-year-old Bridget Stapleton. His early successes included Abundance, winner of the 1902 Australian Jockey Club Derby and the 1903 Victoria Racing Club and A.J.C. St Leger stakes, and Little Toy which won the 1906 Doncaster Handicap. He trained Prince Foote for 'J. Baron' [q.v.7 John Brown]; the horse won the A.J.C. and Victoria Derbys (1909), the Melbourne Cup (1909) and both St Legers (1910). McGrath later maintained that the prize-money he collected early in his career provided him with the 'kick along' to sustain him through the inevitable lean years.

Despite rarely having more than twenty horses in training, McGrath prepared the winners of many major events, among them the Epsom Handicap (Amounis 1926, 1928), Caulfield Cup (Amounis 1930, Denis Boy 1931), Metropolitan Stakes (Denis Boy 1932, Beau Vite 1940), A.J.C. Derby (Tanami 1910, Peter Pan 1932, Pandect 1940) and W. S. Cox Plate (Beau Vite 1940, 1941). His greatest horse was R. R. Dangar's Peter Pan. In addition to taking numerous V.R.C. and A.J.C. weight-for-age trophies, Peter Pan overcame severe interference to win the 1932 Melbourne Cup (returning to scale with grass-stains on his nose), and ploughed through the mud carrying 9 st. 10 lb. (62.6 kg) to 'blitz' the 1934 Melbourne Cup field. Supported by experienced racing officials and some seasoned jockeys, McGrath always maintained that Peter Pan was a better two-miler than Phar Lap.

McGrath was never accused of malpractice by any of the principal club committees. He was always willing to provide advice to young trainers, and to extend a helping hand to those who had fallen on hard times (during the Depression he often 'forgot' to collect the rent from tenants of the cottages he owned). In 1941 he was elected president of the New South Wales Breeders', Owners', and Trainers' Association. He retired in 1945, handing over his stables to his son, Frank junior. Survived by his wife, two sons and three of his four daughters, McGrath died on 28 October 1947 at his Kensington home and was buried in Waverley cemetery. His estate was sworn for probate at £15 537.

Herald & Weekly Times Ltd, *Turf Men and Memories* (Melb, 1912); N. Penton, *A Racing Heart* (Syd, 1987); J. Pollard, *Australian Horse Racing* (Syd, 1988); M. Painter and R. Waterhouse, *The Principal Club* (Syd, 1992); *Aust Jockey Club Racing Calendar*, Sept 1989, p 11, Oct 1989, p 9; *SMH*, 16 Sept 1940, 28 Oct 1941, 28 Oct 1947; *Smith's Weekly*, 28 June 1941; *Daily Mirror* (Syd), 28-29 Oct 1947; information from Mr F. McGrath, Kensington, Syd.
RICHARD WATERHOUSE

McGRATH, VIVIAN ERZERUM BEDE (1916-1978), tennis-player, was born on 17 February 1916 at Merrendee, near Mudgee, New South Wales, fourth child of native-born parents Herbert Francis McGrath, hotel-keeper, and his wife Florence Sophia, née Smith. Vivian was recognized as a tennis prodigy while at Sydney Boys' High School, where he also excelled at cricket. He won the special singles event at the State championships in 1931, the Australian junior singles in 1932 and the French junior singles in 1933. A member of the Davis Cup squad from

1933 until 1937, he made several overseas tours, but never played in a Challenge-round final.

Good looking, with a dark complexion and hazel-coloured eyes, McGrath was 5 ft 10 ins (178 cm) tall, slightly built and a 'terrier' on the court. He worked his double-handed backhand, which opponents regarded as a weakness, into his trademark. Seemingly indifferent to training, he was criticized for modelling himself on his great friend Jack Crawford. A habit McGrath developed early was to drop one ball if his first serve went in; since no one protested, it was ignored by the umpires. Although he had beaten many leading players overseas, including Fred Perry, Christian Boussus and Ellsworth Vines, he had more success at home: with Crawford, he won five consecutive New South Wales doubles titles (1933-37) and the Aus-tralian doubles in 1935. His greatest victory came in the Australian singles in 1937 when he defeated John Bromwich in five sets.

McGrath was generous in his commitment to the sport, playing many exhibition games for his employers—A. G. Spalding & Bros (N.S.W.) Pty Ltd—and at weekends in local Badge matches in Sydney. World War II inter-rupted his career. He silenced his critics by enlisting in the Australian Imperial Force on 19 November 1941 and serving in transport units in Australia, mainly in the Northern Territory; he was allowed leave to play exhibi-tion matches with visiting American service-men. After Sergeant McGrath was discharged on 14 May 1946, he never recaptured his previous form. Constant tennis-playing in his youth had caused a run of injuries; he was plagued by arthritis in his wrist and feet, and by bouts of asthma. He continued to work for Spalding Bros until the late 1950s when he started tennis-coaching. Based in the Southern Highlands, he taught in private schools at Bowral and Moss Vale. For many years he travelled to Canberra once a week to coach at the Japanese Embassy. He also had more time to pursue his interest in horse-racing and follow the Dragons (St George Rugby League team).

Promising at an early age, McGrath was called the 'Wonder Boy', but failed to fulfil ex-pectations. He died of a coronary occlusion on 9 April 1978 at Chevalier College, Bur-radoo, and was buried with Catholic rites in Botany cemetery.

P. Metzler, *Great Players of Australian Tennis* (Syd, 1979); J. Shepherd, *Encyclopaedia of Aus-tralian Sport* (Adel, 1980); Aust Soc for Sports Hist, *Bulletin*, Dec 1995; *SMH*, 17 Oct 1931, 8, 18 Feb 1932, 17 Oct, 23 Dec 1933, 2 Oct, 28 Nov 1934, 1 Feb 1937, 3 Aug 1939, 28 Aug 1940, 21 Nov 1941, 11 July 1944, 13 Apr 1978; information from Mrs M. Dig-nam, Greenacre, Syd.   KERRY REGAN

McGREGOR, SIR JAMES ROBERT (1889-1973) and **HAROLD WADDELL** (1898-1978), woolbrokers, were born on 1 October 1889 and 9 December 1898 at Hindmarsh, Adelaide, eldest and third sons of Scottish-born James Wigham McGregor, woollen manufacturer, and his wife Mary Twaddle, née Waddell. Trained in Scotland, James senior had arrived in Adelaide in 1882. He later established the Torrenside woollen mills at Thebarton and represented Bradford buyers, especially W. & J. Whitehead; he also owned pastoral properties and had plantation interests on Bougainville. As a member of the Federal government's advisory committee, he helped to devise a table of types and limits in 1916 to value the Australian wool clip for wartime sale to Britain. James junior and Harold were both educated at Prince Alfred College. They entered their father's firm, gained experience at Whitehead's topmaking and spinning busi-ness, and acquired an outstanding technical knowledge of wool. Like their father, they were to profit by setting up testing plants in wool-selling centres to estimate the clean value of the product.

About 1908 James established a branch of J. W. McGregor & Co. in Sydney, concen-trating on the markets there and in Brisbane. His technical and trading skills, enhanced by contacts with Whitehead's and other over-seas buyers, soon made him wealthy. On 22 December 1916 he was appointed wool appraiser for the New South Wales committee and buyers' representative for the Queens-land committee, both of which served the Commonwealth Central Wool Committee. In the following year he became wool appraiser for the national body. At St Stephen's Presby-terian Church, Sydney, on 10 August 1921 he married Alice Constance Taylor, a steno-grapher; they were to remain childless. With Harold, he set up companies in the Channel Islands to control the firm's substantial top-making interests in Europe, though they held their Australian interests separately after their father's death in 1925.

James centred his business on his well-known office in Bond Street, Sydney, and travelled abroad regularly. Renowned for his expertise, he again played a leading role (including framing the table of limits) in the Central Wool Committee which was re-established in September 1939 to control wartime wool disposal. Its chairman praised him in 1945 for his 'almost super-human efforts'. In peacetime McGregor traded ex-tensively, expanding his activities and offices during the Korean War wool boom, increas-ing his shareholding in the Bougainville plan-tations and becoming known as Australia's largest wool-buyer—at one Brisbane series he bought a third of the offering for about £1.9 million. McGregor's staff and overseas clients esteemed him highly. A small, dark-haired man of forthright opinions, he was un-ruffled, well organized and courageous. His ability and charm impressed others and won him the friendship of (Sir) Robert Menzies [q.v.] who described him as 'the great Aus-tralian wool authority' and 'one of the best men I ever knew'. In 1956 McGregor was appointed K.B.E. When entertaining at his home, Neidpath, at Darling Point, he shared his love of fine wine and food.

McGregor's wealth, good taste and knowl-edge of art enabled him to build an outstand-ing collection of sculptures and paintings, including works by Australian, English and French artists. Friendly with (Sir) William Ashton, Sir Lionel Lindsay, Sir Daryl Lindsay and Adrian Feint [qq.v.7,10,14], he extended patronage to several artists and donated works to galleries. In 1929-58 he served as a trustee of the National Art Gallery of New South Wales. For him, appreciating art re-quired an imaginative understanding similar to the capacity to judge what a sample of wool might yield. While travelling in the United States of America, Sir James died on 3 August 1973 at St Francis Memorial Hospital, San Francisco, and was cremated; his wife pre-deceased him. His estate was sworn for pro-bate at $935 348.

Based in Adelaide and buying out another brother's holding in the family business, Harold McGregor focused on the more difficult South and Western Australian wool markets, and operated in the Victorian mar-ket jointly with James. His widespread com-mercial activities involved much overseas travel. At St Columba's Church, Chelsea, London, on 12 April 1934 he married Suzanne Marie Régine Scamps with the forms of the Church of Scotland. Harold's business flair and attention to detail, together with rising wool prices, enabled him to do well. His skill in judging wool led to his appointment as con-trolling appraiser for South Australia during World War II. For most of the Korean War he and James operated together and their extensive trading proved very successful. From 1950 Harold had developed large land holdings, the most significant being Bal-quhidder in South Australia, and Glenalpine and Toonambool in Victoria; he also held interests in real estate in Adelaide and other businesses. Like James, he played a leading role in the Australian Council of Woolbuyers and was a discerning collector of art, but in temperament he was more reticent and no *bon vivant*. Respecting the Scottish traits of quiet service and private giving, and having often needed hospital accommodation himself when beds were short, Harold took up the cause of Adelaide's St Andrew's Hospital, a private institution associated with the Presby-terian Church. He organized a family do-nation of £25 000 to its building fund in 1952 and gave large sums of money himself; he harried a reluctant government to help, advis-ing it that he was 'somewhat weary of digging deep into my own pocket and pressing my family and friends to give'; and he guaranteed, personally and anonymously, the hospital's large mortgage for its new building in 1961. As board chairman (1960-71), he worked tirelessly for the expanding hospital as it assumed a large training role. For many years he was an elder of Adelaide's Scots Church, to which he and James gave an outstanding set of stained-glass windows by Lawrence Lee in memory of their parents. As a young man Harold had been a competent yachtsman. Ill health dogged his final years. Survived by his wife, son and two daughters, he died on 26 January 1978 at St Andrew's Hospital and was cremated. His portrait by (Sir) Ivor Hele hangs in the hospital.

R. M. Gibbs, *Not for Ourselves* (Adel, 1994); C. Fyfe, *Gentlemen's Agreements* (Perth, 1996); *Art in Aust*, 15 Nov 1934; *Advertiser* (Adel), 16 Mar 1925; *Aust Financial Review*, 8 Aug 1973; H. W. McGregor papers (held at St Andrew's Hospital, Adel); family papers held by Mr R. McGregor, Adel; information from Mr J. D. Robertshaw, Paddington, Syd, and Mr R. McGregor, Adel.   R. M. GIBBS

McGREGOR, KATHARINE ELIZABETH (1903-1979), lawyer, was born on 16 May 1903 in South Brisbane, second of three children of Queensland-born parents John George McGregor, solicitor, and his wife Katharine Elizabeth, née Ferguson. Her 7-year-old brother Ian was killed when he was struck by a tram in 1909. Katharine and her sister re-ceived a strict and conservative upbringing. Their father, whose firm acted (from 1893) for the Presbyterian Church, instilled in them a keen interest in their Scottish forebears. Educated at Brisbane Girls' Grammar School, Katharine was awarded the languages prize in 1917, 1918 and 1919. In her final year she came second in the class and won an open scholarship to the University of Queensland (B.A., 1923; M.A., 1925).

There she studied classics in the honours school, with Miriam Jones and Cecil McDonnell. A nervous, softly spoken young woman, McGregor avoided university social life and spent most of her time with her family, reading and studying. She graduated with first-class honours, completed a thesis on 'The Island of Samos' for her masterate, and served as honorary secretary of the short-lived Queensland Classical Society.

Persuaded by her father to carry on the family's legal tradition, McGregor sat the Barristers' Board examinations. On 1 October 1926 she was admitted as a solicitor by the

Supreme Court of Queensland; on 5 October she became the first woman in the State to be admitted as a barrister. One newspaper report described her as 'a good looking girl, without the dowdiness and plainness associated with a blue stocking's career. She has been a constant attendant at Court, getting atmosphere and experience'. Another observed that she 'looked a picturesque figure in the traditional wig and gown'.

Miss McGregor joined her father's firm, practised as a solicitor and was soon a partner in McGregor, McGregor, Given & Capner. In September 1935 she set up on her own. From March 1939 Queensland lawyers were required to choose whether they wished to be enrolled as solicitors or barristers. Although Katharine wrote to the Queensland Law Society on 31 March stating that she wanted to remain a barrister, she worked for the rest of her life as a private tutor in Greek and Latin, and as an examiner in classics at secondary and tertiary levels.

Since 1928 McGregor had looked after her widowed mother. The two women were avid readers. Katharine accepted this quiet existence and rejected any increase in her teaching commitments. According to one informant, she found a measure of contentment in home-making, gardening and needlework. McGregor died on 25 June 1979 at Mount Olivet Hospital, Kangaroo Point, and was cremated with Anglican rites. In 1980 several of her friends donated $6000 to the University of Queensland's department of classics and ancient history to commemorate her by a postgraduate scholarship and a prize for introductory Greek or Latin.

Brisb Girls' Grammar School Mag, June 1921, June 1923, Dec 1927; BGGS, Annual Report, 1917-19; Univ Qld, *Univ News*, 8 Apr 1981, p 6; *Queenslander*, 17 Mar 1923, 16 Oct 1926, 31 May 1928; K. E. McGregor scrap-books (Fryer L); personal information. CATHERINE KENNY

McGROWDIE, NOEL LEONARD (1920-1961), jockey, was born on Christmas Day 1920 at Breakfast Creek, Brisbane, fifth child of native-born parents Charles Christopher McGrowdie, a jockey who had become a racehorse-trainer, and his wife Alice Josephine, née Brown. After his father moved his business to Toowoomba, Noel helped around the stables. At the age of 7 he started to win show events and from 11 drove cattle during his holidays. He completed his schooling at St Mary's Christian Brothers' College and was apprenticed as a 14-year-old to Les Roberts, a horse-trainer at Toowoomba. His indentures were later transferred to the leading Brisbane trainer George Anderson. McGrowdie was so small and thin that Anderson 'set him to dig-

ging in the garden every spare moment to build up his muscles—and the other boys soon lighted on the name Digger'.

The nickname stuck among the racing fraternity, and the digging paid off. McGrowdie became a 'pocket dynamo' of a jockey. In 1936 he won his first race, leading all the way on Thought Reader in the Tattersall's Handicap. He was rejected for military service in World War II because of his size; the manpower authorities put him to work on the wharfs and allowed him to ride locally. Keen to try his fortune in Sydney, he moved there on being released from duties in 1943. At the Church of Our Lady of the Sacred Heart, Randwick, on 7 September 1946 he married Marcia Therese Simon with Catholic rites.

A vigorous, lightweight jockey, McGrowdie was first past the post in most of Australia's top races, over all distances. In Brisbane he won the Doomben Cup (1943), Doomben Ten Thousand (1947, 1951 and 1952), Brisbane Cup (1947 and 1950) and Stradbroke Handicap (1952). In Sydney he took the Epsom Handicap (1943), Metropolitan (1944, 1945 and 1957), Australian Jockey Club Derby (1947), Sydney Cup (1951, 1952 and 1958) and Doncaster Handicap (1955 and 1958). And in Melbourne he was victorious in the Oakleigh Plate (1948, 1954 and 1956) and the Victoria Racing Club's Newmarket Handicap (1954). Riding Straight Draw (which started at 13/2), he won the Melbourne Cup in 1957. He triumphed in twenty-seven other cup races on tracks between Rockhampton in Central Queensland and Wagga Wagga in southern New South Wales.

Having contracted to ride in Singapore and in the Malayan cities of Ipoh, Kuala Lumpur and Penang, McGrowdie took his family to Singapore in January 1961. His fifty-nine victories in his first season—including the Singapore Gold Cup and the Selangor Cup—established him as the top jockey on the circuit. He won the sultan's gold vase at Ipoh in September 1961 and was heading the premiership in his second season when he was killed in a road accident on 9 September 1961 at Parit Buntar, Malaya. Survived by his wife, son and daughter, he was buried in Randwick cemetery, Sydney. His estate was sworn for probate at £20 028.

Aust Jockey Club Racing Calendar, Jan 1991, p 16; information from Mr M. J. McGrowdie, Maroubra, Syd; personal information. W. BOYAN

McGUFFOG, JAMES STEEL DORAN (1889-1963), marine engineer and naval officer, was born on 9 April 1889 at Walcha, New South Wales, second of four children of John McGuffog, a shipowner from Scotland,

and his native-born wife Mary Jane, née Steel. The family lived at Chatsworth on the Clarence River. Educated at the local public school, James served his apprenticeship at the Harwood mill (owned by the Colonial Sugar Refining Co. Ltd) and went to sea in C.S.R. ships. After he obtained his second engineer's certificate, he joined (1911) McIlwraith, McEacharn [qq.v.10] & Co. Pty Ltd which operated a line of coastal steamers. He was awarded his chief engineer's certificate (1915) while serving as a junior engineer in the *Karoola*; he then sailed in the *Katoomba* as second engineer. At the Presbyterian Church, Malvern, Melbourne, on 14 October 1919 he married Ivy Adelaide Moore.

In 1920 McGuffog was appointed chief engineer of *Katoomba*. Qualifying as chief engineer (diesel) in 1934, he travelled to Belfast to stand by construction of the firm's new motor liner, *Kanimbla*. He reached Sydney in May 1936 as her chief engineer. The ship was requisitioned by the Royal Navy and converted into an armed merchant cruiser in 1939. H.M.S. (later H.M.A.S.) *Kanimbla* was to be crewed principally by reservists of the Royal Australian Navy, among them McGuffog who was appointed temporary engineer commander, R.A.N.R., on 23 September. *Kanimbla* served on the China and East Indies stations—patrolling, hunting German raiders and escorting allied convoys. Despite falling ill, McGuffog kept her engines running and was mentioned in dispatches (1941).

In August 1941 *Kanimbla* reached the Persian Gulf and prepared to lead a flotilla against the port of Bandar Shapur. For fostering cohesion and high morale in the force —during training and in operations that captured the port on 25 August—McGuffog was again mentioned in dispatches (1942). One of *Kanimbla's* duties was to seize enemy merchant ships at Bandar Shapur. When the crew of a German vessel, *Hohenfels*, scuttled their ship, she had to be beached to prevent her sinking. McGuffog was made technical officer-in-charge of salvaging *Hohenfels*. He improvised 'ingenious' gear, worked indefatigably, took risks when necessary and succeeded in saving the prize. In 1942 he was appointed O.B.E. Back in Australia, *Kanimbla* was again converted (April-October 1943)— into a landing ship, infantry.

Following a term (1944-46) as principal naval overseer, Victoria, McGuffog returned to *Kanimbla*. He was demobilized on 18 January 1951. *Kanimbla* reverted to her peacetime role and McGuffog continued as her chief engineer. Understanding and supportive, he got on well with his sailors, but he had a watchful eye and demanded professionalism of them. He frequently reminded the men: 'If you don't know it, say so. Ask questions'. About six feet (183 cm) tall and 12 stone (76 kg) in weight, he had an upright bearing and a quiet but commanding voice. He was gifted with a strong will and a sense of humour, and kept himself to himself. In 1955 he retired. Survived by his wife and son, he died on 5 January 1963 in North Sydney and was cremated; his estate was sworn for probate at £48 296.

G. H. Gill, *Royal Australian Navy 1939-1942* (Canb, 1957) and *1942-1945* (Canb, 1968); J. Bastock, *Australia's Ships of War* (Syd, 1975); P. Sherman, *Cry Havoc* (Melb, 1994); information from Mr R. McGuffog, St Georges, Adel, Mr N. McCartney, Tathra, and Mr C. Cannon, Ambarvale, Campbelltown, NSW, and Mr F. Newman, Toorak, Melb.
J. S. SEARS

McGUIRE, DOMINIC MARY PAUL (1903-1978), author and diplomat, was born on 3 April 1903 at Petersburg (Peterborough), South Australia, ninth son of James McGuire, superintendent of local railway traffic, and his wife Mary, née O'Sullivan, a former schoolteacher. When James was promoted commissioner of railways in 1917, the family moved to Adelaide. Paul had attended Christian Brothers' College, Wakefield Street, from 1914. He earned pocket money by writing paragraphs for the *Bulletin*, 'anything up to five bob or ten bob a week when I was eleven years old'. Aged about 12, he began to have verse accepted and to think of himself as a writer. His adolescence was marked by recurrent mourning—three brothers in the Australian Imperial Force were killed, a fourth died of wounds, another of consumption; and his only sister Mary Genevieve died shortly after childbirth, with her infant. The dramatic and repeated experience of loss as a boy was mirrored in the intense depressions McGuire suffered as a man, as well as in continuing themes of the fragility of life and happiness in his writing.

At the University of Adelaide from 1923, he read history under Professor George Henderson [q.v.9], whom he admired and credited with confirming that 'history was not looking back; history was essentially deciding where we are'. McGuire was foundation president (1924-25) of the Adelaide University Dramatic Society, editor (1925) of the university magazine and a debater in the team that met visitors from Oxford. He left university to work as a journalist. At St Laurence's Catholic Church, North Adelaide, on 18 November 1927 he married Frances Margaret Cheadle, three years his senior. He had met her at the university while she was launching a research career in biochemistry. Their engagement stunned their friends, but the marriage was a meeting of minds, passions and aspirations. Margaret—a Congregationalist whose family moved in the best of Adelaide's Protestant circles—converted to Catholicism. They set up house in Adelaide, and then in a shooting-hut at Belair, writing for the *Bulletin* and running a literary page in the diocesan Catholic weekly, *Southern Cross*, while Paul taught history and English as a casual lecturer for the Workers' Educational Association of South Australia. Next year they left for London.

In contrast to Irish-Catholicism in Adelaide, McGuire was dazzled by the intellectual, and cheerfully counter-cultural, circle of English Catholic writers around G. K. Chesterton and Hilaire Belloc. McGuire's training in London with the Catholic Evidence Guild equipped him for 'Speakers' Corner' at Hyde Park, where the guild promoted a Catholic world-view based on traditional doctrine, 'Chester-belloc' philosophy (including Distributism) and the social encyclicals. He also read and, in 1937, eventually met, the Belgian priest Fr Joseph Cardijn, founder of the Jeunesse Ouvrière Chrétienne (Young Christian Workers). Like Belloc, Cardijn impressed him with hearty and good-humoured spirituality. McGuire was inspired by the challenge to be 'a fool for Christ' and flourished in a self-consciously Catholic atmosphere charged with intellectual endeavour and a mission to reform the modern state. He wrote poetry with a sense of vocation, and made contacts with literary and Catholic periodicals that would later carry his articles. His direct encounter with Cardijn and his clear understanding of Jocist Catholic Action set him apart from later Catholic activists in Australia.

In 1932 McGuire was welcomed back to Australia by the *Bulletin* as a model for other authors seeking to publish in London. In Adelaide he continued to write. The poetry he had penned in England was included in anthologies and collected in *The Two Men and Other Poems* (1932). To pay 'the butcher and baker (and in honesty . . . the brewer)', he wrote detective stories (as he had done in London), sometimes two or three a year, claiming they took three weeks to complete (though once as little as four days). His fifteen mystery novels were published by 1940. Two in particular cemented his reputation as a 'most satisfying person with whom to go a murdering': *Burial Service* (London, 1938) and *The Spanish Steps* (London, 1940). His non-formulaic plots gave the characters range to express opinions; and heroes were often in tune with his philosophy.

Appalled to find the 1931 papal encyclical, *Quadragesimo Anno*, was difficult to buy in Australia in 1932, Paul, Margaret and Fr James O'Dougherty founded the Catholic Guild for Social Studies to raise awareness of Catholic principles so that ordinary members of the Church could 'win the world'. Their patron 'saints' were St Thomas Aquinas and the then uncanonized layman Sir Thomas More. The first members were mostly unemployed young people. The guild's four-part programme of prayer, study, social action and recreation attracted two thousand participants in the first year as groups formed in parishes, in the railways and post offices, and among nurses in hospitals and schoolboys at C.B.C. The guild prompted the foundation of a Catholic library in Adelaide, and provided its initial stock. Links were made with developing groups in other States, and in 1934 McGuire spoke on Catholic Action to the meeting of Catholic intellectuals held in conjunction with the National Eucharistic Congress, Melbourne.

In addition to running courses for the guild, McGuire lectured for the W.E.A. on literature and history. In 1936 the guild swung to the right (with much of Western Catholic thought) in support of General Franco's cause in the Spanish Civil War. McGuire travelled to Spain as correspondent for the *Catholic Herald* (London), and wrote passionately of the children displaced by the conflict and the damage done to the Catholic culture of Europe. With Fr John Fitzsimmons, he published *Restoring All Things* (London, 1939), a discussion of the wide-ranging aims of Catholic Action. It attracted international attention. The American Catholic benevolent society, the Knights of Columbus, invited McGuire to lecture on 'The Christian Revolution' across the United States of America; his tour of 1939-40 regularly attracted crowds of 3500, and was credited with precipitating the Christian Family Movement.

Aiming to introduce Australia to non-specialists, McGuire had published *Australian Journey* (London, 1939). The Australian delegation in Washington requested copies to give as gifts, and R. G. (Baron) Casey wrote to introduce him to Prime Minister Curtin [qq.v.13] as one 'who has a lot more useful work up his sleeve'. Although McGuire freely admitted in retirement that his mind had never been 'exact enough' for history, a system of research support—led by Margaret, Emilie Woodley and Betty Arnott—provided accurate details for several works blending history and public comment. *Westward the Course!: the New World of Oceania* (New York, 1942) proved a best seller, given Americans' interest in the Pacific after the bombing of Pearl Harbor. *The Price of Admiralty* (Melbourne, 1944), written with Margaret, told the story of H.M.A.S. *Parramatta* and her commanding officer J. H. Walker.

Commissioned on 12 August 1942 in the Royal Australian Naval Volunteer Reserve, McGuire performed intelligence duties in Melbourne as deputy-director of psychological warfare, Far Eastern Liaison Office. He was demobilized as lieutenant on 4 May

1945, but was to remain in the R.A.N.V.R. until 1958, retiring as an honorary commander. Sent to Europe in 1945 as a war correspondent, he covered the work of the United Nations International Children's Emergency Fund and promoted the emigration of British ex-servicemen to Australia. He also claimed to have carried out 'special intelligence operations'.

In 1946 McGuire again lectured in North America, and toured northern South Australia with (Sir) Thomas Playford, forging a long-standing friendship over bottles of milk for the premier and whisky for himself. In 1947 he began discussions with Oxford University Press about editing a series on Australian social history. Although the proposal was never realized, he published two books as preliminary instalments, *The Australian Theatre* (Melbourne, 1948) and *Inns of Australia* (Melbourne, 1952), both with Margaret and Arnott.

Two works of social analysis at the close of the 1940s lifted McGuire into a fuller public role. In *The Three Corners of the World* (London, 1948) he argued that the British Commonwealth's model of co-operation between states should be adopted in the free world, with the United States moving to the hub. *There's Freedom for the Brave* (London, 1949) advocated an urgent increase in moral power and the restoration of true community (symbolized by freer trade) as a cure for the postwar crisis of the West. The book was favourably reviewed, and prompted (Sir) Robert Menzies [q.v.] to make McGuire a personal adviser for the 1951 British Commonwealth prime ministers' meeting in London. McGuire was appointed C.B.E. (1951).

Discussions at that meeting gave shape to plans for a non-party political campaign to revitalize Australian moral life and strengthen the bulwarks against communism. McGuire drafted a statement on the steps of St Peter's Basilica during a stopover in Rome, and contacted Sir Edmund Herring, a former chief justice of Victoria, who agreed to lead the campaign which became 'A Call to the People of Australia'. A flurry of semi-secret meetings between business leaders and ex-servicemen provoked questions in the Senate about McGuire's role in a sinister 'New Guard'. The government answered the question with a statement on spiritual renewal. Broadcast on 11 November 1951, with signed support from State governors, chief justices and church leaders, the 'Call' urged a return to values of civic duty, loyalty and moral strength. To maintain the momentum of overwhelming support, standing committees were established and McGuire directed the national campaign until 1953.

Named Australian ambassador to Ireland in April that year, McGuire was a delegate to the session of the United Nations' General Assembly in New York which opened in September. Following a dispute over his 'letters of credence', his appointment to Dublin was cancelled in January 1954. He served instead as minister (1954-57) and ambassador (1957-59) to Italy. He gloried that he was Australia's special ambassador and envoy to the Holy See for the funeral of Pope Pius XII and the coronation (1958) of Pope John XXIII, but seems to have fretted at being 'a minor organ of the body politic'. For many years he belonged to the Savile and Athenaeum clubs in London, and the Naval, Military (and Air Force) Club in Melbourne. He was appointed (commander) to the Order of Merit of the Republic of Italy in 1967.

The McGuires had returned to Adelaide in 1959 with plans for more books. Writing was impossible while Paul underwent two operations to treat the retina in his eye. In the 1960s and 1970s he wrote television scripts for the Rank Organisation in Britain, and began a series of interviews with South Australian sportsmen, but a round of public-speaking engagements replaced the stream of articles and books. He also worked with the Good Neighbour Council of South Australia. Appointed (grand cross) to the Order of St Sylvester in 1959, he valued his papal knighthood as much for the tradition it endorsed as the achievements it recognized. McGuire was surprised at the talk of crisis in the Church following Vatican Council II. He saw the issues as grim moral and intellectual problems in society—not simply in the Church—and as part of a cycle of centuries.

McGuire died on 15 June 1978—the year of celebrations for the five centuries since Thomas More's birth—at Calvary Hospital, North Adelaide, and was buried in Brighton cemetery. Tributes noted that More's commemoration would have been unthinkable without wide acceptance of McGuire's belief in the value of an intellectual apostolate and the significance of lay people in the Church. His wife survived him, and in 1979 donated his collection of 180 books on maritime subjects, with funds for maintaining them, to establish the Paul McGuire Maritime Library at the State Library of South Australia. In 1980 she prompted the posthumous publication of a selection of his best poems.

C. Steinbrunner and O. Penzler (eds), *Encyclopedia of Mystery and Detection* (New York, 1976); S. Sayers, *Ned Herring* (Melb, 1980); M. I. Zotti, *A Time of Awakening* (Chicago, 1991); K. Massam, *Sacred Threads* (Syd, 1996); *SMH*, 12 Nov 1951, 25 Apr, 13 Aug, 2 Sept, 27 Nov 1953, 15, 18 Jan, 16 Mar 1954, 13 May 1959; *Advertiser* (Adel), 18 Aug 1967, 17 June 1978; B. Duncan, From Ghetto to Crusade: a study of the social and political thought of Catholic opinion makers in Sydney during the 1930s (Ph.D. thesis, Univ Syd, 1987); H. de Berg, Paul McGuire (taped interview, 29 Oct 1966, NL); Paul and Margaret McGuire papers (NL); Margaret McGuire papers (Mort L).   KATHARINE MASSAM

McGUIRE, JAMES RANDAL (1937-1980), rough-rider, was born on 12 July 1937 at Ripley, Queensland, second of three children of Michael McGuire, a native-born dairy-farmer, and his Irish-born wife Mary Josephine, née Moynihan. The children attended the convent school at Booval. They rose early to help milk the cows, and had to knuckle down to additional chores after their father was killed in a horse-riding accident in 1946. Jim rode poddy calves around the yard, without a surcingle. He was infatuated by rodeos: he had an unsuccessful first ride on the steers at Fernvale and was bucked off an outlaw horse in Tex Morton's travelling show when only 10 years old.

Tired of dairying, and with no wish to enter the Ipswich coalmines, McGuire moved west to Taroom at the age of 17. He quickly became a first-class stockman, but his goal was to follow the rodeo-circuit full time. In 1956 he joined the Australian Rough Riders Association and by the early 1960s had become prominent at Queensland's major rodeos. His name appeared in the official riders' standings of the A.R.R.A., and he displayed versatility and toughness as a competitor. On 2 July 1960 at Holy Trinity Church, Taroom, he married with Anglican rites Margaret Isabel Clarris, an 18-year-old housemaid.

McGuire soon competed throughout Australia. The National Finals Rodeos, held at the end of each season, featured the top fifteen contestants in five major events: saddle 'bronc' riding, bareback bronc riding, bull riding, steer wrestling, and roping. In 1967-76 McGuire set a remarkable record by qualifying each year in all five categories. He won the title of All-Round Champion Cowboy five times (1967, 1969, 1970, 1975 and 1976)—another record. What was more, he gained the national saddle (1968) and bareback (1969) bronc-riding titles, and was Australian steer-wrestling champion in 1968, 1969, 1970 and 1972. He won twenty-three trophy saddles and twenty State titles, and was victorious at every major rodeo in the country. Being narrowly beaten by Bill Nichols in the 1975 bull-riding championship was his sole regret. McGuire was saddle bronc-riding director (1970-71) on the executive-committee of the A.R.R.A.; the association made him a life member in 1979.

Songs were written about McGuire, and his strength and tenacity became legendary. Two severe accidents in bull-riding events slowed him only slightly; due to arthritis in his riding hand, he had to use a dangerous grip. Widely known as the 'Iron Man of Rodeo', he endured crippling injuries: he suffered from an arthritic back, eight pins had been inserted to repair fractures of his right arm, and his right shoulder was held together by a screw. He died of cancer on 1 January 1980 at Ipswich and was buried with Catholic rites in Taroom cemetery; his wife survived him, as did their son Daniel and daughter Sharon. Margaret (a drover's daughter) and Sharon won national titles in the Girls' Rodeo Association (Women's Professional Rodeo Association). Danny was the world champion steer wrestler in 1978 and Australian champion in 1981, and national calf-roping champion in 1982 and 1984.

P. Poole, *Rodeo in Australia* (Adel, 1977), and (comp), Rough Riders' Browsing Book (ts, and additional entries added at Aust Stockman's Hall of Fame, Longreach, Qld); *Hoofs and Horns*, Jan 1970; *Courier-Mail*, 2 Jan 1980.   PETER N. POOLE

McGUIRK, GEORGE THOMAS (1896-1967), tramway worker and trade unionist, was born on 3 December 1896 at Quirindi, New South Wales, eldest of five children of native-born parents Edward Thomas McGuirk, maintenance man, and his wife Rebecca, née Worboys. George was educated at St Joseph's Convent and Quirindi Superior Public schools until the age of 15 when he was employed as a book-keeper at J. L. Tebbutt & Co.'s general store. Steeped in his father's Catholicism and political principles, he joined the Quirindi Labor League and opposed conscription. On 12 December 1916 he married Estell Veronica Barnett at St Bridget's Catholic Church, Quirindi.

In 1921 McGuirk moved to Newcastle to take a job with the New South Wales Government Railways and Tramways. He worked as a tram-conductor, then as a driver, and joined the local branch of the Australian Tramway Employees' Association. In the mid-1920s he and his family moved from Mayfield to Tighes Hill. McGuirk retained his job through the Depression, and remained loyal to J. T. Lang [q.v.9] in the internecine struggles which convulsed both the local and wider Labor movements. A member of the Tighes Hill branch of the Australian Labor Party, in the late 1930s McGuirk was branch returning officer, a delegate to the A.L.P.'s New South Wales and Federal electorate councils, and briefly a member of the Lang-dominated central executive of the State Labor Party. Recognizing Lang's impending downfall, McGuirk represented his branch at the unity conference, held in Sydney on 26 August 1939, which led to the end of Lang's leadership; he then helped to negotiate the amalgamation of the rival 'Lang' and 'Heffron' [q.v.14] parties at Tighes Hill.

After World War II, McGuirk and his family sought to align Tighes Hill with the A.L.P. industrial groups. In 1948 he won the branch vice-presidency. His youngest son Kevin was secretary-treasurer (1949-55); his eldest son George was a Labor alderman on Newcastle Municipal Council. At branch level the McGuirks' endeavours were opposed by a left-wing faction led by the brothers C. K. and S. B. Jones. With the demise of the industrial groups in the State A.L.P. in 1955-56, McGuirk again made his peace with the victors, supporting Charlie Jones's successful bid (1958) for the Federal seat of Newcastle. From 1955 until his death, McGuirk was re-elected—unopposed each year—as president of the Tighes Hill branch.

A critic of the private banking system, McGuirk staunchly supported employee co-operatives and mutual insurance. He was a member (from 1913) of the Hibernian Australasian Catholic Benefit Society. In the 1950s, with ministerial support, he successfully promoted building-society initiatives among Newcastle bus and tramway employees, and was founding secretary of five of them. Following his retirement from the tramways in 1961, he was appointed to the New South Wales Board of Health, on which he served until 1966. Of social-democratic temperament, McGuirk was by nature better adapted to local-branch politicking than to the bigger challenges of high union or party political office. He died of cancer on 13 January 1967 at New Lambton and was buried in Quirindi cemetery; his wife, three sons and two daughters survived him.

Quirindi Advocate, 7 Feb 1967; *Newcastle Morning Herald*, 3 Mar 1967; ALP, Tighes Hill Branch, Minute-books, 1937-67 (Newcastle Region Public L); ts of interview with Mrs M. Hallinan, 4 Aug 1987 (NSW Bicentennial Oral Hist Collection, ML); information from Mr G. E. McGuirk, Boronia Park, Mr V. Hallinan, Beverly Hills, Syd, and Mrs C. Timoshenko, Clarence Town, NSW.

JOHN SHIELDS

McILVEEN, SIR ARTHUR WILLIAM (1886-1979), Salvation Army officer, was born on 29 June 1886 at Brodies Plains, near Inverell, New South Wales, son of native-born parents William McIlveen, farmer, and his wife Annie Lucinda, née Lockrey. At the age of 14 Arthur left the local public school to join his father as a tinminer at Tingha. Shortly afterwards William fell ill, and Arthur and his brother Alex supported the family. In a lonely bush camp Arthur made a commitment in 1910 to serve the Salvation Army. He trained (1911-12) in Melbourne where he was dux of his session of 132 cadets.

Undertaking pastoral work in the city, McIlveen soon demonstrated his skills as a public speaker, especially during street-meetings. On 12 January 1916 he married a fellow officer Elizabeth Mary Mundell at the Salvation Army Hall, Richmond. McIlveen's superiors refused him permission to go abroad with the Australian Imperial Force in World War I. He finally took matters into his own hands and enlisted on 9 July 1918, but the war ended while he was *en route* to Britain. Following his discharge in January 1919, he was appointed to Dubbo, New South Wales, where he and Lizzie assisted families suffering from Spanish influenza. The McIlveens were given a 'tumultuous' farewell on their departure in 1921. Posted to country towns in New South Wales (1921-24 and 1935-37), and to Sydney (1924-28, 1930-34 and 1937-39), Brisbane (1928-30) and Toowoomba (1934-35), 'Mac' earned admiration for his dedication and generosity. He was promoted brigadier in 1938.

On 26 February 1940 McIlveen was appointed welfare officer to the 18th Brigade, A.I.F. He sailed for Britain in May and reached Egypt in December. Forging a close relationship with the 2nd/9th Battalion, he also served as unofficial padre to other units in the Middle East. In April-August 1941, during the siege of Tobruk, Libya, he attended to the welfare of Australian servicemen, and Italian and German prisoners of war. He gained special affection for playing his records on a battered phonograph, and for braving enemy fire to visit soldiers in the trenches and perimeter posts. The phonograph and collection of records were later donated to the Australian War Memorial, Canberra.

Returning reluctantly to Australia in March 1942, McIlveen was the Salvation Army's secretary for prison-work in New South Wales until his retirement on 29 June 1951. He won the respect of many convicts for his principles and beliefs. In 1967 he was admitted to the Order of the Founder, the Salvation Army's highest award. The Rats of Tobruk, with whom he maintained strong links, acquired a house for him and his family at Bexley, Sydney. Appointed M.B.E. in 1961, he was knighted in 1970. His career was the subject of a television documentary screened by the Australian Broadcasting Commission on the night before Anzac Day, 1977. Survived by his son and two daughters, Sir Arthur died on 1 May 1979 at the Repatriation General Hospital, Concord, and was buried in Woronora cemetery with full military honours. The Salvation Army named its museum and research centre at Bexley North after him.

N. Dunster, *Padre to the 'Rats'* (Lond, 1971); P. Everson (comp), *The McIlveen Family* (Syd, 1986); *Reveille* (Syd), Feb 1970, July 1979; *SMH*, 1 July

1951, 1, 2 Jan 1970, 2, 5 May 1979; *Daily Telegraph* (Syd), 8 Jan 1970; AWM records; McIlveen collection (Salvation Army Heritage Centre, Bexley North, Syd).   DARRYL MCINTYRE

McINNES, GRAHAM CAMPBELL (1912-1970), diplomat and author, and COLIN CAMPBELL (1914-1976), writer, were born on 18 February 1912 and 20 August 1914 at South Kensington, London, sons of James Campbell McInnes, singer, and his wife Angela Margaret, née Mackail [q.v.12 Thirkell]. The boys' parents were divorced in 1917. In the following year Angela married Captain G. L. A. Thirkell, a Tasmanian-born engineer who was serving in the Australian Imperial Force. The family sailed for Australia early in 1920 and settled at Malvern, Melbourne.

From that year Graham and Colin Thirkell happily attended Scotch College where both were prominent in debating, literary and dramatic societies. They enjoyed Scouting and country holidays. Angela insisted on nightly readings in literature (comics being banned). In 1929 Graham was a school prefect, in 1930 Colin a probationer. Each of them won a government senior scholarship: Graham had first-class honours in British history, English and economics, Colin in British history and economics (exhibition). In November 1930 their mother abandoned her unemployed husband and left for England with their son Lancelot George (1921-1989) who was to become a senior officer in the British Broadcasting Corporation.

Residing in Ormond [q.v.5] College, University of Melbourne (B.A., 1933), Graham graduated in history and English with first-class honours. He had at last learned of his father's whereabouts and was determined to seek him out, but delayed throughout 1933 as an Ormond tutor. In the following year he sailed for Canada and located his father, with whom he got on well, as did Colin. Both reverted to their father's surname. Graham went on to England where his mother judged that Australia had given him an incorrect set of values. Returning to Canada, he worked as a journalist and broadcaster, wrote *A Short History of Canadian Art* (1939) and became an extension lecturer for the University of Toronto. He wooed his old flame Joan Cecile Burke by letter after five years apart, and married her on 28 September 1938 at the register office, Kensington, London.

Employed by the Canadian National Film Board as a producer (from 1942), McInnes joined Canada's Department of External Affairs in 1948: he was successively first secretary in New Delhi and Wellington in 1952-54, chief of protocol in Ottawa, counsellor and

minister in London in 1959-62, high commissioner to Jamaica, and (from 1965) minister, permanent delegate and finally ambassador to the United Nations Educational Scientific and Cultural Organization in Paris. He had published *Canadian Art* (Toronto, 1950) and two novels.

In the mid-1960s Graham McInnes launched out on autobiography, or, rather, 'works of literary art, resting on fact . . . but not bound by fact', which led to four books. *The Road to Gundagai* (London, 1965), with Hal Porter's *The Watcher on the Cast-Iron Balcony* (London, 1963) and Donald Horne's *The Education of Young Donald* (Sydney, 1967), made up an outstanding trio of Australian autobiographies of boyhood. It was about Melbourne and its suburbs, the Bay and the bush, trains and trams, Scotch College, escapades and encounters with the police, Scouting, camping, hiking and fruit-picking, murders of the day, and Allan Wilkie's [q.v.12] productions (the family saw nineteen Shakespearian plays). McInnes's writing was more than attractively lively and comic: a few acute comments such as 'the mingling [at school] of war and religion and Empire', the parody of (Sir) Nikolaus Pevsner in describing his Malvern surrounds, and the chapter on his mother stand out. Though conveying his embarrassment at Angela's detestation of Australia, he was respectful and compassionate. He explained to his friend, the Canadian novelist Robertson Davies, 'in spite of everything, I loved her. I couldn't help it, though she was so awful!'

The Road to Gundagai sold at least 20 000 copies, broadly equally in Britain and Australia. McInnes had scores of enthusiastic letters from contemporaries, thankful for such evocative recall of growing up in the 1920s. *Humping my Bluey* (London, 1966), on university days, was flippant about the Depression period, but full of lively material on *Farrago*, theatre, jazz and debating. *Finding a Father* (London, 1967) detailed his discovery of and adoption by Canada. In *Goodbye Melbourne Town* (London, 1968) the vein ran thin.

Davies described McInnes as 'a warm, generous, merry man' who, like his father, 'was at all times battling with a thrawn, angry man who longed to overturn tables and shout at fools'. Tall (6 ft 2 ins, 188 cm), spare, urbane, courteous, impeccably dressed, and moustached, McInnes visited Australia in 1969. Survived by his wife, daughter and two sons, he died of cancer on 28 February 1970 in hospital in Paris.

Colin MacInnes (as he spelt his name) had joined his mother in England in 1931. He soon broke with her, worked in an office in Brussels, studied at art schools in London and served in the army during World War II. After the war he became a celebrity for his varied work in radio broadcasting. Much of his best writing was as an essayist, but his novels, *City of Spades* (1957) and *Absolute Beginners* (1959), won wide attention. In middle age he lived largely as a nomad in London's new bohemian underworld of rock music, drink, drugs and homosexuality; he was bisexual and did not marry.

Retaining a strong sentimental interest in Australia, MacInnes set two of his novels there—*June in her Spring* (1952), his favourite, and *All Day Saturday* (1966)—but they won little appreciation. He contributed to *Sidney Nolan* (1961) by Kenneth (Lord) Clark and others. The Australian sections of his *England, Half English* (1961) are perhaps the best of his comments on the country. In 1964 he visited Australia for Time-Life, but his contribution to *Australia and New Zealand* (New York, 1966) was out of touch. He died of cancer on 22 April 1976 at Hythe, Kent, and was buried at sea.

T. Gould, *Inside Outsider* (Lond, 1983); G. McInnes, *The Road to Gundagai* (Lond, 1985), intro by R. Davies; *Meanjin Q*, 1969, no 4, p 522, 1970, no 1, p 115; *Age* (Melb), 29 May 1965, 25 July 1969; *The Times*, 2 Mar 1970; G. McInnes papers (NL).

GEOFFREY SERLE*

McINTOSH, HILDA HAYWARD (1886-1958), schoolteacher and postmistress, was born on 4 December 1886 at Yarrunga, near Berrima, New South Wales, fourth child of native-born parents Samuel Hayter, sawyer, and his wife Ann Matilda, née Webb. The family later lived at Burrawang, where Hilda attended school. On 17 March 1908 she was appointed to teach at Queanbeyan Public School; her salary was £84 a year. At St John's Anglican Church, Moss Vale, on 30 December 1912 she married Hector Gordon McIntosh. A 23-year-old carpenter and joiner who was engaged in the building trade in Canberra, he belonged to a pioneering family which had settled at Majura in 1838. Hector and Hilda moved into the house attached to the Canberra Post Office, on the Yass-Canberra road, Federal Capital Territory. Established in 1863, the post office was one of the oldest in the district and was called Canberra long before the city was so named.

After resigning from her teaching post, Hilda McIntosh replaced Mrs Priscilla Murty as Canberra postmistress on 15 March 1913. She was paid only £30 5s. a year, and took in a lodger to make extra money. With the city's growth and the opening of a new Canberra Post Office at Acton, the McIntoshes renamed their post office Ainslie, after the nearby mountain. The name was officially used from 2 June. In 1913 the postmistress and one

assistant handled 33 800 letters (carried by Royal Mail coaches) and 297 telegrams—a telling example of an old form of transport coexisting with modern technology. Revenue for the year totalled £59: postal £44, telegraph £7, telephone £5 and postal notes £3. Hilda also relayed crucial messages about bushfires and accidents.

Although the land was dry and exposed, she and her husband were keen gardeners. They built a windmill, sank a well and installed a pump; and they cooked gooseberry jam in their detached slab-kitchen. Hector enlisted in the Australian Imperial Force in August 1918, but was demobilized because of the Armistice. Between 1920 and 1923 the McIntoshes took up soldier-settlement blocks at Callum Brae, Symonston. Hilda left the postal service in 1925. Believing—incorrectly as it turned out—that the city would soon absorb their holding, they sold it and in 1934 moved to Glendon, a sheep-property near Murrumbateman, New South Wales.

Well known for her good singing voice and hearty laugh, Mrs McIntosh was active in the Murrumbateman branch of the Agricultural Bureau of New South Wales, of which her husband was founding president (1936). She devoted time to the Junior Farmers' Club and to the Presbyterian church, and taught sewing at the primary school. In 1948 Hector served as president of the Goodradigbee Shire Council. After his death in 1957, Hilda moved to Yass. Survived by her son and daughter, she died on 8 April 1958 in the district hospital, Yass, and was buried with Presbyterian forms in the local cemetery.

Yass Tribune, 10 Apr 1958; Cwlth of Aust, Post Master General's Dept, General Post Office, Syd, letter to Mrs H. H. McIntosh, 12 Mar 1913 (copy held by Mrs D. Holden, Queanbeyan, NSW); information from Mr J. G. McIntosh, Ainslie, Canb.

JILL WATERHOUSE

MACINTOSH, NEIL WILLIAM GEORGE (1906-1977), professor of anatomy and anthropologist, was born on 27 December 1906 at Marrickville, Sydney, only child of native-born parents Gregory Grant John Macintosh, art teacher, and his wife Darcy Emma, née Pratt. Neil attended (1920-25) Fort Street Boys' High School; he gained honours in history and English, and won an exhibition. At the University of Sydney (M.B., B.S., 1933), he studied medicine and received Blues for swimming in 1928, 1929 and 1930. He interrupted his course to spend two years jackerooing in western New South Wales.

After graduating, Macintosh served at Lewisham Hospital as registrar (1934-35) in the neurosurgical unit and as medical superintendent (1936-37). During 1937-39 he undertook postgraduate courses in Edinburgh, London and Budapest. The last months of peace were spent in general practice at Bathurst and Newcastle. Macintosh was mobilized in the Royal Australian Naval Reserve on 2 September 1939 and saw active service as surgeon lieutenant-commander in the Indian and Pacific oceans in H.M.A. ships *Swan* (1940-41) and *Manoora* (1941-42). In June 1942 he ceased full-time duty owing to illness. He remained in the R.A.N.R. until 1950. On 6 June 1942 at Christ Church, South Yarra, Melbourne, he had married 22-year-old Barbara Jean Cooley with Anglican rites; they were to be divorced in 1945.

Macintosh joined the department of anatomy at the University of Sydney as a demonstrator (1943), and was subsequently lecturer (1945-47) and senior lecturer (1948-49). He gained a diploma in anthropology from the university in 1950 for a thesis entitled 'Critical studies on the antiquity of Man in Australia; in addition, some facts relating to the possible origin, migration and affinities of Australians and Tasmanians'. Promoted to reader that year, he was appointed Challis [q.v.3] professor of anatomy in 1955 and held the chair until 1973.

A lover of boats and ships and their ways, Macintosh wrote in his private correspondence of the 'so-called primitive' craft of low-technology societies and asked whether such craft might have enabled long migrations. During his war service he had criss-crossed the waters between Australia and Indonesia, which Australia's Aborigines had traversed to reach the southern continent. Those wartime memories helped to shape his scholarly work on the antiquity, migrations and place in human history of the indigenous people of Australia. Extensive and tenacious field-trips were the milestones of his research. He brought to them not only his energy and vision as a scholar, but also an extraordinary personality. An upright figure, open-faced, charismatic, sometimes abrupt, but one whose anger never lasted, he gave a sense of moment to all his ventures. A generation later the men he trained on these trips still recall 'When I was with Mac'.

Macintosh produced over fifty scholarly publications and made important contributions to the knowledge of three features of Aboriginal history—its antiquity, its rich variation over time and place, and its origins in migratory arrivals. He studied every significant ancient bone and artefact available, and discovered or documented several of major significance. On 19 February 1965 at the registrar general's office, Sydney, he married Ann Margaret Scot Skirving, a granddaughter of Robert Scot Skirving and Sir Edmund Barton [qq.v.11,7]. She became his

assistant and 'companion in his later work'. In a series of expeditions to Queensland in the 1960s Macintosh established the geological context of the fossilized Talgai skull which had been found near Warwick in 1886, and studied and publicized by (Sir) Edgeworth David and J. T. Wilson [qq.v.8,12]. Macintosh drew on the most modern techniques available to estimate the age of the skull at c.14 000 years, greatly enhancing its significance. In 1970 at Lake Nitchie, New South Wales, he and his technical officer Ken Smith excavated the 7000-year-old skeleton of a 6 ft 2 ins (188 cm) male. Macintosh and his team reassembled a necklace in which the profusion of *Sarcophilus* (Tasmanian Devil) canine teeth (162 from perhaps 100 animals) showed the importance of the deceased, suggested the practice of elite burials, and indicated that the region was more fertile than in recent times. Rarely seen without a pungent cheroot, Macintosh brought presence to two television films, both centred on human skeletal remains. *The Talgai Skull* (1968), a documentary film made by the Australian Broadcasting Commission, received the Australian Film Institute's Golden Reel award. For the British Broadcasting Corporation's *The Long, Long Walkabout* (1975) he acted as linkman for sites around Australia and South East Asia.

His work and publications on the dingo extended over several decades, and revealed the same ability to strike a new scholarly path. He showed the morphology of a 3000-year-old dingo skeleton to be indistinguishable from a modern skeleton. Having set up a breeding colony of dingoes, he confirmed their resistance to domestication and training, helping to characterize their place in Aboriginal culture.

As an educator, 'Black Mac' was a dynamic teacher. He loved his subject and was illuminating in the dissecting-room and lecture theatre. His innovations in teaching anatomy, particularly his system of surgeon-demonstrators, earned him honorary fellowships of the Royal Australian College of Dental Surgeons (1971) and of the Royal Australasian College of Surgeons (1972). An honorary consultant, he assisted the Criminal Investigation Branch of the New South Wales Police in attempting to unravel a number of bizarre murders. Macintosh was a foundation member of the council (1967-73) and editorial committee of the Australian Academy of Forensic Sciences. He was also associate-editor (from 1966) of the journal, *Archaeology and Physical Anthropology in Oceania*. As an administrator, he left a lasting heritage in the J. L. Shellshear [q.v.] Museum of Comparative Anatomy and Physical Anthropology, established at the University of Sydney on his recommendation in 1958, and named in honour of his mentor.

A foundation member (1961) and chairman (1966-74) of the Australian Institute of Aboriginal Studies, Macintosh was president (1951) of the Anthropological Society of New South Wales, and a foundation member (1963) and president of the Anatomical Society of Australia and New Zealand (life member 1971). He supported the visits to Australia of Czech biological anthropologists at a time when cultural exchanges with communist countries were difficult. In recognition of his outstanding contributions to the study of the origins of man, he was awarded the Hrdlicka medal—which was presented to him in 1970 in the Czech city of Humpolec (Hrdlicka's birthplace)—and the Anthropos medal (1970) by the Moravian Museum in Brno, Czechoslovakia.

Macintosh belonged to the Imperial Service and Tattersall's clubs. Survived by his wife, he died of cancer on 27 November 1977 at his Bellevue Hill home and was cremated. He had no children. A review of his work on the dingo was published by B. C. W. Barker and Ann Macintosh in 1978. An American colleague wrote of the contrast between Macintosh's lively personality and his laborious scholarship: 'He was the right man at the right time: it is not easy to imagine . . . one person, in the future, through his own vigour, application, broad view, and natural wisdom, keeping so many of the reins of the subject in his hands and driving it ahead so far'.

A. P. Elkin (ed), *Collected Papers, In Memoriam —N. W. G. Macintosh*, Oceania monographs (Syd, 1979), *and* for publications; *PIM*, no 9, Jan 1972; *Mankind*, 11, no 4, 1978, p 484; *Archaeology & Physical Anthropology in Oceania*, 13, nos 2 and 3, July and Oct 1978, p 85, 14, no 1, Apr 1979, p 78; *MJA*, 11 Aug 1979, p 138; *SMH*, 18, 25 Jan 1961.

JONATHAN STONE

McINTYRE, WILLIAM KEVERALL (1881-1969), gynaecologist, and MARGARET EDGEWORTH (1886-1948), community worker and politician, were husband and wife. Keverall was born on 13 January 1881 in Hobart, son of John McIntyre, barrister, and his wife Adeline Janetta, née Langdon. Educated at The Hutchins School, he served (1900-01) in the South African War as a member of the 2nd (Tasmanian Bushmen) Contingent. In 1904-07 he read engineering at the University of Sydney (B.Eng., 1921); he then worked as an assayer in Tasmania, at Mount Bischoff and Zeehan. At St John's Anglican Church, Ashfield, Sydney, on 28 September 1909 he married Margaret Edgeworth David; they were to have four children.

Margaret was born on 28 November 1886 at West Maitland, New South Wales, eldest daughter of (Sir) Tannatt William Edgeworth David [q.v.8], a geological surveyor from Wales, and his English-born wife Caroline Martha, née Mallett [q.v.13 David]. She was educated privately and at the University of Sydney (B.A., 1907). Having experienced at first hand the dangers and difficulties of confinements in remote mining centres, her husband determined to study obstetrics and took his family to Scotland where he enrolled at the University of Edinburgh (M.B., Ch.B., 1915; M.D., 1919).

During World War I McIntyre joined the Royal Army Medical Corps and rose to major. For his service in Macedonia, he was awarded the Military Cross (1917) and appointed to the Greek Order of the Redeemer (1918). After being discharged from the army, he became a resident medical officer at the Edinburgh Royal Maternity and Simpson Memorial Hospital. Back in Tasmania, he entered general practice at Launceston.

His wife involved herself in communal and welfare activities. A member of the National Council of Women of Tasmania, New Education Fellowship, Young Women's Christian Association and Launceston Youth Movement, she was also a commissioner (1940-48) of the Girl Guides' Association. In the late 1940s she helped to establish the G. V. Brooks [q.v.7] Community School; its curriculum, initiated by the Launceston Progressive Educational Association, aimed at providing pupils with a range of practical skills, responsibility in running the school, and education for constructive leisure.

Mrs McIntyre was appointed O.B.E. in 1948. That year, standing as an Independent, she won the division of Cornwall in the Legislative Council: she was the first woman to be elected to the Tasmanian parliament. Conscious that women should take a greater interest in government, she believed that every effort should be made to prepare all young people for citizenship. On 2 September 1948, less than four months after her parliamentary career began, she was killed when the Australian National Airways Dakota in which she was travelling crashed into a mountain near Quirindi, New South Wales. She was buried in Tamworth cemetery. Margaret McIntyre House, Launceston, was opened by the Girl Guides' Association in 1950.

Her husband had made obstetrics his speciality. At the Queen Victoria Hospital, Launceston, he was honorary obstetrician for thirty-seven years and an honorary lecturer (1925-57). McIntyre drew on his engineering training to build a negative pressure respirator at a time when infant resuscitation was in an early stage of development. During World War II he worked tirelessly in his private practice and devoted long hours to hospital administration. Towards the end of his career he estimated that he had performed about 8000 deliveries, averaging 600 a year in 1940-45. He was a member (1939) and fellow (1945) of the Royal College of Obstetricians and Gynaecologists, London, a member of the British Medical Association and president (1934 and 1955) of its Tasmanian branch. In 1950 he was appointed C.M.G. Devoted to music, both light and classical, he belonged to the Launceston Players' Society, of which his wife had been a founding member.

Survived by his two sons and two daughters, McIntyre died on 16 February 1969 at Launceston and was cremated. A nurses' home at the Queen Victoria Hospital was named (1950) after him, as was an oration, established in 1955 by the State committee of the R.C.O.G.

V. Veale, *Women to Remember* (priv pub, St Helens, Tas, 1981); *MJA*, 21 June 1969; *Mercury* (Hob), 4, 6 Sept 1948; *Examiner* (Launc), 17 Feb 1969; *Sunday Tas*, 25 Feb 1996; M. Campbell-Smith, Mrs Margaret Edgeworth McIntyre OBE BA 1886-1948 *and* A. Godfrey-Smith, Margaret Edgeworth McIntyre 1886-1948 (tss on ADB file); information from Prof A. K. McIntyre, Dr E. D. McIntyre, Mrs M. E. Waterworth and Dr L. Hardy-Wilson, Launc, Tas; personal information.   R. A. FERRALL

MACK, SIR RONALD WILLIAM (1904-1968), accountant and politician, was born on 20 May 1904 at Warrnambool, Victoria, son of Victorian-born parents Frederick David Mack, wool and skin buyer, and his wife Elizabeth Edith, née Hatton. Ron's grandfather Joseph Mack had arrived at Warrnambool in 1851, practised as an accountant and served as shire secretary. Macks occupied the same sandstone house in the town for more than a century. Ron was educated at Warrnambool High School. He practised (from 1927) as an accountant, soon operated the local branch of Young & Outhwaite (which he eventually bought), and was a fellow of the Institute of Chartered Accountants. At the registry office, Collins Street, Melbourne, on 16 February 1935 he married Helen Isabel Janet Lindsay, née Nicol (d.1957), a 38-year-old divorcee. He joined the Militia and in 1939-40 was a city councillor.

On 29 May 1940 Mack enlisted in the Australian Imperial Force. Based in the Middle East from March 1941, he rose to sergeant and was twice mentioned in dispatches for his work with the 9th Division Special Group which trained reinforcements. He was transferred to the 2nd/24th Battalion in September 1942 and promoted acting company sergeant major. On 25 October, at the battle of El Alamein, he was severely wounded in the face. Repatriated in December, he spent most of the following year in hospital and eventually lost his right eye. He

was discharged from the A.I.F. on 7 December 1943.

Returning to his home town, Mack became secretary of the Warrnambool Permanent Building and Investment Society and resumed the practice of accountancy, forming Mack, Lohrey & Purcell. He involved himself heartily in civic and sporting activities, and was secretary (later president) of the Warrnambool Club. As president of the local branch of the Liberal Party, he was endorsed in 1947 as its candidate for the seat of Warrnambool in the Legislative Assembly, but withdrew in favour of the Country Party nominee. Elected in May 1950, Mack lost the seat in December 1952. In June 1955, however, he was elected to the Legislative Council for Western Province. He was chairman of committees (1958-61) and chairman (1959-61) of parliament's population distribution committee. As minister for health (from 26 July 1961 to 14 September 1965) in (Sir) Henry Bolte's governments, he chiefly concerned himself with the mentally ill and the aged. He then succeeded Sir Gordon McArthur [q.v.] as president of the Legislative Council and in 1967 was consequently knighted, Warrnambool's first.

About 5 ft 7 ins (170 cm) tall, with a fair complexion and blue eyes, Mack was dapper and energetic. He spoke in a manner variously described as rich, manly, booming, and provocative of interjections. Yet, he was popular as a parliamentarian, considerate to his opponents, neither bitter nor acrimonious, but tolerant and full of common sense. His chief recreations were fishing and shooting.

On 20 September 1958 at St James's Old Cathedral, West Melbourne, Mack had married with Anglican rites Winifred Helen Crutchfield, née Campion, a 49-year-old widow and a teacher of commerce. Sir Ronald died of cancer on 12 February 1968 in his flat at Hawthorn; he was accorded a state funeral and was buried in Warrnambool cemetery. His wife survived him, as did the son of his first marriage.

C. E. Sayers and P. L. Yule, *By These We Flourish* (Melb, 1969); C. E. Sayers, *Of Many Things* (Olinda, Vic, 1972); *PD* (Vic), 20 Feb 1968, p 3209; *Age* (Melb) and *Warrnambool Standard*, 13 Feb 1968.
                                        GEOFFREY SERLE*

McKAY, CECIL NEWTON (1899-1968), businessman, was born on 9 October 1899 at Ballarat, Victoria, fourth child of Victorian-born parents Hugh Victor McKay [q.v.10], machinery manufacturer, and his wife Sarah, née Graves. Cecil, the only one of five sons to enter the business (three died young and one became a farmer), was educated locally at a small private school and (from 1911) at Scotch College, Melbourne, where he was school captain in 1918. Enlisting in the Australian Imperial Force on 11 July that year, he trained with the Australian Flying Corps before being discharged on 24 December. He returned to Scotch (resuming as school captain) and stroked the first VIII to victory in the 1919 'Head of the River'.

In 1920 Cecil began work at his father's Sunshine factory. He gained his shop-floor experience as a 'clockie', checking the workers' piece-work rates, before being transferred to the office. Five years later he became a director of H. V. McKay Pty Ltd. Following his father's death in 1926, he inherited a substantial fortune and ultimate responsibility for the business. At the Presbyterian Church, Toorak, on 10 March 1927 he married Marjory Valentine Shaw; they lived at Sunshine until 1938 when they moved to Toorak.

McKay remained prominent in rowing circles. A member of Mercantile Rowing Club and president (1944-47) of the Victorian Rowing Association, he had stroked the V.R.A.'s VIII to victory in the King's Cup (1930). His other enthusiasm was flying. Chairman of the Victorian branch of the Australian Aero Club (1928) and of the Associated Australian Aero Clubs (1929-39), he competed in the Sydney to Perth air race in 1929. That year he was a member of the Commonwealth committee which investigated the circumstances surrounding the disappearance of the *Southern Cross* and the deaths of two searchers.

At Sunshine the old generation was passing: Cecil's uncle Nathaniel McKay died in 1924, George in 1927, and Samuel in 1932. His cousin, the factory superintendent Ralph McKay [q.v.], left the firm in 1931 to found his own engineering business. Cecil became managing director of the company (H. V. McKay Massey Harris Pty Ltd from 1930) in 1937 and chairman in 1947. These years of recovery from Depression and drought, and of transfer to wartime production, proved demanding yet buoyant ones. In 1940 McKay flew to London to negotiate the supply of agricultural machinery to an embattled Britain. Regretting that, at 40, he was too old to fly in Britain's defence, he presented a cheque for £6000 for the purchase of a Spitfire, subsequently named after him.

In 1942 McKay joined with prominent Melbourne businessmen alarmed by resurgent socialism to form the Institute of Public Affairs, which was launched in the following year. A councillor (from 1943) of the Victorian Chamber of Manufactures and chairman (1943-47) of its engineering and allied trades' division, he led the engineering industry during the metal-trades dispute of 1946-47.

Employers admired his steely determination and skilled chairmanship; the Labor leader John Cain [q.v.13] accused him of protracting the dispute. Attempting to blunt worker militancy, McKay formed at Sunshine a council of employees, and supported the Sunshine Housing Co-operative Society. As president of the Victorian Chamber of Manufactures (1947-49), of the Associated Chambers of Manufactures of Australia (1949-50) and of the Royal Agricultural Society of Victoria (1947-51), he campaigned against Federal Labor's cradle-to-grave welfare socialism, paid for by oppressive taxation of business. His presidential address to the Victorian Chamber of Manufactures on Empire Day 1949 called on trade unions to respect the arbitration system, and accept incentive payments in industry: 'the man who regulates his own output and receives commensurate return for his effort, living in conditions which permit him to own his own home, educate his children, and inculcate in them an industrious and moral outlook, is going to be poor material for Socialist and Communist designs'.

When the twenty-five-year merger of H. V. McKay Pty Ltd with the Australian interests of Massey Harris was due to end, the McKay family interests were sold to the Canadians in 1954. Their name was dropped in the following year when the subsidiary company became Massey Ferguson (Australia) Ltd. McKay thereafter kept a city office, from which he administered the H. V. McKay Charitable Trust, created under his father's will, and the Sunshine Foundation. His company directorships included the Bankers and Traders Insurance Co. Ltd, National Mutual Life Association of Australasia Ltd, Union Trustee Co. of Australia Ltd, Consolidated Industries Ltd, Lakes Oil Ltd, Frome-Lakes Pty Ltd and Pilkington Bros (Australia) Ltd.

An intensely private man, McKay was handsome in a patrician way, formal and gentlemanly in manner, plain and direct in speech, and possessed of a dry wit. Fellow captains of industry admired him for his steadfastness and reliability. Some employees—staff and workers—found him stiff, even aloof, courteous but wanting the common touch. Survived by his wife, son and two daughters, he died of cancer on 25 January 1968 in East Melbourne and was cremated. His estate was sworn for probate at $3 945 439.

Cecil's only sister Hilda Mabel (1893-1987) was educated at Clarendon College, Ballarat, and Presbyterian Ladies' College, Melbourne. She married in 1916 Cleveland James Kidd (d.1923) and in 1936 Colonel George Ingram Stevenson (d.1958). Always close to her father, Hilda acted as his hostess when H. V. McKay entertained politicians and businessmen at The Gables, Sunshine, and Rupertswood, Sunbury. She was a founder and trustee of the Sunshine Foundation, which she chaired after Cecil's death. A generous benefactor, notably of Presbyterian Ladies' College, the Royal Children's Hospital (where in 1958 she endowed the chair of child health, named after her), the University of Melbourne (Hon. LL.D., 1973) and the Victorian Arts Centre, she was appointed O.B.E. (1958), and elevated to C.B.E. (1963) and D.B.E. (1968). Dame Hilda's portrait is held by the department of paediatrics, University of Melbourne.

Their cousin SAMUEL STUART MCKAY (1908-1975), exporter, was born on 29 July 1908 in Buenos Aires, elder son of Samuel McKay, manufacturer, and his wife Helen Stuart, née Howe. Educated at Scotch College, Melbourne, Stuart (as he was known to distinguish him from his father) worked in the machine-tool division of McPherson's Pty Ltd. He went to Sunshine in 1930 to join H. V. McKay's experimental department under Headlie Taylor [q.v.12]. In 1937 he was placed in charge of Australian sales and service of the improved Massey Harris tractor distributed by the new Australian company.

Stuart McKay was sent to England in 1942 as managing director of the Sunshine Harvester Co. Ltd to supervise the supply of machinery sent to boost wartime food production. Returning home in 1946, he was appointed general sales manager and a company director, positions he retained with Massey Ferguson (Australia). Dissatisfaction with the Canadian management's control over Sunshine workers and country agents led him to resign in 1956.

President of the Agricultural Engineering Society of Australia and of the Tractor Trade Association of Australia, McKay was vice-president of the Institute of Export. He was an enthusiastic skier who presided over the Ski Club of Victoria. At the Congregational Church, Strathfield, Sydney, on 19 October 1935 he had married Jeanette Emily Herron. Survived by his wife and four daughters, he died of a coronary occlusion on 22 March 1975 at South Yarra, Melbourne, and was cremated; his estate was sworn for probate at $143 693. The S. S. McKay memorial medal honours his thirty years service to the Royal Horticultural Society of Victoria.

M. McKay, *Cecil McKay* (Melb, 1974); D. McNeill, *The McKays of Drummartin and Sunshine* (Melb, 1984); Vic Chamber of Manufactures, Presidential Address, 1949; *IPA Review*, Mar 1968; J. Lack, 'The Legend of H. V. McKay', *VHM*, 61, Aug 1990, p 2; *Table Talk*, 6 Sept 1928; *Argus*, 3, 28 Sept 1940; *Footscray Advertiser*, 31 Jan 1968; *Sunshine Advocate*, 8 Feb 1968; *Herald* (Melb), 19 Nov 1974; H. V. McKay/Massey Ferguson Iseki Archives (Univ Melb); family information.

JOHN LACK
DOROTHY MCNEILL

MCKAY, CLAUDE ERIC FERGUSSON (1878-1972), newspaper proprietor, was born on 19 July 1878 at Kilmore, Victoria, fourth of seven children of Scottish-born parents Ronald Donald McKay, stock and station agent, and his wife Emily Knight, née Kennedy. Claude was educated at Kilmore State School, and in Melbourne at Brunswick College and Brighton Grammar School. He started work at the *Kilmore Advertiser* where he wrote editorial copy, and helped to set the type, print the paper and distribute it on horseback. After gaining experience on several other newspapers and studying mineralogy at the Working Men's College, Melbourne, he joined the *Brisbane Courier* in 1902 and soon became deputy theatre and music critic. His reporting of a complex legal judgement caught the eye of Sir Samuel Griffith [q.v.9] who, remarking that while he did not expect a literary press he would like a literate one, encouraged McKay to read widely from his library.

Moving to Sydney about 1905, McKay contributed to the *Evening News* and *Daily Telegraph* while writing advertising copy for theatrical entrepreneurs. At the age of 28 he joined the 'maestro of melodrama', William Anderson [q.v.7], who was developing Wonderland City—'the Coney Island of Australia'—above Tamarama Beach. Despite weekly stunts, such as the 'Elaborate Oriental Marriage' of a Sydney couple on an elephant, Wonderland City was slow to return a profit and some of the mobile assets were transformed into the Wonderland circus with McKay as part-owner and advance agent. The circus toured the Queensland coast and northern New South Wales.

McKay went back to newspapers before becoming J. C. Williamson's [q.v.6] secretary, house writer and press agent. On New Year's Eve 1907 at St Stephen's Presbyterian Church, Sydney, he married Dorothy Hope Sidney, an actress from an English theatrical family. Williamson gave him 300 shares in 'the Firm'. Visiting North America with Hugh Ward [q.v.12] to scout for shows and talent for Williamson, McKay met William Randolph Hearst, and attracted and cultivated an ever-widening network of friends, acquaintances and professional connexions. He remained in the wings of theatrical events until 1919, writing and rewriting lyrics for Williamson's imported musicals.

While seconded to promote the conscription referendum campaign in 1917, McKay formed an enduring friendship with W. M. Hughes [q.v.9]. In directing publicity for the 8th war loan he worked directly to (Sir) Joynton Smith [q.v.11], whom he casually told that he would like to start a weekly newspaper. Smith later offered to back him with £20 000. Smith bought 100 tons of newsprint, and McKay asked R. C. Packer [q.v.11] to join them.

Smith's Weekly was launched on 1 March 1919 as a twopenny broadsheet. It championed returned soldiers, scourged war profiteers, and quickly developed a brash, irreverent style which made it the spiritual successor of the *Bulletin*. With Smith's encouragement and money, the paper built up an outstanding team of journalists and artists. As it grew profitable, Smith assigned one-third of the equity to each of himself, McKay and Packer. They decided to launch a new morning daily newspaper. Smith and McKay went to London to buy a cable service and ended up with that of the *Manchester Guardian*. The new *Daily Guardian* was launched on 2 July 1923, with McKay editor-in-chief of both papers. To boost flagging sales, he and Packer introduced the London practice of offering free accident insurance to subscribers, and, in 1926, sponsored the first Miss Australia competition. Sales rose strongly.

Relations between the three founders were becoming strained. McKay refused Smith's request to stop disclosing rigged contests in the wrestling boom then sweeping Australia. More important was the growing tension between McKay and Packer. In 1927 McKay sold his shares to Smith for £70 000, payable over five years, and agreed not to engage in journalism in Australia for this period. He went to Britain to play golf (mainly at the Wentworth Club, Surrey), to travel and to enjoy club life in London.

Following Packer's departure in 1931, McKay returned to Sydney to be managing director and editor of *Smith's*. The newspaper continued its crusading journalism, but was in financial difficulties when McKay retired again in 1938. Next year the paper was leased to a syndicate led by Sir Victor Wilson [q.v.12]; McKay returned as managing director. *Smith's Weekly* resumed its role as the diggers' paper, 'vital, tenacious, independent and impudent'. Taking the side of the private soldier, it offended military authorities, censors and the Commonwealth government. McKay's uninhibited flair for showmanship was belied by his appearance. George Blaikie described him as 'the perfect picture of a cultured English gentleman. He was tall and slim and handsome, if you like rather narrowed eyes. His clothes were always in perfect taste and he even smoked cigarettes —which he bought wholesale and puffed endlessly without inhaling—with a highly polished elegance'.

Smith's Weekly returned to prosperity during World War II, but profits fell in peacetime, there were boardroom clashes and McKay again retired. The paper was published for the last time on 28 October 1950. McKay bought a property, Collingwood, near Exeter, bred dairy-cattle, and continued writing occasional articles for, and letters to, Sydney newspapers. An enthusiastic golfer, he belonged to the Killara and Elanora Country clubs in Sydney. He died on 21 February 1972 at Bowral and was cremated with Anglican rites; his wife and two sons survived him. In his autobiography, *This is the Life* (Sydney, 1961), McKay fondly recalled how Griffith had allowed him to use his library; he also remembered the words of the American humorist Artemus Ward: 'Literature being at a low ebb I went into show business'.

H. Julius, *Theatrical Caricatures* (Syd, 1912); G. Blaikie, *Remember Smith's Weekly?* (Adel, 1966); R. S. Whitington, *Sir Frank* (Melb, 1971); R. B. Walker, *Yesterday's News* (Syd, 1980); *British A'sian*, 19 Mar 1908; *SMH*, 9 Feb 1907, 24 Feb 1972; *Punch* (Melb), 14 Mar 1918; Papers on Wonderland City, Waverley Municipal L; information from Mr T. S. McKay, Exeter, NSW.   V. J. CARROLL

MACKAY, DONALD BRUCE (1933-1977), furniture store proprietor and anti-drugs campaigner, was born on 13 September 1933 at Griffith, New South Wales, third and youngest child of Australian-born parents Lennox William Mackay, house furnisher, and his wife Phyllis, née Roberts. The family moved to Sydney in 1943. On leaving Barker College, Hornsby, Don worked for furniture companies, studied accountancy and completed national-service training. In 1955 he returned to Griffith to help his brother run the family business.

At St Martin's Anglican Church, Killara, on 6 April 1957 Mackay married Barbara Vincent Dearman, a physiotherapist. After ten years as an external student of the University of New England (B.A., 1969), he began to study law, attended Italian classes and took flying lessons; 6 ft 3½ ins (192 cm) tall and 15 stone (95 kg) in weight, he was an A-grade squash player and a keen jogger. Mackay was also a devout Christian, involved in Anglican and then in Methodist church activities. Secretary of the Griffith Pioneer Lodge committee, he founded the local branches of the Sub-Normal Children's Welfare Association (later Challenge Foundation) and the Australian Birthright Movement. He was secretary, president and district governor of the Apex Club of Griffith.

Mackay unsuccessfully contested the State seat of Murrumbidgee as a Liberal Party candidate in the elections of 1973 and 1976. At the Federal elections in 1974 he stood for Riverina; his preferences helped to unseat the Labor minister for immigration, A. J. Grassby. While campaigning, Mackay became aware of the drug problem at Griffith. He was concerned about the effect of marijuana on young users, the corrupting influence of illegal profits, and the capacity of laundered money to undermine fair competition in the economy.

As her husband did not want his views on drugs to be seen as an electoral ploy, Barbara Mackay wrote anonymously to the *Area News* in June 1974, questioning the justice of a decision in May when two local farmers received small fines for growing cannabis. Another letter, next February, carried her signature. Meanwhile, Mackay passed information to the Drug Squad in Sydney, thereby precipitating the raid on 10 November 1975 on a cannabis plantation at Coleambally; the police found the largest single crop yet discovered in Australia. The case did not come to court until 7 March 1977 when Mackay's covert role may have been revealed. Disgusted with the lenient sentence, he launched a public campaign of reform. He wrote to the *Area News* on 23 March and organized a petition, signed by two thousand people, which was presented to State parliament in May.

About 6.30 p.m. on Friday 15 July 1977 Mackay left the Hotel Griffith and vanished. His bloodstained vehicle was located seven hours later in the hotel car park. Three spent .22 cartridges lay nearby. Public indignation at the failure of the police to find Mackay's body led the premier Neville Wran to appoint Justice Philip Woodward royal commissioner to inquire into drug trafficking. He reported in 1979 that Mackay was murdered by a 'hit man' on behalf of the Griffith cell of *N'Dranghita* (The Honoured Society). In 1984 the local coroner found that Mackay died of 'wilfully inflicted gunshot wounds'. His wife, two sons and two daughters survived him.

In 1986 James Frederick Bazley, who protested his innocence, was sentenced to life imprisonment for conspiracy to murder Mackay. The report in 1987 of a special commission of inquiry into the police investigation of the death of Donald Bruce Mackay named police officers, politicians and 'Society' members. Few, if any, doubt that Mackay was murdered in 1977, but many questions concerning his disappearance remain unanswered.

L. Hicks, *The Appalling Silence* (Syd, 1979); P. M. Woodward, *Report of the Royal Commission into Drug Trafficking* (Syd, 1979); A. W. McCoy, *Drug Traffic* (Syd, 1980); J. F. Nagle, *Report of the Special Commission of Inquiry into the Police Investigation of the Death of Donald Bruce Mackay* (Syd, 1987); B. Bottom, *Shadow of Shame* (Melb, 1988); *Area News*, 5 June 1974, 3 Feb 1975; information from Mrs B. Mackay, Griffith, NSW.　　C. A. GREGORY

MACKAY, SIR IVEN GIFFARD (1882-1966), army officer, was born on 7 April 1882 at Grafton, New South Wales, eldest of three children of Isaac Mackay, a Presbyterian minister from Scotland, and his Canadian-born wife Emily Frances, née King. Iven was educated at Grafton Superior Public School, Newington College and the University of Sydney (B.A., 1904). He opened the batting for the university's cricket team, won Blues for Rugby Union football and rowing, and demonstrated in physics in his final year. After teaching (from 1905) at Sydney Church of England Grammar School (Shore), he returned to the university in 1910 as an assistant-lecturer in physics, 'glad to resume an academic career'.

At Newington, Mackay had been a sergeant in the school cadets. Although he showed no interest in the university regiment as an undergraduate, he became a lieutenant (1911) in the cadet corps instituted under the universal military training scheme. In July 1913 he transferred to the Militia as adjutant to the 26th Infantry Battalion, commanded by Lieutenant Colonel H. N. MacLaurin. During 1913-14 Mackay studied military science at the university. Promoted captain in June 1914, he volunteered for service with the Australian Imperial Force on the outbreak of World War I. On 27 August he was posted as adjutant to the 4th Battalion in MacLaurin's 1st Brigade. Eight days later, on 4 September, at St Philip's Anglican Church, Sydney, he married Marjorie Eveline, the 23-year-old daughter of J. B. H. Meredith [q.v.10].

Prevented by a riding accident from embarking with his unit, Mackay sailed for Egypt in December with reinforcements for the 13th Battalion. In February 1915 he was posted back to the 4th, which landed at Gallipoli on 25 April. The duties of military transport officer prevented him from joining the battalion until 8 May 1915. Heavy casualties in the early fighting saw him promoted major in July and placed in command of a company in August. Wounded at Lone Pine that month, he was evacuated to Malta and thence to England. He was mentioned in dispatches for his work at Gallipoli. In February 1916 he rejoined the 4th Battalion in Egypt.

Mackay accompanied the unit to France in March. Next month he was promoted lieutenant colonel and given command. He led his battalion in action at Pozières (July) and Mouquet Farm (August). During the second battle of Bullecourt in May 1917, he held temporary command of the 1st Infantry Brigade. For his service in this period he was awarded the Distinguished Service Order (December 1916), a Bar to the D.S.O. (June 1917) and the French Croix de Guerre (1919); he was again mentioned in dispatches. He commanded the 1st Machine-Gun Battalion from March 1918. Promoted temporary brigadier-general, he took command of the 1st Infantry Brigade in June. He was appointed C.M.G. for his conduct at Hazebrouck (June-July) and on the Somme (August-September), and was mentioned in dispatches twice more.

Following the Armistice, Mackay entered the University of Cambridge to study physics. He returned home early in 1920 and lectured in that subject at the University of Sydney before accepting administrative posts: between 1922 and 1932 he was student adviser; from 1925 he was also faculty secretary. In 1933 he was appointed headmaster of Cranbrook School. (Sir) Kenneth Street [q.v.] and other members of the school council blamed him for Cranbrook's relatively slow recovery from the Depression, and he left in acrimonious circumstances in February 1940. Mackay had continued to serve in the Militia, and had held several brigade commands in the 1920s and 1930s. Assuming command of the 2nd Division in March 1937, he was promoted major general in July and was thus one of the most senior officers in the army when World War II began in September 1939.

The decision to raise a second division for the A.I.F. and the consequent elevation of Lieutenant General Sir Thomas Blamey [q.v.13] to command I Corps led to Mackay being selected in April 1940 to replace him as general officer commanding the 6th Division. The troops nicknamed him 'Mr Chips', a reference to his peacetime profession, and to the initial impression he gave of being cool, reserved and strict. Some of his senior regular officers had reservations about him. Colonel George Vasey [q.v.] asserted that Mackay lacked the ruthlessness to remove Militia officers who were not performing well.

Such doubts soon disappeared with the commitment of the division to the campaign (January-February 1941) in Libya against the Italian Tenth Army. In a short contest of rapid movement over considerable distances, Mackay demonstrated careful planning and recognized the need to reinforce success; he also impressed others with the way he cared for soldiers' lives. 'Not only do I want Tobruk quickly', he told his senior officers before the battle, 'but I ... want it cheaply'. His British superior in Libya, General Sir Richard O'Connor, wrote that 'behind a rather diffident and shy manner [Mackay] possessed an extremely strong and resolute character'. The war historian Gavin Long [q.v.] thought that Mackay's tenacity of purpose bordered on obstinacy. At the end of the fighting Mackay cracked down on indiscipline among his troops (an outbreak of 'civilianism', as he termed it). Mindful of the reputation which Australians had acquired in the Middle East in World War I, he was particularly offended by looting. Yet, while he was stern, he was also fair and approachable. For his leadership, 'outstanding gallantry and efficiency' he was appointed K.B.E. (1941).

Mackay led the 6th Division through the débâcle in Greece (April 1941), during which he further earned the respect of his men for sharing their conditions in the field, for his lack of interest in creature comforts, and for his courage and coolness under air-attack. One staff officer 'never forgot the way Mackay would stand round during bombings, looking down calmly (but not critically) on people crouching behind cover or in slit trenches'. Awarded the Greek Military Cross and mentioned in dispatches, he relinquished command of the division in August 1941 and returned to Australia. Next month he was promoted lieutenant general and appointed general officer commanding-in-chief, Home Forces.

In seeking to prepare Australia for defence against the Japanese, Mackay submitted an appreciation in February 1942 which gave rise to the 'Brisbane Line' controversy. In the event of invasion, he proposed to concentrate his forces in locations between Brisbane and Melbourne, without reinforcing strategic peripheries such as North Queensland. Later suggestions that areas north of Brisbane were to be abandoned, and the brigades based there withdrawn, are untrue, as is the notion that a line was drawn on the map. Mackay later stated that he had never known the term 'Brisbane Line' until it appeared in newspapers. The problems he faced in 1942 stemmed from neglect of Australia's defence in the interwar years. Although on paper he commanded a force of five divisions, in practice he had manpower for only three. Moreover, the chiefs of staff had directed that the region between Port Kembla and Newcastle was vital, and that, so long as it was held, Australia could continue to fight the war.

Mackay's appreciation was current for only a few weeks. It was superseded by the knowledge that two divisions of the A.I.F. were returning from the Middle East. Thereafter, the 'Brisbane Line' became 'the plaything of American propagandists and Australian politicians'. General Douglas MacArthur [q.v.] used it to reinforce his image as the saviour of Australians allegedly prey to defeatism; the Australian Labor Party member for East Sydney E. J. Ward [q.v.] mounted attacks in 1942 and 1943 on (Sir) Robert Menzies [q.v.] and (Sir) Arthur Fadden [q.v.14], claiming that their governments were responsible for the 'Brisbane Line' strategy.

Following a reorganization of Australia's defences in early 1942, Mackay was given command of the Second Army in April. Between January and May 1943 he was based in Papua and New Guinea as commander of New Guinea Force. The fighting for Wau took place during this period. Blamey sent him back to New Guinea in August to orchestrate the capture of Finschhafen, and the early stages of the battles for Sattelberg and the Ramu Valley. Mackay's second tenure of command in New Guinea was marked by disagreements with the Americans over the movement of reinforcements by sea to Finschhafen, which led to delays in the capture of Sattelberg. Major General Vasey and Lieutenant General Sir Edmund Herring believed that Mackay was wanting in forcefulness. Herring thought that Mackay should have moved more quickly to enlist Blamey's support in resolving the difficulties over shipping. Mackay appears to have been disinclined to refer such matters to his commander-in-chief, with whom he enjoyed excellent relations.

Aged 61, Mackay—in Herring's words—was 'getting older [and] a bit slower'. By this stage he probably lacked the mental and physical robustness needed for the rigours of campaigning in New Guinea. In January 1944 he relinquished command of New Guinea Force and the Second Army. One month later he took up an appointment as Australia's first high commissioner to India. His duties, until the war ended, were more military than diplomatic. On 27 February 1946 he retired from the army. He promoted trade between India and Australia, and fostered a plan for Indian students and technicians to study and train in Australia. His term as high commissioner ended in May 1948.

Retiring to Sydney, Sir Iven chaired (1950-52) the New South Wales recruiting committee which was set up by the Federal government to increase enlistment in the armed forces. He became active in ex-servicemen's organizations. In 1952 he represented Australia at the unveiling in Athens of the British Commonwealth memorial to those who fell in the Greek campaign; he again visited that city in 1961 for the dedication of the Commonwealth war cemetery at Phaleron. The University of Sydney appointed (1950) him honorary esquire bedell and conferred (1952) on him an honorary doctorate of laws. Survived by his wife, son and two daughters, he died on 30 September 1966 at his East Lindfield home and was cremated with Presbyterian forms. (Sir) John Longstaff's [q.v.10], (Sir) Ivor Hele's and Joshua Smith's portraits of Mackay are held by the Australian War Memorial, Canberra.

I. D. Chapman, *Iven G. Mackay* (Melb, 1975); *Aust Army J*, no 218, 1967, p 3; Mackay papers (AWM); G. Long, notebooks and diaries (AWM); Vasey papers (NL).   JEFFREY GREY

MACKAY, KATHERINE ADA (1901-1975), policewoman, was born on 10 December 1901 in Colombo, Ceylon (Sri Lanka), daughter of Robert Mackay, merchant, and his wife Emma, née Foord. The family lived in New Zealand and New South Wales before settling in Melbourne. On 27 April 1922 Kath joined the motor registration branch of the Victorian Public Service as a typiste and stenographer; later that year she moved to the Victoria Police and worked in the chief commissioner's office. On 15 April 1930 she became one of eight serving policewomen. Initially assigned to the plain clothes branch, by 1935 she was attached to the Criminal Investigation Branch at Russell Street headquarters.

In June 1943 Mackay was promoted senior constable and given charge of the policewomen's section which operated from Russell Street. There were only fifteen policewomen, but their role was enhanced because of the number of men absent from the force on active service. Although Mackay's role and function were largely restricted to welfare and domestic issues, and to cases involving women, she received official commendations in April 1942 for her part in the conviction of a man for incest and in April 1945 for helping to solve a murder case. She was regarded by her superiors as 'well conducted, efficient and reliable'.

Having passed the required examinations, Mackay was eligible for promotion to sergeant in 1953. Unlike its New South Wales counterpart, the Victorian police hierarchy was unwilling to give a female authority over male colleagues. When two men were promoted ahead of her, Mackay appealed to the Police Classification Board. In March 1954 the case was dismissed on the ground that a sergeant in charge of a station might be expected to fulfil duties for which the board felt that Mackay was unfitted. The ramifications of the decision were extensively canvassed in the newspapers.

The Police Association suggested that, since the number of policewomen had increased to thirty-four, a reorganization of the women's section of the Victoria Police was overdue. This proposal was implemented in 1956, providing the opportunity to make Mackay a sergeant. On 22 August that year she became the first woman in Victoria to achieve such rank when she was appointed officer-in-charge of the new Women Police Branch. Her effect on the force was long-standing. In June 1959 she and her younger brother Sergeant Alexander Mackay were each presented with the Police Long Service and Good Conduct medal. She was superannuated from the Victoria Police on 10 December 1961, on reaching the age of 60.

Katherine Mackay was 5 ft 7 ins (170 cm) tall, with hazel eyes and a deep-throated chuckle. She was a practising Presbyterian who enjoyed gardening at her Elwood home and reading biographies. In her retirement she served as secretary of the Victorian

Society for the Prevention of Cruelty to Children, and maintained working links with the Young Women's Christian Association, the Melbourne City Mission and the Melbourne Ladies' Benevolent Society. She died on 15 June 1975 at Brighton and was buried in St Kilda cemetery; her estate was sworn for probate at $75 855.

R. Haldane, *The People's Force* (Melb, 1986); C. Woolley, *Arresting Women* (Melb, 1997); *Police Life*, Dec 1961, Apr 1963; *Truth* (Melb), 13 Mar 1954; *Age* (Melb), 17 Mar 1954; *Sun News-Pictorial*, 17 Mar 1954, 18 June 1975; *Argus*, 18 June 1955; Vic Police, record of conduct and service, K. A. Mackay (held at Vic Police Headquarters, Melb).

GARY PRESLAND

McKAY, RALPH (1885-1959), engineer and industrialist, was born on 19 May 1885 at Numurkah, Victoria, second son of Nathaniel Breakey McKay, schoolteacher, and his wife Emma, née Thompson, both Victorian born. Nathaniel was a brother of Hugh Victor McKay [q.v.10], who gave employment at his Sunshine Harvester Works to four of his eight brothers and most of their eleven sons. Educated at state schools at Mildura and Ballarat, Ralph completed a fitting-and-turning course at the Ballarat School of Mines.

He entered his uncle's employment at Ballarat in 1898 as part of the office staff. Later, while working as an expert setting up machines in the field, he displayed an ingenuity which H. V. McKay quickly recognized. Ralph joined the engineering department and became a foreman. By 1907, when the factory had been relocated at Braybrook Junction (Sunshine), Melbourne, Ralph was in the experimental shop, and in 1910 he was made engineer-in-chief. An energetic doer and thinker, he always had notepad, pencil and eraser at the ready. His experiments with internal combustion engines, harvesters, seed-drills and ploughs led to numerous patents, taken out jointly with his uncle.

In 1913 Ralph visited Europe with H. V. McKay. He enlisted in the Australian Imperial Force on 11 March 1916, but his uncle secured his release for war-work, and sent him to the United States of America to study new technology and to buy advanced machine tools. On his return, Ralph installed and supervised Australia's first seamless brass-and-copper-tubing plant, and assisted in setting up a mild steel shafting-mill. He was appointed factory superintendent in 1921. That year he made another trip to the U.S.A. and Europe to examine the latest assembly-line technology and labour-management practices. The modernization of the Melbourne factory appears to have been substantially his

work. In 1922, on the basis of his observations overseas, he introduced female labour to the production line.

Following H. V. McKay's death in 1926, tensions increased between Ralph and other members of the family and firm, especially his uncle Sam McKay (1871-1932), who had become managing director. Ralph opposed the 1930 merger with the Australian interests of rival Canadians, Massey Harris. Differences with Headlie Taylor [q.v.12], inventor and production supervisor of the header harvester, came to a climax in 1931. Ralph resigned, and was paid £1500 for the manufacturing rights to his joint patents.

With insufficient capital to initiate full-line production, McKay created for himself a lucrative niche in the industry by supplying specialist parts to large firms, a pattern he had observed in the U.S.A. At Ascot Vale he established a plant to manufacture plough discs and circular coulters, items previously imported. Skilled tradesmen followed him from Sunshine, the firm gave him some plant, and he added salvaged materials, including a boiler purchased from scrap dealer 'Ma' Dalley [q.v.13]. Cecil McKay [q.v.], general manager of H. V. McKay Massey Harris Pty Ltd from 1932, arranged to buy the firm's disc requirements from Ralph.

A 'workaholic', Ralph McKay was engineer, plant manager, sales director, purchasing officer and quality controller. Regarded as a demanding and strict but fair employer, he held less uncompromising attitudes towards trade unions than H. V. McKay. In 1935 he established a new factory at Maidstone, which benefited from tariff protection, the stimulus of World War II, and the opportunity to re-equip cheaply at war's end.

McKay had married Hilda Ada McGrath on 21 April 1908 at Allendale with Methodist forms; they were divorced on 9 September 1926. He married Gladys May Stuart Sinclair on 6 May 1927 at Norwood, Adelaide. Stocky and powerfully built, the youthful oarsman, squash player and wrestler became in middle age a keen shooter, fisherman and yachtsman. His blunt and somewhat abrasive manner mellowed with the years, and he grew more relaxed, holidaying (from 1942) with his family on their property, Barwood, at Nagambie. He was also at various times active as a Braybrook shire president, and in the Footscray Football and Rotary clubs.

In 1950 McKay formed his enterprise (reputedly the largest privately owned engineering business in Australia) into a public company as Ralph McKay Ltd. One-quarter of the shares went to his brother Oscar (1893-1971), who had joined Ralph as factory manager after working at Sunshine and farming in Western Australia. Oscar assumed daily management of the business in the 1950s. Their brother Victor Rex (1887-1953) also held a directorship.

Ralph McKay died on 6 August 1959 at Nagambie and was cremated with Anglican rites. His wife, and their daughter and son survived him, as did the two daughters and three sons of his first marriage. The *Sunshine Advocate* claimed that, apart from H. V. McKay himself, 'possibly no other person made such an impact on the activities of the Sunshine Harvester Works'. His own company, renowned for the quality of its products, further testified to his prodigious abilities and energies.

M. Heagney, *Are Women Taking Men's Jobs?* (Melb, 1935); D. McNeill, *The McKays of Drummartin & Sunshine* (Melb, 1984); *Sunshine Advocate*, 1 Dec 1928, 13 Aug 1959; Ralph McKay Ltd *and* Massey Ferguson Iseki papers (Univ Melb Archives); family information.   JOHN LACK
                                             D. KERVILLE

MACKAY, RONALD REAY (1905-1963), radio engineer and educationist, was born on 22 December 1905 in East Melbourne, son of Victorian-born parents Hugh Mackay, civil servant, and his wife Eleanor, née Nonmus. Ronald was educated at Princes Hill State School, at Scotch College briefly, and at the Working Men's College (Melbourne Technical College from 1934) where, after taking some courses in electrical engineering, he was appointed a laboratory demonstrator in 1923 and a lecturer in 1925.

Teaching himself, largely from technical magazines, Mackay specialized in wireless. By 1930 he was in charge of all electrical trade classes; in 1940 he was formally—and belatedly—appointed head of radio and electrical trades. From 1928 he had advised schools on the reception of broadcasts; from 1931 he had developed courses in motion-picture sound-projection. Mackay paved the way for the Victorian Education Department's visual-education branch and for the State Film Centre. He planned the first radio network for the Forests Commission in 1938. Plans for diploma courses in radio and communications engineering were in train (by 1936) and a new building (1938-42) was soon known as the Radio School. At Scots Church, Melbourne, on 3 January 1940 he married Dorothy Perry (d.1947); they were to have one son.

Mackay had been commissioned in the Australian Military Forces. In 1939 he joined the Royal Australian Air Force as temporary flight lieutenant and took charge of defence training at the college, especially intensive short courses in radio communication, primarily for the R.A.A.F. An estimated 23 000 trainees passed through his hands. In 1943 he was appointed honorary squadron leader. Immediately postwar he undertook part-time supervision of diploma courses under the Commonwealth Reconstruction Training Scheme. In 1948 when the teaching of engineering was reorganized, the Radio School, which had grown considerably in staff and equipment, became one of four divisions. Mackay demonstrated educational uses of television in 1950-51.

Innovative, resourceful and a talented lobbyist, he succeeded Frank Ellis [q.v.14] as principal of the college in 1952. Mackay's lack of formal academic qualifications roused jealousy and resentment among some of his colleagues, but he was soon generally accepted as leader of the college. Burly and balding, highly perceptive and obsessively devoted to his work, he had many outside contacts. His enthusiasm and sense of humour helped him. He treated all staff as equals, and his door was always open.

In 1954 Mackay brought about the addition of 'Royal' to the name of the college; in 1960 it became the Royal Melbourne Institute of Technology. During his term the college developed fast, both in the quality of its engineering core and in areas such as architecture, surveying, photography, marine and air navigation, librarianship, and business studies. The number of students reached 20 000, of whom almost half were part time. A strong technical university development committee earned some government support, but Sir Keith Murray's Commonwealth committee on the future of Australian universities recommended the foundation of a second general university in Victoria, squashing the college's ambition. Thus Mackay's period of office was basically frustrating and also marked by fluctuation in relations with the Education Department. R.M.I.T.'s development was further delayed by the long gestation (1961-65) of the report of Sir Leslie Martin's committee on the future of tertiary education, of which Mackay was a member.

Secretary (from 1933), fellow (1940) and councillor (1958) of the Victorian branch of the Institution of Radio Engineers, Australia, Mackay served as federal president in 1961-62. He was also a fellow of the Australian Institute of Management, a member of the Council for Adult Education and of the councils of the Zoological Board of Victoria and the Australian Industries Development Association, and honorary secretary of the Australian Productivity Council. In addition, he was a Rotarian and a justice of the peace.

On 4 December 1963 Mackay returned to his North Carlton home and was shot dead by his 23-year-old son. Following a funeral service at the Presbyterian Church, Toorak, he was cremated. Bayne Reay Mackay was tried for murder, acquitted as insane and committed to custody. His father had named him as heir and executor of an estate which was sworn for probate at £28 871.

S. Murray-Smith and A. J. Dare, *The Tech* (Melb, 1987); RMIT Archives (Melb).

GEOFFREY SERLE*

MACKAY, RONALD WILLIAM GORDON ('KIM') (1902-1960), lawyer, politician and political theorist, was born on 3 September 1902 at Bathurst, New South Wales, fifth child of Alexander William Gordon Mackay, Irish-born governor of Bathurst gaol, and his wife Mary Knight, Tonga-born daughter of Rev. J. E. Moulton [q.v.5]. The Mackays lived at Summer Hill and were a bookish family. Kim was educated at Sydney Grammar School and the University of Sydney (B.A., 1923; LL.B., 1926; M.A., 1929) where he was a founder of the Public Questions Society. Admitted as a solicitor by the Supreme Court on 19 November 1926, he joined the firm of Sly & Russell and by 1929 was a partner specializing in commercial law.

At the chapel of St Paul's College, University of Sydney, Mackay married Mary Barker Hassall on 21 February 1928 with Anglican rites; they were to have two children before being divorced. While waiting for his practice to grow, he tutored (1926-32) part time at the university. He published a 42-page pamphlet, *Commonwealth Conciliation and Arbitration Act* (1928), which examined recent industrial laws, and a book, *Some Aspects of Primary and Secondary Education* (1929), which attacked the quality of compulsory education in New South Wales. In 1932 he was the leading founder of the Australian Institute of Political Science, a non-party forum for the study of social, political and economic problems.

As one of its first activities, the A.I.P.S. held a summer school in January 1933 on reforming the Australian Constitution. Mackay argued for a redistribution of legislative powers to favour the Commonwealth, an outcome which was largely achieved during and after World War II. The A.I.P.S. summer schools proved popular and the institute published a journal, *Australian Quarterly*, from 1935.

Mackay was convinced that the Constitution and the power of the States in Australia precluded the socialist programme he advocated. He emigrated to England in 1934 and joined the British Labour Party. Developing a successful commercial law practice in London in partnership with Herbert Oppenheimer, Harry Nathan and Arthur Vandyk, he began to put himself forward as a candidate for the House of Commons. His books, *Federal*

Europe (London, 1940) and *Peace Aims and the New Order* (1941), claimed that European countries could avoid war by federating and establishing free trade; *Coupon or Free?* (1943) was a critique of the British electoral system.

Elected as Labour member for Hull North-West in 1945, Mackay joined his party's delegation to the Council of Europe. He remained a socialist, but his interest in Europe became consuming. His speeches urged the surrender of national sovereignty and the establishment of a common market. Further books —*Britain in Wonderland* (1948), *Western Union in Crisis* (Oxford, 1949), *Heads in the Sand* (1950), *European Unity* (1951) and *Towards a United States of Europe* (London, 1961)—expanded his arguments for economic and eventual political union. *Whither Britain?* (1953) regarded it as axiomatic that none of the countries of Western Europe could survive in isolation, let alone achieve socialism, because their markets were too small. Mackay envisaged that 'the old white Commonwealth countries' would be part of a federated Europe.

On 15 August 1946 at the register office, St Pancras, London, Mackay had married 28-year-old Doreen Mary Armstrong. In 1950 he successfully contested the division of Reading North in the House of Commons, but was defeated in the following year. Quick, capable, resourceful and industrious, pleasant in manner and generous by nature, he was widely respected among Australian and British political and economic thinkers, but it was said that he could only appreciate a joke if he were notified in advance by telegram. Although he was frustrated when his views were not immediately accepted, he managed to impress his ideas on the people he cultivated and to exert some influence on the movement towards European unity. Mackay died of coronary vascular disease on 15 January 1960 at his St Marylebone home; his wife survived him, as did the son and daughter of his first marriage.

J. Goldring, 'A Prophet Unheeded: Kim Mackay and the development of two federations', *Aust Q*, 68, no 3, 1996, p 99.   JOHN GOLDRING

McKEAN, LORNA CRAWFORD (1914-1963), soprano, was born on 13 August 1914 at Arncliffe, Sydney, youngest of three daughters of native-born parents Robert Crawford McKean, schoolteacher, and his wife Jane, née McManus. Lorna received early piano tuition from her mother and formal education at Bexley Public, Cleveland Street Intermediate High and St George Girls' High schools. She left school to concentrate on full-time piano studies with Elizabeth Coleman and singing lessons with Ruth Ladd.

A talented actress who performed at (Dame) Doris Fitton's Independent Theatre, McKean loved music. She studied singing at the New South Wales State Conservatorium of Music, giving lieder recitals and performing operatic roles such as Pamina in Mozart's *The Magic Flute* and Eurydice in Gluck's *Orpheus and Eurydice*. McKean was awarded a Layman Martin Harrison scholarship, and in 1936 gained teacher's and performer's diplomas in singing. Shortly afterwards she accepted an invitation to join the Australian Broadcasting Commission's wireless chorus, conducted by Joseph Post [q.v.].

On 9 August 1938 at the district registrar's office, Rockdale, Lorna married Leo Denis Vaughan Hanly, a 21-year-old violinist and a fellow student at the conservatorium; they were to have three children. Hanly had been assisting-artist during Richard Tauber's Australian tour and the Taubers attended the wedding. The newlyweds completed a national broadcasting tour for the A.B.C. before settling in Perth, where Hanly was appointed (1939) leader of the A.B.C.'s local orchestra. His wife soon became active in music circles in the city. When World War II broke out she undertook extensive touring and concert work throughout the State to assist the war effort.

In 1948 Lorna McKean (as she continued to be known professionally) travelled to London with an introduction to the soprano Elisabeth Schumann. She auditioned successfully for the British Broadcasting Corporation and fulfilled a number of engagements, including radio recitals and public performances. In 1949 she returned to Western Australia. Her work in London had impressed (Sir) John Barbirolli, conductor of the Hallé Orchestra. In accepting an invitation to tour Australia for the A.B.C. in the summer of 1950-51, he stipulated two conditions: that the tour take place when the English cricket team was in Australia, and that she should appear as soloist in some of his concerts. Barbirolli's tour established McKean in the front rank of Australian musicians.

She continued her singing career, tackling new compositions, adding to her repertoire, and introducing works by composers such as Claude Debussy, Paul Hindemith and Edgar Bainton [q.v.7] to Perth audiences. During the 1950s and early 1960s McKean occupied a prominent position in Perth's music world. Survived by her husband, daughter and one of her two sons, she died of a cerebral tumour on 26 October 1963 at Royal Perth Hospital and was cremated with Congregational forms. John Farnsworth Hall, the conductor of the West Australian Symphony Orchestra, de-scribed her as 'a superb artist who was deeply appreciated'.

Broadcaster, 24 Sept-1 Oct 1938, 29 July 1939, 27 Feb 1946; *West Australian*, 19 Apr 1939, 2, 28 Oct 1963; *SMH*, 15 Jan 1951; family records (held by Mr V. Hanly, Sth Perth).   BRIAN POPE

McKELLAR, GERALD COLIN (1903-1970), farmer and politician, was born on 29 May 1903 at Gulgong, New South Wales, second child of native-born parents Gerald Murdoch McKellar, a carrier who turned his hand to farming, and his wife Margaret Jane, née Travis. Educated at Gilgandra, young Gerald farmed a succession of wheat- and sheep-properties in the district. At the Presbyterian Church, Dulwich Hill, Sydney, on 24 July 1926 he married Florence Emily Smith, a 27-year-old schoolteacher.

Commissioned lieutenant in the Militia in 1936, McKellar commanded the Gilgandra troop of the 6th Light Horse Regiment. He gained a part as an extra in Charles Chauvel's [q.v.7] film, *Forty Thousand Horsemen* (1940), and rode in the dramatic cavalry charge. After serving full time with the 6th Motor Regiment (from October 1941), he was appointed major in the Australian Imperial Force in September 1942. He was posted to the 26th Motor Regiment before being placed in command (June 1945) of the 1st Australian Ordnance Vehicle Park. On 4 April 1946 he transferred to the Reserve of Officers.

Prominent in farming organizations, McKellar was a director (1951-59) of the Dubbo Pastures Protection Board and a councillor (1960-64) of the New South Wales Sheepbreeders' Association. He also chaired Gilgandra Newspapers Pty Ltd for two years. Committed to the Country Party, he led its Lawson and Castlereagh electorate councils for two decades before becoming chairman (1957) of the New South Wales division. In 1958 he was elected to the Senate. He chaired the federal party's rural finance committee until his appointment as minister for repatriation on 22 December 1964.

McKellar's military experience influenced his administration of the portfolio. He insisted on travelling to the Republic of Vietnam (South Vietnam) to spend Christmas with Australian servicemen in 1966 and 1967, and regularly visited repatriation hospitals to discuss veterans' needs. Forced to reconcile the demands of the Returned Services League of Australia with cabinet's efforts to curtail costs, he found himself at times in heated conflict with the R.S.L. In July 1968 Bruce Ruxton accused McKellar of intimidating members of independent tribunals into reducing pension entitlements for ex-servicemen. The Victorian State conference of the R.S.L. carried a vote of no confidence in the minister. By October, however, the row appeared to have subsided: the Victorian branch president Sir William Hall moved a vote of thanks to McKellar at the R.S.L. national congress.

As minister representing the minister for air (Peter Howson) in the Senate, McKellar was subjected in 1967 to increasing Opposition pressure that stemmed from the 'V.I.P. flights affair'. Unlike other ministers, he was never accused of dishonesty throughout the controversy. Labor's Lionel Murphy later recalled that all senators had been 'convinced of one thing, the complete integrity of Senator McKellar'.

Frank and straightforward, sometimes brutally so in parliamentary or party debates, McKellar was committed to integrity and fairness. For twenty-five years he was an elder of the Presbyterian Church. Senator Frank McManus, his regular opponent at billiards, described him as one 'who would do you a good turn if he could and who would never try to do you a bad turn'. He was at his best 'when he took up a cause in which he believed and in relation to which he felt there was a fight that had to be fought'. Gifted with a sense of humour, he was a keen sportsman who played cricket, tennis and polo in his youth and turned to bowls in later life.

McKellar relinquished his portfolio on 12 November 1969 because of illness. On 13 April 1970 he dined at the Australia Hotel, Sydney, with members of the Graziers' Association of New South Wales. He told friends that his health had improved and that he was looking forward to returning to parliament, but he collapsed at 8.30 p.m. and died of coronary vascular disease. Survived by his wife and three sons, he was cremated. His estate was sworn for probate at $101 380.

P. Sekuless and J. Rees, *Lest We Forget* (Syd, 1986); *PD* (Senate), 14 Apr 1970, p 741; *SMH*, 21 Dec 1967, 25, 30 July 1968, 14 Apr 1970.

RUSSELL SCHNEIDER

McKENNA, CLANCY (WARNTUPUN-GARNA) (1909-1979), Aboriginal activist, was born about 24 September 1909, probably at Meentheena station, north-east of Nullagine, Western Australia, son of Maurice McKenna, an Irish-born station manager, and Nyamalangu ('Nellie'). She and her husband Frank Djungunbuna belonged to the Nyamal people and worked on the property. Maurice evicted the family at gunpoint when Clancy was about 3 years old. He was raised by his mother on Coongan, Bungalow and other stations in the Marble Bar area.

McKenna became an itinerant contractor, building fences and sinking wells in the Pilbara region. According to custom, he was allocated a Ngarla wife, Uni, twenty years his senior. Tall and powerfully built, he was outspoken in his relations with White employers. In the early 1940s he met Don McLeod, a contractor from Meekatharra, who was determined to improve conditions for Aboriginal pastoral workers in the Pilbara. With McKenna and Dooley Bin Bin, McLeod sought a minimum wage of 30 shillings per week and planned a mass withdrawal of labour on 1 May 1946. In the week of the industrial action, the magistrate at Port Hedland found McKenna guilty of inciting natives to strike and sentenced him to three months hard labour. Bin Bin was arrested and imprisoned for a similar offence. McLeod was also arrested, but won an appeal.

Undeterred, McKenna and Bin Bin organized some 800 strikers who decided in August not to return to work, despite the offer of better wages and conditions. When McLeod was again arrested, McKenna led a mass march on the Port Hedland police station. The initial wave of strikes lasted until late 1948. Meanwhile, McKenna helped to establish a co-operative which collected pearl-shell, hunted kangaroos and feral goats for their skins, and dry-panned for minerals. At the district registrar's office, Port Hedland, on 18 August 1950 he married Topsy Dougall (d.1975), a 27-year-old domestic servant. He subsequently joined McLeod in various mining ventures of the 'Pindan mob' and supplemented his income by station work. By 1960, when the mob split, McKenna had abandoned his support for McLeod. He worked at Mundabullanga station, and with the Nyamal co-operative set up by Ernie Mitchell and Peter Coppin at Wadangine. Although he had found it demeaning to apply for what was called a 'dog licence', he was granted a certificate of citizenship in 1954. After his son Roy contracted pneumonia, the family moved to Port Hedland where McKenna worked on the wharves. When Topsy and Clancy eventually parted, his life consisted of a 'tedious roundabout of station work, contracting, drinking, gaol and unemployment'.

A 'Law-man' among the Nyamal, McKenna had a special ability to interpret and explain Aboriginal culture to Europeans. At the same time, he suffered the slur of being a 'half-caste' and a 'mudamuda', accused of being 'a whitefella today and a blackfella tomorrow'. His unfulfilled ambition was to be a lawyer in the White man's system. His life story, told to Kingsley Palmer, was published as *Somewhere Between Black and White* (Melbourne, 1978). McKenna died of acute bacterial endocarditis on 20 August 1979 at Wine Tree Camp, Marble Bar, and was buried in Port

Hedland cemetery; he was survived by at least three of his children.

M. Brown, *The Black Eureka* (Syd, 1976); R. M. and C. H. Berndt (eds), *Aborigines of the West* (Perth, 1979); D. W. McLeod, *How the West was Lost* (Perth, 1984); S. Morgan, *Wanamurraganya* (Fremantle, 1989); *West Australian*, 3, 18 May 1946; J. M. Wilson, Authority and Leadership in a 'New Style' Australian Aboriginal Community (M.A. thesis, Univ WA, 1961); family and personal information.							R. H. W. REECE

McKENNA, NICHOLAS EDWARD (1895-1974), politician and lawyer, was born on 9 September 1895 at Carlton, Melbourne, second son of John McKenna, a prison warder from Ireland, and his Victorian-born wife Alice, née Darcy. John was later deputy-governor of Pentridge gaol. Nick attended Christian Brothers' College, North Melbourne, with Arthur Calwell [q.v.13], a future leader of the Australian Labor Party in Federal parliament. In July 1912 McKenna joined the Commonwealth auditor-general's office as a clerk. While studying at the University of Melbourne (LL.B., 1923), he lived briefly in Newman College where he took a prominent part in social functions and excelled as a baritone. He played Australian Rules football (possibly for North Melbourne) until he was about 30, but not at the top level.

From 1924 McKenna was employed as a public accountant, initially at Townsville, Queensland, and then in Melbourne. Admitted as a barrister and solicitor on 1 March 1928, he practised locally before moving to Hobart in 1929. He joined the firm of Albert Ogilvie [q.v.11], a future Labor premier of Tasmania. At St Patrick's Cathedral, East Melbourne, on 9 January 1930 McKenna married Kathleen Mary Coghlan, a 25-year-old telephonist; they were to have a son and daughter.

McKenna was elected to the Senate in 1943 as one of Tasmania's three Labor representatives; he entered that chamber on 1 July 1944 and was to be returned in 1949, 1951, 1955 and 1961. In his maiden speech he expressed the sentiments which guided him throughout his career:

> the Senate has for its objective the true welfare of the people of Australia . . . I am certain that we shall have differences of opinion as to how that end may be attained, but I submit that so long as we all keep that high objective well before our minds we should be able to pursue our way without undue acrimony.

Joining J. B. Chifley's [q.v.13] ministry on 18 June 1946, McKenna held the portfolios of health and social services until Labor lost power in December 1949. At various times he also acted as treasurer, attorney-general and minister for the interior when his colleagues were absent. In the Senate he was deputy-leader (1946-49) of the government, and deputy-leader (1949-51) and leader (1951-66) of the Opposition. He was also a member and chairman of numerous parliamentary committees.

With Chifley, J. J. Dedman and H. V. Evatt [qq.v.13,14], McKenna had been one of federal Labor's 'Big Four' in the mid- to late 1940s. He was a close confidant of Chifley and Evatt. McKenna campaigned strongly in support of the 1946 referendum on social services, marketing and industrial employment. Following the success of the social services proposal, he oversaw the government's efforts to introduce measures for national health and free medicine. While in the Opposition he supported Chifley's attempt—foiled by the A.L.P.'s federal executive—to have civil-rights safeguards inserted in the Communist Party dissolution bill (1950). After the legislation was disallowed by the High Court of Australia, McKenna took part in Evatt's crusade to defeat the 1951 referendum on banning the Communist Party of Australia.

Before the Labor Party split in 1955, McKenna remained close to Evatt. Ten years later he and Senator P. J. Kennelly conducted secret negotiations with B. A. Santamaria in an endeavour to reunite the A.L.P. and the Democratic Labor Party. In 1960 McKenna had led moves that secured E. G. Whitlam's election over E. J. Ward [q.v.] as deputy-leader of the federal parliamentary party. Retiring from the Senate on 30 June 1968, McKenna said that the highlight of his career had been the fight against attempts to proscribe communism: it had ended 'when Australia decided not to become a police state'.

McKenna's wife and son both died in 1969. He continued to live in Sydney and saw his party return to government under Whitlam. Survived by his daughter, he died on 22 April 1974 at Crows Nest and was buried in Northern Suburbs cemetery. Parliamentary colleagues remembered him for his courtesy, kindness, knowledge of the Senate's standing orders, and the care with which he prepared and presented arguments in debate. Tall and fatherly in appearance, he never entered the Senate without a copy of the standing orders under his arm; he spoke on questions of procedure, both to instruct his peers and to give the presiding officer time to take advice on any difficult matter. In a chamber where disorderly interjections are common, he was noted for his close attention to the speeches of others and for his disinclination to interrupt. The Liberal senator (Sir) Reginald Wright said that McKenna had 'ennobled this place and contributed to its operation with ability and . . . genuine interest'.

L. F. Crisp, *Ben Chifley* (Lond, 1960); R. Murray, *The Split* (Melb, 1970); A. A. Calwell, *Be Just and Fear Not* (Melb, 1972); R. McMullin, *The Light on the Hill* (Melb, 1991); *PD* (Cwlth), 17 July 1944, p 12, (Senate), 10 July 1974, p 29; *Aust Financial Review*, 22 July 1966; *SMH*, 28 July 1968, 24 Apr 1974; information from Mrs J. Percival, Lane Cove, Syd.   PETER BAUME

MACKENZIE, AUBREY DUNCAN (1895-1962), civil engineer, was born on 3 January 1895 at North Carlton, Melbourne, son of Duncan Mackenzie, a Scottish-born draughtsman, and his wife Emma, née Surman, who came from England. Educated at Melbourne Continuation (High) School, Aubrey joined the Victorian Public Works Department as a pupil-architect in 1912, changing in the following year to pupil-engineer. On 14 April 1915 he enlisted in the Australian Imperial Force. He served at Gallipoli with the 6th Field Ambulance and on the Western Front in a number of supporting roles. Discharged in Melbourne on 6 July 1919, he rejoined the Public Works Department. On 2 August 1924 at Scots Church, Melbourne, he married Marjorie Kiel with Presbyterian forms.

In December 1934 Mackenzie was promoted to chief engineer of the department, with particular charge of ports and harbours. He had already been responsible for construction of the Yarra Boulevard and the Mount Donna Buang, Acheron Way and Ben Cairn roads, and for the surroundings of the Shrine of Remembrance. Chairman of the State Tourist Committee, the Motor-Omnibus Advisory Board and the Foreshore Erosion Board, he was vice-president of the marine board, and a member of the committees for rivers and streams and for Mount Buffalo National Park. From 1938 to 1940 he was a full-time commissioner of the Country Roads Board.

In July 1940 Mackenzie was appointed (from a field of twelve applicants) executive-chairman of the Melbourne Harbor Trust, at £1500 a year. He was to be reappointed three times. After stagnating in the interwar period, the port of Melbourne saw unprecedented development over the next twenty years. Under wartime conditions the Commonwealth government enabled extensive shipbuilding and repairing by the trust, initially at the Alfred Graving Dock complex. Merchant vessels were armed and others converted to minesweepers, some forty all told. Naval anti-submarine vessels, freighters and cargo barges were soon under construction; new slipways, fitting-out berths, mobile cranes and workshops were developed. In 1942 Melbourne was the chief American supply port; traffic that year broke all records. Having become chairman of the permanent committee of the Australian Port Authorities' Association, Mackenzie visited Darwin, Fremantle, Western Australia, and Whyalla, South Australia, to advise on urgent harbour improvements.

His achievements during the war won Mackenzie respect which he maintained, and his enthusiasm, determined drive and creative imagination as an administrator took him far. Of medium build, he was a good 'staff man' who habitually made a morning round to talk to the labour force.

Under Mackenzie's administration, Melbourne remained the best mechanized Australian port, especially for bulk-loading. Construction of the Appleton Dock (opened in 1956) was a highlight, the Tasmanian car-ferry a notable innovation, and oil wharves on the River Yarra a lasting problem. So was the Waterside Workers' Federation, bedevilled by years of ruthless exploitation; turn round of goods improved very little. Mackenzie retired on 3 January 1960 and, strangely, received no honour.

A member of the Institution of Engineers, Australia, and the Institution of Civil Engineers, London, Mackenzie was commodore (1947-57) of the Sandringham Yacht Club, of which his father had been a leading founder. He died of heart disease on 21 March 1962 in his Hampton home and was cremated. His wife, son and daughter survived him, and his estate was sworn for probate at £15 460.

O. Ruhen, *Port of Melbourne, 1835-1976* (Syd, 1976); *Port of Melbourne Q*, Jan-Mar 1960, Apr-June 1962; *Herald* (Melb), 19 Dec 1934; *Argus*, 1 Mar 1938, 17 May 1949; *Sun News-Pictorial*, 27 Aug 1955; *Age* (Melb), 23 Mar 1962.   GEOFFREY SERLE*

MACKENZIE, KENNETH IVO BROWNLEY LANGWELL ('SEAFORTH') (1913-1955), poet and novelist, was born on 25 September 1913 in South Perth, son of Australian-born parents Hugh Mackenzie, farmer, and his wife Marguerite Christina, née Pryde-Paterson. After his parents were divorced in 1919, Kenneth was raised by his mother and maternal grandfather. Educated at South Perth and Pinjarra state schools, and (as a boarder) at Guildford Grammar School, he took no interest in sport and studied only when he felt inclined. At 16 he ran away from school and refused to return. Finding Muresk Agricultural College even more uncongenial than boarding-school, he entered the University of Western Australia in 1932 to read law. He gained a reputation for spasmodic brilliance and eccentricity, and left before the end of his first year.

Following occasional employment as a journalist on the *West Australian*, Mackenzie travelled to Melbourne in 1933. In the height of the Depression he took a job as a scullery-assistant and survived on the charity of his father's sisters. He moved to Sydney in the following year. There he reviewed books, films and drama for the *Sydney Morning Herald*, wrote for *Fox Movietone News* and contributed to *Smith's Weekly*, through which he met Kenneth Slessor [q.v.]. Impressing Norman Lindsay [q.v.10], he was admitted to his Bohemian circle: wherever Mackenzie was, 'wild comedy and wild adventures tended to break out'. He was strong, muscular and blonde, and immensely attractive to certain women. On 24 December 1934 at the registrar general's office, Sydney, he married Kathleen Bartlett, née Loveday; born in England, she was a 25-year-old widow who had taken a job as a pastry-cook.

His first novel, *The Young Desire It*, was published (1937) under the pseudonym 'Seaforth' Mackenzie by Jonathan Cape in London; sensitive, vital and erotic, it was to win the Australian Literary Society's prize in 1939. A sense of moral ambiguity and impending chaos, evident in Mackenzie's second novel, *Chosen People* (London, 1938), began to invade his own life as he became addicted to alcohol. The outbreak of World War II destroyed what vague plans he had to make a name as a writer in England. Mobilized in the Australian Military Forces, he began full-time duty on 8 April 1943, but was rejected for active service because of poor eyesight. Mackenzie was posted to the 22nd Garrison Battalion at Cowra prisoner-of-war camp. In August 1944 he witnessed the Japanese break-out, the subject of his third novel, *Dead Men Rising* (New York, 1951). Two collections of his poetry were published in his lifetime, *Our Earth* (Sydney, 1937) and *The Moonlit Doorway* (Sydney, 1944). Medically unfit, he was discharged from the army on 11 June 1945. His drinking habits (claret with breakfast) and lack of qualifications meant that he was virtually unemployable.

In 1948 the family moved to Kurrajong at the foot of the Blue Mountains where Kate had bought 14 acres (6 ha) with her child-endowment money. When they failed to make a living there, she returned with the children to Sydney. Left alone, Mackenzie devoted himself to his writing. He was awarded a Commonwealth Literary Fund fellowship for that year and for 1955; he edited (1951-52) *Australian Poetry* and published another novel, *The Refuge* (London, 1954). None the less, his financial situation and personal life were fast deteriorating. He was accidentally drowned on 19 January 1955 while bathing in Tallong Creek, near Goulburn; survived by his wife, daughter and son, he was cremated with Anglican rites. Douglas Stewart edited the *Selected Poems of Kenneth Mackenzie*

(Sydney, 1961), and Evan Jones and Geoffrey Little co-edited a further anthology in 1972.

E. Jones, *Kenneth Mackenzie* (Melb, 1969); D. Stewart, *Norman Lindsay* (Melb, 1975); *Southerly*, 9, 1948, p 214, 25, 1965, p 75, 26, 1966, p 25; *Meanjin Q*, 13, 1954, p 503, 24, 1965, p 298; *Aust Q*, 36, no 2, June 1964, p 70; *Westerly*, 3, 1966; *West Australian*, 29 Jan 1955; Mackenzie papers (BL).

VERONICA BRADY

MacKENZIE, WILLIAM FREDERICK (1897-1972), Presbyterian missionary, was born on 16 February 1897 at Ambrim (Ambrym) Island, New Hebrides (Vanuatu), son of Rev. John William MacKenzie, a Canadian-born missionary, and his second wife Alicia Rosa Bertha, née Roberts, who came from Sydney. Young Bill attended (1911-12) Otago Boys' High School, Dunedin, New Zealand. He studied at the University of Sydney in 1916 before enlisting in the Australian Imperial Force on 8 October. Five ft 7¾ ins (172 cm) tall and 10 st. 8 lb. (67 kg) in weight, he served (from July 1917) as a gunner with the 54th (renamed 1st) Siege Battery on the Western Front. On 10 April 1918 he was taken prisoner at Messines, Belgium.

After being repatriated and discharged in Sydney on 27 June 1919, MacKenzie read theology at Ormond [q.v.5] College, University of Melbourne (B.A., 1923). He helped J. R. B. Love [q.v.10] at Mapoon Presbyterian mission, Queensland, at Christmas 1921 and was influenced by the way that Love mixed compatible Aboriginal cultural practices with Christianity. Appointed superintendent of Aurukun Presbyterian mission on western Cape York Peninsula in December 1923, MacKenzie returned to Melbourne late in 1924 to complete his theological studies and was ordained on 13 October 1925. At St Matthew's Anglican Church, Prahran, on 8 October 1925 he had married Geraldine Adelaide Propsting Storrs, a 25-year-old schoolteacher; they were to remain childless.

On 27 November 1925 the young couple arrived at Aurukun. About seventy-five Aborigines lived permanently at the mission; many more followed their traditional lifestyle south of the Archer River. Aurukun had no wireless communication with the outside world until 1937; before that year the MacKenzies' only contact with other missions was by lugger. Patrols of the mission reserve were conducted on horseback. In her reminiscences, *Aurukun Diary* (Melbourne, 1981), Gerrie wrote of the Aboriginal people and their country: 'I had learnt admiration for their hardiness, their cheerfulness in the face of odds that would have flattened me ... The spaciousness and unhurried peace of the land they lived in had claimed both of us'. Mobilized in the Militia in

1942-44, Bill remained at Aurukun as a coast-watcher during the war in the Pacific.

Queensland legislation made missionaries responsible for the health, education, employment and behaviour of those living on Aboriginal reserves. On occasions MacKenzie's rough justice—which included cutting off girls' hair for alleged impropriety, and chaining men to trees in cases of domestic violence —incurred criticism from visitors, particularly anthropologists. Ian Peinkinna, an Aurukun elder, recalled that MacKenzie was authoritarian, 'but he made a good man and woman out of that. He had discipline'.

Although the MacKenzies took a keen interest in improving Aboriginal health and reducing infant mortality, they also endeavoured to develop a cattle industry and to create a school curriculum adapted to Aboriginal requirements. Gerrie published a set of illustrated English primers, using 'words, experiences and situations' from the everyday life of Aboriginal children: *The First Australians' First* [to *Sixth*] *Book* (Melbourne, 1951-52). While English was taught in the school, the MacKenzies did not discourage the use of Aboriginal languages.

In 1949-50 MacKenzie served as moderator of the Presbyterian Church of Queensland. The Church and the State government came to regard him as a leader among missionaries, and sought his advice on issues such as the unrest at Mapoon in 1953. He was appointed M.B.E. (1958) and elevated to C.B.E. (1963). Sir Henry Abel Smith, the governor of Queensland, noted that MacKenzie and his wife 'by their example of joyous service, generate and radiate happiness to all around them. Their aim has not been to destroy the tribal customs, but to preserve all that is good in them'.

Strongly built, MacKenzie spoke deeply and deliberately. In middle age he developed a limp, but did not allow it to impede him. He preferred manual labour and practical mission management to office-work, yet his correspondence and reports were expressed with clarity. The MacKenzies retired to Melbourne in 1965. He died on 29 June 1972 at Forest Hill and was cremated; his wife (d.1980) survived him. They are commemorated by an annual prize-giving night at the Aurukun State school.

Presbyterian Outlook (Brisb), vol 4, no 65, Jan 1924, p 18, vol 5, no 85, Nov 1925, p 5, vol 32, no 12, June 1949; R. M. Kidd, Regulating bodies: administrations and Aborigines in Queensland 1840-1988 (Ph.D. thesis, Griffith Univ, 1994); J. M. Stuckey, Unpublished biog of W. F. and G. A. P. MacKenzie (held by Mr G. Wharton, Holland Park, Brisb); Cte on Missions to the Aboriginals *and* Aboriginal and Foreign Missions Cte correspondence files *and* Rev F. White, interview with Ian Peinkinna, 24 Sept 1992, ts (Qld Presbyterian Hist Records, Fortitude Valley, Brisb); MacKenzie papers (Aust Inst of Aboriginal and Torres Strait Islander Studies, Canb); information from Mrs L. Haughton, Surrey Hills, Melb, Lady Hibberd, Somers, Vic, Mrs J. Adams, Cairns, Mrs M. Little, Miles, and Mrs G. Tybingoompa, Aurukun, Qld.

GEOFF WHARTON

McKEON, GWLADYS YVONNE (1897-1979), biologist, was born on 23 August 1897 at Llanelly, Carmarthenshire, Wales, youngest of seven children of George James, schoolmaster, and his wife Frances, née Hart. The Jameses had emigrated to Queensland in 1885 and were revisiting Wales. They returned to the colony in 1899. George was headmaster of Albert State School, Maryborough, which Gwladys attended in 1903-09. Proceeding to Maryborough Girls' Grammar School, she held a Queen Victoria Diamond Jubilee scholarship (1910-12), won a Melville bursary (1913), became a prefect and was dux. Another scholarship took her to the University of Queensland (B.Sc., 1918; M.Sc., 1920). Studying biology under T. H. Johnston [q.v.9], Miss James was one of the university's few female graduates and among the first trained parasitologists in the State.

Soon after graduating, she was appointed scientist-in-charge of the Tick Biology Station, West Burleigh. The Cattle Tick Dip Committee, Brisbane, chaired by Johnston, operated the facility for the Commonwealth Institute of Science and Industry. James followed meticulous procedures in collecting data. Recording temperature and humidity, she monitored engorged ticks to determine the nature of their egg-laying and hatching, their larval and adult life spans, and the patterns of their distribution.

After the tick station closed, James moved to Nambour in May 1920 and joined the Australian hookworm campaign as a microscopist. One of a team of seven, she was less isolated than she had been at West Burleigh. An attractive, dark-haired woman, 5 ft 3 ins (160 cm) tall, she was responsible for the preparation and dispatch of treatments to patients infected with hookworm. She also became adept at determining the presence of malarial and filarial parasites in human patients and at collecting and identifying mosquitoes.

On 12 June 1923 at St Paul's Anglican Church, Maryborough, Gwladys married Peter Cecil Egbert Connolly McKeon (d.1969), a soldier settler who farmed at Woombye. The McKeons grew fruit—mainly pineapples and bananas—and Gwladys won prizes at the local show for her crayon, pen-and-ink and chalk drawings. The Depression drove them off the land in 1930. They settled at Toowoomba where Cecil managed an office of the State Wheat Board. When he retired in the late 1950s, they shifted to Point Vernon, Hervey Bay. An avid observer, Gwladys studied seaweeds and marine invertebrates, sending her collections from the shallow and intertidal areas of Hervey Bay to specialists throughout Australia. Her handbook, *Life on the Australian Seashore* (Brisbane, 1966), was lavishly illustrated with her pen-drawings and water-colours. She donated the royalties to Women's College, University of Queensland.

Mrs McKeon was gentle, kind, thoughtful and industrious. After raising five children and helping her husband—at first on their farm, then by designing displays for the Wheat Board—she took up her new professional interests with energy and enthusiasm, making a significant contribution to the study of marine biology. She died on 15 August 1979 at Kedron, Brisbane, and was cremated; her two sons and three daughters survived her.

Cwlth Advisory Council of Science and Industry, *Annual Report*, 1917-18; A10046/1, item A3/1 (AA, Canb); family papers (held by Mrs P. V. J. McKeon, Salisbury, Brisb).   PATRICIA MATHER

McKEOWN, MAURICE ROBERT (1884-1972), mining engineer, was born on 29 March 1884 at Darlinghurst, Sydney, son of native-born parents George Maurice McKeown, estate agent, and his wife Emmeline Mary, née Mayhew. Keith Collingwood McKeown [q.v.10] was his brother. The boys grew up on Wollongbar Experimental Farm where their father was officer-in-charge. Maurice attended Fort Street Model School (while boarding with his uncle Robert McKeown, vicar of St Mary's, Waverley) and later Sydney Technical College.

During the great drought of 1901-02 McKeown worked with a railway survey team in north-western New South Wales. In 1904 he took a post at Broken Hill with Broken Hill Proprietary Co. Ltd; six years of mining and milling experience, with part-time study at the Broken Hill Technical College, enabled him to gain his mine-manager's certificate. After a year as mill superintendent with Phillips River Gold & Copper Co. Ltd in Western Australia, he returned to Broken Hill as mill super-intendent (1911-14) at the large operations of North Broken Hill Ltd. On 16 August 1913 at St Andrew's Kirk, Ballarat, Victoria, he married Margaret McKenzie with Presbyterian forms. He turned to farming in the Joadja Valley, near Newnes, New South Wales, in 1914, but went to Emmaville in 1917 to be assistant-manager of the Vegetable Creek Tin Mining Co. (N.L.).

Determined to establish himself as a consultant mining engineer, McKeown moved to

Melbourne in 1922. He was first retained by the gold-mining interests of A. Victor Leggo [q.v.10]. McKeown gave expert advice covering metalliferous, coal and oil deposits, often in remote places, and wrote at least 255 reports on mining properties. Several small mining firms benefited from his advice, especially during Depression times of 'penny-a-month' calls on their shares. He was made a director of twelve companies, including Deborah Gold Mines (N.L.), Renison Associated Tin Mines (N.L.), and Technical Developments Ltd.

McKeown was a member (from 1912), councillor (1945-68) and vice-president (1948-49 and 1953-54) of the Australasian Institute of Mining and Metallurgy. Honorary editor (1946-54) of its *Proceedings*, he also edited the volumes of the Fifth Empire Mining and Metallurgical Congress (1953). He published in the *Proceedings* a definitive paper (1942) on the new Tennant Creek goldfield, Northern Territory, with which he was associated. In addition, he edited (1939-45) the *Chemical Engineering and Mining Review* and co-authored (with H. S. Elford) *Coal Mining in Australia* (Melbourne, 1947). A member (from 1946) and vice-president of the Victorian Chamber of Mines, he served as chairman of the board of examiners for the metalliferous and coal mine-managers' certificate in Victoria, and as an external examiner for the mining school at the University of Melbourne.

Of average height, somewhat heavy build and balding in middle age, McKeown had kindly eyes which bespoke warmth and quiet charm. Bowls was his only recreation, although he never lost his youthful enthusiasm for steam-trains. He belonged to the Hannans (Kalgoorlie) and Melbourne Scots clubs. Predeceased by his wife, he died on 27 September 1972 in East Melbourne and was buried in Burwood cemetery. His son survived him.

J. Dew (comp), *Mining People* (Melb, 1993); A'sian Inst of Mining and Metallurgy, *Procs*, Mar 1973, *and* records (Parkville, Melb); M. R. McKeown reminiscences (ms held by Univ Melb Archives); information from the late Dr M. McKeown.

D. F. FAIRWEATHER

McKERIHAN, SIR CLARENCE ROY (1896-1969), banker and worker for voluntary societies, was born on 6 May 1896 at Tenterfield, New South Wales, fifth child of Edward McKerihan, a draper from Ireland, and his native-born wife Elizabeth Jane, née Gillespie. Educated at Tamworth, Tenterfield and Casino, Roy excelled at all sports, particularly swimming, tennis and cricket. He began work in 1912 as a junior in the Casino branch of the

Government Savings Bank of New South Wales and was moved to Grafton in 1913. Enlisting in the Australian Imperial Force on 26 May 1915, he served at Gallipoli with the 4th Battalion, and in Egypt, France and Britain with the Australian Records Section. He rose to warrant officer, class one (1917), and was awarded the Meritorious Service Medal (1919). He was known as the first Australian soldier to climb Mont Blanc, during leave in 1916.

Discharged in Australia on 7 September 1919, McKerihan was soon appointed loans officer at the head office of the Government Savings Bank in Sydney. He was transferred to the rural bank department on its creation in 1921 (chief clerk 1928). On 17 August 1921 he married Dorothy Juanita McCallum at St Stephen's Presbyterian Church, Sydney. Following the closure of the Savings Bank in 1931, the Rural Bank of New South Wales was formed from its remnants. McKerihan was appointed commissioner of the new bank in 1933 and president in 1934. He guided the bank out of the Depression. Called 'the banker with the human touch', he displayed tact and compassion, as well as a capacity for hard work. He believed that the bank should assist small holders to increase the number and quality of their stock, and chatted with his clients at such events as the Royal Easter Show, which he regularly attended.

During World War II McKerihan was honorary general secretary (honorary federal administrator 1940-46) of the Australian Comforts Fund for servicemen and women. As the key central co-ordinator, he ensured the organization's success by placating the often competing pressures of State and Federal governments and voluntary organizations. He allowed the A.C.F. executive-committee to hold its Sydney meetings in the board-room of the Rural Bank headquarters in Martin Place, and provided clerical and administrative assistance through his staff.

McKerihan was a board-member (from 1938) and president (1945-53) of the Women's Hospital, Crown Street. A public-spirited man, he was active in many organizations, including the Freemasons, the Rotary and Legacy clubs of Sydney, the Big Brother Movement, and the Boy Scouts' and Girl Guides' associations; he also raised money for the St John Ambulance Brigade. He held numerous honorary positions: president of the State branch of the National Trust of Australia, councillor of the Australian-American Association, treasurer of the Australian Association for the United Nations, trustee of Kuring-gai Chase, federal director of the Arts Council of Australia and founder of the War Veterans' Home, Narrabeen. Deeply religious, he was an elder of St Stephen's Presbyterian Church, Macquarie Street.

In 1959 McKerihan was criticized for the bank's loans to a failing cement company. When he retired in 1961 the bank had 134 branches across New South Wales. He was awarded King George V's silver jubilee medal in 1935, appointed C.B.E. in 1958 and knighted in 1961. Sir Roy belonged to the Australian, Royal Sydney Golf and Rose Bay Bowling clubs. Survived by his wife and two daughters, he died on 28 December 1969 at St Luke's Hospital, Darlinghurst, and was cremated. His estate was sworn for probate at $58 733.

C. O. B. Jackson, *Proud Story* (Syd, 1949); *Banker*, May 1961, p 11; *Sun-Herald* (Syd), 23 Sept 1956; *SMH*, 11 Jan 1958, 30 Sept, 5, 22 Oct 1959, 1 Jan 1967, 29 Dec 1969, 4 Jan 1970; M. Oppenheimer, Volunteers in Action: Voluntary Work in Australia 1939-1945 (Ph.D. thesis, Macquarie Univ, 1997); Dept of Defence Co-ordination files, A817/1 item 141, McKerihan correspondence Aust Comforts Fund, 1 Jan 1940-31 Dec 1946 (AA, Canb); State Bank of NSW Archives, Syd.

MELANIE OPPENHEIMER

MACKERRAS, IAN MURRAY (1898-1980) and MABEL JOSEPHINE (1896-1971), medical scientists, were husband and wife. Ian was born on 19 September 1898 at Balclutha, Otago, New Zealand, elder son of James Murray Mackerras, a New Zealand-born farmer, and his Sydney-born wife Elizabeth Mary, née Creagh. His parents separated and Elizabeth raised the boys in Sydney. Educated at Sydney Grammar School, Ian overstated his age and enlisted in the Australian Imperial Force on 13 December 1915. He served as a laboratory attendant in the hospital ship, *Karoola*, before joining (December 1917) the 13th Field Artillery Brigade on the Western Front. He was gassed in May 1918 at Villers-Bretonneux, France, and subsequently admitted to hospital in England. Returning to Australia in February 1919, he entered the University of Sydney (M.B., Ch.M., B.Sc. Hons, 1924); he graduated with the university medal in zoology and shared the John Coutts scholarship.

Josephine was born on 7 August 1896 at Deception Bay, Caboolture District, Queensland, elder child of Thomas Lane Bancroft [q.v.7], an English-born medical practitioner, and his Brisbane-born wife Cecilia Mary, née Jones. Initially educated at home by her mother, Jo enhanced her knowledge of plants, animals and insects by assisting her father in his research projects at their Deception Bay property. She proceeded to Brisbane Girls' Grammar School (where she won prizes in mathematics) and the University of Queensland (B.Sc., 1918; M.Sc., 1930). In 1918-20 she held a Walter and Eliza Hall [qq.v.9] fellowship in economic biology. During this period she collaborated with her honours supervisor T. H. Johnston [q.v.9] in research that led to fourteen joint publications.

While Josephine was at the University of Sydney (M.B., 1924) she met Ian Mackerras. There was an immediate attraction of kindred spirits. Sailing and fishing at weekends, they did not eat their catch until they had examined its blood for haematozoa. The first paper they published together recorded the blood parasites of Australian marine fish. Ian and Jo were married with Anglican rites on 5 April 1924 at Grosvenor Flat, Eidsvold, Queensland; theirs was to prove one of the most productive and distinguished husband-and-wife partnerships in the history of Australian science. Jo completed twelve months residency at Royal Prince Alfred Hospital, Sydney, then combined a small private practice with a part-time appointment at the Rachel Forster Hospital for Women and Children. When her son was born in 1926, she suspended her professional career.

In 1925 Ian had been appointed Linnean Macleay [q.v.5] fellow in zoology at the University of Sydney, where he came under the influence of Professor Launcelot Harrison [q.v.9]. After two years as assistant-microbiologist in the New South Wales Department of Public Health, Mackerras was offered a position with the Council for Scientific and Industrial Research's division of economic entomology, Canberra. Starting on 1 December 1928 as senior entomologist (later principal research officer), he was thrust into the fields of veterinary entomology and parasitology. He organized and guided a successful research team, and increased knowledge of the control of sheep blowfly, buffalo fly, tick fever, and ephemeral fever in cattle. In 1930 Josephine joined the unit as assistant-entomologist. Her research on blowfly infestation and ephemeral fever led to nine papers, five of them joint publications with Ian.

On 13 October 1939 Ian was appointed major, Australian Army Medical Corps, A.I.F. In January 1940 he sailed for the Middle East. Employed as pathologist with the 2nd/1st Australian General Hospital, he was sent to North Africa to advise on the prevention of diarrhoeal disease. Josephine joined the A.A.M.C. as captain on 7 February 1942 and was posted to the Sydney area. Ian returned to Australia in May; in October he was appointed director of entomology, Land Headquarters. Promoted lieutenant colonel in May 1943, he made numerous visits to Papua and New Guinea, developing control measures for malaria, dengue fever and scrub typhus.

With 25 000 servicemen suffering from malaria in the South-West Pacific Area by June 1943, Mackerras, H. K. Ward and E. V. Keogh [q.v.] proposed an organization 'solely devoted to the scientific investigation' of the disease. That year the L.H.Q. Medical Research Unit was established under (Sir) Neil Fairley [q.v.14] at Cairns, Queensland. Josephine was attached to the unit as entomologist from mid-1943 and promoted major in March 1944. She bred and maintained a stock of infected mosquitoes for testing on volunteers. Her work reduced the incidence of infection in the armed forces, and provided a secure scientific basis for studying the effects of drugs on the malarial parasite. After the unit was disbanded in March 1946, she published eight important papers in collaboration with her former colleagues.

While holding office as adviser in parasitology (1944-45), Ian toured Britain and the United States of America. As malariologist (June to December 1945), First Australian Army, he again visited New Guinea. For his wartime services he was twice mentioned in dispatches. In 1953-56 he was to command the 1st Mobile Malaria Control Company in the Citizen Military Forces. Having been demobilized, the Mackerrases resumed their work with the C.S.I.R. in February 1946. They moved in April to the Yeerongpilly laboratories, Brisbane, where Ian was engaged in studies on the control of the cattle tick and Jo began work on the Simuliidae (blackflies). In 1947 Ian was appointed founding director of the Queensland Institute of Medical Research. His interests focussed on zoonoses (parasitic diseases normally found in animals but able to be transmitted to humans, frequently by arthropods). He achieved a happy balance between his administrative duties and his research.

Josephine began work at the Q.I.M.R. as senior parasitologist in September 1947. Among the various projects on which she was engaged, her chief contribution to scientific knowledge came from her study of the parasites of Australian mammals. She elucidated the life history of the rat lung-worm, later shown to be the aetiological agent of eosinophilic meningitis in the people of the Pacific islands. This lung-worm was named *Angiostrongylus mackerrasae* after her. Husband and wife directed their combined efforts to such endeavours as an examination of the role of cockroaches in the transmission of salmonella (especially to children), a series of studies on the taxonomy and life histories of Australian Simuliidae, and definitive works on the haematozoan parasites of Australian birds, frogs and fishes. They produced 17 joint publications, and 66 under individual authorship or with other colleagues.

In 1961 Ian and Josephine retired from the Q.I.M.R. They returned to Canberra as research fellows in the Commonwealth Scientific and Industrial Research Organization's division of entomology. Jo began a detailed study of cockroaches, while Ian edited and wrote sections of a monumental volume, *The Insects of Australia* (Melbourne), to which Josephine contributed a chapter. The book was published in 1970 and a supplement appeared in 1974. Ian also pursued his long-term study of *Tabanidae*. The Mackerrases continued to share a love of boating, fishing and the sea. They liked company, conversation and classical music, and many young scientists enjoyed cheerful evenings at their home. Foundation members of the Canberra Aero Club, Ian and Jo each held a pilot's licence. Jo's real delight, however, was in collecting specimens on field-trips.

Both Mackerrases were elected (1957) members (later fellows) of the (Royal) College of Pathologists of Australia (Australasia). Both were members of the Royal Society of Queensland, she from 1924 until 1958 when she was made life member; he was president in 1952. They served on the Great Barrier Reef Committee and helped to establish the Marine Research Station on Heron Island. Josephine presided over the Queensland Medical Women's Society and the Women Graduates' Association. Awarded the (W. B.) Clarke [q.v.3] medal of the Royal Society of New South Wales in 1965, she was elected a fellow of the Australian Society of Parasitology in 1966. The University of Queensland conferred an honorary doctorate of science on her in 1967, but she was too ill to attend the ceremony.

Ian served on the faculty of medicine, University of Queensland (1947-61), the medical research advisory committee of the National Health and Medical Research Council (1954-57), and the advisory council of the School of Public Health and Tropical Medicine, University of Sydney. He was president (1961-62) of the Australian Society for Microbiology, a foundation member and fellow of the Australian Society for Parasitology, and founder, president (1965-67) and honorary member (1969) of the Australian Entomological Society. In 1950 he had been awarded the Clarke medal. He held fellowships of the Royal Australasian College of Physicians (1950), the Australian Academy of Science (1954), the Australian and New Zealand Association for the Advancement of Science (1957) and the Royal Entomological Society, London (1958). A.N.Z.A.A.S. awarded him the Mueller [q.v.5] medal in 1961; the University of Sydney conferred on him an honorary doctorate of science in 1971.

Josephine died on 8 October 1971 in her home at Turner, Canberra, and was buried in Canberra cemetery. Ian pressed on with his revision of the *Tabanidae* of Australia, 'the taxonomy of the old, indigenous and probably predominantly marsupial-feeding tribe, the *Diachlorini*'. He died on 21 March 1980 in Canberra and was cremated. Their only child,

David, a reader in electrical engineering at the University of Queensland, became a noted authority on lightning.

Josephine Mackerras was a dedicated scientist, meticulous in her observations and attentive to detail. Her research—recorded in more than eighty papers—contributed to entomology, veterinary medicine and medical science. Characterized by her wisdom and strength of character, she also possessed a serene charm, a placid smile and a shy, self-effacing manner. Quietly and unobtrusively, she fostered young scientists and won the esteem of her senior colleagues. Her portrait by Nora Heysen is held by the Australian War Memorial, Canberra.

Known affectionately and respectfully as 'Dr Mac', or simply 'Mac', Ian Mackerras was a sympathetic, stimulating and critical researcher who gave time and often financial support to young scientists. He instilled in his teams the qualities of trust, goodwill, and genuine pleasure in learning and discovery. Mackerras wrote that: 'Research for its own sake fosters, as nothing else can, the urge always to explore, without which initiative is lost and no research institution can live'. He published more than 130 papers. During his tenure the Q.I.M.R. won an international reputation. The institute holds his portrait by Graeme Inson.

J. Priest, *Scholars and Gentlemen* (Brisb, 1986); L. M. Williams, 'The Prepared Mind', in J. Pearn and L. Powell (eds), *The Bancroft Tradition* (Brisb, 1991); Qld Inst of Medical Research, *Second Annual Report*, 1947; *MJA*, 18 Mar 1972, 1, p 604; *International J of Parasitology*, 2, 1972, p 181, 10, 1980, p 329; *News Bulletin of the Aust Entomological Soc*, May 1980, p 50; *Hist Records of Aust Science*, 5, no 2, 1981; *Canb Times*, 12 Oct 1971; I. M. Mackerras (ms, Basser L, Aust Academy of Science, Canb); priv papers (held by Dr D. Mackerras, Taringa, Brisb). LESLEY WILLIAMS

MACKEY, JOHN BERNARD (1922-1945), baker's mate and soldier, was born on 16 May 1922 at Leichhardt, Sydney, only son and eldest of four children of native-born parents Stanislaus Mackey, baker, and his wife Bridget Catherine, née Smyth. After attending St Columba's School, Leichhardt, and Christian Brothers' High School, Lewisham, Jack moved with his family to Portland in 1936. Aged 14, he finished his formal education at St Joseph's Convent School that year.

Because jobs were scarce, young Mackey was apprenticed in his father's bakery. Of average height, stockily built and weighing about 13 stone (83 kg), he had blue eyes, reddish hair, and a humorous and exuberant nature. He played Rugby League football for the local junior team (and later for his battalion) and proved an excellent swimmer, but he disliked working in the bakery and living in the country. His relationship with his father became strained, particularly after his mother died in 1939. Defying his father, Jack overstated his age and enlisted in the Australian Imperial Force on 4 June 1940. Stanislaus reluctantly accepted the situation.

Posted to the 2nd/3rd Pioneer Battalion, Mackey served in Darwin in 1941 before being sent to the Middle East where he saw action in the battle of El Alamein, Egypt (October-November 1942). He returned to Australia in February 1943, then sailed for Papua in August. During operations around Finschhafen, New Guinea, he was promoted acting corporal in October (substantive June 1944). His company commander described him as an outstanding junior leader who exhibited moral and physical courage. Mackey was hospitalized with malaria in November 1943-January 1944, and again in May-June and August-September 1944. With his battalion, he embarked for the invasion of Tarakan Island, Borneo, in April 1945 and landed on 1 May.

On 12 May 1945 Mackey led his section in an attack on a place code-named 'Helen'. This well-defended position dominated the surrounding vicinity and had to be approached along a precipitous spur, thick with jungle and barely wide enough for two men. Accompanied by his second-in-command, Lance Corporal A. R. 'Yorky' Riedy (who was to be awarded the Distinguished Conduct Medal for his part in the action), Mackey scrambled up the ridge, throwing a smoke-grenade to mask their approach. For reasons best known to themselves, the Japanese held their fire and dragged both Australians into the first position they reached—a light-machine-gun post. In the ensuing fight the two men accounted for four enemy soldiers, but Riedy was wounded. Mackey then killed the remaining Japanese in the post, and dealt with a heavy-machine-gun and its crew in an adjacent bunker. Taking Riedy's Owen gun, he moved towards another heavy-machine-gun nest, farther up the slope. He reached and silenced this post, but was mortally wounded.

Buried where he fell, Mackey was finally laid to rest in Labuan war cemetery. He was posthumously awarded the Victoria Cross. His sister Pat received the decoration from the governor-general, the Duke of Gloucester [q.v.14]; it was later presented to the Australian War Memorial, Canberra.

J. A. Anderson and G. Jackett, *Mud and Sand* (Syd, 1994); L. Wigmore (ed), *They Dared Mightily* (Canb, 1963); information from Mrs K. Middleton, Mornington, Vic, Mr J. Williams, Portland, Col C. Knott, Wagga Wagga, and Mr B. Burton, Lithgow, NSW, Mr W. Bentley, Oatley, and Mr J. Ryan, West Pymble, Syd.   HARRY TAPLIN

MACKINLAY, MARY BARR (1910-1974), Dominican Sister, was born on 28 August 1910 at Temora, New South Wales, third of five children of Australian-born parents John Barr Mackinlay, farmer, and his wife Ellen Theresa, née Duffy. Mary's father remained a staunch Presbyterian; her mother was a Catholic. In 1905 John had settled at Pucawan and named his property Linton. Mary and her six siblings (two of whom were adopted) were educated at the small bush school nearby. In later years she often referred to the excellent grounding and love of learning she had received from dedicated teachers in a one-teacher school.

In 1925 Mary was sent to the Dominican Convent, Santa Sabina, at Strathfield. There she was taught by Sister Anselm O'Brien [q.v.11] who encouraged her to pursue higher studies in English literature. At the 1929 Leaving certificate examination, Mary obtained first-class honours and topped the State in English, while gaining A-level passes in Latin, French, mathematics and history. She had also represented the school in basketball and tennis. In 1930 she entered Sancta Sophia College, University of Sydney (B.A., 1933; M.A., 1935). She majored in English and modern history. After teaching for a year at St Dominic's Convent school, Tamworth, she entered the Dominican novitiate at Maitland on 25 January 1934. In a significant departure from normal Catholic practice for novices, she completed her thesis on 'Mysticism in Modern English Poetry' during her postulancy.

Professed on 28 November 1936, she adopted the religious name Alphonse Marie and took her final vows on 28 November 1939. Sister Alphonse Marie taught in the Order's schools in Maitland, Tamworth and Melbourne, as well as at Santa Sabina, Sydney, and the inter-congregational St Anne's High School, Newcastle. She was an enthusiastic teacher, keenly interested in her pupils with whom she maintained friendships over many years.

Sister Alphonse Marie held the office of provincial directress of studies (1963-69) in the Dominican Congregation and served on the Provincial Council (1963-69 and 1973-74). She managed to combine academic excellence with practical skills and a great exuberance for life. Her conversation, broad in its scope, was enlivened by a trenchant wit and an elegant turn of phrase. Retaining her love of study, she pursued further academic courses virtually all her life. In 1972 Macquarie University conferred on her the degree of master of arts in education for her research into teaching the deaf. At the time of her death she was researching the characteristics of Dominican spirituality through the ages.

The motto, 'Watch and Pray', which she had chosen at profession, influenced her spiritual life. None the less, she was no plaster saint. Sister Alphonse could be caustic and outspoken: she was most critical of the numerous 'hobbles' that seemed to characterize religious life of her time. In early November 1974 the Mackinlay clan held a large family gathering at Santa Sabina. A week later, on the 10th, Sister Alphonse suffered a severe stroke from which she never regained consciousness. She died on 13 November 1974 in Lewisham Hospital and was buried in Rookwood cemetery.

SMH, 27, 29 Jan 1930; Dominican Archives (Santa Sabina Convent, Strathfield, Syd); information from, and papers held by, Mr L. Mackinlay, Holbrook, NSW.   MARGARET CARMEL LEAVEY

McKINNEY, JACK PHILIP (1891-1966), bushman, soldier and author, was born in 1891 at Numurkah, Victoria, son of William Graham McKinney, a Victorian-born journalist, and his wife Lucy Jane, née Burke, who came from England. Educated initially at the local state school, Jack was sent to Scotch College, Melbourne, when his father accepted a senior post with the *Argus*. Jack subsequently joined that newspaper (as a cadet journalist), but resigned in 1912 to embark on a series of jobs in the bush. He rode a bicycle to Broken Hill, New South Wales, went opal gouging at White Cliffs and in 1915 drove cattle from Charleville, Queensland, to Victoria.

McKinney enlisted in the Australian Imperial Force on 6 September 1915 and embarked for Egypt in November. Sent to France and promoted sergeant in March 1916, he served with the 1st Anzac Cyclist Battalion (later the Australian Corps Cyclist Battalion). On 2 November 1917 he gained the rank of company sergeant major. Suffering from shell-shock and gastric illness, he returned to Australia in 1919 and was discharged in Melbourne on 10 February 1920. He was mentioned in dispatches.

On 19 February 1921 at the Presbyterian Church, St Kilda, McKinney married 31-year-old Myrtle Sarah Gallagher, a former member of the Australian Army Nursing Service. She accompanied him to Queensland where he had obtained a post as manager of a maize plantation near Kingaroy. Taking up a small soldier-settlement block at Kumbia, he set out to become a dairy-farmer and pig-breeder. The hard work of clearing, fencing and building was exacerbated by the anxiety of having to care for four children in the Depression and led to a recurrence of his war-related illness.

Leaving the farm, McKinney took his family to Surfers Paradise. He freelanced as a journalist, and wrote short stories and radio serials. One of his scripts, 'The Noonan Family', about the adventures of Irish-Australian farmers, had a large audience. His war novel, 'Over the Top', later entitled *Crucible* (Sydney, 1935), was awarded a prize of £150 by the Victorian branch of the Returned Sailors' and Soldiers' Imperial League of Australia, allowing him to buy a cottage at Surfers Paradise where he wrote and worked until 1945. He later moved to North Tamborine. His marriage eventually ended in divorce.

From the outbreak of World War II, McKinney reflected on the question of why advances in Western thought failed to prevent further and more deadly wars. Untrained, he read philosophy, beginning with the ancient Greeks and devoting the rest of his life to the task. He contributed articles to major journals, published a preliminary book, *The Challenge of Reason* (Brisbane, 1950), and completed a more substantial work, *The Structure of Modern Thought* (London, 1971). Professor J. J. C. Smart praised the latter book for its 'fresh and original' presentation of the 'striking and important idea that knowledge is an interpersonal thing'.

McKinney was helped by his second wife Judith Arundell Wright McKinney whom he married on 13 June 1962 at the general register office, Brisbane. Survived by his wife and their daughter, and by the two sons and two daughters of his first marriage, he died on 6 December 1966 at Greenslopes, Brisbane, and was cremated with Presbyterian forms.

SMH, 25, 26 Apr 1935; Judith Wright McKinney letters (NL); information from Mrs M. Roxburgh, Macksville, NSW, Mrs L. Ellnor and Mr G. A. Greening, Pialba, Qld; personal knowledge.
                                      JUDITH WRIGHT McKINNEY

MACKINNON, CLAIRE ADAMS (1896-1978), film actress and benefactor, was born on 24 September 1896 at Winnipeg, Manitoba, Canada, daughter of Stanley Wells Adams, a Welsh-born accountant, and his Canadian wife Lillian, née Kennedy. Although her given names were registered as Beryl Vere Nassau, she was always known as Claire. Educated in Canada and England, she worked briefly as a Red Cross nurse during World War I. She visited New York and did the rounds of the studios, hoping to break into the motion-picture industry as an actress. In 1920 she signed a five-year contract with Benjamin Bowles Hampton, a 44-year-old producer from Hollywood. She moved to California where she acted in more than forty silent films, including melodramas, comedies and westerns.

Described as 'patricianly beautiful', Claire worked with many of Hollywood's leading actors. She starred in at least four movies with Tom Mix, appeared with Wallace Beery and Lon Chaney, and in 1923 was Rin Tin Tin's leading lady in *Where the North Begins* (she maintained that Rin Tin Tin was her favourite 'leading man'). The best-known film in which she acted was *The Big Parade* (1925), directed by King Vidor, in which she played John Gilbert's American sweetheart. At Hollywood on 18 September 1924 Claire married Ben Hampton; they had no children. He died in 1932, leaving her very wealthy.

DONALD JOHN SCOBIE MACKINNON (1906-1974), grazier and sportsman, was born on 25 March 1906 at Prahran, Melbourne, second child and eldest son of Lauchlan Kenneth Scobie Mackinnon [q.v.10], a Scottish-born solicitor, and his Victorian-born wife Margaret Jessie, whose father John Simson owned the Western District property, Trawalla. Known to family and friends as Scobie, Donald was educated at Melbourne and Geelong Church of England Grammar schools. In October 1925 he entered Jesus College, Cambridge; two years later he was captain of boats. He read history and law, but did not take a degree.

On his return from England in 1928, Mackinnon took up residence at Mooramong, a grazing property bought for him by his father, near Skipton in the Western District. He led a bachelor's life until 1937 when he met Claire at a party in London. They married three weeks later, on 1 April, at Christ Church, Mayfair, and remained childless.

After a protracted honeymoon, in March 1938 Donald brought Claire to Victoria. The couple divided their time between their country house and their town house at 220 Domain Road, South Yarra. They entertained often at Mooramong, which they transformed from a staid Victorian homestead into a jazz-age folly with Art Deco cocktail bar, swimming pool, games room, and a bathroom reminiscent of a film star's dressing-room. On their frequent trips to Melbourne to attend the races, the cinema and innumerable cocktail parties, they travelled in their Silver Ghost Rolls Royce. Wearing smart hats and chic outfits, and often adorned with her diamonds, Claire was an exotic figure at Government House functions and at the race-course.

Donald inherited his father's devotion to horse-breeding and racing: his most successful horse was Contador, winner of the Victoria Racing Club's Grand National Hurdle in 1962. Mackinnon served on the Ripon Shire Council, and he and Claire were life governors of Skipton hospital. A devoted animal lover, she was vice-president of the Lort Smith [q.v.] Hospital for Sick Animals, North Melbourne. Donald Mackinnon died of a coronary occlusion on 22 December 1974 at South Yarra and was cremated; his estate was sworn for probate at $2 111 729. Claire died on 25 September 1978 at Windsor, Melbourne; she, too, was cremated. After generous bequests to friends, family members and animal-welfare bodies, she left the remainder of her estate to the National Trust of Australia (Victoria) for the creation of a wildlife sanctuary and flora and fauna park at Mooramong. The property now has many rare species of plants and provides a habitat for the endangered eastern barred bandicoot. Judy Cassab's portrait of Donald reveals a distinguished-looking man, with a moustache and self-deprecating smile; Reshid Bey's portrait depicts Claire wearing furs and jewels; both paintings are held at Mooramong.

Photoplay, Dec 1924; *Film Index*, no 3, 1970, p 12; *Classic Images* (Muscatine, Iowa, US), no 179, May 1990, p 44; *Argus*, 1 Apr 1937; *NY Times*, 18 Oct 1978; D. Hellier, Social History Report on Mooramong, Skipton (1989) *and* Mooramong Collection (National Trust of Aust, Vic Branch, Melb); Mackinnon albums, National Trust Collection (SLV); information from Mrs J. Mercer, Derrinallum, Vic.
                                        VIRGINIA MAXWELL

MACKINNON, DONALD (1892-1965), pastoralist and diplomat, was born on 30 April 1892 at Prahran, Melbourne, eldest of six children of Victorian-born parents Donald Mackinnon [q.v.10], barrister, and his wife Hilda Eleanor Marie, née Bunny. His grandfathers were Daniel Mackinnon and Frederick Bunny [qq.v.5,3]; Rupert Bunny [q.v.7] was his uncle. After attending Melbourne Church of England Grammar School, young Donald boarded at Geelong Church of England Grammar School where he won prizes for Latin and Greek, edited the school magazine and was a prefect. He enrolled in law at the University of Melbourne and entered Ormond [q.v.5] College in 1910. From 1911 to 1913 he read classics at New College, Oxford, but did not graduate.

Having served (from 1911) in the ranks of the King Edward's Horse, Mackinnon was commissioned in March 1914. He was sent to the Western Front in April 1915. Wounded on 29 March 1916, he was evacuated to London. In 1916-17 he commanded reserve units in Ireland. He returned to France as a captain in 1918 and, following the Armistice, again embarked for Ireland. At All Saints Church, Grangegorman, Dublin, on 12 June 1917 he had married Minella Beatrice Seymour with the rites of the Church of Ireland.

By 1919 Mackinnon was back in Australia. He drove cattle on his uncle's property, Marion Downs, near Boulia, Queensland, then moved to Melbourne where he completed (by correspondence) a course in accountancy. Failing to secure management of any of the family properties, and spurred by his wife's unhappiness in Melbourne, he took her to England in 1924. He worked for the Union Cold Storage Co. Ltd in London's Smithfield market. Following his divorce, he married Mary Hindle James, a 27-year-old physiotherapist, on 10 September 1927 at the register office, St Marylebone.

When the meat merchants, Vestey Bros Ltd, offered Mackinnon an opportunity to represent their interests in Argentina, he sailed for Buenos Aires in 1929. Appointed a director (1937) of Anglo Frigorifico, he was widely respected in commercial circles. During World War II he was a member of 'Los Tamberos', a clandestine organization formed to combat the activities of Germans in Argentina. Despite his British connexions, he retained a strong sense of his nationality and wanted to expand trade between Australia and South America. He later claimed that he had 'been selling Australia in one form or another since 1929'.

In 1946 Mackinnon returned home. Settling on the family property, Marida Yallock, near Terang, Victoria, he soon became involved in local politics and was elected president of the Terang branch of the Returned Sailors', Soldiers' and Airmen's Imperial League of Australia. He joined the State executive of the Liberal Party and was its vice-president in 1948. That year cabinet appointed him to the Victorian Inland Meat Authority. In August 1949 he won the presidency of the Liberal and Country Party of Victoria. He was a co-opted member of the Commonwealth Scientific and Industrial Research Organization's advisory council in 1952-57.

Mackinnon had gained extensive knowledge of South America's primary and secondary industries, of its politics, and of the international trade in meat. This expertise, and his knowledge of Spanish and Portuguese, proved assets when he was posted (1957) as Australian minister to Brazil. In 1958 he was appointed C.B.E. and promoted ambassador. His 'unusual but completely effective' approach to diplomacy was praised. Returning to Victoria in 1960, he led the Australian trade mission to South America in 1962.

A tall man of military bearing, Mackinnon had a purposeful manner, a quiet sense of humour and an ability to communicate ideas. He was forthright, energetic and gentlemanly. Initially a small 'l' Liberal, he grew suspicious of government subsidies and in 1964-65 opposed the introduction of a reserve-price scheme for wool. At the same time, however, he feared that the Liberal Party would be unduly influenced by big business. Described as a 'driving force' in the party, he worked closely with leading members of the parliamentary wing, including Sir Robert Menzies

[q.v.]. Mackinnon advised the Federal treasurer Harold Holt [q.v.14] on rural policy and lent his support to the aspiring Andrew Peacock.

A director of Trufood of Australia Pty Ltd, Mackinnon was a member of the Australian Primary Producers' Union and president (1964) of the Melbourne Club. His newspaper articles (1960-62) provided a lively commentary on South American trade, politics and social issues. He died on 2 May 1965 at Terang and was buried in the local cemetery with Presbyterian forms; his wife, daughter and two sons survived him, as did the daughter of his first marriage.

M. H. Mackinnon, *For all that time has held* (priv print, Yamba, NSW, 1993); *Pastoral Review*, 17 May 1965, p 469; *Age* (Melb), 26 Oct 1948, 1 Jan 1958, 7 Dec 1961, 3 May 1965, 25 May 1966; *Sun News-Pictorial*, 4 Aug 1949, 3 May 1965; *SMH*, 13 Oct 1949, 3 May 1965; D. Mackinnon letters and reports, 1950-65 (NL).   SUZANNE L. G. RICKARD

MACKINNON, DONALD DE BURGH D'ARCY (1900-1963), pastoralist, was born on 17 December 1900 at Madras, India, son of Victorian-born parents Donald de Burgh d'Arcy Mackinnon, businessman, and his wife Edith Mary, née Orr. His father, a kinsman of (Sir) Lauchlan Mackinnon [q.v.10], was a bloodstock-dealer and horse-trainer at Madras who returned to Melbourne and established the firm of Mackinnon & Cox Pty Ltd which reputedly sold the racehorse Bernborough to A. O. Romano [q.v.11].

Young Donald, known as 'Dan', was privately tutored before attending Geelong Church of England Grammar School in 1915-17. He returned to the family's Western District property and later went jackerooing in the Riverina, New South Wales. In the mid-1920s he arrived in Western Australia as overseer of Edjudina, a sheep-station near Leonora. Appointed manager (1926) of Pinnacles station—part-owned by (Sir) Chester Manifold [q.v.]—in the vicinity of Lawlers, he was responsible for converting the 760 000-acre (308 000 ha) cattle-run to a sheep-station. The run was fenced, windmills erected, and quality breeding rams were imported from M. S. Hawker's North Bungaree station, South Australia. At St Columba's Presbyterian Church, Cottesloe, on 15 January 1934 Mackinnon married Marion Adeline ('Angie'), daughter of Robert Bunning [q.v.7].

Pinnacles became recognized as one of the best improved properties in the region, renowned for its superior wool clip, its training of jackeroos and its cricket matches. Jackeroos were taught station-management, and expected to behave like gentlemen. They stood as women entered the room and dressed for dinner, wearing properly knotted bow-ties; they also learned to converse on all subjects, and to play cricket and tennis. Mackinnon gave his sons similar instruction. When they came home from school they shook hands with all the station staff, and did the same again when they left.

Mackinnon was a leader in the Leonora district. He served on the Lawlers Road Board (chairman 1928-29) and the reconstituted Leonora Road Board (chairman 1954-56). In 1947 he acquired a share in Pinnacles Pty Ltd, but his family did not own the station until after his death. As vice-president of the Liberal and Country League and chairman of its Kalgoorlie division in the mid-1950s, Mackinnon campaigned vigorously throughout the constituency in support of L.C.L. candidates. He was also an executive-member (1957-62) of the Pastoralists' (and Graziers') Association of Western Australia.

A small man with a touch of red in his hair that matched his forthright and sometimes fiery nature, Mackinnon gave of his best and expected others to do likewise. He was passionate about sport, keen on reading and staunch in argument. His relationship with one particular bishop was characterized by a long-running difference of opinion over ownership of the bell from the old Lawlers Church which Mackinnon had acquired and refused to return. At Murchison and in the North-West, he regularly organized cricket matches; Pinnacles had its own cricket pitch, tennis-court and swimming-pool. Mackinnon died of cerebrovascular disease on 31 January 1963 in Perth and was cremated; his wife, daughter and three sons survived him.

Elders-GM Weekly (Perth), 7 Feb 1963; *Pastoralist and Grazier* (Perth), 12, no 19, Feb 1963; *Countryman* (Perth), 21 Feb 1963; Pinnacles station papers (BL); family papers, held by Mr D. Mackinnon, Peppermint Grove; information from Mrs M. A. Mackinnon, Mosman Park, Perth.

JENNY MILLS

MACKINOLTY, GEORGE JOHN WILLIAM (1895-1951), air force officer, was born on 24 March 1895 at Leongatha, Victoria, second child of Australian-born parents James Mickleburg Mackinolty, labourer, and his wife Mary, née Windover. Educated at state schools to merit certificate level, George completed a course at the Central Business College, Melbourne, while working as a coach and motor-body builder. On 17 August 1914 he enlisted in the Permanent Military Forces. The practical skills he had acquired facilitated his allocation to the Aviation Instructional Staff as an air mechanic. Regarded as 'a timber expert', he quickly earned pro-

motion to sergeant and was placed in charge of the A.I.S. woodworkers.

On 1 August 1915 Mackinolty transferred to the Australian Imperial Force. That month he led a group of mechanics who were sent to reinforce Australian airmen fighting in Mesopotamia. Employed as a senior rigger in No.30 Squadron, Royal Flying Corps, in 1915-16, he was promoted flight sergeant and mentioned in dispatches. He served in the Middle East in 1916-17 with No.68 (Australian) Squadron, R.F.C. (later renamed No.2 Squadron, Australian Flying Corps), then completed a series of postings in England. Described by one commanding officer as a sober, capable, conscientious and hard-working individual who was 'a particularly good organizer' and an 'excellent' leader, Mackinolty was commissioned in the A.F.C. in March 1918 as an equipment officer.

In April 1918 he was appointed officer-in-charge of an aeroplane-repair section at Minchinhampton, Gloucestershire. In December 1919 he moved to Hendon, Middlesex, to supervise the packing and preparation for shipment of 128 aircraft which the R.A.F. donated to the nascent Australian air force. Mackinolty also found time to complete specialist aeronautical-engineering training before returning to Melbourne in October 1920. His A.I.F. appointment terminated on 4 January 1921. He took a job as a motor-accessories agent and studied (by correspondence) internal combustion engines. Following the establishment of the (Royal) Australian Air Force as an independent service in March 1921, he was appointed flying officer, 'Q' List (Stores and Accounting Branch), on 8 August. He gained field-experience with No.1 Aircraft Depot, Point Cook (1921-24), and No.3 Squadron, Richmond, New South Wales (1925-29), and did staff work at R.A.A.F. Headquarters, Melbourne (1924-25). At Christ Church, South Yarra, on 20 November 1924 he married with Anglican rites 20-year-old Eileen Fairbairn Moore.

By the time Mackinolty left No.3 Squadron he had acquired an exceptional knowledge not only of stores and accounting but also of explosives, barracks management, mechanical transport and technical equipment. Yet it was as a staff officer at R.A.A.F. Headquarters that he made his distinctive contribution to the air force. Appointed director of transport and equipment as a flight lieutenant in 1929, he held the posts of director of equipment from 1935 and director of supply from 1940, and was again director of equipment from 1941. He rose steadily in rank to group captain (1940).

In 1929-40 the R.A.A.F.'s senior equipment post of air member for supply had alternated between two pilots, Air Commodore W. H. Anderson and Group Captain A. L. T. Cole [qq.v.13]. As their right-hand man for over a decade, Mackinolty took much of the load and provided the specialist advice they needed. In 1930 a confidential annual report noted that he had carried 'the bulk of the supply work for the R.A.A.F. for over a year'. Other reports recorded his 'conspicuous ability' across the range of supply tasks. He was appointed O.B.E. in 1937.

Confident in his ability and calm under pressure, Mackinolty was approachable and well liked. His professional competence was complemented by his impressive presence: he was 6 ft 0½ in. (184 cm) tall, with dark brown hair, hazel eyes and slightly prominent features. In June 1942 he was promoted acting air commodore and appointed air member for supply and equipment in his own right. R.A.A.F. personnel increased fiftyfold between 1939 and 1945. It was Mackinolty's responsibility to equip and sustain every individual, to resupply every unit, and to provide spare parts for every aircraft. His success in so doing was one of the R.A.A.F.'s great and unsung achievements of World War II.

Mackinolty was promoted acting air vice marshal in January 1947 and to the substantive rank in October 1948. In addition to his duties as A.M.S.E., he was honorary treasurer (1941-51) of the Returned Sailors', Soldiers' and Airmen's Imperial League of Australia. He died of cancer on 24 February 1951 at the Air Force Hospital, Laverton, Victoria; his wife, son and daughter survived him. Widely respected, and effectively head of the R.A.A.F.'s supply system for twenty-two consecutive years, Mackinolty was one of the few who had made a substantial contribution to the development of both the A.F.C. and the R.A.A.F.

D. Gillison, *Royal Australian Air Force 1939-1942* (Canb, 1962); F. M. Cutlack, *The Australian Flying Corps*, intro G. Odgers (Brisb, 1984); C. D. Coulthard-Clark, *The Third Brother* (Syd, 1991); A. Stephens, *Going Solo* (Canb, 1995); information from Air Marshal Sir Valston Hancock, Nedlands, Perth, and Air Cdre C. W. Probert, Runaway Bay, Qld.   ALAN STEPHENS

MACKINTOSH, ANNE JOSEPHINE; *see* ELDER

MACKINTOSH, GRACE (1890-1954), headmistress and college lecturer, was born on 5 September 1890 at Aberdeen, Scotland, daughter of John Mackintosh, bookseller and historian, and his wife Grace Smith, née Knight. Her father was a doctor of laws, the author of *The History of Civilisation in Scotland* (four volumes, 1878-88) and other works on Scottish history. Young Grace attended the University of Aberdeen (M.A., 1914), graduating with second-class honours in English language and literature. Having completed a teacher's training certificate at the University of Cambridge in 1915, she taught at the Royal Academy, Inverness, and at the Central School, Aberdeen (later Aberdeen Academy).

In 1930, during the Depression, Miss Mackintosh was appointed principal of Columba Girls' College, Dunedin, New Zealand, a Presbyterian day- and boarding-school. Her health deteriorated in the cold climate of the South Island and she was afflicted with rheumatoid arthritis. She found it difficult to make decisions, even to the point of worrying over the marks to be awarded to each girl. After only three years she applied successfully for the position of principal of Presbyterian Ladies' College, Pymble, Sydney, where she succeeded Nancy Jobson [q.v.9].

Tall, with short hair which was greying by the time she had arrived in the antipodes, Mackintosh experienced great difficulty in adjusting to life as a headmistress in Australia, just as she had in New Zealand. At both schools she faced declining enrolments due to uncertain economic conditions. Despite her academic attainments, she found it hard to relate closely to the staff and girls. The younger pupils, in particular, could not understand her Scottish brogue. Believing that the fall in enrolments provided opportunities for new ideas, she tried a number of educational experiments, such as instituting an ex-students' weekend.

To many at both Columba and P.L.C. Pymble, Mackintosh appeared deeply religious—almost mystical in her outlook—as she endeavoured to interpret Presbyterianism for a twentieth-century audience. At P.L.C. she introduced a new college prayer: written in the form of a Collect, and based in part on a Greek hymn to Zeus, and on the words of St Paul and St Augustine, it attempted to bind the girls to centuries of religion and to emphasize the bonds of faith as the basis of education. Revealingly, it was the loss of her own Christian faith that finally led to her decision to resign from P.L.C. in 1936.

Following a visit home, Mackintosh came back to Sydney and taught in state secondary schools. She was seconded from North Sydney Girls' High School in 1943 to act as lecturer in English literature at Teachers' College, Sydney, replacing the long-serving Elizabeth Skillen [q.v.11], and remained as an acting-lecturer on temporary appointments until 1 March 1953. Although she was by then beyond middle age, several of her colleagues believed that she was a good lecturer, but she made little impact on the overall life of the college. Returning to Scotland to live with her brother John, Grace Mackintosh died of cancer on 23 March 1954 at Aberdeen.

DNB, supp, 1912-21; V. A. Sheddon, *Columba College* (Dunedin, NZ, 1965); M. Coleman, *This is Pymble College 1916-1991* (Syd, 1991); *Mag of the Presbyterian Ladies' College*, Pymble (Syd), 1935; *Pymble Ex-Students' Magazine*, 1935-36; *Aberdeen University Review*, 35, 1953-54, p 439; Teachers' records, Dept of Education (NSW) archives, Syd; personal information.   G. E. SHERINGTON

McLAREN, ROBERT KERR (1902-1956), army officer and veterinarian, was born on 27 April 1902 at Pathhead, Fifeshire, Scotland, son of James Bryce McLaren, chemist, and his wife Annie Maxwell, née Kerr. Emigrating to Australia (probably in the 1920s), Bob practised as a veterinary surgeon around Bundaberg, Queensland. Although he belonged to the Church of Scotland, he married 40-year-old Catherine Ahearn with Catholic rites on 18 June 1938 at the Sacred Heart Church, Childers.

On 12 March 1941 McLaren joined the Citizen Military Forces; on 23 April he transferred to the Australian Imperial Force. He was then 5 ft 11 ins (180 cm) tall, lean and sharp-featured, with fair hair and blue eyes. In January 1942 he sailed for Singapore with the 2nd/10th Ordnance Field Workshops. When the Japanese took the island in the following month, he became a prisoner of war at Changi. Within days he escaped with two other Australians and headed to the north-west. Betrayed by some Malayans, they were captured by the Japanese. The three men were made to face a firing squad on six successive mornings at Seremban before being taken to Pudu Gaol, Kuala Lumpur. By September they were back in Changi.

As part of 'E' Force, McLaren was among five hundred British and five hundred Australian prisoners transferred to Borneo in March 1943. The Australians were taken to a camp on Berhala Island, at the entrance to Sandakan harbour in British North Borneo. McLaren and Lieutenant Rex Blow made contact with Filipino guerrillas who helped them and five others to escape in June. Another Australian, already at large, joined the group which then sailed to the island of Tawitawi in the Philippines. Attaching themselves to an American-led guerrilla force, the men sailed for Mindanao in October. McLaren had been promoted sergeant in July. He was to serve with distinction in the Philippines, receiving a field commission (January 1944) and the rank of temporary captain (April 1945).

From September 1944 McLaren skippered an armed whaleboat off Mindanao. He attacked Japanese small craft and coastal installations with dash and aggression, qualities he also displayed when commanding combat patrols on land. On 2 April 1945 he and Blow headed elements of the guerrilla force's 108th Division in an assault on the last Japanese stronghold in Lanao province. Lieutenant Colonel Charles W. Hedges, the American divisional commander, recorded that the fighting ended with the capture of the garrison and the destruction of about 450 enemy troops. For his efforts at sea and on land, McLaren won the Military Cross and was mentioned in dispatches. His M.C. citation read: 'throughout the whole of his service with the Guerilla Forces, Captain McLaren displayed outstanding leadership in battle and had no regard for his personal safety. His cheerful imperturbability was an inspiration to all with whom he came into contact'. The Americans awarded him the Philippines Liberation ribbon.

Ordered home in April 1945, McLaren joined the Services Reconnaissance Department, a section of the Allied Intelligence Bureau which was largely Australian-manned. On 30 June he led four S.R.D. operatives in a pre-invasion parachute operation near Balikpapan, Borneo. One man was injured on landing, another was taken in an ambush, and the Japanese captured their supplies and radios. McLaren, however, carried on with his task and slipped through enemy lines on 6 July to report to 7th Division headquarters. His deeds earned him a Bar to his M.C. His last wartime mission, code-named Agas 5, saw him (as a substantive captain) lead an eight-man team to Talasai, British North Borneo, on 27 July. After World War II had ended, the party remained to administer to civilian needs until 10 September. McLaren returned to Australia on 5 November and transferred to the Reserve of Officers on 15 January 1946.

A natural leader and a man of driving energy, McLaren found no satisfactory occupation in Australia and accepted a post as a government veterinary officer in the Territory of Papua-New Guinea. In early 1956 he left the public service and took over a coffee plantation near Wau. On 3 March that year he accidentally backed his Jeep into a pergola and was killed when struck by falling timber. Survived by his wife, he was buried in the European cemetery at Wau.

H. Richardson, *One-Man War* (Syd, 1957); S. Ross, *And Tomorrow Freedom* (Syd, 1989); A. Powell, *War by Stealth* (Melb, 1996).

ALAN POWELL

McLAREN, WILLIAM ALEXANDER (1898-1973), public servant, was born on 8 May 1898 in Sydney, elder son of Australian-born parents William McLaren, carpenter, and his wife Esther May, née Manning. Educated at Woollahra Public and Sydney Technical High schools, Bill studied (1917-18) science at the University of Sydney until he was struck down by pneumonic influenza. In 1920 he joined the New South Wales Public Service. He worked with the Department of Audit (1920-24) and the State Superannuation Board before becoming (1936) an inspector with the Treasury. At St Peter's Anglican Church, Watsons Bay, on 14 September 1935 he married Doris Elsie Josephine Brooks (d.1951), a 31-year-old dancing teacher; they were to have two children.

When it launched a War Service Land Settlement scheme in 1945, the Federal government was determined to avoid problems encountered by the State schemes after World War I. It aimed to settle fewer men, but to settle them 'properly'. McLaren was appointed director. His division examined State-initiated proposals, and funded training courses, living allowances and credit arrangements. Although some States (New South Wales in particular) chafed at Commonwealth intervention, the undertaking was largely successful.

In 1949 the scheme came under the control of the Department of the Interior, of which McLaren was appointed secretary. His department had many diverse functions, including administering the Australian Capital Territory and managing public service transfers from Melbourne to Canberra. (Sir) William Dunk, chairman of the Commonwealth Public Service Board, was so frustrated by slow progress with the transfers that he damned the Department of the Interior for showing 'neither activity nor imagination'. None the less, the blunt McLaren did drive his staff hard. Some found him an easy man with whom to have an argument, and his deputy H. A. Barrenger [q.v.13] was often obliged to act as peacemaker. McLaren had little time for the National Capital Planning and Development Committee or for the A.C.T. Advisory Council: 'You get sick and tired of waiting for decisions from these committees'. He was equally forthright in defending his department against adverse reports by the auditor-general. Under McLaren, householders lost benefits such as free water and hedge-clipping. In 1954 he was appointed C.B.E.

McLaren was unenthusiastic about Walter Burley Griffin's [q.v.9] plan for the national capital; in his eyes an art gallery and an opera house would be 'white elephants' in Canberra. In 1953 the Department of the Interior made a hasty attempt to restrict Griffin's 'West Lake' to a 'ribbon of water': the proposal was abandoned in the face of parliamentary criticism. A strong and independent National Capital Development Commission was established in 1958. Rankled by this initiative, McLaren responded to the N.C.D.C.'s early requests for assistance with such comments as 'Pig's arse' and 'Find your own bloody office', but a satisfactory working relationship gradually developed.

At the Church of St John the Baptist, Canberra, on 23 April 1952 McLaren had married Phyllis Maude Coles, a 39-year-old manageress. He was an active member of the Royal Canberra Golf and Canberra Bowling clubs. Soon after his retirement in 1963, he moved to Moruya, New South Wales. Survived by his wife, and by the son and daughter of his first marriage, he died on 30 September 1973 at Moruya and was cremated.

Dept of Post-war Reconstruction, *The Farmer was a Fighting Man* (Canb, 1949); W. Dunk, *They Also Serve* (Canb, 1974); J. Gibbney, *Canberra 1913-1953* (Canb, 1988); E. Sparke, *Canberra 1954-1980* (Canb, 1988); J. Overall, *Canberra* (Canb, 1995); *Canb Times*, 19 Mar 1963, 1 Oct 1973; J. J. Dedman papers (NL).   IAN CARNELL

McLARTY, DAVID LYON (1889-1962), engineer and dockyard director, was born on 22 September 1889 at Penang, Straits Settlements (Malaysia), son of Farquhar Matheson McLarty, mechanical engineer, and his wife Wilhelmina, née Lyon. Educated at the Collegiate School, Greenock, and at the Glasgow and West of Scotland Technical College, Lyon was apprenticed to Scott & Sons, shipbuilders and repairers. He transferred to the firm's drawing office, joined John Brown & Co. Ltd, shipbuilders of Clydebank, and became assistant works manager with Barclay, Curie & Co. Ltd, shipbuilders. On 2 April 1921 at St Mary's Cathedral, Glasgow, he married with Episcopalian rites Meta Dusha Tucker, an office manageress; they were to have no children, but gave ready affection to those of friends. From 1922 McLarty was based in China as assistant general manager of the Shanghai Dock & Engineering Co. Ltd. Reaching Sydney in 1925, he joined the staff of Cockatoo Island Dockyard. He managed the engineering firm of Morison & Bearby Ltd at Newcastle in 1927-37 and Robison Bros & Co. Pty Ltd in Melbourne in 1937-39, and was a director (1939-40) of Malleys Ltd in Sydney.

Due to the exigencies of World War II, the McKell government decided in 1941 to build a State dockyard at Newcastle, using much of the plant and buildings from the Walsh Island Dockyard and Engineering Works which had ceased operations eight years earlier. McLarty was appointed director. The dockyard at Carrington launched its first vessel in July 1943. By 1945 it employed 1329 people and had built two vessels for the Royal Australian Navy and twenty-two for the United States; it had also repaired six hundred ships and completed other engineering projects. At the end of 1957 the vessels built numbered forty-seven and the site had grown to 30 acres (12 ha), well equipped with workshops, berths and a floating dock. Total turnover was £22.5 million. The £3 million turnover in 1956-57 included a profit of £1.4 million, available for interest repayment and a share at 10 per cent among the 1700 employees.

Appointed O.B.E. in 1954, in the following year McLarty urged his staff to appreciate their workplace and what they produced: 'especially does this apply to the creation of a ship [beyond] which there is no more interesting and comprehensive product of man'. He retired in 1957, declaring that he had been fortunate in his life and colleagues. Former staff and neighbours recalled his outgoing personality, leadership, considerate nature, and his modest residence amid the Newcastle establishment on The Hill overlooking the harbour. They also remembered his lively speeches and social skills at many ship-launching ceremonies. Tall and genial, he enjoyed playing golf and bowls, and belonged to the Newcastle Club, the Royal Automobile Club of Australia and the Rotary Club of Newcastle.

McLarty also practised as a part-time consulting engineer and was founding chairman of the Newcastle Industrial Promotion Panel. He was president (1947-48) of the Newcastle division, Institution of Engineers, Australia, and a member of the Institution of Engineers and Shipbuilders in Scotland, the North-East Coast Institution of Engineers and Shipbuilders, England (1946-62), and the New South Wales Electricity Commission (1950-57). His support for technical education and public service continued into his retirement. He had joined the Technical Education District Council in 1944 and was a director (1956) of the Hunter Valley Research Foundation. A council-member (1957-62) of the University of New South Wales, he was foundation chairman (1962) of the council of Newcastle University College.

Five days after his wife's death, McLarty died on 30 November 1962 at Royal Newcastle Hospital and was cremated. He had left an indelible mark on the industry and city. His constant faith in the enterprise and the workmanship of his staff suggests an antipodean version of M'Andrew, Rudyard Kipling's Scots marine engineer: 'Predestination in the stride o' yon connectin'-rod'.

J. Armstrong (ed), *Shaping the Hunter* (Newcastle, NSW, 1983); EJE Group, *Record of the State Dockyard* (Newcastle, 1993); State Dockyard (NSW), *Annual Report*, 1953-57 and *Shipshape*, Dec 1955, June 1957; *SMH*, 21, 22 Aug 1941, 10 June 1954, 1 Dec 1962; *Newcastle Sun*, 24 Jan 1956; *Newcastle Morning Herald*, 1 Dec 1962, 2 May 1972, 23 Sept 1976; personal information.
L. E. FREDMAN

McLARTY, SIR DUNCAN ROSS (1891-1962), pastoralist and premier, was born on 17 March 1891 at Pinjarrah, Western Australia, youngest of seven children of Edward McLarty, a Western Australian-born farmer and grazier who became a member of the Legislative Council, and his wife Mary Jane, née Campbell. Educated at Pinjarra State School and the High School, Perth, Ross worked on his father's property. On 12 January 1916 he enlisted in the Australian Imperial Force. He fought on the Western Front (from November 1916) and won the Military Medal in January 1918. Commissioned in May, he was promoted lieutenant in August and wounded in action that month. His A.I.F. appointment terminated in Perth on 22 August 1919.

After the war McLarty returned to farming. At St John's Anglican Church, Pinjarra, on 25 October 1922 he married Violet Olive Margaret Herron. He served (from 1925) as a justice of the peace and belonged to the Returned Sailors' and Soldiers' (and Airmen's) Imperial League of Australia. As a Nationalist candidate, he campaigned on the slogan, 'A Practical Farmer for a Farming Electorate', and won the Legislative Assembly seat of Murray-Wellington in 1930. In parliament, he focused on rural issues. During World War II he commanded the 4th Battalion, Volunteer Defence Corps. When (Sir) Ross McDonald [q.v.] resigned as leader of the Liberal Party and the Opposition in December 1946 to make way for a rural leader, McLarty succeeded him. On 1 April 1947, following a surprise election victory, he became premier, heading a coalition of the Liberal Party and the Country and Democratic League.

As premier McLarty held various portfolios: he was treasurer (until 23 February 1953), and minister for housing (until 5 January 1948), forests (until 5 January 1948, and from 7 October 1949 to 24 October 1950) and the North-West (until 24 October 1950, and from 17 January 1952 to 23 February 1953). McDonald—even in his retirement from politics—remained McLarty's most influential adviser, but McLarty also drew on the knowledge of senior public servants, chiefly under-treasurer (Sir) Alexander Reid and Ralph Doig, under-secretary to the Premier's Department. During his six-year premiership three million acres (1.2 million ha) were opened for farming, the Kwinana industrial area was established, housing shortages were alleviated, and transport and power supplies were improved. Troubled by postwar shortages, the government delayed the lifting of wartime controls. McLarty was criticized by some younger Liberals for being too cautious, and relations between his government and the party organization often proved difficult. Yet he strengthened the cohesion of his administration by his patience and genial manner, and got on well with the deputy-premier Arthur Watts [q.v.]. Knighted in January 1953, he lost the elections one month later, but continued to lead the Opposition.

McLarty travelled home to Pinjarra most weekends, served as chairman of the Murray District Hospital Board and held a number of pastoral investments, including a controlling interest in Liveringa station, near Derby. Violet McLarty was also active in electorate and community affairs as State president (1953-55) of the Country Women's Association, governor of Fairbridge [q.v.8] Farm School and commissioner (1953-58) of the Western Australian branch of the Girl Guides' Association. Sir Ross resigned as leader of the Opposition in March 1957 and from parliament (because of ill health) in May 1962. Survived by his wife and three sons, he died on 22 December 1962 at Pinjarra and was buried in the local cemetery. His estate was sworn for probate at £65 411.

K. West, *Power in the Liberal Party* (Melb, 1965); *West Australian*, 13 Feb 1957, 19 May, 24 Dec 1962; M. McLarty, Sir Duncan Ross McLarty, K.B.E., M.M. (BL); McLarty family papers, 1887-1969 (BL); Sir Ross McLarty, political ephemera, PR3597/1-10 (BL); R. Jamieson, interviews with R. Doig, oral history transcript, 1984-86, OH2144 (BL).
LENORE LAYMAN

McLEAN, CAROLINE MARY (1883-1965), pony-breeder, was born on 8 May 1883 at Murrumburrah, New South Wales, second child and elder daughter of English-born parents George Charles Knight Gregson, bank clerk and later grazier, and his wife Charlotte Louise, née Hughes. Charlotte had attended a finishing-school in Switzerland and supervised her children's education. Caroline was raised at Cunningham Plains station, near Harden, and became an expert horsewoman. On 18 January 1912 at St Paul's Anglican Church, Murrumburrah, she married Stephen Norman McLean (d.1955), a surveyor and engineer. She accompanied him to Papua where he was appointed assistant government surveyor. In 1914, pregnant with her elder daughter, she returned to Sydney. Her husband transferred from the Militia to the Australian Imperial Force and sailed for Egypt in 1915, soon after their second daughter was born. Captain McLean served with the 2nd Light Horse Regiment and returned to Australia on 4 March 1919.

Having bought a house at Burradoo in 1917, Caroline moved there with her daughters. In 1922 she and Stephen acquired the residue of a ninety-nine-year lease of Burradoo Park, 173 acres (70 ha) on the Wingecarribee River. Mrs McLean separated from her husband—who had returned to Papua to search for oil—in 1928; they were to be divorced in 1943. In 1930 she established a pony stud at Burradoo. She had two good, unregistered pony mares and purchased another, Fraser's Dolly, whose parentage was recorded.

Mrs McLean mated Dolly with Retford Prince, a colt bred by Sir Samuel Hordern [q.v.9] from the imported Welsh sire, Greylight, and an Australian mare. The colt, Burradoo Rex (foaled 1930), was to be an influential force in the establishment of the 'Standard of Excellence' for the Australian pony. He sired numerous champion progeny, and won many awards at local shows and in Sydney. Mrs McLean experimented successfully with close- and line-breeding. Burradoo Gay, by Burradoo Rex out of another of his fillies, Burradoo Bonny, was outstandingly successful, both in the show ring and at stud. A prolific sire of sound ponies, Burradoo Rex died in the autumn of 1963. His last crop of foals was born in the following spring.

Throughout 1930 Mrs McLean worked to assist in the formation of the body which, in 1931, became known as the Australian Pony Stud Book Society. She remained a member until her death. Caroline and her elder daughter Jean (who had developed her own Berrima pony stud) helped to arrange the export of Australian ponies to the United States of America, where Burradoo Rex lines were highly prized. They also exported to New Zealand. There were Burradoo ponies in studs throughout the mainland States.

Caroline McLean died on 29 March 1965 at her Burradoo home and was buried in the Anglican section of Bowral cemetery; her daughters survived her. The Mrs C. M. McLean trophy, presented to the supreme champion Australian pony at the Royal Easter Show, Sydney, commemorates her work. The stud was dispersed in 1977.

Aust Pony Stud Book, 1, 1936, 2, 1942, 3, 1947, 4, 1949; L. Howlett, *Ponies in Australia* (Syd, 1979), and *Complete Book of Ponies* (Syd, 1984, 1986, 1989); information from Mrs L. Howlett, Gerringong, NSW.
ZITA DENHOLM

McLEAN, CHARLES (1889-1978), police magistrate, was born on 5 December 1889 at Goornong, Victoria, second of six children of Charles McLean, a schoolteacher from Scotland, and his Victorian-born wife Mary Louisa, née Hay. Educated (from the age of $3\frac{1}{2}$) at his father's schools, first at Goornong and then at Mortlake, young Charles proceeded to Grenville College, Ballarat. He entered the clerical division of the State public service in 1906 and began work in the Department of Public Instruction. In 1909 McLean joined the courts branch of the Crown Law Department and was appointed to the Melbourne City Court. The derelict building was draughty and the coir-matting on the floors stank of tobacco-spittle. Having passed the clerk of courts' examination, he transferred in 1910 to South Melbourne, where he was responsible for the Court of Petty Sessions at St Kilda and at Port Melbourne. In August 1913 he was appointed clerk of courts at Rushworth.

Enlisting in the Australian Imperial Force on 27 July 1915, McLean served with the 24th Battalion on the Western Front from September 1916. He was commissioned in May 1917 and twice wounded in action (May 1917 and August 1918). His A.I.F. appointment terminated in Melbourne on 9 November 1919. On his demobilization he returned to the Crown Law Department. After a year in relieving positions, he took over the court at Beechworth. He was promoted by seniority to Hamilton (1923), Melbourne (1924), and Prahran and Richmond (1928). In 1930 he was made a police magistrate and posted to Warrnambool. He was appointed an examiner for the clerk of courts' examination in 1935 and for the police magistrates' examination in 1937.

In June 1936 McLean commenced his eighteen-year career as metropolitan police magistrate at the Melbourne City Court. There he presided with a 'stern' sense of duty. Promoted to senior metropolitan police magistrate in 1939, he later supervised country police magistrates in addition to their metropolitan counterparts. In 1948 his title became chief stipendiary magistrate. The Western Australian government appointed him a royal commissioner to inquire into trotting (1946) and betting (1948). Back in Melbourne, he sat (from 1950) on the Metropolitan Fire Brigades Appeal Tribunal.

Following his retirement as chief stipendiary magistrate in 1954, the Federal government invited McLean to chair the Commonwealth Public Service Appeals Board for Victoria and Tasmania. The State government used his services as a justice of the peace (1954), as chairman of the Indeterminate Sentences Board (1955-57) and as a member of its successor, the Adult Parole Board (1957-66); as a one-man board of inquiry, he investigated the break-out from Pentridge gaol in 1955, the living conditions of Aborigines in Victoria (1955-57) and alleged bribery on the Richmond City Council (1957). He was appointed C.B.E. in 1956.

A member of the Naval and Military Club and of the Kingston Heath Golf Club (president 1938-43, club captain 1943-45, life member 1960), McLean accompanied the Australian Amateur Golf Team which toured Britain in 1954. He died, unmarried, on 14 January 1978 at Armadale and was cremated; his estate was sworn for probate at $302 816.

W. J. Harvey, *The Red and White Diamond* (Melb, 1920); *Sun News-Pictorial*, 26 Mar, 2 Dec 1954; *Herald* (Melb), 8, 9 Apr 1954, 1 Feb 1956; *SMH*, 5 Oct, 17 Dec 1955, 2 Jan 1956, 31 Jan 1957; W. J. Cuthill, taped interview with C. McLean c1970 (held by author, Camberwell, Melb). W. J. CUTHILL

McLEAN, DONALD JAMES (1905-1975), schoolteacher and educationist, was born on 18 January 1905 at Broken Hill, New South Wales, third child of Australian-born parents Neil McLean, insurance agent, and his wife Mary Winifred, née Clune. At the age of 7 Donald lost his left arm when a detonator which he was investigating exploded. He was educated at Broken Hill Superior Public and Broken Hill High schools, and was trained (1922-23) as a primary school teacher at Teachers College, Sydney. After short postings to Coogee, Alma (Broken Hill) and Milparinka, he was appointed (June 1924) to Broken Hill North Public School where he taught until 1935, except for brief spells at Alma (1932) and Burke Ward Public School (1934). On 23 December 1930 at St Philip's Anglican Church, Broken Hill, he married Kathleen Thelma Arthur, an infants' schoolteacher. Of middle height and medium build, he had a striking personality and was a superb teacher.

In December 1935 McLean was transferred to the primary school at Curlwaa, near the junction of the Murray and Darling rivers. There, for two years, he expanded his knowledge of the far-west country of which he later wrote with great affection and humour in his novels, *The Roaring Days* (London, 1960) and *Treasure from the Earth* (Melbourne, 1963). In 1938 he moved south to a school at Barham on the Murray River; in the following year he was appointed headmaster of Griffith Public School. Posted to Sydney at the end of 1942 as headmaster of St Peters Public School, he took charge of North Newtown Boys' Intermediate High School in 1945. He moved in 1948 to the headmastership of Bankstown Central, Sydney's largest school, and in 1952 took over as head of Darlinghurst, another large school in an underprivileged area. Seconded to the Child Welfare Department in 1955, he returned to the Department of Education in January 1961 and remained editor of publications until he retired in June 1965.

McLean wrote extensively on education and child care. He completed six books describing aspects of his progressive approach to schooling and the upbringing of children, among them *The Education of the Personality* (London, 1952), based on his experiences at Bankstown, *Nature's Second Sun* (Melbourne, 1954), *Your Child and the School* (Melbourne, 1968) and *It's People that Matter* (Sydney,

1969). His views on education were sane, well balanced and persuasive, but not always popular with his administrative superiors. Schools, he argued, should be as much concerned with developing personality as with the intellect. Teachers had the fundamental tasks of understanding children's behaviour, and of providing an environment in which emotional and intellectual problems could be studied and solved. Two vital elements in the educational process were the growth of strong teacher-parent relationships, and the encouragement of pupils in the kind of active, creative work which would enrich their aesthetic and intellectual experiences.

In addition, McLean wrote three textbooks on the teaching of English, five on social studies and three on Australian history; he also published three novels, a sketchbook on Broken Hill and several journal articles. He was education correspondent for the *Sydney Morning Herald* in 1965-75, and State and national president of the New Education Fellowship. Widely appreciated by progressive educationists, he contributed to international conferences and served on the executive of the World Education Fellowship. In 1953-54 he visited Europe, toured eastern and southern parts of the United States of America on a Carnegie grant, and lectured in South Africa. Following a trip to southern Asia in 1972, he edited *The Changing Orient* (Sydney, 1974). He died of basilar artery thrombosis on 28 April 1975 at Hunters Hill and was cremated; his wife and son survived him.

R. Ward, *A Radical Life* (Melb, 1988); *New Era*, 56, no 6, July-Aug 1975, p 162; *Hemisphere*, 20, no 7, July 1976, p 12; *Inside Education*, 70, no 2, 1976, p 19; *SMH*, 24 Jan 1953, 29 Apr 1975; L. T. Hall, Donald McLean, an Australian Progressive Educator (M.Ed. thesis, Univ New England, 1986); H. de Berg, Donald McLean (taped interview, 23 Sept 1965, NL); staff card, D. J. McLean (NSW Dept of Education L, Syd); information from Dr D. J. McLean and family, Syd.   W. F. CONNELL

MACLEAN, DORA (1892-1978), horse-breeder, was born on 12 April 1892 at North Fitzroy, Melbourne, second of four children of Samuel William Gibson, draper, and his wife Mary, née Marshall, both from Glasgow, Scotland. Samuel had come to Victoria with his wife in 1889 to join his uncle William Gibson [q.v.8]; in 1908 he became manager of the Collingwood branch of Foy [qq.v.4,8] & Gibson Pty Ltd. Dora grew up at Kew and was educated at Presbyterian Ladies' College, but she was a country girl at heart and much preferred to be at Fenwick, her father's 320-acre (130 ha) property at Yan Yean. He had bought this farm in 1903 and named it after the small village of his Scottish childhood. At Fenwick he bred Clydesdales. On his death in 1918, his surviving daughters Eva and Dora inherited the property.

The sisters established a Corriedale sheep stud and exhibited with success at major shows until Eva's death in 1923. Their mother died in the same year. Dora accompanied her younger brother James on an extended tour of Europe and Britain, during which she confidently selected foundation stock from which to breed Arabian horses and Shetland ponies. She had an eye for a good horse and could pick the potential of a foal long before others could see it. Between 1924 and 1960 Dora imported nineteen Shetlands from the foremost studs in Britain. She also imported eighteen purebred Arabians, sixteen of them from the Crabbet Stud. On 1 December 1925 at the Presbyterian Church, Toorak, she married Alexander David Dick Maclean, a 29-year-old engineer who had arrived from Scotland that year to join the family firm.

All Mrs Maclean's stock was registered in stud books kept in Britain. Recognizing the need for local records, she became a foundation member of the Australian Pony Stud Book Society in 1931. She was elected to the initial committee of its Victorian branch in 1947, and later made an honorary life member. Dora was also a founding member (1956) and patron (1975-78) of the Arab Horse Society of Australasia (Arabian Horse Society of Australia), and helped to establish (1962) its Victorian branch. Highly respected in both organizations, she did more than any other to promote proper recording in the national stud books. She persistently tried to have Arabian blood formally recognized by the A.P.S.B.S., believing that the qualities it had contributed to Australian ponies in the past should be retained as an out-cross for breeders.

Before World War II Fenwick had been run by a predominantly male staff. When girls from the Australian Women's Land Army arrived to work the property, Dora liked the way they handled the horses; after the war she employed only females. The thorough training given by Mrs Maclean in stud management and show preparation guaranteed employment in the industry and assisted workers to establish their own studs. In the 1960s there were almost one hundred Shetland ponies and more than seventy Arabians sharing the property (by then 640 acres) with beef cattle.

Gifted with character rather than beauty, Dora Maclean was quite short, with clear, lively eyes her best feature. Although forthright and determined, she was a person of integrity and kindness who shared her knowledge of Arabians and Shetlands. She died on 14 September 1978 at Toorak and was cremated; her husband, daughter and two sons survived her.

The Arabian Horse in Australia (Syd, 1980); M. Costello, *Australian Pony Stud Book Society, its Growth and Development* (Melb, 1981); information from Miss V. Maclean, Whittlesea, and Hon R. Maclellan, MLA, San Remo, Vic.

HEATHER B. RONALD

MACLEAN, HECTOR (1885-1968), Presbyterian minister and theologian, was born on 2 February 1885 at Lismore, New South Wales, fourth child of Charles Maclean, a carpenter from Scotland, and his London-born wife Mary Ann, née Teideman. In 1888 the family moved to Port Chalmers, near Dunedin, New Zealand. Hector received his secondary education at Otago Boys' High School, Dunedin (dux, 1903), and won a scholarship to the University of Otago (B.A., N.Z., 1907; M.A., 1908; M.Sc., 1909); a leader in student affairs, he played Rugby for the university and graduated in 1908 with first-class honours in philosophy.

Awarded a travelling scholarship in 1910, Maclean enrolled at the United Free Church College, Glasgow, Scotland, where he was introduced to the historical, linguistic and critical scholarship then transforming biblical studies. He became a tutor in Hebrew at the college and assistant (1914-15) to Professor W. B. Stevenson, under whom he also learned Semitic languages. In 1914 he obtained a B.D. from the University of London.

The outbreak of World War I prevented Maclean from studying in Germany. Returning to New Zealand in 1915, he was ordained and inducted as minister of Knox Church, Invercargill. He enlisted in the New Zealand Expeditionary Force in October 1916, served on the Western Front with the 4th Battalion, New Zealand Rifle Brigade, and rose to sergeant. In July 1918 he was sent to England and appointed a chaplain to the forces. While on leave in Scotland, he married Agnes Hunter Stewart on 31 October that year at Crossmichael, Kirkcudbrightshire, with the forms of the Church of Scotland. He was demobilized in New Zealand in May 1919 and went back to Invercargill. Called to St Andrew's Church, Dunedin, in 1920, he developed an enduring interest in students and in the theological education of future ministers.

In 1927 Maclean was appointed to the chair of Old Testament studies at the Theological Hall of the Presbyterian Church of Victoria, Ormond [q.v.5] College. He held that chair and, from 1942, the principalship of the hall, until his retirement in 1957. Moderator (1943-44) of the Presbyterian Church of Victoria, he was concerned with the reconstruction of life in church and community when World War II had ended. He was best known as a teacher —of Hebrew and of the Old Testament

prophets—who used language meticulously. He led theological studies through a period of severely restricted resources, and, with Professor M. D. Goldman [q.v.14] of the University of Melbourne, founded the Fellowship for Biblical Studies. In 1951 the University of Edinburgh awarded him an honorary D.D.

Maclean's excursions into public life included speaking out against the attempt in 1951 to ban the Communist Party of Australia. His belief in freedom of expression of opinion and his passion for social justice gained him some critics and antagonists inside and outside the Church, but his arguments were cogent and influential. To the end of his life he retained an interest in sport, and enjoyed gardening. He died on 27 May 1968 in East Melbourne and was cremated; his wife, three sons and two daughters survived him. A portrait by Archibald Colquhoun is held by Ormond College.

Presbyterian Messenger, 30 Sept, 14 Oct, 18, 25 Nov 1927, 28 May 1943, 26 Feb, 17 Nov 1944; *Aust Presbyterian Life*, 8 June 1968; *Age* (Melb), 28 May 1968; Presbyterian Church of Vic Archives (Collins St, Melb); records of Claremont United Free Church, Glasgow, Scotland, *and* Knox Church, Invercargill, New Zealand.

DAVIS MCCAUGHEY

McLEAN, MICK (IRINYILI) (c.1888-1976), Aboriginal 'clever man', was born about 1888 near Pirlakaya well, Simpson Desert, South Australia. Irinyili belonged to the Wangkangurru people. Because his paternal grandmother was lower southern Arrernte, he learned to speak the languages of both tribes. He lived in the Poolowanna area, north of Lake Eyre, until 1900 when his group travelled south to Kallakoopah Creek. They settled in the vicinity of the nearest stations, Old Karlamurina and Cowarie on the Diamantina River. It was there he first encountered White people, European food and clothes, and horses and bullocks.

Displaying an intense interest in songs and customs, in 1901 Irinyili accompanied other young people to Goyder's Lagoon where he participated in the Mudlunga (Molonga) ceremony which involved spectacular dancing and singing, brought from the Georgina River in Queensland. Soon after, he and his immediate family moved to Arabana country (west of Lake Eyre) where they lived near the Peake telegraph-station, run by Archie McLean. Irinyili adopted his surname and was known by the given name 'Mick'. He recalled J. W. Gregory's and (Sir) Baldwin Spencer's [qq.v.9,12] visits to the district in 1901-02 and 1903 respectively. Mick McLean married Kathleen Heel Arabalka who came from Anna Creek; they were to have four daughters.

On 29 December 1921 McLean joined the Police Department in Adelaide. Paid 7s. 6d. a day, he became an outstanding tracker and was twice mentioned in the *South Australian Police Gazette* for his work. He resigned in December 1925 and was employed as head stockman on Stuart Creek station. Later, he took a job as a drover. In 1971 he retired to Port Augusta.

McLean's main interest lay in the songs, stories and totemic geography of the people of the northern Lake Eyre basin. With marked perseverance and against considerable odds, he acquired a vast store of traditional knowledge from the few remaining Aboriginal 'clever men'. Caught in a changing world, these men were reluctant to pass on their knowledge, preferring to see their traditions disappear rather than hand them to the unworthy or the unappreciative. Through his enthusiasm and intelligence, McLean managed to persuade them to teach him. He gradually became a 'clever man', the last *minbaru* from the desert. On a trip to Innamincka (to the east of the country he loved best) he once said: 'I don't like this country, it is dead men's country, nobody knows it now'. He was desperate that the culture of the northern Lake Eyre basin should not die out. Committed to its preservation, he learned the languages, customs, history and songs of the Aborigines in the region. A senior researcher from the Australian National University did extensive field-work with him over twelve years. Recordings of her interviews with McLean are held by the Australian Institute of Aboriginal and Torres Strait Islander Studies, Canberra.

Tall and thin, McLean was essentially a cheerful, if rather reticent, man. He died on 7 August 1976 at Port Augusta and was buried in the local cemetery; his wife and children survived him.

R. M. Berndt (ed), *Australian Aboriginal Anthropology* (Perth, 1970); L. A. Hercus, 'Mick McLean Irinjili', *Aust Inst of Aboriginal Studies Newsletter*, no 7, 1977, p 27, *and* 'How we danced the Mudlunga; memories of 1901 and 1902', *Aboriginal Hist*, 4, 1980, p 5, *and* 'Leaving the Simpson Desert', *Aboriginal Hist*, 9, no 1, 1985, p 22.

LUISE HERCUS

MCLEAN, WILLIAM JOHN (1918-1963), air force officer, was born on 9 July 1918 at Katanning, Western Australia, son of Australian-born parents William Willmott McLean, farmer, and his wife Rita Pearl, née Bennett. Jack was raised on the family property near Gnowangerup. Awarded a scholarship to Albany High School, he was captain of the school, and of its football, cricket and swimming teams. In 1937 he taught at Palmyra State School. Next year he entered Teachers' College, Perth. He played for Claremont in the West Australian National Football Association and was the competition's leading goal-kicker in 1938.

On 15 August 1940 McLean enlisted in the Royal Australian Air Force. He completed pilot training and received his wings on 10 February 1941. Commissioned in April, he embarked for the Middle East and in July joined No.117 (Transport) Squadron, Royal Air Force. The unit operated from bases in North Africa and Italy before being sent to India in October 1943. As a flight commander, McLean led six unarmed Dakotas on an urgent supply-dropping mission over Burma in May 1944. Fearing interception by Japanese fighters, he ordered the other aircraft back to base, continued on alone and reached his objective. In June he was promoted acting wing commander and placed in command of the squadron.

In the office of the senior marriage registrar, Calcutta, on 26 February 1945 McLean married Elfida Mary Bruce, née Ahlborn, a 28-year-old divorcee; she was a Red Cross representative at a hospital to which he flew wounded soldiers. Returning to Australia in June 1945, he was appointed commander of No.243 (Transport) Squadron, R.A.F., which was stationed at Camden, New South Wales, and operated in the Pacific theatre. His final posting (1946) was to R.A.A.F. Headquarters, Melbourne. He resigned on 7 January 1947. For leadership and courage in action he had been awarded the Air Force Cross (1944), the Distinguished Flying Cross (1944) and the Distinguished Service Order (1945)—rare honours for a transport pilot. In 1953 he was to receive the Queen's commendation.

McLean accepted a permanent commission in the R.A.F. on 7 July 1947. He served at headquarters, Transport Command, and at the Air Ministry. A member of the British bobsled team in the 1948 Winter Olympics at St Moritz, Switzerland, he played Rugby Union football and cricket for the R.A.F. He commanded No.47 Squadron (1949-51), and completed R.A.F. and joint-services staff courses. In the mid-1950s he spent three years in West Germany with the United States Air Force. Promoted group captain (1960), he was posted as R.A.F. station commander, Changi, Singapore, in December 1962, but in 1963 became seriously ill and was evacuated to England. He died of cancer on 9 November that year in Princess Mary's R.A.F. Hospital, Halton Camp, Wendover, Buckinghamshire, and was buried in the R.A.F. section of Halton churchyard. His wife and four daughters survived him, as did his stepson. Compassionate and modest, McLean got on well with all ranks, inspiring loyalty and affection.

G. Odgers, *Air War Against Japan 1943-1945* (Canb, 1957); AWM 168 and AWM 65 (AWM); information from Mrs E. McLean, Kalamunda, Perth.

MARK LAX

McLEAY, GEORGE (1892-1955), politician and businessman, was born on 6 August 1892 at Port Clinton, South Australia, son of George McLeay, farmer, and his wife Marguaretta, née Barton. The McLeays were a pioneering family, prominent in local politics. Raised on his parents' wheat-farm near Clinton Centre, young George was educated at Port Clinton Public School until 1906 when he and his three brothers were sent to Adelaide. He attended Unley Public School, took a commercial course at Muirden [q.v.10] College and began work as a clerk. Rejected for the Australian Imperial Force in 1914, he undertook civilian war-work for the duration.

George and his younger brother Jack (Sir John) went into business as accountants and agents. In time McLeay Bros Ltd became wholesale and retail merchants (specializing in furnishings and hardware) and George left most of the management to his brother. He honed his public-speaking skills as a debater in the Australian Natives' Association, joined the Freemasons and worshipped at St Andrew's Presbyterian Church, Unley. At the age of 20 he had become a member of the Unley branch of the Liberal Union. He was chairman of the Liberals' organizing committee for eleven years and was to be a permanent executive-member of the Liberal and Country League. His first effort to enter Federal parliament—standing in 1922 for the seat of Adelaide in the House of Representatives—was unsuccessful. On 21 October 1924 at St Andrew's he married 27-year-old Marcia Doreen Weston.

In September 1934 McLeay was elected a senator for South Australia; he was re-elected in 1940, defeated in 1946, and re-elected in 1949 and 1951. A member (1935-38) and chairman (1937-38) of the Senate Standing Committee on Regulations and Ordinances, he quickly rose to government whip in the Senate (1937) and led the government in that chamber from November 1938 to October 1941. Prime Minister J. A. Lyons [q.v.10] appointed him vice-president of the Executive Council in November 1938; he held this office until March 1940 and again from October 1940 to October 1941.

As minister for commerce (April 1939 to March 1940) and minister for trade and customs (March to October 1940), McLeay was a member of the War Cabinet (September-November 1939) and the Economic Cabinet (from December 1939). He held the portfolios of postmaster-general and repatriation (October 1940 to June 1941) and supply and development (June to October 1941). In the early years of World War II he shouldered responsibility for matters that ranged from censorship to wheat exports. From 1941 to 1947 he was leader of the Opposition in the Senate. In this capacity, in 1945, he attended the United Nations Conference on International Organization, held at San Francisco, United States of America, as an assistant to the Australian delegation. McLeay was prepared to speak well of H. V. Evatt's [q.v.14] leadership during the negotiations, and Evatt valued his help.

When the Liberal and Country parties came to office on 19 December 1949, McLeay was appointed deputy-leader of the government in the Senate and minister for shipping and fuel; transport was added to his portfolio in March 1950 and fuel was removed in May 1951. A vigorous minister, he entered into intensive bargaining with shipowners and trade-union leaders in the major Australian ports in an effort to reduce the turn-round time of shipping. He was widely regarded as an effective, genial and forthright politician. Despite (Sir) Robert Menzies' [q.v.] occasionally overbearing manner towards him in cabinet, he remained a faithful and somewhat undemanding supporter.

McLeay lived in the Adelaide suburb of Glenelg; he belonged to golf, lacrosse, tennis and cricket clubs, and was a keen racegoer. Suffering from diabetes mellitus and from the strain of excessive travelling, he died of ischaemic heart disease on 14 September 1955 at Calvary Hospital, North Adelaide. He was accorded a state funeral and was buried in Centennial Park cemetery. His wife, son and daughter survived him.

One of South Australia's best-known and most popular members of Federal parliament, McLeay was remembered for his sparkling wit and quick repartee. Menzies, who was shocked by his early death, said that he had 'never known a man of higher spirit, a man of more infinite good nature' who could 'take knocks, and give knocks, and always remain infinitely good tempered'. McLeay enjoyed the affection of political friends and foes alike. Evatt recalled that he was thought of as 'Mr Pickwick' because of his genial fellowship, simplicity, humanity, lovability and absence of guile. (Sir) John McEwen [q.v.] regarded him as a close friend who could be outspoken without provoking 'an atom of bitterness'.

K. Perkins, *Menzies* (Adel, 1968); D. Gardner, *The Minutes are Confirmed, 1878-1978* (Arthurton, SA, 1978); D. Day, *Contraband and Controversy* (Canb, 1996); *PD* (H of R *and* Senate), 14 Sept 1955; *Observer* (Adel), 11 Sept 1909, 17 June 1916; *News* (Adel), 13, 14, 16 Sept 1955; *Advertiser* (Adel), 15-17 Sept 1955.

ERIC RICHARDS

McLEISH, BERYL ELIZABETH (1902-1974), public servant and State superintendent of the Australian Women's Land Army, was born on 6 February 1902 at Gympie, Queensland, eldest child of Gympie-born parents Walter Henry King, engine driver, and his wife Alice Mary, née Marshall, a music teacher. Educated locally, Beryl passed the junior public examination, travelled to Brisbane and joined the Queensland Public Service about 1920. She worked as private secretary to W. H. Austin and F. E. Walshe, successive under-secretaries of the Department of Labour and Industry, and developed her knowledge, skills and political acumen.

On 5 August 1939 at All Saints Church, Wickham Terrace, Beryl married with Anglican rites Edward Francis Pender, a 28-year-old solicitor. They lived at Barcaldine and were to remain childless. Beryl embraced the interests of country women and served as secretary of the local branch of the Australian Comforts Fund (Queensland division) until Ted enlisted in the Australian Imperial Force in 1941. They were to be divorced in 1946.

Prompted by the wartime shortage of labour, Beryl accepted a post in the office of the premier, William Forgan Smith [q.v.11]. When the Australian Women's Land Army (Queensland) was established on 27 July 1942, she was appointed its administrative officer. Annabel Philp [q.v.], founder of the privately sponsored Queensland Land Army, was made field supervisor. Dissatisfied with these arrangements, Philp resigned within twelve months and Pender was appointed State superintendent on 20 July 1943.

An excellent administrator known for her tenacity, efficiency and wide social contacts, Pender worked tirelessly. She recruited 'land girls', improved their conditions of employment and endeavoured to overcome the scepticism of farming communities. A familiar presence in the press and on radio, she was quick to acknowledge that 'replacing men effectively in scores of jobs . . . in pre-war times would have been regarded as revolutionary'. After the A.W.L.A.(Q.) was disbanded in December 1945, she retained a lively interest in her 'LAGs', assisting with arrangements for a 30-year reunion and compiling a short history of the organization.

At the Ann Street Presbyterian Church, Brisbane, on 31 October 1946 Beryl married Daniel Matthew McLeish (d.1973), a 74-year-old grazier. Their relationship proved difficult. At first they lived on Tumbar, a cattle property near Jericho, before shifting in 1951 to Wacol. In the late 1950s Beryl moved to Auchenflower, Brisbane, and worked as an administrator at Building & Industrial Suppliers Pty Ltd. She retired in her mid-sixties.

Beryl McLeish was a tall, vivacious brunette. She left various impressions: that of an avenging angel rescuing a 16-year-old girl from the amorous advances of a north-coast farmer and declaring 'you needn't look at him again'; that conveyed in a letter to Baroness Elliot of Harwood in 1972, recalling the aftermath of an official inspection at Redland Bay when the two had paddled in the sea to ease the visitor's mosquito bites; that of the competent bureaucrat who 'might have been a general'; and that of the private, romantic and at times flamboyant woman who was interested in astrology. She died on 10 January 1974 at Auchenflower and was cremated with Anglican rites.

C. Lack (comp), *Three Decades of Queensland Political History, 1929-1960* (Brisb, 1962); P. A. Carlton, The Australian Women's Land Army in Queensland, July 1942-December 1945 (M.A. thesis, James Cook Univ, 1980); Aust Women's Land Army, Doris Child collection (OL); information from Mrs T. M. Service, Fig Tree Pocket, and Mr J. Service, Waterford, Brisb.   HELEN TAYLOR

MACLEOD, ALTON RICHMOND (1887-1951), newspaper proprietor and rifleman, was born on 14 July 1887 at Clear View, Richmond River, New South Wales, eldest son of native-born parents William Alexander Macleod, farmer, and his wife Augusta Caroline, née Hermann. Alton left North Codrington Public School at the age of 13 to help on his father's mixed farm. Apprenticed to a coachsmith at Lismore in 1903, he transferred to a Mullumbimby firm in the following year. From 1907 he worked in Queensland at mining-fields on the Atherton Tableland and the Roper River, but suffered a bout of malaria which affected his health thereafter.

While employed at the Hambledon sugar-mill in 1908, Macleod attended the mill's night-school where he was tutored by an old journalist; using the pseudonym 'Magpie', he had a string of contributions published by the *Bulletin*. From May 1909 he studied privately in Sydney until his health again broke down. He joined Massey-Harris Co. Ltd to supervise experiments with a new harvesting machine. After giving a demonstration at Manilla, near Tamworth, he decided to settle in the district and bought the local Massey-Harris agency in 1911. On 18 June 1913 he married Lily Hall with Methodist forms in her father's home at Gunnedah. Having conducted the agency profitably, in January 1919 Macleod bought the *Manilla Express*, a bi-weekly newspaper which he edited from October 1923. He was an executive-member (1920-39) and president (1933-34) of the New South Wales Country Press Association, and a vice-president (1933-36) of the Australian Provincial Press Association.

A rifleman of note, in 1917 Macleod had represented Country against Sydney. In 1927 he won the Country championship and captained the New South Wales rifle team on its New Zealand tour. Next year he was a member of the State team which won the Gordon Highlanders' trophy in Perth. 'Mac' set an Australian record in 1929 by scoring 22 consecutive bull's-eyes at 900 yards (823 m) in the Weinholdt aggregate and the King's prize in Brisbane. He was a councillor (1924-50), life-member (1935) and vice-president (1946-50) of the National Rifle Association of New South Wales.

In 1919 Macleod had been elected to the Manilla Municipal Council: he served as an alderman (1919-21 and 1926-50) and mayor (1930-34 and 1942-50). He was an initiator of the town's sewerage, water and beautification schemes, and was active in more than a score of community organizations, including the Parents and Citizens' Association, hospital board, show committee and Caledonian Society. A drinking-fountain was erected (1934) at the Municipal Chambers in recognition of his community service. He was also founding president (1936-38) and secretary (1939-50) of the Manilla Bowling Club.

'Whatever he did, he put his heart and soul into it.' Macleod believed in work, and in relaxation—through gardening, sport and reading, particularly poetry. After selling the *Express* in 1947, he wrote a history of Manilla, *The Transformation of Manellae* (1949). Survived by his wife, son and two daughters, he died of myasthenia gravis on 8 July 1951 at Manilla and was cremated.

C. H. Cromack, *The History of the National Rifle Association of New South Wales, 1860-1956* (Syd, 1956); *Glen Innes Examiner*, 29 Oct 1923; *Australasian*, 12 Oct 1929; *Newspaper News*, 1 Feb 1935, p 2; *Northern Daily Leader*, 24 May 1948, 23 Nov 1949; *Manilla Express*, 13 July 1951; information from Mrs M. Bignall, Manilla, NSW.

ROD KIRKPATRICK

McLEOD, GERTRUDE EVELYN (1891-1971), golf administrator, was born on 1 June 1891 at Spring Hill, Brisbane, seventh child of Daniel Walker McLeod, a Scottish-born auctioneer, and his wife Sarah, née Slade, who came from England. Gertrude was educated at the Normal School and Brisbane High School for Girls. Although she took up golf with enthusiasm, she was only an average player and her handicap never fell below sixteen. On 26 October 1934 she was elected president of the Queensland Ladies' Golf Union. She introduced country championships, raised money for interstate competitions by imposing a levy on associate-members of golf clubs, and in 1938 took the first Queens-

land women's team to Sydney. During World War II the Q.L.G.U. gave financial support to patriotic bodies, and equipped and maintained the Australian Red Cross Society's convalescent home at Chelmer: the society was to award McLeod honorary life membership in 1962.

As president (1949-54) of the Australian Ladies' Golf Union, McLeod promoted international competitions. (Dame) Joan Hammond gave two concerts in Sydney and two in Melbourne to raise money for the A.L.G.U. to send a team to the 1950 British Ladies' Open Championship. Before that year Australian women had entered the Open as private individuals. During McLeod's presidency regulations controlling the amateur status of players came under discussion as a result of the changing social background of women golfers. Prior to 1945 most competitors had been wealthy women. By the early 1950s 'working girls formed a large percentage of the personnel of interstate teams' and needed help with travel and accommodation expenses. It was difficult for State unions to meet these costs without jeopardizing the amateur standing of the players. Another contentious issue was that of dress. Under McLeod, the A.L.G.U.'s council ruled that it did 'not approve the wearing of slacks except in wet weather'.

An associate-member of the Royal Queensland and Indooroopilly golf clubs, McLeod once said: 'I enjoy every minute of my time that has to do with golf. My greatest pleasure is to visit golf clubs and play with other associates'. She retired from the Q.L.G.U. in 1963, having seen it 'grow from a very small body, to one of over 100 affiliated clubs'. Although in her mid-seventies, she supported a committed group of women who established at Mount Ommaney, Brisbane, the first golf club in Australia—and one of the few such clubs in the world—to be wholly administered by women. The owners of the land on which the course was to be built stipulated that the word 'women's' was not to appear in its name. To solve this problem, and as a tribute to Gertrude, the title McLeod Country Golf Club was chosen.

McLeod was a member of the Victoria League and the Royal Empire Society. Generous, determined and practical, she enjoyed motion-picture photography, motoring and bridge. She died on 21 May 1971 at Loch Earn, her home in Gregory Terrace, and was cremated with Presbyterian forms.

A Biographical Record of Queensland Women (Brisb, 1939); P. Perry (comp), *From Green to Gold* (Syd, 1975); H. Gregory and M. Kowald, *Women on Course* (Brisb, 1993); information from the Qld Ladies' Golf Union and McLeod Country Golf Club (ADB file, Canb).

MARGARET KOWALD

McLUCAS, ALLEN ERNEST (1909-1967), headmaster, was born on 24 February 1909 at Amosfield, New South Wales, son of native-born parents Joseph McLucas, selector, and his wife Suzanne, née Harriman. His parents were of Ulster Scottish descent, and ran a store at Stanthorpe, Queensland. Allen boarded (1920-26) at Scots College, Warwick, where he excelled at sport and studies, and was school captain for two years. Influenced by the principal W. W. V. Briggs, he abandoned his wish to become an architect and turned to teaching. He was an assistant-master for three years at Methodist Boys' College, Stanthorpe, while studying externally at the University of Queensland (B.A., 1937; M.A., 1945; B.Ed., 1948). In 1930 he returned to Scots as boarding-master, but in 1935-36 lived at Emmanuel College, Brisbane, to complete his honours degree in English full time. After a further two years at Scots, he joined Brisbane Boys' College as senior English master. At the Methodist Church, Lutwyche, on 7 October 1939 he married Beth Amy Beeston, a brilliant fellow language student who was to prove a faithful supporter.

On 19 May 1941 McLucas was mobilized in the Militia as a lieutenant and posted to headquarters, Northern Command. Transferring to the Australian Imperial Force in January 1943 as temporary major, he served as a staff officer at brigade, divisional and corps headquarters in Australia, Netherlands New Guinea and Borneo. On 18 January 1946 he transferred to the Reserve of Officers. He had written his M.A. thesis on Thomas Hardy while stationed on Cape York Peninsula, Queensland, and subsequently enrolled in education. Having again taught at Brisbane Boys' College, in 1949 McLucas was named principal of the fledgling Scots School, Bathurst, New South Wales. In May 1953 he was appointed headmaster of Brisbane Grammar School; there he increased enrolments and promoted building projects, just as he had done at Scots, Bathurst.

In February 1956 McLucas was invited to apply for the position of principal of Scots College, Sydney. He took up duties on 27 August. A Presbyterian elder (from 1950), he was strongly committed to Christianity as the basis of 'true' education. He also held egalitarian and progressive educational ideas which cut across entrenched traditions and offended their hard-nosed custodians. A number of senior teachers, old boys, parents and—eventually—college council-members saw McLucas's attitudes as threatening. In his Christian vocation, some perceived him as too traditional; in his educational philosophy, as too revolutionary. His undiplomatic handling of people (including staff) and his alleged poor decisions made him an easy target. An atmosphere of subversion eventually spread throughout the school community and led to his forced resignation at the end of 1965.

McLucas reverted to classroom teaching, at Barker College, Hornsby. He belonged to the United Service Club, Brisbane, and the University Club, Sydney, and enjoyed reading, fishing and tennis. Survived by his wife, son and two daughters, he died suddenly of coronary artery disease on 22 April 1967 at his Avalon home and was cremated with Presbyterian forms.

K. Willey, *The First Hundred Years* (Melb, 1968); B. Shaw, *The Lion and the Thistle* (Warwick, Qld, 1993); G. Sherington and M. Prentis, *Scots to the Fore* (Syd, 1993); Scots College (Warwick, Qld), *Clansman*, June 1940, p 26, *and* (Bathurst, NSW), *Lion*, 1957, p 12, *and* (Syd), *Scotsman*, Aug 1956, p 5, 1965, p 21, 1967, p 44; Scots College Old Boys' Union (Syd), *Lang Syne*, Oct 1956, p 1, Jan 1959, p 4, Aug 1967, p 1.   M. D. PRENTIS

MacMAHON, JOHN STEPHEN (1899-1968), surgeon, was born on 17 September 1899 at Cootamundra, New South Wales, third child of Australian-born parents Thomas Patrick MacMahon, solicitor and farmer, and his wife Mary Ellen, née O'Donnell. John attended St Patrick's College, Goulburn, and was dux of the school. After several years running the family farm, he entered the University of Sydney (M.B., Ch.M., 1926). Graduating with first-class honours, he was appointed resident medical officer at Royal Prince Alfred Hospital. He so impressed his seniors that he was reappointed annually—with increasing seniority—and was deputy medical superintendent in 1932-36. MacMahon displayed rare surgical talent; he also made full use of the opportunities provided by ten years in residence to develop his skills and clinical judgement, and to acquire administrative experience.

In February 1932 MacMahon was elected a fellow of the Royal Australasian College of Surgeons. Granted overseas leave for one year, he studied the latest developments at leading surgical clinics in Britain and Europe (especially in London and Vienna). In December 1932 he was admitted a fellow of the Royal College of Surgeons, England; he was the first Australian to win the Hallett prize for topping the primary fellowship examination.

On returning to Sydney, MacMahon resumed his post at R.P.A.H., which became his permanent base, and was honorary assistant surgeon (1936-46), honorary surgeon (1946-59), honorary consulting surgeon (1959-68), director (1950-68) and vice-chairman of the board (1962-68). He had a private consulting practice in Macquarie Street, served as a consultant at St Joseph's Hospital, Auburn, and operated regularly at Lewisham Hospital. In

1942-43, as a temporary major in the Militia, he was surgeon at the 102nd Australian General Hospital, Tamworth.

MacMahon had a particular interest in the developing field of thoracic surgery and became consultant to the thoracic unit at the Page [q.v.11] Chest Pavilion. None the less, his range was wide: he excelled in abdominal surgery and remained a generalist. His superb technique and rapid, smooth performance of well-planned procedures won the admiration of his colleagues. In classroom teaching he was clear, practical and concise. In the less formal setting of the operating theatre those who studied his methods were well rewarded.

A handsome, athletic man, MacMahon seemed to devote his whole being to surgery, with horses, boxing and rifle-shooting (but little else) for relaxation. He belonged to the Australian Jockey Club. Although he sometimes appeared brusque and curt, those who broke through the barrier he built around himself discovered a friendly but naturally shy man who had his own 'fine, pawky, dry humour'. His marriage to 29-year-old Marie Rita Fagan at St Mary's Catholic Cathedral on 22 May 1948 was followed by a noticeable softening of his manner; he was devoted to his wife and children. He died suddenly of coronary vascular disease on 23 January 1968 at his Vaucluse home and was buried in Rookwood cemetery. His wife, daughter and three sons survived him.

MJA, 17 Aug 1968, p 331; *SMH*, 19 Dec 1962, 27 Nov 1965, 24 Jan 1968; Roy A'sian College of Surgeons Archives, Melb; information from Mrs M. MacMahon and Dr F. H. Mills, Darling Point, Dr D. Bye, Lane Cove, and Dr B. D. Leckie, Strathfield, Syd.   G. L. McDonald

McMAHON, PATRICK REGINALD (1912-1978), wool technologist, was born on 11 August 1912 at Havelock, Pelorus Sound, New Zealand, son of New Zealand-born parents John McMahon, farmer, and his wife Eva, née Mills. Pat was educated at Massey Agricultural College (M.Ag.Sc., 1935) and won the Farmers' Union scholarship. Proceeding with his studies in England, he held the McMillan-Brown and Sir James Gunson research scholarships at the University of Leeds (Ph.D., 1937). In 1938 he returned to New Zealand where he was appointed wool metrologist, Department of Scientific and Industrial Research. On 17 December that year at the Church of San Antonio, Rona Bay, Wellington, he married with Catholic rites Jean Ellen Fortescue Wright. In 1947 McMahon was appointed lecturer-in-charge of the sheep and wool school, Sydney Technical College.

Four years later he was transferred to the New South Wales University of Technology (University of New South Wales from 1959) as head of the school of wool technology and foundation professor.

A pioneer in the application of quantitative genetics to sheep breeding, McMahon had undertaken research to estimate genetic parameters in the New Zealand Romney, which he published in 1943. His active encouragement facilitated the many distinguished contributions in theoretical and applied aspects of sheep breeding made by staff, students and graduates of the school of wool and pastoral sciences. Conscious of the need to assist stud masters to apply sound genetic principles in the sheep industry, he established and promoted the university's flock-testing service.

McMahon initiated research into the objective measurement of wool and its industrial application. His knowledge and experience of the textile industry made him keenly aware that the introduction of measurement of the properties of raw wool offered many benefits to sheep-breeders. He enthusiastically expounded his views and encouraged colleagues, students and others in the research which eventually led to the introduction of objective measurement in wool-selling in the early 1970s. In addition, his foresight in establishing university level education in wool technology provided graduates who could implement and develop wool metrology throughout the industry.

During his career Professor McMahon was involved in numerous assignments for the Food and Agricultural Organization of the United Nations. He investigated wool production in the Territory of Papua and New Guinea in 1953; he spent ten months abroad in 1960 when he attended conferences at Harrogate, England, and Venice, Italy, and visited thirty countries, including four behind the Iron Curtain; and he acted as an adviser in Argentina in 1964. He showed a special concern to educate students from developing nations.

Interested in foreign languages, McMahon also enjoyed woodwork, farming, sailing, food and wine. He was elected a member (1947) of the Royal Society of New South Wales, and a fellow of the Australian Institute of Agriculture Science (1975) and of the Australian Society of Animal Production (1976). In July 1977 he retired. Survived by his son and three daughters, he died of cancer on 15 January 1978 in St Vincent's Hospital, Darlinghurst, and was cremated.

J of Aust Inst of Agr Science, Dec 1975; *Procs of Aust Soc of Animal Production*, 11, 11th biennial conference, Adel, 1976; Roy Soc of NSW, *J*, 111, 1978; *SMH*, 8 June 1951, 13 Dec 1960, 18 July 1978.   John Kennedy

McMILLAN, FLORENCE ELIZABETH (1882-1943), nursing sister, was born on 21 January 1882 at Burwood, Sydney, second child of (Sir) William McMillan [q.v.10], a merchant from Ireland, and his Victorian-born wife Ada Charlotte, née Graham. Her parents were divorced in 1891. On 29 August 1892 at Glasgow, Scotland, William married HELEN MARIA (1863-1937), the widowed daughter of Rev. William Gibson, a Wesleyan minister. Born on 5 March 1863 in England, Helen had been educated partly in France. She had married Archibald O'Reilly (d.1891) on 18 August 1885 in Paris and had accompanied him to Sydney where he practised medicine.

Recognized for her public spirit, sincerity and unselfish commitment to the 'cause of women and children', Helen McMillan had a profound influence on her step-daughter Elizabeth, with whom she had an exceptionally close relationship. Lady McMillan held office in many organizations, including the National Council of Women of New South Wales (president 1918-19), the Women's Club (president 1923-26), the women's auxiliary of Sydney Hospital, the State branch of the Girl Guides' Association, the Royal Society for the Welfare of Mothers and Babies, and the Victoria League. She was also a member of the Alliance Française and the State Children Relief Board. After Sir William's death (1926), she married with Presbyterian forms Andrew Watson Munro [q.v.10] on 27 May 1930 at Dulwich Hill. Survived by the two daughters of her second marriage, she died on 29 October 1937 at Woollahra and was cremated.

Elizabeth attended Claremont College, Randwick. Between 1899 and 1902 she studied art in Paris, mainly at the Académie Julian. She also visited the United States of America and Ireland, and stayed in South Africa in 1906-07. Possibly prompted by her father's financial difficulties, she reacted against her years of 'relatively aimless activity' and began training as a nurse at Royal Prince Alfred Hospital, Sydney, in 1909. She was registered by the Australasian Trained Nurses' Association on 12 November 1913 and qualified as a sister in 1914.

Following the outbreak of World War I, McMillan was one of six nursing sisters who sailed in the hospital ship, *Grantala*, to support the Australian Naval and Military Expeditionary Force in German New Guinea. She transferred to the Australian Army Nursing Service, Australian Imperial Force, in April 1915 and served with the 3rd Australian General Hospital on Lemnos during the Gallipoli Peninsula campaign. Her letters home contained graphic descriptions of the harrowing conditions she experienced. She wrote: 'I could weep hysterically now it is all over ... I may write other letters, but not

another about these first days. I shall try to forget them'. Her correspondence also revealed an affectionate, idealistic and devout disposition. Arriving in England in October 1916, she worked (1917-18) in Australian hospitals on the Western Front.

In London in 1919 McMillan attended lectures at the Babies of the Empire Society where she trained in (Sir) Truby King's 'Plunket Mothercraft Method' before returning to Australia where her A.A.N.S. appointment terminated that year. She completed her obstetrics certificate at the Royal Hospital for Women, Paddington. King then asked her to take charge of the New Zealand Plunket Society's main training school at Dunedin. In 1922 McMillan was back in Sydney, directing the Tresillian Mothercraft Training Centre which had been established by the Royal Society for the Welfare of Mothers and Babies to train nurses for baby clinics.

A 'resolute and fixed determination (often called obstinacy) to carry out to the letter the teaching of ... Truby King' found Sister McMillan at odds with Sydney physicians. She refused to resign and her dismissal in February 1923 caused 'something of a stir in medical and nursing circles'. As the result of a public meeting in March, the Australian Mothercraft Society was formed with the backing of her father and stepmother. Elizabeth became its director. A small, serious woman, with large brown eyes and dark hair, she had 'a quiet air of authority' and marked sincerity. She was devoted to her work, supervising nurses at Karitane (the society's training school at Coogee) and corresponding with country mothers.

At St Andrew's Anglican Cathedral, Sydney, on 8 November 1929 Elizabeth married Dudley Percy Davidson, a Queensland Air Navigation Co. Ltd pilot who was fifteen years her junior. They lived in Brisbane. Dudley was killed on 31 December 1930 in an air crash at Maryborough. By 1934 Elizabeth had returned to Sydney to teach the Plunket mothercraft system. She died of an aortic aneurysm on 9 February 1943 at her Woollahra apartment and was buried in Waverley cemetery.

P. M. Gunnar, *Good Iron Mac* (Syd, 1995); M. Sear, *The National Council of Women of NSW* (Syd, 1996); *Ladies Sphere*, 20 July 1923; *Herself*, 17 Sept 1929; *Daily Telegraph* (Syd), 16 June 1915; *SMH*, 23 Feb, 3 Mar 1923, 20 Oct 1925; *Truth* (Syd), Dec 1925; *Smith's Weekly* (Syd), 1 Oct 1927; P. Gunnar, A Family Companion (ts, extracts held by Dr A. Tate, Annandale, Syd); F. E. McMillan correspondence, 1914-16 (ML).   AUDREY TATE

McMORRAN, DOROTHY VICTORIA (1897-1974), Canadian community leader, was born on 2 November 1897 at Vancouver,

Canada, daughter of William McCusker and his wife Kathryn, née Cooke. Dorothy attended Magee High School and the University of British Columbia before qualifying as an elementary teacher at Vancouver Normal School. Musically inclined, she studied singing part time and had a lovely contralto voice. On 1 March 1923 she married Norman Roy McMorran (d.1982). Coming from a close-knit family, Dorothy resented her husband's posting to Australia as a representative of the Canadian Pacific Railway Co. When she learned that the posting was expected to last only three years, she followed Roy to Sydney, arriving early in 1924. A daughter was born in June, and the family continued to live in New South Wales.

The interest of Canadian companies in Australian markets led the Canadian government to establish trade commissions in Sydney and Melbourne in 1936. Roy McMorran and Roy Miller were prominent in the growing Canadian community; the 'two Roys' and their wives became close friends and remained proudly Canadian. That year Dorothy McMorran (honorary secretary) and Wanda Miller founded the Canadian Women's Association of New South Wales. They established a supportive social and financial network of fifty members, and also helped to care for Canadian ex-servicemen. Following the outbreak of World War II, the Women's Association began its successful 'Canadian Day' (held on Wednesdays) in the Church Hut at St Andrew's Cathedral, Sydney. Australian friends were called on to help. Aided by money from Canada, the association established a therapy hut at the 113th Australian General Hospital, and presented a utility truck, with maple-leaf emblem, to the Sydney Mission to Seamen.

The problems associated with the arrival in Australia of Canadian 'war brides' (wives, fiancées and widows of Royal Australian Air Force personnel from the Empire Air Training Scheme) prompted the Commonwealth government to ask the association for help. Many war brides encountered difficulties that stemmed from the suddenness of their marriages, perceived differences in living standards, and family and cultural adjustments. Under Mrs McMorran's leadership, the association assisted with welcoming arrangements and filled an important social function by giving women the opportunity to hear a familiar accent; it also facilitated assimilation by showing Australian documentary films and providing speakers on topics ranging from literature to home-cooking. Greater prosperity and dispersal to spreading suburbs decreased the need for the association which was disbanded in the 1960s.

Mrs McMorran was dynamic in nature. About 5 ft 6 ins (168 cm) tall, and slender in build, she had brown hair, grey eyes and olive skin. She cooked well, enjoyed entertaining and filled her home with people, particularly during the war. Gifted with 'a rollicking sense of humour', she made a good story out of any misadventure. Her skills included dressmaking, knitting, crocheting, and making Christmas decorations (which she sold) and patchwork quilts. Two of her quilts are held by the Pioneer Women's Hut, Tumbarumba. Survived by her husband and daughter, Dorothy McMorran died on 23 August 1974 at Hunters Hill and was cremated.

J. Bennett and I. Fry, *Canadians in Australia* (Canb, 1995); *SMH*, 3 Mar 1935, 3 Oct 1936, 16 Oct 1942; *Montreal Star*, 21 June 1947; N. McMorran, Canadian Women's Association of N.S.W. (ms, copy held in ADB file); information from Miss N. McMorran, Hunters Hill, Syd.

JOHN ATCHISON

McNAIR, WILLIAM ALLAN (1902-1979), market researcher, was born on 10 January 1902 at Ponsonby, Auckland, New Zealand, eldest of six children of New Zealand-born parents William Peter McNair, farmer, and his wife Laura, née Mitcham. Educated locally, William won a scholarship to Auckland Grammar School. He worked for a major exporter of dairy-foods and for two importers while attending night-classes at Auckland University College (B.Com., N.Z., 1926; M.Com., 1928). From 1928 he taught at Takapuna Grammar School, but teaching was not his forte. At the Church of Christ, Auckland, on 27 March 1929 he married Elizabeth Wilson Feeney (d.1977), a 21-year-old saleswoman. McNair's studies led him 'to explore ways in which social and psychological research might be applied commercially'. He gained a diploma of social science from the university in 1930.

Early that year McNair visited Australia and talked to representatives of the American advertising agency, J. Walter Thompson Co. In May he accepted an invitation to join (as an accountant and research manager) their New Zealand branch to be opened in Wellington under Michael Stiver, an American. Although Thompson's major clients were large British and American companies, the sums spent on market research were small. Besides writing the questionnaires and survey reports, McNair selected the people to be interviewed and conducted the interviews. J.W.T. soon closed its Wellington branch. Stiver, put in charge of its Australian activities, invited McNair to join him as a director, accountant and research manager.

When McNair arrived in Sydney, at the end of 1931, economic conditions were still deteriorating. Within a year General Motors

Corporation had faded as a client and in New York J.W.T. was discussing whether to pull out of Australia. Local support—from William Arnott [q.v.3] Ltd, the *Daily Telegraph* and (from 1933) the *Australian Women's Weekly*—was not enough. The agency was saved by attracting new business, notably from Kellogg (Australia) Pty Ltd, and by the staff agreeing to salary cuts; none the less, McNair's assistant Sylvia Ashby [q.v.13] resigned.

Although advertisers knew how many Australian homes had licensed receivers, they barely understood the nature of the growing radio audience in the early 1930s. Between 1934 and 1936 McNair attempted to establish —by age, sex and breadwinner's occupation–who was listening to what, each quarter-hour of every day, as well as their favourite artists, stations and types of programmes. First, he tried interviewing by telephone, but, whereas 50 per cent of Sydney households owned a wireless, only 15 per cent had telephones. Searching for an alternative method, he was allowed by the Department of Education to distribute questionnaires to Sydney schools so that the listening habits of 2500 primary school children might be documented. Subsequently, he conducted another large-scale telephone survey, distributed questionnaires to workers in various city offices and factories (most of whom failed to fill them out), and conducted a separate and much more successful survey using personal interviews and aided recall.

In 1937 McNair published *Radio Advertising in Australia*. It included the results of surveys of 'the radio audience', with his observations on 'the principles of advertising' and Australian 'broadcasting facilities and methods'. In his foreword A. H. Martin [q.v.] wrote that the book summed up Australian radio advertising 'better ... than any other such work attempts to do for any other country'. Not only was this the first book about any aspect of Australian radio, for the next twenty years it was the only book. To McNair's disappointment, however, the examiners in England to whom the University of New Zealand submitted the manuscript did not recommend that it be awarded a doctorate.

World War II brought new challenges for McNair: surveys farther afield in Brisbane, Adelaide and Melbourne, recruitment for the Women's Auxiliary Australian Air Force, a study of the reasons for the United Australia Party's defeat, and, in 1944, the establishment of McNair Survey Pty Ltd. This new organization was designed to service a wider range of advertising agencies. In radio, McNair's biggest competitor was the Anderson Analysis of Broadcasting, established by G. H. Anderson [q.v.13] that year. Previously, radio surveys had been conducted mostly *ad hoc* for single clients; now audiences were to be

monitored by McNair every two months and the surveys syndicated. In 1947 Anderson switched from personal interviews to diaries, but McNair continued to use the assisted recall method—those being asked what they had listened to were shown the previous day's programmes. By the late 1940s staff of McNair Survey were interviewing in all mainland capitals. This work involved McNair himself in a good deal of travel to select and train interviewers, appoint supervisors to audit their work, and call on current and prospective clients around Australia and occasionally New Zealand.

In 1952 McNair Survey, with a full-time staff of thirteen, became an independent entity; McNair and Gwen Nelson were the directors and principal shareholders. The move away from J.W.T. was encouraged by the Australian Association of Advertising Agencies which largely underwrote the radio surveys. After 1956 television was added. There were also studies of newspaper and magazine readers. From 1958 a monthly McNair-Starch survey was conducted on the extent to which advertisements in the *Women's Weekly* were noticed.

Although McNair was best known for his radio and television work, his business encompassed surveys for individual manufacturers and advertisers, and research on public opinion. In 1954, when International Research Associates was formed in America to facilitate market research internationally, McNair was invited to represent Australia and New Zealand. I.N.R.A. brought business opportunities and international travel. For McNair, one member's motto had particular appeal: '1. Do a good job. 2. Have fun. 3. Make money. In that order'. In 1966 McNair and Nelson sold the goodwill and assets to Ian Muir, Ian Pilz and McNair's son Ian (who had joined the staff in 1953 and later become a director). William McNair stayed on as a consultant.

McNair had been a member (from the 1930s) of the Australian Institute of Political Science; he found that the institute's publications and speakers 'prompted many useful questions' for his public-opinion surveys. He also belonged to the Australian Institute of Industrial Psychology, Sydney, from which he learned about questionnaire design and personnel management; he edited (1944-46) its journal, *People at Work*. A member of the Constitutional Association of New South Wales and the Australian Institute of Sociology, he was a founding member (1955) of the Statistical Society of New South Wales.

In 1950 McNair published *Starland of the South*, a book on the night sky as seen from the southern hemisphere; it was 'highly commended' in 1951 by the State branch of the Children's Book Council of Australia and later reprinted. Rights to the main star charts were purchased in 1961 by Unity Life Assurance Ltd for use in a calendar. In retirement, McNair wrote a book, *In Search of the Four Musketeers* (1972), and his unpublished reminiscences. His other interests included photography, reading, gardening and the Presbyterian Church. He collapsed while playing bowls on 30 August 1979 and died that day in the Mater Misericordiae Hospital, North Sydney. Survived by his three sons, he was cremated.

R. R. Walker, *Communicators* (Melb, 1967); *Newspapers News*, 1 Aug 1944, 15 Dec 1945; *SMH*, 14 Oct 1972, 1 Sept 1979; W. A. McNair (ed), Some Reflections on the First Fifty Years of Market Research in Australia 1928-1978 (ts, np, nd, copy on ADB file, Canb); information from Mr I. McNair, Castlecrag, Syd.   MURRAY GOOT

McNEILL, CHARLES ARTHUR HENRY (1888–1974), lawn bowler and insurance representative, was born on 7 June 1888 at Emigrant Creek, Richmond River, New South Wales, eldest of six children of native-born parents Charles McNeill, farmer, and his wife Wilhelmina, née Drent. Educated locally, Charlie worked as a grocer at Ballina. On 2 August 1911 he married Una Beatrice Gould at St Mary's Anglican Church, Ballina. By 1916 he had moved with his family to Newcastle where he was employed as an insurance representative.

Joining the Hamilton Bowling Club in 1919, McNeill became a committee-member in his first year. He won the club singles title for the first time in 1921 and for the eighteenth in 1964. In 1929 he was elected vice-president of the Newcastle District Bowling Association. As a team-member, he was victorious in the district fours in 1924, 1926 and 1927, and the State fours in 1925. With Aubrey and Harold Murray and Thomas Kinder, he was one of a team known throughout Australia as the 'Big Four': they won the State title in 1936, 1939 and 1943, and represented Australia at the 1938 British Empire Games in Sydney, winning a bronze medal. McNeill also won the State pairs with Kinder in 1934, 1935 and 1938, and in 1954 (with C. Comins); he took the State Singles Championship in 1928, 1931 and 1944, and represented New South Wales more than one hundred times.

A close friend described McNeill's greatest bowling strengths as the forehand shot and his 'deadly drawshot'. Following McNeill's win in the Australian Singles in 1955, the Hamilton Bowling Club—of which he was a member for fifty-five years—hosted a celebratory 'Victory Dance'. He became club patron and a life member in the 1950s, and was Champion of Champions twice in the 1960s. His name appeared eighty-five times

on the club's honour board. In 1973 he was awarded the British Empire medal.

Described as a true gentleman, meticulous in both dress and speech, McNeill was a softly spoken man with a kind word for everyone. Tall and slim, he retained his athletic build throughout his life. His extensive volunteer work as coach and administrator was a sign of the pleasure he received from bowls, and a way of returning something to the sport. He also expressed his love of the game in a history of the Hamilton club which he co-authored in 1965. In his retirement he was Newcastle representative for the Henselite Bowls Co. (N.S.W.) Pty Ltd, and helped many of his fellow bowlers to select appropriate playing equipment.

McNeill died on 12 September 1974 at Waratah and was cremated; he was survived by his two daughters and his son (Sir) James McNeill, managing director of Broken Hill Proprietary Co. Ltd. An obituarist commented that Charles McNeill's bowling record 'was unequalled by any other individual bowler in this State and possibly in Australia'. His club named its No.1 green after him in 1976 and introduced the C. A. H. McNeill memorial two-life pairs tournament in 1993.

History of the Newcastle District Bowling Association, 1898-1972 (Newcastle, NSW, 1973); Hamilton Bowling Club Cooperative Ltd, *Celebrating 100 Years of Bowling 1896-1996* (Newcastle, NSW, 1996); *Newcastle Morning Herald*, 13 Sept 1974; information from Messrs M. Croft, Kingscliff, NSW, L. Shean, Burleigh Heads, Qld, and the late R. Foreman.   LOUELLA MCCARTHY

McNULTY, CLARENCE SYDNEY (1903-1964), journalist and editor, was born on 12 August 1903 in Perth, son of Thomas Sydney McNulty, accountant and public servant, and Caroline Hall. Raised by Thomas and his wife Maude, née Westhoven, Clarrie was educated at St Ildephonsus' College, New Norcia, and Scotch College, Perth. He began his newspaper career in Perth and moved to Sydney in 1920, working briefly on *Truth* and the *Daily Mail*. At Holy Cross Church, Woollahra, on 29 August 1924 he married with Catholic rites Winifred Thelma Attwood, a 21-year-old typist. Their son was born next year. Following a short sojourn on the *Daily Telegraph*, McNulty returned to Truth & Sportsman Ltd. A 'crack reporter', he became chief sub-editor of the Brisbane *Truth* and editor in 1929. From 1930 he was, in turn, editor of the Perth and managing editor of the New Zealand editions of *Truth*.

Back in Sydney in 1936, McNulty joined the *Daily Telegraph* which had been acquired by Consolidated Press Ltd, controlled by (Sir) Frank Packer [q.v.] and E. G. Theodore [q.v.12]. As chief sub-editor he was part of the young and dynamic team which revitalized the ailing newspaper. In the rumbustious, bohemian atmosphere of the *Telegraph* office McNulty fraternized with journalists such as Syd Deamer [q.v.13], Cyril Pearl and Richard Hughes. He was appointed news editor in 1937 and editor in 1939. Under his leadership the *Telegraph*'s progressive liberalism and patronage of modern art continued.

'Mac' was a devotee of the 'new journalism': all the publications with which he was involved were tightly edited and boldly laid out. Despite his Catholic associations, he was an agnostic. A keen student of international affairs, French and the classics, he admired the work of the Impressionists and of Van Gogh. His taste in music ranged from Beethoven to Gilbert and Sullivan, and his political sympathies lay with the left. *Smith's Weekly* described him as level-headed, good-humoured, cheerful and courteous, and as one of the fastest men ever to trim or head a story. Slim and of middle height, he had brown hair and heavy spectacles; his movements were quick, as if he were always in a hurry.

Editor-in-chief for Consolidated Press from 1941, McNulty supervised the vigorous forums and feature articles which characterized the wartime *Daily Telegraph* and *Sunday Telegraph*. He joined an Australian press delegation to the Dutch East Indies and Singapore in August 1941, visited the United States of America in 1942 to investigate Consolidated Press's cable service, and played a vital role in the company's challenge to censorship authorities.

By this time, however, McNulty's private life was in turmoil. On 9 January 1943, after leaving a woman friend, he was arrested in a men's public lavatory at Lang Park, near Wynyard Station. He gave a false name and occupation to protect his family, but his identity was soon revealed. Packer intervened; W. J. MacKay [q.v.10], the New South Wales police commissioner, agreed to drop the charge; and an investigation was launched into the activities of the two arresting officers. The Police Association of New South Wales and some rival newspapers condemned MacKay's actions, and the State government ordered that a summons be issued against McNulty. The charge (obscene exposure) was dismissed on the ground that the prosecution had failed to prove its case beyond reasonable doubt. Although Consolidated Press executives and journalists gave McNulty unqualified support during the affair, his reputation had been dealt an irreparable blow. Late in 1943 he again visited the U.S.A. on business.

In January 1945 McNulty took charge of Consolidated Press's London bureau and co-ordinated the coverage of the last months of the war in Europe. In 1950 he suggested that a Consolidated Press subsidiary should purchase a London publishing firm, Frederick Muller Ltd; McNulty acquired a substantial shareholding and became chairman of the board. Despite his executive responsibilities, he remained a dynamic journalist. In reporting the death of King George VI in 1952, for example, he made the longest radio-telephone call between London and Sydney to that time.

Divorced in 1949, McNulty married Veronica Margaret Vousden, née Beswick, a 40-year-old divorcee, on 19 December 1952 at the register office, Chelsea. In the early 1960s, overweight and drinking heavily, he became increasingly anxious about making appropriate provision for his retirement. Financial concerns contributed to a falling-out with his employer. A few months after reluctantly succumbing to Packer's pressure to retire, McNulty died of a coronary occlusion on 3 June 1964 at his Chelsea flat and was cremated. He was survived by his wife and by the son of his first marriage, who was also a journalist.

E. Barcs, *Backyard of Mars* (Syd, 1980); *Journalist*, 15 Mar 1926; *Newspaper News*, 1 Feb 1936, 1 Mar 1941, 12 June 1964; *Bookseller* (Lond), 10 Apr 1954; *Smith's Weekly* (Syd), 7 Oct 1939; *SMH*, 22 Jan, 2 Feb 1943; *Truth* (Syd), 24 Jan, 7 Mar 1943; *Daily Telegraph* (Syd), 29 Jan, 7 Mar 1943, 4 June 1964; Cassidy papers (ML); A472/1 item W10525, A1608/1 item AY65/1/1 (AA, Canb); papers held by, and information from Mr F. McNulty, Gladesville, Syd, and Mrs V. McNulty, Uckfield, Sussex, Eng; information from Messrs T. Gurr, Waitara, A. Deamer, McMahons Point, and J. A. Morley, Lane Cove, Syd.   BRIDGET GRIFFEN-FOLEY

McPHERSON, WILLIAM EDWARD (1898-1950), industrialist, was born on 12 December 1898 at Hawthorn, Melbourne, second child of (Sir) William Murray McPherson [q.v.10], iron merchant and later premier, and his wife Emily, née Jackson. Educated at Scotch College, he passed the junior public examination in 1915. 'W.E.', as he became popularly known, began his working career in McPherson's Pty Ltd, his father's Melbourne hardware and machinery business, founded in 1860 by his Scottish immigrant grandfather, Thomas McPherson.

After qualifying with the Commonwealth Institute of Accountants (Australia), McPherson studied commerce at the University of Melbourne but did not graduate. On 1 September 1924 at All Souls Church, St Marylebone, London, he married Ethel Margaret McKaige with Anglican rites. When his father retired in 1929, 'W.E.' succeeded him as governing director of McPherson's. An Adelaide branch was opened in 1930. In 1929-32 the company's bolt works at Richmond, Melbourne, supplied six million rivets, some up to 6 lb. (3 kg) in weight, totalling 3000 tons in all, for construction of the Sydney Harbour Bridge. An additional bolt works was established at Alexandria, Sydney, in 1934.

As the 1930s progressed, McPherson feared an impending international war and looked to the development of Australian secondary industry for the manufacture of products previously imported. In 1937 his company acquired an interest in Patience & Nicholson Ltd, makers of engineers' cutting tools, and provided the base capital for production of twist drills. Next year, with 'W.E.' sponsoring the project and McPherson's supplying the capital, the Wiltshire File Co. Pty Ltd was launched in association with (Sir) Frederick Wiltshire.

In 1938 McPherson travelled to Europe and the United States of America to discuss the manufacture in Australia of grinding wheels, files, lathes, small tools, bolts and hacksaw blades. His report announced a redirection of his firm's policy: 'more emphasis on manufacturing and less on merchandising'. Despite initial resistance, agreement was reached for a joint venture with American and British companies which led to the establishment of Australian Abrasives Pty Ltd. That year McPherson's acquired the Tool Equipment Co. Pty Ltd; a new company, Associated Machine Tools Australia Pty Ltd, was formed to separate McPherson's machine-tool manufacturing interests from its merchandising activities. In 1939 a foundry and pump manufacturing plant was established at Tottenham, Melbourne, and the Ajax Bolt & Rivet Co. Pty Ltd commenced manufacture in New Zealand.

While sponsoring these developments, McPherson was associated with an informal committee of industrial leaders, including Sir Colin Fraser, Essington Lewis, W. S. Robinson [qq.v.8,10,11], (Sir) Lindesay Clark and (Sir) Laurence Hartnett. He would see to the production of basic hand and machine tools, they to the provision of raw materials and large-scale component manufacturing. Owing to their foresight, isolated Australia was able to produce during World War II most of the country's munitions needs, small arms, artillery, landing craft, pontoons, trucks, Bren-gun carriers, larger assault tanks and aircraft, to the benefit of herself and her allies. The firm made its designs, plant, and personnel of the lathe-manufacturing works available to the Department of Munitions for the war effort. On 5 December 1944 McPherson's converted to a public company, McPherson's Ltd, with 'W.E.' chairman of directors. In 1948 the Ajax pump foundry opened at Kyneton,

Victoria. The company's overall sales increased from £2 813 000 in 1945 to £5 884 000 in 1950.

Described as a 'shy, modest man who enjoyed his books, his private workshop and the company of a friend', McPherson was respected as a philanthropist and humanist. He lived at Kingussie, a house with a two-acre (0.8 ha) garden in Mont Albert Road, Canterbury. On inheriting (1932) his father's home, Invergowrie, at Hawthorn, he donated it to the Headmistresses' Association of Australia, which used it as a homecraft hostel. At McPherson's, a pension fund was established in 1929 and 'W.E.' extended profit sharing (introduced by his father) to hundreds of employees in four States. In 1939 he introduced a works council scheme, giving each employee the right to have a grievance or problem discussed by an elected representative and the management. Survived by his wife, son and three daughters, he died of a cerebral haemorrhage on 18 January 1950 at the Alfred Hospital, Melbourne, and was cremated. His estate was sworn for probate at £405 540.

Modern Engineer, Feb 1950; McPherson's Ltd records (Univ Melb Archives); information from Mrs B. Hamer, South Yarra, Mrs M. Billson, Toorak, and Mr W. Eady, Camberwell, Melb.

FRANK STRAHAN

MACQUEEN, KENNETH ROBERTSON (1897-1960), artist, was born on 8 April 1897 at Ballarat East, Victoria, eldest of four children of Rev. William Sweyn Macqueen, a Presbyterian clergyman from Scotland, and his second wife Rachel Cecilia Corio, née Robertson, who was Australian born. The family moved to Brisbane in 1898 and Kenneth was sent to Bowen House School. In 1909 the Macqueens shifted to Sydney. Kenneth completed his schooling at Scots College and attended weekly drawing-classes conducted by Alfred Coffey.

In 1914 Macqueen obtained a post as a clerk at the Pyrmont works of the Colonial Sugar Refining Co. Ltd. He enlisted in the Australian Imperial Force on 3 May 1916 and served (1917-18) on the Western Front with the 12th (Army) Brigade, Australian Field Artillery. After the war he studied at the Slade School of Fine Art, University of London, and at the Westminster Technical Institute and School of Art. Returning to Australia, he was discharged from the A.I.F. on 7 November 1919. For the next three years he worked on sheep-stations in New South Wales, at Trangie and Queanbeyan. In 1922 he settled at Mount Emlyn, near Millmerran, in south-eastern Queensland, where he divided his time between water-colour painting and farming.

On 2 April 1927 Macqueen married with Presbyterian forms Olive Kathleen Crane (1895-1935) in her home at Wollstonecraft, Sydney. A gifted illustrator and etcher, she supported her husband's early artistic interests. They had a daughter Marion and a son Revan. Within a few months of Revan's birth, Olive died of meningitis and her sister Mildred took over the household.

Macqueen's work first came to public attention in 1926 when it was included in the seminal exhibition, A Group of Modern Painters, held in Sydney. This showing led to the formation of the Contemporary Group, with whom he was to display his paintings throughout the 1930s. His water-colours frequently appeared in the annual exhibitions of the Society of Artists, Sydney, and had done so from the early 1920s. Having joined the Australian Watercolour Institute in 1928, he contributed to its yearly showings until the late 1950s. Macqueen held many solo exhibitions, mainly in Sydney where he was more widely known than other Queensland artists. His 'Cabbage Gums and Cypress Pines' (1940) was purchased for the Metropolitan Museum of Art, New York, in 1941, well before most Australian public galleries began collecting his water-colours. In 1953 he was awarded Queen Elizabeth II's coronation medal. He served as a trustee (1959-60) of the Queensland Art Gallery.

An unassuming and genial man with a strong affinity for the land, Macqueen was drawn to the undulating landscape of the Darling Downs and to the coastal region adjoining Moreton Bay which provided the principal subjects for his work. His water-colours are noted for their simplicity, and for their lyrical and decorative qualities. Shape, structure and colour played a dominant role in his art, engendering a bold and dynamic expression which infused vitality into the prevailing academicism of Australian water-colour painting. Macqueen's approach—which strove to reduce the landscape to a formalized, semi-abstract pattern of translucent washes—closely aligned his output with that of leading early-modernist painters. Unlike many of his contemporaries, however, he attempted to render the landscape in a more direct and expressive manner, accentuating design and rhythm as the dominant elements in his work. 'Design in landscape interests me tremendously', he wrote in his book, *Adventure in Watercolour* (Sydney, 1948); and he described his creative process as emanating from his response to the shapes and patterns in nature.

Macqueen preferred to work in his studio rather than in the open air. Technically he was a traditionalist, who based his approach chiefly on the early nineteenth-century British practice of water-colour painting, emphasiz-

ing the transparent-wash method and the luminosity of the paper as the distinctive qualities of the medium. His technical facility, sensibility and insight established his reputation as one of Australia's foremost water-colourists of the first half of the twentieth century.

Survived by his two children, Macqueen died of a coronary occlusion on 21 June 1960 at Millmerran and was cremated. His work is represented in the National Gallery of Australia, all State galleries, major regional and university collections, and in public galleries in New Zealand and the United States of America. In November-December 1981 a retrospective exhibition was held at the University of Queensland's art museum, Brisbane.

S. Rainbird, *Kenneth Macqueen*, exhibition cat (Brisb, 1981); K. Bradbury and G. Cooke, *Thorns and Petals* (Brisb, 1988); J. Campbell, *Australian Watercolour Painters 1780 to the Present Day* (Syd, 1989); A. Sayers, *Drawing in Australia* (Melb, 1989); S. Rainbird, 'Kenneth Macqueen', *Art and Aust*, 19, no 4, 1982, p 422; newspaper clippings on Aust art 1937-40, John Cooper Collection (Fryer L, Univ Qld).

STEPHEN RAINBIRD

McRAE, CHRISTOPHER RALPH (1901-1976), university professor and educationist, was born on 25 February 1901 at Glenpatrick, near Avoca, Victoria, second of four children of Victorian-born parents James McRae [q.v.10], schoolteacher, and his first wife Margaret Louisa, née Tuck. Educated at Melbourne High School, Chris proceeded to Melbourne Teachers' College and the University of Melbourne (B.A., 1922; Dip.Ed., 1923; M.A., 1924), graduating with first-class honours in Latin and French. Before he had the chance to teach in schools, he was seconded by the college principal John Smyth to work as an assistant to Kenneth Cunningham [qq.v.12,13] in the newly established 'psychological laboratory'. In 1923 McRae went abroad and gained a '*Diplôme de Français*' from the University of Dijon. That year he enrolled at the London Day Training College, University of London (Ph.D., 1925), under (Sir) Percy Nunn, and worked with the internationally known psychologists Charles Spearman and (Sir) Cyril Burt. McRae's doctoral thesis investigated the effects of educational and social opportunity on intelligence tests. Spearman cited McRae's results at length in his own publications, but, much to McRae's chagrin, always spelt his name incorrectly.

Having returned to Melbourne, McRae lectured (1925-27) at the teachers' college. On 15 July 1926 at St John's Anglican Church, East Malvern, he married Lydia Frances Trembath. At this time he espoused his most controversial views on intelligence and social status. He compared the test results obtained in 'poor' industrial areas with those of 'good' residential areas and found scores to be generally higher in the better neighbourhoods. This work led him to conclude that genetics were the main factor in achievement, and he suggested that schools in industrial areas should only follow a modified curriculum specializing in vocational work. His conclusions accorded with those of other academics of the day (particularly Burt), but gave little consideration to environmental factors.

McRae was appointed lecturer in educational psychology at Teachers' College, Sydney, in February 1928. His major publication, *Psychology and Education* (Melbourne, 1929), outlined a number of psychological theories and showed ways of applying them to education. He visited North America on a grant from the Carnegie Corporation of New York in 1932 and in the following year published *An Australian Looks at American Schools* (Melbourne). *Concerning You and Me* (Melbourne, 1934) was a study of human instinct and the psychology of humour. After serving in 1939 as an inspector of schools in the Albury district, in May 1940 McRae obtained the joint position of professor of education at the University of Sydney and principal of Teachers' College. Throughout his career he emphasized the need for college students to develop intellectual interests in addition to teaching skills. Despite the shortage of paper in 1942, he revived the college journal as the *Forum of Education*, and remained its chief editor until 1948. He developed the faculty of education and introduced a new master of education degree, open to all teachers, whatever their academic background. Promoted full-time professor of education in February 1948, he chaired the professorial board in 1952.

In July 1955 McRae became the first deputy vice-chancellor of the university, responsible for academic matters and liaising with the professorial board and staff. He again visited North America on a Carnegie grant in 1957, and in 1960 chaired a State government committee of inquiry into the need for a fourth university in New South Wales. Among his other endeavours, McRae was an active member (1940-64) and president (1959-60) of the Australian Council for Educational Research, and associate-editor (1957-64) of its *Australian Journal of Education*. He was considered a fine lecturer, with a keen sense of humour, a sharp mind and an incisive style. 'No one used the limerick more effectively as a teaching aid or bettered his collection of limericks'.

The weight of his responsibilities, however, undermined McRae's health and forced him to retire in 1961. He lived at Newport Beach. For many years his chief relaxation had been playing tennis. He served (1961-62) on the Commonwealth government's committee on the future of tertiary education in Australia, chaired by Sir Leslie Martin. McRae died on 21 July 1976 at Manly and was cremated; his wife, daughter and son survived him.

C. Turney (ed), *Pioneers of Australian Education*, 3, (Syd, 1983); B. Williams, *Education with its Eyes Open* (Melb, 1994); *Education Gazette and Teacher's Aid*, 27 Apr 1926, p 129, 20 July 1926, p 241; Aust Council for Educational Research, *AR*, 1976, p 1; *Forum of Education*, 25, no 3, Sept 1976, p 1; *Aust J of Education*, 1976, 20, no 3, p 325; Univ Syd, *Gazette*, Feb 1977, p 21; staff record, Dept of Education (NSW) Archives, Syd.

BRIAN WILLIAMS

McRAE, WILLIAM ALEXANDER (1904-1973), sportsman and psychotherapist, was born on 18 June 1904 at Geelong, Victoria, eldest of four children of Alexander McRae, a Scottish-born commercial traveller and later real-estate agent, and his wife Caroline Lilia, née Lamb, who came from New Zealand. When Bill was aged about 7, Caroline left her husband, taking the two girls. He and his brother Arthur were raised by their father. A sickly child, Bill was taught to run to build up his strength. He boarded at Haileybury College, Melbourne, where, in 1921, he was school captain, dux, and captain of the cricket and football teams. He worked for the hardware firm, James Hardie & Co. Pty Ltd, continued to play cricket and Australian Rules football, and served as a youth leader in the Young Men's Christian Association.

McRae travelled to Western Australia and played for West Perth Cricket Club in 1924 before moving to Adelaide in the autumn. Back in Perth in 1927, he worked for Clarksons Ltd, and played thrice for Western Australia—scoring a century against Victoria (1928)—and once for an Australian XI against the touring Marylebone Cricket Club (1929). He also captained West Perth Football Club briefly in 1928. In the following year he went to the United States of America to attend the International Y.M.C.A. College (B.S., 1932), Springfield, Massachusetts, and Yale University (B.D., 1935), Connecticut. He was made a minister of the Congregational Church on 18 June 1935. While studying psychology at Columbia University (M.A., 1937), New York, he experienced persistent headaches which led him to consult a psychoanalyst who relieved his pain. McRae became interested in the connection between emotional problems and physical illness.

Returning to Perth in 1937, he served as a minister of the North Perth Congregational Church. McRae soon left the Church and set up in private practice at 224 St George's

Terrace as a psychotherapist, specializing in psychosomatic complaints. At the Congregational Church, Leederville, on 31 July 1939 he married Anne Millicent Davey, a 23-year-old commercial artist. During World War II he helped to treat returned soldiers suffering from shell-shock, battle fatigue and other war neuroses; he also assessed the fitness of trainee pilots for combat. His book, *About Ourselves and Others* (Melbourne, 1941), was based on his lectures at the University of Western Australia's adult education classes. He published four more books in Melbourne in quick succession: *Sex, Love and Marriage* (1941), *The Psychology of Nervousness* (1942), *Adventures in Self-Understanding* (1945) and *The Foundations of Behaviour* (1945). His writings showed the influence of leading psychoanalysts, particularly Alfred Adler, Sigmund Freud, Carl Jung and Georg Groddeck.

At Zurich, Switzerland, McRae worked with Dr Liliane Frey-Rohn at the C. G. Jung-Institut in 1958-59. In the 1960s he was persuaded by the orthopaedic surgeon (Sir) George Bedbrook and Archbishop (Sir) George Appleton of Perth to set up a three-year training programme in psychotherapeutic methods for doctors and clergymen. He published his last book, *My Pain is Real*, in 1968, and in 1972 began to appear regularly on television.

Sturdy and full-chested, McRae had luminous brown eyes and a warm smile. He had again played (1937-46) for W.P.C.C. and was State squash rackets champion in 1947, 1948 and 1949. Survived by his wife, son and three daughters, he died of cerebrovascular disease on 25 July 1973 at St John of God Hospital, Subiaco, and was cremated with Anglican rites.

West Australian, 26 July 1973; family papers held by, and information from, Mrs A. Fischer, Maddington, Perth; information from Mrs L. Deperas, Claremont, and Mr R. Smith, Perth.

MARION DIXON

MACROSSAN, NEAL WILLIAM (1889-1955), judge, was born on 27 April 1889 at Lutwyche, Brisbane, eighth and youngest child of Irish-born parents John Murtagh Macrossan [q.v.5], politician, and his wife Bridget, née Queely. Hugh Denis Macrossan [q.v.10] was his elder brother. Educated at the Normal School, Brisbane, and St Joseph's College, Nudgee, Neal played in the first XI and first XV, and won prizes for swimming, handball and rifle-shooting. At the junior public examinations conducted by the University of Sydney in 1904, he was awarded the T. J. Byrnes [q.v.7] medal for obtaining the highest pass in Queensland; at the senior in

1906, he again topped the State. He gained the university's silver medal for Greek at both public examinations. In 1907 he was Rhodes scholar for Queensland.

Macrossan read law at Magdalen College, Oxford (B.A., 1910; M.A., 1914). On his return to Queensland, he obtained a temporary post in the office of Thomas William McCawley [q.v.10], the crown solicitor. Macrossan passed the Barristers' Board examinations and was admitted to the Bar on 27 August 1912. He contested (1915) the Legislative Assembly seat of Cairns for the Liberal Party, but was defeated by William McCormack [q.v.10]. In Brisbane on 14 December 1921 he married with Catholic rites Eileen Elizabeth (d.1954), the 25-year-old daughter of T. C. Beirne [q.v.7].

Building up a strong civil practice, Macrossan acted for McCormack in the Mungana case which was heard in the Supreme Court of Queensland in 1931. McCormack's fellow defendants E. G. Theodore [q.v.12] and two others were separately represented, but Macrossan led the overall argument for the defence. Following an unusually long 21-day-trial, the jury found in favour of the defendants. In 1932-33 Macrossan appeared in the High Court of Australia for the appellant in *Peanut Board v. Rockhampton Harbour Board*; under section 92 of the Australian Constitution, the court ruled in favour of freedom of trade for peanut-growers.

On 29 June 1940 Macrossan was sworn in as a judge of the Supreme Court. The appointment was warmly received, the *Courier-Mail* describing him as an eminent scholar and a profound lawyer, and referring to his industry and to his tenacity in cross-examination. He was immediately appointed senior puisne judge, thus overtaking a number of his fellows who had been on the court for many years, notably Edward Douglas [q.v.14]. During World War II Macrossan twice acted as chief justice. When Sir William Webb [q.v.] moved to the High Court, Macrossan became chief justice on 25 April 1946—the second of the sons of the redoubtable John Murtagh to be so appointed, the first having been his brother Hugh. Neal Macrossan was to die in office.

From 1940 Macrossan had served as warden of the council of the University of Queensland. Concerned for young children, he was president (1931-55) of the Playground (and Recreation) Association of Queensland. He was also president of the Twelfth Night Theatre Company, and patron of the Queensland Authors and Artists Association. In addition, he served in an honorary capacity as official visitor to the internment camp at Enoggera.

Macrossan was by nature a reserved man. Some even thought that his temperament was austere. He made the transition from the rough and tumble of jury advocacy to the stricter values required of him on the bench. The years of his chief justiceship saw the emergence of Queensland's modern legal profession which is almost entirely a product of university law schools. Survived by his son and four daughters, Macrossan died of complications arising from emphysema and asthma on 30 December 1955 in South Brisbane; he was accorded a state funeral, at which Archbishop (Sir) James Duhig [q.v.8] officiated, and was buried in Nudgee cemetery.

H. Bryan, *John Murtagh Macrossan* (Brisb, 1958); *Courier-Mail*, 28 June 1940, 25 Apr 1946, 31 Dec 1955; information from Mr J. B. Macrossan, Clayfield, Mrs L. Sweeney, Ascot, Brisb, and Mrs J. O'Connor, Toowoomba, Qld.

P. D. CONNOLLY

McVEY, SIR DANIEL (1892-1972), public servant and industrialist, was born on 24 November 1892 at Carronshore, Stirlingshire, Scotland, son of Daniel McVey, ironmoulder, and his wife Jeanie, née Kay. Educated at Falkirk High School, young Daniel emigrated to Australia with his family in 1910. After working as a jackeroo in rural Queensland, he moved to Brisbane and joined the Commonwealth Public Service on 5 March 1914 as a clerk in the Postmaster-General's Department. On 21 February 1916 he enlisted in the Australian Imperial Force. He served (1917-18) on the Western Front with the 12th (Army) Brigade, Australian Field Artillery, rose to regimental sergeant major and was mentioned in dispatches. In 1919 he was commissioned and promoted lieutenant. His A.I.F. appointment terminated in Australia in September that year.

On 5 September 1919 McVey married with Presbyterian forms Margaret (Peggy) Gardiner Packman in her father's house at Yeerongpilly, Brisbane. He completed electrical-engineering training with his department and was employed as a communications engineer. Promoted assistant-superintendent (1930) and superintendent (1933) of mails for New South Wales, he was second assistant-commissioner (1937-38) on the Commonwealth Public Service Board before being appointed a national insurance commissioner. In May-December 1939 he was secretary of the new Department of Supply and Development.

As director-general of posts and telegraphs (from December 1939) and director of war organization of industry (from November 1941), McVey played a key part in marshalling Australia's postal, telecommunication and economic resources for the war effort. When he became secretary of the Department of Aircraft Production in January 1942, the *Sydney Morning Herald* described him as 'one of the three ablest men in the Commonwealth Public Service'. It was in this post that he made his greatest contribution to national defence and the prosecution of the war. Asked by J. J. Dedman [q.v.13], the minister for war organization of industry, to explain his success in obtaining manpower for his factories, McVey replied half-jokingly that he had broken all the W.O.I. rules and regulations which he had devised as director.

Deputy-chairman of the aircraft advisory committee, McVey visited the United States of America and Britain in January-May 1943, leading a mission charged with deciding on a fighter and a bomber for manufacture in Australia. The 'McVey Mission' chose the Mustang and the Lancaster. His influence as departmental head and as chairman (1942-46) of the Radiophysics Advisory Board proved decisive in facilitating commercial production of radar equipment in Australia. Shortly before Essington Lewis [q.v.10] resigned as director-general of aircraft production in May 1945, he recommended McVey as his successor. The appointment was made that month.

From February 1944 McVey had also held the post of director-general of civil aviation. In this role, and as a member (February-June 1946) of the Australian National Airlines Commission, he implemented major reforms which transformed domestic travel. Sir Hudson Fysh [q.v.8] regarded J. B. Chifley [q.v.13] and McVey as the 'true architects' of immediate postwar developments in air transport. Moreover, as a director (1947-61) of Qantas Empire Airways Ltd, McVey helped to establish Australia as a force in international aviation.

McVey resigned from the public service on 10 June 1946 to enter private industry. He was chairman and managing director of Standard Telephones & Cables Pty Ltd (Australia) in 1946-49, and managing director of Metal Manufactures Ltd and Austral Bronze Co. Pty Ltd in 1949-62. His longest commercial association was with Dunlop Rubber Australia Ltd, of which he was a director (1947-72), chairman of directors (1956-68), and president and deputy-chairman (1968-72).

A resourceful man of energy and determination, and a tiger for work, Dan McVey had an incisive and inventive mind. His geniality and affability made him many friends. As a public servant, he was liked and respected by his colleagues, and by his political masters—both Labor and conservative. His personal qualities and organizing ability ensured his success and popularity as a leader of industry. In recognition of his achievements, the

University of Melbourne awarded him the (W. C.) Kernot [q.v.5] medal for 1945. He was appointed C.M.G. in 1950 and knighted in 1954. Sir Daniel's chief recreation was golf. Survived by his wife, daughter and two sons, he died on Christmas Eve 1972 in East Melbourne and was cremated. His estate was sworn for probate at $420 622.

D. P. Mellor, *The Role of Science and Industry* (Canb, 1958); H. Fysh, *Wings to the World* (Syd, 1970); S. J. Butlin and C. B. Schedvin, *War Economy 1942-1945* (Canb, 1977); G. Blainey, *Jumping over the Wheel* (Syd, 1993); *Aust Financial Review*, 3 Mar 1960; *SMH*, 27 Dec 1972; information from Sir Brian Massy-Greene, Molong, NSW, Mr I. McVey, Carlton, and Mr G. Vanthoff, Doncaster, Melb.
DEREK DRINKWATER

MADDEN, HORACE WILLIAM ('SLIM') (1924-1951), soldier, was born on 14 February 1924 at Cronulla, Sydney, son of Australian-born parents Charles Bernard Madden, labourer, and his wife Pearl Ellen, née Clemson. Giving his occupation as fruiterer's assistant, Horace was mobilized in the Militia on 26 May 1942 and posted to the 114th Australian General Hospital, Goulburn. He transferred to the Australian Imperial Force in August 1943, and served in New Guinea with the 8th Field Ambulance and on Bougainville with the 5th Motor Ambulance Convoy Platoon. His next unit, the 253rd Supply Depot Platoon, was stationed on Morotai before being sent to Japan as part of the British Commonwealth Occupation Force. After his discharge in Sydney on 2 June 1947, Madden was employed as a male nurse at Morisset Mental Hospital for about two years and then as a moulder. On 19 August 1950 he enlisted for service in Korea with the 3rd Battalion, Royal Australian Regiment.

Joining 3RAR as a driver in November 1950, Madden volunteered to become a linesman in the Signals Platoon which worked in below-freezing temperatures to maintain communications with forward elements of the battalion. On the evening of 23 April 1951 the Chinese attacked 3RAR's positions near Kapyong. Concussed by enemy fire, Madden was surrounded on the following day and forced to surrender. Corporal Bob Parker and Private Keith Gwyther were also captured during the battle. For the next few days the three of them were forced to recover wounded Chinese soldiers and were exposed to attacks by United Nations Command aircraft.

'Slim' Madden was 6 ft 0½ ins (184 cm) tall and—as his nickname indicated—of slender build. Although suffering the effects of concussion, he recovered quickly and helped Australian and other U.N. prisoners of war on their arduous march to the notorious 'Bean Camp'. He showed defiance and refused to co-operate with the Chinese. They beat him repeatedly and subjected him to other forms of maltreatment, but he remained cheerful and optimistic. His health deteriorated, and his condition was exacerbated by his willingness to share the little food he had with men in a worse state than he. Madden was among the sick and wounded prisoners moved to 'the Caves' at Kangdong. In late October the Chinese forced them to march to Pingchong-Ni, a distance of some 140 miles (225 km). Madden collapsed and had to be transported by cart. Although he survived the journey, he died of malnutrition sometime between late November and early December 1951. After the Korean War had ended, his remains were reburied in the United Nations memorial cemetery, Pusan.

Gwyther said of him: 'Slim was a real hero —and didn't know it. He became a sort of legend. He didn't try to be like that—it was just the way he was made. Nothing could make him co-operate with the enemy'. In 1955 Madden was posthumously awarded the George Cross. Parker and Gwyther had made repeated attempts to escape before their release in August 1953; both of them were mentioned in dispatches. The courage shown by these three Australian soldiers in the face of terrible hardships and threats of death was sustained by their indomitable spirit.

A. Farrar-Hockley, *The Edge of the Sword* (Lond, 1954); L. Wigmore (ed), *They Dared Mightily* (Canb, 1963); P. J. Greville, 'The Australian Prisoners of War', in R. O'Neill, *Australia in the Korean War 1950-53*, 2 (Canb, 1985) *and* 'The Unfinished Story of Slim Madden, George Cross', *Duty First*, 2, no 2, Mar 1996.
P. J. GREVILLE

MADDOCKS, SYDNEY AUBREY (1881-1963), public servant, was born on 16 February 1881 at Surry Hills, Sydney, third child of Aubrey Sydney Maddocks, a native-born public servant, and his first wife Emily, née Dalley, who came from England. Educated at Fort Street Model School until the age of 14, Sydney worked in 'commercial life' before he joined the Colonial Secretary's Department on 20 May 1901. He rose quickly to correspondence clerk (1914) and chief clerk (1916) in the office of the inspector-general of police. At St Paul's Anglican Church, Rothbury, on 1 December 1915 he married Hilda Evelyn Campbell; they were to have a son and three daughters.

While secretary (from 1920) of the police department, Maddocks was appointed investigating officer (1928) for the Metropolitan Transport Services. He visited State capitals and New Zealand to inspect their public transport systems, and studied law at the University of Sydney (LL.B., 1930). On 4 June 1930 he was admitted to the Bar. He worked closely with Colonel (Sir) Michael Bruxner [q.v.7], the minister for local government, in preparing a bill based on their conviction that transport should be 'a public utility, not a source of private profit'. Maddocks was soon attacked by business interests for favouring an expanded public tramway system over private buses, but had strong political support from Bruxner. Between April and September 1929 Maddocks visited Europe and North America. His *Report on Transport and Traffic Control Abroad* was published in 1930. Under the Transport Act (1930), he was appointed commissioner of road transport, with control of the tramways and extensive powers to regulate the private bus system. His office was abolished in March 1932.

Following the Lang [q.v.9] government's fall, Bruxner became minister for transport and, with Maddocks's help, drafted the Transport (Division of Functions) Act (1932) which created three departments headed by powerful commissioners. On 30 December 1932 Maddocks was gazetted commissioner for road transport and tramways, on a salary of £2500 per annum. One year later he claimed to have turned disastrous losses on the tramways into a profit, while investing in new rolling stock, reducing fares and retrenching debt. He had a lined but handsome face, thick dark hair, and the broad smile and dapper dress of a bon viveur. Fond of golf, tennis and surfing, he lived in Bower Street, Manly; he was also a talented violinist and producer of amateur theatricals.

Maddocks was a powerful figure surrounded by public controversy and private tensions. Early in 1937 he became involved in a dispute with elements of the police department over control of a road safety campaign at a time when he was also implementing changes to bus routes and services which threatened job losses. On the day the changes came into effect (1 March 1937) Maddocks was arrested in his car in secluded bushland at Northwood with an 18-year-old, unemployed houseboy named Mikiel John Adams, alias 'Peterson'. Both men were naked. Maddocks was charged with indecent assault and 'attempting to commit an unnatural offence'. He was suspended from the public service by the governor and later disbarred.

Although he denied the charges, Maddocks was convicted at the Sydney Quarter Sessions on 8 April 1937 and sentenced to eighteen months imprisonment. Adams, who had made a prior arrangement with police to lay the trap, was not indicted. Maddocks's defence counsel W. J. Curtis described Adams as 'an effeminate degenerate' who had stolen personal items from Maddocks as part of a plan to blackmail him.

Onlookers in the public gallery wept as Maddocks sobbed frequently during his speech from the dock, in which he attributed his behaviour to stress, overwork and heavy drinking. In Sydney the case was a *cause célèbre*. The *Daily Telegraph* and the *Bulletin* were relatively sympathetic to Maddocks, but he was pilloried by *Truth* which condemned his sentence as too lenient and attacked Police Commissioner William MacKay [q.v.10] for appearing as a character witness for his friend and colleague of twenty years standing.

After his release in May 1938, Maddocks eventually formed a partnership with his son in a shop at Manly. He died on 31 October 1963 at his home and was cremated; his wife and children survived him.

D. Aitkin, *The Colonel* (Canb, 1969); G. Wotherspoon, *City of the Plain* (Syd, 1991); *SMH*, 16, 22 Dec 1927, 9 Apr, 21 June, 10, 16 Sept, 4, 5 Oct, 14 Nov 1929, 9, 28 Nov 1933, 9, 10 Apr, 13 Aug 1937; *Sun News-Pictorial*, 4 Apr 1932, 6 May 1938; *Daily Telegraph* (Syd), 3 Mar, 3, 7, 9-10, 12 Apr 1937; *Truth* (Syd), 7, 21 Mar, 11, 18 Apr 1937; *Bulletin*, 10 Mar, 14 Apr 1937; S. A. Maddocks, staff card (State Transit Corporate & Resources Payroll Bureau, Syd); Chief Secretary's correspondence, 8/384, 4/7798-801, 5/8132 (NSWA).   MICHAEL FLYNN

MADGWICK, SIR ROBERT BOWDEN (1905-1979), educationist, was born on 10 May 1905 in North Sydney, second of three sons of native-born parents Richard Chalton Madgwick, an Anglican clergyman's son who became a tram driver, and his wife Annie Jane, née Elston. Robert attended Naremburn Public and North Sydney Boys' High schools. He entered the University of Sydney (B.Ec. Hons, 1927; M.Ec., 1932) on a Teachers' College scholarship, took some history subjects and shared the first university medal in economics with (Sir) Herman Black. While studying at Teachers' College, he partnered Black and (Sir) Ronald Walker in a successful debating team. Walker and Madgwick later wrote an economics textbook for schools, *An Outline of Australian Economics* (Sydney, 1931).

After teaching at Nowra (1927) and Parkes (1927-28) intermediate high schools, Madgwick was appointed (1929) temporary lecturer in the faculty of economics at the University of Sydney. Professor R. C. Mills's [q.v.10] work on E. G. Wakefield [q.v.2] and 'systematic colonization' influenced his research. With Mills's help, he obtained a Rockefeller Foundation fellowship in 1933 and enrolled at Balliol College, Oxford (D.Phil., 1936); his thesis was published as *Immigration into Eastern Australia 1788-1851* (London, 1937, Sydney, 1969). He returned to

Sydney in 1935 as an 'economist who saw the light' and turned to history. In January 1936 he took up a lectureship in economic history at the university. On 19 May 1937 he married Ailsa Margaret Aspinall (d.1967) at St Stephen's Presbyterian Church, Sydney.

Madgwick helped to found the Sydney University Lecturers' Association. From 1938 he was secretary of the University Extension Board. After World War II broke out, he was involved in planning an army education scheme (known as the Australian Army Education Service from October 1943). He had wanted to serve abroad with the Australian Imperial Force, but on 1 March 1941 was mobilized as temporary lieutenant colonel and sent to Army Headquarters, Melbourne, to head the new service. In July 1943 he was promoted temporary colonel and given the title of director of army education.

The A.A.E.S. had mixed objectives: to build morale, to educate for citizenship, to provide a diversion from forward or staging-area tedium, and to prepare servicemen and women for demobilization. There were some 10 million attendances at A.A.E.S. classes. About 250 000 personnel read its journal, *Salt*. Its *Current Affairs Bulletin* had a smaller circulation. Always controversial, the A.A.E.S. was accused of politicizing the army, of harbouring left-wing, 'subversive' instructors, and even of 'owning' a number of grand pianos. Such allegations were deflected by Madgwick's repeated assertions that the scheme provided education, not propaganda.

An exceptional administrator, Madgwick played a major part in establishing the Commonwealth Reconstruction Training Scheme. He also sat (1943-46) on two interdepartmental committees which set out the future role of the Commonwealth government in education. Transferring to the Reserve of Officers on 19 April 1946, he worked (from October) as secretary of the interim council of the Australian National University. He continued to champion the cause of adult education, but his claims for a Commonwealth-funded national system were thwarted by lack of support from either the Federal government or the Opposition.

In February 1947 Madgwick accepted the wardenship of New England University College, Armidale, New South Wales. When the institution became the University of New England in 1954, he was appointed vice-chancellor. He spent a good deal of energy in developing the university to meet the cultural and scientific needs of the local community. The U.N.E. adopted new directions in agricultural economics, rural sciences, regional history, educational administration and adult education. Madgwick forged close personal links between 'town and gown' through his committee-work for Armidale's public and

private schools, the Anglican synod, community organizations and the New England Cricket Association. In 1954-56 he served as an alderman on Armidale City Council.

As vice-chancellor, Madgwick worried over student amenities and performance in an isolated campus that suffered extreme winters. He defended academic freedom and collegial democracy, while lamenting that universities were obsessed with committees. His style of management was diplomatic and liberal, but, as the university grew, his approach became —in his own words—'a sort of quaint paternalism'. In 1955 the U.N.E. introduced degree courses for external students. As chairman (1964-66) of the Australian Vice-Chancellors' Committee, Madgwick successfully rebutted the conclusion of (Sir) Leslie Martin's committee on the future of tertiary education in Australia that the provision of 'distance education' was not a university function.

In December 1966 Madgwick retired. He decided against returning to economic history because it had become 'too highly esoteric in content and often too mathematical in technique'. The Federal government sought his advice on grants to teachers' colleges, and chose him to succeed (Sir) James Darling as chairman of the Australian Broadcasting Commission. Madgwick took up this post on 1 July 1967. He saw his role as akin to that of a university leader, with the A.B.C. managers resembling professors and the producers analogous to younger, strident academics. Resisting government interference, especially in current affairs programmes, he once informed (Sir) Alan Hulme, the minister responsible for the A.B.C., 'for every letter you can put on the table ... criticizing *This Day Tonight* I can put ... fifty saying how good it is'. After two terms, he was keen to secure a third, but E. G. Whitlam's Labor government replaced him in 1973. He chaired the Australian Frontier Commission in 1974-76.

Appointed O.B.E. in 1962, Madgwick was knighted in 1966. That year he was granted the freedom of the city of Armidale. Honorary doctorates were conferred on him by the universities of Sydney (1961), Queensland (1961) and New England (1969). At St Andrew's Anglican Church, Wahroonga, Sydney, on 12 January 1971 he married a widow Eileen Hilda McGrath, née Wall. Sir Robert died on 25 March 1979 at Hornsby and was cremated; his wife survived him, as did the three daughters of his first marriage. Madgwick's contribution to education had been distinctive: he pioneered a massive scheme of adult education and regional higher education. A reserved, unruffled administrator, he believed that Australia could only overcome its 'highly developed inferiority complex' by heavy public investment in its educational and cultural institutions.

A. D. Spaull, *Australian Education in the Second World War* (Brisb, 1982); K. S. Inglis, *This is the ABC* (Melb, 1983); L. Foster, *High Hopes* (Melb, 1986); D. Dymock, *A Sweet Use of Adversity* (Armidale, NSW, 1995); *SMH*, 27 Mar 1979; R. B. Madgwick, unpublished memoir (ADB file, Canb).

ANDREW SPAULL

MADIRAZZA, SPASOJE (1898-1969), medical practitioner, was born on 18 January 1898 at Drnis, Dalmatia, Austria-Hungary, son of Ivan Madirazza, and his wife Luisa, née Vilicic. His father and grandfather had a well-established medical practice at Split. Spasoje studied medicine at the University of Zagreb (M.D., 1926), married Nada Babich on 3 June 1926 and joined the staff of the university's public hospital. In 1929 he went into general practice at Jasenovac, Slovenia, and in 1932 gained a diploma of public health. Madirazza became involved in politics as an advocate of unity between Croats, Serbs and Slovenes. In March 1941 he was called up for service in the Royal Army, but in April, following the German occupation, moved to Budinscina as a civilian.

Some of his wife's family were murdered by the pro-Nazi Ustashi. Madirazza regarded members of the Ustashi government of Croatia as 'bloodthirsty beasts without any trace of humanity'. In June 1941 he was barred from holding public office. He was later condemned to death. Such was his popularity in the town of Budinscina that he was subsequently reprieved. Sent to Pag in the Adriatic Sea, he saw the remains of thousands of civilians who had been killed in the Slana concentration camp before Italian troops occupied the island. He gave medical aid to the islanders, including the anti-fascist partisans, but was anti-communist in his views.

Attempting to escape to Italy, Madirazza, his wife and four children reached Slovenia, after their ship sank. They settled at Logatec, where he worked in the local hospital among typhus sufferers. In March 1945 he caught the fever and was bedridden for months in British hospitals in Italy. He was appointed chief doctor of the Yugoslav Chetnik hospital under British military command at Mercatello, Italy, in September 1945 and emigration medical officer at Diepholz, Germany, in April 1947. Emigrating to Australia as a labourer, he reached Sydney on 19 November 1948 in the *Castelbianco*. He spent eight months with his family at the Bathurst migrant camp, working as a caretaker; he then served as a medical orderly at the Scheyville holding centre before running a milk bar with his family at Surry Hills, Sydney.

Industrious, conscientious and humane, Madirazza approached life with the attitude: 'Do not give in to misfortune but on the con-

trary go forward the more bravely where your fortune permits'. In 1952—at the age of 54—he enrolled in medicine at the University of Sydney; he passed fourth, fifth and final year subjects, and was registered to practise on 2 June 1954. He was naturalized in the same year. During his studies he grew interested in the depression syndrome affecting some of his fellow immigrants, and opened a private practice at Petersham. There he was respected and revered.

Fluent in Serbo-Croatian, Italian and English, Madirazza also spoke German, French and Spanish. He loved music, mathematics and history, especially the history of Dalmatia. After several years of hectic private practice, he died on 29 July 1969 in Lewisham Hospital and was buried with Catholic rites in Rookwood cemetery. His wife, daughter and three sons survived him.

MJA, 24 Jan 1970, p 184; naturalization file, A435/1, item 49/4/5627 (AA, Canb); information from Dr J. Madirazza, Petersham, Syd, who holds a copy of his father's curriculum vitae.

BARRY YORK

MAGNUS, EVERETT RANDALL (1907-1967), dentist, was born on 6 January 1907 at Burwood, Sydney, elder of twins and only son of Frank Douglas Magnus, a medical practitioner from New York, and his native-born wife Robinetta Millicent, née Allan. After graduating in dentistry in the United States of America (like his brother Everett Randall), Frank rose to be a prominent oral surgeon. Young Everett attended Sydney Grammar School where he played cricket ('a fair left hand bowler'), captained the shooting team and became a prefect. At the University of Sydney (B.D.S., 1930; D.D.Sc., 1936), he was president of the dental undergraduates' association, and graduated with honours and the A. J. Arnott [q.v.13] prize for general anaesthesia and clinical surgery. He began practice at Guyra and served as a board-member (1931-32) of the Armidale and New England Hospital.

Having decided to specialize in oral surgery, Magnus took up a post at the United Dental Hospital of Sydney. In 1934 he was appointed an honorary dental surgeon and clinical instructor in periodontia. His doctoral thesis was entitled 'Some observations on acute osteomyelitis of the mandible'. At the Presbyterian Church, Armidale, on 4 June 1935 he married Dulcie May Hutton, a 24-year-old music teacher. He opened consulting rooms in Macquarie Street, Sydney, in 1937, and practised as an oral surgeon. From March 1938 he was an honorary dental surgeon at Royal Prince Alfred Hospital until he accepted a consultancy in January 1967.

Throughout his life Magnus contributed to his profession and the wider community, following the examples set by his father and uncle. He was honorary secretary (1937-41), vice-president (1947-49) and president (1950-51) of the Australian Dental Association; he also chaired (1951-56) the New South Wales branch's defence committee. He sat on the Dental Board of New South Wales (from 1951), represented his profession on the Poisons Advisory Committee (1953-67) and was president of the Australian and New Zealand Society of Oral Surgeons (in the 1960s). Magnus demonstrated his expertise in 1944 when he was called as a witness in the re-opened 'Pyjama Girl' case. His evidence helped to correct an error in the dental description of the murdered victim Linda Agostini, leading to the arrest and conviction of her husband Antonio Agostini [qq.v.13].

In numerous addresses to new graduates of dentistry, Magnus argued that, if high standards were to be maintained and advanced, dentists should continue to study throughout their professional lives. As president of the Australian Dental Association, he lectured in country towns on new developments in his field. His generous prologue to the 1958 Annie Praed [q.v.11] oration showed that he was ahead of many of his generation in recognizing women as equals in the profession. In 1962 he was appointed O.B.E.

Magnus suffered from diabetes, but did not allow it to affect his life. His practice filled his days, and his evenings were often taken up with meetings. What spare time he had was spent playing bowls, or fishing, or at Royal Sydney Golf Club. He was highly regarded for his characteristic gentleness, ethical practice, and consideration for his fellow practitioners. Survived by his wife, daughter and son, he died of a lung abscess on 4 December 1967 at his Double Bay home and was cremated with Anglican rites. It was a sad irony that press comment on his death stressed his part in the notorious 'Pyjama Girl' case, almost to the exclusion of all his other public service.

R. W. Halliday, *A History of Dentistry in New South Wales 1788 to 1945*, A. O. Watson ed (Syd, 1977); R. Coleman, *The Pyjama Girl* (Melb, 1978); *Sydneian*, no 234, July 1919, no 260, Apr 1926, no 360, July 1968; *Aust Dental J*, vol 3, no 4, Aug 1958, p 253, vol 7, no 4, Aug 1962, p 345, vol 13, no 1, Feb 1968, p 102; *SMH*, 2 June 1962, 6 Dec 1967.

RACHEL GRAHAME

MAGNUS, WALTER (1903-1954), restaurateur, was born on 26 June 1903 at Dortmund, Westphalia, Germany, eldest of three children of Sigmund Magnus, cigar manufacturer, and his wife Sophie, née Edelstein. Sigmund died in 1909 and Sophie remarried. On poor terms with his stepfather, Walter spent four years at a Jewish rabbinical school where he acquired fluency in Hebrew, though he was never too particular about observing his religion. He was a keen amateur boxer, and enjoyed cycling, tennis and soccer. After completing an apprenticeship to a dentist, he practised at Dortmund and in Berlin. When Adolf Hitler came to power in 1933, Magnus travelled to Switzerland, Italy and France before setting up as a dentist at Barcelona, Spain. There, he claimed, he once treated (Sir) Winston Churchill. On 10 October 1934 at Barcelona he married German-born Hedwig Lisser Zinner. In 1936, driven out by the civil war, they went in turn to Czechoslovakia, Holland and England. With Walter's sister and Hedy's brother they reached Sydney in the *Orford* on 8 April 1937.

Refused registration to practise his profession, Magnus sold his dental equipment and bought the Claremont Café at Kings Cross. He relished cooking and specialized in continental food. Featuring murals painted by Elaine Haxton, the Claremont attracted artists, actors and Bohemians, among them Peter Finch [q.v.14], Brian Penton [q.v.], (Sir) Russell Drysdale and Donald Friend. In World War II Magnus, who was declared medically unfit for service, supported the Stage Door Canteen. With Harry Jayton (formerly Hans Jacobson) he formed a company, La Palette Pty Ltd; they opened La Palette, Double Bay (1940), and in 1941 took over the catering for the Journalists' Club. In 1943, as Universal Caterers Pty Ltd, they established Le Coq d'Or, Ash Street, near Martin Place and George Street. The cafés came under surveillance as the war brought foreign patrons, in addition to American and British servicemen, including Prince Philip (later Duke of Edinburgh) who became an acquaintance. Magnus was naturalized on 7 December 1945.

In 1946 the partners opened the Savarin, a fashionable city restaurant in George Street, which boasted a kosher licence, a band and a gipsy violinist. Magnus commissioned (Sir) William Dobell [q.v.14] to paint his portrait ('Chez Walter', now in the National Gallery of Australia) and to decorate the Savarin with a mural, 'Carnival'. Other enterprises included the Elite Caterers and Almora House Pty Ltd, Mosman, for private parties. Magnus made radio broadcasts, wrote newspaper articles about food, advised Gordon Edgell [q.v.8] & Sons Ltd and other processing firms, and for some years ran the Australian Wine Producers' Association's restaurant at the Showground.

The gregarious Magnus collected Australian paintings, loved classical music and enjoyed horse-riding; he also dressed impeccably—often in a morning-suit—and wore a monocle. Five ft 8 ins (173 cm) tall, he had become heroically corpulent by the 1950s—his 24½-stone (156 kg) globular frame topped by 'a happy, smiling moon of a face'. He spoke several languages, English with a thick German accent. The partnership with Jayton came to an end. In 1951 Hedy divorced Walter and took over the businesses. Magnus opened The Pier restaurant at Rose Bay. A wine connoisseur, beer quaffer and cigarette smoker who indulged all his pleasures, he died of a cerebral haemorrhage on 5 February 1954 at Royal Prince Alfred Hospital and was buried with Jewish rites in Northern Suburbs cemetery. His two sons survived him. A distinctive 'New Australian', Magnus had helped to broaden Sydney's culture and improve its cuisine.

S. D. Rutland, *Edge of the Diaspora* (Syd, 1988); *Hotel and Cafe News*, 1 Sept 1949, Nov 1952; *People* (Syd), 25 Apr 1951, p 22; *SMH*, 19 Nov 1994; B. Lewis, The Jewish Connections to *Kashruth* in New South Wales since World War Two (B.A. Hons thesis, Univ NSW, 1995); H. Magnus, dossier C123/0 item 10398 (AA, Syd); papers held by and information from Dr P. and Mr M. Magnus, Syd; information from Mr O. Shaul, Syd.
CHRIS CUNNEEN

MAGOFFIN, ANN MARGARET (1918-1971), chartered accountant, was born on 14 May 1918 at Echuca, Victoria, eldest of four children of Victorian-born parents Richard Magoffin, grazier of Ardbrin, North Queensland, and his second wife Josephine Lillian, née Williams. Peg had three half-brothers and a half-sister. Her mother died when she was 12. Richard's family were pioneers in the Winton district of Queensland and Ardbrin's isolation led to Peg's schooling being irregular. Her education from the age of 9 at the Convent of the Sacred Heart, Rose Bay, Sydney, was interrupted by the Depression and by illness.

Leaving school, Peg returned to Ardbrin where her father persuaded her to develop costings for the property's wool output. She pursued her interest in financial management on her return to Sydney in the 1940s and worked for Thom & Smith Pty Ltd, radio manufacturers, as a cost-clerk. After holding similar jobs elsewhere, she was employed by the accounting firm of D. P. Dickson & Son, Bridge Street. She completed accountancy training at night and was admitted to the Institute of Chartered Accountants in Australia on 9 November 1951.

Dickson's had many country clients for whom Peg Magoffin's interest and experience in the wool industry proved useful. In time, she was responsible for many of the firm's pastoral accounts, which she purchased when she left in 1956 to establish her own public accountancy firm, A. M. Magoffin & Co. Well known for her expertise in taxation—largely through her monthly column (1953-71) in *Rydge's* business journal—she wrote a text-book on the subject, and lectured for the Australian Mutual Provident Society and for the faculty of law at the University of Sydney. She also studied economics as an evening student at that university (B.Ec., 1967).

Miss Magoffin chaired (1951-70) the finance committee of the Australian Association of Business and Professional Women's Clubs. During her term as the association's president (1966-70), she oversaw a major restructuring of the organization which led to the creation of State divisions. She worked tirelessly for the B.P.W., spending many week-ends attending meetings in Victoria and in country towns in New South Wales. In 1969 she prepared and presented the B.P.W.'s submission when the association was granted leave to intervene in the Equal Pay cases before the Commonwealth Court of Conciliation and Arbitration. Next year she was appointed to the National Labour Advisory Council's committee on women's employment.

Her role as financial adviser to the Society of the Sacred Heart of Jesus, a French Order, was due to the impact of the Second Vatican Council on the Catholic Church. Even in Australia the Society had kept all its records in French. Under Magoffin's guidance a double-entry accounting system was introduced, individual convents became accountable for their own affairs, and records began to be kept in English. In 1967 she joined the council of Sancta Sophia College, University of Sydney. In spite of suffering from ischaemic heart disease, Magoffin still maintained her hectic pace. She died of myocardial infarction on 7 August 1971 in the home at Arcadia that she owned with Mary Julia Susan Patterson.

P. R. Thoms (comp), *The First 25 Years, B.P.W. Australia* (Melb, 1972); *Chartered Accountant in Aust*, Sept 1971, p 52; *Rydge's*, 44, no 9, Sept 1971; Provincial Archives of the Society of the Sacred Heart, Convent of the Sacred Heart of Jesus, Rose Bay, Syd; information from Mrs F. Cobham, Springwood, NSW, Mr P. Davidson, David B. Dickson & Co, Syd, Mr S. Harrison, Inst of Chartered Accountants in Aust, Syd, and Mr D. Magoffin, Paddington, Syd.
ANN EYLAND

MAGUIRE, BERNARD JOSEPH (1897-1957), public servant, was born on 4 June 1897 in Brisbane, eldest child of Irish-born parents Peter Maguire, baker, and his wife Maria, née Gannon. Educated at Chermside State School and St Joseph's College, Gregory Terrace, Bernard entered the Queensland Public Service on 19 July 1915 as a junior draftsman in the survey office, Department of

Public Lands. At Holy Rosary Church, Bundaberg, on 8 September 1924 he married Veronica Josephine Blake (d.1956) with Catholic rites. Promoted assistant notings officer in 1926, he served as secretary to electoral boundaries commissions for local authorities (1928 and 1933), the Commonwealth (1931 and 1934) and the State (1932 and 1935). In July 1939 he was appointed principal electoral officer. He was to supervise Queensland's general elections in 1941, 1944, 1947 and 1950.

In 1949 the Hanlon [q.v.14] Australian Labor Party government enacted legislation which divided Queensland into four zones and increased the number of electorates from sixty-two to seventy-five. The measure discriminated in favour of electorates in the outback and provincial cities where Labor enjoyed strong support. One of three commissioners appointed to carry out the ensuing redistribution, Maguire was the principal architect of the changes which gave the A.L.P. a majority of nine seats, even though the party received only 46.87 per cent of the votes at the general elections on 29 April 1950.

Labor's R. J. Gardner had defeated the Liberal Party candidate J. E. Hamilton by forty-four votes to win the Legislative Assembly seat of Bulimba. (Sir) Alan Mansfield [q.v.], judge of the Elections Tribunal, declared Gardner's election void. He found that eleven fraudulent absentee ballot papers—submitted before polling day at the chief electoral office and purporting to cast votes for Gardner—had been substituted for papers containing valid votes for Hamilton. In parliament the Liberal Party leader (Sir) Thomas Hiley named Maguire as the person most likely to have perpetrated the fraud. Inspector F. E. Bischof [q.v.13] investigated the allegations and charged Maguire with eight counts of forging ballot papers.

Maguire was suspended from duty on 8 March 1951. Between April and September he was tried three times in the Supreme Court of Queensland. T. M. Barry and Dan Casey appeared for the defence. On each occasion the jury failed to agree on a verdict. The crown prosecutor entered a *nolle prosequi* and Maguire was discharged on 7 September. Handwriting experts, whose evidence was central to the case, gave conflicting accounts. Lax security procedures at the chief electoral office could have allowed other persons to gain access to the ballot papers. Maguire's friends raised funds to meet his legal costs.

Cabinet lifted his suspension and in December he was appointed registrar of co-operative societies, Department of Labour and Industry. Maguire was a devoted family man and a practising Catholic. Thin and of average height, he smoked heavily and long suffered from coronary disease. He died of acute heart failure on 21 November 1957 at his Wooloowin home and was buried in Lutwyche cemetery; his two sons and three daughters survived him.

C. Lack (comp), *Three Decades of Queensland Political History, 1929-1960* (Brisb, 1962); *PD* (Qld), 1951, p 1792; *Telegraph* (Brisb), 8 Mar 1951, 21 Nov 1957; *Courier-Mail*, 19 Apr 1951; staff file (QA); information from Mr P. Maguire, Gordon Park, Brisb.   MANFRED CROSS

MAHONEY, WILLIAM JAMES (1894-1967), vaudevillian and theatre manager, was born on 5 February 1894 at Helena, Montana, United States of America, son of Michael Fitzgerald, rancher, and his wife Mary, née Moran. When Will was 2 years old his father died. His mother supported him—and her children from a previous marriage, Frank and Mary Mahoney—by cooking in shanty towns and logging camps. Will first performed on stage in 1902. He and Frank ('The Mahoney Bros') devised an act and eventually played on the vaudeville circuit. By 1914 they had toured North America and Mexico, and had visited Melbourne.

At the age of 21 Will married Iva Gibbs. After Frank left the stage, Will designed a xylophone platform, 17-ft (5.2 m) long, on which he danced with small mallets attached to his shoes, the tunes matching his rapid patter and slapstick comedy. His acrobatics demanded concentration and skill, and attracted public and critical acclaim. George Gershwin wrote music for him. Mahoney toured England in 1926 and appeared in three Hollywood films. After his wife died, he married Lillian Wilson with Catholic rites on 2 July 1928 at Manhattan, New York; their marriage ended in divorce.

Single-minded, and a perfectionist, Mahoney was said to be the highest-paid variety star in America, allegedly earning $5500 per week by the early 1930s. He and his partner Bob Geraghty worked in Britain in 1934-38. Their shows, *Radio New York*, *Why Be Serious* and *Bats in the Belfry*, featured an American artiste, Vina Evelyn (Evie) Hayes. She was aged 25 when Will married her on 26 March 1938 at the register office, Westminster, London. That year Frank Neil, managing director of the Tivoli vaudeville circuit in Australia, brought Mahoney, Hayes and Geraghty to Melbourne.

Their first performance at the Tivoli Theatre on 22 August 1938 marked the beginning of seventeen successful tours of Australasia. As part of their contract, they appeared in Cinesound Productions Pty Ltd's 1939 film, *Come Up Smiling* (renamed *Ants in his Pants*). In January 1943 Mahoney joined Geraghty in the management of the Cremorne Theatre,

Brisbane. Popular with American and Australian servicemen, the theatre attracted entertainers from overseas, among them Mahoney's friends Jack Benny, Bob Hope, Gary Cooper, Larry Adler and Artie Shaw. Following the end of World War II, variety shows attracted smaller audiences and the Cremorne began to lose money.

In 1948 Mahoney closed his theatre and returned to the U.S.A. to revitalize his career. His reception was overwhelming and he was acclaimed as 'the most versatile variety artist in the world'. Accepting another Tivoli contract, he came back to Australia in April 1959. He and Evie settled in Melbourne, played in musicals and taught young performers. They appeared together in *Funny Girl* during 1966 until Mahoney collapsed on stage in November. He died on 9 February 1967 in South Melbourne and was buried in Melbourne general cemetery; his wife survived him, as did the son of his first marriage and the daughter of his second. Local and international media paid tribute to the 'little American leprechaun with the laughing blue eyes, endearing smile, black bowler hat and magic dancing feet'.

B. Carroll, *The Australian Stage Album* (Melb, 1975); K. Brisbane (ed), *Entertaining Australia* (Syd, 1991); J. Crampton, *Evie Hayes* (Syd, 1992); P. Parsons (ed), *Companion to Theatre in Australia* (Syd, 1995); Cremorne Theatre, Brisb, programmes and notices (OL).

JENNIFER RADBOURNE

MAIDEN, ALFRED CLEMENT BORTHWICK (1922-1979), public servant, was born on 21 August 1922 at Taree, New South Wales, son of Australian-born parents Alfred William Borthwick Maiden, a salesman who became a public accountant, and his wife Florence Ethel, née Rudder. Young Alf attended Taree High School before studying history and economics at New England University College, Armidale (B.A. Hons, 1942). A full-time militiaman from December 1941, he transferred to the Australian Imperial Force on 9 October 1942. At St James's Anglican Church, Sydney, on 20 March 1943 he married Norma Couper Sneesby, a 21-year-old schoolteacher. He served in Port Moresby in 1943-44 as a bombardier with the 555th Light Anti-Aircraft Battery and was demobilized in Australia on 4 December 1945.

In 1946 Maiden obtained a post as a research officer in the Bureau of Agricultural Economics, Department of Commerce and Agriculture, Canberra. He gained valuable experience as secretary to a committee which calculated the costs of production for wheat—the basis of the stabilization plan implemented in 1948. From 1951 he was commercial and agricultural attaché at the Australian Embassy, Washington. Returning home, he was appointed assistant-director of the B.A.E. in April 1954 and assistant-secretary (tariff division), Department of Trade, in July 1956. In the following year he again went to Washington, as commercial counsellor and Australian government trade commissioner. Back in Canberra, in 1959 he was made director of the B.A.E., which had been transferred (1956) to the Department of Primary Industry. On 27 October 1962 he was promoted secretary of the department.

By the 1960s subsidies and price-stabilization schemes for primary products, such as wheat and dairy goods, had led to overproduction and were proving costly to the Commonwealth government. Plans to modify these measures called for inventiveness and fine judgement on the part of ministers and their chief advisers. Maiden was adept at handling these and other politically sensitive issues of agricultural policy. He also gained a reputation as a capable representative of his country at meetings of international economic bodies, particularly those of the United Nations Food and Agriculture Organization.

In 1968 Maiden resigned from the public service to become managing director of the International Wool Secretariat, a post he took up in London in 1969. The I.W.S. had been established to carry out international research and promotional activities for the wool industries of its member countries—Australia, New Zealand and South Africa—at a time of increasing competition from synthetic fibres. Australia initially contributed about two-thirds of the I.W.S. budget. Maiden's management and leadership provided effective and economical administration of the organization's programmes. On 30 July 1973 he was appointed (for a five-year term) full-time chairman of the new Australian Wool Corporation, Melbourne; he also accepted chairmanship of the I.W.S.

Maiden's responsibilities proved demanding. Market fluctuations in the price of wool were extreme. In an attempt to protect producers from the adverse effects of this volatility, the Wool Corporation introduced a minimum reserve-price scheme in September 1974. As a result, the corporation accumulated large quantities of wool (ranging from 1.9 million bales in late 1975 to 350 000 bales in June 1979) and engaged in extensive borrowing to pay for the stockpile. The Wool Corporation also allocated substantial funds for research and promotion, and studied production and marketing methods, such as innovative shearing techniques, sale by sample, the objective measurement of wool and the use of larger bales.

To succeed, Maiden needed the confidence of politicians, growers, buyers, brokers, trade unionists, financiers and other people in the industry. A tall, dark-haired man who enjoyed tennis, war history and operatic music, he gave 'the impression of solidarity, decency and honesty'. His calmness, confidence and openness inspired trust. Appointed C.B.E. in 1965, he was named 'Man of the Year in Australian Agriculture' in 1976. Twelve months into his second term as chairman of the Wool Corporation, he died of a coronary occlusion on 30 July 1979 at his Toorak home and was cremated; his wife, son and daughter survived him. Michael Noakes painted two portraits of Maiden: one is held by the I.W.S. in London, the other by the family.

W. Ives, *The Australian Wool Corporation* (Melb, 1994); *Aust Parliamentary and Legislative Review*, 10 Oct 1968, p 21; Australian Wool Corporation, *Annual Report* 1973-79; *Canb Times*, 1 Jan 1969; *Australian*, 31 July 1979; information from Mrs N. Maiden, Forrest, Canb.

ROBERT S. SWIFT

MAIDMENT, GEORGE; *see* THORNTON, ALEXANDER GEORGE

MAIN, JOHN MURDOCH (1893-1967), director of public works, was born on 24 July 1893 in Sydney, son of William Main, a publican from Scotland, and his Irish-born wife Bridget, née Flannery. Jack was educated at Parramatta, St Joseph's College (1907-08), Hunters Hill, St Mary's Cathedral High School (1909-10), Sydney, and Marist Brothers' High School, Darlinghurst. He failed to matriculate at the senior public examination in 1911, but succeeded in December 1912. At the University of Sydney (B.E., 1917), he graduated with first-class honours in civil engineering.

Joining the Forestry Commission on 11 April 1917, Main served as a forestry engineer. He transferred to the Department of Public Works in 1920 and became a supervising engineer on the reconstruction of the Parramatta Road. At St Mary's Catholic Cathedral on 28 March 1921 he married Myra Alphonsa (Phonsie) Grace; they were to remain childless. He moved to Bourke in 1922, then served at Dubbo (1924-27), Coffs Harbour (1927-30) and Broken Hill (1930-34). His experience of public works was extraordinarily broad. He managed harbour works; he oversaw railways and roads, using both horse and camel teams in the western district; and at Dubbo he was responsible for construction of the town's sewerage scheme and the Narromine water works. As manager of the Broken Hill Water Supply and district engineer, he controlled 270 men, supervised the construction of pumping-stations, roads, railway lines, bridges and public buildings, directed the maintenance of river locks over an area which stretched from the Victorian to the Queensland borders, collected revenue and ran the office at Broken Hill. In referring to his responsibilities for water supply, *St Joseph's College Magazine* noted that 'Jack was always able to save the thirsty population from the necessity of a little trip up to the corner'. In the years 1917 to 1933 he took not a single day of sick leave, and often worked in the evenings and at weekends. His file was endorsed 'a most efficient officer'.

In 1934 Main returned to Sydney and head office. He was seconded to the Department of Labour and Industry in 1935-36 as consulting engineer to the Unemployment Relief Council. Back at the Department of Public Works, he prospered, becoming assistant principal engineer (1936) and principal designing engineer (1938). In 1942 he was appointed chief engineer, responsible to the minister for co-ordinating all technical matters arising in the various professional sections. He was appointed director of public works and permanent head of the department in 1950.

Throughout his career Main was prepared to take on additional responsibilities. He served (1944-50) on the Crown Employees (Land Surveyors) Conciliation Committee, chaired the State Committee of Testing Authorities, and was a councillor (*ex officio*) of the National Association of Testing Authorities. Of the many committees of investigation on which he sat, the most notable were the inquiry into the establishment of a deep-water port at Iluka, and the Snowy River Investigation Committee which was appointed by the State government in December 1941. Under his chairmanship the latter committee endorsed the Water Conservation and Irrigation Commission's plans to dam and divert the Snowy. When the Snowy River scheme began, Jack Main, as director of public works in New South Wales, was responsible for constructing Adaminaby Dam. He was also a member (1947-50) of the Commonwealth-State Snowy River Investigation Committee.

Main's interest in port development was shown by his involvement in harbour works at Port Kembla, Newcastle, Coffs Harbour and Iluka. As departmental head, he was an astute manager of resources, buying surplus earth-moving equipment cheaply from the Joint Coal Board for use on public-works projects. In 1956 Main defended his staff working on the Adaminaby Dam against allegations of maladministration and malpractice (such as using departmental vehicles for private purposes); in doing so, he showed knowledge of and sympathy for the isolation and difficult working conditions. In 1957 he was appointed C.B.E. He retired in December 1958.

Active in the Institution of Engineers, Australia, Main contributed to its *Proceedings* and in 1966 organized its national conference. In retirement, he joined (1961) the advisory board of St Vincent's Hospital, Darlinghurst, and chaired its works and property committee until his death. He belonged to the New South Wales Club. Music was one of his lifelong enjoyments. Although he played golf in middle age, he later took to bowls and joined the Double Bay club. Survived by his wife, he died on 30 October 1967 in St Vincent's Hospital and was buried in Rookwood cemetery.

St Joseph's College Mag, Dec 1934, p 96; Dept of Public Works Staff Assn (NSW), *Stateworks*, 3, no 6, 1958, p 5, 13, no 1, 1968, p 7; St Vincent's Hospital (Syd), *Annual Report*, 1968; *SMH*, 12 Dec 1912, 21 Sept 1954, 16 Jan 1956, 1 Jan 1957, 31 Oct 1967; *Sun-Herald*, 5 Feb 1956; Archives, St Joseph's College, Hunter's Hill, Syd; J. M. Main, personal file, Dept of Public Works 10/49869 (NSWA); information from Mr B. McPherson, Double Bay Bowling Club Ltd, Syd. RACHEL GRAHAME

MAIRINGER, FRANZ (1915-1978), equestrian, was born on 11 December 1915 in Vienna, son of Franz Kurth Mairinger, locksmith, and his wife Theresia, née Zemlicka. When his father died in 1935, young Franz abandoned his plans to study engineering and enlisted in the Austrian cavalry. He was stationed for two years in Hanover where he received a thorough training in steeplechasing, jumping and cross-country riding. At an international horse show in Hanover in June 1939 his horsemanship so impressed the director of the Spanish Riding School of Vienna that he was offered (and accepted) a position there. In 1942 Mairinger was promoted instructor. He had married Ernestine Wilhelmine Pracan in Vienna on 24 August 1940; they lost most of their possessions during World War II.

To save the fare to emigrate, Mairinger gave private riding-lessons (from 1951) in Switzerland. Sponsored by R. M. Williams, he arrived in Adelaide in 1952 and worked successively on Williams's sheep-farm, as a labourer in Elder, Smith [qq.v.4,6] & Co. Ltd's wool store, and in the upholstery factory of A. J. Higgins, who owned thoroughbred show horses. Soon Mairinger was buying and training horses for Higgins and winning prizes at the Royal Adelaide Show. Higgins lent him the money to bring out his wife and two children in 1953; the family was be naturalized in 1959.

In 1954 Mairinger was appointed coach of the Equestrian Federation of Australia (founded 1952). He prepared the first Australian equestrian team to compete in the Olympic Games (Stockholm, 1956). The team finished fourth. In 1957 he became permanent instructor of the E.F.A., operating from Samuel Hordern's [q.v.14] Retford Park, Bowral, New South Wales. Under Mairinger's coaching, the Australian team dominated the Badminton Horse Trials in England in 1960 and provided his greatest triumph at the Olympic Games in Rome that year: in the three-day event the Australians won the team gold medal, Laurie Morgan the individual gold, and Neale Lavis the individual silver. Mairinger coached the Australian equestrian team at six Olympics and was training a seventh team at the time of his death. The team gained bronze medals in Mexico City in 1968 and at Montreal, Canada, in 1976.

Mairinger was a gentle man, with a keen sense of humour, who enjoyed photography and playing chess. A perfectionist and a tough disciplinarian, he had the ability to blend European skill and technique with the raw talent of Australian riders, and to train them in show-jumping, to grand prix level in dressage, and for three-day events. In 1965 he coached apprentices for the Australian Jockey Club; in 1967 he opened an indoor riding-school at Bowral for the E.F.A. to provide for all types of show-riding. Morgan thought there 'has not been, and there is never likely to be, any person in Australia who could psychoanalyse a horse better than Franz'. Lavis regarded Mairinger as a philosopher who 'knew men as well as horses'.

Survived by his wife, son and daughter, Mairinger died of cancer on 10 May 1978 at Bowral and was buried with Catholic rites in the local cemetery. His book, *Horses are made to be Horses* (Adelaide, 1983), was edited by his wife Erna with the assistance of Kay Irving.

R. and M. Howell, *Aussie Gold* (Brisb, 1988); *Hoofs and Horns*, Jan 1979, p 8; *SMH*, 1 Feb 1957, 26 Oct 1967; *Sun* (Syd), 28 June, 20 July 1965; *Bulletin*, 21 Oct 1967; 'This is Your Life: Franz Mairinger', ATN-7 television, 31 Mar 1977 (video, ts and research notes held at National Film and Sound Archive, Canb). R. I. CASHMAN

MAITLAND, ALAN CATHCART (1898-1979), managing director, was born on 18 November 1898 at Braidwood, New South Wales, fifth child of Ernest Leslie Maitland, an English-born police magistrate, and his wife Marion Loyalty, née Doyle, who came from Maitland. Alan was educated at King's College, Goulburn, and The King's School, Parramatta. The family's financial situation obliged him to leave school at the age of 14. He worked briefly for a bank at Parramatta and for a small insurance company at Newcastle before being employed (from 15 May 1916) as a junior clerk at the Mercantile Mutual Insurance Co. Ltd, Sydney. On 3 January 1917 he enlisted in the Australian Imperial Force; he served on the Western Front with the 34th Battalion and the 4th Machine-Gun Battalion.

Discharged from the A.I.F. on 30 October 1919 in Sydney, Maitland was made Mercantile Mutual's inspector for the Northern Rivers. In 1923 he was posted to Sydney where he rose to chief clerk in 1935, company secretary in 1942 and manager in 1947. His reliability and quickness won him the confidence of superiors and colleagues. At St Philip's Anglican Church, Sydney, on 6 October 1923 he had married 19-year-old Sybil ('Betty') Iredale Brennand; they lived at Strathfield and were to have three children before being divorced in 1948. Maitland was a Freemason, captain (1943-45) of Strathfield Golf Club and active in the Returned Soldiers' and Sailors' Imperial League of Australia.

Following his appointment as managing director of Mercantile Mutual on 1 April 1948, Maitland engineered the friendly takeover of Australian General Insurance Co. Ltd and also served as its managing director. In seventeen years at the helm, he brought about considerable change in Mercantile Mutual. He took a particular interest in diversifying into life insurance, and in enlarging and improving the investments, income from which increased twenty-fold while premium income multiplied by almost ten and company assets by seventeen. He made judicious promotions and appointments, and dealt with crises (such as reinsurance treaties) with tact and skill. Maitland demonstrated diligence, foresight in his investments, and loyalty to the company. On one occasion the board had to force him to take a holiday. Active in the Insurance Institute of New South Wales, he was a council-member (from 1948), a fellow (1952) and president (1952-53) of the Australian Insurance Institute. He was also a director (1949-71) of the Church of England Insurance Co. of Australia Ltd.

At St Anne's Anglican Church, Strathfield, on 2 April 1948 Maitland had married 40-year-old Marcia Eadith Walker. They moved to Bellevue Hill in 1958. He was interested in horse-racing and belonged to the Australasian Pioneers', the Union and Royal Sydney Golf clubs; after a back injury he took to bowls. He loved orchids and cultivated them by the hundred. Although he retired on 31 October 1965, he continued as a director (1966-71) of Mercantile Mutual. President (1949-51) of The King's School Old Boys' Union, he donated the Alan Maitland cup for music. He died on 13 May 1979 in St Luke's Hospital, Darlinghurst, and was cremated; his wife survived him, as did the son and younger daughter of his first marriage.

H. Mayfield, *Servant of a Century* (priv pub, Syd, 1978); P. C. Wickens, *Insurance Institutes in Australia 1884-1984* (Syd, 1984); Maitland papers (The King's School Archives, Parramatta, Syd); information from Mr I. H. Maitland, Norwood, New Jersey, US, and Mr M. C. Davis, Castle Cove, Syd.

M. D. PRENTIS

MAKINSON, RICHARD ELLISS BODENHAM (1913-1979), physicist and communist, was born on 5 May 1913 at Burwood, Sydney, second son of native-born parents Patrick Raymond Makinson, bank manager, and his wife Kathleen Marion, née Bodenham. Dick attended Sydney Church of England Grammar School (Shore) and obtained first-class honours in English and physics at the 1930 Leaving certificate examinations. Enrolling in engineering at the University of Sydney, he gained eight high distinctions in two years, then switched to science (B.Sc., 1935). Having won the Norbert Quirk prize, and the Barker and the Deas Thomson [qq.v.1,2] scholarships, he graduated with first-class honours, the John Coutts scholarship, and university medals for mathematics (1934) and physics (1935). In England he undertook postgraduate research at St John's College, Cambridge (Ph.D., 1939), and became a fellow of the Institute of Physics. With fascism threatening democracy, he joined the Communist Party of Great Britain and, on his return home in 1939, that of Australia.

Makinson took up an appointment as assistant-lecturer in physics at the University of Sydney on 1 February 1939. His field was solid state physics, but his interests and talents were wide, encompassing work and published papers on nuclear physics and quantum theory, radiophysics (especially on radar during World War II), the photo-electric effect and the theory of diffraction. An accomplished teacher, he was attentive to the needs and possibilities of his students. Despite his mathematical knowledge, he always focused on the physical realities reflected in formulae.

At the district registrar's office, North Sydney, on 16 August 1939 Makinson married Kathleen Rachel White, a science student whom he had met in England; she was to work for the Commonwealth Scientific and Industrial Research Organization. Dick and Rachel were active in the Sydney University Labor Club and the Sydney branch of the Australian Association of Scientific Workers. Aware that they had visited the Soviet Union in 1938, Commonwealth security officers kept them under surveillance. Makinson belonged to the Australia-U.S.S.R. Society (and its forerunners) until his death, and to the Federation of Scientific & Technical Workers; he was also an executive-member of the Australian Peace Council. In 1946 he was favoured to succeed O. U. Vonwiller [q.v.12] as professor of physics, but the university was subjected to pressure to reject him because of his political beliefs. Similar refusals of appointment were made by the universities of Queensland and Adelaide in 1948, and by the New South Wales University of Technology in 1949.

Shortly before the atomic tests at Monte Bello islands, W. C. Wentworth made an intemperate speech in the House of Representatives on 5 June 1952 in which he accused Makinson of 'conducting what was virtually a campaign of treason on the highest level' while holding a lectureship in physics at the university. Such criticism, and the sense of being spied on by intelligence agents, affected Makinson deeply, preventing him from fully developing his research and teaching skills. A man of integrity, he maintained to the end the beliefs he had formed as a young man, despite the regrets he felt at the sullying of those ideals by Stalinism abroad and its echoes at home. He was essentially a rationalist who believed in the ultimate triumph of the scientific method—in politics and economics, as well as in science itself. In 1968 Makinson was appointed associate-professor in physics at Macquarie University, where he was prominent in opposing the Vietnam War. He developed (1978) an electronic calculator for the blind which enabled the results to be read in braille or heard in synthesized speech.

A tall, slim man, with rather broad and slightly hunched shoulders, sandy hair and blue eyes, Makinson had a lively, if rather simple, sense of humour. He loved folk music, estuary fishing, making things in his workshop, and chats with colleagues. Survived by his wife and two sons, he died of cancer on 15 January 1979 in hospital at Wahroonga and was cremated. Macquarie University set up the Dick Makinson physics prize in his memory.

PD (Cwlth), 1952, p 1619; *Aust Left Review*, no 69, June 1979, p 41; *SMH*, 29 Jan, 19 Mar 1931, 28 Apr 1934, 7 June 1952, 16 Jan 1979; ASIO, AG 119/79, item 1219 (AA, Canb); Makinson papers (Univ Syd Archives); personal information.   ERIC AARONS

MALLEY, GARNET FRANCIS (1892-1961), air force officer, warehouse manager and planter, was born on 2 November 1892 at Mosman, Sydney, fifth of six children of Australian-born parents Francis Malley, ironworker, and his wife Clara Ellen, née Merritt. Francis founded the Sydney whitegoods-manufacturing company, Malleys Ltd. Educated at the Church of England Preparatory School, Mosman, at Mount Victoria and at Hawkesbury Agricultural College, Garnet served an apprenticeship as a mechanic in his father's firm.

On 12 October 1915 Malley enlisted in the Australian Imperial Force. Sailing for Egypt in the following month, he was sent to France in March 1916 and posted to the 1st Field Artillery Brigade in May. He transferred to the Australian Flying Corps in April 1917 and was commissioned as a pilot in October. Two months later he flew to France where he joined No.4 Squadron, A.F.C., which was equipped with Sopwith Camel scouts. In March 1918 he was promoted captain and made a flight commander. Frequently in action, he proved an aggressive and able pilot. Although twice wounded, he qualified as an ace, destroying six enemy aircraft and a balloon. He won the Military Cross (1918) and Air Force Cross (1919). From August 1918 he was an instructor with the A.F.C.'s No.5 Training Squadron at Minchinhampton, Gloucestershire, England. There he flew a Camel trainer painted distinctively white.

Back in Sydney, Malley was one of the former wartime pilots selected in August 1919 to tour country areas to promote the Peace Loan. His A.I.F. appointment terminated on 4 October. He rejoined the family firm as warehouse manager in 1921. At the Presbyterian Church, Mosman, on 25 January 1922 he married Phyllis Kathleen Dare. In June 1925 he was commissioned flight lieutenant in the Citizen Air Force. A member of No.3 Squadron based at Richmond, he was promoted honorary squadron leader in January 1928 and held temporary command of the unit in 1928-29. He was also vice-president (1925-28) of the Australian Flying Corps Association.

In 1928 Malley became a specialist flying consultant to Australian National Airways Ltd. After the company encountered financial difficulties in 1931, he and his wife travelled abroad and settled in China. By 1937 he was a respected and influential adviser to Madame Chiang Kai-shek, who was secretary-general of the Nationalist Chinese government's aeronautical commission (which administered the air force). His standing with the commission was bolstered in February 1937 when, in response to a request from the British Foreign Office, he was made honorary wing commander in the Royal Australian Air Force Reserve, though he had severed his connexion with the R.A.A.F.

Malley tended to exaggerate the importance of his role in China. As a result, the R.A.A.F. was initially indifferent to his views on the tactics of Japanese airmen fighting in that country. Recalled to Australia in 1940, he was restored to the R.A.A.F.'s Active List in October as a squadron leader and posted to the intelligence staff at Air Force Headquarters, Melbourne. He was appointed to the Combined Operational Intelligence Centre and promoted deputy to its director, Commander R. B. M. Long [q.v.]. Sir Frederic Eggleston [q.v.8] was named as Australian minister to China in 1941. Malley applied to accompany him as services attaché. His request was refused.

Granted the honorary rank of wing commander in October 1941, Malley succeeded Long as director of the C.O.I.C. in December. He continued in this capacity even after the arrival of General Douglas MacArthur [q.v.] and his American staff, and the establishment of General Headquarters, South-West Pacific Area. Malley became acting group captain in July 1942. Due to illness, he relinquished his post and higher rank in October. MacArthur complimented him on the centre's efficiency, and on his 'foresight, planning and organizational ability'. In 1948 Malley was to be appointed an officer of the American Legion of Merit. He worked in Canberra for the Commonwealth Security Service as officer-in-charge of the Chinese section in 1944-47 and in this period again held the honorary rank of group captain.

The Malleys bought a cruising yacht, the *Royal Flight*, which was hired for the making of the film, *The Blue Lagoon* (1949). In 1950 they moved to Fiji and bought the Nabavatu coconut plantation on Vanua Balavu. Enjoying a relaxed way of life, he listed his recreations as flying, yachting, golf, tennis, cricket, swimming and badminton. He died of cardiac infarction on 20 May 1961 at Nabavatu and was buried at sea with Anglican rites; his wife and son survived him.

C. Coulthard-Clark, *Garnet Malley and the RAAF's Chinese Connection*, Air Power Studies Centre, Paper no 54 (Canb, 1997), and for sources.

C. D. COULTHARD-CLARK

MALMGRON, HELEN DOROTHY; *see* STIRLING, NELL

MALTBY, SIR THOMAS KARRAN (1890-1976), politician, was born on 17 October 1890 at Barnadown, near Bendigo, Victoria, second child of Thomas Karran Maltby, a storekeeper who came from the Isle of Man, and his Victorian-born, second wife Ada Agnes, née Fascher. His father died in 1893 and his mother remarried in the following year. Tom was educated at Camp Hill Central School until the age of 11, when he left to take three concurrent jobs, each earning him 2s. 6d. a week. He then worked as a battery-boy in a local gold-mine and studied at night at the Bendigo School of Mines for the engineer's certificate. His tough early life developed in

him self-reliance, ambition, determination, a strict code of rectitude, and a love of the country and nature.

Moving to Melbourne, Maltby was employed as a tramway labourer. He joined the Militia and earned a commission in 1912 while working as a clerk for Colonial Sugar Refining Co. Ltd. On 29 January 1913 at the Presbyterian Church, Yarraville, he married Eliza Margaret McDonald, a 20-year-old typist. Appointed lieutenant, Australian Imperial Force, on 16 May 1915, he embarked for Egypt in September. Maltby fought on the Western Front with the 5th Battalion from March 1916 and was promoted captain in August. On 8 April 1917 he was wounded when a rifle exploded and part of the bolt-head entered his arm. He was selected as a staff trainee in July 1918. Mentioned in dispatches, he returned to Australia in 1919 and his A.I.F. appointment terminated on 28 June.

Maltby took a job as a storekeeper at Drysdale before becoming an estate agent at Geelong. Thrice president of the local branch of the Returned Soldiers' and Sailors' Imperial League of Australia, and founding president of the East Geelong Progress Association, he was involved in numerous other community affairs. In 1924 he stood unsuccessfully against William Brownbill [q.v.13 Fanny Brownbill] as National candidate for the Legislative Assembly seat of Geelong.

Elected member for Barwon in a by-election on 6 July 1929, Maltby rapidly assumed parliamentary responsibilities as Opposition whip (1929), government whip (1932-33) in the Argyle-Allan [qq.v.7] coalition, secretary to cabinet (1933-34), honorary minister (1934-35), minister for lands and forests (1935), president of the Board of Land and Works (1935), and temporary chairman (1937-45) and chairman (1945-46) of committees. Mobilized in the Citizen Military Forces in 1940-43, he rose to temporary major while on the staff of the assistant adjutant and quartermaster general, Southern Command. He was a vocal opponent of the release of the *Dunera* detainees, whom he considered 'dangerous'. For several months from December 1941 Maltby dissociated himself from his United Australia Party colleagues and sat as an Independent, in protest at their refusal to support a conference seeking reform of the United Australia Organisation. In April 1943 he was appointed general secretary of the U.A.O. in Victoria.

Maltby was one of five politicians—another was (Sir) Archie Michaelis [q.v.]—who voted to defeat the Dunstan-Hollway [qq.v.8,14] Country Party-Liberal Party coalition in September 1945. In the resulting Macfarlan [q.v.] ministry, composed of dissident Liberals, he was—from 2 October to 21 November—chief secretary, deputy-premier and minister for electrical undertakings. Although he was expelled from the Liberal Party, he was re-admitted in 1946. After the Hollway-McDonald [q.v.] Liberal Country Party coalition took office, he served as Speaker (2 December 1947 to 12 April 1950). In 1949 he was knighted. For eight days before Hollway lost office on 27 June 1950, he held the portfolios of electrical undertakings and mines.

On 28 May 1955 Maltby won the seat of Geelong. He was appointed (7 June) minister of works in (Sir) Henry Bolte's first cabinet, where his years of experience were much appreciated. In 1959 he visited Britain, Europe and the United States of America to study road-making and public-building construction. He was closely associated with three major projects: the construction of the Country Roads Board building at Kew, the opening of Kings Bridge and Kings Way, Melbourne, and the building of a highway between that city and Geelong, with a by-pass at Werribee named after him.

'Tall, slim and straight of bearing', dapper in dress and fond of bow-ties, Maltby was a forthright speaker with an eloquent turn of phrase and a crackling wit. Labor's premier John Cain [q.v.13] advised new members: 'When Sir Thomas Maltby speaks, don't interject—he will cut you to shreds'. Fellow parliamentarians on both sides enjoyed his 'puckish charm' and held him in high regard for his earthy wisdom, tolerance, fairness and help to newcomers.

Maltby retired in July 1961 after thirty-two years in parliament. Apart from politics, his interests included angling, walking and reading. He was a member of the Naval and Military Club, the United Services Institute and the Geelong Chamber of Manufactures. An active Presbyterian, he preached occasionally in Geelong churches. In retirement he remained a director of the family company, Geelong Markets Pty Ltd. He died on 2 June 1976 at Geelong and was buried in Footscray cemetery; his wife survived him, as did two of his three daughters and one of his two sons.

K. West, *Power in the Liberal Party* (Melb, 1965); P. Aimer, *Politics, Power and Persuasion* (Syd, 1974); C. Hazlehurst (ed), *Australian Conservatism* (Canb, 1979); C. Pearl, *The Dunera Scandal* (Syd, 1983); *Herald* (Melb), 27 Mar 1933; *Sun News-Pictorial*, 27 July 1934, 12, 19 Apr 1961, 3 June 1976; *Age* (Melb), 3 Dec 1941, 6 Apr 1943, 12 Dec 1946, 1 June 1955, 12, 19 Apr 1961, 3 June 1976; *SMH*, 3, 10 Oct 1945, 11 Dec 1946, 7 June 1955; information from Mr T. Maltby jnr, Geelong, Vic, the Hon L. H. S. Thompson, Glen Iris, and the Hon F. N. Wilkes, Northcote, Melb.   ROBERT MURRAY

MANCHEE, ARTHUR FREDERICK (1874-1956), grazier and company director, was born on 16 May 1874 at Doondi station, St George,

Queensland, fifth son and sixth child of John Charles Manchee (d.1913), an English-born grazier, and his wife Georgina, née Baldwin, who was born in New South Wales. John was of Huguenot descent and had come to the Victorian goldfields in 1852. Arthur, nick-named 'Dick', spent his boyhood on the family's Glen Moan station, 25 000 acres (10 000 ha) at Willow Tree, New South Wales. Sent to The King's School, Parramatta, he excelled at sport, especially Rugby and cricket (captain first XI, 1891-92): while at school he began playing half-back for the famous Wallaroo Football Club; with P. S. Waddy [q.v.12], he played cricket for 'Twenty of Cumberland and District' against Lord Sheffield's visiting English team in December 1891.

After jackerooing for six months on Binne-guy station (32 000 acres, 13 000 ha), Moree, Manchee spent about ten years in Sydney gaining experience in a merchant's office. Before business commitments forced his retirement from Rugby, he represented New South Wales against Queensland (1894) and Victoria (1895). On 28 February 1901 at St Augustine's Anglican Church, Neutral Bay, he married Nellie Sparke. Arthur joined two of his brothers to purchase (1908) Binneguy. From 1914 he was in partnership with his youngest brother Alfred Lionel; they acquired Yamburgan and Cashmere West stations in Queensland, and Ontario and Retreat in New South Wales. On the dissolution of the partnership in 1928, Arthur became sole owner of Binneguy, which was managed by his sons Richard and Alan. He lived at Neutral Bay, Sydney.

Manchee's executive abilities were keenly sought. A foundation board-member (1919-55) of the Graziers' Co-operative Shearing Co. Ltd (Grazcos Ltd from 1949), he was also a director of the Stock Journal Newspaper Co. Ltd, Sydney Meat Preserving Co. Ltd, Country Broadcasting Services Ltd, Globe Worsted Mills Ltd, Cleveland Shoe Co. Ltd, Australian Guarantee Corporation Ltd and Eldorado Tennant Creek Ltd. He was appointed (1925) to represent cattle interests on the Meat Industry Advisory Board, and was for many years an executive-member and spokesman of the Graziers' Association of New South Wales. In 1931 he chaired a special committee to examine J. B. Cramsie's [q.v.8] proposal for a graziers' meat company and chain of butchers' shops in Britain. In 1939 he supported the correct labelling of wool and woollen products sold in Australia.

A plain and forceful speaker, Manchee took a practical interest in his old school; he was a committee-member (1904-09) and town vice-president (1918-44) of The King's School Old Boys' Union, and one of the first representatives (1924-33) of the old boys on the reconstituted school council. He belonged to the New

South Wales, Neutral Bay, Australian Jockey, Manly Golf and Australian clubs. Golf was his chief recreation.

Dick Manchee was endowed with splendid physical powers and mental alertness. Sympathetic and helpful to the deserving, he could be hard and outspoken where weakness of character and human folly were concerned, but, according to one contemporary, in 'all his dealings justice was his watchword and as a result his friends were legion'. Survived by his wife, daughter and two sons, he died on 10 November 1956 at his Potts Point home and was cremated.

Pastoral Review, 17 Oct 1904, 15 Feb, 15 May 1908, 15 May 1909, 15 July 1910, 16 June 1913, 16 Sept 1931, 16 Nov 1955, 16 Feb, 17 Dec 1956, 18 Jan 1957; *The King's School Mag*, Dec 1956, p 51; *SMH*, 18 July 1922, 14 May, 16 Dec 1929, 11 Sept, 6 Nov 1931, 21 Sept, 20 Oct 1933, 3 Aug 1939; The King's School, Parramatta, Syd, Archives; information from Mr L. Manchee, Narrabri, NSW.

G. P. WALSH

MANDALIS, LAZARUS CONSTANTINE (1896-1968), businessman and Greek community leader, was born on 15 January 1896 at Port Said, Egypt, one of seven children of Greek-born parents Constantine Michael Mandalis, engineer, and his wife Ekaterini, née Lazarou. His parents had moved to Egypt from Kastellorizon (Megisti), an Aegean island near Turkey, after Constantine had obtained work with the Suez Canal Co. Educated at church schools in Cairo and at Port Said, Lazarus proved an excellent student of foreign languages, including English, French, Italian, Spanish and Arabic.

At the age of 17 Mandalis emigrated to Western Australia in search of adventure and in the hope of making a better living. He settled in Perth where he was employed as a liquor salesman and waiter. During World War I he acted as a Greek interpreter in the Censor's Office. Mandalis also worked as an interpreter in court and as an accountant, but he was principally an importer of continental foodstuffs. Having helped to found (1918) the Hellenic Club Association to cater for the social and recreational needs of the increasing number of male Greeks in Perth, he became secretary in 1923 of the Hellenic Community of Western Australia, a newly formed pan-Hellenic organization. He was to hold that post for thirty-seven years.

At St George's Cathedral, Perth, on 26 April 1928 Mandalis married with Greek Orthodox rites Marea Auguste, a 21-year-old accountant; she was the daughter of Athanasios Auguste, one of the earliest Kastellorizians to arrive in Western Australia. The marriage strengthened Mandalis's standing in the Greek community in Perth. A dynamic and persuasive orator, he convinced members of the Hellenic Community in 1935 to proceed with building the Greek Orthodox Cathedral of St Constantine and St Helene in Perth. As secretary of the H.C.W.A., he nominated a number of Greeks for admission to Australia and assisted them after their arrival. On 22 September 1941 Mandalis lowered his age and enlisted in the Militia. Transferring to the Australian Imperial Force in November 1942, he was commissioned in the Security Section, Intelligence Corps, in January 1943. He acted as a translator and in 1946 sailed for Italy, guarding prisoners of war who were in the process of being repatriated. His A.I.F. appointment terminated in Australia on 14 March 1947.

Many of Western Australia's State and Federal politicians sought out Mandalis to present their views to Perth's Greek community. He regularly offered counsel to his compatriots. From the late 1930s, as a translator and interpreter, he had been associated with H. P. Downing, the honorary consul for Greece in Western Australia. Mandalis served (from 1951) as a justice of the peace. In 1960 he was appointed to the Royal Order of the Phoenix in recognition of his promotion of Australian-Greek relations. That year he and his wife retired to Sydney to live near their daughters. Survived by his wife, son and three daughters, he died on 6 August 1968 in his Potts Point home and was buried in Botany cemetery.

J. N. Yiannakis, *Megisti in the Antipodes* (Perth, 1996); *SMH* and *West Australian*, 9 Aug 1968; Hellenic Community of WA, Minutes, vols 1 and 2 (Hellenic Community Centre of WA, Northbridge, Perth); Decorations, A1838/265 item 1535/11/14 (AA, Canb); PP14/1 item 16/1/298, PP302/1 item WA 1800, PP6/1 item 1947/H/573 (AA, WA); information from Ms A. Mandalis, Alexandria, Syd, Mr S. P. Michelides, Cottesloe, and Mrs E. Mirmikidis, Dalkeith, Perth.   JOHN N. YIANNAKIS

MANDER-JONES, EVAN (1902-1975), director of education, was born on 6 July 1902 at Homebush, Sydney, fourth child of Australian-born parents George Mander-Jones, physician, and his wife Margaret Fleming, née Arnott. Evan was descended from William Arnott and David Jones [qq.v.3,2]. He attended Sydney Church of England Grammar School (Shore) and the University of Sydney (B.A., 1924; Dip.Ed., 1925), and was employed as an assistant-master (1926-30) and as a house master (1933-38) at his old school. In the years between these appointments he studied at University College, Oxford (B.A., 1933; M.A., 1937).

After serving (from 1922) in the Militia, Mander-Jones was called up for duty as an intelligence officer on 13 November 1939. In May 1940 he transferred to the Australian Imperial Force and in October sailed for the Middle East with headquarters, I Corps. Sent to Sumatra, Netherlands East Indies, in January 1942, he helped Dutch civilians and refugees from Malaya to elude the invading Japanese by taking them from Palembang to Oosthaven and from there to Merak in Java; he then returned to Sumatra and helped to destroy the port of Oosthaven. For this work he was appointed O.B.E. (1943).

Back in Australia, Mander-Jones was promoted lieutenant colonel in April 1942. He served successively on the staffs of the Second Army, First Army, I Corps, New Guinea Force and II Corps. At Scots Church, Melbourne, on 9 June 1943 he married with Presbyterian forms Lois Jessie McDonald, a 22-year-old sergeant in the Australian Women's Army Service. In January 1945 he was raised to temporary colonel and posted as deputy-director, military intelligence, Allied Forces Land Headquarters, a post which entailed extensive travelling in the South-West Pacific Area. He transferred to the Reserve of Officers on 30 July 1946.

In September that year Mander-Jones succeeded C. A. E. Fenner [q.v.8] as South Australia's director of education. During the next twenty-one years he had to deal with a phenomenal growth in education in the State: primary school enrolments doubled to over 150 000 and secondary enrolments increased six-fold to 70 000. The annual percentage of the government's budget spent on education rose from 11.5 in 1947-48 to 24.9 in 1966-67. The director faced two immediate difficulties —a lack of school buildings and a shortage of teachers. As a 'temporary' solution, pre-fabricated classrooms were introduced and schools were consolidated. Staff numbers were increased by the employment of married women and teachers from Britain, by the re-employment of retired teachers, and by a campaign to recruit young people into the profession.

Mander-Jones was an Australian representative at the United Nations Educational, Scientific and Cultural Organization's biennial conference in Paris in 1952. In 1958 he inspected schools in Britain and the United States of America, and attended the twenty-first joint U.N.E.S.C.O. and International Bureau of Education conference in Geneva. A guest of the Federal Republic of Germany in 1965, he observed educational practices in that country, and in Britain and the U.S.A.

He claimed that he had to print the report of his 1958 tour himself because it was 'unpopular with governments' as it proposed 'expensive changes to the existing setup'. In particular, he recommended the establishment of different types of secondary schools, and advocated both vocational and further education. By the 1960s, under Mander-Jones's guidance, technical schools were developing imaginative general courses (rather than concentrating solely on trade skills) and were promoting adult-education classes and vocational-education courses.

Mander-Jones presided over the Education Department with dignity and scholarly concern. He believed that the 'ultimate object of education' was 'to fit every boy and girl to live the most satisfactory life for themselves and for their fellows'. Faced with agitation for curriculum reform and equal pay for female teachers, he claimed that he had 'always found that teachers will proceed further through conference and round-table discussions, than through processions and demonstrations'. He retired in 1967.

A member of the Legacy Club of Adelaide and the Greater Adelaide Planning Commission, Mander-Jones was a council-member of the Flinders University of South Australia and Roseworthy Agricultural College, and a committee-member of the State branches of the Boy Scouts' Association, the Duke of Edinburgh's Award Scheme and the Gowrie [q.v.9] Scholarship Trust Fund. He was president of the State chapter of the Australian College of Education and of the South Australian Public Schools' Music Society. A junior grand warden (1970) of the Grand Lodge of Antient, Free and Accepted Masons of South Australia, he wrote *A History of Craft Masonry in South Australia, 1884-1934* (1976). He belonged to the Adelaide and the Naval, Military and Air Force clubs, and enjoyed chess and mountain-walking. Survived by his wife and three sons, he died on 18 July 1975 while holidaying in Noumea and was buried in Centennial Park cemetery, Adelaide.

C. Thiele, *Grains of Mustard Seed* (Adel, 1975); *Adelaide Legacy Weekly Bulletin*, 28 July 1975; *SMH*, 15 Oct 1937, 12 June, 26 Aug 1942; *Advertiser* (Adel), 29 Aug 1946, 16 Oct 1965, 17, 21 June 1967, 21 July 1975; L. Arnold, ABC radio interview with Evan Mander-Jones, 3 Aug 1969 (Mort L); SA Minister of Education, *Report*, 1965-67, GRG 18 series 23 (SRSA).

M. BLENCOWE

MANESSIS, CHRISTOPHOROS (1898-1980), Greek Orthodox priest, was born on 1 August 1898 at Kallimasia on the Aegean island of Khíos, Greece, eldest son of Constantine Manessis, farmer, and his wife Maria, née Boyatzis. Christophoros was a competent and lively schoolboy. He served in the Greek army during World War I and continued as a non-commissioned officer until he was discharged in August 1923. Deciding to emigrate to Australia, he reached Melbourne in the *Ville de Metz* on 10 April 1924. Manessis eventually found a job in the smelting works at Port Pirie, South Australia, and made friends with some of the Greeks who worked there. On 18 November 1925 at St Paul's Anglican Church, Port Pirie, he married Evangelia Spartalis; she was aged 21 and came from Kastellorizon (Megisti), Greece.

A deeply religious man, Manessis had for many years studied 'ecclesiastical and theological books'. In Melbourne, he was ordained priest on 6 December 1925 by Bishop Knetes [q.v.9]; he returned to take up his appointment 'as rector of the Greek Orthodox Community of Port Pirie, all of South Australia and Broken Hill'. The relocation of Archimandrite Germanos Illiou to South Australia and the diminishing Greek Orthodox population at Port Pirie led to his transfer to Perth in 1926. Manessis performed his religious duties in the Hellenic Hall before a Greek Orthodox church was built. His humble nature and concern for his parishioners contributed to his success and popularity as a priest, and helped to unite the local community.

With the completion and consecration of the Church of St Constantine and St Helene at Northbridge in 1937, Manessis was installed as its priest. He played an important role in spiritual and community activities, assisting fund-raising ventures, advising his parishioners on various matters and teaching at the local Greek school. To bring comfort to the scattered Greek population, he travelled throughout the State, notably to the goldfields and the south-west. In 1943-44 he was a part-time chaplain in the Australian Military Forces and was attached to the army camp at Melville.

Manessis also worked closely with representatives of other religious denominations, particularly Anglican and Catholic clergymen. In 1955 he was involved in a dispute with a number of influential Greeks over the provision of services to country communities and the suggestion that a second Greek Orthodox priest be ordained to lessen his workload. Dismissed from his duties, he moved to Melbourne where he was appointed a relieving priest.

On his return to Western Australia in 1957 he found a second Greek Orthodox church under consideration. In December 1958 Manessis became foundation priest at the Annunciation of Our Lady (Evangelismos) Church, West Perth. From the early 1970s he shared his religious duties with another priest. Manessis retired in 1975. Survived by his wife, four sons and three daughters, he died on 7 June 1980 in his home at Wembley and was buried in Karrakatta cemetery.

M. Tsounis, *Greek Communities in Australia* (Ph.D. thesis, Univ Adel, 1971); J. N. Yiannakis, *The Church of Sts Constantine and Helene—its construction and the community that supported it, 1910-1936* (B.A. Hons thesis, Murdoch Univ, 1986); Hellenic Community of WA (Perth), Minutes, 1923-39, vol 1; information from Ms A. Manessis, Perth.

JOHN N. YIANNAKIS

MANIFOLD, SIR THOMAS CHESTER (1897-1979), grazier and racing administrator, was born on 13 May 1897 at Talindert, near Camperdown, Victoria, second child and only son of James Chester Manifold [q.v.10], grazier, and his wife Lilian Eva, née Curle. Chester ('Chetty' to his friends) was a grandson of John Manifold and a nephew of William Manifold [qq.v.2,10]. He grew up at Talindert (7500 acres, 3035 ha), his father's share of Purrumbete station, and was educated at Camperdown and (from 1912) Geelong Church of England grammar schools. Photographs show a deep-chested schoolboy with dark good looks who excelled at sport. His upbringing inspired in him an understanding of tradition, a sense of duty and an appreciation of outdoor life.

At the end of 1915 Manifold sailed for Britain. Commissioned on 24 September 1916 in the Royal Field Artillery, he served with the 76th Brigade on the Western Front. Serious injuries at Ypres, Belgium, in September 1917 left him in hospital for three months. After the war he entered Jesus College, Cambridge, where he studied agriculture and political economy, and stroked the college VIII that was 'Head of the River' in 1920. Returning to Australia late that year, he worked with the Geelong woolbrokers, Dennys, Lascelles [qq.v.4,5] Ltd, before taking over the management of Talindert in 1922.

At St Paul's Anglican Church, Frankston, on 22 May 1923 Manifold married Agnes Gwendolen, daughter of Harold William Grimwade [q.v.9]; they settled at Gnarpurt, Manifold's sheep-station near Lismore. Immediately he was pressed into public duty as a vestryman, a hospital committee-man, and as a member (1926-40) of the Hampden Shire Council (president 1938). In a wider sphere, Manifold defeated (1929) the Labor incumbent for the Legislative Assembly seat of Hampden, and represented the Young Nationalists at the convention in May 1931 that established the United Australia Party. At the May 1932 election Manifold was unopposed. A minister without portfolio in Sir Stanley Argyle's [q.v.7] coalition government, he was soon disillusioned by its stringent economic policies and was unhappy as a politician, later saying that 'the insincerity was hard to take'. His health broke down in 1933; he resigned from cabinet on 24 November and did not recontest his seat.

The next few years were more congenial. In 1936 Manifold moved back to Talindert with his family and established a racehorse stud. Elected to the Victoria Racing Club committee in 1937, he was to win the V.R.C. St Leger with Arbroath (1953). On 13 February 1940 he was mobilized in the Militia. Transferring to the Australian Imperial Force on 4 August 1942, Major Manifold served briefly in Papua and was mentioned in dispatches. His A.I.F. appointment terminated on 4 May 1943. Promoted lieutenant colonel, he commanded the 7th Battalion, Volunteer Defence Corps, until 21 January 1946.

It was to racing that Manifold next devoted most of his energies, campaigning tirelessly against punitive taxation. As V.R.C. chairman (1951-62), he lobbied for legalization of the off-course totalizator against a powerful alliance of churches and bookmakers. Knighted in 1953, he was by then a solid, imposing figure whose silver hair and bushy eyebrows suggested owl-like wisdom. Sir Chester was a persuasive advocate. Under the premier (Sir) Henry Bolte, Victoria established Australia's first Totalisator Agency Board in 1961, with rigorous restrictions insisted upon by Manifold, who was appointed chairman. Elevated to K.B.E. in 1965, he remained in the post until 1968, and continued on the V.R.C. committee until 1972.

The hospitality of the Manifolds was a by-word, with the sojourn of Princess Alexandra of Kent at Talindert in 1959 a local high point. This regal gloss assured the success of subsequent charitable open days. In the 1960s the Manifolds supported the successful campaign to save nearby Mount Sugarloaf from quarrying. Although Sir Chester reduced his interstate landholdings, he remained active at Talindert. He belonged to the Melbourne, Athenaeum, and Naval and Military clubs. His later years were crowned by the achievements of his champion steeplechaser, Crisp: taken to England for the 1973 Grand National, the gelding finished a courageous second, three-quarters of a length behind Red Rum. Survived by his wife and three daughters, Manifold died on 6 January 1979 at Camperdown hospital and was cremated; his estate was sworn for probate at $1 426 196.

A. Henderson (ed), *Early Pioneer Families of Victoria and Riverina* (Melb, 1936); N. Chapman, *Historic Houses of Western Victoria* (Colac, Vic, 1965); J. Pacini, *A Century Galloped By* (Melb, 1988); A. W. Martin, *Robert Menzies*, 1 (Melb, 1993); J. J. Corfield and M. Collins Persse (comps), *Geelong Grammarians*, 1 (Geelong, Vic, 1996); *Pastoral Homes of Aust*, 1, 1910; *Camperdown Chronicle*, 14 Nov 1929, 23 Nov 1933, 9 Jan 1979; *Australian*, 13 Mar 1968, 20 Nov 1972; *The Times*, 2 Apr 1973; *Age* (Melb), 8 Jan 1979.   ANDREW LEMON

MANNERS-SUTTON, D.; *see* GENTILE, DORIS

MANNING, HENRY JOHN (1889-1978), newspaper manager and proprietor, was born on 6 August 1889 at Gladstone, Queensland, eldest of five children of Australian-born parents William Joseph Manning, journalist, and his wife Charlotte Emma, née Black. Educated at Gladstone State School and the Normal School, Brisbane, Jack served his apprenticeship as a printer before training as a cadet journalist on the *Gladstone Observer*, a newspaper owned and edited by his father. William sold the *Observer* in 1910, and became principal shareholder and editor of the *Daily Mercury*, Mackay. The paper had fallen on hard times, but he turned the business around. Jack worked in the composing room, did stints as a reporter and sub-editor, and was gradually groomed for a managerial role. On 21 March 1916 at the Baptist City Tabernacle, Brisbane, he married Alison Morcom (d.1956).

Preferring management to journalism and editing, Manning took over as the *Daily Mercury*'s business manager in 1918. In the following year he succeeded his father as a board-member of the Queensland Country Press Co-operative Ltd (Queensland division of the Regional Dailies of Australia Ltd from 1968) and was its chairman in 1934-77. President (1928-30) of the Queensland Country Press Association, he led the Australian Provincial Daily Press Ltd (later R.D.A. Ltd) with distinction in 1936-39 and was to serve for forty-one years on that body's central board. He was a delegate (1938) of Queensland's non-metropolitan press at an advertising convention held at Glasgow, Scotland.

In 1943 Manning succeeded his father as chairman and managing director of the *Daily Mercury*. Accepting the challenge with enthusiasm, he employed a 'hands on' approach and stimulated efficiency within his team. 'He relished success', and in failure was 'analytical and reconstructive. He liked to lead and did not shirk the tough decisions'. By 'constantly looking forward' and by modernizing management, production methods and equipment, he kept abreast of the demands of the industry and the community.

When a merger of the Manning, Dunn [q.v.8] and Irwin family interests in regional newspapers was proposed in the mid-1960s, Jack Manning supported the plan. The resulting conglomerate, Provincial Newspapers (Qld) Ltd, was formed in 1968. Manning argued that the amalgamation would prevent predatory metropolitan companies from buying up country newspapers one by one. His nephew Bruce Manning asked him whether he thought that, 'by putting ourselves all together like this we might become just a vehicle for a one-off takeover'. Jack Manning replied: 'No, too big; too big, son'. Nevertheless, an Irish-Australian combination, headed by Dr Tony O'Reilly, gained the controlling interest in Provincial Newspapers (Qld) Ltd in 1988.

Manning had been a founding director (1931) of radio-station 4MK, Mackay. Active in community organizations, he was an elder of St Paul's Presbyterian Church, master (1927) of Caledonia Masonic Lodge No.34, a member (1939-70) and chairman (1940-53) of the Mackay Ambulance Committee, foundation secretary (1926) and president (1932-33) of the local Rotary Club, and president (1946-49) of the Central Queensland District Bowls Association. He was appointed O.B.E. in 1953. At the Presbyterian Church, St Lucia, Brisbane, on 20 February 1958 he married Edith Agnes Lynch, née Clarkson, a 52-year-old widow. That year he retired to Buderim. Survived by his wife and by the two sons of his first marriage, he died on 10 October 1978 at Nambour and was cremated with the forms of the Uniting Church.

B. Boyan, *Jack Manning* (Brisb, 1978); R. Kirkpatrick, *Sworn to No Master* (Toowoomba, Qld, 1984); *Daily Mercury* (Mackay), 11 Oct 1978; *Chronicle* (Toowoomba) and *Nambour Chronicle*, 12 Oct 1978; information from Messrs C. M. Manning, Auchenflower, Brisb, B. Manning, Toowoomba, Qld, and the late W. R. Golding.

ROD KIRKPATRICK

MANNING, SIR JAMES KENNETH (1907-1976), judge, was born on 26 May 1907 in North Sydney, second son of Australian-born parents Herbert William Manning, chemist, and his wife Mary Elsie Stella Mackenzie, née Clarke. Educated at Sydney Grammar School, Manning qualified through Solicitors' Admission Board examinations and was admitted to practice on 14 March 1930. At All Saints Church, Woollahra, on 24 December 1931 he married with Anglican rites Dorothy May Coleman; they were to have one child before being divorced. After brief sole practice, he formed Manning, Riddle & Co., a Sydney law firm. On 25 October 1940 he transferred to the Bar. Manning was commissioned in the Royal Australian Air Force on 2 June 1941. For his service in 1943 as a law officer with No.9 Operational group, Madang, New Guinea, he was mentioned in dispatches. At Air Force Headquarters, Melbourne, he was appointed deputy-director of personnel services in April 1944 and promoted acting wing commander

in October. He was demobilized in January 1946.

Returning to the Bar in Sydney, Manning acquired an extensive practice, but specialized in bankruptcy law. He took silk in 1953. Although he had not graduated, he lectured in bankruptcy at the university, while still a solicitor, and returned as Challis [q.v.3] lecturer in bankruptcy (1952-55). He long retained those associations, and was later president of the Sydney University Law Society; he was also responsible for establishing the university's law extension committee. Manning wrote standard textbooks on bankruptcy law and on the law of banker and customer in Australia. Honorary treasurer (1950-53) of the New South Wales Bar Association, he collaborated with its president (Sir) Garfield Barwick in having Wentworth Chambers in Phillip Street built as a corporate 'home' for the Bar. Events soon outstripped his imagined 'inn of court' as the decentralization of the courts caused an unprecedented dispersal of Bar chambers.

Manning was appointed an acting-judge of the Supreme Court in September 1955 and confirmed in office on 5 December. He sometimes acted as a judge in the Federal Bankruptcy Court. His robust decisions and efficiency in the previously unrecognized area of case management were admired by some, though he was not universally esteemed by practitioners. A 'stickler for correctness' (as he regarded it), he was impatient and acidulous, and overbearing and abrasive in judicial demeanour. He chaired (1966-69) the New South Wales Law Reform Commission. His contribution was perceptive and effective; under his guidance the commission became a model for Australia. In October 1969 he was elevated to the Court of Appeal.

At St Giles Anglican Church, Greenwich, on 16 December 1967 Manning married Sheila Alison Newton, née Barker, a 51-year-old divorcee. He enjoyed playing golf and bowls, and belonged to the Australian, Union and Royal Sydney Golf clubs. For many years a councillor and honorary treasurer of the Royal Blind Society of New South Wales, he was knighted in 1972. Ill health compelled him to retire from the bench on 28 February 1973. Sir Kenneth died of a cerebral vascular accident on 11 August 1976 in his home at Balmoral Beach and was cremated; his wife survived him, as did the daughter of his first marriage. The New South Wales Bar Association holds his portrait by W. E. Pidgeon.

J. M. Bennett (ed), *A History of the New South Wales Bar* (Syd, 1969); J. and J. Mackinolty (eds), *A Century Down Town* (Syd, 1991); *Aust Law J*, 29, Sept 1955, p 293, Mar 1956, p 646, 47, Apr 1973, p 157, 50, Sept 1976, p 487; *SMH*, 12 Aug 1976.

JOHN KENNEDY MCLAUGHLIN

MANSELL, WILLIAM ARTHUR BYRAM (1893-1977), artist and designer, was born on 9 September 1893 at Double Bay, Sydney, son of Benjamin William Mansell, a company secretary from England, and his first wife Ada Mary, née Byram (d.1893), who was born in New South Wales. Byram attended Scots College and Sydney Grammar School; encouraged by his father, he then studied engineering. At St Stephen's Presbyterian Church, Sydney, on 12 November 1913 he married 19-year-old Beatrice Margaret Forman Cameron; they were to have one child before he divorced her in 1919. He was employed (from 1914) in his father's engineering plant at Gore Bay and spent some evenings at Julian Ashton's [q.v.7] Sydney Art School.

In 1921 Mansell attended the Honolulu Academy of Arts, Hawaii, and in that city opened his first art studio. His flower paintings, mounted on black lacquered Japanese screens, proved popular. After briefly studying art, design, textiles and technology in Mexico, he spent two years at the Académie Julian, Paris. He operated a studio in Hollywood Boulevard, Los Angeles, United States of America, worked for Cecil B. de Mille, designed costumes for several film studios and masks for Lon Chaney, and executed over forty commissions to decorate cafés, theatres and cabarets in cities such as New York, Chicago and Los Angeles. One of his commissions contracted him to decorate coaches for the Atchison, Topeka & Santa Fe Railway Co. His interiors showed an influence of Art Nouveau, especially the style of L. C. Tiffany.

By 1925 Mansell had opened a textiles studio in Elizabeth Street, Sydney, where he taught batik-making. On 29 August 1928 at the Congregational Church, Pitt Street, he married Allison Grace Cameron; she was aged 25. During the mid-1930s his painting reflected 'the more conservative qualities of Australian art—Elioth Gruner-like portrayals of Palm Beach and Heysenesque studies of the Macdonald Ranges'. From 1939 to 1947 he conducted a studio at Bowral.

Inspired by materials from Sir Baldwin Spencer's [q.v.12] expeditions, and Charles Mountford's [q.v.] photographs from the Australian-American Scientific Expedition to Arnhem Land, Mansell took up Aboriginal mythology as a theme in his art, and followed the advice of Sydney Ure Smith [q.v.11] to create his own style by adapting rather than by copying Aboriginal techniques. He used parrot feathers as a brush, and natural pigments and cactus juice as binding agents; the simple, graphic impact of his work was largely due to his use of rich colours and patterns. Mansell responded to narrative aspects and design elements of Aboriginal art, and showed some appreciation of their spiritual value. From 1949 he held a series of one-man exhibitions in Sydney, and later in London at Australia House and Qantas Empire Airways Ltd.

In 1954 Mansell became a foundation member of the National (Art) Gallery Society of New South Wales; four years later he was elected a fellow of the Royal Society of British Artists, London, and the Royal Art Society of New South Wales. Drawing on Aboriginal motifs, he executed numerous murals (some in ceramic tiles) for business firms and local councils in the early 1960s, as well as panels for the New South Wales Government Railways, the tanker, *Amanda Miller*, and the ferry, *Empress of Australia*. His work ranged from white earthenware domestic ceramics, through fabric and interior designs to paintings. He grew cacti in the garden of his Killara home and decorated his studio with Japanese armour. Survived by the son of his first marriage and the two sons of his second, he died on 6 August 1977 at his home and was cremated.

R. Black, *Old and New Australian Aboriginal Art* (Syd, 1964); Woolloomooloo Gallery, Syd, *Retrospective Exhibition*, cat (Syd, 1985); *People* (Syd), 31 Jan 1951, p 21; *Woman's Day*, 5 Jan 1953, p 30; *Art and Aust*, 24, no 1, 1986, p 86; *SMH*, 30 July 1924, 18 Oct 1927, 24 Jan 1950, 10 May 1952, 23 Apr 1955, 21 Sept 1964, 15 Aug 1971; *Sunday Telegraph* (Syd), 10 Sept 1950; *Christian Science Monitor* (Boston, US), 20 Aug 1954.   ARIANNE ROURKE

MANSFIELD, SIR ALAN JAMES (1902-1980), chief justice and governor, was born on 30 September 1902 at Indooroopilly, Brisbane, third son of Edward Mansfield (d.1905), a district-court judge from England, and his wife Margaret Elizabeth, née Bird, who was born in Queensland. Sir James Mansfield (1733-1821), chief justice of common pleas in England, was his great-great-grandfather. Awarded scholarships to Sydney Church of England Grammar School (Shore) and St Paul's College, University of Sydney (LL.B., 1924), Alan represented his college in rowing and Rugby Union football.

On 22 July 1924 Mansfield was admitted to the Queensland Bar. He and another junior Tom Lehane rented chambers—which Mansfield described as a 'broom cupboard'—at 27 Adelaide Street, Brisbane, Queensland's first 'Inns of Court'. Finding his early months in practice 'unbelievably tough', he regularly pawned his watch on Mondays and redeemed it on Fridays if someone paid him a fee. His pawnbroker, Mark Isaacs of George Street, gradually became his friend.

Mansfield supplemented his income by private tutoring and by lecturing part time at the Central Technical College. Undefended divorce provided the staple of the junior Bar. Briefs, tied in red tape and marked in guineas, appeared more frequently. Mansfield attributed his success in the matrimonial jurisdiction to the moustache he had grown to make himself look older. Years later he shaved it off in order to appear younger. Unfortunately, his long-unshaven upper lip developed a painful rash, so the moustache returned and remained for the rest of his life.

When the Depression reduced the number of his clients, Mansfield thought of giving up the law and began to study accountancy. He 'worked like a demon' on the few briefs that came to him. In July-August 1931 he appeared for P. L. Goddard and Frederick Reid, two of the four defendants in the Mungana case (the others were William McCormack and E. G. Theodore [qq.v.10,12]). By securing a verdict in their favour, he rose to prominence and his practice burgeoned. At the Presbyterian Church, Stanthorpe, on 16 December 1933 he married Beryl Susan Pain, née Barnes, a 29-year-old divorcee. On 17 May 1940, at the age of 37, he was appointed to the Supreme Court bench. Described as vigilant, shrewd, conciliatory and 'a good analyst of evidence', he also chaired (1942-44) the Land Appeal Court.

In 1945 the Federal government chose Mansfield as a member of the Australian commission of investigation into war crimes and nominated him for the United Nations War Crimes Commission, London. He was chief Australian prosecutor (1946-47) at the trials of war criminals in Tokyo before the International Military Tribunal for the Far East. Back in Brisbane, he was appointed senior puisne judge in March 1947. As chief justice from 9 February 1956, he presided over a court whose resources were stretched by a substantial increase in litigation, and he sought advice from (Sir) Leslie Herron [q.v.14] on how to make his fellow judges work harder. In his spare time he held office in numerous cultural, charitable, community and sporting organizations.

On 25 January 1957 the illness of Governor Sir John Lavarack [q.v.] required Mansfield to act as administrator, an office he was to hold until March 1958. A large number of people urged him to refuse royal assent to the Gair [q.v.14] government's University of Queensland Acts amendment bill (introduced in March 1957). This legislation established appeal boards (with government-nominated chairmen) to review complaints by staff against appointments, promotions or dismissals, and was widely seen as threatening academic freedom. At this time Mansfield was also warden (1956-66) of convocation at the university. He gave assent to the bill, but the Nicklin [q.v.] ministry repealed (1957) the sections of the Act relating to the boards. In 1958 Mansfield was appointed K.C.M.G.

On 21 March 1966 Mansfield was sworn in as governor of Queensland. Appointed K.C.V.O. (1970), he served until 20 March 1972. The University of Queensland, of which he was chancellor (1966-76), awarded him an honorary LL.D. in 1970. His ready courtesy made him a popular public figure. Throughout his career he maintained his friendships. The group with which he had first played poker in 1940 met for regular games until his death. In the 1960s he accepted invitations to speak at the Young Men's Hebrew Association because the requests came from Isaacs. Sir Alan died on 17 July 1980 at Benowa, Surfers Paradise, and was cremated with Anglican rites; his wife, daughter and one of his two sons survived him.

C. Lack (ed), *Three Decades of Queensland Political History, 1929-1960* (Brisb, 1962); *Aust Law J*, 22 Mar 1956, p 646; *Courier-Mail*, 31 Aug 1940, 28 Jan 1966, 3 Dec 1976, 18 July 1980; family information; personal knowledge.

JOHN GREENWOOD

MANSFIELD, JOHN LESLIE STEPHEN (1906-1965), architect, was born on 4 March 1906 at Double Bay, Sydney, only child of native-born parents Leslie McDougall Mansfield, a Lismore solicitor, and his wife Lucie Olive, née Huthwaite. In 1922 Leslie was gaoled for fraudulent misappropriation and his wife suffered a nervous breakdown. Her sister Florence, widow of Sir Henry Stephen [q.v.6], funded John's education at Cranbrook School, Bellevue Hill, and at St Paul's College, University of Sydney (B.Arch., 1929), where he studied under Professor Leslie Wilkinson [q.v.12]. Lady Stephen took him on a European tour (1929-30) during which he found time to join the Royal Institute of British Architects (fellow, 1946) and to complete courses in town planning and interior design at the Architectural Association school, London. In deference to her, he added Stephen to his names. The Stephen family's influence and the connexions made at Cranbrook and St Paul's were important to Mansfield throughout his life.

Back home, there was little work, so Mansfield tutored briefly on a country property. His initial projects as an architect were modest, but academically competent, such as the *Sydney Morning Herald*'s art gallery for the Fairfaxes [qq.v.4,8,14]. As the Depression eased he gained more substantial commissions, including one for a new wing at Tudor House school, Moss Vale. His most important individual design in the late 1930s was a mansion on the waterfront at Vaucluse for his college friend (Sir) Alexis Albert, which combined Georgian and modern themes. A founder (1934) and president (1939) of the

Town and Country Planning Institute of New South Wales, Mansfield joined Joseph Fowell [q.v.14] and Kenneth McConnel in partnership in 1939.

On 22 September 1941 Mansfield was commissioned lieutenant, Royal Australian Engineers; he performed staff and training duties before being seconded in July 1942 to the Australian Imperial Force as a captain. Postings to the headquarters of New Guinea Force and II Corps took him to Papua, New Guinea and Bougainville in 1943-45. He returned to Australia and transferred to the Reserve of Officers on 4 January 1946.

Resuming work with his firm, Fowell, Mansfield, Jarvis & Maclurcan, Mansfield served on the Sydney Fountains Committee and the State branch of the National Trust of Australia. An early believer in the sympathetic adaptation of historic houses, he remodelled Rona, Bellevue Hill, Springfield, Goulburn, and Harrington Park, Narellan. With Leslie Walford he redecorated Sydney Town Hall's centennial hall, and, with (Dame) Helen Blaxland, was responsible for restoring Kirribilli House for the Commonwealth government. He built comfortable new residences and holiday houses for private clients, among them (Sir) Roy McCaughey [q.v.] and G. B. S. Falkiner [q.v.14].

Mansfield undertook numerous commissions ranging from minor alterations to significant new buildings (often in his paredback classical manner) for Cranbrook, Barker College, Hornsby, St Catherine's School, Waverley, and the Kindergarten Union of New South Wales. He used more contemporary themes in the chapels at St Paul's College (with James Kell) and (with Osmond Jarvis) H.M.A.S. Watson, South Head; both featured a bold use of abstract stained glass by Gabriel Loire of Chartres, France. Among Mansfield's final projects (both with Kell) were the Peninsular & Oriental Steam Navigation Co.'s building, sheathed in glass, marble and sandstone, in Hunter Street, Sydney, and the Commonwealth Club, Canberra.

Of middle height, with brown hair and grey eyes, Mansfield was always carefully groomed and neatly dressed. He was a man of taste and a good public speaker. His interests included gardening and heraldry, and he belonged to the Union, Imperial Service and Royal Sydney Golf clubs. A sensitive and somewhat private person, he lived in a large terrace house at Elizabeth Bay, left to him by his father's sisters. Survived by his companion John Lane, Mansfield died of a cerebral haemorrhage on 23 January 1965 at St Luke's Hospital, Darlinghurst, and was cremated with Anglican rites. His estate was sworn for probate at £105 094; he made bequests to Cranbrook, the National Trust, and to St Paul's College, which built a library that bears his name.

St Paul's College, Univ Syd, *Pauline*, 27, 1929, p 16, 63, 1965, p 75; *Old Cranbrookian*, Feb 1965; *SMH*, 28 Jan 1939, 25 Jan, 8 July 1965; P. Martin, Fowell, Mansfield, Jarvis & Maclurcan, 1929-1970 (B.Arch. thesis, Univ NSW, 1988); Mansfield papers held by, and information from, Mr J. Lane, Elizabeth Bay, Syd; Archives of Univ Syd, *and* Cranbrook School, Bellevue Hill, Syd, *and* St Paul's College, Univ Syd, *and* The King's School, Parramatta; information from Dr K. Cable, Randwick, Mr O. Jarvis, Neutral Bay, Mr C. Lucas, Neutral Bay, the late Sir Alexis Albert and the late Mrs T. L. F. Rutledge.

HOWARD TANNER

MANSOM, DOROTHY MARY (1905-1978), equestrienne, was born on 2 June 1905 at Hyde Park, Adelaide, elder child of Arthur James Mansom, a South Australian-born commercial traveller who became a publican, and his wife Anastasia, née Granleese. Dot left school at 15 and pencilled for her father who doubled as a bookmaker at the Supreme Court Hotel. In her spare time she attended the Hyde Park School of Music. Tall, dark-haired and blue-eyed, she took minor roles with the South Australian Opera Company and in 1924-26 studied singing at the Elder [q.v.4] Conservatorium of Music.

In 1927 Mansom appeared in the chorus of *Rigoletto* with the Italo-Australian Grand Opera Company at Broken Hill, New South Wales. She toured with operas to Melbourne and Western Australia, and performed at Adelaide cinemas. On weekends she taught riding, which helped to keep her cheerful. During the Depression she worked in turn at the Port Adelaide Bacon Factory and at Parisian Mantle Manufacturers Pty Ltd, and produced beauty contests and mannequin parades. Transferred successively to Sydney and Melbourne for two years, she returned to Adelaide as buyer and manageress of the mantle department at Miller Anderson Ltd's Hindley Street store, and helped to support her mother and brother.

During World War II Mansom rose from senior manager to investigating officer with the drapery section of the State branch of the Rationing Commission. She made radio broadcasts on rationing and gained equal status with her male colleagues. At the Pirie Street Methodist Church on 30 June 1950 she married Clarence Henry Gray, a manager and a divorcee whom she had loved since girlhood. Dorothy continued to work as a part-time proof-reader with Clem Taylor Advertising Service Ltd until she was 71.

After the war she bought a former race-horse, Antonym, re-formed the South Adelaide Riding Club and served as its secretary. She also became secretary of the Horse Riding Clubs' Association. Having learned all she could about dressage, she popularized it with the riding public. In 1949 she and Tom Roberts established the Dressage Club of South Australia which was to affiliate with the Equestrian Federation of Australia. Dressage events were included in the Royal Agricultural and Horticultural Society of South Australia's 1950 show. On Elkedra, Mansom won a blue ribbon: they executed a figure eight, side passaging, reining back and cantering on a nominated leg, and were judged best turned-out horse and rider.

Mansom was a member of the executive of the local Light Horse Association and numerous other riding clubs. Accustomed to using a megaphone when training riders, she sang operatic airs while exercising her animals in the parklands or on the beach. She helped to organize Australian Olympic Federation horse trials in South Australia and proved an astute judge. The 1978 inter-club competition, which included a Dorothy Mansom trophy, was the last she arranged. Survived by her husband, she died on 6 November that year in Adelaide and was buried in West Terrace cemetery.

G. Couch-Keen (comp), *Equestrienne Australis* (priv pub, Springton, SA, 1990); *Hoofs and Horns*, Jan 1979; information from Mr and Mrs B. Mansom, Millswood, Adel.   SUZANNE EDGAR

MARLAY, ELAINE (1915-1977), dentist and university lecturer, was born on 9 October 1915 at Coorparoo, Brisbane, second daughter of Queensland-born parents Robert Wilson, public servant, and his wife Elsie Daisy, née Preston. Educated at Greenslopes State and Brisbane Girls' Grammar schools, Elaine wanted to study medicine but could not afford to attend the University of Sydney, the nearest institution that offered a medical course. She took the advice of her mentor Professor Ernest Goddard [q.v.9] and enrolled in dentistry at the University of Queensland (B.D.Sc., 1937). After graduating, she practised at Killarney. On 6 August 1943 at St John's Anglican Cathedral, Brisbane, she married Mervyn Marlay, a 24-year-old soldier in the Australian Imperial Force. When the war ended, her husband's employment in banking took them to various country centres where she worked as a part-time or full-time dentist. In the late 1950s they settled in Brisbane.

Appointed a temporary lecturer in the department of dentistry, University of Queensland, in 1961, Mrs Marlay joined the permanent staff in 1965 as lecturer in oral biology. She was awarded a Ph.D. in 1969 for a study of the incidence of dental caries in adolescent girls; her project also contributed 'to knowledge about tests of buffering ca-

pacity of saliva and the ability to predict dental caries increments'. On 1 January 1971 Dr Marlay was made a senior lecturer.

Throughout her professional career Marlay endeavoured to further her education and to promote the role of women in a male-dominated profession. A skilled and persuasive debater, she was president (for two years) of the Amara Study Group, a society of female dentists. In 1975 she contributed a chapter on women in dentistry to a book commemorating International Women's Year. Taking study leave in 1976, she examined 'schemes for the continuing education of women dentists' in the United States of America, Europe and England, and prepared a report recommending that similar measures be implemented in Australia. While abroad, she represented the Australian Committee on Overseas Professional Qualifications as an official visitor to dental schools at universities in Paris.

Following several years of research and consultation, Marlay completed the final draft of *A History of Dental Education in Queensland 1863-1964* (Brisbane, 1979). Despite holding strong views on the changes that had occurred in the university's department of dentistry from the time she had graduated, she refrained from expressing her opinions in writing 'because she was part of the history she recorded'. The department published her book after her death. Of middle height and average build, with a tinge of red in her hair, she was charming, sensitive and enthusiastic. In March 1977 she fell ill and took sick leave. Survived by her husband and two daughters, she died on 3 May that year in Princess Alexandra Hospital, South Brisbane, and was cremated.

G. N. Davies, 'Foreword' in E. Marlay, *A History of Dental Education in Queensland 1863-1964* (Brisb, 1979); *Univ News*, 18 May 1977, 10 Oct 1979; Univ Qld staff file 61/94 (Univ Qld Archives); information from Dr K. Romaniuk, Brisb.
                                        JENNIFER HARRISON

MAROU MIMI (1886-1968), Torres Strait Islands nationalist, was born on 13 November 1886 on Murray (Mer) Island, north-east of Cape York Peninsula. His father was named Marou; his mother's name remains unknown. He attended the island's government school and became a monitor, but at home he learned traditional Meriam ways. In his late teens he joined the crew of the *Miriam*, Murray island's cutter, and gathered *bêche-de-mer*. He then went canecutting in North Queensland and later tried to establish himself as a share-farmer before being 'deported' to Murray Island. After a period at home, he returned to the sea, collecting trochus-shell, *bêche-de-mer* and pearl-shell.

On Murray Island on 16 July 1917 Marou married Wazan Adai; they adopted a daughter and two sons. During the early 1920s he lived on Darnley (Erub) Island where he studied to become an Anglican priest. A diocesan financial crisis interrupted his training and he was forced to go back to Murray Island. After being employed as a teacher and lay preacher, he resumed work in the boats.

In 1928 Marou was elected to the Murray Island local government council. He was to serve as a councillor for seventeen of the ensuing twenty-eight years, and to have several terms (totalling eight years) as chairman. In addition, he spent five years (from 1947) as the council's representative at the biennial conferences of Torres Strait Islands councillors. While chairman, he used his powers fully: he insisted on obedience to by-laws and dealt severely, sometimes idiosyncratically, with infringements and supposed infractions. His periods in and out of office reflected Murray Island's volatile politics, resentment of his autocratic rule, and enmities fostered by his political ambitions.

In 1936 Marou had been one of the leaders of an inter-island strike by the crews of 'Company' boats—vessels communally run, under the direction of the Aboriginal Industries Board. Beginning as a protest over the crewmen's right to control their earnings, the strike led to demands for the islands' autonomy. The Queensland government made some concessions, but Marou was committed to achieving full citizenship for the islanders; he retained a vision of the islands freed of outside control, and possibly independent from Australia. He supported the establishment of the Torres Strait Light Infantry Battalion in World War II to demonstrate that his people deserved greater respect from Whites.

Hoping to advance the islanders' cause, Marou flirted briefly in 1948 with the Communist Party of Australia, which led one Queensland departmental official to nickname him 'old Stalin'. While Marou's confrontational style enhanced his reputation as his people's champion, some Murray Islanders regarded it as counter-productive. As younger, more accommodating and pragmatic local politicians came to prominence in the 1950s, he was supplanted. He lost his place on the council in 1956. The Queensland government had granted him recognition of a sort, appointing him one of the first islander justices of the peace, presenting him to Queen Elizabeth II at Cairns in 1954, and awarding him a certificate of merit for his service.

In his retirement Marou promoted a revival of Meriam culture. From the late 1930s he had kept a diary. Writing in his native language and in English, he recorded his observations on the customs of old Mer. On 23 January 1963 he set down his understanding of the traditional 'Malo's Law' which governed social relationships and land use. Marou died on 28 March 1968 on Murray Island and was buried in the local cemetery; his wife and sons survived him. Information from his diary provided critical evidence in the legal proceedings instituted by Koiki ('Eddie') Mabo and other Murray Islanders to establish ownership of their land. Their action led in 1992 to the High Court of Australia's 'Mabo' decision on 'native title'.

J. Beckett, *Torres Strait Islanders* (Cambridge, 1987); N. Sharp, *Stars of Tagai* (Canb, 1993) and *No Ordinary Judgment* (Canb, 1996); D. Horton (ed), *The Encyclopedia of Aboriginal Australia*, vol 2 (Canb, 1994); *Torres Strait Islander*, 5, 1983.

IAN HOWIE-WILLIS

MARRIOTT, FRANCIS (1876-1957), farmer and politician, was born on 10 July 1876 at Kennington, Surrey, England, son of William Kenaz Marriott, merchant's clerk, and his wife Maria, née Maycock. Like his three brothers, Frank attended Stamford Grammar School, Lincolnshire, then joined the family business as a junior clerk. He disliked city life and went to sea at the age of 19. His travels took him to the United States of America where he worked for five years on road-construction projects. In 1902 he moved to Scotland but within twelve months sailed for Australia. Stranded in Hobart in 1903, he packed his swag, roamed the country and eventually bought a mixed farm near Elliott. At St Paul's Anglican Church, Emu Bay, on 4 April 1907 he married 33-year-old Alice Maud Harrison (d.1950).

Commissioned in the Australian Imperial Force on 1 June 1915, Marriott served in Egypt and France. On 25 February 1917 at Bapaume he was blinded by bullet-wounds to both eyes; he was invalided to Tasmania where his A.I.F. appointment terminated on 22 September. He joined the Returned Sailors' and Soldiers' Imperial League of Australia, worked on repatriation committees and addressed conscription meetings. In 1919 Marriott sailed with his family for England. At St Dunstan's Hostel for Blinded Soldiers and Sailors, London, he learned Braille, typewriting, joinery and poultry-farming. This training gave new purpose to his life. He became a spokesman for St Dunstan's and was received by its patron, King George V, at Windsor Castle in April 1920.

On his return to Tasmania, Marriott was invited by the Nationalist Party to stand for the House of Assembly. He represented the division of Darwin from June 1922 to December 1941. Preparing for his retirement, he moved to Launceston, but was persuaded to contest Bass which he represented until November 1946. As a politician, he drew on a well-developed memory and the devotion of his wife who read aloud to him from the bills listed for debate.

In addition to his work with blind ex-servicemen, Marriott had engaged in numerous charitable and community activities during his political career. He was federal president (1931-34) of Toc H, a member of Legacy and a board-member of the Tasmanian Institution for the Blind, Deaf and Dumb. A committed Anglican layman, he was a long-time member of the Australian synod and of the Tasmanian diocesan council. As chief commissioner of the Boy Scouts' Association, he was awarded (1933) its gold medal of merit. He was appointed C.M.G. in 1934.

Marriott had a resonant voice and was forthright in his speech. A man of quick, incisive wit, he never compromised his integrity for the sake of popularity. He died on 9 February 1957 in Hobart and was cremated. His four sons survived him: Frederick Marriott was a member (1946-61) for Bass and John represented (1953-75) Tasmania in the Senate. A. L. McIntyre's portrait of Francis Marriott is held by the family.

Mercury (Hob), 1 Jan 1934, 11, 12 Feb 1957; *Examiner* (Launc), 6 July 1950, 14 Feb 1957; *Advocate* (Burnie), 9 Nov 1946; P. Hay, Interview with J. E. Marriott, 20 May-20 Dec 1988 (ts of 17 tapes, Cwlth Parliament's Oral Hist Project); E. J. Smith, Time is the Builder—a History of the Royal Tasmanian Society for the Blind and Deaf, 1887-1987 (ms, 1991, held by author, Lenah Valley, Hob); family papers (held by Mrs D. C. P. Brammall, Mount Nelson, Hob).   E. J. SMITH

MARSDEN, MAY (1876-1968), artist and educationist, was born on 6 May 1876 at Church-Stoke, Montgomeryshire, Wales, daughter of Joseph Marsden, engineer, and his wife Charlotte Priscilla, née Kniveton. May studied art at Wirksworth, Derbyshire, under Fred Simmonds, and at the Derby Central School of Art. After gaining a teacher's certificate from the Royal College of Art, South Kensington, London, in 1897, she taught at Wallasey Grange School for girls, near Liverpool.

In 1913 Marsden came to Sydney with her parents. She initially taught at private schools, and then in public ones. Alexander Mackie, who had been introduced to her by Julian Ashton [qq.v.10,7], appointed her a lecturer in art at Teachers' College, Sydney, on 11 October 1915, a post she was to hold until January 1941. During most of her life in Australia she lived in the family home in Harden Road, Artarmon, with her sister Grace, and their brothers Albert and Philip; Bert managed the Anthony Hordern [q.v.4] & Sons' Fine Art Gallery. May had shown her paintings at Derby, Leicester and Liverpool before arriving in Australia; in Sydney she exhibited with the Australian Water-Colour Institute. She spent holidays with her sister and brothers in the country, and some of her paintings were of landscapes around Canberra, Tidbinbilla and Cobbity. She also drew and etched. Four of her works, 'Magnolias', 'Pyrmont Bridge', 'View from Wollstonecraft' and 'Heber Chapel, Cobbity' form part of the University of Sydney's collection.

May Marsden was an inspiring teacher for whom art was a significant aspect of civilized life. With the enthusiastic support of Mackie, she transformed the corridors of the new Teachers' College (built in 1920) into art galleries replete with old-master reproductions and original Australian prints, drawings and paintings. There she regaled her students, gathered in devoted little packs, with her love of visual beauty and her highly informed taste, often to the amusement of less aesthetically inclined passers-by who regarded her as eccentric. She organized sketch clubs for her pupils and became a patron of the Teachers' College Art Club. A champion of the autonomy of art, she chose Clive Bell's maxim, 'The one good thing society can do for the artist is to leave him alone—give him liberty', as the epigraph for the catalogue of the club's first exhibition (1938).

By introducing her students to modernism and modernist artists such as Eleonore Lange, Marsden played a key role in changing the way art was taught in the State's public schools. As a teacher she was influenced by the English art educational reformer William Ablett, and at Teachers' College strongly advocated innovative methods. She encouraged several generations of her students—including 'Rah' Fizelle [q.v.8], James Gleeson and Bernard Smith—to assist in reforming art teaching in New South Wales schools which, until the 1940s, was conducted on extremely conservative lines. Miss Marsden died on 12 July 1968 at her Artarmon home and was buried with Anglican rites in Northern Suburbs cemetery.

Bernard Smith, *The Boy Adeodatus* (Melb, 1984); *Art and Aust*, 15, no 3, Autumn 1978, p 249; teachers' records, Dept of Education (NSW) Archives, Syd; information from Mr J. Gleeson, Northbridge, Syd, Ms P. Bell and Mr A. Bradley, Univ Syd, and the late Mr P. Marsden; personal information.
                                        BERNARD SMITH

MARSHALL, ALAN JOHN (JOCK) (1911-1967), professor of zoology, was born on 17 February 1911 at Redfern, Sydney, youngest of four children of native-born parents Robert Duncan Marshall, tramway fettler, and his wife Violet Ada, née Crowe. As a boy he was given the nickname 'Jock' because of his ambition to become a jockey, though he was soon too tall for such a career. He grew up at Penshurst on the outskirts of Sydney, riding his horse through paddocks, shooting rabbits and becoming imbued with a sense of nature. Educated at Dumbleton Public School, he later impressed English acquaintances by referring to himself as an 'old Dumbletonian'. He was an avid reader of such books as Charles Darwin's *On the Origin of Species* and Thomas Paine's *The Rights of Man*, given to him by his father, but at Kogarah High School he declared himself bored; academically lazy and given to excessive practical jokes, he was expelled without sitting the Intermediate examinations. Marshall was then apprenticed to a motor mechanic.

Careless handling of a shotgun shortly before his sixteenth birthday resulted in the amputation of his left arm, just below the shoulder. He overcame this disability and could, with one hand, achieve what would normally be delicate, two-handed manipulations. Undeterred by the accident, he continued his investigations of bush fauna. His self-gained knowledge of the natural history around Sydney came to the notice of Alec Chisholm [q.v.13], who put him in touch with the Australian Museum (honorary fellow, 1934). Through its good offices, he was invited (1930) to join a Harvard University expedition to northern New South Wales and Queensland. He was a member of University of Oxford expeditions—to Espiritu Santo, New Hebrides (Vanuatu), in 1934, and to the Mandated Territory of New Guinea and Dutch New Guinea (Irian Jaya) in 1936. Next year he worked at Oxford with his fellow explorers, and joined an Austrian expedition to Spitsbergen, in the Arctic Circle.

Marshall's ambition focused on a career in biology. Entering the University of Sydney (B.Sc., 1940) as an unmatriculated student, he was ineligible to undertake an honours degree, but he was appointed a demonstrator in zoology at the university and a resident tutor at St Paul's College. He wrote a column for the *Daily Telegraph* and fulfilled a weekly broadcasting commitment with the Australian Broadcasting Commission, subsequently becoming 'Jock the Backyard Naturalist' for its Argonauts' Club. At the college chapel on 8 March 1941 he married Joy Lyall Wood with Anglican rites.

That year Marshall applied to enlist in the Australian Imperial Force; he was rejected because he only had one arm. Mobilized in the Militia on 13 October 1941, he was commissioned and promoted temporary captain in November. Initially he performed edu-

cation duties. In July 1942 he was accepted in the A.I.F. and in April 1943 joined the intelligence unit at headquarters, New Guinea Force, Port Moresby. Despite his disability, Marshall was able to obtain a posting in November to a fighting unit, the 2nd/2nd Battalion. During the Wewak campaign he led a patrol, known as 'Jockforce', deep into enemy territory in January-February 1945. Shortly before World War II ended, he was posted to 'Z' Special Unit in Brisbane.

Transferring to the Reserve of Officers on 17 October 1945, Marshall applied to enter the University of Oxford (D.Phil., 1949; D.Sc., 1956). He sailed for England in July 1946, leaving his wife and child in Sydney. The couple had agreed to a divorce, which was granted in 1948. Marshall had formed a relationship with Janet (Jane) Graham, whom he had met in 1945 while they were both in military service. She travelled to England in 1946 and they were married on 13 May 1950 at the register office, London. They had three children in what proved a devoted partnership.

At Oxford, Marshall suffered severe bouts of malaria, but applied himself single-mindedly to a research programme on the breeding cycles of birds. This research complemented his desire to explore, and in 1947 he led an Arctic expedition to Jan Mayen island. In 1949 he was appointed reader in zoology and comparative anatomy at Saint Bartholomew's Hospital Medical College, University of London, a position he held for ten years. While he continued an association with journalism through regular contributions to several newspapers, his principal activity was research into the physiology of reproduction, primarily in birds. Although he was based in London, his field-work took him to Africa, Indonesia, Australia and North America, where he held a visiting lecturership at Yale University, New Haven, Connecticut, in 1958 and at the University of California in 1959.

Anxious to 'retribalize' his children in Australia, in 1959 Marshall applied for and was appointed to the foundation chair of biology at Monash University, Melbourne. The name of his department was later changed to zoology and comparative physiology, which better accorded with his interests. In 1961 he was appointed dean of the faculty of science. He influenced university policies in regard to building and landscaping, insisting on the planting of native vegetation.

Marshall wrote one scholarly monograph, *Bower Birds* (Oxford, 1954), and more than eighty articles in scientific journals. He contributed to encyclopedias and edited three scientific compendia—*Biology and Comparative Physiology of Birds* (2 vols, London, 1960-61), *A Textbook of Zoology* (vol 2, London, 1962), and *The Great Extermination* (Sydney, 1966).

The last, a record of the extinction of animal species in Australia from the time of European settlement, formed part of a campaign to encourage the conservation of biological diversity. Marshall's scientific expeditions and collateral scholarship provided him with material for books of a popular nature, *The Black Musketeers* (London, 1937), *The Men and Birds of Paradise* (London, 1938), *Australia Limited* (Sydney, 1942), *Journey Among Men*, with (Sir) Russell Drysdale (London, 1962), and *Darwin and Huxley in Australia* (Sydney, 1970).

Powerfully built, 5 ft 11 ins (180 cm) tall and about 13 stone (83 kg) in weight, Marshall was fair haired and blue eyed, with 'skin permanently ruddy from outdoor living, and a combative nose and jaw'. He was outspoken and at times aggressive, according to one journalist 'a rude rugged improbable academic' and a 'literate, latter-day version of the Wild Colonial Boy'. Yet he loved the visual arts, collected antiquarian books, antique furniture and eighteenth-century glass, and attracted artists and writers as friends.

In 1965 Marshall's chest pains were traced to a malignant growth pressing on his aorta. His health deteriorated, and in 1966 the university relieved him of administrative duties by appointing him research professor of zoology. Though mostly bedridden, he continued to write articles and once attended a professorial board-meeting on a stretcher. His devotion to writing and his sense of history generated an extensive archive of photographs, correspondence and diaries which recorded the life of an intelligent, humorous, kind and occasionally difficult individual.

Jock Marshall died of cancer on 20 July 1967 at Heidelberg and was cremated; his wife and their son and two daughters survived him, as did the daughter of his first marriage. In keeping with his agnosticism, his funeral ceremony was presided over by the president of the Rationalist Society of Australia. A portrait of Marshall by Lina Bryans is held by the family, two sketches by Louis Kahan by Monash University, and another by Drysdale by the National Library of Australia. At Monash University a ten-acre (4 ha) nature reserve, which Marshall had fought to preserve, was named after him.

J. Hetherington, *Uncommon Men* (Melb, 1965) and *Blamey* (Canb, 1973); *SMH*, 21 July 1967; Marshall papers (NL *and* Monash Univ Archives).

JAMES W. WARREN

MARSHALL, ALMA ELIZABETH (1879-1964), political activist, was born on 29 June 1879 at Cawdor, near Camden, New South Wales, sixth child of native-born parents Frederick Nash, farmer, and his wife Betsy Jane, née Boardman. Elizabeth's childhood was spent at Cootamundra in 'a typical middle-class Methodist family "on the land"'. She went to public school, Sunday School and church, and took part in school concerts and Sunday-School picnics. Her father discouraged further education and her mother wanted her at home, but in 1908-09 she taught at Matavelo school for girls, Fiji.

After studying photography with Mina and May Moore [qq.v.10], Miss Nash opened a studio in Melbourne in 1913. At St John's Anglican Church, Toorak, on 15 March 1917 she married Eric Norman Marshall, a 28-year-old schoolteacher who was to be a master at Scotch College for thirty years. Joining the Australian Labor Party, Elizabeth served as its representative for Hawthorn on the women's central executive, and as campaign organizer at Hawthorn and Kooyong. She looked to socialism to provide equality of opportunity. A justice of the peace (from 1930), she read widely on judicial procedure. In 1931 she inspected conditions at Pentridge gaol and obtained remission of sentence for a mentally afflicted woman imprisoned for bigamy. Her proposal that magistrates should check the treatment of children committed to a particular 'church home' was seen as an attack on the churches.

During the Depression, as the A.L.P.'s local branch representative on the Hawthorn citizens' unemployment relief committee, she set up a sub-committee to care for unemployed women and the wives of unemployed men. Mrs Marshall provided practical assistance to individuals and persuaded the government to subsidize rent 'in cases of extreme hardship'. She served as vice-president of the Howard League for Penal Reform, honorary secretary of the Victorian Association for Social and Moral Hygiene (1940-41), and foundation secretary of the Women Justices' Association.

Marshall's international awareness had led her to join the Ethiopian Relief Committee (1935) and the Spanish Relief Committee (1936), and to become a committee-member of, and an interstate delegate to, the national council of the Movement against War and Fascism. She also held the post of honorary secretary of the Society for Cultural Relations with the Soviet Union and of the Australia China Co-operation Association (1939-45). On 1 March 1946 she founded and became honorary secretary of the East-West Committee 'for friendship with Asia'; its vice-presidents included Kathleen Fitzpatrick, Victor James and Frank Dalby Davison [q.v.13] 'whose names were a guarantee of political respectability'. Under the committee's auspices she and her husband wrote a pamphlet, *Asia, the White Australia Policy and you* (1949), and gave a copy to every member of Federal parliament. They also undertook lengthy correspondence with Commonwealth public servants to obtain permanent residence and higher wages for Asian pearl-divers at Broome, Western Australia. Elizabeth arranged the first official celebration in Australia of Indonesian independence and established the Indonesian Medical Aid Committee.

Known affectionately as 'Grannie', Elizabeth Marshall had a keen mind, courage and integrity. She appreciated literature, music and nature, spoke with a 'ladylike English accent' and enjoyed a good chuckle. Survived by her husband, who had supported her in all her activities, she died on 6 September 1964 at Camberwell and was cremated.

E. Marshall, *It Pays to be White* (Syd, 1973); funeral addresses by Judge G. L. Dethridge, and Mr J. Meltzer, Melb (copies on ADB file, Canb).

A. G. THOMSON ZAINU'DDIN

MARSHALL, BARRY RUSSELL (1923-1970), Anglican priest, college chaplain and theological scholar, was born on 18 July 1923 at Darlinghurst, Sydney, son of Alan Russell Marshall, grazier, and his wife Beryl Marion, née Maude, both born in New South Wales. Barry was initially educated at home on his father's property near Coolah before boarding (1935-41) at Sydney Church of England Grammar School. While at Shore he underwent a religious conversion.

Enlisting in the Royal Australian Air Force on 10 June 1942, Marshall served as a wireless operator in New Guinea and the islands nearby. He was demobilized on 20 June 1945 as a leading aircraftman. To prepare for ordination, he entered St John's College, Morpeth, New South Wales, but moved to Trinity College, University of Melbourne (B.A. Hons, 1948), where he gained first-class honours in history. He returned to Morpeth and completed a licentiate of theology (1950), also with first-class honours. Ordained priest on 21 December 1950, he joined the Brotherhood of the Good Shepherd, taking the religious name of Timothy.

In 1952 Marshall went to Christ Church, University of Oxford (D.Phil., 1956), as Lucas Tooth [q.v.6] scholar. There he came under the influence of Anglo-Catholic scholars, such as V. A. Demant, E. L. Mascall, F. L. Cross and Austin Farrer. Following a period as acting-librarian at Pusey House, he returned in 1956 to the Brotherhood of the Good Shepherd and served as priest-in-charge of Bourke, New South Wales. During this time he sustained a near-fatal motorcar accident which left him with chronic pain.

Fr Marshall was chaplain (1961-69) of Trinity College, where he was renowned for his energy, as well as for his clever, and at times sharp, wit. His preaching, always engaging, revealed a legacy of metaphysical insight. He exercised considerable influence over undergraduates and theological students, and over a wider group of clergy and laity beyond the college and university. Meanwhile, he joined the Oratory of the Good Shepherd, a worldwide society of Anglican clergy and lay associates.

In theology and liturgical practice Marshall was Anglo-Catholic, and as a priest highly disciplined, without displaying narrowness of vision. His opposition to infant baptism, however, proved controversial. If some thought him 'too idiosyncratic', many found him a sympathetic and caring pastor, and a few viewed him as a complex and demanding figure who set standards by his own life which they could not emulate. His personality seemed both engaging and elusive. Widely known as an ecumenical figure, a liturgical scholar and a church historian, Marshall published little. He was especially affected by a period of study in 1966-67 at the Institut Catholique de Paris where he encountered (Cardinal) Jean Danielou and observed the modern Roman Catholic liturgical and renewal movement. Marshall brought some of its theology and practices to Australia.

Offered the post of principal of Pusey House, Oxford, in 1969, Marshall assisted at St James's Church, Sydney, for some months, then left for England in May 1970. Before he formally took up his new post, he fell from a ladder at Pusey House and died of a fractured skull on 12 August 1970 at the Radcliffe Infirmary, Oxford. His ashes were interred in Trinity College chapel, Melbourne. A portrait by Dora McRae is held by the college.

Fleur de Lys, 1969, p 7, 1970, p 4; *Univ Melb Gazette*, Sept 1970; *Bush Brother*, 66, no 2, Sept 1970, p 5; *Torchbearer*, 1970; *Anglican*, 20, 27 Aug 1970; Trinity College Archives (Melb); information from Dr R. L. Sharwood, Parkville, Melb.

JOHN MORGAN

MARSHALL, DOROTHY MAY (1902-1961), schoolteacher, war- and welfare-worker, and public servant, was born on 15 May 1902 in Adelaide, daughter of Charles Henry Marshall, a coachman who became a pioneer radiographer, and his wife Helen Cameron, née Grant (d.1906). Like her father, Dorothy was determined, efficient and warm-hearted. Dark eyed, short and sturdy, she excelled at Adelaide High School and Adelaide Teachers' College. She taught at Gawler (1923-24) and Woodville (1924-34) primary schools, then won an exchange position to Bishop Goodwin Girls' and Margaret Sewell Central schools at Carlisle, England. In 1936 she returned to

Adelaide and joined the staff of the girls' department at Croydon Central School. Three years later she was elected to the advisory council of the South Australian Women Teachers' Guild.

In 1941 Miss Marshall was appointed adviser for vocational training to the Education Department, but was soon seconded to assist Adelaide Miethke [q.v.10] with the Schools Patriotic Fund of South Australia. On loan to the Department of Labour and National Service in June, she became foundation secretary of the Women's War Service Council which co-ordinated and managed the war service and training of South Australian women, including their allocation to seasonal work outdoors. She immediately advocated the establishment of a women's land army. In July 1942 the Commonwealth government appointed her State superintendent of the Australian Women's Land Army. Marshall controlled major policy implementation and everyday detail; she selected and managed headquarters staff, appointed field staff, and supervised women volunteers on the land; and she travelled extensively, determining the labour needs of primary producers, recruiting country girls, and inspecting their working and living conditions.

Recruited herself in 1945 as a camp welfare officer by the United Nations Relief and Rehabilitation Administration, Marshall helped displaced persons in the British zone in Germany. By November she had been promoted to divisional welfare liaison officer at U.N.R.R.A.'s headquarters at Menden, Westphalia, which controlled fourteen camps in the area. Within two months she was selected —over four male applicants—as chief welfare officer of the 1st U.N.R.R.A. Corps. She had charge of seventy-four welfare officers who took care of some 102 000 displaced Poles in forty camps. Responsible for securing supplies of basic food and clothing, she also raised the inmates' morale by organizing schools for children, vocational and craft centres for adults, and films and concerts in the camp halls. Occasionally she enjoyed a break and went to dances in the British officers' mess. Appointed director-general of welfare in June 1946, she capably took charge of every camp in the zone.

When U.N.R.R.A. was dissolved in mid-1947, Marshall joined the International Refugee Organization as a welfare officer in the British zone of Germany. In November 1948 she became a child welfare officer and later chief of the child-welfare division which arranged for the 'final establishment' of unaccompanied displaced children. She was responsible for planning and organizing the child programme within the zone, and for supervising the field-officers. On leave in Australia in February 1949, she met A. A. Calwell [q.v.13], the minister for immigration, to discuss the resettlement of five hundred homeless children aged between 16 and 18. He agreed to accept youths as immigrants. To publicize the new policy in Europe, she gave lectures in Austria and Italy. Her work ended with the completion of I.R.O. operations in the British zone in December 1951. She was appointed M.B.E. in 1952.

Returning to Adelaide, Marshall began the fourth phase of her working life. In 1953 the State government appointed her to the Department of Agriculture as organizer of the Women's Agricultural Bureau of South Australia. With her breadth of experience, charm and personality, she revitalized the far-flung organization. She initiated a bi-monthly bulletin, *W.A.B. News*, introduced a long-awaited constitution (1958) and inaugurated agricultural schools for women. She visited rural districts, even places as remote as Pinkawillie on Eyre Peninsula. Meanwhile, she enjoyed her many friendships, membership of the Lyceum Club and playing golf. In the *W.A.B. News* in June 1961 she reflected on 'the spirit of service'. Her own life symbolized that ideal. She died of cancer on 12 July 1961 in hospital at Henley Beach and was cremated. From her estate, sworn for probate at £15 677, she bequeathed money to establish a scholarship for Adelaide Girls' High School students to study at the University of Adelaide.

Education Gazette (SA), 1923-41; *WAB News*, no 1, Dec 1954, p 3, no 36, Oct 1961, p 3; *Advertiser* (Adel), 19 Aug 1942, 9 Jan 1953; *SMH*, 17 June 1946, 5 June 1952; Records of the Ex-Aust Women's Land Army Club, SRG266 (Mort L); ABC Women's Talks, AP1003/10/1, AP1003/10/5 (AA, Adel); Agr Bureau of SA, Women's branches, executive minutes, GRG10/130, SRSA; Agr Bureau of SA, *Women's Agr Bureau Congress*, 1958, p 21; Frances Taylor papers PRG596 (Mort L); information from Mrs E. Eadie, Glen Osmond, Adel.   HELEN JONES

MARSHALL, JOHN BIRNIE (1930-1957), swimmer, was born on 29 March 1930 at Bondi, Sydney, elder son of Alexander St Andrew McLean Marshall, a window dresser and former surf champion from Western Australia, and his Tasmanian-born wife Jean, née Birnie. Shortly after his birth, the family moved to Perth. By the age of 3 John was swimming in the Swan River and riding a pony over jumps. In 1935 the Marshalls shifted to Melbourne. John attended (1943-49) Haileybury College, Brighton, where he became an enthusiastic all-round sportsman, representing the school at cricket, football, athletics and swimming. He was also a prefect, but he did not distinguish himself as a scholar.

A shy, rather gawky youth, with large ears, a wide smile and a drawl, Marshall decided in

1944 to approach Tom Donnett, a coach at Richmond Baths. Donnett's early reaction was that he 'had natural buoyancy, enthusiasm and not much else. I liked his spirit . . . but he would bash along . . . without much idea of co-ordination'. Undeterred, Donnett moulded Marshall's fluid, gliding movement through the water; his kick gave him tremendous propulsion, and his almost languid stroke distinguished him from other swimmers.

Within months Marshall was winning races at the Brighton Beach Baths. He took his first title, the Victorian one-mile (1.6 km) championship, in December 1945; and in Adelaide fourteen months later, when he was still 16, he won every national title from 220 yards (200 m) to 1650 yards (1508 m). At the Olympic Games in London in 1948, he finished second in the 1500 metres and third in the 400 metres. The renowned coach Bob Kiphuth, from the United States of America, offered to train him if he could gain entry to Yale University, New Haven. Back in Australia, Marshall made history in the following summer by capturing every Australian freestyle championship, from 110 to 1650 yards.

After much study, Marshall qualified to enter Yale (B.A., 1953). Under the conditioning régime of Kiphuth, he became bigger and stronger, and at the U.S. national titles in April 1950 broke four world records. Later that year he set fifteen world records within four months—over distances from 200 yards to one mile. In December he won the Helms Athletic Foundation award as Australasia's outstanding amateur sportsman for 1950. By mid-1951 he had set 171 records, including 28 world and 38 American. Then suddenly, inexplicably, he lost form.

Marshall suffered defeats in America, and at the 1952 Olympics in Helsinki he failed even to qualify for the final of the 400 metres (in which he held the world record). He finished last in the 1500 metres final, two laps behind the winner. Returning to Australia in 1954, he went to work for the tyre firm founded by the former Olympic swimmer Sir Frank Beaurepaire [q.v.7]. At St Leonard's Presbyterian Church, Brighton Beach, on 14 September 1955 he married Wendy Patricia Byrne, an 18-year-old diving champion and receptionist.

By his example, Marshall made a huge contribution to the swimming revolution which culminated in Australia's great success at the Olympic Games in Melbourne in 1956. His preparation techniques and callisthenics, based on Kiphuth's teachings, became a blueprint for the visionaries of Australian swimming. In a bid to gain Olympic representation for a third time, he switched to the new stroke of butterfly. Excluded from Australia's 1956 Olympic squad, he forced his way into the team by winning two Games trials and finished fifth in the Olympic 200-metre final.

He later won the Victorian 200-metre freestyle and butterfly championships, both in record times, and was named captain of the State team for the national titles.

On 25 January 1957 Marshall was critically injured when one of the tyres on his motorcar blew out and the vehicle crashed near Clunes, Victoria. He died six days later in Royal Melbourne Hospital and was cremated. His wife and seven-month-old son survived him.

G. Lomas, *The Will to Win* (Melb, 1960); H. Gordon, *Young Men in a Hurry* (Melb, 1961) and *Australia and the Olympic Games* (Brisb, 1994); P. Cerutty, *Sport is My Life* (Lond, 1966); *Walkabout*, Dec 1968; *Age* (Melb), 31 Jan 1957; *Herald* (Melb), 31 Jan 1957, 22 Jan 1958; *Daily Mirror* (Syd), 5 Nov 1976.   HARRY GORDON

MARSHALL, THOMAS CLAUDE (1896-1976), ichthyologist and museum preparator, was born on 2 January 1896 at Red Hill, Brisbane, son of Joseph Walter Marshall, a clerk who came from London, and his Queensland-born wife Rosalie, née Brigg. Educated at Petrie Terrace State School, Tom joined the Queensland Museum on 10 January 1912 and trained as a cadet-preparator. He became a protégé of the ichthyologist J. D. Ogilby [q.v.11] who instilled in him a lifelong interest in fish taxonomy.

In 1915-17 Marshall served full time in the Militia, working at the 13th Australian General Hospital, Enoggera. Returning to the museum, he was promoted artificer in 1919. At Christ Church, Milton, on 29 March 1922 he married with Anglican rites Dorothy Agnes O'Donnell, a 21-year-old shop-assistant. To hone his skills as a preparator, he studied modelling under L. J. Harvey [q.v.9] at the Central Technical College. In the 1920s and 1930s he produced an excellent series of dioramas, displays, and models and casts in the field of natural history. He made two documentary films, *Enchanted Regions of the Great Barrier Reef* (1939) and *Roving Coral Seas* (1940), which featured Queensland's maritime natural history and scenic attractions.

Seconded (1942) to the Queensland Department of Harbours and Marine, Marshall was appointed assistant chief inspector of fisheries in 1943. His principal task was to supervise wartime manpower regulations in relation to the fishing industry. From 1946 he held the post of ichthyologist. With the aim of developing a small scientific section within the department, he collected many specimens of the State's large and varied fish fauna. He began a journal, *Ichthyological Notes*. Using his connexions with museums, he obtained additional material for the library which became one of the most comprehensive of its kind in Australia and was named after him.

Despite his lack of academic training, Marshall was a careful and exact taxonomist, if somewhat conservative. He had a remarkable memory for taxonomic references. His methods of classification were at odds with those of his old friend and colleague Gilbert Whitley [q.v.] of the Australian Museum, Sydney. In their correspondence, they nicknamed each other 'Lumper' and 'Splitter', but without animus. Although he was a keen collector and breeder of fish for aquariums, Marshall opposed the release of exotic species into Australian waters. He particularly fought against the use of *Gambusia* and *Poecilia* for controlling mosquitoes.

For Marshall, the publication of his monograph, *Fishes of the Great Barrier Reef and Coastal Waters of Queensland* (Sydney, 1964), marked the pinnacle of his career as a scientist. Others, however, saw his main contribution as establishing the scientific section in his department, the forerunner of the Queensland government's comprehensive fisheries research services. Marshall retired in June 1962. Survived by his wife, son and three daughters, he died on 30 June 1976 in Brisbane and was cremated with Methodist forms. A pen-and-ink portrait by Percy Eagles is held by the family.

P. Mather et al, *A Time for a Museum* (Brisb, 1986); *Courier-Mail*, 1 July 1976; information from Mrs A. Auckland, Aspley, Brisb.

NOEL M. HAYSOM

MARSTON, HEDLEY RALPH (1900-1965), biochemist, was born on 26 August 1900 at Bordertown, South Australia, third and youngest son of South Australian-born parents Septimus Herbert Marston, telegraph clerk, and his wife Mary Frances Ann, née Bishop, librarian. Hedley attended Unley District High School, Adelaide, where he met (Sir) Mark Oliphant, a fellow pupil; the two later became close friends. Having entered the South Australian School of Mines and Industries at the age of 16, Marston attended the University of Adelaide as a non-graduating student. He attained a standard equivalent to first-class honours in physiology and biochemistry. In 1927 he attempted to matriculate in order to qualify for a B.Sc., but failed Mathematics I. He was to have the distinction of receiving some of science's highest accolades without completing a degree.

A chance meeting with Professor T. B. Robertson [q.v.11] had led to Marston's appointment in 1922 as a demonstrator in the university's department of physiology and biochemistry. On 1 March 1928 he joined Robertson's staff in the division of animal nutrition, Council for Scientific and Industrial Research, Adelaide. He greatly impressed

Robertson, and became the division's acting-chief on Robertson's death in 1930. Following Sir Charles Martin's [q.v.10] term as head of the division, Marston again served (1933-35) as acting-chief.

In 1936 the divisions of animal health and animal nutrition were combined under Lionel Bull [q.v.13]. Marston was designated officer-in-charge of the animal nutrition laboratory. He did not accept the downgrading of his section and gave Bull a very difficult time. With the help of Sir David Rivett [q.v.11], C.S.I.R.'s chief executive officer, Marston eventually gained autonomy. On 14 August 1944 he was appointed chief, division of biochemistry and general nutrition; the inclusion of biochemistry in the division's title reflected Marston's views on the subject's importance.

Robertson, Martin and Professor Archibald Watson [q.v.12] were lasting influences on Marston's life. Over the years he formed a wide and eclectic circle of friends. In the arts they included Elioth Gruner [q.v.9], Arthur Murch, Clive Turnbull [q.v.], and (Sir) William Dobell [q.v.14] whose portrait of Marston is held by the Queensland Art Gallery. Among scientists, he was close to Rivett and R. G. (Dick) Thomas, as well as Oliphant. The companionship of industrialists, such as J. L. Pratt of General Motors Corporation and W. S. Robinson [q.v.11], was important to him. His generosity towards his friends was renowned, and his flattery and gift-giving knew no bounds.

On 17 September 1934 at the Church of the Epiphany, Crafers, Marston married with Anglican rites Kathleen Nellie Spooner; they were to remain childless. She rarely accompanied her husband in public, but did go with him to England when he spent a year (1937-38) at Sir Gowland Hopkins's biochemical laboratory, University of Cambridge. While in England he developed friendships useful to his career.

The most publicized research of Marston's division dealt with deficiencies of trace elements in the soils of South Australia and had led to the discovery that 'coast disease'—a wasting malady of sheep pastured in the south-east coastal region and other areas—was caused by a lack of cobalt in their diet. Marston claimed this breakthrough as his own. His dramatic announcement at the meeting in 1935 of the Australian and New Zealand Association for the Advancement of Science made his reputation. There is overwhelming evidence, however, that the work originally belonged to Dick Thomas and E. W. L. Lines. At first, Marston dismissed their efforts. It was not until he saw ailing sheep dramatically recover through the administration of cobalt salts that he assumed control of the project, probably in mid-1934. Thomas and Lines never gained the credit due to them, and were thereafter excluded from the investigations carried out at the division's research station at Robe.

In Adelaide that year Marston met Eric Underwood [q.v.], who was working in Western Australia on the same problem and was close to obtaining the same result. No collaboration between the two teams eventuated and Marston seems to have conducted a vitriolic campaign against Underwood for many years without provoking any apparent retaliation. Indeed, at Marston's death, Underwood wrote a memoir for the Australian Academy of Science which was considered and fair.

Another important project to bring prestige to Marston and his division was the research, spearheaded by D. S. Riceman and others, into the soils of South Australia's Ninety Mile Desert. Despite having an adequate rainfall, the region only supported poor scrub. The desert's deficiency of trace elements (copper and zinc) was overcome, and an area of some 2 million acres (800 000 ha)—now called Coonalpyn Downs—was brought into productive mixed farming. To illustrate the impact of the research, Marston wrote to Oliphant in 1957 about a farmer who had recently settled in the area: 'He is sowing 8,000 acres more this year to practically complete the 75,000 acres. Last year he shore 30,000 sheep which was all the stock he could acquire, and "they made no impression as the area would hold easily and well five times this number"'.

In 1948 Marston delivered a lecture on the work of his division to the Royal Society, London, which elected him a fellow in the following year. The C.S.I.R. press release announcing his fellowship boasted that the division had brought the desert to bloom. Marston was involved in other projects, the most important of which were his investigation of the metabolic role of vitamin B12 in sheep and the study which he had carried out with Mary Dawbarn in World War II on the nutritional needs of troops. The effort Marston spent in determining the rate of growth of sheep's wool opened the way to further research. He greatly disliked publishing anything until he could announce the whole story, much to the chagrin of some of his staff who felt that this policy impeded their careers. Then he delighted in making a grand announcement in 'the Marstonian style'.

In 1955 Marston agreed, with alacrity, to assist the British in their research into the biological effects of radiation caused by atomic-bomb testing in Australia. His task was to study the radioactive iodine uptake in sheep and cattle. From monitoring the fall-out due to the tests in 1956 on the Monte Bello Islands and at Maralinga, South Australia, he quickly realized that the Atomic Weapons Tests Safety Committee was under-reporting the extent of the contamination of Australia,

and dismissing the associated risks. Marston claimed that the third test (11 October) at Maralinga had contaminated Adelaide. When the A.W.T.S.C. did not acknowledge such contamination in its press release, he mounted a bitter attack on Sir Leslie Martin and (Sir) Ernest Titterton, the two principal physicists on the committee.

The major thrust of Marston's argument was that radioactive iodine found in the thyroids of animals indicated the presence in the food chain of radioactive strontium which would endanger the health of humans, particularly children. His anger led him, uncharacteristically, to make this claim without recourse to empirical evidence. At that time he was the only senior Australian scientist who adopted a hostile attitude towards the British tests. In many private letters on this subject, and in official reports, he claimed that his countrymen were being hoodwinked, and that the A.W.T.S.C. lacked competence and integrity. The controversy went close to ruining his health, threatened his position of influence in the Australian scientific community, and converted him from an Anglophile to an Anglophobe.

The Australian National University awarded Marston a D.Sc., *honoris causa,* in 1957; he was A.N.Z.A.A.S.'s Mueller [q.v.5] medallist in 1958; and the University of Adelaide conferred a D.Sc., *ad eundem gradum,* on him in 1959. As one who had strenuously supported Oliphant and D. F. Martyn [q.v.] in their plan to form an Australian Academy of Science, he revelled in the pomp and ceremony surrounding its inauguration in 1954. Elected founding treasurer of the academy, he was largely responsible for the adoption of the design for its building in Canberra. His considerable fundraising ability and association with the arts made his a powerful voice, but the period he spent helping to administer the academy was marred by acrimony with certain university scientists.

Marston's standing enabled him to run his division as if it were an independent entity. He took little notice of directions from the executive of C.S.I.R. (Commonwealth Scientific and Industrial Research Organization from 1949) and protected his staff, while expecting herculean efforts and total loyalty in return. The awards and respect which went to Marston were in large measure due to the work of the division as a whole. Its research substantially changed Australian agriculture, and had a significant impact on many hitherto marginal lands throughout the world.

South Australia's farming community revered Marston. The Robe Hotel flew the Australian flag whenever he brought visitors to the local research-station. Perry Stout, an American, wrote of Marston and his colleagues: 'I have wondered, in paraphrase, if

Australians shall ever know "how much they owe to so few"?' Early explorers, he went on, 'so highly thought of in Australia, travelled over the land . . . [R]ecent ones have looked underneath its surface to bring forth great new wealth in the form of plants and animals'.

Marston had a complex personality. He was widely read, a polished writer and quick-witted; his lectures were replete with Churchillian prose; and he was wonderful company at social events. Yet few of his surviving colleagues believe that he possessed the essential qualities of a chief of division, as Martin had recognized. Some of his staff remain strongly antagonistic towards him—and in a few cases are still distressed by memories of him—even though many in his division were enabled to travel abroad, and several obtained their doctorates. Whenever possible Marston used his colleagues as his laboratory-assistants. Despite his vision of a scientific ethos providing a model for society and his image of the 'scientific man' as the pinnacle of perfection, he frequently failed to live up to these ideals.

Thomas called Marston a 'bon viveur', and likened him to James Thurber's Walter Mitty and to Alphonse Daudet's Tartarin de Tarascon. Loving to dramatize his life, Marston took on the personae of people he admired, particularly Watson. He suffered numerous illnesses, but as a talking point they seemed to be a source of pleasure. He was a splendid cook, a lover of the arts and a gifted raconteur. Physically, too, he was impressive—he was very large and used his commanding presence to great effect. R. L. M. Synge said of him that, on occasions, 'a kind of euphoria would liberate him from the real world'. Even on his deathbed he played to the audience, claiming that his life was a 'grand story'. Survived by his wife, he died of uraemia on 25 August 1965 at Toorak Gardens, Adelaide, and was cremated.

J. R. McClelland, *Royal Commission into British Nuclear Tests in Australia* (Canb, 1985); *Biog Memoirs of Fellows of Roy Soc* (Lond), 13, 1967, p 267; *Records of the Australian Academy of Science*, 1, no 2, Dec 1967, p 73; R. T. Cross, 'Falling out over Adelaide' (ms, held by author, LaTrobe Univ); Marston papers (AA, Canb, *and* NL, *and* Aust Academy of Science); Oliphant papers (Barr Smith L, Univ Adel); information from Miss S. Allen, Glenside, Mr D. Dewey, Myrtle Bank, Dr I. Jarrett, Linden Park, Adel, Dr I. McDonald, Cherrybrook, NSW, and Sir Mark Oliphant, Griffith, Canb.

ROGER CROSS

MARTIN, ALFRED HORATIO (1883-1953), psychologist, was born on 9 May 1883 at Cosham, Hampshire, England, third son of Edwin Paddon Martin (d.1891), a master linen draper, and his wife Frances Mary Ralph, née Green. In 1886 the Martins emigrated to Sydney where Edwin opened a mercery and drapery store at Petersham. With his death, the family was impoverished. Alfred left school at the age of 13 and worked briefly in the Treasury before being employed as a pupil-teacher, from June 1898 at Camdenville Public School. In 1902 he attended Fort Street Training School. He taught in Sydney, and at Narrabri (1907-11) and Glen Innes (1911-13). At St Cyprian's Anglican Church, Narrabri, on 16 September 1911 he married Bertha Christina Ross, a fellow schoolteacher.

Posted to Granville Public School in 1913, Martin became a part-time student at the University of Sydney (B.A., 1917; M.A., 1919). He twice graduated with first-class honours and the University medal in philosophy. Awarded the James King [q.v.2] of Irrawang travelling scholarship in 1919, he studied experimental psychology under E. L. Thorndike and R. S. Woodworth at Teachers College, Columbia University (Ph.D., 1921), United States of America. Martin returned to Sydney in 1921 and joined Henry Tasman Lovell [q.v.10], associate-professor of psychology at the university; he was given responsibility for teaching experimental psychology, and for setting up an experimental laboratory.

A foundation member (1923) and general secretary (1923-28) of the Australasian Association of Psychology and Philosophy, Martin was a prolific contributor to its journal. In October 1926, with the assistance of the Sydney Chamber of Commerce, he established the Australian Institute of Industrial Psychology. Under his directorship it pioneered—especially during the 1930s—the construction and application of aptitude tests for vocational guidance and selection. He used the institute as an adjunct to his work at the university: many of the theories which he expounded to his students were put into practice at the institute. He encouraged the A.I.I.P. to provide a number of community services, including a 'Worry Clinic' for young job-seekers and their parents, lectures and radio broadcasts on basic and applied psychology, and a range of pamphlets. The institute's role declined during World War II due to its failure to procure army contracts.

Martin was an imposing figure, barrel chested and square chinned, with a sharp wit and quick mind. He was known for his abrasiveness and short temper. In 1947 he accepted a position at the University of Tasmania. Arriving in Hobart early in 1948, he suffered a debilitating stroke in late March and was forced to return to Sydney. He entered the New South Wales Home for Incurables, Ryde. Survived by his wife and two daughters, he died there of complications of cerebral and vascular disease on 31 March

1953 and was cremated. His daughter Leonie became a prominent psychologist in Hobart. Martin was a pioneer in his field. Although not an original thinker, he adapted the best of overseas developments in applied psychology for use in Australia.

People (Syd), 5 July 1950, p 8; P. D. L. Brandon, Alfred Horatio Martin, 1883-1953: educationalist and pioneer in industrial psychology in New South Wales (B.Ed. thesis, Univ Newcastle, 1993); teacher's record (NSWA *and* Dept of Education Archives, Syd); Univ Syd Archives.

PETER BRANDON

MARTIN, CLARENCE EDWARD (1900-1953), schoolteacher, barrister and politician, was born on 9 February 1900 at Ballarat, Victoria, only child of Australian-born parents Edward Henry Martin, bootmaker, and his wife Catherine Josephine, née Burke (d.1919). After her husband deserted her, Catherine married Bartholomew Mulvenney in 1906 and the family moved to Broken Hill. From Broken Hill District School, Clarrie entered Teachers' College, Sydney, on a scholarship in 1917. He taught at city schools and became active in the Teachers' Federation of New South Wales while studying at the University of Sydney (B.Ec., 1923; M.Ec., 1932; LL.B., 1936). Posted to Young District School in 1923, he moved to Newcastle where he was employed (1926-29) by the Workers' Educational Association. He joined the Australian Labor Party and was its State junior vice-president in 1928.

Having defeated a candidate backed by J. T. Lang [q.v.9] in a bitter contest for Labor preselection, Martin won the Legislative Assembly seat of Young in October 1930. In the conflict between Federal and State Labor over economic strategy, Martin supported Lang, seeing him as a better defender of living standards. None the less, he criticized Lang's leadership style and participated nervously in a small, anti-Lang ginger group in caucus. Following Lang's dismissal, Martin lost his seat in the 1932 elections. At the party's State conference in 1933, he helped to organize 'socialisation units': when they unsuccessfully sought to remove Lang from control of the party, Martin's overriding concern was to avoid expulsion from the A.L.P.

At Moore Theological College chapel, Newtown, on 22 December 1933 Martin married with Anglican rites Janet Doreen Wrightson, a 26-year-old nurse; they later lived in Lang Road, Centennial Park. During the mid-1930s he largely disengaged himself from politics, took various jobs and completed his law degree full time. Admitted to the Bar on 20 November 1936, he mixed with (Sir) Garfield Barwick and his friends rather than with Labor lawyers, such as Clive Evatt, towards whom he held some personal animosity. That year Martin was involved in battles against Lang for control of radio 2KY and the *Labor Daily* which brought together the nucleus of the Industrial Labor Party under R. J. Heffron [q.v.14]. Martin's victory in the Legislative Assembly by-election for Waverley in 1939 set off a chain of events which led directly to Lang losing the leadership in September. Under (Sir) William McKell, Martin became caucus chairman. As attorney-general from 1941 until 1953, he had ambitious plans for substantial law reform. His most notable achievement was widening legal aid through establishing the posts of public defender (1941) and public solicitor (1944). In the face of wartime pressures, party hostility and indifference, he failed in his endeavours to abolish the death penalty and to reform the married women's property law.

Hoping to strengthen his political credentials, Martin was commissioned in the Militia in March 1942 and transferred to the Australian Imperial Force on 15 July. In 1943-44 he was staff captain at Port Moresby Base. As a field co-ordinator (1944-45) on the staff of the quartermaster general, Land Headquarters, Melbourne, he rose to temporary major and travelled around the South-West Pacific Area. He was placed on the Reserve of Officers on 18 October 1945. His war service, however, isolated him from politics, even though he had not resigned his portfolio. After Labor's victory in the 1944 elections, he acted as a 'numbers man' for McKell in an unsuccessful bid to prevent Clive Evatt's re-election to cabinet and was surprised by the animus that he caused. When McKell resigned in January 1947, Martin backed Heffron rather than James McGirr [q.v.], who won narrowly. Evatt returned to favour, and Martin's prospects dimmed. After the elections in May, Martin retained his portfolio. Increasingly, he was excluded from power and influence. His health began to deteriorate and he contemplated taking a judicial appointment. On J. M. Baddeley's [q.v.7] retirement in September 1949, he lost the deputy-premiership by one vote to J. J. Cahill [q.v.13].

At the end of 1950 Martin suffered a cerebral haemorrhage, but after several months leave returned to politics and his many activities. As a fellow (1941-53) of the university senate he sponsored adult matriculation and fought hard to obtain recognition for immigrants with professional qualifications from abroad. He was president (1941-53) of the Fabian Society of New South Wales, and a trustee of the Public Library of New South Wales (1948-53) and the Sydney Cricket Ground (1952-53); he was also involved in Australian Rostrum and belonged to Tattersall's Club. Invariably cheerful, courageous and kind, he never forgot a birthday—even when on active service.

Following McGirr's resignation in April 1952, Martin decisively lost the leadership to Cahill, who appointed him minister for transport after the February 1953 election. Martin took some initiatives to deal with his department's large operating losses. He died of a haemorrhage from a duodenal ulcer on 5 September 1953 at his Centennial Park home and was cremated. His wife and 14-year-old son survived him.

PD (NSW), 5, 8 Sept 1953, pp 463, 544; *Aust Highway*, 1953, p 50; *SMH*, 6 Sept 1953; P. White, C. E. Martin: a political biography 1900-1953 (M.Ec. thesis, Univ Syd, 1986); Martin papers (ML); teacher's record, Dept of Education Archives, Syd.

PAUL WHITE

MARTIN, DAVID NATHANIEL (1898-1958), theatrical entrepreneur, was born on 15 August 1898 in Perth, son of David Nathaniel Martin, a traveller from London, and his Western Australian-born wife Mary Richmond, née Christie. Raised in the Jewish faith, David was educated at Perth Boys' School, and toured the world as a flugelhorn player with the Young Australia League boys' band in 1911-12. He described himself as a secretary and organizer when he enlisted in the Australian Imperial Force on 6 July 1918. Demobilized on 24 December, he joined the advertising staff of Lowe's Ltd, men's outfitters in Sydney. He worked for Paramount Pictures in 1919, then as manager (1920-34) for Universal Film Manufacturing Co. (Australasia) Ltd. On 16 September 1922 at Woollahra he married with Presbyterian forms Isla Victoria Hume Chapman Stephens, a 25-year-old stenographer.

In January 1934 Martin, who had been a major distributor of Australian films, told a State government inquiry that 'the combine' (General Theatres Corporation of Australasia Pty Ltd) was trying to make it impossible for independent exhibitors to operate by denying them outlets. He commissioned Bruce Dellit [q.v.13] to rebuild the Liberty Theatre as an intimate, luxury cinema, seating 650. Having achieved success with *One Night of Love* and *Show Boat* which ran respectively for thirty-nine weeks in 1935 and forty-seven weeks in 1936, Martin disposed of the Liberty to Metro-Goldwyn-Mayer in 1937. A large-scale investor in real estate, he was managing director of several development companies, among them the Minerva Centre Ltd (1937-58) which built shops, a nightclub and the Minerva Theatre (designed as a 1000-seat playhouse or cinema) at Potts Point. In 1941 he handed over management of the Minerva to Whitehall Productions before moving to

Melbourne to stage plays at the Comedy Theatre.

Back in Sydney, Martin turned to vaudeville. He became chairman and managing director of the Tivoli Circuit of Australia Pty Ltd in June 1944, and of its subsidiary companies. In 1946 he went abroad on the first of numerous quests for talent—he never booked an act without seeing it. Martin made variety pay by attention to detail, by a 'businesslike, coldly efficient approach', by putting on world-class shows, and by paying top salaries for overseas performers (Winifred Atwell received over £2000 a week). He faced continued protests from the Actors' and Announcers' Equity Association of Australia about replacing Australian artists by visiting performers, and about allowing the Ballet Rambert and the Old Vic Theatre Company to use the Tivoli Theatre.

Despite costing £40 000 to stage, *Ice Follie* (1950)—which featured skaters from 'fourteen different countries'—proved so popular that it led him to establish (1951) David N. Martin Pty Ltd, concert managers, to import shows and leading artists, including the whole *Folies Bergère* production from London (1953), the Vienna Boys' Choir (1954), the pianists Jose Iturbi (1954) and Julius Katchen (1955), the Hohner Symphony Accordion Orchestra (1955), the Don Cossack Chorus and Dancers (1956), and Katherine Dunham and Her Company (1957). He believed that it 'was a simple matter of economics' to give the audience what it wanted: in Sydney 15 000 people had paid to see the New South Wales National Opera while 600 000 flocked to *Ice Follie*.

A 'rather bald, dark, medium-built man with a liking for gay ties', Martin neither drank nor smoked; he had 'two strong dislikes—off-colour comedians and fat chorus girls' (he kept diet sheets in his desk for the latter). He belonged to the Sydney Savage Club and the Green Room Club, Melbourne, and enjoyed spending Saturday afternoons at the races, when work permitted. From 1955 he was a director of Television Corporation Ltd. While seeking new talent in the United States of America, he died of coronary artery disease on 2 March 1958 at the Clift Hotel, San Francisco, and was cremated. His wife, son and daughter survived him. A memorial service was held at St Mark's Anglican Church, Darling Point, Sydney.

J. West, *Theatre in Australia* (Syd, 1978); *ABC Weekly*, 15 Nov 1952, p 28; *SMH*, 28, 30 Dec 1933, 3 Jan 1934, 24 June 1944, 24, 26, 27 Dec 1945, 7 Jan, 23 Apr, 20 Aug 1947, 6 Jan 1948, 1 Nov 1952, 5, 8, 11 Mar, 10 Oct 1958; *Sun* (Syd), 4 Jan 1946; *Smith's Weekly*, 6 May 1950; *Herald* (Melb), 4 Mar 1958; *Age* (Melb), 5 Mar 1958; *Sun-Herald*, 9 Mar 1958; information from Mrs S. Ferguson, Epping, Syd.

MARTHA RUTLEDGE

MARTIN, ERIC WALWYN ORMSBY (1900-1973), solicitor and mayor, was born on 22 April 1900 at Taree, Manning River, New South Wales, eldest of eight children of Lewis Ormsby Martin [q.v.10], a Victorian-born solicitor, and his wife Lucy Danvers, née Maund, who came from Queensland. Eric grew up in a community-spirited family dedicated to learning, public service and conservative politics. He was educated at Taree District School, The King's School, Parramatta, and St Paul's College, University of Sydney (B.A., 1922; LL.B., 1925). Admitted to practice as a solicitor on 28 August 1925, he returned to Taree and joined his father's firm, which became L. O. Martin & Sons when his brother Lewis joined it in 1936. In December 1937 Eric was elected to Taree Municipal Council. He belonged to the local sailing club and played district cricket for many years.

An Empire man and a patriot, Martin enlisted in the Australian Imperial Force on 10 October 1939. He sailed for the Middle East with the 2nd/2nd Battalion in January 1940 and was posted to the Military Hostel, Jerusalem. In January 1941 he was sent to A.I.F. Headquarters and made sergeant. He transferred to the Royal Air Force as a pilot officer in the Administrative and Special Duties Branch on 3 March that year in Cairo. Promoted flying officer twelve months later, he served in Egypt, Palestine and (from November 1944) England. He returned to Sydney in May 1946.

After resuming his practice at Taree, Martin re-entered local politics in 1950. A man of wide public interests, he had deep roots in the local community, especially in terms of his legal work for the dairy industry. He had two terms as mayor (1951-52 and 1956-65) and also served (1950-65) on the Manning River County Council. 'At all times he was a thorough gentleman' who abided 'by the wishes of the majority' throughout his public life. During his second term as mayor, new council chambers—resembling a 'magnificent, solid Peerless butter box'—were opened. He sat on the Taree-Wingham Water Board, and was sometime chairman of the Oxley Regional Development and the Manning-Forster Tourist committees. Gifted with 'foresight' and 'the highest principles', he retired from the municipal council in 1965 and was appointed C.B.E. in 1967.

Martin was president of the Taree Literary Institute, the Manning River District Cricket Association and the Manning River Aquatic Association; he was also a founder of the Manning River Aero Club. In Sydney he belonged to the Royal Sydney Golf, University and United Services clubs. He died on 14 January 1973 at the family home, Ormsby House, Manning Street, and was cremated with Anglican rites. Martin had never married. As a son he had only left home to complete his education and to serve in World War II.

J. Ramsland, *The Struggle against Isolation* (Syd, 1987); *Manning River Times*, 16, 17 Jan 1973.
                                              JOHN RAMSLAND

MARTIN, JEAN ISOBEL (1923-1979), sociologist, was born on 21 June 1923 at East Malvern, Melbourne, third daughter of David Craig, a civil servant from Scotland, and his Victorian-born wife Elizabeth, née Alexander. Jean attended Abbotsleigh Church of England School for Girls, Sydney, and studied anthropology under A. P. Elkin [q.v.14] at the University of Sydney (B.A., 1943; M.A., 1945), gaining first-class honours and the university medal for her master's degree. In 1943-47, 1949-50 and 1956 she was employed as a lecturer at the university. Elkin encouraged her to move from anthropology to sociology. One of her earliest pieces of research was on women in a Sydney hosiery factory; her M.A. thesis was on dairy-farmers in New South Wales. Obliged to travel abroad for formal training in sociology, she briefly attended classes at the London School of Economics (1947) before studying in 1947-48 at the University of Chicago, United States of America. She was influenced by W. Lloyd Warner, whose blend of a qualitative and quantitative approach to sociology became her hallmark, although her own work had in addition a strong focus on policy. In 1954 she graduated Ph.D. from the Australian National University.

At St Andrew's Presbyterian Church, Eastwood, on 13 August 1955 Jean married Allan William Martin, a university lecturer in history and future biographer of Sir Henry Parkes [q.v.5] and Sir Robert Menzies [q.v.]. Her later career was 'somewhat idiosyncratic'. For nine years after her first child was born, she either worked part time, or carried out unpaid research. In 1965, at the age of 42, she obtained her first tenured, full-time university post, as foundation professor of sociology at La Trobe University, Melbourne. She resigned in 1974, after experiencing ill health, and obtained a senior fellowship in the Department of Sociology, Research School of Social Sciences, A.N.U., where she remained until her death.

Despite this relatively short period of full-time employment, Martin was influential in the academic community. Her work in seven Australian universities had included short periods as a research-assistant to such prominent scholars as Professors W. D. Borrie, S. F. Nadel and R. M. Crawford. She served on the advisory board of the Melbourne-based Institute of Applied Economic and Social Research with Professor Ronald Henderson; he wrote to her in 1977 saying that working with her had been 'a sociological education'. Her influence on the first poverty survey and the later commission of inquiry into poverty in Australia was considerable. Martin corresponded with colleagues and students throughout Australia. By a process of detailed comment and criticism, she taught a generation of social scientists to think and write sociologically.

Her own research centred around a number of interrelated areas, particularly migration, social policy, family and kinship ties, social welfare, and education. Her Ph.D. was a study of refugees in New South Wales, published as *Refugee Settlers* (Canberra, 1965). Other books included *Community and Identity* (Canberra, 1972) and *The Migrant Presence* (Sydney, 1978), studies of Eastern European refugee groups in Adelaide and institutional attitudes to migration. Her longitudinal investigation of Australia's earliest Vietnamese refugees, unfinished at the time of her death, was completed in 1985 by Frank Lewins and Judith Ly, and published as *The First Wave* (Sydney, 1985). *The Ethnic Dimension* (Sydney, 1981), a collection of her papers on ethnicity and pluralism, was edited by Solomon Encel.

Quiet and modest, Martin did much of her sociological work 'behind the scenes'. She played a significant role in the Commonwealth government's publication, *Girls, School and Society* (Canberra, 1975), and was an active researcher for the book, *Who Cares? Family Problems, Community Links and Helping Services* (Melbourne, 1977). A committed public intellectual, she contributed to several parliamentary inquiries and served on numerous policy committees. For a time she chaired the social studies committee of the Australian Population and Immigration Council. She was also a member of the Social Welfare Commission's research advisory committee, a consultant to the royal commission on human relationships, and a member of the National Committee on Social Science Teaching. From its foundation in 1963, she took a leading role in the development of the Sociological Association of Australia and New Zealand (president 1969-71). In 1971 she was elected a fellow of the Academy of the Social Sciences in Australia.

Survived by her husband and two sons, Jean Martin died of cancer on 25 September 1979 at Mona Vale, Sydney, and was cremated. The Australian Sociological Association's biennial award for the best Australian doctoral thesis in one of her research fields is named after her. A portrait by Mollie Wilson is held by the family.

K. Richmond et al, 'Jean Martin: a tribute', *Aust and NZ J of Sociology*, 15, no 3, 1979, p 2, *and* for publications; La Trobe Univ, *Record*, 13, no 6, Nov-Dec 1979, p 2; *SMH*, 17 Feb 1975; J. I. Martin papers (Noel Butlin Archives); information from Prof A. W. Martin, Reid, Canb; personal knowledge.

KATY RICHMOND

MARTIN, MARY MAYDWELL (1915-1973), bookseller, was born on 20 July 1915 at Norwood, Adelaide, eldest of four children of South Australian-born parents Ernest Montgomerie Martin, engineer, and his wife Lorna Gledstanes, née Jacob. She came from Dissenting families on her father's side. They were practical people—chemists, engineers, and vignerons like Henry Maydwell Martin of Stonyfell. The maternal branch of the family was a curious mix of orthodox Anglicans (the Wollastons [qq.v.2,12]) and radical thinkers (the Jacobs [q.v.9]). Mary's liberal-minded parents allowed their children to enjoy an unusual degree of freedom. Her formal education began at Rose Park, in a private school run on progressive lines by Miss E. W. Dunn. Proceeding to Girton Proprietary School, she passed the Intermediate certificate (1931) and was chosen as a prefect (1932). She entered Kindergarten Training College in 1933, but did not qualify.

Granted conditional entry under the proviso that she pass Latin I, Miss Martin enrolled in 1936 as a part-time student at the University of Adelaide. She met Max Harris (later editor of the journal, *Angry Penguins*), became a foundation member of the South Australian branch of the Contemporary Art Society of Australia, and enjoyed the company of writers and artists. During the late 1930s she attended tutorial-classes in English run by Gordon Biaggini [q.v.13] in conjunction with the Workers' Educational Association. In 1939 she won the Tormore prize for English Literature. While studying, she pursued a relatively independent life, living in a self-contained cottage in the garden of her parents' home. She made some money by ordering and selling postcard reproductions of the paintings of old masters, working as a packer in factories, and teaching briefly at the Wilderness School run by Margaret Brown [q.v.7] and her sisters. After eight years of study she completed an honours course in English, but was unable to graduate because she had not passed Latin I.

Martin was a small, dark-eyed woman who dressed simply in plain colours and 'cared more for ideas than appearance'. She was described as 'a little brown wren'. Her appeal lay in her willingness to listen and in her absolute sincerity. Early in 1945 she turned to what interested her most and established the Mary Martin Book Shop in a rented room in the Brookman [q.v.7] Building, Grenfell

Street. The shop specialized in mail orders, sold books cheaply (some bought from the publishers at cost) and eventually entered the remainder market. Prints from abroad cluttered the walls, but space remained for local artists to hang their work. Martin encouraged her customers to browse, served them coffee and attracted a loyal clientele. In 1947 she invited Harris to become a partner in the bookshop, which had moved to Alma Chambers, 13 Commercial Place. Under their joint management, the business expanded.

That year the celebrated dancer Shivaram and his company brought Indian dance to Australia. Martin attended several performances in Adelaide and was struck by seeing 'dance used religiously and seriously'. She arranged for Shivaram to visit her bookshop. Well read in Indian art and temple architecture, she began to study the history of Indian dance. In 1952, encouraged by Harris, she went to India and spent two months travelling through the sub-continent by public buses and in third-class railway carriages. She stayed in railway rest-rooms, Young Women's Christian Association hostels and 'Dak' cottages; while she focused her attention on Hindu temples, she also began to understand the people and to learn a little about their customs. The experience marked a watershed in her life.

Meanwhile, the bookshop continued to flourish and its mail-order business increased. Larger premises were required. By 1955 the shop had moved to 75 Rundle Street; by 1957 it occupied a large part of the first floor of the Da Costa Building, Gawler Place. Harris produced a news-sheet, *Mary's Own Paper*: intended as a monthly, but issued erratically, it provided an outlet for his opinions on a range of subjects. His presence dominated the bookshop. Martin withdrew more and more, preferring to work in a back room where her clients, among them Indian students and others connected with the Colombo Plan, could usually find her. She became obsessed by India and all things Indian. By the early 1960s it was clear that the partnership was not working smoothly. The principals had different aims and philosophies.

Martin had made trips to India in 1952, 1957 and 1961. She decided in 1962 to live there permanently. Harris was left to manage the bookshop. In 1963 Martin sold her interests in the firm to Max and Yvonne Harris, who paid her in instalments over the next few years. She lived initially at Bombay, then moved to Bangalore where she set up an Indian mail-order book business, with her sister Florence overseeing the finances from Adelaide. Developing a sideline in artefacts and crafts, she bought from village craftsmen and sold to Community Aid Abroad. At first, both ventures brought little profit; shipment of goods was erratic, and it was often months before she received any return. She lived frugally, and gradually built up a core of customers.

Although short of money, Martin was persuaded to take as a servant T. R. Kesavamurthy, a young Brahmin. She encouraged him to complete his studies and trained him to take over the day-to-day management of her book-selling business. On 10 November 1965 she moved with him to Kotagiri in the Nilgiri Hills, seeking a better climate because of her asthma. She rented several rooms in the house of an English widow, setting up home and office there. She spent her days ordering, receiving and posting books, and worked at night as a volunteer with the Nilgiris Adivasi Welfare Association. Led by Dr S. Narasimhan, members of the N.A.W.A. journeyed to makeshift clinics in the jungle to provide medical attention for tribal people. Appointed the association's honorary treasurer, Martin wrote its *Newsletter*. When she devoted more of her time to helping Narasimhan, 'Murthy' became responsible for the book business, which by then employed a number of Indians.

Martin visited Australia in 1969. She saw her family, spoke to community groups about the N.A.W.A., and consulted librarians on book orders. Twice she collapsed. Over the next two years she ignored intermittent health problems: her business was thriving and her work with the welfare association was demanding. Following another collapse, she was admitted to the Government General Hospital, Madras. Shortly before Christmas 1972 doctors transferred her to the Christian Medical College Hospital, Vellore. Diagnosed as suffering from insulinoma, she underwent a partial pancreatectomy. She died on 25 January 1973 and was cremated with Hindu rites. Her South Australian estate was sworn for probate at $93 496. She bequeathed most of her assets in India and her extensive library to 'Murthy', made provision for small gifts to her employees, and left her shares to her nieces and nephews.

Mary Martin's ashes were buried in India, beneath a Norfolk Island pine near one of the jungle clinics. A memorial fund to continue her welfare work was established in Adelaide, and a dispensary at Balwadi, India, was named after her. In 1998 there were four Mary Martin bookshops in Australia. The Kesavamurthy family continued to run Mary Martin Booksellers from Coimbatore, India.

J. Lewis, *Mary Martin* (Brisb, 1997) and for bibliog; *National Library of Australia News*, March 1996, p 3; *Adelaide Review*, no 152, May 1996, p 2; *West Australian*, 16 May 1969; *Advertiser* (Adel), 14 June 1967, 19 May 1969, 31 Jan, 29 June 1973, 29 July 1982.						JULIE LEWIS

MARTIN, NORAH MARGARET (1888-1977), mother superior and hospital nurse, was born on 18 June 1888 at Box Creek, near Booligal, New South Wales, sixth and youngest child of Irish immigrants Patrick Martin, grazier, and his wife Mary, née Sullivan. Norah spent her early childhood at Box Creek before joining two of her sisters at the Hillston convent school, run by the Sisters of St Joseph of the Sacred Heart. In 1901 they returned home to help their widowed mother. By 1905 the Riverina property had been sold and the family moved to Sydney.

In June 1908 Norah Martin entered the Little Company of Mary at Lewisham Hospital as a postulant and trainee nurse. She received the habit on 4 July 1909, taking the religious names Mary Bernard, and made her final vows on 6 August 1912. In December 1913 she passed the examinations for membership of the Australasian Trained Nurses' Association. As a specialist in operating-theatre techniques, she was transferred in 1917 to the congregation's Lewisham Hospital, Christchurch, New Zealand. Sister Bernard succeeded Mother Xavier Lynch [q.v.10] in 1929 as provincial superior in Sydney. In accordance with the community's 'six-year rule', she relinquished leadership of the province in 1935; she then served as superior and matron of Lewisham Hospital until reappointed provincial superior in 1941.

Mother Bernard's outstanding leadership of the Australasian Province was recognized in 1947 by her election in Rome as superior general, the L.C.M.'s highest office. She was probably the first Australian woman to head an international congregation. Visits to all of the congregation's houses (of which there were more than forty) took her to North and South America, Southern Africa, Britain, Ireland, Italy, New Zealand and Australia. She helped to initiate the cause for the beatification of Mother Mary Potter, foundress of the Little Company of Mary. During Mother Bernard's years in office fifteen new hospitals were established, and the novitiate at the mother house in Rome was reopened (it had been closed in World War II).

After completing two six-year terms in Rome, Mother Bernard returned to Sydney in 1959. She was local superior at Mount St Margaret Hospital, Ryde, and, in 1965, provincial superior, New Zealand. In 1969 she was appointed O.B.E. That year she returned to Sydney to live in retirement at the Convent of the Maternal Heart, Ryde. At the age of 84 Mother Bernard began writing her unfinished autobiography, 'Footprints in the Sands of Time'. She admitted, regretfully, that her manner may have sometimes produced 'a mistaken idea of personal confidence . . . I did the best I could and put all my trust in Him, knowing that He could work through [me] . . .

this gave me a tranquillity which enabled me to take responsibility . . . but it also caused a degree of misunderstanding to those with whom I worked or had contact'.

Mother Bernard was an extremely able, meticulous and determined woman who demanded strict conformity to what she considered to be unquestionable standards. Although she enjoyed competition, she was a rather ungracious loser. She generally evoked respect—even awe—rather than warmer sentiments, and yet she was generous, friendly and concerned in the company of her patients and closest colleagues. She died on 25 August 1977 at Mount St Margaret Hospital, Ryde, and was buried in Rookwood cemetery.

SMH, 21 May 1947, 20 June 1969, 7 Aug 1972; *Catholic Weekly* (Syd), 8 Sept 1977; Little Company of Mary Archives, Calvary Hospital, Kogarah, *and* Dalton Gardens, Ryde, Syd, *and* Little Company of Mary Generalate Archives, Tooting-Beck, Surrey, Eng.
                                                        J. C. H. DEWDNEY

MARTIN, SIR NORMAN ANGUS (1893-1978), farmer, grazier and politician, was born on 24 April 1893 in Port Melbourne, son of Victorian-born parents Angus Martin, tram conductor, and his wife Ruth, née Gale. Norman attended school at Werribee and began to farm at Lucernvale, Cohuna. Enlisting in the Australian Imperial Force on 20 January 1916, he served with the 8th Field Artillery Brigade on the Western Front. In September 1917 he was gassed at Passchendaele. While recuperating in England, he met Gladys Violet Barrett, a nurse and daughter of an English officer, Captain Walter Barrett, M.C. They were married on 29 January 1919 at the parish church, Warminster, Wiltshire. After Sergeant Martin was discharged on 13 October 1919, he returned to Cohuna and became prominent in community affairs. A foundation member (1922) and president (1930-31, 1939-40) of the Cohuna Shire Council, he joined the Country Party and was president of its Leitchville branch for fifteen years.

Henry Angus's death on 2 April 1934 occasioned a by-election for the Legislative Assembly seat of Gunbower. The United Country Party endorsed J. G. Matheson as its candidate; he had the backing of the party's central council and its president A. E. Hocking [q.v.14]. Martin was encouraged to contest the seat by local supporters and members of the parliamentary Country Party resentful of Hocking's political influence. He ran as 'unendorsed Country Party' candidate and defeated Matheson in a two-way contest by 927 votes. Despite a declaration by central council on 1 May 1934 that 'Mr Martin is no longer a member of the Country Party', he was admitted to the parliamentary Country Party, a decision unanimously denounced by central council. Following a partial reconciliation of the organization and the parliamentarians, Martin's party membership was restored at the Victorian Country Party conference in 1935. He retained Gunbower uncontested until 1945.

Elected Country Party whip in 1937, Martin wanted to retain the post when he was appointed to the ministry on 26 April 1938, but a protest by party backbenchers led him to surrender it. He served as minister without portfolio (April 1938 to June 1943), and as minister of agriculture and of mines (June to September 1943), in (Sir) Albert Dunstan's [q.v.8] minority government. He again held the agriculture portfolio in the Dunstan-Hollway [q.v.14] coalition from September 1943 to October 1945, and was vice-president of the Board of Land and Works. Martin's parliamentary and ministerial career was solid rather than spectacular. After Gunbower was abolished by redistribution, he resigned from parliament in 1945 to become Victorian agent-general in London.

Martin proved an energetic agent-general: encouraging British emigration to Australia, coaxing British industries to establish branches in Victoria, urging Victorians to send food parcels to Britain, and assisting Victorians in Britain to secure shipping-berths home. His term of office expired in 1949, the year he was knighted. Back in Victoria, he maintained four successful properties in the Cohuna district and lived in a two-storey house, Longleat, at South Yarra, where he and his wife displayed their collection of English and European antique furniture. Stockily built and of middle height, he belonged to the Australian club, played golf at the Kew and Peninsula clubs, enjoyed swimming, and fished from a 20-foot (6 m) boat which he moored by his cottage at Long Island in Westernport Bay.

His appointment in 1950 as vice-president of the Victorian division of the Australian Publicity Council allowed Martin to continue his efforts to encourage industries to come to Victoria. Having conducted an inquiry into its operations, he was selected by the Liberal premier (Sir) Henry Bolte to be part-time chairman (1958-73) of the Victorian Inland Meat Authority. Martin was also active in a wide range of voluntary associations, such as the Guide Dogs for the Blind Association of Victoria and the Shrine of Remembrance committee, and was chairman of Victoria's Australia Day Council (1947-70). An unabashed patriot, he publicly lamented the lack of enthusiasm for Australia Day celebrations and regularly berated the media for ignoring them. In addition to his community work, he was a director of numerous companies, including Ball & Welch Ltd (chairman 1952-

70), Holeproof Ltd and Thomas Cook & Son (Australasia) Pty Ltd. Survived by his wife, daughter and son, Sir Norman died on 8 October 1978 in East Melbourne; he was accorded a state funeral and was buried in St Kilda cemetery.

PD (Vic), 10 Oct 1978, p 4366; *Cohuna Farmers' Weekly*, 27 Oct 1978; *Age* (Melb), 11 May 1945, 9 May 1958, 24 Aug 1978; *Herald* (Melb), 4 Mar 1950, 27 Jan 1968, 17 Jan 1969; Vic Country Party, Annual Report, 1934 *and* Central Council, Minutes, 20 May, 19 June, 20 July 1934, 5 Feb 1935 (Country Party Office, Melb).   B. J. COSTAR

MARTINOVICH, KRISTÉ (1903?-1966), chiropractor, was born probably on 20 July 1903 on Brac, an island off Dalmatia, Austria-Hungary, son of Ivan Martinovich, farmer, and his wife Mariza, née Yaksich. He worked as a farmer before emigrating to Western Australia in 1922.

Having lived in Perth for several years, Martinovich moved to Boulder and took a job in the gold-mines. At All Hallows Catholic Church, Boulder, on 21 December 1927 he married 18-year-old Mary Pincetich who came from Dalmatia. During the 1930s the family stayed briefly in Perth before returning to the goldfields. Employed as a gardener and as an underground miner at Wiluna, Martinovich occasionally used the chiropractic techniques he had learned from his father. By 1947 he was back at Boulder, working in the Lake View and Star mine. Meanwhile, as a part-time masseur, he treated local footballers and his reputation soared. Having contracted silicosis, he retired from mining in 1953 to become a chiropractor. His lack of formal qualifications, and successful treatment of people whom doctors had failed to cure, led to mounting opposition from the medical profession, but he received support from the Goldfields Football League and the Chamber of Mines of Western Australia.

Martinovich was a tall, lean, quietly spoken man. Apart from bowls and cards, he had few outside interests and worked long hours each day. His method was simple: he examined a patient and applied a linseed poultice to the injury; next day he manipulated the bones and muscles, and applied a poultice containing egg-white; two days later the poultice was removed; he then used a tennis ball or the rubber core of a golf ball wrapped in towelling to assist with manipulation, and was reputed to 'press hard'. Instead of billing his patients, he asked for a donation. In the 1950s dramatic improvements resulting from his care were described in Australian newspaper articles with headings such as 'Wonder Healer' and 'Miracle Man'. The prominence of a number of his patients enhanced his fame, as did the way in which he defied his critics.

In 1957 Martinovich moved to South Fremantle to teach others his methods and to serve his large metropolitan clientele. He established a successful clinic and trained three of his sons as chiropractors. Following the report of a royal commission into the provisions of a bill to regulate the activities of natural therapists, the State government established the chiropractors' registration board in 1964. Registration was confined to those who had gained a formal qualification, but long-time practitioners were granted exemption.

After his legs had been amputated in 1960 due to Buerger's disease, Martinovich ceased practice. By then his name was synonymous with the chiropractic profession in Western Australia. Many revered him for his extraordinary healing abilities. When pressed to discuss his gifts, he replied simply, 'I'm only here to help people'. He died of chronic myocardial ischaemia on 21 June 1966 in Bethesda Hospital, Claremont, and was buried in Karrakatta cemetery; his wife, two daughters and four sons survived him.

Weekend Mail (Perth), 23, 30 July 1955, 20 Oct 1956; *West Australian*, 31 Dec 1955, 23 June 1966; *A'sian Post*, 31 May 1956; information from Messrs E. and I. Martinovich and Mrs M. Martinovich, South Fremantle, Perth.   E. JAGGARD

MARTYN, DAVID FORBES (1906-1970), physicist, was born on 27 June 1906 at Cambuslang, Lanarkshire, Scotland, son of Harry Somerville Martyn, ophthalmic surgeon, and his wife Elizabeth Craig Allan, née Thom. David attended Plymouth College, England, and Allan Glen's School, Glasgow, which was noted for its commitment to the teaching of science. In 1923 he entered the Royal College of Science, London, to study physics. He graduated with first-class honours (B.Sc., University of London, 1926) and was made an associate of the college.

While registered as an external student of the University of London, Martyn took up a research scholarship at the University of Glasgow in 1926. He investigated the triode oscillator circuit, both experimentally and theoretically, successfully tracing its puzzling instability to a hitherto neglected flow of current to the valve's grid. For this work he was awarded a Ph.D. by the University of London in 1928. He remained at Glasgow, supported by a William Houldsworth research studentship, until mid-1929 when he was one of four research officers selected to join the Australian Radio Research Board, established under the Council for Scientific and Industrial

Research. This appointment transformed his career.

Martyn's early work with C.S.I.R. was largely experimental, but it soon became evident that his real strength lay in theory. Initially, he was attached to the R.R.B. group which worked in T. H. Laby's [q.v.9] laboratory at the University of Melbourne. There, with R. O. Cherry, he investigated the fading of signals from local radio stations. In 1932 he transferred to the R.R.B.'s other group, in (Sir) John Madsen's [q.v.10] electrical-engineering laboratory at the University of Sydney. That year Martyn made substantial technical contributions to a Federal government inquiry into Australia's broadcasting services.

While surveying available data on the propagation of medium waves in the ionosphere, Martyn developed a useful theorem, now named after him, by which mathematical expressions relating to waves incident obliquely on the ionosphere could be obtained from those for vertical incidence. With V. A. Bailey [q.v.13], he also formulated a theory to account for the 'Luxembourg effect', the modulation of a passing radio signal by an intervening powerful source. Their analysis depended on the novel idea that the mean velocity of the electrons in a region of the ionosphere, and hence the absorbing power of the ionosphere in that region, could be significantly affected by a powerful radio signal passing through it. The theory quickly won wide acceptance.

Martyn's work evolved into a more general investigation of waves reflected from the ionosphere, leading to a study of the properties of the ionosphere itself. In 1936, with O. O. Pulley, he published an important paper on conditions in the upper atmosphere. Perhaps their most striking conclusion was that the temperature of the F_2 layer of the ionosphere was 1000°C or more. Soon afterwards, in collaboration with G. H. Munro and J. H. Piddington, Martyn perfected a 'pulse-phase' technique that yielded continuous data on the polarization of reflected radio waves and hence on changes taking place in the layers of the ionosphere from which they were being reflected—data that he was able to use to resolve a debate over which dispersion formula applied in the case of ionospheric reflections. He also became interested in the connections between ionospheric disturbances and solar phenomena.

As early as 1930, in an unpublished R.R.B. report, Martyn had pointed out the advantages of using ultra-high frequencies for long-distance communications and for obtaining information about objects from which the beam was reflected. During a visit to Britain in 1936, he at once guessed the nature of secret research on radio-location being carried out by (Sir) Robert Watson-Watt and his colleagues. On his return, he successfully urged that U.H.F. work be initiated in Australia. He was the natural choice when, in February 1939, the British government invited Australia and the other dominions each to send a scientist to England to learn the secrets of what became known as radar. After he came back to Australia, he was appointed in September head of the new radiophysics laboratory, established by C.S.I.R. at the University of Sydney to contribute to this vital new technology.

Martyn's period in this post was an unhappy one. Although his letter of appointment accorded him the status of chief of a C.S.I.R. division, he was never given full control of his laboratory's affairs, but instead had to share responsibility with his former mentor Madsen, chairman of the Radiophysics Advisory Board. This arrangement sometimes led to difficulties. Martyn also alienated many of the officials with whom he had to deal. Moreover, a proposed overseas trip had to be abandoned when the security service reported unfavourably on his relationship with Ella Horne, a German woman he had indiscreetly befriended. His duties were more and more assumed by (Sir) Frederick White, who, in October 1941, was placed in sole administrative control of the laboratory. The office of chief was temporarily abolished and Martyn's position downgraded. In May 1942 he was seconded to the army to head an operational research group with special responsibility for problems associated with radar. The group's study of 'super-refraction' of radio waves in the atmosphere brought about significant improvements in operational efficiency.

At the district registrar's office, Paddington, on 12 May 1944 Martyn married Margot Adams, a 30-year-old secretary; they were to remain childless. He was transferred in December to the Commonwealth Observatory, Mount Stromlo, Canberra, and resumed his theoretical studies of the ionosphere. In 1956 he was appointed officer-in-charge of the R.R.B. station at Camden, New South Wales. Two years later it became the independent upper atmosphere section, specially created for him within the Commonwealth Scientific and Industrial Research Organization.

Soon after arriving at Mount Stromlo, Martyn had formulated a theory of temperature radiation from the sun. He predicted radiation from the corona corresponding to a black body at $1\,000\,000°C$ at wavelengths of about 1 metre, and also limb brightening at centimetre wavelengths. Both forecasts were rapidly confirmed.

During the following decade Martyn made a series of fundamental contributions to knowledge of the ionosphere and of the way in which changes occurring there are linked with changes in the earth's magnetic field. His starting point was the identification of large solar and lunar tides in the upper atmosphere. He developed a modified 'dynamo' theory, according to which horizontal winds due to these tides gave rise to motions of electrons along the lines of the earth's magnetic field. These motions had a vertical component that could, he suggested, account for the observed semi-diurnal variations in both the ionization of the upper atmosphere and the earth's magnetic field itself.

When it was argued that the conductivity of the upper atmosphere appeared to be too low to fit the requirements of the theory, Martyn proposed a mechanism to overcome this objection, one that he and W. G. Baker showed was in full quantitative agreement with the phenomena. They also showed that there should be a narrow zone of still greater ionospheric conductivity near the magnetic equator that should give rise to an intense equatorial electrojet, the existence of which would explain the recently discovered strong enhancement of the daily magnetic variations in equatorial regions. Such an electrojet was, at about the same time, observed directly using a rocket-borne magnetometer. As a result of this work, the dynamo theory came to be regarded as securely established.

In 1936 the University of London had conferred a D.Sc. on Martyn for his researches on radio propagation. The importance of his work on the ionosphere was recognized by the award of the (Sir Thomas) Lyle [q.v.10] medal (1947) of the Australian National Research Council, the Sidey medal (1947) of the Royal Society of New Zealand, the Walter Burfitt [q.v.7] prize and medal (1950) of the Royal Society of New South Wales, and the Charles Chree medal (1955) of the Physical Society, London. Martyn was elected a fellow of the Royal Society of London in 1950.

With (Sir) Mark Oliphant, Martyn provided the driving force behind the formation of the Australian Academy of Science in 1954. He took on most of the negotiations with the Australian National Research Council, especially concerning the transfer to the academy of responsibility for maintaining Australia's international scientific connexions. He also played a pivotal role in drafting the academy's statutes and rules, and in obtaining its royal charter. The academy's first secretary (physical sciences), he was its president in 1969-70.

In his later years Martyn became deeply involved in international scientific affairs, where he displayed the same diplomatic skills as he had done in the formative stages of the Australian Academy of Science. He was especially active in the International Radio Science Union (U.R.S.I.) and the Committee on Space Research. He was at different times president of two U.R.S.I. commissions, on radio astronomy and on the ionosphere, and vice-president (1950-54) of U.R.S.I. itself. Martyn was instrumental in persuading the union to hold its 1952 general assembly in Australia. He was a principal organizer of Australia's contribution to the 1957-58 International Geophysical Year. From 1962 until his death he chaired the United Nations Scientific and Technical Committee for the Peaceful Uses of Outer Space, playing a major part in framing the Treaty on Outer Space.

Martyn was a complex man, touchy and secretive, yet excellent company and endowed with a sense of humour. A connoisseur of wine, food and cigars, he was also an enthusiastic trout fisherman. He never lost his Scottish accent. Perhaps his greatest strength, in both his science and his committee-work, was his mastery of detail. In his international activities he could be extraordinarily patient and tactful, but he never forgave White or E. G. Bowen (White's successor as chief of the radiophysics laboratory) for the wrongs he believed they had done him. He successfully blocked the election of both men to the Royal Society for many years and took evident pleasure in demonstrating the statistical inadequacies of work on rainfall records published by Bowen in the 1950s. Late in life, Martyn became deeply concerned about the degradation of the environment, and his fear of impending disaster contributed to the depressed state of mind that led him to commit suicide on 5 March 1970 at his Camden home. Survived by his wife, he was cremated.

W. F. Evans, *History of the Radiophysics Advisory Board, 1939-1945* (Melb, 1970) and *History of the Radio Research Board, 1926-1945* (Melb, 1973); C. B. Schedvin, *Shaping Science and Industry* (Syd, 1987); R. W. Home and S. G. Kohlstedt (eds), *International Science and National Scientific Identity* (Dordrecht, Netherlands, 1991), pp 181-204; *Biog Memoirs of Fellows of the Roy Soc* (Lond), 17, 1971, p 497; *Records of the Aust Academy of Science*, 2, pt 2, 1971, p 47; Martyn papers (AA, Canb).

R. W. HOME

MARUFF, ALLAN PETER (1911-1979), tea-planter and medical practitioner, was born on 14 February 1911 at Ferozepore, Punjab, India, son of Frederick William Maruff, assistant civil surgeon, and his wife Margaret Amy, née William. Allan attended the University of Calcutta and won a gold medal for botany. On 20 May 1935 he was appointed assistant-surgeon, fourth class, in the Indian Medical Department. At St Francis Xavier's Church, Calcutta, on 21 March 1936 he married Dorothy Enid Haenon with Catholic rites.

During World War II Maruff served as a medical officer in the Indian Army. In 1946 he

sailed to Britain where he became a member of the Royal College of Surgeons, England, and a licentiate of the Royal College of Physicians, London, in 1948. He emigrated to Australia in 1949. After a term as a Commonwealth medical officer in Port Moresby, he moved to Queensland and settled at Innisfail in 1954. Gaining a reputation as an expert in tropical diseases, he gave his time generously and travelled long distances to visit his patients.

Between 1883 and 1918 the Cutten brothers had struggled to establish a tea-plantation at Bingil Bay. In 1936 the Queensland Bureau of Tropical Agriculture began experimenting with tea at South Johnstone. It was Maruff, however, who demonstrated the feasibility of a commercial tea-growing industry in North Queensland. In 1959 he bought a block of land at Nerada, near Innisfail. He planted 15 000 seedlings in 1960, but lost most of them in a drought. Installing an irrigation system, he tried again with a more drought-resistant strain. By 1968 he had invested $300 000 in the project. Four men worked full time on the plantation, caring for more than 2.5 million trees on 100 acres (40 ha). Maruff engaged local engineering firms to improve the design of a mechanical harvester; as a result of this initiative, Australian machines were later exported to Malaysia and South Africa.

To raise capital, Maruff went into partnership in 1970 with Burns, Philp [qq.v.7,11] & Co. Ltd to form Nerada Tea Estates Pty Ltd. The new company built a factory at Nerada which had an innovative monorail system for conveying bins of green leaf to the withering-troughs. Problems with mechanical harvesting, marketing and cash flow caused the firm to lose money and production ceased on 30 June 1972. In the following year the plantation and factory were sold to Tea Estates of Australia, which operated them successfully. Maruff began an experimental tea, coffee and pepper plantation near Brisbane. He visited his new venture regularly, but continued to live and work at Innisfail.

Actively involved in the local community, Maruff was a Johnstone shire councillor (1976-79), president of the Innisfail branch of the Australian Labor Party, a member of the Returned Sailors', Soldiers' and Airmen's Imperial League of Australia and a supporter of the Queensland Society for Crippled Children. He died of cirrhosis of the liver on 19 July 1979 in Brisbane and was buried in Pinaroo lawn cemetery, Aspley; his wife, three daughters and two sons survived him.

R. J. Taylor, *The Lost Plantation* (Cairns, Qld, 1982); *Walkabout*, Feb 1968, p 27; information from Mrs C. Allan, Chatswood, Syd.

DAWN MAY

MARX, OTTO (1897-1974), herd-tester, was born on 3 August 1897 at Hamburg, Germany, son of Carl Marx, businessman, and his wife Lina, née Steinwehr. Otto was of part-Jewish descent. He fought (from 1914) as a sergeant with the German Army and won the Iron Cross before being made a prisoner of war. Released in 1920, he returned to Hamburg. On 5 July 1923 he married Minna Mollnitz-Schier. While working as a merchant banker with a coffee importing company, he realized the imminent danger facing Jews in Nazi Germany. Leaving his Aryan wife behind, he managed to escape to England in August 1939. He was interned in 1940 and shipped to Australia as an enemy alien in the *Dunera* which reached Sydney on 6 September that year.

Sent to internment camps at Hay, New South Wales, and Tatura, Victoria, Marx was released as a refugee alien with other '*Dunera* boys' to supplement the wartime labour shortage. He joined the Militia on 25 April 1942, served with the 8th Employment Company and was discharged on medical grounds on 20 December 1943. Through a Quaker connexion, Marx was hired as a herd-tester by the co-operative at Maffra. With little knowledge of the dairy industry, he was required to visit farms and stay overnight for the evening and morning milking—a potentially difficult situation for a German in 1944. The milk samples he collected were tested to monitor individual cows' production and butter fat content. He soon procured a caravan which also served as a mobile office. On 3 November 1945 he was naturalized.

Maffra became his home, and that of his wife and her sister, with both of whom he was re-united after the war through the efforts of the International Red Cross Society. Marx worked (1950-53) in the laboratory of Nestlés Food Specialties (Australia) Ltd, but in 1953 returned as secretary to the Maffra and District Herd Improvement Association and began to extend the herd-testing services. With help from progressive local farmers and the Department of Agriculture, he established a service in 1956 for inseminating cows with frozen semen from proven bulls to improve genetic stock and boost milk production. Marx devised a method of combining herd-testing and artificial-insemination resources, and offered artificial breeding on a commercial basis. Thorough, meticulous and forceful as an administrator, he used these attributes to overcome many technical difficulties to implement the new service. The system he established at Maffra became the model for other dairying centres throughout Victoria, and led to an immediate boost in milk production and a decline in cattle disease. He was joint vice-president (1960-66 and 1970-71) of the Artificial Breeding Association of Victoria.

Described in a radio broadcast as having a 'searching and dogmatic persistency', Marx capitalized on his chance arrival at Maffra to become an influential figure who helped to shape the direction of the dairy industry and of farmer co-operatives in Victoria. He retired in 1972. Survived by his wife, he died on 24 March 1974 at Sale from injuries he received in a motorcar accident.

F. Pearce, *The history of herd testing and artificial breeding in the Maffra district* (Boisdale, Vic, 1983); R. Broome and T. Dingle, *The Victorians* (Syd, 1984); M. Fletcher, 'Dairying personalities: Otto Marx', *H. I. Farmer*, May 1989, p 17; *Maffra Spectator*, 14 Feb 1956, 12 Nov 1968, 27 Mar 1974; Otto Marx Collection, Local Hist Collection, Maffra Branch, Wellington Shire L, Vic; naturalization file, A435/1 item 44/4/1705 (AA).

MEREDITH FLETCHER

MASEL, PHILIP (1908-1972), businessman, writer and army officer, was born on 25 May 1908 in Perth, fourth child of Russian-born parents Esor Masel, merchant, and his first wife Leah, née Cohen (d.1919), both of whom were Jewish. Esor had emigrated to South Australia in 1887 and hawked shoelaces before moving to Western Australia. In 1925 the family established Worth's store, a menswear business in Perth. Philip was educated at Highgate State School and Christian Brothers' College, Perth. Although he wanted to become a professional writer, he joined Worth's as its advertising manager. He adopted the maxim that marketing was 'not a life-and-death battle, but an honest expression of the desire to gain the purchaser's goodwill and permanent patronage—even at the cost of losing an occasional sale'.

Active in the Jewish community, Masel co-edited (from 1929) the *Westralian Judean*. The monthly newspaper covered community events, and attracted articles and short stories from around Australia. Using his own name—and the pseudonyms 'P.M.' and 'Philm'—Masel contributed articles to the *Judean*, as well as to the *Bulletin* and *Smith's Weekly*. At the Synagogue, Perth, on 28 July 1931 he married Marian Mendelson, a 21-year-old concert singer. During the early 1930s he competed in Jewish debating teams, served as an adjudicator for the Debating League of Western Australia and co-authored *The Art of Debating* (Melbourne, 1934). In 1935 he published the handbook, *Improve Your Salesmanship* (Melbourne). A keen actor in local Jewish theatre, he wrote an unpublished play, 'Cloth Model', and a novel, *In a Glass Prison* (London, 1937), and worked as drama critic for the *National Theatre News*. The Masels were in London in 1937-38 on a working holiday; Philip wrote articles and scripts for the British Broadcasting Corporation, while Marian studied under Mark Raphael.

In 1938 Masel joined the Citizen Military Forces. He was commissioned in the Australian Imperial Force on 20 July 1940. Posted to the 2nd/28th Battalion, he was mentioned in dispatches for his work at Tobruk, Libya, in 1941, and commended for gallantry in action around El Alamein, Egypt, in 1942. In the following year he was promoted temporary major while serving as an instructor (1943-44) at the Land Headquarters Tactical School, Beenleigh, Queensland. Rejoining his old unit in May 1945, he participated in operations in British North Borneo. As 'Peter Mike', he had also acted as a war correspondent for the *West Australian*. Masel continued to serve with the C.M.F., commanding the 11th-44th Battalion in 1951-54 and the 13th Brigade (Royal West Australian Regiment) in 1959-61. He wrote the history of his battalion, *The Second 28th* (1961), and in 1963 was transferred to the Retired List with the rank of brigadier.

Masel published *The Story of the Perth Hebrew Congregation* (1946) and contributed regularly to the anti-Zionist journal, *Australian Jewish Outlook*. With Harold Boas [q.v.13] and others, he helped to found (1952) the Liberal Jewish Group in Perth which established the Temple David Congregation; Masel recorded its progress in two pamphlets, *The First Decade* (1962) and *The Second Decade* (1972). In 1953 he was appointed O.B.E. He was president (1951) of Perth Legacy, a long-time member of the Australian Jewish Historical Society, a trustee (1956-66) of the Western Australian branch of the Boy Scouts' Association, chairman of the ceremonial committee for the 1962 British Empire and Commonwealth Games, and a member (1962-67) of the Western Australian division of the Duke of Edinburgh's Award Scheme. In addition, he served (1962-67) on the Australian Broadcasting Commission's talks advisory committee for Western Australia. When his elder brother Samuel died in 1966, Philip became general manager of Worth's Stores. He was appointed a commissioner of the A.B.C. in 1967 and a member of the Western Australian Arts Advisory Board in 1970.

Correct in his appearance, bearing and address, Masel had a highly developed sense of duty and responsibility. Loyalty and public service were the hallmarks of his life. Returning from a holiday in England, he died of coronary thrombosis on 26 February 1972 in the *Arkadia*, off Vancouver, and was buried at sea. His wife and daughter survived him.

D. Mossenson, *Hebrew, Israelite, Jew* (Perth, 1990); *Daily News* (Perth), 6 Mar 1967; *SMH*, 29, 30 May 1967, 5 June 1970; *West Australian*, 20, 28, 29 Feb 1972; *Canb Times*, 28 Feb 1972; *Jewish Week* (Perth), Mar 1972; papers held by, and information from, Mrs J. Arkwright, Crawley, Perth; personal knowledge. DAVID MOSSENSON

MASON, (GEORGE) WILLIAM RICHARD STANLEY (1908-1975), accountant and general manager, was born on 25 February 1908 at Bow, London, son of George Robert Mason, music-hall vocalist, and his wife Emily, née Waters. Young George was educated at Margate—at St Dunstan's College and Chatham House School for Boys. An uncle reputedly paid his school fees when the Masons fell on hard times; George changed his name to William. In 1923 the family emigrated to Sydney. Bill obtained employment in 1926 as a cashier with the fledgling National Roads and Motorists' Association. He studied accountancy at night, was admitted (1931) to the Commonwealth Institute of Accountants and rose steadily through the management ranks of the N.R.M.A. At St Stephen's Anglican Church, Woollahra, on 19 July 1930 he married Phyllis Janet Barclay.

Mason was appointed district superintendent at Lismore (1932) and Newcastle (1937). Enlisting in the Militia on 6 July 1940, he was commissioned lieutenant in December. On 14 August 1942 he transferred to the Australian Imperial Force. In 1943 he served in Papua at I Corps and New Guinea Force headquarters; in September he was promoted captain. Attached to the 165th General Transport Company in 1944-45, he became a familiar figure at Lae, New Guinea, and Jacquinot Bay, New Britain; he was usually accompanied by the unit mascot, a dog called Tiger.

Transferring to the Reserve of Officers on 5 December 1945, Mason was again successively placed in charge of the N.R.M.A. branches at Lismore and Newcastle. He studied the operation of other Australian motoring organizations in 1956 and was asked to reorganize the N.R.M.A.'s metropolitan road service branch. Popular with his subordinates, he was 5 ft 7½ ins (171 cm) tall, with fair hair and blue eyes; his dapper appearance and educated English accent belied an egalitarian streak. In 1959 he was appointed assistant-secretary of the N.R.M.A. Following an extensive overseas tour investigating motoring organizations, he was promoted general secretary in 1963.

As spokesman for the N.R.M.A., Mason supported its traditional opposition to new motoring taxes and charges, and urged that more money be spent on roads. With road safety becoming an important public issue, he increasingly found himself invited to comment on ways of reducing the escalating road toll. The N.R.M.A. supported the introduction of a blood-alcohol limit for drivers (1968) and the compulsory fitting of seat-belts in new cars (1969), but opposed the compulsory wearing of seat-belts (1971). Membership of the N.R.M.A. almost doubled during Mason's term as general secretary, reaching one million in 1972.

The demands of his successful career, and the enforced separation of war, strained the relationship with his wife. Although a daughter was born in 1947, the marriage remained an unhappy one and both partners increasingly found solace in drink. Mason belonged to the Imperial Service and Balgowlah Bowling clubs, and to the Legacy Club of Sydney; his other outlets were his dogs, gardening, bowls and fishing. He retired in 1973 and moved to Korora. Survived by his wife and daughter, he died of cancer on 2 June 1975 at Coffs Harbour District Hospital and was cremated.

R. Broomham, *On the Road* (Syd, 1996); *Open Road*, 53, no 4, Aug 1975, p 8; *SMH*, 12 Nov 1962, 11 Feb 1963, 22 Dec 1967, 4 Mar 1968, 18 July 1972; information from Mrs N. J. James, Turramurra, Syd.   JOHN KNOTT

MASON, PAUL EDWARD ALLEN (1901-1972), planter and coastwatcher, was born on 30 April 1901 in North Sydney, third child of Frederick Mason (formerly Mikkelsen), a Danish-born master mariner, and his native-born wife Margaret, née Robinson, who had been widowed before she married Frederick. The family was contented and domesticated, principled but not overtly religious, and valued practical skills such as sailing and horse-riding. Paul briefly attended Fort Street Boys' High School and was afterwards a keen but cursory autodidact. With his father disabled, he left in January 1916 for the Shortland Islands, British Solomon Islands Protectorate, to ease the family burden and to assist his half-brother Tommy, a trader.

An unprepossessing, short, bespectacled youth, with fair, tousled hair and somewhat prominent teeth, Mason intrepidly managed labour-lines of recently contacted warriors. He returned home in 1919 to help his family work an orchard at Penrith, but the tropics lured him again. In 1925 he accepted a job managing Inus plantation on Bougainville, after his predecessor had been hacked to death by labourers. He tramped the island to recruit workers, picking up unrivalled knowledge of the terrain and familiarity with custom. A relieving manager and inspector for Associated Plantations Ltd (which owned Inus), he became an expert navigator. Before World War II, however, he was regarded as an ill-kempt, unlettered eccentric, most genial but gauche and shy, with the taint—through Tommy's marriage—of having mixed-race relations, and distinguished only by navigational and ingenious mechanical skills, particularly with wireless.

Consequently he was invited to join Eric Feldt's [q.v.14] coastwatching team. Although Mason was scoffed at for military service —'overage, undersized, slightly deaf, a bit shortsighted', with a malaria-induced slight impediment in his speech—he remained on Bougainville in 1942 after most officials and planters had scuttled. To safeguard him in the event of capture, he was made petty officer, Royal Australian Naval Volunteer Reserve. He was told to create observation posts behind Kieta, and then inland from Buin in the south.

With forces of the United States of America poised to invade Guadalcanal, Mason and Jack Read (his fellow coastwatcher in the north) were ordered to report all enemy aircraft and ships proceeding south-east. On 7 August Mason's celebrated signal, 'Twenty-four bombers headed yours', brought disaster to the Japanese as American fighters swooped on them. Only one Japanese aircraft returned. Unsuspecting until too late why such losses continued, the Japanese had their air cover destroyed. 'Tokyo Express' warships steaming down the Solomons 'Slot' subsequently encountered a similar reception. (Fleet) Admiral William Halsey, U.S. Navy, said that the coastwatchers 'saved Guadalcanal' and Guadalcanal 'saved the South Pacific'. In November Mason was promoted sub lieutenant and learned that he had won the U.S. Distinguished Service Cross.

Eventually alert to the danger that Europeans posed on Bougainville, the Japanese moved to corral them. A squad of local 'Black Dogs', under Japanese command, harried Mason's party as he fled northwards, eventually reaching Read at Aravia after a gruelling trek through mountainous jungle. Mason arrived with merely 'what he stood up in— shorts and singlet—plus haversack and revolver at belt; and barefooted', wrote an admiring Read. Only his audacity and his rapport with villagers had saved him.

Fresh instructions came to set up another station in the south. Mason wanted to go alone: he was exasperated by soldiers whom he regarded as inexperienced and less resourceful—and he was exhilarated by his own unanticipated physical and moral fibre in spite of age and infirmities. But Read insisted that he be accompanied. In June 1943 Mason's men were ambushed *en route* and had to flee. An epic climb over the 5000-ft (1500 m) Keriaka plateau saved them. By July U.S. submarines had evacuated the remaining Europeans, with the coastwatchers the last to leave. From Sydney, Mason returned to duty in late November. He was selected to take a party of Black scouts to Treasury Island, a hazardous and unsuccessful sally from which he contracted near-fatal pneumonia. He was invalided to Australia in March 1944. In Bougainville villages, rumours spread that he was dead.

Mason's unexpected return in November 1944 impressed locals, wavering in their opposition to the Japanese, with his possible indestructibility. He recruited a small partisan band which terrorized the enemy and was credited with a record body count of 2288. Always he put his scouts' welfare before his own. His daring rescues were notable for the care taken of former prisoners, especially missionaries, and the lack of vindictiveness towards collaborators. His continued wrangling with headquarters over supplies and the deficiencies of regular soldiers probably led to his transfer home in May 1945 before final victory. He was awarded the D.S.C. In December 1951 he was promoted lieutenant commander, R.A.N.V.R. (Special Branch), a matter of deep pride to him.

After the war Mason grew into a self-confident celebrity. On 13 November 1947 at Rabaul he married Noelle Evelyn Taylor, a 30-year-old arts graduate in psychology and a journalist. He returned to Inus. Associated Plantations had rewarded him with shares. The plantation flourished with his recruitment of labour from the Highlands, where he and his wife founded a retail enterprise, Buka Stores, and the Chimbu Lodge. Becoming a spokesman for his 'Cinderella district', he sat on its advisory council and wrote articles for *Pacific Islands Monthly*. In 1961 he stood successfully for the Territory's reconstructed Legislative Council in order to oppose the emergence of political parties which he thought undemocratic. Although listened to respectfully, he was a political nonentity. By 1972 he had accepted the inevitability of early national independence, but feared the outcome.

While not a flag-waver, Mason belonged to the Imperial Service Club, Sydney, and the New Guinea branch of the Returned Sailors', Soldiers' and Airmen's Imperial League of Australia. He died on 31 December 1972 at Greenslopes, Brisbane, and was cremated; his wife, daughter and son survived him. Appropriately for a non-dogmatic Christian, panegyrics were delivered by both Methodist and Catholic clergymen. The Australian War Memorial, Canberra, holds his portrait by Olive Kroening. For the Catalina pilots who had supplied him, Mason 'represented the upper limit of continuous bravery' and was 'their No 1 hero of World War II'.

R. Stuart, *Nuts to You!* (Syd, 1977); J. Griffin, 'Paul Mason: planter and coastwatcher', in J. Griffin (ed), *Papua New Guinea Portraits* (Canb, 1978), and for sources; A. B. Feuer (ed), *Coastwatching in the Solomon Islands* (NY, 1992); A. McNab, *We Were The First* (Syd, 1998); personal information.

JAMES GRIFFIN

MASSEY, CLAUDE (1889-1968), public servant and inventor, was born on 1 November 1889 at Footscray, Melbourne, second son of Victorian-born parents Herbert John Massey, draper, and his wife Fanny, née Tolson. Claude left Footscray College at the age of 15 and was employed in the accountancy branch of the Victorian Railways. On 11 May 1905 he transferred to the Commonwealth Public Service. Joining the new naval administration in July 1911, he shifted to Sydney in 1914, but found that his duties prevented him from enlisting in the Australian Imperial Force. He studied at night, gaining a diploma in economics and commerce (1919) from the University of Sydney and qualifications in factory inspection and public health from Sydney Technical College.

In November 1917 Massey was promoted assistant victualling store officer, Royal Edward Victualling Yard, Darling Harbour. At St Peter's Anglican Church, Sydney, on 7 December 1918 he married Dorothy May Broadbent. He became officer-in-charge of the R.E.V.Y. in 1923. The yard bought goods from Australian growers and manufacturers, and supplied food, mess kits and clothing to naval ships and establishments. During the Depression, when the R.E.V.Y. was threatened with retrenchments and other cuts, Massey stressed its importance to Australia's security and independence.

Massey had studied naval logistics in Britain, Europe and the United States of America in 1923-25. He was seconded to Navy Office, Melbourne, as acting-director of victualling in 1926-28, and again from 1938. Early in World War II he invented a life-jacket which could be rapidly inflated and worn comfortably in most situations. Described as the 'Australian "Mae West"', the jacket had a large flotation area around the chest which gave its wearers 'something of a pouter pigeon appearance'. His 'Mae West' saved the lives of countless Australian and allied servicemen. Massey donated the patent rights of his invention to the Commonwealth.

As chairman of the defence services foodstuffs committee (later defence foodstuffs advisory council), Massey advised the government in 1941 against purchasing the Abbco Bread Co. Pty Ltd; a royal commission dismissed allegations that he had demanded bribes to approve the sale. On loan to the Department of Commerce, in June 1943 he was appointed deputy controller-general of food and director-general of food supply. He helped to manage the production of food and its distribution to civilians and armed forces personnel.

In March 1946 Massey became Australian commissioner for Malaya, based in Singapore. He urged the Australian government to assume a larger role in the region, and advocated that the White Australia policy should be modified to allow limited Asian immigration. Appointed Australian minister to Egypt, he arrived in Cairo in March 1950. The plight of Palestinian refugees attracted his attention and he felt that world peace might be endangered if they were not found a homeland.

By late 1952 Massey had begun to show the first signs of Parkinson's disease. He left Egypt in April 1953 and spent his retirement in Sydney. In 1957 he was master of the Lane Cove Masonic lodge. Survived by his wife, son and three daughters, he died on 21 May 1968 at Collaroy and was cremated.

E. R. Walker, *The Australian Economy in War and Reconstruction* (NY, 1947); G. H. Gill, *Royal Australian Navy 1942-1945* (Canb, 1968); MP 472/1, items 19/17/9030 and 19/21/8018, *and* MP 692/1, item 569/219/144 (AA, Melb), *and* CRS A4231, ministerial dispatches from Singapore and Cairo (AA, Canb); information from Mr D. Massey, Longueville, Syd.   CHRIS TAYLOR

MASSOLA, ALDO GIUSEPPE (1910-1975), museum curator, was born on 9 September 1910 in Rome, son of Carlo Massola, racing-car driver and mechanic, and his wife Erminia, née Vaccaneo. Carlo drove for Diatto of Turin and competed on the Australian circuit in 1922. After his contract expired, he emigrated with his family to Melbourne in 1923. Aldo was educated by the Christian Brothers at St Thomas's school, North Fitzroy. He entered the restaurant service, rose to head waiter and witnessed the heyday of prominent restaurants, working at the Florentino, Navaretti's and the refurbished Savoy Plaza, and then with the Vigano [q.v.12] family at Mario's for twenty years. His friendly, confident manner and loving knowledge of wines were assets. On 28 January 1932 at St Mary's Catholic Church, West Melbourne, he married 24-year-old Marian Zaccari.

An interest in numismatics, ethnography and Tibetan culture was stimulated by Dr Leonhard Adam [q.v.13], from whom Massola received unofficial tuition. Massola accumulated a private collection and an excellent wine cellar at his Montrose home. From June 1954 he was employed as temporary assistant (anthropology) at the National Museum of Victoria, presumably on Adam's advice. His appointment as curator of anthropology, level C, became permanent in June 1956. He commenced his new profession enthusiastically, tidying jumbled collections which had been largely neglected since 1927. While cupboards contained rubbish, artefacts littered the floor. Massola located invaluable Oenpelli bark paintings which had been used as trestle-tables. Although later accused of pilfering artefacts, he saved much from deterioration.

He also developed more systematic records and bibliographies.

Massola revived the moribund Anthropological Society of Victoria (president 1959-61). At a time when the University of Melbourne neglected anthropology, he conducted fruitful excursions in search of Aboriginal rock paintings, located several and published notes in the *Victorian Naturalist*. Victorian Aborigines were then virtually ignored, but Massola visited many communities, won their respect and collected information. He assembled oral, written and pictorial material, and published a dozen books or bibliographies on Aboriginal subjects. Despite their lack of documentation and rigour, they demonstrated the research potential and remain significant for Aboriginal Victorians.

In those impecunious years, Massola doubled as honorary numismatist for the then co-located National Gallery of Victoria. On 6 December 1963 he was charged with the theft of rare coins. Convicted in 1964 on three counts of larceny, he received a two-year gaol sentence, but was released on parole after twelve months. On 6 January 1965 he was dismissed from the museum. In the following year he was charged with six further counts of theft from the National Gallery. Again convicted on three counts, he was fined $110 and costs. According to the sympathetic stipendiary magistrate, Massola was 'an obsessed collector rather than a thief in the ordinary sense'.

Archaeologists knew Massola from the late 1950s as an expedition cook, notable for his wine supplies, exotic meals, and his cheerful and generous company. He typified the rising amateur interest in Aboriginal society before the advent of university professionalism. Survived by his wife and daughter, he died of cancer on 6 July 1975 at Fitzroy and was cremated. His estate was sworn for probate at $50 881.

Aust Author, Oct 1975, p 40; *Age* (Melb), 17, 19 Dec 1964, 28 Oct 1966; Museum of Vic records; information from Mr S. Massola, East Brighton, Melb; personal knowledge.   D. J. MULVANEY

MASTERS, JAMES WILLIAM (1892-1955), soccer player and coalminer, was born on 21 May 1892 at Balgownie, New South Wales, seventh of thirteen children of Alexander George Masters, a miner from Nova Scotia, Canada, and his Sydney-born wife Frances Eliza, née Campbell. He was nicknamed 'Judy', possibly because his mother chose the name during pregnancy, but probably due to his gentleness which contrasted with his three boisterous elder brothers. Many British miners reared on Association football were employed on the coalfields around Wollongong. Judy attended Balgownie Public School where soccer dominated the playground. He captained his school team and, at the age of 12, displaying precocious talent, joined the Balgownie Soccer Club.

Entering first grade at the age of 15, Masters played for Balgownie (1904-11, 1919-29), and for the Sydney clubs, Newtown (1912-13) and Granville (1914-15). About 5 ft 7 ins (170 cm) tall and weighing only ten stone (64 kg), he was all muscle and bone. His toughness, honed by hewing coal, for he had followed his father into the mines, did not equate with roughness. He was never cautioned by a referee in more than 400 club and representative games. As centre forward, Masters was an instinctive player who valued teamwork. Although naturally shy, he was also a leader, progressively captaining Balgownie, South Coast, New South Wales and Australia.

Masters enlisted in the Australian Imperial Force on 1 June 1915. Serving with the 19th Battalion, he saw action at Gallipoli and on the Western Front. On 26 July 1916 at Pozières, France, he was wounded in the shoulder. Promoted sergeant in May 1918, he returned to Sydney in August 1919 and was discharged on 31 October. While on leave in England he had met Annie Barraclough of County Durham. They were married at St Michael's Anglican Church, Wollongong, on 23 June 1920 and set up house at Balgownie where they raised two daughters; their son died in infancy.

Between 1923 and 1927 Masters scored 12 goals in 13 international matches, representing Australia against New Zealand (1923), China (1923, 1927), Canada (1924), England (1925) and Czechoslovakia (1927). He was noted for his consistency and netted a total of 351 goals in first-class football. Scoring in the first minute of play for New South Wales against England before 45 000 people in Sydney in 1925 was a high point. He was granted a testimonial in 1928 and hung up his boots in the following year. Having been captain-secretary of Balgownie in 1919-28, he continued to serve the club as secretary, committeeman, selector or coach until 1953.

Masters worked in the Corrimal mine and maintained an interest in local matters. He was bandmaster of the Balgownie Citizens' Band for fifteen years. Following early retirement, Judy (and Annie) visited Britain in 1953 to see Queen Elizabeth II's coronation procession, the Football Association Cup final, and the annual world championship for brass bands at the Crystal Palace, London. Forty years of inhaling coaldust had taken its toll. He died at his Balgownie home on 2 December 1955 of acute haemoptysis brought on by the miner's curse, pneumoconiosis. Sur-

vived by his wife and daughters, he was buried in Wollongong cemetery. Contemporaries deemed Judy Masters the foremost native-born soccer player of his own and any previous era. The Balgownie soccer ground was named after him.

S. Grant (comp), *Jack Pollard's Soccer Records* (Syd, 1974); Balgownie Publications Cte and J. Fletcher, *Balgownie School Centenary, 1889-1989* (Balgownie, NSW, c1989); *Soccer Weekly News*, 16 Aug 1952; *SMH*, 1 June 1925; *Arrow* (Syd), 16 Apr 1926; *Referee*, 27 June, 18 July 1928; *Illawarra Mercury*, 20 Mar 1936, 3, 5 Dec 1955; *Sun-Herald* (Syd), 4 Dec 1955; information from Mrs J. Barwise, Corrimal, NSW.   PHILIP MOSELY

MATHEWS, WRENFORD JOHN OGILVIE HENRY (1874-1954), wool expert and sheepclasser, and **WRENFORD JOHN** (1903-1967), sheepclasser and studmaster, were father and son. Mathews senior, later known as J. Wrenford Mathews, was born on 30 June 1874 at Morrisons, Shire of Ballan, Victoria, son of Wrenford Herbert Mathews, a farmer from England, and his wife Edith Ann, née Bowler, who was born at sea. After gaining a diploma in wool-growing and woolclassing from the Working Men's College, Melbourne, he joined in turn Joseph Gill & Co. and William Haughton & Co. On 29 July 1903 at the Presbyterian manse, Clifton Hill, he married Isobel Catherine Josephine Zevenboom.

From 1905 Mathews was wool instructor at the School of Mines and Industries, Adelaide, and lecturer in sheep-breeding and wool-growing at Roseworthy Agricultural College. In August 1909 he was appointed sheep and wool expert and instructor in the New South Wales Department of Agriculture on an annual salary of £400; he lectured at the Hawkesbury Agricultural College and at various government farm schools throughout the State, and wrote for the *Agricultural Gazette of New South Wales*.

On his retirement in November 1920, Mathews was presented with a gold watch and matchbox by W. F. Dunn [q.v.8], the minister for agriculture. That year he began his own merino stud at Wahroonga, Nevertire, with 400 ewes from E. E. I. Body [q.v.7] of Bundemar, Trangie. In 1921 he joined Bundemar on a retainer-salary as chief classer of its stud and of its clients' flocks throughout eastern Australia. He judged merinos at most leading sheep shows, and was also an authority on British breeds. Survived by his three sons and twin daughters, Mathews died on 11 October 1954 at Killara, Sydney, and was cremated with Anglican rites.

His eldest son Wrenford John was born on 14 July 1903 at Collingwood, Melbourne.

Leaving school at 17, Wrenford jackerooed on Toora, Nevertire, New South Wales, before taking charge of Wahroonga. He enlisted in the Australian Imperial Force on 7 January 1942, served in the Northern Australia Observer Unit (1942-44) and with training battalions, and was discharged on 26 November 1945. At St Philip's Anglican Church, Sydney, on 2 June 1949 he married Edna Patricia Joan Elwin, a 28-year-old nurse.

With an avid interest in genetics, Mathews made a thorough study of wool and paid particular attention to the various requirements of its manufacturers. Under natural conditions, in low-rainfall country timbered with wilga, myall and box, he concentrated on breeding big, plain-bodied rams of great stamina which produced high-yielding, soft-handling, medium-to-strong wool. In addition to classing his own rams and his clients' flocks, he personally selected many of their rams. He also classed at Bundemar, and for its clients. J. Wrenford Mathews & Sons Pty Ltd was formed in March 1954 to take over the Wahroonga stud (Flock no.1961); Wrenford became managing director and his brothers directors. In 1966 the stud's operations were extended by the formation of a partnership with N. M. Kater [q.v.14], styled Mathews Kater & Co. Mathews' unfailing courtesy, loyalty and cheerfulness endeared him to many. Survived by his wife, son and two daughters, he died of a coronary occlusion on 25 March 1967 at Wahroonga, Nevertire, and was cremated with Presbyterian forms.

C. Massy, *The Australian Merino* (Melb, 1990); G. Walsh, *Pioneering Days* (Syd, 1993); *Pastoral Review*, 16 July, 16 Dec 1920, 15 Jan 1921, 16 Nov 1954, 16 July 1957, 19 Apr 1967; *Aust Stud Merino Flock Register*, 42, 1965; information from Mr J. Mathews, Isisford, Qld.   G. P. WALSH

MATHY, MARIANNE HELENE SARA (1890-1978), teacher of singing, was born on 23 June 1890 at Mannheim, Germany, only child of Dr Richard Michael Kahn, lawyer, and his first wife Martha, née Fürth. Marianne was baptized a Lutheran at Trinity Church in 1896, though her father belonged to a wealthy Jewish family. His putative cousins included Robert Kahn, a composer and friend of Brahms, and Otto Hermann Kahn, a banker who financed the Metropolitan Opera Company, New York. The family home, decorated by a pupil of William Morris, was a centre of Mannheim's musical and intellectual activity. There Marianne met many musicians, among them the violinist Joseph Joachim and the conductor Wilhelm Furtwängler.

From the age of 8 she learned the piano and began to attend concerts with her father, a passionate music lover. In spite of his wish that she become a pianist, she took singing lessons at secondary school from Anna Rodre-Heindl. Marianne attended classes in acting (including deportment, breathing and voice projection) at the Städtische Hochschule für Musik and Theater Mannheim. Impressed by the stress that Professor Max Friedländer laid on the importance of the text and its contribution to the emotion of the music, she later emphasized these principles to her Australian students.

One of her earliest concert experiences occurred in September 1910 when she sang in the chorus at the première performance of Gustav Mahler's eighth symphony, which he conducted at Munich. About 1912 Marianne married Colonel Erich Mathy of the Imperial German Army. Following the declaration of war in 1914, he went to the front and she trained as a nurse. After he was seriously wounded, she transferred to a field-hospital to care for him. He was killed in action in 1915.

A coloratura soprano, Marianne Mathy made her operatic début in 1918 as Gretel in *Hänsel und Gretel*. She was soon singing such roles as the Queen of the Night (*Die Zauberflöte*) and Gilda (*Rigoletto*) at Wiesbaden. Deeply interested in the English composer Purcell, she wrote out her own performing copies from material in the Preussische Staatsbibliothek, Berlin, and sang his music in an authentic way, with harpsichord and strings. As well as standard German lieder, she added to her repertoire works by less familiar composers, among them Telemann and Rameau. In Berlin on 12 August 1921 Marianne married Franz Martin Friedenstein (d.1955), a Jewish architect and amateur violinist from Poland. They lived comfortably in Berlin and she continued her career as Marianne Mathy until the ascendancy of the Nazis in 1933. Protected by Furtwängler, they lived under surveillance and she was not allowed to perform. Her students were eventually told that they would not be engaged if they took 'lessons from the Jewess, Mathy'. Through the intervention of Sir Thomas Beecham's secretary Dr Berta Geissmar, Franz was finally permitted to leave Germany in 1938 and Marianne in 1939.

On (Sir) Malcolm Sargent's advice, they decided to emigrate to Australia. Friedenstein reached Sydney in April 1939; Marianne followed in October in the *Siraimedliv*. By that time Sargent was conducting there. He introduced her to members of the Anglican hierarchy with musical connexions, which led to her first concert, at the Australia Hotel on 29 November 1939. A critic noted her 'highly schooled style' and found her 'charmingly fluent' in the 'more florid pieces'. Engagements with the Australian Broadcasting Commission followed—including a concert of

Schumann lieder and as the soprano soloist in Handel's *Messiah*—until the Australian government banned broadcasts of spoken or sung German. Despite restrictions on their movements, the Friedensteins changed their name to Frisdane and were naturalized in December 1944. They had moved into a cottage at 45 Manning Road, Double Bay (which would be her home and studio until her death). Separated about 1951, they were to be divorced in 1952, with Walter Jackson (a member of their *ménage à trois*) named as co-respondent.

Known professionally as Madame Mathy, she had begun to accumulate the first of a distinguished list of pupils, including Alan Light, Eleanor Houston, Margaret Martin, Sergei Baigildin, Lyndon Terracini, Meg Chilcott, and June 'Bronhill' whom she persuaded to change her surname from Gough. Many of her students were to win the *Sun* Aria competition. A council-member (1950) of the short-lived New South Wales National Opera, she started the Mathy Opera Group in 1952 to give her students experience. Their first performance was *Hansel and Gretel* (with Bronhill as Gretel), supported by the Rockdale Municipal Orchestra. Yielding to the persuasions of (Sir) Eugene Goossens [q.v.14], Mathy taught (1954-72) voice production at the New South Wales State Conservatorium of Music. She also taught briefly at the National Institute of Dramatic Art. In 1965 she published *The Singer's Companion*. She long described herself as a 'Professor of Singing'.

Madame Mathy engendered loyalty in many of her students, and hostility in others. They spoke of her grasp of style, and of the skill with which she conveyed her knowledge. She was very affectionate to her favourites: June Bronhill called her 'my second mother'. Terracini found it 'a huge revelation' when Mathy spoke to him 'in artistic language', but he agreed that she was invariably tough and could be 'an absolute vixen'. She 'was very impatient with talented people who did not want to progress as fast as possible' and she was sometimes manipulative and ruthless. In her view, nothing, not even marriage, should stand in the way of a career. Werner Baer, another Jewish refugee, often accompanied her performances. She considered it disloyal when he played for others.

An excellent cook, Marianne Mathy was an elegant hostess who took great pains over her make-up and dress. At the age of 73, fearful of old age and death, she visited the Privat-Klinik Bircher-Benner, Zürich, Switzerland, for 'rejuvenating' injections of 'monkey-glands'. She died on 15 October 1978 in her Double Bay home and was cremated. Her modest estate formed the nucleus of funds used to establish an award for singing known as the Marianne Mathy scholarship.

Aust Musical News, 1 Mar 1950, 1 Jan 1953; *Con Brio*, Mar 1973; *Opera Australia*, 1978; *SMH*, 30 Nov 1939, 17 Jan 1952, 14 Nov 1953, 19 Oct 1978, 3 June 1982; Mathy file 21317 (ABC Archives, Syd); Frisdane, naturalization file A446/184, item 54/13581 *and* A1067/1, item IC46/90/34 (AA, Canb); newspaper-cuttings and photographs held by Mr R. Gridiger, Syd; information from Frau F. Cussnick, Mannheim, Germany, Ms T. McRae, Noosa Heads, Qld, Mr L. Terracini, Lismore, NSW, Mrs M. Tollett, Castle Hill, and Mr S. Baigildin, Strathfield, Syd.
JOHN CARMODY

MATTHAEI, ERNST ARTUR FRANZ JOSEPH (1904-1966), optical microscopist, was born on 21 April 1904 at Trier, Germany, one of six children of Artur Matthaei, civil servant, and his wife Josephine, née Brentrup. The family pronounced their surname 'Mattay'. Artur served as an officer in World War I. During those years Ernst and his brother Hans lived with various relations. When the war ended, Trier was occupied by the allied armies.

Apprenticed to an optician at Trier, Matthaei studied under German masters of classical optics at the University of Jena and at the Institute of Microscopy. By 1926 he was employed as a trainee in the Carl Zeiss works. In the following year he transferred to the 'Opto' department which made spectacles and ophthalmological instruments. He moved in 1929 to E. C. Heyne & Co., which held the Zeiss agency in Melbourne, and arrived there on 25 September in the *Mosul*. In the 1930s he established Ernst Matthaei & Co., dealers in scientific instruments. He visited Germany on business in 1937. At Ridley College chapel, Parkville, on 26 May 1939 he married with Anglican rites Grace Moran Villiers, a 28-year-old journalist who also worked as a librarian in the geology department at the University of Melbourne. In June 1939 he was naturalized.

Following the outbreak of World War II, imports from Germany ceased and Matthaei's business was reduced. In December 1939 Professor (Sir) Douglas Wright offered him a junior position in the physiology department at the university. Matthaei's first major contribution to war-work came in 1941 when he transferred to Professor J. S. Turner's botany department and was put in charge of the annexe which made graticules for sighting telescopes and binoculars. After Japan declared war in December 1941, it was necessary to 'tropic-proof' equipment—even the inside of optical instruments—against fungal infections. In his annexe Matthaei was part of a multi-specialist team that solved this problem.

By 1945 he ran a well-stocked service laboratory and workshop, with many good staff. Matthaei recommended that the faculty of science absorb the annexe as a workshop for opto-mechanical servicing of university equipment. Aided by his constant helpfulness, the workshop proved a success; interdepartmental research flourished, especially in photomicrography and fluorescence microscopy. In 1949 he began one of the first technical courses of lecture-demonstrations, on the optical microscope for research workers. Its immediate popularity caused it to be repeated, and extended to final-year science students; the courses ran every year thereafter. Joining the teaching and research staff as a part-time lecturer in 1950, he remained receptive to new scientific and technical ideas, such as the electron microscope.

Matthaei's devotion to the university and his adopted country was profound. He enjoyed a happy marriage and thoroughly appreciated his work at the university. A friendly and gregarious man, 'Matt' was a foundation member (1953) of University House and convener of its wine committee. Survived by his wife, he died of a cerebral tumour on 15 July 1966 at his Parkville home. The university's Ernst Matthaei Memorial Collection of Early Glass recalls his lifelong interest in glass, and his well-furnished table with good wine and his friends around him.

D. P. Mellor, *The Role of Science and Industry* (Canb, 1958); *Univ Melb Gazette*, Sept 1966, p 7; H. C. Bolton, 'Optical Instruments in Australia in the 1939-45 War; Successes and Lost Opportunities', *Aust Physicist*, 27, no 3, 1990, p 31; Matthaei archive (Univ Melb Archives); naturalization file, A659/1, item 41/835 (AA, Canb).   H. C. BOLTON

MATTHEWS, LIONEL COLIN (1912-1944), soldier and salesman, was born on 15 August 1912 at Stepney, Adelaide, third child of Edgar Roy Matthews, plumber, and his wife Ann Elizabeth, née Jeffery. Lionel was educated at East Adelaide Public and Norwood High schools, then worked as a salesman in a department store. Assistant-scoutmaster (from 1931), 1st Kensington Sea Scouts, he was a powerful swimmer, a lifesaver, and a good amateur boxer. At St Matthew's Anglican Church, Kensington, on 26 December 1935 he married (Lorna) Myrtle Lane, a 21-year-old packer. Under the auspices of the Boy Scouts' Association, he was involved in social work at Pentridge gaol, Melbourne, in 1937-38.

After training as a signalman in the Citizen Naval Forces, Matthews enlisted in the Militia in April 1939. Posted to the 3rd Division Signals, he was commissioned lieutenant in January 1940. On 10 June he transferred to the Australian Imperial Force and in February 1941 sailed for Singapore with the 8th Division Signals. Sporting a clipped moustache, he was nicknamed 'The Duke' because of his re-

semblance to the Duke of Gloucester [q.v.14]. Matthews was athletically built, stood 6 ft 1 in. (185 cm) tall, had a ready smile, and liked to dress well. As signals officer, 27th Brigade, he maintained cable communications while under fire at Gemas, Malaya, and on Singapore (January-February 1942), and won the Military Cross. In January 1942 he was promoted captain. After Singapore fell on 15 February, he was interned in Changi prison.

In July 1942 the Japanese shipped 'B' Force, which comprised 1496 Australians (including Matthews), to Sandakan in British North Borneo. Soon after his arrival he was largely responsible for setting up an elaborate intelligence organization. Contact was made with Dr J. P. Taylor, an Australian in charge of the nearby government hospital, and with European internees on Berhala Island. Matthews and his second-in-command Lieutenant R. G. Wells contacted a number of Asians—some of them were Chinese and others belonged to the British North Borneo Constabulary—who gave them a revolver, maps, information, medical supplies and parts for a wireless receiver.

By September 1942 the intelligence network had been consolidated and extended. All information was reported to Matthews and collated for future use. He got in touch with Filipino guerrillas operating in the Sulu Archipelago and enabled parties of Australian prisoners to escape. In January 1943, when the Japanese transferred the civilian internees to Kuching, unofficial control of the armed constabulary passed to Matthews. He developed a contingency plan to overthrow the Japanese in the event of an allied landing in Borneo. At his direction, work began on the construction of a wireless transmitter.

In July 1943 four Chinese members of the organization were betrayed to the Japanese. Under torture, they admitted supplying radio parts. The Japanese arrested Matthews, Wells, Taylor and those who had helped them. The suspects were interrogated, beaten, tortured and deprived of food before being taken to Kuching. Matthews was sentenced to death, as were two members of the constabulary and six other Asians. Declining a blindfold, he was executed by a firing-squad on 2 March 1944 at Kuching and buried there. In 1946 his body was exhumed and interred in the Labuan war cemetery.

Matthews had encouraged his fellow accused throughout their ordeal. Although he knew the consequences, he refused to implicate or endanger the lives of his associates. Described as a 'prince among men', he was posthumously awarded the George Cross (1947). His wife and son survived him. Robert Anderson's portrait of Matthews is held by the School of Signals, Simpson Barracks, Melbourne. Matthews' brother Geofrey served in the army in World War II and was awarded the Distinguished Service Order.

L. Wigmore, *The Japanese Thrust* (Canb, 1957) and *They Dared Mightily* (Canb, 1963); T. Barker, *Signals* (Melb, 1987); J. F. Hardacre, The Lionel Matthews Story (ts, copy on ADB file); information from Mr L. D. Matthews, Wayville, Adel, and Lieut Col R. Wells, Rushworth, Vic.   R. E. COWLEY

MATTNER, EDWARD WILLIAM (1893-1977), soldier, farmer and politician, was born on 16 September 1893 at Oakbank, South Australia, third of four children of South Australian-born parents William Charles Mattner, gardener, and his wife Emily Louisa, née Hocking. Educated at Adelaide High School, Ted became a pupil-teacher. He attended the Teachers' Training College and the University of Adelaide in 1914, and in the following year was appointed an assistant-teacher at Kadina Public School.

On 7 September 1915 Mattner enlisted in the Australian Imperial Force. Sent to the Western Front in March 1916, he served in the 6th Army Brigade, Australian Field Artillery. At Ploegsteert, Belgium, on 1 June 1917 Corporal Mattner braved enemy shells and exploding ammunition to extinguish fires in the brigade's gun-pits; he won the Military Medal and was promoted sergeant. After his battery commander was hit during heavy German shelling on 26 September at Hooge, he took charge, evacuated the wounded and kept the Australian guns in action; he was awarded the Distinguished Conduct Medal. On 8 October he was commissioned. He won the Military Cross for his actions nineteen days later, at Zillebeke, when he again risked enemy shell-fire and led a party which rescued wounded infantrymen. In January 1918 he was promoted lieutenant. His A.I.F. appointment terminated in South Australia on 27 October 1919.

Buying a farm at Balhannah, Mattner pioneered summer potato-cropping, ran dairy cattle, bred fat lambs and grew subterranean clover. At the Methodist Church, Pirie Street, Adelaide, on 6 October 1923 he married Lorna May Prince (d.1970), a 22-year-old nurse. He was president of the Onkaparinga sub-branch of the Returned Sailors' and Soldiers' Imperial League of Australia and of the Onkaparinga district committee of the Liberal and Country League. In 1941-42 he served in the A.I.F. He rose to temporary major and acted as second-in-command of the 13th Field Regiment, Royal Australian Artillery, in Port Moresby before being invalided home. Having stood unsuccessfully for the Senate, he was chosen by the South Australian parliament as a senator to fill (from 10 October 1944) a casual vacancy. He criticized aspects of the Labor government's conduct of the war, complaining that Australian forces in New Guinea were inadequately equipped.

Defeated in 1946, Mattner was re-elected in 1949. On 12 June 1951 he became president of the Senate. He lost the government nomination in 1953 after some Liberal senators came to believe that he had allowed himself to be unduly influenced by Archie Cameron [q.v.13], the Speaker of the House of Representatives. That South Australians held both the speakership in the lower house and the presidency in the Senate may have occasioned discontent, but coalition politicians also complained about the restrictions Mattner had imposed on the provision of meals and the sale of beer and cigarettes at Parliament House. His relationship with the press gallery was stormy, and his health in the early 1950s was poor.

Mattner served on various parliamentary committees and delegations until his retirement in 1968. Five ft 9½ ins (177 cm) tall, with hazel eyes and dark hair, he was a good all-round sportsman: he had played cricket for his university and football for Sturt; later in life he enjoyed tennis and was active in the racing fraternity. He died on 21 December 1977 in the Repatriation General Hospital, Daw Park, Adelaide, and was cremated; his two daughters and four sons survived him. (Sir) Ivor Hele's portrait of Mattner is held at Parliament House, Canberra.

G. Long, *The Final Campaigns* (Canb, 1963); P. Hasluck, *The Government and the People 1942-1945* (Canb, 1970); Cwlth Parliament, *A Tribute to the Memory of Edward William Mattner* (Canb, 1978); M. Mattner et al, *The Mattners in Australia 1839-1980* (priv pub, Adel, 1981); C. J. Lloyd, *Parliament and the Press* (Melb, 1988); *Advertiser* (Adel), 22 Dec 1977; information from and papers held by Mrs M. Crisp, Wattle Park, Adel.

FRANK BONGIORNO

MAULDON, FRANK RICHARD EDWARD (1891-1961), economist, was born on 17 December 1891 at Woollahra, Sydney, son of native-born parents James Mauldon, clerk, and his wife Eliza, née Merryweather. Educated at Petersham Superior Public and Sydney Boys' High schools, Frank joined the New South Wales Registrar-General's Department as a cadet draftsman in December 1908. After matriculating in 1910, he studied part time at the University of Sydney (B.A., 1916; B.Ec., 1920; M.Ec., 1925). In November 1916 he sailed for Britain as a Young Men's Christian Association representative with the Australian Imperial Force. By June 1917 he was on the Western Front. There he was appointed Y.M.C.A. officer to the 7th Brigade. He was wounded at Sailly-le-Sec, France, in June 1918.

After the Armistice, he took charge of the Australian Y.M.C.A.'s historical records and attended the London School of Economics and Political Science. He returned to Australia in February 1920 as honorary captain, A.I.F.

In 1921 Mauldon was appointed the University of Sydney's resident tutor for the Hunter River district. Based at Newcastle, he gave numerous lectures and organized the activities of the local branch of the Workers' Educational Association of New South Wales. His master's thesis, published as *A Study in Social Economics: the Hunter River Valley* (Melbourne, 1927), was 'the first integrated' analysis of the region's resources and of its social and industrial structure. At the Methodist Church, Muswellbrook, on 6 January 1926 he married Nora Avis Edith Bowles, a 27-year-old schoolteacher.

Next month Mauldon was appointed senior lecturer in economics in the new faculty of commerce at the University of Melbourne, where he joined (Sir) Douglas Copland [q.v.13]. For *The Economics of Australian Coal* (Melbourne, 1929), Mauldon received the university's Harbison-Higinbotham [q.v.4] research scholarship (1928) and a Litt.D. (1929). In 1930, as a Rockefeller Foundation fellow, he chose to study 'structural changes in industrial organisation and public administration' in the United States of America and Canada. He published *The Rationalisation Movement and Australian Industry* (Melbourne, 1932) and a popular booklet, *The Use and Abuse of Statistics with Special Reference to Australian Economic Statistics* (Melbourne, 1933).

In September 1935 Mauldon took up the chair of economics, University of Tasmania, and the associated post of economic adviser to the Tasmanian government. As a member of the State Finance Committee, he prepared cases for the Commonwealth Grants Commission and the Australian Loan Council. He pioneered annual surveys of Tasmania's economy, and published studies of mechanization and of cost structure in Australian industry. In 1938 he moved to Canberra as research director of the Commonwealth Bureau of Census and Statistics.

Accepting the chair of economics at the University of Western Australia in 1941, Mauldon began an analysis of the State's economy and community income. His pamphlet, *Towards Economic Reconstruction* (Perth, 1941), formed part of a series, 'The Christian and the War'. Although his hope for the establishment of a faculty of economics was not fulfilled until 1954, he introduced the study of public administration to the U.W.A. and founded the Western Australian group of the British Institute of Public Administration.

Mauldon was president (1947-49) of the Economic Society of Australia and New Zealand, and a member of the Royal Economic Society and the American Economic Association. He was a prolific author of articles, reviews, pamphlets and technical publications. Temperate but persistent, he was a man of strong religious and humane convictions, with a keen interest in community activities. His 'strength as an economist was in the empirical application of his knowledge, rather than in the refinement of economic theory'. He retired in 1958. Survived by his wife, daughter and two sons, he died of cancer on 14 February 1961 in Perth and was buried in Karrakatta cemetery with Congregational forms.

F. Alexander, *Campus at Crawley* (Melb, 1963); *Economic Record*, 37, no 78, June 1961, p 207; *Gazette of Univ WA*, 2, no 1, 1961; *SMH*, 16 May, 11 Dec 1929, 10 July 1935; *Herald* (Melb), 30 Sept 1938, 23 Jan, 14 Dec 1941; *West Australian*, 16 Feb 1961; *Bulletin*, 22 Feb 1961.

MARGARET STEVEN

MAWBY, SIR MAURICE ALAN EDGAR (1904-1977), industrialist, was born on 31 August 1904 at Broken Hill, New South Wales, son of Charles Curtis Mawby, a grocer's assistant who came from England, and his South Australian-born wife Alice Maud, née Smith. Maurie attended Broken Hill District and High schools, then studied part time at the local technical college on a scholarship. He gained diplomas in metallurgy (1927) and geology (1934), and won the college's bronze medal in 1934. Often seen collecting mineral specimens and gemstones, he was known to members of the Barrier Field Naturalists' Club as 'the boy on the bicycle'. He identified seventeen of the rarer minerals among the 150 individual species around Broken Hill's complex lodes and also became an ardent naturalist, developing expertise in the botany and zoology of the West Darling area.

Mining and metals treatment were the core of Mawby's intense and vibrant working life. In 1921 he served as a junior analyst with the technical commission of inquiry which investigated the prevalence of miners' phthisis and pneumoconiosis in the metalliferous mines at Broken Hill. Next year he joined the Junction North mine as an assayer and analyst. By 1924 he was company metallurgist in charge of some eighty men. Following the closure of Junction North in 1928, Mawby joined the Zinc Corporation Ltd as a surveyor's assistant on a ventilation survey. He gained varied experience in mining engineering and metallurgical practice. At the Sulphide Street Methodist Church, Broken Hill, on 19 March 1929 he married Lena Lillian White. Promoted mill foreman, he met (1935) W. S. Robinson [q.v.11] who influenced him profoundly. Mawby and a workmate (Sir) George

Fisher (later chairman of Mount Isa Mines Ltd) toured North America, Europe and Africa in 1937-38 with Robinson's backing. Their reports shaped the design of the company's underground and metallurgical operations.

With support from Robinson, Mawby sought in the late 1930s to establish 'the green belt', and engaged Albert Morris [q.v.10] to regenerate flora and fauna in the arid, dusty country surrounding Zinc Corporation and its associated line of lode offshoot, New Broken Hill Consolidated Ltd. Other mines and the local council followed his example. As mill superintendent, he oversaw the commissioning (1939) of an innovative all-flotation plant for simultaneous separation of silver, lead, zinc, gold and copper from the Broken Hill ores. Sydney Technical College awarded him a fellowship in 1942 for his thesis on the application of the all-flotation process. During World War II Mawby directed his skills towards the discovery and increased production of strategic minerals and metals. He was technical secretary (1941-44) of the Commonwealth Copper and Bauxite Committee (Australia) which identified on King Island world-class deposits of scheelite—vital as a source for tungsten which was used as capping on anti-tank shells. In 1942 he was a member of a government mission to North America and Mexico to study metallurgical practices. He was appointed manager of New Broken Hill in 1944; he was also chief metallurgist there, and for Zinc Corporation.

Seeking wider experience, Mawby accepted appointment as director of research and development with Broken Hill Associated Smelters Pty Ltd in 1945, which entailed moving to Melbourne. At the behest of Robinson he returned to Zinc Corporation in 1946 as director of exploration and research. In 1949 Zinc Corporation in Britain merged with the Imperial Smelting Corporation Ltd to form Consolidated Zinc Corporation Ltd and an Australian subsidiary, Consolidated Zinc Pty Ltd. Following the transfer of management from London to Melbourne in 1951, Mawby became vice-chairman (1955) of C.Z.P. and a director (1956) of C.Z.C. Robinson's son Lyell was chairman of both companies.

Mawby was keen to exploit millions of tons of high-grade bauxite, the ore for refining to alumina, recently discovered by a C.Z.P. geologist at Weipa, Cape York Peninsula, Queensland, under the direction of the Australian subsidiary. L. B. Robinson, however, favoured a C.Z.C. initiative in association with the British Aluminium Co. Ltd. In December 1956 the Commonwealth Aluminium Corporation Ltd was registered in Queensland. Over the next four years complicated takeover moves from powerful American companies and counter-manoeuvring occurred. In September 1960 C.Z.P. consented to acquire the B.A.C.

component of Comalco's finance. Meanwhile Mawby and (Sir) Donald Hibberd had been negotiating (from 1958) on behalf of C.Z.P. with the Kaiser Aluminum & Chemical Corporation of the United States of America. On 12 October 1960 Kaiser agreed to enter a fifty-fifty partnership—Comalco Industries Pty Ltd was registered on 15 December—and accepted that management of Comalco would be Australian-based. On the death of L. B. Robinson in July 1961, Mawby became chairman of C.Z.P. and of Comalco, with Hibberd managing director of the latter.

In 1962 Mawby was made a director of Rio Tinto Zinc Corporation Ltd (formed by the merger of C.Z.C. with Rio Tinto Co. Ltd, London), a company with worldwide metals and metallurgical interests. Conzinc Rio Tinto of Australia Ltd (C.R.A.) was formed at the same time, by a merger of C.Z.P. with the smaller Rio Tinto Mining Co. of Australia Ltd whose main asset was a majority shareholding in Mary Kathleen Uranium Ltd, Queensland. Appointed chairman, Mawby declared that, as to Australia, C.Z.C. 'had lots of deposits, lots of work ahead, lots of development and limited money, and they [Rio Tinto] had lots of money and no projects'.

It was Mawby's strongly held and applied belief that, since the natural resources were Australian, initiative, direction and control of development should be Australian. He was strongly backed by Prime Minister (Sir) Robert Menzies and Deputy Prime Minister (Sir) John McEwen [qq.v.]. The Bell Bay aluminium plant, established in Tasmania by the State and Commonwealth governments during World War II, was acquired and enlarged; a refinery was built at Gladstone, Queensland, and a smelter at Bluff Harbour, New Zealand; at Weipa, the township, port and attendant facilities were developed. Mawby oversaw an intensified search for iron ore in the Pilbara region, Western Australia, and in 1962 a massive ore body was discovered at Mount Tom Price, Hamersley Ranges. A huge open-cut mining operation was established, with a railway connecting to it a port at Dampier. Townships were built at both places. The first shipments of ore from Dampier were made by Hamersley Iron Pty Ltd on 22 August 1966. Twenty-three million tons were extracted in 1973, and a second mine opened and a township built at Paraburdoo, 60 miles (100 km) south of Mount Tom Price.

A major copper enterprise closely followed, presenting another achievement vigorously inspired and nurtured by Mawby. He intensified the exploration of a copper-gold resource in the Panguna Valley on Bougainville Island, Territory of Papua and New Guinea. The metal deposits were of relatively low percentage, yet technological developments in open-cut mining could now render this an economically viable venture. After eight years of exploration, evaluation and construction, again including a township, mining was begun in 1972 by the C.R.A. subsidiary, Bougainville Copper Ltd. Yields would be of prime benefit —through leasing, royalties and dividend payments—to the national economy of Papua New Guinea.

Appointed C.B.E. in 1959, Mawby was knighted in 1963. He chose a wooden poppet-head, a mallee fowl and a desert pea for his coat of arms, graced with the motto of Broken Hill High School: *Palma non sine pulvere* ('no prize is won without merit'). Relinquishing executive responsibilities with C.R.A. in 1969, he remained chairman until 1974. With 23 000 employees, sales revenue of $833.5 million and dividends of $36.1 million, C.R.A. was second only to Broken Hill Proprietary Co. Ltd among Australian companies. Mawby also resigned as chairman of Hamersley Iron Pty Ltd, Bougainville Copper Ltd and Interstate Oil Ltd, and as a director of C.R.A.'s many subsidiary companies. Other directorships that he held included Australian Titan Products Pty Ltd, several insurance companies belonging to the Guardian Royal Exchange Assurance Group, Kembla Coal & Coke Pty Ltd, and the Australian Mines & Metals Association.

A student member of the Australasian Institute of Mining and Metallurgy in 1923, Mawby was president (1952-54, 1958) and received its highest honour, the bronze medal, in 1956. As an honorary member of the Institution of Mining and Metallurgy, London, he represented Australia on its council for some years and was awarded (1964) its gold medal. He was acting-president of the fifth Empire (later Commonwealth) Mining and Metallurgical Congress in 1953, and president of the eighth congress in 1965. The American Institute of Mining, Metallurgical and Petroleum Engineers bestowed honorary membership on Mawby in 1964 for his 'outstanding contribution to the world lead and zinc mining industry and for his able and constructive services in developing the raw materials resources of Australia'. He was a fellow (1969) of the Australian Academy of Science, a life member of the Canadian Institute of Mining and Metallurgy, a member of the Institution of Chemical Engineers, London, the faculty of engineering, University of Melbourne (1962-72), and the Victorian State Committee of the Commonwealth Scientific and Industrial Research Organization, and a foundation member (1967) of the Australian Mining Industry Council.

Mawby was inaugural president (1959) of Australian Mineral Industries Research Association Ltd, which established the Australian Mineral Development Laboratories for comprehensive contract-research to benefit the mining industry. He became first life member of the Australia-Japan Business Co-operation Committee for encouragement of Japanese studies in Australia. Although an early member and councillor (1968-74) of the Australian Conservation Foundation, he decided that the conservation movement leaned towards people whose attitudes were 'based on hearsay, intolerance and sheer emotionalism, with little regard to facts and citizenship responsibilities'. He withdrew from the foundation. Mawby was a multiculturalist and a humanist. 'People', he said, 'are the basis of the mining industry: the technical part is secondary ... Mining engineers don't worry so much about politics and nationalities, mining transcends all boundaries'.

His awards included an honorary doctorate of science (1955) from the New South Wales University of Technology. The University of Melbourne presented him with the Kernot [q.v.5] medal for 1965 'in recognition of his distinguished engineering achievement in exploration, research and development in the mining and metallurgical industry in and beyond the continent of Australia, and his concern for preservation of the environment'. In 1975 the Victoria Institute of Colleges conferred on him an honorary doctorate of arts and sciences. A member of the Athenaeum (Melbourne), Broken Hill, Melbourne and Commonwealth (Canberra) clubs, Mawby enjoyed tennis, swimming, shooting and motoring. He had a soft, smiling face and far-seeing eyes. His successor as chairman of C.R.A., (Sir) Roderick Carnegie, said one of 'Sir Maurice's greatest attributes was his ability to lead and be well liked in the process. He generated enthusiasm in others ... instilling a team spirit in those whom he led'. Mawby believed that in 'the ultimate sense development is concerned with people: the development of human personality and understanding is really the objective of all economic endeavour'. Survived by his wife and son, Sir Maurice died on 4 August 1977 in East Melbourne and was cremated; his estate was sworn for probate at $209 833. The National Museum of Victoria acquired his collection of minerals. His portrait by Peter Zageris is held by Comalco Ltd, Brisbane.

J. T. Woodcock (ed), *Mining and Metallurgical Practices in Australasia* (Melb, 1980); *Hist Records of Aust Science*, Nov 1980; *Herald* (Melb), 8 Aug 1977; CRA Ltd records, Univ Melb Archives; J. Ralph, Sir Maurice Mawby (ts, 1991, held by ADB, Canb); M. Pratt, Sir Maurice Mawby (taped interview, 18 Oct 1971, NL).   FRANK STRAHAN

MAXWELL, ALLAN VICTOR (1887-1975), judge, was born on 12 May 1887 at Balmain, Sydney, younger of twin sons and eighth child of native-born parents Francis Augustus Maxwell, letter-carrier, and his wife Amelia Charlotte, née Ledger. Victor was educated at Fort Street Model School and the University of Sydney (B.A., 1909; LL.B., 1913). On 8 May 1913 he was admitted to the New South Wales Bar. Practising at University Chambers, he regarded Robert Darlow Pring [q.v.11] as a mentor, whose precept of 'relevancy' he adopted. Before juries, in the Common Law jurisdiction in which he appeared chiefly as a trial lawyer, Maxwell was equally as relevant and successful. At St Mary's Catholic Cathedral on 22 October 1919 he married Sadie Margaret Lawless.

Appointed an acting District Court judge in 1927, Maxwell took silk on 19 March 1929. From that year he occasionally acted as a judge on the Supreme Court. Although he was not active in constitutional litigation, he submitted—with six other K.C.s—an unsolicited address to Governor Sir Philip Game [q.v.8] in 1932 concerning vice-regal powers to seek new advisers and so resolve the crisis with Premier Lang [q.v.9]. On 9 August 1934 Maxwell was elevated to the Supreme Court bench. He sat mainly at common law and from 1950 was also judge in Admiralty. By 1955, as senior puisne judge, he frequently presided over appeals in all jurisdictions. His judgements, laconic and unadorned, went immediately to the heart of the issues.

Maxwell's judicial career was interrupted by service as a royal commissioner on several inquiries, Federal and State. The most significant was his inquiry (1952-54) into the liquor laws in New South Wales. Sir Garfield Barwick recalled the liquor commission as a 'witch-hunt of individuals' with 'something of the reputation of the Star Chamber'; he also contended (while defending a witness charged with perjury) that the commissioner's appointment was technically defective. After hearing many witnesses and undertaking comparative investigations abroad, Maxwell produced a monumental report in February 1954. It silenced critics and stimulated a referendum on hotel trading-hours which led to legislation allowing for more civilized drinking practices and facilities throughout the State.

Deciding to retire to pursue commercial interests as chairman of Amalgamated Television Services Pty Ltd (ATN-7), Maxwell was farewelled at a ceremonial court-sitting in August 1955. Chief Justice (Sir) Kenneth Street [q.v.] described him as 'possessed of great legal learning, an acute mind, swift in decision, and with a wealth of experience and wisdom'. The solicitor-general Harold Snelling [q.v.] added that, in Maxwell's court, there 'prevailed a subtle blend of dignity and urbanity' in which summings-up for juries were lucid and simple, yet eloquent, and where 'a sparkle of wit, sometimes accompanied by a

slight if unconscious twitch of the eye, often enlivened a dull case'. Maxwell's passion for relevance in the conduct of cases was well remembered, as was the impatience he often displayed if counsel transgressed.

Maxwell was a supporter, president (1945-61) and vice-patron of the Royal Blind Society of New South Wales, and also president (from 1959) and a life governor of the Australian National Council of and for the Blind. Through these associations he became a friend of the celebrated Helen Keller. He was appointed C.M.G. in 1967. In his youth he had been an oarsman and later a keen golfer, belonging to the New South Wales Rowing Association and Royal Sydney Golf Club.

Survived by his wife, son and three daughters, Maxwell died on 5 October 1975 at St Luke's Hospital, Darlinghurst, and was cremated. His son Victor had been appointed to the Supreme Court bench in 1974.

J. M. Bennett, *A History of the Supreme Court of New South Wales* (Syd, 1974); G. Barwick, *A Radical Tory* (Syd, 1995); *State Reports* (NSW), 55, 1955, 'Memoranda'; *Aust Law J*, 29, 1956, p 292; *SMH*, 1 June 1929, 8 Aug 1934, 13 July 1952, 21, 27 Feb 1954, 23 Feb, 30 Aug, 1 Sept 1955; information from the Hon A. V. Maxwell, Elizabeth Bay, Syd.

JOHN KENNEDY MCLAUGHLIN

MAXWELL, IAN RAMSAY (1901-1979), professor of English, was born on 27 June 1901 at Hawthorn, Melbourne, third child of John Ramsay Maxwell, a banker from Scotland, and his Victorian-born wife Cecile Eleanor Elfie, née Strong. Ian was educated at Scotch College, where he gained distinction as a schoolboy poet, a prefect and editor (1919) of the *Scotch Collegian*. He matriculated with first-class honours in English and entered the University of Melbourne (B.A. Hons, 1923; LL.B., 1925). Admitted to the Bar on 16 July 1926, he practised as a barrister until 1931, an occupation which contributed to the fluent persuasiveness of his subsequent teaching. On 18 December 1926 at Queen's College chapel, Parkville, he married with Methodist forms Beatrice Muriel, daughter of Professor R. J. A. Berry [q.v.7]. She was a first-class literary scholar who tutored in English at the university and taught with distinction at several Melbourne schools. A woman of strong political convictions, she later acquired great proficiency in Russian and travelled widely.

In the pit of the Depression, Maxwell quit the law and went to Balliol College, Oxford (B.Litt., 1935). His study of the relations between French and English drama in the Renaissance became in time a book, *French Farce and John Heywood* (Melbourne, 1946).

A fellow Oxford student remembered him in these strong terms: 'he was a lion and we were mice'. In 1934-36 he taught as docent in English at the University of Copenhagen. There, he was memorable for his 'easy manner of presentation' and for his ability at wrestling. His public lecture on 'The Ring and the Book' proved not to be about Robert Browning but about literary accounts of boxing.

Maxwell was appointed in 1936 to the Department of English at the University of Sydney where he remained until 1945. He was president of the university union in 1939. His teaching combined a concern for linguistic and grammatical precision—in which he had enjoyed lively exchanges with C. A. Bodelsen while in Copenhagen—with enthusiastic illumination of a wide range of literature. During World War II he became air-raid precautions warden in the Great Quad, in which role he grew tomatoes atop the tower. In 1942 his family retreated to The Hermitage, in the hills beyond Healesville, Victoria, and Maxwell frequently spent whole weeks in his university study.

For a man who communicated his love of literature so powerfully, Maxwell wrote few poems. They included the often-sung ballad, 'Good Rum's Me Darlin', and the rhythmically haunting lyric, 'Vespers', which was used by H. M. Green [q.v.14] to open his influential anthology, *Modern Australian Poetry* (Melbourne, 1946). There was also a ballade, with the oddly typical refrain, 'Brown ale, spring onions, and a slice of cheese'.

In 1946 Maxwell returned to his native Victoria, having been appointed to the chair of English language and literature at the University of Melbourne. He was dean of arts in 1948-50 and one of the leading academic opponents, with Professor (Sir) Roy Wright, of the proposal (1950) to ban the Communist Party of Australia. It was a source of great pride that he could work in the department of English with A. D. Hope, whose loss to the new chair at Canberra University College in 1951 he felt very keenly.

Although his teaching interests ranged back to French romances, the Border ballads and Milton, Maxwell was particularly notable for expanding the modern offerings in the English course; he gave enchanting lectures, for instance, on W. B. Yeats and T. S. Eliot, E. M. Forster and Aldous Huxley. Maxwell's bravura performance of Robert Burns's 'Tam o'Shanter' was famous, as was the occasional shedding of an emphatic tear. Only late in the piece did he realize that one could lecture on a poem without knowing it by heart. At informal gatherings he would sing affectingly.

Maxwell held his chair at Melbourne until the end of February 1968, surviving sturdily into the new Leavisite era of literary moral-ism. He published little, being chiefly famous for his spellbinding lectures and for his latterly acquired enthusiasm for Old Icelandic language and literature. His study in the Old Arts building was legendary for its aged furniture, bookbinding equipment, overproof rum and 'deliquescent bananas', though few colleagues could be persuaded to sample the slab of dried shark which he brought back from one trip to Iceland. In 1966 he was appointed (chevalier) to the Icelandic Order of the Falcon. He derived joy from his remote bush camp at Howqua, whence came the story of his climbing a tree with a knife between his teeth, seeking to cut the throats of cormorants. His enthusiasm for axemanship was pronounced, and in one letter he wrote: 'some swine stole my axe, and I had a mild headache for a day and a half as I thought out what I should like to do to him'.

After his retirement, Maxwell was widely said to spend six and a half days at the university instead of seven. His clubbable, informal reading groups in the Norse sagas continued unabated, and there was a private edition of his useful pamphlet on rhythm and metre, *Scansion Scanned* (Melbourne, 1967). Survived by his wife, two sons and two daughters, he died on 4 September 1979 at Heidelberg and was cremated. His old friend A. D. Hope had justly immortalized him in a sonnet:

The man of action in the scholar's chair,
Like Gunnar gentle and like Ari wise.

G. Turville-Petre and J. S. Martin (eds), *Iceland and the Mediaeval World* (Melb, 1974); H. Dow (ed), *Memories of Melbourne University* (Melb, 1983); *Age* (Melb), 21 June 1952; Maxwell papers *and* Vice-Chancellor George Paton's files (Univ Melb Archives); Maxwell mss (LaTL); family papers (held by Mr M. Maxwell, Balwyn, Melb).

CHRIS WALLACE-CRABBE

MAXWELL, MAY (1876-1977), actress and journalist, was born on 8 October 1876 at Sandhurst (Bendigo), Victoria, eldest of nine children of David Johnston Moorhead, a stockbroker from Ireland, and his Melbourne-born wife Madeline, née Hannah. Baptized Mary and known to her family as Maisie, she took music and elocution lessons, recited in public from the age of 10, and attended the Corporate High School.

About 1895, yearning for the more vibrant life of the city, Miss Moorhead left Bendigo for Melbourne to try her luck on the stage. She earned money for lessons with the actress Mrs G. B. W. Lewis by working as a nursery governess and as a lady's companion to 'impossible women seated on high chairs with skirts all around them, drinking tea with their gloves on'. More to her spirited taste were the lessons she herself gave in elocution or swinging the clubs at a shilling a time. Adopting the stage-name 'Maisie Maxwell', she toured as a soubrette, *ingénue* or comedienne. She played with A. E. (Bert) Bailey and William Anderson's [qq.v.7] company at the Lyceum in Sydney and the Theatre Royal, Melbourne.

In mid-1907, while on tour with Anderson, Maisie began writing regular contributions for Perth's *Sunday Times* and soon realized that journalism was a more stable career than the theatre. After a season at the Theatre Royal, she changed her name—yet again—to May (more suitable for a by-line) and took a substantial cut in pay to join *Table Talk* at ten shillings a week. In 1910 she was invited to edit the Melbourne *Herald*'s weekly page for women, which had been started by Katharine Susannah Prichard [q.v.11]. At the end of 1921 (Sir) Keith Murdoch [q.v.10] asked her to make the page a daily feature.

Maxwell wrote with independence, intelligence, good sense and an impatience with silly social niceties. Her journalism was characterized by initiative and plain talking. Although she covered the high-society round of balls, parties and royal tours, she insisted on writing her notes openly, and on being allowed to wear evening dress and to mingle with guests at Government House. She interviewed female prisoners, campaigned to have nurses' training cut by one year, and championed those women in public life who did more than go to parties. Throughout her twenty-four years with the *Herald*, she was closely associated with the National Council of Women.

In 1911, within four months of its foundation, Maxwell had joined the Australian Journalists' Association as its second female member. She served (1925-27) on the A.J.A.'s Victorian committee and became an honorary life member (1960). In 1969 she was awarded the British Empire medal for her services to journalism. But the honour that must have pleased her most was the rare printers' rally she had received at the *Herald* when she retired in May 1934.

After leaving daily journalism, Maxwell continued to work as a freelance writer and broadcaster for radio-stations 3XY, 3UZ and 3KZ. On the eve of her 100th birthday—still sharply alert but having long given up her trademark red wig for a cap of silver hair—she wrote in longhand a cheerful and candid column of reminiscence. The *Herald* published it next day, virtually unedited. She died on 24 July 1977 at Jolimont and was buried in Box Hill cemetery.

Herald & Weekly Times House News, May 1934; *Age* (Melb), 27 June 1969, 6, 9 Oct 1976; *Herald* (Melb), 1 Mar 1973, 8 Aug, 12 Nov 1974, 7 Oct 1975, 8 Oct 1976; *Australian*, 8 Oct 1976; Maxwell papers (held by Ms M. Maxwell, East Melb).

SALLY A. WHITE

MAY, ALAN WALTER SYDNEY (1916-1966), entomologist, was born on 22 June 1916 at Ipswich, Queensland, third child of Australian-born parents Sydney Lionel May [q.v.10], music teacher, and his wife Mary Ellen, née Williams. Mary's forebears had been among the first settlers in the Brisbane Valley. After attending West Ipswich State and Ipswich Grammar schools, Alan entered Emmanuel College, University of Queensland (B.Sc.Agr., 1939; M.Sc.Agr., 1948; Ph.D., 1961). In 1936 he was granted leave of absence from the faculty to work as a temporary assistant in the entomology section of the Queensland Department of Agriculture and Stock. Returning to the university in 1937 on a (W. B.) Slade [q.v.11] scholarship, he graduated with first-class honours and later studied part time.

On 1 April 1939 May was appointed assistant research officer in the Department of Agriculture and Stock (Primary Industries). At St Andrew's Presbyterian Church, Brisbane, on 4 April 1942 he married Beryl Eileen Short, a 23-year-old clerk. He served at Normanton, Nambour, Gayndah and (from 1947) at Toowoomba where he was promoted senior entomologist in 1954. Transferred to administrative duties, he was posted to Brisbane in 1961 as assistant to W. J. S. Sloan, the director of plant industry. In January 1966 he became assistant to Dr J. M. Harvey, director-general of primary industries.

May's research on tropical fruit-flies (*Tephritidae*) won international acclaim for his understanding of the biology of these insects and their native-host relationships. He worked untiringly on the systematic connections of Australian and New Guinea species of the pest, and his taxonomic descriptions remain valid. His extensive knowledge of entomology spanned the bionomics of the newly introduced buffalo-fly, as well as pest-management strategies for citrus and deciduous fruits, cereal crops, cotton and pastures. As sole or senior author, he published fifty-two scientific papers on fruit-flies and other insects of importance in agricultural entomology.

Held in high esteem professionally and in the wider community, May was president (1960) of the Queensland Entomological Society, foundation secretary (1965) of the Australian Entomological Society and a member of the Royal Society of Queensland. In addition, he presided over the Toowoomba Naturalists' Club for some years and was a committee-member of the Queensland branch of the Australian Institute of Agricultural Science. He was an excellent companion and a valued mentor of younger entomologists; his ethical standards were exemplary, and he expected his junior and senior colleagues to share them.

May's interests included music, literature and natural science. He also enjoyed propagating native plants and incorporating them in his well-ordered garden. Powerfully built, he had rowed stroke in the university IV; he was a good tennis-player and subsequently became an above-average golfer. He died of leukemia on 2 April 1966 at the Princess Alexandra Hospital, South Brisbane, and was cremated; his wife and four daughters survived him.

Aust Entomological Soc, *News Bulletin*, 2, pt 2, 1966, p 51; *Courier-Mail*, 4 Apr 1966; information from Mrs B. E. May, St Lucia, Brisb; personal knowledge.   NEIL HEATHER

MAYNARD, CHARLES FREDERICK (1879-1946), Aboriginal activist, was born on 4 July 1879 at Hinton, New South Wales, third child of William Maynard, an English-born labourer, and his native-born wife Mary, née Phillips. His grandmother, Mary, was a Wonnarua woman from the Hunter River who had married Jean Phillipe (anglicized as Phillips), an emigrant from Mauritius. After their mother's death in 1884, Fred and his sisters were raised with strict discipline by a Protestant minister at Maitland. Fred read voraciously. He worked as a bullock-driver, drover and photographer, travelling as far as the Kimberleys, Western Australia.

By 1914 Maynard had become a wharf labourer in Sydney and an active member of the Waterside Workers Federation of Australia. He spent much time at the Domain and other public-speaking venues. In the early 1920s he united with his countrymen from the Hunter to make a public protest against the assault on Aborigines' rights; they spoke at local meetings, and lobbied the Sydney and regional press. Maynard contacted a White woman, Elizabeth McKenzie-Hatton. She was prominent in establishing (1923) a refuge at Homebush to protect Aboriginal 'apprentices' who had absconded or been branded 'incorrigible'. Bitterly opposed by the Aborigines Protection Board and kept under police surveillance, the 'Home' functioned for two years. Early in 1925 Maynard and others helped Aboriginal families at Nambucca Heads to rescue their own children from Stuart Island where they were in the board's custody.

In 1925 Maynard launched the Australian Aboriginal Progressive Association. Initially, its office-bearers were all men from the mid-north coast, except for McKenzie-Hatton who was organizing secretary. The group protested against the revocation of north-coast farming reserves; they also demanded that children no longer be separated from their families, or indentured as domestics and menial labourers. The A.A.P.A. advocated that all Aboriginal families should receive inalienable grants of farming land within their traditional country, that their children should have free entry to public schools, and that Aborigines should control any administrative body affecting their lives.

Members of the association made lengthy organizing trips; meetings in coastal towns attracted numerous Aborigines. Maynard and McKenzie-Hatton wrote letters to the press and to politicians. With Jane Duren, an Aboriginal leader from Batemans Bay, Maynard participated in debates with missionaries and public figures who were proposing changes to the administration of Aboriginal affairs. He wrote to Aborigines throughout the State who had been injured by the board's policies, such as young girls who had been raped while indentured.

The Depression undermined the A.A.P.A.'s ability to continue its campaigns into the 1930s. At Darlinghurst, Sydney, on 14 June 1928 Maynard had married with Methodist forms Minnie Critchley, a 32-year-old English-woman and the daughter of a miner. He gradually withdrew from public life to provide for his growing family. An injury on the docks in the 1930s made it increasingly difficult for him to work. He died of diabetes mellitus on 9 September 1946 at the Mental Hospital, Rydalmere, and was buried with Presbyterian forms in Rookwood cemetery; his wife, two sons and two daughters survived him.

H. Goodall, *Invasion to Embassy* (Syd, 1976); S. Baldwin (ed), *Unsung Heroes and Heroines of Australia* (Melb, 1988).   HEATHER GOODALL

MAYNARD, FARNHAM EDWARD (1882-1973), Anglican clergyman, was born on 15 November 1882 at Islington, London, fifth child of Charles Dudley Maynard, surgeon, and his wife Emily Darell Louisa, née McAdam. Farnham attended St Paul's School, London, and studied engineering at the University of London (B.Sc., 1904). After teaching at Ely Grammar School, he prepared for holy orders at Ely Theological College. He was made deacon in the Church of England on 23 December 1906 and ordained priest on 22 December 1907. His first appointment was to the parish church of St Michael and All Angels, Bell Green, Sydenham, London.

Recruited by Bishop Halford [q.v.14] for work in the diocese of Rockhampton, Maynard arrived in Brisbane in March 1910 and was immediately sent to minister at Gladstone.

After two years there, he was made rector of St Mary's, Mount Morgan. He withdrew from the regular exercise of his priesthood for three months and became a goldminer in order to experience at first hand the conditions of such workers; during this brief interval he joined the Queensland branch of the Australian Workers' Union and received permission from Halford to act as a mission priest of the diocese. In 1921-26 Maynard served in the diocese of Brisbane, for most of the period as rector of All Saints, Wickham Terrace, to which he was appointed by Archbishop Sharp [q.v.11].

From 1926 to 1964 Maynard was vicar at St Peter's, Eastern Hill, Melbourne. There he became well known as a leader of the Anglo-Catholic movement within the Church of England in Australia. His approach to liturgical matters was always controlled by his theology and scholarship. Inheriting a somewhat flamboyant pattern of worship from his predecessor E. S. Hughes [q.v.9], he at once sought to restrain it. He experienced considerable opposition from the parish's mission church, St Mary's, Fitzroy, whose congregation he thought did not properly fulfil its ministry to the poor. His attempt to settle this problem by installing Father Gerard Tucker [q.v.12] proved unsuccessful and he eventually handed the mission over to the Community of the Holy Name.

Popularly known as 'F.E.M.', Maynard was deeply and widely read in theology, ecclesiology, history and philosophy. His concern with liturgy and worship was kindled by leaders of the Anglo-Catholic movement, while he traced his interest in history to Mandell Creighton, bishop of London. Bishop Charles Gore's determination to apply Catholic principles to social problems and contemporary issues influenced him throughout his life. Much in demand as a preacher and speaker within and without the Anglican Church, 'F.E.M.' reached a wide circle of people through his preaching and pastoral counselling. He exercised further scholarly influence as editor of the *Australian Church Quarterly*. His own publications included *Economics and the Kingdom of God* (1929) and *The Continuity of the Church of England* (1939), as well as numerous articles and essays. In 1941 he was made a fellow of the Australian College of Theology. He was rural dean of Melbourne in 1940-50 and a canon of St Paul's Cathedral in 1942-64.

Apart from his ecclesiastical reputation, Maynard was recognized for his interest in politics, although he remained strictly unaligned with any political party. An outspoken protagonist of socialism, he feared that Australia would be swamped by fascism during the 1930s. In World War II he supported the struggle against fascism, but was passionate in his desire for peace, and to this end was willing to work with communist organizations and to speak on platforms with fellow travellers. He arranged a series of talks in 1944 on socialism, held in the chapter house at St Paul's Cathedral, and was one of three main speakers. The addresses were published as *A Fair Hearing for Socialism*. It was a controversial initiative, as were his visits to the Soviet Union and China in 1952.

Maynard was a minor patron of artists. For many years his great friend Arthur Nickson [q.v.] was organist and director of music at St Peter's, Eastern Hill. Maynard also encouraged and employed Napier Waller [q.v.12] and Andor Mészáros [q.v.], as well as local goldsmiths, silversmiths and embroiderers. Trained as an engineer, he had a practical side to his nature: while in Queensland he had patented a machine for making blinds and developed an orchard at Yeppoon. His early diaries recorded his fondness for walking, bathing and gymnastics. In 1964, in failing health, Canon Maynard retired from St Peter's, Eastern Hill. He died on 24 January 1973 at Hawthorn and was cremated.

R. S. Gibson, *My Years in the Communist Party* (Melb, 1966); J. Handfield, *Friends and Brothers* (Melb, 1980); C. Holden, *From Tories at Prayer to Socialists at Mass* (Melb, 1996); *Aust Church Q*, Easter 1973; *Age* (Melb), *Herald* (Melb), *Sun News-Pictorial*, 26 Jan 1973; F. E. Maynard papers (St Peter's, Eastern Hill, Archives); personal knowledge.   ALBERT B. MCPHERSON

MAYO, SIR HERBERT (1885-1972), judge, was born on 3 June 1885 in Morphett Street, Adelaide, fourth child of George Gibbes Mayo, a South Australian-born civil engineer, and his Scottish-born wife Henrietta Mary, née Donaldson. George and Helen Mayo [qq.v.10] were his eldest brother and eldest sister. Herbert was educated at the Collegiate School of St Peter, Trinity College, University of Melbourne, and the University of Adelaide (LL.B., 1909). He was admitted to the South Australian Bar on 17 December 1909. At her father's Aldgate home on 17 May 1911 he married Clarice Gwendoline Thomson Melrose (d.1957); they were to have five children. Mayo practised as a solicitor at Lameroo and Pinnaroo before co-founding (1914) Mayo, [(Sir) Stanley] Murray [q.v.] & Cudmore [q.v.13]; he maintained practices in the city and the country until 1919 when he settled in Adelaide. Sir Josiah Symon [q.v.12] later entered the partnership. In 1929 Mayo became a partner in Magarey, Finlayson, Mayo & Astley. He took silk in the following year.

A council-member (1924-41) of the Law Society of South Australia, Mayo served as president in 1932-33, 1934-35 and 1939-41, and sat on many of its committees. He worked tirelessly for the creation of a national body to represent the legal profession. His advocacy led to the formation (1933) of the Australian Council, of which he was foundation president (1933-34); after it became the Law Council of Australia, he was vice-president (1940-42) of that body. He was joint-editor for South Australia of the *Australian Law Journal*. At the University of Adelaide he examined (1919-24) in the law of contracts, and lectured in jurisprudence (1925 and 1927-37) and commercial law (1929-34)—a heavy load for a busy practitioner. His material was very good and he was one of the first to issue printed notes, but he spoke in a monotone which impaired the concentration of his students.

On 30 March 1942 Mayo was appointed a judge of the Supreme Court of South Australia, replacing (Sir) Mellis Napier [q.v.] on his becoming chief justice. Mayo's appointment preceded the institution (1944) of a retiring age and he continued to serve until 30 June 1966. Knighted in 1948, he acted as chief justice from 18 May to 10 December 1957 and deputized for the governor on twenty-five occasions. A fine equity lawyer, he was courteous and pleasant to appear before, although he customarily inserted in most of his written judgements at least one word not in common usage, which sent counsel scurrying for their dictionaries.

On 3 June 1958 at the Presbyterian Church, Tusmore, Mayo married Gwen Alister Brookes, née McInnes, a 49-year-old widow. He was president of numerous religious, charitable and learned organizations, including the British and Foreign Bible Society and the State branch of the Royal Geographical Society of Australasia. In addition, he was chancellor of the Anglican dioceses of Adelaide and Willochra. Survived by his wife, and by the three daughters and a son of his first marriage, Sir Herbert died on 1 October 1972 at his Hyde Park home and was cremated. His other son Lieutenant Eric Mayo was killed when H.M.A.S. *Sydney* was sunk in 1941.

Aust Law J, 15, 13 Mar 1942; *News* (Adel), 30 June 1966; *Advertiser* (Adel), 2 Mar 1942, 10 June 1948, 13 Aug, 22 Dec 1965; Law Soc of SA Archives *and* Supreme Court of SA Archives, Adel, *and* Univ Adel Archives; information from the Very Rev D. Richardson, Adel; personal knowledge.

HOWARD ZELLING

MAYOR, BERYL ANNEAR; *see* BRYANT

MEAGHER, JAMES ANTHONY (1894-1975), solicitor and raconteur, was born on 10 June 1894 in Dublin, son of Philip Meagher,

grocer, and his wife Mary, née Maher. Educated at Clongowes Wood College, Kildare, and at University College, Dublin (B.A., 1914; LL.B., 1916, National University of Ireland), Jim won the Solicitors' Apprentices' Debating Society's silver medal for oratory. He was admitted as a solicitor of the Supreme Court in Ireland on 7 December 1916 and practised in a partnership in Westmoreland Street. A classicist and fluent linguist, he moved in literary circles and signed reviews with his initials, becoming known to his intimates as 'Jam'. Meagher spent a good deal of time on the Continent, including six months in Prague where he taught Esperanto. Frequenting Paris, he was one of the admirers surrounding James Joyce, who once punned about his absence: *Malhereusement, jam est marmalade*. At the Holy Cross Church, Glasgow, Scotland, on 25 March 1926 Meagher married Angelina (Angela) Valentine Kemp with Catholic rites.

Problems within the partnership led him to emigrate to New South Wales. Admitted as a solicitor by the Supreme Court on 28 October 1926, he practised at Tamworth, Sydney (1930) and Tumut (1931) before settling at 107 Liverpool Street, Sydney, in December 1931. He took A. R. De Coek into partnership in 1933. Meagher's most lucrative clients included the madam Tilly Devine [q.v.8], as well as Kings Cross prostitutes and criminals. His wit enlivened the courts. On one occasion, two bruised and battered prostitutes sued each other for assault. The magistrate, unable to decide who was at fault, said in exasperation to the opposing solicitors: 'Surely this can be settled outside the court?' 'With respect', replied Meagher, 'in view of my client's appearance, I don't think she could possibly go another round!' He appeared for Fergan O'Sullivan—formerly H. V. Evatt's [q.v.14] press secretary—before the royal commission on espionage in 1954. As honorary solicitor for the Fellowship of Australian Writers he saved D'Arcy Niland [q.v.] from having to pay most of a literary prize in taxation. Meagher enjoyed the company of women, and was among the first to employ female articled clerks.

Often the centre of an animated and laughing group, he loved to converse (and lecture) in 'his soft Dublin accent' on his favourite subjects—Joyce, W. B. Yeats, George Moore, and their Dublin. Some people claimed that Jimmy Doyle in Joyce's story, 'After the Race', in *Dubliners* (London, 1914) was based on Meagher, but the tale had previously appeared on 17 December 1904 in the *Irish Homestead*. A familiar figure at Pakie's [q.v. A. Macdougall] Club, Meagher belonged to the Kabeiroi of the University of Sydney and regularly invited young admirers to dine at the Millions Club. He took part in the

Australian Broadcasting Commission's radio programmes, 'Spotlight on Literature' and 'Quality Street', and later as a panellist on its television programme, 'Would You Believe?'

Through his love of books, Meagher met writers who became his friends. Angela was a splendid cook. At Neutral Bay they held regular Sunday evening 'at-homes', attended by—among others—Constance Robertson, Sydney Tomholt, Frank Dalby Davison, Flora Eldershaw [qq.v.11,12,13,14] and Marjorie Barnard. The only visitor permitted to sit in his favourite wing-chair was Miles Franklin [q.v.8]. Meagher loved the stage and helped May Hollinworth [q.v.14] to establish the Metropolitan Theatre (1946). He was president (1959-60) of the English Association, and a founding council-member (1954-75) and president (1957-58) of the Aisling Society of Sydney which was established to promote Irish culture. His own writings were few: he contributed occasionally to *Southerly* and *Meanjin*, and in 1966 published a translation in rhyming couplets of Ovid's *The Art of Love*.

Meagher's varied interests included golf, playing chess with Cecil Purdy [q.v.] and Gregory Koshnitsky, and bridge with Lionel Murphy, solving crossword puzzles and 'fighting the odds'. Knowledgeable about Japanese prints, he was asked by James Lawson [q.v.10] to authenticate signatures on pieces for sale. Meagher was 'short and portly', with smooth, pale hair. A vain man, he wore 'dark and very well tailored suits', a buttonhole and a monocle, and carried a cane or tightly-furled umbrella. His liberal-mindedness did not extend to his family, whom he expected to behave with Victorian propriety. He moved to Double Bay and, after retiring in 1974, acted as a consultant. Survived by his wife, daughter and younger son, he died on 23 July 1975 at Calvary Hospital, Kogarah, and was cremated. His diaries were deliberately destroyed.

N. Keesing, *Riding the Elephant* (Syd, 1988); *Southerly*, Dec 1975, p 441; Clongowes Wood College, Kildare, Ireland, *Clongownian*, 1976, p 153; *SMH*, 2 Sept, 2, 3 Oct 1954, 22 Aug 1966; information from, and papers held, by Mrs I. Meagher, North Adel; information from Dr R. Curnow, Univ Syd, Mrs M. Prill, Paddington, and Mr P. Tesoriero, Cremorne, Syd.   MARTHA RUTLEDGE

MEAGHER, SIR THOMAS WILLIAM (1902-1979), medical practitioner and lord mayor, was born on 26 March 1902 at Menzies, Western Australia, son of Victorian-born parents Philip Meagher, cordial manufacturer, and his wife Annie, née Jennings. The family moved to West Leederville and Tom attended (1911-19) Christian Brothers' College, Perth. After completing first-year science at the University of Western Australia

in 1920, he studied medicine at the University of Melbourne (M.B., B.S., 1925). During his four years at Newman College he competed in its athletics, football, swimming and rowing teams. He rowed bow, winning college colours in 1923. In addition, he was a member (1923-24) of the Newman students' general committee.

Returning to Western Australia, Meagher worked as a house surgeon at the Perth (1925) and Children's (1926) hospitals before establishing a general practice at Victoria Park in 1927. At the chapel of Christian Brothers' College, Perth, on 8 March that year he married Marguerite Winifred Hough (d.1952), a schoolteacher; they were to have six children. In 1937 he was elected to represent Victoria Park Ward on Perth City Council. In 1939 he was appointed lord mayor. An honorary captain in the Australian Army Medical Corps Reserve, he was declared unfit for service in World War II.

As a close friend of Prime Minister Curtin [q.v.13], Meagher was acutely conscious of the nation's perilous situation and Perth's wartime vulnerability. He used his position to organize and publicly lead the city's war effort. He ensured that most of the war funds set up in Perth were initiated at council chambers, with the provision of secretarial and financial assistance. In 1941-42 the city council prepared to face the threat of a Japanese invasion by concentrating its works programme on the maintenance of essential city services and building air-raid protection for the people of Perth. Meagher was active in about twenty patriotic and philanthropic war organizations, a commitment which saw him attending two or three functions on any night. In 1945, when announcing that he would not stand for re-election, he declared that his mayoralty had been 'a war-time measure'. He was knighted in 1947.

On 18 November 1953, again at C.B.C. chapel, Meagher married Doris Ita Walsh, a clerk. The pace and scope of his public activities did not decrease after the war. From the mid-1940s to the early 1970s he played a key role in a wide range of state and civil organizations. He was not only a figurehead, but an active office-bearer and skilled chairman, keen to foster development, well-informed and astute in his judgements, and prepared to use his considerable influence in Perth's government and professional circles to benefit the organizations he led. He was fortunate that his energy and public spirit were exercised through almost three decades of postwar prosperity which provided opportunities for improved urban amenities and public events.

Sir Thomas lent his status as patron to several ex-service organizations, including the State branch of the Totally and Permanently

Disabled Soldiers' Association of Australia and of the Ex-Prisoners of War and Relatives Association. He was president (1955-58) of the Western Australian branch of the Royal Empire Society. While president (1945-47) of the Royal Automobile Club of Western Australia, he helped to set up R.A.C. Insurance Pty Ltd and the National Safety Council of Western Australia. He was also president (1954-79) of the Kings Park Board and oversaw the introduction of new attractions to the park: a children's playground, botanic garden, annual wildflower exhibition, floral clock, memorial to pioneer women, barbecue facilities, viewing tower and lakes, as well as the completion of the State war memorial. A councillor of the Order of St John, Meagher was appointed a knight of grace in 1955. He also became involved in the management of Karrakatta cemetery (trustee from 1951, chairman 1971) and Pinnaroo Valley memorial park (trustee from 1962, chairman 1971).

As chairman of trustees (1959-73) of the Western Australian Museum, Meagher worked closely with its director David Ride to develop the museum. A new building was constructed in Francis Street to enlarge the Perth complex, the museum expanded to new sites at Fremantle and regional centres, an Aboriginal sites department was opened and maritime museum work began. Meagher remained involved in sport, particularly in the administration of amateur athletics. President (1947-71) of the Western Australian division of the Australian Olympic Federation, he served as vice-president of the State division of the Australian British Empire and Commonwealth Games Association. He was an official timekeeper for athletics at the 1956 Olympic Games in Melbourne and chief timekeeper for athletics at the 1962 British Empire and Commonwealth Games in Perth.

In the course of all these public activities Meagher continued to practise medicine. He enjoyed fishing, yachting and gardening, and was vice-patron of the National Rose Society of Western Australia. He travelled as often as he could, making twenty-nine voyages, mainly to Asian ports, as ship's doctor. Survived by his wife, and by the four sons and two daughters of his first marriage, he died on 27 June 1979 at Shenton Park and was buried in Karrakatta cemetery.

D. Dettman, *A Brief History of the Royal Association of Justices of Western Australia (Inc), 1916-1967* (Perth, 1967); Newman College, Univ Melb, *Newman* (Melb, 1925); Perth City Council, *Annual Report*, 1939-45; WA Museum, *Your Museum*, 2, no 1, 1973; *Road Patrol*, 18/33, Aug 1979, p 5; *West Australian*, 14 Dec 1943, 12 June 1947, 16 Feb 1959, 29-30 June 1979; information from Ms Sara Meagher, Mosman Park, Perth.

LENORE LAYMAN

MEARES, MARY EMMA GOLDSMITH (1889-1964), welfare worker, was born on 29 August 1889 at Yule Station, near Roebourne, Western Australia, third of nine children of Western Australian-born parents John Goldsmith Meares, grazier, and his wife Emily Ellen, née Withnell (d.1946). Emma Mary Withnell [q.v.6] was her grandmother. Mary was educated privately and at Shelford Ladies' College, Melbourne. She joined the fledgling Western Australian division of the Australian Branch of the British Red Cross Society in 1914, served in a Voluntary Aid Detachment and became a member (1915) of the Soldiers' Welcome Committee. Devastated after the deaths of her sweetheart and her twin brother Douglas in World War I, she devoted herself to the welfare of wounded and blinded servicemen. The Returned Sailors' and Soldiers' (and Airmen's) Imperial League of Australia awarded her a certificate of merit in 1921.

With adequate private means to accommodate her natural generosity, Meares lived with her mother in the family home at West Perth. She belonged to the Perth Repertory Club, liked city life and was fond of people. Her world centred on meetings, hospital visits, Christmas parties, bridge evenings, jumble stalls, raffle tickets, poppy sales and flower days. Appointed M.B.E. in 1935, she was awarded King George V's silver jubilee (1935) and King George VI's coronation (1937) medals. In 1937 she commanded No.507 V.A.D. which won the inaugural McWhae Cup for efficiency.

During World War II Meares joined (1944) the British Young Women's Christian Association and served as a welfare worker in Ceylon (Sri Lanka). Appointed a welfare officer with the rank of captain in the British Army, she spent a year at Assam, India, and was later engaged by the Indian Army to manage a club at Ranchi for recuperating prisoners of war. Back in Perth, she was elected the Red Cross's local director of hospital visiting. As foundation president (1948-58) of the Western Australian ex-servicewomen's sub-branch of the R.S.S. & A.I.L.A., she was proud when it won the Newdegate [q.v.11] Cup in 1953. She was the first woman to be elected a member (1949-59) of the State executive of the R.S.S. & A.I.L.A. and was the only woman on its medical appeal board.

Considered 'plain' (until she smiled), Meares was of average height and solid build; she had fairish hair and pale blue eyes, and wore spectacles. She intimidated young V.A.D.s, but self-styled 'wingies and stumpies' adored her. Each Anzac Day, for forty-one years, she organized transport for incapacitated ex-service men and women. On other occasions she arranged outings to the theatre, the races, and to football and cricket matches. In 1949 she was elevated to O.B.E. Meares was made a life member of the State branches of the Maimed and Limbless Ex-servicemen's Association, the women's auxiliary of the R.S.S. & A.I.L.A. and the South African and Imperial Veterans' Association. She died on 23 June 1964 in her West Perth home and was buried with Anglican rites in Karrakatta cemetery.

N. Stewart, *As I Remember Them* (Perth, 1987); *Listening Post*, Aug 1964; *Western Mail* (Perth), 15 Dec 1930; *West Australian*, 1 Jan 1935, 30 Sept 1949, 24 June 1964; *Daily News* (Perth), 1 Jan 1935; WA Premier's Dept, Acc 1704 77/35 (PRO, WA); Ex-Servicewomen's sub-branch RSL minutes, Jan 1948-Jan 1955 (ANZAC House, Perth); personal knowledge.   WENDY BIRMAN

MEDLEY, SIR JOHN DUDLEY GIBBS (1891-1962), vice-chancellor, was born on 19 April 1891 at Oxford, England, eldest of seven children of Dudley Julius Medley, a tutor at Keble College who became professor of history at the University of Glasgow, and his wife Isabel Alice, née Gibbs. His paternal grandfather had been a major general and engineer in the Indian Army. Many of his maternal ancestors had been merchants and bankers.

From the start his parents called him Jack. An exceptionally intelligent child, he was pushed inexorably towards an intellectual career. After attending four preparatory schools, he won a scholarship in 1904 to Winchester College. Presumably suffering from osteomyelitis, he underwent several operations and spent little time at Winchester in his first two years. At home he read voraciously and began to collect books, Kipling and Dickens especially. The following four years were triumphant: successive prizes in English and classics, acting in a Shakespearian group, editing the *Wykehamist*, joint school captain and a scholarship to New College, Oxford.

Medley's physical condition did not prevent him from playing tennis, cricket and golf. He took *Literae Humaniores* ('Greats'), and one of his tutors was Gilbert Murray [q.v.10]. Jack frequented the Murray household, meeting eminent men, and was taken to Italy in a family party. 'I owe him more than I can ever express', Medley recalled. Here lay one major source of his critical, liberal outlook. In 1914 he took a B.A. with first-class honours (although the degree, and his M.A., were not conferred until 1938) and was awarded a research fellowship at Corpus Christi College, Cambridge, which had to be postponed because of World War I.

Medley immediately enlisted in the British Army and was commissioned on 15 October 1914 in the 6th (Glamorgan) Battalion, Welch Regiment. His lameness became obvious and

early in 1915 he was appointed a railway transport officer in France and Belgium. As a staff officer under Major General (Sir) Thomas Bridges [q.v.7], he witnessed the mass slaughter of the Somme offensive. He was a liaison officer at French headquarters from late 1917 and ended the war as a major. Medley treasured a booklet of verses he strung together to vent his frustration and contempt for the stupidity of senior base officers. Inevitably, most of his friends and acquaintances having been slain or maimed, he felt guilty as a survivor, and was tortured by doubts.

On 15 September 1916 at Southwark Cathedral, London, Medley married EMMELINE MARY (MOLLY) (1891-1977), daughter of (Sir) Francis Newbolt and niece of the poet Sir Henry Newbolt; her mother Alice (Lady) Newbolt was an outstanding worker in baby welfare. In 1920 Medley joined the family firm of Antony Gibbs & Sons, London. Assuming an early return, he cheerfully accepted a move to the Australian branch, Gibbs, Bright & Co., and reached Melbourne in March 1920. From 1922 to 1925 he managed the small Adelaide branch until he was transferred to the Sydney head office. His standing was uncertain: he was apparently on approval for a junior partnership, but lacked the necessary capital and was plagued by ill health. He fell out with his colleagues and early in 1930 was dismissed on generous terms.

Attracted by the prospects of country life and of working together, the Medleys took over Tudor House, an Anglican preparatory school at Moss Vale, New South Wales, which catered principally for the sons of rural landowners. During the Depression the school reached the point of collapse. The Medleys opened in 1931 with nineteen pupils. Six years later there were seventy-five boarders and a long waiting-list, substantial building additions had been made, and Tudor House had become an establishment showplace. The Medleys enjoyed 'a cheerful hardy life' and governed with imagination and energy.

Early in 1938 the University of Melbourne sought a successor to (Sir) Raymond Priestley [q.v.11], its first full-time vice-chancellor. Most of the professorial board supported Professor (Sir) Douglas Copland [q.v.13], for a long conflict between professors and all-powerful council had come to a head. Council could not find a strong alternative candidate until (Sir) Russell Grimwade, Sir Alan Newton [qq.v.9,11] and (Sir) James Darling suggested Medley. He seemed an unlikely candidate, yet he moved freely in vice-regal, Anglican, United Australia Party and pastoral and business circles, belonged to the best clubs and was a sportsman. A first-class Oxford graduate, he had done his duty during the war and was a gentleman of style, wit and charm. The council's selection committee recommended Copland, but after an angry debate Medley was elected by one vote (of 29).

Neither side was adequately informed. Medley turned out to be not a bandbox aristocrat but a liberal, indeed a radical. Within a year he plotted successfully to have the interventionist chancellor Sir James Barrett replaced by Sir John Latham [qq.v.7,10]. Within three years, aided especially by Professors (Sir) Kenneth Bailey [q.v.13] and (Sir) Samuel Wadham and by a new chancellor (Sir) Charles Lowe [qq.v.], he negotiated basic shifts of authority from council to professors.

Medley became a first-rate public speaker. Witty and self-deprecating, he soon had audiences 'in a simmer of chuckling appreciation'. He spoke fervently about high ideals and the sacred duties of teachers, explicitly expounding liberal principles. In 1940 Melbourne University Press published his *Addresses 1939-40* and his Smyth [q.v.12] lecture, 'Education for uncertainty' (*Australian Educational Studies*, second series).

World War II brought university development to a full stop. Student numbers dwindled; many senior staff undertook national tasks; teaching suffered; scientists massively contributed to the war effort; major building had to be abandoned. The Australian Broadcasting Commission called on Medley in mid-1940 to give a series of talks aimed at raising national morale. In later talks he was among the first to discuss postwar reconstruction, advocating a planned society based on co-operation.

Medley was already active in the Educational Reform Association, and in the Australian Council for Educational Research (president 1948-59) which in 1943 published his pamphlet, *Education for Democracy*. As chairman (from 1941) of the Australian Services Education Council, he was much more than a mere figurehead. In June 1942 he became a commissioner of the A.B.C. From 1940 he had been a trustee of the Public Library, museums and National Gallery of Victoria. He was also elected president of the Melbourne Club for 1942-43. Late in 1942 he broke down and took three months leave.

Determined to treat students as adults, Medley earned unusual affection and respect, as he did from most of the staff. John Foster [q.v.14], the able and gregarious registrar, was a close companion and guide. Medley grew in decisiveness, balancing strong leadership with sensitivity; his even-handedness and keeping of promises were recognized. He brought about 'newspaper chairs' in fine arts and architecture, and was an active talent-spotter for staff recruits.

For a decade Medley chaired the Vice-Chancellors' Committee. It met regularly in 1943-44 to consider the activities of the newly founded Universities Commission and the planning of the Commonwealth Reconstruction Training Scheme. The committee made a fractious bullock-team. During the uncertainty about when the war would end, 1945 was a year of desperate planning in the knowledge that the Commonwealth inevitably had to finance emergency expansion. In 1946 Melbourne established its temporary branch at Mildura; in 1945 it had introduced the Ph.D. degree. Medley was a key adviser to prime ministers Ben Chifley [q.v.13] and (Sir) Robert Menzies [q.v.] on national policy on universities. In 1946-51 he was deputy-chairman of the interim council of the Australian National University.

Medley at last was able to take long leave abroad in 1947. In 1948 he was knighted, made an honorary D.C.L. (University of Oxford) and elected a fellow of the Royal Society of Arts. That year he led the Melbourne delegation to the Congress of the Universities of the British Empire, held at Oxford, and was prominent throughout. He had always lived on his nerves, was prone to go under when stressed, and increasingly suffered from lumbago and sciatica. His annual escape was to fly-fish in distant mountains. By 1950 he had to be helped up the stairs at home. Sir John arranged for his formal retirement in mid-1951, after six months leave. His colleagues paid heartfelt tributes, for he left a university high in morale and confidence. In April the university conferred on him an honorary LL.D.

In retirement the Medleys lived in Wickham, their *pisé* house at Harkaway, originally acquired as a weekend retreat. Jack moved the toast to the University of Melbourne at its centenary banquet. He remained an A.B.C. commissioner until 1960, working with chairman Sir Richard Boyer [q.v.13] to insist on intellectual and cultural quality. He chaired the National Gallery Trust in 1952-57 and resigned in 1958 from what he had once unguardedly referred to as 'an inferno of unbridled passion'. He remained active in the A.C.E.R., the Australian Red Cross Society, the Good Neighbour Council and other bodies. His occasional verse was privately published as *Stolne and Surreptitious Verses* (1952), followed by *An Australian Alphabet* (1953). In his last years he enjoyed making colloquial translations of Horace and Catullus. His most astounding activity was to write for the Saturday *Age* nearly 500 weekly essays, about anything and everything, which won a devoted public. He constantly defended the young and was determined not to become an angry old man.

Survived by his wife, son and daughter, Jack Medley died suddenly on 26 September 1962 at Harkaway and was cremated. His portrait by Max Meldrum [q.v.10] is held by the university. Molly Medley had been entirely supportive of her husband. A skilled hostess and president (for ten years) of the Lady Huntingfield Free Kindergarten, she read poetry well, and occasionally contributed to the *Age*. They were precisely of that generation which suffered to the full from two world wars and were deeply saddened, after their golden youth, by the terrible damage Britain had sustained. They had wondered why they had several times decided to remain in Australia. Molly concluded that there was 'some innate kinship with the people which we could not do without'.

G. Serle, *Sir John Medley* (Melb, 1993); Medley papers (Univ Melb Archives).

GEOFFREY SERLE*

MEDWORTH, FRANK CHARLES (1892-1947), artist, was born on 22 August 1892 at Southwark, London, son of Charles Joseph Medworth, journeyman carpenter, and his wife Lilian Rachel, née Rickward. Frank attended school at Brighton and was apprenticed to an advertiser. From 1912 he studied at the Camberwell School of Arts and Crafts where his closest associates were David Jones and H. F. W. Hawkins [q.v.14]. On 2 September 1914 he enlisted in the East Surrey Regiment. He served on the Western Front (where he received a severe head wound) and with the King's African Rifles in East Africa. Demobilized on 1 July 1919, he continued his studies, at the Westminster Technical Institute and School of Art. He taught at that school (1923-34) and at the City of Hull College of Arts and Crafts (1934-38). Alert to the needs of students, he published three books, *Animal Drawing* (London, 1934), *Perspective* (London, 1936) and *Figure Drawing* (London, 1940).

Medworth exhibited principally with the South London Group, the Royal Society of British Artists, the English Wood Engraving Society and the Royal Academy of Arts. Combining high technical skills with a wide-ranging means of expression—at times humorous and at others mildly Modernist—he was a satirist, illustrator, craftsman, muralist and portraitist. He also undertook many painting tours in Spain and France. At the register office, Hammersmith, London, on 5 July 1929 he married Muriel Doris Anderson. With other artists he held studio and home showings, including two with his wife. His first one-man exhibition, in March 1930 at the Goupil Gallery, comprised fifty-six drawings on the theme of 'Mother and Child', mostly of Muriel with their daughter Diana.

On 23 December 1938 Medworth left England with his family to take up the post of lecturer-in-charge of the art department at East Sydney Technical College. He expanded the staff, and brought a dynamism similar to that of its first principal, Lucien Henry [q.v.4]. It was part of Medworth's policy to act as 'a sort of mild irritant amongst his staff and even amongst his students'. In addition, he gave radio broadcasts for the Australian Broadcasting Commission, wrote articles, and lectured on design in modern living. In 1944-45 Medworth was also acting-director of the National Art Gallery of New South Wales. A small, animated man, of 'restless enterprise and fecundity of expression', he was an inspiring teacher who thought the best thing that could be taught was a sense of self-criticism.

His exhibition of 120 works in June 1939 had taken Sydney's art critics by surprise because of its unexpected versatility. Medworth belonged to and exhibited with the Society of Artists, the Contemporary Group, the Royal Art Society of New South Wales, the Australian Academy of Art, the Contemporary Art Society of Australia, and the Australian Water-Colour Institute. He also shared two exhibitions with Muriel (1941 and 1947). His position as vice-president of the People's Council for Culture led in October 1947 to allegations in the Commonwealth and State parliaments that he was a communist when he was named as an Australian delegate to a United Nations Educational, Scientific and Cultural Organization conference in Mexico City.

Medworth committed suicide by slashing his wrists on 11 November 1947 in the Reforma Hotel, Mexico City. His wife and two daughters survived him. In London his works are represented in the Victoria and Albert Museum and the British Museum; in Australia they are held by most of the major public galleries. The A.G.N.S.W. has drawings of Medworth by Hawkins (1922) and Douglas Dundas (1940).

B. Dolman (ed), *A Dictionary of Contemporary British Artists* (Lond, 1929); H. Badham, *A Study of Australian Art* (Syd, 1949); B. Stratton (ed), *Douglas Dundas Remembers* (Syd, 1974); *PD* (Cwlth), 23 and 24 Oct 1947, pp 1232, 1346, 3 Dec 1948, p 3970; *PD* (NSW), 19 Nov 1947, p 1287; *Technical Gazette of NSW*, 27, pt 1, 1939; *SMH*, 10 Apr 1939, 14, 25 Oct, 7, 13 Nov 1947; Medworth file, History Unit (Dept of Technical and Further Education, Syd); Art Gallery of NSW Archives; Medworth file, A3300/7, item 625 (AA, Canb); information from Mrs D. McCartney-Filgate, Georgica, NSW.

CAMERON SPARKS

MEEHAN, ARTHUR VINCENT (1890-1955), orthopaedic surgeon, was born on 12 July 1890 at Marrickville, Sydney, seventh child of native-born parents Joseph Meehan, letter carrier, and his wife Elizabeth, née Poole. Arthur was educated at St Mary's Cathedral High School and the University of Sydney (M.B., 1914). He then served as a resident medical officer at Sydney Hospital.

On 1 March 1916 Meehan was appointed captain, Australian Army Medical Corps, Australian Imperial Force. In December he joined the 9th Field Ambulance on the Western Front. Promoted major in April 1917, he was transferred next month to the 11th F.A. On 13 October he was wounded at Passchendaele, Belgium, which led to the amputation of his right foot. He was posted to the staff of the 2nd Australian Auxiliary Hospital, Southall, England, in March 1918 and mentioned in dispatches in May. After gaining orthopaedic experience with (Sir) Robert Jones at the Royal Southern Hospital, Liverpool, Meehan was elected a fellow (1919) of the Royal College of Surgeons, Edinburgh. His A.I.F. appointment terminated in Australia on 19 July 1919. As a temporary lieutenant colonel he commanded (1919-21) the 27th A.A.H., Brisbane, on a part-time basis.

On 14 June 1919 at St Vincent's Catholic Church, Ashfield, Sydney, Meehan married Marion Kenny. Moving permanently to Brisbane in 1920, he took up private practice in Wickham Terrace. That year, in the Brisbane Children's Hospital, he set up an orthopaedic unit which he was to supervise until 1931. At Brisbane General Hospital, he was honorary orthopaedic surgeon from 1922 to 1928. At the Mater Misericordiae, he was associated with the children's hospital (from 1931) and with the hospital for adults (from 1938); he resigned in 1950 and joined the honorary consulting staff. During World War II he had been a consultant to the Australian Military Forces and the Royal Australian Air Force, and orthopaedic surgeon at the 112th Base Hospital, Greenslopes.

Regarded as the doyen of orthopaedic surgeons in Queensland, Meehan was the first in the State to devote himself solely to the speciality. His enthusiasm and skill attracted many disciples. He was a fellow (1928) of the Royal Australasian College of Surgeons, a fellow (1935) of the British Orthopaedic Association, and a founding member of the Australian Orthopaedic Association which he served as vice-president (1937) and president (1942-44). A frequent contributor to the *Medical Journal of Australia*, he served (1948-50) on the British editorial board of the *Journal of Bone and Joint Surgery*. As an honorary member of, and consultant to, the Queensland branch of the Limbless Soldiers' Association, he was noted for his compassion and understanding.

Meehan was honest, sincere, and a devout Catholic. He enjoyed music, the theatre, swimming and tennis (in spite of his dis-

ability). A deranged former patient shot and killed him on 1 December 1955 in his rooms in Wickham Terrace. Survived by his wife, four daughters and two sons, Meehan was buried in Nudgee cemetery. Both his sons became medical practitioners.

H. Barry, *Orthopaedics in Australia* (Syd, 1983); R. Patrick, *A History of Health & Medicine in Queensland 1824-1960* (Brisb, 1987); R. L. Doherty (ed), *A Medical School for Queensland* (Brisb, 1986); *MJA*, 10 Mar 1956, p 423. M. JOHN THEARLE

MELLOR, DAVID PAVER (1903-1980), professor of chemistry, was born on 19 March 1903 at Launceston, Tasmania, eldest of four children of Joseph Frederick William Mellor, a miner from England, and his Tasmanian-born wife Amy Florence Sarah, née Russell. David was educated at Launceston State High School and the University of Tasmania (B.Sc., 1926; M.Sc., 1928; D.Sc., 1945). After he graduated, he was employed as a chemist at the Electrolytic Zinc Co. of Australasia Ltd, Risdon, and in 1927 was the company's research scholar. In the following year he held a research fellowship at the Commonwealth Solar Observatory, Mount Stromlo, Canberra. He was appointed assistant-lecturer in chemistry at the University of Sydney in 1929. At St Chad's Anglican Church, Cremorne, on 17 August that year he married Nina Hilda Moses, a kindergarten teacher.

Mellor's research interests were mainly concerned with the properties and structures of metal complex (coordination) compounds, a field to which he made significant contributions. In 1938 he spent a period of study-leave as a research fellow with Professor Linus Pauling at the California Institute of Technology, Pasadena, United States of America. He returned to the University of Sydney with a fresh outlook on inorganic chemistry which was to have a notable effect on two young men, Frank Dwyer [q.v.14] and (Sir) Ronald Nyholm [q.v.]. Mellor wrote numerous scientific papers and produced three books: *The Role of Science and Industry* (Canberra, 1958), *The Evolution of the Atomic Theory* (New York, 1971), and *Chelating Agents and Metal Chelates* (New York, 1964) which he edited with Dwyer. He also wrote for the *Australian Dictionary of Biography*.

Promoted reader in 1948, Mellor was appointed to the second chair of chemistry at the New South Wales University of Technology (University of New South Wales) in 1955. He was head (1956-68) of the school of chemistry and dean (1968-69) of the faculty of science. Beyond the university, he made considerable contributions to chemical education as chief examiner in chemistry for the Leaving certificate and chief examiner in science for the Higher School certificate, and as a member of the Secondary Schools Board, the council of the U.N.S.W. and the interim council of Macquarie University. In addition, he chaired the publications committee of the *Australian Journal of Science* and the United Nations Educational, Scientific and Cultural Organization's Australian committee for natural sciences. He was president of the Sydney University Chemical Society and of the Royal Society of New South Wales (1941).

Mellor received a number of honours and awards: the Royal Australian Chemical Institute's H. G. Smith [q.v.11] and Leighton medals in 1949 and 1975 respectively, the R.S.N.S.W.'s medal (1954) and the University of New South Wales Chemical Society's Dwyer memorial medal (1969). In appreciation of his work the U.N.S.W. endowed in 1970 the David Mellor chemical education fund for a lecture and medal. He delivered the Liversidge [q.v.5] lecture in 1951 for the Australian and New Zealand Association for the Advancement of Science, and the inaugural E. E. Kurth memorial lecture in 1977 at the University of Tasmania.

Although barely of middle height, Mellor had a distinguished bearing. If he had a fault, it was a lack of decisive action. An earnest, kindly and quietly spoken man, not without a sense of humour, he was held in affection by his former students and staff. One of his unusual interests was the synthesis of gems; he was patron of the Gemmological Association of Australia. Following his retirement in 1969, he lived at Lindfield and enjoyed photography. He died on 9 January 1980 at Royal North Shore Hospital and was cremated; his wife and two daughters survived him.

G. B. Kauffman (ed), *Coordination Chemistry* (Washington, DC, 1994); *J and Procs of the Roy Soc of NSW*, 113, 1980, p 103; *Chemistry in Aust*, 47, no 3, 1980, p 115; *Polyhedron* (Oxford), 1985, p 1337; *Univ Tas News*, no 39, 30 Sept 1977, p 7; *SMH*, 22 Aug 1958.   STANLEY E. LIVINGSTONE

MELROSE, ALEXANDER (1865-1944), solicitor, writer and patron of the arts, was born on 16 May 1865 at Mount Pleasant, South Australia, eighth child of Scottish-born parents George Melrose, sheep-farmer, and his wife Euphemia, née Thomson. (Sir) John Melrose [q.v.10] was his elder brother; Charles James Melrose [q.v.10] and (Sir) Stanley Murray [q.v.] were his nephews. Alex was educated at Prince Alfred College (1877-82) and the University of Adelaide (LL.B., 1886). Articled to (Sir) Josiah Symon [q.v.12] in 1883, he was admitted to the Bar on 23 July 1886 and practised (from 1890) as a solicitor, initially with Robert Homburg [q.v.9] and later

with Homburg's son. The partnership continued almost until Melrose's death.

A bespectacled, quiet and retiring bachelor, Melrose joined the Adelaide Club in 1898. He was a lively writer whose literary heroes were Thomas Carlyle, George Bernard Shaw and G. K. Chesterton. Melrose's early work appeared in Adelaide newspapers. As 'A. [or Alex] Somerville', he wrote plays, *A Woman Unknown, The Prince Peter's Half-mile, The Usual Three*, and *The Adventure of an Adventuress* which was performed by the Adelaide Repertory Theatre company on 17 November 1917 in the Queen's Hall and published that year in Melbourne. He was a governor of the Botanic Garden, Adelaide (from 1927), and of the Public Library, Museum and Art Gallery of South Australia (1928-40). In 1929 Melrose was commissioned by the State government to report on literature and the fine arts in North America, Europe and Britain. He wrote a number of poems about his travels and expressed his homesickness in 'The Sound of Water Running in the Tank' and 'Nostalgia'.

After Melrose returned to Adelaide, he became president (1930) of the South Australian branch of the Royal Institution for the Blind; his brother John had lost his sight in 1898. During the 1930s Melrose adopted the pseudonym, 'Bill O'C', and wrote verse for the *Bulletin* that was characterized by a racy larrikinism; he also published *Song and Slapstick* (1934) which included a satirical view of the law. In 1936 he composed the centenary tribute, *To the Pioneers*, a fund-raising publication for the Pioneers' Association of South Australia, of which he was elected vice-president (1937). From 1921 Melrose had donated money for annual prizes that were presented under the auspices of the (Royal) South Australian Society of Arts. He gave £10 000 in 1934 for extensions to the newly constituted National Gallery of South Australia and chaired (1940-44) its board. In 1936 he was awarded the medal of the Society of Artists, Sydney, in recognition of his services to art.

Miss Alice Effie Ferguson, Melrose's niece, lived with him and cared for him at Chiverton, Wattle Park. He died there on 2 September 1944 and was buried in the Church of England cemetery, Mount Pleasant; his estate was sworn for probate in South Australia and New South Wales at £279 906. He bequeathed most of his collection of paintings to the N.G.S.A. Every three years between 1949 and 1967 the society awarded the Melrose prize for portrait or figure painting.

Bd of Governors of Public Lib, Museum and Art Gallery of SA, *Annual Report*, 1928-29; National Gallery of SA, *Bulletin*, 6 (1944), no 2, 11 (1949), no 1; Art Gallery Bd of SA, *Annual Report*, 1945-46; *Advertiser* (Adel), 19 Nov 1917, 4 Sept 1944; *Mail* (Adel), 2 Sept 1944; *Chronicle* (Adel), 7 Sept 1944; National Gallery of SA, Minutes, 1944-49; Adelaide

Repertory Theatre, programmes (Performing Arts Collection, Adel Festival Centre).

SUZANNE EDGAR

MELVILLE, GERTRUDE MARY (1884-1959), housewife and politician, was born on 7 October 1884 at Hamilton Saw Mills, Port Macquarie, New South Wales, second child of native-born parents John Joseph Day, sawyer, and his wife Mary Ann, née Dunbar. Gertrude attended St Peter's convent school, Surry Hills, Sydney, run by the Sisters of the Good Samaritan. At St Patrick's Catholic Church, Sydney, on 2 December 1903 she married Arthur Melville, a 33-year-old labourer from New Zealand; they were to have five sons after 1915.

Introduced to politics by her husband, Mrs Melville joined the Paddington branch of the Australian Labor Party in 1904. She remained a stalwart member of the party, campaigning throughout her life for the rights of women and children. Child endowment in New South Wales is said to have originated in a motion she moved at her local branch (Randwick) in 1918. She served (1922-26 and 1950-52) on the party's central executive. In 1925 she gained A.L.P. pre-selection, but was defeated for the Legislative Assembly seat of Eastern Suburbs by five candidates, including Millicent Preston Stanley [q.v.11]. When J. T. Lang [q.v.9] split the party, Melville joined the Federal Labor Party and campaigned against Lang in the 1932 elections.

Melville was a justice of peace, a member (from 1943) of the Board of Health, an alderman (1944-48) on the Cabramatta and Canley Vale Municipal Council, a director of Fairfield District Hospital, and vice-president of the Cabramatta branch of the Country Women's Association. She was also an executive-member of the State divisions of the New Settlers' League of Australia and its successor, the Good Neighbour Council. While president (1947-56) of the Labor Women's Central Organising Committee, she contributed to its *Souvenir of Golden Jubilee Conference* (1954) and opposed the industrial groups when they attempted to control the Labor Party in the upheavals of the 1950s.

In September 1952 Mrs Melville had been elected to fill a casual vacancy in the Legislative Council occasioned by the death of E. H. Farrar [q.v.8]. A 'staunch advocate of women's rights', she committed herself to being a 'Parliamentary spokesman [sic] for the women'. She achieved a political status that belied her small stature and homely appearance. Eventually known as 'the grand old lady of the Labor Party', she was well respected as an energetic battler who believed that the party stood for justice and repre-

sented 'the little people'. In parliament she fought for housing, hospitals, child welfare and equal pay for women. She became the centre of a controversy in 1958 when she accused some members of the police force of brutality, and asserted that they had made wrongful arrests and given false evidence. Her party loyalty, however, was so strong that she voted against a motion for a judicial inquiry into the police force because it was moved by the Opposition.

Survived by her husband and sons, Gertrude Melville died on 21 August 1959 at Prince Henry Hospital, Little Bay, and was buried in Randwick cemetery. Her portrait by Miriam MacRae is held by the Legislative Council.

M. Sawer and M. Simms, *A Woman's Place* (Syd, 1993); *PD* (NSW), 12 Aug 1953, 6 Apr 1954, 22 Mar, 26 Oct 1955, 2 Aug 1956, 27 Aug, 4 Sept 1958, 25 Aug 1959; *SMH*, 7 May 1925, 11 Sept 1952, 28 Aug-8 Sept 1958, 22, 25 Aug 1959; *Sun-Herald*, 25 Nov 1956.

LEONORA RITTER

MENDELSOHN, OSCAR ADOLF (1896-1978), polymath, bon vivant and public analyst, was born on 12 July 1896 at Nanango, Queensland, sixth child of Saul Mendelsohn, a storekeeper from Berlin, and his Brisbane-born wife Abigail, née Rosensweig. Educated at All Saints Grammar School, Melbourne, and at Petersham Superior Public School, Sydney, Oscar studied chemistry at Sydney Technical College where he was influenced by (Sir) Ian Clunies Ross [q.v.13]. He found work as a shift-chemist with G. & C. Hoskins [q.v.9] Ltd, Lithgow, and then as a teacher at All Saints College, Bathurst. On 29 December 1915 he enlisted as a gunner in the Australian Imperial Force. Based in England (from September 1916), he was found to be medically unfit for general service. Mendelsohn was discharged from the army on 27 May 1917 to take up an appointment as chemist in the Chief Postal Censor's Department, London. In December he returned to Australia and obtained a post at Army Headquarters, Melbourne, as an assistant-censor specializing in the chemistry of espionage.

At St Andrew's Anglican Church, Summer Hill, Sydney, on 14 April 1916 Mendelsohn had married 18-year-old Merle Winifred Todd; they were to be divorced in 1932. In 1919 he enrolled at the University of Melbourne (B.Sc., 1923); there, he was impressed by Professor W. A. Osborne [q.v.11], 'the first true food scientist I met'. On graduating, he borrowed money to set up an analytical laboratory; over the next decade he developed an unrivalled knowledge of the food industry and of alcoholic beverages. O. A. Mendelsohn & Co., public analysts, gradually expanded

349

from Flinders Street, Melbourne, to Sydney, Brisbane and Adelaide.

Mendelsohn represented the Commonwealth government at the World Dairy Congress in London (1928) and undertook a mission abroad for the Victorian government to investigate the potato industry (1929). He travelled extensively between the wars, particularly to the United States of America. In 1929 and at a by-election in the following year he stood unsuccessfully as a Nationalist candidate for the seat of Caulfield in the Legislative Assembly. On 7 December 1939 he married Edna Millward Smale at the Church of Christ, Swanston Street, Melbourne; she was aged 23.

During World War II Mendelsohn served (1942-45) in the Royal Australian Air Force; he rose to acting squadron leader as a staff officer and chemical adviser at Air Force Headquarters, Melbourne. From 1947 to 1959 he ran a grazing property at Lara, near Geelong, previously owned by the Armytage [qq.v.1,3] family. In his later years Mendelsohn was professionally known for his work in forensic chemistry, and as an expert graphologist and consultant on disputed documents. His monograph, *Suspected Documents and Outrageous Liars* (Melbourne, 1976), was crammed with anecdotes of human frailty.

Outside his professional field, Mendelsohn had wide interests. He gained a national reputation for promoting civilized attitudes to eating and drinking, and founded the long-running Fellowship of Trenchermen. Among his many works were *The Earnest Drinker* (London, 1950), *Drinking with Pepys* (London, 1963), *The Dictionary of Drinkers and Drinking* (London, 1965) and *From Cellar and Kitchen* (Melbourne, 1968). One curious work included 1187 synonyms for the adjective 'drunk'. He possessed an excellent palate for wine, detested 'Black Velvet' (stout and champagne) and favoured Calvados.

Under the name of Oscar 'Milsen', Mendelsohn composed and published songs and other musical pieces. He conducted the Royal Australian Air Force choir (1943-46), and founded and conducted the Pentridge gaol choir (1961-64) and the South Melbourne Choral Society. His book, *A Waltz with Matilda* (Melbourne, 1966), advanced the now discounted theory that Australia's alternative anthem was written not by A. B. Paterson [q.v.11] but by Harry Nathan, organist at the Anglican Cathedral, Townsville, Queensland. An art collector and friend of artists such as Max Meldrum and Percy Leason [qq.v.10], Mendelsohn donated many works to the National Gallery of Victoria.

As State president (1964-71) of the Fellowship of Australian Writers, Mendelsohn presided over an increase in membership from fifty to five hundred, and played a major part in the establishment of a range of literary prizes, including the Barbara Ramsden [q.v.] and the Victorian short story awards. He was an inveterate contributor to reviews and newspapers, and a familiar voice on Australian Broadcasting Commission programmes. Described as a man who flourished on controversy and enjoyed being a lone voice, he delighted in public speaking and was good at it. As honorary vice-president of the Humanist Society, he attacked—through the *Rationalist* —efforts to introduce religion in state schools. From World War II he was an active member of the Australian Labor Party.

Oscar Mendelsohn was foundation president of the Australian Association of Consulting Chemists, a founding member (fellow 1962) of the Royal Australian Chemical Institute, a councillor of the Australian Consumers' Association and the initiator of the Australian Pure Food Society. In 1975 he was appointed O.B.E. Survived by his wife, their son and two daughters, and by the two sons of his first marriage, he died on 5 January 1978 at Heidelberg and was cremated.

R. D. Magoffin, *Fair Dinkum Matilda* (Charters Towers, Qld, 1973); *Epicurean*, June 1968, p 60, Feb-Mar 1975, p 57; *Meanjin Q*, 35, no 2, 1976, p 211; *Aust Author*, 10, no 2, Apr 1978, p 39; *Chemistry in Aust*, 45, no 7, July 1978, p 243; *Herald* (Melb), 14 Nov 1959, 19 Jan 1967, 11 Jan 1978; *SMH*, 7, 12 Sept 1966, 1 Jan 1975, 3 Aug 1976; *Age* (Melb), 7 Jan 1978; Mendelsohn papers, MS 1857 (NL).

RAY MARGINSON

MENHENNITT, CLIFFORD INCH (1912-1979), judge, was born on 30 October 1912 at North Fitzroy, Melbourne, eldest of four children of Victorian-born parents Frederick William Inch Menhennitt, manufacturing chemist, and his wife Mabel Clara, née Wilkins. Cliff attended Moreland State School and Scotch College. He matriculated with first-class honours in history and in economics, gained several scholarships and entered Ormond [q.v.5] College, University of Melbourne (LL.B., 1933; LL.M., 1935). In 1933 he won the Supreme Court Judges' prize and the E. J. B. Nunn scholarship. On 1 May 1935 Menhennitt was admitted to practise as a barrister and solicitor of the Supreme Court of Victoria. He was articled to W. B. Pearce of Alexander Grant, Dickson & Pearce, in which he later became a partner. In 1942-44 he served as a Commonwealth assistant-director of road transport.

At Scotch College chapel on 26 October 1940 Menhennitt had married with Presbyterian forms Elizabeth Lois (d.1975), sister of his close friend Howard Norman. They remained childless, and enjoyed shared interests in music, art and architecture. He retained his association with the university where he lectured (1935-38 and 1945-47) in constitutional law, and served as a member (1941-65) of the standing committee of convocation, warden (1965-68) of convocation and a member (1968-73) of council.

As a barrister-at-law (from 26 July 1946), Menhennitt read in D. M. Campbell's chambers and quickly gained recognition for his scholarship and competence. In 1948 he was briefed as junior counsel for the Commonwealth government in the Bank nationalization case before both the High Court of Australia and the Privy Council. He subsequently took on many suits involving interstate transport and Commonwealth employees' compensation issues. Gazetted a Q.C. for Victoria in 1957 and for New South Wales in 1958, he appeared in constitutional cases before the High Court and the Privy Council. His practice extended over wide areas of civil law, in which his reputation for thoroughness of preparation and clarity of presentation and expression were often favourably commented upon by opposing counsel. He was a member (1965) and vice-chairman (1966) of the Victorian Bar Council, and an executive-member and treasurer (1965-66) of the Law Council of Australia.

On 27 April 1966 Menhennitt was appointed an acting-judge of the Supreme Court of Victoria. He was confirmed in office on 17 October. His application to his responsibilities was marked by scholarship, industry, thoroughness in research of historical authorities, and development of legal doctrines to meet changing social and economic conditions. Although by temperament he was quick in thought and expression—as well as physical movements—as a trial judge his patience and courtesy with counsel and witnesses appeared unlimited. He speedily identified the basic issues between litigants. After working during the luncheon recess and into the early hours of the morning, he frequently delivered his well-considered judgement immediately upon the conclusion of the trial, thereby avoiding delays and uncertainty for contending parties.

Menhennitt's zeal for the supremacy of the rule of law and for the protection of the rights of the individual was evident when he adjudicated conflicts between the state and the citizen. He developed and reformulated several old common law doctrines. Foremost, perhaps, was his ruling in *R.* v. *Davidson* (1969) that an abortion was lawfully justified if it were (a) 'necessary to preserve the woman from a serious danger to her life or her physical or mental health (not being merely the normal dangers of pregnancy and childbirth)' and (b) 'in circumstances not out of proportion to the danger to be averted'. Known among lawyers as the Menhennitt ruling, it

became binding in all cases of a person tried in Victoria for having unlawfully used an instrument with intent to procure the miscarriage of a woman.

Throughout thirteen years of judicial office, Menhennitt loyally served the law, regardless of his own convenience and well-being. A member of the Supreme Court library committee, he initiated and encouraged the extension of the collection to include works of historical interest. He also served on the Chief Justice's Law Reform Committee, and as a member of the Victoria Law Foundation did much to advance its standing. Menhennitt belonged to the Australian Club. His short vacations were spent walking along the foreshore of the south coast of New South Wales where he gained considerable knowledge of local history. He died of hypertensive heart disease on 29 October 1979 at his North Balwyn home and was cremated; his estate was sworn for probate at $963 937.

Cwlth Law Reports, 76, 1948, p 1, 79, 1950, p 497; *Aust Law J*, 40, 29 July 1966, p 106, 31 Oct 1966, p 215; 54, no 3, 1980, p 107; *Vic Law Reports*, 1969, p 667, 1979, p vii; *Age* (Melb), 18 Oct 1966; Scotch College (Melb) Archives.   WILLIAM KAYE

MENZIES, SIR DOUGLAS IAN (1907-1974), judge, was born on 7 September 1907 at Ballarat, Victoria, second child and eldest son of Ballarat-born parents Francis Menzies, Congregational minister, and his wife Annie Wilson, née Copeland. Frank and (Sir) Robert Menzies [qq.v.] were his cousins. Douglas moved with his family to Tasmania, and was awarded a bursary to Samuel Clemes's [q.v.8] Leslie House School, Hobart; he later attended Hobart and Devonport high schools, and was dux of the latter. Proceeding to the University of Melbourne (LL.B., 1928; LL.M., 1969), he won the Jessie Leggatt scholarship (1927), and the J. B. Nunn scholarship and Supreme Court Judges' prize (1928). In 1929, at Queen's College, he was awarded the oratory medal endowed by the William Quick [q.v.5] Club. Menzies was to become patron (1966) of the club and to provide funds for the continuation of the award. He was president of the Law Students' Society of Victoria in 1930-31.

Completing his articles with E. C. Rigby [q.v.11], Menzies was admitted as a solicitor on 1 May 1930. Due to the Depression, he postponed his application and was not admitted to the Bar until 16 February 1932, after which he read in the chambers of E. H. Hudson. During the 1930s Menzies developed a practice in commercial and taxation law, gaining a reputation as a 'junior with great promise'. His ability to master sophisticated arguments and issues, coupled with his enormous capacity for work, made him one of the leading advocates of his generation. On 18 December 1936 at the Presbyterian Church, Canterbury, he married Helen Jean Borland (d.1966), who was also the child of a clergyman.

With Bernard O'Dowd [q.v.11], Menzies wrote *Victorian Company Law and Practice* (Melbourne, 1940), a text that became the standard in the field. In 1941-45 he acted as secretary to the Defence Committee and the Chiefs of Staff Committee; his legal training enabled him to formulate submissions to the War Cabinet and Advisory War Council in a way which earned the 'warmest praise'. Meanwhile, he lectured in procedure, evidence and company law at the University of Melbourne.

When World War II ended, Menzies' legal practice expanded rapidly. In 1948-49 he represented the State of Victoria in the High Court of Australia and the Privy Council, London, in the Bank nationalization case. He took silk on 22 November 1949. Over the next nine years he made fifty appearances in the High Court. A member of a small Australian Bar that established itself at the Privy Council, he travelled to London almost every year to argue appeals from Australian jurisdictions. Later in life, he expressed his hope that the ties with the Privy Council would be preserved, as a means of 'giving fresh life to organic links which are rooted in history, in tradition, in loyalty, and in the common endeavour'. Menzies' constant opponent and companion in London was (Sir) Garfield Barwick. The two became lifelong friends. In *Newton* v. *Federal Commissioner of Taxation* (1958), Menzies inflicted on Barwick his greatest defeat before the Privy Council.

The Boilermakers' case in the High Court (1956) tested Menzies' skill in advocacy. He knew that, to win, he would have to reverse Chief Justice Sir Owen Dixon's [q.v.14] strong view on the doctrine of the separation of powers. After rejecting Menzies' argument, Dixon paid him the compliment of saying that he had caused him to change his thoughts on a paper he was to deliver at Harvard University, but, Dixon added, 'the alterations are, of course, minor'. Menzies argued the appeal unsuccessfully in the Privy Council.

Menzies was a director (1948-58) of the Australasian Temperance and General Mutual Life Assurance Society Ltd. In 1954-57 he was an honorary area commissioner of Toc H, Victoria. President of the Law Council of Australia in 1956-58 and of the Medico-Legal Society of Victoria in 1957-58, he chaired the Victorian Bar Council in 1958. He was to be president of the National Heart Foundation of Australia (1965-66) and of its Victorian division (1961-62).

Sir William Webb [q.v.] retired from the High Court in 1958. The Federal government chose Menzies to fill the vacancy from 12 June. Newspaper reports noted his family connexion with the prime minister, but the appointment occasioned no controversy. Menzies was sworn in on 25 July and appointed K.B.E. three months later. In February 1963 he was sworn of the Privy Council. In 1964 he sat in London on a number of cases.

Menzies arrived on a bench that was dominated by Dixon. As Menzies himself noted, 'To differ from him was a course always taken with hesitation and never without foreboding'. He sat with Dixon for six years until Dixon was succeeded by Barwick. By disposition Menzies was conservative, and many of his judicial opinions reflected that conservatism, though he brought to his deliberations openness and logic. As a judge, he often had a 'unique perspective on things'. One example was his judgement in *Dennis Hotels Pty Ltd* v. *State of Victoria* (1960), a case which involved the validity of two types of victualler's licence under section 90 of the Constitution. Menzies drew a 'strange' distinction, holding one licence valid and the other not. While his judicial ability was considerable, his mark on Australian law was not as striking as that of some of his contemporaries.

Menzies' personality offered much to an institution whose workload and solemnity could tend to boredom. His wit and humour during argument often helped relieve the monotony of a long day's sitting. It was a humour that was not without its edge. A solicitor-general once finished part of his address to the court with the words, 'That concludes the first branch of my argument'. Menzies rejoined, 'would not "twig" be a more appropriate word?' As something of a raconteur, he entertained his colleagues with his considerable knowledge of English literature and poetry, which he could recall at will. He was described as the 'laughing Cavalier' of the High Court. The dinners he organized were a highlight of the court's austere corporate life. When dressed in his formal judicial garb, Menzies 'conjured up an impression of the Regency and the world of nimble wit'. His dark hair and youthful face belied his age. He sparkled, and had the ability to fill a room.

A council-member (from 1966) of Monash University, Sir Douglas Menzies was installed as its second chancellor in April 1969. He was described as an 'ideal Chancellor—wise, urbane, dignified and influential; detached from day-to-day affairs but deeply concerned with the long-term development of the university'. In 1972 he was made an honorary bencher of the Inner Temple, London. At the annual dinner of the New South Wales Bar Association, held on 29 November 1974, Menzies collapsed. He died that night in Sydney Hospital of coronary vascular disease and was cremated; his son and three daughters survived him. Kevin Connor's portrait of Menzies is held by Monash University.

G. Fricke, *Judges of the High Court* (Melb, 1986); *Aust Law J*, Feb 1975, p 99; *Monash Univ Law Review*, 2, Sept 1975, p 1; *Melb Univ Law Review*, 20, 1995, p 273; *Bulletin*, 17 Sept 1958; *SMH*, 2, 4 Dec 1974.   JOHN M. WILLIAMS

MENZIES, FRANK GLADSTONE (1892-1978), lawyer and public servant, was born on 3 January 1892 at Ballarat, Victoria, second of five children of Australian-born parents James Menzies, a coach-painter who became a storekeeper, and his wife Kate, née Sampson. (Sir) Robert Menzies [q.v.] was his younger brother; (Sir) Douglas Menzies [q.v.] was their cousin. Educated at state schools at Jeparit and Ballarat, and at Grenville College, Ballarat, Frank moved to Melbourne where he was appointed a clerk (on probation) in the Victorian Department of Lands and Survey on 5 August 1909. From 1910 he attended evening classes in arts and law at the University of Melbourne (LL.B., 1920). In the following year he transferred to the Victorian Law Department as clerk of Petty Sessions and on 1 January 1913 to the Crown Solicitor's Office. Menzies enlisted in the Australian Imperial Force on 20 October 1915 and was commissioned in January 1916. Embarking for Egypt in March, he was sent to the Western Front and joined the 24th Battalion in August. He performed regimental and staff duties, rose to captain in December 1917 and was gassed on 2 March 1918. His appointment terminated in Melbourne on 22 May 1919. He resumed work in the Crown Solicitor's Office, completed his degree, and was admitted as a barrister and solicitor of the Supreme Court of Victoria on 3 May 1920.

The Menzies family was proud of its Scottish heritage. In Melbourne in 1909 Frank had professed his faith in the Presbyterian Church. On 22 June 1922 at the Presbyterian Church, Kew, he married Ruby Avery Friend, a 31-year-old nurse. Their eldest son Neville was tragically drowned at Mentone in 1929; their twin sons were born the same year. In the early 1920s Menzies conducted prosecutions in courts of Petty Sessions, acted as a legal-assistant before boards of inquiry and royal commissions, and began to acquire those professional skills that made him a talented lawyer and public service adviser. On 9 April 1926 he was gazetted crown solicitor.

Quick in understanding and responding to problems, Menzies was noted for the confidence with which he gave professional opinions, whether solicited or unsolicited.

Sometimes, however, he returned requests from departments for his views with a handwritten note saying that the subject raised no legal issue and should be dealt with as an administrative matter. Responsible for conducting criminal prosecutions and for advising government departments and instrumentalities, he superintended a wide range of litigation in the Supreme Court and the High Court of Australia, including Victoria's representation in the Uniform Tax case (1942).

Menzies' political sympathies were conservative, but he served his political masters in a non-partisan manner and preserved the independence of the office of crown solicitor. In 1920 he had unsuccessfully stood for Nationalist pre-selection for the Legislative Assembly seat of Toorak. Upright and honest, he amassed vast experience and coped well with the problems that came with the State's eleven changes of government between 1943 and 1955. In the leading constitutional case, *McDonald* v. *Cain* (1953), he instructed (Sir) Henry Winneke, Q.C., who successfully opposed the Country Party's application to the Supreme Court for an injunction to restrain the presentation of the Cain [q.v.13] government's electoral reform bill for royal assent. Menzies supported Winneke's appointment in 1950 as senior counsel to the Victorian attorney-general and in 1951 to the new position of solicitor-general as a full-time, non-political statutory officer.

Appointed C.B.E. in 1951, Menzies retired as crown solicitor in December 1954. Thereafter, he worked for the welfare of war veterans and for community organizations. He was associated with the financier Staniforth Ricketson [q.v.] and became a director of several public companies. An accomplished tenor, he sang with the Royal Victorian Liedertafel for twenty years. In 1955 he was nominated by the Federation of Rhodesia and Nyasaland to the three-member commission established to advise on the siting of the colony's capital. In 1959 he accepted an appointment by the British government to the advisory commission, chaired by Viscount Monckton, which reviewed the constitution of Rhodesia and Nyasaland; its report helped to enable Northern Rhodesia and Nyasaland to emerge in 1964 as the independent states of Zambia and Malawi. Survived by his wife and twin sons, Menzies died on 31 August 1978 at his Balwyn home and was cremated. His estate was sworn for probate at $160 332. The La Trobe [q.v.2] Library holds his reminiscences.

R. Coleman, *Above Renown* (Melb, 1988); A. W. Martin, *Robert Menzies*, 1 (Melb, 1993); *Cwlth Law Reports*, 65, 1941-42, p 375; *Vic Law Reports*, 1953, p 411; *Age* (Melb), 3 Nov 1955, 12-13 Jan 1956, 6 Dec 1975, 25 Mar, 2 Sept 1978; *SMH*, 18 Dec 1959; Sir

Robert Menzies papers MS4936 *and* interview with F. G. Menzies, Oral Hist Project, 1169/350 (NL); information from the Hon J. Cain, Univ Melb, Mr J. Downey, Camberwell, Mr D. Menzies, Burwood, the Hon Sir John Young, Malvern, Melb, Mrs H. Henderson, Yarralumla, Prof A. Martin, Reid, Canb, and the late Mr J. Finemore.

LAURENCE W. MAHER

MENZIES, SIR ROBERT GORDON (1894-1978), prime minister and barrister, was born on 20 December 1894 at Jeparit, Victoria, fourth of five children of Australian-born parents James Menzies, storekeeper, and his wife Kate, née Sampson. The forebears were Scots on the paternal side and Cornish on the maternal. James, originally a skilled Ballarat coach-painter, had become Jeparit's general storekeeper and community leader, a lay preacher in the local Nonconformist church and prominent in activities ranging from organizing sport to presidency of the Dimboola Shire Council. In 1911-20 he held the seat of Lowan in the Victorian Legislative Assembly.

Though lacking much formal education themselves, Menzies' parents were anxious that their children should have the best that could be afforded. Thus the eldest four—Les, Frank [q.v.], Belle and Bob—were sent in turn to Ballarat's Humffray Street State School, boarding with their father's redoubtable Scots mother, the widowed Elizabeth. Bob did best, topping the State scholarship examination in 1907, and studying in consequence for two years at Grenville College, a Ballarat private school. It opened the way to another scholarship, which Menzies took at Wesley College, Melbourne. Success there won him an exhibition to the University of Melbourne (LL.B., 1916; LL.M., 1918). A brilliant undergraduate career followed, with a galaxy of prizes. He was also prominent in student affairs, being in 1916 editor of *Melbourne University Magazine* and president of the Students' Representative Council.

Admitted to the Bar on 13 May 1918, Menzies read with (Sir) Owen Dixon [q.v.14], then the leading Victorian junior. He quickly built up a good general practice. His specialist leaning was towards constitutional law, which he had studied under an admired university teacher (Sir) Harrison Moore [q.v.10]. In 1920, as advocate for the Amalgamated Society of Engineers, he won in the High Court of Australia a case which proved a landmark in the positive reinterpretation of Commonwealth powers over those of the States. The court's verdict brought Menzies 'sudden fame'. More important, it gave him, as a young man of 25, the required status, and the means, to marry. His fiancée was (Dame) Pattie Maie, daughter of John William Leckie [q.v.10], a manufacturer and politician; they were married on 27 September 1920 at the Presbyterian Church, Kew.

His work in this early period brought Menzies into close touch with industrial courts, and indirectly caused his first practical involvement in politics. In 1926 the Federal government of Prime Minister S. M. (Viscount) Bruce [q.v.7], exasperated at continuing industrial disputation, sought at a referendum to augment the powers of the Federal Arbitration Court, and to obtain additional Commonwealth powers over trade unions, employers' associations, trusts and combinations in restraint of trade. The Engineers' case notwithstanding, Menzies disliked Commonwealth inroads on State powers and joined a short-lived 'Federal Union' which was in Victoria a major influence in defeating Bruce's proposals. With a natural bent for public speaking, he soon drifted into more regular politics.

This period was one of ferment in Melbourne, principally among young and respectable men, who, in organizations like the 'Constitutional Club', promoted study groups, speaking-classes, libraries and a model parliament. They wanted to bring a new sense of public responsibility to State politics, then notoriously moribund. Menzies imbibed the atmosphere of the time, and as a successful young professional, with a reasonable income, decided that he had a responsibility to undertake 'a certain amount of public work'.

Under the aegis of a friend, (Sir) Wilfrid Kent Hughes [q.v.], Menzies became active in the Victorian branch of the National Party. In 1928 he entered the Legislative Council, having won a by-election for the province of East Yarra. For eight months in 1928-29 he was a minister without portfolio in Sir William McPherson's [q.v.10] government. At the 1929 general elections, he stood successfully for the seat of Nunawading in the Legislative Assembly. He and Kent Hughes had already begun to form a new ginger group, the Young Nationalist Organisation, dedicated to reform of the party by improving the calibre of its parliamentary representatives and rescuing it from the control of the National Union, a cabal centred on the Melbourne Club and believed to serve primarily the interests of big business. Leader of the 'Young Nats' in 1931, Menzies won the presidency of the National Federation, the peak public body at the head of the party apparatus. The victory symbolized a substantial inroad into National Union power. In 1932 Menzies became attorney-general and minister for railways—the first 'Young Nat' to receive full cabinet rank—in the government of Sir Stanley Argyle [q.v.7].

Meanwhile, he had been indirectly drawn into the federal political conflict arising from the crisis of the Depression. In the hot debates

Menzies stood firmly on the side of ortho-doxy: for balanced budgets, for strict adher-ence to the letter of the law in all contracts, and against expansion of credit. 'Honest' Joe Lyons [q.v.10], acting-treasurer in the Federal Labor government in late 1930, had the same views. Defying a caucus motion to defer the payment of a £28 million loan falling due in December, Lyons insisted on floating a con-version loan. Financiers and businessmen rallied to his support. In Melbourne a 'Group of Six' became the chief organizers of the con-version campaign. Menzies was one of the six; the group was headed by his friend Staniforth Ricketson [q.v.], a stockbroker. The 'Young Nats' were also prominent in the crusade, and the loan was oversubscribed.

Soon after these events came an extra-ordinary mushrooming in all States of citi-zens' leagues, a kind of populist movement through which 'responsible' elements from most (though predominantly the middle) levels of society gave expression to their fears of civil dislocation as the Depression bit. Menzies was among those who saw Lyons as the natural candidate to lead a movement of salvation. In 1931 Menzies and 'the Group' persuaded him to leave the Labor Party and assume leadership of the new United Aus-tralia Party. A Federal election in December installed him as prime minister.

Concurrently, Menzies kept his law prac-tice going—he had taken silk in 1929—and also attended effectively to his ministerial duties in Victoria. A decisive change, how-ever, came in 1934 when he was urged to stand for the Federal seat of Kooyong. Taking this blue-ribbon U.A.P. seat with ease (at the elections on 15 September), Menzies was appointed (12 October) attorney-general and minister for industry in Lyons's government. Among inducements to his transferring to Commonwealth politics was a promise that at the next elections Lyons, who was by this time tired and ill, would step down as leader of the party, and therefore as prime minister, in Menzies' favour. The undertaking was not honoured. Lyons was to stand as prime min-ister in the elections of 1937 and 1939: 'Honest Joe' was a proven election winner, and the party managers insisted that he not give place to the less popular and more abrasive Menzies.

In 1935, accompanied by his wife, Menzies made his first trip to England, one of a small party of Australian ministers visiting London primarily to take part in the silver jubilee cel-ebrations of King George V's reign. Menzies was also involved in official trade talks. He found these tedious and British negotiators obscurantist, but nothing could dim his joy in experiencing, as he put it, the reflections which 'can so strangely . . . move the souls of those who go "home" to a land they have never seen'. For weeks he revelled in the actu-ality, in stones and architecture, countryside and ceremony, of the Britain his education had taught him was also his. He met political notables, travelled widely, was entertained at Buckingham Palace, and won plaudits as a public speaker.

Subsequent official visits to Britain in 1936 and 1938, again largely for trade talks, en-hanced Menzies' reputation and confirmed his affection for British culture, but evoked aversion to the ruthlessness of English busi-nessmen. During the 1938 trip he paid an official visit to Nazi Germany, where he ad-mired the régime's efficiency and wondered at a philosophy that 'has produced a real and disinterested enthusiasm which regards the abandonment of individual liberty with some-thing of the same kind of ecstasy as that with which the medieval monk donned his peni-tential hair shirt'. But he noted that Adolf Hitler was only spoken of 'with the respect which one attaches to a legal fiction' and he told Hjalmar Schacht that 'the suppression of criticism would ultimately destroy Germany'.

Menzies' necessary involvement, as Lyons's attorney-general, in certain domestic dis-agreements became important for the first use of his name, in traditional left-wing de-monology, as emblematic of stern conser-vatism. Two examples were his part in the attempt in 1934 to prevent the Czech com-munist Egon Kisch [q.v.] from entering Australia to appear at a Melbourne peace con-ference, and his resistance in 1938-39 to a waterside workers' ban on exports of pig-iron to Japan. In both cases the facts were more complex than anti-Menzies propaganda allowed. Yet, in the first, the prohibition on Kisch's entry had been imposed, not by Menzies, but by the Country Party minister for the interior Thomas Paterson [q.v.11]. Antipathy to communism—assumed, as that was, on Menzies' side of politics—made it mandatory that he uphold the government's position. There is, nevertheless, no indication that he did so unwillingly. In the second case, which earned him the permanent sobriquet of 'Pig-Iron Bob', Menzies again presented the government view: in this instance that the making of Australian foreign policy could not be surrendered to a minority organization like the Waterside Workers' Federation. Strikers had refused to load a cargo of pig-iron for Japan, a nation they correctly branded as an aggressor in China and predicted as an enemy of Australia. In the heat of contem-porary and subsequent disparagement of Menzies it was not noted that the proposed export was a one-off and very limited con-tract, that Menzies went to great lengths to negotiate with the unions concerned, and that there was clear internal union disagreement on the issues at stake.

More personal was Menzies' embroilment in the artistic controversies of the mid-1930s when, in developing the notion that Australia needed an academy of art, he fell foul of modernist painters and their supporters, one of whom was H. V. Evatt [q.v.14]. Contemporary critics saw Menzies' dislike of modernism as yet another expression of his conservatism, which was undoubtedly true. The claim that he was also an artistic philistine is more debatable.

On Lyons's death in April 1939, the U.A.P. elected Menzies to party leadership. Sir Earle Page [q.v.11] announced that in consequence the Country Party would no longer work in coalition with the U.A.P., and launched on Menzies an attack described by the *Sydney Morning Herald* as 'a violation of the decencies of debate without parallel in the annals of Federal Parliament'. Page asserted that, with war threatening, Menzies was incapable of leading the nation, because he had been disloyal to Lyons and because he had failed to serve in World War I. Though the reasons for this animus are not altogether clear, Page was probably stung by the waspish comments Menzies had made about him behind his back. It is, however, extremely doubtful that —despite the failure of the promises made to him—Menzies was disloyal to Lyons, and that his behaviour was a factor in the latter's collapse. Dame Enid Lyons, whose hostility to Menzies simmered over many years, made the allegation covertly and, in the end, explicitly. Page shared her grief at Lyons's death, and believed the unproven story that Menzies was partly responsible for it.

On 26 April 1939 Menzies became prime minister with a new, all-U.A.P. cabinet. Without any dissenting voices, in September parliament accepted Menzies' assumption that Britain's declaration of war against Germany involved an identical declaration by Australia. Through the National Security Act (1939), the government took the first steps to put Australia on a war footing, announcing the recruitment of a volunteer military force (which at once became 'the second Australian Imperial Force') for service in Australia or abroad, and the calling up of Militia drafts for local defence.

Menzies resisted the demand of 'minds which are heavily indoctrinated in the "old soldiers" … point of view' that the A.I.F. should be sent forthwith to Britain's aid. To him Australia's circumstances were completely different from those of 1914. Then Japan had been an ally. Now, especially given Britain's failure to develop Singapore as an adequate Pacific bastion, 'upon the Japanese relationship and prospects … must depend absolutely the part other than defensive which Australia will be able to take in the war'. But the British government unilaterally arranged scarce shipping for transporting troops; the New Zealand government, without consulting Australia, announced that it would send an expeditionary force; and R. G. (Baron) Casey [q.v.13], then in London, virtually promised the dispatch of a matching A.I.F. division. Menzies furiously noted that the British had shown 'a quite perceptible disposition to treat Australia as a Colony and to make insufficient allowance for the fact that it is for the Government to determine whether and when Australian forces should go out of Australia'.

He was, none the less, like all Australians, proud of the exploits in North Africa of the first troops to fight abroad, those of the 6th Division. *En route* to England in February 1941, he traversed their recent battlefields and celebrated their successes with them. Menzies' purpose in making this trip was to press the British about the parlous position of Singapore. Yet, with German invasion seemingly imminent, he could hardly hope for immediate British help in the Pacific. (Sir) Winston Churchill admitted Menzies to the British War Cabinet while the latter was in London. Menzies was thus privy to the discussions which led to the ill-starred Greek campaign of 1941, in which Australian and New Zealand troops suffered grievous losses. He objected to the lack of a proper military appreciation of the expedition's chances, fought for promises of full equipment for the troops, and altogether proved a thorn in Churchill's side.

Menzies further antagonized Churchill by visiting Ireland to confer confidentially with Eamon de Valera ('that wicked man', as Churchill called him) in the brave but naive hope of winning an end to Irish neutrality in the war. Wartime security requirements and, subsequently, Menzies' own sense of propriety, prevented any of these actions receiving publicity. Meantime, Menzies' horror at the air-raids he had seen in London and Bristol provoked sensitive speeches in England and Australia, and an emotional scarring that never left him.

The end of the 'phoney war' in May 1940 and the fall of France (June) had elicited from Menzies' government legislation and propaganda for full Australian mobilization. Much was achieved, but Menzies suffered a heavy loss when an air-crash near Canberra in August killed three close friends and ministers, G. A. Street, J. V. Fairbairn and Sir Henry Gullett [qq.v.12,8,9]. The results of the Federal elections in September suggested that the nation was not solidly behind the government: the restored coalition and the Labor Party emerged with even numbers, and Menzies held office by the grace of two Independents. In this precarious position he had made his English visit, having vainly suggested to Labor leader John Curtin [q.v.13] the formation of a national, all-party government. It was an open secret during Menzies' absence in England that some ministers and others in the U.A.P. were plotting against his leadership. He was not good—as his political opponent but personal friend Curtin once put it—'at handling his men', and he had alienated, through his social position, intelligence and sometimes arrogant ways, sections of the electorate.

Although welcomed on his return to Australia in May 1941 by great public meetings to which he gave rousing patriotic addresses, Menzies soon came to feel that under his leadership the U.A.P. could not prosper and the war effort might suffer. He offered Labor more proposals for a national government, and, when these were rejected, called an emergency cabinet meeting at which a majority of his ministers agreed that a new leader was desirable. On 29 August Menzies resigned the prime ministership to offer what he called 'real prospects of unity in the ranks of the Government parties'. For him it was a deep personal blow; and for the coalition parties it was an ineffectual move. Before the year was out Labor was in office, and Menzies on the Opposition benches.

After Japan's attack, Menzies seconded most of Curtin's initiatives, though as the crisis waned he was indignant about Labor extremists' allegations that the Curtin government had inherited a nation which was virtually defenceless. He called attention to key appointments his administration had made which Labor subsequently embraced (the most important was that of Essington Lewis [q.v.10] as director-general of munitions, with virtually unlimited authority), and fought bitterly against E. J. Ward's [q.v.] unproven allegations that the Menzies ministry had accepted a strategic plan by which, in the event of Japanese invasion, northern Australia would be abandoned almost as far south as Brisbane. By contrast, (Sir) Frederick Shedden [q.v.], head of the Department of Defence and trusted right-hand man to wartime governments of both colours, wrote privately to Menzies in 1942: 'It was a great experience to be associated with you in the transition to a war footing and the first two years of the war administration … Tribute has yet to be paid to the great foundations laid by you at a time when you lacked the advantage of the effect on national psychology and morale of a war in the Pacific'.

Menzies showed remarkable resilience after the first shock of resignation. W. M. Hughes [q.v.9] succeeded him as U.A.P. leader, but was doomed when Labor won a landslide victory at the elections in 1943. The U.A.P. re-elected Menzies as leader, though it was evident that, with the passing of the Depression which had given it birth, the party

was in decline. Confidential 'post-mortems' on the 1943 defeat counselled a new start, in which a party, freed from the legacy of the recent past, might stand for genuine liberalism. Its immediate tasks would include critical scrutiny of the plans which Labor and a J. M. (Baron) Keynes-inspired bureaucratic elite were already developing for postwar reconstruction. Thus in 1944-45 was formed the Liberal Party, in whose gestation Menzies' influence was the most prominent.

Despite his importance in its foundation, Menzies' position in the party was for some years equivocal. A hope that Labor would be defeated in the elections of 1946 proved badly astray, and in despair Menzies toyed with the idea of leaving political life altogether. But Prime Minister J. B. Chifley's [q.v.13] decision in 1947 to nationalize the private banks gave the Opposition leader a new focus for the 'anti-socialist' cause which he and his colleagues by then saw as a key political issue. Taking the high moral ground, Menzies conducted against bank nationalization a fight whose vigour clinched his leadership of the Liberals. He confirmed this early in 1948 by successfully heading the 'No' case when Chifley's government sought through a referendum an extension of its wartime powers to control rents and prices. Later that year, tired and unwell, Menzies went with his wife and daughter on a holiday to England. 'This', he wrote to a friend, 'is to be a refresher course for me, spiritually, mentally and physically, and I hope to come back "fighting fit"'.

Reaching London in July 1948, Menzies was in time to experience at first hand the tense atmosphere created by the Soviet blockade of Berlin, the most dangerous event of a rapidly escalating Cold War. Even level-headed people, they found, were steeling themselves, only three years after the end of World War II, for another conflagration. Prime Minister Clement (Earl) Attlee told Menzies that he would not have communists in confidential posts in the civil service, 'but [Attlee] otherwise thinks (as I do but my party now does not)' that communists should not 'be martyred by special legislation'. After absorbing the current sense of crisis, and having earnest conversations with (Sir) Anthony Eden (Earl of Avon) and other Conservative friends, Menzies left England wholly converted to the changed views of his party. The parliamentary Liberals had adopted as one of their objectives the dissolution of the Communist Party of Australia. Supposed 'red' initiatives in the chronic industrial unrest of 1947 partly explained this change of heart. It was also a reaction to widespread shock at the death (March 1948) in Prague of Jan Masaryk after a communist *coup*.

Menzies had always used denunciations of communism in domestic industrial upsets as part of his political stock-in-trade, and he continued to do so. Yet his fears took on a new dimension in 1947-48, as he absorbed from experience abroad a sinister sense of communist parties being potential fifth columns. This sense did not leave him, bolstering his acceptance of the Cold-War belief that communist plans for the destruction of capitalism were worldwide and directed by Joseph Stalin and the Soviet dictatorship. That from this view Menzies grasped political advantage does not negate the depth of the belief or Menzies' feeling that he, as prime minister, carried a heavy responsibility to Australia. The frequently reiterated view that he built his subsequent career on cynically 'kicking the communist can' is a shallow one.

Returning to Australia with new anti-communist fears, rhetoric and resolve to fight, Menzies worked assiduously in the run-up to the 1949 Federal elections. Ironically, his cause was helped by Chifley's determination to contain union demands and curb inflation. Most damaging for Chifley was the communist-led coal strike which culminated in the government's use of troops to work open-cut mines. Anti-communist feeling was rife: in Victoria the 'revelations' of a C.P.A. defector Cecil Sharpley brought a royal commission on communism, and in the Melbourne *Herald* Denis Warner gave the 'domino' theory one of its earliest airings. In the election campaign Menzies and the Opposition were frank about their determination to stamp out the communist movement, and to fight in the interest of free enterprise against what they chose to call Labor's 'socialistic' measures. Lesser issues were of importance, especially the Opposition's undertakings to counter inflation, extend child endowment and end petrol rationing. The government stood on its record and suffered a decisive defeat. The Opposition transformed a minority of 40 per cent in the House of Representatives to a majority of 60 per cent. It was notable that, of the fifty new coalition members in the House, thirty-four had served in the recent war, at least thirty of them as officers. By contrast, only about 10 per cent of new Labor members had been in the armed forces. Whatever else Menzies' victory represented, his anti-communism and stress on free enterprise had captured a new and formidable element in postwar Australian society. His second term as prime minister began on 19 December.

Communism was predictably the dominant issue in the first phase of the new government's life. In April 1950 a Communist Party dissolution bill was amended in the Senate (where Labor had a majority) in ways unacceptable to the government. Menzies withdrew it, and in September guillotined through the House of Representatives an identical version which, on the orders of its federal executive, Labor allowed the Senate to pass. The Korean War had begun, anti-communist feeling in the community was high, and it was clear that the Menzies government would insist on a double dissolution if the measure were rejected. In March 1951 the High Court declared the Act invalid. The government then engineered a double dissolution on another issue, banking legislation, and at the elections on 28 April gained a majority in the Senate. Five months later the government held a referendum asking for constitutional powers to deal with communism in the same terms as the nullified Act. The referendum was narrowly defeated, despite government anti-communist 'mandates' at two elections.

Menzies' anti-communist legislation of 1950-51 provoked deep controversy, arising chiefly from its reversal of the accepted principle in British law that an accused person is innocent until proven guilty. It was, and is, a puzzle to explain satisfactorily why Menzies —a lawyer deeply identified with British principles of justice—condoned draconian measures which required 'named' communists to prove their innocence. His own explanation was that, on experience elsewhere, and given the Stalinist rhetoric of some Australian communists, the Communist Party was a potential fifth column. Visits to England and the United States of America in 1950 and 1951 and discussions there with men of affairs confirmed the Cold-War fears bred by his 1948 experience.

On his return from the 1951 trip Menzies warned the nation of the possibility of a third world war within three years. In view of that danger, he presented his attempted breach of civil rights as the lesser evil required of a responsible leader. Ordinary court procedures would require witnesses to testify against the accused, but the revelation of the identity and methods of members of the security services was too dangerous to contemplate. Menzies' most bitter enemies seized on this 'sinister' link as the foundation for a grotesque but long-lived allegation that, in league with Brigadier (Sir) Charles Spry, the head of the Australian Security Intelligence Organization, he was planning to destroy the industrial unions through the establishment of a police state.

The high emotion stirred by these events exploded again in 1954 when, on the eve of Federal elections which some pundits thought Labor had a chance of winning, Vladimir Petrov and his wife defected from the Soviet embassy in Canberra with alleged evidence of Russian spying activities. Supported by the Opposition, the government decreed a royal commission to investigate the case. The coalition victory in the elections in May brought a charge which, though now discredited, has passed into much Labor mythology: that the defection was engineered by Menzies and

A.S.I.O. to smear the Labor Party. Evatt's paranoiac belief in this plot, the sad product of decay in a brilliant mind, brought a degree of self-destruction and gave the more poised and ruthless Menzies the means to crush his opponent. One element in the aftermath of the Petrov affair was the Labor split, chiefly precipitated by Evatt, which was to produce the staunchly anti-communist Democratic Labor Party. No D.L.P. candidate ever won a seat in the House of Representatives, but the cleavage in Labor's ranks was an important factor in Menzies' subsequent election successes. Meantime, the royal commission did not uncover sufficient evidence of espionage in Australia to sustain local prosecutions, though non-Australian sources have provided testimony that the material produced by Petrov's defection was of value to Western intelligence as a whole.

In 1950 Menzies had believed, with most British and American strategists, that the main communist threat was to Europe, and that in the event of world war Australia would provide forces to guard the Middle East. His first two ministers for external affairs (Sir) Percy Spender and Casey, however, saw South East Asia as the crucial area for Australia's defence, a belief given substance by the signing of the Australia-New Zealand-United States treaty (1951) and the formation of the South-East Asia Treaty Organization (1954). Menzies soon accepted the aim of such agreements: to sustain the United States' commitment to the region and look for security through 'great and powerful friends'. He also formally agreed in 1955 to Australian participation in the British-organized Far East Strategic Reserve; in consequence, Australia was involved in conflicts arising from the Malayan Emergency and Indonesia's policy of Confrontation. Henceforth the Menzies administrations were committed to the concept of 'forward defence', a notion which, when combined with increasing dependence on the United States, led almost inexorably to involvement, near the end of Menzies' prime ministership, in the Vietnam War.

Menzies' second prime ministership lasted a record sixteen years, and was to end in his voluntary retirement on 26 January 1966 at the age of 71. Over this time he won seven general elections. There was a serious hiccup in 1961-63 when the government, after providing the Speaker, had a majority of only one in the House. Following the emergence of the D.L.P., Labor's disarray was an important element in consistent Liberal election successes. For all that, Menzies enjoyed formidable support in his own right. In a series of celebrated broadcasts, beginning after his fall in 1941, he had appealed effectively to the 'Forgotten People'—the broad middle class (and especially its women)—rendered powerless, he said, by its lack of wealth on the one hand, and of organization on the other.

The period of Menzies' dominance was also marked by extraordinary economic growth. This 'long boom' was experienced in most advanced economies, but the Menzies governments' stability, their declared policies of 'development' and their continuance of the ambitious immigration programme initiated by Labor were factors in a transformation of Australian material life, as indicated by markers as various as growth in population and home ownership, the ubiquity of white-goods, and a great jump in motor-vehicle ownership.

In the years after 1958, when the minister for trade (and industry) (Sir) John McEwen [q.v.] was leader of the Country Party and deputy prime minister, promotion of Australian production and export through protection, tariff manipulation and aggressive international trade negotiations became characteristics of the Menzies era. McEwen's department was sometimes at odds with the Treasury, occasionally to Menzies' displeasure. This was the case in 1965, for example, when Menzies rejected—on Treasury's advice—the report by Sir James Vernon's committee of economic inquiry, a document understood to embody the views of McEwen's public service lieutenants, in particular his former departmental secretary Sir John Crawford. Nevertheless, though temperamentally different, Menzies and McEwen saw eye to eye on most matters. On the eve of one Federal election in the 1960s Menzies could write to McEwen: 'There never has been such a partnership as this in the political history of Australia'.

Preservation of the Liberal-Country Party coalition was in fact one of the three achievements on which, near the end of his parliamentary career, Menzies looked back with most pride. Given the natural tensions that had always existed between the two parties, this accomplishment reflected the great political acumen and prestige of the mature Menzies. The other two feats he nominated as memorable were the extension of Federal involvement in education and the physical development of Canberra as the national capital. The highlight of the first was the appointment in 1956 of Sir Keith Murray's committee to inquire into the financial plight of Australian universities, and Menzies' insistence that the committee's recommendations be fully implemented for the provision of life-giving funds by government under conditions which preserved university autonomy. The highlight of the second was his insistence in 1960 that money be appropriated for the construction of the long-delayed lake that Walter Burley Griffin [q.v.9] had originally made the centre-piece of his design for Canberra.

Menzies belonged to a generation for whom to be Australian was automatically to be British. That outlook involved veneration for inherited institutions like parliament and the courts because they were the creation of time and history, and respect for the Crown as the focus of loyalty to hold a family of disparate British societies together. Irreverent anachronists lampoon these beliefs and highlight passages of Menzies' career in which his almost sentimental Britishness had regrettable overtones. The prime example was his support of the Eden government's actions in the Suez crisis of 1956.

In the 1950s and 1960s Menzies became at Commonwealth prime ministers' conferences something of the 'Grand Old Man' of the 'Empire' (a description of the Commonwealth into which he often instinctively slipped), but he was unhappy with a situation in which hitherto subject peoples increasingly became the equals of the old 'White' self-governing dominions. Although his good friend Harold Macmillan (Earl of Stockton) tried gently to lead him to accept 'the winds of change', Menzies, at least privately, never quite did so. Yet in his prime he had a shrewd understanding of the way in which superiority was routinely assumed at the metropolitan centre. Occasional diaries and personal letters make it clear that Menzies meant it when he told family and other intimates: 'You've got to be firm with the English. If you allow yourself to be used as a doormat they will trample all over you'.

Menzies' veneration for ancient imperial honours was fired when Queen Elizabeth II appointed him K.T. (1963), and when (Sir) Harold (Baron) Wilson nominated him to succeed Churchill as constable of Dover Castle and warden of the Cinque Ports (1965), ceremonial titles which gave him a uniform and a residence at Walmer Castle. He had been appointed a privy counsellor in 1937 and C.H. in 1951. Among many additional awards and distinctions, he was appointed to the U.S. Legion of Merit in 1950.

Having retired from politics at the peak of his power, Menzies delivered by invitation at the University of Virginia a series of lectures later published as *Central Power in the Australian Commonwealth* (London, 1967), and periodically visited old friends in England. He wrote two volumes of reminiscences, *Afternoon Light* (Melbourne, 1967) and *The Measure of the Years* (Melbourne, 1970). Among his influential earlier collections of speeches and broadcasts, the most important were *"To the People of Britain at War" from the Prime Minister of Australia* (London, 1941) and *The Forgotten People and Other Studies in Democracy* (Sydney, 1943).

In 1971 Menzies suffered a severe stroke which incapacitated him physically and put limits on his remaining public appearances. He died on 15 May 1978 in his home at Malvern, Melbourne; he was accorded a state funeral and was privately cremated. Dame Pattie survived him, as did their son Kenneth and daughter Heather; their younger son Ian had died in 1974. Sir Robert's estate was sworn for probate at $201 306; it included generous legacies to four universities. In June 1996 his ashes were buried with those of his wife in the newly established Prime Ministers' Memorial Garden in Melbourne general cemetery.

Portraits of Menzies include two by Charles Wheeler—one in King's Hall, Old Parliament House, Canberra, from 1946 until slashed in 1954, the other in the Western Australian Art Gallery. Of four by (Sir) Ivor Hele, one won the Archibald [q.v.3] prize (1954) and was given to Menzies, one is held by Parliament House, Canberra; the other two were commissioned by Gray's Inn, London, and the Victorian Bar Council. Of four by (Sir) William Dargie, one is in the Clothworkers' headquarters, London, and the others are in the possession of the University of Melbourne, the Menzies Foundation, East Melbourne, and the Menzies family. The Melbourne Savage Club has a portrait by Sir John Longstaff [q.v.10]. (Sir) William Dobell's [q.v.14] portrait, commissioned by *Time* magazine in 1960, was later given to the New South Wales Art Gallery. Busts include two by V. E. Greenhalgh (in the Liberal Party's headquarters, Canberra, and in the Savage Club, Melbourne), one by Barbara McLean (outside the Liberal Party's headquarters, Canberra), and one by Wallace Anderson [q.v.13] (in the Ballarat Botanical Gardens). A plaque by Peter Latona is in Sir Robert Menzies Square, Jeparit.

Large framed and handsome, Menzies had a ready wit and superb command of language. His outward imperiousness did not simply betoken a sense of intellectual and political superiority. It also covered a certain shyness. Intimates knew a man of great good humour and kindness. Life for him was a gift to be enjoyed with gusto: he took pleasure in food and drink, revelled in letting his hair down at his favourite Savage and West Brighton clubs in Melbourne, and indulged himself in spectator sports, being a connoisseur of the art of cricket. After Alfred Deakin [q.v.8] and before Gough Whitlam, Menzies was probably the most well-read prime minister Australia has had, though he was not given to parading his erudition. He enjoyed the classical nineteenth-century English novels, could quote hundreds of lines of Shakespeare, and on boring train and aeroplane trips loved to fill in the time with 'whodunits'. An intensely private man, he strictly separated personal matters, like his family life, from public affairs. Sir Paul

Hasluck, who knew Menzies well, wrote of him: 'I think the sort of tribute he would have appreciated most would not have been praise of his great talents or a recital of what he had accomplished but rather a statement that he was a man of character, honourable in conduct and decent in behaviour. He was that and I offer the tribute'.

C. Hazlehurst, *Menzies Observed* (Syd, 1979), *and* (ed), *Australian Conservatism* (Canb, 1979); P. Hasluck, *Sir Robert Menzies* (Melb, 1980); C. Bell, *Dependent Ally, a Study in Australian Foreign Policy* (Melb, 1988); J. Bunting, *R. G. Menzies, a Portrait* (Syd, 1988); G. Souter, *Acts of Parliament* (Melb, 1988); J. Brett, *Robert Menzies' Forgotten People* (Syd, 1992); P. Edwards with G. Pemberton, *Crises and Commitments* (Syd, 1992); A. W. Martin, *Robert Menzies*, 1 (Melb, 1993); S. Prasser et al (eds), *The Menzies Era* (Melb, 1995); Menzies papers (NL).

A. W. MARTIN

MEREDITH, WINIFRED BARBARA (1895-1979), medical practitioner, was born on 17 September 1895 at Merino, Victoria, fourth child of Ewen Cameron, grazier, and his wife Emma Harriet, née Nunn, both Victorian-born. Her Scottish grandfather had settled in the area in 1838; her father represented Portland (1900-04) and Glenelg (1904-06) in the Legislative Assembly. Barbara was educated at Presbyterian Ladies' College, Kew, and the University of Melbourne (M.B., B.S., 1921; B.A., 1947). After a year at the Melbourne Hospital, she moved in 1923 to the Queen Victoria Memorial Hospital for Women and Children as medical superintendent. On 6 October 1931 at St George's Church, Malvern, she married Charles William Meredith, a widowed Anglican priest. She continued to work with out-patients at the hospital's department of obstetrics and gynaecology until the birth of her daughter in 1937. Like many other married women doctors, she undertook some medical work at schools. She also raised two stepsons, and supported her husband's pastoral duties in parishes at Murrumbeena and Malvern.

Widowed in 1944, Dr Meredith resumed her professional career in the following year as an ante-natal medical officer in the maternal and child hygiene section of the Department of Health. Concern about maternal deaths, still-births and neo-natal mortality prompted the establishment of municipal ante-natal clinics. On the death of Dr Vera Scantlebury Brown [q.v.11] in July 1946, Meredith took over as acting-director (director from 1947) of maternal, infant and pre-school welfare. Through a period of rapid development, she contended with the instability of postwar conditions and the impacts of the baby boom and immigration. In 1950 she visited North America, Britain and Europe on a World Health Organization fellowship; she returned further convinced of the value of preventive health work, and of the importance of monitoring and supporting the early stages of child development. That year she initiated a special migrant infant welfare service. She served (from 1955) on a new Child Welfare Advisory Council established to assist the minister of education (Sir) Arthur Rylah [q.v]. In 1959 she was an Australian representative to a W.H.O. conference on maternity care, held in the Philippines.

During her term of office the number of infant welfare centres in Victoria doubled (from 296 to 600), pre-schools increased from 185 to 458 and municipal prenatal clinics grew tenfold to 30. Meredith's annual reports reflected recurrent problems of insufficient trained staff and a shortage of building materials in the early 1950s. They also revealed a long-standing attempt to manage the complex relationship between the department and voluntary organizations. Her determination to maintain departmental control over such issues as training of kindergarten teachers, infant feeding and supervision of maternal weight in pregnancy did not always ensure popularity with peers and those outside the department.

Meredith was appointed O.B.E. in 1960, the year of her retirement. In August she travelled to Istanbul, Turkey, to attend a meeting of the International Council of Women as a delegate of the National Council of Women. She belonged to the Lyceum and Soroptimist clubs. Her later years were marred by ill health, but she enjoyed gardening and remained closely involved with the Anglican Church. Survived by her daughter, she died on 28 July 1979 at Camberwell and was cremated.

Barbara's eldest sister MAUD MARTHA CAMERON (1886-1973) was also educated at P.L.C. and the University of Melbourne (B.A., 1908; M.A., Dip.Ed., 1911). She was headmistress (1911-54) of Firbank Church of England Girls' Grammar School, Brighton, and president (1936-37) of the Victorian Association of Headmistresses. In 1955 she was appointed M.B.E.

L. Gardiner, *The Free Kindergarten Union of Victoria 1908-1980* (Melb, 1982); Vic Dept of Health, *Health Bulletin*, no 82, 1943, p 2204, *and* Annual Report of the Director of the Maternal and Child Health Branch, 1959-60, *and* correspondence files (Vic Dept of Health records, Melb); *Age* (Melb), 1 Mar 1945, 26 Feb 1947, 7 Apr 1958, 6 Aug 1960, 31 July 1979; *Argus*, 19 July 1950; information from Firbank Anglican School for Girls, Brighton, Melb, and the late Dr A. E. Wilmot.

KERREEN M. REIGER

MERRYLEES, WILLIAM ANDREW (1900-1969), philosopher, grazier and lobbyist, was born on 13 December 1900 at Charlton, Victoria, eldest of four children of Victorian-born parents William Andrew Merrylees, farmer and Methodist lay preacher, and his wife Jane Alice, née Pearse. Bill 'could handle machinery and mend anything', but his father aspired to have him ordained. From Charlton Higher Elementary School and Wesley College he proceeded to Queen's College, University of Melbourne (B.A., 1921; M.A., 1923; D.Litt., 1935). He rowed for his college and was influenced by W. R. Boyce Gibson [q.v.8], the Idealist philosopher. Gibson's Idealism was not incompatible with Christian belief, and Merrylees only gradually abandoned institutional religion. Awarded the 1921 Rhodes scholarship for Victoria, he read philosophy at Oriel College, Oxford (B.Litt., 1923). Back home, he married Margaret Annie O'Hara, half-sister of J. B. O'Hara [q.v.11], at Queen's College chapel on 26 June 1924. He briefly managed a family property, Groongal station, Hay, New South Wales, then embarked on further study at the University of Heidelberg, Germany, in 1925. In the following year he was appointed senior lecturer in philosophy at the University of Melbourne.

Slowly spoken, intensely serious and reserved, Merrylees disliked lecturing and wandered deviously through Bernard Bosanquet and F. H. Bradley. Their Absolute Idealism had few Australian followers, but he was drawn to Bosanquet's political altruism; his own writings on public affairs revealed him as a social liberal and disciple of J. M. Keynes. He published prolifically in the *Australasian Journal of Psychology and Philosophy* and, while convalescing from pneumonia in 1933, wrote a substantial monograph, *Descartes: An Examination of Some Features of His Metaphysics and Method* (1934), which earned him his doctorate. Expected to succeed to Gibson's chair, he was deeply hurt when the professor's son Alexander [q.v.14] gained preferment. To his siblings' dismay, Merrylees insisted on taking over Groongal in partnership with his brother Joe. During his last year at the university in 1935, he attended Melbourne Technical College on Friday mornings to learn woolclassing.

Merrylees was eager to diversify production on the 37 470-acre (15 164 ha) sheep run on the Murrumbidgee River. He taught himself surveying and began to lay out irrigation channels, initially on the border-check principle and later using his own controlled wild-flooding system. His scheme to convert Groongal into a huge mixed farm alarmed his brother who wanted to build up a merino stud and to use irrigation simply as drought insurance. Undeterred by Joe's opposition and their bankers' misgivings, Bill formed a separate partnership with Annie to irrigate the property's western portion, Coonara. The burning of their two-storeyed wooden homestead in 1944 proved but a temporary setback: he circumvented postwar restrictions by enlisting his children and employees to build a nineteen-room concrete replacement, and installed fire-alarms. From there he dispensed hospitality to visiting parties of farmers, politicians and bureaucrats who were attracted by reports of quadrupled carrying capacity and unorthodox practices like winter watering.

Broad shouldered and over six feet (183 cm) tall, with sandy brown hair, blue eyes and a sun-ravaged complexion, Merrylees looked and sounded like a countryman. Yet he was never conventionally country-minded, being conscious of the disadvantages of rural life and eager to advance regional social-policy objectives. He served on Carrathool Shire Council (1951-68, deputy-president 1956-68) and on Murrumbidgee County Council (1955-68, deputy-chairman 1960-68), promoting libraries and rural electrification, but opposing the proliferation of intensive irrigation settlements.

In 1952 Merrylees founded the Riverine University League and won national prominence with his campaign for a rural university. A formidable controversialist and pamphleteer, he relentlessly attacked the binary policy championed by Sir Leslie Martin and Senator (Sir) John Gorton, and almost secured the establishment of a Riverina university college in 1966. When the Federal government offered to finance a college of advanced education at Wagga Wagga, he persuaded the State government to make it a multi-campus institution serving the entire region. His contribution to establishing the Riverina College of Advanced Education was to be acknowledged in 1981 when the library at the Riverina campus of Charles Sturt University was named after him.

Diagnosed with angina in 1964, Merrylees died of myocardial infarction on 17 August 1969 while digging a utility truck out of dry sand at Coonara. He was buried with Methodist forms in Griffith cemetery; his wife, three daughters and two sons survived him.

A. Watt, *Australian Diplomat* (Syd, 1972); H. Dow (ed), *More Memories of Melbourne University* (Melb, 1985); D. Boadle, *Selling the Rural University* (Wagga Wagga, NSW, 1986), and for bibliog, *and* 'The Idealist as Lobbyist: W. A. Merrylees and his campaign for an Australian Rural University', in *Melbourne Studies in Education, 1989-90*, D. Stockley ed (Melb, 1990) *and* 'Critics of Australia's Binary Policy: the Riverina University College Debate, 1965-67', *Hist of Education Review*, 23, no 2, 1994, p 18; Riverine Univ League papers (Charles Sturt Univ Regional Archives); Blake & Riggall records (Univ Melb Archives); information from the Merrylees and Diss families.

DONALD BOADLE

MÉSZÁROS, ANDOR (1900-1972), architect and sculptor, was born on 1 September 1900 in Budapest, son of Alexander Mészáros, solicitor, and his wife Bertha, née Grunsberg, who was a sculptress. Educated at the local Gymnasium, Andor served in the Hungarian cavalry in 1918, but World War I ended before he saw action. Between 1919 and 1927 he studied building engineering at the Technische Hochschule, Vienna, sculpture at the Académie Julian, Paris, and architecture at the Budapesti Müszaki Egyetem. In Paris, L. Henri Bouchard and P. M. Landowski introduced him to abstract and cubist forms; at night he learned carving in Jószef Csáky's studio.

After two years training as an architectural draftsman with Móric Pogány and as an architectural engineer with Jószef Vágó, Mészáros was admitted to the Hungarian Chamber of Architects. Working as an independent architect, he aimed 'to escape from the all-pervasive influence of the Bauhaus [school], and to adapt modern technology to the Hungarian character'. He formed a close relationship with the sculptor and medallist Ede Telcs, and designed architectural mounts for several of his fountains. On 1 December 1932 he married 22-year-old Erzsébet Back at the registrar-general's office, Budapest. To avoid involvement in an impending war, he emigrated to Australia, reaching Melbourne on 21 June 1939. In the following year his wife and son joined him.

During his first year in Melbourne, Mészáros was employed by the architectural firms of J. V. T. Ward and Marsh & Michaelson. In 1940 he began to make a living from sculpture and secured commissions with the assistance of such influential friends as Professor W. E. Agar and (Sir) Herbert Schlink [qq.v.7,11]. His early works included a series of three carved stone figures for Royal Prince Alfred Hospital, Sydney: 'Maternity' (1944), 'The Surgeon' (1945) and 'King George V' (1946). He also illustrated Oswald Barnett's [q.v.7] book of poetry, *I Hear the Tramp of Millions* (Melbourne, 1945). In 1949 he went to England where he was commissioned to sculpt the altarpiece for St Anselm's Chapel in Canterbury Cathedral and to complete 'The Canterbury Series', fourteen medallions depicting the Stations of the Cross. After some months, when prospects appeared unpromising, he returned to Australia.

Unusually versatile in the range of his sculptural modes, Mészáros was a dramatic narrative artist in a period when style mattered more than subject. His uncommissioned pieces embraced timeless themes—the story of Jesus, maternal love, man's need to adapt in a hostile world, endurance in adversity—which were expressed with a sturdy masculinity in stylized, figurative forms. Among his larger commissioned works were 'The Resurrection', a sandstone carving forming the reredos in the chapel of Sydney Church of England Grammar School (Shore) (1954), the hanging rood in the transept of the Cathedral Church of St Peter, Adelaide (1955), and 'Christ Accepts His Cross', a bronze figure in All Saints Church, Brisbane (1962). Mészáros's bas-reliefs in stone and bronze adorn many buildings, among them the Shrine of Remembrance, Brisbane, the Supreme Court, Darwin, and Sydney's international air-terminal with his memorial to Charles Ulm [q.v.12].

When bigger commissions were lacking, Mészáros turned his hand to designing medallions, of which he produced more than one thousand. He made medals for the Victorian Artists Society (1947), for the Olympic Games (1956), and for Australian and New Zealand servicemen who fought in the Vietnam War (1968). In 1951 he received 'the highest award' at the International Medallion Exhibition, Madrid; in 1964 he won the 'purchase prize' at the International Medallion Competition, Arezzo, Italy. A sensitive artist with a fine eye for line and composition, he believed that 'the medallion is to sculpture' what 'the sonnet is to poetry'. He regarded medals as 'the chamber music of the pictorial arts'.

Mészáros was a member of the International Federation of Medallists, the Amici Della Medaglia, Italy, the Victorian Sculptors' Society (president 1954-55, 1962-63) and the Association of Sculptors of Victoria (president 1968). From 1970 he worked with his younger son Michael. Survived by his wife and two sons, he died on 1 May 1972 in South Melbourne and was cremated. Telcs, Paul Vincze and Michael Mészáros struck his likeness on medallions; L. S. Pendlebury's portrait of Mészáros is held by the family.

K. Semmens, *Andor Meszaros* (Melb, 1972); K. Scarlett, *Australian Sculptors* (Melb, 1980); T. Wachtel, *Andor Meszaros* (Budapest, 1987); *People* (Syd), 1 Aug 1951, p 24; *Aust Women's Weekly*, 28 Oct 1959; H. de Berg, Andor Meszaros (taped interview, 3 Dec 1965, NL); naturalization file, A435/1, item 47/4/2638 (AA, Canb); E. Meszaros, The Artist's Recollections (ms held by Mrs E. Mészáros, Kew, Melb).   KELMAN SEMMENS

METCALFE, ARTHUR JOHN (1895-1971), medical practitioner and public servant, was born on 26 June 1895 at Hamilton, New South Wales, son of English-born parents Rev. John Ewan Metcalfe, Methodist clergyman, and his wife Annie, née Kessell. Educated at Fort Street Model (Boys' High) School and the University of Sydney (M.B., Ch.M., 1918; D.P.H., 1926), Arthur worked as a resident medical officer at Sydney Hospital and the

Renwick [q.v.6] Hospital for Infants. He joined the Commonwealth Quarantine Service in September 1919 and was posted to Newcastle soon afterwards. At the Methodist Church, Mosman, Sydney, on 2 October 1920 he married Kathleen Mary McCauley.

Based at Townsville, Queensland, in 1920-22, Metcalfe served as acting-director of the Australian Institute of Tropical Health and helped to contain an outbreak of bubonic plague. While posted to Thursday Island (1922-23) he was involved in combating beri-beri and hookworm. He was sent to Brisbane in 1924 and to Sydney in the following year. In October 1926 he was transferred to the administrative staff of the Department of Health, Melbourne, where he was employed under J. H. L. Cumpston [q.v.8]. Metcalfe surveyed Federal and State methods of recording medical statistics and the treatment of infectious diseases. His report eventually led the States to adopt uniform recording practices. Appointed chief quarantine officer, Sydney, in 1927, he was made senior medical officer, New South Wales, in 1932. He moved to Canberra in 1944.

After Frank McCallum [q.v.] died in September 1946, Metcalfe acted as director-general of health until he was confirmed in the post in October 1947. That year he studied government health policies in the United States of America, Canada, Britain and Europe. Under the ministerial direction of N. E. McKenna [q.v.] and Sir Earle Page [q.v.11], Metcalfe's department implemented the hospital, pharmaceutical and medical benefit schemes consolidated by the National Health Act (1953).

During Metcalfe's term as director-general the Department of Health expanded significantly. The Australian Institute of Child Health and the National Biological Standards Laboratory were established and added to the scientific organizations—including the Commonwealth Serum Laboratories, the Commonwealth X-ray and Radium Laboratory, the Commonwealth Acoustics Laboratory, and the School of Public Health and Tropical Medicine—for which Metcalfe was responsible. He chaired the National Health and Medical Research Council (1948-59) and the National Tuberculosis Council. To check the health of potential immigrants, he kept medical officers in Britain, Germany, the Netherlands, Greece, Denmark, Italy and Austria. As chief Australian delegate, he attended World Health Organization assemblies in 1951, 1953 and 1954. He was appointed to the assembly's executive-board in 1957, chaired technical discussion meetings in 1958 and headed the executive-board's standing committee on administration and finance in 1960.

In 1954 Metcalfe had been appointed C.B.E. A quiet and unassuming man who did not seek the limelight, he retired in 1960, moved to Sydney and helped with community work. He died on 24 March 1971 at Harbord and was cremated with Anglican rites; his daughter and two sons survived him.

Health, 10, no 3, Sept 1960, p 67; A 1928/1 item 1020/90 section 1 (AA, Canb).

W. D. REFSHAUGE

MEWTON-WOOD, NOEL CHARLES VICTOR (1922-1953), pianist, was born on 20 November 1922 at Hawthorn, Melbourne, son of Frederick William Myles Wood, a secretary from England, and his Victorian-born wife Dulcie Maie, née Mewton. Noel attended Carey Baptist Grammar School, Kew. From the age of 9 he studied under Waldemar Seidel [q.v.] at the University Conservatorium of Music. In 1935, aged 12, he made his first public appearance as pianist with the Australian Broadcasting Commission's Melbourne Symphony Orchestra conducted by (Sir) Bernard Heinze.

In 1937 Mewton-Wood was accepted by the Royal Academy of Music, London. He gave a farewell concert at the Melbourne Town Hall on 8 May. Supported by a public fund, he travelled with his mother to London, where he met his cousin W. J. R. Turner [q.v.12], a well-known poet and music critic. At the academy he studied piano with Harold Craxton and composition with Theodore Holland; then, at Turner's instigation, he spent the summer of 1938 taking lessons at the home of Artur Schnabel at Tremezzo, Italy.

After Mewton-Wood's successful performances at Glasgow late in 1939, Turner contacted Sir Thomas Beecham, who agreed to audition the young pianist. On 31 March 1940 Mewton-Wood made his début with Beecham at the Queen's Hall, London, playing Beethoven's *Piano Concerto No.3*. Beecham described him as 'the best talent I've discovered in the British Empire for years'. He subsequently played as soloist at the Mendelssohn-Schumann concert, conducted by Beecham in London in 1943. His concert tours included one to Australia for the A.B.C. in 1945, and others to South Africa (1950) and Europe. He toured Britain at various times with Richard Tauber, (Dame) Joan Hammond and Ida Haendel. Among the works of which he gave the first performance were Benjamin (Lord) Britten's piano concerto, played at a Cheltenham Festival and conducted by Britten himself, a piano concerto by (Sir) Arthur Bliss, played at a London Promenade Concert in 1949, a piano sonata written by Bliss especially for Mewton-Wood and first performed in public at the St Ives Festival on 7 June 1953, and Prokofiev's eighth piano sonata. He wrote many musical compositions, including the incidental music for the film *Tawny Pipit* (1944). Besides his music, he showed an interest in atomic physics and collected modern paintings.

During his short career Mewton-Wood established a reputation as an outstanding interpreter of modern works, especially those of Stravinsky, Bartok, Prokofiev, Bliss, Britten, Busoni and Hindemith. A friend and admirer of Hindemith, Mewton-Wood played his *Ludus Tonalis* in London in 1946. In October 1952 he played a Hindemith piano concerto with the City of Birmingham Symphony Orchestra; critics praised his 'controlled and expressive artistry' and 'rare musical intelligence'. He became one of the most frequent performers of Hindemith's work, and in January 1953 played his *Sonata for Horn and Piano* with Dennis Brain.

That year Mewton-Wood performed at the Coronation Promenade Concerts and at three major festivals: Edinburgh (with the violinist Max Rostal), Aldeburgh—where he presented with the tenor (Sir) Peter Pears works for voice and piano by Britten—and St Ives. Distressed by the recent death of his close friend William Fedrick, Mewton-Wood committed suicide by swallowing prussic acid on 5 December 1953 in their home at Notting Hill Gate, London, 'while the balance of his mind was disturbed'.

I. Moresby, *Australia Makes Music* (Melb, 1948); C. W. F. McKenna, *W. J. Turner* (Syd, 1990); *Canon*, 4, 1951; *Gramophone*, Jan 1954; *Herald* (Melb), 21 May 1938, 29 Mar, 20 May 1940, 28 Feb 1941, 7 Dec 1953; *The Times*, 7-8 Dec 1953; *Age, Argus* and *Sun News-Pictorial*, 8 Dec 1953.

C. W. F. McKenna

MICHAELIS, Sir ARCHIE REUBEN LOUIS (1889-1975), businessman, politician and Jewish leader, was born on 19 December 1889 at St Kilda, Melbourne, eldest child of Australian-born parents Frederick David Michaelis, merchant, and his wife Esther Zillah, née Phillips. Moritz Michaelis [q.v.5] was his grandfather. His aunt Alice Michaelis was a founder (1912) and president (1944-46) of the Lyceum Club, Melbourne. The close-knit family gathered at Linden, the Michaelis mansion in Acland Street, St Kilda, on Friday nights to observe traditional ceremonies and rituals in preparation for the Sabbath. Archie attended Wesley College, Prahran, and Cumloden School, East St Kilda; in 1903 his parents took him to England and enrolled him at Harrow School.

Returning to Melbourne in 1908, he entered the family tannery business, Michaelis, Hallenstein & Co. Pty Ltd. In 1912 he was sent to England to gain experience in the firm's London office. He served (from 1914) in the Honourable Artillery Company and went with his battery to the Middle East. After being commissioned (1916) in the Royal Field Artillery Special Reserve, he was posted to Ireland and Greece. He trained for the Royal Flying Corps in Egypt in 1917, but contracted malaria and influenza and was repatriated in 1919. Archie's brother and three first-cousins had died or been killed in World War I, and the family required his active involvement in the business. On 14 January 1920 at Tusculum, Potts Point, Sydney, he married his cousin Claire Esther Hart (d.1973).

In the late 1920s Michaelis began to take an interest in politics. He became associated with the Australian Legion and later the Young Nationalist Organisation, and valued his life-long friendship with (Sir) Robert Menzies [q.v.]. In 1932 he was elected to the Victorian Legislative Assembly for the United Australia Party, wresting what had been the safe seat of St Kilda from the Australian Labor Party. During the 1935 election campaign anti-Semitic pamphlets were distributed in St Kilda. In parliament, Michaelis was the foremost advocate of legislation (1939) that made third-party motorcar insurance compulsory; towards the end of World War II he worked to prevent the transfer of vital powers from the States to the Commonwealth. In 1945, with (Sir) Thomas Maltby [q.v.] and three other dissident Liberals, he helped Labor to defeat the Dunstan-Hollway [qq.v.8,14] government. From 2 October to 21 November he was minister without portfolio in Ian Macfarlan's [q.v.] 'stop-gap' government. He rejoined the Liberal Party in December 1946. Elected Speaker in 1950, Michaelis served in that role until his retirement in 1952. He was knighted that year.

Chairman (1948-65) of the family firm and of its parent company, Associated Leathers Ltd, Michaelis was a generous supporter of charities. As treasurer of the Emergency Relief Committee, he had helped Jewish victims of the 1929 riots in Palestine. He was a member (1940-70), president (1945) and chairman (1947-51) of the Patriotic Funds Council of Victoria, and a board-member (1935-72) and vice-president of the Alfred Hospital. He also chaired the Victorian branch of the Australian Jewish Historical Society and served on the board of the Melbourne Jewish Philanthropic Society.

Like his father and grandfather before him, Michaelis was president and a trustee of the St Kilda Hebrew Congregation. He was a friend and disciple of its rabbi, Jacob Danglow [q.v.8], whose wife was his aunt. Michaelis became a defender of the Anglo-Jewish establishment within the Australian Jewish community. As founding president (1939-40) and spokesman of the Victorian Jewish Advisory Board, he resisted attempts to secularize the

Jewish community's leadership. Opposed to Zionism, he publicly defended Sir Isaac Isaacs's [q.v.9] anti-Zionist letters and articles. When some member of the Jewish community condemned Isaacs and his supporters, Michaelis declared that he would not be 'dragooned into silence'. In 1947-48 he helped to fund the short-lived anti-Zionist journal, *Australian Jewish Outlook*. Like Danglow, he later made his peace with the independent state of Israel.

In retirement, Sir Archie maintained a lively interest in community affairs and wrote frequent letters to the press. He relinquished his membership of the Victoria and Peninsula golf clubs and his social games of tennis, but continued to enjoy a weekly game of poker, crossword puzzles and reading (he was vice-president of the Kipling Society, London). In 1966 he published a brief memoir, *Before I Forget*. Survived by his three daughters, he died on 22 April 1975 at South Yarra and was buried in St Kilda cemetery.

The Michaelis, Hallenstein Story 1864-1964 (Syd, 1964); P. Aimer, *Politics, Power and Persuasion* (Syd, 1974); W. D. Rubinstein, *The Jews in Australia*, 2 (Melb, 1991); *PD* (Vic), 23 Apr 1975, p 5299; *Aust Jewish Hist Soc, J*, 8, pt 1, 1975; *SMH*, 22 Feb 1935, 3, 10 Oct 1945, 11 Dec 1946; *Age* (Melb) and *Sun News-Pictorial*, 23 Apr 1975; family papers (held by Mr D. Salek, Melb).   J. S. LEVI

MIDDLETON, RAWDON HUME (1916-1942), airman, was born on 22 July 1916 at Waverley, Sydney, son of native-born parents Francis Rawdon Hamilton Middleton, station-manager, and his wife Faith Lillian, née Millar. Rawdon was educated at Dubbo High School and worked as a jackeroo on Leewong, a station at Yarrabandi, near Parkes, managed by his father. Nicknamed 'Ron', he was a keen cricketer and footballer, despite being slightly built. He was a good-looking young man, very quiet and a little moody, with a strong 'streak of honest determination'.

On 14 October 1940 Middleton enlisted in the Royal Australian Air Force under the Empire Air Training Scheme. He learned to fly at Narromine and received further instruction in Canada. Arriving in Britain in September 1941, he was promoted flight sergeant in December and posted to No.149 Squadron, Royal Air Force, in February 1942. After gaining experience as second pilot in Stirling bombers, he became first pilot and captain in July. Next month he was posted to No.7 Squadron, R.A.F. He returned to No.149 in September.

By 28 November 1942 Middleton had completed twenty-eight operational flights. Three of his crew had already flown their quota of thirty and could have left, but decided to stay through loyalty to Middleton. Their sortie that night was to Turin, Italy. Over the target they were hit by flak. One shell exploded in the cockpit wounding Middleton. His right eye was destroyed and the bone above it exposed; he was probably also wounded in the body and legs.

With his aeroplane severely damaged, Middleton rejected the options of flying to Africa or bailing out over German-occupied France and insisted on returning to England for the sake of the crew. The flight lasted more than four hours, during which he was in constant agony. He could barely see and suffered further pain when he spoke. On reaching the English coast, he flew over land so that his comrades could parachute safely. Five of them reached the ground and survived. He then turned back towards the English Channel to avoid crashing in a populated area. Two of the crew remained with their captain, parachuted into the sea and drowned. Middleton was too weak to leave the Stirling which crashed into the sea on the morning of 29 November 1942, killing him. He was posthumously awarded the Victoria Cross and promoted pilot officer (with effect from 15 November).

Middleton's body was washed ashore at Shakespeare Beach, Dover, in February 1943 and buried in St John's churchyard, Beck Row, Suffolk, with full air force honours. He was 26 and unmarried. He had won the first V.C. awarded to a member of the R.A.A.F. in World War II. His father said, 'My son did his duty'. In 1978 Middleton's V.C. was presented to the Australian War Memorial, Canberra, which holds his portraits, painted by Harold Freedman and Norman Carter after his death.

J. Herington, *Air War Against Germany and Italy 1939-1943* (Canb, 1954); J. F. Turner, *V.C.'s of the Air* (Lond, 1960); L. Wigmore (ed), *They Dared Mightily* (Canb, 1963); S. Bill, *Middleton VC* (Melb, 1991).   LEIGH EDMONDS

MIGHELL, SIR NORMAN RUPERT (1894-1955), company director and public servant, was born on 12 June 1894 at Mackay, Queensland, second son of Alfred William Mighell, an accountant from England, and his Queensland-born wife Mary Anne, née O'Donohue. Educated at St Joseph's College, Brisbane, Norman worked as an articled clerk at Gordonvale and studied law. He was mobilized in the Militia in August 1914 and served briefly with the garrison on Thursday Island before enlisting in the Australian Imperial Force on 3 November. Five ft 11 ins (180 cm) tall and weighing 10 st. 6 lb. (66 kg), he had grey eyes and light brown hair. As a sergeant in the 15th Battalion, he was among the first Australian troops to land at Gallipoli on 25 April 1915, sustaining severe wounds which plagued him for the rest of his life. He was admitted to hospital in England in June, repatriated in November and discharged from the A.I.F. on 14 June 1916.

Admitted as a solicitor on 30 April l918, Mighell practised at Innisfail (until 1925) and then in Brisbane. At her Cairns home on 23 June 1920 he had married with Catholic rites Marjorie, daughter of A. F. J. Draper [q.v.8]; they were to have a son and daughter. Mighell was a foundation member (1928) of the Brisbane Legacy Club and president (1928-29) of the Queensland branch of the Returned Sailors' and Soldiers' Imperial League of Australia. On 16 July 1929 he was admitted to the Bar. That year he became chairman of No.1 War Pensions Assessment Appeal Tribunal.

In 1935 Mighell was appointed chairman of the Repatriation Commission, Melbourne. Fearing that ex-servicemen and women might lose more than they gained, he resisted moves in the late 1930s to reform repatriation legislation, particularly the proposal to subject war pensioners to a means test. In addition, he opposed the Menzies [q.v.] government's decision (1940) to remove the pension entitlement of an ex-serviceman's de facto wife when his lawful wife received or claimed the benefit. Mighell took a special interest in the education of the children of deceased or disabled veterans. During World War II he warned the government against permitting people with disabilities to enlist in the armed forces because they might later qualify for pensions.

Appointed Commonwealth coal commissioner in August 1941 (head of the Coal Commission, 1942-44), Mighell held responsibility for the production and distribution of coal until 1946. He endeavoured to increase yields and to handle the many industrial problems which plagued the industry. In 1943 he chaired the committee whose recommendations on the resettlement of armed services personnel formed the basis for the Commonwealth Reconstruction Training Scheme. Australia's deputy high commissioner in London in 1946-49, he returned to Melbourne in 1950. Mighell had been appointed C.M.G. in 1939. In 1951 he was knighted. He chaired the British Memorial Fund and the Melbourne branch of the Overseas League.

In the 1950s Mighell was chairman of Sulphide Corporation Pty Ltd, Standard Telephones & Cables Pty Ltd, Consolidated Zinc Pty Ltd and the Melbourne board of Atlas Assurance Co. Ltd. As chairman of Territory Enterprises Pty Ltd, he played an important part in developing, on behalf of the Commonwealth government, the uranium deposits at Rum Jungle, Northern Territory. Sir Norman was a director of Zinc Corporation Ltd, New Broken Hill Consolidated Ltd and Anglo-

Australian Corporation Pty Ltd. Survived by his wife and son, he died on 13 April 1955 in the Mercy Hospital, East Melbourne, from injuries received in a motorcar accident and was buried in Melbourne general cemetery.

S. J. Butlin and C. B. Schedvin, *War Economy 1942-1945* (Canb, 1977); C. Lloyd and J. Rees, *The Last Shilling* (Melb, 1994); A5954/1 item 52/1, A649/6 item 183/600/3 (AA, Canb); information from Mrs S. Martens, Glen Iris, Melb, *and* from the Returned & Services League of Aust, Canb (held in ADB file).   RICHARD KINGSLAND

MILES, JOHN BRAMWELL (1888-1969), stonemason and communist leader, was born on 5 September 1888 at Wilton, Roxburghshire, Scotland, son of William Miles, journeyman mason, and his wife Louisa, née Wiggins. Jack attended an elementary school in Edinburgh before being apprenticed to a stonemason in the north of England. He found a job, first at Newcastle, and next at Consett, County Durham, where he joined the Independent Labour Party. At the register office, Lanchester, on 9 October 1911 he married Elizabeth Jane Black.

They emigrated to Queensland, reaching Brisbane on 31 March 1913 in the *Orama*. Miles worked at his trade, but admitted that he had remained 'stuck in the mud politically' until R. S. Ross [q.v.11] recruited him to the Queensland Socialist League in 1918. He then helped to conduct the Workers' School of Social Sciences, established in 1919. When the Communist Party of Australia was formed in Sydney at the end of 1920, he joined its Brisbane branch. Employed (1920-23) in a meatworks, he represented the Australasian Meat Industry Employees' Union and subsequently the United Operative Stonemasons' Society of Queensland on the Trades and Labor Council. He became increasingly influential in the Communist Party, though only residents of Sydney were eligible for senior positions.

In the late 1920s Miles emerged as a critic of the national leadership of the Australian Labor Party and an advocate of unyielding opposition to its 'social fascist' politicians. With Bert Moxon and Lance Sharkey [q.v.], he won control of the C.P.A. at the conference in December 1929. He moved to Sydney early in 1931 as national secretary and exercised absolute control of a party that had been thoroughly 'bolshevised'. The central committee determined policy, enforced its implementation and expelled any who resisted. Especially critical of middle-class converts to communism, Miles censured F. W. Paterson [q.v.] and castigated his fellow Scot, Professor John Anderson [q.v.7]. The threat to the legality of the party compounded Miles's preoccupation with security; he operated mostly in a semi-clandestine manner as a vigilant, driving administrator.

Following his visit (1934-35) to the Soviet Union, and with the turn to the united and popular fronts in 1935, Miles was required to play a new role, that of a model proletarian leader. At the end of that year he embarked on a national tour designed to promote him as a far-sighted patriot of unbending rectitude. The transformation was not easy. Miles was a slight man with a pronounced Scottish burr. During the early 1930s he had formed an illicit relationship with the writer Jean Devanny [q.v.8]. Her encomium—'To hear him analysing a situation, stripping every unessential from it, laying bare its core, is an experience a Communist can never forget'—had an unfortunate ambiguity. Noel Counihan's cartoon in the party press softened Miles's legendary harshness. A profile (1937) claimed that he worked a twelve-hour day, but relaxed at the cinema, where he preferred Joe Brown to Clark Gable, and Popeye to Hollywood he-men. He also enjoyed light fiction, claiming 'It's a big jump from Lenin to Edgar Wallace, but I do it, easily'.

The C.P.A. was banned in 1940 for its anti-war policy. Miles again went underground, and issued fierce polemics under the pseudonym, 'A. Mason'. After the Soviet Union entered the war he emerged to rehabilitate the party, but was increasingly overshadowed by Sharkey, who replaced him as general secretary in 1948. Miles continued to work for the C.P.A. and frequently toured outlying branches to rebuke members for their inadequacies. Often known as 'J.B.M.', he had unsuccessfully contested five State and Commonwealth parliamentary seats between 1929 and 1952. An Australian Security Intelligence Organization officer reported in 1953 that the 'Grand Old Man of Australian Communism', Jack Miles, had 'developed into a kindly little man, aging and whimsical . . . [but] still holds the fire of battle in his eyes. They are sharp, brilliant and magnetic, a strange contrast to the light, grey hair and wrinkled, puckish face'.

In contrast, a visiting Comintern official told Devanny, 'He's got exceptional capacities, but he's too hard on the comrades. He hurts too often and too much'. She found him tense, volatile, cutting, with a powerfully intuitive intelligence. Yet the characteristics that best served his cause were probably the frugality and methodical persistence that sustained an organization where such qualities were sorely needed. None of the later revelations about the Stalinist régime shook his dogmatism. Survived by his daughter and four of his five sons, Miles died on 17 May 1969 at Naremburn and was cremated without a religious service.

C. Ferrier (ed), *Point of Departure* (Brisb, 1986); S. Macintyre, *The Reds* (Syd, 1998); *Communist Review*, Feb 1937, p 6; *Workers' Weekly*, 26 Apr 1929; ASIO files, A6119/79, items 884-886; R. Coates, J. B. Miles (taped interview, held by author); J. N. Rawling papers (ANUABL).

STUART MACINTYRE

MILFORD, EDWARD JAMES (1894-1972), army officer, was born on 10 December 1894 at Prahran, Melbourne, third son of English-born parents James Emery Milford, a pharmacist who had emigrated to Australia in 1885, and his wife Mary Sophia, née Gibbon. Edward was educated (1908-12) at Wesley College. Its headmaster L. A. Adamson [q.v.7] encouraged senior boys to apply for admission to the newly established Royal Military College, Duntroon, Federal Capital Territory. Milford entered Duntroon in 1913, one of the college's third intake. A fellow Wesleyan, George Vasey [q.v.], joined with him and became a lifelong friend. Their class was to produce some of Australia's outstanding wartime commanders: six of them became generals.

Graduating sixth out of thirty-six in 1915, Milford was reported as being 'excellent at mathematics' and 'fair at riding', with 'good personal characteristics'. He was commissioned lieutenant, Australian Imperial Force, in November and sailed for the Middle East with the 4th Field Artillery Brigade. In March 1916 he was sent to the Western Front where he served in a number of regimental and staff postings before being promoted major in September 1917. That month he was wounded in action and evacuated to hospital in London. Returning to duty with the 4th F.A.B., he was awarded the Distinguished Service Order and mentioned in dispatches for his work as a battery commander and brigade major in operations in France and Flanders.

World War I established Milford's reputation as a regimental officer. He chose to stay in England to take a specialist course in ordnance, at Woolwich. On 13 November 1919 at Holy Trinity Church, East Finchley, Middlesex, he married with Anglican rites his childhood sweetheart Wynnie Ray Gray. Following ordnance and equipment-related appointments in Australia and Britain, he attended the British Army Staff College, Camberley, in 1930-31. He was at Army Headquarters, Melbourne, in 1936-40 as assistant-director, then director, of artillery. In April 1940 he was promoted temporary brigadier and posted as commander, Royal Australian Artillery, to the 7th Division.

After four weeks (November-December) in the Middle East, Milford flew back to Australia. On 1 January 1941 he was promoted temporary major general and appointed master-general of the ordnance. The country was gearing up for a protracted struggle, and the M.G.O. post was important in directing the acquisition of equipment for a very much expanded army. Milford's background fitted him well for the task. Vasey acknowledged as much in a letter to his wife, but ungraciously added a comment that 'Teddy' should not flatter himself with his early preferment.

With Japan's entry into the war and northern Australia threatened with invasion, by mid-1942 Milford found himself at Townsville, Queensland, commanding the 5th Division. In January 1943 the division moved to Milne Bay, Papua, where Milford performed excellent work, organizing the defences and reducing the incidence of malaria. He and his men saw action in New Guinea in August-September; they cleared the enemy from the Salamaua area with the aim of developing the township as a major base. Lieutenant General Sir Edmund Herring used the word 'magnificent' to describe the division's work in difficult terrain and under trying conditions. Salamaua was found to be unsuitable for a base. Under Milford's supervision, the Lae area was developed instead.

By November 1943 Milford was major general, general staff, at headquarters, New Guinea Force. For his performance in this post, and for his earlier period in command, he was appointed C.B.E. (1945); the citation praised him as an officer of all-round ability and as a far-sighted planner. He was again mentioned in dispatches. In 1944 Vasey fell ill while in command of the 7th Division. In July that year General Sir Thomas Blamey [q.v.13] appointed Milford to take his place. Vasey's removal was considered premature in some quarters, but Blamey reportedly said that Milford deserved his chance to command an A.I.F. division. Milford did not enter into the controversy. Back in Australia, he spoke briefly but generously at a 7th Division memorial service for Vasey following his untimely death in March 1945.

In May Milford moved to Morotai to conduct final planning for the landing at Balikpapan, Borneo. Begun on 1 July, the successful operation was 'the largest amphibious attack carried out by Australian troops'. The Japanese were well-trained and equipped, and fought 'with their usual fortitude'. But they were overwhelmed by superior firepower. As an artilleryman, Milford determined that the operation would be a lesson in this regard. He was appointed C.B. (1947) for his services at Balikpapan.

At noon on 8 September 1945 Milford accepted the surrender of all Japanese troops in Borneo, Netherlands East Indies, from Vice Admiral Michiaki Kamada on the quarterdeck of H.M.A.S. *Burdekin*. This ceremony marked the high point of his military career.

He stayed on as commander of the 7th Division and of Morotai Force until March 1946 when he became deputy-chief of the General Staff, Melbourne. In May he was appointed adjutant-general (and second member of the Military Board). Wrongly diagnosed as having prostate cancer, he was placed on the Retired List on 23 April 1948.

Milford made a major contribution in senior staff and command appointments. The first Duntroon officer to achieve the rank of general, he might have been expected to advance further. He was unfortunate that his illness occurred at a critical time. Only 5 ft 6 ins (168 cm) tall, strict, strong-willed and opinionated, he was a widely read, decent and upright man. Blamey said that Milford was the equal of Vasey, yet it seems that he did not possess Vasey's charisma as a leader, nor, despite his achievements, is he similarly remembered. None the less, he was the sort of person whom Australia was fortunate to have on hand to accept the responsibilities of senior command during the dark years of World War II. Milford died on 10 June 1972 at Macleod and was cremated. He was survived by his son John who had graduated from Duntroon in 1944; John's son Michael also graduated from Duntroon in 1983.

G. Long, *To Benghazi* (Canb, 1952), and *The Final Campaigns* (Canb, 1963); D. McCarthy, *South-West Pacific Area—First Year* (Canb, 1959); D. Dexter, *The New Guinea Offensives* (Canb, 1961); J. Hetherington, *Blamey, Controversial Soldier* (Canb, 1973); D. M. Horner, *General Vasey's War* (Melb, 1992); P. Dennis et al (eds), *The Oxford Companion to Australian Military History* (Melb, 1995); information from Major M. J. Milford, Point Lonsdale, Vic.   S. N. GOWER

MILJANOVIC, DRAGAN (1922-1974), charity worker, was born on 3 September 1922 at Bunic, Lica, Yugoslavia, third of five children of Djuro Miljanovic, a small farmer, and his wife Sava. Educated locally, Dragan was raised by his grandmother after his parents moved to France to seek employment during the Depression. He worked as a shepherd until 1937 when he joined his parents and became a labourer in the north of France. Following the outbreak of World War II he served in the resistance movement, but in 1940 was conscripted into a Nazi labour camp in the Ruhr valley, Germany. He escaped and made his way to Munich, only to be stricken with rheumatic fever. Miljanovic later worked at a hospital and a warehouse. When the war ended he spent two years in Germany in a displaced-persons' camp, run by the United Nations Educational, Scientific and Cultural Organization. His care of the sick and hungry was widely appreciated: known as 'Francuz' ('the Frenchie'), he was able, against all odds, to find food from a range of sources.

It was difficult for Miljanovic, an anti-communist, to return to Yugoslavia. In 1948 he emigrated to Sydney. After a term in the immigration centre at Bathurst, he spent four years in a similar camp at Woodside, South Australia. Five ft 8 ins (173 cm) tall, with blue eyes and dark brown hair, he drove for the Department of Supply before being naturalized on 25 August 1953. At the Congregational Church, Stirling West, on 22 May 1954 he married Tamara Kutschuk, a 21-year-old nurse. They lived at Stirling in the Adelaide Hills where Miljanovic found a job as a gardener. He began twenty years of unselfish service to others, initially through the Good Neighbour Council of South Australia which helped immigrants to assimilate. With his donkey, Don Pedro, he patrolled Adelaide beaches in 1961-62, collecting money for the surf life-saving movement; he also gave children rides on Don Pedro at charitable functions. He often dressed in a tasselled pillbox hat, red scarf, white shirt and riding-breeches, and sang folk-songs while accompanying himself on a shepherd's lute, a tamboritza or a gusla.

By 1963 Miljanovic was employed as a monotype-operator in Adelaide. That year he won the Gertrude Kumm [q.v.] award for citizenship, presented annually to an immigrant who had made an outstanding contribution to the community. In the same year, to assist young artists, he opened the Don Pedro Gallery in a nineteenth-century cottage which he had restored at Stirling. Miljanovic demonstrated his concern for the underdog by establishing the Independent Youth Club; his passionate interest in the conservation of the Adelaide Hills led him to found the Mount Lofty Ranges Association.

Late in life Miljanovic worked as a surveyor's assistant. Survived by his wife and daughter, he died of septicaemia and peritonitis on 17 November 1974 in Royal Adelaide Hospital and was cremated. His formidable drive and eccentricity had made him a compassionate and colourful figure. In 1975 a plaque in his memory was unveiled at the Heart Centre, Adelaide.

T. Dyster, *Dragan* (Adel, 1992); *Advertiser* (Adel), 20 Mar 1961, 27 May 1963, 24 Oct 1966, 19 Nov, 6, 10 Dec 1974, 19 Dec 1975; *Mount Barker Courier*, 12 Dec 1962; *Canb Times*, 3 June 1963; naturalization file, A435, item 1949/4/3156 (AA, Canb); information from Mr G. Grachanin, Medindie, and Mrs T. Miljanovic, Stirling, Adel; personal information.

TOM DYSTER

MILLER, GODFREY CLIVE (1893-1964), artist, was born on 20 August 1893 at Wellington, New Zealand, second of three children of Thomas Tripney Miller, a bank accountant from Scotland, and his New Zealand-born wife Isabella, née Duthie (d.1896). Thomas married Isabella's sister Eliza Jane in 1897; they were to have four children. Godfrey inherited a share of his grandfather's extensive ironmongery business, John Duthie & Co. Ltd, Wellington. He attended state schools at Hawera and Palmerston North before boarding (on a scholarship) at Otago Boys' High School, Dunedin.

At the age of 17 Miller was apprenticed to J. Louis Salmond, an architect of Salmond & Vanes, Dunedin; he attended classes at the School of Art and Design, Dunedin Technical School, and worked on construction sites. On 20 October 1914 he enlisted in the New Zealand Expeditionary Force. He served as a signalman at Gallipoli where he was severely wounded in the upper right arm on 6 August 1915; as a result of the injury, he suffered musculospiral nerve palsy and neurasthenia. Discharged from the army on 30 May 1916, he was registered by the New Zealand Institute of Architects on 25 July 1917.

Before World War I began, lessons with Alfred O'Keeffe had sharpened Miller's interest in painting, and during 1917 they worked together once more. Miller had early success in 1918 with a prize-winning student drawing submitted to the New Zealand Academy of Fine Arts, but did not exhibit again until 1952. Shyness and a nervously uncertain disposition underlay his reluctance. From the 1930s he was essentially reclusive, yet he took pleasure in company and was 'a prodigious letter writer'. Meanwhile, he worked on each of his paintings for years.

Journeying to Melbourne, Miller enrolled for 1918 under William McInnes [q.v.10] at the National Gallery schools, re-enrolling there for a second year from mid-1923. He travelled in the Far East in 1919 and was fascinated by Asian thought and culture. Between 1918 and 1929 he lived mainly in Victoria, painting at Warrandyte, and in New South Wales. He mixed with a group of artists who in the early 1920s revived the Australian Art Association. About this time he developed an enthusiasm for romantic and symbolist literature. In 1929 he joined the Victorian Artists Society.

For the next decade Miller was based principally in London. He entered (1929) the Slade School of Fine Art, and gained a certificate (1931) for sculpture. In 1933 he rejoined the Slade, moving from Paddington digs to more permanent rooms nearby. By 1934 the school had lost all appeal to him, beyond its unsupervised life-drawing sessions. Throughout his career, Miller drew on other artists' approaches in the belief that the art of the past, and of the present, held the keys to future creativity. Erudite and widely read, he was so enthralled by metaphysics that he joined the British Institute of Philosophy. In the late 1930s he found that theosophy met his mystical inclinations, and he joined the Anthroposophical Society in Australia. He had arrived in London a conservative naturalistic painter, grounded in nineteenth-century artistic traditions. He left a fully-fledged modernist. After moving quickly through Impressionism and Post-Impressionism, he had developed a geometrical, classical style based on the abstraction of natural forms.

Returning to Australia via New Zealand early in 1939, Miller boarded in central Sydney until 1954 when he bought a house at Paddington with an outlook across to Rushcutters Bay, a view occasionally seen in his paintings. He lived frugally (as always) and painted alone until he began teaching part-time at East Sydney Technical College in 1948. Students were awed by his dedication and aesthetic sensibility. In 1952 he agreed to exhibit paintings, with the Sydney Art Group. Next year his work was shown in London, the first of several successful overseas appearances, from one of which the Tate Gallery in 1961 acquired 'Triptych with Figures' (1938-54). Miller held four solo exhibitions, the second a retrospective mounted by the National Gallery of Victoria in 1959. In all, he only ever showed about forty paintings. He published a pamphlet (1959) elaborating the philosophical stance reflected in his paintings, and a book, *40 Drawings by Godfrey Miller* (Sydney, 1962).

Miller died on 10 May 1964 at his Paddington home and was cremated with Anglican rites. His estate was sworn for probate at more than £114 000. A hoard of his paintings was discovered in his house and formed the basis of the Godfrey Miller Memorial Exhibition, held in Sydney in 1965. Miller's achievement lay in melding early twentieth-century practices and theories of picture-making with symbolic traditions to express an enigmatic, poetical mysticism.

J. Henshaw (ed), *Godfrey Miller* (Syd, 1966); G. Dutton, *The Innovators* (Melb, 1986); D. Edwards, *Godfrey Miller: 1893-1964* (Syd, 1996); *Antique News and Sales*, 1, July 1975; *Sunday Telegraph* (Syd), 17 May 1964, 21 Feb 1965; *SMH*, 6 Apr 1996; A. Wookey, The Life and Work of Godfrey Clive Miller, 1893-1964 (Ph.D. thesis, La Trobe Univ, 1994); Miller file (Art Gallery of NSW Archives); G. C. Miller, Letters to G. Sweet, 1938-61 (copies held by author); Miller papers (ML).

ANN WOOKEY

MILLER, HENRY LAWRENCE (1913-1972), boxing promoter and stadium manager, was born on 9 April 1913 at Torquay, Devon,

England, son of Sydney Miller, a petty officer, and Sarah Beatrice Ireland, a barmaid. Harry arrived in Sydney about 1922. He had sundry jobs, which may have included working as an office-boy for Hugh McIntosh [q.v.10] and as a caddy at Royal Sydney Golf Club, before he was engaged in 1936 as manager of the Stadium at Rushcutters Bay by John Wren's [q.v.12] Stadiums Ltd. At St Michael's Anglican Church, Vaucluse, on 5 June 1940 Miller married Veronica Victoria Mecham, a 21-year-old hairdresser; they were to be divorced in 1948.

For more than thirty years Miller proved an energetic and successful promoter of boxing and wrestling. Gregarious, loquacious, and tough when it was required, he established good relations with the press, with American and European fight promoters and managers, and particularly with Ern McQuillan, a leading boxing-trainer in Sydney. Under Miller's auspices, Australian fans were able to see world-rated fighters, such as Archie Moore, Freddie Dawson and Emile Griffith, as well as Tommy Burns's comeback fight in 1946. Miller furthered the careers of Australian boxers, including Ranold ('Ron') Richards [q.v.11], Dave Sands [q.v.] and Vic Patrick.

Cigar-smoking Miller became part of the atmosphere at the Stadium. When the main event started he was in his accustomed seat, hob-nobbing with political, sporting and show-business celebrities. He regularly held parties in his office after the fights, and frequented Sydney's restaurants and nightclubs. On 21 June 1960 at the registrar general's office, Sydney, he married Dawn Kathleen Hall, née Todd; she was a 29-year-old usherette and a divorcee.

Opinions on Miller's professional integrity and character differed sharply. Those associated with McQuillan thought Miller shrewd, but fair; the wrestling champion Len Holt noted his over-fondness for drink and women, but believed that he combined brilliance as a promoter with honesty and loyalty. On the other hand, those who felt excluded from the favoured circle criticized Miller for showing bias against trainers (other than McQuillan) and for exploiting raw fighters, and accused him of sexual deviance. Portly, immaculately dressed and speaking in a high voice with an English accent which sounded affected to Australian ears, Miller conveyed to many people a suggestion of sexual ambivalence.

As interest in boxing declined, Miller brought show-business stars to the Stadium, among them Nat King Cole (1957), Frank Sinatra (1959), Sammy Davis junior (1959), Judy Garland (1964) and 'The Beatles' (1964). When the building was demolished in 1970 to make way for the eastern suburbs railway, Miller was disappointed to receive no 'golden handshake' from Stadiums Ltd. Depressed after a string of misfortunes—the failure of his marriage, his non-appointment as a promoter at the showground, and the death of his dog—he drank heavily and talked of suicide. Sometime between 21 and 24 November 1972 he shot himself in the head at his Elizabeth Bay flat. His funeral at Northern Suburbs crematorium was attended by Wren, McQuillan, Patrick, Jimmy Carruthers and other members of the sporting fraternity. He was survived by his wife. Both marriages were childless.

SMH, 27 July 1964, 9 June 1970, 25, 29 Nov 1972, 17 Feb 1973; *Sun* (Syd), 8 Feb 1968, 27 Nov 1972; *Age* (Melb), 25 Nov 1972; *Daily Telegraph* (Syd), 27 Nov 1972; information from Mr L. Holt, Maroubra, Syd.   PETER CORRIS

MILLER, DAME MABEL FLORA (1906-1978), politician, was born on 30 November 1906 at Broken Hill, New South Wales, second child of South Australian-born parents Joseph Christian Goodhart, draper, and his wife Alice Mary, née Humphries. Brought to Adelaide as a child, Mabel was educated at Girton House Girls' Grammar School. She attended a finishing school in Paris before entering the University of Adelaide (LL.B., 1927). Admitted to the South Australian Bar on 17 December 1927, she pursued her profession in London and Sydney before settling in Tasmania. At St George's Anglican Church, Hobart, on 24 July 1930 she married Alan John Richmond Miller (d.1965), a 31-year-old chemist.

Appointed acting section officer, Women's Auxiliary Australian Air Force, on 30 August 1941, Miller rose to temporary squadron officer while serving (1942-43) in Melbourne as deputy director, W.A.A.A.F. In December 1943 she was posted to Townsville, Queensland, as staff officer, North-Eastern Area. Her appointment terminated in Hobart on 3 October 1944.

After World War II Miller was involved in the Australian Red Cross Society, the Queen Alexandra Hospital and the Mary Ogilvy Homes Society. As president (1952-54) of the National Council of Women of Tasmania, she heard a number of complaints about municipal mismanagement and decided to stand for the city council. In her campaign she stressed the advantages of having a woman's view on services, amenities and the spending of ratepayers' money. She was elected to the Hobart City Council in May 1952, becoming its first female member. Increasingly influential, she chaired the finance, health and building, and town planning committees, and served as deputy lord mayor in 1954-56 and 1964-70. Throughout her period in office she

performed with ability, dignity and charm. Rejecting claims that she was a feminist—and professing to be as 'interested in roads and drains' as women's affairs—she sought the position of lord mayor in 1970. She failed in her bid and retired from the council in 1972.

In a larger political arena Miller had attracted the attention of the Liberal Party. Although she unsuccessfully contested the division of Queenborough for the Legislative Council in 1953, she headed the poll for Franklin in February 1955 and thereby became the first woman to be elected to the House of Assembly. The *Mercury* reported that she would continue her domestic duties 'like any other housewife', but Miller was no stereotype. To the contemporary press she gracefully combined 'a skilled executive's poise and confidence' with 'the chic of a mannequin, and the charm and kindliness of a wife and mother'. In a confident maiden speech she criticized 'ill-planned Government housing subdivisions, which for lack of ordinary common amenities would undoubtedly degenerate rapidly into slums'. When speaking in the assembly on the Hobart corporation bill (1955) she defended the city council from attacks, misrepresentation and government intrusion. Miller supported law, education, health and welfare reforms, and measures designed to protect children from neglect, maltreatment and disease. In 1961 she was elected federal vice-president of the Liberal Party.

Surprisingly defeated at the polls in May 1964, Miller never re-entered State politics. She maintained her association with community bodies, among them the United Ex-Service Women's Homes Association and the Tasmanian division of the Right to Life Association. An effective fund-raiser, she helped to establish (1955) the Women's and Children's Memorial Rest Centre, Hobart. She also sat on the interim council of the Australian National Gallery (from 1968) and on the Metric Conversion Board (from 1970).

In 1967 Miller was appointed D.B.E. Early that year she represented her country on the United Nations' Status of Women Commission. As a rapporteur of the 21st session, she helped to draft and push through declarations on the elimination of discrimination against women. Later in the year she was an Australian delegate to the General Assembly of the United Nations.

Opposed to 'feminine screaming and flag-waving', Dame Mabel had found that 'choosing a goal and going after it with quiet determination nearly always works'. She was a slim, attractive and energetic woman who dressed in the latest fashions and whose photograph regularly appeared in Tasmanian newspapers. Even in her seventies she was still driven by lifelong concerns for personal efficiency and effectiveness. Survived by her daughter, she died on 30 December 1978 in a nursing home at New Town and was cremated.

J. A. Thomson, *The WAAAF in Wartime Australia* (Melb, 1991); M. Sawer and M. Simms, *A Woman's Place* (Syd, 1993); *Sun News-Pictorial*, 5 Apr 1955; *Mercury* (Hob), 20 Apr 1955, 19 Nov 1969, 7 June 1972, 22 Aug 1974; *Advertiser* (Adel), 31 Aug 1957; Miller papers (TA).   STEFAN PETROW

MILLER, ROBIN ELIZABETH; *see* DICKS, ROBIN

MILLER, SIR RODERICK WILLIAM (1911-1971), company director, was born on 12 November 1911 at Balmain, Sydney, second of three sons of Robert William Miller [q.v.10], a lighterman from Scotland, and his native-born wife Annie May, née Kieran. Educated at Scots College, Roderick represented the school at Rugby, rowing and athletics, and later played Rugby Union for New South Wales. He joined R. W. Miller & Co. Pty Ltd at the age of 17 and, in 1931, became sales manager and a director. At St Stephen's Presbyterian Church, Sydney, on 27 October 1934 he married Enid Marie Stevenson; their son and daughter were to predecease him, and the marriage ended in divorce on 17 January 1957. Miller enlisted in the Australian Imperial Force on 30 May 1941. He served in the Middle East with the 2nd/1st Anti-Aircraft Regiment from July 1941 to January 1942. Returning to Australia, he was commissioned lieutenant in June 1942 and seconded to Docks Control duties. From February to May 1944 he carried out this work in Papua and New Guinea. His A.I.F. appointment terminated in Australia on 10 October 1944.

Miller worked closely with his father, sharing a capacity for hard work, toughness and enterprise. He was prominent in building up the company's collieries, hotels and 'sixty-miler' colliers. On 15 February 1957 at the Fullerton [q.v.4] Memorial Church, Sydney, he married Elizabeth Shaw, née Barberie, a 28-year-old divorcee. He succeeded his father as managing director in 1958; R. W. Miller (Holdings) Ltd was registered as a public company in 1962.

Vice-chairman (from 1958) of the Northern Collieries and Independent Steamship Owners' Association, Miller deliberately set out to reduce the influence of overseas monopolies. In June 1963, as owner of the Australian-registered tanker, *Millers Canopus*, he asked the British Petroleum Co. to load petroleum and kerosene at Kwinana, Western Australia. This experiment, he claimed, would lead to cheaper

petrol for motorists. In addition, Miller submitted a plan to order four tankers from Australian shipyards, provided that the Federal government, in the meantime, allowed him to import four tankers. He hoped that these moves would force the government to develop a national fuel policy.

His move into the tanker business involved a political struggle with oil companies, and, surprisingly, with (Sir) Robert Menzies' [q.v.] government. Following a year of overseas visits, international deals and complex negotiations, in July 1964 Miller won approval to import the tankers, *Björdholm* (*Millers McArthur*) and *Storheim* (*R. W. Miller*), on condition that he contract for two tankers with Australian shipyards within a year and for a third tanker within two years, and that he place a written undertaking with the collector of customs. Miller saw this concession not only as a victory over Australian and world oil interests, but also as an effort to save the coal trade (fuel oil carried in foreign tankers with foreign crews had an unfair freight advantage over coal). In his efforts to force the full manning by Australian seamen of ships flying the Australian flag, he resorted to section 288 of the Navigation Act (1913) which specified that such vessels receive priority. Although he thought that this manoeuvre would be welcomed by the government, cabinet subsequently rejected his requests to import a fourth tanker.

The eventual establishment of the fleet followed disputes between the Seamen's Union of Australia and the departments of Labour and National Service and of Shipping and Transport. Miller's strong support from the union earned him the description, 'the working man's folk hero tycoon'. His success stimulated other shipowners and the shipbuilding industry, but it also raised costs significantly and enabled Miller to determine whose cargo was carried, and when.

An influential member of the New South Wales Combined Colliery Proprietors' Association and of the Australia-Japan Business Co-Operation Committee, Miller helped to stabilize the State's coal industry by gaining markets in Victoria and South Australia. By 1968 he had bought the vessel *Karoon*, renamed her *Elisa Miller*, and converted her into a modern bulk-carrier. He pioneered the coal trade with Japan (and later with Europe) and in 1969 won the then largest New South Wales contract with Japanese steel-mills for coal worth $65 million. In that year he accepted a tender from Broken Hill Proprietary Co. Ltd to build a 62 000-ton tanker, the *Amanda Miller*, at Whyalla, South Australia.

Although R. W. Miller had disposed of its brewery to Tooheys [qq.v.6] Ltd in 1967, it retained its forty hotels and by 1971 had added road transport, insurance and engineering to its collieries and ships. Miller had revolutionized the coastal shipping trade by bulk-handling coal in chartered ships and by establishing an Australian tanker fleet to carry oil. He had emerged as one of Australia's most flamboyant businessmen, a 'thrusting, energetic individualist' with a strong, if unpredictable, personality. In 1962 he was appointed C.B.E. In 1970 he was knighted. A florid, thickset man, 'gravel-voiced and tough faced', he remained keen on boating, fishing and swimming, and was patron of Eastern Suburbs Leagues Club. He was a Freemason, and belonged to the Royal Automobile Club of Australia, Tattersall's, the Royal Motor Yacht, Manly Golf, Sydney Turf and the Victorian clubs.

Suffering from emphysema, Sir Roderick died of coronary thrombosis on 26 April 1971 at his Vaucluse home and was cremated. He was survived by his wife, and by their two sons and two daughters. His estate was sworn for probate at about $646 000. In tribute, Justice F. H. Gallagher of the Commonwealth Conciliation and Arbitration Commission said that Miller had always been ready to assist others 'without any fuss or ostentation' and had 'endeavoured to maintain cordial relations with the unions'. Walter Smart, of the Miners' Federation, saw Miller as courageous, idealistic, forthright and scrupulously honest. Following a prolonged takeover battle, Howard Smith [q.v.6] Ltd, Ampol Petroleum Ltd and Bulkships Ltd emerged in 1973 as the major shareholders in R. W. Miller. In 1979 the firm became a subsidiary of Howard Smith.

SMH, 1 Jan 1962, 17, 25, 31 Oct 1963, 4, 7 July, 15 Sept 1964, 11, 17, 20, 23, 25 Mar, 1 Apr, 30 June, 6, 26 Oct 1965, 21 Nov 1966, 2 July 1968, 11 Mar 1969, 1 Jan 1970, 27 Apr, 2 Nov 1971, 7 July 1972; *Sun-Herald* (Syd), 18 Aug 1963; *Australian*, 27 Apr 1971; *Newcastle Morning Herald*, 28 Apr 1971; information from the Rt Hon I. McC. Sinclair.

JOHN ATCHISON

MILLINER, BERTIE RICHARD (1911-1975), politician and trade unionist, was born on 17 July 1911 at Kelvin Grove, Brisbane, sixth son of Queensland-born parents Arthur Milliner, glazier, and his wife Ellen, née Batchelor. Bertie attended the local state school, served an apprenticeship as a compositor at the Queensland Government Printing Office and became a linotype-operator. On 26 March 1938 at the Ann Street Presbyterian Church, Brisbane, he married Thelma Elizabeth Voght, a schoolteacher.

Joining the Queensland Printing Employees' Union (later the Printing Industry Employees' Union of Australia and from 1966 the Printing and Kindred Industries Union), Milliner was elected in 1934 to the board of

management. He was the union's industrial officer and secretary-treasurer in 1949-66 and national vice-president in 1951-68. A delegate to the Trades and Labor Council of Queensland, he was a member of the executive (from 1952) and treasurer (1960-67). He also sat (1948-61) on the Queensland Printing Trades Group Apprenticeship Committee. As trade-union adviser on the Australian delegations, he travelled to Geneva to attend the thirty-seventh (1954) and forty-eighth (1964) sessions of the International Labour Conference.

Milliner represented Small Unions (1947-50) and his own union (from 1950) on the Queensland central executive of the Australian Labor Party. An active and influential State party manager, he chaired the rules committee, held office as vice-president for a term, and was to be president in 1963-68. At the meeting called in April 1957 to consider the situation of V. C. Gair [q.v.14], he moved that there be further negotiations before the premier's expulsion from the A.L.P. was discussed; when his proposal was rejected, he voted with the T.L.C. group to expel Gair.

As party president, Milliner worked closely with two able State secretaries, Jim Keeffe and Tom Burns. They endeavoured to overcome problems arising from the A.L.P.'s period in Opposition, to repair relations with the powerful Australian Workers' Union, and —in concert with J. E. Duggan—to foster cooperation with the Queensland Parliamentary Labor Party. Milliner was a competent chairman, courteous and fair. He tried to achieve unity, to broaden the party's electoral base, and to encourage the involvement of women and the young. His leadership proved decisive in winning party support in Queensland for Gough Whitlam in his confrontation with the A.L.P.'s federal executive in February 1966.

In 1962 Milliner had unsuccessfully sought party nomination as one of two candidates to be considered by the Legislative Assembly for a casual vacancy in the Senate. At the 1967 elections he won a seat in the Senate. His term began on 1 July 1968 and he served exactly seven years. Friendly and well informed, he was a vigorous debater, with a reputation for 'good humour, wisdom and integrity'. He sat on ten parliamentary committees. Chairman (from 1973) of the Senate publications committee and of the joint committee on the Australian Capital Territory, he was appointed temporary chairman of committees in the Senate on 10 July 1974.

Milliner was a Freemason. He assisted numerous community organizations, among them the South Queensland Prisoners' Aid Society, the Queensland Board of Adult Education, the Industries' Sheltered Workshop Committee and the State committee of the Winston Churchill Memorial Trust (Australia). He enjoyed Rugby League football and supported Western Suburbs. Survived by his wife, two sons and two daughters, he died of myocardial infarction on 30 June 1975 in his Brisbane office and was cremated. (Sir) Joh Bjelke-Petersen's government replaced Milliner with Albert Field, an action which enabled the Senate to defer appropriation bills in October, thereby contributing to the dismissal of the Whitlam government. Milliner's son Glen was a member (1977-98) of the Queensland Legislative Assembly.

PD (HR), 9 July 1975, p 3549; *PD* (Senate), 9 July 1975, p 2687; *PD* (Qld), 27 Aug 1975, p 207, 3 Sept 1975, p 387; Trades and Labor Council of Queensland records (Fryer L, Univ Qld); ALP records (OL).

MANFRED CROSS

MILLINGTON, TASMAN MALCOLM (1896-1963), soldier and war graves curator, was born on 16 June 1896 in Hobart, seventh of ten children of William James Millington, surgical bootmaker, and his wife Alice, née Baker. Tasman left Battery Point State School at the age of 14 to be apprenticed as a bricklayer with Gillham Bros. A senior cadet in the 36th Fortress Company (Australian Engineers), he enlisted in the Australian Imperial Force on 26 April 1915. He was posted to the 26th Battalion, which landed at Gallipoli in September. Suffering from dysentery, Millington spent periods in hospital in Malta (October) and in England (from November). Between April 1916 and September 1918 he served on the Western Front and was twice wounded in action.

After World War I had ended, Millington studied at the British School of Telegraphy, London. On 22 September 1919 he married Ruth Evelyn Martin (d.1956) at the parish church of St Martin in the Fields. He joined the Imperial (Commonwealth from 1960) War Graves Commission as a staff sergeant on 7 September and was discharged from the A.I.F. on 14 November. The I.W.G.C. sent him to take charge of its motorboats and water transport in the Dardanelles and the Sea of Marmara, some of which also sailed between Turkey and the islands of Lemnos, Imbros, Tenedos (Bozca) and Lesbos.

While war cemeteries were being built on the Gallipoli Peninsula, Millington and his wife lived there, at Kilya. In the early 1920s he supervised work on former battlefields to locate the remains of the dead and transfer them to war graves. When construction of the cemeteries was completed in the late 1920s, he moved to the commission's headquarters at Canakkale. About 1930 he was promoted area superintendent with responsibility for the maintenance of thirty-six cemeteries and memorials on Gallipoli, and three in Istanbul,

commemorating 34 000 soldiers and sailors of the British Empire who died in the Dardanelles campaign.

Millington found it difficult to maintain the cemetery gardens on the peninsula: water was scarce, the climate harsh, and travel arduous. His staff of Turks and White Russians respected him and affectionately called him Millington Bey. He became proficient in the Turkish language and, with tact and good humour, established excellent working relationships with the local authorities. Millington and his wife looked after the many relations, friends and dignitaries who made pilgrimages to the cemeteries. All of them were made welcome, and helped to identify and reach the grave sites. In 1934 Millington was appointed O.B.E. He was also appointed to the Légion d'honneur (1950) for his assistance in tending a French war cemetery. During World War II he held the honorary rank of major and maintained the commission's work, though largely cut off from the outside world.

In April 1961 Millington retired to England. As a result of diabetes which led to gangrene, both his legs were amputated. He died of coronary thrombosis on 10 December 1963 at West Byfleet, Surrey, and was buried in Sidcup cemetery, Kent. He was survived by his son, who was baptized on 25 April 1922 at Anzac Cove and served in the Royal Air Force in World War II.

P. Longworth, *The Unending Vigil* (Lond, 1967); *Reveille* (Syd), 1 Aug 1933, 1 July 1934, 1 Feb, 1 July 1935; *The Times*, 4 June 1934, 31 Dec 1963; *Star* (Melb), 5 Jan 1935; *SMH*, 20 June 1935; information from Messrs S. T. Grady, Kassandria, Greece, G. R. Moore, Herne Hill, Lond, B. Millington, North Tuddenham, Norfolk, and O. Stolt, Sherborne, Dorset, Eng.

ALISON PILGER

MILLS, ANDREW AGNEW NEILSON (1881-1967), grazier and studmaster, was born on 1 May 1881 at Uardry station, near Carrathool, New South Wales, fifth child of Scottish-born parents Charles Mills [q.v.5], squatter, and his wife Margaret, née Ainslie. Neilson was educated privately, save for a final year (1896) at Sydney Church of England Grammar School (Shore). On the death of his eldest brother Ainslie in 1908, he took charge of the property, then mortgaged for £100 000 due to the depression, the 'long drought' and a rabbit plague. He improved the stud flock by judicious infusions of Boonoke, Haddon Rig and Wanganella blood, and soon discharged the debt.

After his father died in 1916, Mills became chairman of Charles Mills (Uardry) Ltd, and in 1919 bought part of Old Burrabogie station. He renamed it Pembelgong and in February 1921 formed the Uardry-Pembelgong stud, based on Wanganella rams. In 1926 the company acquired the adjacent Burrabogie station (21 000 acres, 8500 ha) for £60 000, enabling Mills to develop Uardry as a major parent stud. During this time he popularized the term 'Peppin' [q.v.5] for sheep with Boonoke or Wanganella blood. At the Presbyterian Church, Hay, on 6 April 1921 he had married 20-year-old Frances Mary ('Toby') Gleeson.

Mills soon had outstanding success at the Sydney Sheep Show: he won grand championship ram (1923, 1925), ewe (1927) and in 1932 'Uardry 0.1' was champion strong wool and grand champion ram. This famous merino's effigy adorned (1938-66) the reverse of the Australian one-shilling coin. In 1932, using Uardry merinos, Mills founded Wahwoon Nos 1 and 2 studs which traded as A. A. Neilson Mills & Son from 1936 and bred the 1946 grand champion ram. Although he studied genetics, he depended in part on the advice of such friends and notable classers as J. C. Darke, W. J. McCarthy and Harold Watson.

Separation of the family interests in Charles Mills (Uardry) Ltd took place in 1938. Neilson received 56 per cent of the company's assets. Moving to Burrabogie, he established Burrabogie (Flock No.844) and Mulbogie (Flock No.859) studs, respectively from the division of the Uardry and Pembelgong stud flocks. He continued to breed Uardry-type sheep and his studs were influential well into the 1950s. In 1961 he was appointed O.B.E. His ill health forced the dispersal and deregistration of the Wahwoon-Burrabogie studs in October 1966 when the stock grossed $280 000: the top price ($1300) for a ram was paid by Charles Mills (Uardry) Ltd.

Tall, handsome and athletic, Mills played cricket and polo in his youth. He was an early member of the Waradgery Club, Hay, and a founder (1900) of the Riverina Picnic Race Club. As a member (1911-34) and president (1912-15 and 1922-23) of Carrathool Shire Council and president of the Pastures Protection Board, Hay district, he successfully opposed moves to carve up the strategic Booligal-Deniliquin stock route. He also opposed the ban on the export of merino rams. Survived by his wife and son, he died on 16 January 1967 at Hay and was buried in the local cemetery. Mills bequeathed to woolgrowers a valuable source of Peppin genes that produced high quality, dense wool.

C. Massy, *The Australian Merino* (Melb, 1990); G. Walsh, *Pioneering Days* (Syd, 1993); NSW Sheepbreeders' Assn, *The Australian Merino* (Syd, 1955) and *Aust Stud Merino Flock Register*, 33, 1956; *Pastoral Review*, 16 Oct 1923, 15 Dec 1928, 16 June 1944, 18 July 1962, 15 Sept, 18 Oct 1966, 24 Feb 1967; *Australasian*, 15 June 1912, 19 Apr 1919, 23 Oct 1920, 28 June 1924, 20 June 1925; *Land* (Syd), 19 Jan 1967, 21 May 1992, 16 Mar 1995.

G. P. WALSH

MILLS, BERYL LUCY (1907-1977), Miss Australia, was born on 3 January 1907 at Walkaway, near Geraldton, Western Australia, fifth child and fourth daughter of Australian-born parents Frank Ernest Mills, grazier, and his wife Kitty, née Gibbons. After attending Geraldton District High School, Beryl won a bursary to Perth Modern School where she became a prefect. Awarded a scholarship to the University of Western Australia in 1924, she studied English and French, won swimming and diving championships, and captained the hockey team. In 1926 she was admitted to the Training College, Claremont.

Beryl's father submitted a photograph of her (wearing a bathing costume) to the inaugural 'Miss Australia' contest, initiated by Claude McKay [q.v.] and R. C. Packer [q.v.11] to promote the *Daily Guardian*. After becoming 'Miss Westralia', she won the national title in June 1926 at a lavish ceremony in Sydney. She admitted 'I like a hard fight'. When she obtained leave from university, one academic commented that her reason was 'unworthy of a serious student'.

Amid a blaze of publicity, Mills—who was 5 ft 6½ ins (169 cm) tall, weighed 9 st 11 lb (60 kg), had short dark hair, a round face and brown eyes, and eschewed make-up—toured retail establishments and attended civic receptions. The 'Miss Australia' selection criteria had included education, sporting ability and poise. Natural, wholesome, healthy and athletic, Mills was presented as the ideal Australian girl. She embarked on a carefully orchestrated promotional tour of the United States of America. Chaperoned by her mother, McKay and (Sir) Frank Packer [q.v.], Mills was greeted by mayors, attended balls, visited movie studios, started baseball matches, gave swimming exhibitions, placed wreaths on war graves and made speeches with a 'modest earnestness'. She was a guest of the Miss America pageant at Atlantic City. Back in Sydney in November, she undertook a lecture tour.

At St Michael's Anglican Church, Vaucluse, on 19 March 1928 she married Francis Keith Davison (d.1946), a journalist on the *Daily Guardian*. That year she established the Beryl Mills Advertising Service. In the early 1930s they shifted to Melbourne where Frank joined the *Herald*; their daughter Judith was born in 1935. Beryl had returned to Sydney by 1941 and became librarian at Packer's Consolidated Press Ltd. She met an American, Major Leslie Garland Calder, whom she married with Methodist forms on 19 December 1946 at Drewry's Bluff, Virginia, U.S.A.

The couple, joined by Judith, bought a 19-acre (7.7 ha) run at Richmond and renovated the ramshackle house. While Leslie worked as a factory supervisor for E. I. Du Pont de Nemours & Co., Beryl joined the American

National Red Cross, taught first aid, presided over the Chesterfield Home Demonstration Club, belonged to the Huguenot Republican Women's Club, helped to start a volunteer rescue service, played golf and swam. She was naturalized on 8 June 1955. In the following year she visited Perth. Still regarding herself as an advocate for her native country, she gave talks about Australia to schoolchildren in Virginia, with a toy koala perched beside her.

On Leslie's retirement, they moved to Florida. Survived by her husband and by the daughter of her first marriage, Beryl died on 13 July 1977 in the Medical Center Hospital, Punta Gorda, and was cremated.

C. McKay, *This is the Life* (Syd, 1961); *Newspaper News*, 1 May 1928; *Aust Women's Weekly*, 17 Sept 1949; *Daily Guardian* (Syd), 28 June 1926; *Richmond Times-Dispatch*, 27 Mar 1949, 16 July 1977; *SMH*, 24, 26 Sept 1968, 23 July 1977; *Daily Telegraph* (Syd), 26 Apr 1971; *Richmond News Leader*, 15, 18 July 1977; Univ WA Archives; family papers held by Ms M. J. Brooke, South Perth.

BRIDGET GRIFFEN-FOLEY
MARION BROOKE

MILLS, FREDERICK JOHN (1876-1952), writer, broadcaster and welfare worker, was born on 14 November 1876 in Adelaide, one of four children of John Mills, a carter from England, and his South Australian-born wife Ellen Jessie Bruce, née Watson. Educated at Sturt Street and Yongala public schools, Fred left at the age of 13 and became a messenger-boy at the Yongala post office. He trained as a telegraphist and spent some years as a junior operator at Eucla, Western Australia, during the gold rushes. In 1913 he transferred to the administration branch at the General Post Office, Adelaide; he resigned in 1923 when he was appointed State secretary of the Boy Scouts' Association. At her father's home at Kadina on 23 January 1901 Mills had married Louisa Symons; they were to have a son and a daughter.

Undeterred by his limited formal education, Mills began to pursue his literary bent. By 1908 he was a committee-member of the South Australian Literary Societies' Union and a contributor to its journal. Using the pen-name, 'The Twinkler', he edited 'Sundry Scintillations' for the *Saturday Evening's Journal*. He was noted 'for his candour and incisiveness in attacking hoary superstition and advocating progressive ideas'. As vice-president of the St John's Young Men's Society, he was regarded as a 'humorist of no mean order'.

After World War I began, Mills was vice-president (1915) of the Cheer-Up Society, founded by Alexandra Seager and (Sir) William Sowden [qq.v.11,12] to provide 'general comfort, welfare, and entertainment' for soldiers. He served (1919-20) on the committee of the Rejected Volunteers' Association of South Australia, and founded and edited the magazine of the Returned Soldiers' Association of South Australia. In 1915 he had also helped to set up Violet Remembrance Day; he subsequently became executive-officer of the Wattle Day League. His first publication, *The Cheer-Up Book* (1915), was followed by *Dinkum Oil* (1917) and *Square Dinkum* (Melbourne, 1917); Mills donated the proceeds to the R.S.A.S.A. In 1917 he was awarded a certificate of merit by the Returned Sailors' and Soldiers' Imperial League of Australia.

In July 1926 Mills inaugurated the 'Twinkler's Boys' Club' on radio 5CL as an adjunct to the scouting movement; he was to manage the programme until 1945. The club boasted 7000 members, enjoyed vice-regal patronage and raised 'thousands of pounds' for the Adelaide Children's Hospital by 1933. Mills's relationship with 5CL was often stormy, but the loyalty of his youthful supporters—and their parents—was beyond doubt. They bought him a second-hand motor-car to use in his charitable work; the vehicle was duly named 'The Snodger or Invalid's Delight'. He retired from the Boy Scouts' Association in 1937: a public testimonial raised £600 and the Children's Hospital made him a life governor. In 1938 he was appointed M.B.E. Mills went on to publish *The Bonzer Place* (1942), *The New Dinkum Oil* (1944) and *The Wisdom of Happiness* (London, 1952). Survived by his wife and son, he died on 10 December 1952 at his Eden Hills home and was buried in Centennial Park cemetery. His estate was sworn for probate at £469.

Literary Societies' J, 10 June 1908; *Radio Programme J*, 29 July 1932; *Radio Call*, 21 Oct 1937, 6 Jan 1938, 17 Dec 1952; *Advertiser* (Adel), 11 Dec 1952; Personalities Remembered, ABC radio talk, 5CL, 7 Feb 1971, Hedley Cullen (Mort L).

PETER STRAWHAN

MILLS, THOMAS (1908-1978), soldier, tin-miner and businessman, was born on 2 April 1908 at Charters Towers, Queensland, son of Thomas Mills, mining engineer, and his wife Hettie Mary, née Millican, both of whom were born in that town. Educated at Newington College, Sydney, young Tom completed his compulsory military training and worked as a woolclasser before becoming a tinminer at Emmaville during the Depression. Enlisting in the Militia in 1933, he served with the 12th Light Horse Regiment and was commissioned lieutenant in 1935. On 13 October 1939 he was appointed to the Australian Imperial Force and posted to the 6th Divisional Recon-naissance (later Cavalry) Regiment.

At the Methodist Church, Crows Nest, Sydney, on 17 December 1939 Mills married Iris Irene O'Loan, a 26-year-old hairdresser. Twenty-three days later he embarked with his regiment for the Middle East to undertake further training in Palestine. On 4 January 1941, the second day of the Australian assault on Bardia, Libya, Mills commanded three troops of Bren-gun carriers which conducted a reconnaissance of the town. He showed coolness and courage in organizing attacks against isolated strong-points and was awarded the Military Cross.

The Australian-led invasion of Syria began on 8 June and the 6th Divisional Cavalry probed the enemy's positions on the coastal road towards Sidon. On 10 June they encoun-tered a strong Vichy French position near Sarafend. Mills armed himself with a Thomp-son sub-machine-gun and, with three of his men, moved through rocky terrain to the top of a ridge that overlooked the enemy. Breaking cover, he fired his weapon, inflicting several casualties before his gun jammed. The French began shooting at him, but he continued to advance with his jammed weapon. After several bursts of supporting fire from Sergeant R. T. Cramp, forty-five French soldiers (with two anti-tank guns and three machine-guns) surrendered to Mills. He won a Bar to his Military Cross, the first of only fifteen such awards to members of the Australian army in World War II.

Rising to captain (June 1941) and major (February 1942), Mills returned to Australia in March 1942 and joined the 2nd/11th Armoured Car Regiment. In March 1943 he was promoted temporary lieutenant colonel and placed in command of the 2nd/5th Armoured Regiment. On 11 May 1944 he took over the 2nd/4th Armoured Regiment which was sent to Madang, New Guinea, in August. Two squadron groups were subsequently detached, one to support the 6th Division in the Aitape-Wewak campaign, and the other to assist the 3rd Division on Bougainville where the main body of the 2nd/4th also served from May 1945. Mills travelled extensively to visit his outlying forces. He came home in December 1945, relinquished his command in February 1946 and transferred to the Reserve of Officers on 27 March.

Lieutenant Colonel F. J. Mulally, who had served with Mills, described him as a tough man who was admired by everyone. After the war Mills owned and operated a pest-control business at Surfers Paradise, Queensland. Quiet and unassuming, he enjoyed reading and fishing. He died of myocardial infarction on 29 July 1978 at Ocean Beach, Moreton Island, and was cremated; his wife and daugh-ter survived him.

G. Long, *To Benghazi* (Canb, 1952), *Greece, Crete and Syria* (Canb, 1953), and *The Final Campaigns* (Canb, 1963); *Tank Tracks* (Syd, 1953); S. O'Leary, *To the Green Fields Beyond* (Syd, 1975); R. N. L. Hopkins, *Australian Armour* (Canb, 1978); AWM 67, item 2/46 and AWM 88, item AMF 12/M (AWM); information from the late Lt-Col F. J. Mulally.

ANTHONY STAUNTON

MILNE, FRANK KENNETH (1885-1980), architect, was born on 18 July 1885 at Tus-more, South Australia, seventh of eight chil-dren of Adelaide-born parents John Milne, land agent, and his wife Lucy Edith, née MacGeorge. Sir William Milne [q.v.5] was his grandfather. Educated privately, and at Glenelg and North Adelaide state schools, Kenneth was introduced to drawing by Miss Mary Overbury at Mrs Kingston's school, New Glenelg. A bachelor uncle, William Milne, paid for his secondary education and provided the £350 necessary to have him articled (1903-06) to the Adelaide architect William Alfred Wells. He came under the tute-lage of Stuart Clark, the firm's chief drafts-man. In 1906 he joined G. B. Robertson & T. J. Marks [q.v.10] in Sydney as an architectural draftsman; he claimed that he learned more there than he might have 'in thirty years' in Adelaide.

Returning home 'full of ideas' in April 1909, Milne set up a practice in Grenfell Street. His designs became increasingly eclectic, using idioms as diverse as Art Nouveau, *beaux-arts* classicism, bungalow, Art Deco, Gothic, and Italian renaissance. He prepared designs for banks, hotels, churches, houses, woolstores, swimming-pools and picture-theatres. Among his early commissions were the Hampshire Hotel (1910), Grote Street, and the South Aus-tralian Cricket Association scoreboard (1911), Adelaide Oval.

At Chalmers Church, North Terrace, on 12 March 1913 Milne had married Hazel Muir Fotheringham (d.1968) with Presbyterian forms. One year earlier he had contracted with the South Australian Brewing Co. Ltd to supervise construction on its properties. This work constituted a large part of his operations until 1920, and he was retained by the com-pany until 1946. As business expanded, he was joined in partnership by J. R. S. Evans (1920) and C. A. Russell (by 1929). During the 1920s many of the firm's principal commercial buildings were commissioned, including the Edments [q.v.8] building, Rundle Street, and Lister House, North Terrace. Early in 1930 the partnership of F. Kenneth Milne, Evans & Russell was dissolved.

On a study-tour of Britain and Europe in 1933-34, Milne renewed an interest in Georgian architecture, in particular the work of the Adam brothers. This style was reflected in Arbury Park (1934), Bridgewater, a house he designed for (Sir) Alexander Downer, in his own home, Sunnyside (1936), North Adelaide, and in offices for Goldsbrough, Mort [qq.v.4,5] & Co. Ltd (1935) and H. C. Sleigh [q.v.11] Ltd (1955), both in Adelaide. Milne considered these buildings his best work. He was president (1937-39) of the South Australian Institute of Architects and received its award of merit (1944) for Sunnyside.

From the late 1940s a number of associates had joined Milne in partnership: L. C. Dawkins and R. V. Boehm (1946), R. S. Ellis (1947), F. P. Bulbeck (by 1957), J. R. N. Twopeny (1960) and James Hodge (by 1964). Milne promoted his profession by giving public addresses on architecture and by helping to establish a school of architecture at the University of Adelaide. In 1955 his firm donated £1000 to the university; in 1958 he gave £5000 for the Kenneth and Hazel Milne travelling scholarship in architecture. In semi-retirement from 1957, he continued to undertake alterations to buildings he had previously designed and other work for established clients (such as the Angas [qq.v.1,3,13] and Kidman [q.v.9] families) until he retired in 1973. He was made a life fellow (1970) of the Royal Australian Institute of Architects.

Active in the English-Speaking Union and the Liberal and Country League of South Australia, Milne was small in stature, physically fit and mentally alert. He belonged to the Adelaide Rowing Club, the Amateur Sports Club and the South Australian Rugby Union. To celebrate his ninety-first year, he stroked an A.R.C. VIII on the River Torrens, with three family members in the crew. He died on 3 October 1980 at Calvary Hospital, North Adelaide, and was cremated. His only child Kenneth Lancelot, founding president (1977) of the South Australian division of the Australian Democrats, sat in the Legislative Council in 1979-85.

D. L. Johnson et al, *F. Kenneth Milne* (Adel, 1984); *SA Master Builder*, July/Aug 1975, p 23; *Advertiser* (Adel), 24 Sept 1924, 2 Apr 1937, 5 May 1939, 21 July 1959, 4 Oct 1980; *Daily News* (Adel), 4 June 1970; F. K. Milne collection (Architecture Archives, Univ SA).

MILSON, COLIN GEORGE MACALISTER (1919-1975), air force officer and grazier, was born on 16 June 1919 at Longreach, Queensland, son of James Arthur Milson, station-manager, and his wife Valerie Aeneas, née Morgan-Reade, both Queensland born. A direct descendant of James Milson [q.v.2], Arthur managed Springvale, one of the family's cattle-stations near Winton. Colin attended Cranbrook School, Sydney, and

All Souls Church of England Boys' School, Charters Towers, Queensland, which he represented in swimming, athletics, cricket (first XI) and Rugby League football (first XIII). He worked for six months on Springvale before becoming a jackeroo at Bundemar, near Trangie, New South Wales.

Enlisting in the Royal Australian Air Force on 19 August 1940 under the Empire Air Training Scheme, Milson proceeded to Rhodesia in November. He qualified as a pilot in April 1941, was commissioned in the following month, and arrived in Britain in October. After further training, he was posted (May 1942) to No.39 Squadron, Royal Air Force, based in the Middle East. The squadron flew Beauforts against German and Italian ships. In September 1942 and March 1943 Milson led attacks on enemy supply ships which were heavily protected by destroyers and aircraft. For these and other actions, in which he 'invariably displayed courage and determination', he won the Distinguished Flying Cross.

In May 1943 Milson was sent to London. Next month he began work at the Air Ministry. Following a brief attachment to No.144 Squadron, R.A.F., he was posted in December to No.455 Squadron, R.A.A.F., which was stationed alternately at bases in Scotland and England. John Herington [q.v.14] described its commanding officer, J. N. Davenport, and flight commanders, A. L. Wiggins and Milson, as 'three of the most pugnacious and inspiring tacticians thrown up in the evolvement of Coastal Command's anti-shipping campaign ... each in other times and circumstances would have been an outstanding cavalry leader'. Providing the 'anti-flak element' of a strike wing, the crews of No.455 Squadron operated Beaufighters fitted with cannons and rockets. They engaged the most heavily armed ships so that torpedo-carrying aircraft could get a clear run at the targets.

Fair, lean, and clear-eyed, Milson led with determination and set an example. He was described as 'tough and charismatic'. Seemingly contemptuous of danger, he always drove home his attacks at low level and took every opportunity to inflict damage on enemy ships. On 15 June 1944 he was prominent in the largest assault Coastal Command sent against a German convoy, located off Ameland, the Netherlands, and was awarded a Bar to his D.F.C. In another sortie, on 29 August, his aircraft was severely hit and he had to fly 300 miles (480 km) back from Heligoland, Germany, on only one engine. He wrote to his father: 'It didn't worry me in the slightest as I was out on "ops" again the next day and also the following one'. Milson was awarded the Distinguished Service Order.

He enjoyed squadron life and operational service, and rejected the opportunity for less arduous work or a transfer to a training unit. In October 1944 he was appointed to command No.455 and promoted acting wing commander. Although Milson was increasingly office-bound, he continued to find opportunities to fly, even in winter when operations proved particularly hazardous. On 9 February 1945 he led a large formation against a naval force in Fördefjord, Norway. For his skill and courage, in what was described as a 'brilliantly executed operation', he won a Bar to his D.S.O. On 14 April his rockets damaged a U-boat in Jössingfjord.

Demobilized back home on 17 April 1946, Milson joined Thomas Borthwick & Sons (Australasia) Ltd as a cattle buyer. He advanced to higher positions in Brisbane and moved to Sydney in 1953 as State manager of the firm. In June 1955 he left the company and took over the management of his family's cattle-stations. Recognizing the potential of light aircraft in the cattle industry, he resumed flying for business purposes. He was elected to the Diamantina Shire Council and served a term as shire president.

On 9 October 1947 at All Saints Anglican Church, Brisbane, Milson had married Sheila Margaret Tonkin, a 32-year-old beautician. He was a gregarious but modest man who read widely on history and politics; Sheila and he enjoyed travel. In 1973 they moved to Darling Point, Sydney, where he remained involved in business. Survived by his wife and two sons, he died of cancer on 14 July 1975 at St Luke's Hospital, Darlinghurst, and was cremated. His medals and his portrait by Harold Freedman are held by the Australian War Memorial, Canberra.

F. Johnson (ed), *R.A.A.F. Over Europe* (Lond, 1946); J. Herington, *Air Power Over Europe 1944-1945* (Canb, 1963); I. Gordon, *Strike and Strike Again* (Canb, 1995); RAAF biog records AWM 65 (AWM); information from Mr S. Milson, Bondi Beach, Syd.   PETER BURNESS

MINGAY, OSWALD FRANCIS (1895-1973), radio engineer, soldier and publisher, was born on 1 July 1895 at Peak Hill, New South Wales, son of 17-year-old Elizabeth Mingay. Ossie was educated at Lithgow District School and Sydney Technical College. He joined the Postmaster General's Department as a telegraph messenger on 1 March 1908 at Lithgow. Moving to Sydney, he was appointed a junior mechanic in the electrical engineers' branch in July 1914. When he enlisted in the Australian Imperial Force on 14 September 1915 he was 5 ft 4 ins (163 cm) tall, with a dark complexion, blue eyes and brown hair. He served on the Western Front, first with the 5th Field Artillery Brigade (March-December 1916) and then with the 2nd Divisional Signal

Company. In March 1918 he was promoted corporal.

After the Armistice, Mingay led a party of post office technicians which reconstructed the civil telephone exchange at Charleroi, Belgium, where he also acted as an instructor at the Université du Travail. In 1919 he gained experience with engineers of the General Post Office, London. Mentioned in dispatches, he returned to Sydney and was discharged from the A.I.F. on 16 January 1920. He resumed duties as a mechanic at the P.M.G.'s central exchange and wrote the wireless column for the *Daily Telegraph*. At St Clement's Anglican Church, Marrickville, on 26 July 1920 he married Winifred Helen Nimmo Esdon (d.1971).

Mingay joined the wireless branch of Burgin Electric Co. in 1922 and became manager of its radio-station 2BE in 1924. He resigned in September 1925, but, instead of visiting England as planned, formed Mingay's Wireless Manufacturing Ltd. In 1930, as the principal and proprietor, he established the Australian Radio College. That year he persuaded a publisher to bring out the *Radio Retailer of Australia* (1930-33). His critical and provocative editorials embraced politics, economics, education, and humanity. When asked to confine his comments to the trade, Mingay resigned as managing editor, formed the Mingay Publishing Co. Ltd to buy the paper and continued his editorials. He was quick-witted, humorous, thoughtful and knowledgable. His other publications included *Broadcasting Business* (1933-48) and *Mingay's Electrical Weekly*. He retired as managing director in 1961 when the firm was sold to the Thomson Organisation Ltd, London.

A member (from 1922) of the State division of the Wireless Institute of Australia, Mingay and (Sir) Ernest Fisk [q.v.8] had provided the drive to found the Institution of Radio (and Electronics) Engineers, Australia, in 1932; he was its secretary until 1940. During World War II he served (1941-42) as a signals officer in the 1st Cavalry Division, Militia, and rose to temporary captain. In May 1942 he transferred to the Ministry of Munitions, 'where his experience of the radio industry, his pertinacity and his irrepressible attitude' were valued. He was a representative at Lend-Lease discussions in Washington.

In 1965 Mingay retired from business. He was appointed M.B.E. in the following year. A long-time member of the Imperial Service Club, the Royal Automobile Club of Australia, the Legacy Club of Sydney, and the Roseville Golf and Killara Bowling clubs, he helped to set up the Broadcasting Radio Electrical Industries Fellowship Club. On 10 October 1972 at St Mark's Anglican Church, Darling Point, he married a widow Theodora Florence Lippmann, née Wills. Survived by his wife and the son of his first marriage, he died on 8 August 1973 at his St Ives home and was cremated.

Mingay's Electrical Weekly, 4 Dec 1964, 26 Feb 1965; *Mingay's News,* 17 July 1972; *Procs of the IREE,* Aug 1973; *Monitor,* Dec 1982; Mingay papers (ML).

JIM SYMES

MITCHELL, SIR ANGUS SINCLAIR (1884-1961), grain broker and Rotarian, was born on 1 April 1884 at Shanghai, China, second son of James Alexander Mitchell, a master mariner from London, and his Victorian-born wife Elizabeth, née Anderson. James settled at Williamstown, Melbourne, in 1885, joined the Port Phillip pilots and helped to found the Victorian Stevedoring Co. Ltd. Angus was educated at Scotch College. In 1905, with his brother-in-law J. B. Bellair, he established Mitchell & Bellair, mercantile and grain brokers. When William Lees of the Corn Exchange Trade Association, Liverpool, England, joined the partnership in 1924, the firm was one of the largest of its kind in Australia. At the Menzies Hotel, Melbourne, on 5 October 1910 Mitchell had married with Presbyterian forms Teenie Robertson MacKenzie. He retired from his firm in 1936 and accepted directorships of several public companies, among them Australian Cement Ltd and Noske Industries Ltd.

A public-spirited man with a strong Presbyterian background, Mitchell gave much of his time to community work. During the Depression he had initiated the Port Melbourne settlement for unemployed youth, later the Young Men's Christian Association Port Melbourne Youth Centre, of which he was chairman. In 1931 he joined the State executive and finance committees of the Boy Scouts' Association (treasurer 1940-61). He was also a sponsor of the Lord Somers' [q.v.12] Camp for boys, and president (1951-61) of the Victorian Society for Crippled Children (and Adults).

Mitchell contributed to international understanding through his membership of Rotary. Having joined the Rotary Club of Melbourne in 1927, he was its president in 1931-32. He was governor (1934-35) of Rotary District 65 (which covered the whole of Australia, except for Queensland and New South Wales north of the Riverina). While a director (1937-38) of Rotary International, he led a goodwill mission of sixty-four Australian Rotarians to the Philippines, China, Hong Kong, Japan, Malaya and the Dutch East Indies (Indonesia). Three days before the outbreak of World War II, Mitchell wrote to his friend Paul Harris, founder of Rotary, that 'friendliness, understanding, and goodwill were the only lines upon which nations could settle their differences'. Throughout the war Mitchell planned

for reconciliation with Rotarians in Germany and Japan. As president (1948-49) of Rotary International, he travelled 100 000 miles (160 000 km), visiting Rotary clubs in the Americas, Africa, Europe and Oceania. His warmth, simplicity and sincerity made a deep impression on all who met him. Before his presidency ended, five clubs in Japan and two in Germany were readmitted to Rotary International. Mitchell was knighted in 1956.

Sir Angus was tall and well built, with close-cropped hair. He was tolerant and wise, and dispassionate in considering problems. After his wife died in 1947, he lived at the Hotel Windsor. He enjoyed trout fishing at Tawonga, and rarely missed a Test match or a football final at the Melbourne Cricket Ground. Survived by his three daughters, he died on 16 August 1961 at Malvern and was cremated. Mitchell's portrait by (Sir) William Dargie is held by the Rotary Club of Melbourne, which established an annual oration in his memory; the library at International House, University of Melbourne, is named after him.

H. Hunt, *The Story of Rotary in Australia, 1921-1971* (Syd, 1971); *Age* (Melb), 2 Jan 1956; Mitchell papers (LaTL); Rotary Club of Melbourne papers (Univ Melb Archives); information from Mr J. Bellair, Upper Beaconsfield, Vic.

OWEN PARNABY

MITCHELL, BESSIE JEAN; *see* GUTHRIE

MITCHELL, GEORGE DEANE (1894-1961), soldier, author, politician and lifelong larrikin, was born on 30 August 1894 at Caltowie, South Australia, one of five children of George Deane Mitchell, railway porter, and his wife Annie, née Smith. Young George was a clerk in Adelaide when he enlisted in the 10th Battalion, Australian Imperial Force, on 5 September 1914. He served at Gallipoli from 25 April 1915 until he was evacuated with enteric fever on 6 August. Rejoining his battalion on 9 September 1916 in Belgium, he was transferred to the 48th Battalion on 31 October and promoted lance corporal on 17 March 1917.

On 11 April, after six hours of bitter trench fighting in the first battle of Bullecourt, France, Mitch covered his comrades' retreat, then shouldered his Lewis gun and strolled through heavy enemy fire to his lines. He won the Distinguished Conduct Medal and was promoted second lieutenant. His walk entered A.I.F. legend, and C. E. W. Bean's [q.v.7] official history used it to characterize Mitchell's brigade in the battle. On 28 March 1918 Mitchell's platoon held an exposed hillside at Dernancourt. On his right the enemy broke through. He ran to the break, waving a pistol, and captured about thirty soldiers. He was awarded the Military Cross. In May 1919 he returned to Australia an A.I.F. rarity, having survived four years of front-line service unwounded.

Mitchell wrote the A.I.F.'s most evocative diary, with a knack of seeing significance in events. 'We had come from the New World for the conquest of the Old', he observed at the Anzac landing. 'They all bore the hall mark of the Cog', he remarked of Londoners in 1916. 'I feel that I have lost touch with any life but this one of war', he wrote in 1917, it 'is hard to recall Australia, and apart from my people nothing stands out vividly. I feel an outsider. We are lost in the magnitude of our task'.

In peace he could not settle. In South Australia until 1922, he grew potatoes and was an army area officer at Mount Gambier; in Victoria until 1926 and Queensland until about 1936, he worked as an estate agent, garage-owner and motorcar salesman; and in New South Wales until 1940, he was a journalist and author. Although Mitchell was a Militia officer in 1920-26, he never liked officers, but he was proud of his war service and from 1934 wrote about it for *Reveille*, then for *Smith's Weekly* and in a book, *Backs to the Wall* (Sydney, 1937). Convinced of the importance of defence to his country's future, he wrote *The Awakening* (1937), a novel describing the invasion of an unprepared Australia, and *Soldier in Battle* (1940), a handbook for front-line infantry. In 1939 he edited and toured with *We of the A.I.F.*, an official film on 1914-18, for which he provided a vivid commentary. He became a State councillor of the Returned Sailors' and Soldiers' Imperial League of Australia. He ran as an Independent for the Legislative Assembly seat of Oxley, losing in 1938 and winning in 1941. Because of war service, he was present for only three sitting days, and lost the seat in 1944.

Having been appointed captain, Reserve of Officers, on 8 July 1940, Mitchell trained militiamen. He was promoted major on 1 September. At St Michael's Anglican Church, Vaucluse, on 30 July 1941 he married Thelma Agnes Bell, a 20-year-old New Zealand-born stenographer. In north-west Australia in 1942-43 he led an independent guerrilla force which lived off the land for weeks while searching for Japanese and training local resistance. Transferring to the A.I.F., he commanded the 43rd Landing Craft Company. With equipment vastly better than at Anzac Cove, he landed troops under fire at Dove Bay, near Wewak, New Guinea, on 11 May 1945. He returned to civilian life in February 1946 and worked for the T. B. Sailors, Soldiers and Airmen's Association. In his retirement he listed his recreations as swimming, hiking, experimenting and writing. He died of cancer

on 11 January 1961 at Darlinghurst, Sydney, and was cremated with Methodist forms. His wife and son survived him.

C. E. W. Bean, *The A.I.F. in France*, 1918 (Syd, 1937); B. Gammage, *The Broken Years* (Canb, 1974); *Reveille* (Syd), Mar 1936, Feb 1961; *People* (Syd), 18 June 1952; G. D. Mitchell, Diary 1914-18 (AWM).

BILL GAMMAGE

MITCHELL, JOHN WESLEY (1891-1969), army officer and public servant, was born on 16 March 1891 at Tarranyurk, near Dimboola, Victoria, fourth child of Australian-born parents Joseph Mitchell, farmer, and his wife Eliza, née Milkins. While working as an engineering cadet at Warracknabeal, Jack served in the Militia and was commissioned (1912) in the Victorian Rangers (later 73rd Infantry Regiment). On 24 August 1914 he was appointed to the Australian Imperial Force. Five ft 9½ ins (177 cm) tall, with dark hair and blue eyes, he was allotted to 'E' Company, 8th Battalion, which embarked for Egypt in October. He was quietly spoken and popular, and able to handle 'all the jobs of a subaltern'.

Landing at Gallipoli on 25 April 1915, Mitchell was wounded that day and admitted to hospital. He rejoined the battalion on 26 May and on the following day became its adjutant. By October he held the rank of temporary captain and was employed as a company commander. He returned to Egypt in January 1916, reached the Western Front in March and was promoted major in June. Absent from his unit in July-October when stricken with influenza, he was away again from January to March 1917 attending the Senior Officers' Course in England. On 14 April 1917 he was promoted lieutenant colonel and placed in command of the battalion.

Mitchell showed great courage in carrying out reconnaissance. In the operations at Lagnicourt and Bullecourt, France, in April and May 1917 (in which he won the Distinguished Service Order) his personal example influenced his men to push ahead and secure tactical positions. On 28 October, although gassed, he remained on duty. During the capture of Rosières Station and the village of Lihons on 9 and 11 August 1918, his battalion suffered heavy casualties; Mitchell twice went forward under fire to reorganize the line; he won a Bar to his D.S.O. For his leadership of the 8th Battalion, he was also awarded the Belgian Croix de Guerre and mentioned in dispatches five times. In October and November he had temporary command of the 2nd Brigade. His A.I.F. appointment terminated in Australia on 5 April 1920.

Employed by the Victorian Department of Lands and Survey as an inspector of land settlement and later as a member of the Discharged Soldiers Settlement Inquiry Board, Mitchell provided practical assistance to former servicemen who settled in the Wimmera and the Mallee. On 2 May 1927 at St John's Anglican Church, Horsham, he married Margaret Blanche West, a 31-year-old nurse; they were to remain childless. He continued to serve in the Militia, commanding the 21st Battalion (1921-22), the 1st Armoured Car Regiment (1934-38) and the 20th Light Horse Regiment (1939).

Following the outbreak of World War II, Mitchell was appointed (13 October 1939) commanding officer of the 2nd/8th Battalion, A.I.F., which embarked for the Middle East in April 1940. The unit saw action in Libya— at Bardia and Tobruk, and in the advance to Benghazi—in January-February 1941. Mitchell was once more mentioned in dispatches. From April he led the 2nd/8th in the arduous Greek campaign and evacuation, relinquishing command on 28 May. He had twice acted as temporary commander (May-June 1940 and February-March 1941) of the 19th Brigade, but clashed with Brigadier G. A. Vasey [q.v.]. Placed on the Sick List in June 1941, he returned to Australia in July. His A.I.F. appointment terminated on 21 September and he transferred to the General List. Next day he was promoted temporary colonel and given command of the 4th Australian Infantry Training Brigade.

Mitchell was detached to Southern Command Training School in November 1941 and to headquarters, Queenscliff Covering Force, in the following month. He returned to the 4th A.I.T.B. (later headquarters, Australian Recruit Training Centre) in March 1942. Again seconded to the A.I.F. from March 1943, he was placed on the Reserve of Officers on 24 November 1944 with the honorary rank of colonel. He joined the Commonwealth Public Service and worked first in Brisbane and then in Sydney before spending his retirement at Seaforth. Survived by his wife, he died on 29 September 1969 at the Repatriation General Hospital, Concord, and was cremated. Mitchell had commanded the 8th Battalion with distinction in some of the most notable operations undertaken by Australian forces in two world wars. He was widely recognized as a great soldier.

D. M. Horner, *General Vasey's War* (Melb, 1992); R. J. Austin, *Cobbers in Khaki* (Rosebud, Vic, 1997); *Smith's Weekly* (Syd), 17 Feb 1940; information from Mr K. Hill, Chirnside Park, Brig K. V. Rossi, Ivanhoe, Melb, and Mrs L. M. Millar, Lorne, Vic.

JAMES WOOD

MITCHELL, SIR MARK LEDINGHAM (1902-1977), biochemist and university chancellor, was born on 13 June 1902 at Fitzroy, Adelaide, younger child and only son of (Sir) William Mitchell [q.v.10], a professor from Scotland, and his South Australian-born wife Marjorie Erlistoun (d.1913), daughter of Robert Barr Smith [q.v.6]. Mark attended Queen's School, North Adelaide, and the University of Adelaide (B.Sc., 1923) where he graduated with first-class honours in physiology. Proceeding to the University of Cambridge (M.Sc., 1929), he entered Christ's College and studied biochemistry in the department in which J. B. S. Haldane was reader. In 1927 he returned to the University of Adelaide to lecture in the department of biochemistry and general physiology under Professor Brailsford Robertson [q.v.11]. Mitchell was lecturer-in-charge (1933-37) of the department while the chair was vacant. He also worked as an editor of the *Australian Journal of Experimental Biology and Medical Science*, and as editor-in-chief (1936-63) nurtured its growth and international recognition.

On 29 July 1937 his father, by then vice-chancellor, offered the university £20 000 to endow a chair of biochemistry. The proposal was accepted at a council-meeting on the following day. Appointed to the chair in 1937, Mitchell held it until 1962. As professor, he undertook little research, but was widely regarded as a 'competent and conscientious' teacher. He supervised a few postgraduate students, and taught biochemistry to dental, medical and science undergraduates. By 1949 he had expanded his *Handbook of Practical Biochemistry* (1934) into a *Manual of Practical Biochemistry for Medical Students*. He understood and supported his staff, and represented Australian university medical schools on the National Health and Medical Research Council. Much of his time was spent on administration. A member (1949-65) of the university council and deputy vice-chancellor (1951-65) during the controversial tenure of A. P. Rowe [q.v.], he demonstrated a 'rare ability to create in negotiations an atmosphere of mutual understanding, respect and complete trust'.

Mitchell was a long-time director and later life member of the Young Men's Christian Association of Adelaide; in addition, he presided over the National Fitness Council of South Australia (1952-73) and the South Australian Council of Social Service (1954-73). A keen promoter of health and sport for young people, especially boys from disadvantaged backgrounds, he organized activities for them at the university, in his homes in North Adelaide and on his properties on Kangaroo Island. The boys played football and tennis in Saturday competitions which he arranged and sponsored, and learned bush skills on the island. He donated a number of sporting trophies, notably the Mark Mitchell shield (1923) for a football competition between the State's public schools. In 1961 he became a vice-president of the South Australian National Football League. His own love of the outdoors found expression in travelling through inland South Australia, coastal fishing and yachting.

Tall, dark and slim, he had continued to live with, and in the shadow of, his father who died in 1962 at the age of 101. Mark Mitchell was instinctively shy, but affable in company. A member of the Adelaide Club, he entertained larger parties of his guests at the South Australian Hotel and kept them amused with his anecdotes. In 1957 he was knighted. He was a benefactor and chairman (1959-74) of the South Australian Museum which established the Mark Mitchell Research Foundation for museum research. The University of Adelaide, to which he had given money unobtrusively for almost forty years, appointed him emeritus professor in 1962. Accepting an invitation (1966) to be the first chancellor of the Flinders University of South Australia, Sir Mark filled the office with dignity for a term of five years. He died on 8 July 1977 at the Regal Park Motel, North Adelaide, and was cremated. His estate, sworn for probate at $1 854 884, was divided between family, friends, charitable organizations and the two universities he had served. The University of Adelaide named its Centre for Physical Health after him. His portrait by Robert Hannaford is held by Flinders University.

A. E. Simpson, *The National Fitness Council of South Australia* (Adel, 1986); *Aust J of Experimental Biology and Medical Science*, 56, pt 4, 1978; Flinders Univ *and* Univ Adel Archives; information from Dr E. Neville, Sandy Bay, Dr J. Sallis, Univ of Tas, Hob, Em Prof E. S. Holdsworth, Margate, Tas, Prof P. H. Karmel, Yarralumla, Canb, Dr D. L. Hilliard, Flinders Univ, Mrs J. Paton, Beaumont, and Mr N. Reynolds, Adel.   JOHN JENKIN

MITCHELL, STANLEY ROBERT (1881-1963), ethnologist, mineralogist, metallurgist and businessman, was born on 12 February 1881 at St Kilda, Melbourne, eldest of eight children of James Davidson Mitchell, a commercial traveller and amateur mineralogist from Scotland, and his Victorian-born wife Jane Frances, née Warren. Taken to the Centennial International Exhibition (1888), Stan was impressed by the display of Aboriginal artefacts and developed a lifelong interest in ethnology. His interest in minerals grew from accompanying his father on collecting trips around the basalt quarries near Melbourne. After attending Armadale State School, he was employed (from 1898) as a metallurgist and industrial chemist in a smelting works at Footscray. At South Yarra on 26 February 1906 he married with Methodist forms Beatrice Anna Pay (d.1922), a 22-year-old music teacher; they were to have two sons

and two daughters. He studied at night at the Working Men's College, gained the 'Geologists' Expert's Certificate' in June 1911 and joined the part-time staff as junior assistant (1912) in the department of metallurgical geology and mineralogy; he was promoted assistant (1914) and instructor (1915).

In 1911 Mitchell had set up his own business as a gold-assayer. From the mid-1920s S. R. Mitchell & Co. Pty Ltd operated as a major refiner of precious metals. He also established (1930) the very profitable Mitchell's Abrasives Pty Ltd to manufacture sandpaper, using crushed glass from the nearby Abbotsford Brewery. A consultant to mining ventures in Australia and abroad, he was a member (from 1915) of the Australasian Institute of Mining Engineers (Australasian Institute of Mining and Metallurgy) and a foundation member (1917) of the (Royal) Australian Chemical Institute. On 9 July 1924 at St Paul's Anglican Cathedral, Melbourne, he married 29-year-old Ila Victoria Davies; they were to have a son before being divorced in 1946. He married a 54-year-old widow Bessie Alice Annie Terry, née Crick, on 28 June 1946 at the Congregational Church, Davey Street, Hobart. His three sons joined the family business.

Mitchell built up major collections of minerals and rocks, and of Aboriginal artefacts which he housed in a special building at his Frankston home. He was honorary mineralogist (1931-63), honorary ethnologist (1949-63), and a trustee and treasurer (1945-54) of the National Museum of Victoria. In the 1930s and 1940s he belonged to a distinguished group of 'amateur' ethnologists and collectors who gathered around Sir Baldwin Spencer [q.v.12]. They collected massive numbers of Aboriginal implements and championed the value of field-work over 'armchair theorists'. They believed that the raw geological material was the dominant factor in determining the forms of stone implements and that these forms had not changed from earliest times to the period of European contact. By the early 1960s such views had been largely superseded by growing evidence from the use of stratigraphy by professionally trained anthropologists to document cultural and environmental change. Mitchell wrote numerous articles on mineralogy, geology and Aboriginal artefacts. His major work, *Stone-Age Craftsmen*, published in 1949 to mixed reviews, was generally recognized as a pioneering effort.

President (1936-37) of the Field Naturalists Club of Victoria, Mitchell was co-founder of field naturalist clubs at Hawthorn and Frankston. In 1955 he was awarded the Australian Natural History medallion. He was also a founder (1934) and president (1940, 1942-43) of the Anthropological Society of Victoria.

Late in life he grew increasingly deaf, but maintained an active interest in ethnology. Survived by his wife, sons and a daughter, he died on 22 March 1963 in East Melbourne and was cremated. His collection of minerals is held by the Museum of Victoria, his collection of artefacts by the National Museum of Australia, Canberra, and his unpublished manuscripts and correspondence by the Australian Institute of Aboriginal and Torres Strait Islander Studies.

T. Griffiths, *Hunters and Collectors* (Melb, 1996); *Vic Naturalist*, 73 (1956), p 1, 80 (1963), p 119; Roy Soc Vic, *Procs*, 77 (1963), p 618; *Artefact*, 3 (1978); J. Carter, S. R. Mitchell and Archaeology in Victoria (M.A. thesis, Univ Melb, 1980); information from Dr A. W. Beasley, Balwyn, Melb.

J. F. LOVERING

MOCKRIDGE, EDWARD RUSSELL (1928-1958), cyclist, was born on 18 July 1928 in South Melbourne, second son of Victorian-born parents Robert Glover Mockridge, engineer, and his wife Aileen Claire, née Riley. In 1931 the family moved from Laverton to Geelong. Russell attended Geelong College and gained his Leaving certificate before joining the *Geelong Advertiser* as a cadet journalist. Seeking 'a little healthy exercise', he entered his first bicycle race with the Geelong amateur club in 1946: though unprepared and pedalling an old roadster, he won the event. He then progressed rapidly. A close third in the Melbourne to Castlemaine handicap on 9 August 1947 earned him selection for the Victorian team in the Australian road championships. He won the 125-mile (200 km) road title on 30 August at Centennial Park, Sydney.

At the 1948 Olympic Games in London, Mockridge had the misfortune to have his tyre punctured twice in the 194.6-km road race, which pushed him back to 26th in a field of 101. By the time of the 1950 Empire Games at Auckland, New Zealand, he was Australia's premier cyclist, winning gold medals in the time trial and the 1000-metre sprint, and silver in the 4000-metre individual pursuit. After he returned home, he created a sensation by quitting the sport and his job to prepare for the Anglican ministry. Having matriculated through Taylor's Coaching College, he enrolled in arts at the University of Melbourne; beset by doubts about his calling, he returned to the track within fourteen months.

Mockridge reached the final of the World Amateur Sprint Championship in Italy in 1951. Next year he won the Open Grand Prix, riding as an amateur against an embarrassed world professional champion Reg Harris. Mockridge's place in the team for the 1952 Helsinki Olympics appeared certain until the Australian Olympic Federation required athletes to sign a £750 fidelity bond to remain amateur for two years after the Games. Keen to turn professional, he refused to sign. Bervin Purnell, the mayor of Geelong, eventually broke the impasse by guaranteeing the money if the A.O.F. would reduce the amateur term to a year. In Helsinki Mockridge won a gold medal in the 1000-metre time trial and another on the same day—paired for the first time with Lionel Cox—in the 2000-metre tandem.

As a novice professional in Europe, Mockridge did not perform well. He abandoned track racing and made a modest living in kermesse (road) and critérium (closed circuit road) races. At the Church-in-the-Grove, Sydenham, London, on 26 September 1953 he married Irene Pritchard with Congregational forms. In 1955 he teamed with Roger Arnold and Sid Patterson to win the Paris six-day event. Returning to Australia after an acclaimed solo ride in the Tour de France, he signed a contract with the promoter Ted Waterford. Over the next three years he became the most celebrated Australian cyclist of his generation, frequently winning from scratch in both track and road races.

The congenitally shortsighted Mockridge was an introspective loner. An abstemious non-smoker, he eschewed performance-enhancing drugs. Less gifted opponents resented his occasional refusals to share major prize-money. Nevertheless, in his posthumously published autobiography, *My World on Wheels* (London, 1960), he wrote candidly about various 'arrangements' to which he had been party.

On 13 September 1958, shortly after the start of the Tour of Gippsland, Mockridge was struck by a bus and killed on the Princes Highway at Clayton, Melbourne. Survived by his wife and 3-year-old daughter, he was cremated. His estate was sworn for probate at £3000. With a world speed record in the Warrnambool to Melbourne classic in 1956, and a string of formidable performances over the next two seasons, Mockridge had seemed set for a triumphant return to Europe. Early jibes that he was a 'china doll' or 'little Lord Fauntleroy', too delicate for robust competition, had been silenced. Already an international star, he died with great potential unfulfilled.

H. Gordon, *Young Men in a Hurry* (Melb, 1961); J. Shepherd, *Encyclopedia of Australian Sport* (Adel, 1980); M. Andrews, *Australia at the Olympics* (Syd, 1996); *People* (Syd), 24 Sept 1952; *Aust Cyclist*, 4, no 6, Oct 1988.

CAMERON HAZLEHURST
SALLY WHITEHEAD

MOFFLIN, ALICE MAUDE (1878-1961), community worker, was born on 26 May 1878

385

at Blackwood, Victoria, second child of English-born parents Rev. William Burridge, Wesleyan minister, and his wife Margaret Alice, née Nale. Alice attended Methodist Ladies' College, Kew, then moved to Western Australia where she assisted her father with his parish work at Fremantle and Claremont. At the Wesleyan Church, Claremont, on 15 August 1906 she married Horace Elgar Mofflin (d.1939). He was a 39-year-old widower from New Zealand who had four children from his first marriage. A well-known merchant and philanthropist, he served on the Fremantle Municipal Council and was mayor (1909-11) of Claremont. Horace and Alice were to have eight children of their own.

From 1910 Mrs Mofflin helped to raise money for the establishment of the Methodist Home for Children, Victoria Park. While waiting for the provision of suitable buildings, she and other Methodist women brought the children into their homes. On 14 October 1922, at the opening of the M.H.C.'s first cottage, Mofflin unveiled the dedication tablet. As president (1921-54) and life president (from 1954) of the ladies' committee appointed by the Methodist Church to manage the children's home, she organized fund-raising activities, assisted with administrative chores, and frequently acted as 'house mother' or matron to relieve the staff.

Mofflin devoted much of her time to various departments of the Methodist Church, but was particularly involved in youth activities and work for missions overseas. She helped to promote the youth department and the Sunday-School movement. Making light of primitive conditions, she participated in Easter camps at Glen Forrest for at least twenty years: as 'camp mother', she counselled young campers, and cooked and served hundreds of meals. She joked that, when 'called to higher service', she might be asked by St Peter whether she had brought a cooked tongue.

For more than thirty years Mofflin served as State president of the Methodist Church's Women's Auxiliary to Foreign (Overseas) Missions. She frequently entertained guests from India, Africa and the Pacific Islands, and attended national conferences of Methodist overseas mission-workers. Her assistance was acknowledged when the Methodist church at Rabaul, Territory of Papua-New Guinea, was rebuilt after World War II. She was also a founder and office-bearer of the Methodist Women's Federation in Western Australia. In 1958 she was appointed M.B.E.

The children's home was renamed 'Mofflyn' in 1959 in honour of Mofflin and R. J. Lynn [q.v.10], each of whom had donated £500 towards its establishment. Although she retired as president of the women's auxiliary that year, she continued to serve on the M.H.C. council. Survived by her six daughters, she died on 23 March 1961 at her Mount Lawley home and was cremated; her two sons predeceased her. Members of the Methodist Church remembered Mrs Mofflin as a woman who dedicated her life 'to the welfare of children'.

Western Methodist (Perth), Dec 1939, p 20, May 1961, p 8; *Old Wesleyan*, no 38, Dec 1990; *West Australian*, 12 June 1958, 24, 25 Mar 1961; Methodist Church of Australasia, Western Australian records, MN172, *and* Uniting Church in Australia, Western Australian records, MN659 (BL); records, Mofflyn Child and Family Care Services, Cannington, Perth; family information.   LEONIE STELLA

MOFFLIN, FLORENCE TURNER BLAKE; *see* BLAKE

MOIR, FRANCIS OAG; *see* HULME-MOIR

MOIR, JOHN KINMONT (1893-1958), book-collector and literary patron, was born on 24 November 1893 at Normanton, Queensland, son of James Alexander Moir, a Scottish-born station-manager, and his wife Olive Adelaide, née Ferguson, who came from New South Wales. The family moved to Melbourne about 1902 when his father was appointed managing agent for a firm with large pastoral holdings. They moved again when James took over as manager of a station at Wellington, New South Wales. Educated at state schools and by private tutors, Jack worked as a jackeroo. From 1912 he was employed as a book-keeper in southern New South Wales, first with (F. A.) Wright [q.v.6], Heaton & Co. Ltd and then with McCulloch & Co. Ltd at Albury. On 18 January 1916 he married Constance Ruby Tratt with Anglican rites at Christ Church, South Yarra, Melbourne; they were divorced in 1930. He married Myrtle Elizabeth Green on 24 January 1931 at the Presbyterian Church, Ascot Vale; this marriage also ended in divorce.

By 1927 Moir was employed in Melbourne as an accountant by Bon Marché Ltd; eight years later he became credit manager for its retail store, Payne's Bon Marché Pty Ltd, in Bourke Street. In the early 1940s his secretary and assistant was the novelist Doris Kerr [q.v.]. Moir lived alone, cultivating the image of a lifelong bachelor. About 1945 he bought as a home a disused pawnbroker's shop at 474 Bridge Road, Richmond. His willingness to open his house and library—described by a contemporary as 'a veritable Aladdin's cave'—to researchers and students was legendary.

One of the twelve founders of the Bread and Cheese Club in June 1938, Moir was appointed its knight grand cheese. He remained president until 1950, and was subsequently made a life-member and named the club's Oknirrabata ('wise old man', in the Arrernte language). He was also an energetic member of most Melbourne literary and historical societies. In 1939 he had donated the Field Naturalists Club of Victoria's Australian Natural History medallion, which was awarded annually at his expense. 'J.K.M.', as he was affectionately known among the Bread and Cheesers, was not popular with those on the left, especially during the Cold War years of the early 1950s: his avowedly anti-communist views led him to lobby against Commonwealth Literary Fund grants to known left-wing writers, and he was an executive-member of the Australian Committee of the Congress for Cultural Freedom.

Funding his book-collecting passion by astute investments, Moir attempted to acquire every novel or book of verse by an Australian author. He also collected photographs of literary figures, corresponded with authors, and subscribed to a press-cuttings service on Australian books and writing. An accumulator of books rather than a reader of them, he was a prolific letter-writer who saw his role as that of a proponent and publicist for Australian literature. Judah Waten once mockingly described him as 'the Governor-General of Letters', but the appellation was apt.

In 1952 Moir was appointed O.B.E. He donated (1954 and 1957) his collection of over ten thousand items to the Public Library of Victoria. In 1957 he retired from Payne's Bon Marché due to ill health. Survived by the daughter of his first marriage, he died of coronary vascular disease on 28 June 1958 at Elsternwick and was cremated with Methodist forms.

Bohemia, Apr 1939, Aug 1958; *People*, 23 Apr 1952; J. Arnold, 'An Extraordinary Man: John Kinmont Moir', LaTL J, 12, nos 47-48, 1991, p 100; *Argus Weekend Mag*, 20 June 1952; *Age* (Melb), 24 Apr 1954; Moir collection (SLV).   JOHN ARNOLD

MOLESWORTH, BEVIL HUGH (1891-1971), educationist and broadcaster, was born on 17 January 1891 at Thompson Estate, Brisbane, son of Hugh Thomas Molesworth, an Anglican clergyman from England, and his Queensland-born wife Alice Marian, née Deshon. Bevil was educated at state schools and (on scholarships) at Brisbane Grammar School and the University of Queensland (B.A., 1915; M.A., 1917). He graduated with first-class honours in history and economic science. A travelling scholarship took him to Balliol College, Oxford, where the university committee for workers' tutorial classes se-

lected him to lecture in mining districts. He long remembered the miners' hunger for knowledge, their generosity and their warmth. Adult education, which he regarded as essential for democracy, became the dominant interest of his working life.

On 19 June 1918 at St Philip's Anglican Church, Thompson Estate, Molesworth married Maud Margaret ('Mall') Mutch; they had one son (d.1960). Mall was the Australasian women's singles tennis champion in 1922-23. Molesworth had taken a post in 1918 as lecturer in history at the University of Tasmania; he also conducted workers' tutorial classes. In 1920 the University of Sydney appointed him staff-tutor at Broken Hill where he taught Marxism and economic history. The surest tribute to his integrity and skill as a teacher was that the miners 'came back, week after week, for more'.

In 1921 Molesworth returned to the University of Queensland as director of tutorial classes for the Workers' Educational Association. He also lectured (from 1932) in economic history and geography. Seeing radio as a means of bringing adult education to rural districts, he broadcast on stations 4QG and 4BK, and joined the Queensland talks advisory committee of the Australian Broadcasting Commission. While travelling on a Carnegie Corporation grant in 1934, he visited the British Broadcasting Corporation and gathered useful ideas for programmes which he would later use at the A.B.C. Back home, he published *Adult Education in America and England* (Melbourne, 1935).

On the advice of G. V. Portus [q.v.11], the A.B.C. offered Molesworth in 1937 the post of federal controller (later director) of talks. 'Moley' moved to Sydney and began work at Broadcast House, with one typist. To make 'talks' more accessible and interesting, he replaced some of the commentary with interviews, discussions and dramatic interludes. He also introduced literary talks, and readings of poetry and short stories. For young people, he initiated programmes such as 'Young Ideas' and 'The Voice of Youth', and (from 1939) weekly discussion groups led by G. I. Smith. Molesworth found the women's sessions an 'aimless mixture of talk and light music', but seemed unable to improve them greatly. His responsibilities in the area of religion involved him in producing the broadcast of the requiem Mass for Joseph Lyons [q.v.10].

'Talks' were designed to inform, stimulate discussion, and offer a range of views on politics and foreign affairs. The main speakers —who usually came from universities— included William Macmahon Ball, W. G. K. Duncan, W. J. Dakin, Portus and (Sir) Walter Murdoch [q.v.10]. 'News Review', 'News Commentary', 'Guest of Honour', 'Nation's

Forum of the Air' and 'Popular Science' met with general approval. In World War II new and improved technology allowed listeners to hear the voices of men at the front and the sounds of battle.

The war placed a heavy strain on Molesworth who had to reconcile the public's demand for information with the Federal government's censorship and propaganda regulations. He strove to maintain balance and objectivity, but politicians (like J. A. Beasley, H. V. Evatt and W. M. Hughes [qq.v.13,14,9]) accused the A.B.C. of bias and threatened to have its funding withdrawn. Molesworth also had to contend with those who were offended by the mention of subjects such as contraception and homosexuality. Although he tried to avoid giving offence, he welcomed debate and said that he was 'pleased that controversy had become so established a part of A.B.C. broadcasting'. Rivalry and competition for funds sometimes brought him into conflict with (Sir) Charles Moses, the A.B.C.'s general manager, and Keith Barry [q.v.13], the controller of programmes.

Molesworth was 'a frail, quiet man ... humane, loyal to his staff and formidable as an advocate'. Following his retirement from the A.B.C. in 1955, he and his family formed a company which owned and operated squash courts. Survived by his wife, he died on 12 August 1971 at his Lindfield home and was cremated with Presbyterian forms.

A. Thomas, *Broadcast and be Damned* (Melb, 1980); C. Semmler, *The ABC—Aunt Sally and Sacred Cow* (Melb, 1981); K. S. Inglis, *This is the ABC* (Melb, 1983); *Aust J of Adult Education*, 11, no 3, Nov 1971, p 151; ABC Document *and* Radio Archives, Syd; information from Mrs P. Martin, Lindfield, Syd.   MARION CONSANDINE

MOLVIG, HELGE JON (1923-1970), artist, was born on 27 May 1923 at Merewether, Newcastle, New South Wales, and registered as Helge John, only child of Helge Molvig, a Norwegian-born sailor who became a steelworker, and his Australian-born wife Bernardine Ivy, née Ward (d.1924). Young Helge was cared for by his maternal grandmother Isabella Ward (d.1932), then by an aunt Eleanor Malley. Educated at Newcastle and briefly at Quirindi, he showed some artistic ability but left school in 1936. He worked in a garage and later in the Newcastle steelworks.

On 12 February 1942 Molvig was called up for full-time service in the Militia. In July he arrived in Port Moresby with the 14th Field Regiment, Royal Australian Artillery. Next month he transferred to the Australian Imperial Force. He contracted malaria and in February 1944 was sent to Australia where he twice went absent without leave. After

working (1945) in prisoner-of-war reception camps on Morotai and in Manila, he was discharged in Australia on 26 June 1946. His early interest in art had been rekindled during his army service when he saw sketches by a fellow soldier, Stanislaw Payne. Changing the spelling of his name to Jon, Molvig enrolled in 1947 under the Commonwealth Reconstruction Training Scheme at the Strathfield annexe of East Sydney Technical College. He exhibited with the Strath Art Group during the years 1949-54, but, being an intensely private man and a committed individualist, never participated in another organized group.

With some college friends, Molvig spent 1949-52 in Europe and encountered the modernist paintings he had known only in reproductions. The German and Norwegian expressionists, whose work he viewed at the Nasjonalgalleriet, Oslo, were to influence him markedly. Back in Australia, he visited Brisbane in 1953 where the underlying looseness of the art of W. G. Grant and his followers reinforced Molvig's own expressionist leanings. He established an individual style in paintings such as 'Crucifixion' (1953, private collection).

Settling permanently in Brisbane two years later, Molvig produced (1956-57) a series of expressive, figurative works—for example, 'Bride and Groom' (Art Gallery of New South Wales) and 'A Twilight of Women' (Queensland Art Gallery)—remarkable for their aggressiveness and intensity. His output from 1955 to 1961 dazzled James Gleeson, who wrote:

No one in Australian art has painted so nakedly as Molvig did at that time. There was no covering to his emotions. He had torn away the last skin of reserve and painted the world he knew in his blood, his nerves and his heart. In a sense it was orgiastic—a great dionysian acceptance of those ecstatic storms that sometimes blow up from the subconscious with such violence that the government of reason is overwhelmed. Even the paint looks as if it has been blown on the canvas by tremendous gusts of passion.

In November 1955 Molvig had taken over his friend John Rigby's classes, held in a studio beneath St Mary's Anglican Church hall, Kangaroo Point. The studio became a focus for a closely knit group of students and fellow artists, and a centre of innovatory painting practice. Molvig was seen as the exemplar of the committed artist. He did not impose his style on his pupils, but created an atmosphere in which they could establish their own. Some were profoundly influenced, among them John Aland, Maryke Degeus, Gil Jamieson, Mervyn Moriarty, Joy Roggenkamp, Andrew Sibley and Gordon Shepherdson. The school lasted for two years, after which Molvig conducted life-drawing classes on and off at a number of premises from 1956 to 1967. He was appreciated as a consummate draftsman; according to Andrew Sibley, he promoted 'the malleability of line and mass to create the pulse of the line'.

Among Molvig's associates were his first dealers Brian and Marjorie Johnstone, with whom he exhibited in 1956-59. The critic Gertrude Langer was a staunch supporter throughout his career, though she acknowledged the unevenness of his production. Another patron was Laurie Thomas [q.v.], director of the Queensland Art Gallery: as sole judge, he awarded Molvig the 1963 Perth prize for contemporary painting (for 'The Family'), the 1964 (Thomas) Finney [q.v.4] art prize (for 'Underarm Still Life No.2'), the 1966 Corio Five Star Whisky prize (for 'Portrait of a Publican'), and the 1969 Gold Coast City art prize (for 'Tree of Man X'). Molvig also won the Lismore art prize (1955 and 1956), and the Rowney drawing exhibition (1960).

His work was characterized by radical shifts of style. In 1958 he toured Central Australia with Degeus. The trip inspired his 'Centralian' series at the Johnstone Gallery in 1959. Although some of these paintings depicted the dispossession and alienation of the Aboriginal people, the series was more colourful than the preceding work—Langer even described it as lyrical. Shortly afterwards the Sydney dealer Rudy Komon contracted Molvig to his gallery with a monthly retainer which provided a stable income. Komon held exhibitions of his work in 1960, 1962, 1964, 1966, 1968, 1978 and 1984, and organized showings at other venues: in Melbourne at the Argus Gallery (1962), and in Brisbane at the Grand Central Gallery (1966), the Kennigo Street Gallery (1966), the Johnstone Gallery (1972) and the New Central Gallery (1977).

The 'Eden Industrial' series (1961-62) marked a further shift, into images of Molvig's childhood at Newcastle. To employ a means of expression appropriate to his subject, he used a blowtorch on the oil paint to create eroded surfaces on some paintings. This technique was sensationalized in the press. In 1961 he won the inaugural Transfield art prize —at that time the nation's richest award—for his painting 'City Industrial'. Another important work was 'Eden Industrial: The Garden' (Queensland Art Gallery).

Molvig's emphasis on figuration continued in his 'Pale Nude' series (to 1964), although the rendering was attenuated. His work veered towards abstraction in 'Tree of Man' (1967-68), the last major series he produced. These paintings, comprising target shapes and skeletal forms (described by Langer as 'expressive symbolism'), may have a connection with Patrick White's book, *The Tree of Man* (1955).

The variation in Molvig's technique is even more obvious in his justly famous portraits. Among these works are the hewn massiveness of 'Self Portrait' (1956, Queensland Art Gallery), the spidery elegance of 'Portrait of Janet Mathews' (1957, private collection), the grim monumentality of 'Russell Cuppaidge Esq.' (1959, Queensland Art Gallery), and the voluptuousness of 'Portrait of Joy Roggenkamp' (1963, private collection). He entered portraits for the Archibald [q.v.3] prize from 1952, but it was not until 1955 that one was hung. Reviewers thought that he deserved the award on several occasions; after he finally succeeded in 1966 with 'Portrait of Charles Blackman' (Art Gallery of South Australia), he ceased submitting entries.

On 26 August 1963 at the general registry office, Brisbane, Molvig had married Cornelia Agatha Johanna ('Otte') van Gilst, a 22-year-old secretary and former art student; they were to remain childless. The Transfield prize enabled him to purchase land at Carbrook, about 20 miles (32 km) south-east of Brisbane, where he devoted much of his time to building the house into which he and Otte moved in 1967. Molvig's output decreased as he became seriously ill. He had suffered from nephritis in childhood. Heavy drinking, and the malaria which he had contracted in World War II, probably exacerbated his chronic renal disease. Following the rejection of a transplanted kidney, he died on 15 May 1970 in Princess Alexandra Hospital, South Brisbane, and was cremated. His wife survived him.

The generating impulses behind Molvig's art can only be conjectured, for he was notoriously reticent, and frequently confrontational, in discussing his work. Although his *oeuvre* is highly regarded, especially by artists, it has still to achieve the prominence it merits, despite the retrospective exhibition (curated by Bronwyn Thomas for the Newcastle Region Art Gallery) which toured nationally in 1978.

B. Churcher, *Molvig* (Melb, 1984), and for bibliog; G. R. Cooke, *A Time Remembered* (Brisb, 1995).

GLENN R. COOKE

MONAHAN, SIR ROBERT VINCENT (1898-1975), barrister and judge, was born on 11 April 1898 at Swan Hill, Victoria, son of Victorian-born parents Patrick Martin Monahan, grazier and butcher, and his wife Mary Frances, née Nolan. Due to protracted drought, the family fell on hard times and was close to poverty by 1902. Encouraged by his mother to study hard, Rob was educated at St Patrick's College, Ballarat, and Newman College, University of Melbourne (LL.B., 1921).

He was admitted to practice on 1 June 1922 and worked with F. C. Mueller, a solicitor at Echuca, before signing the bar roll on 30 April 1923. In Melbourne he read with L. B. Cussen.

At St Patrick's Catholic Cathedral, Melbourne, on 7 September 1929 Monahan married Lillie Elevia Bowman, a 26-year-old hairdresser. He established himself in Equity Chambers in 1931. By the end of the decade he was well known as a defence counsel and as a persuasive advocate in personal injury cases. He always studied his cases closely and was instantly able to marshal any relevant detail. Emotional and sincere, with an actor's sense of timing, he proved a masterful cross-examiner, probing swiftly with penetrating questions. He ordinarily achieved more by courtesy than belligerence. The hardships of his early life had given him a deep understanding of the minds of common people and he expressed complicated matters with simple eloquence so that juries tended to identify with him. Above all, he could influence, charm and dominate a court.

Appointed K.C. on 14 January 1947, Monahan appeared in a succession of sensational trials in the 1940s and early 1950s. In 1944 he had been prominent in the coroner's inquest into the identity of the 'Pyjama Girl' (Linda Agostini [q.v.13]). In the 'Whose Baby' case (commencing December 1948), Monahan acted for Mrs Alberta Morrison who claimed that her daughter had been confused with that of Jessie Jenkins, and accidentally switched on 22 June 1945 when the two babies were born within five minutes of each other at Kyneton hospital. Justice (Sir) John Barry [q.v.13] was satisfied that a switch had occurred and awarded Mrs Morrison custody of Nola Jenkins. On appeal, the Full Court set the order aside, a decision upheld by the High Court of Australia.

In 1950 Monahan defended John Bryan Kerr, a radio announcer charged with the murder by strangulation of a young woman at St Kilda beach. His conduct of the defence was so masterly that many lawyers came to watch in the crowded public galleries. In the first two trials the jury failed to agree, only serving further to heighten public interest, but in the third trial—before Sir Charles Lowe [q.v.]—a 'guilty' verdict was finally obtained. Appeals to the Court of Criminal Appeal and the Privy Council failed. In all, Monahan conducted more than one hundred murder trials; only one of his clients Tommy Johnson, a mental defective, went to the gallows (1939).

Monahan was appointed an acting-judge of the Supreme Court on 3 March 1955 (confirmed on 31 October). As a barrister he had been a persuasive advocate rather than a lawyer steeped in legal knowledge, but as a judge his talents lay primarily in an ability to conduct and control a trial proficiently. For the most part he sat in the criminal court, in personal injury cases, and in the divorce jurisdiction. Almost invariably he was courteous, patient, enthusiastic and sympathetic. Criminal trials before him were conducted with scrupulous fairness to the accused, but his love for the underdog could produce some imbalance in his charges to juries, especially when injured workers sued wealthy employers. In 1967 he was knighted. He retired on 10 April 1970.

Above average height, Monahan had red hair and a distinguished appearance. Peter Coldham, Q.C., said that he looked like 'what a great advocate ought to look like: the clear and piercing eye, the hawk nose, the commanding presence . . . the master of mannerism'. Monahan lived well. He and his wife and children enjoyed a succession of luxurious and elegant homes at East St Kilda, Heidelberg, Kew, Eaglemont, Toorak and South Yarra. A devout Catholic, he often slipped down to St Francis's Church for quiet prayer. He was a genial companion, and was gregarious, kindly and generous to a fault. Sir Robert belonged to the Australian, Athenaeum, Victoria Racing, Victoria Amateur Turf, Moonee Valley Racing and Victoria Golf clubs, and the Lawn Tennis Association of Victoria. In his spare time he enjoyed golf, game-shooting, fishing, and playing the piano. Horse-racing was his passion. The not inconsiderable amount he had lost on racehorses over the years was more than recouped in 1962 when Monahan and Albert Smith, a Melbourne bookmaker, won the Irish Derby sweepstakes (£50 000).

Monahan's last years were spent in a large apartment in Spring Street, Melbourne, but were marred by glaucoma and ill health. Survived by his wife, daughter and three sons, he died on 10 May 1975 at Fitzroy and was buried in Melbourne general cemetery. His portrait by Paul Fitzgerald is held by the family.

K. Anderson, *Fossil in the Sandstone* (Melb, 1986); *Aust Law J*, 49, no 5, May 1975, p 252; *Sun* (Melb), 16 Jan 1947, 8 Dec 1952, 9 May 1970, 29 Nov 1972; *Age* (Melb), 2 Oct 1949; *SMH*, 2 July 1962; *Herald* (Melb), 12 May 1975; Sir Robert Monahan's farewell, ts, (Supreme Court L, Melb); family papers held by and information from Mrs C. Monahan, South Yarra, Melb.

CHARLES FRANCIS

MONEY, WILLIAM ALFRED (1895-1958), soldier, plantation-owner and gold prospector, was born on 9 August 1895 at Holborn, London, son of George John Money, waiter, and his wife Edith Eveline, née Francis. Bill and his brother Charles emigrated to Victoria in 1914 and worked on a farm in the Mallee.

On 19 September Bill enlisted in the Australian Imperial Force: he gave his religion as Anglican, and was recorded as being 5 ft 8½ ins (174 cm) tall, with a ruddy complexion. In February 1915 he joined the 5th Battalion in Egypt.

During the Gallipoli landings on 25 April, Money was wounded in the chest and shoulder; taken to Alexandria, Egypt, for treatment, he returned to his unit in July. He was posted to the 57th Battalion in February 1916, sent to the Western Front in June and promoted sergeant in July. On the night of 14/15 February 1917 at Gueudecourt, France, he 'showed great courage' while leading a raid; his good judgement saved many lives in the subsequent withdrawal through an artillery barrage. Although recommended for the Distinguished Conduct Medal, he was awarded the Military Medal.

Commissioned in September 1917, Money 'displayed coolness and initiative' throughout the operations at Villers Bretonneux on 24-28 April 1918. With a handful of men, he captured a German officer and fifty soldiers. He won the Military Cross and was promoted lieutenant. On 8 August, at Wiencourt railway bridge, he again demonstrated his fighting spirit when two platoons under his command routed German gunners who had halted the advance of Canadian troops.

Money returned to Australia in December, but was unable to settle down. In January 1919 he transferred to the Australian Naval and Military Expeditionary Force and sailed for Rabaul. When his appointment terminated on 9 May 1921, he became a district officer in the civil administration of the Mandated Territory of New Guinea. He resigned in 1923, established copra plantations on Umboi Island and elsewhere, and built up a flotilla of small boats for coastal trade. One of the 'Big Six' who struck gold at Edie Creek, Bulolo district, in 1926, he was soon reputed to be worth more than £50 000.

At Wau on 30 January 1942 Money enlisted in the New Guinea Volunteer Rifles. In February-March he ferried soldiers and civilians from New Britain to Australia in a small boat, the *Gnair*. Promoted lieutenant in April and posted two months later to the Australian New Guinea Administrative Unit, Port Moresby, he collected intelligence from behind enemy lines as a member of Eric Feldt's [q.v.14] coastwatching organization. Money was mentioned in dispatches for 'exceptional courage in the field' and commended by General Sir Thomas Blamey [q.v.13]. In August 1943 he was seconded to 'M' Special Unit and promoted captain. He spent a week on Japanese-occupied Umboi Island in October, observing enemy activity. In November 1944 he reconnoitred the north coast of New Britain by barge.

A confirmed bachelor and a rugged individualist who savoured the hardship, adventure and independence of life in New Guinea, Money thrived on irregular warfare, in which he was unfettered by strict military discipline. From June 1945 he served with the British Borneo Civil Affairs Unit. His army appointment terminated on 1 April 1946 and he went home to the Territory of Papua-New Guinea. He died of cancer on 8 February 1958 at Lae and was buried in the local cemetery.

C. E. W. Bean, *Official History of Australia in the War of 1914-1918*, 6 (Syd, 1942); E. Feldt, *The Coast Watchers* (Melb, 1946); L. Wigmore, *The Japanese Thrust* (Canb, 1957); D. Dexter, *The New Guinea Offensives* (Canb, 1961); G. Long, *The Final Campaigns* (Canb, 1963); J. K. McCarthy, *Patrol into Yesterday* (Melb, 1963); A. Powell, *War by Stealth* (Melb, 1996); J. Sinclair, *Golden Gateway* (Bathurst, NSW, 1998); information from Mr J. Birrell, Helensvale, Qld and Col J. Godwin, Canb.

PETER HOHNEN

MONK, ALBERT ERNEST (1900-1975), trade union leader, was born on 16 September 1900 at Waltham Abbey, Essex, England, son of Ernest George Monk, munitions worker, and his wife Ada Kate, née Dennis. About 1910 the family emigrated to Melbourne where Ernest helped to establish the Commonwealth Government Cordite Factory at Maribyrnong. Albert was subjected to 'anti-Pommy' bullying at Moonee Ponds West State School. He later recalled, 'I think that what happened to me in the sixth grade helped to start me on my rebellious career'. After leaving school, he attended a business college. By the age of 18 he had become an accomplished shorthand writer, a skill which was to serve him well in his subsequent career.

At 19 Monk took a clerk's position with the Carters' and Drivers' Union. He joined the Australian Labor Party and was soon appointed secretary to the Conference of Federated Unions. In 1924 he was employed on the staff of the Melbourne Trades Hall Council. His shorthand earned him the job of minute secretary at the 1927 All-Australian Trade Union Congress which established the Australasian (Australian) Council of Trade Unions. He was promoted assistant-secretary of the T.H.C. in 1929. The political and industrial turmoil at the onset of the Depression pushed him into increasingly prominent roles. Spurred by the growing influence of the communist-led Unemployed Workers' Movement, the T.H.C. executive established the Central Unemployment Committee in 1930, with Monk as secretary. Tensions between the rival organizations often erupted into violence. On one occasion, in the Trades Hall courtyard, Monk was bashed to the ground and kicked.

Like other union leaders in the Depression, he found himself in the uncomfortable position of representing the rank and file in dealings with the ineffectual Labor governments of Premier E. J. Hogan and Prime Minister J. H. Scullin [qq.v.9,11]. Monk's proposals for public works were approved by A.L.P. conferences, but little heeded by Labor governments. His appointment in 1931 to Victoria's Unemployment Relief Works Board increased his involvement in the conflict between the labour movement and its politicians. He supported union objections to the pay and conditions associated with relief work, especially the 'work for sustenance' scheme. But, when militant members of the C.U.C. demanded that State Labor parliamentarians who breached party policy on these issues should lose their endorsements, he sought a more conciliatory approach. In 1934 he became chairman of the Victorian State Relief Committee, a post he was to hold until 1944, and again in 1954-75. He emerged from the Depression with an enduring anxiety about mass unemployment, tempered by a preference for compromise rather than confrontation in working to prevent it.

Following the death of W. J. Duggan [q.v.8] in 1934, Monk took over as T.H.C. secretary and part-time president of the A.C.T.U. Combined with his various positions in the Federated Clerks' Union of Australia, these offices brought him a heavy workload. At this time the labour movement was divided and demoralized. In his quiet, practical and methodical way, he worked to consolidate the organization of which he was titular head. His expanding range of responsibilities left him little time for private life, apart from a day at the races and an occasional drink. In 1938 he relinquished the T.H.C. secretaryship after being appointed union representative on the Victorian Workers' Compensation Board. He joined the Federal Labor Advisory Committee, through which representatives of the A.L.P. federal executive, the federal parliamentary party and the A.C.T.U. conferred on industrial matters. By the outbreak of World War II, he proudly wore the 'triple crown' as president of the A.C.T.U., the T.H.C. and the Victorian branch of the A.L.P.

Monk attended the 1941 International Labour Conference in New York and was a party to its resolutions. His views on the need for co-operation between nations to secure full employment and better living standards were consistent with the objectives of the International Labour Organization. He also endorsed the I.L.O.'s policy of encouraging collaboration between unions, employers and governments in the development of policies affecting workers. In 1945 he represented Australia at conferences of the I.L.O. and the World Federation of Trade Unions, held in Paris. For most of his postwar career he served as a member of the governing body of the I.L.O. and of the executive-board of the International Confederation of Free Trade Unions. He made more than sixty trips abroad. In 1969, at Geneva, he was elected vice-president of the fiftieth anniversary session of the I.L.C.

In 1943 Monk had given up the presidency of the A.C.T.U. and his place on the Victorian Workers' Compensation Board, and had taken the new, full-time, paid post of A.C.T.U. secretary. On 6 October that year at the office of the government statist, Melbourne, he married Frances (Frankie) Mary Fealy, a 33-year-old munitions worker; they were to remain childless.

As A.C.T.U. secretary, Monk had to tread warily in negotiations with factions in the union movement, and with the Federal Labor governments of John Curtin and J. B. Chifley [qq.v.13]. In general, however, he and the A.C.T.U. executive tended to favour pragmatic reform by cautious negotiation rather than radical change by militant tactics. Hostilities between Curtin's government and the Miners' Federation escalated at the end of 1944. The A.C.T.U.—through Monk—declared that it would act as an intermediary in the dispute, but soon backed the government. It was clear to the miners' leaders that Monk placed the Labor government's continuance in office above their union's demands. The A.C.T.U.'s subsequent decision to support Chifley in the 1949 coal strike was typical of its responses to activism by its militant left-wing affiliates.

Nevertheless, there were occasions—such as the fight with the Chifley government in 1946-47 over its wage-pegging regulations—when Monk and the A.C.T.U. executive appeared to back their industrial constituency against their political allies. Many of Monk's views were expressed in the declaration of the 1947 national tripartite conference on industrial peace, signed by Chifley, Monk and an employers' representative: it endorsed free enterprise, advocated greater production and rejected 'unauthorised' strikes.

In 1941-49 Monk's statements and actions showed him to be a committed supporter of the A.L.P.'s broad Keynesian approach as expressed in its white paper on full employment in Australia. The pursuit of full employment in a mixed capitalist economy, with systematic government intervention along broadly social democratic lines, was congenial to his personal inclinations and consistent with I.L.O. resolutions. Within that framework, he believed that sustained economic growth was the best guarantee of jobs for all. Accordingly, it was not surprising that, despite misgivings in the union movement, he resolutely defended the Chifley government's postwar immigration programme which aimed to expand the size of the workforce and so stimulate economic growth. From the late 1940s he was an active member of the Immigration Advisory Council and the Immigration Planning Council (chairman from 1973).

When the A.C.T.U. presidency became a full-time post in 1949, Monk replaced P. J. Clarey [q.v.13] in the position and R. R. Broadby assumed the secretaryship. (Sir) Robert Menzies [q.v.] was elected prime minister that year. Monk faced the challenge of establishing a working relationship with the new conservative government during a rapidly intensifying Cold War. Despite his personal views on communism, he opposed the government's plan in 1950 to ban the Communist Party of Australia. None the less, on traditional matters of wages and conditions an accommodation was finally reached. Having gained a 40-hour week in 1947, the A.C.T.U. concentrated on wages. The 1950 basic-wage case linked minimum earnings to the capacity of the economy to pay. Monk responded by pressing the government to reintroduce price controls, and by urging joint action by government, employers and unions to increase production.

Over time he developed a relatively cosy, interdependent relationship with Harold Holt [q.v.14], the minister for labour and national service, and with (Sir) Henry Bland, Holt's departmental secretary. The A.C.T.U.'s official historian has suggested that, when the department recognized the A.C.T.U. as the sole voice of the union movement and the A.C.T.U. spoke only with the department, the arrangement served to bolster each party within its respective constituency. The A.C.T.U. was able to obtain easy, if informal, access to departmental research, which it could not conduct with its own resources.

The co-operative approach of the government and the A.C.T.U. found organizational form in the Ministry of Labour Advisory Council. Established in 1952 to provide advice to the government, the council included representatives of the government, the A.C.T.U. and the employers. The A.C.T.U. grew concerned that its participation involved a conflict of interest since some members of the A.C.T.U. executive were A.L.P. office-holders. Despite Monk's opposition, the A.C.T.U. decided to withdraw from the M.L.A.C. in 1958. This action simply forced Monk, Holt and Bland into closer consultation. Leslie Bury, a later minister, was to revive formal, tripartite discussions by setting up the National Labour Advisory Committee in 1967. Monk was appointed C.M.G. in 1966. Bland acknowledged in 1975 that he and Monk had been 'partners for 25 years in seeking solutions to industrial relations problems'.

Monk's uneasy dealings with the A.C.T.U.'s more radical left-wing elements continued. Jim Healy's [q.v.14] accusation that the A.C.T.U. executive had betrayed the Waterside Workers' Federation of Australia in the 1956 strike was a case in point. When the metalworkers, seamen, miners and waterside workers challenged the A.C.T.U. executive's authority in 1957, the matter was resolved through changes to the A.C.T.U.'s constitution. Despite pressure from the militants in 1962 and 1964, Monk hesitated to confront the penal powers in the Commonwealth's Conciliation and Arbitration Act. In 1965 he refused A.C.T.U. support for proposed stoppages by seamen and waterside workers in protest against the Vietnam War. He took a similar position on conscription.

Although Monk often opposed political action by left-wing unions, he did not ignore their industrial interests. Between November 1965 and April 1967, in the face of a threat by the Federal government to reform the stevedoring industry, he and Harold Souter, the A.C.T.U. secretary, helped W.W.F. representatives to win permanent employment for their members without loss of pay.

Not all of Monk's trade-union difficulties came from left-wing affiliates. During the late 1940s and 1950s he had to deal with some disruptive tactics from 'grouper' unions. Among his most persistent critics on the right were officials of the Australian Workers' Union, especially its general secretary Tom Dougherty [q.v.14] who had refused to join the A.C.T.U. and denounced it as a hotbed of communism. Irritated by Dougherty's truculence, Monk observed that the A.W.U.'s admission to the Federal Labor Advisory Committee in 1951 put 'a premium on trade union isolationism'. After increasing co-operation from the A.W.U. in industrial campaigns, and extensive negotiations by the A.C.T.U.'s industrial advocate R. J. L. Hawke, Monk finally welcomed the A.W.U. into the fold in 1967. In the early 1960s Monk had prevented a split in the A.C.T.U. when some right-wing unionists objected to funding trade-union trips to the People's Republic of China.

With about 1.5 million members, the A.C.T.U. was by 1968 the undisputed peak council of the trade union movement. Monk retired on 31 December 1969 due to poor health. He had represented Australian workers at home and abroad, presided over the boisterous growth of the A.C.T.U. and guided it through numerous crises in a quiet, self-effacing, but resolutely determined way. He did not have the charisma of his successor, Bob Hawke. Monk was a reserved, rotund, bespectacled man and an unimpressive public speaker who preferred patient, behind-the-scenes negotiation to declamatory confrontation.

In retirement Monk lived quietly at Moonee Ponds, maintaining contact with old friends and working for some of his 'good causes'. In 1970 Monash University conferred on him an honorary LL.D. Survived by his wife, he died on 11 February 1975 at Fitzroy and was cremated. Hawke delivered the eulogy at his funeral.

L. F. Crisp, *The Australian Federal Labour Party 1901-1951* (Lond, 1955); L. J. Louis, *Trade Unions and the Depression* (Canb, 1968); R. J. Hawke, *In Memoriam, Albert Monk* (eulogy, 13 Feb 1975) and *The Hawke Memoirs* (Melb, 1994); R. M. Martin, *Trade Unions in Australia* (Melb, 1975); J. Hagan, *The History of the A.C.T.U.* (Melb, 1981); T. Sheridan, *Division of Labour* (Melb, 1989); M. Beasley, *Wharfies* (Syd, 1996); M. Hearn and H. Knowles, *One Big Union* (Cambridge, 1996); *Age* (Melb), 29 Aug 1964, 12 Feb 1975; *Australian, SMH* and *Sun News-Pictorial* (Melb), 12 Feb 1975.

PETER LOVE

MONSON, RONALD AUSTIN (1905-1973), journalist and war correspondent, was born on 21 February 1905 at Kookynie, Western Australia, third child of John Christian Monsen (d.1916), a fireman from New Zealand, and his Victorian-born wife Laura Tomsey, née Creech. Moving to Perth about 1913, the family changed its surname to 'Monson' as 'Monsen' seemed too German. After her husband died of wounds while serving in World War I, Laura operated a boarding-house. Ron attended Perth Modern School and the University of Western Australia (B.A., 1928). He became a cadet on the *West Australian* in 1925 and was city roundsman by 1928.

In September 1928 Monson and E. A. Cooke set out to trek through Africa from the Cape of Good Hope to Cairo. When Cooke withdrew, Monson was joined by another Australian, J. H. Wilson; they reached Cairo in December 1929. Monson's reports were cabled to the *West Australian*. His account of physical endurance, British colonialism and an attempt to conquer Mount Kilimanjaro appeared as *Across Africa on Foot* (London, 1931).

At St Mary's Anglican Church, West Perth, on 11 June 1932 Monson married Stella McLaren. He lived as an inmate of the Harvey unemployment camp to write about the conditions there and he also covered the riots at Kalgoorlie for the *West Australian*. In 1934 he travelled to England with the State's secessionist delegation. Joining the London *Daily Telegraph* that year, he reported on a diver's descent to the wreck of the *Lusitania*. In 1937 he covered the Spanish Civil War and the Sino-Japanese War, sending back stories about Japanese atrocities and the fall of Nanking

(Nanying). He flew to Sydney in 1938 to report on the opening of the Empire flying-boat service.

In October 1939 Monson went to the French front, representing the Sydney *Daily Telegraph*, the Melbourne *Argus* and some English newspapers, including the *Daily Express*. He described the evacuation of Dunkirk and the Blitz on London, and supported Kenneth Slessor's [q.v.] complaints about delays in cable transmissions to Australia. Monson's account of the Greek campaign (April 1941) for the British Ministry of Information led him to publish *The Battle of Greece* (Melbourne, 1941). In May 1941 he was mentioned in dispatches for swimming across the Euphrates River under Iraqi fire to rescue a wounded British soldier. Slessor persuaded him in March 1943 that he was more valuable as a propagandist than a soldier. Monson next reported from Burma, and then from Alexandria, Egypt.

Despite being dubbed the 'Prince of Press Adventurers', Monson wished that the war would soon be won so that he could rejoin his family. He covered the Normandy landings on D-Day (6 June 1944). In 1945 he accompanied a medical team which entered the Bergen-Belsen concentration camp in Germany; he was devastated by what he saw, and punched the first German he encountered. Anxious that his two sons should grow up in Australia, he became a top feature writer on the *Daily Telegraph* and *Sunday Telegraph*, Sydney. His boys' escapades inspired a column, 'Bringing up Father'. Five ft 10 ins (178 cm) tall and slim in build, with brown hair, blue eyes and a moustache, Monson was a 'good rough and tumble bloke'. While he could be somewhat dour, he had a larrikin sense of humour and a thirst for adventure.

A 'battlefront correspondent by choice and conviction', Monson covered the Arab-Israeli conflict in 1948, asserting that the government's support of the partition of Palestine threatened to create an unfriendly barrier of Muslims between Australia and Britain. In articles from Indonesia and Malaya he urged Western powers to 'put food in the empty bowls of Asia' to halt communist expansion. Returning from the early stage of the Korean War, he reminded the United Nations that it could, if necessary, use the atom bomb on Chinese bases. Late in 1951 in Cairo he was attacked by a mob who thought that he was a British spy. He returned to Egypt in 1956 to report on the Suez crisis. In 1958, when war correspondents were included for the first time among the dead commemorated on Remembrance Day, he was chosen to lay the wreath at Sydney's Cenotaph. One Anzac Day, a drunk declared that Monson was a 'phoney': 'No man alive could have accumulated that mass of campaign ribbons'.

Although Monson contributed editorials, features and book reviews to the *Telegraph*s, he had been downgraded by 1967. In 1969 he was appointed publications officer at the Australian War Memorial, Canberra. Forced into retirement by a stroke in 1972, he died of congestive cardiac failure on 29 April 1973 at Canberra Hospital and was cremated; his wife and sons survived him.

T. C. Bridges and H. H. Tiltman, *Recent Heroes of Modern Adventure* (Lond, 1932); C. Semmler (ed), *The War Diaries of Kenneth Slessor* (Brisb, 1985) and *The War Despatches of Kenneth Slessor* (Brisb, 1987); D. Horne, *Confessions of a New Boy* (Melb, 1985); *Newspaper News*, 1 Nov 1939, 1 June 1951, 1 Jan 1952; *West Australian*, 17 July 1928, 30 Apr 1973; *Cape Times*, 23 Dec 1929; *Sunday Telegraph* (Syd), 6 May 1973; series 1838/1, item 1520/4/12, A2908/15, item S170/3, pt 1, A5954/1, item 1979/91 (AA, Canb); Monson papers, PR89/152 (AWM); information from, and family papers held by, Mr and Mrs B. Clifton, Scarborough, and Mr and Mrs R. J. Monson, Darlington, Perth.

BRIDGET GRIFFEN-FOLEY

MONSOOR, HASSAN ALI ('HARRY') (1883-1959), hawker, was born on 1 March 1883 at Beit Meri, Lebanon, then part of the Ottoman Empire. His father's name was Alie Monsoor. Hassan emigrated to South Australia in 1901 and found work at the Port Pirie lead smelters. Three years later he set up as a hawker, with a small van pulled by donkeys. Based (from about 1908) at Leigh Creek, he toured the Flinders Ranges selling haberdashery; by 1918 he owned a bigger van, hauled by six mules. He was naturalized in 1924. Visiting Lebanon, he married Maheeba Ali Solomon in 1926, then returned to South Australia.

That year Monsoor bought a Graham Bros truck with a large van body. He and his wife hawked their wares in the Flinders Ranges, using Adelaide for provisions and stock. The family (a daughter was born in 1927) slept in the van. They moved to Copley in 1929 before settling in Adelaide in 1934. Throughout this period 'Harry' continued to make his runs. In 1938 the family (by then there were three children) opened a general store at Beltana whence Harry regularly departed on trips that lasted six weeks. His 680-mile (1100 km) journeys took in Leigh Creek, Marree, the Strzelecki track to Mount Hopeless, Arkaroola, Nepabunna mission and every settlement *en route*. After a fortnight at Beltana to restock and service the van, he set off again. His visits to railway towns were timed to coincide with paydays; similarly, he tried not to miss outback race-meetings or the arrival of drovers bringing cattle from Queensland. He also sought out his many Aboriginal customers. On the rough tracks he had to be his own mechanic. At night he removed the steering-wheel and slept in the cab.

Harry was a short, jovial individual whose visits were eagerly awaited. For children in isolated areas, he was the sole source of sweets (Minties, jubilee mixture and almond rock), and for their mothers, bolts of cloth and sewing materials. Men bought tobacco, boots and razor-blades. He was said to have anything one needed: 'I got the pretty bloomer today', he shouted to lady customers, and, to potential condom purchasers, 'I've got the overcoat for the mad dick'. For some, Monsoor's truck was the first motor-vehicle they ever saw. For many, he was the only visitor, month in, month out. His arrival brought news and gossip from along the track, and his boisterous, self-deprecating humour ensured his popularity. He enjoyed gambling at cards or a wager on his remarkable physical strength.

At the age of 66 Monsoor suffered a heart attack. He endured three months sedentary life before saying, 'A bloke might as well be dead', and going back on the road. In 1954 Maheeba's ill health forced the family to return to Adelaide and led to Harry's retirement. The Monsoors managed delicatessens until Maheeba died in 1957. Harry then returned to Leigh Creek. Survived by his daughter and two sons, he died there on 20 May 1959 and was buried in Centennial Park cemetery, Adelaide. His estate was sworn for probate at £4716. Monsoor's van is on display at the National Motor Museum, Birdwood.

G. Aird, *Beltana, the town that will not die* (Beltana, SA, 1984); P. Rajkowski, *In the Tracks of the Camelmen* (Syd, 1987); application for naturalization, D1915/0, item SA853 (AA, Adel); naturalization file, A242 428, item 1924/8372 (AA, Canb); Graham Bros file (National Motor Museum, Birdwood, SA).   JON CHITTLEBOROUGH

MONTGOMERY, JOHN NORRIS (1889-1963), geologist and oil explorer, was born on 1 September 1889 at Wedderburn, Victoria, son of Australian-born parents William Alexander Montgomery, bank manager, and his wife Isabel Ellinor Dorothy, née Shimmin. John was educated at Pleasant Street State School, Ballarat, and at the Ballarat School of Mines (on a scholarship). After studying metallurgy, mining engineering and geology, and working as a geological-assistant, he obtained an assayer's certificate in 1910. Next year he moved to the Bairnsdale School of Mines where he lectured in mathematics and demonstrated in chemistry and assaying.

In 1917 Montgomery joined an exploration party to Upoia, Papua, which was sponsored by the Commonwealth government and led by Arthur Wade [q.v.12]. The search for oil in Papua and New Guinea became his life's work. A member of the Anglo-Persian Oil Co.'s geological expedition in 1920, he began detailed mapping of the Hohoro area; he later surveyed the coastal region of the Gulf of Papua—working north-westward from Yule Island—and a large part of the country between Madang and the border with Netherlands New Guinea. At the Independent Church, Melbourne, on 12 October 1920 he had married Violet White with Congregational forms.

Montgomery transformed his basic geological training with on-the-job experience in Albania, Yugoslavia, Venezuela and Persia (Iran). He studied at the Royal College of Science, London, then returned to Papua in 1929 as second-in-command to B. K. N. Wyllie of Anglo-Persian; they carried out an intensive examination of the region around Port Moresby, inland as far as Rouna Falls, and along the coast from Bootless Inlet to Yule Island. When the Australian government decided to suspend geological investigations in Papua, Montgomery left Port Moresby in November. Employed (from 1934) by Oil Search Ltd, he worked for that Australian firm in the Mandated Territory of New Guinea. In 1938 he was appointed deputy chief geologist of the newly formed Australasian Petroleum Co. Pty Ltd.

Small, rather fussy, and precise in manner, 'Monty' (as he was nicknamed) was one of the tiny band of Australians who became petroleum explorers in a period when it was believed that there was little prospect of discovering oil in Australia. Their long search in the rugged jungles did not prove very successful, but it did engage the interest and capital of oil companies for many years, and contributed significantly to an understanding of the geology of Papua and New Guinea. During World War II Montgomery worked in Australasian Petroleum's Melbourne office, compiling and reviewing data; he also acted as a technical adviser to the United States Army. He stayed with the company until his retirement in 1959.

Montgomery was joint author of two important publications on the geology of Papua and New Guinea. In 1945 he was elected to the Royal Society of Victoria. Survived by his wife and younger son, he died on 3 November 1963 in Melbourne and was cremated. His elder son John was killed in action in 1944 while serving with the Royal Australian Air Force.

The Oil Exploration Work in Papua and New Guinea conducted by the Anglo-Persian Oil Company on behalf of the Government of the Commonwealth of Australia, 1920-29, vol 1 (Lond, 1930); Roy Soc Vic, *Procs*, 77 (1964); *SMH*, 12 June 1929, 3 July 1936, 15 Nov 1938; information from Prof S. W. Carey, Hob, Mrs A. Montgomery, Melb, Prof E. A. Rudd, Adel, Mr F. K. Rickwood and Mr J. Zehnder, Syd.

ROBERT MURRAY

MOONLIGHT, MICHAEL (c.1889-1970), Aboriginal stockman, was born about 1889 at Mount Merlin station, near Boulia, Queensland, son of King Baly and his wife Mammie. King Baly's people, the Kalkadoon, had resisted European attempts to take their lands until a force of settlers and Queensland Native Mounted Police defeated them in battle near Kajabbi in 1884. Michael long remembered how his father was treated: 'They brought him in from the bush and "quietened" [pacified] him'. Moonlight worked as a stockman on stations around Boulia, including Strathelbiss and Marion Downs, before being employed on nearby Chatsworth where he acquired his own house and horses. As a young man, he married Lizzie Cherigsue. Later, he married Lardie Roberts.

In 1955 it was decided that the Moonlights should be sent to Palm Island Aboriginal Settlement where Lardie was to receive medical treatment. Percy, their 13-year-old son, accompanied them to Townsville. The local press reported the family's arrival in the city and their transfer to the island by boat. Moonlight was intrigued by the sights and sounds of the busy streets; since it was the first time he had seen the sea, he was afraid of the last leg of the journey to Palm Island. Twelve months later he asked permission to return home to Chatsworth station.

A western Queensland identity, Moonlight was a hard worker who was respected by his family, his employers and the community. Some Whites gave him an ornate metal gorget inscribed, 'Moonlight—King of the Burke' [region]. The office of the protector of Aborigines managed many aspects of his life and he endorsed documents with his thumbprint. Like numerous other Aborigines, he had contributed to the development of pastoralism in western Queensland. By helping linguists and historians, he was to do much to preserve the cultural heritage of his people.

Moonlight lived in retirement at the Aboriginal camp outside Boulia. From the mid-1960s he and his wife assisted Barry Blake to record the Kalkatungu language. Blake learned about tribal boundaries, place names, songs and grammar. From 1970 Lardie continued working with Blake and another linguist, Gavan Breen. Audiotapes (1966-75) of the Moonlights speaking Kalkatungu are held at the Australian Institute of Aboriginal and Torres Strait Islander Studies, Canberra. Michael and Lardie also provided information to R. E. M. Armstrong who studied the experiences of the Kalkadoon people after European settlement.

During a visit to comfort relations—whose son had been drowned while mustering stock on Davenport Downs station—Moonlight died on 29 September 1970 at Dajarra and was buried in Boulia cemetery with Methodist forms. He was survived by his wife, their three sons and one of their three daughters, and by two daughters and one of the three sons of his first marriage. Once his funeral expenses had been paid, his estate amounted to $97. Leslie Campbell's portrait of Moonlight and Lardie is held by the Stone House Museum, Boulia.

R. E. M. Armstrong, *Kalkadoons* (Brisb, nd); B. Rosser, *Dreamtime Nightmares* (Canb, 1985); *Nth Qld Register*, 19 Nov 1955, 3 Oct 1970; *North-West Star*, 30 Sept 1970; *Townsville Bulletin*, 3 Oct 1970; Dept of Family Services and Aboriginal and Islander Affairs (Brisb), file 8L/260, Lardie Moonlight (QA); information from Ms D. Hoskings *and* annotated collection index (Aust Inst of Aboriginal and Torres Strait Islander Studies, Canb); information from Mrs D. Prowse, Mt Isa, and Mr A. Sanders, Boulia Shire Council, Qld.   YSOLA BEST

MOORE, ARTHUR CLAUDE (1898-1978), public servant and businessman, was born on 1 March 1898 at Strathbogie, Victoria, eighth child of Ballarat-born parents Reuben Edward Moore, farmer, and his wife Mary, née Davis. After Mary's death, Arthur and his sister Marguerite were brought up by 'Granny Andersen' at Moonee Ponds, Melbourne, where they attended state school. Arthur began work as a junior clerk in the Victorian Railways and studied accountancy at night (licentiate Commonwealth Institute of Accountants, 1924). In May 1917 he joined the New South Wales office of the Commonwealth Department of Trade and Customs as a clerk in the statistical branch. He enlisted in the Australian Imperial Force on 21 May 1918 and joined the 7th Australian Light Horse Regiment. The unit occupied the Gallipoli Peninsula from December 1918 to January 1919.

Discharged in Sydney on 19 August 1919, Moore returned to Trade and Customs, transferred to the landing branch in 1922 and moved to central staff, Melbourne, in 1924. At St Brigid's Catholic Church, North Fitzroy, on 14 February 1925 he married Stella Helena Hogan, a 24-year-old saleswoman; they were to have three children (only one of whom survived infancy). He was among the first public servants to move to Canberra; the family home at Ainslie was the second in that suburb and was surrounded by bush.

By July 1932 Moore was a third division clerk in the accounts branch, but his work while accompanying the delegation to the Imperial Economic Conference, Ottawa, ensured him a prominent part in ensuing trade negotiations. He went with Attorney-General (Sir) John Latham's [q.v.10] mission to Japan in 1934, and became principal adviser to Sir Henry Gullett [q.v.9], minister in charge of trade treaties. Moore helped to write the trade requests—rejected by the United States of America in February 1935—that set off the trade diversion crisis. Promoted assistant comptroller-general (tariff) in March 1935, he advised trade delegations to London, led by Prime Minister Lyons (1935) and (Sir) Earle Page [qq.v.10,11] (1938). The latter delegation signed a bilateral agreement with Britain in July 1938. Moore was appointed C.B.E. that year. Gullett observed: he 'has at least held his own with the ablest men of the various British public services with whom he had so much contact'.

As well as carrying out his customs duties, Moore was director (1941-46), division of import procurement, which also administered Lend-Lease. He oversaw the flow of essential industrial goods and war matériel. The War Cabinet approved his plan for a shipping supply council to put to better use ships, wharfs, transport and stores. He replaced L. R. Macgregor [q.v.10] as director-general, Commonwealth of Australia War Supplies Procurement, in Washington in 1944. With the end of Lend-Lease, settlement negotiations with the U.S.A. reached a stalemate by early 1946: Moore and R. V. Keane [q.v.14], minister for trade and customs, argued that Australia had incurred no debts from the wartime agreement. Keane's death in April allowed direct intervention by Prime Minister Chifley [q.v.13], who rapidly reached a compromise settlement.

Moore claimed to have married Olga Badik (d.1978), a 28-year-old Canadian, on 15 April 1946 in New York. After resigning from the public service in July, he persuaded the Coca-Cola Export Corporation to sell its New South Wales bottling franchise which was bought next year by a Sydney firm; Moore was chairman and managing director of the renamed company, Coca-Cola Bottlers (Sydney) Pty Ltd, until December 1954. His other business interests included a carbon processing factory and fertiliser plant at Chullora, and a bauxite and dolomite mine at Mount Fairy. He was a consultant (1955-57) to Ezra Norton's [q.v.] Truth and Sportsman Ltd.

President (1958) and a life member of the Wine and Food Society of New South Wales, Moore was friendly with well-known Sydney artists, among them John Olsen and (Sir) William Dobell [q.v.14], and the dealer Rudy Komon. He belonged to the Cronulla Returned Servicemen's League Memorial Club and the Australian Jockey Club. In his seventies he drove from Nowra to Sydney on race-days; he owned racehorses and brood mares in partnership with Anthony Hordern [q.v.9]. He had played Australian Rules football in his twenties, and was later a weekend golfer. Survived by the two sons by his second wife, Moore died on 4 October 1978 at St Vincent's Hospital, Darlinghurst, and was cremated with Anglican rites.

E. Page, *Truant Surgeon*, A. Mozley (ed) (Syd, 1963); R. A. Esthus, *From Enmity to Alliance* (Melb, 1965); S. J. Butlin and C. B. Schedvin, *War Economy 1942-1945* (Canb, 1977); *SMH*, 1 Jan 1938, 5 May 1939, 1 July 1945, 1, 2 July 1946, 6, 7 Oct 1978; G. Nelson, 'History of Coca-Cola in Australia' (Coca-Cola Amatil Ltd archives, Syd); A. C. Moore papers CP117/3 (AA, Canb); family papers (held by Mr J. T. Moore and Ms H. D. Pearson, Randwick, Syd); information from and papers held by Mrs S. Jorgensen, Deniliquin, NSW.   ANDREW HONEY
ROGER BELL

MOORE, MALCOLM STEWART (1888-1969), engineer and industrialist, was born on 8 February 1888 at Milton, Brisbane, son of John James Moore, a Queensland-born ironmonger, and his wife Amelia Sarah, née Shaw, who came from Melbourne. William Moore [q.v.10] was his uncle. Malcolm attended a Brisbane state school and Caulfield Grammar School, Melbourne; he then studied mining and civil engineering at the University of Melbourne (B.M.E., 1911; B.C.E., 1912). During World War I he worked in Britain as assistant general manager (1915-16) of the National Projectile Factories, Glasgow, and director (1917-18) of the National Ordnance Factories Section, London, both of which came under the control of the Ministry of Munitions.

Back in Melbourne, he established Malcolm Moore (Industries) Ltd in 1921 and advertised his services as a manufacturer's agent and engineer. At the Presbyterian Church, Kew, on 14 November 1922 he married Anna Victoria McCowan; they were to remain childless. In 1927 he set up his firm's manufacturing centre in Williamstown Road, Port Melbourne. Branches were later opened in every State capital and several provincial centres. Appreciating the need for increased productivity in many areas of industry, he made his firm a specialist in the design and manufacture of mechanical-handling and construction equipment. In 1953 he retired to devote himself to his educational and philanthropic interests.

Moore and a number of other industrialists had asked the Education Department in 1937 to introduce courses for foremen and to hold these classes at the Melbourne Technical College. In 1939 he was a foundation member of the M.T.C. Foremanship Association: it changed its name to the Industrial Management Association of Australia in 1940, to the Institute of Industrial Management of Australia in 1941 and to the Australian Institute of Management in 1949. Moore served on the national council and was president in 1956-58. A generous benefactor to the institute and its State divisions, he gave £25 000 in 1961-64 to help to build Management House, Brisbane. In World War II he had been an engineering consultant to the Commonwealth Department of Supply and Development (Shipping) and a member of the Australian Army Mechanisation Board.

A man of integrity and compassion, Moore was active in the Australian Inland Mission's aerial medical service and in establishing (1942) the (Royal) Flying Doctor Service of Australia. He was a long-time councillor and president (1947-51) of the Victorian section of the R.F.D.S., and served on the federal council as secretary, treasurer, consultant and president (1956-58). In 1958 he was appointed C.B.E. He was awarded the Australian Institute of Management's (Sir) John Storey [q.v.] medal (1963), Rotary's vocational service award (1965), and the Institution of Production Engineers' Jack Finlay national award.

Moore belonged to the Athenaeum Club. He was also a member of the Australasian Institute of Mining and Metallurgy, the Institution of Engineers, Australia, the Institution of Civil Engineers, London, and the I.P.E., London. Survived by his wife, he died on 24 November 1969 at Toorak and was cremated. He left 30 per cent of his estate as a bequest to promote management education. His portrait by Paul Fitzgerald is held by the Australian Institute of Management, Queensland division.

J. Bilton, *The Royal Flying Doctor Service of Australia* (Syd, 1961); J. Fogarty, *Leaders in Management* (Melb, 1991); *Memo to Management*, Jan/Feb 1970; *SMH*, 20 Aug 1945, 1 Dec 1948, 24 Jan 1953, 12 June 1958, 20 Nov 1963; *Age* (Melb), 13 Apr 1949, 25 May, 4, 24 Sept 1965, 26 Nov 1969; membership registers, A'sian Inst of Mining and Metallurgy (Melb) *and* Inst of Engineers, Aust (Canb).

E. F. SPREADBOROUGH

MOORE, MAX LYALL (1897-1979), sports administrator, was born on 3 June 1897 at Ipswich, Queensland, fifth child of Tasmanian-born parents Albert Phillip Moore, tailor's-cutter, and his wife Mary Louisa, née Briant. Brought to Tasmania as an infant, Max was educated at Goulburn Street State and Hobart High schools. He became foundation secretary (1915) of the Old Hobartian Association. In 1919 he began an apprenticeship as a journalist with the *Mercury*. He later obtained an auctioneer's licence and worked with A. G. Webster & Sons Ltd where he established a sporting club for fellow employees. At St John's Anglican Church, Hobart, on 9 December 1939 he married Phyllis Pott, a 30-year-old ledgerkeeper.

An active swimmer, Moore was secretary (1922-49), president (1949-72) and a life member (1972) of the Tasmanian Amateur Swimming Association. He frequented the Sandy Bay Baths, a ramshackle wooden structure open to the swells of every tide and the cold winds off the Derwent River. These spartan conditions made him determined to ensure that Hobart had a suitable heated swimming-pool in which to hold State and national championships. While the Amateur Swimming Union of Australia threatened to bypass Tasmania for want of appropriate facilities, he petitioned local and Federal politicians for financial support. It was not until swimming was televised (1956) at the Olympic Games in Melbourne that his campaign received strong community backing, culminating in the opening of the Hobart Olympic Pool in 1958.

Driven by boundless energy, Moore served a wide range of community groups, especially those representing youth. Chairman (1944-62) of the Associated Youth Committee (later Youth Council of Tasmania), he founded (1950) and presided (1951-78) over the Youth Hostels Association of Tasmania which built a chain of hostels throughout the State. As chairman (1944-75) of the Tasmanian branch of the National Fitness Council, he helped to provide programmes to cater for the accelerating demand for recreational pursuits; largely due to his initiative, seaside camps were established at Barnes Bay, Rheban, Port Sorell and Port Esperance, snow and adventure camps were set up in the central highlands, and indoor sporting stadiums were built at Montagu Bay, Launceston, Devonport, Burnie and Moonah.

Moore was honorary secretary (1938-63) of the Tasmanian Olympic Council, and a member of the organizing committees for the British Empire (and Commonwealth) Games (from 1934) and for the 1956 Olympic Games. He was also a State secretary (1948-61) of Empire (British Commonwealth) Youth Sunday, chairman (1953-54) of the sport and youth committee for the Tasmanian sesquicentenary celebrations and honorary secretary (1962-75) of the Tasmanian branch of the Duke of Edinburgh's Award Scheme. A justice of the peace, he served as a special magistrate in the children's court. In 1964 he was appointed O.B.E.

With a phenomenal memory for names and faces, Moore had a warm personality and a friendly smile. His leadership and service encouraged many volunteers to join him in furthering sport and recreation in Tasmania. Survived by his wife and two sons, he died on 12 March 1979 in Royal Hobart Hospital; his body was bequeathed to the faculty of medicine, University of Tasmania. The Max Moore Memorial Stadium was opened at Moonah in 1984.

Youth Hostels Assn of Tas Inc, *Tangara*, June 1979, p 6; *Mercury* (Hob), 19 July, 9 Sept 1972, 8 May 1976, 14 Mar 1979; information from Mrs P. Moore, New Town, and Mr B. Moore, Rose Bay, Hob, and Mr W. Moore, Cambridge, Tas.

ROBIN K. HOOD

MOORE, SIR RICHARD GREENSLADE (1878-1966), blacksmith and mayor, was born on 21 June 1878 at Neereman, near Eddington, Victoria, seventh of fifteen children of English-born parents John Moore, blacksmith, and his wife Anne, née Greenslade. Educated at Eddington State School, Dick learned his father's trade, then travelled to Western Australia in 1900. He reached Kalgoorlie on 18 March and worked on the goldfields.

At the Methodist Church, Menzies, on 22 April 1902 Moore married Margaret McIntyre (d.1952), a 25-year-old, New Zealand-born Salvation Army officer. They settled at Broad Arrow, where he had established his own smithy. Following the death of her infant son in 1903, Margaret visited her family in New Zealand. Dick worked as a coach-builder at Subiaco and as a miner on the goldfields. After his wife returned, he set up as a blacksmith at Kalgoorlie. In 1906 he contracted typhoid fever which confined him to bed for three months. One year later he again fell ill with typhoid and went home to convalesce in Victoria. By 1908 he had returned to Kalgoorlie. In 1912 a cyclone flattened his premises; with the help of local blacksmiths, the shed was rebuilt and named the 'Cyclone Coach Factory'.

In 1925 Moore was elected to the Kalgoorlie Municipal Council. A member of the Nationalist Party, he represented (1932-36) North-East Province in the Legislative Council. In 1937 he was elected mayor of Kalgoorlie, a position he held until his death at the age of 88. Described as a hard-working, non-smoking, teetotal but tolerant man, he was highly respected and affectionately regarded in a town renowned for its drinking and gambling, as well as its gold. As mayor, he opened the Olympic pool (1938), guided the council's electricity undertaking to a profit, jointly chaired the district patriotic fund which raised £70 000 during World War II, and welcomed members of the royal family to Kalgoorlie in 1954 and 1958. He was a long-time adherent of the Methodist Church, and served as a lay preacher and Sunday School superintendent.

Known to all goldfielders as Dickie Moore, he was a wiry man, with a thin face, biggish ears, straight grey hair and a moustache. He held office in the local Mechanics' Institute, and in branches of the Travellers' Aid Society, Fresh Air League, Silver Chain District (and Bush) Nursing Association, Liberal Party, Australian Red Cross Society, Young Men's Christian Association, Royal Flying Doctor Service of Western Australia and St John Ambulance Association (life member). A widower, on 31 January 1953 at Wesley Church, Kalgoorlie, he had married Rose Sarah, née Howlett, widow of Rev. Herbert Fennell. He was appointed O.B.E. in 1951 and knighted in 1960. Two years later the Kalgoorlie council named the sports centre after him. Sir Richard Moore died on 15 September 1966 at his Kalgoorlie home and was buried in the local cemetery; his wife survived him, as did two of the four sons and the two daughters of his first marriage.

J. Ellen, *The Hammer and the Anvil* (Melb, 1992); *People* (Syd), 4 Nov 1953; *Kalgoorlie Miner*, 1 Jan 1951, 4 Jan 1952, 2 Feb 1953, 1 Jan 1960, 16 Sept 1966, 19 Mar 1971; *West Australian*, 1 Jan 1960, 16 Sept 1966.   TESS THOMSON

MOORE, ROBERT CLIFTON (1932-1979), television broadcaster and producer, was born on 16 December 1932 in Adelaide, son of John Moore, butcher, and his wife Dorothy, née Clifton. After attending Adelaide Boys' High School, Bob entered the University of Adelaide (B.A. Hons, 1956) where he studied history and political science, led (1952-55) the debating team and edited (1954) *Adelaide University Magazine*. He worked on a temporary basis with the Australian Broadcasting Commission's talks department, then took up a travelling scholarship and in 1956-58 read politics at the University of Oxford (B.Phil., 1968).

Joining the British Broadcasting Corporation in 1958 as a trainee, Moore soon became a current-affairs producer for radio, in the general overseas service. In 1960 he completed a production course in television and assisted the producers of the programmes, 'Panorama', 'Lifeline' and 'Face to Face'. On 8 March that year at St Michael's parish church, Highgate, London, he married Darlene Fraser Johnson, a 24-year-old actress; they were to have a daughter before being divorced. By December Moore had returned to Sydney as talks-assistant with the A.B.C. A reporter with 'Four Corners' from 1963, he was the programme's executive-producer in 1965-67. He won a Harkness fellowship to travel and study in the United States of America in 1968, and obtained a master's degree from the graduate school of journalism, Columbia University, New York.

By the late 1960s television had proved to be a dominant medium of political reporting. News bulletins covering each day's events reached mass audiences. A smaller number of people watched current-affairs programmes which featured questions and commentary. Moore produced serious programmes aimed at this market. He interviewed prominent figures with civility and a measure of detachment, revealing his liberal-humanist values in the process. His most important guests included Richard Nixon in 1965, Harold Holt [q.v.14] in 1967 and (Sir) John Gorton in 1968. Ten of his conversations with intellectual, re-

ligious, industrial and trade-union leaders (telecast in 1970) were published in *Profiles of Power* (Sydney, c.1970).

Moore found a vehicle for his talents in 'Monday Conference', which he hosted and produced for the A.B.C. through 290 editions in 1971-78. 'Monday Conference' was described as an 'occasion for controlled conflict' in which Moore 'played the role of mediator, endeavouring to be fair to the participants but anxious to [draw out] ideas for the benefit of the audience'. The programme retained its format of a question-and-answer session before a studio audience, with guest speakers offering different opinions on topics of current and controversial interest. Moore quickly grasped the issues, and directed the discussion in a low-keyed and good-natured way. Despite the programme's formulaic repetitiveness, and the rather bland personality and nervous mannerisms of its compere, 'Monday Conference' did relatively well in the ratings.

Converting to Hinduism, Moore married Sheila Chewoolker, an air hostess, on 6 May 1970 at Bombay, India. Back in Sydney, he embarked on a series of interviews, 'Faces of the Eighties'. He died suddenly of coronary vascular disease on 5 December 1979 in Melbourne and was cremated; his wife survived him, as did the daughter of his first marriage.

ABC, *Scan*, 29 Jan 1980; *National Times*, 16-22 Dec 1979; biog notes on R. Moore, ABC Document Archives (Gore Hill, Syd); programme research material for 'Monday Conference' *and* Robert Moore correspondence files, CA251, Series C1341, C1172, C324 (AA, Canb).   MARGOT KERLEY

MOORE, ROBERT HENRY (1872-1964), Anglican clergyman, was born on 8 June 1872 at Mullingar, County Westmeath, Ireland, son of Joseph Henry Moore, civil engineer, and his wife Elizabeth Jane, née King. Robert's grandfathers were Church of Ireland clergymen. He was educated at Drogheda Grammar School and at Trinity College, Dublin (B.A., 1894; M.A., 1911), where he went on to read theology. Made deacon on 14 June 1896 and ordained priest on 13 June 1897, he served at St Luke's Church, Belfast, in a densely populated parish.

In 1897 Moore responded to an appeal by Bishop Riley [q.v.11] for additional clergy to minister to Western Australia's goldrush population. He reached Fremantle in the *Oruba* on 1 June 1898 and held appointments at Kanowna (1898-99), Mount Morgans (1899-1901), Boulder (1901-05) and Northam (1905-10). Although he retained his strong brogue, he adapted rapidly to his new surroundings and introduced liturgical practices characteristic of the Oxford Movement. He supported the idea of a goldfields diocese, and promoted the building of churches and the creation of larger parish structures. On ecclesiastical issues, he aligned himself with such clergymen as Bishop F. W. Goldsmith [q.v.9] who pressed for greater autonomy for the Church of England in Australia. At the Chapel of the Cross, Bishop's House, Perth, on 8 May 1901 he had married Jane Josephine Watterson (d.1916).

Recognition of Moore's energy and leadership came in 1910 when he was appointed a canon of St George's Cathedral, Perth, and in 1911 when he was assigned as priest to St John's Church, Fremantle. Commissioned chaplain, Australian Imperial Force, on 23 November 1917, he served with the 3rd Light Horse Brigade in the Middle East in 1918-19; after he was discharged from the A.I.F. he returned to Fremantle. At St George's Cathedral on 14 September 1921 he married Margaret, the 31-year-old daughter of Archbishop Riley. Archdeacon of Northam and rural dean in 1921-29, Moore was elected dean of Perth in October 1929, under Archbishop Le Fanu [q.v.10].

Moore maintained the cathedral's position as Western Australia's leading Anglican church. He favoured the reservation of the sacrament and wore a biretta, but did not transform St George's into an overtly Anglo-Catholic centre. Due to his efforts, a free-standing altar (west of the roodscreen) was set up and used for a regular liturgy centred on young people; another innovation was the monthly broadcast of a sung Eucharist. Financial constraints imposed during the Depression and lack of support-staff thwarted his intention of creating a large-scale ministry to the working class. As Western Australia's representative on the Anglican and Eastern Churches Association, he encouraged relations with the Greek community and invited Orthodox prelates to the cathedral on special occasions.

In 1947 Moore resigned as dean. He played an active role in the development of the parish of Scarborough as its rector (1947-54), remaining stubborn and intellectually vigorous, and championing the position of modern biblical criticism in debates over evolution. Reports of post-revolutionary society in China fascinated him. Survived by his wife, and their daughter and two sons, and by the daughter and elder son of his first marriage, he died on 20 February 1964 at Subiaco and was buried in Fremantle cemetery.

F. Alexander (ed), *Four Bishops and their See, Perth, Western Australia 1857-1957* (Perth, 1957); J. Tonkin (ed), *Religion and Society in Western Australia* (Perth, 1987); C. Holden, *Ritualist on a Tricycle* (Perth, 1997); *Western Mail* (Perth), 26 Nov, 3 Dec 1910, 18 Feb 1911; *SMH*, 2 Nov 1929, 12 June 1961; *Sunday Times* (Perth), 2 June 1963; *West Australian*, 8 June 1963, 22 Feb 1964; Anglican Church of Australia, Western Australia records, 1834-1990, MN614 3568A/24/7 *and* Moore papers, 1872-1964, MN129 (BL).   COLIN HOLDEN

MOORE, TOM INGLIS (1901-1978), writer, critic and editor, was born on 28 September 1901 at Glenmore, New South Wales, fifth of seven children of native-born parents John Edward Moore, grazier, and his wife Elizabeth, née Inglis. The family property, Ellensville, near Camden, had first been farmed in 1854 by Tom's emancipist great-grandparents Edward and Elizabeth Moore. Educated at Sydney Grammar School and St Paul's College, University of Sydney (B.A., 1923), Tom graduated with first-class honours in English, history and philosophy. He was awarded a James King [q.v.2] of Irrawang travelling scholarship and studied politics, philosophy and economics at The Queen's College, Oxford (B.A., 1926; M.A., 1933).

Tall and good-looking, Moore represented Queen's in rowing, lacrosse and athletics, and won the Walter Many essay prize. He also formed close friendships with Herbert Burton and P. R. Stephensen [q.v.12]. Hoping for a closer 'understanding of the modern world', he began his teaching career in 1926 at Phillips Academy, Andover, Massachusetts, United States of America. At the parish church of St Peter in the East, Oxford, England, on 27 July 1927 he married Peace Flavelle Little, a 29-year-old pharmacist from Sydney. Returning to America, he became an instructor in English at the University of Iowa.

In 1928-31 Moore was associate-professor of English at the University of the Philippines, Manila. He contributed to local literary life, writing reviews, articles, poems, a novel, and a play which was performed by students. As an Australian rather than one of the colonizing Americans, he was a valued mentor to creative writers and was later remembered as 'the father of Filipino writing in English'. His interest in the Philippines continued after he returned to Australia, and he was warmly welcomed on a research-trip to Manila in 1948.

Having arrived in Sydney in 1931, Moore took tutorials and acted as sub-warden at St Paul's (1932-34) before working as a leader-writer and literary reviewer for the *Sydney Morning Herald* (1934-40). He was active in the Sydney branch of the Fellowship of Australian Writers and served as president (December 1934 to June 1935) for a politically fraught term. Frank Dalby Davison [q.v.13] described him as 'the hardest-working president the Fellowship ever had. He made it a publicly and journalistically recognised literary society'. During Moore's presidency, the F.A.W. stimulated interest in Australian literature among the general public and schoolchildren by introducing Authors' Week and by running a competition on Australian authors. The latter initiative led to the gazetting of a recommended list of Australian books for study for the Intermediate and Leaving certificates.

On 3 July 1940 Moore enlisted as a gunner in the Australian Imperial Force. Commissioned in May 1941, he served in New South Wales, Queensland, Papua and New Guinea with the Australian Army Education Service and rose to temporary major. His appointment terminated on 15 January 1945. That year he began lecturing in Pacific studies to diplomatic cadets at Canberra University College, which was later amalgamated with the Australian National University. In 1954 he introduced the first full-year university course in Australian literature (approved as a degree subject, 1955). He was promoted associate-professor in 1959 and retired in December 1966.

A member (1945-71) of the advisory board of the Commonwealth Literary Fund, Moore championed the cause of hundreds of authors and numerous literary journals, and acted as an advocate for left-wing writers in the 1950s. As a C.L.F. lecturer to universities, he travelled extensively. In 1947 he became president of the Canberra branch of the Institute of International Affairs; in 1947-62 he was an associate-editor of the institute's journal, *Australian Outlook*. A founder (1950) of the Australian Capital Territory branch of the F.A.W., he was elected chairman (1956) of the first Commonwealth Council of Fellowships of Australian Writers. In 1958 he was appointed O.B.E. for his services to Australian literature.

Besides the critical and creative work which he contributed to journals, Moore gave talks for the Australian Broadcasting Commission on literary topics. The poems in his three collections, *Adagio in Blue* (Sydney, 1938), *Emu Parade* (1941) and *Bayonet and Grass* (1957), were lyrical and resilient, with many fine images. Romantic heroism, sensitivity and realism were the keynotes of his writing, epitomized in *We're Going Through* (broadcast 1943, published 1945); this verse-play dramatized the struggle between Australian and Japanese soldiers in Malaya. *Love's Revenge*, a comedy set in Manila, appeared in *Philippine Plays* (Manila, 1930). His novel, *The Half Way Sun: A Tale of the Philippine Islands*, was serialized in the *Philippine Magazine* and published in Sydney in 1935; it dealt with the interaction between Kalatong, a hero of the Ifugao and Bontoc peoples, and the American, Captain Jeff Gallman.

Moore's criticism was informed by a wide knowledge of English literature and by his training in political theory and philosophy. He was neither an apologist nor a propagandist for Australian literature. His careful study of the sources and his close contact with living authors gave him both perspective and sympathetic involvement. These attributes were evident in his scholarly introduction to *Selected Poems of Henry Kendall* (1957) and his major critical monograph, *Social Patterns in Australian Literature* (1971). He edited *Best Australian One-Act Plays* (with William Moore, 1937), *Australian Poetry 1946* (1947), *Australia Writes: An Anthology* (Melbourne, 1953), *A Book of Australia* (London, 1961), *Poetry in Australia: From the Ballads to Brennan* (1964) and *Letters of Mary Gilmore* (with W. H. Wilde, Melbourne, 1980). Among his other critical works were *Six Australian Poets* (1942), *Rolf Boldrewood* (Melbourne, 1968) and *Mary Gilmore: A Tribute* (with Dymphna Cusack and Barrie Ovenden, 1965).

A keen gardener, Moore spent his retirement growing prize-winning roses, working for the F.A.W., reading and publishing manuscripts, and advising writers. From 1956 he suffered intermittently from severe rheumatoid arthritis. Survived by his wife and daughter, he died on 23 July 1978 in Canberra and was cremated.

Fellowship of Aust Writers papers, MSS 2008 (ML); Tom Inglis Moore papers, MS 8130 (NL).

ELIZABETH PERKINS

MOORHEAD, MARY; *see* MAXWELL, MAY

MORENO, STEPHEN (1889-1953), Catholic priest and musician, was born on 16 January 1889 at Corella, Navarra, Spain, and baptized Antonio, eldest of four sons of Juan Moreno, watchmaker, and his wife Juana, née Escudero. Introduced to music by his father, Antonio was later taught to play the piano by Dom Resa, organist at the local church. At the age of 15 he entered the Benedictine abbey of El Miracle, near the Pyrenees; in 1906 he began his novitiate at San Juliano d'Albaro, Genoa, Italy. He was professed and took the religious name Esteban (Stephen), then travelled to Rome in 1907 to further his musical education. Dom Moreno studied for a year under Signore Boezzi and met Lorenzo Perosi who encouraged him in his initial efforts at composition. While in Rome he was recruited to the Benedictine Community of New Norcia, Western Australia.

On 7 December 1908 Moreno reached New Norcia to begin his preparation for the priesthood. He acted as assistant-organist and choirmaster, and wrote sacred music for the community, before being ordained by Bishop Fulgentius Torres on 20 September 1913. For sixteen months in 1921-22 he studied performance and composition under Walter Braunfels and Huber Anderach at Munich, Germany. Acting under the instructions of Abbot Anselm Catalan [q.v.13], he arranged for Albert Moser to construct a two-manual pipe-organ and supervised its installation (1923) in the Abbey Church, New Norcia. In 1927 he helped to install another pipe-organ, at the mother house of the Sisters of St Joseph of the Sacred Heart, North Sydney. During the early 1930s he journeyed interstate and to New Zealand to train choirs and supervise performances of his liturgical music; these trips provided opportunities for the publication and recording of his works. Concerts of his music were held at New Norcia, and he arranged music to celebrate the centenary of the monastery in 1946.

Moreno was recognized throughout Australia for his efforts to restore 'music proper to the Catholic ritual' and his work was well received in Europe. Guided by Pope Pius X's 'Motu Proprio' (1903) which established norms for liturgical music, he composed more than twenty Masses, numerous motets and litanies, four *Te Deums*, offertories for the liturgical seasons and for feasts of the saints, and presentations and adaptations of Gregorian chant. 'Modern church music', Moreno wrote, 'has a right to represent the modern mind in what is noble and dignified'. He also provided a musical setting for twenty poems from 'John O'Brien's' [q.v.9 Hartigan] *Around the Boree Log*, wrote eighty pieces for New Norcia's Aboriginal boys' brass band, and composed chamber and orchestral music.

Despite suffering from ill health in the early 1950s, Moreno continued to compose his music. In February 1953 he left New Norcia to visit Spain, Germany, England and the United States of America, hoping to publish his work and find help for his increasing deafness. He died on 6 March that year at Marseilles, France, and was buried in the cemetery of the Benedictine abbey of En Calcat.

St Ildephonsus' College Mag, 1953, p 15; *New Norcia Studies*, 2, June 1994, p 75; *Catholic Press*, 13 Sept 1934; *Catholic Weekly* (Syd), 10 July 1953; S. Sayers, The Life and Works of Dom Stephen Moreno, O.S.B. (Music thesis, 1968, Graylands Teachers' College, Perth); R. G. Revell, The Musical Compositions of Dom Stephen Moreno (ts, 1986) *and* E. Ros, Music at New Norcia (bound ts, nd, c1970-76) *and* D. Barry, Dom Stephen Moreno (ts, 1992) (Benedictine Community of New Norcia, Archives).   JUDITH M. WOODWARD

MOREY, ELWYN AISNE (1914-1968), psychologist, was born on 17 September 1914 at Stawell, Victoria, eldest of three daughters of Victorian-born parents Robert Leslie Morey,

mechanic, and his wife Ida Ellen, née Corbett. Edward Morey [q.v.5] was her great-grandfather. Educated at Elwood Central School, St Michael's Church of England Girls' Grammar School, St Kilda, and the University of Melbourne (B.A. Hons, 1935; Dip.Ed., 1936; M.A., 1939; B.Ed., 1940), she taught in secondary schools in Victoria and England, and was a research-assistant for the Australian Council for Educational Research.

After completing an award-winning Ph.D. (1947) at the University of California at Berkeley, United States of America, Dr Morey became a lecturer in psychology at the University of Western Australia in 1948. With Patrick Pentony, she developed landmark diploma courses in child, educational and clinical psychology—and an exploratory course in therapeutic techniques—while she was involved in extensive, enterprising extramural work for and with children. Appointed lecturer in psychology at the University of Melbourne in 1957, she moved to Monash University as senior lecturer in education in 1961 and was promoted associate-professor in 1965. She was a fellow of the British Psychological Society, the Australian Psychological Society and the International Council of Psychologists, honorary psychologist to seven hospitals and organizations, and a member of the Australian College of Education and the Family Welfare Advisory Council (Victoria). A committee-member of the Victorian Group of Australian Pre-School Associations, she also served on the education advisory committee of the Aborigines Welfare Board. 'There was scarcely an organization concerned with child welfare that she had not addressed or served'. Her publications—which included *Children Need Teachers* (1947), with K. S. Cunningham [q.v.13]—were chiefly expository.

Elwyn Morey was 'probably the best-known child psychologist in Australia'. Her enthusiasm, dedication and energy promoted more enlightened attitudes and practices in mental health, the change from large institutions to cottage homes, and advances in child psychology and parent education. She showed that handicapped children could have unrealized potential, and she developed assessment techniques to discern that potential. She was a prime mover in founding Rossbourne House, Hawthorn, a school for slow-learning children, and the Monash Child Study Centre, now named after her, for which she had visionary aims. She gave her psychological and educational services unstintingly to countless children and families. Morey was an excellent teacher, a popular broadcaster, and a counsellor who inspired by encouraging. She knew her students personally, and they spread her influence. Young people blossomed in her company and she welcomed them in her open home.

Her appearance and her personality were large, motherly, and efficient. She was 'organised, determined, laughing, warm, caring, unshockable, unflappable, fun—and loving', with humanity, wide interests and a gift for friendship. Not everyone liked her or her communist sympathies which were driven by compassion. Some perceived her as bossy, opinionated, egoistic, liking to be the centre of attention, enjoying the gratitude she received, and encouraging dependants. But it was characteristic of her that, when a crying baby embarrassed a young mother in a public audience, Professor Morey took the child and continued her lecture with the baby contented in her arms. She died on 19 January 1968 from injuries received in a motorcar accident on the Princes Highway at Dunmore, New South Wales, and was cremated with Anglican rites.

Aust Psychologist, 2, no 3, Mar 1968; *Univ Melb Gazette*, Mar 1968; S. Wiencke, A Distinguished Australian (ts, held at Elwyn Morey Child Study Centre, Monash Univ, Melb); information from Prof R. Day, Dept of Psychology, Monash Univ, Melb, Mrs S. Wiencke, Woori Yallock, Prof S. Dunn, Pakenham, Vic, and Mrs E. Luci, Sylvania Heights, Syd.   VALERIE YULE

MORGAN, AGNES HELEN (1883-1969), hospital matron, was born on 9 December 1883 at Berwick, Victoria, daughter of Victorian-born parents William Llewelyn Morgan, stationmaster, and his wife Helen, née Williams. After training (1906-09) at the Homoeopathic Hospital, Melbourne, Agnes served as matron at the Ovens and District Hospital before returning to the Homoeopathic as assistant-matron in 1925. She became matron in 1935, a year after it was renamed Prince Henry's Hospital.

As matron, Morgan was responsible for the care of patients, general nursing services and nurse training; she supervised domestic staff, the laundry, catering and even the purchase of the linen. Before expansion in the 1950s, the hospital was small and intimate, and run in an informal way, and Morgan's influence was exercised at a personal level, through persuasion and shrewd diplomacy. She had an excellent relationship with the hospital auxiliaries. In 1949 she was appointed O.B.E.

Agnes Morgan was a petite figure, remembered by her nurses as a firm—but not rigid—disciplinarian, and as approachable and considerate, and much concerned with their welfare and comfort. She appointed her own nursing staff, and pressed for the appointment of a caterer and dietitian in 1940, and a tutor sister in 1941. For the new nurses' home, completed in 1950, she insisted that proper sitting-rooms, smoking-rooms and a modern dining-room be provided to avoid the old institutional atmosphere. She was, primarily, a good practical nurse, concerned above all with the humane treatment of patients; during her four decades at Prince Henry's the hospital was respected for the quality of its care.

The pitiful salaries paid to matrons often made indefinite postponements of retirement necessary for financial reasons. When Morgan retired in 1966, at the age of 82, she was appointed nursing adviser. She left a large teaching hospital in which the nursing staff had grown to some 400. She had not sought, nor embraced readily, a greater role for matrons in the general running of the hospital. Nor was she an academic matron. In the latter years of her long reign she was criticized by tutor sisters for failing to keep pace with changes in the profession.

A wing added to the hospital in 1965 had been named after Morgan and in 1967 her portrait by Alan Martin was unveiled in the nurses' home. In 1969 she was awarded a Prince Henry's Hospital centenary medallion. A foundation member of the Hospital Matrons' Association of Victoria and a member (1950-56) of the State council of the College of Nursing (Australia), she was also a member (1934-62) and vice-president (1949-62) of the Council of the Royal Victorian College of Nursing. For twenty years she was a member (president 1961-69) of the committee of Airdrie, the Society for Aged and Incapacitated Nurses. Endowed with an independent spirit and a keen sense of humour, Matron Morgan enjoyed life, regularly going to the theatre and the Moonee Valley racecourse. She died on 12 August 1969 at South Melbourne and was cremated with Presbyterian forms.

J. Templeton, *Prince Henry's* (Melb, 1969); Homoeopathic Hospital *and* Prince Henry's Hospital (Melb), *Annual Report*, 1869-1969, and Minute-books, 1869-1962 (held at Monash Medical Centre, Melb).   JACQUELINE TEMPLETON

MORGAN, SIR EDWARD JAMES RANEMBE (1900-1977), judge, was born on 25 March 1900 at Warwick, Queensland, second child of Edward Ranembe Morgan, a sheep farmer from South Australia, and his wife Jean Macmillan, née Brown, who was born in India. Sir William Morgan [q.v.5] was his grandfather and William Morgan [q.v.] his cousin. Edward spent his early years at Strathgarvie station on the Darling Downs. When a mortgage on the property was foreclosed, his father became a stock-and-station agent at Warwick. This business also failed, and in 1907 the family moved to Adelaide.

There, the Morgans were perhaps the least wealthy of the leading families; Edward later recalled 'we were all our relations' poor relations'. He was educated (on a scholarship) at the Collegiate School of St Peter and the University of Adelaide (LL.B., 1920). With Charles Jury [q.v.14] and Vernon Knowles, Morgan published an anthology of poetry, *Lamps and Vine Leaves* (Melbourne, 1919); he also won (1921) the Bundey prize for verse. He had enlisted in the Australian Imperial Force on 18 October 1918, but was discharged soon after the Armistice. Although he held some reservations about a legal career:

> Papers and deeds will make our winding sheet,
> Decay will darken all our watching eyes . . .
> Within the ruin of the law we've got,
> We'll sit upon our chairs, and rot and rot,

he was admitted to practice as a barrister and solicitor on 20 April 1921.

On 4 March 1924 at All Souls Church, St Marylebone, London, Morgan married Dorothy Millar, the 26-year-old granddaughter of Peter Waite [q.v.6]. In 1925 he joined the Adelaide Club. After his own legal practice proved unsuccessful, he became a partner (1927) in Norman, Waterhouse & Morgan, took charge of the Port Adelaide office and laboriously built his career from small, unexciting cases. In addition, he served (from 1934) as a stipendiary magistrate in the Police Court, Adelaide. He was honorary secretary (1930-33) of the Port Adelaide Institute, Museum and Art Gallery, founding secretary (1932) and chairman (1949) of the Friends of the Public Library, and a foundation board-member (1940) of the National Gallery of South Australia.

In 1941 Morgan was appointed president of the State's Industrial Court and of the Board of Industry. He was knighted in 1952. That year he accepted a justiceship in the Commonwealth Court of Conciliation and Arbitration, Melbourne. Punctilious and grave in his approach, he possessed a prodigious memory for precedent. While he shared the sympathies of his class in regard to employers, he prided himself on his even-handedness and discretion, and refused to talk to any party about a case unless the opposing party was present. He recorded with relish that the family of a cabinet minister, whose overture he had declined, thereafter called a total rebuff a 'Sir Edward Morgan'.

In the *Metal Trades Employers Association* v. *the Amalgamated Engineering Union (Australian Section) and others* (1952), the applicants sought compliance with the metal trades' award. The case led to a redefinition of the powers of the Commonwealth arbitration court, specifically that the court could no longer exercise both arbitral and judicial functions. In 1956 the court was replaced by the Commonwealth Conciliation and Arbitration Commission and the Commonwealth Industrial Court. Given the choice, Morgan accepted a judgeship in the new court. In 1958 he was also appointed to the Supreme Court of the Australian Capital Territory. He held both positions until his retirement in 1960.

Returning to Adelaide, Morgan became president of the National Trust of South Australia in 1960 and a trustee of the Australian Cancer Society in 1961. He continued his work for the N.G.S.A. and, as chairman (1945-55 and 1963-70), was respected for his 'magisterial attentiveness' and 'guiding taste'. His enthusiasm for the applied arts helped the gallery to build up its collections, especially of silver, furniture and porcelain. In his retirement he wrote a history of the Adelaide Club, a collection of short stories based on accounts of his family, and an unpublished autobiography; he co-authored two books on Adelaide architecture and contributed five entries to the *Australian Dictionary of Biography*.

In 1970 the Art Gallery of South Australia named its gallery of applied arts after Morgan and commissioned a bust by John Dowie. Survived by his wife, daughter and two sons, Sir Edward died on 11 September 1977 in North Adelaide and was cremated.

Art Gallery of SA, *Bulletin*, Apr 1970; *Advertiser* (Adel), 21 Aug 1941, 1 Jan, 1 Aug 1952, 3 Nov 1955, 14 Sept, 8 Oct 1977; *SMH*, 20 Aug 1952, 13 Aug 1956, 2 June 1960; *Sunday Mail* (Adel), 8 Nov 1960; Morgan papers (Mort L); information from Mr P. R. Morgan, Walkerville, Adel.   JULIE-ANN ELLIS

MORGAN, FREDERICK GRANTLEY (1891-1969), medical scientist and administrator, was born on 4 July 1891 at New Glenelg, Adelaide, son of Sydney Morgan, tailor's-cutter, and his wife Jean, née Skinner. The family moved to Victoria. With the help of a benefactor outside his kin, Grantley was educated at Geelong Church of England Grammar School and the University of Melbourne (M.B., B.S., 1916). Diligent and intelligent, he served as a resident medical officer at the Melbourne Hospital. He was Stewart lecturer in pathology at the university (1917-19), junior pathologist at the Melbourne Hospital, tutor in medicine and surgery at Ormond [q.v.5] College and—importantly for his later career—assistant to Sir Harry Allen [q.v.7], honorary director of the Walter and Eliza Hall [qq.v.9] Institute for Research in Pathology and Medicine. For a short period in 1920 Morgan held the post of assistant medical officer at the Mental Diseases Hospital, New Norfolk, Tasmania. Later that year he travelled to Mackay, Queensland, to take part in a Rockefeller Foundation filaria survey.

In February 1921 Morgan was appointed assistant-bacteriologist at the Commonwealth

Serum Laboratories, Melbourne. Next year J. H. L. Cumpston [q.v.8], director-general of health, sent him to Nauru to investigate leprosy. Morgan's reputation was enhanced by the excellent report he presented on his clinical and bacteriological work. Back in Melbourne, he supervised C.S.L.'s early manufacture of insulin. From 1925 he collaborated with (Dame) Jean Macnamara [q.v.10] on the production of a means of passive immunization against poliomyelitis by using human immune serum; he published an article on their research in 1927. Meanwhile, he had shown his skills at the bench in a wide range of other work at C.S.L. involving human and animal vaccines. He became assistant-director to W. J. Penfold [q.v.11] in 1925; when Penfold left, he spent a year as acting-director before being appointed director on 3 March 1927.

One of the early successes of C.S.L. had been the preparation of a toxin-antitoxin prophylactic against diphtheria. Morgan played a central role in that achievement. On 27 January 1928 at Bundaberg, Queensland, twenty-one children were given C.S.L. diphtheria toxin-antitoxin mixture. Eighteen of them became ill and twelve died. This calamity immediately overshadowed the organization and especially its new director. A royal commission investigated the events and found that staphylococci had contaminated the contents of one multi-dose, rubber-capped bottle. Supplied without an antiseptic additive, the prophylactic had been kept unrefrigerated while being used over a number of days. The offending container (the contents of which were certainly sterile on leaving C.S.L.) had been inadvertently dispatched without a notice warning against multiple use of the product on different days. Judicious and fair, the report of the royal commission did not leave C.S.L.'s director unscathed. Evidence showed that the method of supplying the preparation had been unsound.

At All Saints Church, St Kilda, on 4 June 1930 Morgan married 22-year-old Dorothy Lewin with Anglican rites. That his marriage occurred relatively late in life may have stemmed from his wish to repay the costs of his education. The laboratories flourished under his leadership and he wrote or co-authored many scientific papers. During World War II the staff at C.S.L. did vital work in blood processing, in the production of blood-grouping serum and pooled human serum, and in rapidly manufacturing large quantities of penicillin.

By the time Morgan retired on 3 July 1956, C.S.L. had begun to produce poliomyelitis vaccine. He had been in charge for twenty-nine years. His style of administration was conservative and cautious. It reflected his experience as a working medical scientist and especially that of the Bundaberg tragedy. He

was just as concerned that no harm should come from any of C.S.L.'s products as he was with the good that should come from them. Always accessible to his staff, he showed percipience in judging people and their abilities. A notably successful administrator, he was appointed C.B.E. in 1955.

Morgan was of average height and stocky in build. His nature was calm and gentlemanly. He and his family lived in the director's residence in the grounds of C.S.L. Leading a somewhat cloistered life, he acted as C.S.L.'s 'personal custodian', bringing important visitors home to lunch and receiving its telephone calls at night. A number of his colleagues saw him as a lonely man who invariably went to his home for morning tea rather than joining other senior staff in their common-room.

Nevertheless, there was another side to him. He formed close friendships with (Sir) Macfarlane Burnet and Dr George Simpson [q.v.], and the three families spent holidays together at Anglesea. Morgan had a pleasant speaking voice, deliberate and measured when appropriate, and a very good singing voice of considerable range. A capable pianist, he accompanied his own vocal efforts at home and sang in public concerts. He belonged to the Melbourne Cricket Club, supported the Melbourne Football Club, and played golf at the Royal Melbourne and Kingston Heath clubs.

Proud to have been a foundation fellow (1938) of the Royal Australasian College of Physicians, Morgan became a member (1956) of the College of Pathologists of Australia and a trustee (1945-64) of the Baker [q.v.7] Medical Research Institute. He returned to full-time work (from 1961 to 1965) in the BCG section of the Victorian Department of Health with evident enjoyment and was no longer restricted to the role of a cautious administrator of 'reserved public face'. At a relatively early age he suffered from a mild form of Parkinson's disease which progressed slowly and took over when he was in his seventies. He died on 24 December 1969 at Kew and was cremated; his wife and three sons survived him.

G. L. McDonald (ed), *Roll of the Royal Australasian College of Physicians*, 1, 1938-75 (Syd, 1988); A. H. Brogan, *Committed to Saving Lives* (Melb, 1990); Roy com of inquiry into fatalities at Bundaberg, Report, *PP* (Cwlth), 1926-28, 4, pt 1; biog details sheet (Roy A'sian College of Physicians L, Syd); information from Mr D. Morgan, Glen Iris, Melb, and Dr D. T. Oxer, Dromana, Vic.

BRYAN EGAN

MORGAN, JAMES (c.1901-1968), Aboriginal singer and activist, was born about 1901 at Casino, New South Wales, son of Aboriginal parents Ralph Morgan, labourer, and his wife Alice, née Williams. Jim was educated at South Kyogle Public School. From the age of 13 he worked in the district as a farm hand before moving to Queensland cattle-stations. Although proud of his ancestry, Morgan accepted the need to have a good command of the English language 'in what was rapidly becoming an English-speaking world'. As a young man he enrolled in a correspondence course in English, and later earned a reputation as a writer and public speaker. Having overcome disadvantages in early life by diligence and determination, he was equally proud of his intellectual achievements (his favourite author was Charles Dickens [q.v.4] and his favourite book, *Pickwick Papers*) and of his ability to 'compete with anyone doing "hard work", such as splitting fencing posts'.

Morgan was living at Lismore when he married with Anglican rites 18-year-old Eileen Anderson on 21 June 1937 at Cabbage Tree Island Aboriginal Station. He spent the years of World War II on cattle-stations in Queensland. Returning to Kyogle, he soon moved to Coraki where he was employed as a maintenance worker by the Department of Public Works in 1947-67. He described his appointment to permanent employment in the Public Service as 'the proudest moment of my life'.

Considered to be knowledgeable about his ancestral culture, Morgan spoke his native Bundjalung language and was 'well known as a storyteller and singer' of Aboriginal legends learned from his grandfather 'King Morgan'. Through the Richmond River Historical Society, he made a number of broadcasts about Bundjalung culture with the journalist Mildred Norledge on radio-station 2LM, Lismore. *Dawn* magazine published the texts of two of his broadcasts, as well as articles by Morgan, among them 'The Old Women who turned into Birds' (1956), 'Aboriginal Folklore and People' (1958), 'Aboriginal "Criminal Law"' (1960) and 'Aboriginal Place Names: Nimbin —What it Means' (1961). He contributed twelve legends of the 'Dryaaba' people to Norledge's *Aboriginal Legends from Eastern Australia* (Sydney, 1968) and was an occasional lecturer for the University of New England's extension courses.

In 1964 Morgan was elected to the New South Wales Aborigines Welfare Board as one of two full-blood representatives. In 1967 he was re-elected unopposed. His manuscript entitled 'Report to the Aborigines of New South Wales', dated 27 October 1964, criticized the existing assimilation policy, called for greater government commitment to Aboriginal advancement, and recognized the need for Aboriginal ownership of land.

Morgan died of cardiac infarction on 10 July 1968 in the Civic Hall, Casino. A Christian who also retained Aboriginal beliefs, he was buried with Pentecostal forms in Casino cemetery. His wife, five of his seven sons and two of his three daughters survived him. The large number of people (including the president of the Kyogle Shire Council, the mayor of Casino, the secretary of the A.W.B. and a local member of parliament) who attended his memorial service at Box Hill Aboriginal reserve, Coraki, indicated his standing in the community.

NSW Aborigines Welfare Bd, *Dawn*, 1959, 8, no 1, 1964, 13, no 3, 1967, 16, nos 10-12, 1968, 17, no 10; Richmond River Historical Society, *Bulletin*, no 47, 1968; *SMH*, 19 Feb, 2, 3, Nov 1964.

STEPHEN WILD

MORGAN, WILLIAM MATHESON (1906-1972), mining engineer, was born on 9 November 1906 in Adelaide, son of South Australian-born parents Alexander Matheson Morgan, medical practitioner, and his wife Myrtle Ellen, née Green. Sir William Morgan [q.v.5] was his grandfather and (Sir) Edward Morgan [q.v.] his cousin. Like his father, Bill boarded at Geelong Church of England Grammar School, Victoria. He studied civil engineering at the University of Adelaide (B.E., 1930). At school he captained (1924) the VIII that won the 'Head of the River' and at university he 'regenerated' rowing.

Morgan worked as an underground surveyor for the Zinc Corporation Ltd at Broken Hill, New South Wales. In 1931 he joined Gold Mines of Australia Ltd's Mount Coolon mines in Queensland. Before World War II he also gained experience with Nargovissi Co. N.L., New Guinea, Bendigo Mines Ltd, Victoria, and Lake George Mines Pty Ltd, Captains Flat, New South Wales. In 1940 he was seconded to the State Electricity Commission of Victoria to manage the Kiewa tunnelling operations for its hydro-electric scheme. He remained in the Ovens Valley with Adelong Gold Estates. At St Andrew's Anglican Church, Walkerville, Adelaide, on 25 March 1935 he had married Agnes Margaret Davis. During the years they spent near the snow country, he and his family became keen skiers.

Commissioned in the Royal Australian Air Force on 16 March 1942, Morgan served with No.2 Mobile Works Squadron which built airfields in northern Australia, Papua and New Guinea. He was demobilized on 11 October 1944 as a flight lieutenant and returned to the S.E.C., directing coal exploration for its new La Trobe Valley fuel and power projects. As engineer for coal production from 1949, he revitalized and restructured brown-coal mining management; by the late 1950s the S.E.C. was recognized as a world leader in technology and low-cost mining methods.

Invited to join Western Mining Corporation Ltd in 1956, Morgan was appointed general manager of the struggling gold-mining company in 1957; he succeeded (Sir) Lindesay Clark as managing director in 1962. He was also a director of Alcoa of Australia Pty Ltd, Goldmines of Kalgoorlie (Australia) Ltd and Central Norseman Gold Corporation N.L. During the decade and a half of his leadership of W.M.C., the company diversified its mineral exploration and metal production projects. Recognizing the future importance of Japanese markets, he introduced profitable marketing strategies with small financial risks and major benefits to Australian shareholders. Following the discovery (1956) of high-grade nickel deposits at Kambalda, Western Australia, W.M.C. was one of the world's top three nickel producers by the late 1960s. The company had added aluminium and iron ore to its gold interests, and became involved in exploration for coal, petroleum and uranium.

Morgan was noted for his ability to pick the right man for the right place. He had a searching mind, and followed matters that caught his imagination with relentless energy. Having perceived the dominance of Germany in brown-coal mining, he learned (after the age of 40) to speak and write the language, and acquired sufficient mastery to address the Deutsche Bergbau Verein in German. In the mid-1950s he not only learned Japanese, but made himself conversant with Japanese culture, basic beliefs and conduct of business, thereby gaining further respect in Japanese industrial circles. He was a founding member and vice-president of the Australia-Japan Business Co-operation Committee and a member of the Pacific Basin Economic Co-operation Committee.

In addition, Morgan was an executive-member and president (1970) of the Australian Mining Industry Council, a director of Australian Mineral Industries Research Association Ltd and a council-member (from 1969) of the Australasian Institute of Mining and Metallurgy. He served (1962-70) on the advisory council of the Commonwealth Scientific and Industrial Research Organization, and sat on the science and industry forum of the Australian Academy of Science and the general court of directors of the Royal Humane Society of Australasia. He wrote and presented numerous papers on mining-related matters.

A tall, elegant man, Morgan had a wry sense of humour. He belonged to the Melbourne, Adelaide and Weld (Perth) clubs, and to the Royal Melbourne and Barwon Heads golf clubs. One of his favourite pastimes was restoring antique furniture. In 1971 he was appointed C.M.G. and awarded the medal of the A.I.M.M. In November that year he resigned as chief executive because of ill health.

Survived by his wife and two sons, he died of cancer on 2 February 1972 at his Toorak home and was cremated. His estate was sworn for probate at $226 847.

A'sian Inst of Mining and Metallurgy, *Procs*, June 1972; *SMH*, 8 Dec 1966, 13 June 1971; *Australian*, 27 May 1967; *Age* (Melb), 8 Feb 1968; *Herald* (Melb), 5 Feb 1972; Western Mining Corporation Archives (Melb); family information; personal knowledge.

E. D. J. STEWART

MORIARTY, BARBARA ('BIDDY') IERNE (1902-1979), Red Cross field representative, was born on 13 April 1902 at Ipswich, Queensland, second daughter of Travers Robert Goff, an English-born bank manager, and his wife Margaret Agnes, née Morehead, who came from Sydney. 'Biddy' was educated at the Bowral branch of Sydney Church of England Grammar School for Girls before being employed as a secretary. At St James's Anglican Church, Sydney, on 26 December 1927 she married Orpen Boyd Moriarty, a 21-year-old clerk; they were to remain childless.

Commissioned in the Australian Imperial Force in October 1939, Boyd Moriarty sailed for the Middle East with the 6th Division in 1940. His wife followed him as a representative of the Australian Comforts Fund and worked in camps in Palestine. She held the post of cipher officer with the Royal Navy for six months at Alexandria, Egypt. Her husband was killed in action on Crete in May 1941. Two months later Mrs Moriarty joined the Australian Red Cross Society's field force attached to the 2nd/2nd Australian General Hospital at Kantara, Egypt. Returning to Australia in February 1942, she performed Red Cross duties in New South Wales, Victoria, the Northern Territory and North Queensland, and was promoted superintendent in December.

Moriarty was sent back to the Middle East in 1943 to deal with recovered prisoners of war. In August she was made senior superintendent. Promoted commandant in April 1944, she joined the Australian Army Staff in London to prepare for the reception of Australian prisoners of war expected to be liberated when the Allies invaded Western Europe. She was attached to the A.I.F. Reception Group which repatriated large numbers of men after Germany surrendered in May 1945. One of her thoughtful gestures was to distribute sprigs of 'wattle' (mimosa) to the freed Australians.

Having arrived in Sydney with a shipload of liberated men in August 1945, Moriarty went on leave. She was recalled to take charge of women in the Australian Red Cross contingent which reached Singapore in September to assist the 2nd P.O.W. Reception Group.

With the last of the released troops, she came home in November. For her distinguished work with the Red Cross she was awarded the Florence Nightingale medal in July 1947. According to one of her colleagues, she was 'full of energy and charm. She had beautiful, shining golden hair and eyes like aquamarines. Even in uniform she dressed with flair . . . She was very good at achieving the impossible . . . The day after we arrived in Singapore . . . she acquired a jeep . . . Biddy was a wonderful boss . . . dignified and serene when necessary but full of fun and extremely popular with all ranks'.

On 30 July 1946 Moriarty was discharged from the Red Cross. In September she was elected to the council of the War Widows' Craft Guild of New South Wales. Joining the staff of David Jones [q.v.2] Ltd, Sydney, in July 1947, she worked first as a copy-writer in the advertising department and then as a clerical assistant (until February 1965). She died on 11 January 1979 at the Wybenia Nursing Home, Neutral Bay, and was cremated.

Women's Weekly, 24 Feb, 8 Sept 1945; *Sun News-Pictorial* (Melb), 10 May 1947; David Jones Ltd, Syd, Archives; copy of Red Cross record of service *and* ts description by Mrs J. A. Rutherford, Claremont, Perth (held by author, Campbell, Canb).

A. J. HILL

MORONEY, JAMES VINCENT (1898-1965), public servant, was born on 17 December 1898 at Bochara, near Hamilton, Victoria, son of Australian-born parents Daniel William Moroney, schoolteacher, and his wife Jane Cecilia, née Silver. Educated at St Patrick's College, Ballarat, Jim entered the Commonwealth Public Service in Melbourne on 14 March 1916 as a clerk in the Prime Minister's Department. In 1925 he transferred to the Department of Markets and Migration; eight years later he was promoted to the marketing branch of the Department of Commerce (and Agriculture, 1942-56).

After a ten-year engagement, on 4 November 1939 at St Christopher's Catholic Church, Canberra, Moroney married Ivy Florence ('Billie') Davis, a 32-year-old typist. Appointed senior investigation officer (primary industry) that year, he became chief marketing officer in 1946 and assistant-secretary, marketing, in 1949. His rise in 1953 to first assistant-secretary, marketing, confirmed him as one of the right-hand men of (Sir) John Crawford, the secretary of the department. On 16 February 1956 Moroney was gazetted secretary of the new Department of Primary Industry. He held this position until 25 October 1962 when he accepted the chairmanship of the Australian Wheat Board, a post he was to retain until his death.

During his career Moroney participated in the activities of numerous marketing authorities, boards and committees involved with primary produce. Secretary (1943-51) of the Australian Agricultural Council, he was a member of the Australian Wine Board (1950-57), the Standing Committee on Agriculture (1956-62) and the Export Development Council (1959-62). He also served as chairman (1958-62) of the Central Tobacco Advisory Committee. In recognition of his service as deputy-chairman (1941-48) of the Australian Rabbit Skins Board and as chairman (1952-55) of the Australian Hide and Leather Industries Board, he was voted honoraria by those bodies in 1942 and 1954 respectively, although in both instances considerable persistence was called for on Moroney's part and that of his superiors to overturn Public Service Board objections.

When World War II had ended, Moroney was involved from the outset in international trade initiatives. In 1946 he visited London and attended the first session of the United Nations Economic and Social Council's committee which produced a draft compact, subsequently modified and approved (1947) as the General Agreement on Tariffs and Trade. He led Australia's delegations to the international wool conference in Washington in 1951, and to the United Nations Food and Agriculture Organization's conferences held in Rome in 1955, 1957 (vice-chairman), 1959 and 1961. In 1961-62 he represented Australia at negotiations in Britain and Europe over Britain's proposed entry into the European Economic Community.

As secretary of the Department of Primary Industry, Moroney helped to develop price stabilization and marketing plans for many Australian agricultural commodities, most notably wheat. He chaired the wheat quality conference which reported to the Australian Agricultural Council in 1960 on production and marketing. While chairman of the wheat board, he negotiated sales which disposed of three record harvests to the Soviet Union, the People's Republic of China and South East Asian countries. He was, as well, an architect of the 1963 wheat industry stabilization scheme. He was appointed O.B.E. in 1956 and elevated to C.B.E. in 1960. (Sir) Charles Adermann [q.v.13], the minister for primary industry, described him in 1962 as 'Australia's leading authority on the marketing of primary commodities'.

Moroney's strengths lay in negotiation and administration rather than policy formulation. Unconventional in attitude and behaviour, he was a colourful individual who cut a distinctive figure among the senior public servants of his day. Pugnacious, determined, tough and shrewd, he was gruff—even combative—in manner, given to strong language, and nonconformist by nature. He was also a gregarious man who relished a drink. For one who taxed his energies relentlessly, he enjoyed robust health. As a young man he had been an accomplished Australian Rules footballer and a champion snooker-player. In later life he played golf and lawn bowls. Survived by his wife, two sons and two daughters, he died of cancer on 30 August 1965 at his Forrest home and was buried in Canberra cemetery.

Trends (Syd), 6, no 2, Dec 1963, p 6; *Wheat Bd Gazette*, 17, no 4, Sept 1965, p 1; *Canb Times*, 31 Aug 1965; A2974/1, P74/254: Moroney, J. V. (AA, Canb); information from Mr E. Hoffman, Red Hill, Mr A. McGoldrick, Campbell, Dr W. Saw, Forrest, and Mrs C. Wood, Stirling, Canb.

DEREK DRINKWATER

MORPHEW, ESSIE ADELE; *see* ACKLAND

MORRIS, BASIL MOORHOUSE (1888-1975), soldier, was born on 19 December 1888 in East Melbourne, ninth of eleven children of William Edward Morris, who came from England and was registrar of the Anglican Diocese of Melbourne, and his wife Clara Elizabeth, née French, who was born in India. William Morris [q.v.] was his elder brother. Their maternal grandfather was Major John French and their uncle was (Sir) John French [q.v.8]. Basil attended Melbourne Church of England Grammar School (where he rose to sergeant in the cadets) and spent one year at the University of Melbourne before joining the Melbourne Cavalry. He was commissioned in the Royal Australian Artillery on 1 December 1910 and served in coastal defence establishments.

In May 1915 Morris was appointed lieutenant, Australian Imperial Force, and posted to 'O' Siege Brigade. Arriving in England, the brigade was renamed the 36th (Australian) Heavy Artillery Group. It had two batteries, the 54th and the 55th; Morris joined the latter. He served on the Western Front from February 1916 and was transferred in November 1917 to the headquarters of the 5th Divisional Artillery as a staff captain. Promoted major, he took command of the 114th Howitzer Battery in September 1918. The 114th fought at Hargicourt and Bellicourt, and in the advance to the Hindenburg line (September-October). For his leadership during this period, Morris was awarded the Distinguished Service Order. He was thrice mentioned in dispatches.

Returning to Australia in 1919, Morris transferred to the Staff Corps and held a variety of artillery, command and staff appointments. At St Luke's Anglican Church, Christ-

church, New Zealand, on 27 August 1921 he married Audrey Lewis Cogan, the 20-year-old daughter of an accountant. In 1937 he was appointed to Army Headquarters, Melbourne, as director of supplies, transport, movements and quartering. Promoted colonel in November 1939, he was chosen that month to command the Australian Overseas Base. In December he was seconded to the A.I.F. as temporary brigadier. Arriving in Palestine in January 1940, he established the base at Jerusalem and remained there until June. He was appointed Australian military liaison officer, Bombay, India, in August and established cordial relations with military authorities in India and Ceylon (Sri Lanka).

In May 1941 Morris became commandant of the 8th Military District, with headquarters at Port Moresby. He was promoted temporary major general in January 1942. Although provided with inadequate supplies and raw, young troops, he continued to oppose the Japanese until August when Lieutenant General (Sir) Sydney Rowell [q.v.] arrived to take over a greatly augmented New Guinea Force. Morris was transferred to command the New Guinea Lines of Communication Area; from December he also directed the Australian New Guinea Administrative Unit, a body he had been prominent in establishing. Before the civil administration had been suspended on 14 February 1942, he drafted a plan to continue most of its functions in a military organization. He subsequently posted many of the conscripted officers of the Papuan and New Guinean public services to A.N.G.A.U.

Shortish, solidly built and fitter than most leaders of his generation, Morris was a resolute but tolerant commander. G. A. Vasey [q.v.], a harsh judge of his fellow generals, described him as 'a good scout—no brains but very honest and stout hearted'. Yet most of the decisions Morris was required to make during the critical eight months of his command in Port Moresby seem to have been both wise and practical. Under his direction, A.N.G.A.U. made a conspicuous contribution to the success of the allied campaigns; for the remainder of the war it maintained law and order among the civil population, managed primary production and provided indigenous labourers required by the armed services—a lifeline without which they could hardly have operated.

Inevitably, there were criticisms of Morris's leadership, but in wartime these are often easier to make than to sustain. Claims that he had acted with 'undue precipitancy' in conscripting men for military service and that he had deliberately brought about the end of civil government were dismissed by (Sir) John Barry [q.v.13] in his commission of inquiry (1944-45). General Sir Thomas Blamey [q.v.13] shielded Morris from censure for failing to halt the widespread looting of Port Moresby that occurred after the first Japanese air-raids in February 1942. Morris had 'set about his impossible task with courage and determination' and was hamstrung by 'those responsible for providing him with inadequate and incompetent forces'.

Morris retired from the army on 19 October 1946. In the following year he was appointed C.B.E. Living at Upper Beaconsfield, Victoria, he engaged in 'country pursuits'. In 1947 and 1950 he stood unsuccessfully for the Legislative Assembly as the Liberal Party candidate for the seat of Gippsland West. Survived by his wife and five daughters, he died on 5 April 1975 at Upper Beaconsfield and was cremated.

R. Paull, *Retreat from Kokoda* (Melb, 1958); D. McCarthy, *South-West Pacific Area—First Year* (Canb, 1959); P. Hasluck, *The Government and the People, 1942-1945* (Canb, 1970); J. Hetherington, *Blamey* (Canb, 1973); P. Brune, *Those Ragged Bloody Heroes* (Syd, 1991); D. M. Horner, *General Vasey's War* (Melb, 1992); AWM 123, item 619 (AWM).

A. J. SWEETING

MORRIS, EMANUEL SYDNEY (1888-1957), public health administrator, was born on 22 October 1888 at Marrickville, Sydney, sixth child of Russian-born parents Aaron Morris, jeweller, and his wife Bertha, née Lippman. After attending Sydney Grammar School, he studied medicine at the University of Sydney (M.B., 1911, Ch.M., 1912; M.D., 1926). At the Great Synagogue on 30 November 1909 Syd married 30-year-old Alice Sarah Cashmore. He was appointed junior medical officer, Hospitals for the Insane, Victoria, on 27 February 1913, and medical superintendent, Hospital for the Insane, New Norfolk, Tasmania, in December 1915. Following the death of his wife in 1918, he was commissioned captain in the Australian Army Medical Corps, Australian Imperial Force, on 25 June. He served in the Middle East after the Armistice, mainly with the 4th Light Horse Field Ambulance. His A.I.F. appointment terminated in Sydney on 17 September 1919.

Morris belonged to a generation of health administrators who emerged from World War I with grand ambitions for social reform, seeking to strengthen Australia by implementing sound, professional measures of national hygiene. He completed a diploma of public health at the University of Sydney in 1920 and returned to Tasmania as chief health officer (from 1 May). On 16 February 1921 he married with Methodist forms Irene Totten Rabone (d.1956) at Strathfield, Sydney; they were to have three children.

In 1924 Morris settled in Sydney as senior medical officer and director of maternal and baby health. He brought to his position a new emphasis on research and administrative reform. His essay, 'Salus Populi Suprema Lex', was based on a major survey which demonstrated that the fall in infant mortality rates had been offset by a significant rise in maternal mortality and morbidity. He recommended more thorough training in midwifery for medical students and the integration of private practice with public health administration. His study was awarded the Melbourne Permanent Committee for Post-Graduate Work's annual prize of 150 guineas in 1925 and gained him a doctorate in the following year. Under his control, the State's baby health centres were greatly expanded, with the co-operation of the Country Women's Association in rural areas.

In 1934 Morris was promoted director general of health. His dominance over the department was complete. A Quaker, he used 'Brother' as a mode of greeting 'into which he could inflect with unmistakable clarity the amount of familiarity that he would permit in speech'. One of his officers recalled that he was 'never self-effacing'. Morris was president (1934) and a fellow (1938) of the Royal Sanitary Institute in New South Wales, and a foundation fellow (1938) of the Royal Australasian College of Physicians.

A member (1936-52) of the National Health and Medical Research Council, Morris helped to turn its attention to problems of 'national fitness', arguing that the state 'is slowly but surely taking upon itself the management of the physical life of the individual'. In 1941 he denounced fee-for-service medicine and argued that national survival depended on making the birth rate the central issue of national health policy to avoid 'racial extinction'. Like many of his colleagues, he became disillusioned when Federal governments paid little heed to the N.H.M.R.C.'s public health objectives. He withdrew from public debate, playing no part in the battles between the British Medical Association and the Chifley [q.v.13] government. He was by then the senior member of the N.H.M.R.C., but had lost interest in using the council as a vehicle for social reform.

Having been asked to report on the future of public health administration in New South Wales in 1941, Morris recommended that all functions should be concentrated in one department, under a minister for health. His report was implemented in 1942, but, to his disappointment, he was not made permanent head of the new department. He continued as director general and as president (from 1937) of the Board of Health; he also served as inspector general of mental hospitals, chaired numerous boards and committees, and was vice-president of the Royal Society for the Welfare of Mothers and Babies. Morris returned to psychiatric administration with little enthusiasm. After he retired in 1952, he continued to work as medical officer at the Reception House, Darlinghurst.

At his Mosman home, Morris enjoyed tennis, gardening and handicrafts. Suffering from a painful bone condition, he died of cardiac disease on 31 August 1957 at Royal Prince Alfred Hospital and was cremated with the forms of the Society of Friends. His son and two daughters survived him.

G. E. Hall and A. Cousins (eds), *Book of Remembrance of the University of Sydney in the Great War, 1914-1918* (Syd, 1939); C. J. Cummins, *A History of Medical Administration in New South Wales, 1788-1973* (Syd, 1979); G. L. McDonald (ed), *Roll of the Royal Australasian College of Physicians*, 1, 1938-75 (Syd, 1988); J. A. Gillespie, *The Price of Health* (Melb, 1991); *SMH*, 14 Nov 1924, 20 Aug 1925, 17 Dec 1952.   JAMES GILLESPIE

MORRIS, ISACK (1881-1951), rabbi, was born on 10 October 1881 at Zagare, Lithuania, Russia, one of five children of Samuel Selig Monteviersky, storekeeper, and his wife Yarcha Frida, née Yosef. Isack qualified at a Yeshivah college, went to Britain in 1900 and anglicized his surname to Morris. After two years in the Cape Colony where he was naturalized on 2 April 1903, he reached Sydney on 11 July 1904 in the *Geelong* and was appointed reader of the Newtown synagogue. Late in 1905 he was guaranteed a salary by George Judah Cohen [q.v.8] to begin services for the Newcastle Hebrew Congregation.

At the Synagogue, Bourke Street, Melbourne, on 28 March 1906 Morris married Rosie Falk (d.1915); they were to have four sons. In the same synagogue on 6 February 1917 he married Rachel Grinblat; she typed his correspondence and bore him two sons. From 1910 he had served the tiny Jewish congregation in Hobart; to augment his meagre salary, he made chocolates and hawked them in a billycart. He had a considerable impact in Tasmania, but clashed with the congregation's president Samuel Benjamin when religious and lay matters overlapped. In 1921 Morris agreed to return to Newcastle where the congregation had promised to provide a synagogue. It was built in 1927 and dedicated in September.

As a Jewish minister, Morris was reader, preacher, teacher, visitor, *mohel* and *schochet* for his small congregation. He made weekly visits to the abattoirs, using his bicycle for transport. He also travelled to preach in Sydney, and to conduct services for scattered communities. In May 1933 he organized and addressed a large public meeting at Newcastle to protest against Nazi persecution of his co-religionists in Germany. During the Depression he took a cut in his modest salary;

the congregation depended on (Sir) Samuel Cohen [q.v.8] and David Cohen & Co. Ltd for financial support.

In 1922 Morris had been re-naturalized. Active in the wider community and able 'to communicate beyond religious boundaries', he was president of the Newcastle branches of the Australian League of Nations Union and the Kindergarten Union of New South Wales. He was also an executive-member of the local Boy Scouts' Association, Free Library Movement (he was an avid reader), Newcastle Boys' High School Parents and Citizens' Association and the Australian Comforts Fund. A fervent Freemason from his Newtown and Tasmanian days, in New South Wales he was a past master, and past grand chaplain of United Grand Lodge and of Mark Master Masons, past grand inspector of works, Royal Arch Chapter, and past commander, Royal Ark Mariners.

Although from the *Ostjuden*, Morris had quickly developed characteristics of Anglo-Jewry—public service, adaptability, versatility, and moderate orthodoxy in observance. He was presented with illuminated addresses —on leaving Newtown (1905) and Hobart (1921), and for thirty years service at Newcastle (1946). When he retired in 1949 his colleagues—through the chief rabbi of the British Commonwealth—conferred on him the title of rabbi. Survived by his wife and six sons, Morris died of hypertensive cerebrovascular disease on 12 March 1951 at Royal Newcastle Hospital and was buried in Sandgate cemetery.

L. Fredman, *Newcastle Synagogue Jubilee, 1927-1977* (Newcastle, 1977), and *Newcastle Synagogue 70th Anniversary* (Newcastle, 1997); Aust Jewish Hist Soc, *J*, 3, no 5 (1951), 11, no 6 (1993); *Tas Mail*, 10 July 1919, 5 May 1921; *Newcastle Morning Herald*, 22 Apr 1950, 13, 16 Mar 1951; Newcastle Hebrew Congregation archives; naturalization file, A1/1, item 21/24329 (AA, Canb); family information.
L. E. FREDMAN

MORRIS, SIR JOHN DEMETRIUS (1902-1956), judge and university chancellor, was born on Christmas Eve 1902 at Hawthorn, Melbourne, third child of James Demetrius Morris, a civil servant from New Zealand, and his Victorian-born wife Margaret Jane, née Smith. Educated at St Patrick's College, East Melbourne, and the University of Melbourne (B.A., 1924; LL.B., 1925; M.A., 1926), he was admitted to the Victorian Bar on 7 November 1927. At St Dominic's Catholic Church, East Camberwell, on 28 May 1930 he married Mary Louisa McDermott, a 29-year-old clerk. They moved to Hobart where he was admitted to the Tasmanian Bar on 24 October. He joined the firm of A. G. Ogilvie [q.v.11] which became Ogilvie, McKenna [q.v.] & Morris in 1931. Within a few years the firm's major court work was being handled by Morris: Ogilvie chose to devote more time to his political career in the House of Assembly; McKenna was to do likewise when he was elected to the Senate in 1943.

Possessing a keen social conscience, and political acumen no less acute, Morris quickly established a reputation as a legal all-rounder. With his sharp intelligence, verbal skill in interrogation, and human understanding, he had few rivals in criminal cases beyond Eric Johnson and the rising star, Reginald Wright. From June 1934 Morris observed and appreciated the efforts of the premier, his erstwhile senior partner, to lead Tasmania out of the Depression, and was moved to share in the drive to raise the social and cultural standards of the community. The high value he placed on the extension of knowledge made the University of Tasmania's law school, headed by Professor K. O. Shatwell, his special interest. By the end of the decade Morris was the inspiration of many young barristers. He was inspired to work for others, but preferred to work alone. To this end he had left the partnership in 1938 to set up his own legal practice.

Following the sudden death of Ogilvie in June 1939, Morris's career and prospects were transformed when Edmund Dwyer-Gray [q.v.8], the Labor premier, raised him to the Supreme Court bench in July as acting chief justice. His appointment was confirmed by (Sir) Robert Cosgrove [q.v.13] in April 1940. Socially established (which pleased him and his wife greatly), he bought a spacious home, Winmarleigh, at Taroona, and loved to entertain. As administrator on occasion, he also received at Government House. He mixed equally well with conservative families, intellectual leaders and trade-union officials. He dressed well, had a natural charm and social ease, spoke learnedly and talked with wit. His persuasive ways won most people over, though in some he aroused fear or jealousy. Nervous tension lay beneath his easygoing manner.

While the work of the Supreme Court increased, the number of judges did not. The attorney-general Roy Fagan was a friend and supporter, but Cosgrove thought his chief justice over-sensitive to the prestige of his office. In 1947 a royal commission found that a case of alleged corruption had been made against the premier. Charged with bribery, corruption and conspiracy, in February 1948 Cosgrove stood trial in the Criminal Court presided over by Morris. The chief justice instructed the jury to lay political considerations aside and reminded it that 'evidence of an accomplice is always regarded with the greatest suspicion'. The jury by 10 to 2 acquitted Cosgrove on all counts and he resumed his premiership.

Although Morris's Jesuit mentors had developed his social conscience, he was not a practising Catholic in Hobart. His library was graced by an impressive bust of Voltaire, symbolizing his liberal outlook and values. He translated these principles into his work on the bench and in furthering educational reforms. It was no surprise when he turned his attention to a State library suffering from many years of abject poverty and neglect. Following an inquiry and with support from the treasurer Dwyer-Gray, parliament set up and funded a statutory board of which Morris was chairman (1943-56). Improvement was striking and immediate. He then moved to replace the voluntary Workers' Educational Association (for which he had much sympathy) with a government-sponsored and -funded Adult Education Board. Again he served as foundation chairman (1949-56). It caused jealousy and gave rise to criticism that he was spreading his activities too widely. But, in fighting apathy, sloth and indifference, no one did more than he in those postwar years of penury and shortages to improve the cultural life of Tasmania.

As chancellor (from 25 February 1944) of the small and deprived University of Tasmania, he sought to redress grievances, but met resistance from a conservative council and received little support from a State government that had other priorities. In the face of such adversities, Morris managed to increase staff, to improve salaries and conditions, and to commence building on the university's new site at Sandy Bay. In 1949 he had Professor Torleiv Hytten [q.v.14] appointed as the university's first full-time vice-chancellor. The two co-operated well in the face of a tradition-bound council, a professoriate critical of any interference in academic matters, and a staff association clamouring for reforms. Morris fought council on behalf of a staff member Ken Dallas who was being denied study-leave on the ground that he was a communist sympathizer. He overruled the professorial board to admit a brilliant student Christopher Koch who had failed to matriculate in mathematics. Both sides accused the chancellor of excessive intervention and of domination. It was said that he influenced appointments to the Adult Education Board and the university. Fateful was his influence in the appointment (1952) of Sydney Sparkes Orr [q.v.] to the chair of philosophy, believing that he would contribute to adult education in the community. Morris's idealism sometimes clouded his judgement of men, but he did not easily take advice and he disliked interference by others.

Morris was knighted in 1943 and elevated to K.C.M.G. in 1952. Accompanied by Hytten, he attended the Congress of the Universities of the British Commonwealth, held at

Cambridge, England, in 1953. They also visited universities in the United States of America where Morris was appalled by McCarthyite agitation. Back home, he was distressed by the factional strife and sectarian split in the Labor Party on the communist issue. By 1954 troubles at the university were coming to a head. The chancellor was accused by the staff association—including Orr—of dominating council. The staff then persuaded the Opposition in parliament to seek an inquiry. A royal commission sat early in 1955 and made recommendations to improve relations between council, the professorial board and the faculties. Although it recognized the chancellor's contribution to the university, it was critical of him.

The strain of these conflicts, exacerbated by a staff association call that he step down, undermined Morris's health which had already been affected by over-exertion. Calls for his resignation hurt him deeply and he withdrew from society, save for the company of a few close friends. In the following year, when allegations of misbehaviour were made against Orr which ended in his dismissal, the chancellor virtually remained aloof. Sir John died of a coronary occlusion on 3 July 1956 at his desk in the Supreme Court, Hobart. He was accorded a state funeral and was buried in Cornelian Bay cemetery. His wife and son survived him. A portrait (1950) by Jack Carington Smith [q.v.13] is in the family's possession.

R. Davis, *Open to Talent* (Hob, 1990); W. A. Townsley, *Tasmania* (Hob, 1994); *Aust Lib J*, July 1956; *Univ Tas Gazette*, Aug 1956; *Mercury* (Hob), 4 July 1956; interview (1963) by author with Mr Justice William Douglas, Supreme Court, Washington D.C., US; information from Messrs J. P. Morris, Taroona, G. Stilwell, West Hobart, F. C. Mitchell, Sandy Bay, and F. J. Wilmhurst, South Hobart.

W. A. TOWNSLEY

MORRIS, SIR KENNETH JAMES (1903-1978), politician, businessman and farmer, was born on 22 October 1903 at Paddington, Brisbane, eighth child of James Reuben Morris, an English-born farmer, and his wife Christina McKenzie, née Grant, who came from Victoria. Educated at Ithaca Creek, Yeppoon and Mapleton state schools, and at Brisbane Grammar School, Ken directed the family's boot-manufacturing company and other subsidiary firms. At the Presbyterian Church, Ithaca, on 1 October 1931 he married Ettie Louise Dunlop, a 22-year-old typiste. In 1938 he stood unsuccessfully for the Legislative Assembly seat of Ithaca as the United Australia Party's candidate.

On 13 October 1939 Morris was appointed lieutenant, Australian Army Service Corps,

Australian Imperial Force. He served in Britain (1940) and—with the 9th Division—at Tobruk, Libya (1941), and El Alamein, Egypt (1942). After returning to Australia, he was attached to A.A.S.C. units in Papua and New Guinea in 1943-44, and rose to major. His A.I.F. appointment terminated in Queensland on 9 June 1944. Eight weeks earlier he had been elected to the Legislative Assembly as the Queensland People's (later Liberal) Party member for Enoggera (Mount Coot-tha from 1950). Following terms as party whip (1944-50) and deputy-leader (1950-54), he became leader on 17 August 1954.

A coalition of the Country and Liberal parties led by (Sir) Frank Nicklin [q.v.] took office on 12 August 1957. Morris was appointed deputy-premier, and minister for labour and industry. As part of his campaign to attract investment and new industries to Queensland, he and a delegation of businessmen visited Britain, Europe, Canada and the United States of America. They persuaded some overseas companies to license their products to Queensland manufacturers. Morris helped to develop tourism as a major industry by visiting more than fifty resorts in his first fifteen months as minister and by establishing Queensland tourist agencies abroad. To cope with the increasing use of cars in Brisbane's inner city, he implemented a traffic plan involving a system of co-ordinated traffic lights and a network of one-way streets.

In March 1961 Morris introduced a bill to amend the State's conciliation and arbitration laws. The legislation aimed to provide additional incentive for foreign companies to invest in mining. One of the bill's provisions removed the power of industrial authorities to award bonus payments to employees. Claims for increases in bonuses paid to employees of Mount Isa Mines Ltd were about to be heard in the State Industrial Court. The court abandoned proceedings. On 11 April the bill was proclaimed as an Act, leading to a two-month strike (from September) at Mount Isa.

A hard worker, Morris had a dynamic and, at times, aggressive personality. He once advised a group of Liberal candidates: 'When you see a head, hit it'. The junior partner in the coalition contrasted with the more easy-going Nicklin, for whom the peppery Morris was at times a trial. Although it was a custom to deal with cabinet submissions in order of receipt, Morris pestered Nicklin now and again to consider his submissions first. For the sake of coalition harmony, Nicklin let him have his way. While Morris wanted his party to increase its numbers in parliament and exert more influence in government, he was a staunch coalitionist who remained loyal to Nicklin.

Overwork took its toll on Morris's health. Stepping down as party leader and deputy-premier on 23 August 1962, he resigned from the ministry on 28 December and did not contest the elections in June 1963. He moved to a property north-west of Cooktown, where, thin from illness but 'jaunty as a boy in his khaki shorts', he cultivated legume seed. His health restored, he won a seat in the Senate in December as an ungrouped Liberal candidate. The victory was a 'remarkable electoral feat'. Morris aimed to promote 'the interests of the north specifically and those of Queensland generally'. He claimed to enjoy the Senate's 'broader canvas', but his years in Federal parliament were quiet. In mid-1967 he lost Liberal endorsement, and took the rejection calmly: 'I'm content. You've got to be big about these things'. Appointed K.B.E. in January 1968, he left the Senate in June and returned to Cooktown where, in the early 1970s, he ran a milk-delivery service. Sir Kenneth died on 1 June 1978 at Chermside, Brisbane, and was cremated; his wife, daughter and three of his four sons survived him.

Morris was slightly built and 5 ft 7 ins (170 cm) tall. Shy, and a diffident speaker early in his career, as a minister he frequently embarrassed his colleagues by putting personal integrity before political expediency. According to Katharine West, he also discomfited the government with his 'loose, publicity-conscious tongue, which often was too far ahead of his sound but slow-thinking brain'. If his mercurial personality and occasional bombast diminished his effectiveness, his probity, dedication, determination and energy were seldom questioned.

C. Lack (comp), *Three Decades of Queensland Political History, 1929-1960* (Brisb, 1962); K. West, *Power in the Liberal Party* (Melb, 1965); D. J. Murphy (ed), *The Big Strikes* (Brisb, 1983); *PD* (Qld), 1 Aug 1978, p 1458; Qld Government Public Relations Bureau, *News Bulletin,* 3 Feb, 14 Nov 1958; *Truth* (Brisb), 4 Aug 1957, 30 July 1967; *Qld Liberal,* 1 Feb 1960, Sept 1963; *Courier-Mail,* 3 Mar 1961, 18 Dec 1963, 3 June 1978; information from the late Sir Gordon Chalk and the late Sir Thomas Hiley.   BRIAN F. STEVENSON

MORRIS, WILLIAM PERRY FRENCH (1878-1960), Anglican clergyman and headmaster, was born on 21 October 1878 at Brighton, Melbourne, eldest son and third of eleven children of William Edward Morris, who came from England and was deputy-registrar (later registrar) of the Anglican diocese of Melbourne, and his wife Clara Elizabeth, née French, who was born in India. The godson of Bishop Perry [q.v.5], young Will was raised in the upper echelons of Melbourne society. In an uncommonly urbane household, the Morrises upheld the traditions of Church,

Queen and Empire. Will's sisters Mary and Edith became co-principals of Merton Hall. (Major General) Basil Morris [q.v.] was his younger brother.

Entering (1886) Wadhurst Preparatory School, Morris soon proved to be a solid, all-round pupil. At Melbourne Church of England Grammar School he played (1895-96) Australian Rules football for the first XX and became a prefect. From Trinity College, University of Melbourne (B.A., 1900; M.A., 1915), he proceeded to Ridley Hall, Cambridge, where he read theology, and church and medieval history, and was influenced by the notion of 'muscular Christianity'.

Throughout his career Morris was to be an assertive and persuasive representative of the Victorian idea of equilibrium, evoking in his teachings the interrelationship of church and nation. Archbishop Rayner remembered him as 'a broad churchman whose religious understanding focused on the "crises of humanity"'. Morris was suspicious of dogma and eschewed emotional displays of Christian belief. On 22 December 1901 he was made deacon in the Church of England.

He chose to serve as assistant-curate at Whitechapel, London, because, in his words, he had taken holy orders 'to do social work on a religious basis, instead of doing religious work on a social basis'. It was a moral approach and one which, with his disregard for institutional expressions of faith, would bring him occasionally into conflict with Church authorities. Ordained priest on 7 June 1903, he returned to Melbourne soon after. On 3 January 1905 at St John's Church, East Malvern, he married Ethel Ida Remfry, a graduate of the University of Melbourne (B.Sc., 1903; M.Sc., 1905; M.B., B.S., 1911) and a teacher at Merton Hall; they were to remain childless. As vicar of the parish of St Barnabas, South Melbourne, Morris suffered a blow to his ministering zeal when Archbishop H. L. Clarke [q.v.8] refused to sanction special missions to wharf labourers and their families.

The young cleric found his real vocation in teaching, serving an 'apprenticeship' and earning headmasters' accolades as resident master and honorary chaplain at Geelong Church of England Grammar School (1907-08) and as assistant boarding master and chaplain at the Collegiate School of St Peter, Adelaide (1909-11). He was soon advocating the value of small classes and the educational importance of a teacher focusing on the individual pupil.

Late in 1906 Ethel Morris had returned to Merton Hall and to her studies, beginning a separation from her husband that would endure, except for a few weeks in 1912, until her death in London in 1957. Their differences were aesthetic and fundamental. An ardent classicist, Morris viewed life from uncompromisingly romantic, heroic and idealistic perspectives. He abhorred socialism, for example, for its abnegation of the individual and the spirit. His personal requisites were Spartan, and he found intellectual enjoyment in reading literature and writing poetry. For recreation, he favoured outdoor pastimes and team sports such as rowing, Rugby Union football and cricket. By contrast, Ethel Remfry-Morris was a modernist and a feminist, who eventually turned to painting, finding her future in artistic circles in London.

On 8 February 1912, during their brief reunion, the Morrises established a small private school, St Magnus Hall, in a house called Ardencraig at Toowong, Brisbane. With the support of Archbishop Donaldson [q.v.8] and leaders of the Anglican lay community, Morris was able to capitalize on the Church's wish to become more involved in education in Queensland. In 1913 synod decided to amalgamate St Magnus Hall with St John's Day School, under Morris's headmastership. Next year the school was established, adjacent to St John's Cathedral, as Brisbane Church of England Grammar School for Boys. In 1915 it acquired Bowen House Preparatory School. Wartime austerity restricted enrolments, but in his quest for a permanent site for the school, Morris won widespread support.

Governor Sir Hamilton Goold-Adams [q.v.9] officially opened the Church of England Grammar School at its new location, Oaklands Parade, East Brisbane, on 10 June 1918. Within ten years it approached the front rank of the country's independent schools. Its spectacular rise owed much to the qualities of its founding headmaster. By the time he retired at the end of 1946, more than 3000 boys had passed through 'Churchie'.

Recognizing the importance of a stimulating environment in 'framing character', Morris transformed the school site into a rural sanctuary amid the bustle of the city, and into a place where country boys could feel at home and learn. 'Churchie' was a functioning farm which contributed savings to the school budget and reflected the headmaster's austere notions of self-sufficiency. Such frugality enabled the young school to weather the Depression and two world wars, keep fees at a low level, and attract pupils from country and city. Morris decried the creeping exclusiveness of some 'Great Public Schools'.

His appeal to parents derived from a passionate commitment to what he termed 'the purpose of education', namely, 'the training of character on the foundation of Christian faith as taught by the Church of England'. At once both visionary and autocratic, he frequently reminded parents that the Church of England Grammar School was established 'to teach, not to proselytise; our concern being especially with moral issues'. Speech nights were occasions to issue strictures against contemporary political, social and cultural trends, particularly declining moral purpose.

Despite the Depression, Morris completed his building programme by the late 1930s. It was in creating an educational ethos, however, that he was most outstanding. In the Morris school, scholasticism never usurped character formation as the essential product of education. Learning through experience and inspiration were critical tenets. He tried to induce in each boy a desire to strive and perform to his best. 'Finish hard, boy, finish hard', was the headmaster's salutary edict to students running distance races or rowing on the Brisbane River.

Known as the 'Boss' and true to the persona, Morris withstood any encroachment which reduced his authority or the autonomy of the school. The Church was no exception. He regarded intrusions by diocesan administrators and the synod in the same light as interference by the Industrial Court and trade unions. All were tactfully but fiercely resisted. Morris's appointment as an honorary canon on 1 September 1935 was tacit recognition by the diocese of the broad pastoral impact he made on hundreds of Queensland families. Not that the Church was ever pre-eminent in the 'Churchie' ethos during Morris's tenure. In a High-Church diocese, the school was conspicuous for its interdenominational constituency and its rejection of Anglo-Catholic forms of worship.

Seeking to inspire young minds, Morris gave his school a Biblical motto, *Alis Aquilae* ('On the Wings of an Eagle'), from a text in Isaiah. As he grew older, especially in World War II when he was stricken by infirmity and illness, and had to struggle with the privations of shortages, he transcended the epical lessons of his beloved classics and become the hero himself. To his charges, he would always be the model of a man of formidable courage, exemplifying stoicism, self-sacrifice and service. He was what he taught.

In the 1930s Morris had stridently opposed pacifism and appeasement. Despite synod's objections, he insisted on maintaining the school cadet unit, not only because of its contribution to discipline and boyhood development, but also because he believed that 'Those who have the greatest advantages should be the readiest to serve'. And serve they did. Almost one thousand old boys fought in World War II; one in ten of them was killed in action or died of wounds.

After his retirement Morris lived quietly in Brisbane, writing his memoirs, *Sons of Magnus* (1948), and privately publishing a collection of poems, *Havenhome and Other Verses*. In 1955 he was appointed O.B.E. He died on 21 May 1960 in Brisbane and was cremated.

J. R. Cole, *The Making of Men* (Brisb, 1986); *Courier-Mail*, 23, 25 May 1960.   JOHN COLE

MORRISON, ALLAN ARTHUR (1911-1975), historian, was born on 23 November 1911 at Mount Morgan, Queensland, second son of Queensland-born parents Alexander Morrison, schoolteacher, and his wife Alice Ethel, née Jackson. Sent to Lockyer State High and Ipswich Grammar schools, Allan won the Lilley [q.v.5] medal in 1925, the (T. J.) Byrnes [q.v.7] medal in 1927 and a State open scholarship (1929) to the University of Queensland (B.A., 1933; M.A., 1935) where he graduated with first-class honours in history. He completed teacher-training, and was posted to Charleville State School in 1935. At the Albert Street Methodist Church, Brisbane, on 15 August 1936 he married Pauline Lucelle Joice.

After joining the university staff in 1945 as an assistant-lecturer in history, he rose to lecturer (1948), senior lecturer (1957) and reader (1971). He encouraged and promoted the work of the (Royal) Historical Society of Queensland as a member (1945), councillor (1945-48), president (1948-53) and fellow (1963). During his presidency he also served on the board of trustees of Newstead House. A member (1948) and chairman (1968-75) of the Oxley [q.v.2] Memorial Library advisory committee, he fostered co-operation between the library and the R.H.S.Q.

In 1954 a Carnegie Corporation grant enabled Morrison to visit Britain and North America. He, Eunice Hanger [q.v.14] and Roger Joyce travelled throughout Queensland in 1957-59, identifying government and semi-government records which were held in regional centres. Their work helped in the foundation of the Queensland State Archives. Morrison served on both the board and the committee established by the State's Place Names Act (1958). He chaired (1961-75) the Australian Dictionary of Biography's Queensland working party and contributed twenty-seven articles to the project. Colleagues appreciated his friendly manner and co-operative approach.

Gentle, modest and hard working, Morrison published works on local government and regional history, and was interested in class relations and class conflict. He suffered two personal blows in his academic career. His Ph.D. thesis on 'Liberalism in Queensland' (1842-1915) did not satisfy the examiners in 1955, and he was not commissioned to write a general history of Queensland for the centenary in 1959. A generation later one historian considered Morrison's thesis to be 'still the major work on Queensland history in the colonial period'.

Morrison's outstanding chapter on the long years (1915-57) of Australian Labor Party dominance in Queensland appeared in *The Government of the Australian States* (edited by S. R. Davies, Sydney, 1960). His study of colonial society in 1860-90—another pioneering work—was published in *Queensland Heritage* (1966). He collected sources for a general history of Queensland and had almost completed the manuscript when he fell ill. Survived by his son and two daughters, he died of cancer on 30 April 1975 in Brisbane and was cremated with Anglican rites.

Qld Heritage, 3, no 4, 1976, p 3; RHSQ, *J*, 17, no 3, 1986, p 285.   RUTH S. KERR

MORRISON, FRANK RICHARD (1895-1967), chemist and museum director, was born on 14 April 1895 at Randwick, Sydney, third child of native-born parents Alexander John Thomas Morrison, tinsmith and later chemist, and his wife Blanche Agnes, née Moss. Frank was educated at Sydney Technical High School and (part time) at Sydney Technical College where he gained a diploma in chemistry (1922). Employed as an assistant in the chemical laboratory of the Metropolitan Board of Water Supply and Sewerage from 20 July 1912, he transferred to a similar post in the Technological Museum in April 1916. He enlisted in the Australian Imperial Force on 2 July 1918 and arrived in Britain after the Armistice. In 1919 he served at the Australian Staging Camp in France.

Discharged in Sydney on 28 October that year, Morrison returned to the museum. He assisted the economic chemists—Henry George Smith until 1920 and then Arthur de Ramon Penfold [qq.v.11]—in the museum's long-running programme of scientific research into Australian natural products, particularly plants, to foster the economic exploitation of the country's natural resources. Morrison gained an excellent apprenticeship in laboratory methods of organic chemistry. His own research contributions, almost entirely in phytochemistry, were linked with those of Penfold. He also undertook field-work to collect and study experimental material, which involved extensive travel in rural areas of eastern Australia.

Morrison's first research publication (1921) was on the occurrence of the flavonoid substance rutin in various species of *Boronia*, but the major part of his work was on volatile plant oils in Australian flora. Many of his scientific papers (which numbered nearly fifty) were written with Penfold; thirty-four were published in the *Journal and Proceedings* of the Royal Society of New South Wales. Morrison also wrote reviews and articles dealing with historical matters, and (with

Penfold) technical bulletins issued by the museum. Their most important joint contribution was to demonstrate the existence of chemical variation within a plant species: their findings refuted the assertion of their predecessors, R. T. Baker [q.v.7] and Smith, that chemical constancy prevailed throughout a species to the extent that it could be used as a diagnostic feature in taxonomy. The Penfold-Morrison discovery was of great chemical, biological and commercial significance.

At St David's Anglican Church, Arncliffe, on 25 February 1928 Morrison had married Pretoria Beryl Macdonald; they were to have two children. He gave extensive support to scientific and professional bodies as honorary secretary (1922-54) and president (1931-32, 1955) of the Sydney Technical College Chemical Society (and its successor), and as a councillor (1942-51), secretary (1946-47), vice-president (1948-49, 1951) and president (1950) of the R.S.N.S.W. In 1951 he was elected a fellow of the Royal Australian Chemical Institute.

After succeeding Penfold in 1946 as economic chemist at the renamed Museum of Applied Arts and Sciences, Morrison became deputy-director of the museum in 1949 and succeeded Penfold as director on 1 January 1956. In his administrative posts he continued a strong tradition of vigour and foresight. As a United Nations Educational, Scientific and Cultural Organization fellow, Morrison made an extended inspection of museums in North America, Britain and Europe in 1952. The R.S.N.S.W. awarded him its medal in 1958. He retired in 1960. In spite of funding stringency, he left the museum well prepared to undertake future challenges.

A 'cheerful colleague of the utmost integrity', Morrison was a splendid raconteur. He kept fit by swimming, playing golf, exercising in the gymnasium and cultivating the garden at his Wahroonga home. Survived by his wife and only son, he died on 2 October 1967 in Hornsby hospital and was cremated.

Roy Soc NSW, *A Century of Scientific Progress* (Syd, 1968) and *J and Procs*, 102, 1969; Roy Aust Chemical Inst, *Procs*, 35, 1968; *SMH*, 7 Sept 1933, 23 July 1936, 17 Jan 1939; J. L. Willis, From palace to power house. The first one hundred years of the Sydney Museum of Applied Arts and Sciences (ts, 1982, Museum of Applied Arts and Sciences L).

H. G. HOLLAND
H. H. G. McKERN

MORRISON, PHILIP CROSBIE (1900-1958), naturalist, was born on 19 December 1900 at Hawthorn, Melbourne, eldest child of James Crosbie Morrison, a Hawthorn-born draper, and his wife Grace Evelyne, née Cass, who came from New Zealand. The family was solid, respectable, Congregationalist and musical, but not wealthy. Near their home lay open, grassy ground and a municipal drain. There the young Morrison discovered the fascinations of natural history. He later recalled that the arrival of twin brothers when he was aged 6 meant that 'I had to amuse myself to a greater extent. This took the form of watching grasshoppers. They have very interesting faces . . . before long I could tell the difference between the types'. He began his formal education at Auburn State School and won a scholarship to University High School, where he impressed the principal M. S. Sharman [q.v.11] and gained honours in chemistry in the Leaving certificate examinations.

In 1918 Morrison was appointed to the staff of Wesley College's preparatory school as a chemistry demonstrator, with teaching and house duties. He joined the Field Naturalists Club of Victoria that year and became its honorary secretary in 1919. While at Wesley he was persuaded of the need for a university degree in order to become an industrial chemist. To raise funds, he spent eighteen months on Kangaroo Island, South Australia, with a firm that extracted resin from the local 'grass-tree', *Xanthorrhoea tateana*. Matriculating in 1921, he was admitted to the University of Melbourne (B.Sc., 1924; M.Sc., 1926). His career in zoology at Melbourne was described as a 'triumphal procession' of prizes and scholarships. Influenced by his professor W. E. Agar [q.v.7], Morrison enthusiastically embraced a Darwinian view of biology and genetics. Marine biology became his major interest. In 1925 he won a scholarship to carry out research on reef organisms, especially plankton. The ensuing six months on Queensland's Great Barrier Reef, collecting from naval and trading vessels, saw him rapidly mature. A visit to the Commonwealth Prickly Pear Board facility at Sherwood, near Brisbane, where the South American insect, *Cactoblastis cactorum*, was being bred in a successful attempt to control Queensland's prickly pear outbreak, helped to shape his views on biological control.

Trained in photography by his father, a gifted amateur, Morrison had taken a large-format camera to Queensland. His photographs of coral, of Aborigines spearing turtles, and of dugongs and other marine life were published in *The Times* and the *Illustrated London News*, with his own descriptive articles or captions. In April 1926 a letter of recommendation from his faculty brought this material and its author to the attention of (Sir) Edward Cunningham [q.v.8], editor of the Melbourne *Argus*. Cunningham offered Morrison a three-year cadetship in journalism at a starting salary of thirty shillings per week. Morrison worked out his cadetship in three months and became, successively, a general reporter, shipping roundsman, town-hall roundsman, Federal roundsman, State roundsman, leader of the State parliamentary press gallery, and a member of the literary staff, responsible for second editorials and special supplements. On 8 March 1930 at All Saints Church, Sandringham, he married Lucy Frances Washington with Anglican rites. In July 1937 he took over a long-established boys' page and a column of natural-history notes when A. H. Chisholm [q.v.13] became editor of the *Argus*. After allowing his membership to lapse, Morrison rejoined the Field Naturalists Club (president 1941-43), and in 1938 also joined the Royal Society of Victoria (president 1949-51) and the Royal Australasian Ornithologists Union.

In 1938 Sir Keith Murdoch [q.v.10], influenced by (Sir) Russell Grimwade [q.v.9], poached Morrison from the *Argus*—where he had progressed to senior special staff writer, deputy leader-writer, editor of special supplements and sometime acting-editor of the *Australasian*—and appointed him editor of a new magazine, *Wild Life*. Launched in October and priced at sixpence, the copiously illustrated magazine, with its various regular sections mostly written by Morrison under a pseudonym, was enthusiastically received. To publicize the new monthly, it was agreed that the *Herald*'s radio-station 3DB-3LK would run a short series of weekly broadcasts by Crosbie Morrison.

Six 'Wild Life' talks were programmed for 6 p.m. on Sundays, an unpopular timeslot which lacked a commercial sponsor. But, in less than a month, Morrison's warm, well-modulated voice, with an accent neither offensively Australian nor obviously 'cultured', became required listening for thousands. The broadcast opened with a burst of kookaburra laughter, then the throbbing tones of a Sherbrooke Forest lyrebird, next the introduction of 'Mr Crosbie Morrison, Master of Science, editor of *Wild Life*', followed by the familiar, friendly, 'Good evening, listeners'. Before the programme was five years old, a survey found that 78 per cent of all Victorian radios switched on at that time on Sunday evening were tuned to Morrison. In the following year the programme was relayed throughout Australia and New Zealand. Later, it was extended to South Africa. It ran for over twenty years and continued after Morrison's death.

On the outbreak of World War II Morrison —still broadcasting and editing *Wild Life*— was made State publicity censor; his role was to oversee war news and items suitable for publication. The office was subsequently transferred to the Department of Information, whose minister Sir Henry Gullett [q.v.9] appointed Morrison director of the broadcasting division, with the task of organizing an overseas service (later Radio Australia) to put forward Australia's view of the war. Morrison attacked the task with typical dispatch: within ten days of his appointment the service made its first broadcast—a statement by Prime Minister (Sir) Robert Menzies [q.v.] of Australia's reasons for involvement in the war. Morrison soon found that his views on suitable subject matter 'failed to coincide' with those of his departmental colleagues. In January 1940 Gullett agreed to his request to release him.

Reasoning that the reassurance and solace offered by the natural world were doubly important in a nation undergoing the stresses of war, Morrison threw himself into *Wild Life*, his broadcasts and his writing. His crowded small office at the Herald & Weekly Times Ltd in Flinders Street had become legendary. Anything from a redbacked spider to a dead lizard was likely to arrive in the morning mail. He typed on a desk cluttered with books, files, papers, cigarette-lighters, ashtrays, and sundry tins, jars and matchboxes containing both live and obviously dead specimens. Smokers who visited him soon learned not to open any stray matchbox.

Morrison proved to be a popular part-time lecturer (1939-51) in natural history for the Melbourne University Extension Board (Council of Adult Education) and an even more popular panellist on 3DB-3LK's programme, 'Information Please', in which his particular and general knowledge shone. In 1942 he was appointed an honorary lecturer in the Australian Army Education Service. He visited troops in Victoria, in the Northern Territory and in occupied Japan to show films and to talk about wildlife to Australian servicemen and women. In 1947 he was awarded the Australian Natural History medallion by the Field Naturalists Club.

His commitments expanded with his reputation. He addressed a wide range of organizations, and gave fund-raising lectures for such causes as the United Nations Appeal for Children, the Russian Welfare Society, and, frequently, for the (Royal) Children's Hospital. Always a cheerful extrovert, Morrison joined the Rotary Club of Melbourne, and the Bread and Cheese, the Savage and the Beefsteak clubs. To the extent that his income permitted, he was becoming something of a man about town, who wore a black homburg and invariably had time for a quick chat and often a shaggy-dog story.

A trustee (from 1945), vice-president and chairman (1955-58) of the National Museum of Victoria, Morrison carried the fight for a new museum to successive State governments. As chairman of the building trustees representing the Public Library and National Gallery, as well as the museum, he hosted numerous state functions held at the gallery, particularly at the time of the 1956 Olympic

Games. One of his innovations (1951) was a monthly series of Friday-night lectures.

At the end of World War II Morrison and others had pressed for a reorganization of Wilson's Promontory (he was a member of its committee of management) and all Victoria's neglected national parks. He wrote a rousing editorial to that effect in the May 1946 issue of *Wild Life*: 'if we do not have a postwar New Deal for the fauna and flora, the birthright of coming generations will have gone, and, once gone, it can be replaced by neither money nor toil nor tears'. The Field Naturalists Club subsequently convened a series of conferences of interested community bodies (chaired by Morrison) which advocated the creation by the Victorian government of a permanent, adequately funded, national parks authority. To further this aim, in 1952 the conference formed the Victorian National Parks Association, again with Morrison as chairman. For a further four years he led repeated delegations to Victorian premiers and development committees, urging the creation of the authority. Through *Wild Life* (until its demise early in 1954), in the press, on radio and in countless addresses to community organizations, Morrison maintained the pressure.

After various unsuccessful attempts by different political parties to introduce national parks legislation, (Sir) Henry Bolte's Liberal government passed the National Parks Act in October 1956. On 8 May 1957 the government announced the creation of the long-awaited National Parks Authority, with Morrison as its first director. In its care were thirteen national parks, totalling some 467 000 acres (188 990 ha), less than one per cent of the area of Victoria. Morrison faced the challenge with a small budget, few staff, and some entrenched committees of management. Despite suffering high blood pressure, he also kept up his punishing schedule of responsibilities, including his duties as chairman of trustees at the museum, his regular schools' programmes for the Australian Broadcasting Commission, his special consultancies for government and his Radio Australia broadcasts.

Crosbie Morrison died of a cerebral haemorrhage on 1 March 1958 at his Brighton home and was cremated; his wife and two sons survived him. Victoria's national parks system—his legacy—was by 1998 one of the finest in the country, with thirty-five national parks, three wilderness parks, thirty-two State parks, eleven marine or coastal parks and nearly three thousand conservation reserves, totalling more than 9.25 million acres (3.75 million ha) and covering 16 per cent of the State.

G. Pizzey, *Crosbie Morrison* (Melb, 1992) and for sources; *People* (Syd), 1 July 1953; *Vic Naturalist*, 75, June 1958, p 21, Nov 1958, p 113; *Emu*, 58, May 1958, p 161.   GRAHAM PIZZEY

MORRISON, WILLIAM SHEPHERD; *see* DUNROSSIL

MORROW, SIR ARTHUR WILLIAM (1903-1977), physician, was born on 12 July 1903 at East Maitland, New South Wales, only child of native-born parents Arthur John Morrow, commercial traveller, and his wife Helonar, née Harkin. Educated at Newington College, Sydney, Bill coxed the winning VIII in the 'Head of the River' regatta (1921) and won an exhibition at the Leaving certificate examinations. He entered the University of Sydney (M.B., B.S., 1927) and graduated with first-class honours. A contemporary, writing in the *Senior Year Book* (1926), noted his 'livewire' personality and 'rapier like intelligence'. Morrow was active in student affairs and had a range of interests beyond medicine; he was adept at bridge and ballroom dancing, and enjoyed sailing and tennis.

Appointed a junior resident medical officer at Royal Prince Alfred Hospital in 1927, Morrow held the post of deputy clinical superintendent in 1932, but left that year for London where he was admitted to membership (1933) of the Royal College of Physicians (fellow 1949). In 1944 he rejoined R.P.A.H. as an honorary assistant-physician. At St Stephen's Methodist Church, Sydney, on 24 November 1937 he married Jean Buchanan Brown (d.1971); they were to live at Bellevue Hill.

In 1929 Morrow had been commissioned captain, Australian Army Medical Corps. On 1 May 1940 he was seconded to the Australian Imperial Force. That month he was promoted lieutenant colonel and placed in charge of the medical division of the 2nd/5th Australian General Hospital, which sailed for the Middle East in October. The 2nd/5th arrived in Greece on 12 April 1941, but ten days later began to withdraw due to the German invasion. Morrow led a party which embarked for Crete where he administered command of the reassembled unit. In mid-May the 2nd/5th was evacuated to Egypt. For his leadership, organization and calmness in the face of enemy aerial attacks, he was awarded the Distinguished Service Order and mentioned in dispatches.

Returning to Australia in March 1942, Morrow commanded (from May) the 121st A.G.H. at Katherine, Northern Territory. In March 1943 he was appointed assistant director general of medical services at Land Headquarters, Melbourne. Next month he was promoted temporary colonel. As consulting physician attached to Advanced L.H.Q., he visited operational areas in New Guinea, New Britain, Bougainville and Borneo in 1945. He transferred to the Reserve of Officers on 23 December.

Morrow came back to R.P.A.H. as he had left it—an honorary assistant-physician. To the senior medical staff he was still 'young' Morrow. He was to be appointed an honorary physician in 1952 and a consultant in 1963. He also became a consultant at the Repatriation General Hospital, Concord, and at Canterbury District, Marrickville and Western Suburbs hospitals. While he achieved many of his ambitions, perhaps his most enduring success lay in persuading a reluctant administration and senior medical staff at R.P.A.H. to agree to the formation of a gastroenterology unit. In 1949 a compromise was reached in which the unit was awarded consultative status although denied admission rights. A single room was made available and, with the support of his friend Philip Bushell [q.v.7], funds were provided for a trainee registrar and secretary. Morrow and Stanley Goulston, an enthusiastic younger colleague, soon began to raise the standards of practice in gastroenterology, and other hospitals in Australia and New Zealand began to send aspiring gastroenterologists for training. Further private funding led to a larger area, a well-equipped laboratory, and the establishment of research programmes.

Rebuilding his consultant practice, Morrow filled the role of the 'compleat' physician with ease and style. Physically he was not a large man, but he had a dignified presence which was accentuated by close attention to his tailoring. Many of his younger colleagues felt, for a time, either inhibited or disconcerted by this aura. Patients found him courteous and often charming. His concern and tolerance made him a ready listener and he was quick to pick up clues leading to successful diagnoses. Decisiveness was an integral part of his professional life. Remarkably self-disciplined, he rose before daybreak to write letters, read medical journals and prepare for early morning consultations. He felt a particular obligation to meet the requests of doctors and their families.

The intellectual satisfaction of diagnosis was not enough for Morrow. He always wanted to cure or at least relieve. From 1935 to 1963 he lectured in therapeutics at the University of Sydney. He excelled at teaching medical students. His tutorials were relaxed and drew on his wide clinical experience. The hint of a frown at an inattentive student was a potent means of refocusing attention. He frequently took part in courses arranged for general practitioners and specialists, and chaired the Postgraduate Committee of Medicine of the University of Sydney. During meetings, 'he was never aggressive and won through by persuasion that caused no offence and left no hurt'. He invariably acknowledged the importance of successful teamwork in his achievements.

A foundation member (1938) of the Royal Australasian College of Physicians, Morrow wielded great influence. As a member (1950-66) of its board of censors, and as censor-in-chief (1962-66), he proved an excellent examiner, being aware of the necessity to maintain standards while remaining consistent and fair-minded. As president (1966-68) of the college, he inspired loyalty, respect and affection. He was also president (1957-58) of the State branch of the British Medical Association. In later years he was appointed a member (1963) and chairman (1967) of the Commonwealth government's Australian Drug Evaluation Committee; he was also a member of its Pharmaceutical Benefits Advisory Committee.

Morrow's achievements in gastroenterology were widely recognized in Australia and abroad. In 1959 he was knighted. Foundation president (1957-58) of the Gastroenterological Society of Australia, he prevailed on the Bushell Trust to establish a lectureship so that distinguished overseas gastroenterologists could be invited to attend national meetings. In 1961 the directors of R.P.A.H. agreed that the gastroenterology unit should be called the A. W. Morrow department of gastroenterology.

Sir William had numerous friends and acquaintances outside his profession. He valued his membership of the Australian Club and served as president (1973-75) at a time when the club's premises in Macquarie Street were demolished and rebuilt. The governor-general, Field Marshal Sir William (Viscount) Slim [q.v.], periodically sought his opinion on public issues by asking 'what does the Australian Club think of that?' A member of the Royal Sydney Golf and Australian Jockey clubs, Morrow regarded weekend golf with friends as an imperative and found the racecourse another welcome diversion. On 31 July 1974 at St Mark's Anglican Church, Darling Point, he married Margaret Mary Chauvel, née Fairfax, a 64-year-old widow. Survived by his wife and by the three daughters of his first marriage, he died on 22 August 1977 in St Luke's Hospital, Darlinghurst, and was cremated with Anglican rites.

In 1994 the A. W. Morrow chair in medicine was established at the University of Sydney. Portraits of Morrow by Howard Barron and by Graeme Inson are held respectively by the R.A.C.P., Sydney, and R.P.A.H.

A. S. Walker, *Middle East and Far East* (Canb, 1953) and *The Island Campaigns* (Canb, 1957); *Lives of the Fellows of the Royal College of Physicians of London*, 7 (Lond, 1984); J. R. Angel, *The Australian Club 1838-1988* (Syd, 1988); G. L. McDonald (ed), *Roll of the Royal Australasian College of Physicians*, 2 (Syd, 1994); Sydney University Medical Society, *Senior Year Book* (Syd, 1926); *MJA*, 13 Jan 1979; *SMH*, 23 Aug 1977; Sir George Stening, funeral oration (ts, held by Roy A'sian College of Physicians L); information from Prof C. R. B. Blackburn, Darling Point, Dr S. J. M. Goulston, Chatswood, and Dr C. Morrow, Randwick, Syd.

NEIL GALLAGHER

MORROW, JAMES CAIRNS (1905-1963), naval officer, was born on 6 February 1905 at Brunswick, Melbourne, son of Australian-born parents James Ernest Morrow, implement-maker, and his wife Marion Agnes, née Cairns. James Morrow [q.v.5] was his grandfather. Young James attended Melbourne Church of England Grammar School and entered (1919) the Royal Australian Naval College, Jervis Bay, Federal Capital Territory. Chief cadet captain in 1921, he gained colours for cricket and Rugby, and won the King's medal on graduating in 1922. As a midshipman (1923-25) and an acting (1925-26) and confirmed (1926-28) sub lieutenant, he trained at sea and completed courses in Britain.

Returning to Australia, Lieutenant Morrow served as navigator of H.M.A.S. *Marguerite* (1927-29) and as a watch-keeper in H.M.A.S. *Australia* (1929-31) before joining the staff of the R.A.N.C. (then at Flinders Naval Depot, Westernport, Victoria). From 1933 to 1935 he was attached to the Royal Navy. His marriage (probably on 13 April 1935) ended in divorce. He was promoted lieutenant commander in 1936, while executive officer of H.M.A.S. *Vendetta*. In April 1938 he took command of the destroyer, *Voyager*, which was deployed to the Mediterranean shortly after World War II began.

On 13 and 14 June 1940 *Voyager* damaged two Italian submarines near the port of Alexandria, Egypt; within a fortnight she helped to sink another about 100 nautical miles (185 km) south-east of Crete. Morrow was awarded the Distinguished Service Order for his part in these actions and promoted commander that month. In July his ship screened the aircraft-carrier, *Eagle*, in the battle of Calabria. Between December 1940 and April 1941 *Voyager* operated for extensive periods off the North African coast. Maintaining sea communications and bombarding shore positions, she supported the British and Australian drive westwards across Libya and covered the subsequent withdrawal to Tobruk. Her commanding officer was mentioned in dispatches for this work.

During the evacuation of British Commonwealth forces from Greece in late April 1941, *Voyager* carried soldiers and nurses to safety. In the last three weeks of May she helped to reinforce Crete. Earlier that month she had made her first run as part of the 'Tobruk Ferry', a shuttle-service of destroyers which supplied the fortress from Egyptian ports.

Resuming that role, *Voyager* transported troops, ammunition and stores until she sailed for Australia in July. Morrow left the ship in November and in March 1942 assumed command of the newly built destroyer, H.M.A.S. *Arunta*. On 7 August the Japanese submarine, RO 33, sank a passenger vessel, the *Mamutu*, in the Gulf of Papua; its crew then machine-gunned the survivors—men, women and children. Encountering RO 33 off Port Moresby on 29 August, *Arunta* attacked the submarine with depth-charges and destroyed it. Morrow won the Distinguished Service Cross.

Although employed primarily on convoy-protection work in eastern Australian and Papuan waters, *Arunta* landed the 2nd/12th Battalion on Goodenough Island in October 1942 and carried Lancer Force from Timor in January 1943. Posted ashore in August, Morrow commanded escort forces in Sydney and (from January 1944) at Milne Bay, Papua. He joined the cruiser, *Shropshire*, as executive officer in May 1945; she sailed to Tokyo Bay for the Japanese surrender ceremony in September.

Morrow's outstanding record as a captain of destroyers in wartime stemmed from his gifts as a seaman and leader. He was a 'superb shiphandler'. Friendly and convivial, he won the affection of his men as well as their respect. His piercing eyes and ringing voice complemented his strength of character. Of middle height, he was nicknamed 'Copper' because of the colour of his hair. At St Mark's Anglican Church, Darling Point, Sydney, on 11 September 1946 he married 27-year-old Dulce McWhannell.

As an acting and (from June 1947) substantive captain, Morrow commanded H.M.A.S. *Bataan* in 1946-48. He served as Australian naval attaché, Washington (1948-51), commanding officer of H.M.A.S. *Australia* (1951-52) and commodore superintendent of training at Flinders Naval Depot (1952-55). Made commodore, first class, and appointed chief of naval personnel in January 1955, he had little aptitude or liking for staff duties. In 1956 he was appointed C.B.E. Following a posting (1956-59) as naval officer-in-charge, Western Australia, he retired from the navy on 6 February 1960. He worked in 1960-61 as chief executive officer, Melbourne metropolitan area, for World Refugee Year and later held a post in Sydney with the Australian National Travel Association. For recreation, he watched cricket and football, and went to the races. He died of cancer on 8 January 1963 at his Vaucluse home and was cremated; his wife and their two sons survived him.

F. B. Eldridge, *A History of the Royal Australian Naval College* (Melb, 1949); G. H. Gill, *Royal Australian Navy 1939-1942* (Canb, 1957) and *Royal Australian Navy 1942-1945* (Canb, 1968); A3978/9,

Morrow, J. C. (AA, Canb); information from Mrs D. Morrow, Vaucluse, Mr S. Morrow, Bondi, and Mr J. Morrow, Rose Bay, Syd, Rear Admiral A.G. McFarlane, Queanbeyan, NSW, Mr R. Hyslop, Yarralumla, and Mr J. McEntee, Hackett, Canb.

DARRYL BENNET

MORSHEAD, SIR LESLIE JAMES (1889-1959), soldier and businessman, was born on 18 September 1889 at Ballarat East, Victoria, sixth child of William Morshead, a miner from Cornwall, and his South Australian-born wife Mary Eliza, née Rennison. Leslie attended Mount Pleasant State School, belonged to Ballarat's Christ Church Cathedral choir, and captained its football and cricket teams. Having qualified at Melbourne Teachers' College, he taught in the country at Fine View State School, near Jung, and at The Armidale School, New South Wales. In 1914 he moved to Melbourne Church of England Grammar School where he commanded the cadet corps, as he had done at Armidale.

On 13 September 1914 Morshead was appointed lieutenant, Australian Imperial Force. Posted to the 2nd Battalion, he served as a captain at the Gallipoli landings on 25 April 1915 and as a major in the bitter fighting at Lone Pine in August. His reputation for calmness and organization brought him promotion to lieutenant colonel and command (April 1916) of the 33rd Battalion, which he raised in Australia and trained there and in England. He made the battalion 'one of the very best' and took it to France in November. As the 33rd was part of the 3rd Division, Morshead developed under the eye of (Sir) John Monash [q.v.10]. A successful leader in the battles of Messines (June 1917) and Passchendaele (October) in Belgium, and Villers Bretonneux (April 1918) and Amiens (August) in France, Morshead was awarded the Distinguished Service Order (1917) and mentioned in dispatches five times; in 1919 he was appointed C.M.G. and to the French Légion d'honneur.

Monash included Morshead in his staff when he took charge of demobilizing the A.I.F. in England, an operation notable for its efficiency. Morshead reached Sydney in December 1919 and his appointment terminated on 15 March 1920. Intending to begin life on the land, he applied for a grant under the soldier-settlement scheme. While he waited, he worked as a jackeroo at Merriwa. After obtaining a large block near Quilpie, Queensland, he soon realized that he had neither the knowledge nor the capital to make a success of it. At Scots Church, Melbourne, on 17 November 1921 he married 23-year-old Myrtle Catherine Hay Woodside, whom he had known since his days at Melbourne Grammar.

Morshead obtained a job in Sydney, working for a committee representing overseas shipping lines, which led in 1924 to a post with the Orient Steam Navigation Co. Ltd. Next year he was sent to England to familiarize himself with the head office. Thereafter he moved between Sydney, Melbourne and Brisbane in positions of growing responsibility, becoming branch manager in Sydney in 1936. His special interest lay in the development of Pacific cruises. In 1937 he again visited England; part of his time there was spent observing British army training. He had been active in the Militia, commanding in turn the 19th and 36th battalions. Promoted colonel (1933) and temporary brigadier (1938), he led the 14th (1933), 15th (1934-36) and 5th (1937-39) infantry brigades.

On 13 October 1939 Morshead was appointed to the A.I.F. and given command of the 18th Brigade which sailed for Britain in May 1940. He spent five months training the 18th and leading it in operations while Britain came under attack by the *Luftwaffe* and faced the threat of invasion. It was a stimulating preparation for battle. In January 1941 he was appointed C.B.E. Moving to the Middle East, he was promoted major general in February and placed in command of the 9th Division. He faced a grim prospect. There were insufficient weapons and equipment, his men were relatively untrained, and one of his brigades was short of a battalion. As his own gunners were not ready, he was given British artillery. Within three weeks he was ordered to move this improbable collection to Cyrenaica, Libya, to join the weak force under Lieutenant General Sir Philip Neame guarding the desert flank of the Middle East.

Of middle height, trim in build, and dark haired, Morshead was vigorous and resolute. His insistence on discipline and hard work brought him the nickname, 'Ming the Merciless', which in time became 'Ming'. While it was rare for him to remove an officer, he could be hard and unforgiving. He had a capacity for dealing bluntly with senior officers. On one occasion he tackled Neame about the anti-Australian tone of a letter on the behaviour of Australian soldiers in Cyrenaica. When he met General Sir Archibald (Earl) Wavell, the commander-in-chief, Morshead spoke frankly about the dangerous position allotted to his leading brigade and suggested moving back to a defensible position east of Benghazi. Wavell ordered Neame to make the change.

During the withdrawal to Tobruk in April 1941, Morshead was the only general officer of Cyrenaica Command to avoid capture. That his division reached Tobruk almost exhausted but still an organized force and eager 'to have a go', was a commendable performance. Initially, he came under the command of Major General (Sir) John Lavarack [q.v.].

Morshead's task was to hold the perimeter defences which he had inspected closely in January. 'There'll be no Dunkirk here', he told his principal officers, 'There is to be no surrender and no retreat'. He also issued instructions that, if German tanks penetrated the perimeter, the infantry should not engage them but deal with enemy infantry following the tanks which would be stopped by his own artillery. These tactics, new to the Germans, led to the failure of their assault on 14 April.

That day Morshead succeeded Lavarack as commander of the fortress at Tobruk. He maintained an aggressive defence, based on ceaseless patrolling and—in the early days—frequent raids, and made it clear to all that 'we should make no-man's land *our* land'. Whenever the enemy gained ground, he refused to leave it in their hands. His policy sometimes proved costly and was disliked at brigade and unit level.

As the siege dragged on, Morshead agreed with the medical authorities that the physical condition of his men was declining. He supported Lieutenant General Sir Thomas Blamey [q.v.13] in his efforts to have the 9th Division and its supporting troops relieved. Morshead's plea for more periodical decorations and mentions in dispatches for the whole garrison was granted. The determination of Blamey and of successive Australian governments eventually brought about the relief of the Australians, beginning in August. After visiting the British gunners and others who were to remain, Morshead unveiled a memorial and left Tobruk on 22 October 1941 in H.M.S. *Endeavour*.

Morshead and his mixed force of Australian, British, Indian and Polish troops had won an important defensive battle. Not only had they denied the Axis powers the port of Tobruk, but they had also compelled General Erwin Rommel to hold a significant part of his army back from the Egyptian frontier for six months. They had shown that the Nazi juggernaut could be stopped. It was a heartening success in an otherwise gloomy year. Morshead was appointed K.B.E. (1942) as a modest recognition of his achievement, and the Poles awarded him the Virtuti Militari. On Blamey's departure for Australia, Morshead took command of the A.I.F. in the Middle East in March 1942 as a temporary lieutenant general (substantive in September). He continued as commander of the 9th Division, which trained in Palestine and Syria until June when it was ordered to Egypt.

Morshead had to fight for essential equipment and transport, and to resist the penchant of senior British officers for breaking up divisions. In a famous confrontation with General Sir Claude Auchinleck in early July, Morshead flatly refused to give him one of his brigade groups. Only when it was agreed that the entire 9th Division would move to El Alamein under his command would Morshead permit the temporary detachment of a single brigade group. He closely watched how the British prepared to use that brigade in operations and remonstrated with Auchinleck about its lack of artillery protection. On 15 July, when he learned that his 20th Brigade had been moved without any reference to him, Morshead protested vehemently to Auchinleck who agreed to its return.

July 1942 was a testing time for Morshead and his men who in three searing weeks tasted everything from triumph on the 10th to disaster on the 27th when the whole 2nd/28th Battalion was lost. Nevertheless, the spirit of the division was strong, and there was a growing trust between the troops and their commander. Morshead was critical of Auchinleck and his staff, and, like all the infantrymen, had a deep distrust of the armoured regiments and brigades.

Before the battle of El Alamein (23 October-5 November) Morshead told his commanders, 'We must regard ourselves as having been born for this battle'. He argued strongly for the retention of the 10 p.m. zero-hour in the face of a proposed earlier time, understanding the needs of the men in the attacking companies, and the importance of getting their vehicles and gear into position. During the fighting he went forward to see his brigadiers (often twice in a day) and battalion commanders to encourage them and get the 'feel' of the battle. Nor did he neglect the wounded in the field ambulances.

After the initial assault, Morshead's series of attacks northwards threatened to cut off and destroy a German division. This pressure drew upon the 9th Division almost the whole *Afrika Korps*, thus helping to create a situation favourable to Lieutenant General (Sir) Bernard (Viscount) Montgomery's final thrust. Montgomery visited Morshead on 4 November to congratulate him. Morshead was appointed K.C.B. a few weeks later. Like Monash, Morshead drove 'his troops to the extreme limit of their endurance'. His own practical, undramatic outlook was revealed at his conference after the battle when he urged his commanders not to forget 'to say a good word to the cooks'. To a corps commander's congratulations, he replied: 'Thank you, General. The boys were interested'.

In February 1943 Morshead and the 9th Division came home. Next month he was appointed commander of II Corps. Although this role placed him farther from the battle front than at El Alamein, it did not entirely remove him from operations. At the height of the Japanese counter-attack at Finschhafen, New Guinea, on 17 October, his grasp of the situation caused him to signal urgently for the 26th Brigade to move from Lae to reinforce the 9th Division. After commanding the Second Army in January-July 1944, Morshead took over I Corps. In May 1945, when American planners sought to change the location of the 7th Division's landings at Balikpapan, Borneo, he supported Major General E. J. Milford's [q.v.] choice of beaches. Morshead travelled constantly and regularly visited subordinate headquarters; on 1 July 1945 his Catalina broke up when alighting on rough waters off Balikpapan and all on board had to be rescued.

Morshead's wife shared his burdens in a seemingly endless war. Theirs was a deeply happy marriage in which they sustained each other by their letters through four campaigns. In the field, Morshead played shove-halfpenny for relaxation; he had his own board which always went with him. Arriving in Sydney in September 1945, he reluctantly agreed to chair a military court of inquiry into Major General Gordon Bennett's [q.v.13] escape (1942) from Singapore. The court sat in October. Its findings against Bennett led to (Sir) George Ligertwood's [q.v.] appointment as commissioner to investigate the affair. In essence, he reached the same conclusions. Morshead was thrice mentioned in despatches for his service in World War II and awarded (1948) the American Medal of Freedom with Silver Palm.

The former schoolmaster and lieutenant of cadets was famous, but looking only for the peace of his home and his imminent return to civilian employment. He was to decline offers of military and diplomatic posts, and the governorship of Queensland. Placed on the Reserve of Officers on 1 January 1946, he went back to the Orient Line one day later as its New South Wales manager. In 1948 he became general manager in Australia. Maintaining links with the army, he gave lectures to young officers and belonged to the Australian Battles Nomenclature Committee. There were also the special occasions—Anzac Day, El Alamein dinners and unit reunions—when he was received with acclaim, including the extraordinary 'Ho Ho' cry of the 9th Division which had begun on the Atherton Tableland in 1943.

Morshead was president of the Bank of New South Wales, chairman of David Jones [q.v.2] Ltd and of the Bank of New South Wales Savings Bank, and a director of Mutual Life & Citizens' Assurance Co. Ltd and other firms. He was also president of the Boy Scouts' Association of New South Wales and the Big Brother Movement, and a trustee of the Gowrie [q.v.9] scholarship trust fund. From 1950 he headed 'The Association', a secret organization prepared to oppose communist attempts at subversion. It was quietly disbanded in 1952. Morshead had had a brief connexion with a similar movement in the mid-1920s. A gifted organizer in war and peace, he was appointed (1957) chairman of a committee which reviewed the group of departments concerned with defence. The Federal government accepted the committee's recommendation that Supply and Defence Production be amalgamated, but dropped the key proposal that Defence absorb Army, Navy and Air.

Golf and membership of the Sydney Cricket Ground gave Morshead respite from the cares of business, but in 1957 he began to show signs of strain. Survived by his wife and daughter, Sir Leslie died of cancer on 26 September 1959 at St Vincent's Hospital, Darlinghurst, and was cremated with Anglican rites. He had been accorded a military funeral and the cortège passed through streets lined with former soldiers of the 9th Division. (Sir) Ivor Hele's portrait of Morshead is held by the Australian War Memorial, Canberra.

C. E. W. Bean, *The A.I.F. in France*, 5 (Syd, 1937); D. Dexter, *The New Guinea Offensives* (Canb, 1961); G. Long, *The Final Campaigns* (Canb, 1963); B. Maughan, *Tobruk and El Alamein* (Canb, 1966); D. M. Horner (ed), *The Commanders* (Syd, 1984); D. Coombes, 'The Greatest Rat': a biography of Lieutenant General Sir Leslie Morshead (Ph.D. thesis, Univ Syd, 1997); Morshead papers (AWM).

A. J. HILL

MORTIMER, REX ALFRED (1926-1979), solicitor, communist and academic, was born on 11 February 1926 at Mordialloc, Melbourne, third of four children of Victorian-born parents Alfred Thomas Mortimer (d.1928), a horse-trainer who had served in the Australian Imperial Force, and his wife Marjorie Estella, née Reaby. Uncertain about his future at the racetrack, but certain that his wife would receive a pension, Alfred killed himself by driving his motorcar into the Yarra River. Rex remembered his childhood darkly. To live in the family home came his mother's parents and several relations, besides paying boarders. His mother's generosity was exploited. His grandfather, a businessman unemployed since being sacked for embezzlement, laid down the law to him. Rex reacted by being independent, studious and rebellious, leading the local church choir out on strike to obtain payment for rehearsals.

After attending Malvern State School, Mortimer won scholarships to Melbourne High School and to the University of Melbourne (LL.B., 1947) where he joined the Freethought Society of Australia, the Melbourne University Labor Club and the Communist Party of Australia. His friends included Ian Turner [q.v.], Ken Gott, Amirah Gust and Margaret Ince. In 1948 he was joint-editor of *Melbourne University Magazine*.

Mortimer was articled to Cedric Ralph, a solicitor whose firm he joined, and on 1 March 1949 was admitted to practice, both in accord with the C.P.A.'s wishes. For the next decade he worked alongside, and under the spell of, the communist barrister and official Edward (Ted) Hill: in 1949-50 before the royal commission of inquiry into the Communist Party in Victoria, in 1951 in a challenge to the Communist Party Dissolution Act in the High Court of Australia, in 1954-55 before the (Petrov) royal commission on espionage, and as a paid functionary (1952-54) of the party. At the registry office, Queen Street, Melbourne, on 30 October 1953 Mortimer married Margaret Doris Robertson, née Ince, a 30-year-old journalist and a divorcee; their marriage was to end in divorce. In 1957 Hill selected him to study in China; his wife was not permitted to accompany him.

Nine months in China made Mortimer aware of 'the benefits of a liberal education', as he recalled in *Meanjin* in 1976. His adoption of China's freer approach to communism would at first propel him into the leadership of the party and, eventually, out of it altogether. Between 1960 and 1963 Mortimer was part of the group that ousted Hill and his followers (who identified with the new hard-line China in the Sino-Soviet dispute) from the party. As his share of the spoils, Mortimer gained the editorship of the Victorian communist weekly, the *Guardian*. In 1964 he was elected to the central committee of the C.P.A. He became spokesman for the Euro-communists or 'Italian liners' who sought a new revolutionary agent to replace the industrial working class. As a founder of *Arena*, a non-party journal of Marxist analysis, Mortimer re-established links with ex-communist critics of the C.P.A. and in 1965 publicly attacked Soviet anti-Semitism. He extended communist support to the student 'New Left', and, at the twenty-first congress of the C.P.A. in 1967, supported the 'Coalition of the Left' strategy. Always a persuasive speaker, he was by then a good listener, widely known in radical intellectual circles for his tolerance and good humour.

Increasingly repelled by the narrowness of the old guard in the communist movement, Mortimer resigned his editorship of the *Guardian* in 1965 to undertake full-time study at Monash University (Ph.D., 1971), working with Professor Herbert Feith. On 6 September 1967 at the registrar-general's office, Sydney, he married Mary Eleanor Johnston, a 23-year-old schoolteacher. While they were visiting Europe in 1968, Soviet troops invaded Czechoslovakia. In the following year he left the Communist Party and returned to Monash. His doctoral thesis on the Indonesian Communist Party drew on two visits to Indonesia in 1964. He became an acknowledged expert on communism in Australia and Indonesia;

his break with the C.P.A. did not alter the fundamental line of his analysis, which proposed the peaceful route to power in both countries, but doubted its chances of success.

In the last decade of his life Mortimer had a successful academic career. Appointed in 1970 to the department of government and public administration at the University of Sydney, he was soon at the forefront of forces for reform in the department. He took leave in 1974-76 to fill the chair of politics and administrative studies at the University of Papua New Guinea. There, too, he was a force for change, associated with moves to harness expatriate idealism in the university for educational and social reform in the emerging nation. He returned to Sydney as associate-professor and became dean of the faculty of economics in 1979. Of his six books, the most important was *Indonesian Communism under Sukarno* (New York, 1974), which aroused controversy as much for its scepticism about the United States of America's Central Intelligence Agency's line on the 1965 uprising as for its sympathy with the Indonesian communists. Mortimer also broke new ground as co-author of *Development and Dependency: the Political Economy of Papua New Guinea* (Melbourne, 1979), which drew on underdevelopment theory. A posthumous collection, *Stubborn Survivors* (Melbourne, 1984), was edited by two of his colleagues. Survived by his wife and their son and daughter, he died of cancer on New Year's Eve 1979 at Royal North Shore Hospital and was cremated. At the memorial gathering at Monash University, his friends recalled his 'cosmic pessimism and day to day good cheer'.

A. Davidson, *The Communist Party of Australia* (Stanford, California, US, 1969); J. Sendy, *Comrades Come Rally* (Melb, 1978); B. Taft, *Crossing the Party Line* (Newham, Vic, 1994); A. Inglis, *The Hammer & Sickle and the Washing Up* (Melb, 1995); *Biography* (Honolulu), 6, no 3, 1983; ASIO, A6119/78, items 1131-35 (AA, Canb); Dept of Govt files, Univ Syd Archives; Mortimer papers (held by Ms Mary Mortimer, Campbell, Canb).   T. H. IRVING

MORTLOCK, JOHN ANDREW TENNANT (1894-1950), benefactor and pastoralist, and DOROTHY ELIZABETH (1906-1979), philanthropist, were husband and wife. He was born on 30 March 1894 at Mintaro, South Australia, second of five sons of South Australian-born parents William Tennant Mortlock, grazier, and his wife Rosina Forsyth, daughter of Andrew Tennant [q.v.6]. William Ranson Mortlock [q.v.5] was his grandfather. Jack was educated at the Grammar School, Glenelg, the Collegiate School of St Peter, Adelaide, and Jesus College, Cambridge. After his father's death in 1913, he returned to South Australia to take control of the family estate, which included Martindale Hall, a Georgian-style house near Mintaro, and stations in the vicinity of Port Augusta and Port Lincoln, as well as property in Western Australia, Victoria and England.

A member (from 1915) of the Adelaide Club, Mortlock drove fast cars, owned race-horses and greyhounds, and enjoyed shooting. He became a successful pastoralist and stud Merino breeder, and chaired the Yudnapinna Pastoral Co. Ltd and Yalluna Pty Ltd. His employees and neighbours spoke of his 'charm' and 'kindly disposition', yet he was essentially a bookish, withdrawn and solitary individual who did not make friends easily.

In 1926 Mortlock donated £2000 to the Waite [q.v.6] Agricultural Research Institute, University of Adelaide. In 1936 he and his mother gave a further £25 000 to establish the Ranson Mortlock Trust for research into soil erosion and pasture regeneration. An active member of St Peter's Anglican Church, Mintaro, he was also a keen yachtsman, an amateur film-maker and an orchid exhibitor. By this stage, however, he had developed a serious drinking problem.

Dorothy was born on 5 October 1906 at Clapham, London, daughter of Ernest Robert William Beech, pawnbroker's assistant, and his wife Elizabeth Lillian, née Beauchamp. The family emigrated to Adelaide where she was employed (from 1940) as secretary to Ernest Scarfe, who managed Mortlock's estates and finances. When Scarfe died in 1947, she took over Mortlock's accounts. On 7 December 1948, soon after he was diagnosed with cancer, Mortlock married Dorothy at St Peter's Cathedral, Adelaide. He died on 15 March 1950 in North Adelaide and was buried in North Road cemetery. His South Australian estate was sworn for probate at £1 148 124. He left over £73 000 to cultural organizations and charities. The balance, held in trust by his wife, was divided between the Waite institute and the Libraries Board of South Australia. In 1986 the Mortlock Library of South Australiana was established as part of the State Library of South Australia.

Mrs Mortlock had become a committee-member (1961) and vice-president (1979) of the Friends of the S.L.S.A. She gave generously to a host of charities. Shy and reserved, and to some degree a loner like her husband, she was a woman of dignity who held strong opinions, but seemed to lack confidence. She died on 10 August 1979 in Adelaide and was cremated.

Who's Who South Australian Centenary, 1936 (Adel, 1936); D. Whitelock (ed), *The Mid North of South Australia* (Adel, 1977); E. Warburton, *The Bowmans of Martindale Hall* (Adel, 1979); *Greater than their Knowing* (Adel, 1986); *Northern Sportsman* (Adel), 25 Sept 1924; *Advertiser* (Adel), 16 Mar 1950, 18 Aug 1979, 5 May 1984; Mortlock family papers, PRG 717 (Mort L); information from Misses Y. L. and B. S. Scarfe, Dulwich, Adel, and Prof P. Howell, Flinders Univ.   VALMAI A. HANKEL

MOSELEY, HENRY DOYLE (1884-1956), magistrate, was born on 7 September 1884 in Perth, son of Francis Arnold Moseley, registrar of titles, and his wife Lucy Darling, née Johnson. Born in the Bahamas, Francis had emigrated to Western Australia with his wife in 1881; he was to become registrar of the Supreme Court in 1899. Henry was educated at the High School and Scotch College, Perth. He began work as a clerk in the Supreme Court in 1900 before joining the crown solicitor's office as clerk-librarian in 1913.

At Christ Church, Claremont, on 14 October 1908 Moseley had married 30-year-old Blanche May Durbridge (d.1924) with Anglican rites. Enlisting in the Australian Imperial Force on 19 May 1916, he was commissioned on 15 May 1917; he joined the 51st Battalion on the Western Front in August 1918, but saw little action because of illness and was discharged in Perth on 16 August 1919 with the rank of lieutenant. Resuming his former post, he transferred to the solicitor general's office in 1921 and acted as usher of the Black Rod in State parliament in 1923. He served as a stipendiary magistrate at Carnarvon (1924-26) and Northam (1926-28), and as a police magistrate in Perth (from October 1928). On 24 January 1929 at St Mary's Anglican Church, Perth, he married Margaret de Castilla, the 22-year-old grand-daughter of A. P. Bussell [q.v.3].

Moseley's sentencing policy gained him the nickname 'Thirty Days'. Perceived as a fair and decisive adjudicator of decent common sense, he found himself in demand as a commissioner for difficult or controversial public inquiries. In 1934, accompanied by (Sir) Paul Hasluck, he travelled extensively as royal commissioner to investigate the treatment of Aborigines. His report largely upheld the authority of the Aborigines Department under A. O. Neville [q.v.11] and reflected contemporary prejudices against 'half-castes', but it did urge mild reforms, such as granting permanency to Aboriginal reserves and substituting district protectors for police. In 1938, as royal commissioner examining the administration of Heathcote Mental Reception Home, he unravelled a tedious history of personality clashes; he recommended that the matron be moved and that clearer lines of communication be established. He also inquired into the situation of mortgaged wheat-farmers and chaired the Western Australian Railways' appeal board.

On 20 December 1939 Moseley was appointed temporary lieutenant colonel and seconded for full-time duty in the Militia as an intelligence and security staff officer at head-quarters, Western Command. Early in 1942 he authorized the arrest of four members of the Australia First Movement; this action led to the internment of members in other States and to two convictions for sedition. Appointed deputy-director of security in May, he was transferred to the Retired List in November 1944. As royal commissioner (1947-48) to in-quire into alleged malpractices in the State housing commission, he found little evidence of impropriety and concluded that the com-mission had performed reasonably, though not outstandingly. He retired in May 1948.

Squarely built and 5 ft 7 ins (170 cm) tall, Moseley was a patron of the State branches of Toc H and the Young Men's Christian Association. He died on 6 October 1956 at his Claremont home and was cremated with Presbyterian forms. His wife survived him. The son of his second marriage predeceased him; the son of his first marriage, a flight lieutenant in the Royal Australian Air Force, was killed in action in 1942.

B. Muirden, *The Puzzled Patriots* (Melb, 1968); G. C. Bolton, *A Fine Country to Starve in* (Perth, 1972); P. Hasluck, *Mucking About* (Melb, 1977); T. Austen, *Something Worth While* (Perth, 1992); *Cygnet*, vol 17, no 3, 1956; *West Australian*, 8 Oct 1956; personal knowledge.   G. C. BOLTON

MOSES, MARGARET VERONICA (1940-1975), Sister of Mercy, teacher and orphanage administrator, was born on 5 February 1940 at Launceston, Tasmania, second of seven chil-dren of Australian-born parents Harry Moses and his wife Margaret Elizabeth, née Bourke, both schoolteachers. Margaret attended St Thomas More's parish school, Newstead. Fol-lowing her parents' separation, her mother took the children to Adelaide. Margaret was taught (1955-56) by the Sisters of Mercy at St Aloysius' College, Wakefield Street. In 1957 she entered the Convent of Mercy, Angas Street; professed on 16 January 1960, she took the religious name Miriam. She studied French and English at the University of Adelaide (B.A., 1963). After graduating, she was sent to Mater Christi College, Mount Gambier, where she proved a gifted teacher. In 1968, exhausted from overwork, she left the Order.

At first, Moses had difficulty in adjusting to lay life. Although bandy-legged and pigeon-toed, she was an attractive, vivacious woman, with pale skin, black hair and grey eyes; her thoughtful manner and cultured voice im-pressed people. She was employed (1968-70) at Port Adelaide Girls' Technical High School; there she encouraged her pupils—many of whom came from disadvantaged backgrounds

—to express themselves through poetry and diaries. In 1970 she was appointed to two of the Public Examination Board's subject com-mittees, which developed an English syllabus that included less literature and more popular material. Moses was motivated by a strong sense of social justice, and saw her role as pastoral as well as educational, an attitude that was not approved by the South Australian Education Department. Disillusioned, she resigned.

In March 1971 Moses joined her friend Rosemary Taylor, who was based in Saigon running orphanages for an American organiz-ation, Friends of the Children of Vietnam. It had been formed to rescue children who were orphaned or abandoned during the Vietnam War and to place them with families in Western countries. Taylor found 'Margaret's organiz-ational talents, her eloquence, her humour, and her very good French' real assets. Moses came to know plumbers and politicians, mili-tary police and milk-distributors; she inter-preted for English-speaking nurses and French doctors; and she escorted children to Europe and the United States of America. She was best-known as a mediator who was diplo-matic and charming, but able to discern hypo-crites at a glance. Throughout her life she expressed her philosophy and her doubts in letters and poetry. Some of her most poignant verse, written while she kept vigil over sick babies, was to be published in *Turn My Eyes Away* (Boulder, Colorado, U.S.A., 1976). She wrote: 'I never got over the horror of children who had never lived, dying'.

As the communist forces drew closer to Saigon in 1975, Taylor and her colleagues evacuated children from the four orphanages in their care. On 4 April she accepted an offer of 250 places on an American airforce Galaxy C-5A. In a last-minute switch of responsi-bilities, Moses boarded the aeroplane. Soon after take-off the aircraft lost its cargo door and crash-landed, killing seventy-eight chil-dren and their seven escorts, including Moses and a South Australian nurse, Lee Makk. Lockheed, the aircraft's manufacturer, made a settlement which provided money to the prospective parents; the relations of the dead volunteers received lesser amounts. Mrs Moses used her settlement to establish the Margaret Moses Memorial Fund which helps mothers in Vietnam, Thailand and Cambodia to raise their own children.

R. Strobridge (ed), *Turn My Eyes Away* (Boulder, Colorado, US, 1976); R. Taylor, *Orphans of War* (Lond, 1988); *Education Gazette* (SA), Apr 1970; *Newsweek*, 14 Apr 1975; *News* (Adel), 4, 5, 7 Apr 1975; information from Ms R. Young, Sth Franklin, Tas, Mrs M. Morrison, Salisbury, and Mr D. Moses, Rostrevor, Adel.   CARMEL FLOREANI
                                                   SUZANNE EDGAR

MOSS, WILLIAM LIONEL (1891-1971), grazier and Country Party organizer, was born on 9 October 1891 at Kaarimba, near Numurkah, Victoria, seventh child of Victorian-born parents Frederick George Moss, farmer, and his wife Isabella, née Spiers. Educated at local state schools, Bill began farming on his parents' property. He enlisted in the Australian Imperial Force on 1 February 1917 and served on the Western Front as a gunner in the 12th Army Brigade, Australian Field Artillery. Having been severely gassed in October 1918, he was sent home in December and discharged from the A.I.F. on 19 February 1919.

Moss resumed wheat- and wool-growing at Numurkah, and joined the newly formed Victorian Farmers' Union. Vice-president of the Victorian Wheat Growers' Association, he visited Canberra in July 1930 to lobby (unsuccessfully) for the passage of wheat-marketing legislation. Despite expressing admiration for Labor Prime Minister James Scullin's [q.v.11] stand on the wheat-marketing issue, Moss joined the Victorian (United) Country Party and was elected to its central council in 1931. He served a second term as vice-president of the V.W.G.A. and in 1934 organized rallies at Numurkah in support of orderly marketing.

In August that year the central council of the U.C.P. ruled that all party members must sign a pledge not to enter coalition governments without permission. Rather than sign, William Caldwell Hill (the member for Echuca) decided not to contest the Federal election which was held on 15 September 1934. Moss stood as an Australian Country Party candidate (opposed to the pledge) against the U.C.P.'s endorsed candidate (Sir) John McEwen [q.v.]. Although (Sir) Earle Page [q.v.11], the federal Country Party leader, visited the electorate to offer qualified support to Moss (and stronger endorsement to another Australian Country Party candidate Galloway Stewart), McEwen secured the seat comfortably on Australian Labor Party preferences. When McEwen was expelled from the Victorian Country Party in April 1938 for accepting a portfolio in the Lyons [q.v.10]-Page coalition, Moss chaired a protest meeting and joined the splinter Liberal Country Party which was formed at the meeting. After the rift was healed in 1943, he helped to redraft the federal party's constitution. He gained pre-selection for the Senate in 1946, but was not elected. In 1949-52 he was chief president of the V.C.P.

In 1951 the McDonald [q.v.] Country Party government appointed Moss a commissioner of the State Savings Bank of Victoria (chairman 1958, 1963 and 1968). He chaired the Goulburn Regional Committee and the No.2 Region Murray Valley Development League (1944-54), and also served (1939-55) on the

Numurkah Shire Council (president 1943). On 17 December 1953 at the Presbyterian Church, Batesford, he married Dorothy Gertrude Hill; he was aged 62 and she was 28.

As federal president (1962-68) of the Australian Country Party, Moss was an active propagandist who regularly contributed articles to the *Countryman* and other newspapers. While remaining a grazier, he expanded his business interests and was company chairman of Enterprise of New Guinea Gold and Petroleum Development. He played golf and tennis, and belonged to the Victorian Amateur Turf and the Moonee Valley Racing clubs. In 1965 he was appointed C.B.E. Survived by his wife and daughter, he died on 4 June 1971 in his Camberwell home and was buried in Numurkah cemetery.

G. H. Mitchell (comp and ed), *Growers in Action* (Melb, 1969); R. Murray and K. White, *A Bank for the People* (Melb, 1992); P. Golding, *Black Jack McEwen* (Melb, 1996); *Countryman* (Melb), 10 Aug, 7 Sept 1934, 15 June 1971; *Age* (Melb), 4 Apr 1951; *Herald* (Melb), 17 Nov 1955.   B. J. COSTAR

MOTEN, MURRAY JOHN (1899-1953), army officer and banker, was born on 3 July 1899 at Hawker, South Australia, elder son of John Moten, an Australian-born railway porter, and his wife Maude Mary Sophia, née Murray, a nurse from Ireland. Educated at primary schools at Port Augusta, in Adelaide and at Mingary, and at Mount Gambier District High School, Murray started work as a messenger-boy at the Mount Gambier post office in January 1915. Within six months he was employed as a clerk in the local branch of the Savings Bank of South Australia. In 1918 he was transferred to head office, Adelaide.

After being commissioned (August 1916) in the Commonwealth Military Cadet Corps, Moten had enlisted in the Australian Imperial Force on 23 August 1917. Immediately sent on leave (apparently because of flat feet), he was discharged as medically unfit in January 1918. He studied accountancy at the University of Adelaide in 1924. At St Mary's Catholic Church, Port Adelaide, on 16 January 1926 he married Kathleen Meegan, a 28-year-old musician. President (1934-35) of the Bank Officials' Association of South Australia, by October 1938 he was sales clerk in the bank's mortgage department.

Moten had resigned from the cadets and been appointed provisional lieutenant, 48th Battalion, Militia, in July 1923. He rose to major in 1929. Promoted lieutenant colonel, he commanded the 43rd-48th Battalion (1936-39) and the 48th (1939-40). Despite diminished sight in one eye, he was seconded to the A.I.F. as commander of the 2nd/27th Battalion on 26 April 1940. Five ft 9½ ins (177 cm) tall, with hazel eyes, brown hair and a ruddy complexion, he gave his religion as Anglican. In October he embarked for the Middle East.

The 2nd/27th trained in Palestine before moving in April 1941 to the fortress at Mersa Matruh, Egypt. There, the men suffered frequent air bombardment, gained valuable operational experience and improved their physical fitness. The battalion fought in the Syrian campaign, capturing Sidon on 15 June and taking part in the successful battle of Damour on 6-12 July. For his leadership and gallantry, Moten was awarded the Distinguished Service Order and mentioned in dispatches. Promoted colonel and temporary brigadier on 27 December (substantive 1949), he 'quietly and efficiently' took over the 17th Brigade from (Sir) Stanley Savige [q.v.].

Having garrisoned Ceylon (Sri Lanka), the 17th reached Australia in August 1942 and two months later embarked for Milne Bay, Papua. Air-lifted to Wau, New Guinea, in January 1943, the brigade absorbed Kanga Force and later that month withstood an enemy assault at Wandumi. Moten launched a counter-attack and gained the initiative; by March the opposing Japanese force was virtually annihilated. He won a Bar to his D.S.O. In May-June the 17th repulsed Japanese thrusts at Mubo and Lababia Ridge. Following the capture of Komiatum and Mount Tambu in August, Moten was appointed C.B.E. (1944) and again mentioned in dispatches. He and his soldiers rested and trained in Australia, then returned to New Guinea for the Wewak campaign (November 1944-August 1945).

From 18 November 1945 Moten administered command of the 6th Division. He was transferred to the Regimental Supernumerary List on 17 January 1946 in Adelaide and resumed his civilian career. In June he led the Australian army component of the Victory March in London. Next year he became a member of the War Graves Advisory Council. While commanding (1948-52) the 9th Brigade, Citizen Military Forces, he was appointed honorary colonel of the 27th Battalion in 1952. He was promoted general manager of the Savings Bank of South Australia in December that year.

Perhaps not as popular as Savige, Moten had earned the respect of his men, to whom he was deeply loyal, sharing with them 'the blood, the sweat, the tears, the laughter' of campaigning. Some officers considered him unduly harsh for removing a number of their peers who did not attain the standards he expected. Although rather overweight for operational service, he performed brilliantly as a commander at battalion and brigade levels.

Moten died of myocardial infarction on 14 September 1953 at Royal Adelaide Hospital and was buried in Centennial Park cemetery with Anglican and Catholic rites and full military honours; his wife, daughter and two sons survived him. His son John was director-general of the Australian Security Intelligence Organization in 1988-92. Geoffrey Mainwaring's portrait of Moten is held by the Australian War Memorial, Canberra; another portrait, by Ingrid Earns, is in the family's possession.

A. R. Ross (ed), *The Seventeenth Brigade Magazine* (Melb, 1944); G. Long, *To Benghazi* (Canb, 1952) and *Greece, Crete and Syria* (Canb, 1953); J. H. Burns, *The Brown and Blue Diamond at War* (Adel, 1960); S. Trigellis-Smith and J. McAllester, *Largely a Gamble* (Syd, 1995); *Advertiser* (Adel), 15 Sept 1953; State Bank of SA records; 3DRL5043 and PR 91/002 (AWM); information from Major H. P. Boland, Pymble, and Maj-Gen C. M. I. Pearson, Northbridge, Syd, Lieut-Col O. L. Edwards, Moss Vale, NSW, Mr J. M. Moten, Aranda, and Miss D. V. Thompson, Turner, Canb.   R. SUTTON

MOULD, JOHN STUART (1910-1957), naval officer and architect, was born on 21 March 1910 at Gosforth, Northumberland, England, son of Stuart Mill Mould, architect and surveyor, and his wife Ethel Kate, née Robinson. The family emigrated to Australia when John was aged 2. Educated at Sydney Grammar School and subsequently in London, he became an associate of the Royal Institute of British Architects in 1934. That year he returned to Sydney and joined his father in private practice. At the Presbyterian Church, Mosman, on 29 April 1935 he married Phyllis Sarah Palmer; they were to have one child before being divorced.

On 14 June 1940 Mould enlisted in the Australian Imperial Force. He contracted bronchial pneumonia and, while recuperating, qualified through the Yachtsmen Scheme for appointment as sub lieutenant, Royal Australian Naval Volunteer Reserve. Discharged from the A.I.F., he was mobilized in the R.A.N.V.R. on 14 September and sent to England for training at H.M.S. *King Alfred*. With Hugh Syme [q.v.], H. D. Reid and J. H. H. Kessack, he volunteered for 'special duties ashore'—service in the Royal Navy's Rendering Mines Safe section. He was provisionally promoted lieutenant in December and posted to H.M.S. *Vernon*.

The R.M.S. section had been established to assist in disarming the large number of unexploded bombs and mines strewn across Britain by German aircraft. Although most of the work involved bombs, the R.M.S.'s naval personnel were primarily concerned with 'delousing' German sea mines which had been dropped on land or washed ashore. Mould performed 'outstanding work on dock clearance operations and those resulting in the stripping of the early German mine Type G'. He received a commendation for bravery in June 1941 and won the George Medal in April 1942.

Among numerous assignments, Mould recovered, rendered safe and investigated 'the first German magnetic acoustic unit and moored magnetic mine'. The successful dismantling of such weapons allowed British scientists to identify their triggering mechanisms and thus devise countermeasures. In addition to the usual hazards of handling explosives, Mould and his colleagues had to contend with booby traps set to detonate the mines if attempts were made to disarm and disassemble them. He was awarded (November 1942) the George Cross for 'great gallantry and devotion to duty'.

Promoted acting lieutenant commander in January 1943, he began work with Professor Jack Haldane to develop a diving-suit with an independent air supply. Later that year Mould, Lieutenant Leon Goldsworthy, R.A.N.V.R., and Lieutenant Commander J. L. Harries, Royal Canadian Navy, trained groups of men known as 'P' parties in preparation for the invasion of Western Europe. These units were to be dispatched to newly captured harbours to clear them of booby traps, mines and other obstructions. Declining the opportunity to command one of the parties, Mould chose instead to continue training men who would serve in them. Following the German surrender in May 1945, he was sent to Ceylon (Sri Lanka) and Australia to assess the requirement for 'P' parties in the Far East and Pacific theatres. He was designated commander of two of the parties about the time that World War II ended.

Mould's R.A.N.V.R. appointment terminated on 26 November 1945 in Britain. He obtained a post as an architect with the allied military government in Germany and helped with that country's reconstruction. On 28 May 1947 at the Presbyterian Church, Bayswater, London, he married Margaret Agnes Massey, née Heeps, a 32-year-old divorcee. He returned to Australia in 1948. After working as an architect with the Department of Public Works, he was appointed chief architect to the Housing Commission of New South Wales in 1950. The amount of construction increased dramatically during his tenure, and he was responsible for the design of housing estates and shopping centres. His most conspicuous buildings are the Greenway [q.v.1] apartment blocks in Ennis Road, Milsons Point, immediately east of the northern approach to Sydney Harbour Bridge. He died of peritonitis on 9 August 1957 in Royal North Shore Hospital and was cremated; his wife, and their son and daughter survived him, as did the son of his first marriage.

J. F. Turner, *Service Most Silent* (Syd, 1955); I. Southall, *Softly Tread the Brave* (Syd, 1960); G. H. Gill, *Royal Australian Navy 1942-1945* (Canb, 1968); P. Firkins, *Of Nautilus and Eagles* (Syd, 1975); L. Wigmore (ed), *They Dared Mightily*, second ed revised and condensed by J. Williams and A. Staunton (Canb, 1986); *SMH*, 30 Nov 1946, 10 Aug 1957; information from Ms M.-C. Mould Tierny, Bexley, Syd.   ALASTAIR COOPER

MOUNTFORD, CHARLES PEARCY (1890-1976), anthropologist, was born on 8 May 1890 at Hallett, South Australia, son of South Australian-born parents Charles Mountford, farmer, and his wife Arabella, née Windsor. He attended public schools at Hallett, Georgetown and Moonta, and began working for his father at the age of 10. After the family moved to Adelaide, 'Monty' (as he was nicknamed) took a job as a tram conductor in 1909 and began correspondence courses in mechanics and engineering at the South Australian School of Mines and Industries. Appointed an electrical mechanic with the Municipal Tramways Trust, he moved to the Postmaster-General's Department in 1913. At the Methodist Church, Thebarton, on 18 March 1914 he married Florence Julge Purnell, a 23-year-old clerk; they were to have two children.

In 1920 Mountford was promoted senior mechanic and sent to the Darwin Post Office. Contact with Aborigines at the Kahlin Compound sparked his interest in their ceremonies and lore. He also began to investigate the region's natural history. Returning to Adelaide, he experienced personal loss with the death of his wife in 1925 and consoled himself by making tracings of Aboriginal rock-carvings near his parents' Peterborough farm. In 1926, with Norman Tindale of the South Australian Museum, he published a paper on the carvings; in 1928 he spoke on the subject at the conference of the Australasian Association for the Advancement of Science.

Mountford and his father had become foundation members (1926) of the Anthropological Society of South Australia. Encouraged by its president Frederic Wood Jones [q.v.9], he surveyed engravings around Panaramittee and Mount Chambers Gorge. On 28 October 1933 at the Gartrell Memorial Methodist Church, Rose Park, he married Bessie Ilma Johnstone, a 42-year-old civil servant. In 1935 he was appointed secretary of a board of inquiry to investigate allegations of ill-treatment of Aborigines in the Northern Territory, at Hermannsburg and Ayers Rock. Later that year he joined Tindale, C. J. Hackett, a physical anthropologist, and E. O. Stocker, a cine-photographer, on an expedition (under the auspices of the University of Adelaide's board for anthropological research) to the Warburton Range, Western Australia. He worked as stills-photographer and art recorder, and returned with many photographs and over 400 crayon drawings depicting sites and dreaming-tracks.

After accompanying the board's expedition to the Granites, Northern Territory, in 1936, Mountford joined another to Nepabunna Mission, Flinders Ranges, South Australia, in 1937. He revisited Nepabunna several times: his photographs, recordings, and notes on mythology, material culture and social customs constituted an unmatched ethnographic record of the Adnyamathanha people. In 1938 he went with (Sir) Grenfell Price's [q.v.] expedition to Mount Dare station to investigate an alleged sighting of the remains of Ludwig Leichhardt's [q.v.2] party. An accomplished Workers' Educational Association lecturer in ethnology, Mountford had published several scientific papers and a series of newspaper articles, and completed two years as an honorary assistant in ethnology at the South Australian Museum. In the P.M.G.'s Department, he had also conducted successful research into the corrosive effects of electrolysis on underground cables.

In mid-1938 Mountford took a years leave from the department to work as acting-ethnologist at the museum. He planned a camel expedition from Ernabella to Ayers Rock to examine the art of the Pitjantjatjara and Yankuntjatjara. A. P. Elkin [q.v.14] dissuaded the Carnegie trust from funding Mountford's project on the ground of his amateur status, but he was supported by the board for anthropological research and private sponsors. The four-month expedition in 1940, with Lauri Sheard and the cameleer Tommy Dodd [q.v.14], resulted in a detailed survey of the art and mythology of Ayers Rock and the Olgas. Mountford's exhibitions of photographs, his book, *Brown Men and Red Sand* (Melbourne, 1948), and his prize-winning film of the same name became springboards for his later career. In 1942 he travelled through the MacDonnell Ranges, documenting the art of sacred objects and recording the journey in his film, *Tjurunga*. He also made another influential film, *Namatjira the Painter*, which accompanied his illustrated book, *The Art of Albert Namatjira* (Melbourne, 1944).

Mountford's ease as a speaker and enthusiasm as a presenter of his films and photographs led to his engagement as a lecturer by the Commonwealth Department of Information. His tours (1945, 1946) of the United States of America brought Aboriginal art to the notice of an international audience and made him influential friends. Invited to apply to the National Geographic Society for an ethnological research grant, he led a N.G.S.-funded field-trip to Arnhem land, Northern Territory, in 1948. He published a detailed account of the region's art and produced three more films. Collections of bark-paintings gathered on this trip were distributed among the country's art galleries and museums, influencing future acquisition policies. He went on further expeditions to Arnhem Land (1949), to Yuendumu, Northern Territory (1951), and to Melville Island (1954).

In the 1950s and 1960s Mountford published several books based on his journeys and photographs. They included *The Tiwi* (London, 1958), which recorded their ceremonial and artistic life, and *Winbaraku* (Adelaide, 1967), which documented the Central Australian dreaming-track of the 'Mulga Snake' Jarapiri. Mountford retired from the Commonwealth Public Service in 1955 and was appointed O.B.E. that year. Supported by the Nuffield Foundation, he entered St John's College, Cambridge (Dip.Anthrop., 1959), wrote a thesis on Aboriginal art and inspected museum collections in Europe. His final expeditions to survey rock art in the regions of Port Hedland, Western Australia, and Cape York Peninsula, Queensland, were undertaken in 1963 and 1964 respectively.

The thesis which Mountford submitted at the University of Adelaide (M.A., 1964) was subsequently published as *Ayers Rock, its people, their beliefs and their art* (Sydney, 1965). He and the artist Ainslie Roberts became widely known for their joint publications —*The Dreamtime* (1965), *The Dawn of Time* (1969) and *The First Sunrise* (1971)—dealing with Aboriginal mythology. In 1973 Mountford donated his manuscripts and his collection of 13 000 photographs to the State Library of South Australia. Concentrating his efforts on an illustrated analysis of Central Australian Aboriginal art and mythology, he worked from his office in the museum and, at the age of 86, completed his magnum opus, *Nomads of the Australian Desert* (1976). The book contained images of restricted Aboriginal subjects and was withdrawn from sale soon after publication.

Mountford had been presented with the Australian Natural History medallion (1945) by the Field Naturalists Club of Victoria and the Franklin L. Burr award (1949) by the National Geographic Society; in 1955 the South Australian branch of the Royal Geographical Society of Australasia awarded him its John Lewis [q.v.10] gold medal and the Queensland branch awarded him its Thomson [q.v.12] gold medal; he won the Sir Joseph Verco [q.v.12] medal (1971) of the Royal Society of South Australia, and received an honorary Litt.D. (1973) from the University of Melbourne and a D.Litt. (1976) from the University of Adelaide. His tallish, stooped figure and his courteous manner belied that combination of physical energy and scepticism of the academic establishment which had underpinned his life's work. Survived by his wife, and by the son and daughter of his first marriage, he died on 16 December 1976 at Norwood and was cremated.

M. Lamshed, *'Monty'* (Adel, 1972); *People* (Syd), 11 Oct 1950, p 24; *Aust Inst of Aboriginal Studies Newsletter*, no 7, Jan 1977; *Advertiser* (Adel), 5 Apr, 17 Dec 1976; Mountford-Sheard Collection of Ethnology (SLSA).   PHILIP JONES

MOWLL, HOWARD WEST KILVINTON (1890-1958), Anglican archbishop, was born on 2 February 1890 at Chaldercot, near Dover, Kent, England, eldest son of Henry Martyn Mowll, solicitor and later mayor of Dover, and his wife Gertrude Emily, née Worsfold. Howard attended Dover College junior school and, from 1903, King's School, Canterbury. He was an earnest boy, uninterested in games, but an industrious scholar and a keen debater. From childhood, he had learned from his parents a deep and abiding evangelical faith. In 1909 he entered King's College, Cambridge (B.A., 1912; M.A., 1916) to read history, in which subject he kept a lifelong interest. Much of his thought was to be couched in historical terms. As president (1911-12) of the Cambridge Inter-collegiate Christian Union, he battled the liberal Student Christian Movement, emerging as a doughty leader and controversialist.

After theological training (though he was never a systematic theologian) at Ridley Hall in 1913-14, Mowll was made deacon for colonial service on 21 September 1913 by the evangelical Bishop E. A. Knox of Manchester, and appointed to the theological staff at Wycliffe College, Toronto, Canada. As a tutor (1913-16) and professor of history (1916-22) at Wycliffe, he acquired a lasting interest in Canada and a passion for travel. Mowll visited England to be ordained priest on 7 June 1914 by the archbishop of Canterbury, on the putative title of curate of Dover. He served (1918-19) as an army chaplain on the Western Front. His work in Canada and his reputation in England led to an invitation to become assistant-bishop of West China. He was consecrated on 24 June 1922 in Westminster Abbey, London.

Civil disorder in his western Szechwan (Sichuan) province of China made mission work hard to sustain: on one occasion Mowll and his party were taken hostage by bandits. There were policy differences between the support organizations—the Church Missionary Society and the China Inland Mission—over the degree of leadership to be given to native Christians. Mowll championed local autonomy and it was with C.M.S. support (which he was to repay by his patronage in later years) that he became diocesan bishop in 1928. He soon appointed two Chinese assistant-bishops.

Mowll had married Dorothy Anne Martin on 23 October 1924 with Anglican rites at Mienchu Sze, and on 17 December that year at the British Consulate General, Chengtu (Chengdu). She had worked in the mission field at Sintu (Xindu) and supplied the linguistic skill that Mowll lacked. The marriage was childless, but they were a devoted couple, united in a strong sense of Christian purpose and complementing each other in personality and bearing. The towering Howard was stately, measured and reserved; Dorothy was sprightly and vivacious, and more practical. In 1930-32 they made journeys to India, Europe, North America and Australasia. Mowll's extensive travels widened his reputation as a mission bishop. Although, as he said, he would always think of himself as an Englishman, in March 1933 he agreed to consider election to the see of Sydney, following the death of Archbishop J. C. Wright [q.v.12]. He was elected next month and arrived in Sydney on 1 March 1934.

Determined to galvanize his diocese, still suffering from the Depression and (as he believed) weakened by a lack of clear evangelical purpose in the 1920s, Mowll worked prodigiously and expected others to do likewise. His clergy did not always take kindly to telephone calls in the very early hours. He visited every parish, using his remarkable memory for names and faces to good effect. His sermons, delivered with grave emphasis, but always simple and direct, were heard by many. The Home Mission Society was overhauled and Moore Theological College (under a new principal, T. C. Hammond [q.v.14]) expanded. Missions to the beaches and to children and youth were initiated. Money was sought for new churches. In 1936 Mowll presided at the centenary of W. G. Broughton's [q.v.1] consecration as bishop of Australia, using it as a means to increase an appreciation of Australian Church history. Not all his initiatives succeeded. He could never wholly persuade his diocese that a new cathedral should be built on the George Street site, even though the government's wish to resume the land had been deflected. But the young archbishop did much to make Sydney an efficient diocese and a leader among the evangelical dioceses in the Anglican communion.

Mowll's activity was prompted, in part, by the urge to vindicate himself and his school of churchmanship. Archbishop Lang of Canterbury had told him that he possessed neither the gifts nor the training for Sydney. Governor Sir Philip Game [q.v.8] complained to Lang that Mowll seemed averse to giving his Church high social prominence. The Australian bishops, by a single vote, declined to elect him primate, an office held by all his predecessors since Frederic Barker [q.v.3]. It was Mowll's churchmanship rather than his inexperience which decided the issue. The rebuff strengthened his determination to consolidate Sydney's evangelical character. Some influential liberal clerics had already broken with the dominant Anglican Church League to form the Anglican Fellowship. In 1938 A. H. Garnsey [q.v.8] and others presented the 'Memorial', a protest to Mowll, complaining of a conservative evangelical monopoly of key diocesan positions. Mowll was badly advised and did not handle the occasion well, thus causing public controversy. It did not, however, shake his spirit of determination.

World War II changed the atmosphere, holding Sydney Anglicans together and offering Mowll, newly returned from a visit to Britain, the chance to prove his leadership on a broader front. He set up the Church of England National Emergency Fund, which ran clubs for servicemen. The Anglican Building Crusade planned new churches and there was encouragement for those involved in postwar reconstruction schemes for social betterment. It was significant that one of Mowll's first actions when hostilities ceased was to visit war-torn China. In 1948 he was elected, without opposition, as primate. He had come to be acknowledged by his fellow bishops as the natural leader of the Church in Australia.

In 1947 Mowll had delivered the Moorhouse [q.v.5] lectures on 'Seeing all the World' which stressed the need for Australia's involvement in worldwide mission. A seasoned traveller, he had been to International Missionary Council conferences in India (1938) and Canada (1947). As president (1946-51, 1954-55 and 1957-58), he was the leading figure in the Australian council of the World Council of Churches, and attended meetings of the world body in the Netherlands (1948) and the United States of America (1954), serving on its central committee. This ecumenism was not without its conservative critics in his own diocese. His duties as primate took him far and wide, in Australia and New Guinea and beyond. He attended the Lambeth Conference in 1948, Queen Elizabeth II's coronation in 1953 and the Anglican Congress at Minneapolis, U.S.A., in 1954. He had long sought modification of the immigration regulations in the interests of Asian students in Australia; the Colombo Plan of 1951 allowed him to give substance to his policy with an international friendship centre in Sydney.

As an unswerving upholder of evangelicalism, Mowll revived the local Church Missionary Society and forwarded its work in Africa and India. He was a consistent patron of the minority Church of England in South Africa, world president of the Scripture Union and a vice-president of the Evangelical Alliance. In 1957 he invited Billy Graham to conduct a long crusade in Australia. Mowll

inherited, and maintained, Sydney's policy of caution towards the creation of a constitution for the Australian Church, fearful of consequent theological and liturgical change. He gave tacit support to Hammond in the famous 'Red Book' case before the Supreme and High courts. The triumphal Australian visit of Archbishop Fisher of Canterbury in 1950 led to Mowll's recognition that there was a way forward. He and Hammond became supporters of a modified constitution which, despite opposition, was accepted by the general and Sydney synods and took effect in 1962.

Mowll's commitments allowed him less time with his own diocese in the 1950s. In a period of large-scale material expansion he promoted extensive church-building and encouraged lay action for church growth. Imperial immigration found in him a ready supporter. He was appointed C.M.G. in 1954 and his wife O.B.E. in 1956. They made an official visit (1956) to China, a memorable occasion for them both. Dorothy Mowll was responsible for the genesis of the 'retirement village' plan which eventually became the Mowll Memorial Village, Castle Hill. She died on 23 December 1957. Howard became ill from overwork and strain. He died of myocardial infarction on 24 October 1958 at St Luke's Hospital, Darlinghurst, and was cremated. His ashes, mingled with those of his wife, were placed beside the episcopal throne in St Andrew's Cathedral, Sydney. The cathedral holds his portrait by F. O. Salisbury.

M. L. Loane, *Archbishop Mowll* (Lond, 1960); S. Judd and K. Cable, *Sydney Anglicans* (Syd, 1987); Syd Diocesan Synod Reports, *Yearbook*, 1933-58; C of E (NSW), *Procs of General Synod*, 1935-55; *The Times*, 25 Oct 1958; *SMH*, 26 Oct 1958; Lang *and* Fisher papers (Lambeth Palace L, Lond).

K. J. Cable

MOYES, JOHN STOWARD (1884-1972), Anglican bishop, and ALBAN GEORGE ('JOHNNY') (1893-1963), journalist and cricket commentator, were born on 25 July 1884 at Koolunga, South Australia, and 2 January 1893 at Gladstone, second and sixth children of John Moyes, schoolteacher, and his wife Ellen Jane, née Stoward, both from New South Wales. Educated at the Collegiate School of St Peter, Adelaide, the three Moyes brothers were all called 'John'; 'Johnny' stuck to Alban who detested his given name. John Stoward Moyes studied psychology and logic at the University of Adelaide (B.A., 1905; M.A., 1907) and became president of the university branch of the Australian Student Christian Movement; he later wrote that the S.C.M. had introduced him to a Christianity of 'grace and love', not merely 'law and commandments'.

Entering St Barnabas' Theological College, he was made deacon on 22 December 1907 and ordained priest on 21 December 1908 by the bishop of Adelaide.

His first appointment (1907) was to a curacy in the parish of St Paul's, Port Pirie. At St Cyprian's Church, North Adelaide, on 22 April 1909 he married Helen Margaret (d.1970), daughter of (Sir) Richard Butler [q.v.7]. In 1911-13 Moyes worked as assistant-curate in the London parish of Lewisham. The extreme poverty he witnessed there, and that which he had seen at Port Pirie during the 1908-09 lockout, consolidated his commitment to a social application of the gospel. He returned to South Australia in 1913 and took up the rectorship of St Cuthbert's, Prospect. Reappointed to Port Pirie in 1919, he helped in 1921 to mediate the end of a two-year strike at Broken Hill Associated Smelters Pty Ltd. While Moyes was rector (1921-29) of St Bartholomew's, Norwood, the parish grew; many were attracted to Sunday-evening services by his powerful preaching. From 1925 he was also archdeacon of Adelaide.

Consecrated on 30 November 1929 as bishop of Armidale, New South Wales, Moyes used his episcopacy as a platform for his political and social views. He aroused opposition when he criticized banking policy during the Depression, advocated closer settlement in 1935-36, supported waterside workers who refused to ship iron ore to Japan in 1938, and defended striking coalminers in 1942. He spoke out against (Sir) Robert Menzies' [q.v.] proposal to outlaw the Communist Party of Australia, backed the movement to reform the White Australia policy and opposed the Vietnam War. Moyes was chairman of the General Synod's social questions committee (1933-63) and of the Christian Social Order Movement (1943-51).

In 1941 Moyes had delivered the Moorhouse [q.v.5] lectures in Melbourne—published as *Australia: The Church and the Future* (1942)—in which he criticized Australian institutions, including the Church, for being characterized by 'individualism and no sense of divine calling'. Once again he 'created a storm'. He spoke frequently on the importance of education, chaired the boards of the New England Girls' School and The Armidale School, and was a founding member (1953) of the council and deputy-chancellor of the University of New England (Hon. D.Litt., 1961).

Moyes travelled extensively throughout the diocese and abroad, attending the Lambeth conferences of 1930, 1948 and 1958, and visiting North America in 1943, 1948, 1954, 1958 and 1963 as chairman of the social questions committee and as a representative of the World Council of Churches. He published *American Journey* (Sydney, 1944), *In Journeyings Often* (Melbourne, 1949), *America Re-*

visited (Sydney, 1955) and *Third Time of Asking* (Sydney, 1959).

Bishop Moyes was disappointed in his wish to be promoted to a metropolitan see. Despite accusations that he was a communist sympathizer, his politics were essentially liberal. In 1965 he published a critique of communism, *The Communist Way of Life and the Christian's Answer* (Sydney). He attributed his 'radical outlook' in part to the snobbish manner in which his parents had been treated by a number of South Australian pastoral families. Sometimes seen as aloof or vain, he acted according to clear-cut perceptions of right and wrong, believing that he had 'a duty to oppose what is wicked'. In 1962 he was appointed C.M.G. Moyes retired to Vaucluse, Sydney, in 1964. He enjoyed cricket and music, and wrote his memoirs. On 30 August 1971 at St Peter's Church, Hornsby, he married Mary Scott Pentreath, née Holland, an 87-year-old widow. Survived by his wife, and by the four sons and two daughters of his first marriage, he died on 29 January 1972 at Hornsby and was cremated.

His brother 'Johnny' studied science at the University of Adelaide before joining the Australian Imperial Force on 13 July 1915. Commissioned two months later, he served with the 48th Battalion on the Western Front, was twice wounded and won the Military Cross (1918). In November 1918 Major Moyes sailed for Melbourne. After his A.I.F. appointment terminated, he took a job with the Repatriation Commission. At St Paul's Anglican Church, Fairfield, on 28 June 1919 he married 30-year-old Frederica Sophia Honor Christensen. Late in 1921 he moved to Sydney where he worked as a correspondent for Melbourne's *Sporting Globe*.

A promising young cricketer, Moyes had represented (1912-15) South Australia (making a century on début), been chosen (1914) for Australia in a tour (cancelled due to World War I) against South Africa, and played for Victoria in 1920. In Sydney, he achieved one of the highest individual scores in grade cricket when he made 218 runs in 83 minutes for the Gordon District Cricket Club in 1922. Presented with an engraved silver ball to honour 'his captaincy and the good fellowship he inspired', he served as a New South Wales selector (1926-27) and wanted (Sir) Donald Bradman to play for the State.

By 1927, when Moyes joined the State branch of the Australian Journalists' Association, he was a senior reporter for the *Globe*. He became news editor for the *Daily Telegraph* about 1928, but soon transferred to the *Daily Guardian*. Having joined Associated Newspapers Ltd in 1931, he was sporting editor of the *Sun* for fifteen years. In 1941-44 he commanded the 7th Australian Garrison as a lieutenant colonel, and remained involved in casual sporting journalism. From 1946 to 1951 he edited Associated Newspapers' magazine, *Sporting Life*. His thirteen books on cricket included accounts of Test tours, the biographies, *Bradman* (1948) and *Benaud* (1962), and *Australian Cricket* (1959).

In 1949 Moyes had begun broadcasting sporting sessions for the Australian Broadcasting Commission. In 1950-51 he covered his first Test series, against England. In 1955 he received a full-time contract. As a cricket broadcaster, he became a household name in Australia and New Zealand in the 1950s and early 1960s. His pithy and authoritative commentaries, delivered in a 'dryly-humourous voice', won thousands of listeners to the A.B.C. He was renowned for his summaries of the day's game which, he wrote, should be 'factual and yet not dull'. Sir Charles Moses described him as 'a scrupulously honest communicator'. Moyes's 'infectiously hysterical' description of the last over of the tied Test between Australia and the West Indies in December 1960 was replayed many times by popular request.

Moyes was appointed M.B.E. in 1959. He and his wife were active members of the congregation of St Stephen's Anglican Church, Willoughby. Bradman, who had worked with him as a junior on the *Sun*, described him as 'most considerate and helpful . . . a fine-living man'. Survived by his wife and two sons, Johnny Moyes died of coronary vascular disease on 18 January 1963 at his Chatswood home and was cremated.

K. Grose and J. Newall (eds), *So Great a Heritage* (Syd, 1990); C. Jones, *Something in the Air* (Syd, 1995); *Reveille* (Syd), Mar 1963; *J of Religious Hist*, 13, no 4, 1985; *Aust Hist Studies*, no 107, Oct 1996; *SMH*, 23 Nov, 2 Dec 1929, 12 Dec 1935, 6 Dec 1938, 12 May 1950, 13 June 1959, 1 Jan 1962, 19 Jan 1963, 31 Jan 1972; *Daily Telegraph* (Syd), 19 Jan 1963; *North Shore Times*, 23 Jan 1963; Gordon District Cricket Club, *Annual Report*, 1921-22 (NSW Cricket Assn L); D. H. Ingrouille, John S. Armidale: an account of the public life of John Stoward Moyes with particular reference to his ministry as Bishop of Armidale (B.Litt. thesis, UNE, 1976); J. S. Moyes papers (ML); information from Miss M. Moyes and Mrs H. Corell, Daw Park, Adel, and Mr A. G. Moyes, Wahroonga, Syd, who also holds family papers.   ANNE O'BRIEN

MOYSEY, ANNIE (d.1976), Aboriginal matriarch, was born probably in the 1870s near the junction of the Warrego and Darling rivers, New South Wales, daughter of Tom Kega, a European labourer, and a Gunu mother who died soon afterwards. The Gunu were a northern affiliation of the Barkindji tribes. Although Annie and her sisters were reared by their Gunu grandmother among the 'station blacks', they became deeply versed in tribal lore. While travelling, sometimes far to the north and west, Annie learned several Aboriginal languages. English, necessary only for communicating with the Whites, was of secondary importance: 'Barkindji's our lingo so we'll use it'.

If the youthful Annie's performance of the 'garombarn' (quivering of the legs) enlivened tribal dancing, she needed all her strength and vitality for the long years of toil that followed, mostly as sole provider for an ever-growing family. Her first husband Norman Clark did not help in raising their children, or the other children who came to her camp; her heart went out to any homeless child, whether her own kin or not. A river steamer abandoned near Louth made a roomy houseboat. The family fished from a bark canoe, kept goats for milk and meat, hunted, and gathered wild food in the bush. With her wagonette and horses, Annie worked on Toorale and other stations to earn money for their additional needs.

About 1920, a shortage of rural employment apparently forced Annie to take the children downriver to the Pooncarie Aboriginal reserve. To ensure her independence, she set up camp beyond its borders. A former Pooncarie nurse recalled her as a 'splendid woman' who worked tirelessly to make a decent living for her children. Moving to Wilcannia, Annie claimed to be aged 45 when she married Leonard Alfred Moysey, a 25-year-old European labourer, on 11 October 1930 at St James's Anglican Church, Wilcannia. Throughout the Depression years and onwards she remained the chief breadwinner.

They transferred to the Menindee Mission Station in 1933, but had returned to Wilcannia by 1939. Still active and hard-working, Annie was a forceful and outspoken member of a community that included her sisters, some of her own married children and numerous other relations. Again widowed, and growing old, she became known as 'Grannie Moysey', and was revered—and also feared—as a matriarch and keeper of the tribal laws, which were sadly neglected, especially by the younger generation. If her verbal chastisement missed its mark, she gave a 'walloping' with her walking-stick. She was believed to have knowledge of the occult mysteries of the 'mekigar' (Barkindji witch doctor) and on one occasion helped the victim of a lightning strike to regain his consciousness and vision. Anthropologists, linguists and historians consulted her intermittently.

Late in life Grannie Moysey was to be seen seated on the shady veranda of the Wilcannia and District Hospital, smoking her trusty pipe. She died on 2 February 1976 in that hospital and was buried with Catholic rites in Wilcannia cemetery; four sons and eight daughters survived her.

B. Hardy, *Lament for the Barkindji* (Adel, 1976); P. Memmott, *Humpy, House and Tin Shed* (Syd, 1991); E. Crawford, *Over My Tracks* (Melb, 1993); *Encyclopaedia of Aboriginal Australia* (Canb, 1994); *Papers in Aust Linguistics*, 10, 1976, p 33; information from Mr B. Bates, Broken Hill, NSW, Prof J. Beckett, Univ Syd, and the late Mrs Murkins.

BOBBIE HARDY*

MUDIE, IAN MAYELSTON (1911-1976), poet, was born on 1 March 1911 at Hawthorn, Adelaide, younger child of South Australian-born parents Henry Mayelston Mudie, bank accountant, and his second wife Gertrude Mary, née Wurm. Ian was educated (1920-26) at Scotch College, Adelaide, but showed more interest in extracurricular reading than in study and left without gaining his Leaving certificate. At the office of the registrar-general, Adelaide, on 30 October 1934 he married Renee Dunford Doble. From his early twenties writing was Mudie's chief activity, although the difficulties in providing for his family as a freelancer forced him to try his hand as a wool-scourer, furniture-dealer, grape-picker, and as a salesman of insurance and real-estate.

Mudie published his first poem in 1931, but it was not until P. R. Stephensen [q.v.12] included his work in the *Publicist* in October 1937 that his career as a poet began to flourish. Attracted by Stephensen's nationalism, he moved to Sydney where he was elected to the executive-committee of the Australia-First Movement at its inaugural meeting in October 1941. He was committed to the organization's second aim—'To encourage the development of a distinctively-Australian National Culture in Australia'—and there is no evidence that he showed sympathy for the German or Japanese governments. Stephensen and fifteen other A.F.M. members were arrested on 10 March 1942 on suspicion of collaborating with the Japanese. Mudie, by chance, had returned to Adelaide before the arrests.

Encouraged by Stephensen's interest in him, by a close friendship with Miles Franklin [q.v.8] and by praise from literary figures such as Xavier Herbert, Mudie rapidly produced *Corroboree to the Sun* (Melbourne, 1940), *This Is Australia* (1941), *Their Seven Stars Unseen* (1943), *The Australian Dream* (1943)—winner of the W. J. Miles [q.v.10] prize—and *Poems* (Melbourne, 1945). He was almost six feet (183 cm) tall and of wiry build, and was once described as looking like a shearer. Gregarious and fiercely egalitarian, Mudie embodied much of the traditional version of Australian identity that he celebrated in his best-known poem, 'They'll Tell You About Me'. A deep love of the land and its inhabitants are recurrent themes in his poetry; so,

too, are harsh criticisms of the Europeans for the way they treated the indigenous people and desecrated the environment.

At this time Mudie's nationalism and concern for Aborigines found an outlet in a loose association with Rex Ingamells [q.v.14] and the Jindyworobak poets. He contributed (from 1939) to their anthologies, joined (1941) their club and edited the *Jindyworobak Anthology* (1946). Having been called up for full-time duty in the Militia in 1942, he served in anti-aircraft units and ordnance depots in Australia. He edited the anthology, *Poets at War* (Melbourne, 1944), and, on being discharged in 1945, took up a Commonwealth Literary Fund fellowship to carry out research into paddle-steamers on the Murray and Darling rivers. His gift for establishing rapport allowed him to collect many stories from old-timers and eventually to publish *Riverboats* (1961). His other writing included two histories, *Wreck of the Admella* (1966) and *The Heroic Journey of John McDouall Stuart* (Sydney, 1968), numerous newspaper articles and short stories, productions such as *Glenelg Sketchbook* (1974), a children's story, *The Christmas Kangaroo* (1946), and several edited books, including *Australian Poets Speak* (1961) on which he collaborated with his friend Colin Thiele.

After a decade in which the riverboats were sometimes an obsessive preoccupation, Mudie again turned to poetry, publishing *The Blue Crane* (Sydney, 1959), *The North-Bound Rider* (1963)—winner of the Grace Leven prize—*Look, the Kingfisher!* (Melbourne, 1970) and *Selected Poems 1934-1974* (Melbourne, 1976). While the poems from this period retain his earlier commitments and often colloquial style, they are less strident, and place more emphasis on personal reflection and city life.

Mudie was a keen evangelist for Australian literature. He was active in the Australian Society of Authors, national president (1959-60) of the Fellowship of Australian Writers, editor-in-chief (1960-65) of Rigby Ltd, publishers, and an organizer of Writers' Week at the Adelaide Festival of Arts from its inception in 1960 until 1972. A great communicator, he lectured to adult education classes at the University of Adelaide, taught at the South Australian School of Arts and conducted speaking tours for the Commonwealth Literary Fund. Survived by his wife and two sons, he died of a coronary occlusion on 23 October 1976 in London and was cremated; his ashes were scattered on the Murray River.

B. W. Muirden, *The Puzzled Patriots* (Melb, 1968); J. Tonkin, *Ian Mudie* (Adel, 1970); B. Elliott (ed), *The Jindyworobaks* (Brisb, 1979); C. Munro, *Wild Man of Letters* (Melb, 1984); Miles Franklin *and* P. R. Stephensen papers (ML); Mudie papers (Mort L).

PHILIP BUTTERSS

MUIR, ALAN HOLMES ('BONNIE') (1907-1977), wrestler, was born on 28 November 1907 at Jolimont, Melbourne, son of Victorian-born parents Edwin Holmes Muir, dentist, and his wife Alice May, née Horan. Educated at Melbourne Church of England Grammar School (1915-25), he played for three years in the first XI, and was a prefect in his final year. 'Bonnie' (a nickname he had acquired as a baby) was 'one of those kids who didn't know what to do with himself'. He took a job in the accounts department of J. C. Williamson [q.v.6] Ltd. Having boxed at school, he was encouraged to take up amateur wrestling by a visiting American grappler, Mike Yokel, who was impressed by the young man's 6 ft 1½ ins (187 cm) muscular physique. Muir soon showed promise, winning the Victorian amateur heavyweight championship (1929 and 1930) and being runner-up for the Australian championship (1930). He also worked out with some visiting American professionals brought to Australia by John Wren [q.v.12]. After Muir was thrown out of work in 1930, Ed 'Strangler' Lewis suggested that he might make a career as a wrestler.

Muir travelled to the United States of America to learn his craft. For his initial bout, at Seattle in October 1930, he received $40 and the first of his cauliflower ears. When he was back in Australia in 1932-33, the journalist Norman McCance commented on the 're-markable progress' he had made, and noted that he had 'developed ... clean-limbed, supple strength and vigorous aggression'. Leaving Australia again, Muir wrestled his way through Europe before—more adventur-ously—trying his luck in North Africa. At Casablanca, Morocco, he fell ill; having lost much weight, he spent two years out of the business, living in Paris.

In October 1939 Muir was welcomed back at West Melbourne stadium. At the office of the government statist, Queen Street, on 13 December that year he married Moyra Geraldine Hayes Marco, a 30-year-old di-vorcee. He lost a bout with Chief Little Wolf in June 1940 but 'gave a display of wrestling that for all-round effectiveness has not been surpassed by any visitor in recent years'. Enlisting in the Militia on 9 October, he rose to captain, Australian Imperial Force, as an instructor in physical training and unarmed combat. His appointment terminated in April 1945. Muir returned to the ring, but by 1950 had given up wrestling to officiate as a referee. He worked for the National Fitness Council and Percy Pearce's gymnasium before man-aging the Oasis gymnasium. By this time he was something of a Melbourne identity.

A capable wrestler, Muir had acquired the skills of a performer, necessary in a profession that had been transformed into an enter-tainment. Characteristically, he was always 'the good guy' in the ring, never making the transition to a 'heel', as did so many older wrestlers. In 1973 he expressed his distaste for the further changes wrought by television. The vulgarity of the televised spectacle offended him: while the sport of his day had involved much 'acting', its exponents were technically skilled as wrestlers. A genuine enthusiast for wrestling, Muir saw it as a natural sport, unlike boxing.

Outside the ring, Bonnie was quiet and gentle in manner, well spoken, fluent in French, a reader and conversationalist, with friends from diverse backgrounds. He died of cancer on 12 June 1977 at Hawthorn East and was cremated; his wife, son and stepson sur-vived him.

Melb C of E Grammar School, *Liber Mel-burniensis* (Melb, 1965); *Argus*, 31 Oct 1932, 23 Oct 1939, 3 June, 13 July 1940; *Sun News-Pictorial*, 14 June 1977; information from Mr C. Muir, Syd.

JOHN RICKARD

MULGA FRED (c.1874-1948), Aboriginal buckjumper, was born about 1874, probably near Port Hedland, Western Australia. His parentage is unknown. Called Fred Wilson and also Fred Clark, he became an expert drover and horse-breaker, but never learned to read or write. After travelling to Adelaide by cattle-ship about 1905, he joined 'Broncho' George's rodeo troupe; he later toured with the Mulder brothers and with Billy Kinnear, riding in shows throughout south-eastern Australia. Nicknamed 'Mulga Fred', he gave outstanding performances at a buckjumping rodeo held at the Melbourne Hippodrome in June 1911, and subsequently won several Victorian titles.

By the 1920s Mulga Fred's 'beat' lay in the Wimmera and Western districts. From Lake Condah Aboriginal mission in the south, he toured as far north as Kaniva, Dimboola and Swan Hill; in addition, he regularly appeared at the Melbourne Royal Show. Kinnear re-garded him as one of the greatest rodeo riders of their day. Fred was rarely thrown; he could vault on to a moving horse; and he could ride from 'head to tail'. He continued to ride buck-jumpers professionally until the 1930s, then turned to giving exhibitions: his last, for ten seconds at Swan Hill in 1948, brought him thunderous applause and a shower of coins. In old age he concentrated on rural labouring, and on subtle horse-taming as distinct from crude horse-breaking. He was also an expert at stockwhip-cracking and boomerang-throwing. Crowds at the football and the show frequently saw him whip a cigarette paper from the hands and lips of a volunteer. While lying on the ground, he could even use a stockwhip to crack paper from his own mouth.

In 1917 the clothing manufacturers J. K. Pearson and J. L. G. Law had renamed their firm Pelaco Ltd. The company's advertising soon depicted a bare-legged and bare-foot Aboriginal man striding along in a pristine white Pelaco dinner-shirt and exclaiming: 'Mine Tinkit They Fit'. A. T. Mockridge drew the original sketch. By the 1930s 'Pelaco Bill' sported a monocle and cigar, or stood resplendent in shirt, tie and trousers beneath the Australian flag. What began as a racist play on civilization and savagery had become something more inclusive. Pelaco Bill proved popular for almost forty years and contributed to the company's rising fortunes. Mulga Fred always maintained that he was the model for Pelaco Bill. Although the company acknowledged his claim by sending him shirts, it has oscillated (from 1948) about its connexion with him.

Mulga Fred was 5 ft 10 ins (178 cm) tall, full-bearded and softly spoken; in later life he walked with a limp, a legacy of rodeo work. A favourite with children, he was respected by adults, even when cadging a 'shillin'. He never married and spent his earnings on his drinking mates. Between 1927 and 1940 he was gaoled fifteen times for drunkenness: he reacted sometimes with defiance, sometimes with gentleness and sometimes with wit. *En route* to an appearance at the Dimboola Regatta, he was killed when hit by a train on the night of 2/3 November 1948 at Horsham station. He was buried in the local cemetery with Catholic rites. His tombstone is engraved with a stockwhip and boomerang, symbols of the two cultures he mastered.

Vic Police Gazette, 1927, p 260, 1934, p 468, 1936, p 914, 1938, pp 51, 291, 429, 928, 1007; *Age* (Melb), 23 June 1911; *Horsham Times*, 5 Nov 1948; *Coleraine Albion*, 4 Feb 1960; Aborigines Protection Bd (Vic), personal file, CRS B337/0, item 551 (AA, Vic); Inquest no 1704, VPRS 24, box 1605 (PRO, Vic); Stock Exchange of Melb papers, box 880-881 (Univ Melb Archives); information from Messrs D. McCabe and N. Flack, Horsham, Vic.

RICHARD BROOME

MULLENS, PHYLLIS KATHERINE FRASER (1908-1962), nurse, was born on 19 September 1908 at Mosman, Sydney, second daughter of English-born Harold Weymouth Mullens, Anglican clergyman, and his wife Adeline Maud, née Fraser, who came from New Zealand. Educated at Holmer girls' school, Parramatta, and Woodcourt College, Marrickville, Phyllis trained at Prince Henry Hospital, Little Bay, and was registered by the Australasian Trained Nurses' Association on 1 June 1932. She remained at Prince Henry as a staff nurse until becoming matron at Bexhill Private Hospital, Maroubra. In 1939 she joined the Sydney District Nursing Association.

Mobilized on 9 October 1940 in the Australian Army Nursing Service, Mullens was posted to Darwin in the following month. From December 1941 she worked at the 113th Australian General Hospital, Concord, Sydney. Appointed to the Australian Imperial Force in September 1942 as a sister (captain 1943), she joined the hospital ship, *Wanganella*, and tended wounded soldiers from the Middle East and South-West Pacific Area. In 1945 her duties included the care of prisoners of war who were being repatriated in the ship. Attached to the British Commonwealth Occupation Force, she served (from March 1946) in Japan, at Kure and in Tokyo. She returned to Sydney in September 1947, transferred to the Reserve of Officers and spent two years farming with her brother-in-law at Mount Tootie, near Bilpin.

Miss Mullens was a skilled nurse with extensive experience across a wide range of illness, disease and injuries. She chose to devote her life to the sick poor of Sydney and rejoined the S.D.N.A. in September 1950. Within three months she was made deputy-matron, with a staff of twenty-three nurses. A brisk, efficient and cheerful woman, round-faced and small in stature, she was appointed acting-matron in November 1954. She proved a capable administrator, coping with the increased demand for home care (that stemmed from the compulsory tuberculosis X-ray programme), engaging more nurses, and encouraging the establishment of a central sterilizing depot to increase efficiency. In October 1955 she became matron. Under her direction, care of the aged and chronically ill increased, and district nurses were regularly accompanied by student nurses and almoners. Following a stroke, she underwent surgery in January 1957, but was back at work by the end of April. She was always mindful of her patients' welfare, and provided hospital-type beds and tripod walking-sticks for their use.

In 1957 the rehabilitative side of district nursing was commended by social workers from Lidcombe State Hospital and Home. By 1961 Mullens was in charge of forty-seven nurses ministering in thirty-six districts. That year her lecture on 'Domiciliary Care' was published, and overseas delegates from the International Council of Nurses visited the Glebe headquarters of the S.D.N.A. Mullens played an important role in retaining the original stonework and iron railing that contribute to the historic and heritage value of the Glebe property. A member of the Nurses' Club, she enjoyed reading and gardening.

Phyllis Mullens died of subarachnoid haemorrhage on 18 September 1962 at Royal North Shore Hospital and was buried in the cemetery of St Stephen's Anglican Church, Kurrajong, where her father had once been rector.

Lamp, Jan 1961; *Daily Mirror* (Syd), 25 June 1962; Syd District Nursing Assn, Annual Report, 1938-41, 1950-62, Monthly Board Meeting Minutes, 1950-62 *and* Matron's Monthly Report Book, 1955-62; War diary, Hospital Ship *Wanganella* (AWM); information from Mrs M. Cordia, Artarmon, Mr B. Hambly, Botany, and Mrs B. McLeod, Dee Why, Syd.   VILMA PAGE

MULLEY, DANIEL STERN (1891-1964), surveyor-general, was born on 19 February 1891 at Kogarah, Sydney, fourth child of English-born parents Daniel Mulley, gardener, and his wife Anna Louisa, née Stocks. Educated at Kogarah Superior Public School, young Dan entered the Department of Lands on 7 April 1908. After serving as a cadet draughtsman, he was articled in 1911 as field-assistant to L. S. Ferrier and R. A. Holmes. He was gazetted as a licensed surveyor on 21 October 1914. On 20 March 1916 Mulley enlisted in the Australian Imperial Force. Commissioned in September, he sailed for England two months later. He served with the 1st Pioneer Battalion on the Western Front from April 1917 and was mentioned in dispatches. Following the Armistice, he was promoted temporary captain and posted as an instructor, A.I.F. Survey School, Southampton. He shared with his old mentor Ferrier the teaching of computations, astronomy and geodesy. From a class of seventy-five young surveyors emerged one Commonwealth, four State and one Malay States surveyors-general.

Mulley's A.I.F. appointment terminated in Sydney on 27 September 1919. At St George's Anglican Church, Hurstville, on 17 December that year he married Winifred Welch. Returning to the Department of Lands, he was in turn staff surveyor (1919-26) at Orange and senior surveyor (1926-41) at Grafton. With the outbreak of war in the Pacific, he led the civilian organization which carried out mapping of the coastal strip for defence purposes under the emergency mapping programme, a task necessitating close liaison with H. P. G. Clews and A. M. Allen [qq.v.13]. While employed as district surveyor (1942-46) at Goulburn, Mulley mapped the snow belt and enjoyed 'long days on horseback inspecting the vast area in his charge'.

Succeeding Allen as surveyor-general and chief mining surveyor on 14 August 1946, Mulley also became director of mapping in 1951. The Survey Co-ordination Act (1949) and the survey co-ordination branch stemmed from his initiatives, as did the Central Mapping Authority of New South Wales. He reorganized the mapping branch and installed modern equipment with the latest techniques in photogrammetry and geodetic surveying. In 1948 he had sent John Middleton abroad to acquire familiarity with best international practice. Despite the Public Service Board's opposition to Mulley, his achievements were long lasting. He was an able president of the Board of Surveyors, a member of the National Mapping Council of Australia and the Commonwealth Electoral Redistribution Committee for New South Wales, chairman of the National Parks Committee and deputy-chairman of the Kosciusko State Park Trust. A tall, solid man, he was genial and energetic, noted for his integrity, ability and willingness to assist fellow-surveyors. He particularly fostered the careers of 'digger' surveyors.

In May 1953 Mulley was obliged to retire on grounds of ill health. He later surveyed Lord Howe Island for titles allocation. Bowls was his main recreation, and he remained interested in the activities of the State division of the Institution of Surveyors. Survived by his wife and two daughters, he died on 10 July 1964 at his Killara home and was cremated.

Aust Women's Weekly, 16 Mar 1946, p 9, 14 Sept 1946, p 10; *Aust Surveyor*, Mar 1955, p 182, Sept 1964, p 229; *SMH*, 2 Oct 1953; information from Messrs C. C. Bradley, Armidale, NSW, and L. N. Fletcher, Gordon, Syd.   JOHN ATCHISON

MUMARING; *see* BINDI, DAISY

MUNGOMERY, REGINALD WILLIAM (1901-1972), entomologist, was born on 11 March 1901 at Childers, Queensland, fourth child of Queensland-born parents John Mungomery, blacksmith, and his wife Julia, née Sale. Reg developed a love of science, especially biology, at Childers State School (dux 1915). He continued to excel at Maryborough Grammar School (Melville gold medallist 1917) and at the Charters Towers School of Mines where he was awarded Browne memorial medals and gained a diploma in metallurgical engineering, chemistry and mining surveying (1920).

Lack of prospects in his field obliged Mungomery to work on the family farm. He found a job with the Commonwealth Prickly Pear Board at Rockhampton about 1923 and with Mount Isa Proprietary Silver-Lead Ltd in 1924. Next year he joined the entomology division of the Queensland Bureau of Sugar Experiment Stations and was posted to Meringa, near Cairns. He took charge of a new laboratory at Bundaberg in 1926. At Christ Church, Bundaberg, on 10 December 1930 he married with Anglican rites Martha

Nicolson Clement, a music teacher. Again based at Meringa from the mid-1930s, he moved to Brisbane in 1945 as officer-in-charge of the division of entomology and pathology. In 1964 he was promoted assistant-director of the B.S.E.S.

Although he had no formal tertiary training in biological sciences, Mungomery made a major contribution to research into controlling pests and diseases of sugar-cane. Particularly notable were his studies of *Perkinsiella saccharicida*: in 1933 he and Arthur Bell proved that this leaf-hopper was the vector which transmitted Fiji disease. Before the advent of chlorinated hydrocarbon insecticides, grubs and other soil-inhabiting insects were fumigated with carbon disulphide. Mungomery explored ways of mechanizing and improving the process. In 1945 he began laboratory- and field-experiments with benzene hexachloride; the preparation proved to be successful and cheap, but it was withdrawn for environmental reasons in the 1980s.

Despite his success with insecticides, Mungomery preferred taking biological measures to control pests. In 1929 he had recommended that research be undertaken on the use of parasitic fungi to kill cane-grubs, but detailed work was not initiated until the 1970s. He was sent to Hawaii in 1935 to collect specimens of the giant American toad, *Bufo marinus*, for breeding and testing in Queensland as a predator of insect pests in sugar-cane fields. The toad proved less useful than had been hoped, and itself became a pest. Following his transfer to Brisbane, Mungomery oversaw the operations of the regional Cane Pest and Disease Control boards.

Mungomery was a perfectionist who loved his work. He expected his staff and associates to have similar standards, and was always willing to help and encourage junior colleagues. As a child he had stuttered; he overcame the affliction by sheer determination, but in later life lapsed into a slight stammer when engaged in vigorous debate. A runner, high-jumper, footballer and cricketer in his youth, he later enjoyed gardening, photography and playing the violin. He retired in 1968. Survived by his wife and two daughters, he died on 25 March 1972 in Brisbane and was cremated.

Annual Report of Bureau of Sugar Experiment Stations, *PP* (Qld), 1926, 1927, 1929, 1930, 1935, 1936, 1944-45, 1946, 1952; Mungomery papers (Bureau of Sugar Experiment Stations L, Brisb); information from Mrs J. Weil, Townsville, Qld; personal knowledge.   K. C. LEVERINGTON

MUNRO, CRAWFORD HUGH (1904-1976), civil engineer and university professor, was born on 23 March 1904 at Toowoomba, Queensland, second child of Toowoomba-born parents Robert Henry Munro, commission agent, and his wife Grace Agnes, née Nelson. Crawford attended Sydney Technical High School and studied civil engineering at the University of Sydney (B.E., 1926). Joining the Metropolitan Water, Sewerage and Drainage Board in 1926, he worked as resident engineer and research officer. At Hawthorn, Melbourne, on 26 July 1937 he married with Presbyterian forms Emily Grace Metcalf, a 38-year-old kindergarten teacher.

In 1936 Munro was appointed lecturer-in-charge, department of mechanical and civil engineering, Sydney Technical College. Attached (1941-45) to the Commonwealth Department of Munitions as State supervising engineer, he oversaw the design and production of armoured fighting vehicles and small ships. He was commissioned major, Royal Engineers, in June 1945 and was stationed with the British Army in Burma. Returning to S.T.C. in the following year, he became head of the department of civil engineering and assistant-director of technical education. He contributed to the establishment (1949) of the New South Wales University of Technology (University of New South Wales). There he was promoted to associate-professor in 1951 and to the chair of civil engineering in 1954.

Surrounded by enthusiastic staff and students, Munro was determined to achieve an international reputation for his department. He planned a specially outfitted building at the university's new Kensington site, as well as a water research laboratory at Manly Vale. Convinced that 'research must go hand in hand with teaching', he introduced new courses, encouraged practising engineers to return for further education and helped undergraduates to engage in research. His most enduring contribution was to hydrology. Water was his passion: he saw it as 'the lifeline upon which Australia must depend . . . for survival as a white nation'. He helped to establish (1955) the Water Research Foundation of Australia to raise funds for water engineering, participated in State and national committees, and served as a consultant on numerous projects. Pleading primary industry's need for water, he deplored the large quantities wasted on suburban domestic gardens.

Munro's dominating nature, magnified by an imposing physique and loud voice, meant that some found him overbearing, but his manner was down-to-earth, with larrikin touches. He relished a good argument, enjoyed social occasions and could tell an entertaining story. A number of people remembered him as the professor who, on hot days, wore 'the Bond's singlet of a construction worker'.

A council-member (1962-74) of the Institution of Engineers, Australia, Munro was a fellow of the Royal Society of Arts, London, and the Royal Society of Health. He was also a member of the Art Gallery Society of New South Wales, and of the Imperial Service and Hunters Hill Tennis clubs. After he retired in 1969, he continued to undertake consultancies and published a textbook, *Australian Water Resources and their Development* (1974). Survived by his wife and three daughters, he died on 21 September 1976 at his Hunters Hill home and was cremated. The I.E.A. inaugurated the C. H. Munro memorial oration. At the U.N.S.W. the centre for civil and environmental engineering was named (1992) after him.

D. P. Mellor, *The Role of Science and Industry* (Canb, 1958); Inst of Engineers, Aust, *Hydrology Symposium*, 1977; Inst of Engineers, Aust (Civil Engineering), *Trans*, CE26, 1984, p 210; Univ NSW, *University News*, 1969, p 4; E. B. and P. MacDonald, Reminiscences of C. H. Munro, *and* R. H. Myers, Memorial address, 15 Oct 1976, BRF-Munro, *and* Munro, C. H., Personnel file CN968/7 (UNSW Archives).   JULIA HORNE

MUNTZ, JEAN (JANE) EILEEN (1903-1969), nurse, was born on 14 March 1903 at Alexandra, Victoria, youngest of seven children of Victorian-born parents William Jamison Muntz, civil engineer, and his wife Alice Elizabeth, née Irvine. The family moved to Kew where William was town (later city) surveyor in 1912-24. Jean attended Ruyton Girls' School from June 1917. After passing four subjects at the Intermediate certificate examinations, she left in December 1919, apparently intending to enter a business college. Little trace remains of her activities over the next decade.

She qualified at the Royal Melbourne Hospital in 1934 and held various nursing positions. To her disappointment, hypertension prevented her from joining the Australian Army Nursing Service during World War II. Muntz gained an infant welfare certificate in 1938, joined the Victorian maternal and child hygiene branch of the Victorian Department of Health in 1942, and became an infant welfare inspector in 1943. The Victorian government seconded her in 1946 to establish a State bureau to recruit and place nurses. Two years later Jane, as she called herself in adult life, was awarded a British Council bursary to study nursing trends abroad.

With a growing reputation in her field, Muntz was the first nursing adviser (1951-68) to the Victorian minister of health. In 'Nursing —Professional Responsibility', her 1954 Marian Barrett memorial lecture, she expressed some of her ethical views. She served on the Nurses Board (1953-58) and its successor, the Victorian Nursing Council (1958-68). The council—which formulated policy, set educational standards and controlled the registration of nurses—was established under the *Nurses Act* (1956), legislation she had done much to shape and which, according to Vance Dickie, minister of health, was perhaps her 'greatest monument'. In 1957 she was appointed O.B.E. She sat on the minister's committee of inquiry into nursing, set up in 1966, but died before its work was completed.

Miss Muntz was a co-founder and fellow (1950) of the College of Nursing, Australia, a council-member (1946-67) and president (1953-58) of the Royal Victorian College of Nursing, and a council-member (from 1950) and president (1961-66) of the Royal Australian Nursing Federation. She was also a foundation member and vice-president of the War Nurses Memorial Centre (from 1953 the Nurses Memorial Centre) and a member of the national Florence Nightingale Committee of Australia. Seeing herself as a citizen of the world, she served on both the grand council and board of directors of the International Council of Nurses, and attended several of its congresses: in 1965 she was a keynote speaker at Frankfurt, Germany.

Well groomed and dignified, Muntz was short, with a neat figure, even features, brown hair, direct blue eyes and a slightly florid complexion. For more than twenty years she shared a flat in East Melbourne with her close friend Jill Morey. Two of her many hobbies were reflected in presents from colleagues on her retirement—a tumbler for polishing semi-precious stones and binoculars for bird-watching. She died of an intracerebral haemorrhage on 30 November 1969 in South Melbourne and was cremated with Anglican rites.

M. K. Minchin, *Revolutions and Rosewater* (Melb, c1977); J. and B. Bessant, *The Growth of a Profession* (Melb, 1991); *UNA*, Nov 1954, p 336, June 1957, p 162, July 1965, p 218, June 1968, p 163, Sept 1970, p 21; information from Miss M. Menzies, Nunawading, Miss M. E. Patten, Ashburton, and Mrs J. Dean, Melb.   JAN BASSETT*

MUNZ, HIRSCH (1905-1979), scientist, businessman and man of letters, was born on 21 April 1905 at Krynki, Poland, then part of the Russian empire, son of Moses Munz, businessman, and his wife Mirjam, née Iwenitzki. Hirsch was educated at a Hebrew high school and a Jewish seminary at Lemberg (Lvov), Austria (Russia), before working as a schoolteacher. Assisted by his cousin Alfred Lipshut, he emigrated to Australia, arriving in Melbourne on 15 December 1927.

While working as a commercial traveller for the Benjamin Gross knitting mills, Munz studied woolsorting at the Working Men's

College and commerce at the University of Melbourne. He then gained first-hand experience as a jackeroo on Merungle station, New South Wales, and as a woolsorter for the Australian Mercantile, Land & Finance Co. From 1931 to 1935 he was employed as a research officer with the Council for Scientific and Industrial Research in Adelaide, investigating the microscopic structure of wool fibre. He was naturalized in February 1933. After moving to Sydney in 1936, he joined (Sir) Ian Clunies Ross's [q.v.13] team at the F. D. McMaster [q.v.10] Animal Health Laboratory and attended classes in wool technology at Sydney Technical College.

Munz was a gifted linguist, with a passion for literature. He lectured in Hebrew and tutored in contemporary European literature at the Workers' Educational Association, Adelaide, and taught university extension classes in Sydney and Melbourne. In the mid-1930s he was foreign editor of the literary quarterly, *Manuscripts*, to which he contributed articles on French literature, Polish Romanticism and Post-Revolutionary writing in Russia. His work also appeared intermittently in the Melbourne *Age*, the *Sydney Morning Herald* and the *Bulletin*.

Based at the University of Melbourne from 1940 to 1942, Munz continued to research the properties of wool. On 13 August 1942 he was mobilized as sub lieutenant (later lieutenant), Royal Australian Naval Volunteer Reserve. He served in Brisbane with the Allied Intelligence Bureau. Proficient in German and Japanese, he interrogated suspected war criminals in the Netherlands East Indies and Singapore. His appointment terminated in April 1946. At the Synagogue, South Yarra, on 14 December 1943 he had married Estra Rosenblatt, a 27-year-old physiotherapist. He established an exporting firm (H. Muntz Wool Trade Co.) when World War II ended, published *The Australian Wool Industry* (Sydney, 1950) and devised the 'Munz Scale', a simple means of correlating international descriptions of wool fibres.

Munz was prominently involved in Jewish cultural circles, notably in the Yiddishist Kadimah in Melbourne and the *Poale Zion* (Labour Zionist) movement, and as co-founder of the Jewish Council to Combat Fascism and Anti-Semitism. He had made a lasting impact on Australian-Jewish historiography with his pioneering monograph, *Jews in South Australia* (Adelaide, 1936). A founding committee-member (1938) of the Australian Jewish Historical Society, Sydney, he co-edited the *Second Australian Jewish Almanac* (Melbourne, 1942) and edited the Yiddish-language supplement of the *Australian Jewish News* in the 1950s.

After suffering a stroke in 1965, Munz retired from business. Survived by his wife and son, he died on 22 April 1979 at St Kilda and was buried in the Chevra Kadisha cemetery, Springvale.

S. D. Rutland, *Edge of the Diaspora* (Syd, 1988); H. L. Rubinstein, *The Jews in Australia*, 1 (Melb, 1991); Aust Jewish Hist Soc, *J and Procs*, 8, 1979, p 475; *Aust Jewish News*, 1 June 1962, 27 Apr 1979; ASIO file, A6119/79, item 1304 (AA, Canb); naturalization files, A1/1, item 1933/792 (AA, Canb); B741/3, item V/5127 (AA, Melb); information from Mr M. Munz, Bondi, Syd.

MALCOLM J. TURNBULL

MURAKAMI, YASUKICHI (1880-1944), Japanese storekeeper, was born on 19 December 1880 at Tanami, Wakayama prefecture, Japan, second son of Jòubei Murakami and his wife Yasu. At the age of 16 Yasukichi joined the flow of Wakayama younger sons to the Australian pearling towns, arriving at Cossack, Western Australia, aboard the *Saladin* in August 1897. Some three thousand of his countrymen were then in Australia. He worked with a carter, delivering water, but soon secured permanent employment with Takazò Nishioka, a Japanese storekeeper, with whom he moved to Broome in 1900.

On Nishioka's death in 1901, the enterprise passed to his widow Eki, née Yamaguchi, whom Murakami married on 11 May 1906 at the district registry office, Broome. She was fifteen years older than he and they remained childless. Under their direction, business expanded. They operated as importers, wholesalers and retailers; the store also served as a photographer's studio and a savings bank for Japanese residents and pearling crews. Murakami became one of the leaders of his community. When, during the annual lay-up in December 1907, violence broke out between Japanese and Malay crewmen, he helped to restore peace between the two groups. From about 1911 he was in financial difficulties. A local slump in 1915 led many of the divers and crewmen to withdraw their deposits and he was forced to close the business. The pearler A. C. Gregory then employed him to manage the Dampier Hotel in return for a half-share of the profits.

In April 1918 Murakami was declared bankrupt. His wife had left him two months earlier, having first collected for herself book debts amounting to some £500. She died in Japan in December. At the district registry office, Broome, on 3 February 1920 he married (Theresa) Shigeno Murata (d.1981); she was aged 23, the daughter of Japanese parents and Australian born. It was generally believed that Gregory had received financial assistance from Murakami to enter the pearling industry and that he secured the best of the Japanese divers and crews through Murakami's good offices. In 1921 he entered into a joint venture with Murakami to produce cultured pearls.

Alarmed that the price of natural pearls would fall, the West Australian Pearlers' Association persuaded the State government to prohibit the scheme.

At considerable cost, Murakami designed and patented (1926) a diving suit. Less buoyant and lighter than the conventional type, it afforded the diver greater mobility. It was not, however, a commercial success. In 1936 Gregory helped Murakami and his family to move to Darwin where he established a successful business as a photographer. On 30 August 1939 he applied to be naturalized. His application was rejected on the ground that 'it is the established policy of the Government not to naturalize Asiatics or other coloured persons'.

When Japan entered World War II in December 1941, Murakami and his family—with the rest of the Japanese community—were interned. He died of 'chronic myocarditis' on 26 June 1944 at Tatura internment camp, Victoria, and was buried with Catholic rites in the local cemetery. His wife, and their six sons and three daughters survived him. Murakami's remains were later reinterred in the Japanese cemetery, Cowra, New South Wales.

M. A. Bain, *Full Fathom Five* (Perth, 1982); D. Carment et al, *Northern Territory Dictionary of Biography*, 1 (Darwin, 1990); Aust Patents and Patents Application records, no 1525/26 (Patents Office, Canb); A1, item 1925/13328 *and* A659, item 39/1/12989 (AA, Canb); WA Bankruptcy file, WAS 165, consignment 3560, item 1918/10 (WAA).

D. C. S. SISSONS

MURPHY, SIR ALEXANDER PATERSON (1892-1976), physician and cardiologist, was born on 25 October 1892 at Teneriffe, Brisbane, only child of George Sylvester Murphy, a London-born accountant, and his Queensland-born wife Jessie Watson, née Raff. Alex attended Bowen House Preparatory and Brisbane Grammar schools, and was a champion rifle-shooter and long-distance runner. He entered St Andrew's College, University of Sydney (M.B., Ch.M., 1916; M.D., 1947), and spent a year as a junior resident medical officer at Royal Prince Alfred Hospital.

On 1 March 1917 Murphy was appointed captain, Australian Army Medical Corps, Australian Imperial Force. One year later he joined the 1st Field Ambulance on the Western Front. From 23 to 26 August 1918, while attached to the 12th Battalion at Péronne, France, he operated under fire, treating wounded Australian and enemy soldiers; although he was hit in the face by shell fragments, he remained at his post for a further twenty-four hours and was awarded the Military Cross.

When his A.I.F. appointment terminated in Sydney on 19 June 1919, he resumed his residency at R.P.A.H.

Returning to Brisbane, Murphy began general practice in 1920 and became a visiting physician at Brisbane General Hospital. On 8 October 1921 at St Luke's Anglican Church, Toowoomba, he married Esmé Park Hobson; their only son, one of four children, suffered from Down's syndrome and died at the age of 21. In 1928 Murphy set up as a specialist physician at Ballow [q.v.1] Chambers, Wickham Terrace, where he continued to have rooms until his death. At Brisbane General Hospital he was appointed a senior visiting physician in 1938 and cardiologist in 1953.

As a lieutenant colonel in the A.A.M.C. Reserve, Murphy worked as a consultant physician at the 112th Military Hospital, Greenslopes, during World War II. After lecturing (from 1937) in the University of Queensland's medical school, he was foundation professor of medicine in 1946-50. In 1954 he was knighted. He was visiting consultant in cardiology and medicine at the South Brisbane (Princess Alexandra) Hospital from 1957, and continued to teach until he retired from his hospital appointments in 1962.

A foundation member (1938) and president (1952-54) of the Royal Australasian College of Physicians, Murphy was also president (1933) of the Queensland branch of the British Medical Association and vice-president (1969) of the Australian Medical Association (Queensland branch). The Royal College of Physicians, London, elected him a fellow in 1954, as did the A.M.A. in 1964; the University of Tasmania awarded him an honorary D.Sc. (1958) and the University of Queensland conferred on him an honorary M.D. (1967). He served on the Commonwealth government's Pharmaceutical Benefits Advisory Committee and was patron (1967-76) of the Australian Postgraduate Federation in Medicine.

Murphy delivered the presidential address at the seventh session of the Australasian Medical Congress in 1950 and the Bancroft [q.v.3] oration in 1954. A director of several companies, including the Brisbane Gas Co. Ltd (1942-71), he belonged to the Queensland, United Service (Brisbane), Union (Sydney) and Royal Queensland Golf clubs. Sir Alexander died on 1 October 1976 at his Hamilton home and was cremated; his wife and three daughters survived him. As a clinician, he was superb; as a teacher, he had a dry and sometimes acerbic wit, and examined his students firmly and fairly.

Lives of the Fellows of the Royal College of Physicians of London (Lond, 1984); G. L. McDonald (ed), *Roll of the Royal Australasian College of Physicians*, 2, 1976-1990 (Syd, 1994); information from Dr R. Goodwin, Rochedale, Dr B. Hirschfeld,

Wickham Terrace, Dr O. W. Powell, Yeronga, and Mrs L. Worthington-Wilmer, Hendra, Brisb.

G. R. C. McLEOD

MURPHY, ISLA VICTORIA (1913-1967), lawyer and army officer, was born on 17 July 1913 at St Kilda, Melbourne, eldest of ten children of Victorian-born parents Thomas Murphy, medical practitioner, and his wife Victoria Sarah, née Noonan. Educated at the Presentation convent school, Windsor, where she was dux, and at the University of Melbourne (B.A. Hons, 1933; LL.B., 1934; M.A., 1935), Isla was admitted to the Bar on 1 May 1936. She practised with her uncle's firm, Luke Murphy & Co., and was hailed as 'the best man in the office'. During these years she also served on the Victorian committee of the St Joan's Social and Political Alliance, an international organization committed to an active role in society for lay Catholic women. Eager to contribute to the war effort, she joined the Australian Women's Army Service on 21 November 1941.

One of the twenty-nine women chosen by the controller Sybil Irving [q.v.14] to form the nucleus of the service, Murphy attended the first A.W.A.S. officers' course, held at Yarra Junction. With the rank of captain (January 1942), she was second-in-command to Major M. K. Deasey [q.v.13] at A.W.A.S. headquarters, Southern Command, Melbourne. Interviewing and enlisting recruits was one of her main responsibilities. On 1 March 1943 she was promoted major and appointed deputy assistant adjutant-general (women's services) at Land Headquarters. There she played a key role in drafting A.W.A.S. regulations. In September 1944 she replaced Kathleen Best [q.v.13] as assistant adjutant-general (women's services) and was made temporary lieutenant colonel (substantive in September 1945). Murphy was responsible 'for advice and staff duties in all matters of policy in the administration of the Women's Services'; her subordinates included officers from the Australian Army Nursing Service and the Australian Army Medical Women's Service.

As a member of officer pre-selection boards, Murphy frequently travelled interstate. In January 1946 she accompanied Colonel Irving on a tour to inspect A.W.A.S. personnel serving at First Army headquarters, Lae, New Guinea. Murphy assisted with the rehabilitation of servicewomen before transferring to the Reserve of Officers on 7 September 1946. With the intention of resuming her legal career, she attended a refresher course at the University of Melbourne, where she met Horace Arthur Wimpole, a 38-year-old solicitor; he had served with the 8th Division, Australian Imperial Force, and been a prisoner of war. They were married on 16 September 1947 at St Mary's Catholic Church, East St Kilda. An intellectually-gifted, generous, compassionate and dedicated woman, Isla devoted most of her time to caring for her husband (whose health had been impaired by his prisoner-of-war experience) and raising their two children.

In 1957-60 Mrs Wimpole was vice-president of the Lyceum Club. As acting-president in 1959, she supervised the club's move from Flinders Lane to Ridgway Place, off Collins Street. An increase in the number of members in the late 1940s had necessitated changes to the club's articles of association and she helped to revise the constitution. Survived by her husband, daughter and son, she died of cancer on 4 January 1967 at Toorak and was buried in St Kilda cemetery.

J. M. Gillison, *A History of the Lyceum Club* (Melb, 1975); L. Ollif, *Women in Khaki* (Syd, 1981), and *Colonel Best and her Soldiers* (Syd, 1985); P. Adam-Smith, *Australian Women at War* (Melb, 1984); S. Kennedy, *Faith and Feminism* (Syd, 1985); D. Martin (ed), *Backing Up the Boys* (Bandiana, Vic, 1988); A. Howard, *You'll be Sorry!* (Syd, 1990); AWM 54, item 88/1/1, pt 9 (AWM); information from Mr D. Wimpole, Hawthorn, Melb.

MAREE REID

MURPHY, JAMES FRANCIS (1893-1949), public servant, was born on 12 March 1893 at North Carlton, Melbourne, second son of Irish-born parents Peter Murphy, police constable (later sergeant), and his wife Winifred Mary, née Sheane. Educated at Christian Brothers' colleges in South and East Melbourne, Frank joined the Commonwealth Public Service in 1910 and was appointed to the Department of External Affairs. He studied commerce part time at the University of Melbourne. On 25 February 1922 at the Church of Our Lady of Victories, Camberwell, he married with Catholic rites Beatrice Emily McClounan, a 31-year-old typist.

Seconded to the staff of the Development and Migration Commission in 1927, Murphy transferred to the Prime Minister's Department in 1930. He served as secretary of the Australian delegation to the Imperial Economic Conference, held in Ottawa in 1932, and that year was made assistant-secretary, Department of Commerce (Commerce and Agriculture from 1942). Aged only 41, he took over as departmental secretary on 17 December 1934 and was to occupy that position until November 1945. He moved to Canberra in 1936 with the department's central administration. In the following year he was appointed C.M.G.

From 1939 Murphy was a member of numerous government bodies established to

445

administer wartime controls. Chairman of the Australian Hides and Leather Industries Board and of the Australian Potato Committee, he was vice-chairman of the Shipping Control and the Wheat Industry Stabilization boards. In February 1943 he became deputy-chairman of the Rural Reconstruction Commission. After Japan entered (1941) World War II, the Australian armed forces increased in size and large numbers of American servicemen arrived in Australia. Food was officially declared a munition of war. The Federal government saw the need for a central authority to regulate the growth, production, manufacture, processing, distribution, disposal and use of food, foodstuffs, fertilizers and fodder. In May 1943 the office of controller-general of food was established in Melbourne. Murphy held the post until two months after hostilities ended.

In November 1945 Murphy was appointed chairman of the Australian Wool Realization Commission, Commonwealth wool adviser, and economic adviser to the minister for commerce and agriculture. The Wool Realization Commission was the Australian participant in United Kingdom-Dominion Wool Disposals Ltd (of which he was a director), a body which was established jointly by the British, Australian, New Zealand and South African governments to manage the disposal of stocks accumulated during the war and to market future clips. The commission instituted a reserve-price scheme for wool and quickly reduced the Australian portion (almost seven million bales in July 1945) of the stockpile.

Suffering from hypertension, Murphy died of a cerebral haemorrhage on 18 January 1949 at his Balwyn home and was buried in Melbourne general cemetery; his wife, two sons and two daughters survived him. A tall, handsome, bespectacled man with a hearty laugh, a booming voice and an imposing presence, he was forthright and dominating in manner. His colleagues on the commission praised his 'conspicuous ability' and 'masterly understanding', and felt the loss of 'an able Chairman, a lovable personality and a wise leader'.

S. J. Butlin, *War Economy 1939-42* (Canb, 1955); D. P. Mellor, *The Role of Science and Industry* (Canb, 1958); Rural Reconstruction Com, *Report*, Jan 1944-Aug 1946; *Herald* (Melb), 9 Feb 1933, 10 Feb 1936, 25 May 1943, 19, 20 Jan 1949; *Advocate* (Melb), 27 Jan 1949; United Kingdom—Dominion Wool Disposals Ltd records (PRO, mf copy, NL); family information.   ROBERT S. SWIFT

MURPHY, RICHARD JAMES FRANCIS (1875-1957), Jesuit priest, was born on 24 April 1875 at Kingstown, Dublin, one of ten children of Richard James Murphy, merchant,

and his wife Mary Josephine, née Burden. Dick attended Clongowes Wood College and entered the Society of Jesus at Tullamore at the age of 17. He completed philosophy studies at Maison St Louis, Jersey, Channel Islands, and Stonyhurst College, England, in 1898. Arriving in Sydney in September, he taught at St Ignatius' College, Riverview, and from 1901 at St Patrick's College, Melbourne, where he also organized the work of the Professional Men's Sodality of Our Lady. In 1904 he returned to Dublin. After studying theology at Milltown Park, he was ordained priest on 26 July 1908.

In Sydney again, Murphy taught (1910-11 and 1915-16) at St Aloysius' College. An outstanding tennis player, he was responsible for forming the Catholic Lawn Tennis Association of New South Wales. In 1911 he was transferred to Loyola, Greenwich, to direct retreats for laymen. He developed a strong commitment to medico-moral issues and lectured to nurses at St Vincent's Hospital, Darlinghurst. In 1912 he was a founder of the Catholic Federation of New South Wales. Launched into parochial duties in 1916 as parish priest (superior) at Toowong, Brisbane, he was appointed to Richmond, Melbourne, in 1919. He spent four months in hospital with pneumonia and serious heart problems, but unexpectedly recovered.

Back in Sydney, Murphy was bursar (1920-21) at Riverview for the college and the entire Sydney Mission before returning to pastoral duties at North Sydney (1921-22) and Lavender Bay (1922-24). He lectured on medical ethics to students at the University of Sydney. His book, *The Catholic Nurse* (Milwaukee, 1923), led him to found the Catholic Nurses' Guild of New South Wales. While superior (1924-33) at Toowong, he supervised the construction of St Ignatius' Church. Between 1933 and 1953 he was based in the parish of North Sydney. With Dr H. M. Moran [q.v.10], he inaugurated the Catholic Medical Guild of St Luke in 1933; he edited its *Transactions*, in which he published (1943) two articles, 'Catholic Hospitals of Australia' and 'The History of Nursing in Australia'. A council-member of the Newman Association of Catholic Graduates, Murphy founded the Campion Society in Melbourne in 1934 and introduced it to Sydney, where its autonomy was initially suppressed because Archbishop Kelly [q.v.9] 'liked to keep a tight rein on his lay societies'. Murphy established the Catholic Chemists Guild of St Francis Xavier. He also set up the Teachers' Guild of New South Wales for the religious education of Catholic children in state schools.

Although described as a 'diffident' superior, Fr Dick was an enthusiastic, zealous and energetic man who saw the Catholic laity as 'the draught horses of the Church'. He, Dr

Sylvester Minogue (a psychiatrist) and others founded Alcoholics Anonymous in Australia in July 1945. Minogue (overlooking Fr Dunlea [q.v.14]) noted that with 'the exception of Father Murphy . . . no other clergyman takes any active interest', and observed that he was 'the only one of us with any practical commonsense'. Lillian Roth, the actress, acknowledged the help she had received from Murphy.

In 1955 Murphy retired to Canisius' College, Pymble. He died on 13 November 1957 in Lewisham Hospital and was buried in Gore Hill cemetery.

L. Roth, *I'll Cry Tomorrow* (Lond, 1955); D. Coleman, *Priest of the Highway* (Syd, 1973); C. Jory, *The Campion Society and Catholic Social Militancy in Australia 1929-1939* (Syd, 1986); St Aloysius' College (Syd), *The Aloysian*, 1957, p 24; St Ignatius' College, Riverview (Syd), *Our Alma Mater*, 1958, p 184; *Catholic Weekly* (Syd), 18 Sept 1952, 21 Nov 1957; AA Assn papers (Alcoholics Anonymous Archives, Croydon, Syd); Fr R. J. Murphy, SJ, papers (Society of Jesus Archives, Hawthorn, Melb).

JUDITH NOLAN

MURPHY, ROBERT KENNETH (1887-1972), chemical engineer, was born on 29 July 1887 at Newark, New Jersey, United States of America, one of five children of William Augustus Murphy, paper-mill proprietor, and his wife Georgia, née Hunt. At the age of 7 Robert was sent to a school near Niagara Falls, Ontario, Canada. His later schooling at Ridley College, St Catharines, was interrupted by acute peritonitis and long spells in hospital. After attending Horace Mann School, New York, he studied chemical engineering at Columbia University (Chem.E., 1910). To build up his strength, Murphy spent much of his spare time playing sport: he was stroke of the university VIII, captain of the ice-hockey team and vice-captain of the football team. In 1910 he entered Grossherzogliche Technische Hochschule zu Darmstadt (Dr.Ing., 1913), Germany. Aided by his friend George Merck, he visited many of that country's chemical plants. Late in 1912 he was invited to join the staff of Columbia University.

At Columbia Murphy had met Dr Percival Cole [q.v.8], vice-principal of Teachers' College, Sydney. He accepted Cole's invitation to investigate the possibilities of establishing professional training in industrial chemistry and chemical engineering in Australia, and reached Sydney on 30 September 1914. Although he found James Nangle [q.v.10], director of technical education, to be a sound administrator, he encountered many obstructions in establishing his courses. On 20 January 1915 he was appointed lecturer-in-charge of chemistry and head of the science depart-

ment at Sydney Technical College for an initial term of five years. At St Andrew's Anglican Cathedral, Sydney, on 30 September that year he married Gladys Ruth Gray (d.1963). They lived at Mosman.

From the beginning, Murphy insisted that entrance standards for his several diploma courses should be the same as at the University of Sydney and that the associateship of S.T.C. should have 'guinea value'. In time the associateship was recognized by the Royal Institute of Chemistry of Great Britain and Ireland as an acceptable qualification for its A.R.I.C. Murphy's appointment was confirmed in 1920, following an inquiry into complaints Nangle had received about the science department and the lecturer-in-charge. Described as 'a young, energetic foreigner', Murphy found himself 'in charge of a department starved of funds and equipment, accustomed to a gentlemanly and undemanding style of supervision, under which the senior teachers had carved out their own little empires'. He was seen as brash, 'with a flair for showmanship and a marked ability to upset his fellow-workers'. On one occasion he attracted his students' attention by throwing sausages (frozen in liquid nitrogen) which exploded when they hit the floor. He never lost his impatience with what he termed Australians' 'lackadaisical approach to life'.

An excellent administrator and lecturer, Murphy attracted many capable scientists to his staff, among them Frank Dwyer [q.v.14] and (Sir) Ronald Nyholm [q.v.]. His students learned how to make chemical and metallurgical products, such as aluminium, carborundum and red ceramic glazes, in demonstration plants which they built themselves. They were also given practical knowledge in other fields—microscopy, metallurgy, photography, economics and marketing.

Murphy was awarded King George V's jubilee medal (1935) and a Carnegie medal and grant (1939). He was a founder (1917), president (1936) and fellow (1945) of the (Royal) Australian Chemical Institute, and a committee-member (1928-52) and president (1934-35) of its New South Wales branch. Naturalized in 1936, he was refused leave in 1941 to join the Australian Military Forces as chemical warfare officer, General Staff, Eastern Command, with the rank of captain, but was a chemical adviser to the army during World War II.

From 1921 Murphy had campaigned for a degree-granting institute of technology. He was appointed principal of S.T.C. in 1950. The New South Wales University of Technology, of which he was a councillor (1948-52), awarded him an honorary D.Sc. in 1957. Following his retirement as principal in December 1951, he lectured in the school of chemical engineering at the N.S.W.U.T. until 1956. He was a founder of the Australian Welding Institute; after many years he retired as its federal and New South Wales secretary in 1960.

Known as 'the Doc', Murphy retained his rich American accent, 'infectious laughter' and charming personality. He belonged to Warringah Bowling Club for fifty years, and regularly met friends and past students at the County Clare Hotel, Broadway. Survived by his son and three daughters, he died on 31 May 1972 at Royal North Shore Hospital and was cremated.

N. Neill, *Technically & Further* (Syd, 1991); Univ NSW, *University News*, Nov 1940, July 1972; *Chemical Engineering in Australia*, June 1990, p 9; *SMH*, 13 Dec 1935, 13 Dec 1944, 5 Jan 1945, 5 Dec 1951; *Sunday Herald*, 11 June 1972; naturalization file A659/1, item 1941/1/3120 (AA, Canb); R. K. Murphy, series 13/9329, item 49/P26/90766 (AA, Syd); Dept of Education (NSW) Archives, Syd, staff file; H. de Berg, R. K. Murphy (taped interview, 20 Aug 1966, NL); information from Mr R. Murphy, Avoca, NSW; personal knowledge.

NEVILLE WHIFFEN

MURRAY, HAROLD JOHN JOSEPH (1898-1968), army officer, planter and businessman, was born on 13 November 1898 at Balmain, Sydney, third son of native-born parents James Francis Murray, a general indent agent, and his wife Rachel Esther, née Gray. Harry worked as an order-man in a timber-yard. He raised his age by two years, enlisted in the Australian Imperial Force on 11 May 1915 and saw action with the 2nd Battalion towards the end of the Gallipoli campaign.

Proceeding with his unit to the Western Front in March 1916, Murray was promoted corporal in the following February. During an assault on 9 April 1917 against German positions at Hermies, France, his platoon commander and sergeant were wounded. Murray took charge and captured a strongly defended trench; for his leadership he was awarded the Distinguished Conduct Medal and immediately made a sergeant. He was commissioned in June 1918 and promoted lieutenant in November. In June 1919 he returned to Australia. His A.I.F. appointment terminated on 10 August, but he continued to serve as an acting area officer until he moved to the Mandated Territory of New Guinea in February 1921. Living in the Kavieng area of New Ireland, he developed copra and coffee plantations, traded in timber, and bottled mineral water. At St Bede's Anglican Church, Drummoyne, Sydney, on 11 March 1930 he married Florence Irene Johnston.

When the Japanese invaded Kavieng on 23 January 1942, Murray and sixteen others escaped by sailing a small boat to Oro Bay, Papua. In August the Inter-Allied Services

Department, a section of the newly formed Allied Intelligence Bureau, recruited him, gave him the rank of lieutenant in the A.I.F., and sent him to Cairns, Queensland, for training. Having established an I.S.D. base in Darwin in December, he remained there as camp adjutant. In March 1943 he transferred to the North Eastern Area Section of the A.I.B. in search of action. First he set up and commanded a training camp at Tabragalba, near Beaudesert, Queensland. Next he led a bold and successful reconnaissance mission to Cape Bun Bun, New Ireland, in November 1943. In the following month he took an American party on a pre-invasion survey of Boang Island; they fended off Japanese attackers with a skilful ambush and withdrew unscathed. Radio-network supervision and further intelligence collecting in the New Ireland area kept Murray busy until World War II ended.

Cool-headed, aggressive and independently minded, Murray was almost the archetype of the 'Islander' Australians whose field leadership placed his section of the A.I.B. at the forefront of intelligence-gathering and guerrilla-warfare organizations. His exploits won him a captaincy (February 1944), the Military Cross (March 1945) and the American Silver Star (June 1945). He transferred to the Reserve of Officers in February 1946 and returned to Lakuramau plantation, near Kavieng. A widower, he married Mary Morrison, a 24-year-old sales manager, on 8 March 1950 at St Canice's Catholic Church, Elizabeth Bay, Sydney. In 1960 he retired to Queensland. Survived by his wife, he died of cancer on 22 October 1968 at Innisfail and was cremated with Anglican rites. He had no children.

M. Murray, *Escape* (Adel, 1965) and *Hunted* (Adel, 1967); E. Feldt, *The Coast Watchers* (Melb, 1975); A. Powell, *War by Stealth* (Melb, 1996), and for bib; AWM 54, item 423/9/39, part 1 (AWM).

ALAN POWELL

MURRAY, HUBERT LEONARD (1886-1963), public servant and colonial administrator, was born on 13 December 1886 at Watsons Bay, Sydney, second surviving child and eldest son of Australian-born parents James Aubrey Gibbes Murray, a draftsman in the surveyor-general's office, and his wife Marian Edith, née Lewis. Sir Terence Murray [q.v.2] was his grandfather. Educated at Fort Street Model School, Leonard joined the Commonwealth Department of Trade and Customs as a clerk in 1905.

His father was (Sir) Hubert Murray's [q.v.10] half-brother, and that relationship was critical in Leonard's career and people's expectations of him. In 1908 Hubert, the new lieutenant-governor of Papua, asked that

Leonard, in whom he had 'implicit confidence', be appointed without advertisement as his assistant private secretary. Leonard arrived in Port Moresby in February 1909. He became private secretary in 1913 and official secretary in 1916. In his many travels (along the coast and on inland patrols) with Hubert, he gained a detailed knowledge of Papua. A champion swimmer (said to have narrowly missed Olympic selection), a member of the Bondi Life Saving Club and a keen sailor, Leonard served as navigator in the government ship, *Elevala*, and as master of the *Merrie England* and the 150-ton *Laurabada*. He wrote *Territory of Papua: Sailing Directions* (Port Moresby, 1923 and 1930). Dignified and 'naturally pleasant', he was good looking, but, at middle height, overshadowed by his uncle Hubert. On 24 February 1915 at St John's Anglican Church, Port Moresby, Leonard married Pauline Anna Schomburgk, daughter of the deputy chief judicial officer C. E. Herbert [q.v.9].

From 1925 Leonard was a member of both the Executive and Legislative councils in Port Moresby. He was appointed C.B.E. in 1936. Hubert, who had turned 70 in 1931, wrote about retiring—if he could be sure Leonard would succeed him. Believing that his benign Papuan policies were at risk, Hubert nominated Leonard as a member of the committee to report to Federal parliament in 1939 on whether the territories of Papua and New Guinea should unite. Leonard argued effectively against amalgamation.

Hubert died in office in February 1940. Leonard was appointed administrator in December, on a salary of £1500 per annum. Mission leaders applauded the choice, hoping he would maintain the 'Murray tradition'. Although some businessmen had wanted a 'complete change' and the promotion of economic development by Europeans, they praised Leonard's personal qualities. When he outlined his policy, he said that he would 'keep doing ... what the old Governor would have done'; but, even as he took office, the Papua he knew was being transformed. By March 1941 Murray informed Canberra that bush shelters had been built inland where civilians might seek 'doubtful security' if Port Moresby were attacked. On 5 December the Papuan administration publicly advised all White women and children to consider leaving the Territory. After the cabinet decision of 12 December ordering compulsory evacuation, Murray reported that he and his officials were working night and day in 'vile weather' to get the six hundred women and children away.

On 23 December Murray complained to the Department of External Territories about the powers being assumed by Brigadier Basil Morris [q.v.], commandant of Australian troops in Papua and New Guinea. Morris—

thinking he was acting on a cabinet decision —called up all able-bodied civilians on 24 January 1942, effectively closing businesses and civil government. When the minister for external territories instructed Murray to continue civil affairs, Morris refused to release sufficient men. Through the weeks of the dispute between Murray and Morris, both men were 'formally harmonious and correct'. After Port Moresby was bombed for the second time on 5 February, soldiers looted stores and defied officers and military police who proved 'worthless'. Cabinet finally decided that civil administration would end. Murray was told that he was subject to Morris, and to show Morris this instruction. Finding the transfer of power 'extremely humiliating', Murray conformed, but pressed for clear instructions before surrendering his full responsibilities. With the formal declaration of military rule on 14 February, he and his senior officials left for Australia next day, 'like whipped dogs', according to the government secretary H. W. Champion [q.v.7].

In 1945 (Sir) John Barry [q.v.13] was appointed commissioner to inquire into the suspension of civil government in Papua. His report criticized Murray for frequently referring matters to Canberra during an emergency and for being prepared to close out-stations, thereby leaving villagers without police, courts and welfare services. The charge of ignoring the needs of Papuans on the eve of the Japanese invasion was damning for a man whose reputation rested on the Murray record of promoting the interests of Papuans. Murray's defence was that he thought Morris would be totally committed to fighting the Japanese, and that an orderly withdrawal from the out-stations was preferable to abandoning them. The ill discipline and looting by troops (an army matter) had led to the investigation, but the inquiry which Murray had welcomed left the impression that the civil authorities had been guilty of dereliction of duty.

Settled in Sydney, Murray could not understand why he was ignored by the Federal government, given his knowledge of Papua. He vainly attempted to argue his case, which he was convinced was 'righteous and strong'. Following an approach to General Douglas MacArthur [q.v.], he was employed by the Allied Geographical Section, General Headquarters. He put his name forward in 1945 to become administrator of the Territory of Papua-New Guinea: in spite of support from the Public Service Association of Papua and others, he was passed over in favour of (Sir) Keith Murray [q.v.]. Leonard Murray wrote courteous complaints to the minister about the denigration of his reputation, the failure to pay him for his full five-year commission as administrator of Papua, and his fixed level of superannuation. He received no satisfaction.

Predeceased by his wife (d.1958) and son, he died on 9 December 1963 at his Manly home and was cremated.

F. Clune, *Prowling through Papua* (Syd, 1943); F. West, *Hubert Murray* (Melb, 1968) and (ed), *Selected Letters of Hubert Murray* (Melb, 1970); *PP* (Cwlth), 1937-40, 3, p 711; *PIM*, no 11, Jan 1941, no 15, June 1945, no 35, Jan 1964; *Papuan Courier*, 13, 20, 27 Dec 1940; *SMH*, 27 Dec 1940; CP389/1, items 1, 24 and 25, AA series A1, item 1909/2763, A56/1, A452 1959/6182, A518 16/2/1, M2104/12 and 14, G69 (mfm) (AA, Canb).   H. N. NELSON

MURRAY, SIR JACK KEITH (1889-1979), colonial administrator and teacher, was born on 8 February 1889 at Middle Brighton, Melbourne, son of Victorian-born parents John Murray, gentleman, and his wife Elinor Marie, née Grant. Jack's parents separated when he was 2. Elinor moved to Sydney, where she supported her son by working as a domestic servant. She was a liberal influence on Murray, who later wrote that he found it 'impossible to pay an adequate tribute to her'. They lived in several suburbs, and Murray attended eleven different schools while Elinor saved the money that enabled him to enter St Joseph's College, Hunters Hill, in 1904.

After an unsettled year at the University of Sydney in 1908 and two years as an agriculture cadet at Cowra, Murray resumed his studies at the university (B.Sc.Agr., 1914; B.A., 1915), served with the Sydney University Scouts (captain 1916) and was awarded a diploma of military science. On 31 May 1916 he enlisted in the Australian Imperial Force. He sailed to Britain as adjutant in the transport, *Kyarra*, returned to Australia and was discharged from the A.I.F. on 3 January 1917. Re-enlisting on 26 November, he was based in France with the Australian Army Veterinary Corps from November 1918 to January 1919. The army gave him leave to attend an agricultural college in Scotland (he topped its diploma course in dairying) and to make vocational visits to North America on his way home. He was demobilized from the A.I.F. on 24 May 1920.

That year Murray was appointed lecturer in dairy bacteriology and technology at Hawkesbury Agricultural College, New South Wales. In 1923 he became principal of the Queensland Agricultural High School and College, Gatton. At Scots Church, Sydney, on 10 July 1924 he married with Presbyterian forms Evelyn Ernestine Pritchard Andrews. An attractive, intelligent woman, nine years his junior, she was—like her husband—a University of Sydney graduate in agriculture. Murray took up a concurrent appointment in 1927 as foundation professor of agriculture at the University of Queensland.

Gatton College, which was severely run down, was transformed into the centre of rural education in Queensland under Murray's direction. He fostered a network of senior officials, premiers and governors to help with the college's development. Murray was well regarded at the university, but the college was the centre of his influence. He lectured regularly on the need for peace, but, as the 1930s advanced, prepared for what he feared was inevitable war. Active in the Militia from 1935, he was promoted temporary lieutenant colonel in 1940 and given command of the 25th Battalion, Darling Downs Regiment. He spent the next three years administering army training establishments in Queensland (as temporary colonel from August 1941).

Murray looked the part. He was fit and wiry, and of middle height and upright bearing. His features were regular, though his nose was a little long. Rather heavy eyebrows accentuated his large, sensitive eyes. He wore a full moustache, clipped at the ends of thin, determined lips. His hair was thick and cut evenly, emphasizing his disciplined carriage. Murray was far more than an enthusiastic citizen-soldier. His sometimes difficult childhood, broad education and wartime experiences were reflected in a complex and even contradictory character.

Although no longer a Catholic, Murray remained deeply interested in Christian ethics. A scientist by profession, he showed a wide understanding of the humanities; he was a strong supporter of tradition, but he had liberal political views; while conscious of his status, he was Spartan in his personal tastes and habits. Murray was reserved in manner and sometimes called 'aloof', yet he was warm and considerate to those who were close to him. He spoke quietly and with authority, considering his words and rarely hesitating. A man of old-fashioned courtesy and impeccable manners, he listened closely and politely.

In 1943 Colonel Murray was sent to Melbourne where, in February 1944, he joined Alf Conlon's [q.v.13] Directorate of Research (and Civil Affairs). After visiting Papua and New Guinea, he was appointed (December) acting chief instructor, Land Headquarters School of Civil Affairs, Canberra, where he trained personnel to administer Australia's territories. He transferred to the Reserve of Officers on 11 October 1945. As the Territory of Papua-New Guinea returned to civil administration, advisers of the minister for external territories, E. J. Ward [q.v.], looked for an administrator who would pursue their reformist aims for the country. Murray was chosen from fifty-three candidates and sworn in on 16 October 1945.

Caught between the competing interests trying to shape postwar Papua-New Guinea— European settlers, missionaries, Canberra bureaucrats, colonial officials fearful of change, and the United Nations—Murray dealt with problems of reconstruction as they arose, paying special attention to the plight of the people in villages devastated by war. Each year he spent months visiting outlying districts, talking with village leaders and missionaries, encouraging his staff, and restoring confidence in the Australian administration. He obtained from Canberra neither policy directions nor decisions on his own proposals, which he set out in his Macrossan [q.v.5] lecture at the University of Queensland in 1946, *The Provisional Administration of the Territory of Papua-New Guinea* (Brisbane, 1949). Action, he thought, could best be taken in Port Moresby, owing to the lack of interest in Australia. Few in Canberra agreed.

In pursuit of a 'new deal' for Papuans and New Guineans, Murray supervised the establishment of village courts and village councils, legislated for the creation of co-operative societies, developed extension courses in agriculture, set up aid-posts, instigated the training of indigenous medical officers and orderlies, and moved the workforce from an indenture system to one of free labour. The local White establishment found Murray's attitude to Papua New Guineans scandalous; when the Murrays invited Papuans to functions at Government House, some Whites boycotted them and Murray was dubbed 'Kanaka Jack'. He had a few able lieutenants, but the lack of support and understanding in Australia and Port Moresby gradually wore him down.

As a Labor appointee, Murray was held suspect by (Sir) Robert Menzies' [q.v.] government, and was offered lesser posts, which he declined. A major rift occurred in 1950 when Murray disagreed with an order from (Sir) Percy Spender, the new minister for external territories, that Papua New Guineans should not speak directly to a visiting mission from the United Nations. Spender was proved wrong, but the conclusion in Canberra was that Murray was overreaching himself. In 1951 (Sir) Paul Hasluck became minister and endorsed a programme of gradual development. His views on policy were similar to Murray's, but Hasluck was determined to take full control. In May 1952, without offering him the opportunity to retire or resign, he had Murray dismissed and replaced by (Sir) Donald Cleland [q.v.13].

Apart from an appointment (1956-57) as a Colombo Plan adviser in Ceylon, Murray lived in retirement at St Lucia, Brisbane. He was a member (1953-68) of the senate of the University of Queensland and, at Hasluck's request, became a mentor to young Papua New Guineans studying in Australia. In 1959 he was appointed O.B.E. The university awarded him an honorary doctorate of science (1967) and made him an emeritus professor (1975).

On the recommendation of the recently independent (1975) Papua New Guinea government, he was knighted in 1978. He and Evelyn gave each other devoted support into old age, as throughout their marriage. Murray died on 10 December 1979 at Jindalee and was cremated with the forms of the Uniting Church. His wife (d.1984) survived him; they had no children.

Sir Keith Murray focused and epitomized reform in postwar Papua and New Guinea. So long as he was administrator, change remained the central issue. By the time he was removed from office, the pattern had been set, and the best policies of the following decades flowed from those he had supported and proposed.

L. P. Mair, *Australia in New Guinea* (Lond, 1948); P. Hasluck, *A Time for Building* (Melb, 1976); I. Downs, *The Australian Trusteeship* (Canb, 1980); R. Cleland, *Papua New Guinea* (Perth, 1983); Territory of PNG, *Annual Report*, 1947-52; *Courier-Mail*, *Newcastle Morning Herald* and *SMH*, 12 Dec 1979; B. E. Jinks, Policy, Planning and Administration in Papua New Guinea, 1942-1952 (Ph.D. thesis, Univ Syd, 1975); J. K. Murray papers (Univ Qld L); External Territories files, A518, 1944-56 (AA, Canb).

BRIAN JINKS

MURRAY, JOHN DAVID (1918-1977), soldier and businessman, was born on 15 May 1918 at Fremantle, Western Australia, fourth child of English-born parents John Murray, engineer, and his wife Mary Isabell, née Smith. Educated at Guildford Grammar School, Jock joined S. J. McGibbon & Co., an accountancy firm in Perth, in 1935.

After serving (from 1937) in the Citizen Military Forces, Murray enlisted in the Australian Imperial Force on 3 November 1939. He sailed for the Middle East in April 1940 as a lieutenant in the 2nd/11th Battalion. Next year he fought in North Africa, Greece and Crete. Following the allied defeat, Cretans hid him from the Germans until he was taken to the Middle East by submarine in August. Returning to Australia in March 1942, he joined the staff of the 19th Brigade and saw action (1944-45) in the Wewak, New Guinea, campaign as brigade major. He was appointed M.B.E. (1944) and O.B.E. (1947). On 15 January 1946 he transferred to the Reserve of Officers.

That year he rejoined McGibbon & Co. and was sent to Albany. There he became associated with Westralian Trawling Co. Pty Ltd and Seafoods Pty Ltd, first as secretary and then as manager. The companies, set up as part of the State government's proposal to establish a fishing industry in the Great Australian Bight, commenced operations in July 1948. By November they were in financial difficulties. In 1949 Anglo-Australian Fisheries Co. Ltd provided two Mersey-type trawlers to assist the venture. Murray was appointed general manager of the three companies. Although packs of frozen fish (trademarked Snowman) were well received on the market, the irregularity of supply and the inefficiency of the coal-fired trawlers forced the companies into receivership in 1952.

Murray moved to another accountancy firm, J. D. Whyte, Reilly & Mitchell, and was appointed manager of Cheynes Beach Whaling Co. Pty Ltd in 1953. He continued his involvement with the C.M.F. On 15 July 1954 he was seconded to the Department of External Affairs to serve as a United Nations military observer in Kashmir. Back home in 1957, he was promoted lieutenant colonel and commanded the 28th Battalion in 1959-60. Reappointed (1959) manager of the Cheynes Beach Whaling Co., he lived on the station at Frenchman Bay, Albany, and guided the firm to prosperity. Profits soared, and a dividend of 60 per cent was declared in 1964. By 1973 the company had secured interests in Fertal Pty Ltd, which manufactured tallow and meat meal, and in Sigma Chemicals Pty Ltd, through which other whale products were marketed.

Nuggety in build, with dark hair, blue eyes and a ready smile, Murray was a gregarious, popular and community-spirited man. He chaired the Albany Port Authority (1964-77) and the Old Farm, Strawberry Hill, committee (1969-77) of the National Trust of Australia, and was active in Rotary, Legacy and the Returned Services League of Australia. Murray died suddenly of heart disease on 6 January 1977 at Albany and was cremated with Anglican rites. In the following year the International Whaling Commission agreed to a moratorium on whaling and a Commonwealth inquiry recommended that it be prohibited in Australian waters.

H. M. Binks, *The 2/11th (City of Perth) Australian Infantry Battalion, 1939-1945* (Perth, 1984); Albany Port Authority, *Annual Report*, 1964-77 (BL); National Trust of Aust (WA), *Trust News*, no 86, Feb 1977; *Sunday Times* (Perth), 22 Aug 1971; *Albany Advertiser*, 11 Jan 1977; Dept of Fisheries (WA) files, AN 108, *and* Dept of Industrial Development (WA) files, AN 183 (WA PRO).   M. MEDCALF

MURRAY, JOHN FRANCIS NOWELL (1900-1978), valuer and chartered surveyor, was born on Christmas Day 1900 in Hobart, eldest son of Tasmanian-born parents John William Murray, grocer, and his wife Emily, née Smith. Educated at St Virgil's College, Hobart, John entered the Commonwealth Public Service in December 1916 as a clerk in the Taxation Office. He worked as an assistant to staff valuers (from 1920), draftsman

(from 1927) and senior valuer (from 1934). On 12 February 1924 he had married Olive Eileen Lottie Davern at St John's Anglican Church, Launceston. By studying part time Murray qualified as an associate (1927) and colonial fellow (1934) of the Surveyors' Institution (Royal Institution of Chartered Surveyors), London. He also graduated from the University of Tasmania (B.A., 1933; D.Litt., 1953).

In 1934 Murray was commissioned in the Australian Field Artillery, Militia. Posted to the 6th Field Regiment in 1941, he was seconded to the Australian Imperial Force in the following year. His appointment terminated on 28 April 1943 when the government requisitioned his services for the War Damage Commission. In 1943-46 he carried out valuation work in Papua, New Guinea and nearby islands. After World War II Murray moved to Sydney, and was employed as Commonwealth chief valuer for New South Wales (1946-49) and as chairman (1949-65) of the Commonwealth valuation appeals boards. From 1957 he was a land commissioner for the Australian Capital Territory. Retiring from the public service in 1965, he set up in private practice.

Murray had contributed significantly to his profession as its focus shifted from local and personal levels to matters of national and theoretical dimensions. At the invitation of the Commonwealth Institute of Valuers, he wrote *Principles and Practice of Valuation* (Sydney, 1949) and *Valuation Practice* (Sydney, 1953); both became standard texts. He lectured and examined for the institute, to which he was elected a life fellow (1955), and contributed to its journal, the *Valuer*. Murray's doctoral thesis—in part published as *Valuation and the National Economy* (Phoenix, Arizona, 1967)—examined the problem of balancing the rights of individuals and the state in land matters, and contained insights which he applied as a technical-assistance consultant to the governments of Singapore (1955), Ghana (1957) and Jamaica (1956, 1957 and 1960). Other assignments followed in Kenya (1960, 1961), New Zealand (1962) and Papua New Guinea (1971), and as a visiting lecturer in Taiwan (1969-74). He also advised numerous Australian organizations and enjoyed the challenge of appearing as an expert witness in complex court cases.

Astute and self-confident, Murray was a fluent communicator, gifted with an excellent memory and an analytical mind. Within his profession he exemplified the effectiveness of the individual practitioner who used the science of measurement and 'the art of determining the value of all descriptions of landed . . . and house property' to offer a fair resolution to conflicts inherent in land use. Murray died on 13 March 1978 at Greens Beach, Tasmania, and was cremated; his wife, daughter and two sons survived him.

Aust Inst of Valuers Inc, *A History 1926-1988* (Canb, 1988); *Valuer*, 10, 1 Oct 1949, p 365, 14, 1 Oct 1956, p 171, 25, July 1978, p 216; *Mercury* (Hob), 14, 15 Mar 1978; *Examiner* (Launc), 15 Mar 1978; Murray papers (NL).   ANN ELIAS

MURRAY, JOHN JOSEPH (1892-1951), businessman and army officer, was born on 26 April 1892 in Sydney, fourth child of John Murray, an Irish-born labourer, and his wife Margaret, née Ferrow, who came from Wollongong. Educated at Catholic schools, young John joined the sales staff of Anthony Hordern & Sons [qq.v.4,8] in 1910. He served for two and a half years in the ranks of the Citizen Military Forces before being commissioned in 1913 in the 33rd Infantry Regiment.

On 6 March 1915 Murray was appointed second lieutenant, Australian Imperial Force. In June he sailed for Egypt. Posted to the 1st Battalion, he was transferred to the 53rd Battalion, 5th Division, in March 1916 when the A.I.F. expanded. Soon after he reached France, he went into action on 19 July in the appalling battle of Fromelles; for his 'courage and tenacity' in leading a charge and holding the position he had captured, he won the Military Cross. He was promoted major in June 1917. In the fighting for Péronne on 1 September 1918, he 'set a fine example' to the company under his command and was awarded the Distinguished Service Order. Twice mentioned in dispatches, he embarked for Australia in May 1919.

After his A.I.F. appointment terminated on 25 August 1919, Murray returned to life in the C.M.F. as readily as he did to business. Active in the Militia from September 1920, he was promoted lieutenant colonel in 1925 and commanded the 56th Battalion (1925-30) and the 53rd Battalion (1930-34). On 4 January 1923 at St Mary's Catholic Cathedral, Sydney, he had married Mary Madeline Cannon. His business affairs prospered and he became well known as head of the delivery department of Anthony Hordern & Sons Ltd. In 1932 he was appointed chairman of the New South Wales Transport Advisory Committee. He held the managing directorship of Associated Transport Services Ltd from 1935. While he was commander (1934-38) of the Australian Army Service Corps, 1st Division, his business and military interests were closely related.

In May 1938 Murray took command of the 9th Infantry Brigade. Mobilized in February 1940, he initially headed the Eastern Command Recruit Training Depot. He joined the A.I.F. in April and was appointed commander of the 20th Brigade which sailed for the Middle East in October and trained in Palestine. The brigade was transferred from the 7th Division to the 9th in February 1941. Although undertrained, and short of weapons

and transport, the 9th Division was sent to relieve the 6th in Libya. The 20th Brigade met the first onslaught of General Erwin Rommel's *Afrika Korps* at Er Regima on 4 April and briefly delayed the enemy's advance. After the successful withdrawal to Tobruk, the brigade repelled Rommel's attack on 14 April, a disastrous day for the Germans. For his leadership Murray was awarded a Bar to his D.S.O.

Murray's experience of raids and night-patrols on the Western Front in World War I proved valuable during the siege of Tobruk. In July, while Major General (Sir) Leslie Morshead [q.v.] visited General Headquarters, Cairo, Murray commanded the fortress. He left Tobruk in November and was mentioned in dispatches. General Sir Thomas Blamey [q.v.13] considered him, at 49, 'unequal to the severe physical trials of … modern warfare' and recommended that he be sent home to direct a recruiting campaign. Murray's return to Australia in January 1942 coincided with Japan's drive southwards. Instead of being given a recruiting job, he was immediately made commander, Newcastle Covering Force, and promoted temporary major general (substantive in September).

Having continued with this force when it was redesignated the 10th Division, Murray was sent to Western Australia in August 1942 to lead the 4th Division which moved to North Queensland during April-May 1943. In October 1944 he became general officer commanding Rear Echelon, First Army, at Mareeba. He commanded Northern Territory Force from March 1945 until January 1946, then transferred to the Reserve of Officers.

Morshead described Murray as 'a pleasant, forceful character; alert, kindly, and cheerful, yet direct and purposeful'. These characteristics prepared Murray for his role as Australian trade commissioner to New Zealand in 1946-49 and Ceylon (Sri Lanka) from 1949. He died of haematemesis associated with cirrhosis of the liver on 8 September 1951 at the Repatriation General Hospital, Concord, Sydney, and was buried with military honours in Frenchs Forest cemetery. His wife, three sons and two daughters survived him.

C. E. W. Bean, *The A.I.F. in France*, 1916-18 (Syd, 1929, 1933, 1937, 1942); D. McCarthy, *South-West Pacific Area—First Year* (Canb, 1959); B. Maughan, *Tobruk and El Alamein* (Canb, 1966); D. M. Horner, *Crisis of Command* (Canb, 1978); *Daily Telegraph* (Syd), 8 Sept 1951; Blamey papers (AWM).

A. J. HILL

MURRAY, SIR JOHN STANLEY (1884-1971), businessman and pastoralist, was born on 27 March 1884 at Rosebank, Mount

Pleasant, South Australia, son of native-born parents John Murray (d.1885), station manager, and his wife Elizabeth Thompson, née Melrose. (Sir) George Murray [q.v.10] and Alexander Melrose [q.v.] were his uncles. Stanley was educated at Queen's School, North Adelaide, Glenalmond School (1897-98), Perthshire, Scotland, and the Collegiate School of St Peter (1899-1902), Adelaide. After studying law at Trinity College, Cambridge (B.A., 1908), he was called to the Bar at the Inner Temple, London, in 1909 and admitted to the Bar in South Australia in the same year. In 1914 Murray joined (Sir) Herbert Mayo [q.v.] and (Sir) Collier Cudmore [q.v.13] in partnership; Murray and Cudmore were to remain partners until Murray retired in 1948. At St Peter's chapel on 8 June 1910 he married Winifred Olive Wigg (d.1964), Cudmore's sister-in-law.

On 19 December 1916 Murray enlisted in the Australian Imperial Force. Commissioned in November 1917, he served on the Western Front with the 1st Divisional Artillery and was promoted lieutenant in December 1918. His appointment terminated in Adelaide on 22 August 1919. He became a leading company lawyer, particularly in mining law, and held directorships of several Western Australian mining companies. Murray also influenced the business world of Adelaide through his appointment to the boards of major firms, including Harris Scarfe Ltd, of which he was chairman. As chairman of directors (from 1939) of the Adelaide Electric Supply Co. Ltd, he resisted Premier (Sir) Thomas Playford's efforts in 1945-46 to nationalize the company, while Cudmore fought against them in the Legislative Council. Although Murray lost the bitter battle, he succeeded in having A.E.S.Co. funds in England returned to the shareholders rather than allowing them to be appropriated by the government. Chairman (from 1936) of News Ltd, he worked closely with Rupert Murdoch who arrived in Adelaide in 1953 to oversee his family's interests in the *News*. Murray was still chairman in January 1960 at the time of the Rupert Max Stuart case when the newspaper and its editor-in-chief Rohan Rivett [q.v.] were charged with publishing seditious libel. Murray appeared as a witness at the trial in March.

Having acquired Rosebank, which had been owned by two of his uncles—Robert Murray and Alec Melrose [q.v.]—Stanley Murray lived on his property and ran it from 1948; his managers were responsible for its continued development as a leading Aberdeen Angus stud. A keen racehorse-owner, he was a committee-member, chairman (1941-47) and vice-chairman (1947-50) of the South Australian Jockey Club.

Murray was president (1955-57) of the Adelaide Club. In 1957 he was knighted. Following the death of his wife, Sir Stanley retired from public life, moved to Walkerville, and concentrated on managing his portfolio of shares. On 2 April 1971 at Gilberton he married Irenie Florence Walpole, his long-time secretary. Survived by his wife, and by one of the two daughters of his first marriage, he died on 30 May 1971 at his Walkerville home and was cremated. His estate was sworn for probate at $417 755.

C. and M. Kerr, *The Vital Spark* (Adel, 1979); S. Cockburn, *Playford* (Adel, 1991); Roy Com on the Adelaide Electric Supply Co, *PP* (SA), (55), 1945; *News* (Adel), 31 May 1971; *Advertiser* (Adel), 1 June 1971.

PETER DONOVAN

MURRAY, PATRICK DESMOND FITZ-GERALD (1900-1967), zoologist, was born on 18 June 1900 at Dorchester, Dorset, England, youngest of three children of Australian-born parents (Sir) John Hubert Plunkett Murray [q.v.10], barrister and later lieutenant-governor of Papua, and his first wife Sybil Maud, née Jenkins, who was living in England while her husband served in the South African War. Pat attended St John's preparatory school, Beaumont, Old Windsor, where he became interested in entomology. In 1914 he entered St Ignatius' College, Riverview, Sydney. He graduated from the University of Sydney (B.Sc., 1922; D.Sc., 1926) with first-class honours in botany and zoology, the university medal for zoology, and the John Coutts scholarship.

Matriculating in 1922 at Magdalen College, Oxford (B.Sc., 1924), Murray studied experimental embryology. He returned to Sydney in 1924 to become Macleay [q.v.5.] fellow of the Linnean Society of New South Wales; the university appointed him lecturer and demonstrator in the department of zoology. At St Mary's Catholic Cathedral on 14 March 1925 Murray married Margery Holland; they remained childless and their marriage was dissolved on 28 July 1966. Having been awarded a Rockefeller Foundation fellowship in 1929, Murray worked at the universities of Cambridge and Freiburg, Germany. From January 1931 until December 1935 he held the Royal Society's Smithson fellowship in natural sciences, at the Strangeways Research Laboratory, Cambridge. His research centred on the morphogenesis of bone and functional aspects of embryonic heart cells in tissue culture. In 1936 he published his first book, *Bones; a Study of the Development and Structure of the Vertebrate Skeleton*.

After demonstrating in zoology at Bedford College for Women, University of London, Murray held a readership in biology and comparative anatomy at St Bartholomew's Hospital medical school in 1939-49. During these years he researched the effects of nutrition, especially vitamin C, on the development and repair of injuries to bones and wrote *Biology* (London, 1950), an introduction to medical studies, which became a popular elementary textbook.

In 1949 Murray was appointed Challis [q.v.3] professor of zoology at the University of Sydney. He was elected a fellow (1954) of the Australian Academy of Science, Canberra, and presided (1957) over section D of the Australian and New Zealand Association for the Advancement of Science. University administration overshadowed his research, which probably contributed to his decision to resign his chair in 1960. He moved to the University of New England as reader in zoology (later, research fellow) where he specialized in experimental embryology.

A modest, kindly, sometimes remote man —though not a recluse—Murray took an interest in public affairs; he criticized the Commonwealth government's Communist Party of Australia dissolution bill (1950) and opposed nuclear weapons. On 9 September 1966 he married Jascha Ann Morgan, a 37-year-old university teacher, in a civil ceremony at Armidale. Intent on continuing his work at Cambridge, he sailed for England in the *Achille Lauro*, but died at sea on 17 May 1967. His body was cremated and his ashes buried at Stoke Poges gardens, Buckinghamshire.

F. West, *Hubert Murray* (Melb, 1962), and (ed), *Selected Letters of Hubert Murray* (Melb, 1970); *Records of the Aust Academy of Science*, 1, no 3, Nov 1968, p 72; *SMH*, 9 Jan 1931, 19 May 1950, 24 Mar 1954; *Armidale Express*, 19 May 1967; *The Times*, 14 June 1967; information from Miss M. Pinney, Bowral, NSW.   BRIAN WIMBORNE

MURTAGH, JAMES GEORGE HILL (1908-1971), Catholic priest, journalist and historian, was born on 20 July 1908 at Waiwakaihi, Taranaki, New Zealand, eldest of five children of George Stedham Hill Murtagh, a meat exporter from Melbourne, and his New Zealand-born wife Martha Quinn, née Kirkwood. The family moved to Melbourne. James was educated at St Monica's School, Essendon, Assumption College, Kilmore, and the Victorian provincial seminary, Corpus Christi Ecclesiastical College, Werribee.

Ordained priest for the Melbourne archdiocese by Archbishop Daniel Mannix [q.v.10] on 17 July 1932, Fr Murtagh served (1933-36) as a curate at North Essendon before being appointed associate-editor of Melbourne's weekly Catholic newspaper, the *Advocate*. He was a diligent editor who enhanced the paper's reputation as a quality religious journal, aimed at readers interested in literary and cultural matters as well as world affairs. Founding president of the Catholic Press Association of Australia and New Zealand, he was elected to the executive of the International Catholic Union of the Press. He also established (1938) and edited the *Australian Catholic Digest*. In 1939 he was briefly national director of the Pontifical Mission Aid Societies.

After Mannix granted him leave, Murtagh studied (1941-43) social sciences, journalism and media at the Catholic University of America (M.A., 1943), Washington, D.C. With the encouragement of the expatriate publisher Frank Sheed, he expanded and published his thesis as *Australia: The Catholic Chapter* (New York, 1946). Revised editions appeared in 1959 and 1969. Critics recognized the book as a significant pioneering work. While its perspective and tone were still somewhat clerical and at times triumphalist, these characteristics were less pronounced than in earlier Catholic histories, notably those of Cardinal Patrick Moran [q.v.10] and (Archbishop) Eris O'Brien [q.v.]. Murtagh focused on the Church's social teaching as applied in Australia and gave due emphasis to religion's part in the nation's development. He also highlighted the contributions of such notable clerics as Dr William Ullathorne [q.v.2], Moran and Mannix, and the importance of lay figures like Caroline Chisholm, Peter Lalor [qq.v.1,5] and B. A. Santamaria. Murtagh was sympathetic to Santamaria's controversial role in the Catholic Social Studies Movement and in the Australian Labor Party split of the 1950s.

His other writings consisted mainly of articles in the *Advocate* over twenty-three years, a dozen or so pamphlets (some devotional and some sociological) and two short books, *Democracy in Australia* (Melbourne, 1946) and *Catholics and the Commonwealth* (Melbourne, 1951). Murtagh was influenced in his attitude to church-state relationships and the democratic ideal by the thinking of a few international Catholic celebrities, among them Jacques Maritain and John Courtney Murray, whose liberal views on social questions and religious freedom were to prevail over the integralist approach of Cardinal Alfredo Ottaviani and his theological school at the Second Vatican Council (1962-65). Murtagh also took a special interest in rural co-operatives.

Following his retirement from the *Advocate*, on 3 September 1959 Murtagh was appointed parish priest at Glen Iris where he showed pastoral concern for those in his charge, especially the sick. He continued to write on public affairs and socio-political questions, and championed Caroline Chisholm's beatification cause, without apparent success. In 1968 Archbishop (Cardinal) James Knox of

Melbourne commissioned him to write an official life of Mannix. Murtagh researched abroad in 1970, staying for several months at St Patrick's College, Maynooth. He interviewed scores of people with memories of Mannix, both in Ireland and Australia. They included ex-President Eamon De Valera, and a number of his subject's relations and former pupils. His research led him to revise some of his views about his hero, but, given his rather timid character and his devotion to Mannix, he would have found it difficult to disturb what Patrick O'Farrell has called 'the stagnancy of unthinking veneration'.

Murtagh died suddenly of coronary thrombosis on 7 June 1971 in his presbytery at Glen Iris and was buried in Melbourne general cemetery. His research notes were lodged with the Melbourne Diocesan Historical Commission.

W. Ebsworth, *Archbishop Mannix* (Melb, 1977); *Hist Studies*, 8, Nov 1958, p 233; *Compass*, Autumn/Winter 1988, p 26, Autumn 1989, p 4; *A'sian Catholic Record*, 68, no 2, Apr 1991, p 131; *New Norcia Studies*, 3, July 1995, p 9; *Tjurunga*, 49, Mar 1996, p 61; *SMH*, 25 Apr 1959; Murtagh papers (MDHC).

MICHAEL COSTIGAN

MYER, SIR NORMAN (1897-1956), businessman, was born on 25 May 1897 (and named Nahum Moshe) at Tatarsk Smolensk, Russia (Byelorusse), son of Jewish parents Yacov Meer Baevski (d.1899), a local manufacturer and trader, and his wife Chaya, née Sitz. His mother remarried. Nahum's uncle Simcha [q.v.10 Sidney Myer] sent in 1908 for his nephew, who reached Melbourne on 7 February 1909 in the *Frederich der Grosse*. Nahum attended Rev. Clifford Nash's [q.v.10] school at Hawthorn and learned English. After the Myer retail business moved (1911) to Bourke Street, Melbourne, he began working there and continued his education at Wesley College. On 8 June 1916 he enlisted in the Australian Imperial Force. Failing to gain entry into the Australian Flying Corps, he served on the Western Front from August 1917 as a driver with the 1st Divisional Ammunition Column. He was commissioned in January 1919 and promoted lieutenant in April.

After investigating developments in retailing in the United States of America, he returned to Melbourne where his A.I.F. appointment terminated on 19 March 1920. Nahum changed his given name to Norman and was naturalized on 21 April 1920. He partnered a wartime friend Arthur Long in offering joy-ride flights over Melbourne and planned other commercial aviation ventures, but Sidney wanted his nephew in the store. Norman was given charge of the hosiery

department. On 14 March 1922 in a civil ceremony at 165 Collins Street he married Gladys Margaret Roche. Following the acquisition of James Marshall [q.v.5] & Co. Ltd, Adelaide, Norman Myer and James Martin were placed in charge in 1928. Despite the Depression, the Myer Emporium (S.A.) Ltd proved a success. In South Australia Norman gained valuable experience in merchandising, store management and administration; Gladys was important in dealings with the Adelaide establishment.

In 1934 the organization was rocked by the death of Sidney Myer. After E. L. Neil [q.v.10] and Elcon Myer died, Norman succeeded as chairman and managing director of the Myer Emporium Ltd, Melbourne, in 1938. Believing in decentralization, he appointed eight directors, giving them autonomy in their fields, while he concentrated on overall policy. Like his uncle, Myer sought to keep things moving on the shop-floor, even if it meant sacrificing profits to sales. Extensive advertising campaigns reflected new ideas and merchandise obtained on his regular trips abroad (the Hudson Co. of Detroit and R. H. Macy & Co., New York, were among the American firms he admired). Myer's strengths were his direct involvement with people and his understanding of customer requirements. A property on the Mornington Peninsula was purchased for staff holidays and named Norman Lodge. During World War II he advised the Menzies [q.v.] and Curtin [q.v.13] governments as a member of the Board of Business Administration, but he was accused of controlling prices and criticized by Arthur Calwell [q.v.13]. Myer was active in the Victorian division of the Australian Red Cross Society and the Australian Comforts Fund.

Myer oversaw the expansion of the firm into a huge retail organization. It remained in the control of male members of the family and selected intimates. He opened additional stores in Brisbane, and at Geelong and Ballarat, Victoria, a furniture factory at Footscray and woollen mills at Ballarat. Myer's had buying offices and agents throughout the world. A director of numerous companies including Bruck Mills (Australia) Ltd and the Overseas Corporation (Australia) Ltd, Norman Myer was a governor of the Corps of Commissionaires (a businessmen's organization) and a sponsor of the Australian Administrative Staff College, Mount Eliza. He was also a founder and chairman of the City Development Association and backed the idea of the Melbourne Moomba Festival, but he foresaw that the future of retailing lay in regional shopping-centres.

Most comfortable in the company of men, Myer dominated the board-room at executive luncheons, with fine cigars and a repertoire of Australian jokes. He belonged to the Naval and Military, Victoria Golf, Victoria Racing and Victoria Amateur Turf clubs. In 1951 he and Gladys were divorced. At the Methodist Church, Caulfield, on 19 April 1952 he married 24-year-old Pamela Margaret Sallmann, a school contemporary of his daughter Pamela.

Knighted in 1956, Myer was chairman of the Sidney Myer charity trust which distributed over £400 000 to charitable and cultural projects. Shortly after announcing the presentation of the Sidney Myer Music Bowl to the people of Melbourne, he died of cancer on 17 December 1956 in his Toorak home and was cremated. His wife and their two sons, and the daughter and two sons of his first marriage, survived him. Sir Norman left control of his estate, sworn for probate at £373 737, to his wife. No longer dominated by one man, the Myer Emporium continued to be managed by the family, but Norman's sons did not follow him into the firm. A posthumous portrait by (Sir) William Dargie is held by Coles [q.v.13] Myer Ltd.

A. Marshall, *The Gay Provider* (Melb, 1961); P. Warrender, *Prince of Merchants* (Melb, 1972); *People* (Syd), 12 Jan 1955, p 41; *SMH*, 22 Sept, 29 Nov 1939, 31 May 1956; naturalization file A1/15, item 20/4310 (AA, Canb); information from Ms S. Barber, Sidney Myer Archival Research Project, South Yarra, Melb.

DAVID DUNSTAN

N

NAMATJIRA, ALBERT (ELEA) (1902-1959), artist, was born on 28 July 1902 at Hermannsburg (Ntaria), Northern Territory, son of Namatjira and his wife Ljukuta. Elea belonged to the western group of the Arrernte people. In 1905 the family was received into the Lutheran Church: Elea (who was given the name Albert) and his father (who took the name Jonathan) were baptized, and his mother was blessed (as Emilie). Albert attended the Hermannsburg mission school. In accordance with the practice of the missions, he lived separately from his parents in a boys' dormitory. At 13 he spent six months in the bush and underwent initiation. He left the mission again at the age of 18 and married Ilkalita, a Kukatja woman. Eight of their children were to survive infancy: five sons— Enos, Oscar, Ewald, Keith and Maurice—and three daughters—Maisie, Hazel and Martha. The family shifted to Hermannsburg in 1923 and Ilkalita was christened Rubina.

In his boyhood Albert sketched 'scenes and incidents around him . . . the cattle yard, the stockmen with their horses, and the hunters after game'. He later made artefacts such as boomerangs and woomeras. Encouraged by the mission authorities, he began to produce mulga-wood plaques with poker-worked designs. Meanwhile, he worked as a blacksmith, carpenter, stockman and cameleer —at the mission for rations and on neighbouring stations for wages. The spectacular scenery of Central Australia, then entering the national consciousness as a symbol of Australian identity, attracted artists to Hermannsburg, among them Rex Battarbee [q.v.13] and John Gardner. During their second visit in 1934 they held an exhibition for an Aboriginal audience. The Arrernte were familiar with illustrations of biblical scenes, but none had seen landscapes depicting their own surroundings.

Motivated by a deep attachment to his country and the possibility of a vocation that offered financial return, Namatjira expressed an interest in learning to paint. In 1936 he accompanied Battarbee as a cameleer on two month-long excursions in and around the Macdonnell Ranges. Battarbee was impressed by his evident talent. In the following year Pastor Friedrich Albrecht, the superintendent of Hermannsburg, displayed ten of Namatjira's water-colours at a Lutheran conference held at Nuriootpa, South Australia. Battarbee included another three of his water-colours in an exhibition with the Royal South Australian Society of Arts, Adelaide. In 1938 the two men went on an expedition, during which Battarbee taught him photography. Later that year Namatjira held his first solo exhibition at the Fine Art Society Gallery, Melbourne. With Battarbee's assistance as teacher, dealer and mentor, a school of artists developed around Namatjira.

Although Namatjira is best known for his water-colour landscapes of the Macdonnell Ranges and the nearby region, earlier in his career his imagery had included tjuringa designs, biblical themes and figurative subjects. He also produced carved and painted artefacts, and briefly painted on bean-wood panels. Superficially, his paintings give the appearance of conventional European landscapes, but Namatjira painted with 'country in mind' and continually returned to sites imbued with ancestral associations. The repetition, detailed patterning and high horizons—so characteristic of his work—blended Aboriginal and European modes of depiction.

Namatjira's initiatives won national and international acclaim. As the first prominent Aboriginal artist to work in a modern idiom, he was widely regarded as a representative of assimilation. In 1944 he was included in *Who's Who in Australia*. He was awarded Queen Elizabeth II's coronation medal (1953), presented to the Queen in Canberra (1954) and elected an honorary member of the Royal Art Society of New South Wales (1955). His quiet and dignified presence belied the underlying tensions in his life.

With fame came controversy. Namatjira's brilliant career highlighted the gap between the rhetoric and reality of assimilation policies. He encountered an ambiguous response from the art world. Some criticized his water-colour landscapes as derivative and conventional; others viewed them as evidence of acculturation and a loss of tribal traditions. Tensions arose between Namatjira and the Aranda Arts Council (chaired by Battarbee) when the council tried to maintain control over the quality and quantity of his work. Namatjira also encountered racial discrimination. He was refused a grazing licence in 1949-50 and prevented in 1951 from building a house on land he bought at Alice Springs. Seeking further means of support for his family, he discovered copper deposits at Areyonga Reserve, but they proved commercially unviable. By the early 1950s he lived independently of the mission in a fringe camp at Morris Soak on the outskirts of Alice Springs.

The citizenship granted to Namatjira in 1957 led to further anomalies. Exempted from the restrictions imposed on other 'full-blooded' Aborigines, he had access to alcohol which he shared with members of his family in accordance with Aboriginal custom. In 1958 he was charged with supplying alcohol to the artist Henoch Raberaba and sentenced to six months imprisonment with labour. Following a public outcry and two appeals, the sentence was reduced to three months. Namatjira finally served two months of 'open' detention at the Papunya settlement in March-May 1959. He died of hypertensive heart failure on 8 August that year at Alice Springs Hospital and was buried with Lutheran forms in the local cemetery. His wife, five sons and one of his daughters survived him.

For a time Namatjira's name drifted into obscurity, his achievements largely eclipsed by the 'dot painting' style developed at Papunya in the 1970s. Recent re-evaluations recognize his influence on Aboriginal artists in Central Australia and elsewhere. In 1994 members of the Hermannsburg Potters, led by his grand-daughter Elaine, acknowledged Namatjira's legacy by producing a terracotta mural for the headstone of his grave. The work is a landscape combining three sites in the Macdonnell Ranges which were the subjects of his paintings.

C. Mountford, *The Art of Albert Namatjira* (Melb, 1944); R. Battarbee, *Modern Australian Aboriginal Art* (Syd, 1951); J. D. Batty, *Namatjira* (Melb, 1963); N. Amadio et al, *Albert Namatjira* (Melb, 1986); J. Hardy et al (eds), *The Heritage of Namatjira* (Melb, 1992); *Herald Weekend Magazine* (Melb), 29 Mar 1947; *Centralian Advocate*, 20 Sept 1985; *Namatjira the Painter* (1974) and *Sons of Namatjira* (1975), motion pictures (NL); information from Mrs H. Burns, Linden Park, Adel, Ms G. Griffiths, Kingston, SA, and Ms N. Sharp, Ntaria (Hermannsburg), NT.

SYLVIA KLEINERT

NANKERVIS, ALFRED ROY (1885-1956), public servant, was born on 10 March 1885 near Kadina, South Australia, third of eight children of Henry Nankervis, accountant, and his wife Mary Elizabeth, née Davis. Roy attended school at Kadina and entered the South Australian Public Service on 23 October 1899 as a telegraph messenger. Transferring to the Commonwealth Postmaster-General's Department in 1901, he moved in 1907 to Melbourne where he worked in the clerical division. On 12 July 1910 at St Columba's Anglican Church, Hawthorn, Adelaide, he married Nellie Ward. In the following year he was appointed a receiver of public moneys and paying officer in the South Australian naval office of the Department of Defence. He joined the Department of the Navy on its formation in 1915 and reverted to Defence when the separate naval administration was disbanded in 1921.

By 1919 Nankervis was serving with the finance branch at Navy Office, Melbourne. He held increasingly senior positions. Early in 1938 he was appointed to the National Insurance Commission, Canberra, but in September was recalled to Navy Office to succeed Ralph Abercrombie [q.v.13] as director of navy accounts and as finance and civil member of the Naval Board. After World War II broke out, the government again divided the Department of Defence. Nankervis was appointed secretary of the new Department of the Navy, established on 13 November 1939. With the enlargement of the Naval Board in October 1940, his finance and civil responsibilities passed to Raymond Anthony. Nankervis continued as an *ex officio* member of the board.

As secretary through the hectic war years, Nankervis kept a close watch on expenditure and worked harmoniously with most uniformed members of the Naval Board. Although his particular strength was finance, he also dealt effectively with policy issues and with political decisions affecting the department. He was at ease in his relations with a string of ministers—Sir Frederick Stewart, A. G. Cameron, W. M. Hughes [qq.v.12,13, 9], N. J. O. Makin, A. S. Drakeford [q.v.14], W. J. F. Riordan [q.v.] and (Sir) Josiah Francis [q.v.14]. Nankervis's style was that of a shrewd businessman: he thought ahead, alert for trouble, and was prepared to act decisively.

Always well dressed in the fashion of a senior public servant, 'Nanky' clung to tradition by wearing spats in winter. He was about 5 ft 11 ins (180 cm) tall and lightly built. In his later years he walked with a stoop. While his demeanour was usually serious, it was enlivened by a puckish sense of humour. Nankervis expected high standards from his staff and was sharply critical when they failed to meet them. He was a good permanent head, but would have been better had he been as tolerant of all his officers as he was of the few he trusted. On 9 March 1950 he retired from the public service. That year he was appointed O.B.E. He was a member of the Royal Automobile Club of Victoria and of the Navy, Army and Air Force Club. Survived by his wife, son and two daughters, he died on 11 July 1956 at his Camberwell home and was cremated.

R. Hyslop, *Aye Aye, Minister* (Canb, 1990); *Age* (Melb), 12 July 1956; information from Mrs J. Cozens, Castlemaine, Vic; personal knowledge.

K. W. MAJOR

NAN KIVELL, SIR REX DE CHAREMBAC (1898-1977), art dealer, collector and cultural benefactor, was born on 8 April 1898 at

Christchurch, New Zealand, son of Alice Nankivell. His Christian name was registered as Reginald. Cornish in origin, the Nankivells of New Zealand's Canterbury Plains were small businessmen, not the patrician land-holders Nan Kivell alluded to in later revisions of his family history. He was raised in the home of his grandparents George and Annie Nankivell whom he sometimes referred to as his parents. His primary education at New Brighton Public School was not followed by study of the classics at Christ's College Grammar School, as he subsequently alleged. In an interview towards the end of his life, he said that his interest in collecting had been stimulated in his childhood by 'Sidney Smith', a dealer in antiquarian books. Nankivell began reading history and geography, especially works on European voyagers in the Pacific.

Overstating his age by two years and describing his occupation as bookbinder, Nankivell enlisted in the New Zealand Expeditionary Force on 31 May 1916. His service in England (1916-19)—on the staff of No.1 New Zealand General Hospital, Brockenhurst, Hampshire, and at the New Zealand Command Depot, Codford, Wiltshire—was undistinguished and marked by delinquencies such as insolence, stealing and using a travel warrant, and masquerading as an officer. Although he claimed to have been gassed on the Western Front, he never saw action. An extended period of leave (October 1917 to May 1918) gave him an opportunity to pursue his growing antiquarian interests. Discharged from the N.Z.E.F. on 13 May 1919 in England, he was employed as a judge's marshal for some years. He worked on the La Tène archaeological excavations in Wiltshire and presented (1930) the objects he unearthed to the Devizes Museum. His subsequent assertion that, for this work, he was appointed to the Danish Order of Dannebrog apparently lacked foundation.

As early as 1918 he had begun to style himself Rex de Charembac Nan Kivell. This form of his name reflected his creation of a new persona. He resolutely discarded his modest antipodean origins to emerge as an up-and-coming gentleman art-dealer in London in the 1920s. He began to visit galleries and exhibitions by contemporary artists, honed his skills of discrimination and connoisseurship, and developed a taste for the best of modern European art. At the same time he began to collect books, paintings, prints, documents, manuscripts and artefacts relating to the history of Australia, New Zealand and the Pacific. These twin interests were to dominate his career.

In 1925 Nan Kivell joined the Redfern Gallery. By 1931 he had assumed control as managing director. His association with the Redfern, maintained in partnership with Australian-born Harry Tatlock Miller, continued until his death. The gallery promoted contemporary art, assisting a number of British artists who became major figures. Nan Kivell helped to bring to England the work of important European painters, and he encouraged some young Australian artists, including (Sir) Sidney Nolan.

Prompted by conversations with Maie, wife of R. G. (Baron) Casey [q.v.13], to whom he was distantly related, Nan Kivell considered making parts of his Australasian collection available for use in Australia. In 1946 he commenced discussions with London representatives of the Commonwealth National Library (National Library of Australia), Canberra. Three years later the first consignment of his pictures, books and other material reached Canberra on loan to the library. Although he was unfailingly generous in honouring his commitment to allow the library full use of his collection, he was cautious in defining any agreement concerning its ultimate disposition, or in stating terms for its donation or sale.

Part of the difficulty was that the collection was not exclusively Australian and that Nan Kivell felt an obligation to the country of his birth. More to the point, the collection represented a bargaining chip in his quest for a knighthood, which he saw as a key to his social and professional advancement in Britain. Eventually, in 1959, he sold his collection to the Australian government for £70 000, a fraction of its true value. This modest price, combined with his later gifts to the N.L.A., established him as one of the country's greatest cultural benefactors. Despite a number of invitations, he never visited Australia and never returned to New Zealand. In 1953 he had donated hundreds of contemporary prints by British artists to New Zealand institutions for the fine arts.

On the recommendation of the Australian government, Nan Kivell was appointed C.M.G. in 1966 and knighted in 1976. He died on 7 June 1977 at Paddington, London, and was buried with Anglican rites in the parish churchyard at West Lavington, Wiltshire. His estate was sworn for probate at £653 747. Bequests included water-colours of natural history subjects to Queen Elizabeth II, and his gold watch and bracelet to his chauffeur. His collection—which includes more than 1600 original drawings and paintings, over 3000 prints and some 5000 books, as well as maps, photographs, manuscripts and artefacts—has exercised a substantial and enduring influence on Australasian historical and artistic scholarship. A number of major paintings from the collection were placed on permanent exhibition in the National Gallery of Australia in 1992. Robert Buhler's and Bryan Kneale's portraits of Nan Kivell are held by the N.L.A.

Sir Rex had lived an extraordinary life, shaped in the grand manner to his own exacting design. An archetypal outsider—illegitimate, homosexual, self-educated and antipodean—he acquired a residence in London, a country house in Wiltshire and a villa in Morocco overlooking the Strait of Gibraltar. Oliver Stead described him as the quintessential expatriate, obdurate in his refusal to return, yet obsessed with images of his birthplace and its region, his whole identity bound up in his colonial past.

J. Thompson, 'Self-Made: Towards a Life of Rex Nan Kivell', in *Paradise Possessed* (Canb, 1998); *Aust Women's Weekly*, 30 Jan 1957; *Art New Zealand*, 66, 1993, p 78; *The Times*, 21 June, 5, 27 Oct, 15 Nov 1977; *Bulletin*, 3 Aug 1982; H. de Berg, Rex Nan Kivell (taped interview, 1970, NL); Nan Kivell papers (NL); information from Mr O. Stead, Auckland, NZ.

JOHN R. THOMPSON

NAPIER, SIR THOMAS JOHN MELLIS (1882-1976), judge, was born on 24 October 1882 at Dunbar, East Lothian, Scotland, third son of Alexander Disney Leith Napier, medical practitioner, and his wife Jessie, née Mellis. The family moved to London in 1887 where Mellis attended the City of London School. In 1896, after the medical superintendent and honorary staff of the Adelaide Hospital had resigned because of a dispute with Charles Kingston's [q.v.9] government, Alexander Napier ignored a British Medical Association black ban, accepted an appointment as the hospital's senior resident physician and emigrated to South Australia with his elder children. The rest of the family followed after Mellis completed his schooling. It was an inauspicious beginning. Dr Napier was ostracized by Adelaide 'society' and never forgiven for his role in keeping the hospital open.

On 17 December 1898 Mellis was articled to Kingston. He studied law at the University of Adelaide (LL.B., 1902; LL.D., 1959) and was admitted to the Bar on 24 October 1903. Managing clerk (1903-05) for the legal firm of Kingston & McLachlan [q.v.10], he joined A. J. McLachlan in partnership in 1906. He first made his mark as junior counsel for the plaintiff in *Billiet* v. *The Commercial Bank of Australasia Ltd*. Continued study and painstaking preparation gave him a 'rapid ascendancy' over his contemporaries at the Bar. At St Andrew's Anglican Church, Walkerville, on 24 October 1908 he had married Dorothy Bell Kay (d.1959).

In 1912-13 Napier and Thomas Poole [q.v.11] resuscitated the Law Society of South Australia; Napier was to become its vice-president (1923). In 1917 he entered the firm of Glynn, Parsons [qq.v.9,11] & McEwin,

which later amalgamated with Baker & Barlow [qq.v.7]. Napier also lectured (1921-22) part time and examined at the university's law school. In 1921 he took silk. He handled several briefs from the crown solicitor to the Barwell [q.v.7] government's satisfaction and in February 1924 was appointed a Supreme Court judge. On the bench, he was noted for the erudition he displayed in Equity and testamentary cases, but he became better known for his view that the law must be 'a servant of the people' and 'adapted to the needs of changing circumstances'.

The Australian Labor Party made bank nationalization a central feature of its Federal election campaign in 1934, claiming that the banking system had been responsible for the Depression. The Country Party joined in criticism of the banks. In 1935 Napier was appointed chairman of a royal commission to inquire into the nation's monetary and banking systems. While bankers like Sir Ernest Wreford [q.v.12] perceived the commission as 'an expedient to stifle Labor and Country Party politicians', Prime Minister Lyons [q.v.10] knew what he was doing.

Napier's fellow-commissioners—J. P. Abbott, J. B. Chifley, R. C. Mills, H. A. Pitt [qq.v.13, 10,11] and (Sir) Edwin Nixon [q.v.]—complemented his talents and he proved an inspirational chairman. The commission examined more than two hundred witnesses and gathered almost 1800 pages of evidence; it also studied the activities of the private and State banks, and those of a range of finance, investment and assurance companies. It recommended the maintenance of a strong central bank to regulate credit, the appointment of an independent governor of a restructured Commonwealth Bank of Australia, selection of its board-members for their 'capacity and diversity of experience and contact, and not as representatives of special interests', and the cementing of ties between the government and the central bank.

The thirty recommendations embodied in the commission's report (presented in July 1937) became the basis of the regulatory system progressively enacted by Federal treasurers between 1939 and 1959. While every commissioner expressed reservations and qualifications about some of the recommendations, it was a measure of Napier's triumph that Chifley was happy to sign the report. They remained firm friends. (Sir) Robert Menzies [q.v.] was also impressed. Although the prime minister was disappointed when Napier refused (1939) an appointment as chief judge of the Commonwealth Court of Conciliation and Arbitration, he used wartime emergency regulations to start implementing the commission's recommendations on banking. Knighted in 1943, Napier was appointed K.C.M.G. in 1945.

Napier had succeeded Sir George Murray [q.v.10] as chief justice of South Australia in February 1942. He ran a relaxed court. He also allowed his colleagues to appear in the streets without their traditional top hats, frock-coats and silver-topped canes, and, for the first time, to dine, smoke and have their hair cut in public establishments. Following Murray's example, he lunched with his puisne judges every weekday to discuss current cases. Consequently it was not until 1960 that one of his judgements was reversed on appeal to the Full Court. Meanwhile, senior counsel concluded that it was necessary to go to the High Court of Australia or the Judicial Committee of the Privy Council to obtain an independent review of his decisions.

In 1959 Napier was appointed chairman of a royal commission to determine whether a case existed for granting a new trial to Rupert Max Stuart, who had been convicted of the rape and murder of a 9-year-old girl near Thevenard. Stuart's lawyers had failed in their attempts to persuade the Full Court, the High Court and the Privy Council to quash the verdict. The case engendered great passion: Stuart was an Aborigine and had a limited command of English; there had been allegations of police brutality; he had been sentenced to death at a time when there was growing opposition to capital punishment; and Premier Sir Thomas Playford had rejected pleas that the sentence be commuted to life imprisonment.

Napier was criticized for his involvement in the commission because he had presided over Stuart's appeal to the Full Court. He defended himself by citing Australian and British precedents. Yet, given the peculiar circumstances, he showed a lack of political acumen in agreeing to sit on the commission. He drew further fire when, on the morning his wife had collapsed from a stroke which proved fatal, he lost patience with Stuart's counsel for relentlessly cross-examining a witness. Napier immediately corrected himself, but he was hounded for the lapse. After Playford finally commuted the death sentence, the situation was defused, and the commission's finding that a new trial was unwarranted met with general acceptance.

Among new colleagues in the 1960s, Napier often found himself in the minority on the Full Court. He retired on 1 March 1967. Throughout his forty-three years on the Supreme Court bench, he sought to ascertain the essential justice of each case that came before him, and then constructed a legal argument to support his decision. The High Court and the Privy Council almost invariably upheld his judgements, a number of which were adopted by English judges as proper developments of the common law.

Short in stature, Napier had a cherubic face, a great sense of humour and a lively interest in community organizations. He was State president (1938-48) of the English Speaking Union, grand master (1928-30, 1935-39) of the Grand Lodge of Antient, Free and Accepted Masons of South Australia, and patron of the National Trust of South Australia. President (K.St.J., 1948) of the St John Ambulance Association from 1942, he promoted the amalgamation of the State's ambulance services and served as president (1950-76) of the St John Council. In 1956 the University of Melbourne conferred on him an honorary LL.D. As lieutenant-governor (1942-73) of South Australia, Napier administered the government on 179 occasions, totalling almost nine and a half years—longer than any governor of the State. He enjoyed presiding over the Executive Council, wearing his ceremonial cocked hat on parade, and living in Government House.

While chancellor (1948-61) of the University of Adelaide, Napier helped to gain additional funding from the State government and backed sweeping reforms demanded by A. P. Rowe [q.v.], the university's vice-chancellor. In 1959-60 Napier frustrated attempts by the council's conservatives to block the appointment of George Rudé, a communist, as senior lecturer in history, and the promotion to reader of K. S. Inglis, who had criticized Napier's role in the Stuart commission. In each case Napier told the candidates' sponsors: 'If you say this is an honest scholar doing his job in an honest way then I will support you'.

Adelaide's gentry had been slow to accept Napier for they did not approve of his work on the banking commission. In 1952, when he was nominated as president of the Adelaide Club, several medical men unsuccessfully lobbied against his election because he was the son of 'that dreadful Dr Napier!' Sir Mellis remained grateful to Kingston, who had given him the chance to study law, and to whose training he attributed his success in drafting statutes such as the Justices Act (1921), the Evidence Act (1925) and a new Supreme Court Act (1926). Survived by two sons, he died on 22 March 1976 at Kingswood; his other son Keith had been killed in 1944 while serving with the Royal Australian Air Force. Napier was accorded a state funeral and was cremated. A building at the University of Adelaide was named after him. John Dowie's bust of Napier stands near the gates of Government House, Adelaide.

L. F. Giblin, *The Growth of a Central Bank* (Melb, 1951); K. S. Inglis, *The Stuart Case* (Syd, 1961); R. Chamberlain, *The Stuart Affair* (Adel, 1973); I. Howie-Willis and B. Fegan, *South Australians and St John Ambulance, 1885-1985* (Adel, 1985); *Aust Law J*, 40, 1967, 50, 1976; *Adel Law Review*, 3, 1967, p 1; *Nation* (Syd), 15 Aug, 12 Sept, 24 Oct, 19 Dec 1959; *Sunday Mail* (Adel), 20 Oct 1962, 25 Mar

1967; *Advertiser* (Adel), 24 Oct 1962, 19 Sept 1968, 23 Mar 1976; Lieut Governor's dispatches and press-clipping books (Govt House, Adel); information from Prof A. C. Castles, Norwood, Prof H. Stretton, North Adel, the Hon H. Zelling, Brighton, the Hon Dame Roma Mitchell and the Hon G. H. Walters, Adel.   P. A. HOWELL

NELSON, EDNA LILLIAN (1896-1948), medical practitioner, was born on 17 November 1896 at Candelo, New South Wales, fifth child of English-born parents Wright Smith, schoolteacher, and his wife Lillian, née Cordingly. Educated at Sydney Girls' High School, Edna gained honours in English and botany at the Leaving certificate examinations and entered the University of Sydney (M.B., Ch.M., 1920). She graduated with first-class honours and won the Dagmar Berne prize 'for proficiency amongst women candidates'. Having worked as a resident medical officer (1920-21) at Sydney Hospital, she practised briefly in the suburbs. On 23 December 1924 at the Congregational Church, Mosman, she married William Thomas Nelson (1894-1954), a medical officer with the Commonwealth Department of Health; they were to have four sons, including twins.

The Nelsons moved to Kalgoorlie, Western Australia, where Tom established a medical centre for miners. After settling in Melbourne with their young family in 1928, Edna set up in general practice. She was appointed honorary medical officer in the venereal diseases department of the Queen Victoria Memorial Hospital and became part-time director of its venereal diseases clinics; Tom worked in the Commonwealth Serum Laboratories and later in the Department of Munitions. In 1936 the Nelsons returned to Sydney. While her husband engaged in private practice in Macquarie Street as a consultant in industrial diseases, Edna was director of the venereal-diseases clinic at the Rachel Forster Hospital for Women and Children. Granted nine months leave for postgraduate study in venereology and dermatology, she travelled in 1939 to London, Edinburgh, Copenhagen and Stockholm, and came home after the outbreak of World War II. At her own request she resumed her directorship of the venereal-diseases clinic on a part-time basis. In 1943 she was appointed a consultant.

Edna Nelson also set up in private practice in Macquarie Street. The war enabled her, as it did other female doctors, to take advantage of professional opportunities that had previously been restricted. From 1941, at Rachel Forster, she was relieving physician for diseases of the skin; in 1946 she gained the substantive post. She was a reserve clinical assistant in the department of dermatology at Royal Prince Alfred Hospital from 1940 until her appointment as clinical assistant in 1946.

Actively engaged in professional and community organizations, Nelson represented the medical staff on the board of the Rachel Forster. She belonged to the Women's Club, Sydney, and the Medical Women's Society of New South Wales, and persistently sought to have women appointed to positions in teaching hospitals. As president (1946-48) of the Business and Professional Women's Club of Sydney, she made her home and garden at St Ives available for fund-raising activities and represented the club on the Australia group of the Liaison Committee of Women's International Organisations. Like many of her fellow members, she was particularly concerned about discriminatory practices in the workplace which denied women the male basic wage and equal pay for equal work and equal qualifications. Conservative in politics and a Congregationalist in religion, Dr Nelson was widely respected as a woman of integrity who 'inspired confidence and affection in her patients'. She died of a coronary occlusion on 25 February 1948 at Sydney Hospital and was cremated; her husband and sons survived her.

Principal Women of the Empire, 1 (Lond, 1940); Rachel Forster Hospital for Women and Children, *Annual Report*, 1935-48 *and* Records (ML); Roy Prince Alfred Hospital, Syd, *Annual Report*, 1940-48; *MJA*, 1948, p 664, 1955, p 55; *SMH*, 16 Jan 1915; Business and Professional Women's Club of Syd, records 1939-77 (ML).   HILARY WEATHERBURN

NEMARLUK (c.1911-1940), Aboriginal resistance leader, was born about 1911 in the central Daly River region of the Northern Territory. He belonged to the Murrinh-patha language group (called the 'Cahn-mah' by Ion Idriess). W. E. H. Stanner described that part of the Territory as a 'barbarous frontier' in the first four decades of the twentieth century, and Nemarluk's life should be seen in this context. By the early 1930s he was a fully initiated man. His shoulders, chest and thighs were deeply cicatrized, his long hair was tied back with a headband, and he wore a belt made of human hair. Idriess (who met him twice) admired his 'magnificent' appearance: broad chested and 6 ft 2 ins (188 cm) tall, he was 'a picture of youth and strength, and of muscles and sinew in rippling relief'. Nemarluk reportedly had five wives, one of whom, Marpu, bore him his only tribal child.

In the 1930s Aboriginal resistance fighters operated on both sides of the border between Western Australia and the Northern Territory. Their tactics were to spear cattle and horses and attack isolated travellers before retreating to rugged terrain and eluding their pursuers. They also engaged in traditional blood-feuds with other Aborigines. Nemarluk led a small band of warriors who lived and camped mainly on the Moyle Plain and around Port Keats. He and his followers armed themselves and painted their bodies red before setting out on forays.

In July 1931 three Japanese shark-fishermen, Nagata Yoshikiya, Yusama Owashi and Ryukichi Yoshida, anchored their rented lugger, *Ouida*, near Port Keats. Nemarluk and his party used Aboriginal women to win the confidence of the fishermen. Days later, they killed the Japanese. News of the murders reached Darwin in October. Idriess romanticized the pursuit of the killers as a duel of wits between Nemarluk and Bul-Bul, an Aboriginal police tracker. Nemarluk's companions —Minemarra, Montespare (also known as Mangul Mangul), Nargoon, Marragin and Mankee—were arrested and taken to Darwin. In March 1933 they were tried, found guilty of the crimes and sentenced to death. The sentences were later commuted to imprisonment for life.

Nemarluk evaded arrest until 4 May 1933 when he was apprehended at Legune Station. While awaiting trial, he escaped from Darwin Gaol and Labour Prison in September and remained at large for six months. After his recapture he was transported back to Darwin and tried in April 1934. Evidence was heard in court that the Japanese had been killed for failing to pay (in tobacco) for the favours of the Aboriginal women. Another explanation is that the fishermen had been murdered for detaining and raping the women. It is part of the oral tradition of Nemarluk's people, however, that he had vowed to kill those who intruded on his country. As was the case with his companions, his death sentence was commuted to life imprisonment. He died (probably of tuberculosis) in early August 1940 at Darwin Hospital.

I. L. Idriess, *Man Tracks* (Syd, 1935), and *Nemarluk, King of the Wilds* (Syd, 1941); K. Willey, *Eaters of the Lotus* (Brisb, 1964); J. Pye, *The Port Keats Story* (Syd, 1973); B. Parry, *The Story of Nimalak* (Batchelor, NT, 1983); D. Carment et al (eds), *Northern Territory Dictionary of Biography*, vol 1 (Darwin, 1990); *Walkabout*, Sept 1973; *Northern Standard*, 10, 13 Apr 1934, 13 Aug 1940; A1, 1933/2852, A1, 1937/5697, A659/1, 1939/1/9949 (AA, Canb).   BRUCE SHAW

NETTLEFOLD, LEONARD (1905-1971), golfer and businessman, was born on 16 October 1905 at Bellerive, Hobart, one of three children of Isaac Robert Nettlefold [q.v.11], a Tasmanian-born assurance agent, and his wife Edith Maria, née Hutchison, who came from South Australia. Len was educated at

The Hutchins School. Encouraged by his father to join him in learning the game of golf on a nine-hole course at Wharncliff (the family property on the Huon River), he developed as a natural left-hander and soon played off low handicaps. In 1926 he won the Australian Amateur championship. One year later he was runner-up in the Swiss and a quarter-finalist in the British amateur championships.

Australian amateur champion again in 1928, Nettlefold combined with Ivo Whitton [q.v.12] to take the national foursomes title in 1932. He captained the Australian team which toured Britain in 1938. Between 1924 and 1947 he won sixteen Tasmanian amateur championships, including eight Open titles (1930-32, 1934-37 and 1947). He had numerous other successes in men's and mixed foursomes, often partnered by his father or his sister Mollie. A prodigious hitter off the tee, he held many Australian club records. In 1927 he had equalled the amateur record for the old course at the Royal and Ancient Golf Club of St Andrews, Scotland. In his later years Nettlefold helped in the administration of his chosen sport. He was president (1947-60) of the Tasmanian Golf Council, a State delegate to the Australian Golf Union for much of the period 1932-56, and president (1944-47 and 1960-64) of the Kingston Beach Golf Club.

At St Clement's Anglican Church, Kingston, on 1 October 1934 Nettlefold had married Beryl Olga Heathorn. In the mid-1930s, when his father became chairman of directors of the family's motor-trade business, Robert Nettlefold Pty Ltd (which held the Tasmanian franchise for General Motors), Len succeeded him as managing director. From May 1943 to March 1944 he served as an intelligence officer in the Royal Australian Naval Volunteer Reserve. Appointed a director of several radio and television companies, he was also a foundation trustee of the Van Diemen's Land Memorial Folk Museum, a councillor (1957-69) and life member (1971) of the Royal Agricultural Society of Tasmania, and a State council-member of the Fairbridge [q.v.8] Society.

Nettlefold was a successful and prosperous businessman who gave generously to philanthropic organizations. He helped young sportsmen financially, but always on the condition that they make some small contribution themselves. An extremely private person, he had accepted community adulation for his sporting achievements, but shunned it fiercely in all other respects. In 1960 he was appointed C.B.E. Survived by his wife, son and two daughters, he died of a heart attack on 4 October 1971 at Honolulu, Hawaii, and was buried in the graveyard of the church where he was married. His estate was sworn for probate at $1 211 676. Nettlefold's name was listed (1988) in the Tasmanian Sporting Hall of Fame, Launceston.

K. Waters, *Kingston Beach Golf Club* (Hob, 1991); *Advocate* (Hob) and *Mercury* (Hob), 5 Oct 1971; *Sunday Examiner-Express*, 9 Oct 1971; information from Mrs O. Braham, Sandy Bay, Mr T. K. Shadforth and Mr O. G. Groom, Hob, and the late Mr W. Barwick; personal information.

R. A. FERRALL

NEUMANN, JOHANNA (1914-1971), mathematician, was born on 12 February 1914 at Lankwitz, Berlin, youngest of three children of Hermann Konrad von Caemmerer (d.1914), historian, and his wife Katharina Elisabeth, née Jordan. Educated at the Auguste-Viktoria-Schule and the University of Berlin, Hanna completed the Staatsexamen in 1936, with distinctions in mathematics and physics. She had intended to study for a doctorate, but, because of her opposition to Nazism, was advised to move elsewhere. In 1937 she became a research student in pure mathematics at the University of Göttingen.

Next year Miss von Caemmerer joined her fiancé Bernhard Herman Neumann in Britain. A Jewish refugee from Germany, he had taken a lectureship in mathematics at the University College of South Wales and Monmouthshire, Cardiff. They were married on 22 December 1938 at the local register office and were to have five children. Hanna enrolled at the University of Oxford (D.Phil., 1944) and completed a thesis on the theory of groups; the university later awarded her a D.Sc. (1955) for her publications. Naturalized as a British subject in 1946, she began her teaching career that year at the University College of Hull (University of Hull from 1954). She was appointed to a lectureship at the Manchester College of Science and Technology in 1958, and was soon promoted senior lecturer. She and her husband spent their study leave at the Courant Institute of Mathematical Sciences, New York University, in 1961-62.

Leaving England in August 1963, Hanna took up a professorial fellowship in the Institute of Advanced Studies, Australian National University, Canberra, where Bernhard had set up the department of mathematics in the Research School of Physical Sciences. On 1 April 1964 Hanna was appointed to the chair of pure mathematics in the university's School of General Studies. In 1965 she helped to organize a successful international conference on group theory, held at the A.N.U. She was president (1967-68) of the Canberra Mathematical Association and a fellow (1969) of the Australian Academy of Science. In 1969-70 she and Bernhard spent their sabbaticals in England, Europe, North America and India.

Hanna was a born teacher. She made abstract ideas accessible through concrete examples and showed that mathematics could be applied to many human endeavours. Within months of becoming a professor, she gave a series of courses to secondary schoolteachers and participated in discussions on new syllabuses for senior students. In 1966 she was elected a foundation vice-president of the Australian Association of Mathematics Teachers. Convinced that mathematical education in Australia was 'lagging behind the rest of the world to a frightening extent', she worked hard to rectify the problem and was made a fellow (1970) of the Australian College of Education. She served as dean of students at the A.N.U. in 1968-69.

Hanna Neumann's research centred largely on group theory, in particular on problems related to free products with amalgamations, embeddings, and varieties of groups. She was invited to lecture at colloquia and universities throughout the world. Her monograph, *Varieties of Groups* (Berlin, 1967), was translated into Russian and is still in print. Most of her thirty-four articles were published in international journals, nine jointly written with her husband, and two with him and their son Peter. D. S. Meek and R. G. Stanton edited the six-volume *Selected Works of B. H. and Hanna Neumann* (Winnipeg, Canada, 1988).

Hanna Neumann found joy and beauty in the study of mathematics. A humble woman, peace-loving, warm, enthusiastic, inspiring and energetic, she had a flair for languages. Her hobbies were cycling, botany and photography. She frequently invited staff and students to coffee-evenings in her Forrest home. By carefully organizing the time she gave to work and recreation, she managed to remain closely involved with her children, four of whom became mathematicians. She held no formal religious beliefs. While on a lecture tour of Canadian universities, she died of a cerebral aneurysm on 14 November 1971 in Ottawa and was cremated; her husband, three sons and two daughters survived her. A building at the A.N.U. was named (1973) after her.

Aust Mathematics Teacher, 29, no 1, 1973, p 1; *Aust Mathematical Soc J*, 17, pt 1, 1974, p 1.

KENNETH F. FOWLER

NEVILE, ROY VIVIAN (1904-1970), judge, was born on 6 April 1904 at Kalgoorlie, Western Australia, son of Vivian Hill Nevile, a civil servant from New South Wales, and his Victorian-born wife Emily Victoria, née Gibbons. Roy was educated at Perth Modern School (on a scholarship) and at the University of Western Australia (B.A., 1924; LL.B., 1930). He briefly taught at the High School, Perth, before being articled to Wallace Unmack.

In 1927 'Spud' Nevile enrolled in the university's new law school. He was founding president (1928) of the Blackstone Society for law students and president (1930) of the Guild of Undergraduates. On 18 March 1930 he was admitted to the Bar. At the Methodist Church, Subiaco, on 31 August 1931 he married Jessie Eversley Cheffins, a 26-year-old schoolteacher. A scholarly man, with a commitment to social causes and a prodigious capacity for work, Nevile was involved in a wide range of activities. He lectured part time in adult-education courses and became a partner (by 1934) in the law firm, Olney, Gibson & Nevile. A board-member (1930-42) of the State branch of the Australian Natives' Association, he stood unsuccessfully in 1939 for the Legislative Assembly seat of West Perth as the Australian Labor Party candidate.

On 15 August 1942 Nevile was commissioned in the Royal Australian Air Force. He served as an intelligence officer in Melbourne, in Darwin and at Townsville, Queensland, and was demobilized on 23 November 1945 with the rank of flight lieutenant. That month he was appointed assistant crown solicitor in Western Australia's Crown Law Department. He moved to the Attorney-General's Department in June 1947 and took silk in December 1954. In January 1955 he was gazetted judge of the Supreme Court and president of the Court of Arbitration. His term at the arbitration court coincided with volatile industrial activity. On occasions, he was vehemently criticized by trade unionists, employers and the government.

In 1963 the Brand [q.v.13] ministry announced its intention to replace the court with a lay tribunal, aiming to bring the system more into line with other States. The Trades and Labor Council attacked the decision on numerous grounds and perceived that its real purpose was to remove Nevile. In October the T.L.C. began a campaign of industrial action. An intense 18-hour debate took place in parliament over three days before the bill reached its second reading. After a further 28 hours of debate, the bill was finally carried amid slow handclapping and a walk-out by some Opposition members. Meanwhile, the T.L.C. called a six-hour general stoppage for 20 November. Nevile warned workers of possible dismissals resulting from strike action. Sackings did occur, and the protests petered out.

Nevile remained a member of the Supreme Court. In 1970 he finished hearing a notorious forgery case against Salvatore Franchina, relating to the Perth City Council elections in the previous year. The judge belonged to the Weld Club, and enjoyed surfing and playing tennis. Survived by his wife, son and daughter, he died suddenly of myocardial infarction on 23 September 1970 at Nedlands and was buried in Karrakatta cemetery.

F. Alexander, *Campus at Crawley* (Melb, 1963); *Aust Law J*, 15 Sept 1955; *WA Industrial Gazette*, 40-43, 1960-63; *Bulletin*, 30 Nov 1963; *West Australian*, 10 Dec 1954, 25 Oct, 23, 25, 27 Nov 1963, 24 Sept 1970; information from Mr B. Collier, City Beach, Perth, and Prof J. Nevile, Randwick, Syd.

SALLY CAWLEY

NEWBOLD, ARTHUR ROGER (1878-1960), industrialist, was born on 12 October 1878 at Willenhall, Staffordshire, England, son of Roger Newbould, brickmaker, and his wife Esther, née Broadhurst. Arthur followed his father's trade. After spending some time in South Africa, he was a local brickworks manager when, on 17 December 1907, spelling his surname 'Newbold', he married Annie Richards (d.1958) at the parish church, Skewan, Glamorgan, Wales. One of his brothers married his wife's sister, Wynne. The Newbolds reached Australia in February 1908. They had two sons, and adopted the daughter of Wynne who had died in childbirth.

With assistance from Charles Hoskins [q.v.9], Newbold set up a small works at Lithgow to make refractories (furnace-bricks). It employed only ten people. Newbold later said that it only survived because he 'went to work early instead of 5 a.m.'. By 1912, the year in which Newbold Silica Fire Brick Co. Ltd was registered, he had established a larger plant at nearby Marrangaroo. In 1918 operations were transferred to the Newcastle suburb of Mayfield. Newbold responded to technological developments in industries requiring high-quality refractories by increasing the range of his products. In 1946 the firm's name was changed to Newbold General Refractories Ltd. Plants were established that year at Thirroul and Port Kembla, and soon after at Wollongong. The company also operated its own mines and quarries, and manufactured building-bricks in Sydney and Melbourne. Special requirements were imported from as far away as Madagascar.

Newbold was fond of saying 'never spoil the ship for a ha'p'orth of paint'. In that spirit he pursued a programme of research and development: he travelled abroad several times himself and regularly sent senior executives overseas to study new processes. By 1960 the Mayfield plant was producing 18 million refractories per year. Newbold's supplied more than seventy different products—including graphite refractories and crucibles, standard clay and silica firebricks, and adhesives—to a wide range of metal industries and to gas, electricity and cement producers throughout Australia. A considerable export trade had also been established.

In his youth Newbold had been a competitive cyclist; he later took up golf, and in the last ten years of his life regularly played lawn bowls at Newbold's Bowling Club, established beside the firm's head office at Mayfield. The club remains a monument not only to his own interest in the sport, but to the firm's good relations with its staff. Newbold was an enthusiastic gardener. The grounds of his New Lambton home, The Gables, were regularly opened to the public to raise funds for charity and became a Newcastle showpiece. A generation later local residents still referred to The Gables as Newbold's.

Newbold never retired as managing director. Survived by his sons, both of whom held senior positions in the business, and by his adopted daughter, he died on 30 August 1960 at the Mater Misericordiae Hospital, Waratah, and was cremated. His estate was sworn for probate at about £108 000. In 1974 the firm was acquired by Broken Hill Proprietary Co. Ltd and renamed B.H.P. Refractories Pty Ltd.

SMH, 9 June 1939, 24 Feb 1961; *Newcastle Morning Herald*, 26 Sept 1959, 1 Sept 1960, 8 Oct 1983; Newbold General Refractories Ltd, *Directors' Report*, 1940-53 and 1961 (ML); information from Mr A. E. McKendry, Bolwarra, NSW.

W. G. McMinn

NEWMAN, HORACE BOHMER (1889-1968), importer and manufacturing agent, was born on 20 November 1889 at Chorlton upon Medlock, Manchester, England, eldest of eight children of Jewish parents of Polish-German descent Levi Newman, commercial traveller, and his wife Mary, née Böhmer. Soon afterwards the family moved to Glasgow, Scotland. On leaving Hillhead High School, Horace was employed as a 'boy' in a drapery business. About 1904 he went to London to work for Raphael Tuck & Sons Ltd, publishers, and was sent to Sydney in 1911. Back in London before World War I, he tried to enlist, but was turned down because of a heart murmur. He returned to Australia and married Ella Katie Lyons on 28 August 1918 at the Synagogue, St Kilda, Melbourne.

Based in Sydney, Newman worked as a commercial traveller until setting up as a merchant in 1926. He went into partnership with his cousin Alfred Newman in 1929 as a manufacturers' agent, importing such diverse products as pens, soap, glue, ink, books and jewellery. In 1931 Felix Benson in London and Harold Ponsford in Melbourne joined the firm; Newman was to be managing director of Ponsford, Newman & Benson Pty Ltd until the early 1960s. During World War II he served as a warrant officer in the Volunteer Defence Corps and was attached to a searchlight unit on South Head. After the war he returned to his business, which was taken over in the late 1960s.

In 1935 Newman had become involved in Jewish communal affairs through his close friendship with Max Freilich and Norman Schureck. Newman was president (1945-48, 1952-60) of the Zionist Council of New South Wales. As president of the Zionist Federation of Australia (1947-49, 1962-68) and of the Executive Council of Australian Jewry (1949-50), he headed the two key national organizations. Perceiving Zionist political activity as 'dangerous', a number of leaders of the Jewish community in New South Wales opposed Freilich and Newman in their attempts (from 1939) to win the support of the Commonwealth government and of the Australian Labor Party for the concept of a Jewish state in Palestine: Dr H. V. Evatt [q.v.14] played a central role at the United Nations in the creation of the Jewish state (1948) and its admittance to the U.N. (1949).

Newman also presided over the New South Wales Jewish Board of Deputies (1952-55, 1957-67) and the Jewish National Fund. Associated with the Great Synagogue for more than fifty years, he served as its vice-president (1958-62). He was a member of the State Opera of New South Wales committee, the Bankers' Club and the Commercial Travellers' Association, and was a Freemason.

Noted for his gentlemanly and dignified approach, and for his command of the English language, Newman set high standards, for himself and others. He lived at Rose Bay, and enjoyed reading, gardening and playing tennis. Survived by his wife, son and daughter, he died on 22 March 1968 at Randwick and was buried in Rookwood cemetery. A portrait by William Pidgeon, submitted for the 1959 Archibald [q.v.3] prize, is held by the Jewish Board of Deputies, Sydney.

J. Staedter and H. Kimmel, *Sydney's Jewish Community*, 2 vols (Syd, 1953); M. Freilich, *Zion in Our Time* (Syd, 1967); *Syd Jewish News*, 13 Aug 1943, 20 May 1952, 29 Mar 1968; *Hebrew Standard of A'sia*, 30 Jan 1953; *Aust Jewish Times*, 28 Mar 1968; Aust Jewish Hist Soc, *J*, 6, no 8 (1970), p 497; information from Dr N. Newman, Sandy Bay, Hob, and the late Mr M. Freilich.

Suzanne D. Rutland

NEWMAN, JAMES MALCOLM (1880-1973), mining engineer and grazier, was born on 20 June 1880 at Caboolture, Queensland, fourth of eight children of Irish-born parents James Newman, a labourer who later became a farmer, and his wife Elizabeth, née Irwin. Malcolm attended Brisbane Grammar School and studied mining and metallurgy at the University of Sydney (B.E., 1901). In 1902 he went to Broken Hill where he worked as a trucker, timberman, miner and assistant-surveyor. Two years later he was employed as a surveyor and mining engineer with Peak Hill Goldfield Ltd in Western Australia; by 1907 he was general manager. At St Andrew's Presbyterian Church, Perth, on 3 October 1908 he married Elizabeth Maud; they were to have one child before being divorced.

In 1908 Newman was appointed a consultant to Mount Morgan Gold Mining Co. Ltd, Queensland. He joined the company's engineering staff and produced (with G. F. Campbell Brown) an authoritative paper on the geology of the Mount Morgan district. Resuming practice as a consultant in 1912, he worked (1913) on the Yodda goldfields in Papua before going to the Malayan tinfields. During World War I he served with the Malay States Guides and trained as an army engineer officer in Australia. He and F. G. Pratten formed Alluvial Tin (Malaya) Ltd in 1923. In the swamplands of lower Perak they discovered deposits of tin-bearing alluvium which could be mined by deep dredging. Their bucket-dredges were soon lifting and treating up to 400 000 cubic yards (365 760 m³) of material per month. After extending their activities to Siam, Borneo and Burma, the partners began to sell Alluvial Tin and its associated companies in 1927.

Newman settled at Caboolture, in a timber mansion with thirty-eight rooms. On 16 February 1927 at the general registry office, Brisbane, he married Gwendoline Nita Stephensen (d.1973), who was sixteen years his junior. He invested extensively in the region between Deception Bay and the Conondale Range, buying dairy-farms, a pineapple plantation, grazing properties and cattle-studs. He also acquired Anthony Lagoon cattle-station in the Northern Territory and used aeroplanes for property management. To increase the carrying capacity of his land, he sank bores and experimented with fertilizers. An office-bearer in the Aberdeen-Angus Society of Australia, he regularly exhibited cattle from his stud at D'Aguilar, Queensland.

In the 1930s Newman formed companies which dredged for gold along the Grey River in New Zealand. He then set up Tableland Tin Dredging N.L. and Alluvial Prospectors Ltd, and introduced bucket-dredges to extract tin from the Mount Garnet district of North Queensland. The Commonwealth government appointed him controller of minerals production in 1942 and asked him to increase local output of strategic minerals, such as tungsten and tin. When he moved temporarily to Melbourne with his family, the Royal Australian Navy took over his house. He subsequently donated the building and 11½ acres (4.7 ha) as a war-veterans' home. Back in Queensland, he lived at Beachmere.

A director (from 1938) and chairman (1949-62) of Mount Morgan Ltd, Newman reformed its mining processes and supplied the growing market for pyrites. He served on the Mount Morgan Technical College committee and supported the introduction of mining engineering at the University of Queensland. In 1957 he was appointed C.B.E. He was awarded the medal of the Australasian Institute of Mining and Metallurgy for 1960. Business acumen and timing had ensured success in his ventures, but at heart he remained a 'bush cocky'. He died on 23 November 1973 at St Lucia and was cremated. The daughter and six sons of his second marriage survived him, as did the daughter of his first.

Presentation of the Australasian Institute of Mining and Metallurgy Medal to J. Malcolm Newman on Thursday June 29th, 1961 (Melb, 1961); J. Kerr, *Mount Morgan* (Brisb, 1982); R. L. Whitmore (ed), *Eminent Queensland Engineers* (Brisb, 1984); *Heritage*, no 18, Sept-Nov 1980, p 22; information from the late Mr I. W. Morley.

RUTH S. KERR

NEWSON, VIVIENNE ELIZABETH (1891-1973), editor, was born on 21 September 1891 at Goulburn, New South Wales, eldest of six children of Victorian-born parents Thomas Dobney, commercial traveller, and his wife Agnes May Fleming, née Browning. By 1900 the family had moved to Wagga Wagga, where Vivienne attended the public school. At the Church of England High School for Girls, Bishopthorpe, Goulburn, she edited the school magazine and passed the junior public examinations.

On 27 October 1915 at St John's Anglican Church, Wagga Wagga, Vivienne Dobney, by then a clerk, married Sergeant Basil William Newson (d.1972), who served (1914-19) with the Australian Imperial Force; they were to remain childless. Vivienne lived at Woollahra, Sydney, and worked as a typist. When Basil returned from France in 1919, he resumed employment with the Bank of New South Wales. Little is known of Viv Newson in the 1920s. She let her house at Mosman and sailed for Europe in 1929. Family letters reveal that she enjoyed life in London. Possessing an adventurous spirit, she travelled to the Arctic circle and trekked along the Rhine in Germany. From Sydney she made a world tour (1938-41) with Basil, and visited upper Burma.

'I have always been a feminist', said Newson in 1938. After joining the United Associations (of Women) in 1933, she was elected to the executive in 1935 and represented the associations on the International Women's Day, International Peace Campaign and Spanish Relief committees. She paid particular attention to working conditions and in 1935 became State secretary of Open Door International. Elected a vice-president of the U.A.W. in 1942, she helped to establish the Council for Women in War Work in New South Wales. In 1944 the U.A.W. launched the *Australian Women's Digest*; Newson was appointed its part-time editor. That year she campaigned for Jessie Street [q.v.] in the Federal election. From 1945 Newson also produced a monthly *News Sheet*, which she brought out single-handed until 1972. Due to insufficient income from advertisements, the *Digest* was sold in 1947.

In 1947-48 Newson was acting-president of the U.A.W. Refused a passport in September 1952 to attend a peace conference in Peking, she sailed one month later for another peace congress in Vienna, returning via the Soviet Union and China. While she was president of the U.A.W. in 1954, a break occurred with the Australian Federation of Women Voters. The U.A.W. maintained its course, though saddened by the split.

Through the *News Sheet*, Newson contributed much to Australian feminism. Energetic, eagle-eyed and 'as much at home at the piano as the typewriter', she kept her colleagues informed and entertained for almost a generation. Three of her particular interests were sexism in the churches, 'protective' legislation and parliamentary representation. She prepared a history of the U.A.W. in 1969. Next year she attended the inaugural meeting of Women's Liberation and Revolution, held in Sydney, and also learned to drive. Diagnosed as suffering from lung cancer, she visited Singapore. She died on 16 August 1973 at Mosman District Community Hospital; her body was delivered to the University of Sydney and later buried in Rookwood cemetery.

H. Radi (ed), *Jessie Street* (Syd, 1990); *PD* (Cwlth), 25 Sept 1952; *Southern Churchman* (Goulburn), Jan 1910; *SMH*, 22 June 1935, 18 July 1938, 18 Sept 1947; *Daily Advertiser* (Wagga Wagga), 7 Sept 1938, 3 Jan 1939; *Tribune* (Syd), 3, 10 Sept 1952, 25 Jan 1953; United Assns of Women papers (ML); Newson papers (NL); ts letters held by and information from Ms S. Webb, Mosman, Syd.

J. I. ROE
MARGARET BETTISON

NEWTON, JOSEPH JOHN; *see* WALLIS

NEWTON, WALTER (c.1889-1963), soldier and stationhand, was born about 1889 at Yancannia, a large pastoral station near Tibooburra, New South Wales, son of Walter Newton, a White stockman, and an Aboriginal woman later known as Maggie Tyler. She was a Wanjiwalgu, a people linguistically related to the Barkindji of the Lower Darling River, but whose country was situated around White Cliffs in the north-west corner of the State.

Deserted by his father, young Walter was raised by his mother among the Aborigines working on the station.

When he was about 10 his mother moved away, leaving him in the care of the manager, Edward Peter Tapp, who employed him in various tasks around Tarrawingee station. Newton maintained a lifelong friendship with Tapp and eventually worked for him as overseer. They both enlisted in the Australian Imperial Force on 5 February 1917 and were allocated to the 9th Light Horse Regiment. On 20 April that year at St Peter's Anglican Church, Broken Hill, Newton married Emily Pantony, a 31-year-old domestic servant from Tarrawingee; the marriage was to be brief and childless. He and Tapp embarked for the Middle East in June. Only some four hundred Aboriginal men, most of them of mixed descent, were accepted by the A.I.F. Newton's experience with horses may have recommended him. His duties mainly involved looking after remounts, although he later stated that he had often been under fire. Discharged from the army on 10 September 1919, he took a job in the Broken Hill mines before returning to stockwork.

Newton had not been initiated as a boy, but he had heard many of the old people's stories, particularly the myths describing the forming of the 'Corner' country in the 'Dreamtime'. He had attended Church of England services while in the army, and was deeply impressed by seeing the Holy Land. Some time after his return, he began to try to reconcile Christianity and Aboriginal lore. Myths that he had heard as a child he retold in the idiom of the Bible, pointing out parallels between them, such as the feeding of the multitudes and the flood. His wartime experiences also seem to have imbued Aboriginal stories of cataclysms with a new force. He dictated his 'history' to an anthropologist in 1957. Its conclusion consisted of the Aboriginal creator, 'the Guluwiru', announcing the coming of White people, and naming the place (after the British Crown) from which he would ascend into the sky. Newton's history of the Corner country put Aboriginal knowledge and people on the same footing and in the same moral dimension as European knowledge and people.

The last years of his working life were spent in solitary occupations like boundary-riding. After World War II he obtained employment with the Broken Hill Municipal Council. Through Tapp's good offices, Newton received a pension. For some years he was the only Aborigine living in the town. He died about 23 July 1963 at his Broken Hill home; the expenses of his burial in the nearby cemetery were covered by the local branch of the Returned Sailors', Soldiers' and Airmen's Imperial League of Australia, of which he had been a member.

J. Beckett, 'Marginal Men: A Study of Two Half Caste Aborigines', *Oceania*, 29, no 2, 1958, p 91 *and* 'Walter Newton's history of the world—or Australia', *American Ethnologist*, 20, 1993, p 675.

JEREMY BECKETT

NEWTON, Sir WILBERFORCE STEPHEN (1890-1956), physician, was born on 27 December 1890 at East Malvern, Melbourne, third son of Victorian-born parents Hibbert Henry Newton, civil servant, and his wife Clara Violet, née Stephen. (Sir) Alan Newton [q.v.11] was his eldest brother. Wilberforce, known as Bill, attended Haileybury College, Brighton, where he was school captain and dux in 1907, and played in the first XI. While studying medicine at the University of Melbourne (M.B., B.S., 1915; M.D., 1921), he represented the university in hockey and Brighton in the Victorian Football Association.

Following his graduation, Newton responded to Lord Kitchener's call for one hundred Australian doctors to aid the war effort. He sailed for England on 16 June 1915 and was appointed temporary lieutenant, Royal Army Medical Corps. Serving on the Western Front, he was promoted captain in 1916. He scorned the incompetence of senior British army medical officers and, after being called a 'bloody convict', 'altered the shape of a British officer's face', giving him 'the biggest black eye' one onlooker had ever seen. His diary described the mud, slush and shelling, the difficulty of lifting wounded men from the trenches, and his lucky escapes from injury. On 30 May 1917 he relinquished his commission.

In September 1917 Newton was appointed a resident medical officer at the Alfred Hospital, Melbourne. He worked as medical superintendent for sixteen months and in 1919 took charge of the hospital's response to the influenza epidemic. Joining the Alfred's honorary medical staff, he became a clinical assistant (1920), physician to out-patients (1924) and physician to in-patients (1933). He was thorough in taking his patients' medical histories and in conducting clinical examinations, and he expected others to maintain the same standards. Always a gentleman, as a clinical teacher he believed in the maxim, 'example is better than precept'. At St Cuthbert's Presbyterian Church, Brighton, on 28 July 1926 he had married Margaret Windeyer Macansh, grand-daughter of John Donald Macansh [q.v.5].

Newton served (1937-56) on the Alfred Hospital's board of management. Having been involved in the Baker [q.v.7] Medical Research Institute from its foundation in 1926, he cherished a vision of the Alfred as an influential teaching institution: he was a driving force behind the introduction of clinical tutors, and became involved with clinical research and thoracic surgery. He was a member (1934-48) of the faculty of medicine at the University of Melbourne and acting Stewart lecturer in medicine (1941, 1946). A foundation fellow (1938), council-member (1944-54) and vice-president (1950-52) of the Royal Australasian College of Physicians, he chaired (1950) its Victorian committee. He was also a member of the Consultative Council on Tuberculosis, the Anti-Cancer Council of Victoria and the Melbourne Medical Postgraduate Committee.

In 1946 Newton was elected a fellow of the American College of Chest Physicians. He retired from the Alfred in 1948 because of ill health. In 1950 he was knighted. Survived by his wife and four sons, Sir Wilberforce died of coronary vascular disease on 3 October 1956 in a private hospital at Fitzroy and was cremated with Anglican rites.

A. M. Mitchell, *The Hospital South of the Yarra* (Melb, 1977); G. L. McDonald (ed), *Roll of the Royal Australasian College of Physicians*, 1 (Syd, 1988); J. C. Trinca, *Neither Hypocrite nor Saint* (Melb, 1994); Alfred Healthcare Group Heritage Cte, *Alfred Hospital, Faces and Places* (Melb, 1996); *MJA*, 26 Jan 1957, p 122; *Herald* (Melb), 1 June 1944, 4 Oct 1956; family papers (held by Mr R. Newton, South Melb); information from Mr G. S. Tolson, Alfred Hospital, Prahran, and Mr I. Collins, Haileybury College, Keysborough, Melb.

JAMES SMIBERT

NEWTON, WILLIAM ELLIS (1919-1943), air force officer, was born on 8 June 1919 at St Kilda, Melbourne, son of Australian-born parents Charles Ellis Newton, dentist, and his second wife Minnie, née Miller. Bill was educated to Intermediate certificate level at Melbourne Church of England Grammar School, where his masters regarded him as having qualities of leadership. Six ft 3 ins (191 cm) tall and 16 stone (101 kg) in weight, he was a fine all-round sportsman who played cricket for the Victorian second XI. He worked in the silk-warehouse of Makower, McBeath [q.v.10] & Co. Pty Ltd before enlisting in the Royal Australian Air Force on 5 February 1940. Newton qualified as a pilot and was commissioned in June. After serving as a flying instructor, he was posted in May 1942 to No.22 Squadron which was based in Port Moresby and equipped with Boston light bombers.

In fifty-two operational sorties—90 per cent of them flown through anti-aircraft fire —Flight Lieutenant Newton displayed exceptional courage and a remarkable determination to inflict the utmost damage on the enemy. Disdaining evasive tactics, he always 'went straight at his objective' to achieve maximum accuracy with his weapons. On one occasion his aircraft's starboard engine failed over the target, but he completed the attack and then flew 160 nautical miles (300 km) to a safe airfield. His exploits earned him the nickname of 'The Firebug': 'Wherever he flew he left a big fire behind him'.

On 16 March 1943, while leading an attack on an enemy base near Salamaua, New Guinea, Newton dived through intense and accurate shell-fire. Although his aircraft was repeatedly hit, he held his course and bombed the target from low level, destroying numerous buildings and supply-dumps. The plane was severely damaged—its fuselage and wings torn, engines hit, fuel tanks pierced and one tyre punctured—but he managed to nurse the machine back home and land it safely.

Despite that harrowing experience, two days later Newton returned to the same locality for another strike. This time his target was a single building, which he attacked through a barrage of fire. At the instant his bombs scored a direct hit on the building, his aircraft burst into flames. With great skill, he brought the aeroplane down in the sea about 1000 yards (900 m) offshore. From the air his squadron colleagues saw two of the Boston's three crew members swim ashore.

Newton was one of the survivors captured by the Japanese. They beheaded him on 29 March 1943 at Salamaua. For his extraordinary fearlessness and leadership he was posthumously awarded the Victoria Cross. He was the only member of the R.A.A.F. to win the decoration in the Pacific theatre. Details of his murder, recorded in a captured Japanese diary, shocked Australians when newspapers reported the atrocity in October 1943. After the war, Newton's remains were recovered and buried in Lae war cemetery.

J. C. Waters, *Valiant Youth* (Syd, 1945); D. Gillison, *Royal Australian Air Force 1939-1942* (Canb, 1962); A. Stephens, *High Fliers* (Canb, 1996); *Aust Women's Weekly*, 30 Oct 1943; *RAAF News*, Mar 1996; *Sunday Sun* and *Guardian*, 29 Mar 1953.

ALAN STEPHENS

NIBBI, GINO (1896-1969), author, art critic and bookseller, was born on 29 April 1896 at Fermo, Italy, son of Pasquale Nibbi, cooper, and his wife Anna, née Spinelli. Raised at Porto San Giorgio, Gino qualified as an accountant in 1915. During World War I he served as a lieutenant in an Italian artillery regiment and was decorated for bravery; by the end of the war he had become a convinced pacifist. On 3 April 1922 at Porto San Giorgio he married Elvira Petrelli, a schoolteacher.

Of middle height, with upstanding black hair, an aquiline nose and dark, penetrating eyes, Nibbi read voraciously and had a retentive memory. He was attracted by the *avant-garde*, and, through his lifelong friend Osvaldo Licini, made contacts in the Paris art world. Emigrating to Melbourne in 1928, he set up the Leonardo Art Shop at 166 Little Collins Street and began importing foreign-language art books and quality prints of works by the Post-Impressionists. He influenced painters such as Arthur Boyd, Donald Friend, John Perceval and (Sir) Russell Drysdale who had previously only seen inferior reproductions.

Fascinated by the life and art of Paul Gauguin, Nibbi visited Tahiti in the early 1930s. He went to Italy for the publication of his book on Tahiti, *Nelle Isole della Felicità* (Milan, 1934), and his short stories of migrant life, *Il Volto degli Emigranti* (Florence, 1937). Meanwhile, his wife Elvira taught Italian at the Melbourne Conservatorium of Music and the Berlitz School of Languages. They later ran a course in Italian for the Australian Broadcasting Commission, for which Nibbi prepared the *Newest Italian-English Reader* (Melbourne, 1936). In 1938 he became a founding member of the Melbourne branch of the Contemporary Art Society of Australia. He was naturalized in February 1939.

When Nibbi's lease on the shop was not renewed and he was unable to find suitable alternative premises, he returned with his family to Italy in 1947 and opened a bookshop and art gallery, Ai Quattro Venti, in Rome. There, in 1952, he held an exhibition of (Sir) Sidney Nolan's and Albert Tucker's work. His shop was much frequented by Australians. After publishing *Oracoli Sommessi* (Florence, 1953), a series of reflections and impressions on a range of topics, he again returned to Melbourne. He visited Italy in 1957 to attend the 52nd Dante Alighieri congress, and worked briefly in Japan in 1961 as art critic for the *Japan Times*. From 1963 he and his wife lived in the hills near Rome.

Nibbi regularly contributed to Italian newspapers—*Il Tempo*, *Il Resto del Carlino*, *Il Giornale d'Italia*—and occasionally to the Melbourne *Herald*, and wrote on Australia and Australian artists in Italian journals. He published *Cocktails d'Australia* (Milan, 1965), another book of short stories set in Australia, and completed a biography of Amedeo Modigliani. He also compiled a glossary of words, phrases and expressions peculiar to the disappearing dialects of the Marche provinces of Macerata and Ascoli Piceno.

Respected as an art critic, Nibbi possessed 'a wonderful mixture of childlike innocence, humour, intellectual brilliance and dedication to the arts'. He did much to make Australia and Italy culturally closer. Survived by his wife, son and daughter, he died on 17 December 1969 in his home at Grottaferrata and was buried in the cemetery at Porto San Giorgio.

A road from Porto San Giorgio to Fermo was named after him.

C. Antognini, *Scrittori Marchigiani del Novecento* (Ancona, Italy, 1971); O. Licini, *Errante, Erotico, Eretico* (Milan, 1974); R. Haese, *Rebels and Precursors* (Melb, 1981); A. Kershaw, *Heydays* (Syd, 1991); D. O'Grady, *Correggio Jones and the Runaways* (Melb, 1995); D. Pupilli, *Il Professore Catalini* (Fermo, Italy, 1995); *Overland*, no 111, June 1988; *Herald* (Melb), 26 Aug 1970.

DESMOND O'GRADY

NICHOLAS, MABEL (1866-1958), Anglican Sister and college principal, was born on 13 July 1866 at Kilburn, Middlesex, England, daughter of John Nicholas, wine merchant, and his wife Mary Ellen, née Hodding. Aged only 4, Mabel had given coins for 'Bun Breakfasts' for pauper children, organized by the Anglican Order of the Community of the Sisters of the Church. An attractive, high-spirited woman, she renounced her comfortable secular life and entered the Order's novitiate at Kilburn on 18 June 1892. She was professed on 3 January 1895, taking the religious name Rosalie. After training as a teacher and community worker, she taught boys at C.S.C. schools in London. She was also encouraged by her superior, Mother Emily Ayckbowm, to develop her natural business acumen.

When asked by the Order's Mother to respond to a call from the Perth diocese, Sister Rosalie obeyed, though with some misgivings. She reached Fremantle in the *Australia* on 20 November 1901, accompanied by Sisters Vera and Susanna. Their tasks were to establish a school, to introduce Sunday mission services and meals for indigent men, and later to support Sister Kate Clutterbuck's [q.v.8] home for orphans. In 1902 the Sisters established Perth Girls' College and its junior school, Cowandilla, and Kalgoorlie High School for Girls. With the arrival of additional Sisters, they opened St George's High School (1908), Perth, Lady Margaret School (1911), Guildford, and St Alban's (1913), Highgate Hill. As Sister Vera's deputy, Sister Rosalie was responsible for securing premises and co-ordinating management of the schools.

The cost of renting each building—and the Sisters' wish to consolidate their girls' schools in Perth—prompted them to settle on a location at Mount Lawley. Assisted by James Fisher, secretary of the diocese of Perth, Sister Rosalie raised money to build a college for boarders and day-girls. While visiting England in 1913-14, she received support from the bishop of London, and persuaded the editors of two newspapers to include an article on the C.S.C.'s appeal for funds. She oversaw the planning of Perth College, its opening in 1916 and the addition of a chapel in 1927.

As principal (1928-47), Sister Rosalie identified with the college's pastoral and community ethos. She subscribed to Maria Montessori's philosophy that 'real education' brought out the 'whole nature of a child'. She worked in conjunction with a lay head-mistress, and took pride in the scholars and community leaders produced by Perth College. Considered fair and never petty, she turned a blind eye to the students' midnight feasts and nocturnal swims, but, when angered, made one recalcitrant feel like 'an absolute worm'. She was a compassionate, worldly and approachable woman, with 'a homely and straightforward way of putting eternal truths'.

In retirement Sister Rosalie remained interested in students and anonymously published *Perth College* (1958), a history of the school. In 1949 she was appointed O.B.E. She died on 16 July 1958 at Mount Lawley and was buried in Karrakatta cemetery. Rosalie House at Perth College was named after her.

E. Ayckbowm, *A Valiant Victorian* (Lond, 1964); *Myola* (Perth), 1913-33 (BL); *Western Anglican*, Aug 1958; *Our Work*, 81, Sept-Oct 1958; C. King, *By the Way* (ts, Perth College Archives).

WENDY BIRMAN

NICHOLLS, CLIFF; *see* WHITTA

NICHOLLS, SYDNEY WENTWORTH (1896-1977), cartoonist, was born on 20 December 1896 at Devonport, Tasmania, son of Hubert George Jordan, watchmaker, and his wife Arabella Cluidunning, née Bartsche. After his parents were divorced, his mother remarried in 1907 and he adopted his stepfather's surname, Nicholls. The family moved to New Zealand. Syd attended schools in New Zealand and New South Wales. He studied in Sydney under Norman Carter and Dattilo Rubbo [qq.v.7,11], and at the Royal Art Society of New South Wales.

The first drawing that Nicholls published appeared in the *International Socialist* in 1912. Soon his work was appearing in the *Bulletin*, *Australian Worker* and *Australasian Seamen's Journal*. His cartoon attacking war-profiteering (March 1916) appeared in the Industrial Workers of the World's *Direct Action* and led to the prosecution of its editor Tom Barker [q.v.7]. Nicholls's art titles for Raymond Longford's [q.v.10] film, *The Sentimental Bloke* (1919), brought him work for other films. In 1920 he visited the United States of America. Back in Sydney, he joined the staff of the *Evening News* in 1923 as senior artist. (Sir) Errol Knox [q.v.9], the editor, asked him to create a comic in colour for the

Sunday News supplement to compete with 'Us Fellers' ('Ginger Meggs' from 1939) drawn by J. C. Bancks [q.v.7] for the rival *Sunday Sun*.

Nicholls produced 'Fat and His Friends', first published on 16 September 1923. 'Initially presented as a Billy Bunterish comedy figure, complete with straw boater, Fatty Finn evolved … into a knockabout schoolboy innocently living out his days in a never-never urban world'. Within a year the strip had been renamed 'Fatty Finn'. It came to be recognized as one of the best-drawn comics in Australia and vied with 'Ginger Meggs' in popularity. Nicholls and Bancks remained rivals and rarely spoke to each other.

Tal Ordell [q.v.11] produced a film in 1927 based on Fatty Finn and his goat Hector; Nicholls made an appearance seated at his drawing-board. Shot at Woolloomooloo and titled *The Kid Stakes*, the film became a box-office success. In 1928-30 Nicholls produced three volumes of Fatty Finn annuals. The strip survived the absorptions of the *Sunday News* into the *Sunday Guardian* (1930) and of the latter by the *Sunday Sun* (1931). Nicholls had thrice tried, in 1928 and 1929, to introduce a dream sequence into 'Fatty Finn', involving pirates, cannibals and highwaymen, but was forced by Knox to return to his original comic style. Believing that there was public interest, Nicholls drew one of the world's first adventure strips, 'Middy Malone', but could find no publisher. In 1931 he went to New York, seeking an outlet for 'Middy Malone'. He recalled in an interview in 1973 that, 'Trying to place my new adventure series I found that any time I tried to compete with the local boys . . . it was a closed shop'.

Back in Sydney, Nicholls again unavailingly offered 'Middy Malone' to a number of news-papers. Sacked without explanation in May 1933, he decided to publish his own comic books. *Middy Malone in the Lost World* appeared in the late 1930s; other Middy Malone adventures and the *Fatty Finn Weekly*, tabloid-sized, sold well. Comic books by other artists quickly followed. Unable to compete with increasing paper costs and cheap, im-ported American comics, Nicholls's publish-ing company was put out of business in 1950. Nicholls and Fatty Finn returned to news-papers, in the *Sunday Herald* in December 1951. Following the merger (1953) of the *Sunday Herald* and *Sunday Sun and Guardian*, they continued in the new *Sun-Herald*. The rivalry with Ginger Meggs was rekindled.

At the district registrar's office, Paddington, on 29 August 1942 Nicholls had married Roberta Clarice Vickery, a 25-year-old com-mercial artist. After being involved in having the Sydney Press Club stripped of its licence, Nicholls was a founder (1939), president (1942-44) and vice-president (1947-49 and 1957-59) of the Journalists' Club. He also chaired the New South Wales authors' and artists' section of the Australian Journalists' Association. From the late 1940s his artwork aided the New South Wales Teachers' Feder-ation in many of its campaigns.

While in a state of mental depression, Syd Nicholls jumped to his death from the tenth-floor balcony next door to his Potts Point apartment on 3 June 1977. His wife and two daughters survived him. Within a few weeks 'Fatty Finn' vanished from the *Sun-Herald*.

I. Turner, *Sydney's Burning* (Melb, 1967); V. Lindesay, *The Inked-in Image* (Melb, 1970); J. Ryan, *Panel by Panel* (Syd, 1979); D. Angel, *The Journal-ists' Club, Sydney* (Syd, 1985); *Education*, 6 July 1977, p 237; *Smith's Weekly* (Syd), 29 June 1946; *SMH*, 21 Jan 1973, 4 June 1977; information from Mr J. Russell, Kirrawee, Syd, Mr M. Wedd, William-town, NSW, and the late Mr S. Clements.

LINDSAY FOYLE

NICHOLSON, ALEXANDER JOHN (1895-1969), entomologist, was born on 25 March 1895 at Blackhall, near Dunboyne, County Meath, Ireland, second of four children of Alexander Nicholson, draughtsman, and his wife Agnes Hannah, née Smith. The family moved to Birmingham, England, where in 1908 John entered Waverley Road Secondary School and joined the Birmingham Field Naturalists' Club. He graduated from the Uni-versity of Birmingham (B.Sc., 1915; M.Sc., 1920) with first-class honours in zoology. Commissioned on 3 November 1915 in the Royal Field Artillery, he served in France and Belgium with the Royal Regiment of Artillery; he was twice mentioned in dispatches and received King George V's commendation for bravery.

In 1919 Nicholson returned to the Univer-sity of Birmingham and carried out research on the development of the ovaries in the mos-quito, *Anopheles maculipennis*. Appointed first McCaughey [q.v.5] lecturer in entomology at the University of Sydney, he visited teaching and research institutions in the United States of America before arriving in Australia in October 1921. Over the next eight years he produced graduates in agriculture who took a broad, 'new approach to economic entomol-ogy'. He rapidly acquired a wide knowledge of Australian insects, built up a notable teaching collection, and took many photographs using a telescopic rangefinder which he had devel-oped to sharpen close shots.

The photographs provided a valuable basis for 'A New Theory of Mimicry in Insects', Nicholson's presidential address in 1927 to the Royal Zoological Society of New South Wales; published that year in the *Australian Zoologist*, it was a major work for which the

University of Sydney awarded him a D.Sc. (1929). The article gave a comprehensive account of Australian insects' capacity for mimicry and concealment, outlined basic principles and hypotheses, and foreshadowed his main research interests thereafter. His central thesis was that 'animal populations could not survive in nature unless their densities were governed by a regulatory (feedback) mechanism that was density-dependent in its operation'.

Nicholson used arithmetical models to explore his ideas further, and collaborated with V. A. Bailey [q.v.13] who provided a more rigorous mathematical treatment which confirmed his approximations. In 1933 Nicholson published a classical paper, 'The Balance of Animal Populations' in the *Journal of Animal Ecology* in which he showed that populations characteristically fluctuated and generally about a mean density. Balance, in this context, was akin to the outcome of the compensatory movements of a tightrope walker, rather than the steady state assumed by a chemical equilibrium.

The Council for Scientific and Industrial Research's division of economic entomology (Commonwealth Scientific and Industrial Research Organization's division of entomology, from 1949) was established in 1928 with R. J. Tillyard [q.v.12] as its first chief. Next year 'Nic' (as Nicholson was by then known) was offered the post of deputy-chief. He began work in Canberra in 1930. Finding that the scientifically distinguished Tillyard was an inept administrator, he requested a transfer to sheep-blowfly investigations and devised ingenious ways to use traps for measuring the efficiency of baits. In 1933 Nicholson became acting-chief. At St Paul's Anglican Church, Kyneton, Victoria, on 28 October that year he married Phyllis Heather Jarrett, a 28-year-old plant pathologist.

Under Nicholson the activities of the division grew steadily in scope and reputation, a judicious balance being maintained between fundamental and applied research. He was a meticulous worker, but took considerable time to develop proposals and to react to memoranda. This irritated C.S.I.R. executives, though they came to respect (even to admire) the clarity and scientific integrity of his advice. On 16 April 1936 he was appointed chief. Biological control and taxonomy remained major divisional activities, but ecology attained equal importance, and studies in physiology, biochemistry and toxicology were added. The scientific staff increased: 16 in 1933, 23 in 1936, and 43 in 1959. Disliking a rigid, pyramidal administrative structure, Nicholson encouraged direct contact with his research staff.

In the early 1950s Nicholson began a long series of important experiments, using caged Australian sheep-blowflies to study the causes of their numerical oscillations. His flair for gadgetry again emerged in the equipment he designed. His ideas on the population dynamics of insects came under criticism from some scientists—in Australia and abroad —who asserted that weather and other non-density-dependent causes were principal factors in regulating numbers. The resultant exchange of views was often far from gentlemanly and caused Nicholson much unhappiness. The controversy resulted in very tardy recognition by his peers of the major importance and relevance of his findings. It was not until 1995, at an international meeting in Canberra to mark the centenary of his birth, that opinion had swung heavily in his favour and the seminal nature of his contributions received due recognition. His chapter in *The Evolution of Life* (edited by S. Tax, Chicago, 1960) clarified what Charles Darwin [q.v.1] and Alfred Wallace meant by natural selection and explained how it might work.

Nicholson retired in 1960 and was appointed C.B.E. in 1961. The Royal Society of New South Wales awarded him the (W. B.) Clarke [q.v.3] medal in 1952, the Royal Entomological Society of London made him an honorary fellow in 1961, and the British Ecological Society elected him an honorary member in 1963. A foundation fellow of the Australian Academy of Science, he was its first secretary, biological sciences (1954-55). He was a council-member (1928-30) of the Linnean Society of New South Wales, president (1950-51) of the Royal Society of Australia, and a foundation member of the Australian Institute of Agricultural Science (1935), the Australian Entomological Society (1965) and the Ecological Society of Australia. Foundation president (1960) of the National Parks Association of the Australian Capital Territory, he presided over section D (zoology) at the 1947 congress of the Australian and New Zealand Association for the Advancement of Science.

Having arrived in Australia a shy young man, Nicholson consistently exhibited a quiet, but sustained, drive to achieve his goals. He remained self-effacing, though capable of entering effectively into debate when the need arose. His search for perfection led him to produce only twenty-five scientific papers and so delayed his writings that he left several incomplete manuscripts. Survived by his wife and two sons, he died on 28 October 1969 in Canberra Hospital and was cremated.

R. B. Floyd et al (eds), *Frontiers of Population Ecology* (Melb, 1996); Aust Entomological Soc, *News Bulletin*, 5, pt 4, 1969, p 78; *J of the Entomological Soc of Aust (NSW)*, 6, 1969, p 57; *Records of the Aust Academy of Science*, 2, no 1, Nov 1970, p 66.

D. F. WATERHOUSE

NICKLIN, Sir GEORGE FRANCIS REUBEN (1895-1978), fruit-grower and premier, was born on 6 August 1895 at Murwillumbah, New South Wales, son of George Francis Nicklin, a Queensland-born journalist and later newspaper proprietor, and his wife Edith Catherine, née Bond, who came from New Zealand. Frank was educated at Murwillumbah Public School and Highfield College, Turramurra, Sydney. About 1910 the family moved to Beerwah, Queensland, where he worked on his parents' banana plantation. He enlisted in the Australian Imperial Force on 5 May 1916 and joined the 49th Battalion on the Western Front in July 1917. Three months later he was promoted corporal. On 5 April 1918 at Dernancourt, France, he took charge when his platoon commander was killed, led his men bravely and won the Military Medal.

Sent to England in June for officer-training, Nicklin was commissioned in January 1919 and promoted lieutenant in April. His A.I.F. appointment terminated in Brisbane on 16 September. He bought a 20-acre (8 ha) pineapple-farm at Palmwoods, near Nambour, under the soldier-settlement scheme. His farming experience and the fact that he paid a large deposit on his block helped him to make a success of his holding. On 22 October 1921 at the Joyful News Mission, Fortitude Valley, Brisbane, he married Georgina Robertson Fleming (d.1960), a 25-year-old dental assistant; they were to remain childless.

In the 1920s Nicklin was connected with local fruit-growing associations, usually as an office-bearer. This involvement led him into politics. On 11 June 1932 he was elected to the Legislative Assembly as the Country Party's candidate for the seat of Murrumba. As an Opposition back-bencher he was unremarkable, except when speaking on agricultural matters. His informed contributions earned praise from Frank Bulcock [q.v.13], secretary for agriculture and stock in the Australian Labor Party government. Nicklin spoke often, and with feeling, about the problems experienced by his fellow soldier settlers. He soon won esteem in his electorate for his 'honesty of purpose and character'. By 1941 he held the safest Opposition seat in the Assembly.

Following the 1941 elections, most members of the Country and United Australia parties in State parliament formed themselves into the Country-National Party. Nicklin became its leader in June. In 1942-46 he commanded the 6th Battalion, Volunteer Defence Corps. When the conservatives resumed their two-party arrangement in 1944, he continued to lead the Opposition. He was to lose five general elections in 1944-56. Although he faced the hurdle of Labor's electoral zoning system after 1949, the conservatives' listless performances usually contributed to their defeat. From 1950 Nicklin held the seat of Landsborough.

After the A.L.P. government split in April 1957, Vince Gair [q.v.14] attempted to retain power as leader of the Queensland Labor Party. He negotiated with Nicklin for parliamentary backing, offering electoral redistribution as an inducement. Perennially good natured but surprisingly naive after a quarter of a century in politics, Nicklin briefly considered the idea until the federal Country Party leader Sir Arthur Fadden [q.v.14] pointed out that Nicklin had an excellent chance to win government himself. Gair's administration fell in June and elections were called for 3 August. Nicklin and the Liberal Party leader (Sir) Kenneth Morris [q.v.] campaigned on the theme of unity, and the coalition won comfortably. While premier, Nicklin held the additional portfolios of chief secretary (1957-63) and State development (1963-68).

To safeguard the coalition's position, the government legislated in 1958 for a new system of electoral zones which favoured the conservatives. In return for additional seats in the Brisbane metropolitan area, the Liberals agreed to retain the principle of zonal weighting in favour of rural regions. Nicklin's direct influence on these negotiations cannot be demonstrated, but the arrangements advanced his interests considerably.

Nicklin was a staunch coalitionist who wisely regulated cabinet decision-making in order to promote harmony between the Country and Liberal parties. He presided over, rather than dominated, his cabinet, though from time to time there were rumours that he used 'the iron fist in private'. His relations with Morris—and with Morris's successors (Sir) Alan Munro, (Sir) Thomas Hiley and (Sir) Gordon Chalk—were invariably good, despite expansionist moves from elements in the Liberal Party in the later years of Nicklin's premiership.

In 1962 the coalition parties had agreed to restore preferential voting. The change gave the Liberals the means and the excuse to mount campaigns in traditional Country Party electorates. Nicklin tried to placate the Liberals, but failed to prevent them from contesting (unsuccessfully) eight 'Country Party' seats at the elections in 1966. While feelings within the coalition were bitter, disaffected Liberals usually exempted Nicklin from their criticisms of his party.

Nicklin could be unyielding when he chose. In 1961 he intimidated the Country Party conference into abandoning plans for a standing committee on hospitals. 'When he thinks it is necessary he cracks the whip hard', the *Courier-Mail* reported. 'He was ... serious and determined [before reverting] to the role he likes best—the friendly leader listening to the problems of his friends'. The conference later authorized him to select his own ministers.

On coming to power, Nicklin had rapidly conciliated Queensland's public servants, whom Labor had alienated by its parsimony. In 1958 all government employees were re-classified and a large salary rise was implemented. The pace of reform later slowed and by 1968 the Queensland State Service Union was complaining that its members' salaries had fallen behind those paid to public servants in other States and the Commonwealth. Nevertheless, the service remained loyal to Nicklin and gave few useful 'leaks' to the Opposition. When he retired, the union described him as a man who could 'say a very firm "No" in a very pleasant manner'.

Nicklin was less adept in his handling of the strikes at Mount Isa in 1961 and 1964-65. Precipitated by legislation in 1961 threatening traditional bonuses paid to employees of Mount Isa Mines Ltd, the strike that year ended when Nicklin proclaimed a state of emergency, ordered the craft unions back to work and directed M.I.M. to negotiate with union leaders on conditions of work. The issue that caused the trouble was not discussed and the dispute ended with an uneasy truce.

In August 1964 the State Industrial Conciliation and Arbitration Commission rejected a bid by M.I.M.'s workers for a pay rise of £4 a week in lieu of an increase in the bonus. The contract miners decided to 'revert to wages', effectively slowing production. After months of fruitless negotiation, the government issued an order-in-council on 10 December directing the men to return to contract work. Four days later the government amended the order, giving M.I.M. the right to dismiss recalcitrant employees. Next day the company sacked 230 underground miners.

By late January 1965, with funds running low, the strikers were close to accepting an offer of a prosperity loading of £3 a week. On the 27th, however, the government issued another order-in-council which incorporated regulations allowing the police to deny access to Mount Isa of any 'undesirable' and to use necessary force to enter any building. Nicklin defended his actions on the ground that the communists had planned a programme of industrial disruption with the aim of reducing Queensland to 'economic chaos'. Faced with overwhelming public disapproval, his government grudgingly withdrew the order on 1 February. The strikers began to return to work soon after.

Despite the misplaced severity he exhibited in the Mount Isa disputes, Nicklin saw his political popularity as being linked to his genial disposition and personal probity. During the 1957 election campaign a senior party official had coined the nickname 'Honest Frank'. The epithet stuck, and for good reasons. When Queensland seemed on the verge of an oil boom in 1962, Nicklin asked members of his cabinet to refrain from investing in oil shares.

Although Nicklin was later shown to have misled the public on two occasions, his image was not unduly tarnished. Both incidents involved suppressing the truth about circumstances relating to a minister's dismissal. In the first instance (1960) Nicklin admitted, 'I wanted to cover up as much as I could for an old friend and an old cobber' (a tax defaulter). Nicklin's action 'sadly disillusioned' Jack Duggan, the leader of the Opposition, without shaking his belief that the premier was 'a man of the highest principles'. In the second instance (1967) Nicklin concealed for a time details of alleged sexual misbehaviour by one of his ministers, but the *Courier-Mail* forgave him for his 'white lie'.

In a fateful step early in 1958 the government appointed Frank Bischof [q.v.13] as Queensland's commissioner of police. When allegations of his involvement in starting-price betting began to circulate, the solicitor-general advised cabinet that nothing could be proved against him. The government believed that it would be difficult to obtain a conviction. With Nicklin's blessing, Hiley confronted Bischof, who capitulated. A continuing pattern of corruption within the police force eventually led to G. E. Fitzgerald's inquiry in 1987-89.

In 1967 Nicklin entered hospital with a serious illness that may have stemmed from being gassed in the trenches during World War I. He resigned as premier on 17 January 1968 and retired from parliament in the following month. The University of Queensland had awarded him an honorary LL.D. in 1960. In 1968 he was appointed K.C.M.G. Sir Francis died on 29 January 1978 at Nambour and was cremated with the forms of the Uniting Church. His estate was sworn for probate at $132 108. (Sir) William Dargie's portrait of Nicklin is held at Parliament House, Brisbane.

Nicklin was a large, personable and ruggedly handsome man with the type of 'bony, angular face that cartoonists used to draw to typify the First World War digger'. At 52 he weighed 14½ stone (92 kg); at 61 he was 'an erect six-footer who would pass for 51'. As a politician he was more subtle, astute and complicated than many realized. On various occasions he demonstrated resilience, conciliation, assertiveness and sternness. He often identified his government with the policy of 'development', but left the fine details to his ministers, especially the Liberal treasurers. The role he filled was that of a trustworthy and honourable leader. He presided over the most tranquil ten years in Queensland politics in the twentieth century.

B. Stevenson, 'George Francis Reuben Nicklin: "Honest Frank"—the Gentleman Premier', in D. J. Murphy et al (eds), *The Premiers of Queensland* (Brisb, 1990); B. Stevenson, 'Frank Nicklin and the Coalition Government, 1957-1968', *JRHSQ*, 13, no 11, 1989, p 401.   BRIAN F. STEVENSON

NICKSON, ARTHUR ERNEST HOWARD (1876-1964), musician, was born on 1 March 1876 at Collingwood, Melbourne, third child of Frederick Thomas Nickson, storeman, and his wife Jemima Hunter, née Snowball, both English born. Arthur was educated at a nearby school. His parents were active members of St Michael's Anglican Church, North Carlton, at which he became Sunday School organist. Ernest Wood, his first organ teacher, taught him at St Paul's Cathedral, Melbourne: the 'beautiful tones' of its instrument, Nickson recalled, had 'ever since made me discontented with inferior sound'.

Appointed organist of St Mark's Church, Fitzroy, in 1893, he demonstrated his considerable talent two years later by winning the (Sir William) Clarke [q.v.3] scholarship to study at the Royal College of Music, London (A.R.C.M., 1899). The chief organ teacher Sir Walter Parratt described him as 'a brilliant executant'. Yet, although Nickson gained a prize for extemporization and had his scholarship extended by a year, his piano teacher complained that he was unpunctual and his industry 'only moderate'. In 1896, while continuing his studies, he became organist and choirmaster of St Andrew's parish church, Farnham, Surrey. There he embraced the mystical, neo-platonic Anglo-Catholicism that was to be the guiding force of his life.

Home again in 1901, Nickson threw himself into church activities, becoming Australian secretary of the Oxford Mission to Calcutta, and organist and choirmaster, first at Holy Trinity Church, Balaclava, then, from 1903, at St Peter's Church, East Melbourne, where he introduced plainsong and personally helped to pay for a new organ. He travelled to London in 1911 to supervise its construction. On returning, he began a series of recitals that did much to familiarize Melbourne audiences with modern composers, especially the German mystic Sigfrid Karg-Elert. At St Peter's on 29 December 1914 he married Beryl Florence Bennie, a 23-year-old student at the University Conservatorium. From 1916 he was organist and choir-master at St John's, Toorak, but he returned to St Peter's, his preferred spiritual home, in the early 1930s and remained there, nominally, until 1947.

Nickson had given private lessons, served (1906-26) as Melbourne Church of England Grammar School organist, choirmaster and music-teacher, and (from 1904) taught organ, piano and theoretical subjects for the University Conservatorium. Stressing the importance of music in preparing a congregation for the sacraments, he urged its study in association with other arts. This, paradoxically, reflected the influence of the aggressively anti-Christian Professor G. W. L. Marshall-Hall [q.v.10], whose Melbourne concerts Nickson had attended when young and whose teaching, he said, 'sent me to the Cathedrals [and] Galleries as well as the Concert Halls' of Europe. Immensely energetic, Nickson also published three booklets, composed songs, enjoyed walking and worked as music critic (1927-47) for the *Age* newspaper. To him, the function of critic was primarily educative. He often gave less attention to evaluating performances than to elucidating the emotional significance of the music and placing it in its historical context.

During his teaching career of almost sixty years, many of Nickson's students achieved distinction. Clive Douglas [q.v.14] and Dorian Le Gallienne [q.v.] studied composition under him; (Sir) William McKie, organist at Westminster Abbey, London, stated that he owed Nickson 'more than I can possibly say'. The University of Melbourne awarded Nickson an honorary doctorate of music in 1959. A fellow (1901) of the Royal College of Organists, he was elected an honorary fellow of the R.C.M. in 1963. But his influence, while potent, was not entirely benign. Dismissing jazz as 'the lowest form of music', he also held that 'the powers of the Artist reach their fullest extension only in the Christian Faith' without which 'our music would be similar to that ... [of] non-progressive races such as India, China & Japan'.

An unashamed elitist, Nickson was convinced that 'appreciation of the sublime ... is denied to all but a few'. Although he was a fundamentally kind man, he was at times stern and irritable in temperament. There were complaints about his brusque, unsympathetic manner as an examiner. None the less, he was partial to fun. One ex-student, though sometimes 'in awe of him', recalled that 'the wry smile and ... hilarious aside were never far away'. Nickson praised Beethoven's eighth symphony for its 'explosive laughter' and 'horse play'. When walking with friends he would interrupt conversations to doff his hat to, or hurl abuse at, statues of people he admired or abhorred. Such eccentricity extended to his clothes. Tall, slim and straight-backed, with prematurely white hair, he continued to wear a Homburg and high Edwardian collar long after both had gone out of fashion. He died on 16 February 1964 at Mont Albert and was cremated; his daughter and two sons survived him.

J. Bazely (ed), *Retrospections A. E. H. N.* (Melb, 1996); C. Holden, *From Tories at Prayer to Socialists at Mass* (Melb, 1996); P. J. Tregear, *The Conservatorium of Music, University of Melbourne* (Melb, 1997); *Univ Melb Gazette*, 10 July 1964; *Vic Organ J*, 7, no 5, Apr 1979; *Age* (Melb), 17 Feb 1964; Nickson Collection (Grainger Museum, Univ Melb).

JOE RICH

NICOL, PHYLLIS MARY (1903-1964), lecturer and demonstrator in physics, was born on 2 March 1903 at Thirroul, New South Wales, eldest daughter of native-born parents Walter George Phillip Nicol, teamster, and his wife Florence, née Reeves. Educated at North Sydney Girls' High School, Phyllis won a bursary in 1921 to the University of Sydney (B.Sc., 1925; M.Sc., 1926). She shared the Deas Thomson [q.v.2] scholarship (1924) and graduated (1925) with first-class honours in physics and in mathematics from a department somewhat unwelcoming to women students. Awarded an 1851 Exhibition science research scholarship, she wrote her thesis on the optical properties of selenium and published her findings in the *Journal and Proceedings* of the Royal Society of New South Wales; she was to join the society in 1935.

In March 1927 Miss Nicol resigned her scholarship. She worked for the rest of her life in the department of physics. A full-time demonstrator (1927-33), reduced to part-time (1933-46), she became a part-time lecturer in 1946 (following the retirement of Professor Oscar Vonwiller [q.v.12]) and a full-time lecturer in 1948 but with 'temporary' status. She had written with her colleague Edgar Booth [q.v.13] *Physics* (1931, 16th edition 1962), a standard text for high-school students and undergraduates.

Nicol unsuccessfully applied in 1952 for the position of senior lecturer. Her status and that of other 'temporary' members of the department was reviewed by a senate committee in July 1953. Although she was damned with faint praise by Harry Messel, the dynamic new professor of physics, who considered that she 'coached' rather than lectured, but was worthy of consideration because she 'had been here for many years', the committee recommended that she be offered a permanent appointment. After almost thirty years of teaching, her reward was the position of 'tutor demonstrator with the status of lecturer'.

Her devotion to the department was equalled only by her attachment to Women's College, where she had lived from 1921 as student, tutor in physics and mathematics, and sub-principal (1933-54). Hindered by a lack of opportunity for overseas research, by limitations within the physics department and by her reluctance to take any public role of leadership, she remained as a subordinate within her department and college, voicing no grudge or criticism of others. The stereotype of the scholarly spinster, untidy, careless of dress and seemingly always running late, 'Phylly Nic' spoke on the benefits of eight hours sleep a night and exhorted her female students to dress in their best for examinations as a means of boosting confidence.

Nicol resigned as sub-principal in 1954 to live with her unmarried sister at Lane Cove. She underwent a mastectomy in 1953 and later suffered severe illness, but continued to work, resigning from the physics department 'due to ill health' only four days before she died of cancer on 13 June 1964 at her home; she was cremated with Anglican rites. Students were her vocation. Her genius was that, through her teaching, the most unpromising candidates could pass physics I, the first hurdle for many university courses. Her legacy was to help others on the path to opportunities she never enjoyed.

D. Branagan and G. Holland (eds), *Ever Reaping Something New* (Syd, 1985); R. Annable (ed), *Biographical Register, The Women's College within the University of Sydney*, vol 1, 1892-1939 (Syd, 1995); W. V. Hole, 'Phyllis Mary Nicol, MSc (1903-64)', Univ Syd, *Record*, 2, 1989, p 2; P. M. Nicol staff file *and* Univ Syd Senate minutes, 6 July 1953 (Univ Syd Archives); Univ Syd *and* Women's College Archives.

ROSEMARY ANNABLE

NICOL, WILLIAM DALZIEL (1907-1978), schoolteacher and puppeteer, was born on 28 April 1907 at Dundee, Forfarshire, Scotland, son of William Dalziel Nicol, master shoemaker, and his wife Jean Fleming, née Mitchell. Educated at Dundee, young Will arrived in Melbourne with his family in 1922 and was apprenticed in the 'wood machinery trade'. On 30 April 1928 he was accepted by the Education Department as a junior teacher (on condition that he pass the Intermediate certificate) and sent to Reservoir State School. After training at Melbourne Teachers' College in 1930, he opened a new state school, Chrome Estate, in the Western District, in January 1931. At the Presbyterian Church, Footscray, on 20 April 1935 he married Emily Catherine Rankin, a 23-year-old schoolteacher.

In January 1937 Nicol was transferred to Hamilton High School where he taught woodwork. Seeking an interesting project for his students, he found plans in an education journal for a wooden marionette, or string puppet. At the next school fête his class performed what Emily described as 'an ambitious affair of pirates, underwater scenes and circus acts' to packed houses at 3d. a head. Nicol's set of charts explaining how to make and manipulate a marionette were displayed at the University of Melbourne. In January 1939 he was appointed temporary assistant (confirmed July 1940) in the art department at M.T.C.; he was to be promoted lecturer in 1951.

Nicol and his students took over a basement workshop in the college and converted it into a theatre. During World War II they formed the Teachers' College Marionette Guild and held shows to raise money for the war effort. Soon they were entertaining wounded servicemen in hospitals and teaching puppetry at army education camps. In 1943 Nicol persuaded the Education Department to accredit puppetry as an examination subject in secondary schools. One of the first students to be examined was Peter Scriven, the puppeteer who created the 'Tintookies'. By 1944 the Marionette Guild had a regular booking, performing for the National Fitness Council of Victoria's holiday play centres in a van fitted out as a mobile puppet theatre.

Early in 1945 ten professionals and enthusiasts formed the Puppet Guild of Australia, with Nicol as president. In April they held a public performance at Kelvin Hall, Collins Place; by June they were housed at the N.F.C.'s training centre in Flinders Lane. 'The Littlest Theatre', with Nicol as director, became the centre of puppetry in Melbourne, opening on Saturdays for morning classes, an afternoon children's show and an evening show for adults. Nicol edited the guild's newsletter, *Australian Puppeteer*, and lectured on puppetry on radio and in country areas. When the centre closed in 1950, new venues were found under the aegis of Gertrude Johnson's [q.v.14] Australian National Theatre Movement. A group of guild members and student-teachers formed the National Theatre Puppet Company and staged seasons of plays directed by Nicol. He wrote *Puppetry* (1962), *Terracotta* (1963) and *Wood* (1966), all illustrated by his daughter Jennifer.

Bill and Emily had visited South Australia in 1953 to investigate Aboriginal children's art; next year he lectured on the subject in Britain. They carried out further research in the Northern Territory in 1966 and collected material for a series of shadow plays about the Dreamtime. After retiring from M.T.C. in mid-1968, Nicol spent three months at Kormilda College, Darwin. He and his wife edited *Aboriginal Children's Stories* (1969). While on a fishing holiday at Phillip Island, he was presumed to have drowned when his dinghy overturned in Western Port Bay on 13 June 1978. His wife and three daughters survived him. Three puppets from the N.T.P.C. production, *The Story of Waltzing Matilda* (1955), are held in the Performing Arts Museum, Melbourne.

M. Vella and H. Rickards, *Theatre of the Impossible* (Syd, 1989); Melb Teachers' College, *Trainee*, 1966, 1968; *Aust Inst of Aboriginal Studies Newsletter*, no 11, Mar 1979, p 35; *Age* (Melb), 25 Mar 1991; Education Dept (Vic) Archives, Series 640, unit 1849, no 3960 (PRO, Vic); Teaching record: W. D. Nicol, Education History Unit, Dept of Education, Melb; E. Nicol, 'Bill Nicol, Notes on His Work', unpublished ms (Performing Arts Museum Archives, Vic Arts Centre, Melb).

MAEVE VELLA

NIELSEN, JUANITA JOAN (1937-1975), publisher and urban conservationist, was born on 22 April 1937 at New Lambton, Newcastle, New South Wales, daughter of Neil Donovan Smith, English-born heir to the fortune of Kathleen Sophia Foy, and his wife Vilma Grace, née Meares, who was born in Sydney. Juanita was a great-granddaughter of Mark Foy [q.v.4]; her father was a major shareholder in Mark Foy's [qq.v.4,8] Ltd. Her parents separated soon after her birth and she was raised by her mother at Killara, Sydney. Educated at various schools, including Presbyterian Ladies' College, Pymble, she obtained her Intermediate certificate in 1952 and worked at Mark Foy's as a glove model before leaving Australia in 1959.

While abroad, she married Jorgen Fritz Nielsen, a Danish merchant seaman. They solemnized their union in 1962 in a Shinto ceremony at Kobe City, Japan, but were to be divorced in 1967. After living in Morocco and Denmark, Juanita returned alone to Sydney in 1965 and opened the 'Gear Box' fashion boutique in Mark Foy's city store. She was briefly estranged from her father for leading an unsuccessful shareholders' revolt against a takeover offer ($4 million) by McDowell's [q.v.] Ltd for Mark Foy's in 1968. Following their reconciliation, her father bought her a terrace house in Victoria Street, Kings Cross, and a local newspaper, *Now*, which she published from her home.

Wearing distinctive clothes and a 'beehive' wig, Nielsen modelled fashions and hair styles for her newspaper's feature pages. She also conducted a vigorous editorial campaign in support of the 'green ban' movement against the redevelopment of Victoria Street by F. W. Theeman's real-estate company, Victoria Point Pty Ltd. With her neighbour and trade-union activist Jack ('Mick') Fowler [q.v.14], she played a prominent role in mobilizing local residents against the demolition of Victoria Street's historic terraces and the eviction of their tenants.

Juanita Nielsen vanished on 4 July 1975 after visiting the Carousel (previously Les Girls)—a transvestite nightclub and underworld haunt at Kings Cross—on advertising business for *Now*. Attempts to find her or her corpse proved fruitless. Despite public outcry, the mystery remained a major case in the annals of unsolved Australian crimes. Over the years some information about the circumstances of her presumed abduction and murder came to light. Two persons connected with the Carousel nightclub were convicted (one in 1981, the other in 1983) on charges of conspiracy to abduct Juanita Nielsen on an earlier occasion. The trials did not directly involve events on the day she vanished.

In July 1983 the Sydney City Council opened a recreation centre in the Juanita Nielsen Building, near her former residence at Woolloomooloo. It was not until 10 November 1983 that a coroner and jury of six declared that Nielsen had died 'on or shortly after 4 July 1975'. They were unable to name 'the place of death or the manner and cause of death', but found 'evidence to show that the police inquiries were inhibited by an atmosphere of corruption, real or imagined, that existed at the time'. In 1994 the Commonwealth Parliamentary Joint Committee on the National Crime Authority further castigated investigative ineptitude in the case and emphasized links between her presumed murder, property developers and the criminal milieu at Kings Cross.

Report, Parliamentary Joint Committee on the National Crime Authority, *PP* (Cwlth), 1994; *Sun-Herald*, 10 Mar 1968; *SMH*, 12 Oct 1974, 19 Jan 1979, 4 July, 11 Nov 1983, 1 July 1995; *National Times*, 5-10 July 1976, p 4; A. King and P. Rees, unpublished ms (held by author, Syd); information from Mr F. Foy, Wahroonga, and Mr Justice James Macken, Syd.   RICHARD MORRIS

NILAND, D'ARCY FRANCIS (1917–1967), author, was born on 20 October 1917 at Glen Innes, New South Wales, eldest of six children of native-born parents Francis Augustus Niland, a cooper who became a woolclasser, and his wife Barbara Lucy, née Egan. The family was of Irish-Catholic ancestry, a background which was to feed into much of Niland's writing. He was named after the boxer Les Darcy [q.v.8], but later spelt his Christian name 'D'Arcy'.

Educated at the convent of the Sisters of St Joseph of the Sacred Heart, Glen Innes, Niland left school at the age of 14, hoping to become a writer. For two years he accompanied his father around the local shearing sheds and had first-hand experience of the effects of the Depression in rural areas. At 16 he gained the position of copy-boy at the Sydney *Sun* newspaper, a potential stepping-stone to a career as a journalist, but he was retrenched after a year. He returned to the country, taking up whatever work was available. By the late 1930s he was back in Sydney, earning his living as a railway porter. He was rejected for military service in World War II because of a cardiac condition. Under the orders of the Directorate of Manpower, he worked in the shearing sheds of north-west New South Wales.

At St Peter's Catholic Church, Surry Hills, on 11 May 1942 Niland married Rosina Ruth Park, a 23-year-old journalist from New Zealand; they were to have five children, including twin daughters. D'Arcy and Ruth determined that they would pursue careers as professional writers, a decision which meant they had to produce material such as short stories, radio scripts and even jingles that would bring immediate financial returns. An account of their efforts is found in their autobiography, *The Drums Go Bang* (1956). D'Arcy established himself as a prolific short story writer. His knowledge of the practicalities of professional writing is evident in his book, *Make Your Stories Sell* (1955).

A significant shift in his career occurred in 1947 when Ruth Park's novel, *The Harp in the South* (1948), won first prize of £2000 in the *Sydney Morning Herald* literary competition. Niland then turned to writing novels. In the 1948-49 *S.M.H.* literary competition he won second prize of £50 in the short story section, and third prize of £500 in the novel section for *Gold in the Streets* (London, 1959). In the 1951 Commonwealth Jubilee literary competition he won second prize of £100 in the short story section (and a special prize of £50) and second prize of £500 in the novel section for *The Big Smoke* (London, 1959). As a result of these prizes, he was awarded £600 in 1952 by the Commonwealth Literary Fund to write a novel.

Niland again took to the road for research. The resulting novel, *The Shiralee* (1955), told the story of a swagman and his 4-year-old daughter. The book proved an international success, and in 1957 was made into a motion picture with Peter Finch [q.v.14] as the swagman. Niland subsequently published the novels, *Call Me When the Cross Turns Over* (1957) and *The Apprentices* (1965), and four collections of short stories, *The Ballad of the Fat Bushranger* (1961), *Logan's Girl* (1961), *Dadda Jumped Over Two Elephants* (London, 1961) and *Pairs and Loners* (1966). The novel, *Dead Men Running* (1969), was completed two days before he died of myocardial infarction on 29 March 1967 at St Vincent's Hospital, Darlinghurst. Survived by his wife, two sons and three daughters, he was buried in Northern Suburbs cemetery. His extensive research for a biography of Les Darcy was used by Ruth Park and Rafe Champion in *Home Before Dark* (Melbourne, 1995).

Although gregarious by nature, Niland was also absorbed in the art and craft of writing. He is best remembered for *The Shiralee* which uses as its title an obscure Australian word of unknown origin for a 'swag'. As metaphor in the novel the shiralee is paradoxical: like the swag, the child is both a burden and a source of living. Niland's writing reveals a man who was profoundly aware of the paradoxical burdens and vitality of the shiralees which all human beings must carry, whether those burdens be (as in *The Shiralee*) the responsibility of fatherhood, or (as in *Dead Men Running*) the responsibility of Irish political history, Australian nationhood and mateship, or (as in his career as a whole) the responsibility of writing.

J. A. Hetherington, *Forty-two Faces* (Melb, 1962); R. Park, *A Fence around the Cuckoo* (Melb, 1992) and *Fishing in the Styx* (Melb, 1993); Armidale and Dist Hist Soc, *J and Procs*, 16, 1973, p 48; *SMH*, 8 Oct 1949, 24 Dec 1951, 26 Feb, 11 Nov 1952, 17 Apr 1955, 31 Mar 1967.   BRUCE MOORE

NILSEN, NILS EMIL (1902-1975), mining engineer, was born on 5 March 1902 at Pequaming, Michigan, United States of America, son of Norwegian-born parents Brent Nilsen, sailor, and his wife Anne, née Ragnhild. After completing high school at L'Anse, Nils qualified as a mining engineer at the Michigan College of Mines (B.Sc., 1925). He worked as a surveyor of mines for the Montreal Mining Co. in Wisconsin until 1926, then became engineer-in-charge of development for the Castile Mining Co. in Michigan. Deciding to seek a warmer climate, he obtained a post in Queensland in 1929 as engineer-in-charge of development with Mount Isa Mines Ltd. In summer the water in his bath 'was so hot from the pipes that ran on the surface of the ground that it had to be left to cool'.

At St Paul's Anglican Cathedral, Melbourne, on 23 August 1930 Nilsen married Gwenyth Ida, daughter of Albert Thurgood [q.v.12]. In 1931 he reportedly told Julius Kruttschnitt [q.v.9], general manager of Mount Isa Mines Ltd, that he was being paid more than he was worth, and resigned on the understanding that, if a position became available where the work equated to the pay, he would return. Following two years as efficiency engineer at the Lake View and Star mine, Kalgoorlie, Western Australia, Nilsen went back to Mount Isa in 1933 as assistant underground superintendent. He helped the company to set new records in 'shaft-sinking, driving and rising'; he also increased mechanization and achieved greater productivity in underground operations.

In 1936 Nilsen was appointed general manager of the Emperor Gold Mining Co. at Vatukoula, Fiji, thus beginning what he regarded as the most important part of his career. Three years later his responsibilities were extended to include management of the nearby Loloma and Dolphin mines. At their peak the three operations yielded some 2.8 tons of gold per year. Production had only begun in 1935. Nilsen's duties therefore entailed building up a skilled workforce and the services needed by a major mining field. The Vatukoula ore contained tellurides from which it was difficult to extract the gold, but many problems in treating the ore were overcome during his years in charge. 'Bruiser' Nilsen fought strenuously against any government impost which reduced profits, his preferred tactic being to threaten to close down the mines.

Before 1935 there had been little knowledge of mining among the peoples of Fiji. Nilsen adopted a policy of employing Euronesians, Rotumans and Fijians; only as a last resort did he engage Indians, who demanded higher wages and seemed less tractable. By 1945 large numbers of Fijian residents had acquired skills as miners, planthands and tradesmen, and the first non-European 'shift bosses' had been appointed. After a further ten years most positions in the production division were filled by locals and there were only a few expatriates in the mining division. Nilsen considered that his 'crowning achievement' was in creating 'an efficient team of miners and mill operators', and in establishing a community at Vatukoula in which he took pride. He proved to his own satisfaction 'that the old gulf between employer and employee can be bridged to the advantage of both'.

Nilsen moved to Melbourne in 1949 as chief general manager of the Emperor group. In 1960 he was made a director. He sat on the boards of several mining companies, including King Island Scheelite Ltd, United Uranium N.L., Western Titanium N.L., and Great Boulder Gold Mines Ltd (chairman from 1968). In 1967 he was naturalized. An active member (from 1948) of the Australasian Institute of Mining and Metallurgy, he was elected to its council in 1958 and awarded its medal for 1970. He died on 17 April 1975 in Perth and was cremated; his wife, son and daughter survived him.

A. Parbo, *Down Under* (Melb, 1992); 'A. Emberson-Bain, *Labour and Gold in Fiji* (Cambridge, 1994); A'sian Inst of Mining and Metallurgy, *Bulletin*, no 344, July 1971, supp; *SMH*, 8 June 1968.   JIM HOWARTH

NILSEN, OLIVER JOHN (1884-1977), radio broadcaster, electrical engineer and lord mayor, was born on 17 August 1884 at Collingwood, Melbourne, posthumous son of Ole Nilsen (d. 26 May 1884), a master mariner from Norway, by his Victorian-born wife Christina, née Alexander. Oliver was raised by his Presbyterian grandparents, John Alexander (d.1906), carpenter, and his wife Margaret (d.1903); they had emigrated to Victoria from the Orkney Islands, Scotland.

Educated at Rathdowne Street State School, Carlton, and the Working Men's College, 'O.J.' (as he was known) started work at T. C. Hyde & Co., electrical engineers, in Flinders Street, Melbourne. At the Presbyterian Church, Fitzroy, on 4 September 1907 he married Ethel Margaret Williams. His aptitude for the burgeoning electrical-engineering profession saw him do well, and he gradually bought out the firm in which he was employed. In 1916 he began his own electrical business, Oliver J. Nilsen & Co. (later Oliver J. Nilsen (Australia) Ltd). By 1924 he had moved his operations to 45 Bourke Street. Slim in build and about 5 ft 10 ins (178 cm) tall, he was a hard-driven and successful man whose personality and dedication engendered loyalty from those who worked for him.

Nilsen's professional expertise and interest in the developing broadcasting industry led him to investigate the possibility of establishing a radio station in Melbourne. On 6 February 1925 he was granted the first commercial broadcasting licence in Victoria. Next month he opened radio-station 3UZ in his Bourke Street premises. 3UZ, 'the Voice of Victoria', became a major station, specializing in live performances by musicians, orchestras, comedians, and actors in serials. Nilsen's peers dubbed him the 'Father of Radio' in Melbourne. In 1944 he won the Australian Federation of Commercial Broadcasters' award.

Like many successful radio broadcasters, he was closely involved with the community he served. Nilsen was a keen football follower, fisherman and racegoer. He belonged to numerous organizations, including the Royal Automobile Club of Victoria, Royal Commonwealth Society and Melbourne Cricket Club; his membership of the Danish Club indicated his interest in his Scandinavian heritage. His community spirit found another outlet through the Rotary Club of Melbourne. After joining Rotary in 1932, he remained a member for the rest of his life: he chaired its club service, introduction and fellowship committees, and was a director for three years. In 1964 the club presented him with its inaugural Vocational Service award.

In June 1934, as a candidate for Gipps Ward, Nilsen had been elected to the Melbourne City Council. His professional expertise was immediately put to use with his appointment to the electric-supply committee, on which he served for thirty years. During this period he represented the council on twenty-five other committees or boards, among them that of the Victorian Civil Ambulance Service. In August 1951 he was elected lord mayor. During his year as mayor he campaigned to have the State government partially fund slum clearance in Carlton; he also established a hospitality organization for the 1956 Olympic Games. He contributed enthusiastically to special committees which made arrangements for royal visits in 1954 and 1958. In 1964 he retired from the council.

A long-standing justice of the peace, Nilsen had been appointed C.B.E. in 1956. Oliver J. Nilsen (Australia) Ltd and its vast number of subsidiary companies continued to prosper in broadcasting and manufacturing. The 1960s and early 1970s saw 3UZ heading the Melbourne ratings, with innovative programming, sporting coverage and leading radio personalities. Nilsen's manufactured goods included such diverse products as transformers, bearings, battery chargers, bells, buzzers and gongs, porcelain ware, fuses, insulators and neon signs. As executive-chairman, he gave particular attention to developing markets in South East Asia.

In 1971, at the age of 86, Nilsen stood down as executive-chairman to become president of his company. His son Vic took charge of day-to-day operations. O.J.'s enthusiasm for his broadcasting, industrial and community interests was unabated, although his involvement in them was restricted by ill health. Survived by his son and daughter, he died on 24 October 1977 in East Melbourne and was cremated. His estate was sworn for probate at $1 845 530.

The Nilsen Story (Melb, nd); Rotary Club of Melb, *A History of Service 1921-86* (Melb, 1986) and *Weekly Bulletin*, 2 Sept 1964, 9 Nov 1977 and *Annual Report*, 1977-78; *Herald* (Melb), 21 Jan 1952, 1 July 1953, 1 June, 1 July, 4 Sept 1964, 21 Feb 1967, 29 Nov 1974, 26 Oct 1977; *Age* (Melb), 14 Nov 1966, 26 Oct 1977; City of Melb, Service on Committees Record Book (held by Melb City Council) and news-cuttings (Vic PRO); information from Mr F. J. Kendall, Burwood, and Mr O. J. Nilsen, Heidelberg West, Melb.   GEOFFREY W. PEEL

NIMMO, WILLIAM HOGARTH ROBERTSON (1885-1970), hydraulic engineer, was born on 10 February 1885 at Torquay, Devon, England, son of William Henry Nimmo, a Scottish-born civil engineer, and his Victorian-born wife Emma Margaret, née Robertson; his parents had left Australia on a world tour. Educated at Cumloden school, East St Kilda, and the University of Melbourne (B.C.E., 1908; M.C.E., 1924), young Nimmo gained experience as a draftsman and engineering surveyor in Victoria, New South Wales and Queensland. In 1913 he joined the Tasmanian Public Works Department. His work included the design of a concrete-arch dam and a reinforced-concrete bridge.

Transferring to the Hydro-Electric Department in 1918, Nimmo studied the hydrology of the Great Lake and, as resident engineer, oversaw the building of the Liawenee diversion canal from the Ouse River to the lake. He also began a lifelong practice of using investigations at construction sites to solve theoretical design problems. The thesis he wrote for his M.C.E. drew on the experience he gained in Tasmania. In 1924 he moved to Brisbane as civil engineer to the Metropolitan Water and Sewerage Board. At St Cuthbert's Presbyterian Church, Brighton, Melbourne, on 17 December that year he married Alice Emily Clark.

In 1927 Nimmo became designing engineer with the Queensland Main Roads Commission, then in its formative years under (Sir) John Kemp [q.v.]. He served (from 1933) on a Bureau of Industry committee which investigated Brisbane's water-supply and flood-mitigation requirements, completing the investigation almost single-handed in about fifteen months. For the economic assessment he derived flood-probability data and unit-hydrographs which he used in conjunction with the flood plan of the city. His efforts led to the establishment in 1934 of the Stanley River Works Board to build the Somerset Dam on the upper reaches of the Brisbane River. He was seconded to the board, initially as designing engineer and later as chief engineer (1935-49). Innovations in design and construction included measures to prevent hydraulic uplift on the base of the dam, and hydraulic models to test the performance of the dissipator and sluice-gates.

When work on the dam ceased during World War II, Nimmo chaired the board of engineers which managed the building (1942-44) of the Brisbane Graving Dock at Colmslie. The board employed personnel and plant from the Stanley River Works Board, the Main Roads Commission and the Department of Harbours and Marine, as well as additional labourers from the Civil Constructional Corps. After the war Nimmo and his staff (who at that time made up the hydraulics branch in the office of the co-ordinator-general of public works) investigated the hydrology of the Channel Country in the south-west of Queensland, and the possibility of scour at the site of the new Burdekin River road and rail bridge. They also conducted a feasibility study of the Burdekin irrigation, hydro-electric and flood-mitigation scheme, designed and took charge of construction of the Tully Falls hydro-electric project, and resumed work on the Somerset Dam in 1948.

On 24 November 1949 Nimmo was appointed commissioner of irrigation and water supply. He held office during a period of increased activity which saw the construction of the Tinaroo Falls Dam and works associated with the Mareeba-Dimbulah irrigation scheme. At the same time he was either chairman or a member of numerous inter-departmental commissions and boards. An engineer-scientist who based his designs and

building techniques on sound theoretical understanding and wide practical experience, he had an unassuming manner, but was definite about what he wanted and adept in devising new approaches to problems of investigation and construction. He gained the confidence, admiration and affection of his staff, and was always ready to provide a useful reference. In 1964 the University of Queensland awarded him a doctorate of engineering for his published work.

A foundation member (1919) of the Institution of Engineers, Australia, Nimmo was chairman (1937) of the Brisbane division, and a national councillor (1938-58) and president (1948). He won the institution's (Sir) Peter Nicol Russell [q.v.6] medal in 1950 and was elected an honorary member (fellow) in 1960. In 1956 he was awarded the W. C. Kernot [q.v.5] medal by the University of Melbourne. He led the Australian delegation to the congress of the International Commission on Large Dams, held in Rome in 1961. In the following year he was appointed C.B.E.

Nimmo had retired from the public service in 1955, but was retained as engineering consultant to the Queensland government and continued to serve as chairman of the Dumaresq-Barwon Border Rivers Commission. He died on 7 May 1970 in South Brisbane and was cremated; his wife, daughter and son survived him.

Inst of Engineers, Aust, *J*, 42, June 1970, p 56; Inst of Civil Engineers (Lond), *Procs*, 48, Feb 1971, p 363, *and* membership records; Nimmo papers (Fryer L, Univ Qld); information from Mrs A. E. Wickham, Albany Creek, Brisb; personal knowledge.

RAYMOND L. WHITMORE
E. RICHARD*

NIVISON, ALEX STRATFORD (1894-1965), grazier and sheep-breeder, was born on 4 March 1894 at The Glen, Walcha, New South Wales, ninth of eleven children of native-born parents James Alexander Nivison, grazier, and his wife Mary Maude, née Perry, grand-daughter of S. A. Perry [q.v.2]. Educated at Walcha Public School and Barker College, Sydney, he joined (1912) his four brothers in running the family property, Ohio. He enlisted in the Australian Imperial Force on 8 September 1915. While serving on the Western Front with the 5th and 7th Field Artillery brigades, he was wounded (April 1916), commissioned (April 1917), promoted lieutenant (August), and recommended for the Military Cross. His A.I.F. appointment terminated on 9 July 1919. Back home, he eschewed politics and never marched on Anzac Day.

In the 1920s, when the family partnership was dissolved, A. S. Nivison received the northern section of Ohio, which he named Mirani. He progressively bought adjoining land until he held 12 500 acres (5060 ha). From 1922 he strove to improve its carrying capacity and to breed bigger-framed, fine-wool sheep by experimenting with pastures, animal health (control of internal parasites) and nutrition. He found that subterranean clover and rye grass did well if superphosphate was added to the soil. At St Stephen's Presbyterian Church, Sydney, on 23 November 1927 he married Grace Gordon ('Nancy'), daughter of Grace and Hugh Munro [qq.v.10].

Nivison founded the Mirani merino stud in 1932 from the Ohio bloodlines with additions from Ravensworth and (Sir) Walter Merriman's [q.v.10] Merryville studs. He classed the stud and wool himself, and gained four world-record wool prices (1934, 1935, 1948 and 1949). In 1944 he founded a poll Hereford stud: he imported cattle from England and the United States of America, and produced champion steers in carcass competitions. Vice-president of the New South Wales Sheep-breeders' Association and the Armidale Pastures Protection Board, he worked closely with members of the Council for Scientific and Industrial Research and the Department of Agriculture. On his travels in New Zealand, Britain, Europe, the Soviet Union, and North and South America he observed various techniques of stock and pasture management.

His attempts to develop broad-scale methods of spreading fertilizers succeeded when he used an aeroplane to drop superphosphate on 1 February 1950. Nivison greatly increased the carrying capacity of Mirani: 17 800 sheep grazing on 4400 acres (1780 ha) produced 672 bales of wool in 1964. The productivity of the New England region doubled and trebled as others followed his methods. He used similar methods to develop both the granite soils of Warrabah, near Barraba, and a mineral-deficient property near Keith, South Australia. Oversowing native pastures with grass seed (and appropriate fertilizers) promoted better results with less environmental disturbance. He delivered a paper on the development of Mirani pastures to a conference of the Australian and New Zealand Association for the Advancement of Science, held in Canberra in 1964.

A gentle and humorous man, Nivison was affectionately known as 'Uncle Poss'. He had played in a family polo team in the 1920s, and belonged to the Union, Royal Sydney Golf and Australian Jockey clubs in Sydney. Survived by his wife, son and two daughters, he died on 28 June 1965 at Mirani and was cremated with Anglican rites.

J. Oppenheimer and B. Mitchell, *An Australian Clan* (Syd, 1989); *Walcha News*, 22 Feb 1935, 20 Dec 1956, 17 May 1962, 27 May, 1 July 1965, 4 Nov 1982, 5 Feb 1987; *Northern Daily Leader*, 11 Oct 1961, 28 June 1965; *SMH*, 24 Jan 1964, 29 June 1965; war diaries 1916-17 and personal papers, held by Mr H. Nivison, Mirani, Walcha, NSW.

JILLIAN OPPENHEIMER

NIXON, SIR EDWIN VAN-DER-VORD (1876-1955), accountant, was born on 31 March 1876 at St Hélier, Jersey, Channel Islands, only child of Thomas Nixon, watch-maker, and his wife Jane, née Vandervord. The family emigrated to Brisbane in 1882. Educated locally, Edwin was appointed a pupil-teacher at South Brisbane State School on 14 April 1891. At the age of 18 he became the head (and only) teacher at Raglan Creek Provisional School. From 1895 he was an assistant-teacher, first at Mount Morgan and then at schools in Brisbane.

After resigning from the Department of Education in 1897, Nixon studied accounting. Admitted as a member of the British Society of Accountants and Auditors in 1901, he moved to Melbourne with his widowed mother and worked for a firm of accountants. On 15 November 1905 at All Saints Church, St Kilda, he married Amy Mabel MacKenzie with Anglican rites. In 1912 he established his own practice. Taking an increasingly prominent role in the profession, he joined (1919) the general council of the Australasian Corporation of Public Accountants and helped to found (1928) the Institute of Chartered Accountants in Australia.

In 1924 Nixon was nominated by the Joint Council of Accountancy Bodies of Victoria to the committee, chaired by (Sir) Douglas Copland [q.v.13], which developed the curricula and regulations for the new faculty of commerce at the University of Melbourne. Accepting an appointment as a part-time lecturer, he supervised the teaching of accounting and auditing subjects until 1929. The lectures which he and (Sir) Alexander Fitzgerald [q.v.14] gave to their professional colleagues were published as *Some Problems of Modern Accountancy* (1928). Edwin V. Nixon & Partners developed into one of Melbourne's leading accounting firms. Its principal devoted an increasing proportion of his time to public affairs. His reputation for financial expertise led to his appointment to the Federal royal commissions on taxation (1932-34) and on the monetary and banking systems (1935-37).

Following the outbreak of World War II, Nixon accepted a number of posts in the departments of Defence Co-ordination, Supply and Development (Supply and Shipping) and the Treasury, working for almost the whole of his time without remuneration. His most important office, which he held from June 1940, was that of director of finance in the

Department of Munitions. He was in his seventieth year when he returned to normal practice and he continued to work a ten-hour day during the last decade of his life. Appointed C.M.G. in 1935, he was knighted in 1951. Sir Edwin died on 19 August 1955 at his Brighton home and was cremated; his wife survived him, as did his daughter and two sons, the younger of whom had become a partner in his father's firm in 1936. Nixon's estate was sworn for probate at £193 260.

Shy and reserved in manner, Nixon displayed a prodigious capacity for well-directed work. When he established his practice he chose the code-word 'Methodical' for his telegraphic address. His professional philosophy was encapsulated in the conclusion to his lecture, *Business Finance* (1930): 'In the long run, the successful business is that which makes fewest mistakes'.

PD (Cwlth), 23 Sept 1932, p 760; *Arthur Young News*, no 42, Feb 1976; *Herald* (Melb), 19 Aug 1955.
IAN CASTLES

NIXON-SMITH, ROBERT ELLERSLEIGH (1890-1947), businessman, was born on 14 April 1890 in South Brisbane, son of John Nixon Smith, an English-born commercial traveller, and his wife Zara Blanche Barbara, née McDonnell, who came from Melbourne. Educated at state and private schools, Robert began work in 1907 with the Australasian United Steam Navigation Co. From 1911 he was employed as a commercial traveller, first with Thomas Heaslop & Co. and then with Thomas Brown & Sons. In 1914 he set up a general broking business with W. H. Espenett. At St Andrew's Anglican Church, South Brisbane, on 3 September 1913 Smith had married Florence Margaret Akes; they had four children before she divorced him in August 1920. Styling himself Nixon-Smith, he married Genevra Mary Mabel Cross on 21 December that year at St Mary's Church, Kangaroo Point.

After becoming a shipping agent for A. H. Hassell, Nixon-Smith had formed a partnership with William Bellgrove on 5 June 1920. The Brisbane City Council leased them sections 2 and 3 of the Circular Quay wharves at Petrie Bight in June 1921. Severing their relationship with Hassell, they took over as agents for James Patrick Steamship Co. Pty Ltd. Nixon-Smith acquired Bellgrove's share of their joint assets, and the partnership ended in December. In 1923 the Nixon-Smith Shipping & Wool Dumping Co. Pty Ltd was established with a capital of £75 000. Next year the firm secured the agency for Messageries Maritimes. Nixon-Smith's company prospered. In 1928 the council extended his

lease to include section 4 of the Circular Quay wharves.

In the 1930s and 1940s the company's business declined. Construction of the Story [q.v.12] Bridge at Kangaroo Point disrupted shipping at Circular Quay, and the wool-trade eventually moved downriver to New Farm, Teneriffe and Newstead. Nixon-Smith had a sharp eye for new opportunities, and pursued them with determination. In addition to being managing director of his shipping firm, he was Queensland manager of James Patrick & Co. Ltd, director of Circular Quay Stevedoring Pty Ltd and the local director of the Liverpool & London & Globe Insurance Co. He was also founder and managing director of the Sumana Pastoral Co. of Central Queensland, and a member of the Brisbane Chamber of Commerce. In October 1934 he was appointed consular agent in Brisbane for France. The French government conferred on him the Palmes Académiques.

Nixon-Smith had entered municipal politics in 1931 at a time when the 'Greater Brisbane' concept had come under attack, the Brisbane City Council had fallen into debt and the Depression had severely cut revenues. Non-Labor forces fragmented into the Civic Reform League, the National Citizens' Party and the Progress Party. Standing for Logan Ward, Nixon-Smith was one of only two National Citizen candidates elected. Although conservative aldermen constituted an overall majority, the Nationalist and Progress parties combined with Labor to keep the Civic Reformers (the most numerous conservative group) out of office. Nixon-Smith was elected vice-mayor and executive-member for the transit, electric-light and power-house departments. Firm and capable, he upheld the interests of the city and the ratepayers. He played a leading role in unifying the non-Labor parties, but was defeated in the 1934 elections.

A big man with an imposing presence, 'Leigh' Nixon-Smith gave the impression of being larger then life, yet he retained the ability to make people feel at ease and important. He was kind and generous to those close to him and equally charitable to strangers in need. A warden of St Stephen's Anglican Church, Coorparoo, and a member of the Brisbane diocesan synod and council, he made fund-raising his forte, especially for the Church of England Grammar School, East Brisbane, of which he was a councillor (1934-47). Nixon-Smith was a keen sportsman: he served on the council of the Queensland Amateur Boxing and Wrestling Union, and belonged to the Royal Queensland Yacht and Brisbane Golf clubs. His other pastimes included fishing and gardening. He died of septicaemia on 22 June 1947 at Beerwah Private Hospital and was cremated; his wife and one of their two sons survived him, as did the two sons and two daughters of his first marriage.

Men of Queensland (Brisb, 1929, 1937); *Queensland and Queenslanders* (Brisb, 1936); G. Greenwood and J. Laverty, *Brisbane 1859-1959* (Brisb, 1959); J. R. Cole, *The Making of Men* (Brisb, 1986); *Telegraph* (Brisb), 23 June 1947; Brisb City Council Minutes, 1920-21, 1928, 1948, 1970-71 (Town Hall, Brisb); Brisb City Council press-cuttings book, 1932-35 (Brisb Central City L); Register of Companies 24/17-34/21, 5 June 1917-5 May 1921, A/18945; Principal Register of Firms, Card Register of Brisb and Country Firms, 1903-42 (QA).

JOHN LAVERTY

NOACK, ERROL WAYNE (1945-1966), fisherman and soldier, was born on 28 March 1945 in North Adelaide, only child of Australian-born parents Walter Heinrich Noack, mechanic, and his wife Dorothy Muriel, née Wilson. Errol's mother 'cleared out when he was just a baby'. Raised by his father and, for a time, by his aunt and uncle, he completed his schooling at Concordia College, Highgate.

After being employed in a number of jobs, Noack joined his father and worked as a tuna fisherman. A good-looking young man, he was 6 ft 1 in. (185 cm) tall, with fair hair, blue eyes, firm features and a brooding expression. He enjoyed spear-fishing and skin-diving. In November 1964 the Federal government introduced a system of national service, whereby 20-year-old males were selected by ballot for two years full-time service in the Australian Regular Army. The conscripts could be sent abroad. Noack did not welcome being called up, but 'decided to make the most of it'. He was among the first intake of national servicemen to be enlisted on 30 June 1965.

Noack settled easily into life as a 'nasho'. His nickname, 'Flex', suggests that he had an easygoing personality. He completed basic training and was posted as a rifleman to the newly raised 5th Battalion, Royal Australian Regiment, based at Holsworthy, New South Wales. While on exercises in Western Australia, he began a relationship with Sandra Harrison, a 17-year-old who lived in Perth. She believed that they would marry when he completed national service. Having belatedly celebrated his 21st birthday with his family in Adelaide on 8 May 1966, he left Australia four days later for the Republic of Vietnam (South Vietnam).

5RAR's first operational task was to clear suspected People's Liberation Armed Forces (Viet Cong) from around Nui Dat, the proposed base for the 1st Australian Task Force. A member of No.5 Platoon, 'B' Company, Noack was flown in by helicopter on the morning of 24 May 1966. The weather was hot and the soldiers struggled to push through the dense scrub in single file. Late that afternoon 'B' Company made camp for the night. With 'A' Company operating close by, a forward listening post was set up to warn if they, or the enemy, approached. Members of No.5 Platoon, including Noack, were chosen for this duty.

As his party moved through the scrub, it was suddenly fired upon. Everyone went to ground and returned fire. During a pause, Noack rose to move to another position and was hit in the side by a bullet from a submachine gun. Whether or not the Viet Cong had initiated the action, it soon became apparent that 'A' Company and 'B' Company were shooting at each other. When the firing stopped, Noack was still conscious. He died in a helicopter on the way to hospital at Vung Tau.

The death of the first national serviceman in Vietnam was bound to provoke controversy. That initial reports attributed Noack's loss to friendly fire only made matters worse. Major General Kenneth Mackay, commander, Australian Force Vietnam, ordered that the 'plug be pulled' on communications with Australia while an autopsy was held and senior officers made a series of urgent visits to the men in the field. On 25 May Mackay reported that Noack 'had been killed by enemy gunfire'. Although Mackay's account became the official explanation, the men of 'A' and 'B' companies remained convinced that Noack died 'as a result of a tragic error'.

In death Noack became a symbol of the small but growing anti-Vietnam War movement in Australia. His uncle said that the family wanted no 'propaganda ... made out of Errol's death'. None the less, protests escalated. On Adelaide's Cross of Sacrifice the following words were written in red paint:

ERROL WAYNE NOACK
aged 21
HIS WAS NOT
TO REASON WHY

On 1 June a large crowd gathered in Adelaide for his military funeral. The army flew Sandra Harrison from Perth so that she could attend. Noack was buried in the Derrick [q.v.13] Garden of Remembrance, Centennial Park cemetery. An emergency accommodation house for Vietnam veterans, at Mitchell Park, was named after him.

I. Mackay, *Australians in Vietnam* (Adel, 1968); R. J. O'Neill, *Vietnam Task* (Melb, 1968); P. King, *Australia's Vietnam* (Syd, 1983); D. M. Horner, *Australian Higher Command in the Vietnam War* (Canb, 1986); F. Frost, *Australia's War in Vietnam* (Syd, 1987); G. Langley, *A Decade of Dissent* (Syd, 1992); T. Burstall, *Vietnam* (Brisb, 1993); I. McNeill, *To Long Tan* (Syd, 1993); *Advertiser* (Adel), 26-28, 30 May-2 June 1966.

JOHN KNOTT

NOLAN, FRANCIS GEORGE (1894-1977), trade-union official and railway clerk, was born on 7 August 1894 at Bridstoon's Dam, Wellshot station, near Longreach, Queensland, third child of Henry Nolan, a Queensland-born carrier, and his wife Delia, née Connell, who came from Ireland. The family moved to Rockhampton where Frank attended school. Although his parents had little money, he enjoyed a happy childhood, playing cricket and football, and swimming in the waterholes on the outskirts of the city. 'At the age of 13 years 7 months' he passed an examination for the post of apprentice clerk, and on 22 November 1909 was appointed to the traffic branch of the Queensland Railway Department. His first job, at Mount Chalmers, involved a daily return trip because he could not afford to live away from home on his meagre wages. On 5 December 1910 he accepted employment in the railway goods office at Rockhampton.

After attending meetings of the Railway Clerks' Association, Nolan joined the 'all-grades' Queensland Railway Union in November 1914. In 1920 the Q.R.U. amalgamated with similar bodies in other States to form the Australian Railways Union. A militant organization with syndicalist elements in its ideology, the A.R.U. preferred direct action to the institutionalized system of arbitration advocated by the Australian Labor Party. In the ensuing years the A.R.U. often came into conflict with Queensland Labor governments. Nolan's career as a union official had begun in the Rockhampton sub-branch of the Q.R.U. In 1917 he was elected its vice-chairman and became a correspondent for the union's journal, the *Militant* (from 1921, as the organ of the A.R.U.'s Queensland branch, it was named the *Advocate*). Nolan spent a short period at Mount Morgan before being transferred back to Rockhampton. He took part in the 1925 railway strike in which the A.R.U. won a resounding victory, forcing W. N. Gillies' [q.v.9] State Labor government to support an increase of five shillings in the weekly basic wage, the amount by which it had been reduced in 1922 at the request of E. G. Theodore's [q.v.12] government. The A.L.P. struck back by excluding A.R.U. delegates—among them Tim Moroney [q.v.10] and George Rymer [q.v.]—from the 1926 Labor-in-Politics Convention. This action precipitated the A.R.U.'s disaffiliation from the A.L.P.

Later that year Nolan was a delegate to the A.R.U.'s conference at Townsville which condemned the A.L.P. He played an active role in the 1927 railway lockout in which the Labor premier William McCormack [q.v.10] sacked the entire Queensland railway staff and forced the A.R.U. to capitulate on the government's terms. In 1929 Nolan unsuccessfully contested Labor pre-selection for the Legislative Assembly seat of Rockhampton against the incumbent G. P. Farrell. He attended the 1930 Red International of Labour Unions conference in Moscow and made an extensive tour of the Soviet Union.

Transferred to Brisbane in 1935, Nolan soon rose through the union's ranks to become State treasurer in 1939. During World War II he served as the employees' representative on the Clerical Classification Board. When Moroney died, Nolan was elected State secretary of the A.R.U. in January 1945. He was immediately embroiled in the union movement's agitation for improvements in wages and conditions. The A.R.U. supported the meatworkers' strike in 1946, then joined other unions in a bitter struggle with Premier E. M. Hanlon's [q.v.14] Labor government over increases in wage margins for skilled workers. In December 1947 Nolan was fined for disobeying an order of the State Industrial Court. The conflict with the government culminated in the railway strike, which began in February 1948. Acting under the government's emergency powers, police resorted to violence in breaking up a railwaymen's march on St Patrick's Day. The government and the A.R.U. reached a compromise settlement after nine weeks.

Prompted by the split in the A.L.P. in 1957, Nolan led the A.R.U. back into the official Labor fold. He later served as a delegate to the party's State central executive and to its federal conferences. Although he continued the A.R.U.'s aggressive style of unionism, he was able, as chairman of the Combined Railway Unions, to muster considerable support from affiliates. In the 1950s and 1960s the Queensland railways underwent substantial change, with redundancies resulting from competition from road transport, the introduction of diesel locomotives, increased use of long trains to transport minerals, and the advent of new technologies. As an executive-member (vice-president 1957-69) of the Trades and Labor Council of Queensland, Nolan helped to organize several mass stopwork meetings in the 1960s over claims for increased wages.

In 1958 Nolan addressed the 42nd session of the International Labour Conference at Geneva. Of average height and solid build, he was self-educated and an avid reader. He never married, and in the latter part of his life lived at Bulimba with his sister and her children. Following his retirement in December 1969, he wrote and published his memoirs, *You Pass This Way Only Once* (edited by Denis Murphy, Brisbane, 1974). He died on 8 October 1977 in Princess Alexandra Hospital, South Brisbane, and was cremated with Anglican rites.

D. J. Murphy et al (eds), *Labor in Power* (Brisb, 1980); D. J. Murphy, *The Big Strikes* (Brisb, 1983);

D. Blackmur, *Strikes* (Syd, 1993); *Militant* (Brisb), 11 Oct 1920; *Advocate* (Brisb), 15 Jan 1945; *Brisb Catholic Hist Soc Procs*, 2, 1990, p 52; information from Mr F. Campbell, Brisb, and Ms A. and Mr G. Edwards, Hawthorn, Brisb.

TIM MORONEY

NOLAN, VIOLET CYNTHIA (1908-1976), writer, was born on 18 September 1908 at Evandale, Tasmania, youngest of seven children of Henry Reed, an English-born and Cambridge-educated grazier, and his wife Lila Borwick, née Dennison (d.1928), who came from the Orkney Islands, Scotland. Her grandfather was Henry Reed [q.v.2]. With her siblings at schools in England and at Geelong, Victoria, from 1911, Cynthia spent a lonely childhood at the family mansion, Mount Pleasant, Launceston, in a household run on lines of strict Nonconformist piety. She was taught by a governess, then boarded (1920-26) at the Church of England Girls' Grammar School (The Hermitage), Geelong. After leaving school she worked in an art shop in Melbourne. In 1929 she travelled to England where her sister Margaret was a medical practitioner at Cambridge. In London, Cynthia attended the theatre, ballet, concerts, exhibitions and lectures on art; by March 1930 she was living with a Jewish family in Germany, studying languages, art and music.

Back in Melbourne, she became a notable player in alternative art and intellectual circles. Maie, wife of R. G. (Baron) Casey [q.v.13], who met Cynthia through (Sir) Daryl Lindsay and Basil Burdett [qq.v.10,7], recalled her as 'tallish, graceful, always beautifully dressed. Her pale face shaded by dark hair was of rare sculptural beauty, her eyes were blue with black lashes, her mouth precisely drawn, sensitive, rather sad'. Friends and intimates included Edward Dyason [q.v.8], the H. V. Evatts, Moya Dyring, Reg Ellery [qq.v.14], Sam Atyeo, (Sir) Bernard Heinze, Peter Bellew, and Sunday Baillieu who married Cynthia's brother John in 1932. She was associated with Fred Ward's furniture shop at 52a Collins Street before opening her own modern interior-design shop and gallery in Little Collins Street. Ward, Atyeo and Mark Bracegirdle designed furniture for her, and Michael O'Connell, fabrics. She showed Atyeo's controversial paintings in June 1933 and held Ian Fairweather's [q.v.14] first exhibition in March 1934.

Cynthia went to Sydney where she studied dance and art. In mid-1935 she left for Hollywood and New York. Deciding to nurse, she trained at St Joseph's Hospital, Chicago, and in London at the Nightingale School, St Thomas's Hospital (from June 1936 to June 1939). During snatched leave she renewed friendships with expatriates such as Atyeo, Dyring, Clive Turnbull [q.v.] and Kenneth von Bibra. In August 1939 she began nursing at the American Hospital of Paris, escaping the German invasion in 1940 by accompanying an elderly invalid to New York. There she attended a course at the Payne Whitney Psychiatric Clinic of the New York Hospital.

Known as Mrs Jan Knut Hansen, she returned to Melbourne at the end of 1940. Her daughter Jinx was born on 6 May 1941 at Heidelberg. Cynthia spent time at Heide with the Reeds, but, following a serious breach with Sunday, moved with Jinx to Wahroonga, Sydney. Her first novel, *Lucky Alphonse* (Melbourne, 1944), based on her experiences at St Thomas's, was later rewritten as *A Bride for St Thomas* (London, 1970). *Daddy Sowed a Wind!* (Sydney, 1947) drew on her Tasmanian upbringing.

In the early 1940s Cynthia had met (Sir) Sidney Robert Nolan at Heide. In 1948 he called on her at Wahroonga. He was aged 30, she 39. Their marriage on 25 March that year at St Stephen's Presbyterian Church, Sydney, marked an estrangement from the Reeds and Heide. Sidney formally adopted Jinx on 7 June 1949. Cosmopolitan and well connected, Cynthia provided both aesthetic guidance and business contacts for Sidney. She believed him to be a genius, and threw herself into organizing and promoting his exhibitions. After touring outback Australia in June-September 1949, the Nolans travelled to England and Europe. They returned to Sydney, but, by late 1953, were again in London, thereafter their base. In 1957 they bought a house by the Thames in Deodar Road, Putney.

Over the next twenty years Cynthia accompanied Sidney on most of his travels, making notes and observations which formed the basis of her books. *Outback* (London, 1962), her account of their first trip, received good reviews. *One Traveller's Africa* (1965) recorded an expedition in 1962. She described travels in the United States in 1959-61 in *Open Negative* (1967); its title referred to her six-month stay in a New York hospital, receiving treatment for tuberculosis. Two trips in 1965, to Asia and New Guinea, provided Cynthia with material for *A Sight of China* (1969) and *Paradise, and yet* (1971). Sidney contributed the dustcover designs, endpapers, illustrations and photographs to her travel books. While of interest for their account of Sidney's creative processes, these books stand on their own for the idiosyncratic and perceptive quality of Cynthia's writing, especially her vocabulary of colour, shape and form. Her chronically poor health was an underlying theme.

The Nolans' circle in London included Kenneth (Lord) Clark and his wife, C. P. (Lord) Snow and his wife Pamela Hansford Johnson, Benjamin (Lord) Britten, Patrick

White and Manoly Lascaris. Cynthia's direct manner and fierce protection of Sidney's professional privacy contributed to her reputation as a 'difficult woman'. In fact she loved to entertain close friends, in her home—which was described by Patrick White as wearing her 'peculiar aura, her simple, sometimes sombre elegance'—and in her garden, which she tended with passion. Elizabeth Harrower remembered her as a complex and contradictory woman, intuitive and intense. In 1974 Cynthia visited Australia for the last time. She died of an overdose of barbiturates on 24 November 1976 in an hotel in London. Her husband and daughter survived her.

The impact of Cynthia Nolan's suicide and the subsequent public feud between White and Sidney detracted from a proper assessment of her, both as a writer and as partner in Nolan's international career. Some recognition has since been accorded her with the republication of her books on Australia, Africa, China and New Guinea as *Outback and Beyond* (Sydney, 1994).

R. Haese, *Rebels and Precursors* (Melb, 1981); P. White, *Flaws in the Glass* (Lond, 1981); E. Harrower, 'Introduction' to Cynthia Nolan's *Outback and Beyond* (Syd, 1994); M. E. McGuire, 'Paradise, and yet: the writings of Cynthia Reed Nolan', *Age Monthly Review*, Apr 1988, p 3; *Australian Style*, issue 10, 1994; *Australian*, 7 Dec 1976; *Age* (Melb), 8 Dec 1976; *SMH*, 4 June 1994; The Nightingale School Probationers' Record Book H1/ST/NTS/C4/25 (Lond Metropolitan A); MSS 3865, letter to Pat Flower (ML); information from Jinx Nolan, Boston, USA, Dr N. Underhill, St Lucia, and Mr S. Bracegirdle, Kelvin Grove, Brisb.

SALLY O'NEILL

NONA, TANU (c.1902-1980), pearler and Torres Strait Islands councillor, was born about 1902 on Saibai Island, one of eleven children of a Samoan seaman known locally as Tipoti Nona and his wife Ugari, a Saibai woman. Tipoti's Samoan name is said to have been Moses Nonga. Soon after Tanu was born the family moved to Badu Island where Tipoti found a job with the mission-run Papuan Industries Ltd. The Nonas became integrated into the Badu community through the traditional mechanisms of adoption and friendship. Like most Torres Strait Islander boys, Tanu had a brief schooling before joining a pearling boat. He quickly revealed the qualities of drive and dominance that were to mark his later career, and at the age of 18 was made a skipper. In 1931 he won a contest among the leading captains of the strait by gathering ten tons of trochus-shell in six weeks. Working the reefs along the Queensland coast from Cape York to Gladstone for months on end, he acquired a detailed knowledge of the sea, the

winds and the tides. He attributed his success to the work ethic:

> You must have a strong captain to make [the] boys work. If they not get much shell I not let them into the dinghy to eat dinner, midday. They got to eat their piece of damper standing on the reef.

On 12 February 1924 at the Court House, Thursday Island, Tanu had married Naianga (d.1964), daughter of Tamwoy, a prominent skipper and Badu community leader. Their marriage laid the ground for Nona's entry into public affairs. Elected to the Badu council in 1929, he was chosen to direct the construction of a new church on the island. While at sea, he drove his men to earn money to pay for the materials; while ashore, he drove the villagers to take on much of the building work themselves. That Badu was able to complete the project and pay off its debts within a few years—despite the Depression—was a remarkable accomplishment, for which Tanu was given much of the credit.

Tanu's achievements as a skipper attracted the notice of the Queensland government's Aboriginal Department (Department of Native Affairs), which managed a pearling fleet on behalf of the Islanders. The department provided him with the best and biggest boats. From the late 1930s he operated these vessels as a family business, assisted by his brothers and, later, his sons and nephews. In time the elder members of the family took luggers and cutters of their own, but remained part of Nona Bros, under the management of Tanu.

Pearling was suspended during World War II. When hostilities ended, the Nonas resumed with only one boat. They soon regained their pre-eminence. In the peak year of 1959 they controlled eight government vessels, all equipped with diving gear, and accounted for well over 50 per cent of the catch of the government fleet. The Nonas and their associates also provided skippers for four boats in the industry's private sector. Badu prospered during those years, and the island's feasts were the most opulent in the strait.

In the 1960s the pearling industry went into decline. Although the Nonas' boats kept working longer than most and some younger members of the family took up other types of fishing, the Nonas lost their economic supremacy. Tanu, however, remained a powerful figure in local government, almost without interruption, until his retirement in 1976. He and his family dominated the Badu council, and, as the representative of the Western Islands group, he ensured that his influence prevailed throughout the region.

When the Queensland government encountered increasing restlessness among the Islanders, Nona remained loyal. In 1972 he was appointed O.B.E. Survived by his daughter and seven sons, he died on 10 December 1980 on Badu Island and was buried with Anglican rites in the local cemetery. A few years later, the ceremony to mark the unveiling of his tombstone was attended by more than a thousand visitors from other island communities and farther afield.

J. Beckett, *Torres Strait Islanders* (Cambridge, 1987); N. Sharp, *Stars of Tagai* (Canb, 1993).

JEREMY BECKETT

NORMAN, ELDRED DE BRACTON (1914-1971), inventor and racing-car driver, was born on 9 January 1914 in Adelaide, second of six children of Australian-born parents William Ashley Norman, solicitor, and his wife Alma Janet, daughter of Daniel Matthews [q.v.5]. Thomas Magarey [q.v.2] was his great-grandfather. Eldred attended Scotch College and made a token effort to study law at the University of Adelaide. In 1938 he set up an engineering workshop and motorcar-dealership in Adelaide. Rejected for military service in World War II because of asthma, he began to make garden tools and to manufacture charcoal-burning gas producers to power vehicles. At the Church of the Epiphany, Crafers, on 15 May 1941 he married with Anglican rites Nancy Fotheringham Cato, a 24-year-old journalist.

In 1946 Norman bought ex-army vehicles and sold them in Adelaide at a profit. While visiting the Territory of Papua-New Guinea, he started to construct a racing-car—the 'double bunger'. Powered by two Ford V8 engines, this large machine had water-cooled brakes which produced spectacular clouds of steam as he applied them. Between 1948 and 1951 he drove the car successfully in hill-climbs and races in three States. While leading in the 1951 Australian Grand Prix, the vehicle broke down. Norman then bought a 1936 Maserati Type 6 CM, for which he made a new engine. Stories abound of how he outpaced police as he tested cars on the road from his workshop to his Hope Valley home.

Norman and his wife pursued a wide variety of interests. With the help of income from his father-in-law, Eldred built an observatory; Nancy worked as a journalist and art critic for the Adelaide *News*, and became a poet and novelist. In 1954 Norman drove a Triumph sports car to Queensland, towing a trailer of racing-fuel. Winning a support race on the morning of the Australian Grand Prix gained him entry into the main race, in which he came fourth. An active member of the Sporting Car Club of South Australia, he often took his children to events, leaving Nancy free to write. During construction of the club's hill-climb at Collingrove, he used a sub-machine-gun to

blast holes for explosive charges. For the 1955 Grand Prix he assembled a new car in ten weeks. The Zephyr Special incorporated proprietary parts and used the engine as a stressed chassis-member.

In 1956 Norman abandoned racing to concentrate on inventing. Many of his prototypes, including a car tow-bar and a photographic device to capture burglars, never reached the production stage. With Nancy, he made a motoring trip in 1961 which took them to the Soviet Union, Poland, East Germany, Iran and Pakistan. Back in Adelaide, he designed and manufactured a supercharger which dramatically improved the performance of Holden [q.v.9] engines; driving an old utility, he took potential customers on public roads and gave them terrifying demonstrations of its power. In 1967 the Normans moved to Noosa Heads, Queensland. Two years later he published *Supercharge!*

Tall and spare, with strong wrists and hands, Norman had dynamism, but often lost the enthusiasm to persevere with projects. While his solutions to engineering problems were frequently audacious, his mechanical work could be crude. Survived by his wife, daughter and two sons, he died of cancer on 28 June 1971 at Noosa Heads and was cremated with Presbyterian forms.

J. B. Blanden, *Historic Racing Cars in Australia* (Adel, 1979); *The Official 50-Race History of the Australian Grand Prix* (Syd, 1986); D. Harrison, *With Casual Efficiency* (Adel, 1994); *Wheelspin*, Apr 1990, p 18; W. H. Hayes, Recollections of the late Eldred de Bracton Norman during the period 1939-1971 (ts held by ADB); family information.

JON CHITTLEBOROUGH

NORMINGTON RAWLING, JAMES; *see* RAWLING

NORRIE, SIR CHARLES WILLOUGHBY MOKE, BARON NORRIE OF WELLINGTON AND OF UPTON (1893-1977), army officer and governor, was born on 26 September 1893 at Brompton, London, son of George Edward Moke-Norrie, barrister, and his wife Beatrice, née Stephen. Willoughby was educated at Eton and the Royal Military College, Sandhurst. He joined the 11th Hussars in 1913 and was in active service from the outbreak of World War I. Wounded four times, he rose to temporary major, and won the Military Cross (1915) and Bar (1916); he was awarded the Distinguished Service Order (1919) and twice mentioned in dispatches.

On 9 June 1921 at Holy Trinity Church, Sloane Street, London, Norrie married Jocelyn Helen Gosling (d.1938). A keen polo-player, fox-hunter and steeplechaser, he was also a successful owner and breeder of racehorses. Gaining steady promotion in the army, he served in India, attended staff college and became a specialist in mechanized warfare. At the parish church of St Peter with St Thomas, Marylebone, London, on 28 November 1938 he married 31-year-old Patricia Merryweather Bainbridge. At the beginning of World War II he commanded the 1st Armoured Brigade. Promoted acting lieutenant general (October 1941), he led the XXX Corps in North Africa with distinction and heroism in 1941-42 and was appointed C.B. (1942). Back in Britain, by 1943 he held the post of major general, Royal Armoured Corps.

Norrie retired from the army in September 1944 on accepting the governorship of South Australia; he was appointed K.C.M.G. Accompanied by his wife, children, an orphaned niece and twelve staff, he sailed to Sydney, travelled by train to Adelaide and assumed office on 19 December 1944. A handsome couple who liked meeting people, the Norries believed that their duty was to keep the 'Empire spirit alive'. Within two years he had visited every local government area and mining district in the State, and as many as three hundred schools, delivering up to ten speeches a day. He made a point of greeting servicemen when they returned from abroad, and calling on former prisoners of war. Lady Norrie and their elder children supported many charitable and patriotic causes, including the Food for Britain Appeal.

Sir Willoughby's confidential reports to the Dominions Office were unusually full and frank. He criticized the 'misguided sentimentality' of the Aborigines' champion, Charles Duguid, but praised the 'sound judgement' and 'honesty of purpose' of Prime Minister Chifley [q.v.13]. He also admired the government of (Sir) Thomas Playford, claiming that —although labelled 'Liberal and Country League'—it was 'what in England would be termed sound Right Wing Labour'. While keeping his views on local politics private, he publicly scorned Winston Churchill's opposition to both independence for India and the revival of assisted immigration to Australia.

During leave in Britain in 1947, Norrie persuaded the Ministry of Food to ease its restrictions on the volume of Australian wine which could be imported; he also induced the Peninsular & Oriental and Orient steamship companies to resume their pre-war practice of allowing some passenger ships to call at Port Adelaide. He expressed 'shock' when Playford's bill to nationalize the Adelaide Electric Supply Co. Ltd was defeated on the casting vote of the president of the Legislative Council. Considering the measure 'very reasonable', he privately exerted influence on its main opponents. When a revised bill was presented in 1946, (Sir) Collier Cudmore [q.v.13] absented himself from the crucial divisions, and it was passed.

In 1948 Norrie's term was extended for four years, but he was allowed to leave in June 1952 to become governor-general of New Zealand. He served in that post from December 1952 to July 1957. Appointed G.C.M.G. (1952) and G.C.V.O. (1954), he was created Baron Norrie of Wellington (New Zealand) and of Upton (Gloucestershire, England) in 1957. In his retirement he was a director (from 1958) of the London branch of the Bank of New South Wales and president (1967) of the British Boys' Movement for Australia. He always claimed his greatest achievement was catching a 2225-lb. (1009 kg) shark with a rod and reel off Port Lincoln, South Australia. Survived by his wife and their son and two daughters, and by the son and daughter of his first marriage, he died on 25 May 1977 at Wantage, Oxfordshire, and was cremated.

People (Syd), 8 Oct 1952; *SMH*, 18 Dec 1944; *Advertiser* (Adel), 28 May 1977; duplicate dispatches and news-cuttings, 1944-52 (Govt House, Adel); information from Baron Norrie, Lond, and (Patricia) Lady Norrie, Leckhampstead, Berkshire, Eng.

P. A. HOWELL

NORTH, EDGAR ALEXANDER (1896-1970), medical scientist, was born on 12 February 1896 at Launceston, Tasmania, son of Alexander North [q.v.11], architect, and his wife Lucy Mariannie Hamilton, née Morgan. Edgar excelled at English in his years at Launceston Church Grammar School. He entered Trinity College, University of Melbourne (M.B., B.S., 1923; M.D., 1948), but interrupted his studies and enlisted in the Australian Imperial Force on 4 April 1916. Wounded in 1917 while serving on the Western Front with the 38th Battalion, he saw out the war, returned to Australia and was discharged from the A.I.F. on 26 April 1919. He worked as a resident medical officer (1923-24) at the Alfred Hospital, Melbourne, before being introduced to psychiatry at the Hospital for the Insane, Sunbury. On 26 June 1924 at Trinity College chapel he married with Anglican rites Jean Alice Cranstoun Andrew. While employed as a medical officer (1925-28) at the Repatriation Mental Hospital, Bundoora, in his spare hours he practised at the Alfred as a physician to out-patients.

Joining the Commonwealth Department of Health in May 1928, North was briefly based at Port Pirie, South Australia. He was appointed medical officer in charge of the Commonwealth health laboratories at Rockhampton, Queensland, in 1929 and at Bendigo, Victoria, in 1935. Transferred (1938) to the

Commonwealth Serum Laboratories at Parkville, Melbourne, of which F. G. Morgan [q.v.]
was director, North was to be promoted
deputy-director and to succeed E. V. Keogh
[q.v.] in 1950 as chief of the research division.

During World War II North was involved in
the manufacture of smallpox vaccine, and of
tetanus toxoid which was of critical importance for the immunization of servicemen and
women. With Keogh and others, he developed
a more efficient vaccine against pertussis
(whooping cough): this project formed the
subject of his M.D. thesis. North also worked
on staphylococcal toxins. He took a leading
role in the production and distribution in
Australia of Bacillus Calmette-Guérin vaccine
to prevent tuberculosis. In the early 1950s he
was a pioneer in introducing triple antigen
vaccine (against diphtheria, pertussis and
tetanus). He published more than forty papers
in these areas.

An avid reader and regular attender of
orations and lectures, North was regarded by
his colleagues as being 'an erudite and courtly
gentleman', quietly spoken and considerate.
To some, he was the archetypal 'absent-
minded professor'. A young scientist once
saw him 'driving his motorcar, at its usual
sedate pace, for several hundred yards along
the footpath after leaving C.S.L., obviously
engrossed in some intellectual problem and
blissfully unaware that he was not on the
road'. North was active in Legacy and in his
local Anglican church. Because of the importance attached to vaccine production, he had
been rejected for the A.I.F. in World War II,
but had served in the Volunteer Defence
Corps.

North was a member (1950) and fellow
(1956) of the Royal Australasian College of
Physicians, and a foundation member (1956)
of the College of Pathologists of Australia. On
his retirement in 1961, he returned to Tasmania, cultivated his garden and developed
a system of 'trickle irrigation'. He died on
4 March 1970 at Launceston and was cremated; his wife and three sons survived him.

G. L. McDonald (ed), *Roll of the Royal Australasian College of Physicians*, 1, 1938-75 (Syd, 1988);
A. H. Brogan, *Committed to Saving Lives* (Melb,
1990); Cwlth Serum Laboratories Archives, Melb;
information from Dr J. North, East Ivanhoe, Melb.

ANTHONY PROUST

NORTHCOTT, CLARENCE HUNTER
(1880-1968), schoolteacher, personnel manager and author, was born on 4 November
1880 at Ulmarra, New South Wales, son of
native-born parents Joseph Northcott, farmer,
and his wife Lydia, née Lee. Clarence attended
Ulmarra Public School and passed (1895)
the junior public examination. A pupil-teacher

from 1897 at three small local schools, he was
transferred to Grafton Superior Public School
in January 1899. He spent 1902 at Fort Street
Training School, Sydney, on a full scholarship
and was awarded another to the University of
Sydney (B.A., 1905; M.A., 1916). While at university, he taught at Forest Lodge (1903-05)
and Fort Street (1905-06) schools.

At the Methodist Church, Grafton, on 5
January 1904 Northcott married Nellie May
Francis. From 1906 he was a master at Sydney
Grammar School. Influenced by Professor
(Sir) Francis Anderson [q.v.7], he advocated
the inclusion of sociology in the university
curriculum, arguing the need for sociological
investigation to furnish data for social planning in Australia. He gave the first sociology
classes for the Workers' Educational Association in Sydney in 1915-16.

Northcott left in 1916 for Columbia University (Ph.D., 1918), New York, to work with
a noted American sociologist Franklin H.
Giddings. His thesis, published as *Australian
Social Development* (New York, 1918), ana-
lysed Australia's 'social laboratory': he surveyed the country's experiments with land,
race, capital, labour, wealth and education,
discerning the working out of the ideal of a
progressive social democracy. A study in
Giddings's theory of 'social efficiency', the
book focused on the industrial sphere. Northcott, who was an active member of the
Methodist Church, believed that social science
should serve a Christian mission. His early
conviction that industrial democracy and co-
operation would produce social efficiency and
an ethical society remained the guiding philosophy of his career.

In August 1919, while working with the
National Industrial Conference Board at
Boston, Northcott was recruited by B. See-
bohm Rowntree as statistical adviser to the
Quaker enterprise of Rowntree & Co., cocoa
and chocolate manufacturers, at York, England. Visiting Australia in 1928, he addressed
church and business groups on Rowntree's
labour initiatives.

A pioneer in personnel management and
industrial relations, Northcott was a founder
(1931) of the Institute of Labour Management
in Britain. He helped to reshape this body into
the Institute of Personnel Management, of
which he was president (1941-43) and director (1949-50); he was also involved in organizing the Balliol management conferences.
Northcott explained his ideas and labour-
management practices in several articles and
in his books, *Factory Organization* (London,
1928) and *Personnel Management* (London,
1945). In *Christian Principles in Industry*
(London, 1958) he developed his belief that
'rightly considered, industry is a venture in
co-operation' in the context of the teaching of
the New Testament.

Northcott remained at Rowntree's as labour manager until he retired in 1946. The Colonial Office appointed him to direct a survey in Kenya and he wrote the report, *African Labour Efficiency Survey* (London, 1949). Survived by his wife and daughter, he died on 26 January 1968 at Scorton, Yorkshire, recognized for his contribution to a new body of professional knowledge, but little remembered for his pioneering sociological study of Australia.

M. M. Niven, *Personnel Management 1913-63* (Lond, 1967); J. D. Bollen, *Protestantism and Social Reform in New South Wales 1890-1910* (Melb, 1972); L. Dunt, *Speaking Worlds* (Melb, 1993); *SMH*, 17 Feb 1917, 18 July 1921, 16, 25 July, 4, 6, 14, 15, 16 Aug, 4 Sept 1928, 7 Feb 1947; *The Times*, 31 Jan, 2 Feb 1968; teachers' records, Dept of Education (NSWA).   HELEN BOURKE

NORTHCOTT, SIR JOHN (1890-1966), army officer and governor, was born on 24 March 1890 at Creswick, Victoria, eldest son of English-born parents John Northcott, storekeeper, and his wife Elizabeth Jane, née Reynolds. His father owned a store in the nearby town of Dean. Young John was educated at Dean State School and Grenville College, Ballarat. An enthusiastic former member of the school cadets, he was commissioned in August 1908 in a Militia unit, the 9th Light Horse Regiment (redesignated the 19th Light Horse in 1912). On 16 November 1912 he joined the Permanent Military Forces as lieutenant, Administrative and Instructional Staff, and was posted to the 6th Military District (Tasmania). He transferred to the Australian Imperial Force in August 1914 and was appointed adjutant of the 12th Battalion which was based at Anglesea Barracks, Hobart.

In October Captain Northcott sailed with his battalion for Egypt. On the morning of 25 April 1915 the 12th landed at Ari Burnu (Anzac Cove), Gallipoli. Almost immediately, Northcott was wounded in the chest by a rifle bullet. He was evacuated to Alexandria, Egypt, and thence to England, and took no further part in the war. On 14 September 1915 at the parish church, Oxted, Surrey, he married Winifred Mary Paton (d.1960), who had travelled to England to join him. His recuperation was prolonged, and he did not return to Australia until 30 December.

Like others in the permanent forces, Northcott had to accept a drop in rank when his A.I.F. appointment terminated on 30 September 1916. Nevertheless, he steadily advanced in his chosen career. He undertook several staff postings in Western Australia before attending the Staff College, Camberley, England, in 1924-25. Back in Australia, he served as staff officer (later director), stores and transport, at Army Headquarters, Mel-

bourne. From 1933 he spent a longer period in England, during which he attended the Imperial Defence College, London, and the Senior Officers' School, Sheerness, and completed an attachment to the Committee of Imperial Defence.

In 1937 Northcott returned to Melbourne. His broad experience in staff appointments gave him an unrivalled knowledge of some areas, particularly transport, important to a future mobilization for war. His assiduity in making contact with people in industry, including influential figures like Essington Lewis [q.v.10], made him as well known outside the army as in it. At the outbreak of World War II he was director of military operations and intelligence, with the rank of brevet colonel. In October 1939 he was promoted local major general and appointed deputy-chief of the General Staff. He accompanied R. G. (Baron) Casey [q.v.13] to the dominions' conference (October-December) in London as his military adviser.

Northcott was one of the regular officers who aspired to field command. In August 1940 the chief of the General Staff, General Sir Brudenell White [q.v.12], died in an air crash. Lieutenant General (Sir) Vernon Sturdee [q.v.] succeeded him. The post of commander, 8th Division, thus became available, but Northcott was excluded from consideration because his knowledge was vital to the new C.G.S. When Major General H. D. Wynter [q.v.] fell ill and Lieutenant General Sir Thomas Blamey [q.v.13] asked in January 1941 for Northcott to command the 9th Division in the Middle East, Northcott was involved in organizing the 1st Armoured Division and the appointment went instead to Brigadier (Sir) Leslie Morshead [q.v.]. Northcott had to settle for command in Australia of the 1st Armoured Division (September 1941 to April 1942) and II Corps (April-September). He was promoted temporary lieutenant general in April 1942 (substantive 1 September).

On 10 September 1942 Northcott was appointed chief of the General Staff. As Blamey's principal non-operational subordinate, he was responsible for administering and training the army. Not only did he discharge his duties to Blamey's satisfaction, he also developed excellent relations with key officers at General Douglas MacArthur's [q.v.] headquarters, and worked harmoniously with members of the Royal Australian Navy and the Royal Australian Air Force. At the end of the war Sturdee was again invited to become C.G.S. He made it a condition of his acceptance that Northcott be given the appointment of commander-in-chief of the British Commonwealth Occupation Force in Japan, an indication of the genuine esteem in which Northcott's service was held. He headed B.C.O.F. from December 1945 to June 1946.

Throughout his army career Northcott was highly regarded as an outstanding staff officer. In contrast, his short periods in command of the 1st Armoured Division, II Corps and B.C.O.F. were noted neither for innovation nor conspicuous success. In two of these three appointments he was followed by (Sir) Horace Robertson [q.v.] who possessed the ebullience and flair that Northcott lacked. Northcott's qualities of correctness, competence and dedication were perhaps best displayed in his role as the first Australian-born and one of the longest-serving governors of New South Wales. Sworn in on 1 August 1946, he gave patronage and support to charitable organizations and to youth, church and citizens' groups. A staunch advocate of the British Empire, he was a widely known and respected figure throughout the State. He retired in July 1957.

Northcott had been appointed M.V.O. in 1927 for his service during the visit of the Duke and Duchess of York that year. He was appointed C.B. (1941), K.C.M.G. (1950) and K.C.V.O. (1954). In 1951 and 1956 he administered the Commonwealth of Australia; while occupying that office he held the honorary rank of general. He was awarded honorary degrees by the University of Sydney (D.Litt., 1952), the New South Wales University of Technology (D.Sc., 1956) and the University of New England (D.Litt., 1956). During his term as governor he was honorary colonel of the 1st-15th Royal New South Wales Lancers. Survived by his two daughters, Sir John died on 4 August 1966 in his home at Wahroonga, Sydney; he was accorded a state funeral with military honours and was cremated with Presbyterian forms.

L. M. Newton, *The Story of the Twelfth* (Hob, 1925); P. Hasluck, *The Government and the People 1939-1941* (Canb, 1952) and *The Government and the People 1942-1945* (Canb, 1970); L. Wigmore, *The Japanese Thrust* (Canb, 1957); D. McCarthy, *South-West Pacific Area—First Year* (Canb, 1959); G. Long, *The Final Campaigns* (Canb, 1963); J. Hetherington, *Blamey, Controversial Soldier* (Canb, 1973); S. F. Rowell, *Full Circle* (Melb, 1974); R. N. L. Hopkins, *Australian Armour* (Canb, 1978); J. Grey, *Australian Brass* (Melb, 1992); *Age* (Melb) and *SMH*, 5 Aug 1966; War Cabinet Minutes 1939-45 (AA, Canb); Northcott papers (ML) and M4069, item 7 (AA, Canb).   H. J. COATES

NORTHEY, JAMES DOUGLAS (1890-1975), Congregational clergyman, was born on 26 March 1890 at Hindmarsh, Adelaide, eldest of four sons of James Northey, stoker, and his second wife Mary Elizabeth, née Davis. When his father died, 12-year-old Douglas left Kyre College and worked as a printer's devil to help support his mother, brothers and half-sister. In 1906 he was apprenticed to a bookbinder.

Raised in domestic piety by a mother who 'lived her faith', Northey began preaching at the age of 16 and was challenged by an old minister to 'take up the Lord's work'. At that time his ambition was to be a professional athlete. Stockily built and possessing extraordinary physical energy, he excelled at every sport he tried: he was regarded as a prospective international cricketer, though he was blind in one eye from a football injury.

When he completed his trade, Northey entered Parkin [q.v.5] Theological College, Kent Town, and studied at the University of Adelaide (B.A., 1919). He was ordained a minister in the Congregational Church on 1 December 1916. At Riverton Methodist Church on 20 December that year he married Eva Janet Hannaford. Parish appointments followed, at Kensington Gardens (1916-21) and Victor Harbour (1921-29).

In 1929 Northey transferred to Canterbury, Melbourne, where he quickly distinguished himself. An indefatigable proponent of the ecumenical movement, by the early 1930s he was advocating organic union between the Congregational, Methodist and Presbyterian churches (eventually achieved, with his active assistance, in 1977). He was chairman (1934-35) of the Congregational Union of Victoria and president (1936-37) of the Council of Churches of Victoria. In 1938 he helped to found the Christian Commonwealth Movement, which sought to interpret the 'kingdom of God' in socio-political terms. A member for twenty-one years of the Melbourne College of Divinity (B.D., 1936), he was its president in 1944-46 and 1957-59.

Northey left Canterbury in 1940 to become principal of the Congregational College of Victoria. A major formative influence on generations of candidates preparing for ordination, he rebuked pietism and the introverted church, narrow-mindedness and inflexibility. As president (1948-50) of the Congregational Union of Australia and New Zealand, he travelled extensively, visiting theological schools and preaching from famous pulpits in Britain and the United States of America.

With a resonant voice which he used to effect, Northey was a popular speaker—not only in pulpits, but at retreats, conferences and secular public events. He rarely spoke without a full handwritten script before him. Having joined the Freemasons in 1921, he had risen to be a grand chaplain with the United Grand Lodge of Victoria. He co-founded Mayflower Lodge (Congregational). His rapport with men was a singular asset. A prolific writer of pamphlets and articles for religious and secular media, he was renowned for his love of the deft phrase, and for his quirky alliteration (which some considered obsessive). For one whose logic and rhetoric could border on the overpowering, he was flexible, tolerant and forgiving. One of his maxims was 'guiding principles are better than prescriptive rules'. In public he was the epitome of dignity, and was often seen in a homburg, black coat and striped trousers. In private he was warm and at times riotously comic. Students goaded him at the dining-table to tell favourite jokes so as to see the tears of uncontrolled mirth before he could deliver the punch-line.

'J.D.', as he was widely known, retired from the college in 1960 and served as a locum pastor for eight years with the South St Kilda congregation. Survived by his son and two daughters, he died on 28 February 1975 at Kew and was cremated.

Aust Congregationalist, Apr 1975; *Age* (Melb), 1 Mar 1975; K. Hammond, Northey Family History (unpublished pamphlet, 1994, held by author, Sunbury, Vic); information from Mr A. E. Steggall, Surrey Hills, Melb, Mr J. D. Gunson, Toora, Vic, the late Mrs G. D. Northey and the late Rev N. Robinson; personal knowledge.

JOHN F. BODYCOMB

NORTHFIELD, ISAAC JAMES (1887-1973), poster artist and painter, was born on Christmas Day 1887 at Ellengerrin station, near Inverleigh, Victoria, third child of Isaac Northfield, overseer, and his wife Louisa, née Everett, both Victorian born. After completing his primary schooling, James trained under George King at the Gordon Technical College, Geelong. He joined a local lithographic firm before moving to Melbourne where he served an apprenticeship with F. W. Niven & Co., one of the city's leading lithographic printers. On 23 December 1913 he married Una Grace Daniel at St John's Anglican Church, Toorak; their only child, a daughter, predeceased them.

About 1932 Northfield set up his own studio in Flinders Street and specialized in hand lithographic work. His understanding of the new process of colour printing in commercial art established his expertise and artistic reputation, and he was commissioned by the Victorian Railways and the Australian National Travel Association to design travel posters. His posters of the Mount Buffalo chalet, the Blue Mountains (New South Wales) and Canberra were displayed in travel offices, used for promotions abroad and presented in reduced format on tourist brochures. Northfield was as much at ease with flora and fauna as with landscapes. He received wider recognition when his poster of Collins Street, Melbourne, published by A.N.T.A. in 1935, was reproduced in a British poster annual.

During World War II, like a number of other artists, Northfield turned his talents to recording and celebrating the war effort. Sir Harold Clapp [q.v.8], head of the aircraft construction branch of the Commonwealth Department of Supply and Development—who had previously employed Northfield on behalf of the Victorian Railways—sought him out again. From the 1930s Northfield had been a part-time instructor at the Art Training Institute, Melbourne; by the early 1950s, slightly balding and with aquiline features, he was its chief director of studies.

In one of the longest careers in Australian commercial art, Northfield tackled a host of subjects and countless images. His graphic and colour skills were superb. He accepted commissions from travel organizations, industrial firms, government bodies, breweries and clothing manufacturers. A committed commercial artist, he produced artwork for Pelaco shirts, Hypol Cod Liver Oil and Abbotsford Invalid Stout; his large-format brewery posters dominated advertising hoardings for years. His clients also included the Triumph Motor Co. of Britain and the Indian Motocycle Co. of the United States of America. In 1956 he designed covers of publications for the Olympic Games. About this time he began to paint in oils and contributed his landscapes to local exhibitions.

With Percy Trompf [q.v.12] and Gert Sellheim [q.v.], Northfield was one of the three best-known poster artists of his generation. His most enduring work, his travel posters of the 1920s and 1930s, have figured in numerous major exhibitions. The National Gallery of Australia and the State Library of Victoria hold many examples of his work. Survived by his wife, Northfield died on 18 March 1973 at East Malvern and was cremated.

Art Training Institute, *Prospectus* (Melb, 1950); G. Caban, *A Fine Line* (Syd, 1983); P. Spearritt (ed), *Trading Places* (Melb, 1991); R. Butler, *Poster Art in Australia* (Canb, 1993); *Art Student* (Melb), 1, no 1, 1932.

PETER SPEARRITT

NORTON, EZRA (1897-1967), newspaper proprietor, was born on 8 April 1897 at Watsons Bay, Sydney, elder child of John Norton [q.v.11], the English-born proprietor of *Truth*, and Ada McGrath who was native-born. John married Ada a few weeks later and may have chosen the infant's name in honour of the scribe in the Old Testament book of Nehemiah. Ezra never recovered from his parents' tempestuous relationship. His birth was legitimized in 1907. By the time he was 15, he had learned how to defend his mother from his father's assaults and to stand up for his own rights in the face of continuing mental and physical abuse. He was educated at Scots

College, Bellevue Hill. There he was ridiculed by a teacher because of his infamous father. As a result, Norton often stayed away from school and was thrashed when he did attend. After he failed to matriculate for the second time, he was sent to Christian Brothers' College, Waverley, where he was treated with kindness.

Ezra worked in his father's business and quickly acquired the basics of newspaper production. John died in 1916. He disinherited his wife and son, and left his estate (sworn for probate at £140 331) to his daughter Joan. In 1920 Ada Norton successfully challenged the will in the Equity Court, receiving a third share of the estate, with the remainder divided equally between Ezra and Joan. At St James's Anglican Church, Sydney, on 30 November 1922 Norton married Lillian Mary (Molly) Willoughby (d.1952), a 29-year-old teacher of dancing; he adopted her son.

On gaining control of his father's company, Norton became managing director of Truth and Sportsman Ltd which published the Sunday paper, *Truth*, in various State editions, and the weekly *Sydney Sportsman*. He tried at first to broaden the *Truth* formula from its staples of divorce reports and sport. Under a new slogan, 'The People's Paper', it waged war against crime in Sydney, added a smattering of culture, and temporarily abandoned columns called 'Sheisms' (about the silliness of women) and 'Prickly Pairs' (about relationships in trouble). They soon returned as *Truth* fell back on its familiar mix of sport, crime and divorce, all told with an alliterative flourish (such as 'From Lounge Lizard to Long Bay Lodger').

Norton frightened his staff, treating reporters and executives alike with calculated rudeness. A stream of abuse was often preceded by a twitching of his nose. Any sign of weakness in his targets encouraged him to greater sarcasm and ridicule. In frequent sacking blitzes, up to twenty reporters were dismissed at a time. Eric Baume [q.v.13] said that Norton 'was never a great editor but he was a genius in newspaper machinery matters. Before you joined him he was all politeness. Once you had joined him it was all fear and you became his body-servant. I loathed every bit of my service with him'. Norton was known as a 'tightwad' in business matters, but in private he was generous to staff who were ill or in financial trouble. Unable to accept gratitude with ease, he turned away thanks as if receiving an insult.

For all his crudity and roughhouse manner, Norton was not uncouth. He was polite to women and sentimental towards animals, especially dogs. Considered enigmatic and a lone wolf, he was a short, trim man, usually clad in expensively tailored suits. He invariably wore a hat and often a camelhair coat,

even on warm days. His manner was furtive, he seldom smiled, and his mouth seemed permanently set at '20 to 4'. He frequently went to the cinema, read history and literature, collected paintings, and was fond of certain operas, operettas, and musical comedies, especially those by Rodgers and Hammerstein. His friends included the politicians Arthur Calwell, (Sir) Eric Harrison [qq.v.13,14] and Eddie Ward [q.v.]. A close friend was Dr Kenneth Smith, a general practitioner of Darlinghurst, who accompanied Norton to the races, and to the boxing at the Stadium. He made other friends through his interests in racing and the Trocadero nightclub which he established in George Street in 1936.

On Derby Day 1939 Norton had came to blows in the members' enclosure at Randwick Racecourse with his 'enemy' (Sir) Frank Packer [q.v.] of Consolidated Press Ltd. Provoked by Packer, who had published unflattering photographs of him in the *Telegraph*, Norton struck the first blow and was forced to apologize to the Australian Jockey Club committee. Maurice Grogan, studmaster at Blandford Lodge, Matamata, New Zealand, selected racehorses for Norton, among them Straight Draw, winner of the A.J.C. Metropolitan Handicap and the Melbourne Cup in 1957, and the Sydney Cup in 1958.

The launch of Packer's *Sunday Telegraph* in 1939 had weakened *Truth*. Norton envied Packer's success and, during World War II, resented his commission in the Australian Imperial Force. For some time *Truth* ran a photograph of 'Captain Frank Packer' enjoying himself at the races, with the comment 'Captain Packer will be leaving for the front shortly'. Norton decided to launch a daily tabloid in competition with both Packer's *Telegraph* and Associated Newspapers Ltd's *Sun*. He lobbied politicians for a licence to import newsprint, despite the Menzies [q.v.] government's decision to introduce newsprint rationing. After setbacks and fierce opposition from his rivals, Norton gained the licence in January 1941, with the help of Harrison who was by then the Federal minister for trade and customs. The afternoon *Daily Mirror* was launched in May; by 1947 its circulation had overtaken that of the *Sun*.

By the mid-1950s the 'news' in *Truth* revolved around 'the Dogs' Home, the race courses, Sydney Stadium, the doings of Mr Justice Dovey [q.v.14], adulterated food, White Australia and the threat of atomic radiation' and what it was doing to the weather. Both the *Daily Mirror* and *Truth* had fallen in circulation, and Norton wanted to quit. In October 1958 *Truth* was replaced by Norton's new *Sunday Mirror*. He considered selling his newspaper interests to the *Daily Mirror* group in Britain and the Herald and Weekly Times Ltd in Melbourne, but instead approached

Rupert Henderson, managing director of John Fairfax & Sons [qq.v.4,8] Pty Ltd, publisher of the *Sydney Morning Herald*. In December 1958 Norton and his associates sold their shares in Truth and Sportsman Ltd to O'Connell Pty Ltd, a company controlled by Fairfax, which in turn disposed of a controlling interest to Rupert Murdoch's News Ltd.

On 11 June 1953 at St James's Church, Sydney, Norton had married Emma Georgina ('Peggy') Morrison, his 38-year-old secretary. They lived at Carmel, Albert Street, Woollahra, where a bust of Norton as a young man was placed in the hall. Peggy believed that her husband sold his newspaper interests because he feared ill health and knew he had no clear successor; moreover, he anticipated that the Matrimonial Causes Act (1959) would proscribe the reporting of evidence in divorce cases. After his retirement Norton said, 'I'm now a piece of cheese with everyone trying to have a nibble at me'. He owned a publishing business, Invincible Press, and a parking station in the city, and he continued to take an interest in the Trocadero. Having sold Carmel, he built a house at Vaucluse, with an Olympic-sized, salt-water swimming-pool.

Driven by his fears and prejudices, Norton was 'a tortured soul seeking inward peace', according to a former employee, Irvine Douglas. Norton loathed Freemasons and despised homosexuals. His alarm at what Cyril Pearl had written about his father led him to attempt to prevent the publication of *Wild Men of Sydney* (1958). It was widely believed that Norton had lobbied the State government to introduce and pass the controversial Defamation Act (1958) which redefined criminal libel to include the dead. He was afraid of travelling by air or in welded ships (as he had heard of Liberty ships breaking up in wartime). Norton was as fond of alcohol as his father had been, and frequented the Australia Hotel where he often drank French champagne.

Still fit in his fifties and early sixties, Norton learned in 1966 that he had cancer. He converted to Catholicism and was received into the Church by Cardinal (Sir) Norman Gilroy [q.v.14]. Grateful to the Sisters of Mercy who had cared for his sister when she was dying, Norton was a benefactor of the Order. Survived by his wife and their daughter, and by his adopted son, he died on 4 January 1967 at his Vaucluse home and was buried in South Head cemetery with Catholic rites. His estate was sworn for probate in Canberra at $3 844 672.

A. Manning, *Larger Than Life* (Syd, 1967); A. A. Calwell, *Be Just and Fear Not* (Melb, 1972); D. McNicoll, *Luck's a Fortune* (Syd, 1979); M. Cannon, *That Damned Democrat* (Melb, 1981); G. Souter, *Company of Heralds* (Melb, 1981); P. Knightley, *A Hack's Progress* (Lond, 1997); *Nation*, 20 Dec 1958, p 8, 3 Jan 1959, p 19, 14 Jan 1967, p 5; *SMH*, 6 Jan 1967, 4 Sept 1982.   VALERIE LAWSON

NORTON, ROSALEEN MIRIAM (1917-1979), painter and self-styled witch, was born on 2 October 1917 at Dunedin, New Zealand, third daughter of Albert Thomas Norton, a master mariner from London, and his New Zealand-born wife Beena Salek, née Aschman. Albert was a cousin of the composer Ralph Vaughan Williams. The family arrived in Sydney in June 1925. Rosaleen was expelled from the Church of England Girls' School, Chatswood, at the age of 14 for producing 'depraved' drawings of vampires, ghouls and werewolves thought likely to corrupt the other girls. She later studied for two years at East Sydney Technical College under Rayner Hoff [q.v.9] who encouraged her 'pagan' creativity.

Norton dabbled as a pavement artist near the General Post Office and worked variously as a kitchen-maid, nightclub waitress, postal messenger, and cadet journalist on *Smith's Weekly*. At the registrar general's office, Sydney, on 24 December 1940 she married Beresford Lionel Conroy, a Duco sprayer; they were to be divorced in 1951. Her first published illustrations—two fantasy works and a pencil study, 'The Borgias'—appeared in the magazine, *Pertinent* (October-November 1941). By 1949 she had met her lover, the poet Gavin Greenlees (b.1930). Norton first attracted controversy when she exhibited a series of pagan, sexually explicit drawings at the Rowden White Library, University of Melbourne, in August 1949. Police raided the exhibition, which included such works as 'Lucifer', 'Witches' Sabbath' and 'Individuation', and Norton was charged with obscenity. The charges were dismissed after she provided the court with detailed explanations of her occult symbolism.

Her work was influenced by British vorticism and has been linked stylistically to that of Norman Lindsay [q.v.10], for whom she occasionally modelled. Norton derived much of her imagery from a type of psychic exploration based on self-hypnosis and from what in occult circles has been described as 'wanderings on the astral planes'. Many of her paintings were based on trance-encounters with archetypal beings whom Norton believed had their own independent existence. She began to compile a series of these mystical drawings which, with poems by Greenlees, appeared in *The Art of Rosaleen Norton* (1952), under the sponsorship of the publisher Walter Glover. This book was even more controversial than her Melbourne exhibition. Glover was charged with producing an obscene publication. The book could only be distributed in

Australia with some of the more sexually explicit images blacked out. In the United States of America copies were burned by customs officials. Greenlees and Norton, who had been financially assisted by Glover, were forced to scrounge a living by other means when he was declared bankrupt.

'Roie', to her friends, was small, wiry and vital, with black hair, arched eyebrows and a face sullen in repose. An occult artist and a Bohemian in the 1950s and early 1960s, she sold her sketches and paintings to anyone who expressed an interest. Known as 'The Witch of Kings Cross', she openly proclaimed her dedication to occult beliefs and the 'Great God Pan', but was falsely accused by the tabloid press of holding Black Masses. On the basis of a series of confiscated photographs of simulated ceremonial rituals, she was charged in 1956 with 'engaging in unnatural sexual acts', and she unwittingly played a part in the downfall of Sir Eugene Goossens [q.v.14], the conductor of the Sydney Symphony Orchestra, who was a member (from 1952) of her occult group.

Norton continued to produce macabre paintings of the supernatural, though they were increasingly lurid and repetitive. She died of cancer on 5 December 1979 in the Sacred Heart Hospice, Darlinghurst. After he emerged from bankruptcy, Glover reissued *The Art of Rosaleen Norton* (1982) and published the *Supplement to The Art of Rosaleen Norton* (1984).

N. Drury, *Pan's Daughter* (Syd, 1988) and for bib; *People* (Syd), 29 Mar 1950, p 26.

NEVILL DRURY

NORWAY, NEVIL SHUTE (1899-1960), writer and aeronautical engineer, was born on 17 January 1899 at Ealing, London, second child of Arthur Hamilton Norway, a clerk in the General Post Office, and his wife Mary Louisa, née Gadsden. In 1912 Arthur became secretary of the Post Office in Ireland. Father and son had first-hand experience of the siege of its Dublin headquarters at Easter 1916. Educated in England at Lynam's (the Dragon) School, Oxford, and Shrewsbury School, Shropshire, Nevil suffered from a stammer which, though it lessened, was still noticeable late in life. It prevented him from being commissioned in the British Army in mid-1918 when he completed training at the Royal Military Academy, Woolwich. He served (from August) in England as a private in the 1st Reserve Battalion, Suffolk Regiment, then entered Balliol College, Oxford (B.A., 1923), where he read engineering.

From an early age Norway showed an intense interest in aeroplanes. While at Oxford he undertook unpaid work for the de Havilland Aircraft Co. in university vacations. He started regular employment with the firm in January 1923. During this time he learned to fly and began writing novels. His father had published several travel books with Macmillan & Co. Ltd at the turn of the century and his grandmother had written children's books. Norway completed his first novel in 1923, and another in the following year, but neither was published. In 1924 he joined Vickers Ltd as chief calculator for the famous inventor (Sir) Barnes Wallis who was in charge of the design and construction of the rigid airship, R100. Norway's account in his autobiography, *Slide Rule*, of the six-year trials and tribulations of the competitive construction of the airships R100 and R101 (built by the government), and the subsequent disastrous crash of R101 in France on its maiden flight to India, revealed his narrative gifts and some of his major preoccupations as a writer—the hubris of governments, bureaucratic paralysis, and the betrayal of individual common sense by large organizations.

As an antidote to the stress of the R100 project, Norway began writing regularly in his spare time. He completed his third novel, *Marazan*, which was published by Cassell & Co. Ltd in 1926. Sensing that his colleagues and Vickers might think that his writing compromised his commitment to his engineering work, he chose to publish as Nevil Shute (a truncated version of his full name), as he did for all his subsequent writing. Despite the pressures of his daily work, Norway continued to write, and *So Disdained* was published in 1928. On 7 March 1931 at St Peter's parish church, Bromley, Kent, he married Frances Mary Heaton, a 28-year-old medical practitioner. That year Norway established his own aircraft construction company, Airspeed Ltd, which became one of the major aircraft-makers in Britain by the outbreak of World War II. So intense was the effort he put into the engineering and business sides of the company that *The Lonely Road*, published in 1932, marked the beginning of a publishing hiatus of six years.

In 1938 Norway recognized that Airspeed was a different company from the one he had founded. The board asked him to resign with a generous settlement that enabled him to devote himself to full-time writing. *Ruined City* appeared in 1938, followed by *What Happened to the Corbetts* (1939), *An Old Captivity* (1940), *Landfall: A Channel Story* (1940), *Pied Piper* (1942), *Pastoral* (1944) and *Most Secret* (1945). The productivity and commercial success which marked Norway's writing career was evident in this period. His books, mostly published by Heinemann Ltd in London, also sold well in the Dominions and in the United States of America, and his early apprenticeship had equipped him to write regularly and easily. His published advice to aspiring novelists often referred to writing as a craft and a business—of learning both the structural formulas and the marketing ploys for publishing success. In many ways his professional life as an engineer and businessman informed much of his writing practice. Commissioned lieutenant and promoted acting lieutenant commander, Royal Naval Volunteer Reserve, in 1940, he worked in the Admiralty's Miscellaneous Weapon Development Department. After World War II his work became even more commercially successful. *The Chequer Board* (1947) preceded *No Highway* (1948), the subject of which—the problems of aircraft design and the effects of metal fatigue—was well-known to him.

In 1948 Norway flew his own plane to Australia. Back home, he felt oppressed by British taxation and decided that he and his family would emigrate. With his wife and two daughters, he settled in 1950 on farmland at Langwarrin, south-east of Melbourne. His greatest successes dated from this time, and most of them had Australian settings: *A Town Like Alice* (1950), *Round the Bend* (1951), which Norway considered his most important work, *The Far Country* (1952) and *In the Wet* (1953). The last caused some controversy. Released in the coronation year, the novel is partly set in a future where the monarch seeks refuge in Australia from an unsympathetic British government. In 1954 he published *Slide Rule* which gave an account of his life to 1938. *Requiem for a Wren* (1955), *Beyond the Black Stump* (1956) and his most famous book, *On the Beach* (1957), were followed by *The Rainbow and the Rose* (1958), *Trustee from the Toolroom* (1960) and *Stephen Morris* (1961), the last two published posthumously. Several of his novels were made into films, the most notable being *A Town Like Alice* (1956), starring Peter Finch [q.v.14], and *On the Beach* (1959), produced by Stanley Kramer.

Described as a 'friendly, nervous, tweedy man . . . with the strong hands of an engineer', Norway died of a cerebral haemorrhage on 12 January 1960 in East Melbourne and was cremated; his wife and daughters survived him. Norway had few literary pretensions, and publicly confessed that he could not finish reading Patrick White's *Voss*. He believed that the subject matter for novels came from direct observation of ordinary people in their own settings. An unambiguous morality of strong heroes and loyal heroines, combined with simple characterization, realistic settings alloyed with the fantastic, and exciting and well-told narratives were the basis of his success. His prose style was plain. If his novels seem ponderous to today's taste, they convey very well the last British imperialist vision of the Dominions, Australia in particular, as societies where English virtues might thrive, away from the decadence of postwar Britain.

J. Riddell, *Flight of Fancy* (Lond, 1950); G. Pawle, *The Secret War, 1939-45* (Lond, 1956); J. Smith, *Nevil Shute* (Boston, 1976); C. Giffuni, *Nevil Shute* (Adel, 1988); *Sun* (Melb), 5 June 1954; *Observer* (Lond), 20 Dec 1959; *The Times* and *New York Times*, 13 Jan 1960; *Age* (Melb), 25 Nov 1960.

JULIAN CROFT

NOSWORTHY, ELLICE MAUD (1897-1972), architect, was born on 25 February 1897 at Neutral Bay, Sydney, second of four daughters of Robert John Nosworthy, who came from England and was secretary to Burns, Philp [qq.v.7,11] & Co. Ltd, and his native-born wife Maud Jane Eliza, née Smith. Ellice attended Redlands Girls' School under Gertrude Roseby [q.v.] and was dux in 1915. At the University of Sydney (B.Arch., 1922) she enrolled in arts in 1917, but transferred to architecture in 1919 and studied under Professor Leslie Wilkinson [q.v.12]. She lived at Women's College, where she won (1919 and 1921) the Dickinson Cup for tennis.

Employed (1922-23) by (B. J.) Waterhouse [q.v.12] & Lake, Nosworthy was registered as an architect on 26 June 1923. After travelling and working in Europe in 1924, she practised from her parents' home at Lindfield and specialized in domestic architecture. She made several extensive study and working trips to North America (1929) and Britain (1935-38), and was employed by the Department of the Interior during World War II. From 1956 she conducted her practice from her own home, built to her specifications in her parents' orchard. Her clientele consisted largely of well-connected North Shore friends and acquaintances. She mostly employed women architects, including Barbara Munro, Louise Hutchinson and Brigid Wilkinson.

As honorary architect (1941-72) for Women's College, Nosworthy provided free advice on the maintenance of its buildings and also designed several substantial alterations, among them an air-raid shelter (1942) under the cloister and the (Mary) Reid [q.v.] wing (1958) which accommodated thirty-one students. She frequently donated her fees for such work to the college's building appeal. In the late 1950s she collaborated with Wilkinson on additions to St Andrew's College, University of Sydney.

Her other non-domestic projects included work for the Australian Mothercraft Society (1942) and the Young Women's Christian Association (1958-59). She designed child-care centres for the Sydney Day Nursery & Nursery Schools Association at Erskineville (1945) and Newtown (1955), and for the Ku-ring-gai Municipal Council at Gordon (1950).

In the 1960s she designed community housing for the Ku-ring-gai Old People's Welfare Association. Nosworthy tended to follow contemporary architectural norms: her early houses exhibited Federation-type spaces and details, while her later work showed a preference for non-decorative, functional, modern design. Her architectural philosophy focused on accommodating her client's complex needs rather than imposing stylish aesthetic solutions: 'The more I plan houses for people the more it is brought home to me that there will never be the perfect house, for the very things that one person thinks so desirable—another would not want at any price'.

Miss Nosworthy was a fellow (1970) of the Royal Australian Institute of Architects and an associate-member (1948) of the Royal Institute of British Architects. A member of the Australian Federation of University Women, she attended the international federation's conference in Mexico City (1964) and visited South America. She died on 7 January 1972 at Killara and was cremated with Congregational forms; her estate was sworn for probate at almost $510 000.

G. Beiers, *Houses of Australia* (Syd, 1948); *Aust National J*, Autumn 1940; Aust Federation of Univ Women (Syd), *Newsletter*, no 40, Mar 1972; *SMH*, 1 Apr 1958, 16 Aug 1964, 10 Jan, 10 Mar 1972; E. M. Nosworthy papers (NL).   BRONWYN HANNA

NOTHLING, OTTO ERNEST (1900-1965), medical practitioner and sportsman, was born on 1 August 1900 at Teutoburg (Witta), near Maleny, Queensland, sixth child of Carl Martin Nothling, a mason from Prussia, and his Queensland-born wife Marie Wilhelmine, née Tesch. Otto won a scholarship from Woombye State School to Brisbane Grammar School. A 'public spirited' boy of 'very fair ability', he excelled at cricket, Rugby Union football (captain first XV, 1918) and athletics. He entered St Andrew's College, University of Sydney (M.B., Ch.M., 1926), where he distinguished himself as an athlete, breaking records in javelin-throwing and shot-putting, and representing the university at cricket and Rugby.

An outstanding Rugby full-back for New South Wales, Nothling played three times against the visiting South Africans (1921), ten times against New Zealand (touring in 1921 and 1923) and six times against Maori teams. (The Queensland Rugby Union was defunct in 1920-28 so the New South Wales team effectively represented Australia and these matches are now recognized as Tests.) H. M. Moran [q.v.10] thought that Nothling 'had every attribute for becoming the greatest footballer in the world, except one: intuition'.

On his retirement from Rugby in 1924, Nothling concentrated on cricket. He played five times for New South Wales in 1922-25. After returning to Queensland in 1926, he represented the State (1927-29) in twelve Sheffield Shield matches, including three as captain. In November 1928 he was chosen for both an Australian XI and a Queensland XI against A. P. F. Chapman's touring Marylebone Cricket Club team. Next month he was selected to replace the young (Sir) Donald Bradman, who was dropped to twelfth man, for the Test against England in Sydney. Nothling's figures of 8 and 44 with the bat, and 0 for 72 off 46 overs of zestful medium pace, were not enough: he was not picked again. In all first-class matches, he scored 882 runs at an average of 24.5 and took 36 wickets at 41 runs apiece.

From 1930 Nothling practised medicine at Maryborough, Queensland. In that city on 1 June 1932 at St Paul's Anglican Church he married Mildred Melville Horsburgh. Appointed major, Australian Army Medical Corps, Australian Imperial Force, on 12 July 1940, he sailed for the Middle East in December as second-in-command of the 2nd/3rd Casualty Clearing Station. He served in Greece and on Crete, but poor health forced his return to Australia; his A.I.F. appointment terminated on 2 October 1943 and he resumed his practice at Maryborough. After obtaining a diploma in dermatological medicine (1949) at the University of Sydney, he set up as a specialist in Wickham Terrace, Brisbane. The first skin specialist appointed to the Brisbane Children's Hospital, he was a council-member of the Dermatological Association of Australia.

Nothling's many interests included farming. He served as an alderman (1933-40) of Maryborough City Council, president (1938-39) of the Maryborough and Wide Bay Club, secretary of the local branch of the British Medical Association, vice-president of the Maryborough Golf Club (1936-40) and the Q.R.U. (1960-65), and president (1964-65) of the Queensland Cricket Association. Of splendid physique and 6 ft 3 ins (191 cm) tall, he could run 100 yards in even time in his youth. According to Dr John Belisario, a friend and colleague, he was 'in many respects a naive, lovable, big overgrown boy, who never grew up'. Nothling was gregarious and ever cheerful. His most outstanding quality was his loyalty to his friends. Survived by his wife, son and daughter, he died of hypertensive heart disease on 26 September 1965 at Chelmer, Brisbane, and was cremated.

H. M. Moran, *Viewless Winds* (Lond, 1939); J. Pollard, *Australian Cricket* (Syd, 1982) and *Australian Rugby* (Syd, 1994); A. Buzo and J. Grant (eds), *The Longest Game* (Melb, 1990); *MJA*, 11 Dec 1965, p 1005; *Daily Standard*, 20 Apr 1936; *Courier-Mail*, 27 Sept 1965; *Age* (Melb), 23 Nov 1987; Brisb

Grammar School Archives; information from Dr M.
M. Nothling, Wickham Terrace, Brisb.

G. P. WALSH

NOTT, LEWIS WINDERMERE (1886-
1951), politician, medical practitioner and
hospital superintendent, was born on 12 February 1886 at Windermere sugar-plantation,
near Bundaberg, Queensland, seventh child
of Frederick Lewis Nott, sugar-planter, and
his wife Jean, née Blair, both from New South
Wales. After attending Maryborough Grammar School, young Lew studied assaying at
the School of Mines, Ballarat, Victoria, and
medicine at the University of Sydney. On
28 July 1913 at Woolwich he married with
Unitarian forms Doris Ashbury, a 20-year-old
student. They travelled to Scotland where he
continued his medical training with the Royal
College of Surgeons, Edinburgh, the Royal
College of Physicians, Edinburgh, and the
Royal Faculty of Physicians and Surgeons,
Glasgow.

At the outbreak of World War I Nott enlisted in the Royal Scots Greys on 7 August
1914 and was drafted to the Lovat's Scouts.
Commissioned in the Royal Horse Artillery in
May 1915, he transferred in October to the
15th Battalion, Royal Scots (Lothian Regiment), in which he was promoted captain and
made adjutant. While serving on the Western
Front in 1916, he was wounded and twice
mentioned in dispatches. His affectionate
letters to his wife, describing conditions in the
field, were edited by his son David and published as *Somewhere in France* (Sydney, 1996).

Relinquishing his commission, Nott returned to Scotland in December 1916, resumed his medical studies and qualified
(L.R.C.S., L.R.C.P. and L.R.F.P.S.) in 1918. He
joined the Royal Army Medical Corps, then
worked as a resident surgeon (1919) at the
Pilkington Special (Orthopaedic) Hospital, St
Helens, Lancashire, England. Returning to
Australia, he took part in the hookworm campaign in Central and North Queensland before
being appointed medical superintendent of
Mackay District Hospital. In 1924-27 he was
mayor of Mackay. On 14 November 1925 he
won the Federal seat of Herbert for the
National Party, defeating E. G. Theodore
[q.v.12] by 268 votes. After he lost Herbert in
1928, he unsuccessfully contested the seats of
North Sydney (1929), Calare (1934) and East
Sydney (1940).

With the relocation of the Commonwealth
parliament in the Federal (Australian) Capital
Territory in 1927, Nott had settled in Canberra. He identified with the community's
aspirations and promoted its interests. In
April 1928 he presented petitions from the
Territory's citizens seeking representation in

Federal parliament and on the Federal Capital
Commission. Although he failed to win the
new position of elected member on the F.C.C.
in 1929, he was returned to the F.C.T. (A.C.T.)
Advisory Council from 1935 to 1949. On 10
December 1949, standing as an Independent,
he became the A.C.T.'s first member of the
House of Representatives; he had limited
voting rights, but could speak on any issue.
He advocated building a road from Canberra
to the New South Wales coast, and the provision of more money and facilities for the
Aborigines at Wreck Bay.

Nott had begun a long association with
Canberra (Community) Hospital in 1928 when
he was appointed to a board of three to inquire
into its administration. In November 1929 he
was gazetted medical superintendent, with
the right to practise privately. He held the post
until 1934 and again in 1941-49. Not only did
he contribute to the development of the hospital and its school of nursing, he also fought
to ensure that patients received the best possible care. His ability to relate to people was
unquestionable, but his touch was less sure
where administration was concerned. He reverted to private practice (1934-40) and criticized the hospital's management, precipitating
another inquiry (1937).

Described as 'a man of an extroverted, even
flamboyant disposition with a strong social
conscience and a compassionate concern for
the underprivileged', Nott had set up and
manned a soup-and-sandwich kitchen in Can-
berra's Causeway area during the Depression.
His interests were varied: he was involved in
Legacy, the Returned Sailors', Soldiers' and
Airmen's Imperial League of Australia, the
Canberra Repertory Society, the Canberra
Philharmonic Society and the Horticultural
Society of Canberra.

In April 1951 Nott was defeated for the seat
of the A.C.T. by Jim Fraser [q.v.14]. Appointed
medical officer at the Newborough Clinic,
Yallourn, Victoria, he flew to Melbourne on 26
October. He had been suffering from leukaemia for a number of years and collapsed on
board the aircraft; he died on 27 October 1951
in Royal Melbourne Hospital and was buried
in Canberra cemetery with Presbyterian
forms. His wife, two daughters and one of his
three sons survived him.

A. Ide, *Royal Canberra Hospital* (Canb, 1994);
A. J. Proust (ed), *History of Medicine in Canberra
and Queanbeyan* (Gundaroo, NSW, 1994); *SMH*,
21 Nov 1925; *Canb Times*, 29 Oct 1951; information
from Mr R. Hohnen, Forrest, Miss N. Morgan,
Braddon, Dr D. Nott, Narrabundah, Canb, and the
late Miss S. Curley.   JOHN FARQUHARSON

NUGAN, FRANCIS JOHN (1942-1980),
lawyer and merchant banker, was born on 30

December 1942 at Griffith, New South Wales, younger twin and third child of German-born parents Alfredo Mariano Nugan (Neugarten), fruit packer, and his second wife Anna Lisa, née Meinhardt. Alfredo had taken Spanish nationality and had arrived in Melbourne in the *Strathnaver* on 13 August 1939 with his wife and the son of his first marriage. Settling at Griffith, he established a small packing company in 1941 and was naturalized in 1945. Frank attended Griffith High School, the University of Sydney (LL.B., 1964) and the University of California at Berkeley (LL.M., 1965), United States of America. After spending some years in Canada, he returned to Sydney in 1968. He was admitted as a solicitor on 22 November and set up practice. In New York on 23 May 1970 he married Charlotte Lee Sofge, who came from Tennessee.

That year Nugan was involved, as a director (1970-72), in floating Meekatharra Minerals N.L. to mine nickel, cobalt and copper in Western Australia; its shares rose to $6.90 then fell sharply. With a New Yorker named Michael Hand, Nugan engaged in land-deals and share-trading. In 1973 they set up a merchant bank, Nugan Hand Ltd, with a nominal paid-up capital of $1 million. Between 1976 and 1979 'turnover' reportedly rose from $30 million to $1000 million; the bank opened offices to accept deposits in Hong Kong, Singapore, the Cayman Islands and Saudi Arabia. Dynamic and assertive, Nugan was disorganized in the way he worked. Using the bank's reserves, he acquired the Orange Spot 'fruit juice concern' in Sydney and a substantial residence at Vaucluse. He was 'a heavy whisky drinker'. Despite the 'aura of . . . success' that surrounded him, 'his wealth was illusory'.

Meanwhile, his elder brother Kenneth had expanded their father's firm, the Nugan Group Ltd, into one of Australia's largest fruit and vegetable distributors; Frank was one of its directors. In 1978 he, Ken and others were charged with conspiracy to defraud the Nugan Group. Frank became preoccupied with the criminal proceedings and 'funded the defence of the charges by simply milking funds of Nugan Hand'.

On Sunday 27 January 1980 Frank Nugan's body was found at 4.20 a.m. in his Mercedes Benz at Forty Bends Road, Bowenfels. According to press reports he had a bullet wound to the head. A coroner's inquest recorded that he had died 'of the effects of a gunshot wound, self-inflicted and with the intention of taking his own life'. Survived by his wife, daughter and son, he was buried in Northern Suburbs cemetery. Subsequently, a reported sighting of Frank in a bistro at Atlanta, Georgia, U.S.A., led to speculation that a drug dealer was buried in his grave. Nugan's body was exhumed, and a second inquest, held in March 1981, confirmed the earlier findings on the basis of dental evidence.

The Nugan Hand bank had become the centre of media attention, with spiralling allegations of international conspiracy, tax evasion, bribery, arms dealing, drug trafficking, money laundering, and links with the Central Intelligence Agency. The bank went into receivership in April 1980 and was investigated by the Commonwealth-New South Wales Joint Task Force on Drug Trafficking. Hampered by deliberate obfuscation of records and the flight of Hand, the Corporate Affairs Commission reported in 1983 that Frank Nugan had been 'involved in massive international and local fraud' and had deliberately falsified the bank's accounts to conceal debt. The royal commission of inquiry (1983-85) into the activities of the Nugan Hand Group uncovered little new information.

Cwlth-NSW Joint Task Force on Drug Trafficking, *Report*, vols 2, 4, Nugan Hand (Canb, 1982, 1983); NSW Corporate Affairs Commission, *Sixth* and *Seventh Interim Reports on the Affairs of Nugan Hand Ltd and Other Companies* (Syd, 1983); Roy Com of Inquiry into the Activities of the Nugan Hand Group, *Interim Report*, 1983, 1984, *Final Report*, 1985 (Canb); *SMH*, 28, 30 May 1978, 29 Jan, 3, 6, 28 May, 31 Aug, 25-27, 29 Sept, 1 Nov 1980, 1-4, 6, 7, 10 Feb, 6, 25 Mar, 22 Apr 1981; *Sun-Herald* (Syd), 3 Feb, 27 Apr, 15 June 1980, 1 Feb 1981; A. Nugan, naturalization file A435/1, item 44/4/4235 (AA, Canb).   FRANK FARRELL

NUNAN, MARJORIE ESTELLA (1910-1963), pensioners' advocate, was born on 27 October 1910 at Wodonga, Victoria, second of five children of Australian-born parents Francis Joseph Nunan (d.1953), coach driver, and his wife Daisy Florence, née Dougherty (d.1973). Marj was educated at St Michael's Catholic School, Deniliquin. Her father was often absent, working as a driver and later as a travelling salesman.

Less than five feet (152 cm) tall, Miss Nunan had straight hair with a deep fringe and wore thick-lensed spectacles. She suffered from the debilitating and ultimately fatal Ehlers-Danlos syndrome, a rare inherited disorder. Although crippled and often ill, she disliked and avoided using a wheelchair. Cheerful and gregarious, she received an invalid's pension and shared a house with her parents when they moved to Brunswick, Melbourne, about 1933. In the early 1940s she became a social activist, particularly concerned to obtain a better deal for pensioners. By this time she was a member of the Communist Party of Australia; she was secretary of its Brunswick branch in 1948-56.

In March 1954 Nunan called a public meeting at the Melbourne Town Hall with the aim of uniting pensioners' associations through-out the State. The meeting led to the establish-ment that year of the Combined Pensioners' Association of Victoria, under her presidency. She used the press extensively to publicize the C.P.A.'s claims for an adequate standard of living, reasonable rent, health care and con-cessions. With indefatigable spirit, she spoke on behalf of pensioners at court hearings, as-sisted them to resist evictions, and organized protest meetings, petitions and deputations, often in the face of considerable opposition. On one occasion, after the Melbourne City Council refused her application to use a public-address system at a picnic-meeting, she ob-tained a vehicle with loudspeakers from the police.

Nunan organized the association's annual conference and led a deputation of pensioners to Canberra each year before the budget was tabled in parliament. The Federal treasurer Sir Arthur Fadden [q.v.14] declined to meet them in 1955 on their first visit. In the follow-ing year they went armed with a petition: it bore 120 000 signatures and demanded a pen-sion equal to half the basic wage. Although it was winter, they threatened to sit overnight on the steps of Parliament House until they were heard. Fadden remained intransigent, but the pensioners received wide publicity. Nunan proved resourceful in retaining the sympathy of the press for the pensioners' cause.

In 1956 she helped to found the Australian Commonwealth Pensioners' Federation. She was appointed its first treasurer, a position she was to hold until her death. From 1959 she produced a bi-monthly tabloid newspaper, the *Combined Pensioners' Association News*; it was initially priced at one penny and had a circulation of 9000. Nunan died of septicaemia and heart disease on 12 January 1963 at Royal Melbourne Hospital and was cremated. Articles in the *C.P.A. News* continued to refer to 'Our Marj' for years after her death. In 1986 the association opened at Thornbury the Marjorie Nunan home for pensioners.

R. Gibson, *My Years in the Communist Party* (Melb, 1966); *CPA News*, Feb-Mar, Apr-May 1963, Jan-Mar 1964, Nov-Dec 1969; *Age* (Melb), 23 June 1955; *Guardian* (Melb), 1 Sept 1955; *Herald* (Melb), 12, 14, 15 Jan 1963; A1533/33, item 56/2853, ASIO, A6119/90, item 2472, A6122/2, item 493 (AA, Canb).
ANTHEA BUNDOCK

NUTT, ERNEST ARTHUR (1911-1974), press photographer, was born on 5 June 1911 at Camperdown, Sydney, third child of native-born parents Arthur Edward Nutt, clerk, and his wife Stella Kezia Maud, née Crundwell. Ernie (or Ern, as he was also known) was edu-cated at Ashfield and Croydon Superior public

schools. In 1916 he joined the Sydney daily newspaper, the *Evening News*, as a copy-boy. Disliking shorthand, he found the lure of the darkroom stronger than that of the journal-ist's desk. When the *News* folded in 1931, he was a second-year photographer cadet. He remained in Sydney, moved to the photo-graphic staff of the *World* and later worked for *Truth*. During the Depression he had a job as a milkman. By the mid-1930s he was em-ployed on the *Daily Telegraph*, part of (Sir) Frank Packer's [q.v.] Consolidated Press Ltd. At the Methodist Church, North Croydon, on 24 August 1935 he married Florence Winifred Francis.

A stocky, affable and talkative man, Nutt was particularly skilled at action photography and at 'thawing frosty interviewees'. As a staff photographer, he was expected to cover news stories, social events, court cases and sport. His specialty was sport, and it was said that he outran wingers as he sprinted along the side-line taking shots of Rugby League football. On 24 September 1936, while on a routine assign-ment for the *Telegraph*, he photographed the collision of the *Kulgoa* and *Kurra-ba* ferries in Sydney Harbour. His 'scoop' was used in the Court of Marine Inquiry's investigation of the incident, at which he demonstrated his speed and expertise by taking pictures with a bulky reflex camera before a startled judge.

In February 1938 Nutt photographed the tragic sinking of the launch, *Rodney*. Like other senior photographers, he contributed to various magazines and newspapers owned by Consolidated Press. He regularly went to the Melbourne Cup for the *Australian Women's Weekly* and in World War II produced some of the *Weekly*'s first coloured photographic covers. Unable to enlist in the armed services due to high blood pressure, he travelled throughout Australia and went abroad, spend-ing time in the Territory of Papua-New Guinea and in Japan. In 1948 he made a picture series on Broken Hill and Lightning Ridge for the monthly magazine, *A.M.*

Press photography had its occupational hazards. Nutt began his career in a period before flashbulbs, when photographers filled rooms with smoke from their magnesium powder flashes. If assigned to a divorce case, he tried to keep an eye on all exits from the court-house. In 1940 he was assaulted and robbed of his camera. In 1952 he was involved in a motorcar accident. Despite his occu-pation, he never owned a camera and relied on the camaraderie of his colleagues when he needed to record a family occasion. Although he took a huge number of photographs during his professional career, his name was seldom acknowledged. He died of cancer on 26 July 1974 at his Croydon home and was cremated; his wife, two sons and two daughters survived him.

D. O'Brien, *The Weekly* (Melb, 1982); *Aust Women's Weekly*, 14 June 1947, 14 Aug 1948; *A.M.*, Aug, Nov 1948, Feb 1949; *Journalist*, Oct 1974; *Daily Telegraph* (Syd), 25 Sept, 4 Nov 1936, 14 Feb 1938; information from Mr R. Berg, Dural, Mrs F. W. Nutt, Croydon, and Mr G. Nutt, Chester Hill, Syd, who also holds the family papers.

KATE EVANS

NYHOLM, SIR RONALD SYDNEY (1917-1971), professor of chemistry, was born on 29 January 1917 at Broken Hill, New South Wales, fourth of six children of Adelaide-born parents Eric Edward Nyholm (d.1932), railway shunter, and his wife Gertrude Mary, née Woods. His paternal grandfather Erik Nyholm, a coppersmith, had emigrated from Finland in 1873. Ron attended Broken Hill High School on a bursary. Dux in 1933, he won a Teachers' College scholarship to the University of Sydney (B.Sc., 1938; M.Sc., 1942). In his third year he was influenced by the lectures on coordination (metal complex) chemistry given by George Burrows, who was to supervise his fourth year. Nyholm investigated iron complexes of arsines and graduated with first-class honours. Thus began his lifelong activity with arsines as ligands (compounds which bind chemically to metal ions).

After a short period in 1938 as a research chemist with the Eveready Co. (Australia) Pty Ltd in Sydney, Nyholm returned to the Department of Education. In May 1940 he was appointed teacher of chemistry at Sydney Technical College. He commenced research on platinum-metal complexes with another member of staff, Frank Dwyer [q.v.14]. Dwyer —with his enthusiasm and experimental skills—and Nyholm—with his keen interest in coordination chemistry and experience with arsines—developed a good working relationship, and a close friendship. Between 1942 and 1947 they reported complexes of rhodium, iridium, and osmium in seventeen papers in the *Journal and Proceedings* of the Royal Society of New South Wales.

In 1947 Nyholm was awarded an Imperial Chemical Industries Ltd fellowship to work with Professor (Sir) Christopher Ingold at University College, London (Ph.D., 1950; D.Sc., 1953). At the parish church, Kensington, on 6 August 1948 he married Maureen Richardson, an Australian-born nurse. Appointed to the staff of U.C.L., he worked on metal complexes of o-phenylenebisdimethylarsine; he showed that this arsine is effective in stabilizing both unusually high and unusually low oxidation states. His important discovery prompted considerable theoretical discussion and led to a search for other ligands that might behave similarly.

In 1952 Nyholm returned to Sydney as lecturer at the New South Wales University of Technology, where his effect on the inorganic chemistry department was immediate and profound. He brought fresh ideas of what he called the 'renaissance of inorganic chemistry' and stimulated a greater enthusiasm for research in coordination chemistry. He was also interested in magnetochemistry, and considerably extended knowledge in that area. Promoted associate-professor in 1953, he was president of the Royal Society of New South Wales in 1954. Early in 1955 he accepted a chair of chemistry at University College, London. In only three years in Sydney he had taken coordination chemistry in Australia out of a rut: from that time this area of research has been vigorously pursued in Australia, largely due to his influence.

At U.C.L. Nyholm soon built a flourishing research group which attracted doctoral and postdoctoral students from Britain, the United States of America, Australia, India, New Zealand and elsewhere. From 1963 he was head of the department. The scope of his research widened and included most areas of the rapidly expanding field of coordination chemistry. His publications numbered 278. A 'vigorous, hard-hitting, yet witty campaigner for reform in science teaching at all levels', he was a moderator in chemistry for the University of London examinations board and chaired the Nuffield Foundation's consultative committee on O-level chemistry. As chairman of the Royal Institute of Chemistry's editorial board, he took a leading part in launching its journal, *Education in Chemistry*; he also served on the editorial board of *Comprehensive Inorganic Chemistry* (1973), which was to be published in five volumes.

A fellow (1958) of the Royal Society, Nyholm valued his Finnish ancestry and was delighted to be elected a corresponding-member (1959) of the Finska Kemistsamfundet-Suomen Kemistiseura (Chemical Society of Finland). He was a member (1967-68) of the Science Research Council, president (1967) of the Association for Scientific Education and a trustee of the British Museum. While president (1968-70) of the Chemical Society, he oversaw its amalgamation with the Faraday Society, the Royal Institute of Chemistry and the Society of Chemical Industry.

Nyholm's many honours included the Chemical Society's Corday-Morgan medal (for 1950), the H. G. Smith [q.v.11] medal of the Royal Australian Chemical Institute (1955), the medal of the R.S.N.S.W. (for 1963), the gold medal of the Societa Chimica Italiana (1968) and the 'Sigillum Magnum' medal of the University of Bologna (1969). He visited Sydney to give the first Dwyer memorial lecture for the University of New South Wales Chemical Society (1963) and to receive an honorary doctorate of science from the U.N.S.W. (1969). He was knighted in 1967.

Nyholm played cricket and was intensely interested in the game. He belonged to the Athenaeum Club. Just under middle height, with fair hair which thinned with the years, he had an infectious smile and, above all, charm. Lord Arran, provost of University College, London, said: 'Ron Nyholm never entered a room, he bubbled into it and exploded into good fellowship, mirth and happiness'. At the height of his career Sir Ronald died on 4 December 1971 in Addenbrooke's Hospital, Cambridge, from injuries received in a motor-car accident. He was cremated after a service at Hinchley Wood, Esher, Surrey, where he had lived. His wife, son and two daughters survived him.

Biog Memoirs of Fellows of Roy Soc (Lond), 18, 1972, p 445; S. E. Livingstone, 'The contributions of David P. Mellor, Frank P. Dwyer, and Ronald S. Nyholm to coordination chemistry', in G. B. Kauffman (ed), *Coordination Chemistry* (Washington, 1994); Roy Aust Chemical Inst, *Procs*, 39, 1972, p 320; Roy Soc NSW, *J and Procs*, 105, 1972, p 54; A. T. Baker and S. E. Livingstone, 'The early history of coordination chemistry in Australia', *Polyhedron* (Oxford), 4, 1985, p 1337; *The Times*, 29 Feb 1952, 6 Dec 1971; *SMH*, 21 June 1954, 11 Nov 1955, 2 Apr 1964, 6 June 1967, 22 Aug 1969.

STANLEY E. LIVINGSTONE

O

OALA-RARUA, OALA (1934-1980), teacher, trade-union leader, politician and diplomat, was born on 12 June 1934 at Pari village, near Port Moresby, son of Oala Oala-Rarua, pastor, and his wife Asi, née Daroa. He received his early education in village mission schools before transferring in 1948 to the Sogeri education centre where he was trained, and then employed, as a teacher. In 1955 he began teaching at Kwato mission, Milne Bay, an outpost of the Moral Rearmament Movement, under whose auspices he visited New Zealand, the United States of America and Europe. In 1957 he joined the Territory of Papua and New Guinea's administration as a teacher. He was headmaster of the Kerepunu school in the Marshall Lagoon area when, in 1962, he was recalled to Port Moresby to become assistant to (Sir) John Gunther, the assistant-administrator. Recognizing his ability, and his fluency in English, Gunther gave him a number of specialized tasks, including appointment (1963) as assistant executive officer for the Commission on Higher Education.

In 1962 Oala-Rarua was elected president of the Port Moresby Workers' Association. He resigned from the administration in 1965 to work full time for the new Territory-wide Federation of Workers' Associations, which he had helped to establish. Within several years, however, both organizations were defunct, and he took a job with a private firm in Port Moresby.

Oala-Rarua stood unsuccessfully for the Legislative Council in 1961 and for the House of Assembly in 1964. In the following year he founded the short-lived New Guinea United National Party. He was a founding member (1967) and co-chairman of the Pangu (Papua and New Guinea Union) Pati, but soon left because of policy differences. In 1968 he was elected to the House of Assembly as member for the Central Regional Electorate and was appointed assistant-minister for the Treasury.

In the House, Oala-Rarua's contributions to debate were forthright, cogent and uncompromising. As a 'straight-out nationalist', he consistently argued for the country's advance towards independence and for 'the betterment of its people regardless of colour, race, or creed'. He was a member of the Select Committee on Constitutional Development which reported in 1971. While urging Papua-New Guinea's development as one nation, he also recognized that there was an imbalance in the allocation of funds which should be redressed in Papua's favour. He persistently advocated the development of Port Moresby as the national capital. Elected president of the Port Moresby Town Council in 1971, he became its first mayor in 1972.

After his defeat in the 1972 election, Oala-Rarua was chosen in 1974 to set up Papua New Guinea's first diplomatic office in Australia. When the nation gained its independence in 1975, he became its first high commissioner to Australia. At the end of his term he returned to Papua New Guinea and stood unsuccessfully as a candidate for the Moresby South Open electorate in the 1977 election. Retiring from politics, he pursued business interests. He died suddenly of hypertensive cerebrovascular disease on 17 May 1980 in Port Moresby and was buried at Pari village; his wife Paruru Rarua, three daughters and two sons survived him.

Able, intelligent, personable and urbane, Oala-Rarua mixed easily with Australians, indigenous Papua New Guinea leaders and his own Motu people. He was part of an elite group who carried the burden of the expectations of Papua New Guineans and Australian government officials as the country approached independence. One of the few Papuans of his generation with education beyond primary level, he was thrust into responsibilities which did not always suit his talents or temperament. (Sir) Michael Somare paid tribute to him as 'one of the pioneers of our nation, a wonderful man and a dedicated . . . nationalist'.

D. G. Bettison et al (eds), *The Papua-New Guinea Elections 1964* (Canb, 1965); A. L. Epstein et al (eds), *The Politics of Dependence* (Canb, 1971); D. Woolford, *Papua New Guinea* (Brisb, 1976); R. R. Premdas and J. S. Steeves, *Electoral Politics in a Third World City* (Port Moresby, 1978); *Aust External Territories*, 9, no 4, 1969, p 28; *Post-Courier*, 19, 21 May 1980; personal knowledge.

MURRAY GROVES

OBERG, DAVID OLOF AUGUST (1893-1975), timber merchant, was born on 24 September 1893 at Coolamon, New South Wales, second child of Joseph Nathanael Oberg (d.1896), a licensed surveyor from Sweden, and his Victorian-born wife Jane (Jean), née Hannah. In 1897 Jean married Sidney Welman; they were to have three children. Ollie's stepfather arranged for him to be raised by a neighbour and then by a friend in Sydney. An outstanding student, he was a school captain (1911) at Sydney Boys' High School, but was forced to leave before sitting the senior public examination to assist his mother, who had again been widowed. His bitter disappointment fuelled a determination to succeed.

Starting work as a timber-yard labourer, Oberg became manager (by 1915) of the lumber firm, A. C. Laman. In 1921 he was appointed general manager of Davies & Fehon Ltd, timber merchants. At the Congregational Church, Petersham, on 3 November 1917 he had married with Methodist forms Dulcie Sutton Druce (d.1974). In 1930 he joined with the Thatcher brothers in establishing a new timber business, Thatcher & Oberg (Pty) Ltd. Oberg chose the firm's motto, 'Quality and Efficiency'. Under his direction the partnership developed as a major importer of American west-coast softwoods. In 1962 the company was to be taken over by Blue Metal Industries Ltd.

Oberg was a member (1931-34) of the Unemployment Relief Council and president (1939-48) of the Citizens' Reform Association. His other offices included presidency of Sydney trade organizations, and of the Timber Development Association of Australia (1938-48) and the Australian Council of Employers' Federations (1943-46). During World War II he was an adviser to the timber controller for Australia and to the deputy-controller of manpower (New South Wales). Co-ordinating timber distribution, he encouraged the development and conservation of forests, and demonstrated how improved kiln-drying techniques could make Australian timber more suitable for building and furniture.

His advisory role with the Australian delegation to the United Nations Conference on International Organization, held at San Francisco in 1945, was the highlight of Oberg's public life. That year he also joined employer delegates at the International Labour Organization's conference in Paris, and was a member (later deputy-chairman) of the Commonwealth Immigration Advisory Council. Politically conservative, Oberg opposed Labor's socialist policies, especially its postwar plans for regulating the building industry. In anticipation of a housing boom, he urged taxation relief for new capital investment, and advocated equality between private and public enterprise in regard to manpower and material. Appointed C.M.G. in 1953, he was State president (1957-61) of the United Nations Association of Australia.

A long-time member of Rotary International (director 1954-55, vice-president 1955-56), Oberg believed in repaying through community service the debt he owed for the opportunities he had received. He was a national council-member of the Boy Scouts' Association of Australia and was also involved with the Young Men's Christian Association. Strong and vital, ebullient and convivial, he was fond of sport, gardening and fishing. He belonged to the New South Wales, Sydney Savage and Concord Golf clubs, and the Royal Sydney Yacht Squadron. Survived by his two daughters and two of his three sons, he died on 15 February 1975 at Bowning and was cremated.

A. G. Mitchell, *The Rotary Club of Sydney 1921-1981* (Syd, 1981) and *District 975 of Rotary International 1927-1983* (Syd, 1984); *Pinion*, Dec 1939; *SMH*, 15 June 1937, 21 Apr 1939, 17 Jan 1941, 13, 14 June, 16 Aug 1944, 19 Oct 1945, 2 Dec 1957, 20 Oct 1958, 24 Oct 1960; information from Mrs J. Greenhalgh, Roseville, Syd.

ALISON PILGER

O'BRIEN, CLAUDE HARDING (1879-1960), sugar-technologist, was born on Christmas Eve 1879 in Sydney, son of Richard William O'Brien, a coach painter from Wales, and his native-born wife Elizabeth Ann, née Barden. The family moved to Glebe and Richard set up as a bootmaker. Although Claude did not matriculate, he was permitted to study first-year science at the University of Sydney in 1900.

In September 1901 O'Brien joined the newly established Queensland Bureau of Sugar Experiment Stations as a junior assistant-chemist. After working in its laboratories at Bundaberg, he went to Fiji in 1903 as chief chemist for the Fiji Sugar Co. Ltd. He returned to Bundaberg in 1905 as supervising chemist at the State's central mills. At St Mary's Catholic Church, Bundaberg, on 2 March 1908 he married Louise Clarissa Marie Nogues. Two months later he became chief sugar chemist at Mossman Central Sugar Mill Co. Ltd. From 1909 he was employed by the Mulgrave Central Mill Co. Ltd where he made his two biggest contributions to the Queensland sugar industry.

First, in 1915 O'Brien designed apparatus that assisted in determining the amount of fibre in the cane being crushed. His patented machine, known as a cane fibrator, became standard laboratory equipment in the State's sugar-mills. Secondly, in the same year he and Dr J. H. Reed were asked by the Cairns Cane Growers' Association to investigate systems of payment for cane. Their investigation followed complaints from growers that it had proved impossible to harvest all their crops at a time when each had maximum juice content and thus its highest value. O'Brien and Reed developed the relative percentage scheme by which growers, no matter when their cane was harvested, suffered no loss. This scheme was eventually endorsed by the Australian Sugar Producers' Association and adopted by mills throughout Queensland as the basis for paying their suppliers.

In October 1915 O'Brien was appointed chemist to the Central Cane Prices Board,

Brisbane. The board was established under the Regulation of Sugar Cane Prices Act (1915) to hear appeals from local bodies (consisting of miller and grower representatives) which set the prices paid for cane. O'Brien wrote numerous dissenting memoranda in which he calculated the costs of cane production and sugar-manufacture differently from other board-members. Despite being described as a 'bit too troublesome', he was reappointed in 1922.

After the A.S.P.A. had received a request from the South African Planters' Association for a qualified sugar technologist to advise their planters on Australia's system of payment for cane, in August 1922 O'Brien was granted six months leave to visit South Africa. His recommendations—which covered the establishment of a sugar experiment station, the types of cane to be grown, and payment for cane by sucrose content—were subsequently implemented in that country. Early in 1925 he left the board to return to his former post at the Mossman mill. In 1930 he rejoined the A.S.P.A. as a technical adviser. Following the retirement of E. J. T. Barton in May 1935, O'Brien also edited the association's monthly publication, the *Australian Sugar Journal*.

O'Brien was a foundation member (1917) and committee-member (1933-35) of the Queensland branch of the (Royal) Australian Chemical Institute, and a founder (1929) and executive-member (1931-37 and 1941-50) of the Queensland Society of Sugar Cane Technologists. He represented the A.S.P.A. at congresses of the International Society of Sugar Cane Technologists, in Brisbane (1935, 1950) and Louisiana, United States of America (1938). His published papers were limited to one address (1934) to the A.C.I.'s Queensland branch and two talks (1930 and 1949) to the Q.S.S.C.T.

Although O'Brien retired as editor in 1950, he continued as the A.S.P.A.'s technical adviser until 1954. At the request of the association's executive he wrote (1951-53) a series of articles on the history of the Australian sugar industry for the *Australian Sugar Journal*. Survived by his wife, daughter and son, he died on 4 November 1960 in East Brisbane and was buried in Hemmant cemetery.

J. Kerr, *Northern Outpost* (Mossman, Qld, 1979); *Aust Sugar J*, 14, no 6, 1922, 14, no 11, 1923, 22, no 1, 1930, 41, no 10, 1950, 52, no 8, 1960; *Producers' Review*, Nov 1960; *International Sugar J*, 63, no 747, 1961; information from Ms B. Poulton, R.A.C.I., Melb.

PETER D. GRIGGS

O'BRIEN, ERIS MICHAEL (1895-1974), Catholic archbishop and Australian historian, was born on 29 September 1895 at Condo-bolin, New South Wales, eldest of three children of Terence O'Brien, a native-born police constable, and his Irish-born wife Bertha, née Conroy. Terence became a publican and a Sydney Municipal Council alderman. His son was baptized Erisford (allegedly after the racehorse, Eridsforde) Norman and called Eris; the adopted second name Michael was both his confirmation name and that of the saint whose feast fell on his birthday. In 1901 the family settled in Sydney. Eris attended primary schools at Camperdown and Chatswood, then studied at St Aloysius' College, Milsons Point.

After training at St Columba's Seminary, Springwood, and St Patrick's College, Manly, O'Brien was ordained priest on 30 November 1918. His parish work in Sydney was to take him to Haymarket (1918-21 and 1929-31), Waterloo (1922), Rose Bay (1922-24), Hurstville (1927-29) and Bankstown (1931-34). He lectured in Australian history at his old colleges (St Patrick's in 1921 and St Columba's in 1924-27), and published *The Life and Letters of Archpriest John Joseph Therry* (Sydney, 1922, also titled *The Foundation of Catholicism in Australia*). *The Dawn of Catholicism in Australia*, the story of Fr Jeremiah O'Flynn [q.v.2], appeared in 1928. Both books were well received. Today they are considered uncritical. O'Brien also published *The Hostage: A Miracle Play* (1928).

Among his archdiocesan appointments, O'Brien was editor (1931-32) of the *Catholic School Paper*. In 1934 he was granted leave to attend the Catholic University of Louvain, Belgium (Ph.D., 1936), and the National University of Ireland, Dublin (M.A., 1936). His aims were to study a topic in social science and political economy, and—at the request of the New South Wales bishops—to collect sources for a biography of Cardinal Moran [q.v.10]. O'Brien's thesis, published as *The Foundation of Australia (1786-1800)* (London, 1937), established his academic reputation. A Sydney edition (1950) was used as a text in Australian universities. He worked on his biography of Moran for many years, but never completed it.

O'Brien returned to Sydney in 1936. Taking up parish duties at Bankstown and later at Neutral Bay (1938-48), he also held the post of diocesan director (1937-40) of Catholic Action, the lay social apostolate. At (Sir) Stephen Roberts's [q.v.] invitation, he lectured part time in Australian history (1947-48) at the University of Sydney; Dr H. V. Evatt [q.v.14] asked him to give courses at the Australian School of Pacific Administration. On 6 April 1948 O'Brien was consecrated auxiliary bishop to Cardinal (Sir) Norman Gilroy [q.v.14]. O'Brien was a member of the Australian delegation to the third session (1948) of the United Nations General Assembly in Paris and to the fifth session (1950) at Lake Success, New York State, United States of America. Evatt presided at the third session and arranged for him to sit on the committee dealing with human rights. O'Brien enjoyed Paris, but not Lake Success where he was at odds with the rest of the Australian delegation over the issue of Jerusalem.

In January 1951 O'Brien was made an auxiliary archbishop in the archdiocese of Sydney. On 16 November 1953 he was appointed archbishop of Canberra and Goulburn. He was enthroned twice on 28 December, first at the cathedral of St Peter and St Paul, Goulburn, and later at St Christopher's Pro-Cathedral, Canberra. In 1955 he moved to Canberra and designated St Christopher's co-cathedral for the archdiocese. During his term the number of Catholic parishes in the Australian Capital Territory increased from one to ten, placing strain on finances and personnel.

After lobbying for assistance, O'Brien accepted the Federal government's offer in 1956 to subsidize interest on money borrowed to build or extend church secondary schools in the A.C.T. Pressures on the New South Wales Catholic school system led to the 'Goulburn School Strike' in 1962, during which O'Brien's auxiliary bishop John Cullinane and a lay committee closed Catholic schools in that city. O'Brien publicly gave his support, emphasizing the right of Catholics to take action as private citizens. Privately he wavered. The schools reopened after five days, but the incident accelerated action to provide state aid for all church schools.

With Gilroy, O'Brien travelled to the Republic of Vietnam (South Vietnam) in 1955. He was an active member of the Social Science Research Council of Australia, the council of Canberra University College, and the Canberra and District Historical Society. In 1957 he was appointed C.M.G. O'Brien had been elected a fellow of the Royal Geographical and the Royal Historical societies, London, in 1935 and of the Royal Australian Historical Society in 1949. He composed church music, translated French, co-founded (1940) the Australian Catholic Historical Society and participated in the Second Vatican Council.

Increasing mental and physical frailty obliged O'Brien to resign his see in 1967. Shifting to Sydney, he lived at St Patrick's College, Manly, and later with his sister Beryl at Crows Nest. He died on 28 February 1974 at the St John of God Hospital, Richmond, and was buried in the crypt of St Christopher's Cathedral, Canberra. Archbishop Guilford Young of Hobart wrote of O'Brien's achievements: 'When we, as a Catholic community, did not have any standing in the world of scholarship . . . you made the break through . . . You showed . . . that the Australian priest valued culture and was not a mere pragmatist'.

J. N. Cullinane, *Goulburn School 'Strike'* (Canb, 1989); *Hist Studies*, 17, no 66, 1976, p 129; O'Brien papers, Veech L, Catholic Inst of Syd; Syd Archdiocesan Archives; Archdiocese of Hob Archives; information from Bishop J. Cullinane, Burwood, Syd.

ELIZABETH JOHNSTON

O'BRIEN, JACK LOCKYER (1909-1965), historian, was born on 30 December 1909 at Adelong, New South Wales, second surviving child of Australian-born parents Richard Thomas Lockyer O'Brien, miner, and his wife Selina Rachel, née Crain. Influenced by his classics master John Gibbs at Sydney Boys' High School, 'John' O'Brien was awarded a scholarship to the University of Sydney (B.A., 1930) where he graduated with first-class honours and won the university medal in classics. He then proceeded to Emmanuel College, Cambridge (B.A., 1932).

In 1932 O'Brien returned to Australia and took up a tutorship at Trinity College, University of Melbourne. Two years later he was appointed a lecturer in the university's department of classics. A lapsed Catholic, he married Joyce Mary Hansen with Anglican rites on 12 December 1936 at Holy Trinity Church, Kew; they were to be divorced in 1956. Following the death of Jessie Webb [q.v.12], he transferred on 1 March 1945 to the department of history as a senior lecturer.

Realistic about teaching undergraduates who generally knew neither Greek nor Latin, O'Brien adopted a broad approach to ancient history and provided extensive translations for his students. His lectures were totally based on primary sources, linking—for example—Athenian tribute lists, other inscriptions, monuments and literary texts. He was a self-effacing and tolerant teacher who encouraged students to assess the reliability of all explanations. His advanced course on Roman Britain was celebrated for its critical examination of the sources, and the theories of R. G. Collingwood. Delivered in a precise, even style, his lectures formed a series, complete with footnotes. The need for concentration and diligent note-taking meant that they were popular only with a minority, yet his originality and humanity pervaded small classes.

O'Brien was a meticulous linguist with a penetrating grasp of the logic and nuances of a language. He completed translations which were models of lucidity, rendering a hieroglyphic text as fluently as one in medieval Latin. When Michael Ventris and John Chadwick claimed the decipherment of the Mycenaen Linear B script, he applied their principles to undeciphered texts published in *Scripta Minoa*; as they passed his test, he abandoned investigations without reporting his innovative successes. None of his basic research was published, probably because his combination of perfectionism and humility discounted his originality. His encouragement of student involvement in Australian archaeology, however, brought positive results.

Late in his career O'Brien developed an unorthodox and consuming interest that stamped him as an innovator in studies in Australian architectural and urban history. In the same spirit of inquiry with which he calculated the cost of building the Parthenon, he applied the principles of archaeological typology and the primacy of original texts to the study of suburban domestic housing. He concentrated on the housing stock of inner Melbourne, much of it then under threat of demolition by the Housing Commission of Victoria. With the solicitor Peter Balmford's collaboration, he used ratebooks, street directories, titles, sub-division notices, tenders and even sewerage connection data to identify the date, pattern of construction and occupation of complete streets. In 1957 O'Brien bought a bluestone house in Hanover Street, Fitzroy, and fiercely campaigned to prevent its demolition. His stand became a symbol of changing social values towards mindless, bureaucratic 'slum' clearance. He took two thousand colour photographs documenting suburban streetscapes, which were subsequently donated to the University of Melbourne's archives.

Slightly built, quietly spoken and wearing distinctive steel-framed spectacles, O'Brien appeared so impassive during lectures that his wry puns and jokes were unexpected. Outside classes his selfless attitude and impish wit made him a character of distinction. At the office of the government statist, Melbourne, on 28 January 1958 he married Laurie Rose Campbell McBriar, née Douglas. He died of emphysema and chronic bronchitis on 13 August 1965 in South Melbourne and was cremated; his wife and their son survived him, as did the son and daughter of his first marriage.

B. and K. Smith, *The Architectural Character of Glebe, Sydney* (Syd, 1973); Fitzroy Hist Soc, *Fitzroy* (Melb, 1989); *Univ Melb Gazette*, Oct 1965; *Mundus Antiquus*, 2, 1978; Univ Melb Archives; information from Messrs P. Balmford, East Ivanhoe, Melb, and R. O'Brien, Claremont, Perth; personal knowledge.

D. J. MULVANEY

O'BRIEN, JOHN WILLIAM ALEXANDER (1908-1980), engineer and soldier, was born on 13 June 1908 at Collingwood, Melbourne, only child of Henry Charles O'Brien, a police constable from England, and his New Zealand-born wife Jean Doris, née Kerr. Educated at St Patrick's College, East Melbourne, and the

Working Men's College, John obtained a job as a draughtsman with the Melbourne and Metropolitan Tramways Board. In August 1928 he was commissioned lieutenant in the 2nd Artillery Survey Company, Militia. On a world tour in 1930-31 he studied artillery survey techniques used by the United States and British armies, and tramped across the battlefields of the American Civil War and World War I.

While employed (1932-35) by United Stevedoring Pty Ltd in Melbourne, O'Brien designed an 'automatic grab' for unloading coal-ships. On 31 March 1934 at St Columba's Catholic Church, Elwood, he married Gwen Victoria Goddard Britton, a 23-year-old saleswoman. He co-founded (1938) and managed an engineering firm, Fleet Forge Pty Ltd. Meanwhile, in the Militia, he had been acting-adjutant (1932-36) of the 10th Field Artillery Brigade and later a battery commander. Promoted major in 1937, he transferred to Army Headquarters in September 1939 as deputy assistant director of artillery.

O'Brien joined the Australian Imperial Force on 1 May 1940 and was posted to the 2nd/7th Field Regiment as second-in-command. In Palestine on 5 March 1941 he was promoted lieutenant colonel and appointed to command the 2nd/5th Field Regiment. His military and engineering experience, and his 'almost youthful dash and enthusiasm', won him the respect of the regiment. He led the 2nd/5th throughout the Syrian campaign during which he repeatedly came under mortar and sniper fire. For his 'courage, driving power and relentless energy' he was awarded the Distinguished Service Order and mentioned in dispatches.

Returning to Melbourne, O'Brien was promoted temporary brigadier in April 1942 and appointed director of artillery in the following month. He was made deputy master-general of the ordnance (army equipment) in January 1943. His role was to manage the acquisition and trial of military equipment, including the short 25-pounder (11.3 kg) field-gun, an adaptation which he had suggested when director of artillery. He also provided a link between the army's material requirements and the manufacturers who supplied them. With his flair for administration, it 'was as if he sat at the centre of an enormous web that covered businessmen, public servants and politicians'.

O'Brien led the Australian Scientific Mission to Japan (1945-46) and headed (1945-51) the science and technology division of General Douglas MacArthur's [q.v.] staff in Tokyo. In 1948-49 he presided over the war crimes tribunal which acquitted Admiral Soemu Toyoda. He wrote *Guns and Gunners* (Sydney, 1950), a history of his old regiment. Transferring to the Reserve of Officers on 31 March 1951, he was accorded the honorary rank of major general while acting as Australia's supply and defence production representative in Washington (1951-54). In both the Tokyo and Washington posts he was 'frustrated and discouraged by bureaucratic wrangling'.

Settling in Sydney, O'Brien worked as director of engineering and sales (1955-59) with Howard [q.v.9] Auto-Cultivators Pty Ltd before founding and managing Contract Tooling Pty Ltd which specialized in precision engineering. In 1971-72 and 1975-76 he was mayor of Woollahra. Energetically involved in cultural and sporting bodies, he supported local charities and gave freely of his time to old comrades. O'Brien was a handsome man, 5 ft 10 ins (178 cm) tall, with brown hair and blue eyes. An altruist and a natural leader, 'able, shrewd and proud', he mixed easily with a wide range of people. He died on 27 May 1980 at Darlinghurst and was buried in South Head cemetery; his wife, son and daughter survived him.

W. G. Rimmer, *In Time for War* (Syd, 1991); *Harry Peck's Post*, Sept 1980, p 34.

A. J. SWEETING

O'BRIEN, LOUISA (1880-1957), hotelier, was born on 1 September 1880 at Naracoorte, South Australia, third child of George Henry Read, racehorse-trainer, and his wife Mary Hannah, née Chaston. In the mid-1880s the family moved to Melbourne where George became publican of Waldock's Hotel, Ascot Vale. Returning to Adelaide, he and Mary managed (from 1890) the Black Bull Hotel in Hindley Street. Louisa was educated at Hardwicke College, East Adelaide; she loved parties, the theatre and meeting people.

At Holy Trinity Church, Adelaide, on 15 July 1911 she married with Anglican rites John O'Brien (d.1922), a 25-year-old jockey. Although her father disapproved of the match and called her husband 'Flash Jack', he helped to secure their lease (1913) of the Young Queen (later Commercial) Hotel, Gawler Place. In 1921 they took over the Black Bull. After John's death she continued to run the hotel and sent her five children to boarding-schools. It was her instinctive and impulsive decision to lease the rundown South Australian Hotel in 1934 that made her the 'grand duchess of the hotel world'. Dating from 1879, this three-storeyed building on North Terrace had broad balconies, elegant columns and a grand cedar staircase.

Gaining control of the hotel on 18 June 1934, O'Brien sacked the kitchen staff (because of the filth in the rat-ridden kitchen) and hired twenty-five unemployed painters and plasterers. Two days later the beautiful white-and-gold dining-room, presided over by head waiter Lewy Cotton [q.v.13], served luncheon (the cost was three shillings). The room could seat up to six hundred people. O'Brien subsequently engaged Kenneth Milne [q.v.] to design alterations to the hotel; four firms furnished its interior. One of the great hotels of the British Empire, 'The South' was her castle. In summer she sat by the window in the foyer and greeted her guests with 'Hullo dear, how are you?' When her children were home, at 6.15 each evening she led them to their table in the dining-room.

With her sculptured hair, piercing eyes and couturier-clothed, ample figure, Mrs O'Brien could be brusque and acidic, though she 'preferred to be kindly'. During the 1939 bushfires she turned the Blue Room into a dormitory for firefighters; in 1941 that room became a staging camp for Dutch refugees; and in World War II American soldiers used part of 'The South' as their headquarters. O'Brien helped the Australian Red Cross Society, the Fighting Forces Comforts Fund and the Cheer-up Society. In 1948 she was appointed M.B.E.

It was O'Brien's ambition to have her children run the hotels she had acquired. Brian managed the Gresham Hotel, King William Street, Olive the Berkeley Hotel (formerly the Black Bull), John the Strathmore Hotel, North Terrace, and Beth was groomed to succeed her at 'The South'. Survived by her three daughters and one of her two sons, Louisa O'Brien died on 16 December 1957 in her beloved South Australian Hotel and was buried in North Road cemetery. Her estate was sworn for probate at £63 949. Ingrid Erns's portrait of O'Brien hangs in Stamford Plaza which now stands on the site of 'The South'.

J. Larkins and B. Howard, *Australian Pubs* (Adel, 1973); J. L. Hoad, *Hotels and Publicans in South Australia 1836-1984* (Adel, 1986); *Advertiser* (Adel), 10 June 1948, 17 Dec 1957; *Sunday Mail* (Adel), 21 Dec 1957; J. Robertson, 'Louisa O'Brien', in Personalities Remembered (radio talk 23 May 1971, Mort L); Mrs O. Bey, scrapbook (held by Mr P. O. A. Bey, Glenunga, Adel); information from Mr and Mrs P. O. A. Bey, Glenunga, Mr G. Ashton, Glenelg, and Mrs B. O'Brien, College Park, Adel.

JOYCE GIBBERD

O'BRIEN, MICHAEL (1900-1967), trade unionist, was born on 15 April 1900 at Toowoomba, Queensland, younger of twin sons of Toowoomba-born parents John Joseph O'Brien, farmer, hotel yardman and Labor member (1904-07) of the Legislative Assembly, and his wife Margaret Mary, née Fahy. Mick was educated at the Christian Brothers' primary school, Toowoomba, and Valley State School, Brisbane. In 1915 he took a job as a clerk in the Queensland Railways and joined the Queensland Railways Union (later the Queensland branch of the Australian Railways Union). A keen sportsman and secretary of the Queensland Railway Institute cricket club, he managed a number of teams that played interstate competitions in Sydney and Melbourne. He also played Rugby League for the Carlton and Valley clubs in Brisbane.

After holding (from 1927) some minor posts in the union, O'Brien was its State president from 1930 until 1952. At St Joseph's Catholic Church, Kangaroo Point, on 31 July 1937 he married Ethel Morrison, a 38-year-old dressmaker; they were to remain childless. He resigned from the Queensland Railways in 1948 when the office of president was made a full-time, paid position.

O'Brien was A.R.U. delegate to the Queensland Combined Railway Unions' committee from its foundation in 1936. He became president in 1944. As president of the Central Railway Disputes Committee, he gained national prominence during the 1948 Queensland railway strike, which lasted nine weeks and challenged the industrial relations policies of the Hanlon [q.v.14] Labor government. At various times he also served on the executives of the Trades and Labor Council of Queensland and the Australian Council of Trade Unions. He represented Australian trade unions at an International Labor Organization conference in Geneva in 1947.

From 1952 until his death O'Brien was based in Sydney as general secretary of the A.R.U. He proved a successful advocate before the arbitration courts and became an expert on the impact of technological change, particularly in the transport industry. Although he was a member of the Australian Labor Party, he championed the right of trade unions to challenge Labor governments if their members' interests were not being met. He defended the civil rights of communists during the Cold War, and criticized interference by A.L.P. industrial groups and the Catholic Social Studies Movement in the internal affairs of trade unions. In supporting H. V. Evatt [q.v.14] as leader of the Federal parliamentary Labor Party, he clashed with Dr Lloyd Ross, the 'grouper' leader of the New South Wales branch of the A.R.U., and briefly took control of that branch in 1955. O'Brien advocated a continuing dialogue with trade unions in the Soviet bloc and the need for Australian unions to assist labour organization in Asian countries.

A powerfully built man with heavy jowls, O'Brien was strong willed, passionate and obdurate. He died of cancer on 21 August 1967 at the Ryde District Soldiers Memorial Hospital and was buried in Nudgee cemetery, Brisbane. His wife survived him.

M. Hearn, *Working Lives* (Syd, 1990); D. Blackmur, *Strikes* (Syd, 1993); ACTU *and* ARU *and* TLCQ records (ANUABL); Public Transport Union records (held at national office, Syd, and Qld branch, Brisb); information from Dr A. Moore, Northbridge, and Dr J. Shields, Univ NSW, Syd.

GREG PATMORE

O'BRIEN, THOMAS PATRICK (1892-1969), flour-miller, was born on 14 August 1892 at Toowoomba, Queensland, second son and sixth of ten children of Irish-born parents Patrick O'Brien (d.1906), storekeeper, and his wife Ellen, née Fitzgerald. His parents founded the Defiance Milling Co. in partnership with George Crisp in 1898. Educated at St Saviour's convent school and St Mary's Christian Brothers' College, Tom joined the family firm in 1908 as an apprentice miller. He spent several years (from 1913) in New South Wales, broadening his experience at Homebush, Sydney, and at Young, before returning to Toowoomba. On 1 April 1918 at the Church of St Michael and All Souls, Toowong, Brisbane, he married Muriel Gladys Josephine Wightman with Catholic rites.

After opening a mill in Brisbane in 1903, Defiance had rebuilt and modernized the Toowoomba plant in 1911 and added extensive grain sheds in 1914. O'Brien (who was medically unfit for military service) succeeded Crisp as manager in 1918 and took over from his mother as chairman of directors in 1924. The mills were deeply in debt and operating at a loss due to government price controls, quotas imposed by the new State Wheat Board, and the dumping of cut-price flour on the Queensland market by manufacturers in the southern States.

In 1920 O'Brien sold the Brisbane mill. He acquired one at Dalby for £6000 in 1924. Located in the heart of the Darling Downs wheat-belt, it proved highly profitable. The Toowoomba mill was further improved when O'Brien returned from a tour of English factories in 1928. Because he used Queensland wheat exclusively and discharged his obligations, Defiance was one of the few Queensland milling companies which remained free from criticism by growers and the Wheat Board in the 1920s and 1930s. The increased demand for flour during World War II led him to expand production.

A 'hands-on manager', O'Brien personally assessed the wheat according to variety and condition, and determined the blend to be used by his millers to produce a flour of the quality required. He had a 'habit of turning up unexpectedly' to carry out some of his inspections. Defiance grew large enough to compete with its national and international rivals. In 1955 the partnership was reorganized as a limited proprietary company: 'T.P.' became governing director and his sons handled day-to-day management. To counter competition from the British-based George Weston Foods Ltd, Defiance produced its own brand of household flour ('Tee Pee') and extended its operations into northern Queensland, buying bakeries in several towns and building a modern mill at Rockhampton.

O'Brien gave long service to diocesan bodies and charitable institutions, especially the St Vincent de Paul Society. Active in Rotary and the Toowoomba Chamber of Commerce, he belonged to the city's golf, turf and bowling clubs, and enjoyed walking. He died on 22 May 1969 at Toowoomba and was buried in the local cemetery; his wife, five sons and three daughters survived him. Defiance endowed scholarships at St Mary's C.B.C. and the University of Southern Queensland to commemorate him.

B. Hinchliffe (ed), *They Meant Business* (Toowoomba, Qld, 1984); *News for the Bread Manufacturers of Qld*, July 1958; *Toowoomba Chronicle*, 27 Mar 1928, 5 Oct 1931, 26 Aug 1932, 23 May 1969; *Courier-Mail*, 7 June 1983.

M. FRENCH

O'BRYAN, SIR NORMAN JOHN (1894-1968), judge, was born on 16 October 1894 in South Melbourne, youngest of six children of Victorian-born parents Michael John O'Bryan, bank manager, and his wife Mary Ann, née Gleeson. Norman was educated at St Peter and Paul's School, South Melbourne, St Patrick's College, East Melbourne, and Christian Brothers' College, Victoria Parade (dux 1910). At the University of Melbourne (LL.B., 1915) he topped his final year and won the Supreme Court judges' prize. While at university he joined the Catholic Debating Society, competed in cross-country events, rowed, and played cricket and tennis. He had been a member of the Melbourne University Rifles since 1913, but his father opposed his enlisting in the Australian Imperial Force until he had completed his articles of clerkship.

Articled to Plante & Henty in 1915, O'Bryan was admitted to practice as a barrister and solicitor on 1 August 1916. Two months earlier he had enlisted in the A.I.F. Commissioned in April 1917, he served in France from April 1918 with the 3rd Army Brigade, Australian Field Artillery. He was promoted lieutenant in June and wounded in September. After spending some months in chambers at the Middle Temple, London, he returned to Melbourne where his A.I.F. appointment terminated on 25 December 1919. He signed the Bar roll on 20 February 1920 and read in the chambers of L. B. Cussen.

At St Patrick's Cathedral, East Melbourne, on 1 June 1921 O'Bryan married Elsa Duncan,

a 24-year-old accountant. One child of the marriage survived, but Elsa died in childbirth in 1928. On 14 December 1929 at the same cathedral O'Bryan married her youngest sister Violet Leila Duncan, who was then aged 28. In his early years at the Bar, he held a part-time lectureship (1929-32) at the university in private international law. Despite the Depression, his practice grew steadily. He was a forceful advocate who prepared his cases thoroughly and excelled at trials, though he also appeared before royal commissions and courts of appeal.

In 1937 O'Bryan took silk. On 2 February 1939 he was appointed an acting-judge of the Supreme Court of Victoria during the absence on leave of Sir James Macfarlan [q.v.10]. His appointment was made permanent in September. He conducted his court particularly well in cases before juries, whether civil or criminal, and was noted for his lucid explanation of the law. Essentially a 'common law' judge, he was quick, invariably courteous, fair, and vigorous in argument. He was equally at home in appellate cases, of which he did an increasing amount in his later years on the bench. His judicial work was always practical and he was popular with the legal profession.

During World War II O'Bryan acted as legal adviser to the minister for the army and as an official visitor to internment camps in Victoria. Knighted in 1958, he retired from the bench in October 1966. Throughout his life he was a devout Catholic who devoted time and energy to charitable work. A member for more than thirty years of the electoral college of St Vincent's Hospital, Fitzroy, he also chaired (1944-63) the hospital's advisory council. In retirement, he became a lay catechist, gave religious instruction at Melbourne High School and worked for a number of religious institutions, contributing to them with his usual enthusiasm.

A tall, well-built and sartorially distinguished man, Sir Norman had a distinctive walk—a long stride with one arm swinging vigorously. He liked sport and served on the committee of the Melbourne Cricket Club. Declining health curtailed his enjoyment of bowls and gardening. Survived by his wife, their daughter and four sons, and by the daughter of his first marriage, he died on 5 June 1968 at his Toorak home and was buried in Melbourne general cemetery. Paul Fitzgerald's portrait of O'Bryan is held by the family.

A. Dean, *A Multitude of Counsellors* (Melb, 1968); K. Anderson, *Fossil in the Sandstone* (Melb, 1986); R. Coleman, *Above Renown* (Melb, 1988); N. M. O'Bryan, *Kinkora* (Vic, 1994); *Age* (Melb), 27 Jan 1956, 12 Nov 1962, 5 Oct 1966, 6 June 1968; family information; personal knowledge.

J. McI. YOUNG

O'CONNELL, DANIEL PATRICK (1924-1979), barrister and professor of law, was born on 7 July 1924 at Auckland, New Zealand, only child of Daniel Patrick O'Connell, clerk, and his wife Magdalen Alice, née Roche. Young Pat (later known as Dan) was educated at the local Sacred Heart College and at Auckland University College (LL.M., N.Z., 1948; B.A., 1953) where he read history and law. On 28 March 1947 he was admitted to the New Zealand Bar. In 1949, with the help of a national scholarship, he entered Trinity College, Cambridge (Ph.D., 1951). At the suggestion of his supervisor Professor (Sir) Hersch Lauterpacht (later a judge of the International Court of Justice), he studied the law of state succession, a field especially suited to his interests in history, legal theory and diplomacy.

After a brief period in private practice with E. L. Thwaites at Auckland, O'Connell unsuccessfully applied for the chair of law at Auckland University College before being appointed (1953) reader in law at the University of Adelaide. The staff of the faculty consisted of only three full-time members: (Sir) Richard Blackburn, the dean and Bonython [q.v.7] professor of laws, O'Connell and G. H. L. Fridman, a lecturer. The appointment (1958) of Professor Norval Morris as Blackburn's successor marked the beginning of a gradual increase in their numbers.

At the Church of St Michael, Berg am Laim, Munich, West Germany, on 21 September 1957 O'Connell married Renate Else Agnes von Kleist. Back in Adelaide, he was promoted in 1962 to a personal chair in international law and served as dean for the two-year interval between Morris's resignation and the arrival of Professor Arthur Rogerson in 1964. O'Connell was elected Chichele professor of public international law at All Souls College, Oxford, in 1972, succeeding Sir Humphrey Waldock. In an unusual arrangement, the council of the University of Adelaide gave him the option of resuming his chair within three years of his departure. With the university's agreement, he returned to Adelaide to teach for one term a year over this period.

For the first three of his treatises on international law, as well as for a prodigious flow of articles in major legal journals, O'Connell was awarded the degree of doctor of laws (1972) by the University of Cambridge. He had also been elected an associate (1967) of L'Institut de Droit International, and a fellow of the Royal Historical Society, London, and of the Academy of the Social Sciences in Australia (1971). In the Sovereign Military Order of Malta he was appointed a knight of honour and devotion. After his move to Oxford he was increasingly engaged as counsel in cases before the British courts, international arbitral tribunals and the International Court of Justice. In 1977 he took silk. He was widely credited with having persuaded the English Court of Appeal by his advocacy in the landmark case, *Trendtex Trading Corporation Ltd* v. *Central Bank of Nigeria* (1977), to return to the eighteenth-century doctrine of the automatic incorporation of customary international law into English law.

O'Connell's command of international law was both broad and authoritative. His systematic treatise, *International Law* (2 volumes, London, 1965), soon came to be regarded as the chief rival to Lauterpacht's edition of Lassa Oppenheim's work, *International Law, a Treatise*, published ten years earlier. The former work alone would have served as a monument to his vision, his industry and his dexterity with sources and examples of state practice, but it came to be equalled by his two-volume treatise, *The International Law of the Sea* (Oxford, 1982), published posthumously. Between these two monumental works of scholarship O'Connell also managed to write an expanded and updated version of his doctoral dissertation, *State Succession in Municipal Law and International Law* (Cambridge, 1967), an historical study, *Richelieu* (London, 1968), and another monograph, *The Influence of Law on Sea Power* (Manchester, 1975).

In all O'Connell's publications, and in his many contributions to the periodical literature of international law, certain characteristics emerged clearly. His approach was deeply informed by history: every principle had a reason grounded in history, and was shaped by juridical, theological, political and practical considerations. He believed that international law should respond gradually to changing needs and circumstances through the classical process of customary law formation, and he regarded with misgiving the politically engineered majorities at international conferences who sought to make radical changes to the law through multilateral conventions. In his view, such proceedings threatened the integrity of the discipline. Indeed, he saw international law as increasingly falling into intellectual disarray.

As a teacher, O'Connell was regarded with considerable awe by his students in Adelaide, a response heightened by his adherence to the old custom of appearing in an academic gown. His delivery was lucid and fluent, and he illustrated topics with examples from matters in which he himself was involved, either as counsel or adviser to governments, or through the work of international committees. To some he may have seemed lofty and detached; he had no time for the uncouth or lazy, but he showed patience with the honest struggler. To his friends he was generous with his time and hospitality, and was a witty raconteur.

Despite his social conservatism and aristocratic inclinations, O'Connell was tolerant of contrary opinions and willing to concede a point. He shared with friends his knowledge of places he had visited, books he had read and people he had met. His interests were wide—music, art, architecture, history and films—and often surprising, as in his passions for bricklaying and building model ships. He took a particular interest in lawyers who emigrated from Europe to Adelaide in the 1950s, and did much to help them to establish professional and personal contacts.

O'Connell's childhood love had been the sea and he had hoped for a career in the navy. As commander, Royal Australian Naval Volunteer Reserve (1966-73) and Royal Naval Reserve (1973-78), he advised the navies of both countries on international law. He studied navigation, tactics, weapons and strategy. In May-June 1968, aboard Australian and American warships, he observed operations off the coast of the Republic of Vietnam (South Vietnam). His book on the influence of the law on sea power has affected operating procedures adopted by Western navies. Awarded the Reserve Decoration in 1973, O'Connell was placed on the Retired List in 1978.

Australia's successful action against France in the International Court of Justice in 1973 over atmospheric nuclear testing in the South Pacific was based on O'Connell's opinion. The Commonwealth Attorney-General's Department had earlier advised (Sir) William McMahon's government that there was no juridical ground on which to bring the case. O'Connell saw a way to base jurisdiction on the dormant and neglected (but not obsolete) provisions of the General Act for the Pacific Settlement of Disputes, concluded at Geneva in 1928, to which Australia and France were signatories. His opinion, commissioned by State Labor attorneys-general in 1972, was passed on to and used by E. G. Whitlam's Federal government. O'Connell appeared as counsel in the case. He was also engaged as a legal adviser to (Sir) Joh Bjelke-Petersen's government in Queensland.

O'Connell was a committed and practising Catholic. His religion guided his personal life and his vision of international law. In a lecture in 1975 he summed up his attitude in a passage in which he lamented the beginning of the decline of the natural-law foundations of international law from the time of the positivist Swiss lawyer Emmerich de Vattel's treatise (1758): 'From the Catholic viewpoint, international law on Vattelian premises is fundamentally flawed, because it offers an insufficient basis for obligation where a superior is not available and because it puts intolerable power in the hands of a majority, merely because it is a majority'.

Shortly after undergoing an operation for hiatus hernia, O'Connell died of a ruptured oesophagus on 8 June 1979 at his Oxford home and was buried in Onehunga cemetery, Auckland. His wife, two daughters and three sons survived him. Sir Michael Havers, attorney-general in the British government, had recommended him for a life peerage in that year's forthcoming honours list.

Aust Law J, 53, Sept 1979, p 679; *Law and Justice*, no 62-63, 1979, p 122; *Adel Law Review*, 7, no 2, 1980, p 167; *British Year Book of International Law* (Lond, 1980), p 1; *Aust Year Book of International Law* (Syd, 1981), p xxiii; *Daily Telegraph* (Lond), 12 June 1979; *Universe* (Lond), 15 June 1979; *Tablet* (Lond), 21 July 1979; 'Daniel Patrick O'Connell, 1924-1979', tributes by colleagues and friends (held at Univ of Adel Law L).   I. A. SHEARER

O'CONNELL, TERENCE JOHN (1916-1977), educationist, was born on 14 February 1916 at Scone, New South Wales, second of seven children of Australian-born parents Timothy Edward O'Connell (d.1932), labourer, and his wife Kathleen Mary Agnes, née Felan. Terry attended Aberdeen Public School and St Joseph's College, Hunters Hill, Sydney, entered (1935) Teachers' College, Armidale, and studied as an external student of the University of New England (B.A., 1961; Litt.B., 1964). His early teaching posts were in primary schools at Bendemeer (1937-38) and Brackendale (1939).

On 11 October 1939 O'Connell enlisted in the Australian Imperial Force. He gave his religion as Catholic and was recorded as being 5 ft 6 ins (168 cm) tall, with hazel eyes and brown hair. In 1940-42 he served in the Middle East with the 2nd/2nd and 2nd/33rd battalions. At St Luke's Anglican Church, Scone, on 7 May 1942, Lieutenant O'Connell married Nancy Aline Barwick, an organist. Transferred to the Reserve of Officers on compassionate grounds in July 1943, he performed part-time duties with the Volunteer Defence Corps until 1945.

O'Connell taught at Tamworth (1943-47), Wagga Wagga (1947-49), Bungwahl (1950-54) and Yass (1954-57). As founding headmaster (principal) in 1958-74 of Ainslie North Primary School, Australian Capital Territory, and as an acting inspector, he gained a national reputation for his methods and ideas. His initiatives included flexible staffing, language development, closed-circuit television, school boards and open-plan education. He saw the role of principal as that of an 'educational catalyst, the one who keeps the professional pot bubbling in the staff-room discussions'. In 1961-65 he presented a schools' radio programme, 'The World We Live In', for the Australian Broadcasting Commission. He also contributed a chapter to *Primary Education in Australia* (edited by G. W. Bassett, Sydney, 1974).

In 1973 O'Connell joined the Common-wealth Teaching Service and the Common-wealth Teachers' Federation (A.C.T.). Next year he played a major role in an inquiry which led to improved salaries for teachers. Having been influential—as a member of Sir George Currie's committee—in setting up an independent education authority in the A.C.T., he joined the office of the Interim A.C.T. Schools Authority in 1975 as acting-head of the curriculum and research branch. He be-came head of the student services branch in 1976, but retired in January 1977 due to ill health.

An active member of the Australian College of Education, O'Connell was a fellow (1968), national councillor (1968-72) and chairman (1972-73) of its A.C.T. chapter. Through the college, and his membership (1969-74) of the Australian Unesco Committee for Education, he participated in conferences on Aboriginal education, and on the teaching of English and music. He belonged to Legacy and the Canberra Workers' Club. A youthful oarsman, he later played tennis and golf, and enjoyed landscape painting. He died of cancer on 15 November 1977 in Canberra Hospital and was cremated; his wife, daughter and son sur-vived him. The O'Connell Education Centre, Griffith, A.C.T., was named (1979) after him.

B. Price, 'Mr ACT Education', *Canb Hist J*, no 39, Mar 1997, p 29; *Canb Times*, 16 Nov 1977; informa-tion from Mrs J. Gregory, Lyons, Dr E. McKenzie, Cook, Mr J. G. Morris, Downer, Mr R. Sandeman, Latham, and Mr W. Simpson, Pearce, ACT.

BARRY PRICE

O'CONNOR, FRANCIS ALEXANDER (1894-1972), public servant, was born on 13 October 1894 at Leongatha, Victoria, fifth child of Alexander O'Connor, a stationmaster from Ireland, and his Victorian-born wife Christina, née McDermid. Educated at Mel-bourne Continuation (High) School, Frank joined the Commonwealth Public Service on 1 January 1912 and worked as a naval staff clerk in the Department of Defence. By 1924 he was employed with the Contract Supply Board (Contract Board) attached to that de-partment. At St Monica's Catholic Church, Essendon, on 15 April 1925 he married Annie Morrison Nunan.

In 1936 O'Connor was appointed secretary of the Contract Board, which from 1939 was administered by the new Department of Supply and Development (Supply and Shipping 1942-48, Supply and Development 1948-50, Supply 1950-74). Promoted assistant-secretary, he became the board's chairman in 1941. He and his colleagues authorized the purchase of stores and equipment (other than munitions) needed by the armed services,

and disposed of surplus material. In 1942, at the peak of its wartime activity, the board authorized 25 419 requisitions for goods valued at £142.3 million. Next year O'Connor was given the additional post of director of supply.

As secretary of the Department of Supply and Shipping from September 1946, O'Connor oversaw the importation, production and dis-tribution of fuel and strategic material (such as aluminium and tin-plate); he also super-vised the purchase of supplies for the armed services and regulated the shipping industry. Reverting to first assistant secretary after a departmental reorganization in April 1948, he assumed the secretaryship once more on 16 April 1953. He worked with British and Australian scientists who were developing the Weapons Research Establishment at Salis-bury, South Australia, and the rocket range at Woomera, and testing atomic weapons on the Monte Bello Islands, off Western Australia, and at Emu and Maralinga, South Australia. His duties were extended in 1958 when the Department of Defence Production was abol-ished and its functions (including the govern-ment's munitions and aircraft factories) were transferred to Supply.

O'Connor was tall and distinguished look-ing, and approachable in manner. A capable and dedicated head of department, he inspired respect and commitment among his staff. The minister he most appreciated serving was a Liberal, (Sir) Howard Beale, who remembered him as an 'old time Labor man and a great friend of Arthur Calwell' [q.v.13]. Yet, at the time O'Connor took over as head of the de-partment, Beale 'knew nothing of his present politics and never asked; all I knew was that he was wise, experienced, [and] loyal to the government he served'. O'Connor's integrity and sense of fairness helped him to maintain harmonious working and personal relation-ships. He was appointed O.B.E. in 1953 and elevated to C.B.E. in 1957.

In 1959 O'Connor retired. His interests included horse-racing—he belonged to the Moonee Valley Racing Club—cards, and gar-dening. A devout Catholic and a dedicated family man, he loved telling stories to his grandchildren. He died on 16 April 1972 at Fitzroy and was buried in Box Hill cemetery; his wife, three sons and one of his two daugh-ters survived him.

H. Beale, *This Inch of Time* (Melb, 1977); S. J. Butlin and C. B. Schedvin, *War Economy 1942-1945* (Canb, 1977); *Herald* (Melb), 6 Sept 1941; family information. HELEN BOXALL

OCTOMAN, JANETTE HANNUM (1879-1971), community worker, was born on 14

November 1879 at Port Lincoln, South Australia, daughter of Caleb Provis, a farmer from England, and his South Australian-born wife Janetta, née Patterson. Named after her mother, Janetta was to change (1940) her name to Janette. She was educated by her grandfather Joseph Provis, a schoolteacher who lived with them. At the Methodist Church, Tumby Bay, on 11 April 1903 she married Charles Mashon Ochtomann (Octoman from 1919), a 32-year-old blacksmith; they were to have four sons. About 1920 the family moved to Marden, Adelaide; Charles worked as a builder and farmer, and the boys furthered their schooling.

Early in 1927 the Octomans returned to the Eyre Peninsula. Mrs Octoman served as a justice of the peace. A member of a policy-forming committee of the Liberal Union of South Australia for the 1927 State elections, she was appointed to the State executive of the Liberal and Country League in 1932. Five years later she unsuccessfully sought endorsement for the Legislative Assembly seat of Flinders. She was a founding member (1933) of the Tumby Bay branch of the South Australian Country Women's Association and president (1937-40, 1943-46) of the Eyre Peninsula division. In 1938 she represented the S.A.C.W.A. on the executive-committee of the Associated Country Women of the World at its meetings in London, and at the Jubilee conference of the International Council of Women, held in Edinburgh.

Concerned to ensure that women had a voice in parliament, Octoman came home and resumed her battle for party endorsement. As a member both of the C.W.A. and the National Council of Women of South Australia, she became known for her efforts to help women and children, and to improve education, transport and postal services on the Eyre Peninsula. During World War II she also threw her energies into the Australian Red Cross Society, the Fighting Forces Comforts Fund, the Wheatgrowers' Protection Association and the Mothers and Babies' Health Association. She again stood for endorsement in 1939, 1940 and 1944 at State level, and in 1943 for the Senate. Despite her ability and perseverance, she never won pre-selection. Her final attempt to enter parliament (in 1944) was as an unendorsed L.C.L. member when she polled only 410 votes.

After her husband died in 1949, Octoman served (1949-52, 1955-56) as State president of the C.W.A. (honorary life member 1954). During her first term of office she visited all 236 State branches, a formidable undertaking for a woman in her seventies. She helped to acquire land for holiday cottages at Port Lincoln and Tumby Bay, and initiated the establishment of homemakers' schools. In 1953 she was appointed M.B.E.

A skilled needlewoman, and a keen gardener and cook, Octoman won prizes at the Adelaide Royal Show where she sometimes had as many as 150 entries. In 1970 the C.W.A. and the Tumby Bay District Council planted an avenue of native trees at Lipson in her honour. Survived by two of her sons, she died on 23 October 1971 at Leabrook and was buried in Lipson cemetery.

H. Parker, *The First Fifty Years* (Adel, 1979); *Farmer & Grazier*, 28 Oct 1971; *Advertiser* (Adel), 1 Jan 1953; information from the late Mr R. Octoman.

PHILIPPA L. FLETCHER

O'DEA, ERNEST CHARLES (1889-1976), trade unionist, politician and lord mayor, was born on 19 February 1889 at Armidale, New South Wales, second child of Martin Bernard O'Dea, a native-born bootmaker, and his wife Kate Augusta, née Gillett, who came from London. In 1896 hard times forced the family to move to Camperdown, Sydney. Ernie attended the Christian Brothers' school at Newtown until he was 14. After being employed as a commercial traveller for his family's boot-manufacturing business, he worked in Edward Fay's Pitt Street shoe store. At St Paul's Anglican Church, Canterbury, on 30 June 1909 he married Elsie May Remfry (d.1927); they were to have a son and daughter.

In 1910 O'Dea joined both the State branch of the Shop Assistants' and Warehouse Employees' Federation of Australia and the Camperdown Labor Electoral League. In 1912 he was elected to the union executive. He rose rapidly through the union's ranks, becoming country organizer (1915), assistant secretary (1917) and a delegate (from 1915) to the Labor Council of New South Wales. Active in the anti-conscription campaigns, he founded a union journal and played a prominent role in persuading the union's country branches to amalgamate. In 1919 he was elected general secretary of the union's New South Wales branch. O'Dea served (1921-23) on the Australian Labor Party's State central executive. A delegate to the party's 1921 federal conference in Brisbane, he was among the minority who opposed the 'socialisation objective'. He served as a Labor alderman (1924-27 and 1930-65) on Sydney Municipal (City) Council. Seeking to expand his political influence, he threw his union's support behind the premier in the 1926 challenge to J. T. Lang's [q.v.9] leadership of the New South Wales parliamentary Labor Party. On 26 October 1927 at St Benedict's Catholic Church, East Brisbane, he married Johanna Ellen Gleeson, née Elliott (d.1960), a 30-year-old widow.

Developing a solid expertise in industrial law and advocacy, O'Dea represented the shop assistants on an investigation (1937) by the Industrial Commission of New South Wales into employment in department stores, and gained award provisions for equal pay for some male and female shop assistants in large retail stores. Although he was a Langite in the internecine struggles of the late 1930s, he had a strong industrial power base which left him well placed to survive Lang's downfall. In 1939 he joined a deputation to the party's triennial federal conference to seek mediation to end the 'blood-letting' in the New South Wales branch. Reappointed to the A.L.P.'s State executive in 1941, he was elected to the Legislative Council for twelve years in December 1942 and again in November 1954. During World War II he consolidated his influence in the shop assistants' union. As federal secretary-treasurer (from 1942), he worked to strengthen the federal organization, and oversaw the affiliation of the Newcastle, northern New South Wales, Queensland, Western Australian and Tasmanian branches. By 1945 he had emerged as a vehement opponent of communist influence within the unions and as a supporter of the anti-communist industrial groups.

In December 1948 O'Dea was elected lord mayor of Sydney by his fellow aldermen. He revelled in the trappings of his office and entertained such visitors as the archbishop of Canterbury and the film star Maureen O'Hara. During his four years in the post, he visited London to supervise the distribution of proceeds from the Food For Britain Appeal, of which he was an unofficial patron. His administration, however, was characterized by political controversy. His insistence on wearing the robes of office, in defiance of Labor Party practice, spurred opponents in the Labor movement to taunt him with the epithet 'Ermine Ernie'. One of his first acts was to ban the use of the Sydney Town Hall by left-wing unions and political groups; he refused to receive deputations protesting against the ban, and clashed publicly over the matter with the colonial secretary Clive Evatt in November 1950. A member (1935-59) of the Sydney County Council, O'Dea was its president in 1958-59.

While his combative style alienated him increasingly from left-wing and moderate elements, O'Dea saw his support from the 'grouper'-dominated State executive and municipal Labor caucus gradually undermined by internal rivalry and rumours of administrative corruption. He averted defeat at the 1951 mayoral pre-selection meeting on a technicality, and did not seek endorsement in the following year. On his departure from office, his opponents publicly accused him of malpractice in issuing development permits, allocating street vendors' licences and leasing council-owned hotels. O'Dea sued his accusers. A subsequent police investigation into the charges proved inconclusive. Having failed to regain Labor's mayoral nomination at the end of 1953, he ran as an 'outside' candidate in a three-way contest in 1956.

His command of a sizeable block of union votes meant that O'Dea continued as a force in the industrial and political spheres. He remained one of the staunchest supporters of the 'groupers' until the eruptions of 1954. He devoted much of his attention to campaigns for compulsory unionism and equal pay, and against Saturday retail trading and late-night shopping. He was an architect of the compulsory unionism legislation introduced by the Cahill [q.v.13] government in 1953. In the early 1960s his intractable opposition to extended trading hours brought him into conflict with Labor premier R. J. Heffron [q.v.14] and the party's State executive.

O'Dea retired as an alderman in 1965. While visiting Athens in 1966, he suffered severe cerebral thrombosis. That year he shared first prize of $200 000 in the Sydney Opera House lottery. His term in the Legislative Council expired in 1967. He relinquished leadership of the federal and State branches of the shop assistants' union early in 1968. Known affectionately as 'The Bull', he had a commanding physical presence, an unembellished mode of public address, and an abiding commitment to the principles and practices of Catholic social conservatism and trade-union mateship. He belonged to the New South Wales National Coursing Association, and enjoyed walking and playing bowls. Survived by the son of his first marriage, and by his stepdaughter and the son of his second, O'Dea died on 21 November 1976 at St George Hospital, Kogarah, and was buried in Northern Suburbs cemetery.

J. Kane, *Exploding the Myths* (Syd, 1989); S. Fitzgerald, *Sydney 1842-1992* (Syd, 1992); *People*, 24 Oct 1951, p 29; *Nation* (Syd), 1 July 1961; *Shop Assistant of Aust*, June 1967; *Voice* (Syd), Jan 1977; *Aust Worker*, 27 Nov 1919; *Daily Telegraph* (Syd), 19 Dec 1948, 11 Dec 1953, 13 June 1957; *SMH*, 7 Dec 1949, 21, 23, 28 Nov 1950, 3 Nov 1951, 6 Dec 1952, 7 Nov, 12 Dec 1953, 20 Sept 1956, 5 Nov 1967, 23 Nov 1976; O'Dea papers, CRS 817 (Syd City Council Archives).   JOHN SHIELDS

O'DEA, PATRICK JOHN (1872-1962), footballer, was born on 16 March 1872 at Kilmore, Victoria, third of seven surviving children of Patrick Flannery O'Dea, a squatter from Ireland, and his Victorian-born wife Johanna, née Crossley. After the family moved to Melbourne, Pat attended Christian Brothers' College, St Kilda, and Xavier College, Kew (1888-89). He was awarded a bronze medallion by the Royal Humane Society of Australasia for recovering a drowned woman from the sea at Mordialloc on 3 January 1888. A lithe six-footer (183 cm) weighing about 12 stone (76 kg), O'Dea was an outstanding Australian Rules footballer, playing for Melbourne in the Victorian Football Association from 1893 to 1895 when he transferred to Essendon. He was described by the *Australasian* as a 'fleet' wingman; his high marking and 'prodigious dropkicks', often accurate from any angle, made him one of the 'cracks' of the competition.

Interrupting his legal studies in 1896 to visit Europe, he detoured through the United States of America to see his brother Andrew, whom he joined at the University of Wisconsin (LL.B., 1900), Madison. A casual display of his skill had led to an immediate invitation to study there and play gridiron. Americans had never seen such explosive kicking: he slammed the ball with a shoulder-high follow-through while his other foot was 6 ins (15 cm) off the ground. The 'Kicking Kangaroo's' punts and drops 'electrified the Mid-West fans' and changed the emphasis of gridiron from 'bone-crushing power plays to cleaner ball-handling and frequent kicking'. In 1898-99, mostly as full-back, he captained the Badgers and made Walter Camp's second All-American team.

His feats became legendary. With the lighter American ball, O'Dea established a punt-kicking record, with wind assistance, of 110 yards (100 m)—the next best was 91 yards. In 1899 he performed 'the most-impossible [place] kick in football history' to defeat Illinois—55 yards, half the length of a gridiron field, into a 20-mile (32 km)-an-hour crosswind. His side-stepping and victorious running goal over the head of his blocker, the great Gil Dobie, is still recalled. In only two seasons O'Dea drop-kicked 32 goals. After graduating, he coached football at the University of Notre Dame, Indiana, in 1900-01 and, later, football, rowing and athletics at Stanford University, California. By 1906 he had married and been divorced.

In 1917 this 'quiet, modest' man disappeared. A futile worldwide search, reaching to Australia, was made. His brother thought that he may have joined the Australian Imperial Force, becoming an 'unknown soldier'. Pat O'Dea later claimed that he had 'wanted to get away from … mere student days' as his fame had made it difficult to establish his law firm at San Francisco; however, a certain Elsie Waters complained in 1919 that he had 'embezzled $3000 and stock valued at $500' from her. By 1920 O'Dea had been naturalized, and was living in Lassen County, California, with his second wife, Emma. In 1934 he was discovered living as 'Charles J. Mitchell', a lumber company statistician at Westwood,

where he was a popular secretary of the Auto Club, treasurer of the Chamber of Commerce and a director of Lassen Volcanic National Park.

Amiable and relaxed, O'Dea received a triumphal homecoming at the University of Wisconsin before he returned to San Francisco where he joined an export business. His last occupation was as office-manager with F. S. Gearhardt & Co., a clothing firm. In 1952 'America's greatest football hero', was given a testimonial banquet by Wisconsin alumni. He deplored the loss of kicking skills in contemporary gridiron: 'the boys don't follow through enough'. In his view, Australian Rules football was the better game: it 'allowed players more spectator appeal with its faster action'. On 3 April 1962 he became the only known Australian elected to the Football Hall of Fame at Rutgers, the State University, New Jersey. Survived by his daughter, O'Dea died next day, 4 April 1962, at the University of California Hospital, San Francisco.

Xavier College, *Xaverian*, 1952, 1962; *Age* (Melb) and *Argus*, 4 Jan 1888; *Australasian*, 18 June 1892; *San Francisco Chronicle*, 6 May 1919; *New York Times*, 20, 21 Sept, 16 Nov 1934, 4, 5 Apr 1962; *SMH*, 21 Sept, 16 Nov 1934; *Herald* (Melb), 13 Jan 1969, 2 July 1977; *Advertiser* (Adel), 14 Sept 1977; *Daily Mirror*, 13 Oct 1978; information from Mr D. Cash, Box Hill, Melb, and Dr R. Joslyn, New York.

JAMES GRIFFIN

O'DONNELL, PATRICK MARY (1897-1980), Catholic archbishop, was born on 2 February 1897 at Fethard, County Tipperary, Ireland, youngest of sixteen children of Thomas O'Donnell, draper, and his wife Johanna, née Sheehan. Schooled by the Patrician Brothers at Fethard and by the Jesuits at Mungret College, Limerick, Patrick studied for the priesthood at All Hallows College, Dublin, and at the Pontifical Urban College of Propaganda Fide, Rome. His fellow students in Rome included the Australians (Sir) Norman Gilroy [q.v.14], who was to became a cardinal, and Matthew Beovich, a future archbishop of Adelaide. O'Donnell's Irish and later Australian loyalties were broadened by an easy relationship with people from other countries. He was ordained priest on 15 April 1922 at the basilica of St John Lateran and sent to the diocese of Sale, Victoria. Its bishop Patrick Phelan [q.v.11] was a family friend.

Appointed to the staff of the cathedral, O'Donnell served as curate (1922-27) and administrator (1927-37). He then served as parish priest at Leongatha (1937-46) and Warragul (1946-49). Learned, genial and witty, he established a reputation as a preacher, and as a raconteur. His stories of all classes of people from farmers to popes were noted for their quirkish insight, pastoral understanding and complete lack of malice. In the quiet country parishes he devoted himself to reading canon law, which suited him for the role of vicar-general (from 1941) to Bishop Richard Ryan. O'Donnell was made a domestic prelate in 1944. His special interest in the care of the Italian community brought him to the attention of Archbishop John Panico, the apostolic delegate.

In 1947 O'Donnell travelled with Panico to Europe where he met Archbishop (Sir) James Duhig [q.v.8] of Brisbane and Archbishop Angelo Roncalli, the future Pope John XXIII. On 8 November 1948 O'Donnell was appointed titular archbishop of Pelusium and coadjutor archbishop of Brisbane with the right of succession. He was consecrated on 17 March 1949 by Cardinal Gilroy in St Mary's Cathedral, Sale. For his sixteen years as coadjutor, O'Donnell stood in the shadow of the formidable Duhig. Occupied locally in minor episcopal functions, he attempted a canonical reform of the Brisbane archdiocese. In this work he was largely frustrated by his principal, but he was more successful with his committee-work in the Australian hierarchy. From 1950 he served on the Federal Catholic Immigration Committee (president 1954-72). He negotiated with Australian and overseas bodies for the financing of immigration, but his main concern was to minister to the new citizens.

O'Donnell sided with Gilroy and the New South Wales party in the episcopal divisions over the Catholic Social Studies Movement and the National Civic Council. Although he differed from Duhig in this regard, they maintained respect for each other's position. In 1956 O'Donnell, Gilroy and Bishop (Archbishop) James Carroll went to Rome to seek intervention in the dispute. O'Donnell attended every session of the Second Vatican Council in 1962-65. His expectations of it were purely canonical before he came to realize the pastoral and theological implications of Pope John's modernizing of the Church. He was disturbed by them, but accepted them, describing his attitude as 'enlightened conservatism'.

On 10 April 1965 Duhig died and O'Donnell became archbishop of Brisbane. Reorganizing the archdiocese, he established agencies that brought a curial style to Brisbane. His oversight was less personal than that of Duhig, but it was thorough. He increased lay participation in the official work of the Church, and he initiated the Archdiocesan Development Fund to create resources for rational expansion. His innate scrupulosity and canonical formation made him nervous of the changes, liturgical and pastoral, required by Vatican Council II. To his credit, he found a technique for handling the situation. He was a skilled chairman, and he chose advisers to recommend and plan the changes. Then he moderated, but generally accepted, their advice. In particular, he took the first, tentative steps to implement the conciliar and post-conciliar decisions on ecumenism. It was indicative of his attitude that he always mispronounced the word. He played little part in public life, but in the background he maintained the connexions established by Duhig.

O'Donnell tendered his resignation when he turned 75. It took effect on 5 March 1973. For the next seven years he lived quietly in his historic home, Glengariff, at Hendra. He died on 2 November 1980 in the Mater Misericordiae Hospital, South Brisbane, and was buried in the vault of St Stephen's Cathedral. Pope Paul VI praised him for being 'a man of dignity ... unshakeable in faith, calm in prosperity, firm and active in adversity'. It was a just, if kindly, estimate.

Acta et Documenta, Concilio Oecumenico Vaticano II Apparando, series 1 (Antepraeparatoria), 2: *Consilia et Vota Episcoporum ac Praelatorum*, pt 7, *America Meridionalis-Oceania* (Vatican City, 1961); F. A. Mecham, *The Church and the Migrants, 1946-1987* (Syd, 1991); *Brisb Catholic Hist Soc Procs*, 3, 1992, p 78; *Catholic Leader*, 24 Mar, 21 Apr, 5 May 1949, 15 Apr 1965, 27 May, 10 June 1973, 9 Nov 1980.
                                                                    T. P. BOLAND

O'DRISCOLL, JOHN XAVIER (1903-1977), barrister, judge and sporting administrator, was born on 6 September 1903 at Coburg, Melbourne, second child of Eugene Andrew O'Driscoll, a clerk from Ireland, and his Victorian-born wife Gertrude Hannah, née Harnetty. John was educated at Christian Brothers' College, East Melbourne, and the University of Melbourne (B.A., 1923; LL.B., 1924; LL.M., 1926).

In 1921 O'Driscoll won the intervarsity mile (1.6 km) in Brisbane (in a time of 4 minutes, 42 seconds) and competed for the combined universities' team against South Africa. While living at Newman College, he won the Dixson scholarship in pure mathematics (1923), a Blue for athletics and the college debating prize. From 1925 to 1933 he was a resident tutor at Newman in pure mathematics and in law; he was president of the Newman Old Boys' Association (1935) and of the university's Newman Society.

Having been articled in 1925 to Luke Murphy & Co., O'Driscoll was admitted to the Victorian Bar on 2 March 1927 and gradually built up a varied practice. On 5 January 1933 at Newman College chapel he married Marie Bridget Canny. He enlisted in the Royal Australian Air Force on 30 March 1942 and was commissioned two months later in the Administrative and Special Duties Branch. For his work as a judge-advocate at courts martial in the R.A.A.F.'s North-Western Area, he was mentioned in dispatches. He was demobilized from the air force on 2 April 1946 as acting squadron leader. Back in Melbourne, he tutored (1947-49) at the university's law school and took silk in 1948. He was admitted to the New South Wales Bar in 1934 and to the Tasmanian Bar in 1953, and was called to the Bar at the Middle Temple, London, in 1952. A popular barrister, he specialized in common law and helped to establish Sir Owen Dixon [q.v.14] Chambers.

O'Driscoll also developed a particular expertise in licensing law: with (Sir) Kevin Anderson, he revised (1952) J. S. Meagher's book, *Licensing Law and Practice in Victoria* (Melbourne, 1935). In 1963 he was appointed a judge of the County Court and chairman of General Sessions. Two years later he was gazetted chairman of the Workers' Compensation Board. As chairman (from 1968) of the newly established Liquor Control Commission, he was asked by Sir Arthur Rylah [q.v.] to visit every hotel in the State. The commission was largely responsible for reforming Victoria's liquor laws after the abolition of the 'six o'clock swill'. Empowered to order publicans to make improvements, the commission did much to transform the appearance and cleanliness of hotels throughout the State.

A tall and fit man, O'Driscoll retained his interest in sport: he was a fine golfer and an A-grade tennis player. He chaired (1928-57) the Victorian Amateur Athletic Association, and was active in the Lawn Tennis Association of Victoria (member 1932-62) and the L.T.A. of Australia (member 1963-68, vice-president 1966-67). In addition, he was a founder (1938) of the Victorian State Council for Physical Fitness (later National Fitness Council of Victoria) and a member (1948 and 1954-77) of the Australian Olympic Federation.

At the request of the lord mayor of Melbourne, O'Driscoll had been an observer at the Olympic Games in Helsinki in 1952. He sat on the committee which oversaw Melbourne's hosting of the games in 1956 and, with his support, the modern pentathlon was included in the programme. In 1960 he captained (as a non-competitor) Australia's modern pentathlon team at the Olympic Games in Rome. Appointed O.B.E. in 1959, he was awarded the International Modern Pentathlon Union's medal of honour in 1966. During his presidency (1954-69) of the Australian M.P.U., the world pentathlon championships were held in Melbourne in 1966.

A devoted Catholic, O'Driscoll retained his love of Newman College, served (from 1955) on its council and rarely missed an old boys' function. In July 1975 he retired from the bench. Survived by his wife and daughter, he died on 19 June 1977 at Toorak and was buried in Springvale cemetery. He bequeathed part of his law library to Newman College. Paul Fitzgerald's portrait of O'Driscoll is held by the family.

E. E. Hewitt, *Judges Through the Years* (Melb, 1984); K. Anderson, *Fossil in the Sandstone* (Melb, 1986); H. Gordon, *Australia and the Olympic Games* (Brisb, 1994); *Aust Bar Gazette*, Oct 1963; *Aust Law J*, 37, 1963, 49, 1975, 51, 1977; *Herald* (Melb), 4 Sept, 3 Dec 1975, 20 June 1977; information from Mr P. Balmford, Monash Univ, Miss J. Carolan, Newman College, Parkville, Dr P. Opas, Caulfield, Mr J. O. Parker, Toorak, and the Hon X. Connor, Balwyn, Melb.   J. NEVILLE TURNER

OFFICER, DORIS LYNE (1898-1967), medical practitioner, was born on 28 June 1898 at Sidcup, Kent, England, daughter of Ernest Alfred Veale, master mariner, and his Australian-born wife Amy, née Glen-Wilson. Doris's parents had met in Sydney. Her maternal grandfather James Glen Wilson, an artist attached to H.M.S. *Herald*, had arrived in Australia in 1853. Doris was educated at Cheltenham Ladies' College, Gloucestershire. Perhaps inspired by a family friend Mrs Elizabeth Garrett Anderson (the first woman to qualify as a medical practitioner in England), she was encouraged in her choice of a profession by her cousin Dr Laura Veale and uncle Dr Ellacott Ward. In 1915 she entered the London School of Medicine for Women (M.B., B.S., 1921).

Doris visited Australia in 1922, and returned the following year. At All Saints Church, St Kilda, Melbourne, on 14 May 1923 she married with Anglican rites Ernest Officer, a 52-year-old grazier. They lived on Zara station, near Wanganella, New South Wales, and were to have three children. Doris learned to ride and shoot; she played the piano, enjoyed hiking and read detective stories. An attractive young woman, she showed little interest in fashion.

In 1927 the Officers sold Zara and settled in Melbourne where Doris joined the Alexandra Club. In 1930 she resumed her medical career. A clinical-assistant in paediatrics (1932-46) at the Queen Victoria Memorial Hospital, she was also honorary medical officer at the Richmond Baby Health Centre.

After her husband died in 1936, Officer threw herself into her work, becoming honorary secretary of the Victorian Baby Health Centres Association, a post she held for thirty years. Tireless in her efforts, she stimulated State-wide interest in establishing baby health centres. She helped to improve existing facilities, introduced a travelling health-centre caravan, addressed meetings, edited the magazine, *Baby Health*, and wrote articles on child health for the *Sun News-Pictorial*. She mediated between voluntary health committees, local councils and the Department of Health's maternal and infant welfare division, and sought increased funding for a voluntary infant-welfare training programme for nurses.

During World War II she served as honorary medical officer to the Red Cross Blood Transfusion Service, and as medical officer at the Australian Women's Recruiting Depot and the Free Kindergarten Union of Victoria (1941-64). Dr Officer was a board-member (from 1943) of the Queen's Memorial Infectious Diseases Hospital (later Fairfield Hospital), lecturer in infant feeding and management at St George's Hospital, Kew, and president (1945-46) of the Victorian Medical Women's Society. Following her persistent submissions, the Carlton Home was transferred to the control of the V.B.H.C.A. and renamed the Queen Elizabeth Hospital for Mothers and Babies. She helped to organize its opening (1958) by Elizabeth, the Queen Mother, and later raised funds to build the Isabella Younger Ross [q.v.11] lecture hall in the grounds. In the 1960s she was patron of the Nursing Mothers' Association of Australia and vice-president of the Children's Welfare Association of Victoria.

Officer was awarded Queen Elizabeth II's coronation medal in 1953 and appointed O.B.E. in 1959. She upheld the adage 'prevention is better than cure' and remained single-minded in promoting family health. Her last words to one of her children were: 'Bother, it's Health Week and I won't be there!' Survived by her daughter and two sons, she died of myocardial infarction on 31 July 1967 at Richmond and was cremated; her estate was sworn for probate at $93 502. At Fairfield Hospital a prize for nursing was named after her. Aileen Dent's portrait of Officer is held by the Queen Elizabeth Centre, Noble Park.

Baby Health, Sept 1967, p 2; *MJA*, 27 Jan 1968, p 150; *Age* (Melb), 13 June 1959, 1 Aug 1967; C. D. Crockett, The History of the Baby Health Centre Movement in Victoria 1917-1976 (M.A. thesis, Monash Univ, 1997); papers held by, and information from, Dr C. Officer, Broadford, Vic.

CHERYL CROCKETT

OFFICER, SIR FRANK KEITH (1889-1969), diplomat, was born on 2 October 1889 at Toorak, Melbourne, son of Victorian-born parents Frank Suetonius Officer, accountant, and his wife Ethel Catherine Marzetti, née Umphelby. Sir Robert Officer [q.v.2] was his great-grandfather. Keith attended Melbourne Church of England Grammar School, lived in Ormond [q.v.5] College while studying at the University of Melbourne (LL.B., 1912), and became an associate to H. B. Higgins [q.v.9].

On 6 December 1914 Officer was commissioned in the Australian Imperial Force.

He served at Gallipoli in June-October 1915 as staff captain, 6th Infantry Brigade. Sent to the Western Front, he was appointed deputy assistant quartermaster-general, 2nd Division, in July 1916, and deputy assistant adjutant-general, I Anzac Corps, in July 1917. Four months later he was promoted major. For his service as a staff officer he was awarded the Military Cross (1917), appointed O.B.E. (1919) and thrice mentioned in dispatches. His A.I.F. appointment terminated on 20 November 1919.

Joining the British Colonial Service, Officer was posted in 1920 to Ankpa, Nigeria, where he supervised 200 000 people in a district as large as Wales. Whenever possible, he relied on local custom and used the existing system of village government to administer the area. After returning to Melbourne in 1923, he was employed in his father's office before obtaining a temporary post with the Department of External Affairs, Canberra, in 1927. Responsible for keeping the department informed of developments abroad, he was a methodical and thorough worker who liked order and routine. He belonged (1924-30) to the Melbourne group of Round Table. In 1928 he accompanied the Australian delegation— headed by A. J. McLachlan [q.v.10]—to Geneva for the ninth assembly of the League of Nations and to Paris for the signing of the 'Kellogg-Briand' pact.

Officer was appointed a permanent member of the Commonwealth Public Service and dispatched to London as external affairs officer in May 1933. He fostered close links with the Foreign Office, the Dominions Office, the Committee of Imperial Defence and the high commissions of other Commonwealth countries. While cultivating this network of contacts, he established enduring friendships. He attended annual assemblies of the League of Nations as adviser to Australian delegations. In 1933 he engaged in 'horse trading' to secure Australia's election to a vacant seat on the League's council. That year he also attended the Disarmament Conference.

In 1937 Officer was appointed Australian counsellor attached to the British embassy in Washington. He kept in constant touch with the State Department over commercial relations between the United States of America and Australia at a time when Australia was on America's 'Black List' of countries denied tariff concessions. When Australia was removed from the list in February 1938, he began discussions to prepare the ground for a trade agreement. He described Washington as 'the greatest listening post in the world', and took advantage of the opportunities it offered to hone his skills as a 'brilliant collector' of information. In February 1940 he was transferred to the staff of the new Australian legation under R. G. (Baron) Casey [q.v.13].

Officer returned to Australia in September 1940. By November he was Australian counsellor in Tokyo. In September 1941 he took over as chargé d'affaires during Sir John Latham's [q.v.10] absence. On 8 December Officer received Japan's formal declaration of war. Following 'a long dull period of confinement', he and his staff returned home in August 1942.

Appointed counsellor to the Soviet Union, Officer arrived at Kuibyshev with the Australian minister William Slater [q.v.] on 2 January 1943. On Slater's departure in April, Officer became chargé d'affaires. Next month the small Australian staff accepted responsibility for representing Polish interests in the Soviet Union. Officer's broad experience and practical approach enabled him to work effectively and to bolster the morale of his subordinates, despite the human misery they daily confronted. None the less, he felt like 'the old man in the wilderness' and wanted to move back to the centre of things—'London, Washington or even Canberra'.

Officer left Moscow in February 1944 and proceeded to Chungking, China, as chargé d'affaires. He found life simple, and the work interesting but full of anxieties. In 1946 Clement (Earl) Attlee, the British prime minister, nominated him to represent Britain, Australia, New Zealand and India on the Allied Council for Japan, but Dr H. V. Evatt [q.v.14] distrusted Officer's conservatism and appointed him Australian political representative (minister) to South East Asia. In February-April Officer held discussions in Batavia (Jakarta) and Singapore, and negotiated a peace treaty with Thailand. In June he took up the post of minister to the Netherlands.

One of Officer's main responsibilities in The Hague was to persuade the Dutch to reach a settlement with the Indonesians. Despite tension resulting from the boycott of Dutch ships by the Waterside Workers' Federation of Australia, he established good relations with the Dutch. In 1946 he attended the peace conference in Paris. Transferred to Nanking as ambassador to China in 1948, he saw the city fall to communist troops on 23 April 1949. Officer was recalled to Australia in November. He was made Australian ambassador to France in February 1950. The work kept him busy and the French political scene was 'never dull'. In 1950 he was knighted. From 21 November 1951, in the absence of Casey, he led the Australian delegation to the sixth session of the United Nations General Assembly.

Sir Keith never married. Although he was a generous and considerate host, each year he looked forward to summer when he escaped in his yacht, *Yarinya*, often accompanied by Crumpet, his pet golden Labrador. Officer had the 'traditional appearance of a professional army officer', with 'London style' clothes, brushed-back hair and clipped moustache. Occasionally he wore a monocle. Following his retirement in 1954, he lived at Blackfield, Southampton, England. A director of the English, Scottish & Australian Bank Ltd and the Australian Estates Co. Ltd, he was chairman of the Solent Protection Society. He died on 21 June 1969 at Southampton; his funeral took place at St Francis's Church, Langley.

Quadrant, Aug 1970, p 30; *SMH*, 29 Jan 1938, 5 Feb 1960, 24 June 1969; Officer papers (NL).
                                        KATHLEEN DERMODY

OGILVY, CLIVE DAVID (1908-1978), broadcasting administrator, was born on 7 November 1908 at Mosman, Sydney, eldest of three children of David Ogilvy, grazier of Airlie Park, near Delegate, and his wife Emma Ann, née Glen. Educated (1921-26) at Sydney Church of England Grammar School (Shore), Clive worked as a jackeroo in Queensland. With the onset of the Depression he joined Sir Hugh Denison's [q.v.8] Associated Newspapers Ltd and became manager of radio-station 2CA, Canberra. Ogilvy was a director of Macquarie Broadcasting Services Pty Ltd (founded by Denison in 1938) which controlled fifteen radio stations in Australia, including 2GB and 2CA. At Fullerton [q.v.4] Memorial Presbyterian Church, Sydney, on 30 July 1938 he married June Adele Munro, a 21-year-old actress.

Appointed temporary captain in the Militia on 9 June 1942, Ogilvy directed the radio campaign for the 'Austerity' war loan. In September he was allocated to the Security Service Intelligence Corps. He was appointed a principal assistant to W. B. Simpson, the director general of security. Promoted temporary major in December 1943, he was seconded to the Australian Imperial Force in May 1944. That year he visited London to liaise with the Radio Security Service, and Washington to work with the Federal Bureau of Investigation. He told his family that for him 'the war is a field which must always remain a closed book'.

Ogilvy transferred to the Reserve of Officers on 14 November 1945 and returned to the Macquarie Network as managing director. He was appointed in 1949 to Prime Minister Chifley's [q.v.13] new Australian Broadcasting Control Board, but resigned in July 1951 owing to a conflict of interests. In that month he masterminded a group, headed by his father-in-law Charles Munro, to buy a controlling interest in 2GB. One of the largest producers of radio programmes in Australia, Macquarie Broadcasting employed such favourites as Eric Baume, Jack Davey, John Dease [qq.v.13] and 'The Quiz Kids'.

As chairman (1946-c.1963) of Macquarie Broadcasting Service Pty Ltd, Ogilvy was appointed executive-member for the consortium, Amalgamated Television Services Pty Ltd, which included John Fairfax & Sons [qq.v.4,8] Pty Ltd. At the royal commission on television in 1953 he led the evidence for Macquarie Broadcasting to acquire a licence, believing the soundest way to launch television and to produce first-class programmes was by private enterprise. Due to his discordant relationship with the chairman Rupert Henderson, Ogilvy was managing director of A.T.S.'s ATN-Channel 7 only until June 1955. In 1964 he unsuccessfully sought an injunction in the Equity Court to remove four directors nominated by Fairfax from Broadcasting Station 2GB Pty Ltd.

In addition to being chairman of Geigy Australasia Pty Ltd and a director of Rothmans of Pall Mall (Australia) Ltd and of several family companies, Ogilvy had business interests in the Netherlands. A friend of (Sir) John McEwen [q.v.] and J. D. Anthony, he was involved in the Federal organization of the Country (National) Party and liked the 'hassle and bustle' of politics. Appointed C.B.E. in 1965, he was a member of the Export Development Council in 1967-68.

Ogilvy was an enthusiastic and efficient councillor (1961-78) of the Royal Agricultural Society of New South Wales. His flair for presentation and promotion took him to the Netherlands in 1968 to buy, on the society's behalf, a calèche with harness and livery for use by the vice-regal party at the Royal Easter Show. A devotee of equestrian sports, he was president (1955-61) of the Pony Club Association of New South Wales and a committee-member (1955-71) of the State branch of the Equestrian Federation of Australia.

Of medium build, with blue eyes and brown hair, Ogilvy was an intriguer with an engaging and gregarious personality, and a sense of fun. He set off his dashing appearance in well-cut suits by wearing a red carnation. A foundation member of the Australian Elizabethan Theatre Trust, he belonged to the Union, Green Room, Tattersall's and Australian Jockey clubs, and was a director (1966-69) of Sydney Hospital. Proud of his Scottish ancestry, he became a keen parishioner and benefactor of St Stephen's Presbyterian Church, Sydney. He died of a coronary occlusion on 18 May 1978 at Woollahra and was cremated; his wife, two sons and three daughters survived him. Graham Inson's portrait of Ogilvy is held by the family.

G. Souter, *Company of Heralds* (Melb, 1981); *SMH*, 22, 28 Jan, 4 Feb, 14 Oct 1949, 7 July, 12 Dec 1951, 2 July 1953, 9, 11 May, 23, 27 Sept, 26 Oct 1954, 2, 3, 22 Feb, 6 June 1955, 20 May 1978; information from Ms R. Bieri, Roy Agr Soc of NSW, Mr A. E. Harris, Vaucluse, Mrs S. Pico-Alapont, Neutral Bay, Mr A. Stephenson, St Stephen's Uniting Church, Syd, and Mr I. Ogilvy, Woodstock, NSW.
                                    CAROLINE SIMPSON

O'GRADY, OSWALD JAMES (1901-1971), businessman, was born on 6 April 1901 at Parkside, Adelaide, son of Thomas Patrick O'Grady (d.1916), motorcar manufacturer, and his wife Violet Isabel, née Fraser. After attending school at Unley and Woodville, Ossie was employed as a clerk by the National Bank of Australasia. In 1918 he moved to the Commonwealth Bank of Australia. Ambitious to improve himself, he disregarded his mother's wish that he become a lawyer and studied commerce at night at the University of Adelaide (Dip.Com., 1923), a decision in part taken to enable him to continue supporting her.

From an early age O'Grady wanted to emulate the business and sporting success of his father. Despite being short and bespectacled, he developed a fierce competitive spirit which helped him to excel in sport throughout his life. He played Australian Rules football for the West Torrens club, represented the State, and in his first season was runner-up (1923) for the Magarey medal; his football career ended when stomach cancer was diagnosed in 1925. He worked as a sports-writer for the *Sunday Mail* and continued to be associated with West Torrens (president 1954-71). Australian dinghy (1930) and 12-metre yachting (1947) champion, he was also a member of the four which won the State lawn bowls title in 1934.

At St Paul's Anglican Church, Adelaide, on 9 October 1926 O'Grady had married Jessie Bartlett Adcock Ellis (d.1967). He left the bank in 1930, allegedly because of lack of promotion. Within months of taking up an offer to manage a small finance company, he was acting as its liquidator, but he had seen the potential of its cash-order business. He established a similar enterprise, Cash Orders Ltd. That the firm succeeded through the Depression was testament to his hard work and business acumen.

Throughout the 1930s O'Grady's cash-order business in linen and Manchester grew, expanding locally and into Western Australia. Careful selection of clients enabled the company to allow its customers flexibility in repayments. Common sense, initiative, local connexions and a desire to succeed kept interstate rivals at bay. None the less, through the war and immediately after, the business endured tight financial conditions. The company, by then named David Murray [q.v.5] (Holdings) Ltd, prospered due to rising immigration, new home building, and consumer demand for such products as electrical appliances.

The seeds of financial collapse, however, were sown when O'Grady followed an American lead and began funding expansion on the basis of debentures rather than retained earnings and direct borrowing. In 1957 David Murray merged with Robert Reid [q.v.11] & Co. Ltd. The late 1950s saw a frantic expansion in Reid Murray Holdings Ltd. The board's small-town mentality and O'Grady's self-confident, but trusting, management style began to lose touch with a nationwide company's diverse interests in finance, retailing and real-estate development.

The collapse of Reid Murray in the credit squeeze of 1961—one of the largest corporate failures in Australia's business history to that time—left O'Grady battered but unbroken. Although he was fined for making loans to finance share issues and for issuing a prospectus with false statements, he was cleared by a parliamentary inquiry of any moral culpability. He maintained that precipitate and ill-judged asset sales by the trustees of debenture holders had increased the firm's losses, as had the opportunism of business rivals. His stoicism masked feelings of betrayal by some trusted social and business associates.

O'Grady's attitude was never particularly materialistic. The loss of a good deal of his personal wealth affected him little. Rather than dwelling on the past, he turned his energy to improving his family's properties in South Australia. While he had been described as 'Australia's most dynamic businessman', he always ensured that he balanced his time between family, work, community obligations and sport.

A generous (and frequently anonymous) donor to charity, O'Grady regarded his involvement in local affairs as a responsibility he owed to others. He helped to establish a youth centre at Woodville, and served as founding president of South Australian Youth Clubs, vice-president (1962-63) of the Kindergarten Union of South Australia, and a governor of the Adelaide Children's Hospital. Survived by his three sons and two of his three daughters, he died of cancer on 27 January 1971 in Royal Adelaide Hospital and was cremated.

T. Sykes, *Two Centuries of Panic* (Syd, 1988); *PP* (Vic), 1963-64, 1, p 807, 1966-67, 1, p 1045; *Sunday Advertiser* (Adel), 18 Feb 1956, 24 Aug 1957; *News* (Adel), 22 Nov 1961; *Sun-Herald*, 4 Aug 1963; *Advertiser* (Adel), 5 Aug, 14 Dec 1963, 7 May 1965, 19 Nov 1966, 26, 28 Jan 1971; O'Grady papers (Mort L); information from Mrs C. Williams, Lockleys, Adel.

MARTIN SHANAHAN

O'HALLORAN, MICHAEL RAPHAEL (1893-1960), politician, farmer and storekeeper, was born on 12 April 1893 at Yan-

yarrie, near Carrieton, South Australia, only child of South Australian-born parents James Andrew O'Halloran, farmer, and his wife Mary Catherine, née Brown. Mick attended Pamatta Provisional and Red Hill Public schools before working on his parents' mixed farm. Meeting 'a fine old Englishman' with 'a library of early Fabian publications', he 'read every one of them' and joined the Australian Labor Party at the age of 15.

After his father died in 1910, O'Halloran supported his mother on the farm at Belton. He won the House of Assembly seat of Burra Burra in 1918, lost it in 1921 and regained it in 1924. Defeated again in 1927, he served as State organizer for the A.L.P. and entered the Senate in 1928. He was deputy-leader of the Opposition in the Senate from 1932 until his defeat at the elections in 1935.

With Labor reduced to a rump of the assembly in the 1933 South Australian elections, O'Halloran was recalled to State politics and won Frome in 1938. Re-elected seven times, he held the seat until his death. At St Gabriel's Catholic Church, Cradock, on 14 May 1924 he had married Mary Frances Rowe; they were to remain childless. Mary handled her husband's electorate work from their Peterborough home during parliamentary sessions. The O'Hallorans ran their own organization, and the party was forbidden to campaign in the vast country electorate which virtually became his private fiefdom. For more than forty years he was Labor's key country advocate, described as 'a bell wether . . . an old and tractable sheep whose services are requisitioned to lead his fellow sheep [the farmers] into the muster yard' of the A.L.P.

In November 1949 O'Halloran became the first Catholic to lead the State parliamentary Labor Party. He consistently rejected sectarianism. His close ties with the Catholic Church and Archbishop Beovich were important in preventing a split in the State branch of the A.L.P. in the 1950s. The rocksolid support of the branch for Dr H. V. Evatt [q.v.14] did much to help him retain Federal party leadership. O'Halloran confronted (Sir) Thomas Playford's ascendancy in South Australia: while often gaining a majority of the popular vote, he lost four general elections. Despite this record, his leadership remained unchallenged.

An effective orator, O'Halloran was a better performer on the stump and in the House than the premier, but seemed content to leave it at that. Playford appreciated his policy of constructive opposition, and consulted and negotiated with him; they sometimes made common cause against Playford's conservative colleagues in the Legislative Council. Reflecting on the progress of the State under his premiership, Playford acknowledged that 'in all those advances Mr O'Halloran played a conspicuous part'. O'Halloran claimed that, given the circumstances, he was able to achieve more of Labor's objectives in opposition than in government. Most of his party concurred.

Of middle height, with a plump face and genial manner, O'Halloran enjoyed a drink, smoked a pipe and spoke in a 'strong, resonant voice with a touch of Irish brogue'. He made no enemies, and was universally liked and respected. This he prized more than office. Survived by his wife, he died of a pulmonary embolism on 22 September 1960 in Calvary Hospital, North Adelaide; he was accorded a state funeral and buried in Centennial Park cemetery.

D. Dunstan, *Felicia* (Melb, 1981); J. Moss, *Sound of Trumpets* (Adel, 1985); S. Cockburn, *Playford* (Adel, 1991); *PD* (SA), 15 Aug 1918, p 247, 4 Oct 1960, p 1092; *PD* (Cwlth, Senate), 4 Nov 1929, p 36; *News* (Adel), 22 Aug 1950, 22 Sept 1960; *Advertiser* (Adel), 23 Sept 1960; J. Medwell, Personalities Remembered, radio talk 5CL, 12 Dec 1971 (Mort L); information from the late D. A. Dunstan.

J. C. BANNON

OKEDEN, RICHARD PARRY; *see* PARRY OKEDEN

O'KEEFE, JOHN MICHAEL (1935-1978), rock'n'roll singer, was born on 19 January 1935 in Sydney, second of three children of Raymond Moran O'Keefe, furniture salesman, and his wife Thelma Edna, née Kennedy, both born in New South Wales. Johnny attended Christian Brothers' College, Waverley, and completed a first-year certificate at the College of Retailing. His father occasionally played in a jazz band. While at school Johnny sang in the choir and studied piano. He began to imitate the emotional singing style of the American pop idol, Johnnie Ray, and appeared on radio 2UW's 'Australian Amateur Hour'.

While working as a salesman in his father's furniture store, R. M. O'Keefe & Co., Pitt Street, O'Keefe enrolled in economics at the University of Sydney. After he heard Bill Haley singing *Rock Around the Clock* in the film *Blackboard Jungle* in 1955, he decided to become a rock'n'roller. In September 1956 he and Dave Owens formed the 'Dee Jays' (Dee was for Dave, and Jay for Johnny). They were joined by Johnny Greenan, Lou Casch, Keith Williams and Johnny 'Catfish' Purser. The band began performing at Stones Cabaret, Coogee. By early 1957 they were playing at four dances a week (at Chatswood, Coogee, Balmain and Petersham) and also appearing on Saturdays in the interval between feature films at the Embassy Theatre, Manly.

After signing with Festival Records Pty Ltd, O'Keefe and the 'Dee Jays' released *You Hit the Wrong Note Billy Goat*, written by Haley, in July 1957. Their second record was *Am I Blue?*, with *Love Letters in the Sand* on the 'flip side'. In October they performed in one of Lee Gordon's [q.v.14] 'Big Shows' at the Stadium with American stars 'Little Richard', Gene Vincent and Eddie Cochran. Five months later O'Keefe released *Wild One*, which he wrote with Owens, Greenan and Tony Withers, a disc jockey; the song was an immediate hit and made him the first Australian rock'n'roller to reach the national charts. *Shout* followed in 1959 and *She's My Baby* in 1960.

Stockily built and 5 ft 7½ ins (172 cm) tall, O'Keefe looked more like a boxer than a singer. Although his appearance was not striking and his vocal talents were unexceptional, most commentators agreed that he had 'presence'. On stage he traded, in part, on an overt sexuality and handled the microphone in a suggestive manner. He once remarked: 'It didn't matter how you sang the song; it mattered what you did'. Despite his image as 'The Wild One', he promoted rock'n'roll as wholesome entertainment, claiming that it was one of 'the greatest barriers to delinquency'. Like most stars of that period, he aspired to be an 'all-round entertainer'; two of his biggest hits were the ballads, *I'm Counting on You* (1961) and *She Wears My Ring* (1964).

At St Therese's Catholic Church, Dover Heights, on 2 August 1958 O'Keefe had married Marianne Renate Willinzik, a 23-year-old hairdresser; they were to have three children before she divorced him in 1966. The marriage felt the strain of his frenetic lifestyle and ambitions. O'Keefe left the family business in 1958. Joining Lee Gordon's record company, he worked as an artist and repertoire man. He recruited singers for the Leedon label, including 'Lonnie Lee', Barry Stanton and 'The Crescents', and wrote songs for them. From 28 February 1959 he and the 'Dee Jays' starred on the Australian Broadcasting Commission's Saturday evening television show, 'Six O'Clock Rock'. O'Keefe soon became the compere, and was closely involved in the show's production. By the beginning of 1960 he also hosted an A.B.C. radio programme, the 'Johnny O'Keefe Show, Rockville Junction', which was broadcast on Friday nights.

O'Keefe regarded success in the United States of America as the ultimate accolade. In November 1959 he had visited America and signed with Liberty Records. Next year he toured thirty-five States and appeared on the television programme, 'American Bandstand', but his reception was far from the triumph he wanted and he returned to Australia. On 27 June 1960 he was involved in a serious motorcar accident on the Pacific Highway near Kempsey. He received sixty-four stitches in his head and another twenty-six in his hands. After only seven weeks he again compered 'Six O'Clock Rock'. In 1961 he hosted the 'Johnny O'Keefe Show' on ATN-7.

That year O'Keefe made another unsuccessful American tour. He flew to London, where he suffered a nervous breakdown. In August 1962 he suffered a further breakdown and spent two months in a psychiatric ward at Royal Prince Alfred Hospital, Sydney. He returned to his television show—renamed 'Sing, Sing, Sing' during his absence—in February 1963, but it ceased production in 1965. Exceptionally energetic and often charming, O'Keefe was subject to dramatic changes of mood and had a tendency to overreact. In November 1964 he was back in hospital, his 'holiday camp' as he jokingly called it.

The rise of 'Mersey beat' music signalled a change in O'Keefe's fortunes. He called 1964, the year in which 'The Beatles' toured Australia, the 'biggest downer of his career'. The production and sale of his records declined. Following a brief return to television in 1967 as host of 'Where the Action Is', he found work largely in tent-shows and at leagues clubs. In 1974 his career underwent something of a resurgence. His show, *The Good Old Days of Rock'n'Roll*, opened at the St George Leagues Club in August that year and continued on tour until his death. His song, *Mockingbird*, recorded with Margaret McLaren, became a hit. On 14 February 1975 (St Valentine's Day) at the Masonic Hall, Waverley, he married with Methodist forms Maureen Joan Maricic, a 29-year-old fashion consultant and a divorcee. They opened a boutique, J. O'K Creations, at Paddington in 1978.

The highs and lows of O'Keefe's life appeared extreme. Apart from numerous breakdowns, he had some run-ins with the police for driving offences and minor drug charges. Generous by nature, he helped to raise funds for the Spastic Centre of New South Wales and the Margaret Reid Orthopaedic Hospital, St Ives. He entertained Australian troops in Vietnam in 1969 and performed at a free concert in cyclone-devastated Darwin in 1975.

After taking pills at his Double Bay home, O'Keefe died of barbiturate poisoning on 6 October 1978 at St Vincent's Hospital, Darlinghurst, and was buried with Catholic rites in Northern Suburbs cemetery. His wife survived him, as did the daughter and two sons of his first marriage. The Australian Variety Artists Association named an award after him. In 1988 his name was included in the Australian Record Industry Association's hall of fame.

B. Rogers (with D. O'Brien) *Rock'n'Roll Australia* (Syd, 1975); J. Bryden-Brown, *JO'K* (Syd, 1982); N. McGrath, *Noel McGrath's Australian Encyclopaedia of Rock & Pop* (Adel, 1984); M. Sturma, *Australian Rock'n'Roll* (Syd, 1991); *Pix*, 11 Apr 1964; *TV Times*, 26 Mar, 2 July, 13 Aug, 24 Dec 1960, 8 Sept, 6 Oct 1962, 26 Jan, 2 Mar, 5 June 1963; *Bulletin*, 13 Oct 1962; *SMH*, 28 Jan 1964, 6 Apr, 6 May, 15 Dec 1966, 7 Oct 1978.   MICHAEL STURMA

O'KEEFFE, KATHLEEN CLARE (1883-1949), public servant and campaigner for equal pay for women, was born on 9 January 1883 at Maitland, New South Wales, second daughter of native-born parents Maurice O'Keeffe, solicitor, and his wife Susan, née Normoyle. Kathleen joined the Department of Mines as a shorthand writer and typist on 28 February 1911, and in 1920 was promoted clerk. In 1922 she gained a diploma in economics and commerce at the University of Sydney, achieving a high distinction in public administration and winning the Sydney Chamber of Commerce prize. Having completed further study at Sydney Technical College in industrial hygiene, sanitary law and health inspection, she transferred to the Department of Public Instruction on 21 June 1929 to work as an inspector under the Child Welfare Act (1923).

A 'staunch feminist' and member of the National Council of Women of New South Wales, O'Keeffe became a strong advocate for women in the Public Service Association of New South Wales. She chaired the women's clerical sub-section and the women's auxiliary, and sat on the clerical management and arbitration committees. In 1929 she was the first woman to be appointed to the P.S.A. executive.

O'Keeffe made good use of these positions to pursue equal pay issues. In 1927 she had played a key role on behalf of the P.S.A. in negotiating the first women's clerical award with the New South Wales government. During 1929 she pushed for the principle of equal pay for equal work to be included in amendments to the Public Service Act (1902). Her efforts in this regard were met with 'evasive replies' by the government and the Public Service Board, and ultimately went unheeded. O'Keeffe also agitated for changes to long-service-leave regulations so that women who left the service on marriage would not be disadvantaged. Throughout the 1930s she joined others, including Dorothy Beveridge [q.v.13], in campaigning for qualified women public servants to be employed as permanent, rather than temporary, staff. In 1936 O'Keeffe was a member of the P.S.A. deputation which met the deputy-premier (Sir) Michael Bruxner [q.v.7] to discuss salary cuts in the Public Service.

At St Mary's Catholic Cathedral, Sydney, on 26 December 1934 O'Keeffe married Albert Nelson Graham, a 54-year-old mining warden; he was to be appointed (1936) under-secretary for mines. Despite the existence of the marriage bar in the public service, she continued to work under her maiden name. It was not until 1 March 1938 that she retired from the Child Welfare Department.

Popular with her colleagues, O'Keeffe was respected for her 'thoroughness, mastery of detail, rapidity and soundness of judgement'. She was fondly remembered for her cheerful disposition, clear thinking and eloquence in debate, and for her willingness to be constantly at the forefront of the battle for her sisters. Survived by her husband, she died of a coronary occlusion on 9 September 1949 at her Mosman home and was buried in Northern Suburbs cemetery.

Red Tape, 5 Oct 1927, 15 Jan, 15 Apr, 25 July, 25 Aug, 25 Oct 1929, 25 Mar, 25 Apr 1930, 25 Apr 1931, 25 May 1935, 25 May 1936, 25 May 1937, Sept-Oct 1949; *Aust Woman's Mirror*, 2 Apr 1929, p 20.

LOUISE CHAPPELL

OLD, ERNEST (1874-1962), cyclist and soldier, was born on 10 July 1874 at Barrys Reef, near Blackwood, Victoria, elder of twins and fourth of nine children of Thomas Spear Old, a Cornish miner, and his Irish-born wife Charlotte, née Mitchell (d.1881). Thomas selected land at Dingee, north of Sandhurst (Bendigo). His children attended Prairie State School, and the boys worked on their father's farms and as contract harvesters.

Ernie was sent in 1896 with two brothers to develop family properties near Swan Hill, but he became more interested in machinery than in farming. He began cycling competitively and won a number of local events. Old finished eighth in the Warrnambool to Melbourne road race in 1901, fourth under handicap in 1903, and was doing well in 1904 before a bad fall. He had not raced in 1902: motivated by the drought and scant harvest, and impelled by a mixture of patriotism and a wish to travel, he enlisted in the 4th Battalion, Australian Commonwealth Horse, and embarked for South Africa. The war ended before he saw action and he arrived home in July.

On 23 February 1905 Old married Marion Patience Grylls at the Dingee Methodist Church. He designed a scarifier with easily replaced tines, sold his farm, bought his father's interest in a smithy, and commenced manufacture. Leaving the business in the care of a brother, he enlisted in the Australian Imperial Force on 22 December 1914. He served at Gallipoli with the 13th Light Horse Regiment and on the Western Front with the 2nd Pioneer Battalion. Badly wounded at Flers, France, in November 1916, he was repatriated in December 1917 and discharged from the army on 22 March 1918.

Old resumed work as a blacksmith and implement-maker, but found that his scarifier had been superseded. He then invented a motorcar steering stabilizer as an inexpensive alternative to replacing worn parts. This device sustained his family through the Depression. During World War II he tried to enlist in the A.I.F. before taking jobs as a blacksmith—on the construction of the Lauriston Reservoir, near Kyneton, and at the Ordnance Factory, Maribyrnong, Melbourne.

In 1945 Old began a series of long-distance cycle rides which were to make him a national figure. That year he completed a 1136-mile (1828 km) return journey from Melbourne to Sydney in nine days. He made a return ride to Adelaide (1138 miles, 1831 km) in eight days in 1946, and to Brisbane (2500 miles, 4025 km) in twenty-three days in 1947. He had ridden 256 miles (412 km) in 24 hours to raise funds in 1946 for the Children's Hospital, Melbourne. Press and radio monitored his feats; crowds and civic receptions greeted him along his routes.

In 1947 Old rode some 6000 miles (9650 km) in 56 days, passing through Adelaide on the way to Darwin, then returning to Melbourne via Mount Isa, Brisbane and Sydney. In 1948 he cycled 4500 miles (7250 km) from Melbourne to Perth and back, and in 1951-52 he travelled 6000 miles (9650 km) in 102 days, first to Fremantle and back, and then via Canberra to Sydney and back. He completed another outback ride in 1957, climbed Ayers Rock (Uluru) at the age of 83, and cycled across Tasmania in 1959.

Old's concern to maintain personal fitness developed into a crusade to demonstrate the connection between clean living, exercise and longevity. The veteran cyclist was an ambassador for the great outdoors of the wide, brown and ancient land he loved. Trim and tanned, with a shock of silver-grey hair, he was a teetotaller and non-smoker. He became a celebrity in an age when the automobile seemed to be assigning the bicycle to the scrap heap. His regular appearances at Anzac Day parades, upright and soldierly in his A.I.F. uniform, excited admiration from public and press. He died on 11 August 1962 in his home at Murrumbeena, Melbourne, and was buried in New Cheltenham cemetery with Unitarian forms; his wife, three daughters and two sons survived him. Ernie had lived by the injunction, 'Love thy neighbour as thyself'. His complex attitudes on the purpose of life, and his decidedly anti-war views, had been largely omitted by the publisher of his autobiography, *By Bread Alone* (Melbourne, 1950).

Sun News-Pictorial, 12 June 1950; *Age* (Melb), 23 May 1952, 13 Aug 1962; *Express* (Launc), 26 Dec 1959; *Herald* (Melb), 1 Dec 1984; information from Mr L. Noye, Altona, Melb; family information.

JOHN LACK

OLDAKER, MAXWELL CHARLES (1907-1972), singer and actor, was born on 17 December 1907 at Devonport, Tasmania, only child of Tasmanian-born parents Charles Edmund Wells Oldaker, farmer, and his wife Alice Mabel, née Wade. He was sent to Devonport High School, but showed no interest in his studies and left early to work in a record shop. Success in music examinations and eisteddfods confirmed his ability as a pianist and singer. The Westminster Glee Singers visited Devonport in 1930 and engaged him as a tenor for their tour of Australia and the Far East; when the company experienced financial difficulties, his contract was broken.

Undeterred, Oldaker travelled to England in search of experience in the theatre. He had good looks, elegance and a natural charm. His fine lyric voice was soon enhanced by professional training and by work that ranged from opera to vaudeville, including broadcasting and recording. On 3 August 1931 at Eastbourne, Sussex, he made his theatrical début in *The Chocolate Soldier*. Joining the D'Oyly Carte Opera Company in the following year, he understudied leading tenors and played small parts in the company's extensive repertoire.

In October 1934 Oldaker entered the Royal Academy of Music, London, on a Walter Stokes free-tuition scholarship. He took jobs in films and on radio to make a living until he graduated in 1936 with the Arnold Bax prize for the best pianist-singer. The academy's conductor (Sir) John Barbirolli predicted that he would have a distinguished operatic career. Declining an invitation from J. C. Williamson [q.v.6] Ltd to join 'the Firm' in Australia, Oldaker was selected in 1937 by (Sir) Noël Coward for the leading juvenile singing role in *Operette*.

The outbreak of World War II and a renewed offer from J. C. Williamson's led Oldaker to return to Melbourne in October 1939. He was received as a celebrity. Over the next decade he became a star performer and a matinée idol. In spite of his triumphs, a combination of diffidence and reserve tended to hamper his otherwise brilliant career.

Although Oldaker registered for military service, he was not called up. He made his contribution to the war effort by involving himself in fund-raising activities. At this time he began to compose works for the piano and was elected a member (1941) of the Australian Composers' Guild; he also appeared in Gilbert and Sullivan operettas, and—with Gladys Moncrieff [q.v.10]—in *The Maid of the Mountains* and *The Merry Widow*. While critical of J. C. Williamson's treatment of its employees, he did not support strikes organized by the Actors' and Announcers' Equity Association of Australia because he felt a duty to the theatre-going public.

After the war Oldaker enjoyed success in *The Desert Song*, *The Dancing Years*, and *Gay Rosalinda*. He visited England in 1948-50, but found postwar theatre very different from that of the 1930s. In 1951-52 he made a national tour with the John Alden [q.v.13] Company; in 1953 he appeared in *White Horse Inn* in major Australian cities. Late in 1957 Oldaker travelled to England and secured the role of understudy to (Sir) Rex Harrison, the leading man in *My Fair Lady*. He was acclaimed for his appearances as Professor Higgins, but was bitterly disappointed when he was not offered the part in the Australian production. Returning to Tasmania in 1959 to care for his invalid parents, he undertook radio and television broadcasting, vocal teaching, acting, producing, and music and theatre reviewing for the Launceston *Examiner*. In addition, he performed in musicals and revues on the mainland, notably at the Phillip Street Theatre, Sydney. Even though he was fully occupied, he continued to feel isolated from professional theatre in England.

Max Oldaker, who was homosexual, died of a coronary occlusion on 1 February 1972 at Launceston and was cremated. Charles Osborne, his biographer, concluded that he was more than a star: 'he was a generous, sensitive and life-enhancing man, with a rare gift for friendship'. A room in the Princess Theatre, Launceston, is named in Oldaker's memory; it contains memorabilia associated with his career, including Grant Macdonald's sketch (1938) of him. A portrait in oils is held by the Launceston Local Studies Library.

C. Osborne, *Max Oldaker* (Lond, 1988); *Tatler* (Lond), 6 Apr 1939; *Examiner* (Launc), 31 Aug 1940, 16 July 1958, 11 Aug 1970, 3 Feb 1972, 21 Sept 1973; Oldaker papers (Launc Local Studies L).

GILLIAN WINTER

OLDHAM, TREVOR DONALD (1900-1953), barrister and politician, was born on 10 March 1900 at St Kilda, Melbourne, eldest of three sons of Victorian-born parents Arthur Eggleston Oldham, solicitor, and his wife Ethel Constance, née Krcrouse. Trevor was educated at Melbourne Church of England Grammar School and the University of Melbourne (LL.B., 1921). A schoolboy cadet and a member of the Melbourne University Regiment, he enlisted in the Australian Imperial Force on 7 November 1918, four days before the Armistice.

Joining the family firm, Oldham & Oldham, he was admitted to practice as a barrister and solicitor on 1 March 1923. In addition to that practice, he was also associated with another that bore his grandfather's name—his uncle's firm of Krcrouse, Oldham & Bloomfield (later

Krcrouse, Oldham & Darvall). A specialist in commercial law, Oldham eventually became vice-chairman of Henry Berry [q.v.3] & Co. (Australasia) Ltd, and a director of Hoadley's [q.v.9] Chocolates Ltd, Ruskin Motor Bodies Ltd and Ensign Dry Cleaners Ltd. At the Presbyterian Church, Toorak, on 25 September 1929 he married Kathleen Norma MacLeod Cooch; they were to have three children.

Oldham had been commissioned in the Royal Australian Naval Volunteer Reserve in March 1926. Promoted to paymaster lieutenant in 1927, he served at Navy Office in August-November 1939. On 29 April 1933 he had been elected to the Legislative Assembly as a United Australia Party candidate for the seat of Boroondara. An approachable and effective local member, he was to be returned in eight successive elections, thrice unopposed: he retained Boroondara until its abolition in the redistribution of 1945 and then won the new seat of Malvern which he held until his death.

Conservative advocacy, a grasp of detail and a flair for debate helped Oldham to rise in the U.A.P. and subsequently in the Liberal (and Country) Party. From September 1943 to October 1945 he was minister without portfolio in (Sir) Albert Dunstan's [q.v.8] cabinet. Attorney-general and solicitor-general from November 1947 to June 1950 in T. T. Hollway's [q.v.14] two ministries, he was also minister for health (3 to 7 December 1948) and chief secretary (19 to 27 June 1950). He served on the statute law revision committee (1937-51), the House committee (1935-37), the library committee (1942-45) and the McPherson's [q.v.10] Ltd pension fund investigatory committee (1950). Temporary chairman of committees from May 1940 to June 1944, he was State delegate to the Commonwealth Parliamentary Association conference (1952) in Ottawa.

As a minister, Oldham earned a reputation for efficient administration, law reform and, more controversially, for his strike-breaking Essential Services Act (1948). As a parliamentarian, he was known to help new members of all parties with procedure and protocol. It was, however, as a party reformer and leader that he was best known. In 1930 he had been a founder of the Young Nationalist Organisation which became a significant faction for change within the Victorian branch of the U.A.P. Later that decade he publicly argued the need to modernize the party's organizational arm. And, until his death, he sought reform of an electoral system that had maintained Country Party dominance of Victorian conservative politics—a case, Oldham declared, of the 'tail wagging the dog'. He insisted that reform would never be achieved 'by sitting down calmly and waiting for something to turn up'.

In November 1945 Oldham was elected Hollway's deputy. Two years later he honoured an earlier agreement and relinquished the deputyship to (Sir) Wilfrid Kent Hughes [q.v.] who had returned from internment as a prisoner of war. When Kent Hughes resigned in October 1949, Oldham again assumed the deputy-leadership of the party and was deputy-premier (November 1949 to June 1950). His frustration over electoral distribution deepened. Despite opposition within his party, he strongly endorsed Hollway's '2 for 1' proposal—by which each Federal seat in Victoria would be divided into two State seats—even though he knew that it would reduce his party's numbers. In December 1951 Hollway and Oldham were replaced as leader and deputy-leader of the Liberals by Leslie Norman and (Sir) Henry Bolte.

Five ft 7 ins (170 cm) tall, dapper and bespectacled, with fair hair and blue eyes, Oldham had been a keen university debater and was later a dedicated gardener. With his wife, he was active in community affairs, especially charities which he unobtrusively assisted as a trustee of the Henry Berry [q.v.3] Estate. He served on the councils of the Old Melburnians (1927-41), the University of Melbourne (1939-53), the Law Institute of Victoria (1942-50) and Legal Education; he was also deputy-chancellor (1949-51) of the university, honorary consul (1930-33) in Victoria for Yugoslavia, president of the Victorian Eye and Ear Hospital, vice-president of the Victorian branch of the Navy League and chairman of the Metropolitan Firewood Supply Committee. Active in the Empire Day Movement, he belonged to the Naval and Military, Yorick and Constitutional clubs.

At the general election on 6 December 1952 Labor won government and Hollway defeated Norman for the seat of Glen Iris. Oldham was elected leader of the Liberal and Country Party. He was widely tipped to be the next premier. As leader of the Opposition he was invited to attend Queen Elizabeth II's coronation. He and his wife embarked for London on 30 April 1953. At Singapore they boarded a British Overseas Airways Corporation Comet which crashed on 2 May 1953 near the village of Jangipara, India, twenty-five miles northwest of Calcutta, killing all on board. On 6 May a state memorial service for the Oldhams was held at St Paul's Cathedral, Melbourne. They were survived by their son and two daughters.

K. West, *Power in the Liberal Party* (Melb, 1965); P. Aimer, *Politics, Power and Persuasion* (Syd, 1974); *PD* (Vic), 8 Sept 1953; Melb C of E Grammar School, *Melburnian*, May 1953; *Univ Melb Gazette*, May 1953, p 34; *Melb Graduate*, 4, no 2, Dec 1953, p 97; *Argus*, 18 May 1938, 24 Jan 1950, 4, 5 May, 2 July 1953; *Age* (Melb), 27 Jan, 4, 5 May, 5 Sept,

25 Nov 1953, 18 Oct 1954; information from Dr
J. Oldham, South Melb.

R. WRIGHT

OLDHAM, WILFRID (1890-1959), university lecturer and historian, was born on 8 June
1890 at Kabakada, near Rabaul, New Britain,
second son of Victorian-born parents Frederic
Bignell Oldham, Methodist minister, and his
wife Alice Edith, née Crothers. In 1894 the
family moved to New Zealand, where Wilfrid
attended state primary schools at Pukekohe
and Gisborne. After his father was transferred
to circuits in South Australia, Wilfrid continued his schooling at Port Augusta and
Naracoorte, and in Adelaide.

In 1908 Oldham became a pupil-teacher at
Balaklava Public School. He entered the University (Teachers') Training College in 1912
and enrolled at the University of Adelaide
(B.A., 1914; M.A., 1920). In 1914 he graduated
with first-class honours and won the Tinline
[q.v.6] scholarship for history. He worked on
his M.A. thesis under the supervision of Professor G. C. Henderson [q.v.9], while taking
undergraduate subjects in economics (1915-
16) and teaching at Adelaide High School
(1916-17). On 11 July 1917 he enlisted in the
Australian Imperial Force. Because of defective vision resulting from a childhood accident, he was allocated to the Australian Army
Medical Corps. He served at headquarters,
A.I.F. Depots in Britain, from June 1918 and
was discharged from the army on 21 June
1919 in Adelaide.

At the Methodist Church, West Hindmarsh,
on 2 April 1920 Oldham married Marjory
Anderson, a 26-year-old schoolteacher; the
service was conducted by a Congregational
minister. That year he was transferred to the
Teachers' Training College and appointed
half-time assistant-lecturer in the university's
department of modern history. He did not
leave the Education Department until 1927,
when he became 'night lecturer in History' at
the university. After securing a fellowship
(1931-32) from the Rockefeller Foundation, he
enrolled at the University of London (Ph.D.,
1933) where he completed a substantial and
well-researched thesis on 'The Administration of the System of the Transportation of
British Convicts, 1763-1793'.

Unfortunately this academic qualification
did not assist Oldham's subsequent career.
He continued to teach at the University of
Adelaide until 1946 on the same salary at
which he had been first employed. Only in
1950, six years before his retirement, was he
promoted to senior lecturer. While careful and
conscientious in his dealings with students, as
a lecturer he was too modest and uneasy in
manner to be a crowd pleaser. His personal

fulfilment came rather from his relationship
with his wife and two children, from gardening and tennis, and from membership of the
Johnian Club and the State branch of the
Royal Geographical Society of Australasia.

Shortly after undergoing surgery for
cancer, he died of a coronary occlusion on
24 July 1959 in Kingswood Private Hospital,
Malvern, and was cremated; his wife, son and
daughter survived him. Oldham's publications
included his Tinline thesis, *The Land Policy
of South Australia* (Adelaide, 1917), *Adelaide
History, Grade VII* (Adelaide, 1922), and a
children's book, *London on the Thames* (Melbourne, 1935). His Ph.D. thesis, edited by his
son Hugh, was published as *Britain's Convicts
to the Colonies* (Sydney, 1990).

W. K. Hancock, *Country and Calling* (Lond,
1954); Johnian Club, *Syllabus*, 1930-62/63 (SLSA);
Staff Book of Pupil-Teachers 1900-19, GRG 18/123,
and Record of Secondary Teachers 1900-65, GRG
109 (SA PRO); Student records, 2351 *and* Staff file
1915/374, 399, 1918/347, 1927/6, 1929/78, 1930/
97, 1945/368 (Univ Adel Archives); papers held by,
and information from, Mr W. H. Oldham, Curtin,
Canb.   WILFRID PREST

O'LEARY, CORNELIUS (1897-1971), director of native affairs, was born on 19 June 1897
at Murwillumbah, New South Wales, fifth
child of John O'Leary, a farmer from Ireland,
and his Queensland-born wife Ellen, née
Dooner. Educated at the Christian Brothers'
College, Ipswich, 'Con' entered the Queensland Public Service on 1 September 1913. He
worked as a clerk—in Brisbane with the Agricultural Bank of Queensland and the Department of Public Lands, at Ipswich in the
office of the labour agent and inspector of factories and shops, and back in Brisbane with
the Marine Department. In November 1922
he was appointed a 'protector of Aboriginals'
and assigned to the district of Somerset,
which encompassed the Torres Strait Islands
and the northern half of Cape York Peninsula.
He was based on Thursday Island where he
also held the post of shipping master.

Keenly aware of the responsibilities of his
joint positions, O'Leary wrote in 1923 to J. W.
Bleakley [q.v.7], chief protector of Aboriginals, seeking a special allowance. Bleakley
supported O'Leary's request and described
him as an officer who displayed 'zeal and ability' in performing 'important and responsible'
duties. When the application was not approved, O'Leary thought that he was unfairly
treated and persisted with his representations.
At the Catholic Church, Thursday Island, on
20 April 1927 he married Frances Catherine
Josephine Bowers.

In March 1930 O'Leary was sent as acting-
superintendent to Palm Island Aboriginal

Settlement. His predecessor had 'run amok' —firing a weapon, burning buildings and terrorizing the inhabitants. By 'tactful management' O'Leary restored confidence in the administration. In October he was transferred to Brisbane as inspector and deputy chief protector of Aboriginals. He toured Queensland in 1935 to familiarize himself with the indigenous communities. The passing of the Aboriginals Protection and Restriction of the Sale of Opium Acts Amendment Act (1934) had aroused fear among Aborigines working on pastoral stations and elsewhere that they were to be rounded up and sent to missions and reserves. O'Leary reassured them that, provided they were well behaved, they would be allowed to remain in their jobs.

After investigating the causes of a strike by Torres Strait Islander seamen, O'Leary was seconded in 1936 to Thursday Island as local protector, shipping master and chairman of the Aboriginal (Island from 1939) Industries Board; he retained his status as deputy chief protector. Under his leadership the industries board maintained throughout the islands the existing system of chain-stores through which people could buy essential goods at fair prices, draw their pensions and child-endowment payments, and operate savings bank accounts.

O'Leary returned to Brisbane in March 1940. One year earlier the Aboriginals Preservation and Protection Act and the Torres Strait Islanders Act had been passed, widening the chief protector's powers and changing his title to director of native affairs. On 8 October 1942 O'Leary succeeded Bleakley as director. He moved his office to Thursday Island in July 1948 to be closer to the majority of those for whom he was responsible. When Saibai Island began to subside, he arranged for its residents to be relocated at Bamaga on Cape York Peninsula. He envisaged 'that Bamaga, when developed, could produce a virile race of islanders to be moulded into a defence force'. His wife became a leader of Thursday Island society; she supported the Catholic Church, and the local branches of the Australian Red Cross Society and the Queensland Country Women's Association. From 1957 O'Leary was again stationed in Brisbane.

Described by some as boisterous, bombastic, dogmatic and authoritarian, O'Leary held attitudes towards Aborigines that were common among Whites at the time, but which have come to be regarded as paternalistic. He saw himself as a father-figure, duty-bound to intervene in Aborigines' private lives to settle domestic disputes. In his view, Aborigines and Islanders needed strict discipline. While they remained obedient, he governed them benignly; yet he also acted swiftly to remove those who opposed the wishes of their White supervisors. He administered the Aborigines Welfare Fund which, though intended to benefit Aborigines, deprived them of access to their wages. Controversy still surrounds the fund, with claims that moneys due have not been paid.

On the other hand, O'Leary's régime has been seen as dynamic and benevolent. He had a genuine interest in the welfare of Aborigines and Torres Strait Islanders, and formulated a number of schemes to improve their lot. Education, he argued, was central to their advancement. His efforts to help both Aborigines and Islanders to become independent members of Australian society led to claims that he was jeopardizing the safety of the Whites in North Queensland. He retired in 1963 and was appointed O.B.E. in 1964. Survived by his wife, daughter and two sons, he died on 6 November 1971 in his home at Holland Park, Brisbane, and was buried in Mount Gravatt cemetery.

H. Wearne, *A Clash of Cultures* (Brisb, 1980); Annual Report of Director of Native Affairs, *PP* (Qld), 1961-62, 1963-64; *People* (Syd), 4 June 1952; *Goondiwindi Argus*, 18 Oct 1935; *World's News*, 3 May 1952; *Telegraph* (Brisb), 31 May 1952; *Courier-Mail*, 1 June 1964; *Daily Telegraph Mirror*, 2 Oct 1992; information from Mr J. O'Leary, Enoggera, Brisb.   Les Malezer

OLIPHANT, KENNETH HENRY BELL (1894-1975), architect, was born on 10 November 1894 at Bendigo, Victoria, fourth child of James Glen Oliphant, a schoolteacher from Scotland, and his English-born wife Hannah, née Bell. Educated at St Andrew's College, Bendigo, Ken trained as an architect in Melbourne. On 10 January 1916 he enlisted in the Australian Imperial Force. He served on the Western Front and rose to corporal in the 10th Field Company, Engineers. After suffering a bullet-wound to the right thigh on 19 April 1918, he was admitted to hospital, and was discharged from the army on 3 December.

Continuing his studies at an atelier in Melbourne, Oliphant showed particular skills in residential design. He was elected an associate of the Royal Victorian Institute of Architects in 1921 and commenced practice that year. His designs for a two-storeyed house (1922), his drawings for a parish hall at Kew (1925-26), and the plans and photographs of three of his completed houses in Canberra (1930) were all published. By 1925 he was employed in the firm of Oakley & Parkes, which had won a Commonwealth competition to design homes for senior public servants at Blandfordia (Forrest), Canberra. Oliphant probably worked on the detailed drawings prepared for their construction; there is a clear connection in style and detail between the Canberra designs of Oakley & Parkes and the built work of Oliphant.

In 1926 Oakley & Parkes sent Oliphant to Canberra to supervise building in the Blandfordia subdivision. His professional association with the firm was apparently a loose one, for he was commissioned later that year to design two private residences in his own name. Oliphant's almost immediate success was deserved but unexpected. Recognizing the risk he was taking in setting up on his own, he left the firm in 1927, reportedly saying that he would rather starve in Canberra than in Melbourne. At St Philip's Anglican Church, Sydney, on 11 November 1935 he married Ruth Betty Moor.

By 1930 Oliphant had designed more than thirty private houses, commercial premises and other buildings in Canberra. The homes varied in style, but they shared a simple grace which in many cases has ensured their preservation virtually intact. He borrowed widely from Georgian and Queen Anne styles, with occasional essays into Tudor, Mediterranean and Art Deco. There was a marked degree of confidence in his siting and building designs, and his houses were finely detailed, beautifully crafted and soundly constructed.

Oliphant's materials included locally made red-brick and terracotta roof-tiles, and smooth or rough-cast plaster for external walls. Many of Canberra's early municipal buildings were similarly clad. A number of churches, hotels and private schools constructed at the same time exhibited the romantic imagery, axiality and garden plantings associated with Oliphant's houses. This use of a consistent but broad design vocabulary at a range of scales established the character of Canberra's original suburbs.

During the Depression, Oliphant designed the impressive Barton Court apartments facing Bourke, Macquarie and Darling streets, Barton, and maintained his practice, despite fewer residential and commercial commissions. Ill at ease with the new styles of architecture which emerged after World War II, he produced little of the spark in his later years that had characterized his earlier work. Although he contributed to the design of the Dairy Farmers' building, Mildura Street, Griffith, in functional modern style, he was more comfortable with traditional forms and materials. He assisted Professor Brian Lewis in planning the vice-chancellor's residence at the Australian National University.

Oliphant was a foundation member (1954) of the Commonwealth Club and an active Rotarian. For many years he served as honorary architect to the Church of St John the Baptist, Reid, to which he added the elegant lich-gates in red mahogany, the sandstone altar and the war-memorial shrine. He retired in 1965. Survived by his wife, son and two daughters, he died on 10 February 1975 in Canberra Hospital and was buried in Canberra cemetery. Oliphant was a tall, distinguished-looking and considerate man. Believing that there is 'art in everything', he expressed delight equally in the skills of tradesmen and labourers. His work exhibited an awareness of place not always found in architecture.

A. H. Body, *Firm Still You Stand* (Canb, 1986); P. Freeman (ed), *The Early Canberra House* (Canb, 1996); *Aust Home Beautiful*, 2 June 1930, p 24; *Canb Times*, 4 Dec 1983, 23 Apr 1995; Kenneth H. Oliphant: His Life and Work, unpublished report, 1996, Register of Significant Twentieth Century Architecture, RAIA/ACT Chapter, ACT Heritage Unit L, Lyneham, ACT; information from Rev D. Oliphant, O'Connor, Mr R. Lilley, Narrabundah, ACT, and the late Mrs B. Oliphant.

ROGER PEGRUM

O'LOGHLEN, JOHN HENRY PATRICK FRANCIS (c.1892–1964), rural and sporting writer, was born about 1892 at Bendigo, Victoria, eldest child of Victorian-born parents Michael Henry O'Loghlen, butcher, and his wife Susannah, née McMahon. Frank was raised on the family's dairy-farm. After leaving primary school, he held various jobs, from rouseabout to trade-union representative. His interest in beef cattle began in New South Wales in 1911 when he encountered a large mob of Herefords on the Deniliquin-Finley road on his way to Tuppal station. He turned down a droving position with the mob as he wanted the 30 shillings a week as a 'rousie' at Tuppal station to earn enough to 'go back to Bendigo—and to night school'. Following a short stint in the local branch of the Bank of Victoria, he joined the staff of the *Bendigo Independent* in 1914. He then worked on newspapers at Bathurst and Dubbo in New South Wales. At St Michael and St John's Catholic Cathedral, Bathurst, on 29 August 1919 he married Irene May Michelsen.

On 3 April 1926 O'Loghlen joined the Sydney staff of *Country Life and Stock and Station Journal* as a sub-editor; he was editor from 1 April 1942 until he retired in 1960. As 'Eurythmic', he produced authoritative articles on racing and horse-breeding; he also wrote on Rugby League and Union football for the *Daily Mail* and Sunday newspapers. He had a deep knowledge of breeding and bloodstock pedigrees. Although a keen follower of the turf, he was only a modest better, specializing in quinellas, which he won with great regularity. In 1945 he published *Champions of the Turf*, a book about Australian thoroughbreds.

O'Loghlen was the confidant of politicians and industry leaders. He made several tours to Britain and the United States of America in the interests of Australian stud stock. In

1954 he went to Britain to ascertain why that country was 'the stud farm of the world'. He interviewed studmasters 'from Cornwall to Inverness, from East Anglia to Hereford' and attended the famous Smithfield Show at Earls Court, London. On his return he wrote: 'Of all theories and practices that impressed me, line-breeding stood out pre-eminently. I have always thought it a sine quo [sic] non of good breeding, but have recognised that it must be done with discretion and judgment'. For fourteen years he travelled around Australia in the interest of the cattle industry with his friend and business associate Frank Johnston. Honorary editor for the Australian Poll Hereford Society, O'Loghlen published the highly regarded *Beef Cattle in Australia* (1948, second edition 1956) and, with Johnston, co-edited *Cattle Country* (1960). He also wrote an unpublished novel, 'The Vet's Victory'.

Forthright, energetic and intolerant of slackers, 'Old Frank' was well liked and respected for the professional advice he gave freely to many in the cattle industry: he made *Country Life* a leading stud-stock journal. Survived by his wife and three daughters, he died on 20 May 1964 at Roseville and was buried in Northern Suburbs cemetery. His only son Patrick had been killed in action over Italy in 1943 while serving with the Royal Australian Air Force.

Country Life, 26 Aug 1960, 22 May 1964; *Bulletin*, 10 Sept 1960; *Meat Industry Bulletin*, 7, June 1964; *SMH*, 22 May 1964; F. O'Loghlen, literary mss and notes (ML).   G. P. WALSH

OLSEN, OLAV TRYGVE (1890-1966), civil engineer, was born on 5 September 1890 at Søgne, near Kristiansand, Norway, son of Peter Olsen and his wife Anne Johanne, née Thomasdatter. Trygve attended Kristiansand Katedralskole, studied engineering (1908-11) at Bergen Tekniske Skole, and became a member (1912) of the Norwegian Society of Chartered Engineers. Employed by the consulting firm of Harald M. Irgens, he was engaged in the investigation, design and construction of several hydro-electricity projects, including the Samnanger, Dale and Osa schemes. In 1924 he took a job as a cook in the steel barque, *Svarvarnut*, and sailed for Australia. His wife Marie, née Schouw, whom he had married in 1918, and their son Lasse followed him by steamship.

Landing at Bunbury, Western Australia, in February 1925, Olsen made his way to Melbourne where he obtained a post as a civil investigations engineer with the State Electricity Commission of Victoria. Survey work for the proposed Kiewa hydro-electricity scheme was by then in progress. Olsen recommended that tunnels should be dug between the water-storages and power stations, and that the tunnels be unlined except where the rock was unsound. His proposal to use closed conduits instead of open channels meant that there would be no ice-blockages in winter; moreover, the operation would have greater flexibility 'as load could be picked up in the time it took to open a valve and bring a turbine up to speed'.

To facilitate hydrological and meteorological studies of the catchment area in the Victorian Alps, Olsen established a research-station on the Bogong High Plains. In 1932 he was naturalized. While resident engineer in charge of the station in 1932-34, he lived with his family in an isolated cottage forty miles (64 km) from Omeo. In winter Trygve skied to the sites of his gauges and instruments. Marie maintained a cosy home at which visitors were made welcome. Lasse did his schooling by correspondence. Olsen was over 6 ft 2 ins (188 cm) tall and weighed about 18 stone (114 kg). He was nicknamed 'Tiny'. Colleagues found him an affable man and a genial host. Posted to Melbourne, he took part in investigations into the Big Eildon scheme.

During World War II politicians and engineers in New South Wales and Victoria considered new plans for using the waters of the Snowy River for power and inland irrigation. About 1944 Olsen proposed diverting the waters of the Snowy to the Murray River by trans-mountain tunnel, thus increasing the project's power-generating potential. He was appointed to the hydro-electric sub-committee of the Commonwealth-States Technical Committee whose reports (1948-49) formed the basis of the Snowy Mountains scheme. In 1950 he joined the staff of the Snowy Mountains Hydro-electric Authority as chief investigating engineer. After retiring in September 1955, he returned to Norway. He died on 5 December 1966 at Stavanger; his wife and son survived him. The S.M.H.E.A. gave him 'a large share of the credit for the general conception' of the Snowy Mountains scheme and noted the passing of an 'imaginative and able' engineer.

G. Napier and G. Easdown, *The Kiewa Story* (Melb, 1993); Snowy Mountains Hydro-electric Authority, Eighteenth Annual Report for Year 1966-1967, *PP* (Cwlth), 1967, 5, p 808; *Snowy News*, no 78, 28 Feb 1967; A446/69 item 58/43782 (AA, Canb); information from Mr M. Lawrence and Mr G. Napier, Mount Beauty, Vic, and Mr M. Olsen, Peregian Beach, Qld.   DARRYL BENNET

O'MALLEY, LOUIS JAMES (1912-1975), public servant and explorer, was born on 23 January 1912 at Hunters Hill, Sydney, youngest of the three sons of native-born parents John Joseph O'Malley, storeman, and his wife Amelia Henrietta, née Nattey. His mother died in 1913. With his brothers, Jim was raised in Sydney by an aunt brought from Perth by their uncle James Thomas O'Malley, later commissioner for native affairs in Papua. The three boys attended Holy Cross College, Ryde, after which Jim worked briefly as a jackeroo near Orange.

Following an offer from Sir Hubert Murray [q.v.10], O'Malley visited Papua in 1929 and took up a temporary position under his uncle as inspector in the Department of Native Affairs. At Kikori in 1931 he met Jack Hides [q.v.9], who was gaining a reputation as an energetic 'outside man'. When O'Malley was appointed patrol officer in the magisterial branch in 1933, he was immediately assigned to accompany Hides to Kairuku. Their first patrol together that year, in the Kunimaipa Valley, won them commendations from Murray and the Prime Minister's Department, Canberra. In 1934 Murray chose Hides and O'Malley to explore the large region between the Strickland and Purari rivers.

The two explorers complemented each other: Hides was slight, O'Malley strongly built; Hides 'restless, impulsive and dashing', O'Malley calm and methodical. The patrol through the southern fringes of the Central Highlands endured harsh conditions and considerable loss of life, capturing the imagination of the press, which lionized Hides and O'Malley on their return to Australia. The quieter O'Malley shied away from the attention. Yet he showed enduring loyalty to Hides, who enjoyed the public adulation, though it was to earn him detractors in Papua.

O'Malley's postings to the stations from which he patrolled the difficult Kukukuku, Goilala and Kunimaipa areas in 1935-38 indicated the esteem in which his superiors held him. Between 1938 and 1940 he was transferred in turn to Misima, Samarai and Baniara. In 1941 he returned to patrol in Goilala, where he remained as assistant resident magistrate until he was mobilized in the Militia on 21 March 1942 as acting lieutenant, Australian New Guinea Administrative Unit. He patrolled extensively in the Kairuku and Kunimaipa areas, and transferred to the Australian Imperial Force in 1943. Promoted major in March 1945, he was placed on the Reserve of Officers on 16 November.

After World War II O'Malley was appointed district officer and magistrate in Port Moresby. There, on 23 June 1949 at the Church of Our Lady of the Rosary, he married Vere Pauline, whose father John Esmond Brien had been Murray's private secretary. Following his marriage, O'Malley was posted to Gulf District as district officer. He served at Kerema and Kikori. In 1958 he was appointed district commissioner, Manus District. He stayed there until he retired to Sydney in 1968. Survived by

his wife, two daughters and two sons, he died of acute myocardial infarction on 10 February 1975 at his Killarney Heights home and was buried in Northern Suburbs cemetery.

J. P. Sinclair, *The Outside Man* (Melb, 1969); F. West (ed), *Selected Letters of Hubert Murray* (Melb, 1970); E. L. Schieffelin and R. Crittenden, *Like People You See in a Dream* (Stanford, California, US, 1991); *PIM*, 22 May 1936, June 1942, July 1949; O'Malley's patrol reports (held by Mrs V. O'Malley, Killarney Heights, Syd).

CHRIS BALLARD

O'MAY, HENRY (1872-1962) and **GEORGE ELWIN** (1876-1956), ferrymasters, were born on 27 February 1872 and 17 June 1876 at Kangaroo Point (Bellerive), Tasmania, sons of Robert O'May (d.1900), a boatman from Scotland, and his wife Ann, née Roberts. Robert and his brothers Thomas and James established (c.1865) O'May Bros ferry service which plied between Hobart Town and Kangaroo Bay.

Harry attended Bellerive State School and Scotch College, Hobart, but left at the age of 11 to work as a wharf-boy. He gained his rivermaster's and engineer's certificates, and in 1889 became skipper of the *Silver Crown*, the firm's fifth vessel. In 1891 George joined O'May Bros as a deckhand. Following the deaths of Thomas and Robert O'May, James took over the management of the company; he was joined in partnership by Harry and George who inherited their father's share of the business. At Bellerive on 17 March 1902 Harry married with Presbyterian forms Frances Isobel Cottrell (d.1921), a 25-year-old dressmaker; they were to have three children.

In 1903 the firm bought the paddle-steamer, *Kangaroo*. This ship, affectionately known as 'The Twins' or 'Old Double Guts' because of her twin hull, carried both passengers and vehicles. Harry was her master. George, who had skippered *Silver Crown*, took charge of the newly built *Derwent* in 1905. A double-ended vessel certified to carry 590 passengers, she cost £6000 and was to make 250 000 river crossings. George married Emily Lavinia Clark with Congregational forms on 2 December 1907 at Nubeena. In 1912, after O'May Bros merged with Rosny Estates, the company acquired 668 acres (270 ha) between Kangaroo Bay and Lindisfarne Bay. Rosny Estates & Ferry Co. hoped to increase patronage of its ferries by encouraging settlement through the sale of cheap land.

James O'May retired in 1921. Harry succeeded him as manager and George became master of the *Kangaroo*. Following the failure of its land sales, the company went into liquidation in 1926. Harry and George reconstructed their old firm as O'May Bros Pty Ltd.

In February 1927 they established a ferry service from Bellerive to Hobart and two years later bought out their main rival, the Reemere Steamship Co. On 6 November 1929 at Chalmers Church, Hobart, Harry married 52-year-old Maud Isabell Fraser. The Tasmanian parliament passed legislation in 1937 which gave the Hobart Bridge Co. Ltd 'sole right of transport across the River Derwent'. On 1 May 1939, when O'May Bros was taken over by that company, Harry and George retired. George died on 30 December 1956 in Royal Hobart Hospital and was cremated; his son and daughter survived him.

Harry O'May published *Wrecks in Tasmanian Waters* (1955), *Wooden Hookers of Hobart Town* (1957) and *Hobart River Craft* (1959). He was a foundation member of the Shiplovers' Society of Tasmania and the Bellerive Yacht Club, patron of the Bellerive Regatta Association, a member (from 1941) of the Royal Society of Tasmania and a trustee of the Narryna Folk Museum. Survived by the son and two daughters of his first marriage, he died on 15 May 1962 in his Bellerive home and was cremated.

The Tasmanian Cyclopedia (Hob, 1931); D. G. O'May, *Ferries of the Derwent* (Hob, 1988); W. T. Davenport, *Spirit of Clarence* (Hob, 1989); Bellerive Hist Soc, *Bellerive Heritage*, vols 1-4 (Hob, 1993-96); *Mercury* (Hob), 16, 18 May 1962; *Examiner* (Launc), 26 May, 2 June 1962.   DAVID DILGER

O'NEILL, JOSEPHINE (1905-1968), journalist and film critic, was born on 15 December 1905 at Dunedin, New Zealand, eldest of four children of Eugene Joseph O'Neill, a New Zealand-born medical practitioner, and his wife Josephine, née Monaghan, who came from England. Young Josephine was educated at St Dominic's College (until 1916) and the University of Otago (B.A., N.Z., 1927). In 1929, soon after her arrival in Sydney, she published nursery rhymes and short stories in local newspapers. She contributed a short story in 1932 to the first issue of *Ink*, edited by Constance Robertson [q.v.11] to raise money for the friendly fund of the Society of Women Writers of New South Wales. O'Neill was appointed a reporter on the *Sun* newspaper that year and moved to the *Telegraph* in 1934.

From 1936, when Consolidated Press Ltd relaunched the *Telegraph* as the *Daily Telegraph*, intending it to be a serious newspaper 'with an independent policy and modern outlook', Josephine O'Neill began to develop her style as a critical reviewer, analysing films as an art-form different from books or the theatre. While she continued to provide unsigned book reviews and items for 'entertainment news' columns, in her critiques she considered whether a film—within its particu-

lar genre—succeeded on the levels of plot, structure, subject matter and the development of its characters. She was forthright about actors' performances, interested in the use of special cinematographic and production techniques, and aware of one film's legacy to another.

Active within the Australian Journalists' Association, O'Neill was, at various times, a member of its house committee at the *Daily Telegraph*, and of the State branch of the A.J.A.'s ethics committee which adjudicated on complaints against member journalists who breached the association's code. She was invited to speak about films to many groups, including radio and television audiences and the Workers' Educational Association. In 1951 she wrote for the short-lived Melbourne magazine, *Woman's Day and Home*. With three others, among them the journalist Elizabeth Riddell, she sat on the panel in Harry Dearth's [q.v.13] radio programme, 'Leave it to the Girls' (1951-55): they offered solutions to problems and questions sent in by listeners. Moving to the *Sydney Morning Herald* in 1957, O'Neill reviewed films and theatre; she also wrote an annual critique of the year's best movies, substantial articles on a range of issues not always to do with cinema, and a regular column, 'Show Business', in the *Sun-Herald*.

Noted for her intelligence, erect posture and dull, plain clothes, Josephine O'Neill made people feel that they had to behave in her company. She wore very thick glasses—her trademark—which led her friends to quip that she was the 'only blind film critic in Australia'. She collapsed and died of myocardial infarction on 28 February 1968 in Castlereagh Street, Sydney, and was buried with Catholic rites in Northern Suburbs cemetery. One obituarist noted that she had been 'something of a legendary figure as a film critic'.

D. Collins, *Hollywood Down Under* (Syd, 1987); I. Bertrand (ed), *Cinema in Australia* (Syd, 1989); *Journalist*, Apr 1968; Aust Journalists' Assn (NSW), *Annual Report and Balance Sheet*, 1930-68; *SMH*, 29 Feb 1968; information from the late Ms E. Riddell.
                JULIA HORNE

O'NEILL, MARTHA MARY (1878-1972), Sister of Mercy and schoolteacher, was born on 18 November 1878 at Cork, County Cork, Ireland, eldest child of William O'Neill, accountant, and his wife Hannah, née O'Regan. The family emigrated to Victoria in 1886 and settled at Kyneton. William worked as a driver for the local brewery. 'Mattie' was educated at the Convent of Mercy girls' school, Kyneton, and taught (from 1898) at St Bridget's School, Maldon. On 26 April

1899 she entered the Institute of Our Lady of Mercy, Geelong. She was professed on 17 February 1903 and took the religious name Patricia.

Transferred to Melbourne, Sister Patricia taught in primary schools at Coburg and North Melbourne before returning to Geelong in 1906. After she had been registered to teach at both primary and secondary levels, she gave classes at the Sacred Heart College and demonstration lessons for Sisters who were training to be teachers. She enrolled as an external student at the University of Melbourne; although she completed the requirements for a diploma of education (1917) and a bachelor of arts degree (1919), she did not have them conferred. In 1917 she became acting-principal of the Mater Misericordiae Novitiate and Training College, Ascot Vale, and head of St Brendan's Infant School, Flemington. Her methods were influenced by watching experienced teachers in state schools and by observing a course at Mary Lush's [q.v.] kindergarten, Carlton. By 1935 she was principal of the training college: she taught all day and gave lectures after hours. In the Ascot Vale convent she was superior of the religious community.

In 1939 Sister Patricia was elected mother-general of the Sisters of Mercy in Victoria and Tasmania, comprising some four hundred members in forty houses. She made the welfare of the communities and the schools her chief priority. Faced with scant resources and large numbers of postwar immigrants, parish priests turned to her for help in staffing their schools. While she acceded to many requests, she worried that her Sisters were being overworked. The Congregation's income was meagre and the community lived in austere conditions, but Mother Patricia never cut down on meals. She adopted a flexible approach to discipline, allowing the nuns relaxation and outings. Her sense of humour and repartee lightened many situations.

During 1953 the Sisters of Mercy in Australia, then in fifteen autonomous groups, were invited to unite under a central administration. Eight groups joined the Australian Union of the Sisters of Mercy. Mother Patricia, a leader in the movement for union, was appointed (1954) superior-general. She lived in St Anne's convent, Canberra, and regularly visited each convent in the union. In 1955, responding to the call of a priest in the Territory of Papua and New Guinea, she commissioned a band of nuns who volunteered to serve as missionaries in that country. She had a wing added (1961) to the convent to cater for Sisters who wished to study in Canberra. In 1966 she retired to the convent at Geelong, Victoria. She died on 25 November 1972 in St Joseph's Hospital, Newtown, and was buried in the convent's cemetery.

M. M. O'Brien, *Mother Mary Patricia O'Neill* (Melb, 1976); *Mercy Teachers' College* (Melb, 1984); M. G. Allen, *The Labourers' Friends* (Melb, 1989); *Advocate* (Melb), 21 Dec 1972; Sisters of Mercy Archives (held at Congregation Centre, Alphington, Melb).   MAREE G. ALLEN

O'NEILL, PATRICK (1886-1968), Christian Brother and schoolteacher, was born on 2 September 1886 at Drumwood, County Tipperary, Ireland, one of eleven children of Owen O'Neill, farmer, and his wife Winifred, née English. Patrick attended a nearby National school. On 29 June 1901 he entered the novitiate of St Mary's Provincialate of the Christian Brothers, Marino, Dublin, and took the religious name of Gildas. He taught for almost four years at St Aloysius', Dundalk, St Vincent's Orphanage, Glasnevin, and Our Lady's Mount, Cork.

Fulfilling a private vow that, if he became a Brother, he would volunteer for the mission field, O'Neill sailed for Australia, reaching Melbourne in the *Omrah* in August 1906. He taught at St Peter and Paul's School, South Melbourne, until the end of that year before being sent to St Francis's School, Elizabeth Street, Melbourne. As a junior Christian Brother, he was transferred from place to place as the need arose. After terms at Ballarat and at a 'practising school' at Burwood, Sydney, he was appointed superior at Balmain in 1913. In his five years there he overcame considerable financial difficulties to renovate the buildings and grounds. He was known as 'a strong teacher'.

O'Neill was next based at Christian Brothers' College, Wakefield Street, Adelaide, where he suffered a detached retina. Following a period of rest at St Mary's Provincialate, Strathfield, Sydney, he was regarded as sufficiently fit in 1921 to be made superior of St Vincent de Paul's Boys Catholic Orphanage, South Melbourne. On 21 June 1926 he bent down to get some money from a drawer in his office at the orphanage. On straightening up, he found that he had completely lost his sight. He retired from St Vincent's in January 1927. Three months afterwards, he travelled to Lourdes, France, hoping for a miraculous cure. He 'became patiently resigned to the will of God'.

That year O'Neill joined the Catholic Braille Writers' Association (later the Villa Maria Society for the Blind), St Kilda, Melbourne. Members transcribed religious books into braille, befriended the blind, and escorted them on their trips to the Victorian Eye and Ear Hospital. In 1931 O'Neill became president of the association; he was to hold office until his death. Under his vigorous full-time leadership the Villa Maria Hostel for the Blind was opened at Prahran in 1938, the Villa

Madonna Hostel for the Blind was established at Windsor in 1948 and St Paul's School for Blind Boys was founded at Kew in 1957.

Often referred to as 'the Blind Brother', O'Neill was a good and courageous man. In 1957 he was appointed M.B.E. Well groomed and courteous, he made his way alone around Melbourne, using public transport. He had remarkable business acumen and 'could charm a bird off a tree', both considerable advantages in his expansion of the Villa Maria Society. O'Neill died on 14 October 1968 at Windsor and was buried at Edmund Rice College, Bundoora. A nursing home, Villa O'Neill, built at Prahran in 1972, was named after him.

K. D. Kane, *The Origin and Growth of the Villa Maria Society for the Blind* (Melb, 1975); D. N. Gallagher (ed), *Christian Brothers' High School, Thames Street, Balmain* (Syd, 1987); P. L. Reynolds, *On Balmain Hill* (Syd, 1988); *Southern Cross* (Melb), 12 Jan 1951, pp 7, 9; Christian Brothers Archives, Parkville, Melb; information from Fr F. Richards, Balwyn, and Bro L. Kelty, East Melb.

KATHLEEN DUNLOP KANE*

ONUS, WILLIAM TOWNSEND (1906-1968), Aboriginal political activist and entrepreneur, was born on 15 November 1906 at Cumeroogunga (Cummeragunja) Aboriginal reserve on the banks of the Murray River, New South Wales, eldest child of William Townsend Onus, drover, and his wife Maud Mary, née Nelson, both of the Wiradjuri people. Bill attended Thomas James's [q.v.14] school at Cumeroogunga until he was 10 and had two further years schooling at Echuca before the family went droving in the Riverina, travelling in a covered wagon. He left home at 16 to go shearing, a trade he followed for the next seven years. At St Andrew's Presbyterian Church, West Wyalong, on 12 May 1928 he married Bella Elizabeth Patten; they were to be divorced in 1941.

In 1929 Onus moved to Sydney. He first worked as a rigger at the Bankstown aerodrome. As jobs diminished during the Depression, he prospected around Bega, then returned to Sydney and drove delivery trucks. A member of the Australian Workers' Union since his droving days, he came under the influence of Michael Olaf Sawtell, a radical unionist who coached him in public speaking. In 1939 Onus joined the Aborigines Progressive Association, formed in 1937 by William Ferguson and John Patten [qq.v.8,11]. Ferguson regarded him as the type of activist the movement needed to achieve citizenship rights for Aborigines and improve living conditions on the reserves. Onus soon became the association's secretary.

From 1941 he worked full time for the association. In the early 1940s he emerged as a principal member of the Committee for Aboriginal Citizen Rights, a body campaigning to reform the Aborigines Welfare Board of New South Wales. The restructuring of the board in 1943 to introduce Aboriginal representation, and Ferguson's election to it in 1944 against official opposition, reflected Onus's skills as an organizer and tactician. He used his trade-union and political contacts to advantage, lobbying politicians and the press to support A.P.A. causes. During this period Onus also worked to foster a sense of community among the disparate Aboriginal families who had migrated to Redfern from rural districts. He organized a weekly dance and used the profits to cover the legal expenses of Aborigines brought before the local courts.

About 1946 Onus moved to Melbourne, where he was employed as a shipping clerk. On 10 June 1947 he married Mary McLintock Kelly at the office of the government statist, Queen Street. Their only child William McLintock Onus later established a reputation as the artist Lin Onus. Among the former Cumeroogunga residents who had settled in Melbourne was pastor (Sir) Douglas Nicholls, with whom Onus and his brother Eric revived the Australian Aborigines League. Both Onus and Nicholls were forceful orators. From the mid-1940s they appeared as guest speakers at public rallies, meetings of community groups and on radio. They used such forums to promote the cause of Aboriginal citizenship rights and civil liberties. With other prominent Aborigines, they formed a nucleus around which the Aborigines Advancement League (Victoria) was to form in 1957.

By the early 1950s Onus was disillusioned with politics. A campaign he and Nicholls had waged in the late 1940s had failed to dissuade the Federal government from constructing the Woomera rocket-testing range on land in South Australia which they regarded as Aboriginal. In 1949 Onus organized and accompanied a twenty-member deputation of Aborigines from New South Wales and Victoria to visit H. V. Johnson [q.v.14], the minister for the interior: the delegation requested a number of civil rights, but gained few significant concessions. Later that year Onus enthusiastically supported Ferguson's unsuccessful campaign as an Independent Aboriginal candidate for the House of Representatives seat of Lawson.

After these disappointments Onus gave up politics (for about fifteen years) to concentrate on his emerging business interests. In 1952 he established Aboriginal Enterprise Novelties to produce boomerangs, woomeras, fabrics and greeting cards imprinted with Aboriginal motifs. He ran it from his small factory and shop at Belgrave in the Dandenong Ranges. To promote his wares he toured widely in Victoria and beyond as a travelling showman, giving demonstrations of boomerang-throwing, which he advocated as a national sport. By the late 1950s he was better known as a boomerang-thrower than he had been as a political activist. He made an occasional public comment, as in 1956 when he attacked (Sir) Paul Hasluck, minister for territories, over the wages paid to Aborigines in the Northern Territory, pointing out that they received only one-eighth of the basic wage.

Onus had appeared in minor Aboriginal roles in several Australian films—*Uncivilised* (1936), *Lovers and Luggers* (1937) and *The Overlanders* (1946). In 1962 he compered the Australian Broadcasting Commission's *Alcheringa* series, twelve short documentary films about traditional Aboriginal life. He also appeared, with Nicholls, in *Forgotten People* (1967), a film which documented Aboriginal living conditions in the Goulburn and Murray valleys.

In 1967 Bill Onus became the first Aboriginal president of the Aborigines Advancement League (Victoria) and its representative on the Victorian Aborigines Welfare Board. He served as Victorian director of the Aboriginal referendum movement, playing a leading role in the campaign for a 'Yes' vote at the 1967 referendum. Following a coronary occlusion, he died on 10 January 1968 at Deepdene and was cremated; his wife and son survived him, as did a daughter of his first marriage.

J. Horner, *Vote Ferguson for Aboriginal Freedom* (Syd, 1974); Aborigines Advancement League of Vic, *Forgotten People*, film (1967) and *Smoke Signals*, Apr 1968, p 16; I. Howie-Willis, 'Onus, W' in D. Horton (ed), *The Encyclopaedia of Aboriginal Australia*, 2 (Canb, 1994); ABC Television, *Alcheringa*, film series, 1962; *Age* (Melb), 11 Jan 1968.   IAN HOWIE-WILLIS

OOM, KARL ERIK (1904-1972), naval officer, was born on 27 May 1904 at Chatswood, Sydney, fourth child of Gustaf Peter Ludwig August Oom, a draftsman from Sweden, and his English-born wife May Isabel, née Le Guay. In 1918 Karl entered the Royal Australian Naval College, Jervis Bay, Federal Capital Territory, as a cadet midshipman. Noted for his individuality and physical fitness, he graduated in 1921. He trained at sea and completed courses in England before returning to Australia in March 1926.

Commencing his career in the R.A.N.'s Hydrographic Branch, Oom joined the survey ship, H.M.A.S. *Moresby*, in May that year. In July 1927 he was promoted lieutenant. He gained respect for his initiative and ability to handle boats, and for the speed and accuracy of his work. These qualities led to his selection as a member of Sir Douglas Mawson's

[q.v.10] British, Australian and New Zealand Antarctic Research Expedition (1930-31), on which his surveys and cartography proved valuable.

In 1932-34 Oom was on loan to the Royal Navy, serving in H.M.S. *Challenger*. He spent most of the next five years either aboard H.M.A.S. *Moresby* or with detached boat-parties, surveying Torres Strait and the seas off Queensland, the Northern Territory, Papua and the Mandated Territory of New Guinea. Again with the R.N. in 1939, he was posted to H.M.S. *Franklin*. On 17 June that year at the register office, Hammersmith, London, he married Evelyn Margaret Stewart Mocatta, née Jeffrey, a 29-year-old divorcee; they were to remain childless. From February 1941 to January 1942 he commanded H.M.S. *Gleaner* and performed well in anti-submarine and escort operations in the North Sea.

Returning to Australia, Oom was posted to command H.M.A.S. *Whyalla* in November 1942. He was ordered to produce reliable charts for ships involved in the allied offensives in Papua and New Guinea. While off Cape Nelson, Papua, on 2 January 1943, *Whyalla* was repeatedly bombed. Spray from near misses washed survey sheets and the plotting-board over the ship's side; the work had to be immediately and painstakingly redone. Oom transferred to *Shepparton* in May 1943 and was promoted commander in June.

Two months later he was appointed officer-in-charge of the Hydrographic Branch and commander, Task Group 70.5, which was responsible for survey operations in the South-West Pacific Area. He sailed in various ships to find and mark safe passages for allied landings in New Guinea, the Philippines and Borneo. For his achievements he won the Gill memorial award of the Royal Geographical Society, London, in 1945, and was appointed O.B.E. and to the United States of America's Legion of Merit in the same year. In March 1945 he conducted a survey off Zamboanga, Philippines, under enemy fire for which he was awarded the U.S.A.'s Bronze Star Medal (1947).

After the war, Oom helped to formulate a new policy by which the Naval Board—through the senior officer, Hydrographic Service—became the charting authority for waters around Australia and the Territory of Papua-New Guinea. From May 1946 he commanded H.M.A.S. *Warrego*. In November 1947 he was appointed to command H.M.A.S. *Wyatt Earp* and to take charge of Antarctic surveys. Captain W. F. Cook described him as a self-assured, imperturbable and splendid seaman, with an impish sense of humour; in other regards Cook found him an enigmatic man who kept his own counsel.

From April 1948 Oom again headed the Hydrographic Branch. He was passed over for promotion to captain in 1951 and in December returned to sea in *Warrego*. In poor health, he was posted ashore in February 1952 and invalided from the navy on 30 October. A widower, he married Jean Miriam Kearney, née Wells, a 42-year-old divorcee, on 14 March 1955 at the registrar general's office, Sydney. They retired to the south coast. Oom suffered from cirrhosis of the liver. He died of pulmonary thrombosis on 22 June 1972 at his Turlinjah home and was buried with Anglican rites in Moruya cemetery. His wife survived him.

F. B. Eldridge, *A History of the Royal Australian Naval College* (Melb, 1949); G. H. Gill, *Royal Australian Navy 1942-1945* (Canb, 1968); A. Savours, *The Voyages of the Discovery* (Lond, 1992); R. J. Hardstaff, *Leadline to Laser* (Syd, 1995); P. G. Law, *The Antarctic Voyage of HMAS Wyatt Earp* (Syd, 1995); *Aust Women's Weekly*, 14 Apr 1945, 8 Nov 1947; *Navy* (Syd), Jan 1948, p 12, May 1949, p 18; *People* (Syd), 15 July 1953, p 17; *Naval Hist Review*, Dec 1978, p 5; A3978/10, K. E. Oom (AA, Canb); information from Capt W. F. Cook, Woollahra, Cmdr R. J. Hardstaff, Northwood, and Mr M. C. Hordern, Warrawee, Syd.   J. S. COMPTON

OPAS, DAVID LOUIS (1936-1980), judge, was born on 30 June 1936 at Waverley, Sydney, son of London-born parents Maurice Opas, commercial traveller, and his wife Bessie, née Hart. Maurice served as a ship's canteen manager and died when H.M.A.S. *Sydney* was sunk in 1941. Educated as a Legacy ward at Sydney Grammar School (1947-53), David did well in English and history, and represented the school at debating. He worked as an articled clerk with the solicitors Pike & Pike, studied part time at the University of Sydney and passed the Barristers' Admission Board examinations. On 26 July 1963 he was admitted to the New South Wales Bar.

As a young barrister, Opas soon established his reputation and moved into chambers in Macquarie Street. Although small, he had a powerful and strikingly modulated speaking voice. He built up a successful practice, dealing initially with criminal and family matters and later exclusively with family law. On 17 December 1970 at the registrar general's office, Sydney, he married Kristin Mary Bisset, née Deck, a 29-year-old assistant-pharmacist and a divorcee. Opas was a devoted husband and father who lived for his family and his work. His interests included reading, listening to classical music and playing tennis.

Opas became known for his humane and patient approach to the law. On 27 October 1977 he was appointed a judge of the Family Court of Australia. He sat at Parramatta. The Family Law Act (1975) required proceedings to be conducted without robes and with minimum formality. Focusing on basic issues, Opas was intolerant of garrulous counsel and of litigants who tried to use the court as a platform for their prejudices.

About 7 p.m. on 23 June 1980, while having dinner with his family, Opas answered a call at the security gate to the courtyard of his Woollahra home. When he opened the gate, he was shot in the abdomen by a single bullet from a .22-inch (5.6 mm) calibre rifle. He died that night in St Vincent's Hospital, Darlinghurst, and was buried with Jewish rites in Rookwood cemetery; his wife, son and daughter survived him. Despite an extensive investigation by the police, his murderer has not been brought to justice. Opas's murder came as a blow to the Australian judiciary: it was thought to be the first occasion in which a judge was killed while holding office in Sydney.

Justice R. S. Watson, Opas's colleague, said of him: 'We miss his infectious laugh, his quick wit, his clear insight, his sheer joy in all things beautiful, lively and challenging, his deep compassion for all people'. Senator Peter Durack, the Commonwealth attorney-general, declared that Opas had met the onerous demands of family law work. These opinions of Opas were widely shared.

Aust Law J, 54, Sept 1980, p 566; *Aust Family Law Cases*, 1980, p xxvii; *SMH*, 28 Oct 1977, 5 Mar 1982; *Sun-Herald*, 13 July 1980.   E. R. BAKER
                                                      P. I. ROSE

OPPEN, MARGARET (1890-1975), artist and embroiderer, was born on 8 July 1890 at Newcastle, New South Wales, daughter of William Arnott, baker, and his wife Mary Eleanor, née Dixon. William Arnott [q.v.3] was her grandfather. Margaret's parents travelled often between Australia and Britain, and she attended school in both countries. Later, she trained at Julian Ashton's [q.v.7] Sydney Art School, and in London at the Slade School of Fine Art and the Grosvenor School of Modern Art. Her woodcut, 'The Backyard', was reproduced in *Art in Australia* in 1924 and some of her linocuts were exhibited at the Younger Group of Australian Artists' 1925 exhibition in Sydney.

At the register office, Steyning, Sussex, England, on 13 April 1928 Margaret married Hans Oppen (d.1972), a man of independent means. With her husband and two sons, she returned to Sydney in 1935. During World War II she assisted with occupational therapy through the Australian Red Cross Society. Becoming interested in embroidery, she worked with Dora Sweetapple and Ann Rees at the Double Bay studio of the Society of Arts and Crafts. In 1949 she held a joint exhibition with her friend Ethleen Palmer before again travelling to London. She studied at the Royal School of Needlework and joined the Embroiderers' Guild.

Back in Sydney, in 1955 Mrs Oppen established the Redleaf Studio at her Wahroonga home where she painted and taught design. She and a few friends determined to set up a branch of the Embroiderers' Guild. After many requests, a letter to its patron, Queen Mary, eventually produced the necessary acceptance by the London guild. In 1957 Margaret Oppen became foundation president of the New South Wales branch. Beginning as a small group sharing a common interest and meeting regularly at her Wahroonga studio, it flourished and soon needed larger premises in central Sydney. A pattern was set of monthly meetings, lectures, classes and advice.

Oppen's work was usually done in simple stitches, directly onto material, without sketch or pattern. She believed that 'the needle can be as much an art medium as the pencil and as creative as the painter's brush'. With Patricia Langford, she produced a book for designers and embroiderers, *Paper Cuts* (1964). In 1966 and 1973 she exhibited paintings and embroideries at the guild rooms. A tall, stylish woman with a direct gaze, she could be intimidating on occasions, but was 'cheerful and dauntless', and highly respected by her fellow members. She refused to accept the words 'I can't', and encouraged her pupils to say 'I'll try'. In 1967 she retired as president, but remained active in the guild's work.

Generous in all things large and small, Oppen always provided biscuits for meetings that she attended, and used her considerable personal, social and financial resources unstintingly in the service of the guild, which she endowed with $3000 in 1969. The Embroiderers' Guild N.S.W. was incorporated in 1971. Margaret Oppen was awarded the British Empire Medal in 1973. Survived by her sons, she died on 17 June 1975 at Royal North Shore Hospital and was cremated. The E.G.N.S.W. named a prize in her honour. Her self-portrait is held by the guild.

Grosvenor Galleries, catalogue Oppen-Palmer exhibition 1949; G. Cochrane, *The Crafts Movement in Australia* (Syd, 1992); *Art in Aust*, Oct 1924; *Aust Women's Weekly*, 4 Oct 1947, 17 Jan 1968; Embroiders Guild, NSW, *Monthly Record*, Apr 1966, Sept 1970, Mar, Apr 1973, Aug 1975, July 1987; *SMH*, 16 Oct 1949, 2 June 1973; information from Mrs P. Langford, Mt Colah, and Mr C. Oppen, Hunters Hill, Syd.　　　RACHEL GRAHAME

ORD, CHARLES ANDREW (1905-1977), banker and stockbroker, was born on 16 June 1905 at Cooma, New South Wales, second child of George William Ord, a bank manager from England, and his native-born wife Grace Elizabeth, née Aiken. Charles spent his childhood mainly in country towns—Cooma, Ulmarra, Maclean and Lismore—before attending (1919-21) Cranbrook School, Sydney. Following his father, he joined (1922) the Australian Bank of Commerce; after the bank was taken over in 1931, he continued with the Bank of New South Wales. He studied accountancy part time and became an associate of the Commonwealth Institute of Accountants. A good cricketer, he also played Rugby Union football for Eastern Suburbs.

At All Saints Church, Woollahra, on 25 June 1932 Ord married with Anglican rites Marjorie Vivienne Elizabeth Lord, a 27-year-old nurse; they were to live at Darling Point. In 1923 he had joined the Militia. On 1 October 1939 he began full-time duty as major, Royal Australian Artillery. Transferred to the Australian Imperial Force in August 1942, he was promoted lieutenant colonel in September. He served in Sydney (1939-42 and 1943-45), Darwin (1942) and Fremantle (1945), commanding coastal artillery and performing staff and instructional duties. In September 1945 he transferred to the Retired List. An assistant (1946-49) to the central inspector of the Bank of N.S.W., Ord helped in the bank's battle against nationalization. In May 1949 he resigned from the bank and joined the Sydney Stock Exchange (committee-member 1966-69).

A tall (6 ft 1 in., 185 cm), imposing man, with piercing blue eyes and a jutting chin, Ord had a forceful personality. Some people were terrified of him; others thought him extroverted and boisterous; family and friends found him kind, fun-loving and courageous, with a zest for life. All agreed that his strengths were his recognition of talent and his receptiveness to ideas. He enjoyed being in authority: honest and straightforward, he insisted on integrity. J. A. M. Minnett, a friend from army days and an experienced broker, joined him in the partnership in 1951, but it was Ord who was the driving force in extending the range of business. He built up a strong firm which combined academically qualified staff and experienced brokers. Ord & Minnett set up a research service (1953) and investment trusts, underwrote several important company flotations, including Lend Lease Corporation Ltd (1958) and Pioneer Sugar Mills Ltd (1960), and entered the semi-government and corporate debenture markets. Ord frequently travelled abroad to make new business connexions.

Strengthened by the acquisitions of A. W. Harvey Lowe & Co. (1960) and T. J. Thompson & Sons (1964), the firm was renamed (1964) Ord, Minnett, T. J. Thompson & Partners and developed into one of Australia's leading brokerage businesses. In 1961 Ord had helped to establish the investment bank, Darling & Co. With Bankers' Trust Co., New York, the firm formed in 1969 (and Ord chaired until 1973) a new merchant bank, Ord-BT Co. Ltd. During the 1960s Ord had been nominated by the Commonwealth government to attend meetings of the World Bank as an observer. In June 1970 he reluctantly retired from Ord Minnett and received a record $85 000 for his stock-exchange seat. It was a mark of Charles Ord's achievements that Ord Minnett was soundly based and survived several stock-market crashes when other firms collapsed.

Ord was appointed M.B.E. in 1975. He was State chairman (1970-71) of the National Heart Foundation of Australia, and a generous benefactor to charities, among them the (Royal) Guide Dogs for the Blind Associations of Australia, the New South Wales Society for Crippled Children, and Royal Prince Alfred Hospital. Vice-president of the State branch of the National Parks and Wildlife Foundation, he was a delegate (1970) to the congress of the World Wildlife Fund, London. He belonged to Royal Sydney Golf Club, and was a Freemason (past master of Lodge Army and Navy), a councillor (1953-68) of Cranbrook, and president (1953-54) of the Old Cranbrookians' Association. (Sir) Russell Drysdale was a friend; Ord bought his painting, 'The Sunday Walk'.

Survived by his wife and two daughters, Ord died on 31 March 1977 at R.P.A.H., Camperdown, and was cremated. His portrait by Jeffrey Smart is held by the family.

R. F. Holder, *Bank of New South Wales* (Syd, 1970); S. Salsbury and K. Sweeney, *Sydney Stockbrokers* (Syd, 1992); R. J. White and C. Clarke, *Cheques and Balances* (Melb, 1995); *Cranbrookian*, June 1977, p 95; *SMH*, 3 Jan 1933, 14 June 1975; *Aust Financial Review*, 20 Aug 1963; Cranbrook School, Syd, archives; information from Mrs E. McCabe, Paddington, Sir Robert Norman, Woollahra, Mr M. Gleeson-White, Woollahra, Mr J. Rothery, Mosman, and Mrs J. Yule, Woollahra, Syd.

KAY SWEENEY

ORR, JOHN (1885-1966), professor of linguistics, was born on 4 June 1885 at Egremont, Cumberland, England, eldest of five children of Peter Orr, joiner, and his wife Lillias Duncan, née Allan. In that year the family emigrated to Australia, settling first at Albany, Western Australia, and then at Launceston, Tasmania. John attended Charles Street School and the High School, Launceston. In 1902 he enrolled at the University of Tasmania. After winning a Rhodes scholarship in April 1905, he entered Balliol College, Oxford (B.A., 1910; B.Litt., 1913).

In 1909 Orr was troubled by ill health. Advised to winter in France, he discovered both an affinity for the language and a future wife. On 5 March 1910 he married Augusta Berthe Brisac (d.1961), daughter of an expatriate French family who were living in St Petersburg. He completed his *licence ès lettres* at the Sorbonne in 1911. Appointed assistant-lecturer in French at Victoria University of Manchester, England, in 1913, he later taught (1915) at the East London College, University of London. In 1916-18, as a second lieutenant in the British Army, he performed intelligence duties with the Admiralty and in France. Returning to the University of Manchester, he held (from 1919) the chair of French language before becoming professor of French at the University of Edinburgh in 1933.

Orr's most penetrating work was in linguistic geography, historical phonetics and etymology. Particularly interested in the mechanism of homonymic collisions, he composed some fascinating studies on the perturbations caused by the clash of obscene and scabrous words with their homonyms. His approach was humanistic, marked by modesty and an engaging sense of humour. He published *Old French and Modern English Idiom* (Oxford, 1962) and two volumes of collected articles, *Words and Sounds in English and French* (Oxford, 1953) and *Essais d'Étymologie et de Philologie Françaises* (Paris, 1963). Appointed to the Légion d'honneur, he was elected a fellow of the British Academy (1952) and awarded honorary doctorates by the universities of Manchester (1938), Caen, France (1945), and St Andrews, Scotland (1955).

Six ft 4 ins (193 cm) tall, with a long, square-jawed face, Orr was a good athlete, a talented artist, and a collector of paintings. He returned only once to Tasmania, in 1928, and contributed to a debate in the *Mercury* about the role of academics in university government. His letter of 12 November that year was courteous and judicious, but was deemed 'paternalistic' by lay members of the council of the University of Tasmania. Over twenty-six years later, the issue was decided by a royal commission, precipitated by another letter to the *Mercury* composed by Orr's homonym, the professor of philosophy Sydney Sparkes Orr [q.v.].

John Orr retired from the University of Edinburgh in 1955. He was president of the Modern Humanities Research Association (1954) and the Fédération Internationale des Langues et Littératures Modernes (1963-66) at Cambridge; he also presided over the Association Internationale des Études Françaises (1955-57) and the Société de Linguistique Romane (1965) in Paris. Orr died on 10 August 1966 at the Royal Infirmary, Edinburgh. His son (and only child) had been killed in June 1944 while serving with the Royal Air Force.

Studies in Romance Philology and French Litera-ture Presented to John Orr by Pupils, Colleagues and Friends (Manchester, Eng, 1953); *Orbis*, 1, 1952; *Student*, Apr 1953; British Academy (Lond), *Procs*, 52, 1967; *Revue de Linguistique Romane*, 31, 1967; *Examiner* (Launc), 6 July 1938, 13 Aug 1966; *The Times*, 15 Aug 1966; papers held by, and information from, Mr A. Orr, Launc, Tas.   I. H. SMITH

ORR, SYDNEY SPARKES (1914-1966), philosopher, claimed to have been born on 6 December 1914 at Belfast, Ireland, son of Tedford Orr, blacksmith, and his wife Elizabeth. However, in giving evidence before the Supreme Court of Tasmania in October 1956, he said: 'My birth is a mystery. It has been a source of great distress to me all my life. I do not know whether my purported parents are my real parents, whether I am adopted or illegitimate'.

Educated at Bedford College and Queen's University of Belfast, Sydney graduated with first-class honours in philosophy (B.A., 1939; M.A., 1941). At Cooke Centenary Church on 22 September 1941 he married Sarah David-son with Presbyterian forms. While employed at Queen's as an assistant-lecturer (1939-44) in philosophy, he began in 1942 to study for his doctorate on 'the relationship between virtue and knowledge in Plato', but was never awarded the degree. He held a temporary assistant-lectureship (from 1944) in the de-partment of logic and metaphysics, University of St Andrews, Scotland.

In 1946 Orr was appointed acting-lecturer in the department of philosophy, University of Melbourne; in the following year he obtained a permanent lectureship. While awaiting his wife's arrival, he formed an intimate relation-ship with a young woman who bore him a child. She later lived with the Orrs in a *ménage à trois*. The affair ended while Orr was still in Melbourne. In 1952 he was appointed professor of philosophy at the University of Tasmania. The choice was surprising, as Orr had published little, and was not as highly regarded as some other applicants for the chair, but he had the support of the chancellor Sir John Morris [q.v.], who believed that he would contribute to adult education in the community and who wanted a philosopher untainted by logical positivism.

During his tenure of the chair Orr played a significant role in seeking reform of an out-dated university administrative structure. The university council was seen by many staff members to be both interfering and obstruc-tionist, involving itself in matters that were properly the concern of academics and not of a body of lay persons. In 1953-54 staff and stu-dents campaigned against the old order. An open letter to the premier, written by Orr and signed by thirty-five fellow academics, was

published in the *Mercury* on 29 October 1954. It called for an inquiry into 'the present ad-ministration of the University of Tasmania' and led (Sir) Robert Cosgrove [q.v.13] reluc-tantly to agree to the appointment of a royal commission.

Headed by Justice James Walker of the Supreme Court of Western Australia, the com-mission opened on 22 February 1955 and delivered its report on 26 May. The report was highly critical of Morris and of the uni-versity council, which it recommended be replaced. The council did not feel obliged to implement all the commission's recommen-dations. A new University Act was passed by parliament in November 1955 and proclaimed on 15 December.

Next day the council authorized the vice-chancellor to establish a committee to con-sider complaints against Orr made by two members of staff—W. A. Townsley, an his-torian, and Dr K. Milanov, a member of Orr's department—and by a mature-age student of philosophy, Edwin Tanner. Following a special council meeting on 2 March 1956, which heard an allegation by Reginald Kemp, a local timber merchant, that Orr had seduced his daughter Suzanne (an undergraduate student of philosophy), a second committee was es-tablished. Both committees found against Orr. The university refused to accept his resignation, and he was summarily dismissed on 16 March 1956.

Orr's significance for historians derives from the circumstances of his expulsion, the subsequent campaign for his reinstatement, and the consequent prolonged debate con-cerning both the propriety of the university's proceedings and the proper relationship be-tween a university and its academic staff. Orr sued the university alleging wrongful dis-missal. The case was heard in the Supreme Court in October and November 1956. The court found that the complaints of Townsley, Milanov and Tanner were not of sufficient gravity to justify Orr's removal, but it did accept the veracity of Miss Kemp's evidence, and found that the university was justified in summarily dismissing him. In May 1957 the High Court of Australia rejected Orr's appeal and supported the findings of the Supreme Court.

That month Orr enlisted the help of Pro-fessor R. D. Wright of the University of Mel-bourne as his academic 'next friend'. Wright devoted energy, time and money to assist Orr until the year of the latter's death. In June 1958 the Orr case gained considerable cre-dence when the Kirk Session of Scot's Church, Hobart, after receiving Orr's application for readmission to the Church, found that he had been convicted on insufficient evidence and that a gross miscarriage of justice had occurred. The session's findings took account of new evidence produced by Orr, and were later endorsed by other church authorities, most notably the Catholic archbishop (Sir) Guilford Young and the Anglican bishop Geoffrey Cranswick [q.v.13].

Support for Orr was not confined to Tasmania. The staff associations of most Australian universities expressed their concern, that of Newcastle University College calling in July 1958 for a 'ban on applications for positions on the Staff of the University of Tasmania'. In August that year the Australasian Association of Philosophy imposed a ban on the filling of the chair of philosophy at the University of Tasmania. There was consistent agitation for reopening the case, either by the court or by a special inquiry, so that the new evidence could be examined. In Hobart the community was divided. Orr's supporters and opponents campaigned vigorously. The strength of feeling was demonstrated when a shot was fired through the window of his home on 23 December 1959. The owner of the rifle from which the bullet was fired was tried early in 1960, but the magistrate dismissed the case. There is still argument as to whether the shooting was an attempted assassination or a ploy to gain sympathy for the former professor.

Orr was widely regarded as a martyr, an antipodean Dreyfus, the victim of a conspiracy by members of a conservative establishment determined to rid the university of a difficult troublemaker by punishing him for the part he had played in bringing about the royal commission and the reform of the university and its council. This view was put most strongly by W. H. C. Eddy [q.v.14], a senior tutor in external studies at the University of Sydney, in his voluminous and passionate book, *Orr* (Brisbane, 1961).

Not all of Orr's supporters saw him as an innocent figure: some simply thought that the charges against him were not proven; others believed that the procedures of the university committees were improper and that due process had not been observed. Professor E. Morris Miller [q.v.10] was not alone in arguing that an affair with a student was a private matter and no proper ground for disciplinary action—even though Orr himself consistently denied having had sexual intercourse with Suzanne Kemp. The Federal Council of University Staff Associations was as concerned with seeing that proper tenure conditions and disciplinary procedures were accepted by the university as with the case itself.

In spite of approaches made on his behalf, Orr was unable to obtain any other academic appointment, and was reduced to dependence on the charity of his sympathisers. Except for short periods when he was employed in unskilled tasks, he devoted the remainder of his life to seeking compensation from the university and reinstatement as its professor of philosophy. In December 1963 the university offered him a cash settlement. The chancellor Sir Henry Baker [q.v.13] and four other council-members resigned in protest. Orr rejected the offer. In May 1966, when his health was failing, he accepted a similar settlement which included compensation of $32 000.

Survived by his wife and their daughter and two sons, Orr died of multiple pulmonary emboli on 15 July 1966 in Royal Hobart Hospital and was cremated. A public appeal was launched to raise funds for his family.

In recent years the Orr case has been re-evaluated, in particular by Cassandra Pybus in *Gross Moral Turpitude* (Melbourne, 1993). Pybus argued that there was no conspiracy, that Orr was guilty, that the shortcomings in the procedures of the University were excusable, and that the seduction of a student by a professor is a serious abuse of a special relationship. She pointed out that—as shown by (Sir) John Kerr and J. H. Wootten in 1958—the new evidence, which long provided the main reason for seeking a rehearing of the case, could only be accepted by denying facts that were conceded by Orr at his trials.

Univ Tas, *The Dismissal of S. S. Orr by the University of Tasmania* (Hob, 1958); W. H. C. Eddy, *Orr* (Brisb, 1961); R. Davis, *Open to Talent* (Hob, 1990); C. Pybus, *Gross Moral Turpitude* (Melb, 1993); J. B. Polya and R. J. Solomon, *Dreyfus in Australia* (Syd, 1996); Roy Com on Univ Tas, Report, *PP*, no 18 (HA, Tas), 1955; *Free Spirit*, 4, Aug 1968; *Mercury* (Hob), 29 Oct 1954, 16, 17 Dec 1963, 7, 9, 27 May, 16 June, 16, 19 July, 6 Aug, 22 Sept 1966; *Sun* (Melb), 17 Dec 1963, 9 Nov 1966; papers relating to Orr case (Univ Tas Archives).

W. D. JOSKE

ORRY-KELLY; see KELLY, ORRY

OSBORNE, DORIS MARGARET (1906-1977), schoolteacher and campaigner for equal rights for women, was born on 22 October 1906 at Glen Innes, New South Wales, only daughter and eldest of three children of native-born parents Herbert Osborne, farmer, and his wife Nellie Winifred, née Souter. Doris grew up on her parents' cattle property and boarded with relations in the town during school weeks. On leaving Glen Innes Intermediate High School, she entered the University of Sydney (B.Sc., 1927; Dip.Ed., 1928). She taught mathematics and physics successively at Yass, Tamworth, Broken Hill and Glen Innes high schools for the next ten years, and was a leading member of the Secondary Teachers' Association of New South Wales.

Later appointments in Sydney led to her first senior promotion (deputy-headmistress,

Fairfield Girls' High School, 1955) and also allowed her to become more active in the New South Wales Teachers' Federation, on whose council she served almost continuously from 1951 to 1968. By the late 1940s the federation was pursuing the goal of equal pay for men and women teachers. At her first meeting as a member of its equal pay committee, Osborne remarked that, although she was deputy-headmistress of a girls' high school, she could not return to her old co-educational school at Glen Innes—except as a lower paid assistant —because women could not be appointed to senior positions at boys' and co-educational schools. Teachers like herself, she said, were professionally ten years behind men with whom they had trained at Teachers' College. At a federation meeting in 1951 she success-fully moved that the words 'and opportunity' be inserted after 'equal pay' in a resolution being moved by Lucy Woodcock [q.v.12] and Vera Leggett.

Miss Osborne worked assiduously towards both objectives, writing and presenting radio talks. She represented the federation at seven Australian Council of Trade Unions' con-gresses and, in 1957, on a deputation to the premier, J. J. Cahill [q.v.13], concerning equal-ity of pay and opportunity. She was senior vice-president (1954-57) of the federation and in 1961 was accorded life membership. As a result of the federation's campaign, supported by other unions, the Industrial Arbitration (Female Rates) Amendment Act (1958) pro-vided, by annual increments over five years, equality of pay for women doing work of the same nature, range and volume as men. Equal-ity of opportunity was also partially intro-duced by negotiation between the federation and Public Service Board. In 1965 Osborne travelled abroad.

Headmistress (from 1959) of Blacktown and (from 1961) of Strathfield girls' high schools, Osborne was appointed in 1966 the State's first woman principal of a co-educational high school (West Wyalong)—an equality of oppor-tunity slightly tarnished by the absence of a vested residence which had formerly gone with the position. She was a tall, handsome woman with a sociable, generous manner. At the local Methodist Church on 21 June 1968 she married Harold Helyar, a 69-year-old store-keeper and a widower. That year Mrs Helyar was appointed to the board of the Wyalong and District Hospital. In 1974, three years after retiring from teaching, she topped the poll for Bland Shire Council. Survived by her husband, she died of coronary artery disease on 27 June 1977 at her West Wyalong home and was cremated with Uniting Church forms.

G. Phelan, *Women in Action in the Federation* (Syd, 1981); J. O'Brien, *A Divided Unity!* (Syd, 1987); *Education*, 12 Apr 1961; *West Wyalong Advocate*, 23 Sept 1974; M. Millar, Justice Versus Tradition: A History of the Campaign for Equal Pay for Equal Work by the New South Wales Teachers' Feder-ation, 1918-1963 (B.A. Hons thesis, Macquarie Univ, 1993); Teachers records, Dept of Education (NSW) archives.
GAVIN SOUTER

O'SHANE, GLADYS DOROTHY (1919-1965), Aboriginal political activist, was born on 22 September 1919 at Mossman, Queens-land, sixth child of Queensland-born parents Edgar Davis, labourer, and his wife Caroline, née Brown. An official pencilled the word 'half-caste' beside her name in the register of births. Gladys's family lived at the Yarrabah mission, near Cairns. She attended primary school for a few years before being employed as a domestic servant. At the Assembly of God Tabernacle, Cairns, on 26 October 1940 she married Patrick James O'Shane. Described as 'well-travelled' and 'well-educated', O'Shane was a 27-year-old militant trade unionist who worked as a canecutter and later as a wharf labourer. The young couple moved to Moss-man, but returned to Cairns about 1946 to give their children the chance of a better education.

Gladys encouraged her children to read newspapers and discuss current affairs. Sent to secondary school, her eldest daughter Pat 'brought home the novels of Charles Dickens' [q.v.4] which she and her mother read and talked over 'for hours'. Gladys took paid domestic work in hotels. She taught her chil-dren that they were 'as good as anybody else'. About 5 ft 10½ ins (179 cm) tall, alert, agile and attractive, she overcame her shyness, joined the women's auxiliary of the Waterside Workers' Federation of Australia and ad-dressed strike meetings. In 1959 she and Pat became members of the Communist Party of Australia.

By 1961 Gladys was president of the Cairns Advancement League, which was affiliated with the Federal Council for Aboriginal Ad-vancement (Federal Council for the Ad-vancement of Aborigines and Torres Strait Islanders). In May that year it was alleged that Pastor Eric Kernick, superintendent of the Hopevale Lutheran mission, Cooktown, had mistreated two young Aborigines, Jim Jacko and Gertie Simon. The league mounted a campaign for an inquiry. J. O. Lee, a magis-trate, was commissioned by the Queensland government to investigate the incident. The league secured Fred Paterson [q.v.] as legal adviser to Jacko and Simon. Mrs O'Shane attended the hearings and asked the govern-ment to widen the terms of reference of the investigation. Lee found Kernick's action in flogging Jacko 'inexcusable'. The affair drew attention to the arbitrary nature of the laws applying to Australia's indigenous people. In 1963 O'Shane helped to circulate a petition throughout the Torres Strait Islands calling for Queensland's discriminatory legislation to be abolished; more than one thousand signatures were gathered. The State government was forced to review the Aboriginals Preservation and Protection Acts (1939-46) and the Torres Strait Islanders Acts (1939-46).

Suffering from renal disease, O'Shane died of cardiac arrest on 29 December 1965 at the Base Hospital, Cairns, and was buried in Martyn Street cemetery; her husband, two daughters and three sons survived her. The 1966 annual conference of the F.C.A.A.T.S.I. noted the passing of one of the 'leaders in Aboriginal advancement'. She had inspired her children to be active in education, law and Aboriginal affairs. Her daughter Pat became a magistrate and chancellor of the University of New England.

S. Mitchell, *Tall Poppies* (Melb, 1984); *Courier-Mail*, 22 Aug 1961; *National Times*, 26 Dec 1982-1 Jan 1983; Federal Council for the Advancement of Aborigines and Torres Strait Islanders, 9th Annual Conference on Aboriginal Affairs, Reports and Recommendations, 1966 (ts, held by Aust Inst of Aboriginal and Torres Strait Islander Studies L).

YSOLA BEST

O'SHEA, MAURICE GEORGE (1897-1956), winemaker, was born on 13 June 1897 in North Sydney, son of John Augustus O'Shea (d.1912), an Irish-born wine-and-spirit merchant, and his wife Leontine Frances, née Beaucher, who came from France. Maurice attended St Ignatius' College, Riverview, and Holy Cross College, Ryde. Sent to a lycée at Montpellier, France, to learn French, he continued his education at the École Nationale Supérieure Agronomique de Grigon, near Paris, before training as a viticulturist and analytical chemist at the University of Montpellier. He lectured at Montpellier, reluctantly declined a post in the United States of America, and returned to New South Wales in 1920 at his mother's request.

Maurice, who was 'extremely French' and undecided about remaining in Australia, began to make wine on the family property at Pokolbin in the Hunter Valley. In 1925 he named the vineyard Mount Pleasant. He did not find the going easy. The public preferred beer, fortified wines and spirits to table wine. Grapes were damaged by hailstorms every second year from 1927 to 1939. During the Depression he was fortunate to sell (in 1932) a half-share in the vineyard to McWilliam's [q.v.10] Wines Pty Ltd; O'Shea became manager and a director of its subsidiary, Mt Pleasant Wines Pty Ltd. Relieved of sales and distribution responsibilities, he was free to concentrate on making fine table wine. In 1941 he sold out completely, but remained manager and winemaker.

Backed by the powerful McWilliam family, O'Shea was a major purchaser of district grapes and wine for resale and blending. Other growers deferred to his expertise. An individualist and an innovator, he broke with tradition by using varietal rather than generic names for his own products, calling fine wines after individual vats, vineyards, friends and relations. He was also knowledgeable about food, and highly regarded by Sydney restaurateurs such as J. K. 'Johnnie' Walker and Henri Renault (after whom his 'Henry' wines were named) who championed his wines. O'Shea had a long association with the Wine and Food Society and was president of its Newcastle branch. Although he was thought by many to be a bachelor, he had married Marcia Singer Fuller on 2 December 1925 at St Peter's Anglican Church, Hamilton; they shared an affectionate relationship, at Cessnock, in Sydney and later at Newcastle. Their son died in infancy.

Physically small, O'Shea suffered from extreme myopia; his thick spectacles had the effect of enlarging his eyes. Max Dupain's photograph of him, peering at a glass of wine, captured him well. He was a much-loved, gentle, talented and cultivated man, with an impish sense of humour, who lived and worked alone in the countryside. Once he had overcome his initial shyness, he made lasting friendships and welcomed visitors prepared to 'rough it' at his Pokolbin shack. Good company, superb wines and food cooked on an old kerosene stove were their reward. Sydney gourmets spoke 'with wonder of his casseroled duck with mushrooms, his baked hares—and bandicoots'. Survived by his wife and daughter, he died of cancer on 5 May 1956 in his flat at Newcastle and was buried with Catholic rites in Gore Hill cemetery, Sydney. His best wine-making efforts have delighted subsequent generations.

J. Thompson, *On Lips of Living Men* (Melb, 1962); M. Lake, *Hunter Winemakers* (Brisb, 1970); *Wine and Spirit News and Aust Vigneron*, 21 May 1956; *Newcastle Morning Herald*, 7 May 1956; *ABC Weekly*, 6 Apr 1957, p 8; *Sun-Herald*, 24 Jan 1971; *Age*, 5 Dec 1989; information from Mrs S. Bryce, Mount Kembla, NSW.

DAVID DUNSTAN

OSMAN, NEILE (1920-1972), educationist, was born on 31 March 1920 in Adelaide, second son of Australian-born parents Laurence Henry Osman, military clerk, and his wife Ethel Rebecca, née Allen. Neile attended the Collegiate School of St Peter and furthered his study of languages at the University of

Adelaide (B.A., 1942; M.A., 1945; Dip.Ed., 1948). In 1940 he returned to St Peter's to teach at the preparatory school. Called up for full-time duty with the Militia on 29 August 1941, he served mainly with the 3rd Field Company, Royal Australian Engineers. Lieutenant Osman transferred to the Australian Imperial Force in October 1942. In July 1943 he was promoted captain and placed on the Reserve of Officers. At his school chapel on 5 December 1942 he had married Margaret Mary Moody, a 22-year-old secretary; they were to have two daughters before being divorced.

On 7 January 1946 Osman joined the Commonwealth Public Service. Next month he was appointed to the Adelaide branch of the Office of Education (Department of Education and Science from 1966). In 1953 he moved to head office in North Sydney where he became officer-in-charge of the migrant education section, responsible for producing materials for teaching English to adults. Building on the work of Richard Crossley and George Pittman, Osman's staff developed the Australian Situational Method which catered for people with different language needs. A.S.M. courses provided books for both teachers and students, with detailed plans for lessons. The books also contained information about the sound-system and structure of the English language. Materials were prepared for shipboard classes and night-schools, and for courses on the radio and by correspondence. A number of pamphlets were distributed on aspects of teaching English as a second language.

Osman privately published *Modern English: A Self-Tutor or Class Text for Foreign Students* (Sydney, 1959). The book was still being reprinted as late as the 1970s, and editions were produced for readers in Japan, South East Asia, the Middle East, Europe, Africa and South America. Osman's next publication was *Word Function and Dictionary Use* (London, 1965), a workbook for advanced learners of English. Meanwhile, he and his team adapted the A.S.M. to a French-language course. *Let's Speak French*: Part I (1963), II (1964) and III (1966) were published in Sydney by Angus & Robertson [qq.v.7,11] for the Commonwealth Office of Education; Part IV (1970) was co-authored by Osman, James Houston and Michel Bocquet. Osman issued disc recordings and manuals to support the course.

On 30 January 1968 at the office of the government statist, Melbourne, he married Berna Zoe Beaumont, a 38-year-old schoolteacher. A member (1963) of the Australian College of Education, Osman joined the Canberra College of Advanced Education in 1969 as founding principal lecturer in English. He died of cancer on 13 October 1972 in Canberra Hospital and was buried in Canberra cemetery; his wife survived him, as did the children of his first marriage.

Cwlth Office of Education, *Annual Report*, 1953-65; *Canb Times*, 20 Oct 1972; ST3531, item S/107 pt 2 (AA, Syd).   BERYL CIGLER

O'SULLIVAN, MICHAEL (c.1866-1950), policeman, was born about 1866 at Grenagh, County Cork, Ireland, son of Denis O'Sullivan, farmer, and his wife Catherine, née O'Callaghan. A minor prank in which he was involved at Blarney Castle led him to emigrate to Queensland. Sailing under an assumed name, he disembarked at Rockhampton in January 1883. He initially worked at clearing land and installing a saw-milling plant.

On 30 May 1883 O'Sullivan was appointed a mounted constable in the Queensland Police Force. His postings included Roma, Dulbydilla, St George, Taroom, Rockhampton, Winton, Mount Morgan, Emerald, Brisbane and Cunnamulla. He dealt with murderers, rapists, horse-thieves, and travellers lost in the bush. In helping to bring law and order to the western frontier, he established a reputation as a persistent and fair officer, and was promoted sergeant in 1899. At St Stephen's Catholic Cathedral, Brisbane, on 30 April 1890 he had married Norah Eveleen Gaine (d.1922), a 23-year-old dressmaker.

O'Sullivan's methods of detection (such as taking plaster casts of horses' hooves to prove the guilt of horse-thieves) impressed Chief Justice (Sir) Pope Cooper [q.v.8]. In 1904 O'Sullivan was transferred to the Criminal Investigation Branch, Brisbane, as second-in-charge. Despite an immediate strike by detectives who objected to the appointment of an outsider, he soon improved the calibre and performance of the branch, which he later claimed was as good as any in the world. He was made head of the branch in 1912. Promoted senior inspector in 1920, he took charge of protecting the Prince of Wales during his visit to Queensland. His precautions included 'detaining' at Boonah a deranged man who was seen as a threat to the prince.

In 1921 O'Sullivan was promoted chief inspector and deputy-commissioner to Patrick Short. His name was mentioned as a possible commissioner, but seems to have been rejected because he was not sufficiently sympathetic to Labor's cause: in 1901-02 he had incurred the wrath of Labor members of parliament for his actions in guarding and escorting non-union shearers; in the 1912 general strike in Brisbane he had stood firmly with Commissioner W. G. Cahill [q.v.7] who led a baton charge against demonstrators; and in 1915 he had opposed the police force being unionized. Some Labor politicians argued that, if he were made commissioner, he would be a 'second Major Cahill'. O'Sullivan responded by criticizing politicians for meddling in police affairs.

Exhausted by years of constant work, cynical about politicians and promotion, and distressed by the death of his wife, O'Sullivan suffered a nervous breakdown in 1922 and retired in the following year. He served as secretary (1923-50) of the Queensland Society for the Prevention of Cruelty, and took up lawn bowls. On 20 November 1924 at St Patrick's Church, Glen Innes, New South Wales, he married Gertrude (d.1949), daughter of K. I. O'Doherty [q.v.5]. In 1935 O'Sullivan published his memoirs, *Cameos of Crime* (Sydney). Survived by the son and three of the four daughters of his first marriage, he died on 5 October 1950 at Clayfield, Brisbane, and was buried in Toowong cemetery.

W. R. Johnston, *The Long Blue Line* (Brisb, 1992); *V&P* (Qld), 1899, 4, p 710; *Queenslander*, 1 Jan 1921; *Courier-Mail*, 19 Apr, 31 Oct 1923, 28 Sept 1935, 6 Oct 1950; O'Sullivan cutting-books, OM 92-85/1-3 (OL); Police staff files, A/47938-9 *and* Immigration passenger lists, IMM 116-7, microfilm Z 1959-60 (QA).   W. ROSS JOHNSTON

O'SULLIVAN, SIR MICHAEL NEIL (1900-1968), politician and solicitor, was born on 2 August 1900 at Toowong, Brisbane, fifth child of Queensland-born parents Patrick Alban O'Sullivan, solicitor, and his wife Mary Bridget, née Macgroarty. Patrick O'Sullivan [q.v.5] was his grandfather; Thomas O'Sullivan and Neil Macgroarty [qq.v.11,10] were his uncles. Young Neil proceeded from Taringa State School to St Joseph's College, Nudgee. He retained a strong interest in the college as a foundation member (1922) and president (1940-41) of the Old Boys' Association. After serving his articles with firms in Brisbane and at Warwick, he was admitted as a solicitor on 5 December 1922. He took over his father's Brisbane practice and later formed a partnership with J. J. Rowell.

On 3 April 1929 at St Stephen's Catholic Cathedral, Brisbane, O'Sullivan married 18-year-old Jessie Margaret Mary McEncroe. As the United Australia Party's candidate, he unsuccessfully contested the House of Representatives seat of Brisbane in 1934 and the Legislative Assembly seat of Windsor in 1941. He was president of the Brisbane Chamber of Commerce (1936-37) and the Property Owners' Protection Association (1937-38). Enlisting in the Royal Australian Air Force on 8 May 1942, he was commissioned and promoted flying officer in June. For the next two and a half years he performed intelligence and administrative duties in Australia and the South-West Pacific Area. His R.A.A.F. appointment terminated on 15 December 1944.

At the 1946 Federal general elections O'Sullivan stood for the Senate as a Liberal Party candidate. (Sir) Robert Menzies [q.v.] described him as the best speaker he heard on the Queensland leg of the campaign. O'Sullivan entered the Senate on 1 July 1947. As one of two Liberals—(Dame) Annabelle Rankin was the other—in the three-person Opposition in the Upper House, he had some claim to the leadership, but left this role to his experienced Country Party colleague (Sir) Walter Cooper [q.v.13]. Following the coalition's victory in the general elections in December 1949, O'Sullivan became leader of the government in the Senate, an office he was to hold for nine years. The government lacked a majority in the Upper House for half that period, yet most of its legislative programme was passed.

O'Sullivan had been appointed minister for trade and customs on 19 December 1949. Playing a significant part in expanding and stabilizing the sugar industry, he set up a committee which in 1952 reviewed the Sugar Agreement between the Commonwealth and Queensland governments. In 1953 he led the Australian delegation to a conference in London (convened by the United Nations) to discuss changes to the International Sugar Agreement which regulated production and marketing. Acting in concert with (Sir) John McEwen [q.v.], O'Sullivan instituted measures to assist the development of the tobacco industry. He and McEwen were joint-leaders of the Australian delegation which travelled to Geneva in 1954 for a special meeting to review the General Agreement on Tariffs and Trade.

Relinquishing the trade and customs portfolio in January 1956, O'Sullivan served as minister for the navy (January-October) and as vice-president of the Executive Council (from 24 October). On 15 August 1956 he had been made attorney-general. Although flattered by this appointment, he believed that the attorney-general, as leader of the Australian Bar, should be a barrister. He resigned from cabinet in December 1958, telling Menzies that it was time 'some of our younger members be given a chance of Ministerial experience'. O'Sullivan chaired (1956-59) the Joint Committee on Constitutional Review. As a general principle, he thought that senators should not be ministers so that the Senate could better exercise its function as a house of review. Appointed K.B.E. in 1959, he retired from parliament on 30 June 1962.

O'Sullivan was a director of several companies, including L. J. Hooker [q.v.14] Investment Corporation Ltd and Queensland Press Ltd. He was a member of the council and the executive-committee of the Royal Flying Doctor Service of Australia (Queensland section), and the council of the Queensland branch of the Australian Boy Scouts' Association. In 1950 a journalist had described him as 'distinguished-looking, diplomatic and friendly ... silver-haired, one of the best-dressed men in politics'. Sir Neil enjoyed golf and tennis; he also liked surfing, but once remarked that he would rather read a telephone directory than go fishing. Survived by his wife and two sons, he died suddenly of a coronary occlusion on 4 July 1968 in the Carlton Rex Hotel, Sydney; he was accorded a state funeral and was buried in Nudgee cemetery, Brisbane. Colleagues remembered him as a 'generous, calm and persuasive' man who gave his name and energy to charitable causes.

A. L. Lougheed, *A Century of Service* (Brisb, 1969); *Queenslander*, 19 July 1934; *Courier-Mail*, 14 July, 26 Aug 1953, 9 Dec 1958, 5 July 1968; O'Sullivan papers (NL).

BRIAN F. STEVENSON

O'TOOLE, THOMAS WILLIAM (1885-1957), coalminer, was born on 28 July 1885 at Chester-le-Street, Durham, England, second of nine children of Edward Toole, a Scottish-born coalminer, and his wife Annie, née Dinning, who came from Newcastle upon Tyne. The Tooles emigrated to New South Wales in 1890 and settled in the Hunter Valley. Edward worked at Stockton colliery. Blacklisted because of his industrial activities, he moved with his family to the Fingal area of Tasmania. There Tommy began work as an underground miner. He changed his surname to O'Toole, returned to the South Maitland field about 1901, and was employed in John Brown's [q.v.7] colliery at Pelaw Main, a 'Geordie' stronghold.

At St Mary's Anglican Church, West Maitland, on 25 April 1906 O'Toole married Margaret MacMillan; they were to have five sons and two daughters. He served (from 1912) as president of the Pelaw Main miners' lodge. In 1924 he was elected secretary of the lodge, and of its funeral and sick funds, a post he held for thirty years. William (Billy) McBlane, secretary of the Richmond Main miners' lodge, and O'Toole emerged as key spokesmen for the Kurri Kurri community during the 1929-30 lockout. They led a rank-and-file movement against the policy of the Australasian Coal & Shale Employees' (Miners') Federation which sought to confine the dispute to certain mines in the northern district. Challenging the coal-owners' attacks head-on, the O'Toole-McBlane breakaway group called for a general stoppage.

O'Toole and McBlane addressed some of the largest meetings ever seen in the South Maitland area, and won the loyal support of local miners. It was said that 'What Tommy O'Toole and Billy McBlane think today, the whole town of Kurri will think tomorrow'. After fifteen months of industrial action, however, the strikers reluctantly accepted the recommendation of the Miners' Federation to agree to a compromise settlement and resume work. Their backdown was criticized by the Militant Minority Movement, a communist-front organization. During the Depression O'Toole helped to establish the Kurri Kurri Citizens' Relief Committee, and served on the miners' central council and northern board of management. Nominated by the Australian Labor Party for the House of Representatives seat of Hunter in 1939, he stood aside in favour of the incumbent, Rowley James [q.v.14].

Although O'Toole survived two cave-ins at the mines, the second (1942) buried him up to his chest, fractured both his legs and left him with a permanently damaged foot. In 1944 he agreed to be appointed as an industrial officer to investigate coal disputes at Newcastle and Maitland, on the condition that he could retain his membership of the Miners' Federation. His findings were fair and practical, and rarely questioned. Throughout his life he opposed overtime for coalminers, arguing that it kept fellow workers unemployed. He retired in 1954.

In 1955 O'Toole helped the northern executive of the Miners' Federation to resist a new code of working conditions sought by employers. At Kurri Kurri he was an executive-member of the Co-operative Society, and a board-member of the district hospital and the workers' club. He belonged to the Grand United Order of Free Gardeners of Australasia. Survived by his sons, he died on 19 June 1957 at Royal Newcastle Hospital and was cremated.

E. Ross, *A History of the Miners' Federation of Australia* (Syd, 1970); A. Metcalfe, *For Freedom and Dignity* (Syd, 1988); *Newcastle Morning Herald*, 20 Aug 1924, 24 Mar, 13 Oct 1942, 6 Jan 1943, 26 Oct 1944, 21 July 1957; *SMH*, 26, 27 Oct 1944; J. Comerford, 'Tommy O'Toole', unpublished ms (held by Coalfield Heritage Group Inc, Kurri Kurri, NSW); family and personal information.

BOB JAMES

OWEN, EVELYN ERNEST (1915-1949), inventor of the Owen gun, was born on 15 May 1915 at Wollongong, New South Wales, fourth of five children of Australian-born parents Ernest William Owen, law clerk, and his wife Constance Elaine, née McMillan. Robert and Percy Owen [qq.v.11] were his uncles; Sir William McMillan [q.v.10] was his maternal grandfather. 'Evo' was educated at Wollongong High School. He showed no interest in scholastic endeavour or in his family's traditional vocations, the law and the army. Raised in an affectionate household, he had an independent spirit and a generous nature. With one of his brothers, he began a ready-mixed mortar business, but the venture failed due to their lack of commercial acumen. Although he had little experience and no technical qualifications, Owen was fascinated by firearms and experimented with them recklessly.

Appreciating that sub-machine guns would be widely used in a future war, Owen designed and built (by 1938) a .22-inch (5.6 mm) calibre prototype, adaptable to a larger bore for military use. His attempt in July 1939 to interest the Australian Military Forces in his invention was rebuffed on the grounds that neither the British nor the Australian armies saw a need for such weapons. On 28 May 1940 he enlisted in the Australian Imperial Force and was posted to the 2nd/17th Battalion. While on pre-embarkation leave in September, he discussed his gun with V. A. Wardell, manager of the Port Kembla plant of Lysaght's Newcastle Works Pty Ltd. Wardell referred the matter to Essington Lewis [q.v.10] who arranged Owen's immediate transfer to the Central Inventions Board, Melbourne. Owen was reluctant and annoyed because he wanted to serve abroad with his brothers.

When Lieutenant C. M. Dyer, the board's secretary, failed to gain approval to produce a model of Owen's gun suitable for military use, he sent Owen to Port Kembla and asked Wardell (unofficially) for assistance. Lysaght's made versions of the weapon with larger calibres, but the Australian military authorities, by then in favour of sub-machine guns, opted for the new, British-designed Sten. (Sir) Percy Spender, the minister for the army, overruled his advisers and instructed the army in June 1941 to order one hundred Owen guns for testing. On the 25th of that month Owen was discharged from the A.I.F. and joined Lysaght's.

Trials conducted in September showed the Owen gun to be more reliable than the American Thompson gun and the British Sten gun. Only after further intervention by Spender and his successor F. M. Forde, a campaign by Brian Penton [q.v.] in the Sydney *Daily Telegraph*, and the courageous support of some army officers, notably Colonel E. W. Latchford, were the Australian armed forces equipped with the 9-mm calibre Owen gun in 1942. Lysaght's produced 45 477 Owen guns in World War II. Soldiers in New Guinea preferred them to similar weapons, and Australians later used them in the Korean War, the Malayan Emergency and the Vietnam War.

Having received about £10 000 in royalties and proceeds from the sale of his patent rights, Owen established a small sawmill at Tongarra, near Wollongong, and lived there, unmarried and usually alone, while experimenting with sporting rifles. He died of cardiac syncope on 1 April 1949 in Wollongong District Hospital and was buried in the local cemetery with Anglican rites.

D. P. Mellor, *The Role of Science and Industry* (Canb, 1958); G. S. Wardell, *The Development and Manufacture of the Owen Gun* (Wollongong, NSW, 1982); *Reveille* (Syd), 36, no 1, 1 Aug 1962, p 9; *Aust Army J*, Sept 1967, p 33; *Daily Telegraph* (Syd), 5 Nov, 21 Nov 1941; John Lysaght (Aust) Ltd, bibliog on the Owen gun (copy on ADB file); family information.

V. A. WARDELL*

OWEN, JOHN EVAN ERIC (1901-1965), Presbyterian minister, was born on 4 April 1901 at Williamstown, Melbourne, second child of John John (sic) Owen (d.1914), a Welsh Presbyterian minister who was born in Wales, and his Victorian-born wife Margot Emily, née Roberts. John served the Welsh Church at Williamstown and in La Trobe Street, Melbourne. Following his father's death, Eric worked for the Victorian Railways to help support the household.

In 1919 Owen decided to become a minister of the Presbyterian Church of Australia. He enrolled at Scotch College, Hawthorn, and, after one and a half terms, matriculated, doing particularly well in Latin and Greek. In 1922 he entered Ormond [q.v.5] College, University of Melbourne (B.A., 1925; M.A., 1927), and studied divinity at the college's Theological Hall (B.D., 1936). He combined study with a love of sport and of acting, and exercised a gift for leadership which remained with him for life. Slight of stature, with freckles and red hair, he was often the centre of activity. At the university he met Mary (Molly) Helen Hamilton. Her maternal grandfather was Sir John Davies [q.v.4]. Eric's marriage to Molly on 27 February 1930 at the Presbyterian Church, Malvern, introduced him to an extended family with different experiences of life in Victoria from those of the Welsh immigrants among whom he had been reared.

On completing his studies, Owen had ministered briefly at Manangatang. Late in 1929 he became assistant-minister to Rev. (Dr) John Walker [q.v.12] in the Canberra parish of the Presbyterian Church. In 1933-54, while minister of St Andrew's Church, Gardiner, Melbourne, he served as acting-master (1944-45) of Ormond College and chairman (1948-54) of its council. During this ministry his three great passions were manifest.

First came his work as a parish minister. Owen was an outstanding preacher, with Welsh eloquence—and love for music. His commitment was infectious: a number of young men from the congregation decided to enter the ministry. He also lectured to deaconesses in training at Rolland [q.v.11] House, Carlton. Among the governing bodies of the Church his ready tongue and passionate manner made him a redoubtable debater. In 1951-52 he was moderator of the Presbyterian Church of Victoria.

Owen's second passion was for world peace. Throughout the 1930s he was a Christian pacifist. He made his position clear to his congregation in 1938 with an address entitled 'If War Comes!', subsequently published as a pamphlet. In doing so, however, he endorsed a current declaration: 'The Church must . . . hold together in one spiritual fellowship those of its members who take different views concerning their duty as Christian citizens in time of war'. St Andrew's congregation stayed loyal to him throughout World War II.

In the postwar years Owen's emphasis changed, from opposition to war to reconciliation between nations. With several leading ministers of the churches, he took part in preparations for the Australian Convention for Peace and War, held in Sydney in September 1953. He and others, including Frank Hartley [q.v.14], were attacked in the press and in parliament by those who believed that the peace movement was a communist front. Owen's account of the convention and of his attempt to persuade the prime minister, (Sir) Robert Menzies [q.v.], to take a different view was given in his book, *The Road to Peace* (1954).

Owen's third passion was for the mission of the Church. In 1938 he had been a delegate to the International Missionary Conference, at Madras, India, one of the precursors of the World Council of Churches. He held senior appointments in the Board of Missions of the Presbyterian Church of Australia, and visited inland Australia and neighbouring churches overseas. In 1955-60 he worked as a missionary in the New Hebrides (Vanuatu); through his membership of the resident commissioner's advisory council, he exerted influence at a critical time in the country's transition to independence.

In 1960 the Owens returned to Victoria and Eric was inducted as minister of the Presbyterian Church at Warrnambool. There he made his characteristic contributions to church and community. He died of asthma (from which he had suffered for most of his life) on 3 May 1965 at Warrnambool and was cremated. His wife, son and two daughters survived him.

Presbyterian Church of Vic, *Messenger*, 27, no 18, Nov 1953; *Age* (Melb), 4 May 1965; *Canb Times*, 5 May 1965; V. O'Byrne, The Peace Parsons: clergy involvement in the peace movement of the fifties (M.A. thesis, Monash Univ, 1984); Presbyterian Church of Vic Archives; family records.

DAVIS McCAUGHEY

OWEN, Sir WILLIAM FRANCIS LANGER (1899-1972), judge, was born on 21 November 1899 at Hunters Hill, Sydney, only son and youngest of three children of (Sir) Langer Meade Loftus Owen [q.v.11], a Sydney-born barrister, and his wife Mary Louisa, née Dames Longworth, who came from Ireland. William was educated at Tudor House, Moss Vale, and Sydney Church of England Grammar School (Shore). He ran away from school and enlisted in the Australian Imperial Force on 31 December 1915, claiming to be aged 18.

Owen served on the Western Front from September 1916 as a sapper in the 7th Field Company, Engineers. He was wounded in September 1917 and gassed in May 1918. Transferring to the Australian Flying Corps in August, he was training as a pilot in England when the war ended. In April 1919 he was commissioned. His A.I.F. appointment terminated in Sydney on 15 November. While studying for the Bar examinations, he acted as associate to Sir William Cullen [q.v.8], the chief justice. At St Mark's Anglican Church, Darling Point, on 11 July 1923 Owen married Joan Bately, daughter of Judge Thomas Rolin. On 2 August that year he was admitted to the Bar.

Fleetingly, in the early 1930s, Owen was politically active—in the Old Guard, and in the United Australia Party for which he unsuccessfully stood for pre-selection for the 1932 State elections. He took silk in 1935 and in April 1936 became an acting-judge of the Supreme Court of New South Wales. On 25 October 1937 he was made a judge of the court, following in the footsteps of his father and grandfather Sir William Owen [q.v.11]. Appointed K.B.E. in 1957, he was elevated to the High Court of Australia on 22 September 1961 and sworn of the Privy Council in the following year. He was regarded as a 'conservative' judge for preferring 'what in legal principle is well-established to that which savours of experiment' and for 'the chill wind of his common sense'.

Owen had also served the Commonwealth in various non-judicial functions. Under John Curtin's [q.v.13] Australian Labor Party government, he chaired (1942-45) the Central Wool Committee during World War II, a full-time occupation for which he declined a salary. He was a member of the Australian delegation to a conference, held in London in 1945, on the disposal of wartime wool stocks. In 1950 (Sir) Robert Menzies' [q.v.] Liberal-Country Party government appointed him chairman of a committee which investigated claims for payment of an allowance to ex-prisoners of war.

In May 1954 Menzies chose Owen to chair the royal commission on espionage (1954-55) in Australia, an investigation that stemmed from evidence provided by Vladimir Petrov, an official from the Embassy of the Soviet Union who had defected. The early proceedings of the commission were monopolized by the efforts of Dr H. V. Evatt [q.v.14], leader of the Opposition, to defend members of his staff who were named in a Petrov document and to depict the defection as a political conspiracy against him. Evatt's excesses eventually moved the commissioners to terminate his right to appear. In 1960 Evatt again intruded upon Owen's life. As senior puisne judge (from 1955) of the Supreme Court of New South Wales, Owen hoped for promotion to chief justice, but the State Labor government appointed Evatt, by then increasingly erratic, to ease his departure from Federal politics. Owen's move to the High Court, where he found himself in congenial company, provided considerable consolation.

About 5 ft 10½ ins (179 cm) tall, with a fair complexion, brown hair (which receded with age) and blue eyes, Sir William wore glasses and had a moustache. He was a member of the Union Club (Sydney), the Royal Sydney Golf Club and the Melbourne Club, and found recreation in golf, fishing and reading.

Although he was shy by nature, he revealed to family and colleagues his warmth, sense of humour, and humanity. A humble man with an 'unremitting devotion to duty', he gained from his upbringing, connexions and career on the bench a demeanour of 'natural authority' and 'an unselfconscious presence'.

In 1967 an aneurysm led to the amputation of Owen's right leg, and his left leg later required arterial surgery. Suffering constant discomfort and frequent pain, he continued his duties with a commitment which his fellow judges regarded as 'heroic'. On 29 March 1972, during a court sitting, he fell ill. He died two days later in St Luke's Hospital, Darlinghurst, Sydney, and was cremated; his wife and daughter survived him.

D. Marr, *Barwick* (Syd, 1980); M. Sexton and L. W. Maher, *The Legal Mystique* (Syd, 1982); G. Fricke, *Judges of the High Court* (Melb, 1986); R. Manne, *The Petrov Affair* (Syd, 1987); A. Moore, *The Secret Army and the Premier* (Syd, 1989); *Aust Law J*, 35, 1961, p 225, 46, 1972, p 251; *A.P.S.A. News*, 6, no 3, 1961, p 5; *Cwlth Law Reports*, 125, 1972; information from Mrs P. Lovell, East Redfern, Syd.

PHILLIPA WEEKS

P

PACKARD, GUY SPENCER (1884-1963), shipping company manager, was born on 7 August 1884 at Burra, South Australia, fourth child of Daniel Spencer Packard (d.1896), solicitor, and his wife Florence Suzanne, née Randall, both South Australian born. Guy was educated at the Collegiate School of St Peter, Adelaide. He joined the Adelaide Steamship Co. Ltd on 20 October 1901 as a junior clerk at head office. Enlisting in the Australian Imperial Force on 6 August 1915, he served in Egypt and—with the 50th Battalion—on the Western Front. He was commissioned lieutenant in February 1917 but, because of illness, was admitted to hospital in the following month and repatriated in September. His A.I.F. appointment terminated in Adelaide on 14 December. At St Peter's College chapel on 13 April 1918 he married with Anglican rites Alison Scott Richardson.

Packard rejoined the A.S.S.Co. in May 1918 and was posted to head office as freight and coal clerk. Rising rapidly within the company, he was appointed Brisbane manager in December 1924. Briefly manager of the Port Adelaide branch in March 1927, he was acting assistant secretary of the company in Adelaide in 1927 and again in 1930. In February 1931 he became assistant-secretary. He acquired a wide knowledge of freight matters generally, and a particular knowledge of the South Australian coastal trade. In 1924, as the company's representative, he had accompanied members of the Eyre Peninsula Transport Commission when they investigated Spencer Gulf and the south-western coast of South Australia.

Appointed manager of the A.S.S.Co.'s Sydney branch in November 1931, Packard became a director of other firms in which his company had a financial interest, including Australian National Airways Pty Ltd, J. & A. Brown [qq.v.3] and Abermain Seaham Collieries Ltd, Newstead Wharves & Stevedoring Co. Pty Ltd and the Waratah Tug & Salvage Co. Pty Ltd. He was chairman of the New South Wales Interstate Shipowners' Association and of the Sydney branch of the Australasian Steamship Owners' Federation (1939-41, 1942-43). During World War II he chaired the Shipping Control Board's Sydney traffic committee.

As general manager from 1 July 1946 until his retirement in 1951, Packard was faced with higher operating costs, as well as with demands by maritime unions which not only added greatly to expenses but also slowed down cargo handling and interrupted sailing schedules. The company's five passenger-ships and twenty-five cargo vessels had to compete with increasing air, rail and road transport. During Packard's term of office, company dividends averaged over $5\frac{1}{2}$ per cent a year, but the A.S.S.Co. had diversified its business and much of its revenue came from subsidiaries unconnected with shipping. The results from shipping were dismal and the company fought a losing battle. Packard delayed the inevitable by keeping the A.S.S.Co. as efficient as possible.

A keen golfer and bridge player, Packard belonged to the Royal Sydney Golf, and the Australian, Newcastle and Adelaide clubs. Survived by his wife, daughter and son, he died on 29 September 1963 at Woollahra and was cremated.

SMH, 15 Oct 1938, 1 Oct 1963; Adelaide Steamship Co Ltd records (Mort L and ANUABL).

G. A. HARDWICK

PACKER, SIR DOUGLAS FRANK HEWSON (1906-1974), media proprietor, was born on 3 December 1906 at Kings Cross, Sydney, elder child of Robert Clyde Packer [q.v.11], a Tasmanian-born journalist, and his wife Ethel Maude, née Hewson (d.1947), who came from Ireland. A mischievous youngster and a poor student, Frank attended Abbotsholme and Turramurra colleges, Wahroonga Grammar School and Sydney Church of England Grammar School (Shore). Despite an accident which caused the loss of most of the sight in his right eye, he was 'strong as a bear, aggressive, full of fight' and participated enthusiastically in Rugby Union football, cricket and rowing. He did not sit for the Intermediate certificate.

In 1923 Packer became a cadet on the *Daily Guardian*, recently launched by Smith's [q.v.11] Newspapers Ltd (a company in which his father held a one-third share). Revelling in schemes to expose corruption, Frank found himself unloading newsprint and working in the engine-room, for his father insisted that he learn every aspect of newspaper production. About 1924 he went jackerooing in the central west of New South Wales; digging up weeds dispelled the appeal of life on the land. His return to Smith's Newspapers in 1926 coincided with the first Miss Australia contest. Frank and Claude McKay accompanied the winner Beryl Mills [qq.v.] on a tour of the United States of America. Back at Smith's, he served as assistant business manager and then as advertising director. Although his financial flair was already obvious, his promotion was resented by a number of people who depicted him as a reckless gambler and playboy.

In 1930 Sir Hugh Denison [q.v.8] acquired the *Daily Guardian* and *Sunday Guardian* for £175 000 and 400 000 preference shares in Associated Newspapers Ltd. The shares were divided among ordinary shareholders in Smith's Newspapers and the Packers received about 173 000 of them. When Sir James Joynton Smith bought out the Packers' shares in 1931, R. C. Packer was appointed managing editor of Associated Newspapers. Frank joined the company in January 1932. The constant boardroom intrigues made his colleagues feel that he was acting as a 'detective' and led to his quick departure.

In October 1932 the journalist G. W. 'George' Warnecke told the Packers of a plan to convert the Australian Workers' Union's daily, the *World*, into a 1d. afternoon newspaper to attract a takeover offer from Associated Newspapers, whose *Sun* was retailing at 1½d. Frank met with E. G. Theodore [q.v.12] who saw a vitality and shrewdness in him. For his part, Frank was to regard Theodore as a father figure. When it became clear that Associated Newspapers was prepared to offer a financial incentive not to publish the *World*, Denison authorized R. C. Packer to 'fix up the matter'. Denison was furious when Associated Newspapers was committed to pay Frank's and Theodore's infant company, Sydney Newspapers Ltd, £86 500 in return for an agreement not to publish a daily or Sunday newspaper for three years. Frank joined Theodore, John Wren [q.v.12] and P. F. Cody in a Fijian gold-mining venture.

Lacking the capital himself, Warnecke suggested to Packer that they publish a women's newspaper with a national focus. Theodore agreed to help to finance the project. The *Australian Women's Weekly*—vigorously promoted, edited by Warnecke and staffed by outstanding contributors like Alice Jackson [q.v.14]—appeared in June 1933. It combined topical features with the traditional contents of women's magazines (such as recipes and patterns), abundant fiction and sophisticated fashion illustrations. In comparison, rival magazines looked staid and matronly. The first issue was phenomenally successful: the sale of 121 162 copies far exceeded the estimated circulation of 50 000.

Packer rushed to England in January 1934 to join his gravely ill father. In April, as he made his way back to the *Weekly*, his beloved father died. Frank inherited most of his share portfolio. At All Saints Church, Woollahra, on 24 July 1934 he married with Anglican rites Gretel Joyce Bullmore, a sister of Mary Hordern [q.v.14]. For some years he had doggedly pursued the beautiful, vivacious and sports-loving Gretel, who was at the forefront of Sydney society. They were to have two sons, (Robert) Clyde and Kerry.

With the 1932 agreement about to lapse, Packer considered launching a daily newspaper. Associated Newspapers was alarmed at the prospect of a new competitor for the *Sun*. The goodwill of its moribund morning newspaper, the *Telegraph*, and that of the *Weekly*, was transferred to a new company, Consolidated Press Ltd, registered in January 1936. Packer and Theodore were, respectively, managing director and chairman. In March the new *Daily Telegraph*—under the control of Sydney Deamer [q.v.13]—appeared; less concerned with partisan politics, the revitalized newspaper posited itself as a forum for progressive and modernist ideas. In 1939, the year in which Packer became president of the Australian Newspapers Conference, the *Sunday Telegraph*, edited by Cyril Pearl, was launched.

Packer was commissioned lieutenant, Militia, in April 1939 and transferred to the Australian Imperial Force on 1 February 1941. Next year Prime Minister Curtin [q.v.13] appointed Theodore director-general of the Allied Works Council. Packer was seconded to serve as director of personnel. The appointments were pilloried by newspaper rivals, old political opponents and some trade unions. An inquiry in 1943 cleared the A.W.C. of charges of corruption and breaching awards. Packer scrutinized the wartime activities of his publications, which were struggling under newsprint and censorship restrictions; on one occasion he was accused of running his papers during government time. In 1944 he resigned from the A.W.C. He served in Australia and New Guinea with the 43rd Landing Craft Company and the 2nd/1st Amphibious Armoured Squadron before transferring to the Reserve of Officers on 14 July 1945.

During a business trip to England in October, Packer asserted that Australia should be consulted in any settlement with Japan, and that an imperial council should be formed to speak for all members of the British Empire and Commonwealth. He feared that the Empire might collapse and that Australia would be left alone, 'a tiny white population on the perimeter of Asia'. New South Wales president (1950-51) of the Australian-American Association, he was also a director (1953-56) of Reuters Ltd and a founding councillor (1954) of the Nuclear Research Foundation within the University of Sydney.

His newspapers supported the Liberal and Country parties after the 1946 election. In 1948, believing that the *Weekly*'s newsprint allocation was discriminatory, Packer accused Prime Minister Chifley [q.v.13] of allowing other publishers to invade the magazine's 'birthright' and openly threatened to intensify his publications' hostility to Labor. Yet, when private companies controlled by Packer were examined by the commissioner for taxation in 1952, his newspapers savaged the treasurer Sir Arthur Fadden [q.v.14] for amendments to income tax laws. Packer then created family trusts and Consolidated Press Holdings Ltd (1954). His interests were to extend from newspaper, magazine and book publishing to printing, television, film distribution, tourist resorts and a piggery. During the Cold War his papers had turned increasingly to the right. On his instructions, the *Daily Telegraph* (7 March 1953) marked Joseph Stalin's death with a sketch of a crocodile crying and the caption, 'POOR OLD JOE'.

In 1955 Packer established an affiliated company, Television Corporation Ltd, which obtained a Sydney television licence. On 16 September 1956 TCN-9 began transmitting experimental programmes. Although he was chairman, Packer never felt as comfortable with television as he did with the press. In 1960 his group purchased a majority share-holding in General Television Corporation Pty Ltd, Melbourne. Packer made regular visits to London and New York, where he stayed at luxury hotels and negotiated deals. Australian Consolidated Press Ltd, as his main company became known in 1957, launched a plethora of publications at this time: the 'radically conservative' *Observer* was the only one of cultural significance.

Despite his working knowledge of newspapers, Packer always remained self-conscious about his limited journalistic experience. The 'Young Master' fiercely defended his father's achievements and reputation. His own achievements were largely due to two exceptional mentors, financial cunning, bravado, prodigious energy and an ability to identify and nurture the talents of others. Packer fell out with several individuals who had participated in his early successes. He resented Warnecke's closeness to R. C. Packer and his belief that he was entitled to a major shareholding in the company; Warnecke maintained that Frank did not want to be seen as 'the playboy son of a rich father' or to share the credit for his achievements. When relations became strained with N. B. Theodore, who had assumed various executive positions held by his father, Packer acquired his family's shareholding in 1957.

Office gossip centred round Packer's latest burst of tyranny. The flurry of memoranda concerning petty cash for models' brassieres, camera bulbs and seating requirements bordered on high farce. He made generous donations to charity on the condition that they were not publicized, bestowed largesse on employees down on their luck and adopted stray dogs while fighting against increases in award wages and indulging in ritual sackings.

Packer had immense charm, when he cared to exercise it, but he was viewed with disdain by some members of the establishment. Few forgot his brawl with Ezra Norton [q.v.] at Randwick racecourse in 1939. Packer was 6 ft 1 in. (185 cm) tall and thickset, with blue eyes, dark brown wavy hair, a jutting jaw and a husky voice. His sense of humour and blustering manner hid his shyness. When choristers performed 'Hark! the Herald-Angels Sing' outside Cairnton, his Bellevue Hill mansion, he offered them money to sing 'Hark! the Telegraph-Angels Sing' outside (Sir) Warwick Fairfax's household.

Knighted in 1959, Packer joined the boards of charities such as the Royal Blind Society of New South Wales and the University of Sydney's Post Graduate Medical Foundation. He was increasingly drawn to traditional Australian institutions: when he acquired the *Bulletin* and attempted to take over Angus & Robertson [qq.v.7,11] Ltd, observers wondered whether St Andrew's Cathedral would be the next property targeted.

In 1960 Packer flew with Gretel to the United States for her heart surgery. He was by her side when she died in the Mayo Clinic, Rochester, New York. Their marriage had endured his roving eye and more than one affair. By this time their sons were working at Consolidated Press, where they were subjected to their father's bullying. On 15 June 1964 at the register office, Westminster, London, Frank married the stylish, half-Russian, half-French, twice-wed divorcee Florence Adeline Vincent, née Porges.

Sport remained Packer's passion. He had won the State amateur heavyweight boxing championship in 1929, and was an accomplished polo player and yachtsman before World War II. He won the 1947 Caulfield Cup with Columnist, bred at his part-owned stud. Packer served on the committees of the New South Wales Amateur Boxing Association, the New South Wales Polo Association, the Australian Jockey Club and the Royal Agricultural Society of New South Wales. He belonged to the Royal Sydney Yacht Squadron and the Australian Golf Club, held Sunday tennis parties, and imported an American golf cart which he used when holidaying at Surfers Paradise, Queensland.

Having commissioned Australia's 12-metre sloop, *Gretel*, to compete in the 1962 America's Cup, Packer (who loved to 'pile on sail and barge straight ahead') adopted a 'hands-on' approach to the challenge, which was unsuccessful. He tried again in 1970: when his syndicate's appeal against the disqualification of *Gretel II* in the second race failed, he commented that appealing against the New York Yacht Club was like complaining to your mother-in-law about your wife. In 1971 he was appointed K.B.E.

Packer candidly admitted that the *Telegraph*s were political bludgeons. His editors and editor-in-chief David McNicoll 'learnt how to sniff the breeze'. Following the award of a libel payment of £30 000 in 1963 to a Labor politician Tom Uren against the *Bulletin* and *Telegraph*s, a six-year legal battle raged until the matter was settled out of court. By late 1969 Packer was campaigning against Prime Minister (Sir) John Gorton and promoting (Sir) William McMahon, the treasurer and an old friend. Although Gorton's administration was dogged by controversy, Packer was dubbed a 'king-maker' for his role in McMahon's accession to the prime ministership in March 1971.

Sir Frank had executed a business coup in 1967 which increased his family's wealth and forced Rupert Murdoch to sell his interest in Television Corporation; Murdoch had once observed that Packer was 'the biggest crook in Australian newspapers, but equally he is the cleverest'. Packer had developed elaborate measures to hide the *Telegraph*s' losses. He had long realized the necessity of producing an afternoon newspaper to use idle printing capacity, but his efforts to acquire a majority shareholding in Associated Newspapers Ltd in 1953 had been thwarted by John Fairfax & Sons [qq.v.4,8] Pty Ltd. Despite impressive sales, the *Daily Telegraph* had never been able to break the *Sydney Morning Herald*'s stranglehold on classified advertising, and had always been subsidized by the *Weekly*. In June 1972, following a printers' strike, Packer finally acceded to his sons' pressure to sell the *Telegraph*s to News Ltd for $15 million.

After taking over K. G. Murray's family interests in Publishers Holdings Ltd, Consolidated Press became the largest magazine publisher in the southern hemisphere. It was of little consolation to Packer, who was devastated by losing his newspapers—'he cried when he spoke of it; his face was pinched and his gaze distracted'. There were two further blows in 1972. Clyde resigned in protest at his father's order that an interview with R. J. L. Hawke, the leader of the Australian Council of Trade Unions, could not be telecast; and the *Weekly*'s editor Esmé Fenston [q.v.14], whom Packer revered, died suddenly.

Despite being fitted with a pacemaker and despite his glaucoma, Packer could not resist one final political foray. During the 1972 elections he forbade the *Bulletin* to run a feature on Margaret Whitlam, the wife of E. G. Whitlam, leader of the Australian Labor Party, and he instructed senior staff to deliver editorials on TCN-9 supporting McMahon. Part of the agreement with News Ltd had been a promise not to start another newspaper for two years. As the second anniversary of the sale approached, Packer ordered offset

presses. Survived by his wife and by the sons of his first marriage, he died of cancer and pneumonia on 1 May 1974 in Royal Prince Alfred Hospital and was cremated. His estate was sworn for probate at $1.3 million; tax minimization schemes meant that the assets under his control were worth much more. Although Clyde had been reconciled with his father, Kerry took charge of the empire; they cancelled the order for the new presses.

Packer took risks and lived fast. His financial deals, political campaigns and sporting efforts were spectacular. As *The Times* noted, he was 'in a real sense a colourful figure, but his colours were always primary ones'. Emery Barcs, the veteran *Telegraph* foreign correspondent, recorded: 'The King is dead. I was fond of that strange buccaneer'. Judy Cassab's portrait (1956) of Packer is held by Australian Consolidated Press Ltd.

B. Griffen-Foley, *The House of Packer* (Syd, 1999) and for bib; *PD* (H of R), vol 219, 1952, p 2314; Prime Minister's Dept, Allied Works Council, A1608, AK27/1/2, *and* Cabinet Secretariat, A4909/XM1, Cabinet Minutes, vol 5 (AA); Dept of Trade and Customs, CP208/1, A37 *and* Dept of Information, SP195/2, 365/25 (AA); John Fairfax Group Pty Ltd Archives, Syd; Barcs family *and* Sir Jack Cassidy *and* Donald Horne *and* Voltaire Molesworth papers (ML); Sir Lloyd Dumas *and* Sir Robert Menzies *and* Alan Reid *and* Sir Ernest White papers (NL); family papers held by and information from Lady Stening, Point Piper, Syd; papers held by Ms I. Buttrose, Double Bay, Syd; G. Warnecke papers held by Mme M. Sordello, Paris; information from Lady Packer, Monaco.   BRIDGET GRIFFEN-FOLEY

PACKER, GERALD (1900-1962), army and air force officer, businessman and government adviser, was born on 14 April 1900 at Brighton, Melbourne, eldest of three children of John William Packer, an English-born accountant, and his Melbourne-born wife Linda Amy Yates, née Woolcott. Educated at Brighton Grammar School (dux 1915) and (on a scholarship) at Melbourne Church of England Grammar School, Gerry entered the Royal Military College, Duntroon, Federal Capital Territory, in 1917. He graduated in December 1920 and won the King's Medal for coming top of his class. Lieutenant Packer trained with British Army units in England and Germany in 1921-22. He returned to Australia in June 1922 and was posted to the 1st Coast Artillery Brigade, centred in Sydney.

In 1923, following a reduction in the military establishment, Packer obtained a secondment (later a transfer) to the Royal Australian Air Force. He completed pilot training at Point Cook, Victoria, in December 1924 and was posted to Air Force Headquarters, Melbourne. After attending the University of Melbourne (B.Sc., 1926), he was sent to England to learn aerial photography. Back at R.A.A.F. Headquarters in 1927, he planned aerial surveys, flew on an expedition around Papua and the Mandated Territory of New Guinea as a photographer, and served (1928) with a detachment at Bowen, Queensland, mapping the Great Barrier Reef from the air.

On 16 May 1929 at the Presbyterian Church, Armadale, Melbourne, Flight Lieutenant Packer married Maida Helen Crawford. In September he was posted to No.1 Squadron at Laverton, where he was a flight commander and unit photographic officer. Problems with his eyesight, wrongly diagnosed as glaucoma, led him to resign in February 1932. Beginning his civilian career as an investment adviser and consultant, he became a public accountant in 1935 and sat on the boards of several companies. He joined the Economic Society of Australia and New Zealand and the Australian Institute of International Affairs, and contributed to their publications. In 1930 he had also joined the Young Nationalist Organisation.

As a captain, then a major, on the army's Unattached List, Packer spent an increasing amount of his time on intelligence and operational planning duties at Army Headquarters in 1937-40. Disillusioned with the complacency of some of his superiors over the threat posed by Japan, he left the army in July 1940. He unsuccessfully sought United Australia Party pre-selection for the House of Representatives seat of Corio. In September he was mobilized in the R.A.A.F. as a flight lieutenant and posted to the Directorate of Operations and Intelligence. Promoted temporary wing commander in April 1941, he was appointed director of intelligence on 18 September. Following Japanese air-raids on Darwin in February 1942, he gave evidence to (Sir) Charles Lowe's [q.v.] inquiry into the state of the R.A.A.F.'s preparedness.

In April 1942 Packer was appointed senior air intelligence officer at Allied Naval Forces Headquarters. On the formation of R.A.A.F. Command within the Allied Air Forces in September, he was promoted acting group captain and dispatched to Brisbane to command Forward Echelon of R.A.A.F. Headquarters. He represented the chief of the Air Staff at A.A.F. Headquarters and was a liaison officer to the headquarters of the allied naval and land forces.

Leaving Brisbane in July 1943, Packer helped to found and taught at the R.A.A.F. Staff School, Mount Martha, Victoria. In October 1944 he was sent to Noemfoor, Netherlands East Indies, as officer-in-charge of administration, No.10 Operational Group (renamed First Tactical Air Force), which soon moved to Morotai. He transferred to R.A.A.F. Headquarters in February 1945 as assistant-inspector of administration. After his

R.A.A.F. appointment terminated on 21 June, he was a member (1945-47) of the war establishments investigation committee.

Packer was made a vice-president of the A.I.I.A. in 1946 and associate-editor of the institute's new journal, *Australian Outlook*, in 1947. He joined (1946) Round Table and contributed unsigned articles to its quarterly. The Federal government nominated him as an observer at the Asian Relations Conference, held in New Delhi in March-April 1947. In that year Dr H. V. Evatt [q.v.14] invited him to serve on a committee which advised the government on terms for a peace settlement with Japan. Packer was disappointed when he failed to gain pre-selection as Liberal Party candidate for Deakin at the 1949 Federal elections.

A member (1950-55 and 1959-62) and vice-chairman (1953-56) of the Australian National Airlines Commission, Packer played a part in formulating the Federal coalition government's two-airline policy. In 1950 he was appointed to the defence services establishments committee. In the following year he visited England as a delegate to a conference of British Commonwealth countries on closer links with Europe; further discussions, organized by the European League for Economic Co-operation, followed in Brussels. The Menzies [q.v.] government placed him on the Commonwealth Immigration Planning Council in 1954. He was appointed C.B.E. in 1959. Later that year he joined a committee which examined Post Office accounts.

Packer was a member of the Australian Institute of Management (councillor, Melbourne division, 1953-55), the Operational Research Society of Victoria, the Australian Industries Development Association, and the Australian Committee (Association) for Cultural Freedom (from 1954). He helped to organize appeals for charities, and promoted civil liberties and Aboriginal welfare. Survived by his wife and daughter, he died of a coronary occlusion on 23 May 1962 in Little Bourke Street, Melbourne, and was cremated.

C. Coulthard-Clark, *Edge of Centre* (Point Cook, Vic, 1992), and for bib.

C. D. COULTHARD-CLARK

PAGE, ROBERT CHARLES (1920-1945), soldier, was born on 21 July 1920 at Summer Hill, Sydney, eldest of four children of Harold Hillis Page [q.v.11], an Australian-born public servant, and his wife Anne Miller, née Brewster, who came from Scotland. (Sir) Earle Page [q.v.11] was his uncle. Educated at Sydney Boys' High School, Bob enrolled in medicine at the University of Sydney in 1940 and joined the Sydney University Rifles. On

15 April 1941 he enlisted in the Australian Imperial Force. He was posted to the 2nd/4th Pioneer Battalion in May and promoted lieutenant in July. In February 1943 he transferred to 'Z' Special Unit, whose members conducted secret operations behind enemy lines in the South-West Pacific Area.

Six feet (183 cm) tall and lean, with fair hair, blue eyes and 'a smile that seemed to splash his face', Page underwent training near Cairns, Queensland. He was selected to take part in Operation Jaywick, a raid on enemy shipping at Singapore. The party left Exmouth Gulf, Western Australia, on 2 September 1943, bound for the Rhio (Riau) Archipelago (near Singapore) in a 70-ft (21 m) motor vessel which had been captured from the Japanese and renamed *Krait*. Before dawn on 18 September Page and five companions were put ashore at Panjang Island. On the night of the 26th they paddled three two-man canoes towards their objectives. Page and Able Seaman A. W. Jones attached limpet mines to three merchant ships, one at Bukum Island and two in Keppel Harbour. Their comrades targeted three freighters and a tanker before all six commandos withdrew. They heard the first explosions at 5.15 a.m. on the 27th as they reached Dongas Island.

The *Krait* picked up Page and his companions at Pompong Island on 2 and 3 October, and returned to Exmouth Gulf on the 19th. In all, the party had sunk or damaged more than 36 000 tons of Japanese shipping. Page won the Distinguished Service Order for his part in the action, but the award was not promulgated until 1945. At St Andrew's Presbyterian Church, Canberra, on 1 November 1943 he married Roma Noelene Prowse, a 21-year-old machinist. He was promoted temporary captain in July 1944 while training for Operation Rimau, a second raid on Singapore.

In September 1944 Page was one of twenty-three men taken by submarine to the South China Sea. There they seized a junk in which they sailed towards Singapore. On 6 October, off Laban Island, they mistakenly fired on a Malay police launch, killing some or all of the crew. With secrecy lost, the mission was abandoned. The commandos scuttled the junk and made their way in rubber dinghies to their base on Merapas Island. For about two months they either evaded or fought off the pursuing Japanese. A British submarine sent to collect them failed to make contact. Page and ten other survivors were eventually captured, taken to Singapore and sentenced to death. With nine comrades, he was beheaded on 7 July 1945 at Ulu Pandan. After the war had ended, his remains were reinterred in Kranji war cemetery. His wife survived him.

N. Wynyard, *Winning Hazard* (Lond, 1947); A. Ind, *Spy Ring Pacific* (Lond, 1958); R. McKie, *The Heroes* (Syd, 1960); G. H. Gill, *Royal Australian Navy 1942-1945* (Canb, 1968); D. C. Horton, *Ring of Fire* (Melb, 1983); S. Lithgow, Special Operations: the Organisations of the Special Operations Executive in Australia and their operations against the Japanese during the Second World War (M.A. Hons thesis, ADFA, UNSW, 1992).

SHIRLEY LITHGOW

PAGE, WALTER (c.1904-1956), Aboriginal activist, was born about 1904 at Lismore, New South Wales, son of Mary Page. He was one of the few Aboriginal children permitted to attend Lismore Public School. Many years later he recalled that the assistant-master Herbert Moffitt had taken a keen interest in him and had said, 'Walter, don't be shy, I will make a good little scholar of you. Some day you may be a great man among your people'. The teacher later became a justice of the Workers' Compensation Commission. After leaving school, Page undertook general farm work, fencing and shearing, particularly for the Armstrong family of Disputed Plains station. He became known as the accomplished rider of Armstrong's hunters and jumpers in show-rings throughout the Northern Rivers district. At St Andrew's Anglican Church, Lismore, on 16 May 1936 he married Charlotte Close; they were to remain childless.

Although Page and the leading Aboriginal activist William Ferguson [q.v.8] were elected on the Aborigines Protection Association's 'ticket' to the Aborigines Welfare Board in November 1943, Page's eligibility was questioned on the grounds that he was not 'a full-blooded Aboriginal'. When he was not permitted to take his seat, a struggle developed between the A.W.B., supported by the colonial secretary J. M. Baddeley [q.v.7], and the Aboriginal electors, who boycotted further nominations. Questions were asked in State parliament and an impasse ensued. Eventually, in January 1946, Page was named as the successful candidate.

A regular attender of the board's monthly meetings, Page deplored the abysmal standard of Aboriginal housing and the lack of educational opportunities for Aboriginal children. Although the government had agreed in 1939 to transfer the responsibility for the education of Aboriginal children to the Department of Education, there were still many Aboriginal schools on A.W.B. stations where the manager, who had no teacher-training, was obliged to instruct the children as part of his day-to-day duties. Page's address to the international conference of the New Education Fellowship in Sydney in September 1946 was published in *Education for International Understanding* (Adelaide, 1948). In January 1948 he and Ferguson toured Aboriginal stations on the north coast; their written report to the board was commended. Later that year they both travelled to Aboriginal stations and reserves in the Riverina and the south-west, and wrote another comprehensive report.

During his visits to Sydney, Page invariably called on 'the judge', as he affectionately referred to Moffitt. In turn, Moffitt introduced him to influential people whom he thought would support efforts to improve the situation of Aborigines. Page continued his work to better the condition of his people in a quiet, unassuming way that won him numerous friends and supporters. He lacked the fiery disposition of Ferguson and was widely regarded as a thorough 'gentleman'. Page did not seek re-election to the board in July 1948 as 'he had no patience to carry on'. Survived by his wife, he died of cancer on 9 March 1956 at the Memorial Hospital, Kyogle, and was buried with Pentecostal rites in the Aboriginal cemetery at Woodenbong.

J. Horner, *Vote Ferguson for Aboriginal Freedom* (Syd, 1974); *PD* (NSW), 14 Mar 1944, p 1632, 6 Mar 1945, p 2354, 8 Mar 1945, p 2502; NSW Aborigines Welfare Bd, *Dawn*, 5, no 3, 1956, p 7; *SMH*, 10 Sept 1946, 15 Feb 1949; Aborigines Welfare Bd, minutes 1945-48; information from Ms V. Close, Woodenbong, NSW.   ALAN T. DUNCAN

PAINE, ARNOLD GERALD STEWART (1897-1979), soapbox orator, was born on 24 June 1897 in Adelaide, youngest of four children of Henry William James Paine, insurance agent, and his wife Rebecca Louisa, née Worley (d.1899). Little is known about Arnold's childhood or youth, except that he may have had a brief flirtation with socialism. When he first came to public notice he was living in lodgings in the Carlton-Fitzroy area of Melbourne, whence he conducted a horse-and-van carrier business, delivering goods such as footwear from Collingwood factories to shops in the inner-northern suburbs. About 1945 Paine became a newspaper-seller, eventually occupying a kiosk in the city near the corner of Russell and Bourke streets. On Friday nights he often addressed passers-by from that corner, usually gathering a modest but interested audience. His natural habitat, however, was the Yarra Bank (adjacent to Batman Avenue) on Sunday afternoons. There, from the late 1930s, he ranged widely over issues of the day, concentrating particularly on the evils of communism.

When Paine stepped onto the mound under the trees on the Yarra Bank, he looked an unprepossessing figure, gaunt and birdlike in a well-worn suit, with a disconcerting in-turned left eye accentuated by thick, horn-rimmed glasses. His usual texts were week-old news-paper articles reporting some recent Soviet infamy, which he denounced in his strident, nasal voice for all to hear. Hecklers or nearby speakers were sprayed with a blast of vitriolic wit, such as, 'Yeww wouldn't have enough brains to be able to lead a willing heifer to the business end of an enterprising bull', and, 'Madam, you've been crook on me ever since I refused to sleep with you'.

In July 1951 Daniel Cody, a regular interlocutor, brought a charge of insulting language against him: it was dismissed, partly because of Cody's behaviour in the witness-box. Paine claimed, on another occasion, that a group of communists threatened to throw him in the river, but he escaped by jumping on a passing tram, promising to return on the following Sunday. He frequently attended May Day marches and other left-wing demonstrations where his taunts and droll humour provoked irritation and good-natured banter.

By the early 1950s Paine was such a well-known eccentric that students at the University of Melbourne invited him to deliver an annual lecture. Only nominally addressing the set topic, his lectures were more theatrical than pedagogical, with Paine seeming to enjoy the heckling and other student pranks: 'I like my listeners to be demonstrative. There's nothing worse than talking to rows of dead cabbages'. His emphasis later shifted from Cold War rhetoric to 'rough-house' repartee. In the early 1970s, when public speaking gave way to television and other entertainment, he left the Yarra Bank 'to the lunatic fringe'. As his health declined, he lived an increasingly reclusive life in a Carlton rooming-house, though he continued to sell newspapers in the city until stricken by lung cancer. He died on 16 July 1979 at Fitzroy and was cremated; his estate was sworn for probate at $67 174.

Herald (Melb), 10, 21 July 1951; *Age* (Melb), 11 July 1951, 25 June 1952, 30 July, 25 Aug 1979; information from Ms L. Hemensley, Westgarth, Mr V. Little, Brunswick, Ms U. Norris, Brunswick East, Mr J. Button, Melb, and the late Mr J. Arrowsmith.
PETER LOVE

PAINE, DUKE DOUGLAS (1892-1960), public servant and army officer, was born on 26 May 1892 at Ballarat, Victoria, second child of Ballarat-born parents William Louis Paine, a commission agent who became a teacher of elocution, and his wife Ellen, née Brown. Educated at Melbourne Continuation (High) School, Douglas entered the Victorian Public Service on 23 July 1909 as a clerk in the statist's office, Department of the Chief Secretary. He transferred to the land tax office, Department of the Treasurer, in 1913. At Christ Church, South Yarra, on 24 September 1914 he married with Anglican rites Alice

Freda (d.1957), daughter of the artist Alexander McClintock.

On 1 July 1911 Paine had been commissioned in the Australian Army Service Corps, Militia. Joining the Australian Imperial Force on 21 August 1914, he served with the 1st Divisional Train in Egypt, at Gallipoli and on the Western Front. In January 1917 he was promoted temporary major (substantive in March) and appointed senior supply officer for the division. He was awarded the Distinguished Service Order for his 'consistent good work' between September 1917 and February 1918. Twice mentioned in dispatches, he returned to Melbourne where his A.I.F. appointment terminated in April 1919.

Paine resumed his career in the public service. In 1923 he was promoted inspector and secretary to the commissioner, Taxation Department. He was general secretary (1933-35) to the Victorian and Melbourne Centenary Celebrations Council before becoming comptroller of stamps in 1936. Meanwhile he had been active in the Militia. For his services (from 1921) as lieutenant colonel commanding the 3rd Divisional Train (A.A.S.C.) he was appointed O.B.E. (1933). He was transferred to the Unattached List in 1935. In 1939 he was made assistant-director of supplies and transport, 3rd Military District base headquarters.

In April 1940 Paine was seconded to the A.I.F. Promoted colonel and temporary brigadier, he was gazetted assistant-director (later deputy-director) of supplies and transport, I Corps. He sailed for the Middle East in October. During the campaign in Greece (April 1941) his work in providing stores and vehicles 'was one of the principal factors in securing the successful withdrawal' of the Anzac Corps; he was elevated to C.B.E. (1941) and awarded the Greek Military Cross (1942). From September 1941 he held the additional post of D.D.S. & T. at A.I.F. Headquarters, Palestine. Returning to Melbourne in November, he was deputy quartermaster general at Army (Land) Headquarters until May 1944. In the following month he was transferred to the Reserve of Officers.

Throughout his military career Paine was known as a man of gruff exterior, but one who always looked to the welfare of his soldiers. In World War I he had established his reputation as a junior commander. One of the dedicated few who remained with the Citizen Military Forces in the lean years of the 1920s and 1930s, he and others like him trained the militiamen who provided the backbone for the second A.I.F., though they might have given junior officers more opportunities to gain command experience. Paine's work as a staff officer and administrator during World War II was highly regarded.

On 1 June 1944 Paine was appointed chairman of the Victorian Public Service Board, a post he held until his retirement in 1957. The Victorian Public Service Association praised him as one who, behind an 'often hard and unrelenting front', consistently acted in the interests of the service, defended the conditions of its members, and rejected 'representations by people in high places seeking preferential treatment for the favoured few'. Following his retirement, he chaired the Trotting Control Board: he proved an effective and principled chairman, and turned out to be a keen punter with his own betting systems. A dedicated family man, he also acted as warden and organist of Christ Church, South Yarra. He died of cancer on 27 February 1960 in East Melbourne and was cremated; his son and two daughters survived him.

N. Lindsay, *Equal to the Task*, vol 1 (Brisb, 1992); *Public Service J of Vic*, June 1957, p 3; *Age* (Melb), 29 Feb 1960; *Herald* (Melb), 1 Mar 1960; A1838/265, file 1535/11/1 (AA, Canb); AWM 43, item A663, and AWM 140 (AWM).

NEVILLE LINDSAY

PAINE, SIR HERBERT KINGSLEY (1883-1972), judge, was born on 26 January 1883 at Gawler, South Australia, second child of Herbert Paine (d.1891), an accountant from England, and his South Australian-born wife Helen, née Milne (d.1885). After his father died of typhoid fever, Kingsley was raised by his guardian, the solicitor S. B. Rudall. Taught at a local school (run by the Misses Lewis) and by a private tutor, he later boarded at the Collegiate School of St Peter, Adelaide, where he won the Farrell open scholarship (1897), the Young exhibition (1899) and the Westminster scholarship (1900). He coached a fellow prefect, Essington Lewis [q.v.10], in Latin and became his lifelong friend.

In 1902 Paine was articled to W. R. Lewis at Gawler and in 1904 to T. R. Bright at Gilberton. Graduating from the University of Adelaide (LL.B., 1904), he was admitted to the South Australian Bar on 19 April 1905. He conducted a general legal practice at Port Pirie and Gawler for three years. By 1908 he was confidential clerk to W. J. Denny [q.v.8] in Adelaide. At St Augustine's Anglican Church, Unley, on 8 October 1912 he married Amy Muriel Pearson; they were to have two sons and two daughters. In partnership with H. W. Uffindell, he practised at Wallaroo, Kadina and Moonta until 1922 when he was employed as a special magistrate at Wallaroo.

Paine was transferred in 1923 to the Adelaide Local Court Department. He was appointed a judge in insolvency (1926) and a judge of the local court (1927). In 1926 he was assigned to a royal commission to investigate allegations that members of the South Australian police force had taken bribes. Although evidence proved difficult to obtain, he concluded that bribery had occurred for some years, involving bookmakers and a number of officers. A member of a range of statutory boards and tribunals, Paine acted as returning officer for various electoral districts and eventually for the State. As chairman of the Farmers' Assistance Board he played 'an important part in the rehabilitation of wheat-growers adversely affected by . . . the depression of the 1930s'. He also served as an adjudicator on wheat contracts.

In 1943 Paine headed the committee of inquiry into South Australia's electricity supply. Its report advocated the development of local sources of fuel, especially at Leigh Creek, and recommended the appointment of a co-ordinating authority to oversee all matters connected with the generation and supply of power. Four weeks after the findings were presented, the State Electricity Commission was established. From 1947 to 1951 Paine chaired the royal commission on transport services in South Australia. Following an extensive survey of the systems operating on land and waterways, the commission recommended the creation of a ministry of transport, with a co-ordinating authority to advise the minister. Paine was appointed C.M.G. in 1944 and knighted in 1953.

After retiring as a judge of the local court in 1948, Paine served as an acting puisne judge of the Supreme Court of South Australia in 1949-50 and 1951-52. For the most part he presided over divorce cases, claims for damages and traffic infringements. Displaying a first-rate mind, he got straight to the issue, even in involved cases. He travelled to work by tram until he was 88.

Sir Kingsley resigned as a judge in insolvency early in 1972. Survived by a son and a daughter, he died on 3 November that year in North Adelaide and was cremated. His elder son Robert had been killed in action (1943) in New Guinea during World War II.

Honorary Magistrate, 31 Dec 1926, p 672; *Observer* (Adel), 30 Oct 1926; *Advertiser* (Adel), 1 Jan 1944, 25 Mar 1949, 1 Jan 1953, 2 Mar 1971, 8 Nov 1972; 'Tributes to His Honour the Late Sir Kingsley Paine' (ts, Bankruptcy Court, Adel); family information.

K. P. McEvoy

PALAZZI, VICTORIA LEONIE ('PAT') (1888-1964), teacher and school inspector, was born on 2 April 1888 at Boman, near Wagga Wagga, New South Wales, third daughter and tenth of eleven children of Swiss-born parents Jean-Baptiste Palazzi, railway-ganger, and his wife Assunta, née Delponte. Jean-Baptiste reputedly left the Italian-speaking canton of Ticino to evade Austrian military conscrip-

tion. He worked in rural New South Wales as a goldminer and on the railways before moving to Sydney to be near his family, 'most of whom had settled there'. Leonie (who detested her first name of Victoria and later settled for 'Pat') attended the Presentation Convent, Mount Erin, and passed the senior public examination in 1904.

Miss Palazzi joined the Department of Public Instruction in July 1907 as a pupil-teacher at Enmore Public School, Sydney, and completed training in 1909. While teaching (1910-15) in primary schools, she attended (part time) the University of Sydney (B.A., 1913) and in 1916-19 taught in turn at Goulburn and at St George Girls' high schools. A tallish, attractive woman, she caught the attention of the Catholic diocese of Maitland. Paid from a sustaining fund willed to the Church, she became in 1920 the diocese's inspector of schools. From the early 1930s she drove her own car, 'Rosebud'. In 1936 she edited the *Roma Poetry Book*, a much-reprinted anthology for school children.

In April 1938 Palazzi returned to the department and taught at Wagga Wagga High School; she also began tutoring novices at Mount Erin convent, and led the local group of a Melbourne-based lay movement for Catholic teachers in public primary and secondary schools. She retired from the department in late 1943 and served as inspector of schools (1945-48) for the Wilcannia-Forbes diocese. Palazzi returned to Sydney (to live at Kings Cross). At the Church of Mary Immaculate, Manly, on 21 May 1948 she married John Joseph ('J.J.') Byrnes (d.1955), a widower and a retired hotel-owner from Wagga Wagga. They lived in Darley Road, Manly.

Age, late marriage and widowhood did not stop Pat's involvement in education. Her Catholic inspectorates had been directed to advancing primary education. At Wagga Wagga, as novices' tutor, she had joined the drive for higher secondary teaching standards. She continued to visit the novices at Mount Erin during her Wilcannia-Forbes inspectorate. In 1956, long financially independent, she was installed as the honorary 'Mistress of Method' to the novices' teacher-training schools at Lochinvar and Singleton convents.

Once a keen golfer, Palazzi divided her last years between training novices, motoring, playing solo and bridge, being a generous and enlivening 'auntie' to her Palazzi nieces and nephews, and reading aloud to 'J.J.'s' grandson the children's literature which her world had inherited. Remembered variously as imperious, bossy, friendly, pleasant and one who enjoyed a beer with the girls, she was a spiritual, intellectual and secular inspirer to two generations of Catholics, religious and lay. She died of myocardial infarction on 12 May

1964 at Manly District Hospital and was buried in Woronora cemetery.

Daily Advertiser (Wagga Wagga), 10 Dec 1912, 6 Oct 1917; Presentation Convent, Mount Erin, Wagga Wagga, archives; information from Mrs K. Hawke and Mrs M. McNair, NSW; family information.

DAVID DENHOLM*

PALMER, HELEN GWYNNETH (1917-1979), educationist, was born on 9 May 1917 at Kew, Melbourne, younger daughter of Edward Vivian ('Vance') Palmer and his wife Janet (Nettie) Gertrude, née Higgins [qq.v.11 Palmer] both Australian-born writers. Helen attended Presbyterian Ladies' College (dux 1934) and won a scholarship to the University of Melbourne (B.A. Hons, 1939; B.Ed., 1952), where she co-edited and wrote for *Melbourne University Magazine*. From 1940 she taught in state schools, first at Port Fairy and then at Terang. On 18 February 1942 she joined the Women's Auxiliary Australian Air Force. She served mainly in Melbourne, at the School of Administration and Air Force Headquarters. Rising to flight officer, she took charge of educational services for W.A.A.A.F. personnel. After being placed on the Retired List on 16 October 1946, she worked in Sydney, briefly for Edwards & Shaw, publishers, and later in the Commonwealth Office of Education. Returning to Melbourne in 1948, she taught in private schools and completed her second degree. In 1952 she joined the New South Wales Department of Education as a casual teacher.

Skilful and creative, Palmer was greatly appreciated by her students. With her friend Jessie Macleod, she wrote a number of books: the two most important were *The First Hundred Years* (London, 1954) and *After the First Hundred Years* (Melbourne, 1961). While academic historians were still talking about the importance of social history she was writing it. Her books emphasized 'the elements of the everyday lives of ordinary people'. Readable and informative, they appealed both to children and adults.

An active member of the N.S.W. Teachers' Federation, Palmer made significant contributions to campaigns for equal pay and improved working conditions. She saw that, for education to continue throughout life, there needed to be an adequate foundation in the instruction of children at the primary and secondary levels, which could only be provided by a strong public-school system. Although she had attended a church school herself, she defended secular and humanist education, believing that teaching which was not directed towards encouraging inquiry was simply indoctrination. 'Human relations', she wrote, 'will fare better in the hands of adults who

have read *Pride and Prejudice, Cry the Beloved Country, The Fortunes of Richard Mahony* and *Catcher in the Rye* than of those whose acquisition of literacy has been interrupted by talks of "life-adjustment" and "how to get on with people"'.

Palmer belonged to the generation which had grown up during the Depression and the slide to war in 1939. She accepted the Marxist view that the economic malaise and the emergence of Nazism were features of a general crisis in world capitalism. Convinced of a socialist alternative, she had joined the Communist Party of Australia while a student and remained a member for two decades. Despite the atmosphere of the Korean War and the opposition of the Australian government, she attended the Peace Conference of the Asian and Pacific Regions, held in Peking (Beijing) in 1952. In a small book, *Australian Teacher in China* (Sydney, c.1953), she wrote warmly about the changes for the better which she thought were taking place in post-revolutionary China. On her return, the Department of Education refused to re-employ her for eighteen months; in 1955 she was appointed a temporary teacher of French and general studies at Fort Street Girls' High School (Fort Street High from 1975).

Her enthusiasm for communism in China was balanced by a growing disillusionment with the Soviet Union. It came to a head with the publication in 1956 of Nikita Khrushchev's secret speech to the 20th Congress of the Communist Party of the Soviet Union. For Palmer, who believed that socialism should lead to the freeing of the human spirit, this was the moment of truth. The leadership of the C.P.A. declared the speech a forgery and banned any discussion of it.

In the two years following the secret speech and the Soviet invasion of Hungary there was a mass exodus from the party by expulsion and resignation. Palmer was expelled after announcing her intention to publish material designed to open up discussion on socialist issues. For her, the discovery of the evils of Soviet communism did not remove the evils of capitalism. In mid-1957, with the support of an editorial board, she began the publication of *Outlook*, an independent socialist journal. From its earliest issues *Outlook* carried articles on the social conditions that were generating revolutionary upheavals in underdeveloped countries. In the complex anti-war movement led by peace groups, students, radicals and civil libertarians, *Outlook* was one of the voices of protest. Palmer did the detailed work of editor, as well as achieving the consensus of an editorial board comprising people with a wide range of specialized knowledge.

An active member of the Sydney committee of the South African Defence and Aid Fund,

Palmer was the object of a scurrilous attack during a committee-meeting in 1963. Although she had been publicly expelled from the Communist Party, she was required to state whether she was a communist. As a matter of principle she refused, and was expelled by the committee, which was itself split by the issue.

From the age of 11 Palmer was an occasional poet. 'The Ballad of 1891', which she wrote (1951) in collaboration with Doreen Bridges (who composed the music), celebrated the struggle of Queensland shearers against the pastoralists and the government. It has become an important part of Australian folklore, albeit often mistakenly assumed to be anonymous and to date from the time of the shearers' strike.

A sturdy woman of middle height, Palmer had green eyes and dark hair. Her brisk and efficient manner belied her warmth, humour and sensitivity. She died of cancer on 6 May 1979 in the Mater Misericordiae Hospital, North Sydney, and was cremated.

D. Bridges (ed), *Helen Palmer's Outlook* (Syd, 1982); H. Radi (ed), *200 Australian Women* (Syd, 1988); *SMH*, 21 Oct 1966; ASIO, A6119/XR, item 178 (AA); Teachers' records, Dept of Education (NSW) archives; V., N., A. and H. Palmer papers (NL).   ROBIN GOLLAN

PALMOS, ANGELOS (1903-1976), forester, was born on 25 May 1903 on the island of Levkados (Levkás), Greece, son of Petros Palmos, ship's captain, and his wife Stamata, née Manzaph. Angelos was married locally. A middle-ranking officer in the Royal Greek Navy, he claimed that he had become a wanted man after killing a senior officer in a pistol-duel. Assisted by fellow officers who had sided with him, he boarded a vessel bound for South Africa, Australia and Japan. When it reached Geelong, Victoria, in 1922, he jumped ship. In his application (1950) for Australian citizenship, however, he stated that he had disembarked from the *Commissare Ramel* in Melbourne in 1929. His wife had died in 1926 in Greece.

Able to speak only Greek and French, Palmos was helped by an Indo-Chinese storekeeper who directed him to some Greeks living in the city. With their help he leased a fruit shop in Sydney Road, Brunswick. At the Presbyterian Church, Brunswick, on 9 December 1933 he married Irene May Fitzpatrick, a 20-year-old saleswoman who worked for him. They were ostracized by family and friends who disapproved of the marriage. Irene taught him English and they opened a new shop in Sydney Road. Following a brief period of relative prosperity, the business was looted and their savings of three years were lost. In 1938 they moved to South Yarra.

During World War II the Directorate of Manpower sent Palmos to the tiny bush town of Noojee, Gippsland. He lived with his wife and four children in a tin hut, with an earthen floor, open fire and hessian-covered windows. His job was to supply wood to the army. After the war ended, he remained at Noojee and worked as a labourer, first for the Victorian Railways and then for the Department of State Forests. Realizing that little was being done to regenerate the forests, he began to propagate thousands of seedlings each year. He planted one million seedlings (mountain ash and pine) in south-east Victoria and was known as the 'Million Tree Man'. This physically demanding undertaking required him to live in tents or huts, and to walk long distances to and from his home. On 27 July 1951 he was naturalized.

Irene raised the children in primitive conditions. Strong-minded and ambitious, she strove to educate herself by taking correspondence courses, and by borrowing books from travelling salesmen and truck drivers who passed through Noojee. A founder of the Neerim and District Progress Association, she helped to preserve the trestle railway-bridges, and to prevent the felling of the area's remaining old trees and the banking of the La Trobe River. In her view, some trees were 'for chopping, others for beauty, others to hold the soil, others for continuing the natural forest'.

The Palmos family left Noojee about 1957. Irene and Angelos were later divorced. From 1975 he lived with his son Paul at Seaford. Survived by his two sons and two daughters, he died on 3 June 1976 at Prahran and was cremated with Anglican rites.

A. Loukakis, 'Angelo & Irene Palmos', in S. Baldwin (ed), *Unsung Heroes and Heroines of Australia* (Melb, 1988); D. Hunt, *Noojee and Neerim* (Melb, 1989); naturalization file, A443/1, item 1951/15/1468 (AA, Canb); family information.
ANGELO LOUKAKIS

PALTRIDGE, SIR SHANE DUNNE (1910-1966), politician, was born on 11 January 1910 at Leederville, Perth, son of South Australian-born parents Archer Dunn Paltridge, bank clerk, and his wife Florence Marjory, née Thomas. Educated at government schools in Western Australia, Queensland and New South Wales (including Fort Street Boys' High School, Sydney), Shane obtained a job with the National Bank of Australasia Ltd. He worked at branches in New South Wales (1926-29) and Western Australia (1929-36) before managing his aunt's hotel at Victoria Park, Perth.

On 12 February 1940 Paltridge enlisted in the Royal Australian Air Force. He failed flying training and was discharged in December 1941. After joining the Australian Imperial Force on 5 January 1942, he completed a number of courses and was posted as a gunner to the 2nd/7th Field Artillery Regiment in November 1944. He sailed to Morotai in April 1945, then served on Tarakan Island, Borneo. Returning to Australia, he was discharged from the army on 5 November. At the Sacred Heart Church, Highgate, Perth, on 21 January 1947 he married with Catholic rites Mary (Molly) Elizabeth McEncroe.

Paltridge was a foundation member (1946) of the Victoria Park branch of the Liberal and Country League of Western Australia, and a member (from 1947) of the State executive. He won pre-selection as a candidate for the Senate and at the general elections on 28 April 1951 narrowly gained the tenth and last place. Having served on two joint committees—public accounts (1952-55) and the broadcasting of parliamentary proceedings (1953-55)—he was minister for shipping and transport (1955-60) and for civil aviation (1956-64) under (Sir) Robert Menzies [q.v.]. He was admitted to cabinet in 1958 and appointed deputy-leader of the government in the Senate in 1959.

In his first years in parliament Paltridge was a stern critic of Australian communists. Describing them as fifth-columnists intent on 'industrial destruction', he strongly endorsed Menzies' efforts to proscribe the Communist Party of Australia. He spoke in support of Western Australia's economic interests, particularly North-West development and the air-beef scheme, and on defence issues, such as the spread of communism in Asia. As minister for shipping and transport, he won a reputation for hard-working competence. The Australian National Line was established, roll-on roll-off shipping was introduced, and services between Tasmania and the mainland were improved. As minister for civil aviation he was involved in the selection of the Boeing 727 and Fokker Friendship aircraft for domestic airlines, and in negotiating reciprocal landing rights with other countries for Qantas Empire Airways Ltd.

Appointed minister for defence in April 1964, Paltridge became leader of the government in the Senate in June. It was his lot to hold the defence portfolio at a time when Australia edged itself into the Vietnam War, and to be responsible for implementing significant and controversial defence decisions. On 8 June he announced that Australia's military presence in the Republic of Vietnam (South Vietnam) was to be expanded, and that Australian army instructors would not only train South Vietnamese soldiers but accompany them into action as advisers. In November 1964 Paltridge brought a paper to cabinet which stated that conscription would probably have to be introduced, but he suggested that the army should be allowed one final chance at voluntary enlistment. Cabinet, however, decided on the immediate introduction of compulsory national service, with conscripts selected by ballot and liable to serve overseas. At a meeting of cabinet's foreign affairs and defence committee on 7 April 1965, Paltridge was one of the 4:2 majority which decided to inform the United States of America that Australia was willing to offer a battalion of troops for service in South Vietnam.

Later that year Paltridge fell gravely ill. He was converted to Catholicism. On 1 January 1966 he was appointed K.B.E. He resigned from the ministry on the 19th. Survived by his wife and two daughters, he died of cancer on 21 January 1966 in South Perth; he was accorded a state funeral and was buried in Karrakatta cemetery. Sir Shane was of middle height, heavily built, and genial and open in manner. One of Menzies's few close confidants, he was also liked and respected by politicians of all parties.

S. Brogden, *Australia's Two-Airline Policy* (Melb, 1968); P. Edwards, *Crises and Commitments* (Syd, 1992); P. Hasluck, *The Chance of Politics* (Melb, 1997); *West Australian*, 22 Jan 1966; family information.

B. K. DE GARIS

PAPATHANASOPOULOS, THEOPHY-LACTOS (1891-1958), Greek Orthodox bishop, was born on the feast of St Basil, 1 January 1891, at Pyrgos, Greece, son of Demetrios Papathanasopoulos and his wife Kaliopi. He was baptized Vasileios (Basil). Having completed his schooling at Pyrgos and Halki, Constantinople (Istanbul), he began his novitiate at the monastery of Stavronikita, Mount Athos, Greece, made his vows as a monk on 2 December 1917 and took the name Theophylactos. He was ordained priest by Bishop Paisios of Nyssa on 24 December. After graduating from the theological faculty, University of Athens, he taught at the Rizareios Ecclesiastical School and proved a popular preacher in the capital's churches.

In February 1928, following the dismissal of Metropolitan Christophoros Knetes [q.v.9], Archimandrite Theophylactos was sent to Sydney as administrator until a new bishop arrived. He served for five years in Sydney and for fourteen in Melbourne. Theophylactos was appointed metropolitan of Australia and New Zealand on 22 April 1947 and was consecrated in Greece on 24 August. Spending some time at the monastery of Stavronikita, he proceeded by slow stages to his new post, reaching Perth on 19 April 1948. He was enthroned in Sydney on 13 June in the presence of a congregation that included Greek, Russian and Syrian clergy.

Despite his initial enthusiasm, Theophylactos encountered long-running disputes over Church administration and dogged opposition from a number of leaders of the old communities who refused to accept the authority of the ecumenical patriarchate in Istanbul. Postwar immigration swelled the number of faithful to over 75 000 and strained the resources at Theophylactos's disposal. Among the newcomers were thousands of prosperous, educated and multilingual Greeks from Egypt. Alarmed at the loss of so many of its subjects, the patriarchate of Alexandria tried to set up exarchates in other jurisdictions, including Australia. *Pantainos*, its official journal, made a series of savage attacks on Theophylactos in 1955, accusing him of neglecting the welfare and education of his flock. It also charged him with scheming to set up an independent Orthodox Church covering all the faithful (regardless of ethnic and jurisdictional origin) in spite of the fact that instructions to do precisely this had been issued to Knetes in 1924 by the patriarchate in Istanbul. These divisive tactics failed in Australia, although they had limited success in the United States of America. Tall and imposing, if somewhat reserved, Theophylactos was widely regarded as a fair and objective administrator, and as a dedicated pastor.

Theophylactos died on 2 August 1958 in the Alfred Hospital, Melbourne, from injuries received in a motorcar accident two days earlier. Following a service presided over by Archbishop Athenagoras of Thyateira at the Cathedral of St Sophia, Sydney, he was buried in Botany cemetery.

Pentekontaeteris, 1924-74 (Syd, 1976); *Threskeutike kai Ethike Enkyklopaideia* (Athens, 1980); H. L. N. Simmons, *Orthodoxy in Australia* (Brookline, Mass, US, 1986); *Pantainos* (Alexandria, Egypt), 47, 1955, pp 95, 137, 155-6; *SMH*, 11 Feb 1928, 14 June 1948, 12 Aug 1958; information from the Abbot of Stavronikita, Mt Athos, Greece, and Protopr. M. Chryssavgis, Syd.

H. L. N. SIMMONS

PARAMOR, WENDY (1938-1975), artist, was born on 12 December 1938 in East Melbourne, daughter of Victorian-born parents John Weston Paramor, company representative, and his wife Lillian Clarice, née Walker. Wendy was aged 5 when the family moved to Sydney. She attended Sydney Church of England Grammar School for Girls, Redlands, Cremorne, and Wenona School, North Sydney, but left at 15 wanting to be an artist. At the insistence of her father she completed a secretarial course before studying art at East Sydney Technical College and the Julian Ashton [q.v.7] School. In 1960 she left for Europe. She remained abroad for three years,

based for much of the time in the south of France. In Portugal for three months on a grant from the Fundação Calouste Gulbenkian, she held solo exhibitions in Lisbon, and at Coimbra and Oporto. She also showed in London and New York.

Returning to Sydney in 1963, Paramor exhibited in group shows with the Contemporary Art Society of Australia (Victoria and New South Wales), and at the Dominion, Barry Stern and Blaxland galleries in Sydney. Her first solo show was held at the Watters Gallery in 1965. Later that year some of her paintings and drawings were displayed at the Bognar Gallery, Los Angeles, United States of America. She joined Central Street Gallery, Sydney, in 1966, confirming that she had moved decisively away from landscape-based work to 'hard-edge', geometric abstraction. From 1966 she lived at West Hoxton, a rural area outside Liverpool, where Philip Cox, a leading architect, designed her house which was built into the ground. In October 1967 her son Luke was born; she never married his father, the painter Vernon Treweeke.

Although Paramor had two sculptures included in The Field exhibition for the opening of the National Gallery of Victoria's new building in 1968, her solo exhibitions at Central Street were neither critically nor commercially successful. Distressed by her apparent failure, she produced very little, apart from paintings for the 'International Young Contemporaries' in Tokyo in 1969. This hiatus was not helped by raising a baby in the relative isolation of West Hoxton. When she resumed work it was with experimental sculpture: her pieces were included in the Mildura Sculpture Triennial exhibitions (1970 and 1973) and the Sculpture Competition, Marland House, Melbourne (1971).

In late 1973 Paramor was diagnosed as suffering from a cerebral tumour. Galvanized into painting again, she returned to figurative and semi-figurative work—still lifes, landscapes and some portraiture—and made plans for a large-scale metal sculpture exhibition. She died on 28 November 1975 at the Wolper Jewish Hospital, Woollahra, Sydney, and was cremated; her son survived her. Remembered by artists of her generation for the vivacity of her personality and the originality of her art, she was independent, warm and generous, despite her limited means. Since her death, her paintings and sculptures have been exhibited from time to time. They are held in collections in Britain, the United States of America, Portugal, France, Italy and Australia.

Other Voices, Aug-Sept 1970, p 17; *Art and Aust*, 14, no 1, July-Sept 1976, p 35; *Sun* (Syd), 21 Nov 1961, 30 June 1965; *SMH*, 13 Nov 1963, 1 July 1965; family information.

PAUL MCGILLICK

PARDEY, EDITH EMMA (1896-1963) and MINNIE LAUREL (1897-1974), pianola-roll pianists, were born on 17 January 1896 at Waverley, Sydney, and on 19 September 1897 at Woollahra, daughters of Australian-born parents Edmund Pardey, carriage-builder, and his wife Minnie, née Cooper, a seamstress. By 1912 their mother was running a boarding-house at Katoomba. Although they were not Catholics, Edith and Laurel attended a Catholic school, probably Mount St Mary's Ladies' College, Katoomba, where their musical gifts were recognized. They also studied in Sydney for examinations of the Associated Board of the Royal Academy of Music and the Royal College of Music. Each of them gained medals.

On Saturday nights at the boarding-house the sisters played popular songs and dances in piano solos and duets. Both improvised skilfully while providing music for dancing or the accompaniment for singing around the piano. Edith also played the organ at St Hilda's Anglican Church. Known by their friends as 'the Girls', they appeared as a piano duet at Sydney Town Hall and often performed during dinner at the Carrington Hotel, Katoomba, where George Horton discovered Laurel's pianistic ability.

Recognizing a large potential market for Australian-made piano rolls, he established G. H. Horton & Co. Ltd and engaged the sisters to record. Laurel made her first commercial piano roll in 1919 for the Duo label; the Mastertouch label was used from 1922. The Pardeys were 'nine-to-fivers' and, as the number of artists who were invited to record increased, Edith was expected to edit their work. The sisters had a distinctive pianistic style which they were able to translate to piano rolls. They generally recorded cover versions of North American and European standard popular repertoire. Laurel was interested in foxtrots; Edith specialized in waltzes. They also recorded rolls designed to support parlour singing and could even transform marches into romantic pieces. Their teamwork as a duo proved very successful in the 1920s. The *Australasian Phonograph Monthly and Music Trade Review* (20 September 1927) claimed that their skills had been 'for years on par with the leading American artists'.

At St James's Anglican Church, Sydney, on 5 November 1924 Edith married Frank Baker Murn (d.1957), a 29-year-old telegraphist. She continued to perform, usually as Edith Murn or Mrs Murn, until her son was born in 1933. In his spare time Frank wrote lyrics for piano-roll music.

Although the production of pianolas and the making of rolls continued through the 1930s and 1940s, the impact of radio, sound recording and 'talkies' led to the industry's slow decline. Laurel carried on during the late 1930s and World War II. She expressed her lingering celebrity by driving a flashy Chrysler 770 coupé. Giving her age as 35, she married John William O'Sullivan, a 28-year-old buyer, on 16 August 1941 at St Andrew's Anglican Cathedral, Sydney; they were to remain childless. The stress of recording and anxiety about her husband who was serving in the Australian Imperial Force caused her to suffer a nervous breakdown.

In the 1940s Edith returned to record for Mastertouch. Whenever the recording machine broke down, she was expected to graph out the music on blank paper which she subsequently turned into a master roll by cutting it out, hole by hole. Barclay Wright remembered her in 1961, 'sitting at a little wicker table', graphing out the master-roll with a music-rule that had been used so often that all the engraved coding had worn off: 'she was virtually doing it from memory'.

Survived by her son, Edith died of cancer on 6 August 1963 at Chatswood and was cremated with Methodist forms. Laurel died on 13 January 1974 in Royal North Shore Hospital and was cremated; her husband survived her. The sisters rarely recorded either light or substantial pieces by classical composers. It was playing of distinction in the genre of their chosen repertoire that made them household names.

A'sian Phonograph Mthly & Music Trade Review, 20 Sept 1927; *Music in Australia*, 25 Apr 1930; information from Katoomba Hist Soc, NSW, *and* Mastertouch Piano Roll Co, Petersham, Syd, *and* Mr P. Murn, St Ives, Syd.   JEFF BROWNRIGG

PARER, DAMIEN PETER (1912-1944), war photographer and cameraman, was born on 1 August 1912 at Malvern, Melbourne, youngest of eight children of John Arthur Parer, an hotelkeeper from Spain, and his Victorian-born wife Teresa, née Carolin. Damien attended Loreto convent school, Portland, St Stanislaus' College, Bathurst, New South Wales (1923-29), and St Kevin's College, Toorak, Melbourne (1929-30). He was apprenticed as a photographer, briefly to Spencer Shier and then to Arthur Dickinson with whom he completed his articles in 1933. Following a spell of freelance work and a period when he was unemployed, he was hired by Charles Chauvel [q.v.7] as a camera-assistant in the making of the film, *Heritage* (1935). At Chauvel's instigation, National Studios Ltd, Sydney, engaged Parer for the shooting of *Uncivilised* (1936), *The Flying Doctor* (1936) and *Rangle River* (1936). Chauvel also hired him for the filming of *Forty Thousand Horsemen* (1940).

Between feature films, Parer made 'home movies' and documentaries, and worked as a studio photographer. His employers included Max Dupain, who was then married to another photographer Olive Cotton; the couple became his friends and collaborators. In late 1938 Parer directed the photography of the short film, *This Place Australia*, which depicted (in two parts) poems by Henry Lawson and A. B. Paterson [qq.v.10,11]. Although the film's camera-work revealed the influence of the cinematographers Tasman and Arthur Higgins [qq.v.9], and Errol Hind, Parer was at his most original and impressive when adapting the styles of Australian still-photographers to motion pictures: Dupain's cityscapes were models for his sequences showing Sydney, and the pictorialists' use of the Australian light in landscape compositions influenced the way he filmed the Blue Mountains.

In January 1940 Parer, by then a photographer with the Commonwealth Department of Information, sailed for the Middle East with elements of the Australian Imperial Force. From the gunboat, H.M.S. *Ladybird*, he filmed the bombardment of Bardia, Libya, on 2 January 1941. With Frank Hurley [q.v.9], he covered the Australian assault on Tobruk on 21-22 January. Three days later he accompanied 'C' Company, 2nd/11th Battalion, in its attack on the aerodrome at Derna, and shot his first film of infantry advancing under fire. Parer took some stills but mainly motion pictures of the Greek (April) and Syrian (June-July) campaigns, and the siege of Tobruk (April-December). While flying with the Australian crew of a Royal Air Force Blenheim bomber he filmed an air-raid. Although dissatisfied with his efforts, he established himself as the outstanding cameraman in the Middle East. His work was seen in newsreels and his name became well known.

When Japan entered World War II Parer returned to Australia. After covering operations by Kanga Force around Wau and Salamaua, New Guinea, in 1942, he filmed the Australian withdrawal along the Kokoda Track in Papua. On 18 September Cinesound Productions Ltd released the newsreel, *Kokoda Front Line*, which used his footage. Introduced by Parer, the film and commentary brought home to Australians the realities of the war in the Pacific. The United States of America's Academy of Motion Picture Arts and Sciences commended the work in 1943 'for distinctive achievement in documentary production' and later awarded an Oscar to its producer Ken Hall.

In 1943 Parer's footage was used in the Cinesound newsreels, *Men of Timor, The Bismarck Convoy Smashed* and—arguably his finest work—*Assault on Salamaua*. Disgruntled with his salary and allowances, and convinced that the Department of Infor-

mation had victimized his colleagues George Silk and Alan Anderson, he resigned in August and joined Paramount News. Thereafter he covered American operations. At St Mary's Catholic Church, North Sydney, on 23 March 1944 he married Elizabeth Marie Cotter, a 22-year-old clerk. On 17 September that year, the second day of the invasion of Peleliu Island in the Palau group, Parer was killed by a Japanese machine-gunner; he was reported to have been walking backwards behind a tank to capture the expression in soldiers' eyes as they went into action. He was buried in Ambon war cemetery and mentioned in dispatches. His wife survived him; their son was born in the following year.

Parer was more than a combat cameraman and propagandist. His films were narratives about the human situation. They reflected his wide reading in the theory of cinema, especially the ideas of John Grierson. Parer's record of the everyday lives of servicemen anticipated the *cinéma-vérité* style of documentary. His images of a caped soldier crossing a stream, and of a Salvation Army officer lighting a cigarette for a wounded digger (framed like a Renaissance altar painting), became part of the Anzac legend. Parer was a self-effacing man and a devout Catholic. Osmar White described him as 'long, stooped, black-headed, sallow-faced, smiling', and remembered his infectious, 'bubbling bass hoot' of a laugh. An exhibition of Parer's photography, Still Action, sponsored by the Orange Regional Art Gallery and the Australian War Memorial, Canberra, toured Australia in 1997-99.

F. Legg, *The Eyes of Damien Parer* (Adel, 1963); N. McDonald, *War Cameraman* (Melb, 1994); N. McDonald and P. Brune, *200 Shots* (Syd, 1998); *Still Action*, cat of exhibition curated by N. McDonald, Orange Regional Art Gallery, 1995.

NEIL McDONALD

PARISH, AUGUSTUS ALBERT (1912-1967), metallurgist, was born on 13 April 1912 at Charlton, Victoria, fifth child of Victorian-born parents George Parish, farmer, and his wife Alice Clara, née Peverill. After attending Charlton High School and Wesley College, Melbourne, Gus studied (1931-33) science and metallurgy at the University of Melbourne, but did not graduate. Moving to New South Wales, he joined Australian Iron & Steel Ltd in 1935 as a cadet in the Port Kembla steelworks, shortly before the firm merged with Broken Hill Proprietary Co. Ltd. At the Methodist Church, Wollongong, on 29 January 1938 he married Agnes Jean Pratt.

During his time at Port Kembla the steelworks expanded considerably. Employment rose from a few thousand to about twenty thousand, including immigrants from more than sixty countries. Parish oversaw the introduction of large blast- and open-hearth furnaces, flat-products manufacturing and a tin-plating line. Research to improve processes and products received his enthusiastic support. He contributed to the Port Kembla plant an unusually keen intellect, energy, decisiveness, foresight and leadership. Rivalry with B.H.P.'s Newcastle steelworks was a natural challenge, and he relished it.

Apart from a year (1948-49) as works manager of Southern Portland Cement Ltd (a subsidiary of A.I.&S.) and a term at the Newcastle steelworks, Parish spent his working life at the Port Kembla steelworks. In 1959 he became general manager and chairman of S.P.C. Seven years later he was appointed general manager of A.I. & S. (excluding coal mines) and a director of the Commonwealth Steel Co. Ltd.

After joining the Australasian Institute of Mining and Metallurgy in 1951, Parish served that organization as a councillor (from 1958) and president (1961). He supported numerous sporting and charitable organizations (especially for the disabled), the Boy Scouts' Association (he was president of the South Coast and Tablelands Area), and the formation of Wollongong University College. Retaining his impish sense of humour and his interest in people, he loved to throw a party for his staff, keeping them up very late, but insisting on top performances at work on the following morning. In stature he was somewhat rotund, as became one who relished entertaining. He lived life to the full and seemed always in high spirits. Owing to a serious injury as a boy on his father's farm and another from football, he had one glass eye. He belonged to the Union (Sydney) and Wollongong clubs, and enjoyed music and an occasional game of golf; in earlier years he had played cricket and sung in a church choir.

Parish was transferred to B.H.P.'s head office in Melbourne in January 1967 as group general manager, subsidiaries. He became a director of several associated companies. Survived by his wife and three daughters, he died suddenly of coronary vascular disease on 22 December 1967 in his Melbourne office and was cremated. Parish had been helping to compile a book on the early development of the steel industry in Australia and the role of the Hoskins [qq.v.9] family of Lithgow and Port Kembla. *The Hoskins Saga*, by Sir Cecil Hoskins, was published in 1969.

BHP Review, 43, Apr 1966, p 25, 45, Autumn 1968, p 29; A'sian Inst of Mining and Metallurgy, *Procs*, no 226, June 1968, p 1; *SMH*, 11 Jan, 23 Dec 1967; information from Mrs J. Parish, Murwillumbah, NSW, and Mr J. W. Thompson, Kew, Melb; personal knowledge.   D. F. FAIRWEATHER

PARKER, KATHLEEN ISABEL ALICE (1906-1979), army nurse, was born on 23 November 1906 at Bathurst, New South Wales, fourth of eight children of Australian-born parents Osborne Holmes Parker, police constable, and his wife Evelyn Athalia, née Booth. Educated at various public schools, Kay (as she was known) gained her general nursing certificate at the War Memorial Hospital, Waverley, Sydney, and her midwifery certificate at the Royal Hospital for Women, Paddington. She worked as a sister at Burnley Private Hospital, and as a senior sister (later matron) at Yass District Hospital. Liberal in outlook, with an 'enormous capacity for fun', she enjoyed company and social occasions.

On 7 January 1941 Parker was appointed to the Australian Army Nursing Service, Australian Imperial Force. Promoted temporary sister, she sailed to Rabaul in April in charge of five staff nurses: Marjory Jean ('Andy') Anderson, Eileen Callaghan, Mavis Cullen, Daisy ('Tootie') Keast and Lorna Whyte. Although the male staff did not welcome them at first, they joined the military hospital which had been established by a detachment of medical officers and orderlies from the 2nd/10th Field Ambulance. Following Japanese air-raids, the hospital was evacuated to nearby Kokopo on 22 January 1942. Next morning a powerful enemy force overwhelmed the small Australian garrison. The hospital's two medical officers reputedly said, 'Every man for himself. You can look after the patients. We're not staying'.

Parker, her nurses, and a number of other women were captured and interned for the remainder of the war. In July 1942 they were transferred to Japan where they were held at Yokohama until 1944 and then at Totsuka. Conditions for the nineteen members of the group deteriorated markedly. Garments and bedding were so inadequate that the army nurses slept in pairs for warmth. The women's tasks included shovelling snow, barefoot, from paths on which Japanese walked 'in their fur-lined boots'. Hunger forced them to cook and eat glue provided for making envelopes. Their medical treatment was negligible.

The nurses suffered from a range of illnesses, including malaria. While at Yokohama, Parker was taken to hospital with severe abdominal pains. On seeing the unhygienic conditions, she refused an operation, preferring the possibility of dying in her own quarters. Gradually, she recovered. When Eileen Callaghan contracted tuberculosis, 'Kay took complete responsibility of caring for her, and as much as possible kept her isolated and did everything for her'. Parker's behaviour in this case typified her conduct throughout the war. Her stature and her composure commanded respect, both from captors and colleagues. She was 5 ft 10 ins (178 cm) tall, with blue eyes, dark hair, and a handsome face that reflected her strong character. The women's survival owed much to her leadership.

With her fellow internees, Parker was recovered from the Japanese on 31 August 1945. She had been given the rank of lieutenant and temporary captain, A.A.N.S., on 23 March 1943. Her A.I.F. appointment terminated in Sydney on 1 April 1946; on the following day she was placed on the Reserve of Officers as an honorary captain. For their service at Rabaul and as prisoners of war in Japan, Parker and Anderson were appointed associates of the Royal Red Cross (1948). Parker succeeded (1947) Hilda Mary Hanton [q.v.14] as matron of the Memorial Hospital, North Adelaide. The 'staff respected both Hilda Mary & Kay as matrons. Hilda Mary they revered from a distance. Kay, they loved'.

In 1949 Parker resigned from the hospital. On 5 March that year at the chapel of the War Memorial Hospital, Waverley, she married with Methodist forms Charles Stanley Sly, a 50-year-old widower and a newsagent. In the early 1950s they moved to Sydney where Stan worked as a driving instructor. As Mrs Sly, Kay lived a quiet life. She did some voluntary hospital work and cared for her sister Ella who suffered from arthritis. Kay and Stan retired to the Gosford area in the 1970s. Survived by her husband, she died on 16 June 1979 at Wyoming Hospital and was cremated. She had no children.

A. S. Walker, *Medical Services of the R.A.N. and R.A.A.F.* (Canb, 1961); C. Kenny, *Captives* (Brisb, 1986); J. Bassett, *Guns and Brooches* (Melb, 1992); M. J. Yates, 'Our Story' (ts held by author); information from Miss W. Haseloff, Highbury, SA, Mr R. Lord, Reservoir, Melb, Miss J. Higgins, West Pennant Hills, Mrs K. Horner, Goulburn, Mr R. Parker, East Gosford, Yass & District Hist Soc, NSW, and Mrs L. Johnston, Auckland, NZ.

JAN BASSETT*

PARKES, COBDEN (1892-1978), architect, public servant and soldier, was born on 2 August 1892 at Hampton Villa, Balmain, Sydney, youngest of five children of English-born parents Sir Henry Parkes [q.v.5], politician, and his second wife Eleanor, née Dixon (d.1895). Raised by his stepmother, Cobden was educated at Fort Street Model School and Rockdale College. He entered the Department of Public Works in 1909 as a cadet in the office of the government architect W. L. Vernon [q.v.12] and studied at night at Sydney Technical College.

Enlisting in the Australian Imperial Force on 27 August 1914, Parkes embarked for Egypt with the 1st Battalion. At Gallipoli, he was promoted lance sergeant in June 1915 and commissioned two months later. On 4 September he was wounded in both hands: his left index finger was severely lacerated and three fingers of his right hand were amputated—a critical impairment for a draughtsman. He was invalided to Australia where his A.I.F. appointment terminated in April 1916. After serving in the Militia, he gained a new commission in the A.I.F. in February 1918. Sailing via Egypt to England, he joined the 34th Battalion on the Western Front in October. His second appointment terminated in Sydney on 4 September 1919.

Parkes rejoined the Department of Public Works in 1920 and had extended periods in country offices. On 19 November 1921 he married Victoria Lenore Lillyman at St Philip's Anglican Church, Sydney. He returned to head office in 1929. Appointed designing architect in charge of the drawing office on 1 February 1930, he succeeded Edwin Evan Smith on 4 October 1935 as government architect, the first to be fully trained within the office. His duties included preparations for the sesquicentenary celebrations in 1938.

Essentially 'a man of considerable stature as an administrator and organiser', Parkes continued the conservative architecture of his predecessors in projects (1939-41) such as the portico and great reading room of the New South Wales Public Library (designed by Samuel Coleman). He recognized the skills of his staff architect E. H. Rembert and gave him *carte blanche* to produce buildings such as the Newcastle Technical College (from 1936) and the Hoskins block at Sydney Technical College (1938), both inspired by the Dutch modernist W. M. Dudok.

In 1939 Parkes accompanied the minister for health on a visit to inspect hospitals in England and North America. He returned to Sydney after World War II began and chaired the technical committee of the National Emergency Services. Following Japan's entry into the war in 1941, he provided support for the Air Raid Precautions and New South Wales Camouflage committees. In the 1950s, as the building trade recovered from postwar shortages of materials and manpower, one of Parkes's innovative measures was to develop co-operative arrangements with private architects to alleviate staff shortages. He also encouraged university training of cadets, who were given office experience on specialized projects in Rembert's 'Design Room' during vacations and on graduating.

Parkes retired on 1 August 1958 and was appointed (full-time) officer-in-charge of building, planning and development at the University of New South Wales, and a member of the planning and co-ordination committees of the Prince of Wales and Prince Henry hospitals. As councillor, honorary architect, president, vice-president or fund-raiser of such organizations as the Women's Hospital, Crown

Street, the Nielsen [q.v.11]-Vaucluse Park Trust, the Legacy Club of Sydney and the State division of the Australian Red Cross Society, he was regarded as a legend. He was a man of character, charm, dignity, understanding and humanity who inspired 'affection in all who knew him'.

A member (from 1924) of the Institute of Architects of New South Wales, Parkes was a foundation member (1929), fellow (1936) and life fellow (1958) of the Royal Australian Institute of Architects; he was president (1942-44) of the State chapter, and a national councillor (1947-54) and president (1950-52). He was also a member (from 1942) and chairman (1949-63) of the Board of Architects of New South Wales, and a member of the Board of Architectural Education. Elected a fellow of the Royal Institute of British Architects (1951), he received the Florence Taylor [q.v.12] award (1955) from the Master Builders' Association of New South Wales. The U.N.S.W. conferred on him a D.Sc. (*honoris causa*) in 1958, the year in which he was appointed C.B.E. In 1964 he received the gold medal of the R.A.I.A. He belonged to the Imperial Service Club.

Survived by his son and two daughters, Parkes died on 15 August 1978 at Blakehurst and was cremated.

G. P. Webber, *E. H. Rembert, the Life and Work of the Sydney Architect, 1902-1966* (Syd, 1982); *Architecture in Aust*, Oct-Dec 1958, Nov 1964; *Building, Lighting and Engineering*, Dec 1964, p 70; *SMH*, 3 Oct 1935, 17 Aug 1978; P. L. Reynolds, The Evolution of the Government Architect's Branch of the New South Wales Department of Public Works, 1788-1911 (Ph.D. thesis, Univ NSW, 1972), vol 2.

PETER REYNOLDS

PARKES, EDWARD (1890-1953), public servant, was born on 8 June 1890 at Glebe, Hobart, son of Edward Parkes, fitter, and his wife Mary, née Richards. Educated at Scotch College, Launceston, young Edward joined the Tasmanian Civil (Public) Service on 1 December 1905 as a clerk in the Lands and Works Department. In 1911 he transferred to the Premier's Office. He enlisted in the Australian Imperial Force on 16 February 1915, sailed for Egypt in June and served at Gallipoli with the 7th Field Ambulance. On the Western Front in 1916-18 he performed clerical duties at 2nd Divisional headquarters. Granted leave in 1919, he worked in London in the office of the agent-general for Tasmania from April to October.

By January 1920 Parkes had returned to Hobart. Discharged from the A.I.F. on 16 March, he was employed in the Chief Secretary's Department and Premier's Office. On 4 March 1924 at St Stephen's Anglican Church, Sandy Bay, he married Gladys Winifred May Lipscombe. In January 1926 he was appointed a salmon and freshwater fisheries commissioner. Three months later he was promoted chief clerk and secretary to the premier. He had a term as official secretary in the agent-general's office, London, in 1927-28, before being gazetted (1 April 1930) head of his department as under-secretary, clerk to the Executive Council, chief electoral officer and secretary to the premier.

Parkes led an 'awkward department bridging two portfolios often held by different ministers'. He provided support to the premier, cabinet and Executive Council, and administered a number of sub-departments and statutory and non-statutory bodies, among them public buildings and transport, State publicity, the governor's establishment and the Cinema Board. The under-secretary was also required to act in several legal capacities. R. L. Wettenhall wondered 'how much time he spent writing himself letters to keep the records straight'. Parkes was appointed I.S.O. (1932), M.V.O. (1934)—for his work as Tasmanian director for the visit of the Duke of Gloucester—and C.M.G. (1941). He served (from 1939) on the executive of the Civil Defence Legion which the government established as a precaution against air-raids.

Slightly more than six feet (183 cm) tall, Parkes combed his hair flat and dressed conservatively. In December 1943 he was seconded for three months to the office of Tom D'Alton [q.v.13], the Australian high commissioner in New Zealand, who shared his love of sport, especially boxing and football. Parkes's political masters found him 'painstaking and pleasant'. Premier (Sir) Robert Cosgrove [q.v.13], a Labor man, relied on him and became a friend; the Liberals' leader R. C. Townley considered him 'most punctilious about official duties'. Serious-minded and respected by his peers, Parkes was a model public servant of the old school. In August 1951 he was relieved of his duties due to ill health. He died of cerebrovascular disease on 24 March 1953 in St John's Hospital, Hobart, and was cremated; his wife, son and daughter survived him.

R. L. Wettenhall, *Evolution of a Departmental System* (Hob, 1967) and *A Guide to Tasmanian Government Administration* (Hob, 1968); *Weekly Courier* (Launc), 23 Apr 1930; *Mercury* (Hob), 1 Jan 1941, 25 Mar 1953; information from Mr F. J. Carter, Lindisfarne, Hob.

DARRYL BENNET

PARNELL, THOMAS (1881-1948), physicist, was born on 15 July 1881 at West Haddon, Northamptonshire, England, third of seven children of Richard Parnell, farmer, and his wife Kate, née Cotterell. His father was the local agent for the Liberal politician, Earl Spencer. Thomas attended the Northampton and County School, from which he won scholarships to the University of Cambridge that allowed him, despite his father's opposition, to enter St John's College.

A good wrestler and boxer, and an excellent marksman, Parnell represented the university in cross-country running and his college in rowing. He studied for the natural sciences tripos and, after two years, completed part I with first-class honours. While preparing for the second part of the tripos, he collaborated with (Sir) Owen Richardson at the Cavendish Laboratory in research on the diffusion of hydrogen through hot platinum. He never sat the part II examinations, but took an ordinary B.A. in 1903 (M.A., 1907) after being appointed a resident tutor in mathematics and physics at Trinity College, University of Melbourne.

Parnell arrived in Melbourne early in 1904 and taught at Trinity until 1911. On 25 March that year he became foundation lecturer in physics at the new University of Queensland, nominally responsible to the professor of mathematics and physics H. J. Priestley [q.v.11], but in fact charged with setting up the teaching programme in his subject. He also became an examiner for the Public Examinations Board and was responsible for a marked improvement in the standard of mathematics and physics teaching in Queensland's schools. At St James's Old Cathedral, Melbourne, on 10 March 1913 he married Hermiene Friederica Ulrich, assistant-lecturer in modern languages at the University of Queensland.

On 29 January 1917 Parnell enlisted in the Australian Imperial Force. He joined the 2nd Field Artillery Brigade on the Western Front in October that year. Commissioned in May 1918, he was appointed to Australian Corps headquarters as gas officer: his duties included defusing unexploded gas-shells. Lieutenant Parnell returned to Brisbane and was demobilized on 5 May 1919. He refunded £437 'excess salary' paid by the university, asking that it be used to help ex-servicemen to undertake tertiary studies.

In Parnell's absence the university had created a separate chair of physics, to which he was appointed with effect from 1 January 1919. He was to remain in the post until his death. Under his leadership the physics department developed a useful service role, both in providing a scientific base for the Queensland hospital system's X-ray and radium services and, during World War II, in operating an ionospheric recorder for the Radio Research Board. Its focus, however, was always firmly on teaching. Parnell himself did effectively no research, his closest approach being to take part in the Melbourne Observatory's solar-eclipse expedition to Goondiwindi in 1922 to test Albert Einstein's theory of relativity.

At the university Parnell was chairman (1919-23) and dean (1928-31 and 1935) of the faculty of science, a member (1932-35, 1938-44) of the senate, and president (1938-44) of the professorial board. He was involved in the protracted negotiations that led to the creation (1933) of a massage school and the introduction (1937) of a diploma in physiotherapy. In 1935 he was a member of the planning committee for the faculty of medicine, and of a delegation to the Queensland government that resulted in the establishment of a separate faculty of dentistry.

While president of the professorial board, Parnell represented the university on the Australian Vice-Chancellors' Committee. He was president of the Royal Society of Queensland (1928-29) and of Section A—Mathematics, Physics, and Astronomy—at the congress of the Australian and New Zealand Association for the Advancement of Science, held in Canberra in 1939. In World War II he was a member of the Radio Research Board, the Queensland Cancer Trust, and the board of visitors of the Commonwealth Solar Observatory, Mount Stromlo, Australian Capital Territory.

Parnell was a smallish but strong man, fluid and precise in his movements, and deft with tools and apparatus. He was a nominal Anglican, but religion played little part in his life. Otherwise of firm views, formal and somewhat shy, he preferred his regular game of bridge with friends to active participation in university social life. He was an enthusiastic fly-fisherman and regularly caught trout in the New England district of New South Wales. Survived by his wife and son, he died of hypertensive cardiorenal failure on 1 September 1948 at Indooroopilly, Brisbane, and was cremated. The university named a building after him.

H. C. Webster, *A History of the Physics Department of the University of Queensland* (Brisb, 1977); H. Gregory, *Vivant Professores* (Brisb, 1987); *Brisb Courier*, 17 Mar 1919; Parnell file, Univ Qld Archives; Univ Qld, Parnell Project, unpublished (held by Prof J. S. Mainstone, St Lucia, Brisb).

R. W. HOME

PARRY OKEDEN, RICHARD GODFREY CHRISTIAN (1900-1978), businessman, was born on Christmas Day 1900 at Turnworth, Dorset, England, seventh child of Uvedale Edward Parry Parry-Okeden, landowner, and his second wife Carolina Susan, née Hambro. Dick was educated at Eton College. Due to family financial difficulties he was unable to proceed to university at Oxford or Cambridge. Through his friendship at Eton with Edward Connor Lysaght, great-nephew of the founder of John Lysaght Ltd, he joined that sheet-steel and galvanized-iron manufacturing firm at Bristol. He went to New South Wales in 1923 to join Lysaght's Newcastle Works Ltd under H. R. Lysaght [q.v.10]. Although he lacked a background in metallurgy or engineering, he was appointed supervisor of the rolling plant in 1926. At St Philip's Anglican Church, Sydney, on 1 March 1930 he married Florence Brown (d.1975), grand-daughter of Harriette McCathie [q.v.10].

From 1940 Parry Okeden was chairman and managing director of Lysaght's Newcastle Works Ltd, and of Commonwealth Rolling Mills Pty Ltd which was established after the opening of the Port Kembla plant in 1937. The Lysaght companies were Broken Hill Proprietary Co. Ltd's leading customer for steel. They made galvanized iron and, increasingly, sheet-steel, products for which there was a growing demand, in particular for housing (roofing and guttering), motor-vehicle bodies, white goods, agricultural equipment and water tanks. During World War II the firm manufactured the Owen [q.v.] gun and other matériel.

Parry Okeden took over as chairman and managing director of John Lysaght (Australia) Ltd in 1946. He was also a director of it parent company, John Lysaght Ltd. After the Australian works were amalgamated and converted into a public company (with the same name) in 1961, he continued as managing director and chairman. Relinquishing the former post in 1964 and the latter in 1967, he remained deputy-chairman until 1970.

His knowledge of economics, like that of metallurgy, had been acquired from study and observation, both involving the application of an acute mind. Parry Okeden strongly opposed the demand from organized labour for the 40-hour week, an issue that affected Lysaght's in 1947-48 through strikes and bans on overtime and weekend work, as well as through labour unrest on the waterfront at Newcastle and Port Kembla. President of the New South Wales Chamber of Manufactures (1951-53) and of the Associated Chambers of Manufactures of Australia (1952-54), he blamed inflation on 'bottlenecks in production', or on supply factors, including 'the shortage of coal, the Communist disruptionists, inadequate transport facilities, and excessive absorption of man-power in Government employ'.

In 1949 Parry Okeden was appointed to the council of the New South Wales University of Technology (later University of New South Wales). In the mid-1950s he was also chairman of the Nuclear Research Foundation within the University of Sydney; that university conferred on him an honorary doctorate of science in 1957. Parry Okeden collected non-executive directorships in companies unrelated to metals manufacture, which he continued to hold after his retirement from Lysaght—they included E.M.I. (Australia) Ltd, the Australian Gas Light Co., Manufacturers' Mutual Insurance Ltd and the Perpetual Trustee Co. Ltd. He was appointed C.B.E. in 1961 and C.M.G. in 1964.

Before his marriage Parry Okeden had been an ardent motorcyclist; he brought with him perhaps the only Scott water-cooled motorcycle to reach Australia, and retained an interest in motorcars and motoring. He was honorary secretary of the Newcastle Golf Club, though his inclinations may have been less towards the fairways and greens than the 19th hole (the bar of the club became known as the 'Okeden Inn'). In Sydney, where he moved with his family in 1948, he belonged to the Elanora Country, Royal Sydney Golf and Australian clubs. He was president (1957-59) of the Union Club and frequently lunched there. As pastimes, he enjoyed fly-fishing, quail-shooting, photography (some of his images of steam locomotives were published) and the history of the iron-and-steel industry in Australia. Parry Okeden's enduring passions were classical music and playing the piano; he had the capacity to play by ear and never learned to read music. Survived by his son and two daughters, he died on 16 December 1978 at his Bayview home and was cremated.

John Lysaght (Aust) Pty Ltd, *Lysaght's Silver Jubilee 1921-1946* (priv print, Syd, 1946), *Lysaght Venture* (Syd, 1955), *The Lysaght Century, 1857-1957* (Bristol, Eng, 1957); P. N. Richards, *Lysaght Enterprise* (Port Kembla, NSW, 1992); *SMH*, 13 Mar, 16 June, 7-8 July, 14, 16, 18, 27, 30 Oct 1947, 20, 23-24 Feb, 27 Aug 1948, 12-13 Jan 1949, 5 Oct 1950, 14, 17 Mar, 5, 27, 29 Sept, 1 Dec 1951, 12, 21, 23 Jan, 27 Nov, 31 Dec 1952, 15-16 May, 21 Aug, 12 Oct, 12 Nov 1953, 29 Mar 1954; information from Mr M. Alcock, Wollongong, Mr A. Stein, New Lambton, NSW, and Mr R. D. Parry Okeden, Hawthorn, Melb.
JOHN PERKINS

PARTRIDGE, FRANK JOHN (1924-1964), soldier, farmer and quiz-champion, was born on 29 November 1924 at Grafton, New South Wales, third of five children of Patrick (Paddy) James Partridge, an Australian-born farmer, and his wife Mary, née Saggs, who came from England. Frank left Tewinga Public School at the age of 13 and worked on the family farm —dairying and growing bananas at Upper Newee Creek, near Macksville. While serving in the Volunteer Defence Corps, he was called up for full-time duty in the Australian Military Forces on 26 March 1943. He was posted to the 8th Battalion, a Militia unit which moved to Lae, New Guinea, in May 1944 and to Emirau Island in September.

From June 1945 the 8th Battalion operated in northern Bougainville, containing Japanese forces on the Bonis Peninsula. On 24 July

Partridge was a member of a patrol ordered to destroy an enemy post, known as Base 5, near Ratsua. The Australians came under heavy machine-gun fire. Despite wounds to his arm and thigh, Partridge rushed the nearest bunker, killing its occupants with grenade and knife, then began to attack a second bunker until loss of blood forced him to stop. He was awarded the Victoria Cross. Of the Australians who won the V.C. in World War II, he was the youngest and the last, and the only militia-man. After visiting London in 1946 for the Victory march, he was discharged from the A.M.F. on 17 October in New South Wales; he was again to travel to England in 1953 for the coronation of Queen Elizabeth II and in 1956 for the Victoria Cross centenary celebrations.

Returning to Upper Newee Creek, Partridge lived with his father in a dirt-floored farm-house. He devoted himself to self-education, reading the *Encyclopaedia Britannica* by kero-sene lamp and developing an extraordinarily retentive memory. In 1962-63 he appeared as a contestant on the television quiz show, 'Pick-a-Box', compered by Bob Dyer; his laconic manner appealed strongly to viewers. Partridge was one of only three contestants to win all forty boxes; his prizes were valued at more than £12 000. At St Stephen's Presby-terian Church, Sydney, on 23 February 1963 he married Barbara Mavis Vyvienne Jenniffer Wylie Dunlop, a 31-year-old nursing sister who lived at Turramurra. The wedding re-ceived extensive media coverage. Barbara re-mained at Turramurra while Frank built a new home at the farm. He drove to Sydney every weekend to see her.

Partridge was an honorary member of the Returned Sailors', Soldiers' and Airmen's Im-perial League of Australia, a life member and patron of the Macksville Ex-Servicemen's Club, and vice-president of the Nambucca district council of the Banana Growers' Fed-eration Co-operative Ltd. Harbouring deep political ambitions, he confidently sought Country Party pre-selection for the House of Representatives seat of Cowper in 1963. His views were regarded as rather extreme, and he lost to Ian Robinson. Partridge agreed to be Robinson's campaign-manager for the elec-tion that year. To supplement the income from his farm, Partridge travelled around the dis-trict selling life assurance. He was killed in a motorcar accident on 23 March 1964 near Bellingen and was buried with full military honours in Macksville cemetery. His wife and three-month-old son survived him.

L. Wigmore, *They Dared Mightily* (Canb, 1963); personal knowledge.   BARRY O. JONES

PASCHKE, OLIVE DOROTHY (1905-1942), army matron, was born on 19 July 1905 at Dimboola, Victoria, third daughter of Australian-born parents Heinrich Wilhelm Paschke, stock-and-station agent, and his wife Ottilie Emma, née Kreig. Educated at Dim-boola State School (where she was a pupil-teacher in 1921), Dorothy helped on her parents' farm, attended the Presbyterian church, and played tennis and golf. In Mel-bourne in 1930 she began training at the Queen Victoria Memorial Hospital for Women and Children and its allied institutions, gain-ing her nursing certificate in 1934. She also qualified for certificates in midwifery and infectious diseases.

Back at Dimboola, Miss Paschke was matron of Airlie Private Hospital for four years before returning to Melbourne as assistant-matron of the Jessie McPherson Community Hospital. She joined the Australian Army Nursing Service on 23 July 1940 as a staff nurse. In January 1941 she was promoted matron and posted to the 2nd/10th Australian General Hospital. Next month the unit travelled by ship to Singapore and thence by train to Malacca, Malaya. The first Australian troops sent to the area experienced a high incidence of sickness; largely due to the efforts of its matron, the 2nd/10th coped efficiently with the resulting admissions. Paschke was popular with her staff, patients and medical officers. She led by example, often working long hours beside her nurses. In November 1941 she learned that she had been selected for promotion to principal matron, Malaya. On 1 January 1942 she was appointed a member of the Royal Red Cross.

Advancing Japanese troops forced the 2nd/10th A.G.H. to withdraw south. On 13 January Paschke was sent to Singapore where she and two nurses began converting an abandoned school, Oldham Hall, into 'a spotlessly clean 200 bed hospital'. As the number of casualties increased, nearby buildings were requi-sitioned. By 31 January the 2nd/10th was caring for more than six hundred patients. Throughout this time Paschke's spirit re-mained undaunted.

Against their wishes, groups of A.A.N.S. personnel were sent back to Australia from 10 February 1942. On the 12th of that month Paschke, Matron Irene Drummond [q.v.14] and sixty-three nurses sailed in the ship, *Vyner Brooke*. The vessel carried some three hundred passengers, mostly women and chil-dren. Paschke helped to cook meals, gave instruction in lifeboat drill, distributed life-jackets, and ordered the nurses to prepare dressings and bandages. On the 14th Japanese aircraft bombed and machine-gunned the *Vyner Brooke*, which sank in Banka Strait. After ensuring that those around her aban-doned ship without panic, Paschke jumped overboard and managed to climb into a life-raft in which there were seven nurses and some civilians. Strong currents prevented them from reaching Banka Island. Two nurses and two civilians entered the water and swam to safety on the 15th, but Paschke and the others in the raft were swept out to sea and were presumed to have drowned. She was posthumously awarded (1951) the Florence Nightingale medal.

In 1949 a sundial was placed in the grounds of Dimboola Memorial High School to commemorate Dorothy Paschke. Each year, about Anzac Day, a pupil at that school tells an assembly of students the story of Paschke's life.

B. Jeffrey, *White Coolies* (Syd, 1954); C. Kenny, *Captives* (Brisb, 1986); R. Goodman, *Our War Nurses* (Brisb, 1988); J. Bassett, *Guns and Brooches* (Melb, 1992); *Dimboola Banner*, 2 May 1949; Aust Army Nursing Service records (Dept of Defence, Canb); Nurses Bd of Vic, records; information from Dimboola Memorial Secondary College L, Mrs G. Irving, Rosebud, and Mr J. Jones, Stawell, Vic.

JANICE MCCARTHY

PASPALIS, MICHAEL THEODOSIOS (1911-1972), businessman, was born on 14 November 1911 on Kastellorizon (Megisti), a Greek island near Turkey, second of six children of Theodosios Paspalis (d.1921), shopkeeper, and his wife Chrisaphina, née Stampoli. In 1917 the family reached Point Sampson, near Port Hedland, Western Australia. Educated at Port Hedland, Mick helped his father in various ventures, including pearling and storekeeping. About 1927 he moved to Darwin.

In 1930, eager to join the local rifle-club, Paspalis sought Australian citizenship, but it was not until 16 June 1933 that he was naturalized. By this time he was employed as a 'motor driver' by a butcher; later he drove his own taxi. On 27 January 1935 at the Hellenic Hall, Northbridge, Perth, he married Chrysamthi (Chrissie) Kailis with Greek Orthodox rites. They ran a café in Smith Street, Darwin, before opening the Rendezvous Café, a Mediterranean-style coffee-house. Paspalis brought fresh fruit, vegetables, ice-cream and chocolates to the town. By 1940 he owned four blocks of land. Following the bombing of Darwin in February 1942, he spent the remaining years of World War II working at the Flying Boat Base, Rose Bay, Sydney.

At the end of the war the Commonwealth government compulsorily acquired all freehold land in Darwin. Paspalis received £34 210 in compensation for his holdings. After obtaining short-term leases, he began to renovate his properties. On 11 April 1947 he successfully tendered for the Hotel Darwin; in 1951 he was granted a ninety-nine-year lease on the premises; in 1957 he leased the

hotel to a brewery. He had built his home on East Point Road by 1956 and subsequently bought another residence in Sydney. In 1962 he was described as a millionaire.

Paspalis had extensive interests in property in Darwin. He built hotels at Fannie Bay and Nightcliff, a number of shops, the Parap Theatre and the city's only drive-in cinema. For many years he represented Peter's [q.v.11] ice-cream in the Northern Territory and was a board-member of Paul's (N.T.) Pty Ltd (later part of Queensland United Foods Ltd). He took charge of the planning of his business undertakings and his wife attended to day-to-day administration. A non-smoker and a moderate drinker, Paspalis was 5 ft 7½ ins (172 cm) tall and remarkably strong. Although he seemed to enjoy 'few pleasures' outside his work and described himself as 'just a simple peasant', he was a more complex and sensitive man than his business associates thought. If he was hard on his employees, he was also fair, and generous.

In the 1960s Paspalis was an honoured benefactor of the Greek Church and community, both in Darwin and Sydney. In the Northern Territory he served (from 1967) as honorary consul for Greece. The St John Ambulance Brigade and Christ Church Anglican Cathedral, Darwin, also benefited from his philanthropy. In 1964 he was appointed M.B.E. He belonged to Rotary, the Darwin Club and Tattersall's Club, Sydney. Survived by his wife and two daughters, he died suddenly of a coronary occlusion on 17 October 1972 in Darwin and was buried in McMillans Road cemetery; his estate was sworn for probate at almost $3 million.

Daily Telegraph (Syd), 8 July 1967; *Daily Mirror* (Syd), 6 Oct 1976; *NT News*, 22 Oct 1959, 10 Apr 1962, 2 Jan 1964, 18, 20 Oct 1972, 1 May 1995; A1 32/10758 (AA, Canb); E37 1957/453, E68 DP440, E68 DP846, F1 1948/119, F1 1950/476, F1 1956/2217, F1 1959/654, F1 1963/1672, F1 1963/555 (AA, Darwin); NTRS226, TS101/2 (NT Archives); information from Mr T. G. Jones, Ainslie, Canb; family information.

HELEN J. WILSON

PATERSON, ESTHER; *see under* GILL, GEORGE HERMON

PATERSON, FREDERICK WOOLNOUGH (1897-1977), barrister and politician, was born on 13 June 1897 at Gladstone, Queensland, sixth of eleven children of William Hunter Paterson, a Scottish-born boarding-house-keeper, and his wife Edith, née Jeffery, a trained nurse who came from England. Fred attended Gladstone State School, Rockhampton Grammar School (on a bursary) and Brisbane Grammar School. He won the T. J.

Byrnes [q.v.7] medal (1913) for coming top in the State in the junior public examinations and an open scholarship to the University of Queensland (B.A., 1920), where he read classics and boarded at St John's College. At school and university he proved a successful athlete and Rugby Union footballer; he served in the cadets and in the Militia. A devout Anglican, he hoped to be ordained after his graduation.

On 7 January 1918 Paterson suspended his course and enlisted in the Australian Imperial Force. He was undergoing training in England when World War I ended. Returning to Brisbane, he was discharged from the A.I.F. on 18 May 1919. His army service had made him a radical and, when he resumed his university studies in June, he became involved in student politics. In early 1920 he took up a Rhodes scholarship (which he had been awarded in 1918) to read theology at Merton College, Oxford (B.A., 1922). Back in Brisbane, in 1923 he joined both the Australian Labor Party and the Communist Party of Australia. He took a job as a schoolteacher, and was also vice-warden of St John's. On 11 April 1924 at St Philip's Anglican Church, Thompson Estate, he married Lucy Ethel Blackman; they were to remain childless and to be divorced in September 1931.

From 1925 Paterson worked on the family pig-farm at Gladstone. That year the Queensland branch of the A.L.P. introduced an anti-communist pledge. Although Paterson resigned from the C.P.A., the Queensland central executive of the A.L.P. overruled his pre-selection as Labor candidate for the Legislative Assembly seat of Port Curtis. He contested two State elections (Port Curtis in 1926 and Paddington in 1929) as an Independent. A member (April 1927-November 1928) of the Gladstone Town Council, he was deputy-mayor and chairman of the finance committee; he supported striking railwaymen and waterside workers.

Paterson enrolled to study for the Barristers' Board examinations and moved to Brisbane in 1928. He bought a piggery near Caboolture in 1929, but the Depression forced him to abandon his farm. In January 1930 he rejoined the C.P.A. and was arrested for making an allegedly seditious speech in the Brisbane Domain. Shortly afterwards, he failed a Bar examination; when he failed two further attempts, he made it known that he would publish his next set of answers in *Smith's Weekly*. He was admitted to the Bar on 18 March 1931 and began practising in offices shared with the Friends of the Soviet Union. At Yerongpilly on 30 March 1932 he married, with the forms of the Churches of Christ, Kathleen Claire, a 23-year-old typist.

In December 1932 Paterson moved to Townsville where he built up a substantial,

though not lucrative, criminal practice. His ingenious defence arguments entered the mythology of the left in North Queensland. From May 1937 he edited the communist newspaper, *North Queensland Guardian*. In 1939-44 he was an active and popular alderman of Townsville City Council. He contested Federal and State elections on every possible occasion, and, when he won the State seat of Bowen on 15 April 1944, became the first communist in Australia to be elected to parliament. On 23 August he delivered his maiden speech, in which he presented a vision of his country free from hunger and poverty. His debating style was calm and courteous, and he scorned interjections. Although he lived in Brisbane from 1944, he worked tirelessly in his electorate which returned him to parliament in 1947.

During the railway strike in 1948, the Queensland parliament passed the Industrial Law Amendment Act. It gave the state sweeping powers to intervene in strikes and to prevent picketing. In introducing the legislation, the Labor premier E. M. Hanlon [q.v.14] described it as the 'Paterson Bill' because one of its aims was to counteract picketing techniques devised by the member for Bowen. On 17 March Paterson was on his way to court to defend some of the railwaymen when he stopped to write notes on the behaviour of police involved in breaking up a procession in Edward Street. Struck by a policeman's baton, he was knocked unconscious and rushed to hospital. Paterson was absent from parliament for three months. His wife believed that the bashing 'accentuated' his asthma; his own view was that his efficiency was 'diminished'. The redistribution of the Bowen electorate in 1949 split his power base. In 1950 he failed to win the seat of Whitsunday. He stood unsuccessfully for the Senate in 1951.

In 1952 Paterson shifted to Sydney. Lacking a parliamentary pension, he developed a practice in industrial law. He appeared in the High Court of Australia in 1950-51 for the C.P.A. in its challenge to the validity of the Communist Party Dissolution Act (1950), and before a Sydney magistrate in 1953 for Adam Ogston in the *Communist Review* sedition case. In 1961 the Federal Council for Aboriginal Advancement retained him to represent two Aborigines at a magisterial inquiry into their mistreatment at Hopevale mission, Cooktown, Queensland. After suffering a coronary occlusion that year, he retired, and eventually lived on an old-age pension.

An idealist and an individualist who rarely compromised his personal beliefs—despite considerable pressure from the left as well as the right—Paterson frequently clashed with leaders of the C.P.A. and took little interest in the party's hierarchy. He was about 5 ft 9 ins (175 cm) tall and slightly built; his features seemed too large for his finely boned face. Quietly spoken, frugal and abstemious, he enjoyed football and gardening, and had a robust sense of humour. While there is no indication that he ever regained his religious faith, he sent his children regularly to Sunday School. Survived by his wife and their two sons, he died on 7 October 1977 in the Repatriation General Hospital, Concord, Sydney, and was cremated.

D. Menghetti, *The Red North* (Townsville, 1981); E. O'Neill, *Popular Front* (Brisb, 1988); Brisb Labour Hist Assn, *Fred Paterson* (Brisb, 1994); R. Fitzgerald, *The People's Champion, Fred Paterson* (Brisb, 1997); *Aust Left Review*, Aug-Sept 1966; A. E. Jones, Electoral Support for the Communist Party in North Queensland: a study of F. W. Paterson's victory in Bowen, 1944 (B.A. Hons thesis, Univ of Qld, 1972); ABC TV documentary, *The Legend of Fred Paterson* (Crow Films, 1996).

DIANE MENGHETTI

PATTEN, ROBERT ANTHONY (1889-1958), veterinary surgeon and zoological-park superintendent, was born on 20 June 1889 at Wellington, New South Wales, second child of Robert Patten, a schoolteacher from England, and his native-born wife Emelia Bridget, née Bernasconi. Bob attended Wellington Superior Public School and Hawkesbury Agricultural College. He began his veterinary education as a private pupil of A. P. Gribben, in Sydney. In 1910 he entered the new faculty of veterinary science at the University of Sydney (B.V.Sc., 1914). On 20 August 1914 he was appointed captain, Australian Army Veterinary Corps, Australian Imperial Force. He served in Egypt and at Gallipoli with the 1st Infantry Brigade, and in Egypt and on the Western Front with the 14th Field Artillery Brigade. In December 1916 he was promoted major. Next year he returned to Australia where his A.I.F. appointment terminated on 4 December.

On 8 May 1918 Patten joined the Department of Trade and Commerce as a customs officer. In May 1920 he was gazetted manager of North Bangaroo horse stud farm by the New South Wales Department of Agriculture. At St Andrew's Anglican Cathedral, Sydney, on 10 September that year he married Eva Aileen Rutherford, a 27-year-old bank clerk. Following the closure of the stud in 1923, he established a veterinary practice at Orange. Employed by the Department of Trade and Customs from 1925, he lectured part time on meat inspection at Sydney Technical College.

In 1936 Patten was appointed superintendent (and later curator) of Taronga Zoological Park, nominally under A. S. Le Souef [q.v.10] who had supervised the development of the zoo at Mosman. Patten found his practice remarkably similar to that of a doctor treating humans: in the course of his duties he 'pulled the teeth of tigers and orang-outangs, performed a Caesarean section on a normally vicious Cape dog, delivered a giraffe that stood 6 ft high a few days after its birth and supervised hormone treatment for "balding" furred animals'. His greatest problem, however, was the careful planning of the diets of some 7000 animals.

By and large, Patten managed to work amicably with the chairman of trustees (Sir) Edward Hallstrom [q.v.14], although he was temporarily out of favour when a giraffe, two hippopotamuses and a rhinoceros died (July-August 1943). In 1941 Keefi, the first chimpanzee born at the zoo, was ignored by her mother. Patten and his wife reared her in their home for a year as if she were one of their children: the chimpanzee sucked from an infant's feeding-bottle, wore nappies and had her own pushchair. An insurance salesman, noticing a bassinet on the verandah, congratulated Mrs Patten on having a new baby, peeped under the net and fled in dismay. It was no small achievement to rear the chimpanzee, and the grateful trustees presented Mrs Patten with a gold watch. In 1947 the Pattens moved from their Roseville home to a flat at the zoo. The more confined space did not deter them from rearing a lion cub that had been attacked by its mother.

In 1947-54 Patten appeared as a panellist on 'Nature Speaks', a wildlife programme chaired by John Dease [q.v.13] on radio-station 2GB. A member of the Royal Zoological Society of New South Wales, Patten published articles in its *Proceedings*, the *Australian Veterinary Journal*, and in local and overseas magazines. He was an innovative, kind and honourable man who served the zoo with distinction and had many close friends inside and outside the profession. Retiring in 1954, he developed a substantial practice at Kellyville. He died of a cerebral tumour on 10 October 1958 in the Home of Peace, Wahroonga, and was cremated; his wife, son and daughter survived him, as did Keefi (d.1966).

I. Bevan, *Keefi* (Syd, 1945?); R. Strahan, *Beauty and the Beasts* (Syd, 1991); Roy Zoological Soc of NSW, *Procs*, 1947-48, p 11, 1957-58, p 5; *Aust Veterinary J*, Dec 1958, p 437; *SMH*, 25 July 1953, 5 July 1954, 20 Oct 1958; Taronga Zoological Park, Bd of Trustees, minutes, 1938-54; information from Dr D. R. Johns, Aust Veterinary Assn, Artarmon, Dr J. D. Kelly and Mrs M. Miller, Zoological Parks Bd of NSW, Mosman, Syd, and Dr A. K. Sutherland, East Malvern, Melb.

ROBERT I. TAYLOR

PATTERSON, GEORGE HERBERT (1890-1968), advertising entrepreneur and businessman, was born on 24 August 1890 in South Melbourne, fourth child and only son of John

Alfred Patterson (d.1899), a comedian from Hobart, and his wife Frances Julia, née Rogers, an actress from Sydney. He was named after his maternal grandfather George Herbert Rogers, who had been well known on the Australian stage. Young George's lifelong love and patronage of the theatre, opera, music and art owed much to his theatrical background. He was educated at Carlton College, Parkville. After their mother died in 1905, the children were sent to live with relations. In the following year George was compelled to earn a living to help support his sisters.

Starting as an office-boy with Thomas McPherson & Son, machinery merchants, Patterson rose to advertising manager by 1908. About 1912 he embarked on the first of many journeys, visiting Britain and working in New York. When World War I began, he returned to Australia to enlist, but was rejected on medical grounds and set up an advertising firm in Melbourne. On 29 June 1915 he succeeded in joining the Australian Imperial Force. He served in Egypt (1915-16) with the Australian Army Medical Corps and on the Western Front (1916-17) with the Australian Army Pay Corps, and rose to sergeant. An agent mismanaged his business and Patterson was permitted to return to Melbourne where he was discharged from the army on 3 January 1918. At St Philip's Anglican Church, Sydney, on 27 August that year he married Maud Rigby, née Raybould (d.1959), who had served overseas with the Australian Army Nursing Service; eight years his senior, she was a widow with a daughter. Maud and George were to have a daughter (d.1919) and a son of their own.

In 1920 Patterson went into partnership with Norman Catts to form the Sydney-based advertising agency, Catts-Patterson Co. Ltd. They acquired the Palmolive Co. Australasia Ltd and Ford Motor Co. of Australia Pty Ltd as clients, and later the Dunlop Rubber Co. of Australasia Ltd, Berlei [Burley, qq.v.13] Ltd, Gillette Safety Razor Co. of Australia Pty Ltd and Pepsodent Co. (Australia) Ltd. In 1934, following a series of disagreements with Catts and a bout of severe illness, Patterson resigned. He bought out the virtually bankrupt Griffin, Shave & Russell Co. Pty Ltd and formed George Patterson Pty Ltd. Although —for ethical reasons—he discouraged his former clients from following him to his new agency, Colgate-Palmolive and Gillette were the first to do so. The personal loyalty that he inspired in his clients and staff owed much to his generosity, gregarious nature and interest in their welfare.

During the 1930s Patterson travelled extensively abroad. He responded to wartime newsprint shortages by developing the Colgate-Palmolive Radio Unit which produced programmes featuring stars such as 'Roy Rene', Jack Davey [qq.v.11,13] and Bob Dyer. During World War II Patterson's used both radio and newspaper advertising to publicize recruiting drives and assist the sale of war bonds. Patterson was an air-raid warden at Bellevue Hill, his home suburb. Committed to the Australian Red Cross Society, he served as a member of its New South Wales divisional council and executive (1940-68), and on the national council (1941-68). He organized and chaired the Red Cross's rehabilitation (social service) and publicity committees, and was made an honorary life member of the national council in 1961.

An astute businessman, Patterson had also been chairman of Gillette Australia, and a director of Colgate-Palmolive, Peek Frean (Australia) Ltd and Phipson & Co. Ltd. His position on the boards of most of his major clients 'made it rather difficult for other agencies to get their foot in the door'. After a period of intense ill health caused by heavy smoking, he retired in 1952, handing over his position to his stepdaughter's husband William Farnsworth. In retirement, Patterson indulged his literary and sporting proclivities. He published his autobiography, *Life Has Been Wonderful* (1956), and two books on trout fishing, *Chasing Rainbows* (1959) and *Angling in the Andes* (1961). Landscape painting, collecting antiques, golf, tennis and fishing were his favourite pastimes. He contributed regularly to *Art in Australia* and was a friend of (Sir) William Ashton [q.v.7]. Patterson belonged to the Royal Sydney Golf, Elanora Country and the Australian clubs.

At St Michael's Church, Vaucluse, on 20 February 1961 he married his nurse Florence Mary Stonelake, née Mason, a 62-year-old widow. Patterson died on 19 December 1968 at Woollahra and was cremated; his wife, stepdaughter and the son of his first marriage survived him. A portrait of him by E. Wright is held by the firm, George Patterson Bates, Sydney.

B & T Weekly, 9 Jan 1969, 9 Nov 1984; *Newspaper News*, 10 Jan 1969; *Parade*, Sept 1977; *SMH*, 1 Jan 1957, 26 Aug 1959, 23 Dec 1968; *Bulletin*, 27 Mar 1957; *Sunday Telegraph* (Syd), 26 Aug 1959, 23 Dec 1968; *Financial Review*, 23 Dec 1968; *Ad News*, 14 Oct 1988; Ashton family papers (ML); information from and family papers held by Ms J. Patterson-Smith and Mr M. Smith, Syd; information from Mr W. Batten, Syd.   KAREN HUTCHINGS

PAUL, TIBOR (1909-1973), conductor, was born on 29 March 1909 in Budapest, son of Antal János Paul, vintner, and his wife Gizella, née Verényi. Tibor studied piano and woodwind instruments at the Liszt Ferenc Zenemüvészeti Föiskola under the composer Zoltán Kodály and the conductors Hermann

Scherchen and Felix Weingartner. In 1930 he founded the Budapest Concert Orchestra which, through his leadership and that of guest conductors, 'rapidly achieved a high standard'. On 9 November 1935 he married Maria Penninger in Budapest; they were to have two sons. In 1939 he began conducting his own orchestra. About this time he became an adviser to the recording firm Durium Products Corporation, recording supervisor of the fledgling Hungarian film institute and a conductor at the Budapest National Theatre. By 1945 he was principal conductor for the Hungarian Broadcasting Corporation.

In 1948, when communist rule was established in Hungary, Paul left for Switzerland. He conducted for the Swiss Broadcasting Corporation and at the opera house in Berne before emigrating to Australia with his family in 1950. Within a year he was a conductor with the New South Wales National Opera and a guest conductor with the Australian Broadcasting Commission. Appointed to teach orchestral and choral conducting at the New South Wales State Conservatorium of Music in 1954, he was also principal conductor for the Elizabethan Theatre Trust Opera Company in 1954-55. On 28 November 1955 he was naturalized.

Paul found that the A.B.C. was unable to offer him sufficient engagements. He regularly corresponded with (Sir) Charles Moses, the general manager, asking to be given more concerts. During his nine years with the commission he worked extremely hard, travelled widely throughout Australia and conducted in every capital city. Meanwhile, he made trips to Britain, Italy, Switzerland, the Netherlands, Denmark, France, Portugal and Austria. A vigorous promoter of Australian composers, he toured Europe and North America in 1958 and included the work of Australians in his concerts.

In 1959 Paul left for Europe with his wife and younger son. He eventually settled in Ireland, where he was principal conductor (1961-67) with the Radio Eireann Symphony Orchestra and director of music (1962-67) for Radio and Telefis Eireann, Dublin. Although he visited Australia from time to time, he was based in Ireland for almost seven years. A versatile and accomplished musician, he had a fiery temperament. At the behest of the Elizabethan Theatre Trust, he returned to Sydney in October 1968 to conduct its orchestra. Over the next six years he divided his time between Australia and Europe.

Appointed conductor of the Western Australian Symphony Orchestra in 1971, Paul led three seasons in Perth. He knew by heart 47 symphonies, 11 operas and numerous other works, and seldom conducted from a score. In January 1973 he conducted the combined West Australian and South Australian symphony orchestras in a performance to inaugurate the Concert Hall, Perth. Survived by his wife and sons, he died of a coronary occlusion on 11 November 1973 in his home at Wahroonga, Sydney, and was cremated with Catholic rites.

Musical Times (Lond), Jan 1974; *Sun-Herald*, 13 Nov 1966; *SMH* and *West Australian*, 12 Nov 1973; naturalization file A446/184, item 53/49125 (AA, Canb); SP613/1, 7/19/5 pts I and II, SP1011/2, Box 76, ST3836/1/0, Box 5, ST1890/1/0, Box 15, C687 T2, Box 6 (AA, Syd); Concert notes, nd, July 1959 and 20 May 1972 (Alexander L).

MICHAL BOSWORTH

PAWSEY, JOSEPH LADE (1908-1962), physicist, was born on 14 May 1908 at Ararat, Victoria, only child of Victorian-born parents Joseph Andrews Pawsey, farmer, and his wife Margaret, née Lade. Gifted with 'an unusually inquiring mind', young Joe attended state schools at Lalkaldarno (Stavely), Coleraine and Camperdown. In 1922 he won a scholarship to Wesley College, Melbourne, where he did well in physics and mathematics. After he graduated from the University of Melbourne (B.Sc., 1929; M.Sc., 1931), he entered Sidney Sussex College, Cambridge (Ph.D., 1935); he worked under J. A. Ratcliffe at the Cavendish Laboratory, investigating the reflection of radio waves by the ionosphere.

In 1934 Pawsey joined the research staff of Electrical & Musical Industries Ltd at Hayes, Middlesex. He gained extensive experience in aerial design and contributed to the introduction of television. At the register office, Uxbridge, on 7 September 1935 he married Greta Lenore Nicoll, a 32-year-old Canadian. Returning to Australia, he began work in Sydney in February 1940 at the radiophysics laboratory which had been established by the Council for Scientific and Industrial Research (Commonwealth Scientific and Industrial Research Organization) to develop and manufacture radar equipment. One group that he led produced a microwave set for the Royal Australian Navy; another, under his direction, investigated the 'super-refraction' of radio waves in the earth's atmosphere.

By the end of World War II the staff of the radiophysics laboratory had grown to more than three hundred; they were encouraged to remain and turn their attention to peacetime projects. Pawsey, the laboratory's most senior and respected scientist, had seen secret reports during the war which described how radar sets had sometimes been jammed by interference from radio waves, probably coming from the sun and possibly related to the appearance of sunspots. He tried to investigate these reports in 1944, using a small aerial mounted outside a laboratory window.

Although this makeshift attempt failed, his curiosity had been aroused.

In September 1945, assisted by Ruby Payne-Scott and Lindsay McCready, Pawsey began new observation of the sun, using a radar aerial at Collaroy. Success came almost immediately with steady radio emissions being recorded, even though it was clear that sunspot activity was not the cause. The emission seemed to indicate that regions of the sun had temperatures as high as one million degrees Celsius. Pawsey's results were greeted with disbelief until it was realized that he and his team had measured temperatures, not on the sun's surface, but in its corona. These studies of the 'quiet' sun marked the effective beginning of a new branch of science which he named 'radio astronomy'.

Pawsey next turned his attention to the strong, variable radio emission which wartime radar operators had suspected was associated with sunspots. The problem confronting him was that no existing radar aerial could pinpoint sunspots as the source of this type of radiation. He devised an instrument known as the sea interferometer—an aerial placed on a cliff-top and facing out to sea. At sunrise, the aerial would pick up two signals, one direct from the sun and the other reflected from the surface of the sea. The two signals could then be combined to form an interference pattern, from which information could be obtained about the size and position of the source of the radiation.

Early in 1946 Pawsey began observations with the sea interferometer at Dover Heights, south of Sydney Heads. The timing was fortunate. Within a few days, one of the largest groups of sunspots ever recorded began its slow transit of the sun's disc, causing major disruptions to radio communications on Earth. Pawsey's early-morning interference patterns proved that the strong radio emission originated from the vicinity of the sunspots. Although cliff-top aerials were soon outmoded, interferometry became the fundamental principle of many of the world's radio telescopes, including the Australia Telescope, completed at Narrabri in 1988. The introduction of interferometry was probably Pawsey's most important contribution to radio astronomy.

Others at the laboratory quickly took up the study of radio emission from the sun; they later investigated waves emanating from more distant celestial objects. Small, relatively independent teams built their own radio telescopes and began operating at field-stations scattered around Sydney. As the officer-in-charge of this research and assistant-chief (from 1951) of the radiophysics division, Pawsey faced the challenge of co-ordinating and guiding the teams which worked in comparative isolation and sometimes in competition with one another. His tall, angular frame soon became a regular sight at the field-stations, where he suggested research projects, helped in the design of equipment and advised on the best observational methods. Above all, he was a dependable critic when it came to analysing data and presenting results for publication. Scientific papers from the teams were expected to meet his high standards of clarity and accuracy.

Straightforward, honest and humble, Pawsey was scrupulous in acknowledging his colleagues' achievements. In the 1950s he published relatively few papers himself, having sacrificed his own research to his duties as leader of the teams. Somehow he found time to write—with R. N. Bracewell—*Radio Astronomy* (Oxford, 1955), the first comprehensive text on the subject. The Australian National Research Council awarded him its Lyle [q.v.10] medal (1953). A foundation fellow of the Australian Academy of Science in 1954, he was elected a fellow of the Royal Society, London, in the same year: he gave the academy's inaugural Matthew Flinders [q.v.1] lecture in 1957 and won the society's Hughes medal in 1960. The Australian National University conferred an honorary D.Sc. on him in 1961.

In December 1961 Pawsey accepted an appointment as director of the recently established National Radio Astronomy Observatory at Green Bank, West Virginia, United States of America. Before taking up the post, he visited the observatory in March 1962 but became seriously ill and returned to Sydney. He died of a cerebral tumour on 30 November that year at the Victoria Convalescent Hospital, Potts Point, and was cremated. His wife, daughter and two sons survived him.

P. Robertson, *Beyond Southern Skies* (Melb, 1992); *Biog Memoirs of Fellows of the Roy Soc* (Lond), 10, 1964, p 229; *Aust Physicist*, Dec 1964, p 137.   PETER ROBERTSON

PAYNE, FRANCES (FRANK) MALLALIEU (1885-1976), artist and illustrator, was born on 7 May 1885 at Kangaroo Point, Brisbane, daughter of English-born parents Arthur Peel Payne, shipping clerk, and his wife Julia Finch, née Batchellor. Frank (as she was known) was educated at All Hallows' Convent and Brisbane Technical College where she trained as a portrait painter under Godfrey Rivers [q.v.11] and learned etching and block-making. She exhibited with the Queensland Art Society. Accompanied by her mother, she sailed for England in March 1905. In Paris for nine months, she enrolled at the Académie Colarossi, then studied at the École Nationale Supérieure des Beaux-Arts. At 'La Grande Chaumière' she was taught black-and-white work by Théophile-Alexandre Steinlen. Back in London, she worked in Frank Brangwyn's studio and did her most serious study there. During the summers she travelled extensively through England (1905), Brittany, France (1906), and elsewhere on the Continent (1907).

For two and a half years Payne had written regular articles for the *Brisbane Courier* about her experiences. Returning to Brisbane in September 1907, she began freelance design work for the *Courier* and the *Bulletin*; she also produced commercial catalogues for Finney [q.v.4] Isles & Co.'s department store and illustrations for the *Queenslander*. The Australasian Union Steam Navigation Co. sent her on cruises so that she could write and illustrate their travel brochures.

By 1916 Payne was living in Sydney. She illustrated catalogues for David Jones [q.v.2] Ltd's and Farmer [q.v.4] & Co. Ltd's department stores, drew covers for the *Australian Woman's Mirror*, and drove her own motorcar. At Neutral Bay on 24 August 1921 she married with Presbyterian forms Andrew Patrick Clinton, a 36-year-old superintendent stevedore from Ireland and a divorcee. They had two sons, but separated in 1928. Continuing to be known professionally as Frank Payne (though often referred to as Mrs A. P. Clinton), she supported herself and her children from her catalogues, magazine covers and part-time work for the *Bulletin*. Reputedly, she was among the nation's highest paid women.

In contact with many prominent women artists, Payne numbered among her friends Jessie Traill, Ethel Carrick Fox and the writer Dorothea Mackellar [qq.v.12,8,10]. She promoted the careers of young artists such as Daphne Mayo and Lloyd Rees. Payne had joined the Society of Women Painters in 1919, served on the society's committees and council for many years, and, from 1921, contributed to every annual exhibition. Her oils and water-colours were frequently studies of children (including her own) in unposed settings, as well as landscape and genre paintings. Founding president (1934) of the Women's Industrial Arts Society, she was awarded King George VI's coronation medal in 1937.

Payne helped W. M. Hughes [q.v.9] in his campaign for the House of Representatives seat of North Sydney in 1946. She continued to paint well into her later years, and held exhibitions at the Morton Galleries, Brisbane, in 1948 and the Grosvenor Galleries, Sydney, in 1952. Survived by her sons, she died on 11 July 1976 at Normanhurst and was cremated.

J. Kerr (ed), *Heritage* (Syd, 1995); *Lone Hand*, 1 Mar 1916; *Telegraph* (Brisb), 2 Apr 1934, 22 Nov 1948; *SMH*, 17 June 1952; A. Philp, The Sydney Society of Women Painters, 1910-1934 (M.A. thesis, Univ Syd, 1988) and for bib.   ANGELA PHILP

PEACOCK, FREDERICK HOOD (1886-1969), businessman, was born on 13 November 1886 at Franklin, Tasmania, son of Charles Morley Moffat Peacock (d.1892), schoolteacher, and his wife Sarah Maria, née Hood. Educated (on a scholarship) at The Hutchins [q.v.1] School, Frederick was apprenticed to a jeweller before being employed as a clerk with George Adams's [q.v.3] Tattersall's lotteries. In his youth he stoked the boiler in his uncle's jam-manufacturing firm, W. D. Peacock & Co. By the time H. Jones [q.v.9] & Co. (Pty) Ltd bought the company in 1920, Peacock was factory manager. At St George's Anglican Church, Hobart, on 9 March that year he married Lydia Cripps.

Sir Henry Jones sent Peacock to manage the company's newest factory at Oakland, California, United States of America. The venture was intended to spearhead Jones & Co.'s entry into the seemingly limitless North American market, but it struggled against the powerful monopoly of local fruit suppliers and jam manufacturers. In 1924, on Peacock's recommendation, the plant was sold; he returned to Tasmania to become head-office manager at the Old Wharf, Hobart. After Jones died in 1926, Peacock was appointed managing director of the firm, which had expanded its interests to include shipping, insurance, hops and timber. He was also a director (from 1927) and chairman (1965-67) of Henry Jones Co-Operative Ltd; it was renamed Henry Jones (IXL) Ltd in 1966.

Peacock was widely acknowledged for his capacity to turn around an ailing business. In the late 1920s he had revived the Australian Commonwealth Carbide Co. Ltd's works at Electrona and become one of the firm's representatives. A director (from 1934) and chairman (from 1965) of the National Executors & Trustees Co. of Tasmania Ltd, he was a local director of the National Mutual Life Association of Australasia Ltd and of the Union Steam Ship Co. of New Zealand Ltd. In addition, he served on the Tasmanian committee of the Commonwealth Scientific and Industrial Research Organization.

Quiet and almost self-effacing in manner, Peacock was humanitarian in outlook, with a genuine interest in the welfare of his workers and suppliers. When a poliomyelitis epidemic had swept through the State in 1937, he helped to found the Tasmanian Society for the Care of Crippled Children, of which he was president and a life member. He was also a Rotarian and sat on the board of St John's Hospital, Hobart. During World War II he was a consultant to the Commonwealth government on industrial and economic matters, and directed much of his factories' production towards the war effort. In 1940 he joined the committee of the Hobart Savings Bank (president 1951-64).

Peacock was well known for the familiar adages which he repeated to his staff and business associates, such as 'don't try to carry the load; ride on top of it' and 'figures never lie, but lies sometimes figure'. He advised State Labor ministers and senior public servants, who chose to visit him at his home. In 1961 he was appointed C.M.G. He retired in 1967. Survived by his wife, daughter and four sons, he died on 29 December 1969 at St John's Hospital and was cremated. His estate was sworn for probate at $300 929.

G. V. Brooks, *30 Years of Rotary in Hobart* (Hob, 1955); B. Brown, *I Excel!* (Hob, 1991); *PTHRA*, 20, no 1, Mar 1973, p 21; *Mercury* (Hob), 10 June 1961, 31 Dec 1969, 6 Jan 1970; *Examiner* (Launc), 30 Dec 1969; information from Mr F. H. and Mr D. H. Peacock, Sandy Bay, Hob.

BRUCE BROWN

PEARCE, CHARLES WILLIAM (1910-1980), air force officer, was born on 1 February 1910 at Kalgoorlie, Western Australia, son of William Snelling Pearce, an Australian-born police constable, and his wife Margaret Mary, née Crowley, who came from Ireland. After attending Christian Brothers' High School, Fremantle, Charles worked as a draughtsman while studying civil engineering at Perth Technical School and later at the University of Western Australia. On 15 January 1930 he joined the Royal Australian Air Force as an air cadet. He completed training at Point Cook, Victoria, and was commissioned on 5 February 1931. Piloting seaplanes, he spent periods in 1934-38 attached to ships of the Royal Australian Navy. In 1939 he qualified as a navigator. British domination of most aspects of Australian defence strengthened his Anglophilia.

In July 1939 Pearce was a member of an elite R.A.A.F. team sent to Britain to bring back nine Sunderland flying-boats which Australia had purchased. When World War II broke out, the Australian government agreed to leave the aircraft and crews in Britain. Pearce and his comrades formed the nucleus of No.10 Squadron, R.A.A.F., and operated the Sunderlands from Wales and southern England. With limited navigational aids and often in bad weather, they hunted German submarines, reconnoitred enemy dispositions in Europe, and provided transport for dignitaries. Appointed temporary commanding officer in February 1940, Pearce won the Distinguished Flying Cross five months later—the first awarded to a member of the R.A.A.F. in World War II—for his leadership and gallantry in the air, especially during an attack on a U-boat in June. His men respected him for his skill as a pilot, and for his courtesy, compassion and kindness.

At Trinity Presbyterian Church, Compton Gifford, Plymouth, on 3 August 1940 Pearce married Vera Madeleine Waldron Axford, née Modley, a 30-year-old divorcee and an officer in the Women's Royal Naval Service. Reverting to flight commander later that month, he was promoted temporary wing commander in January 1941. He returned to Australia in March and in May was appointed commander of No.11 Squadron, R.A.A.F. It was based in Port Moresby and equipped with American Catalina flying-boats. In August he took command of the R.A.A.F. Station, Port Moresby (as acting group captain from January 1942). Holding his unprepared forces together, he introduced air-raid procedures which proved so effective that, despite fifty Japanese attacks, only one person was killed on the ground during his term of command. He was appointed C.B.E. in 1942.

Leaving Papua in June, Pearce held command and staff posts in Australia, New Guinea and Borneo. He was mentioned in dispatches for his work as senior air staff officer, No.10 (Operational) Group, New Guinea (November 1943-July 1944). After the war, he served at home, except for a term (1949-52) as Australian air attaché, Washington. In April 1957 he was promoted acting air commodore (substantive 1 July 1958) and appointed to command the R.A.A.F. Station, Richmond, New South Wales. In 1965 he retired from the air force. He became a director of several firms, including Palgrave Corporation Ltd. Suffering from cancer and cerebrovascular disease, he died on 10 September 1980 in his home at Palm Beach and was cremated. His wife and daughter survived him.

G. Odgers, *Air War Against Japan 1943-1945* (Canb, 1957); D. Gillison, *Royal Australian Air Force 1939-1942* (Canb, 1962); J. E. Hewitt, *Adversity in Success* (Melb, 1980); K. C. Baff, *Maritime is Number Ten* (Adel, 1983); information from Air Commodore W. H. Garing, Turramurra, Syd, Wing Cmdr R. Cresswell, Garran, Sir Richard Kingsland, Campbell, Canb, and the late Air Marshal Sir Valston Hancock.
IAN MACFARLING

PEARCE, EDWARD TOM STANLEY (1914-1980), sugar-industry administrator, was born on 13 January 1914 in South Brisbane, son of Thomas Stanley Pearce, a commercial traveller from England, and his Queensland-born wife Mary Lilith Dagmar, née Hasberg. Dux of Toowong State School, Eddie won the Lilley [q.v.5] memorial medal in 1927. He proceeded to Brisbane Grammar School, where he was awarded gold and silver Lilley medals, then entered the University of Queensland (B.A., 1935; B.Com., 1938).

In August 1934 Pearce joined the Australian Sugar Producers' Association as a junior industrial officer. Promoted to industrial officer one year later, he appeared as the association's advocate in the Industrial Court of Queensland. He regularly visited sugar districts to provide advice to millers and growers, and to stimulate membership of the A.S.P.A. After becoming the association's assistant-secretary in 1937, he began to study law at the university.

On 25 June 1940 Pearce enlisted in the Australian Imperial Force. Allocated to intelligence duties with the 24th Brigade, he sailed for the Middle East in December. In May 1942 he was mentioned in dispatches and commissioned lieutenant. He served at 9th Division headquarters in the South-West Pacific Area in 1943-45 and attained the rank of captain. When F. C. P. Curlewis [q.v.13], the A.S.P.A.'s general secretary, died in March 1945, the association secured Pearce's release from military operations. He took over as general secretary in June 1945.

Working closely with (Sir) Alfred Brand [q.v.13], president of the A.S.P.A., Pearce expanded the association from its Brisbane base into an effective regional organization, with offices spread throughout the major sugar districts. He co-operated with the Returned Sailors', Soldiers' and Airmen's Imperial League of Australia to encourage ex-servicemen to enter the industry under the War Service Land Settlement Agreements Act (1945). To overcome postwar labour shortages, he was involved in an immigration scheme which enabled farmers to select and employ Southern Europeans as canecutters. At St Mary's Anglican Church, Kangaroo Point, on 13 December 1947 he married Edith Jean Ritchie, a 31-year-old social worker.

Pearce urged sugar-growers to introduce machinery and enlarge their holdings so that the industry would be more competitive. A member of the Mechanical Harvesting Committee and the Bulk Handling Consultative Committee, he served on the royal commission (1950) which prepared a long-term plan for the development of the sugar industry. He was a founder (1949) and a director of Sugar Research Ltd, an organization free from government control; its laboratories at Mackay were opened in 1953 and funded by the mill-owners.

Known as 'Mr Sugar', Pearce represented the industry at meetings—in Canberra, London and Geneva—which regularly negotiated renewals of Australian, British Commonwealth and international sugar agreements. Appointed C.M.G. in 1959, he retired in 1977. He was a member of the Queensland, Brisbane and United Services clubs. Survived by his wife and son, he died of cancer on 9 January 1980 at Wesley Hospital, Brisbane, and was cremated with the forms of the Uniting Church. In 1980 the A.S.P.A. named a student bursary after him.

Aust Sugar J, 37, no 3, 1945, 41, no 10, 1950, 69, no 9, 1977, 71, no 10, 1980; Qld Cane Growers' Assn, *Annual Report*, 1980; *SMH*, 9 Dec 1949, 12 Jan 1971, 20 May 1977; *Courier-Mail*, 15 Dec 1977, 12 Jan 1980; information from the late Dr H. W. Kerr.

JOHN D. KERR

PEARCE, MALCOLM ARTHUR FRASER (1898-1979), public servant, was born on 19 April 1898 at Kapunda, South Australia, eldest child of James Smith Pearce, accountant, and his wife Elizabeth Ann, née Moyle. His father was a correspondent for the newspaper, the *Register*; his grandfather James Pearce had been mayor (1868) of Kapunda, and a member of the House of Assembly (1870-75) and the Legislative Council (1877-85). Educated at the local public and high schools, Malcolm began work in 1914 as a junior clerk in the Attorney-General's Department, Adelaide. During World War I he twice tried to enlist in the Australian Imperial Force, but was rejected on medical grounds. After qualifying as an accountant, he was promoted to clerk in April 1920.

At St John's Anglican Church, Adelaide, on 8 December 1922 Pearce married Gladys Myrtle Green (d.1958), a 25-year-old typist; they were to have two children. In 1926 he transferred to the Treasury Department and became confidential clerk to the premier. He worked as personal secretary to five premiers in the years that followed. In 1935 he visited London with (Sir) Richard Butler [q.v.7] for the celebrations to mark King George V's silver jubilee. With (Sir) Thomas Playford, he travelled to the United States of America in 1951 for talks on uranium, and to London in 1953 to attend Queen Elizabeth II's coronation at Westminster Abbey. Pearce had been appointed C.B.E. in 1946.

In 1954 he was made under-secretary of the Chief Secretary's Department, clerk of the Executive Council, secretary to the minister of health, and a member of the public debt commission. Honest, conscientious, diplomatic and gifted with an exceptional memory, he developed his own form of shorthand and spoke little of his job. Premiers and ministers trusted him and relied upon him. 'Leave it to George' (Pearce's nickname) became a popular saying. For his work as State director of Queen Elizabeth II's visit to South Australia in 1954, he was appointed C.V.O. He also directed the visit of the Queen Mother in 1958. On 9 July 1959 at St Michael and All Angels Church, Henley Beach, he married Ivy Beatrice Duffy, a 58-year-old widow. She shared his work for charities and proved a capable hostess when he was South Australia's agent-general and trade commissioner in London in 1961-66.

Pearce was a board-member (1937-61) and chairman (1948-61) of the State Bank of South Australia, a justice of the peace (for forty years), president of the Royal Institute of Public Administration, vice-president of the South Australian branch of Meals on Wheels, chairman (1943-61) of the South Australian Symphony Orchestra committee and a member of the State division of the Australian Red Cross Society. He enjoyed bowls, golf, and gardening at his Erindale home. Survived by his wife, and by the son and daughter of his first marriage, he died on 21 November 1979 at the Burnside Memorial Hospital, Toorak Gardens, and was cremated.

PP (SA), 1954 (25); *Public Service Review* (SA), 28 Nov 1942; *South Australian Year Book*, 1966, p 66; *Advertiser* (Adel), 17 July 1929, 13 June 1946, 18, 19, 23, 25, 26 Mar 1954, 24 Nov 1979; *News* (Adel), 19 Feb, 3, 6, 7 Mar 1958.

TONY BOTT

PEARSON, ERIC JOHN (1918-1977), teacher and trade-union leader, was born on 6 May 1918 at Armidale, New South Wales, seventh child of native-born parents Herbert Henry Pearson, farmer, and his wife Hilda Maud, née Arentz. Eric attended Armidale High School. At Teachers' College, Armidale, he trained (1935-36) for one-teacher bush schools. He was appointed teacher-in-charge of Furracabad, near Glen Innes, in February 1937, and was transferred in May to Duck Creek Upper, which he later referred to as 'Up-a-duck Creek'. After eighteen months he was moved to Wylie Creek where he remained for three years.

On 9 January 1942 Pearson enlisted in the Australian Imperial Force. At the Methodist Church, Liston, on 13 February 1943 he married Evelyn Winifred Crome, a 19-year-old nurse. As an infantryman in the 2nd/33rd Battalion he saw action (September to December 1943) in New Guinea. In 1944-46 he was a sergeant, Australian Army Education Service: attached to 25th Brigade headquarters, he served in Australia and Borneo. He was discharged from the army on 18 January 1946.

After the war Pearson taught in primary schools in Sydney and studied in the evenings at the University of Sydney (B.A., 1952; M.A., 1958). He obtained second-class honours in psychology and a Blue (1948) for Rugby Union; he was to remain a keen supporter of Sydney University Football Club. Promoted deputy-headmaster at Gordon in 1951, he was appointed lecturer in education at Teachers' College, Wagga Wagga, in 1952. Pearson gained his masterate in psychology, then entered Birkbeck College, University of London (Ph.D., 1960). Back in New South Wales,

he lectured (1961-64) at Teachers' College, Armidale. From 1965 until his death he taught at Teachers' College, Sydney, becoming head of education in 1973. A widower, on 9 January 1964 at St Margaret's Presbyterian Church, Turramurra, he had married Joan Pauline Myers, née Roseby, a 42-year-old receptionist and a divorcee.

Throughout his professional career Pearson was a passionate activist in the New South Wales Teachers' Federation. After returning to Sydney in 1965, he led the lecturers' association through a difficult time when teachers' colleges were transformed into autonomous colleges of advanced education. It was also a period of increased radicalism, marked by the teachers' strike in 1968 and several others in the following years. Pearson emerged as a leader of the younger and more radical teachers. He was president of the N.S.W.T.F. (1974-75) and of the Australian Teachers' Federation (1974). He fought his campaigns with integrity and determination. Over six feet (183 cm) tall, he wore small-framed glasses and had a distinctive, if mannered, style of oratory. He frequently used wit and humour to destroy an opponent's case, but was never personal in his attacks.

Pearson's radical public stands against the Vietnam War and the dismissal of the Whitlam government upset many in his beloved Roseville sub-branch of the Returned Services League of Australia. Yet, he was conservative in some ways. He dressed in dark, three-piece suits, and was a traditionalist on most social and moral issues. Survived by his wife, and by the son and daughter of his first marriage, he died of leukemia on 8 June 1977 in Royal North Shore Hospital and was buried in Northern Suburbs cemetery.

B. Mitchell, *Teachers, Education and Politics* (Brisb, 1975); *Education*, 22 June, 6 July 1977; *SMH*, 6, 11 Dec 1973, 10 June 1977; teachers' records (NSW Dept of Education, Syd).

BRUCE MITCHELL

PELENSKY, YEVHEN YULII (EUGENE JULIAN) (1908-1956), literary critic, bibliographer and teacher, was born on 3 January 1908 at Stryi, Galicia, Austria-Hungary (Ukraine), son of Yosyp Pelensky, a justice official, and his wife Albina, née Hummer. An active member (from 1918) of Plast, the Ukrainian scouting association, Yevhen worked on various publications to promote its cause. He studied Slavic philology at the University of Lvov (M.A., 1930; Ph.D., 1933), and taught (1929-39) commerce in secondary schools at Lvov and Cracow, Poland. About 1935 at Stryi he married Iryna Vynnytska, a writer. Pelensky became a fellow of the philological section of the Shevchenko Scientific Society in 1937 and of the Historical-Philological Society in Prague in 1941.

From 1928 Pelensky had published literary criticism, bibliographical and biographical works, anthologies and text books, written mostly in Ukrainian. In the 1930s he edited the literary journals, *Dosvitni vohni*, *Dazhboh* and *Ukraïnska knyha*, and worked (1923-42) on the quarterly, *Bohoslovia*. While at Cracow he was co-founder and director of Ukrainske vydavnytstvo which published books and the newspaper, *Krakivs'ki visti* (*Cracow News*). Soon he established his own publishing company, Bystrytsia; after World War II he set it up in Germany. He was a *docent* at the Ukrainian Free University in Prague (1943-45) and at Munich, Germany (1946-49).

In 1949 Pelensky emigrated to Australia and settled with his family in Sydney. After establishing another printing business, he published (1952-53) the Ukrainian language journal, *Slovo* (*Word*). Eugene and Iryna became intellectual leaders of the Ukrainian community. As co-founder and first chairman of the Association of Ukrainians in New South Wales, he organized the purchase of a community hall. He was founding president (1950-56) of the Shevchenko Scientific Society in Australia. Active in the formation of Ukrainian Saturday schools, he headed their education advisory committee and wrote the first textbook for Ukrainian schools in the State. He helped to establish a Ukrainian credit union in Sydney and led the Plast Youth Association in Australia.

Pelensky was a man of energy, enthusiasm and administrative ability. An individualist, and a polite but stubborn optimist, he was continually planning for the future. A colleague, Professor J. B. Rudnytsky, noted his 'psychological disposition for systematisation and organisation of collective spiritual acquisitions'. Pelensky died of a cerebral haemorrhage on 29 September 1956 in Royal Prince Alfred Hospital and was buried with Catholic rites in Botany cemetery; his wife and daughter survived him.

Iryna Pelenska (1906-1990) was foundation president (1949-56, 1959-62) of the Ukrainian Women's Association in Australia and an executive-member (1951-62) of the Federation of Ukrainian Organizations in Australia. She inherited and ran (1956-62) her husband's printing business, contributed to Australian-Ukrainian periodicals and was vice-president (1956-62) of the Australian chapter of the Shevchenko Scientific Society. In 1962 she moved with her daughter to Detroit, United States of America. She was secretary of the Ukrainian National Women's League of America, an executive-member of the World Federation of Ukrainian Women's Organizations and editor of its journal *Ukraïnka v Sviti*,

and head (from 1970) of the pre-school council of the World Congress of Free Ukrainians.

H. Koscharsky (ed), *Istoriia Ukrainskoho Poselennia v Avstralii* (Syd, 1990); D. H. Struk (ed), *Encyclopedia of Ukraine*, vol 4 (Toronto, Canada, 1993); H. Padokh et al (eds), *Vyznachni Diachi NTSh* (Lviv, Ukraine, 1994); V. Markus (ed), *Entsyklopediia Ukrainskoi Diiaspory*, vol 4 (Kiev, 1995).

HALYNA KOSCHARSKY

PENDER, BERYL ELIZABETH; *see* MCLEISH

PENDRED, EDITH GLADYS (1897-1964), kindergarten teacher, was born on 28 February 1897 at Elsternwick, Melbourne, daughter of Benjamin Pendred, a commercial traveller from England, and his Victorian-born wife Edith Marion, née Chalker. Dux (1915) of Fintona Presbyterian Girls' Grammar School, Camberwell, Gladys studied at the Melbourne Teachers' College and Melbourne Kindergarten Training College (Moorool-beek). In 1925 she became a director with the Free Kindergarten Union of Victoria.

Although children were Pendred's main interest, it was through her work with adults that she was most influential. While principal (1928-41) of the Kindergarten Training College, Perth, she oversaw the education of students at the college and served as a supervisor for the Kindergarten Union of Western Australia. In 1937 she received a grant from the Carnegie Foundation for the Advancement of Teaching: she visited educational institutions in Britain and the United States of America in 1938 and completed a B.Sc. at Teachers' College, Columbia University, New York. After returning to Perth in 1940, she recommended that kindergartens should base their work on new theories of child development from America and Britain.

In 1942 Pendred was appointed field officer for the Nursery Kindergarten Extension Board, Melbourne. She advised parents and politicians on matters relating to young children, spoke on the radio, co-ordinated newsletters, and argued tirelessly for improved funding and services. The establishment (1944) of the Nursery School at Acton, Canberra, owed much to her efforts. Succeeding Christine Heinig [q.v.14] in November 1944 as federal education officer for the Australian Association for Pre-School Child Development (Australian Pre-School Association), Miss Pendred was based in Melbourne and then in Canberra. She travelled widely, conducted reviews of the Lady Gowrie [q.v.9] child centres, organized staff activities and association conferences, encouraged research and arranged exhibitions of pre-school work.

Pendred sat on the Australian Broadcasting Commission's advisory committee for children's programmes. In 1957 she spent time in the Philippines as a consultant for the Colombo plan. She edited the A.A.P.S.C.D. booklet, *Play Materials For Young Children* (Melbourne, 1952), contributed to the Australian Council for Educational Research's *Review of Education in Australia 1955-1962* (Melbourne, 1964), and wrote articles for the *Pre-School Child Bulletin* and the *Australian Pre-School Quarterly*. In 1963 she was appointed O.B.E. In 1964 she was elected a fellow of the Australian College of Education. She belonged to the Canberra Association of University Women, the Soroptimist Club of Canberra, and the Lyceum Club, Melbourne.

Strong, intellectually honest, energetic and committed, Pendred had a direct manner which could intimidate young teachers, yet it was tempered by kindness and a keen sense of humour. Although she proved to be as capable as an administrator as she was as a writer and speaker, she was essentially a teacher who never lost her enjoyment and appreciation of children. Early in 1964 she began to work part time. She died of a coronary occlusion on 30 November that year in Canberra Community Hospital and was buried with Anglican rites in Canberra cemetery. The Australian Pre-School Association established (1965) the Gladys Pendred memorial fund.

R. Kerr, *A History of the Kindergarten Union of Western Australia 1911-1973* (Perth, 1994); Canb Assn of Univ Women, *Newsletter*, Jan 1965; *Aust Pre-School Q*, Feb 1965; *Canb Times*, 2-3 Dec 1964; *West Australian*, 2 Dec 1964; A. Nakano-Jackson, *From the Cradle* ... (ms held by Aust Early Childhood Assn, Canb); information from Mrs A. Farrance, Mornington, Vic, and Dr P. Scott, Armadale, Melb.

ELIZABETH J. MELLOR

PENFOLD HYLAND, GLADYS (1886-1974), businesswoman and collector of antiques, was born on 17 March 1886 at Albury, New South Wales, elder daughter of Australian-born parents George Henry Lethbridge, sheriff's officer, and his second wife Ada Margaret, née Dawson. Gladys had five half-brothers and was a great-granddaughter of Governor King [q.v.2]. She lived with her family in Sydney after 1896, except when she briefly attended a private school in Melbourne. At St Stephen's Presbyterian Church, Sydney, on 10 August 1921 she married FRANK ASTOR PENFOLD HYLAND (1873-1948), governing director (from 1913) of Penfolds Wines Ltd; their only child was born in 1922. A grandson of Christopher Penfold [q.v.5], Frank had opened a branch of Penfolds in Pitt Street

in 1901. He belonged to the Australian Club and was founding president (1918) of the Federal Viticultural Council of Australia. On their frequent trips abroad he did much to publicize Australian wines.

Frank had begun collecting old silver, paintings and antiques while he did his own travelling to promote Penfolds wines. It was a pastime that Gladys took to with enthusiasm. In December 1923 she bought Toft Monks, an ornate, brick, Edwardian mansion at Elizabeth Bay. Over the years the house was furnished with Queen Anne and Georgian pieces, rare eighteenth-century porcelain figurines (mainly from the Bow and Chelsea factories), portraits by Sir Thomas Gainsborough, George Romney and Nicolaes Maes, landscapes by George Morland, J. M. W. Turner, Salomon van Ruysdael and Richard Wilson, and other paintings. The pantry was crammed with valuable silver. The Penfold Hylands found many of their *objets d'art* overseas and bought paintings from Thos Agnew & Sons Ltd in London. Local dealers, including Stanley Lipscombe [q.v.], also enjoyed their custom.

Gladys was a domineering woman who kept tight hold of the family purse-strings. Stocky in build, she generally dressed in beautifully tailored suits, often with initialled brass buttons. She belonged (from 1927) to the Macquarie Club. In the 1930s she helped to raise funds for charities, but usually managed to avoid mention in the social pages of the newspapers. An executive-member (from 1937) of the State division of the Australian Red Cross Society, she served during World War II on its divisional council, and on the military convalescent homes committee, and the publicity and public-relations committee. As president (1941-47) of the Red Cross Day committee she raised over £2 million.

Following Frank's death, Gladys inherited his majority shareholding in Penfolds and was chairman (1948-61) of the board. As she was inexperienced in running a company, she relied on his former secretary Grace Longhurst. Mrs Penfold Hyland was a fair-thinking woman—'apart from every now and then'—and a good listener. Impressed by the special sherry she had asked Max Schubert to make for her, she sent him on a mission to Europe in 1950 to buy different varieties of grapes and equipment, and to learn about winemaking. She endorsed the suggestion that the company should increase its production of uniform, high-quality table wines and was Schubert's ally in his efforts to make a top red wine—Grange Hermitage. At her initiative the company built conspicuous white premises at Tempe. In June 1961 Penfolds was registered as a public company, Penfolds Wines Australia Ltd. Gladys was a director until 1963.

In the 1950s Mrs Penfold Hyland 'never travelled without Bevan the butler or Myrtle the maid'. The chauffeur wore a silver-grey uniform to match her Rolls Royce motorcars. In 1964 she gave antique furniture, porcelain, silver (including an Elizabethan silver-gilt salt) and paintings to the National Gallery of South Australia in memory of her husband; she asked that her gifts—valued at £200 000—'should be shown as a group as far as possible'.

Generous to the State branch of the National Trust of Australia, Mrs Penfold Hyland held 'most enjoyable fund-raising exhibitions of the antiquities' at Toft Monks. In 1967, when the trust took over Old Government House, Parramatta, she gave a number of 'interesting and valuable items', including a 1720 long-case grandfather clock. A life-governor (1960-74) of Sydney Hospital, she made annual donations ($39 000 by 1970) towards a fellowship in gastroenterology. In 1967 she donated a Rolls Royce—with only 200 miles (320 km) on its odometer—to an appeal for the Royal Blind Society of New South Wales.

After a number of paintings (including four by Turner) had been stolen (1965), Mrs Penfold Hyland sold Toft Monks in 1966 and moved to a flat at Edgecliff. In 1967 she was appointed C.B.E. Her last years were spent at Chateau Blanc, her farm near Ingleburn. She died there on 11 July 1974 and was buried in the Church of England cemetery, Denham Court. Her daughter survived her.

O. L. Ziegler, *The Penfold Story* (Syd, 1975); H. Hooke, *Max Schubert, Winemaker* (Syd, 1994); Aust Red Cross Soc (NSW), *Annual Report*, 1937-50; *Ormolu*, Oct 1979, p 18; *SMH*, 10 Oct 1933, 18 Dec 1948, 6 July 1963, 2 July 1964, 16 Nov 1965, 22 Mar, 10 June 1967, 23 July, 1 Aug 1974; National Gallery of SA, Minutes (1964); information from Ms R. Penfold Russell, Paddington, Syd, and Mrs B. Simpson, Leabrook, Adel.

MARTHA RUTLEDGE

PENINGTON, FRANCES EILEEN (1897-1972), social scientist, was born on 5 August 1897 at Malvern, Melbourne, second of five children of Victorian-born parents George Penington, accountant, and his wife Marion, née Moody. Her father was secretary of the biscuit-manufacturing company Swallow [q.v.6] & Ariell Ltd and an active member of the Albert Park Methodist Church. Frances and her brothers attended University Practising (High) School. In 1914 she began as a student teacher with the Victorian Education Department; two years later she enrolled at the University of Melbourne (B.A., 1919; Dip.Ed., 1920; M.A., 1921). Graduating with first-class honours in ancient history and a Dwight [q.v.4] prize, she became a tutor (1920-26) in the history department. In 1924

she undertook field-work in Fiji. At King's College, University of London, she was a research student (1926-27) in Pacific history. After returning to Melbourne, she taught history at Fintona Presbyterian Girls' Grammar School in 1930-35.

The International Federation of University Women awarded Miss Penington a scholarship in 1936 to study in the United States of America at Smith College, Massachusetts. There she was influenced by the psychiatric case-work approach to social work, taught by Jessie Taft. In 1937-38 she visited Britain under the auspices of the Playgrounds Association of Victoria. She lived at the university settlement at Blackfriars, London, and extended her interests in child therapy (at the Tavistock Clinic) and in housing reform. Back in Melbourne, she practised as a child therapist. She helped to develop Winlaton, at Nunawading, as a detention centre for delinquent girls, in whom she took a personal interest, especially after their release.

Penington had been an investigator for an inquiry (1935-36) into slum housing in Melbourne under the direction of the Methodist layman and housing reformer Oswald Barnett [q.v.7]. When the State's first public housing authority was set up in 1938, she was appointed a commissioner, together with Barnett and the lawyer W. O. Burt [q.v.13]. She was one of the few women to gain a senior position in Melbourne's statutory authorities. At the Housing Commission she took responsibility for the social needs of residents in their re-location from inner-city areas to new housing estates. Following the British model, she appointed women housing officers to oversee the adjustment of tenants to their new homes. She worked with the Playgrounds Association to plan community facilities on the Garden City estate at Port Melbourne, advised the commission's architects on house, flat, and estate design, and urged consideration of the requirements of young mothers and their children in suburban developments. Her involvement with the social studies department at the University of Melbourne and her training of housing officers were important initiatives in relating theory and practice in the social-work profession. Although she did not entirely escape the 'redbaiters' who had unjustly persecuted Barnett and Burt before their resignation in 1948, Penington remained with the Housing Commission until 1955, despite growing disillusionment at the neglect of tenants' social needs after Barnett's departure.

Throughout her professional career Penington was active in numerous women's and welfare organizations. She chaired (1938-45) the training committee of the Young Women's Christian Association, and was an executive-member (1941-44) of the National Council of Women and president (1949-50) of the Victorian Women Graduates' Association. As president (1954-56) of the Australian Federation of University Women, she attended meetings of the international body, including the first regional conference in Manila in 1953. Her network of friends and membership of the Lyceum Club, Melbourne, were important to her, as was the extended Penington family. In 1956-58 she was senior history teacher at Presbyterian Ladies' College, Burwood.

Frances Penington embodied a social reform tradition which was strong among Melbourne women. Through her ability to bridge policy and practice, she made an important contribution to the development of the social-work profession, to the direction of public housing in Australia, and to the care of children. She died on 12 July 1972 at Donvale and was cremated with Anglican rites.

R. Howe, *New Houses for Old* (Melb, 1988); Aust Federation of Univ Women, *Newsletter*, no 42, Oct 1972; information from Mrs S. Penington, Balwyn, Mrs V. McCutcheon, St Kilda, and Prof D. Penington, Parkville, Melb.   RENATE HOWE

PENMAN, FRANK (1905-1973), chemist, was born on 20 March 1905 at Collingwood, Melbourne, second of six children of Australian-born parents George Alexander Penman, clerk, and his wife Myra Sidonia, née Cox. Educated at Scotch College (dux 1922) and the University of Melbourne (B.Sc., 1926; M.Sc., 1927), Frank won numerous prizes and scholarships. On 13 May 1927 he joined the Victorian Department of Agriculture as an assistant research chemist. He built his reputation in hydrology and soils. In 1933 he was awarded the Rennie [q.v.11] medal by the Australian Chemical Institute, of which he was elected a fellow (1945).

On 25 April 1931 at Chalmers Presbyterian Church, Auburn, Penman had married Mary Rorke. Mary later fell chronically ill and became drug-dependent, causing them many years of distress: eventually they divorced. Penman was seconded to the Commonwealth Department of Munitions in 1940 and sent to North America in the following year to study the manufacture of explosives. His experience helped in establishing an explosives factory at Mulwala, New South Wales. Recalled to the Department of Agriculture in 1945, he assisted in implementing the soldier-settlement scheme by identifying land suitable for irrigated cropping. In 1948 he was promoted deputy chief chemist.

Penman was appointed chief irrigation officer in the State Rivers and Water Supply Commission on 10 February 1950. Within seven months he moved to the Common-

wealth Scientific and Industrial Research Organization to superintend viticultural and citrus work at research stations at Merbein, Victoria (1950), and Griffith, New South Wales (1954). Developing a rapport with local growers, he advised them on soil analysis, salinity, irrigation, drainage, plant nutrition, and chemicals. He was made chief research officer in 1954. His publications, mostly practical, dated from 1929 and included articles in the C.S.I.R.O. *Bulletin* and the *Journal of the Department of Agriculture of Victoria*.

In the late 1950s Penman's relations with some of his colleagues deteriorated. Although the C.S.I.R.O. gradually shifted the focus of its primary-industry research from regional to national problems, he did not allow Merbein to follow this trend. Strongly committed to local tasks, he was overworked, and exhausted by his wife's illness. Formal complaints were made about his management methods and alleged indifference to long-term research. The C.S.I.R.O.'s executive failed to give him timely guidance and transferred him on 14 April 1961 to head office, Melbourne, to assist 'in the formulation of policies particularly in relation to irrigation research'. At St Andrew's Church, Gardiner, on 7 August 1964 he married Emily Gwen Prosser, née Schmidt, a 48-year-old divorcee.

Five ft 10½ ins (180 cm) tall and robust in build, Penman had a ruddy complexion and curly reddish-grey hair. He was variously seen as decent, companionable and affable, albeit 'a very private person . . . [due to] some deep tragedy in his family life'. While he was a successful practical scientist, he never attained as a research leader the heights fore-shadowed by his early academic performance. He retired in 1970. Survived by his wife, and by the son and daughter of his first marriage, he died of bronchopneumonia on 22 March 1973 in South Melbourne and was cremated.

Aqua, May 1950; *SMH*, 18 Aug 1956; CSIRO Archives, Canb, series 3, PH/PEN/6, 6A and 6B; information from Mr A. Gurnett-Smith, Deakin, Dr J. R. Philip, Campbell, ACT, Mr W. Ives, Neutral Bay, Syd, Mr R. Prunster, Deniliquin, NSW, Mr E. Lawton, Mildura, Mr R. Penman, Blairgowrie, Vic, Dr J. V. Possingham, Unley Park, Adel, Mr D. Walters, Gympie, Qld, and the late Mr M. Sauer.
                                          JOHN P. LONERGAN

PENNEFATHER, HUGH FRANK (1894-1964), sheepclasser, was born on 5 April 1894 at Pyalong, Victoria, third child and eldest son of Melbourne-born parents Hugh Claude Pennefather (d.1951), wool valuer, and his wife Mabel Annie Rose, née Irving. Edward Curr [q.v.1] was his great-grandfather. Hugh Claude joined the Australian Estates & Mortgage Co. Ltd (Australian Estates Co. Ltd from

1936) in 1899 as wool expert. From 1914 he concentrated on sheep-classing. 'Old Penny' travelled about 40 000 miles (64 000 km) a year until the 1930s, classing over forty leading studs and flocks in eastern Australia. Educated at Scotch College, Melbourne, Frank spent two seasons working under his father at the A.E. & M. Co. He jackerooed on Terrick Terrick station, near Blackall, Queensland, for two years, then managed his father's property, Ardsley, near Bathurst, New South Wales.

A member of the 41st Australian Infantry, Militia, Pennefather enlisted in the Australian Imperial Force on 1 June 1915. He served in Egypt, where he was commissioned (March 1916), and in England. In April 1917 he was sent to the Western Front as a lieutenant in the 56th Battalion. Appointed the 14th Brigade's bombing officer, he remained on duty at a critical period in March 1918, despite suffering the effects of gas. In August-September he established and maintained forward dumps while under heavy shell-fire. He was awarded the Military Cross and mentioned in dispatches. After World War I ended he spent some months in England with a Bradford wool firm. His A.I.F. appointment terminated in Sydney on 12 September 1919.

Pennefather ran Widgery Wah, near Trangie, in partnership with his sister, before selling out. At Holy Trinity Church, Kelso, on 7 July 1922 he married Mary Udy Jordan (d.1951) with Anglican rites; they were to have a daughter. Based (1926-58) at Darling Point, Sydney, he travelled extensively, understudying his father who favoured quality, medium wool on a sound frame; like him, he held that sheep-breeding was a total concept. He advised on such interrelated matters as nutrition, pastures, health, management and the special requirements of different areas.

Among the many merino studs and flocks that Pennefather classed were the Australian Estate Co.'s studs Terrick Terrick, Queensland, Raby and Oolambeyan (1930-57), Wanganella (1920s and 1930s), Bairnkine (1946-63), Goolgumbla, Buttabone Stud Park, Deniliquin Stud Park and Uardry, New South Wales, and Mawallok, Victoria. He kept abreast of modern developments by making several trips abroad. Following World War II, he ran a high-class Peppin [q.v.5] merino flock on his property, Llambeda, O'Connell, where he carried out extensive pasture improvement. On 24 September 1953 at St Columba's Church, Woollahra, he married with Presbyterian forms Marion Eleanor Little, née Friend (d.1962), a 48-year-old divorcee.

Quiet, unassuming, sociable but somewhat reserved, Pennefather always wore a tie at dinner and addressed men as 'Mr'. Once asked what he looked for in a ram, he replied—'Lust!' He was a keen tennis player, and a member of the Royal Sydney Golf Club and the Australian Club, Sydney. While at Uardry, Hay, for the classing, he died of a coronary occlusion on 11 March 1964 and was cremated with Anglican rites. The daughter of his first marriage predeceased him.

C. Massy, *The Australian Merino* (Melb, 1990); G. Walsh, *Pioneering Days* (Syd, 1993); *Pastoral Review*, 16 Aug 1922, 16 Mar 1951, 18 Mar, 18 Apr, 17 July, 17 Aug 1964.   G. P. WALSH

PENNEFATHER, REGINALD RICHARD (1905-1957), agricultural scientist, was born on 4 May 1905 at Camberwell, Melbourne, second child of John Francis Pennefather, a Victorian-born clerk of courts, and his second wife Grace Hilda, née Curtis, late Kemp, who came from England. Reg was educated at Wangaratta Agricultural High School, Melbourne Church of England Grammar School (1920-24) and the University of Melbourne (B.Agr.Sc., 1927). After joining the development branch of the Prime Minister's Department as an investigation officer, he examined agricultural conditions in Tasmania, potato marketing, and the transport of sheep. From 1930 he surveyed farms in the chief dairying districts of Queensland, South Australia and Western Australia for the Federal Dairy Investigation Committee.

In 1932 the Council for Scientific and Industrial Research appointed Pennefather a field research assistant at its station at Griffith, New South Wales. He helped to find solutions to the massive problems of salination and declining soil fertility in the Murrumbidgee Irrigation Area. From his investigations of the properties of local soils and the infiltration of water through them, he formulated principles to guide irrigation techniques. In 1940 he became foundation secretary of the C.S.I.R.'s irrigation research and extension committee. He began to put his principles for sustainable irrigation into practice, and much of the region's valuable land was saved from irreparable damage.

Pennefather was made research officer-in-charge of the new soils and irrigation extension service in 1944. He wrote numerous articles in the *Farmers' Newsletter* and regularly broadcast on radio 2RG. Seconded (1945) to the New South Wales Department of Agriculture to organize its M.I.A. agricultural extension service, he tried to improve both the farmers' economic returns and their way of life. On 9 October 1948 he married Norma Margaret Simms Tracy; she had served in the Women's Land Army. Their only child was stillborn in 1950. After a few years they lived apart.

Concerned that the Commonwealth Scientific and Industrial Research Organization's findings were not being widely disseminated, (Sir) Ian Clunies Ross [q.v.13] established an agricultural research liaison section in Melbourne in 1951. Pennefather was persuaded to accept the post of officer-in-charge. His work brought him into contact with many members of the C.S.I.R.O., State departments and university faculties of agriculture. He established closer relations between scientists, farmers and public servants, and narrowed the gap between the results of research and their practical application. The section published the periodical *Rural Research in C.S.I.R.O.* to provide information on its work.

Although Pennefather had an outgoing personality and got on well with people, he was deeply tormented. On 19 January 1957 he was questioned by police about 'his associations with young boys' and warned that court proceedings would probably follow. He committed suicide by inhaling carbon monoxide on or about 2 February that year in a flat at Parkville and was buried in Melbourne general cemetery. His wife survived him.

Farmers' Newsletter, Mar 1957; *SMH*, 26 Jan 1951; *Age* (Melb), 11 Feb 1957; CSIRO Archives, Canb, series 3, PH/PEN 002, pts 1, 2; Inquest deposition file, no 4247, 1957, VPRS 24 (PRO, Vic); information from Mr A. F. Gurnett-Smith, Deakin, Dr R. Milton Moore, Aranda, Dr J. R. Philip, Campbell, and Mr K. Spencer, Lyneham, ACT.

N. KEITH BOARDMAN

PENTON, BRIAN CON (1904-1951), journalist, novelist and polemicist, was born on 21 August 1904 at Ascot, Brisbane, fifth child of English-born parents Reginald Penton, commercial traveller, and his wife Sarah, née Bennett. Brian attended New Farm and Windsor state schools, and Brisbane Grammar School (1918-19). In 1921 he found work as a copy-boy on the *Brisbane Courier*, at the same time as did Ray Lindsay, second son of Norman Lindsay [qq.v.10]. Over the next three years Penton advanced to general reporting.

In the oratory of the Liberal Catholic Church, Ann Street, Brisbane, on 6 January 1924 he married Olga Saville Moss (d.1972); they were to remain childless. Olga was a clever and sophisticated woman, some seven years his senior, who taught Latin and English at Brisbane Girls' Grammar School. Resigning from the *Courier* in 1925, Penton worked his passage to London where he languished in a Bloomsbury 'bedsit' for six weeks before coming home. On his return, the couple moved to Sydney where he obtained a job as a reporter on the *Sydney Morning Herald* and began to make a name for himself as the author (1926-28) of a regular column of satirical commentary on proceedings in the State and Federal parliaments. He used the column, 'From the Gallery', to develop his political views, which he described as those of a 'classical liberal'. In addition, he did some speech-writing for the prime minister S. M. (Viscount) Bruce, and for his predecessor W. M. Hughes [qq.v.7,9] with whom he formed a close bond which lasted many years.

By 1928 Penton's column had angered influential figures in Canberra sufficiently to have him recalled to Sydney. He resigned from the *Herald* soon after and sailed for London, where Olga joined him six months later. They both tried—and failed—to interest British publishers in two comic novels they had written about contemporary life in Sydney. Penton had more success with Norman Lindsay's novel, *Redheap* (1930), which Faber & Faber Ltd had undertaken to publish, and which Penton—by then a close friend of Lindsay—had agreed to shepherd through the process. In London, Penton found himself some reporting and sub-editing with the *Daily Express* and the *Daily Mail*, but his main interest was in the Fanfrolico Press—a small but moderately successful subscription printer and publisher of fine books—which P. R. ('Inky') Stephensen [q.v.12], Jack Lindsay and John Kirtley had established. Soon after his arrival he became its new business manager, ousting Stephensen with whom he long continued to have hostile relations. By 1931 the press had folded, but by this time Olga was earning a good salary teaching Latin at Pitman's College, and receiving substantial royalties on a Latin textbook she had written in her spare time.

While in London, Penton was introduced to the expatriate Australian novelist 'Henry Handel' Richardson [q.v.11]. He and Norman Lindsay, who had arrived in London, visited her at her home, and Penton visited by himself several times and also exchanged letters with her. He was deeply impressed by Richardson's work. The novel he began to write at this time, *Landtakers* (Sydney, 1934), was envisaged as the first part of an Australian historical trilogy modelled on *The Fortunes of Richard Mahony*, and focusing on the same central dilemma of the divided colonial psyche.

The Pentons returned to Sydney towards the end of 1933. Brian had been offered a job as a regular columnist with the *Telegraph*, which had recently been acquired by Associated Newspapers Ltd, publishers of the Sydney *Sun*. The new column, known as 'The Sydney Spy', appeared on weekdays for almost two years. Its distinctive blend of tones and topics —urbane, mocking and iconoclastic, with an extraordinary range of cultural reference— made Penton something of a cult figure in Sydney. His reputation was enhanced by the critical success of *Landtakers*, the story of Derek Cabell, an English immigrant to the

Moreton Bay settlement in the 1840s, though its passionate 'debunking' of the myths of pioneering heroism scandalized some readers —as intended. The sequel, *Inheritors* (1936), completed in Spain two years later, dealt with the lives of the second generation of the Cabell family. It proved less popular and was never reprinted.

In 1935-36 Penton was the defendant in two controversial libel suits (the first of a number in his career) brought by the author Vivian Crockett and the publisher Stephensen of a novel, *Mezzomorto* (1934), which Penton had reviewed unfavourably in the *Bulletin*. Penton lost both suits, which pleased his enemies, such as Miles Franklin [q.v.8], and alarmed admirers, such as Nettie Palmer [q.v.11]. It may have been a turning-point in his career, but it coincided with his employment by Consolidated Press Ltd which had taken over the *Telegraph* in 1936. Under a dynamic new proprietor and managing director, (Sir) Frank Packer [q.v.], Penton began to rise in the company, becoming news editor of the *Daily Telegraph*, then editor in 1941, following Sydney Deamer [q.v.13] and C. S. McNulty [q.v.].

Through the late 1930s Penton had made a major contribution to the distinctive style of the *Daily Telegraph*. That new style, particularly as it appeared in his own articles and reviews, was irreverent, progressive and individualist, critical of 'red tape' and censorship, and seriously committed to improving public awareness and promoting a modern and civilized urban lifestyle. The *Daily Telegraph* of the mid-1940s, under his direction, was a triumph of editorial co-ordination and flair.

Penton's intellectual focus in the early years of World War II was on the complacency, mediocrity and pettiness of much of Australian public life and national culture. With Cyril Pearl, editor of the *Sunday Telegraph* from 1939, and with the implicit backing of Packer, Penton attacked both major political parties, the education system, achievements in art and literature, and the nation's general unreadiness to mobilize effectively for war. Outside Consolidated Press he formed close alliances with Dr H. V. Evatt [q.v.14], Dr Frank Louat [q.v.], W. C. Wentworth and other like-minded people, and conducted an anti-government 'Win-the-War' campaign in the lead-up to the 1940 Federal election. In 1941 Penton published a booklet, *Think—or Be Damned*, and two years later a longer, more reflective book, *Advance Australia—Where?* (London, 1943).

In 1944, as the subject of another portrait by (Sir) William Dobell [q.v.14], Penton was marginally involved in the controversy surrounding the award of the 1943 Archibald [q.v.3] prize to Dobell for his portrait of Joshua Smith; and he was centrally involved in the 'Censorship Crisis' in which the Federal Labor government attempted to muzzle criticism from the press by seizing entire editions of several newspapers in Sydney and some other capital cities, beginning in May with the *Daily Telegraph* and the *Sunday Telegraph*. Penton and Pearl, backed by the three Sydney press proprietors, led the counter-charge against the censors and Arthur Calwell [q.v.13] who sued Penton for £25 000 damages in a libel suit which was eventually settled out of court. Penton wrote a blow-by-blow account of the events in *Censored!* (1947).

In mid-1944 he visited the United States of America and London, and observed the devastation of Normandy, France. On his return, he signalled his increasingly hard anti-union stance by his boots-and-all support for Packer against the Australian Journalists' Association and other unions in the journalists' strike in October. Penton maintained this stance through the industrial conflicts of the late 1940s and in a series of attempts by Consolidated Press to have the A.J.A. deregistered. His, and the paper's, wartime support for the Labor government turned to uncompromising support for (Sir) Robert Menzies' [q.v.] new Liberal Party.

Penton's private life was always controversial: his bohemian appearance and behaviour, his compulsive pursuit of women, and his refusal to defer to convention in the conduct of his two, long-term, extra-marital liaisons with Sadie Bull and Zélie McLeod made him (and them) some enemies. He was a noted bon viveur and an enthusiastic sailor. A member of Royal Prince Alfred Yacht Club, he owned and skippered a cutter, the *Josephine*, winning the first Montague Island race (1947) and competing in the Sydney to Hobart races in the late 1940s.

Brian Penton died of cancer on 24 August 1951 at St Luke's Hospital, Sydney, and was cremated with Anglican rites. He had been one of Australia's great newspaper editors, an important novelist, a passionate but critical Australian nationalist, and a courageous liberal campaigner for what he called 'a civilized mode of social living together'.

J. Lindsay, *Fanfrolico and After* (Lond, 1962); D. Horne, *Confessions of a New Boy* (Melb, 1985); P. Buckridge, *The Scandalous Penton* (Brisb, 1994) and for bib; Penton papers (ML and Fryer L).

PATRICK BUCKRIDGE

PERCY, HAL (1898-1949), actor and writer, was born on 2 October 1898 at Moonee Ponds, Melbourne, and named Percy Ewart, son of Australian-born parents Vernon John Montague Henry, accountant, and his wife Amy Fanny Elizabeth, née Gardiner. He attended All Saints Grammar School, St Kilda, and worked as a motor driver. On 1 July 1918 he enlisted in the Australian Imperial Force. Reaching England after the Armistice, he served in France before being discharged from the army on 28 November 1919. Concert parties for the troops had stimulated his interest in theatre, but, on his return to Melbourne, he bowed to his parents' reservations about such a career and trained as a commercial artist. In 1920 he succumbed to theatrical temptation and joined Phillip Lytton's travelling tent-show company. His two years with the company gave him the broad experience which was to underpin his professional career.

Throughout the 1920s 'Hal Percy' (as he styled himself) was in demand as an actor, often playing in J. C. Williamson [q.v.6] Ltd's companies; among the 'stars' in whose productions he appeared were Maurice Moscovitch, (Sir) Seymour Hicks and Leon Gordon. When the Depression, combined with the advent of 'talkies', devastated professional theatre, he and Brett Randall founded (1931) the Melbourne Little Theatre, envisaged as a repertory company to bridge the gap between amateur and professional theatre. Percy's practical and artistic skills were important in making the best of primitive conditions at the Fawkner Park Kiosk, South Yarra, the theatre's humble premises from 1932. The Little Theatre was cautious in choice of plays, but was committed to the development of Australian drama.

On 23 December 1933 at St Paul's Anglican Cathedral, Melbourne, Percy Henry married Peggy Alice Maud Benson Mitchell, a 28-year-old, London-born beautician who was a member of the company. Deciding to make a career in radio, he became a studio manager for 3UZ and was soon devising variety programmes. He moved into the production of serials and set up his own company, Hal Percy Productions; later he was involved with another company, Legionnaire. The subjects of these popular serials ranged from Lawrence of Arabia ('The Broken Idol') to (Sir) Winston Churchill ('Imperial Leader'). From time to time Percy returned to the Little Theatre to direct and act.

During World War II Percy concentrated on variety. He appeared regularly in the Australian Broadcasting Commission's 'Merry-Go-Round', creating a segment called 'Canteen Capers' in which he played a 'Dinkum Digger'; he continued in this genre in another programme, 'Rola Radio Newsreel', on radio 3XY. Many of his verses, written in a style reminiscent of C. J. Dennis [q.v.8], were later published in *Here's Hal Percy in Verse* (1941) and *Radio Rambles with Hal Percy* (1945), the latter with his own illustrations. While celebrating the decency and humour of the digger, Percy also had a patriotic agenda which emphasized Imperial loyalty and encouraged recruiting.

Hailed by his peers as 'a trouper', Hal Percy—like many professionals of his generation—developed the versatility necessary for economic survival, but was particularly renowned for being equally at ease on radio and the stage, and in variety as much as drama. Cheerful and vigorous in manner, he was solidly built, his gruff voice lending itself to character roles.

In 1945 Percy joined the A.B.C., working first as a variety producer and then as head of 'light entertainment' in Victoria. He was twice acting federal director of variety, in Sydney. Survived by his wife and son, he died suddenly of heart disease on 23 July 1949 at the King's Cross Hotel and was cremated.

R. Lane, *The Golden Age of Australian Radio Drama 1923-1960* (Melb, 1994); *Bulletin*, 9 Dec 1931; *Listener-In*, 23 Oct 1937; *Herald* (Melb), 9 Jan 1932; *Age* (Melb), 3 Dec 1931, 25 July 1949; *Argus*, 25 July 1949; Melb Little Theatre scrap-book *and* H. and P. Percy files (Performing Arts Museum, Vic Arts Centre, Melb); H. Percy papers (NFSA).

JOHN RICKARD

PERIVOLARIS, ANNA (c.1888-1963), schoolteacher, was born about 1888 on the island of Samos, Greece, daughter of Constantine Christodoulis, artist, and his wife Anthea, née Chrysakis. Anna arrived with her family at Port Said, Egypt, probably in 1903. There she married John Boreas in 1912; they were to have three children. In the same city in 1917, as a widow, she married Nicolas Guiseppe Perivolaris, a Greek sailor.

In December 1921 Nicolas emigrated to Australia. He was followed by Anna and the children who reached Sydney in the *Jervis Bay* in March 1923. They lived in Little Bloomfield Street, Surry Hills, and Anna taught Greek. The growing number of children attending the Greek community's after-hours school in Perth prompted her friend Peter Michelides [q.v.10], president of the Hellenic Community of Western Australia, to ask her to move there as a schoolteacher. With her husband and youngest daughter, she had settled in Perth by 1933. Nicolas worked as a machinist for Michelides Ltd and Anna became principal schoolteacher of the after-hours classes. On 9 May 1938 they were naturalized.

For many years the Perivolarises lived in the residential heartland of Perth's Greek community, which centred on Aberdeen and Lake streets, Northbridge. Located in the nearby Greek Hall in Parker Street, the Greek School was open for three hours each evening from Monday to Friday. Mrs Perivolaris instructed children of all ages, and insisted that they wear uniforms. She taught Greek grammar, reading, writing, history and religion; for advanced students, she included classical Greek in the curriculum. In addition, she introduced Hellenic dancing in traditional costume and held regular concerts.

A leader in the Hellenic Women's Association, Perivolaris belonged to a group which met fortnightly to co-ordinate cultural activities, such as those to celebrate Easter Week, and to raise money for the Church and for philanthropic causes. During World War II she organized performances to aid the Greece Fund in support of the exiled Greek government. On 21 November 1943 the Hellenic Community held a concert in her honour as a way of expressing gratitude for her work in teaching 'love for our mother tongue to our children'. After Nicholas retired, Anna continued to work, receiving £5 per week from 1946 for teaching at the school.

Anna Perivolaris was a gentle, neatly groomed and quietly spoken woman. Professional in her approach and concerned for her students, she was respected and well liked by the local Greeks. She became an integral part of that community, helping to maintain and enhance Hellenism in Western Australia for two generations. Survived by her husband, son and two daughters, she died on 27 January 1963 in Royal Perth Hospital and was buried in Karrakatta cemetery with Greek Orthodox rites.

Hellenic Community of WA Inc, *50th Anniversary Commemorative Book* (Perth, 1987); *West Australian*, 28, 29 Jan 1963; naturalization files A435, item 46/4/6398, A446/71, item 55/47485 (AA, Canb), *and* AA SP1122/1, item N1957/13385 (AA, NSW), *and* PP302/1, item WA 12210 (AA, WA); Souvenir Programme, concert in honour of Mrs A. Perivolaris, 21 Nov 1943 (held by Dr J. Yiannakis, Alexander Heights, Perth); M. Kouts (taped interview) 17 Nov 1988 (BL); information from Messrs S., M. and G. Kakulas, City Beach, Mr J. and Mrs N. Pitsikas, Tuart Hill, and Mrs C. Panos, Wembley, Perth.   JOHN N. YIANNAKIS

PERKIN, EDWIN GRAHAM (1929-1975), newspaper editor, was born on 16 December 1929 at Hopetoun, Victoria, elder son of Herbert Edwin Perkin, baker, and his wife Iris Lily, née Graham, both Victorian born. Graham grew up at Warracknabeal and was educated at the local high school. In 1948 he began to study law at the University of Melbourne, but abandoned his course in the following year when he obtained a cadetship with the *Age*. At the Methodist Church, St Kilda, on 6 September 1952 he married Peggy Lorraine Corrie.

As a young reporter, Perkin rapidly acquired a reputation for enthusiasm and restless energy. In 1955 he won a Kemsley scholarship in journalism which took him to London. Returning to Australia as a feature writer, he

shared the Walkley [q.v.] award for journalism in 1959 for an article on pioneering heart surgery. His rise in the newspaper hierarchy was rapid: he became deputy news editor in 1959, news editor in 1963, assistant-editor in 1964 and editor (at the age of 36) in 1966. He was appointed to the additional post of editor-in-chief in 1973.

Under Perkin's editorship, and with the encouragement of his young managing director Ranald Macdonald, the *Age* again set itself to influence the agenda of governments, as it had under David Syme [q.v.6]. Perkin aimed to establish the paper's credibility as a purveyor of reliable information, authoritative analysis and entertaining writing that would be read by the young and the middle class, and that would make politicians sensitive to the needs of their constituency. He succeeded in part by raising the *Age*'s journalistic standards. He recruited ambitious young reporters, a stable of talented cartoonists and photographers, and a group of senior writers to contribute news analysis and comment. He redesigned the typography and layout of the paper, expanded its foreign coverage, appointed a team of investigative reporters and an environmental writer, doubled the space for readers' letters, and began an occasional feature ('We Were Wrong') which explained and apologized for the paper's mistakes.

Despite his gruff, sometimes unforgiving, insistence on accuracy and ethics, and his earlier stint (1961-63) as lecturer in journalism at the University of Melbourne, Perkin did not believe that training alone produced good journalists: 'intuitive ability runs first for me, intellectual capacity second, training third'. He believed in 'creative subjectivity' and said that contemporary newspapers should concern themselves more with 'analysis and interpretation' than with reportage.

Perkin turned the *Age* into a more interventionist and campaigning newspaper. It exposed financial scandals in State governments and corruption in the police force, and attacked Federal governments for suppressing information. In the process, it attracted critics who thought it too 'leftist'. In 1972 the *Age*, which had traditionally supported Coalition governments, advocated the election of E. G. Whitlam's Labor Party. When that government was forced to an early election in 1974, Perkin wanted to support Whitlam again. His stand led to a conflict with the board of David Syme & Co. Ltd, owner and publisher of the *Age*. A compromise, supported by Macdonald, narrowly averted Perkin's resignation. It also reinforced his insistence on editorial independence, subject to the management's right to dismiss an editor in whom it had lost confidence. The *Age* became a more substantial, wider ranging, better written and significantly more influential newspaper.

Perkin's reforms and his willingness to speak out strongly in defence of the paper's policies boosted circulation from a stagnant 180 000 in 1965 to a solid 222 000 ten years later. The company's revenues rose correspondingly.

Graham Perkin was a large man with a large appetite for life. His success as editor owed much to his ebullience, to his infectious enthusiasm for journalism, to his dominant—sometimes domineering—personality, and to his willingness to bear the heat of criticism. That success won recognition for the *Age* as one of the ten great newspapers of the world and for Perkin as one of the most distinguished editors of his time. It also led him into senior roles in the newspaper industry, as a director (from 1966) of Australian Associated Press, its chairman in 1970-72, and a director of Reuters Ltd, London, in 1971-74. Away from his desk, he supported the North Melbourne Football Club, and belonged to the Savage, Victoria Golf and Melbourne Cricket clubs. He died of myocardial infarction on 16 October 1975 at his Sandringham home and was cremated with Presbyterian forms; his wife, son and daughter survived him. An award for the journalist of the year was named (1976) after him.

G. Hutton and L. Tanner (eds), *The Age, 125 Years of Age* (Melb, 1979); M. Walker, *Powers of the Press* (Lond, 1982); *Quadrant*, Oct 1975; *Age* (Melb), 17 Oct 1975, 17 Oct 1985; J. T. Tidey, The Last Syme (M.A. thesis, Monash Univ, 1997); Perkin papers (NL).   CREIGHTON BURNS

PERKINS, HETTY (c.1895-1979), Arrernte matriarch, was born about 1895 at Arltunga, Northern Territory, daughter of Harry Perkins, a White miner from Broken Hill, New South Wales, and his wife Nellie Errerreke, an Aborigine from the Arrernte people of Central Australia. She spent her early years in the Arltunga gold-mining region, east of Alice Springs, a violent frontier which produced people who were resourceful and tough. Hetty's character and intelligence thrived on the hard conditions. Like many other Aboriginal women, she learned to raise a large family unaided, ride horses and camels, skin a bullock, lay a fuse, and dig and assay gold-bearing ore.

At the age of 14 Perkins had been employed at the Crossroads hotel. She then moved to The Garden station, north-west of Arltunga. For a number of years she worked on the property and helped to manage it. She later refused a gift of part of The Garden from Jim Turner, the father of several of her eleven children, because he had abandoned her for a White woman. In 1928 she went to the Jay Creek institution for 'half-castes' where she worked as 'senior dormitory girl'. The insti-

tution was moved in 1932 to the Alice Springs telegraph-station buildings and was thereafter known as The Bungalow. Hetty had charge of the infants' dormitory and supervised the cooking. In the mid-1930s she met the man who was to be the father of her younger children, Martin Connelly, a Kalkadoon from Mount Isa, Queensland.

Dignified in manner and a disciplinarian in attitude, Perkins insisted on clean clothes for herself and her children, whatever the circumstances. She left coins on a table as a test of temptation for her children. The coins gathered dust. 'If you're not doing the right thing you're doing the wrong thing', was her constant refrain. She was one of the few Aborigines not evacuated from Alice Springs during World War II, probably because her organizational and cooking skills were too valuable for the military to lose. By 1950 she was living at Sanitary Camp with one of her sons.

Perkins was born at a time when, according to the anthropologist Sir Baldwin Spencer [q.v.12], the old ways of the Arrernte people seemed almost finished. Her attitude to traditional Arrernte life was ambivalent. She spoke Eastern Arrernte fluently, and passed to her male children the sub-section (skin-name) *perrurle*, the yam and caterpillar dreaming. Yet, four of her children were raised in White institutions, and she explained to her family, 'We were going White way. We bin working'. Late in life she witnessed the revival of Aboriginal self-confidence and pride, and willingly took on the roles of grandmother, nanna and auntie.

Survived by four of her sons and two of her daughters, Perkins died on 8 December 1979 at Alice Springs and was buried locally with Anglican rites. At Alice Springs a nursing home for elderly Aborigines was named after her. Her son Charles was the first Aboriginal secretary (1984-88) of the Commonwealth Department of Aboriginal Affairs; her granddaughter Patricia Turner was the first Aboriginal chief executive officer (1994-98) of the Aboriginal and Torres Strait Islander Commission; and her grandson Neville Perkins was secretary (1987-88) of the Department of Aboriginal Affairs, New South Wales.

J. Larkins and B. Howard, *Sheilas* (Adel, 1976); H. Radi (ed), *200 Australian Women* (Syd, 1988); P. Read (ed), *Charles Perkins, a Biography* (Melb, 1990); Half Caste Home, Alice Springs, series A659/1, 1939/1/996 (AA, Canb); information from Mr C. Perkins, Syd, and Mr N. Perkins, Latham, Canb.
                                                     PETER READ

PERRETT, CHRISTOPHER JAMES (1896-1972), public servant, was born on 26 November 1896 at Moonee Ponds, Melbourne, son of Victorian-born parents William Joseph

Perrett, baker, and his wife Margaret, née Keogh. Chris was educated at St Patrick's College, East Melbourne, and the University of Melbourne (B.Com., 1931; B.A., 1943). Five ft 8 ins (173 cm) tall, he had a 'quick eye' and represented the university in cricket and baseball.

On 24 September 1913 Perrett joined the Department of Defence as a clerk. Enlisting in the Australian Imperial Force on 20 March 1917, he performed pay and administrative duties at headquarters in England and France, and rose to warrant officer (1919). At Westminster Cathedral, London, on 4 June 1919 he married with Catholic rites Charlotte MacDowell (d.1966); they were to remain childless. He was discharged from the A.I.F. on 16 April 1920 in Melbourne. Resuming his job with the Department of Defence, he worked in the finance, accounts and munitions-supply branches. By the 1921-22 season he was playing sub-district cricket for Malvern's first XI. Promoted (1931) investigating officer in the Treasury's taxation branch, he moved to Canberra in 1935 to join the marketing arm of the Department of Commerce. In September 1939 he was appointed secretary of the newly established Australian Wheat Board, which was based in Melbourne.

Succeeding John Thomson as the board's general manager on 1 January 1946, Perrett was responsible for finding additional markets for Australian wheat. He went on numerous missions to Africa, Europe and Asia to contact potential buyers. Having negotiated the first large purchase of Australian wheat by the People's Republic of China, he organized the export of 2 007 000 tons to that country in 1960-61, 1 161 000 tons in 1961-62, and 2 967 000 tons in 1962-63 during a period of record harvests. In the face of opposition to dealing with China from Sir John Teasdale [q.v.], chairman of the A.W.B., and despite rumours that the Chinese resold the wheat to pay for arms, Perrett was named 'Salesman of the Year' by the Australian Sales Representatives' Association in May 1962.

Under his management, Perrett thought that the A.W.B. had achieved a high reputation throughout the world for 'its efficiency and the standard of its trading methods'. In 1962 he was strongly supported by the Australian Wheatgrowers' Federation to succeed Teasdale, but the government appointed Jim Moroney [q.v.]. Perrett blamed (Sir) John McEwen [q.v.] for the decision.

Perrett retired from the board in 1963 and was appointed O.B.E. that year. In 1964 he visited China as a guest of the government. He worked as a business consultant, and wrote *A Record of the Constitutional Developments, Policies and Operations of the Australian Wheat Board, 1939-1965* (Melbourne, c.1966). On 9 June 1967 at the registrar general's office, Sydney, he married Shirley Prior Reid, a 46-year-old 'sales counsellor'. He died on 19 July 1972 at his Seaforth home and was buried with Catholic rites in Northern Suburbs cemetery. His wife survived him.

G. Whitwell and D. Sydenham, *A Shared Harvest* (Melb, 1991); *Wheat Bd Gazette*, 12, no 10, Mar 1961, 14, no 6, Oct 1962, no 9, Jan-Feb, no 11, Apr 1963, 15, no 6, Oct 1963; *Wheat Aust*, Aug 1972, p 1; *Sporting Globe*, 27 Jan 1923; *Land* (Syd), 24 May 1962; Perrett papers (NL).

N. T. McLennan

PERRIER, GRACE (1875-1979), librarian, was born on 18 November 1875 at Rockhampton, Queensland, third of eleven children of Henry Perrier, a Sydney-born railway porter, and his wife Ellen, née Brenan, who came from Ireland. Grace was educated locally at St Brigid's Convent of Mercy school. On 6 November 1889 she commenced work as a junior library assistant at the Rockhampton School of Arts, the main cultural institution in the town. She was trained and deeply influenced by its scholarly librarian N. M. M. Davidson who built up a fine collection of early Australiana.

In 1926 Perrier was promoted to assistant-librarian. With no formal training, but a love of books and a commitment to providing a high standard of service to subscribers, she proved to be an outstanding librarian. She was well informed, knew the tastes of her borrowers and selected their books unerringly. An avid reader of British newspapers and reviews, she provided ready advice and worked long hours. She arrived at work by 7.30 a.m. and called in on Saturday nights with overseas newspapers to ensure that they were available for the readers. In addition to training her staff to be meticulous in their duties, she personally cared for and repaired the library's collection of old and valuable books.

When the Rockhampton City Council took over the School of Arts on 1 July 1947, Miss Perrier became head of the municipal library, a post she held until a formally qualified librarian was appointed in 1950. She retired, reluctantly, on 11 September 1952. A public meeting was held, at which she was made an honorary life member of the library, and presented with a bedroom clock and a cheque for six months salary. W. A. Woolcock, chairman of the library committee, told those present that his most difficult task had been 'to stop her working so hard'. A plaque commemorating her loyal and conscientious service was placed in the School of Arts.

Gifted with an extensive knowledge of the history of Central Queensland, Perrier was a foundation member (1948), honorary librarian (1955-68) and a life member of the

Rockhampton and District Historical Society. For many years she was the only wage-earner in her household, which included two of her sisters, two of her brothers and two nephews. She took responsibility for their welfare and helped to raise her nephews.

Perrier enjoyed excellent health, and was known as a woman of physical strength and some elegance. At Canome, the family home in King Street, she enjoyed gardening: she had a sound knowledge of plants, especially natives, and established a notable garden of trees, shrubs, ferns and orchids in the stony soil. Aged 103, she died on 30 August 1979 in a local nursing home and was buried in North Rockhampton cemetery with Catholic rites. The municipal library's special collection of books on early Australian literature, exploration and travel was named after her.

L. McDonald, *Rockhampton* (Brisb, 1981) and *Delving into the Past* (Rockhampton, 1998); Rockhampton and District Hist Soc, *Annual Report*, 1962-77; *Morning Bulletin*, 14 Aug, 21 Oct 1952, 19 Nov 1975, 3 Sept 1979; Rockhampton City Council, employees' cards; information from Mr J. Perrier, Brisb, Mrs D. Hampson, Mudgeeraba, and Mrs S. Woolcock, Buderim, Qld.   CAROL GISTITIN

PERRY, ADELAIDE ELIZABETH (1891-1973), painter, printmaker and teacher, was born on 23 June 1891 at Beechworth, Victoria, second daughter of Richard Hull Perry (d.1896), solicitor, and his wife Eliza Adelaide, née Reardon, both Victorian born. After Richard's death, Eliza moved with her family to Melbourne. Adelaide attended a private school at Brighton Beach until her mother remarried and they went to Dunedin, New Zealand. Miss Perry returned to Melbourne in 1914 to study at the National Gallery schools under Bernard Hall and Frederick McCubbin [qq.v.9,10]. She exhibited with the Victorian Artists Society. Awarded the National Gallery of Victoria travelling scholarship in 1920, she left for Europe next year to study in Paris and at the Royal Academy of Arts, London. She came under the influence of Charles Sims, Walter Sickert, Gerald Kelly and Ernest Jackson; according to Perry 'they taught me all the art I know'.

Settled in Sydney by 1926, Perry was a member of the Society of Artists and a founder of the Contemporary Group. She exhibited with a group at the Grosvenor Galleries in 1926, and at the Macquarie Galleries in 1927 and 1935. Her 'uncompromising manner, as well as her unswerving commitment to a modernist form of realism', were evident in her 'Nude Study' (1932). She had given private lessons before teaching (c.1927-30) day-classes at Julian Ashton's [q.v.7] Sydney Art School. From 1930 she taught part time at

Presbyterian Ladies' College, Croydon. In 1937 she joined the conservative Australian Academy of Art.

Perry took advantage of the introduction in the 1920s of a soft, close-textured linoleum that was easier to cut than wooden blocks and could produce prints without a press. A major proponent of linocuts, she exhibited her work and taught the medium in Sydney. She focused on the importance of design, apparent in the sharp black-and-white contrasts and the rhythmic lines of hills, trees and waves in her work. In her numerous harbour and coastal views she presented a new and modern interpretation of a very traditional theme, with bold silhouettes and simplified forms.

In the early 1930s she established the Adelaide Perry Art School in Bridge Street, later moving to Pitt Street. She encouraged her students 'to work from the real object, in the traditional manner, and base their work on that of the old masters'. To achieve this end, she took them on painting expeditions into the bush close to Sydney or to Bradleys Head 'to give them rocks and water'. Among her noted pupils were Vera Blackburn and Mary Cooper Edwards.

Soon after the outbreak of World War II, Perry became full-time art mistress at P.L.C. She painted a portrait for the college of Eunice Macindoe, who was headmistress in 1946-56. Perry retired in 1962. Living at Hunters Hill, she continued to paint portraits and still lifes, and landscapes of her views across the Lane Cove and Parramatta rivers. She died on 19 November 1973 at Killara, and was cremated with Christadelphian forms. Admired in the 1930s for her distinctive painting style and draughtsmanship, she was influential as a teacher and printmaker.

C. Deutscher and R. Butler, *A Survey of Australian Relief Prints, 1900-1950* (Melb, 1978); J. Burke, *Australian Women Artists 1840-1940* (Melb, 1980); J. Kerr (ed), *Heritage* (Syd, 1995); H. Topliss, *Modernism and Feminism* (Syd, 1996); *Art in Australia*, Dec 1928, Sept 1929, Nov 1939; *Aurora Australis*, 1962, p 29; *SMH*, 28 July 1927, 15 May 1935; H. de Berg, A. E. Perry (taped interview, 29 Dec 1965, NL).   CHARLOTTE HAYMAN

PERRY, SIR FRANK TENNYSON (1887-1965), industrialist and politician, was born on 4 February 1887 at Gawler, South Australia, son of Rev. Isaiah Perry, a Wesleyan minister from England, and his South Australian-born wife Caroline Marie Paulina, née Roediger. Educated at public schools and at Prince Alfred College, Adelaide, Frank joined his uncle Samuel Perry's foundry business in 1903. The firm moved from its Hindley Street premises in 1913 to a large site at Mile End, near the new railway yards. In 1915, after acquiring James Martin [q.v.5] & Co.'s works at Gawler, it became the biggest engineering firm in South Australia. Perry was appointed manager, and oversaw the manufacture of locomotives and rolling stock until 1928 when the Gawler works closed and production was concentrated at Mile End.

Tall and handsome, with an athletic build, Perry enjoyed tennis, golf, yachting and Australian Rules football. In 1909 he had played for the Norwood Football Club with his brother (Rev.) C. J. 'Redwing' Perry. At the Lutheran Church, Mount Gambier, on 27 December 1911 he married Hildegarde Therese Matschoss; they were to have a son and two daughters. The family lived at Dawley, College Park. Perry served on the council of the Corporation of the Town of St Peters as councillor, alderman and mayor (1932-33). He was also a member of Prince Alfred College's council and the Memorial Hospital's board. When his uncle died in 1930, he became chairman and managing director of the firm, which was registered as Perry Engineering Co. Ltd in 1937.

From an early age Perry had demonstrated organizing ability and a capacity for leadership. These qualities were used to the full as he guided the company through the Depression and its aftermath. He took a leading role in advancing South Australia's industrialization. President of the local Iron Trades Employers' Association (1930-38) and the Metal Industries Association (1940-48), he was a founder (1943) and first president (1943-48) of the Australian Metal Industries Association.

Perry was keenly interested in politics. With Horace Hogben [q.v.14], he was a prominent member of the Young Liberal League. Elected to the House of Assembly as a Liberal and Country League candidate in April 1933, he represented East Torrens until February 1938. Perry, his business colleague (Sir) Edward Holden [q.v.9] and the auditor-general J. W. Wainwright [q.v.12] persuaded the L.C.L. government to shift its focus from supporting primary industry to promoting secondary industry, and were responsible for planning strategies to attract manufacturers to set up in South Australia.

Holden and Perry also pursued these objectives as president and deputy-president respectively of the South Australian Chamber of Manufactures. They formed a secondary industries committee in 1935 and replaced it in 1937 with the Industries Assistance Corporation of South Australia. Both bodies advised the government on industrialization policies, such as setting up the South Australian Housing Trust. The corporation's main objectives were to encourage the development of industry, to provide capital or credit, and to create employment. It succeeded in saving or establishing several companies which became

major employers. Perry was president of the South Australian Chamber of Manufactures (1939-41) and of the Associated Chambers of Manufactures of Australia (1941-42).

The industrialization policies devised by Perry and his colleagues were largely implemented by (Sir) Richard Butler [q.v.7], fully adopted by (Sir) Thomas Playford and given further impetus during World War II. A member of the Federal government's defence panel and manufacturers' representative on a committee appointed to advise the State government on defence contracts, Perry threw himself into securing munitions work for South Australia. At the invitation of Essington Lewis [q.v.10], director-general of the Commonwealth's war supply organization in the Ministry of Munitions, he became honorary chairman (1940-45) of the Board of Area Management for South Australia. In his first three years as chairman he devoted most of his time to the job, attending the office daily and continually visiting contractors to make them increase output or to encourage them to shift to wartime production.

Perry's wartime expertise was put to further use as chairman (1952-55) of the ammunition industry advisory committee for the Department of Defence Production. He was also a member of State government committees on afforestation and on brick production, which sought to meet postwar demand for building materials. His own Mile End works, with its range of mechanical and structural engineering activity, had expanded through wartime production and the acquisition of low-cost munitions factory areas to emerge as one of the largest firms in Australia.

Perry was a member (1930-61) of the State committee of the Council for Scientific and Industrial Research (later Commonwealth Scientific and Industrial Research Organization). He chaired the boards of several companies, served (1949-62) on the council of the University of Adelaide and belonged to the Adelaide Club. In 1951 he was appointed M.B.E. In 1955 he was knighted. Elected to the Legislative Council in 1947 as a member for the Central No.2 electorate, he remained in that House until October 1965, giving 'first consideration to the good of the state rather than a political party'. Sir Frank was leader of the government in the council from 1959 to 1960, but declined nomination as president in 1962 on medical advice.

Survived by his wife and a daughter, Perry died on 20 October 1965 at his Leabrook home and was cremated; his estate was sworn for probate at £213 796. The Australian Metal Industries Association named a lecture in his honour. In 1966 Perry Engineering merged with Johns & Waygood Holdings Ltd, a Melbourne-based firm. Johns & Waygood Perry Engineering Ltd closed the Mile End foundry in 1969 and sold its remaining South Australian plant in 1978.

J. Miles, *A Richness of People* (Adel, 1969); P. F. Donovan, *Between the City and the Sea* (Adel, 1986); G. R. Needham and D. I. Thomson, *Men of Metal* (Adel, 1987); *J of Industry*, Oct 1946, Jan 1947, Mar 1948, Jan 1953; *SMH*, 28 Sept 1939, 21 June 1940, 1 Jan 1951, 1 Jan 1955; *Advertiser* (Adel), 14 Nov 1939, 22 Oct 1965; S. Marsden, Constructing Playford's City: the South Australian Housing Trust and the transformation of Adelaide, 1936-1966 (Ph.D. thesis, Flinders Univ, 1994).

SUSAN MARSDEN

PERRY, PATRICK (1903-1975), naval officer, was born on 14 February 1903 near Oakey, Queensland, second of seven children of Frederick Charles Perry, an English-born farmer, and his Queensland-born wife Catherine, née McGovern. Educated at St Mary's Christian Brothers' College, Toowoomba, Pat joined the Royal Australian Navy as a paymaster cadet on 1 February 1921. Following training at Flinders Naval Depot, Westernport, Victoria, he went to sea in H.M.A. ships *Marguerite* (1921-22), *Melbourne* (1922-24, 1927-28), *Adelaide* (1924-25), *Australia* (1928-29, 1930-31) and *Canberra* (1931). He also served at the Royal Australian Naval College, Jervis Bay, Federal Capital Territory (1925-26), in the Sydney shore establishment, H.M.A.S. *Penguin* (1929-30), on the staff of the captain superintendent, Sydney (1931-33), and at Navy Office, Melbourne (1933-35).

Although Perry performed the usual tasks of a naval paymaster, he was principally employed in secretarial work—supervising a captain's or admiral's office, handling correspondence, and dealing with personnel matters. In this work he became closely associated with a number of admirals, the first of whom were (Sir) George Hyde [q.v.9] and E. R. G. R. Evans (Baron Mountevans). Sent to England in 1936, he was posted to H.M.S. *Ramillies*. He was Australian naval liaison officer, London, in 1937-41, and was to hold this post twice more (1948-52 and 1955). As the senior naval representative at the Australian High Commission, he headed a team which facilitated the Naval Board's contact with the Admiralty, and which handled the administration of R.A.N. personnel attending courses or standing by ships under construction in Britain. At the Church of Our Lady of Victories, Kensington, on 9 November 1938 he married with Catholic rites Barbara Reynolds Riley; they were to remain childless.

Promoted paymaster commander in 1939, Perry joined H.M.A.S. *Australia* in January 1942 as secretary to (Sir) John Crace [q.v.13], the rear admiral commanding H.M.A. Squadron, with whom he was involved in the battle of the Coral Sea in May. After (Sir) Victor Crutchley succeeded Crace in June, he and his secretary Perry saw action off Tulagi and Guadalcanal in August. On the successful completion of the allied assault against Hollandia, Netherlands New Guinea, in April 1944, Perry left the squadron. In 1945 he was appointed O.B.E. From July 1944 to May 1948 he served at Navy Office, Melbourne, as secretary to successive chiefs of Naval Staff—Admiral Sir Guy Royle, Admiral Sir Louis Hamilton and Rear Admiral (Sir) John Collins. He was promoted substantive captain in December 1947.

While again in London as naval liaison officer, Perry qualified as a barrister and was called to the Bar at Gray's Inn in 1952; he was admitted to the Victorian Bar on 29 August. A widower, on 21 March 1951 at the chapel of the Assumption Convent, Kensington Square, London, he had married Margaret Jean Booker, a 33-year-old chartered accountant. Back at Navy Office from 1952 to 1955, he was director-general of the Supply and Secretariat Branch, director of administrative planning and chief naval judge advocate; he was to hold these offices once more in 1957-58. He attended the Imperial Defence College, London, in 1956.

In July 1958 Perry was made commodore, second class, and appointed fourth naval member of the Naval Board and chief of supply. Responsible for providing logistic support to the fleet, he was appointed C.B.E. in 1959 and promoted rear admiral on 18 May 1961. He retired from the R.A.N. in February 1963. Six months earlier he had been granted leave to chair the Department of Repatriation's No.7 War Pensions Assessment Appeal Tribunal, Brisbane. He held that post until 1969.

Perry was 6 ft 1 in. (185 cm) tall, well groomed and very fit: he had boxed in his early years and later played squash and tennis. Reserved, discreet, even sphinx-like, he could give the impression of lacking warmth, but his manner cloaked a forceful personality. He died on 10 May 1975 in his home at Indooroopilly, Brisbane, and was buried in Mount Gravatt cemetery; his wife and their two sons survived him.

W. Perry, *The Naval and Military Club, Melbourne* (Melb, 1981); *Courier-Mail*, 13 May 1975; A3978/10 (AA, Canb); information from Mr K. W. Major, Forrest, Canb, and Mr C. Perry, Indooroopilly, Brisb.

ROBERT HYSLOP

PETERS, CHARLES HAROLD (1889-1951), bookseller and soldier, was born on 25 January 1889 at Collingwood, Melbourne, son of Charles Thomas Peters, a Victorian-born boot importer, and his second wife Katie Gibbs, née Foot, who came from South Australia. Harold attended state schools and took night-classes at the Working Men's College, Melbourne. He was an omnivorous reader, and later claimed that he was educated 'mainly through books'. At the age of 14 he joined Melville & Mullen's [q.v.5] bookshop, where he was trained by Leonard Slade. When he was refused a raise, he crossed to George Robertson [q.v.6] & Co. Pty Ltd, but two years later went back to Melville & Mullen.

Commissioned in the Australian Imperial Force on 6 March 1916, Peters reached the Western Front in November as a lieutenant in the 38th Battalion. He won the Military Cross for leading a patrol against an enemy trench at Armentières, France, on New Year's Eve 1917 and for recovering a wounded soldier from no man's land on the following night. In August 1918 he was promoted temporary captain (substantive in October). Near Bony, in September-October, he commanded two companies which penetrated the Hindenburg line. For his 'dash and judgement' he was awarded a Bar to his M.C. Following leave in London—during which he called on leading publishers—he returned to Melbourne. His A.I.F. appointment terminated on 19 August 1919, by which time he was manager of Melville & Mullen Pty Ltd.

At Scots Church, Melbourne, on 30 September 1919 Peters married Elizabeth Wilson with Presbyterian forms. Unable to renew its lease on the 'The Block' in Collins Street, the firm merged with its old rival, George Robertson, on 1 July 1921 and moved to Elizabeth Street. Peters became general manager of Robertson & Mullens Ltd. Later that year he led a trade campaign to promote books as Christmas gifts. He organized Children's Book Week in 1924 and Australian Authors' Week in 1927. With S. V. A. Zelman [q.v.12] and A. S. Nicholas, he compiled a book of 'digger' songs.

Due to Peters' initiatives, Robertson & Mullens sold 100 000 copies of P. C. Wren's Beau Geste (London, 1924). He published local works and often used the Melbourne printers, Brown, Prior & Co. Each week from 1925 to 1936 he presented 'Books, Wise and Otherwise', a book-review programme on radio-station 3LO. He donated his earnings from the show to the Melbourne Legacy Club, of which he was a member and acting-president (1928). (Dame) Mary Gilmore [q.v.9] called Peters 'that kindest of men' and regarded him as the best sales promoter among local publishers. He wrote the introduction to her book of poetry, The Disinherited (1941).

Peters was appointed managing director of Robertson & Mullens in 1943. Ill health led him to retire in 1948, but he continued as a director of the firm. Short, thickset and convivial, he was president of the Victorian Book-

sellers' Association (1927-48), the Working Men's College (1929-30) and the Australian Booksellers' Association (1949). He chaired the Union Building Society for many years, served on the council of the University of Melbourne (1932-39) and belonged to the Savage Club. Survived by his wife, son and daughter, he died of coronary vascular disease on 10 January 1951 in his Canterbury home and was cremated with Anglican and Masonic rites. His estate was sworn for probate at £15 807.

Aust Booksellers Assn, The Early Australian Booksellers (Adel, 1980); W. H. Wilde and T. I. Moore (eds), Letters of Mary Gilmore (Melb, 1980); private records of C. H. Peters, 1DRL/0545 (AWM); C. H. Peters, ABC radio broadcast, 5 Feb 1950 (ts, ML); Aust Booksellers Assn records, ms 3937 (NL).

J. P. HOLROYD

PETERS, JACK VERNON (1920-1973), organist and teacher, was born on 20 September 1920 at New Brighton, Christchurch, New Zealand, only child of New Zealand-born parents Samuel George Peters, engineer, and his wife Annie Elizabeth, née Bailey. Jack attended Otago Boys' High School, Dunedin, and Canterbury College, Christchurch (Mus.B., N.Z., 1948; Mus.D., University of Canterbury, 1959). He enlisted in the New Zealand Military Forces on 7 October 1941, and served in North Africa and Italy. Twice wounded in action (1943) while attached to the 26th Battalion, he was discharged from the army on 19 December 1945.

At St Luke's Anglican Church, Christchurch, on 3 April 1948 Peters married Barbara Mary Richards; they were to separate in 1963 and to be divorced in February 1968. Awarded a bursary to study at the University of Durham (Mus.B., 1950), England, and at the Trinity College of Music, London, he gained a diploma of choir training and a diploma in church music from the Royal College of Organists, and was elected a fellow of the R.C.O. and of T.C.M. In 1953 he was appointed lecturer and organ teacher at the Elder [q.v.4] Conservatorium of Music, University of Adelaide. He was promoted senior lecturer in 1963 and reader in 1966. An inspiring teacher, he mesmerized his students with the brilliance of his lectures in harmony, counterpoint and orchestration. His compositions included Serenata Fuga for wind quintet, Symphony No. 1 and various songs.

As the university's organist (1955-72), Peters gave numerous recitals, including the demanding organ sonatas of J. S. Bach and the mighty compositions of Max Reger. His extemporization on themes prepared by other musicians produced thrilling works. From 1955 he was also organist and master of choristers at St Peter's Cathedral, Adelaide. He refused to compromise in the way he presented his music. On 10 June 1962 when he could no longer tolerate Canon Loan's out-of-tune chanting, he refused to play, and told the choir to return to the crypt and disrobe. For this action he was dismissed.

On 14 March 1968 at the office of the principal registrar, Adelaide, Peters married 23-year-old Eleanor Frances Nelson; this marriage also ended in divorce. From 1968 until 1972 he was, in turn, organist and emeritus organist at the Pirie Street Methodist Church. In 1967 he became city organist. He had said that the Adelaide Town Hall organ had 'one of the best tones in the world, but playing it is like driving a Rolls Royce without a steering wheel'. In 1968 the Adelaide City Council decided to have the organ rebuilt. At Peters' suggestion the $69 000 contract was given to Laurie Pipe Organs Pty Ltd, Melbourne. Following complaints about the reconstructed organ, a committee found deficiencies which required the services of 'conscientious' and 'skilled' workmen, but no action was taken. Peters was not blamed for the situation.

Of middle height and medium build, with a puckish grin and sense of humour, Peters had a quixotic brilliance and a touch of genius, but was a dreamer who was unable to cope with the difficulties of life. Alcohol dependent and unreliable, he had 'tantrums like a child', but was quick to apologize to those he offended. He died of complications arising from cirrhosis of the liver on 22 February 1973 at St Andrew's Hospital, Adelaide, and was cremated; the two sons of his first marriage survived him.

A. D. McCredie (ed), *From Colonel Light into the Footlights* (Adel, 1988); *Advertiser* (Adel), 25 June 1959, 13 May 1967, 7 Feb 1970, 10 Aug 1972, 23 Feb 1973; Minutes and reports 1967-73, Adel City Council Archives; J. V. Peters correspondence 1952-73 (Univ Adel Archives); information from Mr L. Dosser, Beaumont, Mr D. R. Gallasch, Everard Park, Adel, Mrs E. Lawson, Yarralumla, Canb, and the late Mr W. Cosh.   JOYCE GIBBERD

PETHARD, GEORGE ALBERT (1885-1961), businessman and mayor, was born on 5 December 1885 at Ballarat East, Victoria, second child of George Albert Pethard, an English-born storeman, and his Victorian-born wife Miriam Hurst, née Peatling. After serving in the British Army in India, George senior worked as a storeman for the Phoenix Foundry Co. Ltd, Ballarat, before setting up as a produce merchant at Warragul. He later transferred his business to Kyneton, and then to Numurkah where he established a soft drink factory, producing the brand name of Taraxale.

Educated at Kyneton State School, George junior entered his father's soft drink business in 1898 and moved with the firm to Bendigo in 1909. At Golden Square on 7 July that year he married Hilda Leed with Methodist forms. In 1918 he began working as an auctioneer at Rochester. By 1921 he had returned to Bendigo as a real-estate agent. To publicize and sell blocks at Robinvale, Pethard chartered a train to take buyers to the site. In 1924 he secured the General Motors-Holden's [q.v.9] Ltd franchise for northern Victoria and built a service station at Bendigo. A keen traveller, he visited the United States of America on business in 1927; he returned convinced that Australia was insufficiently promoted abroad.

In 1938 Pethard entered the Bendigo City Council as an alderman for Darling Ward, a division he was to represent for the ensuing twenty years. Elected mayor in 1940, 1947 and 1951, he took a particular interest in tourism, and was responsible for the construction of an information pavilion in the heart of the city. He was prominent in local affairs as president of the Art Gallery (1943), Rotary Club (1945) and District Bowling Association (1946), as chairman (1944, 1947) of the Easter Fair Society, and as a board-member of the Bendigo and Northern District Base Hospital and the Bendigo Benevolent Home.

Pethard proved to be a tireless promoter of local industry. He belonged to the Bendigo Chamber of Commerce and Industries, the Victorian Decentralisation League, the Loddon Regional Committee and the Bendigo Industrial Expansion Committee. In 1956 he toured the U.S.A. as part of a team chosen by Premier (Sir) Henry Bolte to encourage investment in Victoria. Pethard also served on the Provincial Sewerage Authorities' Association of Victoria and the Bendigo Local Repatriation Committee. Dubbed the 'Father of the City Council', he retired from office in June 1958 and became chairman of Tarax Drinks Holdings Ltd.

Known affectionately as 'G.P.', Pethard described himself as a 'real goer'. Others recognized his vision, versatility and 'tremendous capacity for getting a job done quickly'. In 1961 he donated £5200 to build a nurses' home at the base hospital; it was posthumously named (1964) after him. Survived by his wife and one of his two sons, he died on 20 September 1961 at Kurmala Hospital, Bendigo, and was buried in the local cemetery. His estate was sworn for probate at £481 874.

D. F. Jones, *Not by Myself* (Syd, 1976); G. V. Lansell and W. J. Stephens (eds), *Annals of Bendigo*, 5 (Bendigo, 1938); D. Lockwood (ed), *Annals of Bendigo*, 6 (Bendigo, 1981); F. Cusack (ed), *Annals of Bendigo*, 7 (Bendigo, 1988); Tarax Drinks Holdings Ltd, *Annual Report*, 1959-72; *Bendigo Advertiser*, 21-23 Sept 1961; Bendigo City Archives, news-cuttings, 1938-61.   CHARLES FAHEY

PETRIE, WINIFRED MARION (1890-1966), nurse and hospital proprietress, was born on 21 November 1890 at Randwick, Sydney, eldest of three children of Queensland-born parents Fitt Charles Petrie, solicitor, and his wife Marion, née Hescott. Educated at Ravenswood school under Mabel Fidler [q.v.8], Winifred began (1918) to train as a nurse at the Coast Hospital, Little Bay, and was registered with the Australasian Trained Nurses' Association on 15 November 1922. In the following year she obtained a certificate in obstetrics from the Royal Hospital for Women, Paddington. She spent much of 1926 touring Britain with her family.

In 1927 Petrie was appointed sister-in-charge of the obstetric ward at Canberra Hospital, where she again worked with Dr John James [q.v.14] who had served at the Coast Hospital. Within a year she and three other senior nursing sisters handed in their notice. Sister Petrie informed a Federal Capital Commission board of inquiry that the matron should have made better arrangements for their comfort, that night nurses had no crockery or cutlery, and that they had next to nothing for supper. Pressed by the board, the matron resigned. In 1930 Petrie left the hospital to holiday abroad. She resumed nursing next year, at Auberne Private Hospital, Queanbeyan, New South Wales.

On 20 September 1935 Petrie leased a block on the corner of Empire Circuit and Arthur Circle, Forrest, with the aim of building a private hospital in Canberra. Returning to Sydney that year, she gained her mothercraft certificate from the Royal Society for the Welfare of Mothers & Babies. By May 1936 her twelve-bed Allawah Private Hospital had opened. For many years it was the bush capital's only hospital south of the Molonglo River. The building was the product of Petrie's practical experience and the skill of the architect Ken Oliphant [q.v.]. Their unorthodox design incorporated a curved-floor plan, with no right-angle turnings to enable easier manoeuvring of wheelchairs. Each ward had a private balcony. The hospital was equipped with a modern operating theatre with shadowless lighting, and a central steam-heating system. Nurses quarters were detached, and comfortable.

Petrie's economic gamble in the depressed 1930s succeeded, and she discharged the mortgage in 1940. Allawah gained a good reputation with medical practitioners as a general and obstetric hospital. Its patients received first-class care in pleasant surroundings. Petrie ran Allawah firmly and calmly, and became a mentor and friend to her staff. John Curtin [q.v.13], the Duke of Gloucester [q.v.14] and his son Prince William, and (Dame) Alexandra Hasluck were among the hospital's patients.

Wartime shortages, the opening (1943) of new buildings at Canberra Community Hospital and Petrie's failing health forced the closure of Allawah in 1948. Moving to Deakin, she lived at 93 Empire Circuit where she made two rooms available for any of her friends who were convalescing. She died there on 6 May 1966 and was cremated with Anglican rites.

M. J. Cordia, *Nurses at Little Bay* (Syd, 1990); J. Newman and J. Warren, *Royal Canberra Hospital* (Canb, 1993); A. Ide, *Royal Canberra Hospital* (Canb, 1994); B. Knowles, 'Sister Winifred Marion Petrie (1890-1966)', *Canb Hist J*, no 39, Mar 1997, p 11; *Canb Times*, 27 Mar 1930, 27 Feb 1936, 11 June 1966; family papers (held by Mr B. H. Petrie, Northbridge, Syd); family information.

BETH KNOWLES

PHELAN, WILLIAM (1915-1973), businessman and politician, was born on 16 July 1915 at Maryborough, Victoria, second child of Sydney Clifford Phelan, ironmonger, and his wife Letitia Ellen, née Chellew, both Victorian born. Educated at Maryborough High School, Bill joined the family construction company, William Phelan & Sons Pty Ltd. On 22 October 1938 at the Methodist Church, St Kilda, he married Hazel Patten, a 22-year-old saleswoman; they were to have two sons and two daughters. At the age of 24 he succeeded his father as managing director of Phelan & Sons. In 1942 he added a joinery to the business.

Once rationing was eased, the firm flourished during the postwar building boom, producing sash-windows for the Housing Commission of Victoria. The commission invited the company to build dwellings in the Maryborough district and provided a factory at Carisbrook for the construction of transportable homes. In 1950 Phelan & Sons produced its first prefabricated house; by 1953 it had supplied five hundred, at the rate of one per day, to much of western Victoria. Phelans was Maryborough's largest firm, employing three hundred workers, for whom it created a housing estate. When building activity slowed after 1960, it won construction contracts from other State government departments.

A Freemason and a Presbyterian, Phelan was active in a range of local community organizations. He was a member (1944-61) of the Maryborough council (mayor 1954-55), a founding member (1939) of the local Apex club (president 1944-46) and of Maryborough Rotary Club (president 1961), a member (1953-63) and president (1959-61) of the Maryborough Hospital Committee, chairman (1954-55) of the Maryborough Waterworks Trust and the Maryborough Sewerage Authority, and a member of the Central Highlands Regional Committee. He also served as a justice of the peace.

These community connections made Phelan attractive to the Country Party which was keen to dislodge the Liberal Country Party minister of lands and soldier settlement, Keith Turnbull [q.v.], from the Legislative Assembly seat of Kara Kara at the 1961 election. In a four-way contest Phelan finished third, with Turnbull easily defeating the Australian Labor Party's candidate. Phelan served on the Country Party's central council in 1962-64. At the 1964 election he succeeded in defeating Turnbull with the aid of A.L.P. preferences. Although he successfully defended his marginal seat in 1967, he was defeated by Labor in the anti-Country Party landslide of 1970. His brief parliamentary career was undistinguished: he advocated the decentralization of industry and served on the Privileges and State Development committees.

By contrast, 'chubby-faced, wavy-haired, smiling Bill Phelan' was, by the late 1960s, 'one of the most successful country industrialists' in Victoria. He was a fellow of the Australian Institute of Management and an executive-member of the Victorian Employers' Federation. For recreation, he enjoyed tennis, golf, field-shooting and fishing. Survived by his wife and children, he died of cerebrovascular disease on 22 December 1973 at Maryborough and was buried in the local cemetery. His estate was sworn for probate at $179 075.

B. Osborn, *Against the Odds* (Maryborough, 1995); *Maryborough Advertiser*, 28 Dec 1973; *Countryman* (Melb), 20 Apr 1967; *Age* (Melb), 26 Dec 1973.   B. J. COSTAR

PHILIP, SIR WILLIAM SHEARER (1891-1975), accountant and charity worker, was born on 18 August 1891 at Williamstown, Melbourne, second child of William Philip, a master mariner from Scotland, and his Victorian-born wife Catherine Louise, née Lamont. Educated at Scotch College, young William joined Flack & Flack [q.v.8], accountants, in 1909. On 11 November 1915, the day that he completed his accountancy examinations, he enlisted in the Australian Imperial Force.

After sailing to England, he was sent to the Western Front in November 1916 as a company sergeant major in the 37th Battalion. In January 1917 he was commissioned. Southwest of Albert, France, on 9 April 1918 he commanded a section of the front line during an enemy artillery bombardment which lasted twelve hours. His 'foresight and coolness' minimized casualties among his men and he was awarded the Military Cross. In May, near the Ancre flats, he led a party in a bold raid

which 'brought back two prisoners, both of whom fought hard'. That month he was promoted lieutenant. His A.I.F. appointment terminated in Australia on 27 July 1919.

At the Methodist Church, Hawthorn, on 8 December 1920 Philip married Irene Laura Cross, a 27-year-old typist. Having returned to Flack & Flack, he became a partner in 1925, and senior partner in 1935 on the death of Edwin Flack. He oversaw the firm's expansion in Australia and New Zealand. Philip was also a senior partner in the allied firm, Price, Waterhouse & Co., for ten years before he retired from accountancy in 1956. He had joined the Institute of Chartered Accountants in Australia in 1928: he was a member (1936-54) and chairman (1946-48) of its Victorian council, and a member (1944-50) of its general council. In 1940-45 he served as business adviser to the Australian Army Medical Corps. He also served as a member (1942-48) and chairman (1947-48) of the Charities Board of Victoria.

The main focus of Philip's voluntary activities, however, was the Alfred Hospital: he was a member (1935-75), treasurer (1939-48) and president (1948-75) of its board of management. During his presidency he oversaw an expansion of medical services, and an extensive rebuilding programme which included a new block that was named (1963) after him. In 1946 he had established a medical research fund which ensured that outstanding staff would be drawn to the Alfred. His contribution to the health system was motivated by the belief that 'the highest standard of medical care should be made available to all the people', a conviction that others saw as his personal creed.

In 1961 Philip was appointed C.M.G. In January 1975 he was knighted. A member of the Melbourne, Australian and Royal Melbourne Golf clubs, Sir William enjoyed excellent health for most of his life. He had a formidable memory, especially for the 'figures' with which much of his professional career and charitable interests were concerned. Survived by his two daughters and two sons, he died on 25 August 1975 in his home at Toorak and was cremated.

History of Scotch College, Melbourne, 1851-1925 (Melb, 1926); C. E. W. Bean, *The A.I.F. in France, 1914-18*, vol 6 (Syd, 1942); A. M. Mitchell, *The Hospital South of the Yarra* (Melb, 1977); *Chartered Accountant in Aust*, Oct 1975, p 57; information from Mr G. B. Carnham, Kew, Mr W. G. Philip, Toorak, and Alfred Hospital, Melb.

RICHARD TREMBATH

PHILIPP, FRANZ ADOLF (1914-1970), art historian, was born on 29 March 1914 in Vienna, son of Jewish parents Edmund

Philipp, a Czech-born businessman, and his wife Karoline, née Selinko, who came from Hungary. With his two brothers and sister, Franz attended the Bundesgymnasium at Doebling. In 1933 he entered the University of Vienna where he studied art history under Julius von Schlosser. Philipp began his doctoral thesis on 'The Mannerist Portrait in Northern Italy' in 1937, but was interned at Dachau, Germany, on 15 November 1938. He escaped to England in June 1939 and worked as an agricultural labourer in Yorkshire before being detained in 1940 and transported to Australia as an enemy alien. Arriving in the *Dunera* on 6 September, he was interned at Hay, New South Wales, and at Tatura and Shepparton, Victoria. While at Hay he taught art history to fellow refugees. Released in February 1942, he enlisted in the Australian Military Forces on 8 April and served with a succession of employment companies, mainly in Melbourne, until being discharged on 15 February 1946. Fifteen weeks later he was naturalized.

Having enrolled in 1943 at the University of Melbourne (B.A. Hons, 1946), Philipp specialized in Italian Renaissance history under Professor Max Crawford. He graduated top of his class, winning a Dwight [q.v.4] prize, and in 1947 was appointed a senior tutor in Crawford's department. On 13 March 1948 at the office of the government statist, Melbourne, he married June Margaret Rowley, a 22-year-old teacher who later lectured in history. Next year he was made an assistant-lecturer in history and fine arts.

In 1950 Philipp became a lecturer in the department of fine arts, where he was to be promoted senior lecturer (1954) and reader (1964). For those who could cope with his erudition and meet his exacting standards, he was an inspiring and generous teacher who treated his students as his equals. He dressed formally, smoked heavily, and was reasonably tall and thin; his hair was dark and curly, and his thick glasses framed vibrant eyes which lit up when a crucial discovery was made. Arthur Boyd remembered him as 'a gentle, thoughtful soul'. In 1955-56 Philipp was a senior research fellow at the Warburg Institute, London. In 1963 he was awarded a Carnegie Corporation travelling fellowship to the United States of America.

Philipp was best known for contributing to Renaissance scholarship through his teaching, yet his major work was on an Australian painter, Arthur Boyd, whom he believed the most important artist of his generation. In 1947 he had published an article in *Present Opinion* demonstrating Boyd's appropriation of Mannerist motifs from Breughel and other sixteenth-century artists, and seeing his style as a metaphor for the postwar years. Philipp's *Arthur Boyd* (London, 1967) set new

critical standards for scholarship in Australian art history. He wrote for *Meanjin*, *Historical Studies* and the bulletin of the National Gallery of Victoria; with June Stewart, he edited a volume of essays in honour of Sir Daryl Lindsay [q.v.10], published in Melbourne in 1964. While on sabbatical leave in London, Philipp died of myocardial infarction on 30 May 1970 at Hampstead. Survived by his wife and two daughters, he was buried in Melbourne general cemetery.

K. Bittman (ed), *Strauss to Matilda* (Syd, 1988); *Univ Melb Gazette*, July 1970; *Aust J of Art*, 3, 1983; *Art and Aust*, Dec 1970, Winter, 1993; naturalization file, A435, item 1945/4/1955 (AA, Canb); Philipp papers, Univ Melb Archives; information from Yad Vashem Archives, Jerusalem.

JAYNIE ANDERSON

PHILIPS, THEA; *see* PHILLIPS, DOROTHY

PHILLIPS, CLAUDIA PORTIA; *see* BRADLEY

PHILLIPS, DOROTHY JANE ('THEA PHILIPS') (1892-1960), soprano and teacher of singing, was born on Christmas Eve 1892 at Dorchester, Dorset, England, daughter of David Phillips, clothier and outfitter, and his wife Emma, née Chapple. Dorothy made her operatic début at Manchester before she was 20, studied singing with Emma Molajoli at Milan, Italy, and sang at Naples with Tullio Serafin. On 18 July 1916 at the register office, King's Norton, Birmingham, she married Robert Alfred Clement Pike, a 39-year-old divorcee and a lieutenant in the Army Ordnance Department.

After the birth of their three sons, Dorothy embarked on a professional singing career, leaving her husband, from whom she was to be divorced in 1935. Her early engagements included revues and seaside concerts, but she later worked in opera and oratorio. In 1930 she caught the attention of Sir Thomas Beecham and made her London début as Agatha in *Der Freischütz* to excellent reviews. Concert and opera engagements followed in London and the provinces, but the highlight of her career was her appearance before the royal family in May 1932 at Covent Garden, when she replaced Lotte Lehmann as Elisabeth in *Tannhäuser*.

'Thea Philips', as she was by then known professionally, arrived in Australia in 1934 to perform with Sir Benjamin Fuller's [q.v.8] grand opera company in a six-month Melbourne-Sydney season. She sang both lyric and dramatic soprano roles in *Il Trovatore, Rigoletto, Faust, Die Walküre, Lohengrin,*

Tannhäuser, La Bohème and *Die Fledermaus.* Although overshadowed by Florence Austral [q.v.7], she was well received. Further engagements extended her stay to more than three years. She performed in a 1935-36 season of studio broadcast operas, and toured for the Australian Broadcasting Commission and its New Zealand counterpart.

Philips made the first of nineteen appearances as soprano for the (Royal) Melbourne Philharmonic Society in September 1935. In the following year she was soloist in Verdi's *Requiem* with the Sydney Symphony Orchestra. She returned to Britain late in 1938 and sang Marguerite in *Faust* at the Royal Albert Hall, but was back in Australia before the outbreak of World War II. Her professional life for the next decade consisted mostly of appearances in oratorio and recitals, with some adjudication and teaching. She sang with leading Victorian choirs and appeared in Sydney for the A.B.C. At the Congregational manse, Kew, on 4 December 1941 she married Claude Mackay Wallis, a 53-year-old widower and an accountant.

An imposing, well groomed and attractive woman with dark hair and large brown eyes, Philips had a strong, 'theatrical', yet genuinely warm personality, and abundant charm. In April 1944 she gave her first solo public recital in Melbourne; three others took place in 1945. She performed works by local composers, took part in two recitals (1941 and 1945) of songs by Edith Harrhy [q.v.14] and founded the short-lived Thea Philips School of Opera in March 1947. Partiality to alcohol impeded her career. As her public performances tapered off she took on more private pupils. While in Sydney to play a non-singing role in *The Merry Widow*, she died of heart disease on 15 November 1960 in a Goulburn Street hotel and was cremated with Presbyterian forms. Her husband survived her, as did two of the sons of her first marriage.

P. Game, *The Music Sellers* (Melb, 1976); A. Gyger, *Opera for the Antipodes* (Syd, 1990); *Aust Musical News*, Apr, June, Oct 1944, Feb 1947, Mar 1949, June 1951; *Music and Dance*, Dec 1960; *Herald* (Melb), 23 Sept 1935; *Sun News-Pictorial*, 4 Apr 1942, 13 May 1943, 24 Apr 1944, 3 Feb 1948, 16 Nov 1960; *Age* and *SMH*, 16 Nov 1960; information from Miss M. Bertoldini, Perugia, Italy, Ms H. Coutts, Bermagui South, NSW, Mr M. Jost, East Hawthorn, Mr F. Lasslett, South Yarra, and Miss M. Schofield, Kew, Melb. JENNIFER HILL

PHILLIPS, GILBERT EDWARD (1904-1952), neurosurgeon and wine connoisseur, was born on 23 September 1904 in North Sydney, son of Thomas Buckland Phillips, a Sydney-born estate agent, and his wife Edith Katherine, née King, who came from New Zealand. Gilbert was educated at Chatswood Preparatory School, the Blue Mountains Grammar School, North Sydney Boys' High School and the University of Sydney (B.Sc., 1927; M.Sc., 1928; M.B., B.S., 1929; M.S., 1936). He gained first-class honours in science, university medals in physiology, and Blues in rowing and swimming. A champion heavyweight, he boxed under an adopted name, using his purses, and his earnings as a sports journalist, to pay his fees. He served as a board-member (1934-37) and vice-president (1935-36) of the Sydney University Union, and as president of the boxing club (1934-35) and sports union (1951-52).

While holding a Liston Wilson research fellowship (1930-34), Phillips joined the university's department of anatomy, won a Rockefeller Foundation fellowship and sailed for England. In 1931-33 he worked in turn as research-assistant to Sir Charles Sherrington at Oxford and Professor (Lord) Adrian at Cambridge, as clinical clerk at the National Hospital for Diseases of the Nervous System, London, and as surgical-assistant to (Sir) Hugh Cairns [q.v.7]. At the parish church of St Martin-in-the-Fields, London, on 22 June 1932 he married Coralie Ngareta Bloomfield.

Returning to the University of Sydney in 1934, Phillips was appointed assistant-lecturer in surgery (lecturer 1935-37); he also lectured in the anatomy department on neurology and applied neurophysiology. After a period as consulting neurosurgeon at Lewisham Hospital in 1934-36, he resumed his connection with Royal Prince Alfred Hospital where he had been a resident medical officer (1929-31). Regarded as the brilliant protégé of (Sir) Harold Dew [q.v.13], he served (1937-44) as honorary assistant neurosurgeon at R.P.A.H. In 1937 he travelled to England and the United States of America to visit major neurological centres. Next year he became a fellow of the Royal Australasian College of Surgeons.

In 1937-45 Phillips was a part-time consultant with the Royal Australian Air Force, holding the rank of squadron leader (1940). At Cairns's request, he went to England in February 1945 and accepted an emergency commission in the Royal Army Medical Corps. He served in a mobile neurosurgical unit before being made temporary lieutenant colonel and officer-in-charge of the surgical division of the hospital for head injuries, St Hugh's College, Oxford. When World War II ended, Phillips returned to R.P.A.H. as honorary neurosurgeon. From 1947 he endeavoured to have a centre founded in Sydney for the diagnosis of nervous diseases in returned servicemen: the Northcott [q.v.] Neurological Centre was opened in November 1951. During his career Phillips published forty-five articles, many in the *Medical Journal of Australia.*

A founder (1939) and president of the Wine and Food Society of New South Wales, Phillips had been impressed by the activities of a co-operative wine-buying society which he had seen in London. On his return to Sydney, he established (1946) the Australian Wine Consumers' Co-operative Society Ltd. He frequently visited Maurice O'Shea [q.v.] at Mount Pleasant, Pokolbin; with a group of up to a dozen friends, they devoted weekends to discussion and tasting. Phillips's J. K. Walker lecture was published by the Wine and Food Society as *The Appreciation of Wine* (1950). A splendid cook, he created original dishes from ducks reared on his farm at Bilpin.

Phillips had a zest for life. He read widely, enjoyed sailing, played the piano competently and sang well; his erudition was legendary, his often Rabelaisian wit a delight. Well over six feet (183 cm) tall, with brushed-down wavy hair and eyes that saw all, he was described as 'a man's man'. He exercised a profound influence on his peers and inspired his students.

In June 1951, following long-term treatment for skin cancer, Phillips's right leg was amputated below the knee. Within six weeks he was performing operations again, with an artificial leg, and, later, aided by a special chair. He revisited England in January 1952 to continue his work on head injuries, but came back to Sydney in April. Suffering from a secondary melanoma, he died of a pulmonary embolism on 12 September 1952 at his Darling Point home and was cremated with Anglican rites; his wife and four daughters survived him.

G. J. Fraenkel, *Hugh Cairns* (Oxford, 1991); Roy Prince Alfred Hospital (Syd), *Annual Report*, 1936-37, 1942-44, 1952-53; *MJA*, 29 Nov 1952; *SMH*, 7 July 1933, 8 Jan 1937, 14, 20, 21 Sept 1952; *Sunday Telegraph* (Syd), 14 Sept 1952; information from Roy A'sian College of Surgeons; personal knowledge.

MAX LAKE

PHILLIPS, LESLIE WILLIAM (1893-1949), chemist and educationist, was born on 15 April 1893 at Tungamah, Victoria, sixth child of Victorian-born parents William Henry Phillips, baker, and his wife Elizabeth Ann, née Clark. Leslie was educated at Melbourne High School, the Teachers' Training College and the University of Melbourne (B.Sc., 1920; Dip.Ed., 1920; M.Sc., 1923; M.Ed., 1938). On 14 April 1915 he enlisted in the Australian Imperial Force. He served with medical units in England (1915-18) and with the 2nd Field Ambulance in France (1918). Promoted sergeant in 1917 and commended for his services in the following year, he was discharged from the A.I.F. on 24 June 1919 in Melbourne.

He taught in turn at Hamilton High and Footscray Technical schools. In 1920 he took the post of assistant-lecturer in chemistry at Perth Technical School (College).

At Wesley Church, Perth, on 12 July 1921 Phillips married with Methodist forms Mary Matilda Read, a 26-year-old schoolteacher; they were to remain childless. While at the technical school he received a grant from the Australian Science and Industrial Endowment Fund to investigate toxic principles in common poison plants. In 1929 the Department of Education appointed him assistant-superintendent of technical education in Western Australia. Responsible for co-ordinating studies, organization and discipline, he was 'on duty day and night as required'. He continued to maintain his interest in science: he was foundation secretary of the Western Australian committee of the Council of Scientific and Industrial Research, and president of the Royal Society of Western Australia (1931-32) and the (Royal) Australian Chemical Institute (1943).

Phillips gave occasional lectures in chemistry and education at the University of Western Australia. Supported by the vice-chancellor H. E. Whitfeld [q.v.12], he received a Carnegie Foundation fellowship in 1935 to study at the Institute of Education, University of London. While in England, he visited technical institutions, and investigated legislative and administrative developments in vocational training. Back in Perth, he told the 1937-38 royal commission on youth employment and the apprenticeship system that Perth Technical College was so hampered by inadequate funding and cramped facilities that basement storerooms, photographic darkrooms and even a 'washing room' were used for classes. He welcomed the commission's recommendation that a bureau of industry and economic research be established, but was frustrated when an enabling bill was blocked in the Legislative Council.

In 1941 Phillips was promoted superintendent of technical education. For the next eight years he endeavoured to close the gap between industry and education. Against formidable opposition from trade unions and employers, he advocated formal teacher-training for trade instructors, and the provision of advanced technological, administrative and managerial courses. During World War II he advised the armed services on technical education and helped to administer the Commonwealth Reconstruction Training Scheme in Western Australia. With K. S. Cunningham [q.v.13] he wrote *Education for Livelihood* (Melbourne, 1946).

A conscientious and unassuming man who shunned publicity, Phillips was a prominent member of the Perth Legacy Club (president 1941-42), the State School Teachers' Union of Western Australia and the Australian Council for Educational Research. Survived by his wife, he died of coronary vascular disease on 10 May 1949 at his Mount Lawley home and was cremated.

J. P. Dunne, *I Will Arise* (Perth, 1976); M. A. White and W. Birman, 'The Apprenticeship Training System in Western Australia: A History', in S. Murray-Smith (ed), *Melbourne Studies in Education, 1981* (Melb, 1981); *Aust J of Science*, 2, no 2, 21 Oct 1949, p 68; *West Australian*, 11 May 1949; Phillips file, AN 45/5, Acc 1059, file 904/40 (WA PRO); information from the late Prof F. Alexander.

WENDY BIRMAN

PHILLIPS, SIR PHILIP DAVID (1897-1970), lawyer and teacher, was born on 22 March 1897 at Prahran, Melbourne, second child of Melbourne-born parents Morris Mondle Phillips [q.v.11], barrister, and his wife Rebecca, née Ellis. The writer Arthur Angell Phillips was his younger brother; Marion Phillips [q.v.11] was their aunt. Educated at Melbourne Church of England Grammar School and the University of Melbourne (B.A. Hons, 1921; LL.B., 1922), Philip enlisted in the Australian Imperial Force on 31 January 1916 and served on the Western Front as a gunner in the 8th Artillery Brigade. In June 1917 he was transferred to the 3rd Divisional Signal Company. Near Corbie, France, on 30 March 1918 Lance Corporal Phillips braved enemy shellfire to repair telephone lines and won the Military Medal. Returning to Australia, he was discharged from the A.I.F. on 1 June 1919.

After completing his university studies with first-class honours and four prizes, Phillips was admitted as a barrister and solicitor of the Supreme Court of Victoria in 1922. He signed the Bar roll on 21 March 1923. At Holy Trinity Church, East Melbourne, on 13 December that year he married with Anglican rites Leonore Rennick, a 29-year-old architect and daughter of L. O. Lukin [q.v.10]; they were to be divorced on 1 December 1949.

Practising at Selborne Chambers, Phillips never confined himself to the life of a full-time barrister. He lectured part time in the university's arts and law faculties for many years. His wide interest in human affairs was exemplified by his active participation in the Institute of Public Administration, the Australian Institute of International Affairs, the Economic Society of Australia and New Zealand, the League of Nations Union and the Medico-Legal Society of Victoria. He commented on public affairs in the *Age*, *Argus* and *Herald*, joined in public debates, and was a member and chairman (1941-46) of the editorial board of the *Austral-Asiatic Bulletin*. Prominent in the Nationalist Party, through which he came under the influence of (Sir) Frederic Eggleston [q.v.8], he chaired (1934-37) the Victorian Transport Regulation Board at the invitation

of (Sir) Robert Menzies [q.v.]. Phillips served as deputy-chairman (1940-45) of the Commonwealth Liquid Fuel Control Board and as a member (1946-52) of South Melbourne Council. On 16 December 1949 at the office of the government statist, Melbourne, he married Olive Catherine Rosenthal, a 38-year-old secretary.

Phillips (or 'P.D.' as he was widely known in the legal profession) had taken silk on 14 February 1946. He soon became a leader of the Bar in Australia. With the Federal attorney-general H. V. Evatt and the solicitor-general (Sir) Kenneth Bailey [qq.v.14,13] (his close friend from the Young Nationalist Organisation), he was a member of the team of counsel briefed for the Commonwealth in the Bank nationalization case (1948-49). He appeared frequently in constitutional, industrial, tax, commercial and other civil cases in the High Court of Australia, in addition to maintaining an extensive civil practice before the Supreme Court of Victoria where perhaps his most notable appearance was in *McDonald* v. *Cain* (1953). His knowledge of transport regulation was applied on behalf of the Commonwealth which intervened in the test case, *Hughes and Vale Pty Ltd* v. *New South Wales* (1952-54), to support the validity of the State Transport Co-ordination Act (1931-52). He represented R. E. Fitzpatrick [q.v.14] before the High Court of Australia when Fitzpatrick and F. C. Browne were gaoled by parliament for breach of privilege. Again with Bailey, Phillips appeared for the Commonwealth in the Second Uniform Tax case (1957). His familiarity with American jurisprudence and constitutional law was reflected in his teaching, scholarly writing and appellate advocacy. Phillips was widely read and gifted with an exceptional memory; if he had any failings, they probably arose from his extraordinary capacity to talk, a thickness of hide and a resulting impaired capacity to sense when he had said enough.

Renowned for taking a keen interest in his appearance, Phillips could be very good company, but some were put off by his under-developed sense of humour, fondness for patrician forms of speech, and tendency to be self-opinionated and arrogant. While most of his contemporaries in the important constitutional cases of the decade went to the bench, Phillips retired from practice in 1958. He returned to the University of Melbourne as senior (1958-63) and special (1963-70) lecturer in law. For the next decade he conducted the law school's moot-court programme, bringing his considerable talents to the task of introducing students to the world of advocacy.

Phillips resumed public office in 1960 when the Menzies government appointed him chairman of the Commonwealth Grants Commission, a post he held until 1966. In October 1963 the Victorian government, led by (Sir)

Henry Bolte, invited him to conduct a royal commission into the sale and consumption of liquor. This role thrust Phillips, the bon vivant, into the limelight, and gave him the opportunity, which he enthusiastically grasped, to apply his interests in the law and personal freedom, economics, public administration, social policy and the methodology of social research. The recommendations in his three detailed reports were promptly enacted by the government, liberalizing Victoria's liquor laws. Phillips was, however, unable to bring himself to recommend relaxing the laws on Sunday drinking.

Throughout his adult life Phillips contributed to the scholarly literature of law, economics and public administration, with articles in *Australian Quarterly*, the *Economic Record*, *Public Administration*, *Res Judicatae*, the *Melbourne University Law Review* and the *Australian Law Journal*. In 1964 he was appointed C.M.G. Two years later he conducted an inquiry for the Tasmanian government into that State's Sunday observance laws. In 1967 he was knighted. Sir Philip was a company director, a president of the Royal Victorian Bowls Association and a member of the Alcoholism Foundation of Victoria. He co-edited *The Peopling of Australia* (London, 1968), tended the garden of his home at Eltham, played bowls, and made furniture. Survived by his wife, and by the two daughters of his first marriage, he died on 19 September 1970 at Eltham and was cremated.

A. Dean, *A Multitude of Counsellors* (Melb, 1968); W. Osmond, *Frederic Eggleston* (Syd, 1985); A. W. Martin, *Robert Menzies*, 1 (Melb, 1993); *Sun News-Pictorial*, 30 Mar 1927, 15 Feb 1946, 22 Sept 1970; *Herald* (Melb), 13, 24 Sept 1960, 20 Mar 1965, 13 Sept 1969, 21 Sept 1970; *Australian*, 31 Dec 1964, 22 Sept 1970; information from Mr C. B. Christesen, Eltham, Prof H. A. J. Ford, Kew, and Sir John Young, Malvern, Melb.

LAURENCE W. MAHER

PHILLIPS, STANLEY THOMAS (1912-1976), studmaster, was born on 27 July 1912 at Greenview, near Wondai, Queensland, second of seven children of Queensland-born parents Joseph Phillips, farmer, and his wife Anne Catherine, née Jensen. Educated at Greenview State School, Stan worked on the family dairy-farm. Joe established the Sunnyview (later Sunny View) stud of Illawarra Shorthorns which won awards (from the 1920s) at the Brisbane Royal National Exhibition. In December 1938 the family enterprise was named J. Phillips & Sons.

At St Johannes Evangelical Church, Mondure, on 23 January 1937 Stan Phillips had married Gertrude Adell Hansen with Lutheran forms. Late in 1948 the Phillipses sold the Greenview farm and bought land near Kingaroy. Their intention was that Joe would retire, and that Stan and his brother Cyril would grow peanuts and grain on the new property. Their desire to breed and show elite dairy cattle proved too strong. After buying back their stud name and part of the herd, they began to resurrect the stud. Stan showed their stock annually on a circuit that at times extended to Rockhampton. He also bred horses which he raced as trotters.

Stan Phillips was a committee-member (from 1952) of the Queensland branch of the Australian Illawarra Shorthorn Society, but he lived for his stud and the show-ring rather than the committee-room. Like his father, he judged at major shows, including the Royal Easter Show, Sydney (1954, 1957 and 1959). He was an excellent judge and 'managed the big classes with ease'. In 1961 he spent almost four months in hospital and underwent radiotherapy. That year Sunny View Little Princess 30 was champion A.I.S. cow at the Brisbane Royal National Exhibition. This rangy red cow was named Australian dairy 'Cow of the Year' nine times by the *Livestock Bulletin*, and her lifetime production record put her among the world's top ten living cows. Phillips energetically promoted the export of semen carrying her bloodlines in a programme to rejuvenate the American Milking Shorthorn breed.

The Phillips family owned or bred senior, reserve, or production champions in all but five Brisbane Royal National Exhibitions between 1929 and 1975. A genetic analysis of the A.I.S. breed of 1973 showed Sunny View as the most important stud in Australia. Sunny View and Tabbagong (Jamberoo, New South Wales) studs had more influence on the national herd than the next ten studs combined. After Cyril died in 1971, J. Phillips & Sons was dissolved. The dispersal sale on 2 October 1973 grossed $141 250 for 109 head of cattle. Stan helped his son Ray to establish Sunny View Droughtmaster stud; by 1975 its beef cattle were winning ribbons in Brisbane.

Rather stocky in appearance, Stan Phillips was held in affectionate respect by his family and fellow cattlemen. He had an unassuming manner which concealed a painstaking, intensely competitive concern for his stud. Survived by his wife and son, he died of myocardial infarction on 20 May 1976 at the Gympie showgrounds and was buried in Taabinga cemetery with Methodist forms.

Aust Illawarra Shorthorn Soc: Golden Jubilee Souvenir (Kiama, 1980); Kingaroy & Dist Hist Soc, *One Step of Progress* (Kingaroy, 1985); *Qld Country Life*, 26 Oct 1950, 21 June 1956, 29 July 1971, 4 Oct 1973, 3 June 1976; *Aust Dairy J*, Sept, Nov 1973; *Dairyman*, June 1976; *Aust J of Agr Research*, Nov 1977; information from Mr M. R. Phillips, Kingaroy, Qld.

S. J. ROUTH

PHILP, SIR ROSLYN FOSTER BOWIE (1895-1965), judge, was born on 27 July 1895 at Double Bay, Sydney, fourth of seven children of James Alexander Philp, a Scottish-born journalist, and his wife Ellen, née Kilgour, who came from New Zealand. 'Ross' was educated at South Brisbane State School and (on scholarships) at Brisbane Grammar School where he passed the senior public examination. With a helping hand from (Sir) James Blair [q.v.7], he was appointed a clerk in the Queensland Department of Justice on 16 March 1914. He spent one year as associate to Justice (W. A. B.) Shand at Townsville before enlisting in the Australian Imperial Force on 30 September 1916. At St Alban's Anglican Church, Leura, New South Wales, on 7 March 1917 he married Marjorie Alice Hewson ('Peggy') Ferrier.

In June 1917 Philp sailed for England. Four months later he was sent to the Western Front as a gunner in the 12th Army Brigade, Australian Field Artillery. Gassed on 4 November at Ypres, Belgium, he was treated locally and admitted to hospital in England. As a result of the gassing he suffered a recurrent condition known as 'effort syndrome'. He remained in Britain until February 1919, then returned to Brisbane and was discharged from the A.I.F. on 24 April 1919. Resuming his career in the Department of Justice, he studied for the Barristers' Board examinations and was admitted to the Bar on 17 July 1923. That year he was appointed legal-assistant and assistant crown solicitor.

Resigning from the public service in 1926, Philp was State manager of the oil-firm, C. C. Wakefield & Co. Ltd, for two years. From 1928 he developed a large private general practice at the Bar. The Queensland Sugar Millers' Association retained him for some ten years. In 1931 he represented E. G. Theodore [q.v.12] in the Mungana case, heard in the Supreme Court of Queensland, and secured a finding in his client's favour. He gained a reputation in commercial and industrial law, lectured at the University of Queensland and became a member (1939) of the law faculty.

On 4 May 1939 Philp was appointed a judge of the Supreme Court of Queensland. The Australian Labor Party government appreciated his work in the Mungana case and Chief Justice Blair doubtless supported him. Although Philp lacked seniority, his abilities and practice justified his elevation to the bench. Initially, he was unsure whether he could carry the burden, but any doubts were quickly dispelled by his talent for and application to judicial work. He was to show his mastery of probate, criminal, matrimonial and commercial law.

Decisive and clear-minded, Philp made a special study of the Queensland criminal code; his reading included judgements by courts in the United States of America. He led Queensland judges in deriving from the criminal code a coherent body of legal principles rather than a disjointed collection of rules. His decisions were often reported in the press: one newspaper article described him as 'hard on criminals' but not 'callous'. In 1962 a senior police officer suggested that detectives' promotions should depend in part on the number of arrests they made. In a summing-up that year Philp observed that 'it would be a grave matter if a judge could no longer tell a jury . . . that a police officer, prima facie, had no interest in getting a conviction'. His remark led to a ministerial inquiry and to the police commissioner's denial that arrest rates had anything to do with promotion.

Philp's failure to become chief justice stemmed from what he regarded as a matter of principle. When Premier William Forgan Smith [q.v.11] had offered him the position of senior puisne judge in 1940, he had declined it, even after Forgan Smith intimated that the promotion would probably ensure his selection as the next chief justice. Philp felt that he should not be appointed to the position over E. A. Douglas [q.v.14] who had found against E. M. Hanlon [q.v.14] in the Ithaca election case. Neal Macrossan [q.v.] accepted the post and was appointed chief justice in 1946.

Macrossan's elevation left the position of senior puisne judge vacant. Hanlon was by then premier. Douglas was again overlooked. A falling out ensued after Philp's friend (Sir) Alan Mansfield [q.v.] took the post in March 1947. Philp claimed that Mansfield had agreed not to accept it; Mansfield declared that he had made no such promise. They avoided a public rift, though Philp's disapproval was well known. Douglas died in August that year. In 1956, when Mansfield was appointed chief justice, Philp succeeded him as senior puisne judge. He held that office until his death. While his actions had inhibited his advancement, they considerably enhanced his reputation. In 1958 he was appointed K.B.E.

Never a stranger to controversy, Philp had given evidence in 1956 to the royal commission (conducted by K. R. Townley, another Supreme Court judge) into alleged corrupt conduct by T. A. Foley [q.v.14], secretary for public lands. Philp stated that F. M. Bell, a grazier, had told him in 1949 that Foley had demanded £1000 for A.L.P. funds in exchange for granting him a crown lease. During criminal proceedings against Foley in April-May 1956, the magistrate M. J. Hickey ruled Philp's evidence inadmissible and dismissed the charge. Townley, however, found in June that Foley had been guilty of corrupt conduct. Foley resigned his portfolio, but remained in parliament and from the back-benches vilified both Philp and Townley.

At the request of the Federal government, Philp chaired (1939-45) the Queensland advisory committee on aliens, investigated (1945) the loss of a Stinson aircraft in Victoria and headed (1961) a committee of inquiry into the marketing of wool. In 1954-55 he was a member of the Commonwealth royal commission on espionage which found evidence that the Soviet Union was conducting clandestine activities in Australia.

Philp was a trustee (1940-47) of his old school, a member (1955-61) of the Queensland committee for selecting Rhodes scholars, and a patron of the Twelfth Night Theatre Company. He presided over the Queensland Club (1957-58), the State division of the National Heart Foundation of Australia (1959-64) and the trustees of the Queensland Art Gallery (1959-65). A keen golfer and a noted club-man who enjoyed company, conversation, food and wine, he had strong features and an impressive bearing.

In 1964 Philp fell fatally ill. He bore his condition with patience and courage. When he was unable to attend court he delivered reserved judgements from his Wickham Terrace home. Survived by his wife and one of his three sons, he died of cancer on 19 March 1965 at St Martin's Private Hospital, Brisbane; he was accorded a state funeral and was cremated. His son Ross had been killed over Denmark in 1944 while serving in the Royal Australian Air Force.

Sir Owen Dixon [q.v.14] called Philp's death a 'great loss'. (Sir) Joseph Sheehy described him as a 'man of the highest principles'. Sir Harry Gibbs recalled him as 'even-tempered, good humoured, quick to grasp the point of an argument and expeditious in giving judgment'. The Bar Association of Queensland holds J. T. Rigby's portrait (1959) of Sir Roslyn.

R. Johnston, *History of the Queensland Bar* (Brisb, 1979); B. H. McPherson, *The Supreme Court of Queensland 1859-1960* (Brisb, 1989); *PP* (Cwlth), 1954-55, 3, p 187; *PP* (Qld), 1956-57 and 1957, 2, p 733; *State Reports* (Qld), 1939, p 90, 1941, p 56, 1942, p 40, 1943, p 137; *Queensland Reports*, 1965, memoranda of 1965; *Aust Bar Review*, July 1990, p 181; *Courier-Mail*, 24-25 Aug 1940, 1 Jan 1958, 27 Sept 1962, 20, 30 Mar, 23 June 1965; *Sunday Mail*, 14 July 1957, 30 Sept 1962.   JAMES B. THOMAS

PICKWORTH, HORACE HENRY ALFRED ('OSSIE') (1918-1969), golfer, was born on 17 January 1918 at Manly, Sydney, fifth child of Sydney-born parents Harold Thomas Pickworth, stonemason, and his wife Helena Doris Matilda, née Grey. Ossie left school at 14 and, despite admonishment, caddied at Manly Golf Club until he was appointed assistant-professional there in 1934. Fair haired, slim and strong, he practised tire-lessly, but did not win the State assistants' title until 1938.

After seven tournament wins, he enlisted in the Militia on 9 August 1940 and began full-time duty in the Australian Army Service Corps. Transferring to the Australian Imperial Force in July 1942, he trained as a cook and served (from 1945) on Morotai and in British North Borneo before being discharged from the army on 4 February 1946. At St Matthew's Anglican Church, Manly, on 15 December 1942 he had married Lorna Estelle McDougall, a 20-year-old waitress. He often seemed more proud of his cooking and home life than his golfing feats.

In 1946-48 Pickworth became the only golfer to win three Australian Open championships in succession, the last in a play-off with Manly's earlier wonder boy, Jim Ferrier. Following his first Open, Pickworth was invited to a teaching and playing position at Royal Melbourne Golf Club, where his earthy language and camaraderie offended the long-serving incumbent, Arthur Le Fevre, whose retirement in 1948 only softened a nagging embarrassment. Although pleased with Pickworth's successes, many members missed Le Fevre's polite attentiveness; they were also uneasy about Pickworth's frequent tournament absences. Social incompatibility and contractual issues ended Pickworth's stay at Royal Melbourne in 1953. In the following year he accepted the post of professional at the Cranbourne Country Club, won his fourth Australian Open and kept on winning tournaments. Even so, he could not have afforded to represent Australia in the 1957 Canada Cup without a £10 000 Tattersall's lottery win. That, and failing health, changed his life. A committed family man, he decided in 1958 to become licensee of the Railway Hotel, Hawthorn.

Always nonchalant, a cigarette on his lips, Pickworth sized up situations rapidly and played without hesitation. 'My feet ache from walking' was his explanation for his speedy rounds. He was famous for bunker play, fairway woods and fearless putting. He liked to back himself—to break a course record or hole out a ball embedded in a bunker. Never daunted, he was smilingly at ease with galleries; over a beer, he was a born story-teller, with an infectious giggle that anticipated laughter. He gave generous support to charities and served as president (1955-58) of the Professional Golfers' Association of Australia.

Pickworth won every major Australian event: four Opens, three Australian (1947, 1953 and 1955) and four Victorian (1948, 1954-56) Professional championships, six Ampol tournaments (1947-49, 1951 and 1953) and the Victorian Open (1957). He considered his greatest round to be a ten-under-par 63, to beat Bobby Locke's 65, at Royal Melbourne in

1950. That year Royal Melbourne members helped him to visit Britain. The British Open eluded him, but he won the Irish Open, drawing from Henry Cotton the comment, 'the best pair of hands I have ever seen'. In retirement, Ossie played golf socially, but failed to regain amateur status. In 1968 he was made a life member of the P.G.A. He died of chronic hypertensive renal failure on 23 September 1969 at Parkville and was cremated; his wife, daughter and two sons survived him.

C. de Groot, *Pro Golf* (Syd, 1991); J. Johnson, *The Royal Melbourne Golf Club* (Melb, 1991); *Victorian Golf*, Oct 1969; *Herald* (Melb), 17 Feb 1956, 24 Sept 1969; *Sun* (Syd), 27 Sept 1969; *Daily Mirror* (Syd), 28 Apr 1978, 24 Dec 1984.

WESTON BATE

PICOT, JAMES (1906-1944), poet and literary critic, was born on 15 April 1906 at Baldock, Hertfordshire, England, youngest of three children of James Picot, a Wesleyan minister from the Channel Islands, and his Parisian-born second wife Laure, née Ahier. Laure died two days after his birth. With seven children to raise (four from his first marriage), his father remarried. Educated at schools in Lancashire and Cornwall, and on Guernsey, by the age of 8 Jim had begun to read Edward Gibbon's *Decline and Fall of the Roman Empire*. In 1923 he was sent to Queensland under an assisted-emigration scheme. He joined one of his brothers at Montrose, a farm near Goondiwindi, and obtained the first of a series of outback jobs which took him up and down the eastern States.

In 1928 Picot had a poem accepted by the *Bulletin*, and columns by the Melbourne *Age* and *Brisbane Courier*. A small legacy allowed him to move in 1930 to Brisbane, where he attended the Teachers' Training College while continuing to write stories, poems and articles. In 1931 he won the first of several literary prizes, ten guineas in a short story competition run by *Stead's Review*. He studied at the University of Queensland (B.A. Hons, 1936) and became friendly with F. W. Robinson [q.v.11], lecturer in English and modern languages, who recalled his bohemian 'peculiarities', such as attending lectures in dinner-jacket and sandshoes. Graduating with third-class honours in philosophy, he won a Freemasons' scholarship in 1936. Two years later he entered St Francis's (Anglican) Theological College. He left after six months, having decided that 'literature, not the priesthood, is my job'.

In Brisbane, Picot was befriended by Vance and Nettie Palmer [qq.v.11], and by Vance's sister, the poet Emily Bulcock [q.v.7]. Picot's poems were published in British magazines such as *Poetry of Today* and *Poetry Review*. He lectured on modern poetry—on the radio and for organizations like the Queensland Authors' and Artists' Association—and championed T. S. Eliot and Gerard Manley Hopkins. His own poetry, a combination of experimentalism and archaism, was always intense, and often very powerful. In 1939 he befriended an older poet 'Brian Vrepont' [q.v. Benjamin Truebridge]; they gave a series of joint public recitations. Through Vrepont, Picot met Clem Christesen whom he urged to 'revive plans to publish a literary journal'. With Christesen, Vrepont and Paul Grano [q.v.9], he contributed to the first issue of *Meanjin Papers* in December 1940.

Picot enlisted in the Australian Imperial Force on 28 May 1941 and was posted to the 8th Division Signals. He was sent to Singapore in August, captured by the Japanese in February 1942 and interned at Changi. Forced to work on the Burma-Thailand Railway, he died of beriberi on 11 April 1944. His remains were later reburied in Kanburi war cemetery, Thailand. Tributes in *Meanjin* in 1953 praised him for rallying his fellow prisoners by his wit, learning and love of literature. A collection of his poetry, *With A Hawk's Quill* (Melbourne, 1953), was published posthumously.

L. Strahan, *Just City and the Mirrors* (Melb, 1984); Catholic Readers and Writers Soc (Brisb), *Vista*, 1, no 2, 1946; *Meanjin Q*, 12, no 4, 1953, 13, no 1, 1954; *Advocate* (Melb), 3 Mar 1955; Meanjin Archive, James Picot correspondence 1923-c1943 (Baillieu L, Univ Melb); Picot papers, MS 6673 (NL).

PATRICK BUCKRIDGE

PIE, ARTHUR BRUCE (1902-1962), businessman and politician, was born on 18 May 1902 at Coburg, Melbourne, second child of Melbourne-born parents Arthur Savoi Garibaldi Pie, clerk, and his wife Annie Gertrude, née Miller. Bruce was educated at state schools, and at Caulfield Grammar School where he showed ability at cricket, football and swimming. At the age of 15 he found a job with Harrisons, Ramsay Pty Ltd, importers, a firm for which his father also worked. In 1922 he was transferred to Brisbane as the firm's merchandising manager. On 24 June 1925 at Scots Church, Clayfield, he married with Presbyterian forms Jean Margaret Wright.

Immediately he arrived in Queensland, Pie noticed its lack of secondary industry. His passionate belief in the need to develop the manufacturing sector became a driving force in his life. With limited capital, he acquired a few knitting machines and launched Queensland Textile Co. Pty Ltd in 1927. He set up Bruce Pie & Co., importers, in 1935 and the Bruce Pie Bedding Co. in 1943. At Kedron in

1946 he established Bruce Pie Industries Ltd which specialized in spinning and knitting, and in general textile manufacture; by 1948 its annual turnover exceeded £1 million.

Standing as an Independent Democrat, Pie had won the seat of Hamilton in the Legislative Assembly on 29 March 1941, defeating H. M. Russell, the leader of the United Australia Party. In 1942 he was appointed an honorary adviser to the Commonwealth Department of War Organization of Industry. He resigned from this office and from the Queensland parliament in 1943 to contest the Federal seat of Brisbane, but was defeated by George Lawson [q.v.]. Pie was elected to the Legislative Assembly in 1944 as the Queensland People's (later Liberal) Party member for Windsor. After visiting Germany in 1945, he published *Journey into Desolation* (Brisbane, 1946); among other things, the book revealed conditions in Nazi concentration camps.

In March 1946 Pie succeeded (Sir) John Chandler [q.v.13] as Q.P.P. leader. Announcing a 'dynamic reform policy' before the 1947 polls, he promised a 'new deal' for women through a programme which offered them refrigerators, trained home-assistants, and representation on hospital boards. He also urged an investigation into hotel ownership, advocated trade training for ex-servicemen, and supported industrial arbitration. In a fiery debate in the House later that year, he and the Q.P.P. supported a bill to introduce a 40-hour week, despite bitter opposition from the Country Party. In February 1948 he handed over leadership of the Q.P.P. to (Sir) Thomas Hiley. Following an electoral redistribution in 1949, Pie won the seat of Kedron in the 1950 general elections.

Quickly earning a reputation as a robust politician with a heightened sense of propriety, Pie objected to large salary rises for politicians in 1948 and 1950. On this issue he found himself in unlikely alliances with two colourful back-benchers, Fred Paterson [q.v.] and (Sir) Johannes Bjelke-Petersen. Pie resigned from the Liberal Party in 1950 on the principle that it was wrong for parliamentarians to increase their salaries between elections. He had caused a row in the House on 23 November 1949 in a speech demanding an inquiry into allegations that a winning ticket in the State's Golden Casket Art Union had been sold after the lottery was drawn. Refusing to retract his accusation that the government 'would come at anything' to prevent the appointment of a royal commission, he was suspended from parliament for two hours and became involved in a fist-fight with H. H. Collins [q.v.13], the secretary for agriculture.

On 8 January 1951 Pie resigned from the Legislative Assembly, ensuring that the subsequent by-election would be contested at a time when Labor was embarrassed by alleged polling irregularities in the adjacent electorate of Bulimba. President (1958) of the Brisbane Club, he was a member (1943-62) of the Queensland Turf Club and patron (1953-56) of Windsor Australian Rules Football Club. While visiting Sydney on business, he died of coronary artery disease on the night of 30/31 July 1962 at Tattersall's Club and was cremated with Anglican rites. His wife, daughter and six sons survived him.

C. Lack (comp), *Three Decades of Queensland Political History, 1929-1960* (Brisb, 1962); *PD* (Qld), 22 Aug 1962, p 6; *Courier-Mail*, 1 Aug 1962; information from Mr D. Pie, Clayfield, Brisb.
PAUL D. WILLIAMS

PIERCE, JOHN PATRICK (1909-1970), Catholic priest, was born on 24 March 1909 at Footscray, Melbourne, eldest of seven children of Victorian-born parents John Patrick Pierce, ironmoulder, and his wife Anne, née Whelan, both of whom were of Irish descent. Young Johnny was educated at St Augustine's parish school, Yarraville, and at Assumption College, Kilmore, where he was dux in his final year. Having completed his studies at Corpus Christi College, Werribee, he was ordained priest by Archbishop Mannix [q.v.10] on 15 July 1934. Fr Pierce began his ministry as assistant-priest at Daylesford before being sent to Heidelberg.

Following the outbreak of World War II, Pierce joined the Australian Military Forces on 3 October 1939 and served in Melbourne as a chaplain, 4th class. In December 1940 he transferred to the Royal Australian Air Force with the same rank (equivalent to flight lieutenant) and was posted to the headquarters of R.A.A.F. Station, Laverton. Embarking for Singapore in May 1941, he ministered to airmen from his base at Sembawang. There, he was renowned for the vigour with which he played recreational games of Australian Rules football. He was based at Ipoh, Malaya, in December, when Japanese forces approached. Air force personnel were evacuated on the 20th. Purloining a car from a deserted Bentley showroom, he headed for Singapore with five men.

The air force was withdrawn from Singapore to the Netherlands East Indies in January-February 1942. Pierce commandeered a vessel and took sixty men to Palembang, Sumatra, and then to Perth. Following postings in Victoria (1942 and 1944-45) and England (1943-44), he was demobilized in Melbourne on 14 November 1945 as chaplain, 2nd class (wing commander). Airmen admired him for his courage, leadership and concern for their welfare.

After the war Pierce was placed in charge of the Catholic Rehabilitation Office, Melbourne. Appointed immigration chaplain in 1948, he established the Catholic Immigration Office. At this period he was also Catholic chaplain to the deaf; at Mannix's request, he set up a Catholic school for the deaf at Portsea. In 1950 he became parish priest of St Teresa's, Essendon. Keenly interested in a range of sports, he instituted an annual Mass at St Francis's Church for the racing fraternity at the time of the Melbourne Cup. This interest led to his appointment as Catholic chaplain to Melbourne's racing clubs.

Suffering from chronic leukaemia, Pierce retired in 1969. He died of cardiac infarction on 14 December 1970 at Box Hill and was buried in Melbourne general cemetery. Pierce had served airmen, returned servicemen, immigrants, the deaf, his parishoners, sporting friends and all manner of people irrespective of their religion. The Catholic centre for the deaf, at Prahran, was named after him.

Australian Catholic Truth Society, *For This Was I Born* (Melb, 1971); P. A. Davidson, *Sky Pilot* (Canb, 1990); *Teresian*, Dec 1970; *Advocate* (Melb), 24 Dec 1970.   W. J. McCarthy